THE
BOOK
OF THE
STATES

2005 EDITION
VOLUME 37

ISBN 0872928268

9 780872 928268

The Council of State Governments
Lexington, Kentucky

Headquarters: (859) 244-8000
Fax: (859) 244-8001
Internet: www.csg.org

The Council of State Governments

Council Offices

Headquarters:
Daniel M. Sprague, Executive Director
2760 Research Park Drive, P.O. Box 11910
Lexington, KY 40578-1910
Phone: (859) 244-8000
Internet: www.csg.org

Southern:
Colleen Cousineau, Director
P.O. Box 98129
Atlanta, GA 30359
Phone: (404) 633-1866
Internet: www.slcatlanta.org

Eastern:
Alan V. Sokolow, Director
40 Broad Street, 20th Floor
New York, NY 10004
Phone: (212) 482-2320
Internet: www.csgeast.org

Western:
Kent Briggs, Director
1107 9th Street, Suite 650
Sacramento, CA 95814
Phone: (916) 553-4423
Internet: www.csgwest.org

Midwestern:
Michael H. McCabe, Director
641 E. Butterfield Road, Suite 401
Lombard, IL 60148
Phone: (630) 810-0210
Internet: www.csgmidwest.org

Washington, D.C.:
Jim Brown, General Counsel & Director
444 N. Capitol Street, NW, Suite 401
Washington, D.C. 20001
Phone: (202) 624-5460
Internet: www.csg-dc.org

Copyright 2005
The Council of State Governments
2760 Research Park Drive • P.O. Box 11910
Lexington, Kentucky 40578-1910

Manufactured in the United States of America

Publication Sales Department
1(800) 800-1910

Paperback Price: $99.00
ISBN # 0-87292-827-6

Hard Cover Price: $125.00
ISBN # 0-87292-826-8

Foreword

Since its inception more than seven decades ago, The Council of State Governments has promoted the sovereignty of the states, interpreted changing national and international conditions, advocated multistate problem-solving and helped states prepare for the future.

Today, CSG performs the role of a trend tracker for policy-makers and managers in the three branches of state governments through various means, including leadership forums, regional conferences and policy research and publications. *The Book of the States* is one of its core publications and regarded as a most reliable premier reference book on the states.

It is with great pleasure that we publish the 2005 edition of *The Book of the States* with timely information and up-to-date data on many areas of state government. This year is indeed a challenging time for state officials who are faced with external influences, such as international terrorist attacks, federal aid cuts and encroachment upon state authorities. Hopefully, this publication is informative to them, when planning, implementing and evaluating the policies and programs, as well as to researchers who look for reliable comparative data.

May 2005

Daniel M. Sprague
Executive Director
The Council of State Governments

The Book of the States 2005

Editor in Chief	Keon S. Chi
Associate Editors	Audrey S. Wall
	Heather M. Perkins
Production Coordinators	Lisa K. Eads
	Susie D. Bush

Acknowledgements

The editorial and production staff members wish to thank the article authors who graciously shared their expertise and insights, the hundred of individuals in the states who responded to national surveys conducted by The Council of State Governments, national organizations of state officials, federal agencies and think tank organizations who made their most recent data and information available for this volume.

Table of Contents

CONTENTS

CONTENTS

CONTENTS

Chapter Six
STATE POLITICAL PARTIES, ELECTIONS AND ETHICS 329

CONTENTS

CONTENTS

Emerging Trends Shaping State Governments: 2005 and Beyond

By Keon S. Chi

In 2005, governors, legislators and judges and their staff in the three branches of our state governments are faced with unprecedented challenges—political, fiscal and management challenges stemming from both external and internal forces. External forces include global dynamics and terrorist threats, the proposed elimination of, or deep cuts in, some federal aid programs, continuous preemptions and mandates, and federal encroachment upon state regulatory powers. Internal forces are generated by increasing partisan competition in legislative chambers as well as between the three branches of state government, serious structural deficits in budget-making, and growing opportunities and pressures from direct citizen control—initiatives and referenda—in many states.

One broad question state policy-makers should be asking is: "How should we define changing roles of the state to face up with these trends?" Under these external and internal forces, decision-makers are expected to be more innovative, effective and efficient than ever before in managing agencies and delivering services because of high public expectations and growing demands. In order to redefine and prioritize states' roles, policy-makers might want to have an update on what is taking place between the state and the federal government and within the three branches of state government across the nation. For those who are trying to anticipate what might happen in the remainder of this year and in 2006, major trends described in this issue of *The Book of the States* might be helpful guides. What follows in this introductory chapter are highlights of a few external and internal forces that are likely to shape the way state governments are making decisions.

Federalism

New Politics

The topic of federalism and intergovernmental relations will continue to be one of the major external forces affecting the states, especially in implementing some of the most expensive state-federal joint programs, such as homeland security, Medicaid and No Child Left Behind. State officials like to know what they can expect under the Bush administration to tackle these and other federal-state programs in the next few years. The answer might not be very promising.

During the past several years, state policy-makers have experienced continuous federal encroachment upon states' rights when Republicans controlled both the executive and legislative branches of the national government. Clearly, this trend appeared to be contrary to the past patterns of the workings of American federalism under each of the two major political parties. In the past half a century, Republican presidents usually sided with conservatives who favored a smaller role for the federal government with stronger states, while Democratic presidents tended to favor a larger role for the national government, thus drawing criticisms from traditional advocates for state rights and Republicans.

Such a traditional description, however, does not seem to apply to the current Republican administration or Congress. In his article, "The New Politics of Federalism," Paul E. Peterson of Harvard University describes the changing trend in American federalism from a historical perspective and says, "Jefferson is recognized as the spiritual father of the Democratic Party, while Hamilton is at times given comparable status among Republicans. But as political interests changed, so did the positions of the two political parties. Throughout most of the 20th century, it was the New Deal Democrats who celebrated an expansion of the national government in ways Hamilton might have blessed, while conservative Republicans defended states rights that Jefferson had extolled." Peterson continues:

"Today, the parties are returning to their historic roots. In the Spring of 2005, the Republican leadership in Congress asked federal courts to assure jurisdiction in the Schiavo case, which raised issues long thought to be the preserve of state courts. Most Democrats opposed the move. Only weeks earlier, the Republican majority in Congress, at the behest of the president, had passed sweeping legislation that shifted class action suits that transcended state boundaries from state to federal courts, a nationalizing move that harkens back to the days of Hamilton and his close ally, Chief Justice John Marshall. Meanwhile, the vast majority of congressional Democrats fiercely defended the prerogatives of state trial courts—notwithstanding the party's deep-rooted preference for federal over state courts during the Great Society years."

The recent trend in American federalism characterized by Peterson is corroborated by other observers of American federalism, including John Kincaid, former executive director of the U.S. Advisory Commission on Intergovernmental Relations. In his article, "State-Federal Relations: Defense, Demography, Debt, and Deconstruction as Destiny," Kincaid lists examples of continuing "coercive federalism" during the Bush administration with "a shift of federal aid from places to persons, policy conditions and earmarks attached to federal aid, preemptions, federal encroachments on state taxation, federalization of state criminal law, defunct intergovernmental institutions, reduced federal-state cooperation within major intergovernmental programs, and federal court litigation." His prediction is, "Although state activism will generate a kind of competitive state-federal federalism, coercive federalism will be the system's dominant motif and will be exacerbated by the fiscal pressures generated by defense, demography, debt, and deconstruction."

Rebalancing Federal-State Relations

The balance in state-federal relations in the next few years is likely to favor the national government. How should state policy-makers face up with such an imbalance in the years to come? Carl W. Stenberg, former executive director of The Council of State Governments, proposes rebalancing federal-state relations by "working together more strategically and building effective horizontal and vertical networks." He cites the state-led tobacco settlement as an example of vertical network and the Streamlined State Sales and Use Tax as an example of horizontal network.

As John Mountjoy and Melissa Bell describe in their article, "Interstate Compacts: Trends and Issues," The Council of State Governments created the National Center for Interstate Compacts in 2004. This center serves as a national information clearinghouse on interstate compacts, provides training and technical assistance in helping states and manages the compact process. The center also promotes interstate compacts as a tool for cooperative state action, develops standards and provides an adaptive structure for states.

Interstate cooperation itself, however, might not be sufficient to slow down federal encroachment upon the states. In his article, "Interstate Relations Trends," Joseph F. Zimmerman of the University at Albany suggests:

> Compacts, agreements, and enactment of harmonious regulatory laws have been promoted as means to discourage Congress from exer-

cising its powers of preemption removing regulatory authority completely or partially in specified fields from states. Nevertheless, we conclude disparate state regulatory statutes and regulations, increasing globalization of the domestic economy, international trade treaties, lobbying by interest groups, and technological developments will result in Congress enacting preemption statutes.

Congress

To better comprehend federal-state relations, state policy-makers need to pay attention to how the first session of the 109th Congress handles a variety of issues affecting the states. State attorneys general, as their state's chief law enforcement officer, will be testifying before Congressional committees in 2005 as they have done during the last Congress. Major issues they testified about included consumer credit, on-line pharmaceuticals, I.D. theft, banking issues and predatory lending. The issues in consideration during the 109th Congress in 2005 could include: antitrust, Medicare Prescription Drug Improvement and Modernization Act of 2003, drug price competition, prescription drug importation, patient access to health care, antitrust exemption for insurance industry, antitrust enforcement, retail gas prices, bankruptcy, consumer protection, identity theft, "Do Not Call," spam, household goods movers, Fair Credit Reporting Act, cell phone bill of rights, online pharmaceuticals, privacy, rent to own, debt counseling, debt consolidation and debt settlement, predatory lending, anti-pyramid scheme legislation, drug price disclosure, Internet file sharing, protecting older Americans from fraud, and flu vaccine price gouging.

In addition, the first session of the 109th Congress is likely to deal with crime, including cyber crime, end-of-life health care, environment, tobacco and violence against women. There seems to be ample room for further federal preemption of traditional state jurisdictions.

Three Branches

Constitutional Amendments

Although citizen discontent with state government is not likely to disappear any time soon, there might not be any significant changes in public attitudes towards comprehensive constitutional amendments that are designed to radically reform the structure and function of state government. As Janice May's article describes, there were many constitutional amendments proposed in 2004 to change the structure or procedures of all three branches of state government, but these were aimed at minor changes as they have been in recent years.

Of the legislative amendments, attempts to change term limits by extending the number of years legislators could serve were defeated in two states. Virginia voters agreed to modification of reapportionment laws to avoid double or no representation of residents in certain districts. Among the executive branch ballot measures was a Colorado amendment to strengthen the governor's power of appointment, which was rejected. Virginia voters also approved an amendment which increases the number of officers who can succeed to the governor in the event of a terrorist attack and permit the lower house to convene to elect an acting governor and, if necessary, to waive eligibility requirements. State judicial branches were changed very little by amendment in 2004 despite efforts to do so. Voters defeated a South Dakota amendment that would have extended merit selection of judges from the supreme court to the circuit courts. New Hampshire voters defeated an amendment to resolve a separation of powers dispute between the legislature and the judiciary over the authority to make rules on judicial administration and procedures. Voters in Arizona and magistrates in North Carolina passed ballot measures regarding the office of justice of the peace and magistrates, respectively.

During the 2004 elections, 34 states passed approximately two-thirds of the 162 state-level ballot propositions. The most popular issue was the gay marriage issue, with 11 states approving constitutional amendments in November defending traditional marriage between a man and woman. Other high profile issues include marijuana legislation, gambling, election reform, fiscal policies, environment, and health care related matters. In 2004, approximately $200 million was spent for propositions in California alone. Whether spending big money for such ballot measures helps determine the outcome of direct citizen control is not certain, however.

Legislatures

Partisan Politics

State political parties are not only getting stronger but also more competitive, especially in state legislatures. Observers of American politics tend to disagree with the role of political parties at the national or state level. Some have predicted a decline of party

politics in general, while others have taken a contrary view. The current and future trends appear to be a resurgence of party politics at all levels of government. As political scientists Sarah Morehouse and Malcolm Jewell describe in their article, "The Future of Political Parties in the States," many state political parties are becoming stronger, not weaker because they have adapted to the new technology and provide valuable services to state and national candidates. "Far from the predicted decline," the authors argue, "state parties have become parties in service. They provide services such as polling, campaign seminars, advertising and fundraising. State parties maintained their autonomy as they became more professionalized and more durable."

As the state legislative sessions began in early 2005, legislative seats in the 50 states were almost evenly occupied by Democrats and Republicans, and the difference between the two major parties was miniscule. For example, Republicans controlled 20 legislatures, Democrats held 19, and 10 were split with either party having both legislative chambers. Before the 2004 elections, the breakdown was 21 Republican legislatures, 17 Democratic and 11 split. Implications of the party parity in state legislatures are not clear, but there could be more deadlocks and delays during legislative sessions and budget-making processes.

Term Limits

The issue of legislative term limits does not appear to be a major concern to legislators in most states in 2005. Term limits measures, begun in 1990 in three states, had been popular when a total of 21 states adopted them by 2000. Since then, the measure was thrown out by courts in six states and repealed in two states, leaving 15 with term limits in 2005. Only 12 state legislatures presently operate under term limits, and the measure in the remaining three will kick in between 2006 and 2010.

In an effort to assess the effect of term limits, the National Conference of State Legislatures, The Council of State Governments and State Legislative Leaders Forum have conducted a Joint Term Limits Project in the past three years. Jennifer Drage Bowser of the National Conference of State Legislatures reports some preliminary findings of the study project in her article, "The Effect of Legislative Term Limits." She says:

> It is clear that term limits have brought many changes to the legislatures where they are in effect. Term limited legislatures report more

general chaos, a decline in civility, reduced influence of legislative leaders and committees, and in some states, a shift in power relationships. However, the bottom line is that legislatures are resilient and highly adaptive institutions and continue to function efficiently under term limits. Many of the problems experienced by term limited legislatures are the same problems faced by all legislatures; term limits simply tend to amplify and accelerate them. As term limits continue to tighten their hold, and as veteran members continue to cycle out, the term limited legislatures will continue to evolve. As they do, they will provide valuable ideas that all legislatures, term limited or not, can adopt to improve their institutions.

The joint study project is planning to publish two or three products in 2005 or 2006.

Redistricting

Partisan politics has been evident in recent redistricting practices for state legislative elections. Most, if not all, state legislators are elected from single-member election districts, and redistricting in every 10 years has been a great deal of interest to observers of state politics. Ronald E. Weber of the University of Wisconsin-Milwaukee says, "Whereas the redistricting round of the 1990s can be described as the round of racial and ethnic predominance, the 2000 round showed a growing emergence of partisanship as the predominant pattern of conflict." The author elaborates the trend as follows:

The state legislatures were able to take into account race or ethnicity in drawing lines as had been the emphasis in the previous decade; however, since political partisanship of voters correlates highly with the racial and ethnic makeup of populations, the use of race and ethnicity was subordinated to the use of partisan criteria with the 2000 decade proving to be a round of either partisan gerrymandering or bi-partisan protection of incumbent state legislators. Finally, the partisanship surrounding state legislative districting processes of the current round has spurred a renewed interest in citizen initiatives to create less partisan reapportionment boards and commissions in states without them at the present time.

Good Legislatures

To be a good legislature, lawmakers must be responsive to their constituents, must have a balance between deliberative and political aspects during the legislative process and need to have effective leadership. In the past four decades or so, a number of national and regional organizations of state legislators, as well as academic and research groups, have conducted studies aimed at strengthen state legislatures. Some studies have dealt with institutional modernization while others addressed professionalism in legislatures. Of those, the 1971 report by the Citizen's Conference on State Legislatures has been one of the most frequently cited studies of legislative bodies in the 50 states. In the report, CCSL evaluated each state based on five criteria: functionality, accountability, informedness, independence and representativeness (FAIIR). Each state was then ranked by scores in structural and operational factors.

In his article, "The 'Good' Legislature," Alan Rosenthal of Rutgers University offers an alternative to traditional evaluation criteria used by CCSL and other similar studies. The author argues "appearance," "structure" and "product" should not be used as standards by which to make judgments of legislatures. Instead, he argues, state legislatures should be assessed by "the performance of three principal functions: representing constituents and constituencies, lawmaking, and balancing the power of the executive." To be a "good" legislature, Rosenthal argues, there must be three conditions: first, legislators must be responsive to their constituents; second, there must be a balance between the deliberative aspects of and political aspects of lawmaking; and, third, there must be effective legislative leadership in the legislature. Rosenthal says, "Among the many responsibilities of leadership are finding common ground, facilitating compromise, forging consensus, and enabling a legislative majority to find and work its will." The author presents detailed information on the actual workings of legislatures in legislator-constituency relations, legislative processes and relationships between legislators and governors.

Governors

Elections, Powers, Staffing

In 2005, a majority of the states have governors elected for the first time either in 2002 or 2004. The 2004 gubernatorial elections and resignations continued the recent trend of changes in the governorships across the states. In addition to the 11 gubernatorial races, two governors resigned their positions and left office before their terms were up. The results of the 2004 elections brought seven new governors into office, and they were split between the two parties, leaving the Republicans holding a 28 to 22 edge among the governors. Several governors are working in a "divided government" where the executive and legislative branches are controlled by opposing political parties.

In general, governors' powers have increased over the years, but not in all areas. For example, between 1960 and 2005, the overall institutional powers of the of the nation's governors increased, according to Thad Beyle of the University of North Carolina at Chapel Hill. He found that the greatest increase among the individual gubernatorial powers was in their veto power as more governors gained an item veto. On the other hand, the gubernatorial budgetary power actually declined, and there has also been a drop in the gubernatorial party control in the state legislatures.

As gubernatorial responsibilities increased in the past decades, staff support also increased drastically. The growth of staffing at the state level has been very uneven, and staff functions vary from state to state. The staff size ranges from less than 10 (Nebraska and Wyoming) to more than 200 (Florida and Texas). Contributing factors to the staff growth include the increasing complexity of governmental responsibilities, administrative expediency as well as political patronage and public relations.

Gubernatorial Succession

Gubernatorial succession is likely to be a concern in some states, where succession provisions are not clearly provided, especially when dealing with emergency situations, such as a terrorist attacks. Several states have enacted new statutes since the 9/11 attacks. One example is found in Virginia where voters recently overwhelmingly supported a constitutional amendment adding an additional 14 potential successors to a line previously containing only three. Brian J. Gaines of the University of Illinois at Urbana-Champaign and Brian D. Roberts of Principia College, the authors of "Gubernatorial Incapacity and Succession Provisions" recommend: "As officials and scholars revisit the question of how to handle the unthinkable in many states, they would do well also to re-examine their rules for handling an isolated emergency." The question of gubernatorial succession has been raised routinely. In 2003 and 2004, four gubernatorial successions occurred, three due to resignations and one due to death. A lieutenant governor in Nebraska became governor through succession when the previous governor was appointed a cabinet secretary in the federal government.

Governors' Policy Initiatives

Would gubernatorial initiatives proposed in 2005 be adequate to solve current and emerging problems states are faced with? This is a question policy-makers should deal with when addressing long-term solutions. As in the past, governors have announced their policy initiatives in their annual state of the state addresses. Although empirical records show approximately half of such initiatives have not passed the legislatures in the past, it is useful for state policy-makers to take a careful look at them to be better informed of what's going on in other states. Moreover, they can benefit from innovations implemented by other states when attempting to solve the same or similar problems in their own states.

Based on more than 40 state of the state addresses given in early 2005, Katherine Willoughby of Georgia State University summarizes her findings: "In 2005, most governors are promoting economic development through tax cuts and credits in order to be able to light up an 'open for business' sign in their state. Many governors are also calling for spending reductions and/or agency and program reorientations or reorganizations in order to reach budget balance."

These gubernatorial initiatives may be highlighted in two broad areas: revenue enhancement and spending reduction. To increase revenues, for example, they have proposed both traditional and innovative methods such as: initiating tax amnesty programs; accelerating tax payments; joining a multi-state lottery consortium; diverting tobacco settlement proceeds to general fund; and suspending implementation of voter initiative to divert general funds elsewhere.

In order to reduce expenditures, governors have proposed such methods as: early retirement programs; terminating and/or amending state contracts; eliminating funding to non-essential appropriations; suspending transfers from the general fund; delaying scheduled payments to K–12 schools and payments to counties for property tax relief; requiring or increasing employee contributions to health care costs; and monthly agency spending targets.

Other policy areas governors also talked about in the state of the state addresses include: containment of prescription drugs; reducing the opportunities to develop and deal methamphetamines; changing funding relationships with local governments; advancing protection of natural resources, the environment, development of renewable energy resources, and water conservation; strengthening government ethics law; initiating elections reform; negotiating related to tribal gaming; advancing homeland security and public safety and legislating tort reform. Whether governors would be able to persuade legislatures to buy in these proposals this year is not easy to predict.

Courts

Judicial Elections and Dispute Resolutions

Judicial elections in 2005 may be characterized as heavy spending and active involvement by interest groups and trial lawyers if the recent judicial elections are indications. Preliminary figures for 2004 show candidates in 20 states spent more than $39 million on the supreme court contests in 44 states. When final tallies are out, this figure could approach the $45 million mark for 46 seats, the same amount spent in 2000. Political parties and other interest groups spent as much as $10 million, mainly in six states.

In his review of state courts in 2004, David Rottman of the National Center for State Courts uses the phrase "vanishing trial" to characterize the recent trend, caused by insufficient funding and the backlog of cases. He says: "Courts need to anticipate changing demand for their service. Some signs that fundamental changes are taking place in the demand for court services were much discussed during 2004. Attention focused on the implications of what became known as 'the vanishing trial' phenomenon, a sustained decline in the number of trials, both trials by jury and trials by judge, in the state courts." He continues:

> The state courts in 2004 continued to supply their basic service to the public: quietly deciding the nearly 100 million disputes that the public, businesses, and governments bought to them for resolution. During 2004, however, alarms sounded in many states where improving state finances did not translate into adequate funding for the courts, interrupting the services the courts provide. The courts in most states have been left to accommodate the steady rise in their workload without securing a commensurate growth in resources. The losers are the members of the public with disputes for which they cannot obtain resolution. Court reform continued along mainly familiar tracks, including the longstanding movement toward court systems that are more centralized, streamlined, and funded at the state rather than the local level. Still more imaginative ways were found to respond to the needs of the growing number of citizens that prefer to represent themselves in court.

Election Reform

By January 1, 2006, all states are scheduled to set up a voting system that meets requirements under the Help American Vote Act of 2002. Such requirements include notification to a voter if he/she overvotes, or selects more than one candidate for the same race, and gives him or her the opportunity to correct the ballot; production of a permanent paper record with a manual audit capacity; provision of levels of access, privacy and independence to disabled voters that are equal to those available to other voters; and provision of alternative language accessibility.

The 2004 elections are regarded as a "dramatic improvement" over the 2002 elections, as characterized by R. Doug Lewis of The Election Center, and states have been recognized with new initiatives to reform their election laws and practices. More than 11 million new voters participated due largely to increases in voter registration and active campaigns, and the increase in voters ranged 8 percent in Alaska to 27 percent in Florida. According to the National Association of Secretaries of State, many states are planning to focus on statewide voter registration databases, voting equipment, voter education and poll worker training, and the budgets the states included in their plans were largely based on the money allocated under HAVA in 2002.

Finance

State Budgets

Overall, state budgets in 2005 look much better than they did in the past four years. "States are recovering from the recent fiscal crisis," says Donald L. Boyd of the Rockefeller Institute. Based on appropriations for fiscal 2005, Nick Samuels of the National Association of State Budget Officers reports state general fund spending will increase by 4.5 percent; only three states budgeted for less spending. Three states had spending growth of 10 percent or more in fiscal 2004 and appropriated budgets in eight states in fiscal 2005 do as well. As for revenues, 24 states increased taxes and fees for fiscal 2005, mostly from cigarette and other tobacco taxes. On the spending side, 15 states were forced to make cuts in their fiscal 2004 budgets, compared with 38 states in 2002 and 40 states in 2003 that had budget cuts.

Some experts on state finance, including William Fox and LeAnn Luna of the University of Tennessee, blame eroding tax bases for the recent state fiscal crises while others say these crises were in part "self inflicted" by the states because they have failed to address structural deficits. In their article, "State Tax Collections: Eroding Tax Bases," the authors say, "Legislators, with a view towards long-term fiscal stability, need to better understand the fundamental attributes of their revenue sources, why some of their tax bases continue to erode, and some options for stemming the erosion."

Federal Aid Cuts

In 2005 and 2006, state policy-makers should anticipate significant cuts in federal aid. With on-budget deficits of more than $400 billion projected each year through the next five years, states should expect decreasing federal aid. Federal grants to state and local governments were $423 billion in fiscal year 2004, accounting for one quarter of the federal budget for domestic programs. Grants account for approximately 30 percent of all state government revenue. Mandatory federal grants, which amount to approximately one-third of federal grants, include Medicaid, Temporary Assistance to Needy Families, and child nutrition programs; and discretionary programs include Title I education grants for the disabled, special education grants, and various public housing and community development grants. According to Nick Samuels, if President Bush's budget proposal passes Congress in 2005, discretionary grants would be cut by 9.2 percent in real per-capita terms, and grants for mandatory programs other than Medicaid would be cut by 5.8 percent. Combined, these cuts would be equivalent to about a 2.4 percent reduction in state government tax revenue.

Of all the federal aids to the states, Medicaid cuts are likely to have a greater impact on the states. Don Boyd estimates the impact of proposed Medicaid cuts as follows:

The President has proposed $45 billion in net federal Medicaid savings over the next 10 years, reflecting $60 billion of cuts and $15 billion in new initiatives. Most of the federal savings would result in higher costs to states, but some would result in state savings, for a net cost to states of $34 billion over 10 years. The largest changes that would

provide savings to states include reductions in payments Medicaid will make to pharmacies and provisions that would make it harder for people seeking to enter nursing homes to shield assets from Medicaid. The largest changes that would shift costs from the federal government to states include limits on intergovernmental transfers, limits on administrative expenditures, and restrictions on case management expenditures. The President's budget also proposed to increase outreach to and coverage of children, increasing federal and state expenditures. All told, Medicaid changes appear likely to increase state Medicaid expenditures by about 2–3 percent over 10 years.

Federal Tax Reform

Besides the proposed federal aid cuts, state policy-makers also might have to worry about the effect of the proposed federal tax reform. In January 2005, President Bush established the President's Advisory Panel on Federal Tax Reform to simplify tax laws, address equity issues and promote economic growth and job creation. There is a possibility that the federal government will enact a major overhaul of the federal tax system, adopting a retail sales tax, a consumption tax, or a value-added tax. Boyd says: "Whatever the merits of these changes for the federal tax system and the nation's economy, all of these choices could create major—and largely undiscussed—problems for state and local government finances." He offers his scenarios as follows:

"Depending on very important details, these proposals could (a) eliminate the deductibility of state and local income and property taxes, raising the effective cost of state and local services and having dramatically different impacts across states, (b) tread into the traditional state-local terrain of sales taxes, making it difficult for state and local governments to raise revenue from these taxes, (c) make it impractically expensive for states to have their own income taxes if federal tax changes are in place of the existing federal income tax, and/or (d) raise the costs to states of maintaining and improving infrastructure, if municipal bond interest is no longer tax-exempt."

Other experts on state finance, including W. Bartley Hildreth, formerly of Wichita State University, also agree with Boyd's analysis by saying, "state and local budgets face significant impacts from fundamental federal income tax reform, including new budget costs and the effective loss of revenue choices. It is hard to pin down the precise nature of these implications at this time. At the least, any discussion of federal tax reform legislation deserves the careful scrutiny by state and local officials because there are significant fiscal federalism implications."

Retirement Systems

In addition to aforementioned structural deficits and federal aid cuts, state retirement systems also have emerged as one of the major financial issues for state policy-makers to address. State policy-makers need to monitor the performance of state and local government retirement funds so as to avoid the financial pitfalls. The recent recession and current demographic trends, including aging boomers, have had a serious impact on state systems. According to Sujit CanagaRetna, with the Southern Legislative Conference, there are several factors that have contributed to the financial pitfall in the retirement systems. These include "the precarious financial position of private sector pensions and the federal Pension Benefit Guaranty Corporation; the looming shortfalls expected in the Social Security and Medicare programs in coming decades; and the low personal savings rates of most Americans, coupled with the high rates of consumer and household debt."

Over the past decade, according to Frank T. Baumgardner of the U.S. Census Bureau, the number of state administered public employee retirement systems has grown by 28 from the 190 in fiscal year 1993. Currently, there are 218 state retirement systems in the United States with a total 21.2 million active and inactive members. These systems usually extended state retirement benefits to new classes of employees, such as local law enforcement personnel, legislators, judges and local government employees. Local governments employ more than two-thirds of the active employees covered by state systems. In 2003, local government employees account for seven out of 10 active members. The state retirement systems command a total of $1.8 trillion in retirement assets, making them major players in the financial markets.

Management

Increasing revenues and decreasing expenditures, as recommended by governors and legislators, may not be possible unless agency directors and administrators improve the way they manage resources and improve information technology. For example, state treasurers, auditors and comptrollers would have to

provide increased services with a renewed sense of accountability, innovation in technology and strategic partnership initiatives.

State personnel executives would have to have innovative workforce development plans; otherwise they are likely to face a workforce shortage in state governments. Some human resource management organizations call it a crisis. A joint study by the National Association of State Personnel Executives and The Council of State Governments in 2002 estimated that state governments could lose at least 30 percent of their employees in the next few years due to the growing rate of employee retirement, the composition of current workforce with less-trained workers and worsened state budget problems.

State chief information officers would have to increase service delivery and efficiency, both internally and externally, and they will focus on reorganization and consolidation strategies, interoperability and improve the public safety communications infrastructure at the local, state and national levels. In 2005, Congress is expected to rewrite the 1996 telecommunications act, which has been rendered increasingly meaningless by developments in communications technology in recent years.

Foresight and Innovations

The year 2005 may be known, for most states, as a year of fiscal and economic recovery, restructuring and cost-efficiency and multi-state collaboration to solve social and environmental problems. The year may also be seen as a period of coercive regulatory federalism with continuous preemption of state authorities and national standards and intervention. The most serious concern state policy-makers have, however, seems to be the proposed federal aid cuts and pending federal tax reform. Federal deficit-reduction efforts and additional tax cuts will inevitably affect state coffers negatively and put state policy-makers in difficult situations to find alternatives to decreasing intergovernmental transfers.

The external and internal forces summarized above are based on more than 30 articles in Chapter One through Chapter Seven of the 2005 edition of *The Book of the States*. This edition also contains articles on more than 20 other areas in state government, including administration, public policy and programs. Topics of these articles range from libraries, licensure, motor vehicles, parks to homeland security, public safety, education, health care, energy, economic development, science and technology, transportation, parole and probation, welfare and international trade. Each of these articles highlight some of the most recent trends and issues state policy-makers and researchers on state government should be concerned about.

To face up with aforementioned forces and these trends, state policy-makers should keep at least two things in mind: foresight and innovations. They must first realize we are living in a rapidly changing era; what was adequate yesterday might not be sufficient tomorrow. Now more than ever, state leaders and managers need to track the major forces that have the potential to change state priorities and operations. Second, there are compelling reasons for state officials to be more innovative. They may need new and different ways of managing agencies and deliver ser-vices when they determine traditional and ongoing policies and programs are not working as well as they should. State decision-makers are expected to help each other across state borders by sharing their innovations. Moreover, the public expects to do more with less, especially during times of fiscal austerity like 2005 and 2006.

About the Author

Keon S. Chi, editor-in-chief of *The Book of the States*, is a senior fellow for The Council of State Governments and professor of political science at Georgetown College. He has published extensively on state politics, policy and administration.

Chapter One

STATE CONSTITUTIONS

State Constitutional Developments in 2004
By Janice C. May

In 2004 state constitutions played an unusually important role in state and national affairs. A record number of amendments banned same-sex marriage and may have influenced the presidential election. Other significant issues were also addressed. But the long-term trend against comprehensive revision continued.

Many important developments concerning state constitutions occurred in 2004. In retrospect, it was a remarkable year. Most publicized was the historic number of state constitutional amendments prohibiting same-sex marriage. Thirteen, all passing handily, were on the ballot in 2004, 11 in the November presidential election and two in special elections. There was speculation that the popularity of the amendments may have helped George W. Bush win the presidential election, particularly in the battleground state of Ohio where a win by John Kerry would have enabled him to receive enough electoral votes for the majority necessary to be president. Also of relevance to the presidential election was a proposed Colorado amendment to change the state's winner-take-all method of allocating the state's electoral votes to a proportional one. It was rejected but is a reminder that the Electoral College is constitutionally state based. Of national and world interest was the adoption of a California amendment to establish one of the world's largest stem cell research programs. Also of considerable interest were tort reform propositions on the ballots in several states. Fiscal issues also commanded attention. A budget amendment in California was designed to assure passage of a $15 billion bond issue, the largest floated in U. S. municipal bond history. In contrast to specific changes, however, no general revision of state constitutions took place by constitutional convention or other method. Rhode Island voters turned down the only convention call on the ballot.

Use of Authorized Methods

Developments in 2004 appear to be consistent with a downward trend in state constitutional activity observed in recent years. State constitutional amendments proposed or adopted in 33 states, including Delaware where constitutional amendments are not referred to the voters. By comparison, in 2002, a general election year, 35 states participated. Also, the number of amendments proposed in 2004 was 140 compared with 175 in 2002 and 98 were adopted, rather than 118. Table A contains information by which other comparisons can be made. Except for 2004, the figures refer to biennia to facilitate comparison with similar tables published in *The Book of the States* since 1968-1969.

Legislative Proposal and Constitutional Initiatives

As indicated in Table A, the legislative and constitutional initiative methods were the only ones used by the states in 2004. The legislative method, available in all states, continued to dominate the amendment process. The method accounted for over 77 percent of proposals and 82 percent of adoptions.

Table A: State Constitutional Changes by Method of Initiation: 1998–99, 2000–01, 2002–03 and 2004

Method of initiation	Number of states involved				Total proposals				Total adopted				Percentage adopted			
	1998–1999	2000–2001	2002–2003	2004	1998–1999	2000–2001	2002–2003	2004	1998 1999	2000–2001	2002–2003	2004	1998–1999	2000–2001	2002–2003	2004
All methods	46	40	38	33	296	212	232	140	229(b)	154	164	98	77.2 (a)(b)	72.0 (a)	70.6	70.0
Legislative proposal	46	38	36	30	266	180	208	109	210(b)	141	155	81	78.8 (a)(b)	91.0 (a)	74.5	74.3
Constitutional initiative	12	10	11	12	21	32	24	31	11	13	9	17	52.4	40.6	37.5	54.8
Constitutional convention	...	...	...	...	...	...	...	...	...	...	...	...	...	...	...	...
Constitutional commission	1	...	...	...	9	...	...	...	8	...	...	...	...	...	...	...

Source: Survey conducted by Janice May, University of Texas at Austin, January 2005.
Key:
. . . — Not applicable.
(a)—In calculating these percentages, the amendments adopted in Delaware (where proposals are not submitted to the voters) are excluded.
(b)—One Alabama amendment is excluded from adoptions because the election results were in dispute.

However, the constitutional initiative authorized in 18 states, proved to be more popular than usual. The number of states (12), proposals (31) and adoptions (17) were all high and the adoption rate (54.8 percent) was the highest. The boost in numbers can be attributed in large part to the six same-sex marriage initiatives, all of which passed.

Constitutional Conventions and Commissions

In every state, the constitutional convention is the traditional method to draft new constitutions or substantially revise existing ones. But no convention has convened since the Rhode Island Convention of 1986. The prospects for a convention in Rhode Island and Colorado were considered in the last volume of *The Book of the States*. In neither state was a convention approved in 2004.

Rhode Island voters rejected the referendum to call a convention at the November general election by a narrow margin (52 to 48 percent). The Rhode Island Constitution requires a vote on the issue at least every 10 years. At the same election the voters approved an amendment to reshape the constitutional distribution of powers among the three branches of government to a more traditional separation of powers structure. They had approved a nonbinding referendum in 2000 for a convention on the separation of powers issue. It is reasonable to conclude that at least some voters were satisfied with the resolution of the issue and a convention was unnecessary. The campaign focused on issues that might be considered in an unlimited convention. Those in favor supported the possibility of new reforms; those opposed were concerned about costs and undesirable changes.

In Colorado no action was taken on the convention question in the 2004 legislative session. The legislature was deeply divided over the resolution of a serious fiscal crisis and other issues and no consensus for a convention was likely in this political atmosphere. Research underway on conventions was discontinued.

In New Jersey, the prospects for a constitutional convention in the near future were improved with the passage in 2004 of legislation creating the Property Tax Convention Task Force. Property tax reform has been an issue for many years in the state and the idea of a convention has been considered as the best way to bring about needed reforms. Former Gov. James McGreevey, a strong advocate of reform, backed the convention option.

The task force was composed of 15 members, nine members appointed by the governor and the others by legislative leaders. Four were members of the New Jersey Legislature. The body was charged with "considering and developing recommendations regarding the process of conducting a constitutional convention designed to change the existing property tax system." Following an organizational session in September, nine public hearings were held to encourage public participation, among other activities. The final report was submitted on the last day of December.

The task force recommendations were numerous. They began with an emphasis on strictly limiting the convention to property tax reform. They proposed that a vote on the convention call be scheduled for the 2005 general election and at the same election non-partisan election of delegates should take place. The convention should be held as soon as possible after the election and end in July 2006. The convention's proposals were to be submitted at the 2006 general election in the form of a single comprehensive ballot measure in which separate proposals could be incorporated. The most unusual recommendation was the group's preference for convention authority over both statutory and constitutional property tax changes. To implement the recommendation, a temporary constitutional amendment to allow consideration of statutory changes would have to be proposed by the legislature for voter approval.

Creation of a task force to advise the legislature on the process of holding a convention is a fresh approach to constitutional change. Although it performed some of the services of a constitutional commission, it is not regarded as a commission, a common purpose of which is to propose substantive reforms. It is of interest that bills have been introduced in the 2005 New Jersey Legislature to carry out task force recommendations

Table A refers to constitutional commissions as a method of changing state constitutions. The only commissions included are Florida commissions which have the unique power to refer proposals directly to the voters. These commissions are created periodically and none of them were in operation in 2004. In 2004, the only constitutional commission in operation was the Utah Constitutional Revision Commission, which was established on a permanent basis in 1977 (see Table 1.5).

Substantive Changes

Substantive changes in the form of a new constitution were not on the ballot in 2004. Not since the 1980s have new constitutions been proposed or adopted. Also missing was comprehensive revision, either substantive or editorial, of an existing constitution. However, Rhode Island voters approved a substantial change by the adoption of an amendment on separation of powers. The ballot language made clear that the amendment's intent was to ensure the separation of powers among the three branches of government. To this end, four articles were amended. In general the powers of the state legislature were reduced and the governor's power enhanced, most particularly over appointments. In the absence of general revision of constitutions, it is common to propose editorial revision of some kind. In 2004 "clean-up" amendments repealing a few provisions were approved in Colorado and Nevada. Editorial revision is usually non-controversial. Somewhat of a surprise was the defeat of an Alabama amendment that would have deleted provisions on racial segregation in the public schools, prohibiting a right to education and several references to the poll tax. The change was recommended in 2003 by the Alabama Citizens' Constitution Commission. Opponents argued that it would lead to federal intervention and increased taxes. The initial vote was so close that a recount was ordered.

Table B contains information on the number of proposed and adopted state constitutional amendments by articles common to state constitutions. Except for 2004, the figures apply to biennia so that comparisons can be made to tables published in earlier volumes of *The Book of the States*. The table can serve as a rough guide to changes over a period of years in the framework of state government, including rights and elections in addition to the three branches of government and local government, and the various policies that are part of state constitutions.

Framework of Government

Proposals to prohibit same-sex marriage were the most numerous and most significant of amendments pertaining to state constitutional rights in 2004. Eleven were before the voters in the November 2 general election (Arkansas, Georgia, Kentucky, Michigan, Mississippi, Montana, North Dakota, Ohio, Oklahoma, Oregon and Utah) and two in special elections (Louisiana, Missouri). All passed by comfortable to large margins. Adding four measures adopted in previous years, Alaska, Hawaii, Nebraska and Nevada, 16 ban same-sex marriage and Hawaii reserves to the legislature the power to do so. In at least three more states (Massachusetts, Tennessee and Wisconsin) the proposal is expected to be on the ballot in 2005 or 2006. It is widely believed that a key factor in the large number of same-sex amendments in 2004 was a reaction to the ruling in 2003 by the Massachusetts Supreme Judicial Court that prohib-

iting same-sex marriages denies basic rights under the state constitution. This was a signal that only by amending the state constitution could the same-sex marriage prohibition be secure under state law.

Most of the proposals (at least five in 2004 and all four of the earlier ones) have amended the Bill of Rights (or Declaration of Rights) in state constitutions. To those who believe that denial of marriage to same-sex couples is a violation of constitutional rights, this must seem ironic. The location in the Bill or Rights might be simply a directive to the courts that gay marriage is not a right or it may be a return to an earlier view of community rights. Historically, the ban on interracial marriage was placed in the constitutions of six of the 16 states in which the ban was law.[1] In none was the provision in the state bill of rights.

Although the state constitution is the highest state law, it is still possible for a constitutional proposal to violate it. For example, soon after Louisiana voters approved the same-sex marriage amendment, it was declared unconstitutional by a Louisiana court for violating the constitution's single subject rule. The amendment not only prohibited same-sex marriage but also civil unions, two different subjects according to the court. The case is on appeal.

It is more common to argue that the marriage amendments could violate the U.S. Constitution. As reported in the 2004 edition of *The Book of the States*, this was the ruling of a federal district court in a case challenging the Nebraska ban. The court held that the bar amounted to an unconstitutional bill of attainder, among other arguments. The most likely provision of the U.S. Constitution to be relevant, however, is the "equal protection clause" of the 14th Amendment. The marriage prohibition may be in violation of the clause, but even if it is sustained, other provisions of the amendments might violate it. Nine of the laws of the state amendments do more than limit a marriage to one man and one woman (Arkansas, Georgia, Kentucky, Michigan, North Dakota, Ohio, Oklahoma and Utah). They also prohibit other unions or domestic partnerships that give benefits equivalent to marriage. In the case of *Romer v. Evans* (517 U.S. 620 [1996]), the U.S. Supreme Court ruled that persons on the basis of their sexual orientation could not be denied the same rights as others to use politic processes to pursue their political goals. The argument has been made that the nine amendments deny persons the right to use political methods to retain or add benefits of a civil union or domestic partnership without having to amend the state constitutions.

The gay marriage amendments also raise the question of recognizing such marriages from other states or jurisdictions. Whether this is a violation of the "full faith and credit clause" of Article IV of the U.S. Constitution will eventually have to be resolved by the U.S. Supreme Court. To date, the only U.S. Supreme Court action on the issue was to deny review of a U.S. Court of Appeals decision to reject a challenge to the constitutionality of the Massachusetts Supreme Judicial Court's ruling on same-sex marriage based on the "republican form of government clause" of Article IV of the U.S. Constitution.[2]

Litigation is under way in many states either to support or oppose same-sex marriage. The state constitutions and courts will continue to play an important role in its resolution.

Among the amendments of most interest to the states and nation were those proposing reform of the civil justice system, a major responsibility of the states in the federal system. The trend seems to be one of more constitutional proposals to change the system but a mixed record of success. Tort reform amendments to cap non-economic damage in medical malpractice cases, similar to the one approved in Texas in 2004 (see the last volume of *The Book of the States*) failed to pass in Oregon and Wyoming. But a third proposal to remove limits on damages in suits against construction companies failed in Colorado, the effect of which was to retain restrictions. Also defeated was a lengthy constitutional initiative measure in Nevada to punish attorneys for filing frivolous law suits. However a limit on attorney fees in medical practice cases was passed in Florida, as was a Wyoming amendment to allow the legislature

to require alternative dispute resolution or review by a medical panel before suits could be filed against health providers. Three Florida proposals, all passing, were of relevance to medical malpractice. Doctors who had committed three or more incidents of malpractice were barred from the practice of medicine in the state. The other two allowed access to medical records by patients or their families when medical error led to injury or death, and the public was entitled to information on "adverse medical incidents" caused by a health care provider or facility.

The intensity of interest in medical malpractice cases was well illustrated in Oregon by the narrow margin of defeat and also by the numerous arguments for and against printed in the Oregon Voters' Pamphlet. Proponents emphasized the need to reduce the high costs of law suits, high medical insurance rates and the loss of doctors. The opposition was concerned about the erosion of the right to a trial by jury and access to the courts and blamed insurance companies rather than the courts and lawyers for high insurance costs. Both the governor and attorney general opposed the measure.

Contributing to the large number of state constitutional amendments concerned with rights were several others in addition to same-sex marriage and tort reform. The most unique was the right to study stem cell research, adopted in California. More traditional was another California proposal, one that elevated the statutory right of public access to government information to constitutional status; it also passed. The trend toward creating a constitutional right to

Table B: Substantive Changes in State Constitutions: Proposed and Adopted: 2000–01, 2002–03 and 2004

Subject Matter	Total proposed			Total adopted			Percentage adopted		
	2000–01	2002–03	2004	2000–01	2002–03	2004	2000–01	2002–03	2004
Proposals of statewide applicability	162 (a)	191	113 (b)	114 (b)	128	81 (b)	70.3 (a)(e)	67.0	71.6 (b)(c)(f)(g)
Bill of Rights	4	12	12 (f)	1	8	12 (f)	25.0	66.6	100.0
Suffrage & elections	6	6	9	4	3	6	66.6	50.0	66.6
Legislative branch	37	24	14	27	17	6	72.9	70.8	42.8
Executive branch	9	8	4	7	4	3	77.7	50.0	75.0
Judicial branch	7 (a)	19	8	8	11	3	100.0	57.8	37.5
Local government	9	5	2	6	5	2	66.6	100.0	100.0
Finance & taxation	38	65	29	25	39	22	65.5	60.0	75.8
State & local debt	5	10	3	5	5	3	100.0	50.0	100.0
State functions	24	16	14 (b)	17	13	8(b)	70.8	81.2	57.1
Amendment & revision	3	3	1	0	3	1	0.0	100.0	100.0
General revision proposals	0	0	0	0	0	0	0.0	0.0	0.0
Miscellaneous proposals	20 (c)	23 (c)	17 (c)(g)	14	20 (c)	15 (c)(g)	70.0	86.0	88.2
Local amendments	50	41	27	40	36	17	80.0	87.8	62.9

Source: Survey conducted by Janice May, University of Texas at Austin, January 2005.
Key:
(a)—Excludes Delaware where proposals are not submitted to voters.
(b)—Includes Delaware.
(c)—Includes amendments that contain substantial editorial revision.

(d)—Excludes one Alabama amendment in a legal dispute at the time.
(e)—Excludes one Oregon amendment not canvassed by court order.
(f)—Includes a Georgia amendment adopted by voters but in litigation in 2004.
(g)—Includes a Louisiana amendment adopted by voters but in litigation in 2004.

hunt and fish continued with its adoption in two more states, Louisiana and Montana. In Hawaii, four changes in the criminal justice system were passed, among them allowing prosecutors to file charges by information. The only one to reduce rights was a Florida amendment requiring parental notification before a minor could have an abortion. The only one on this list to fail was a South Dakota amendment to extend transportation and food assistance to all school children, including those in religious schools. Also recently adopted (in 2003) was protection of free speech added to the Delaware Bill of Rights. It was inadvertently omitted from the last volume of *The Book of the States*.

The year 2004 turned out to be a significant one for proposals to change election provisions in state constitutions. Because it could conceivably affect the outcome of the current presidential election, a Colorado proposal to change the method of allocating the state's electoral votes for president and vice president was the most significant, nationally. The state's winner-take-all method would be replaced by a proportional distribution of the votes on the basis of the percentage of the popular vote received by each candidate. The new method would have applied, if passed, to the 2004 election. The amendment was soundly defeated. Had it been adopted it undoubtedly would have been challenged as a violation of Section 1 of Article II of the U.S. Constitution, which provides that electors shall be "appointed in such a manner as the Legislature thereof may direct." The Colorado measure was proposed by a constitutional initiative and was not a decision made by the state legislature.

In California the voters decided to retain the closed primary that was challenged by supporters of a modified blanket primary, one distinguishing feature of which was the possibility of two candidates from the same party for a given office to advance to the general election. Oregon voters approved an unusual provision to postpone an election if a nominee for a given office died 30 days before the election. The postponement would enable the voters to elect the replacement instead of having an appointed or a holdover officer serve. Also of importance was the adoption in New Mexico of run-off elections in large cities (over 20,000) to replace the plurality vote currently required.

Other propositions proposed changes to the initiative and referendum. With one important exception the amendments would make it more difficult to use the process by placing new restrictions. The most far-reaching of these was an Arizona amendment. An initiative measure that requires new spending must identify the source of funding, such as a tax increase or fees without drawing from the general fund. The legislature is allowed to make cuts if revenues are insufficient. Opponents argued that it would unduly interfere with the public's right to influence public policy. Supporters contended that the legislature cannot balance the budget when spending is beyond its control. Two other amendments, only one of which passed, set earlier dates for submission of petitions. Voters approved an Alaska measure to increase the number of districts and signatures required to submit a petition. The only exception to the new restrictions was the approval by Nebraska voters of an amendment to increase the effectiveness of an initiative by requiring a two-thirds vote of the legislature to change a measure adopted by the initiative process.

Amendments were proposed in 2004 to change the structure or procedures of all three branches of state government. A little over half were adopted. The Rhode Island reform of separation of powers was the most substantial of the proposals as already noted. In contrast, most of the other significant changes were rejected. Ballot measures that passed tended to fill gaps in existing provisions or clarify confusion over others.

Of the legislative amendments, attempts to change term limits by extending the number of years legislators could serve met with defeat in Arkansas and Montana. Another proposal, also rejected, would have removed the Nebraska lieutenant governor as presiding officer of the unicameral state legislature and power over ties. Although the office is one of little or no legislative power, voters are reluctant to abolish it. Virginia voters agreed to modification of reapportionment laws to avoid double or no representation of residents in certain districts. It allowed state legislators and U. S. representatives to complete their elected terms before newly drawn districts became effective. Also, to fill a gap voters approved a measure to give the Utah Legislature power to call itself into session for impeachment purposes.

Among the few executive branch ballot measures was a Colorado amendment to strengthen the governor's power of appointment over state employees, which was rejected. It would have removed 140 positions from the civil service system, which has enjoyed constitutional status since 1918. To fill a gap in procedures Virginia voters approved an amendment recommended by the governor's Make Virginia Secure Panel, a post 9/11 homeland security body. It enlarges the list of officers who can succeed to the office of governor in the event of an emergency, including a

terrorist attack, and permit the lower house to convene to elect an acting governor and, if necessary, to
waive eligibility requirements. Also passing was an
Indiana proposition to determine who is to serve as
governor when both the office of governor and lieutenant governor are vacant.

State judicial branches were changed very little
by amendment in 2004 despite efforts to do so. Voters defeated a South Dakota amendment that would
have extended merit selection of judges from the Supreme Court to the circuit courts, the second tier of
courts in the unified judicial system. In New Hampshire voters defeated for the second time an amendment to resolve a separation of powers dispute
between the legislature and the courts over authority to make rules regarding judicial administration
and procedures. A majority of voters said yes, but
two-thirds vote is required. Two ballot measures
that passed concerned the office of justice of the
peace in Arizona and magistrates (successors to the
justice of the peace) in North Carolina. One confirmed that temporary justices of the peace do not
have to be attorneys and the other set terms for the
magistrates for the first time.

Major changes in local government structure and
procedures were not the subject of amendments in
2004. The most important change for local governments related to fiscal policy.

Policy

In 2004 fiscal policy was the subject of more
amendments to state constitutions than any other
policy, the trend for many years. Although the performance of the economy improved, budget problems
in the states were common. The most serious state
budget difficulties were faced in California where
deficits have been as high as $62 billion in recent
years. In 2004 the governor and the legislature agreed
to borrow more money to resolve current short-term
problems and to allow some breathing space for a final solution. The result was a proposed bond issue of
$15 billion, the largest floated in municipal bond his-
tory. The bond issue itself, approved by the voters,
was not in the form of a constitutional amendment.
Since 1962, the state's constitution has prohibited the
inclusion of bond issues; they must be proposed to
the voters as statutes or bond acts. But a companion
constitutional amendment, said to "be joined at the
hip" to the bond issue was adopted. Called the Balanced Budget Act, it was not effective unless the bond
passed. It provided for a reserve fund for the purpose
of avoiding future budget crises and a minor change
that requires the final budget to be balanced, not just
the governor's proposed in January.

Four other California amendment proposals were relevant to the budget. Rejected by the voters was a measure to reduce the legislative vote required to pass the
budget from two-thirds to 55 percent. California is one
of only three states with a super-majority vote. Two
competing amendments, one referred to the voters by
the legislature and the other by a constitutional initiative petition, would, if passed, make substantial changes
in state-local fiscal relationships. Their relevance to
the budget is that the state government has been exercising its authority over local taxes to use some of the
revenues to pay for state costs and help reduce state
budget deficits. The amendment proposed by the legislature was adopted. One result is that the state can no
longer rely on local tax revenues to balance the budget,
except in an emergency. The fourth amendment, which
passed, dedicated revenues from the sales of state surplus property to paying interest and principal on the
$15 billion bonds issue.

Constitutional amendments relating to taxes outnumbered others on fiscal policy. No major reforms
to increase taxes comparable to the Alabama amendment defeated in 2003 were on the ballot. (See the
2004 edition of *The Book of the States* for information about the Alabama amendment.) New or increased taxes were notably absent from measures
passed to resolve the budget crisis in California. (The
vehicle license fee was reduced for a loss of $7 bil-
lion.) However, major changes in tax policy were
proposed by the aforementioned California amendments on state-local fiscal relationships. According
to the California legislative analyst, both measures
proposed a substantial reduction of state authority
over local taxes and would over time possibly increase local revenues by billions of dollars with a
corresponding loss of state revenues. All three of the
major local taxes (sales, property and vehicle license
fee) would be affected. In addition changes were
made to lessen the financial burden of state mandates
on local governments. A primary difference between
the two constitutional proposals was that the initiative version, which was rejected, required a statewide vote before the legislature could approve certain local tax changes.

The few constitutional tax increases on the ballot
were limited to specific purposes: in Colorado, higher
taxes on cigarettes and tobacco products to improve
public health; in West Virginia legislative authorization to impose or raise taxes to finance bonds to pay
for bonuses and death benefits to veterans of recent
conflicts; and in California, a surcharge on monthly
telephone bills to help pay for emergency health care.
The California amendment was the only one to be
rejected. Although not a tax increase, Missouri vot-

ers approved a significant dedication of motor fuels tax to highways and roads.

As usual, the property tax measures were the most popular and numerous and invariably reduced rather than raised taxes. All eight on the ballot were approved. Veterans were given exemptions of one kind or another in New Mexico and Oklahoma.

Also congruent with past trends was the approval of bonds authorized by constitutional amendment. In the four states with such amendments all were approved, three were for economic development and one for veteran benefits. Another continuation of past developments was the approval of funds to support specific projects or programs. In 2004, they included noxious weed eradication, a trust fund for lotteries, and promotion of seafood products (all passed).

Gambling enterprises and lotteries are often put forward as alternatives to taxes or as a source of new tax revenue. It seems appropriate to consider them as a component of fiscal policy although other issues are relevant. Nine propositions in six states (California, Florida, Michigan, Missouri, Nebraska and Oklahoma) were on the 2004 ballot, possibly a record number. The two lottery amendments (Nebraska and Oklahoma) were adopted and two of the gambling measures (Florida and Michigan). Oklahoma became the 42nd state to approve a state lottery. Although the lottery itself was adopted as a statute, a companion Lottery Trust Fund was created by constitutional amendment. In common with lotteries in many other states, the revenues are dedicated to education.

All state constitutions contain provisions on public education, a primary responsibility of the states in the federal system. Education provisions are frequently amended, but in 2004 no major reforms were on the ballots. A number of amendments already reviewed contributed to the funding of education, such as the previously mentioned Oklahoma Lottery. North Carolina added proceeds from civil penalties. In response to budgetary difficulties last year, voters gave the first approval to a Nevada proposition to consider education first in the appropriations process. (See the 2004 edition of *The Book of the States* for more information.) But raising school expenditures to the national average failed. Among other proposals already reviewed was the South Dakota measure to provide transportation and food assistance to private schools. Amendments to the Arizona and Utah constitutions would permit intellectual property developed by state universities to be transferred or exchanged for stock in private companies. Only the Utah version passed.

Of the many other policy amendments, the most unusual and significant was the California measure to promote stem cell research. It would establish one of the world's largest stem cell research programs as already noted. A new medical institution would be created. Financing would be provided by the sale of bonds. Projected annual expenditures would exceed current federal government spending on stem cell research and research on human reproductive cloning would be prohibited.

Among other policy amendments were: adoption of a minimum wage in Florida and the first of two approvals in Nevada; repeal of a Florida amendment authorizing a high-speed railroad; approval of a change in alcohol regulation in South Carolina whose constitution contains a separate article on alcohol regulation; repeal of an obsolete Delaware provision on types of consideration received by corporations for stock issues; and defeat of a Arizona amendment to exchange state trust land for federal land to protect open space and help military bases. This was the fifth defeat for a land exchange measure in that state.

Research Note

The Center for State Constitutional Studies at Rutgers University, Camden, continues to provide current information on state constitutions and support research activities and conferences. In 2004 the Center published a series of background papers for the New Jersey Property Tax Convention Task Force. The papers are posted on the Center's Web site, www.camlaw.rutgers.edu/statecon.

Notes

[1]*Loving v. Virginia,* 338 U.S. 1 (1967) p. 6 N. 3
[2]*Largess v. Massachusetts Supreme Court.* U.S. Supreme Court. Case No. 04-420. 73 U.S.L.W. 3318 (Nov. 30, 2004).

References

"Annual Issue on State Constitutional Law." *Rutgers Law Journal.* 20 (Summer 1989) to 34 (Summer 2003).
The Report of the Property Tax Convention Task Force to the Governor and Legislature. A Plan to Hold a Property Tax Convention. Finding a Fairer System. The State of New Jersey. December 31, 2004.
"State Constitutional Commentary." *Albany Law Review.* 67 (2004) 637. (Annual Issue since 1996)
"Symposium on Tomorrow's Issues in State Constitutional Law." *Valparaiso University Law Review.* 38 (Spring 2004) 317.

About the Author

Janice C. May is professor emeritus of government at the University of Texas at Austin, where she specializes in state government and politics. A regular contributor to *The Book of the States*, she is the author of numerous publications on the Texas Constitution and government, including *The Texas State Constitution: A Reference Guide*, and on state constitutional development nationwide. She has served on two Texas constitutional commissions and on the board of directors of the Texas State Bar.

Table 1.1
GENERAL INFORMATION ON STATE CONSTITUTIONS
(As of January 1, 2005)

State or other jurisdiction	Number of constitutions*	Dates of adoption	Effective date of present constitution	Estimated length (number of words)	Number of amendments Submitted to voters	Adopted
Alabama	6	1819, 1861, 1865, 1868, 1875, 1901	Nov. 28, 1901	340,136 (a)(b)(c)	1,063	766
Alaska	1	1956	Jan. 3, 1959	15,988 (b)	41	29
Arizona	1	1911	Feb. 14, 1912	28,876	246	136
Arkansas	5	1836, 1861, 1864, 1868, 1874	Oct. 30, 1874	59,500 (b)	189	91 (d)
California	2	1849, 1879	July 4, 1879	54,645	860	513
Colorado	1	1876	Aug. 1, 1876	74,522 (b)	304	145
Connecticut	4	1818 (f), 1965	Dec. 30, 1965	17,256 (b)	30	29
Delaware	4	1776, 1792, 1831, 1897	June 10, 1897	19,000	(e)	138
Florida	6	1839, 1861, 1865, 1868, 1886, 1968	Jan. 7, 1969	51,456 (b)	135	104
Georgia	10	1777, 1789, 1798, 1861, 1865, 1868, 1877, 1945, 1976, 1982	July 1,1983	39,526 (b)	83 (g)	63 (g)
Hawaii	1 (h)	1950	Aug. 21, 1959	20,774 (b)	123	104
Idaho	1	1889	July 3, 1890	24,232 (b)	204	117
Illinois	4	1818, 1848, 1870, 1970	July 1, 1971	16,510 (b)	17	11
Indiana	2	1816, 1851	Nov. 1, 1851	10,379 (b)	78	46
Iowa	2	1846, 1857	Sept. 3, 1857	12,616 (b)	57	52 (i)
Kansas	1	1859	Jan. 29, 1861	12,296(b)	122	92 (i)
Kentucky	4	1792, 1799, 1850, 1891	Sept. 28, 1891	23,911 (b)	75	41
Louisiana	11	1812, 1845, 1852, 1861, 1864, 1868, 1879, 1898, 1913, 1921, 1974	Jan. 1, 1975	54,112 (b)	189	129
Maine	1	1819	March 15, 1820	16,276 (b)	201	169 (j)
Maryland	4	1776, 1851, 1864, 1867	Oct. 5, 1867	46,600 (b)	254	218 (k)
Massachusetts	1	1780	Oct. 25, 1780	36,700 (l)	148	120
Michigan	4	1835, 1850, 1908, 1963	Jan. 1, 1964	34,659 (b)	63	25
Minnesota	1	1857	May 11, 1858	11,547 (b)	213	118
Mississippi	4	1817, 1832, 1869, 1890	Nov. 1, 1890	24,323 (b)	158	123
Missouri	4	1820, 1865, 1875, 1945	March 30,1945	42,600 (b)	165	105
Montana	2	1889, 1972	July 1, 1973	13,145 (b)	53	30
Nebraska	2	1866, 1875	Oct. 12, 1875	20,048	336 (m)	222 (m)
Nevada	1	1864	Oct. 31, 1864	31,377 (b)	220	132
New Hampshire	2	1776, 1784	June 2, 1784	9,200	285 (n)	143
New Jersey	3	1776, 1844, 1947	Jan. 1, 1948	22,956 (b)	69	36
New Mexico	1	1911	Jan. 6, 1912	27,200	280	151
New York	4	1777, 1822, 1846, 1894	Jan. 1, 1895	51,700	290	216
North Carolina	3	1776, 1868, 1970	July 1, 1971	16,532 (b)	42	34
North Dakota	1	1889	Nov. 2, 1889	19,130 (b)	258	145 (o)
Ohio	2	1802, 1851	Sept. 1, 1851	48,521 (b)	267	161
Oklahoma	1	1907	Nov. 16, 1907	74,075 (b)	335 (p)	171 (p)
Oregon	1	1857	Feb. 14, 1859	54,083 (b)	473 (q)	238 (q)
Pennsylvania	5	1776, 1790, 1838, 1873, 1968 (r)	1968 (r)	27,711 (b)	36(r)	30 (r)
Rhode Island	3	1842 (f) 1986 (s)	Dec. 4, 1986	10,908 (b)	8 (s)	8 (s)
South Carolina	7	1776, 1778, 1790, 1861, 1865, 1868, 1895	Jan. 1, 1896	22,300	672 (t)	485 (t)
South Dakota	1	1889	Nov. 2, 1889	27,675 (b)	219	212
Tennessee	3	1796, 1835, 1870	Feb. 23, 1870	13,300	59	36
Texas	5 (u)	1845, 1861, 1866, 1869, 1876	Feb. 15, 1876	90,000	605 (v)	432
Utah	1	1895	Jan. 4, 1896	11,000	157	106
Vermont	3	1777, 1786, 1793	July 9, 1793	10,286 (b)	211	53
Virginia	6	1776, 1830, 1851, 1869, 1902, 1970	July 1, 1971	21,319 (b)	48	40
Washington	1	1889	Nov. 11, 1889	33,564 (b)	168	95
West Virginia	2	1863, 1872	April 9, 1872	26,000	120	71
Wisconsin	1	1848	May 29, 1848	14,392 (b)	181	133 (i)
Wyoming	1	1889	July 10, 1890	31,800	120	94
American Samoa	2	1960, 1967	July 1, 1967	6,000	14	7
No. Mariana Islands	1	1977	Jan. 9, 1978	11,000	55	51 (w)(x)
Puerto Rico	1	1952	July 25, 1952	9,281	6	6

See footnotes at end of table.

GENERAL INFORMATION ON STATE CONSTITUTIONS — Continued

Source: Janice May, The University of Texas at Austin and The Council of State Governments, January 2005. The constitutions referred to in this table include those Civil War documents customarily listed by the individual states.

(a) The Alabama constitution includes numerous local amendments that apply to only one county. An estimated 70 percent of all amendments are local. A 1982 amendment provides that after proposal by the legislature to which special procedures apply, only a local vote (with exceptions) is necessary to add them to the constitution.

(b) Computer word count.

(c) The total number of Alabama amendments includes one that is commonly overlooked.

(d) Eight of the approved amendments have been superseded and are not printed in the current edition of the constitution. The total adopted does not include five amendments proposed and adopted since statehood.

(e) Proposed amendments are not submitted to the voters in Delaware.

(f) Colonial charters with some alterations served as the first constitutions in Connecticut (1638, 1662) and in Rhode Island (1663).

(g) The Georgia constitution requires amendments to be of general and uniform application throughout the state, thus eliminating local amendments that accounted for most of the amendments before 1982.

(h) As a kingdom and republic, Hawaii had five constitutions.

(i) The figure includes amendments approved by the voters and later nullified by the state supreme court in Iowa (three), Kansas (one), Nevada (six) and Wisconsin (two).

(j) The figure does not include one amendment approved by the voters in 1967 that is inoperative until implemented by legislation.

(k) Two sets of identical amendments were on the ballot and adopted in the 1992 Maryland election. The four amendments are counted as two in the table.

(l) The printed constitution includes many provisions that have been annulled. The length of effective provisions is an estimated 24,122 words (12,400 annulled in Massachusetts, and in Rhode Island before the rewrite of the con-

stitution in 1986, it was 11,399 words (7,627 annulled).

(m) The 1998 and 2000 Nebraska ballots allowed the voters to vote separately on parts of propositions. In 1998, 10 of 18 separate propositions were adopted; in 2000, 6 of 9.

(n) The constitution of 1784 was extensively revised in 1792. Figure shows proposals and adoptions since the constitution was adopted in 1784.

(o) The figures do not include submission and approval of the constitution of 1889 itself and of Article XX; these are constitutional questions included in some counts of constitutional amendments and would add two to the figure in each column.

(p) The figures include five amendments submitted to and approved by the voters which were, by decisions of the Oklahoma or U.S. Supreme Courts, rendered inoperative or ruled invalid, unconstitutional, or illegally submitted.

(q) One Oregon amendment on the 2000 ballot was not counted as approved because canvassing was enjoined by the courts.

(r) Certain sections of the constitution were revised by the limited convention of 1967–68. Amendments proposed and adopted are since 1968.

(s) Following approval of the eight amendments and a rewrite of the Rhode Island Constitution in 1986, the constitution has been called the 1986 Constitution. Amendments since 1986 total eight proposed and eight adopted. Otherwise, the total is 106 proposals and 60 adopted.

(t) In 1981 approximately two-thirds of 626 proposed and four-fifths of the adopted amendments were local. Since then the amendments have been statewide propositions.

(u) The Constitution of the Republic of Texas preceded five state constitutions.

(v) The number of proposed amendments to the Texas Constitution excludes three proposed by the legislature but not placed on the ballot.

(w) By 1992, 49 amendments had been proposed and 47 adopted. Since then, one was proposed but rejected in 1994, all three proposals were ratified in 1996 and in 1998, of two proposals one was adopted.

(x) The total excludes one amendment ruled void by a federal district court.

Table 1.2
CONSTITUTIONAL AMENDMENT PROCEDURE: BY THE LEGISLATURE
Constitutional Provisions

State or other jurisdiction	Legislative vote required for proposal (a)	Consideration by two sessions required	Vote required for ratification	Limitation on the number of amendments submitted at one election
Alabama	3/5	No	Majority vote on amendment	None
Alaska	2/3	No	Majority vote on amendment	None
Arizona	Majority	No	Majority vote on amendment	None
Arkansas	Majority	No	Majority vote on amendment	3
California	2/3	No	Majority vote on amendment	None
Colorado	2/3	No	Majority vote on amendment	None (b)
Connecticut	(c)	(c)	Majority vote on amendment	None
Delaware	2/3	Yes	Not required	No referendum
Florida	3/5	No	Majority vote on amendment (d)	None
Georgia	2/3	No	Majority vote on amendment	None
Hawaii	(e)	(e)	Majority vote on amendment (f)	None
Idaho	2/3	No	Majority vote on amendment	None
Illinois	3/5	No	(g)	3 articles
Indiana	Majority	Yes	Majority vote on amendment	None
Iowa	Majority	Yes	Majority vote on amendment	None
Kansas	2/3	No	Majority vote on amendment	5
Kentucky	3/5	No	Majority vote on amendment	4
Louisiana	2/3	No	Majority vote on amendment (h)	None
Maine	2/3 (i)	No	Majority vote on amendment	None
Maryland	3/5	No	Majority vote on amendment	None
Massachusetts	Majority (j)	Yes	Majority vote on amendment	None
Michigan	2/3	No	Majority vote on amendment	None
Minnesota	Majority	No	Majority vote in election	None
Mississippi	2/3 (k)	No	Majority vote on amendment	None
Missouri	Majority	No	Majority vote on amendment	None
Montana	2/3 (i)	No	Majority vote on amendment	None
Nebraska	3/5	No	Majority vote on amendment (f)	None
Nevada	Majority	Yes	Majority vote on amendment	None
New Hampshire	3/5	No	2/3 vote on amendment	None
New Jersey	(l)	(l)	Majority vote on amendment	None (m)
New Mexico	Majority (n)	No	Majority vote on amendment (n)	None
New York	Majority	Yes	Majority vote on amendment	None
North Carolina	3/5	No	Majority vote on amendment	None
North Dakota	Majority	No	Majority vote on amendment	None
Ohio	3/5	No	Majority vote on amendment	None
Oklahoma	Majority	No	Majority vote on amendment	None
Oregon	(o)	No	Majority vote on amendment (p)	None
Pennsylvania	Majority (p)	Yes (p)	Majority vote on amendment	None
Rhode Island	Majority	No	Majority vote on amendment	None
South Carolina	2/3 (q)	Yes (q)	Majority vote on amendment	None
South Dakota	Majority	No	Majority vote on amendment	None
Tennessee	(r)	Yes (r)	Majority vote in election (s)	None
Texas	2/3	No	Majority vote on amendment	None
Utah	2/3	No	Majority vote on amendment	None
Vermont	(t)	Yes	Majority vote on amendment	None
Virginia	Majority	Yes	Majority vote on amendment	None
Washington	2/3	No	Majority vote on amendment	None
West Virginia	2/3	No	Majority vote on amendment	None
Wisconsin	Majority	Yes	Majority vote on amendment	None
Wyoming	2/3	No	Majority vote in election	None
American Samoa	2/3	No	Majority vote on amendment (u)	None
No. Mariana Islands	3/4	No	Majority vote on amendment	None
Puerto Rico	2/3 (v)	No	Majority vote on amendment	3

See footnotes at end of table.

CONSTITUTIONAL AMENDMENT PROCEDURE: BY THE LEGISLATURE — Continued

Source: Survey conducted by Janice May, University of Texas at Austin and The Council of State Governments, January 2005.

Key:

(a) In all states not otherwise noted, the figure shown in the column refers to the proportion of elected members in each house required for appro val of proposed constitutional amendments.

(b) Legislature may not propose amendments to more than six articles of the constitution in the same legislative session.

(c) Three-fourths vote in each house at one session, or majority vote in each house in two sessions between which an election has intervened.

(d) Majority vote on amendment except amendment for new state tax or fee not in effect on Nov. 7, 1994 requires two-thirds of voters in the election.

(e) Two-thirds vote in each house at one session, or majority vote in each house in two sessions.

(f) Majority vote on amendment must be at least 50 percent of the total votes cast at the election (at least 35 percent in Nebraska); or, at a special election, a majority of the votes tallied which must be at least 30 percent of the total number of registered voters.

(g) Majority voting in election or three-fifths voting on amendment.

(h) If five or fewer political subdivisions of the state are affected, majority in state as a whole and also in affected subdivisions) is required.

(i) Two-thirds of both houses.

(j) Majority of members elected sitting in joint session.

(k) The two-thirds must include not less than a majority elected to each house.

(l) Three-fifths of all members of each house at one session, or majority of all members of each house for two successive sessions.

(m) If a proposed amendment is not approved at the election when submit-ted, neither the same amendment nor one which would make substantially the same change for the constitution may be again submitted to the people before the third general election thereafter.

(n) Amendments concerning certain elective franchise and education mat-ters require three-fourths vote of members elected and approval by three-fourths off electors voting in state and two-thirds of those voting in each county.

(o) Majority vote to amend constitution, two-thirds to revise (revise in-cludes all or a part of the constitution).

(p) Emergency amendments may be passed by two-thirds vote of each house, followed by ratification by majority vote of electors in election held at least one month after legislative approval. There is an exception for an amend-ment containing a supermajority voting requirement, which must be ratified by an equal supermajority.

(q) Two-thirds of members of each house, first passage; majority of mem-bers of each house after popular ratification.

(r) Majority of members elected to both houses, first passage; two-thirds of members elected to both houses, second passage.

(s) Majority of all citizens voting for governor.

(t) Two-thirds vote senate, majority vote house, first passage; majority both houses, second passage. As of 1974, amendments may be submitted only ev-ery four years.

(u) Within 30 days after voter approval, governor must submit amendment(s) to U.S. Secretary of the Interior for approval.

(v) If approved by two-thirds of members of each house, amendment(s) submitted to voters at special referendum; if approved by not less than three-fourths of total members of each house, referendum may be held at next gen-eral election.

Table 1.3
CONSTITUTIONAL AMENDMENT PROCEDURE: BY INITIATIVE
Constitutional Provisions

State or other jurisdiction	Number of signatures required on initiative petition	Distribution of signatures	Referendum vote
Arizona	15% of total votes cast for all candidates for governor at last election.	None specified.	Majority vote on amendment.
Arkansas	10% of voters for governor at last election.	Must include 5% of voters for governor in each of 15 counties.	Majority vote on amendment.
California	8% of total voters for all candidates for governor at last election.	None specified.	Majority vote on amendment.
Colorado	5% of total legal votes for all candidates for secretary of state at last general election.	None specified.	Majority vote on amendment.
Florida	8% of total votes cast in the state in the last election for presidential electors.	8% of total votes cast in each of 1/2 of the congressional districts.	Majority vote on amendment except amendment for new state tax or fee not in effect Nov. 7, 1994 requires 2/3 of voters voting in election.
Illinois (a)	8% of total votes cast for candidates for governor at last election.	None specified. 3/5 voting on amendment.	Majority voting in election or
Massachusetts (b)	3% of total votes cast for governor at preceding biennial state election (not less than 25,000 qualified voters).	No more than 1/4 from any one county.	Majority vote on amendment which must be 30% of total ballots cast at election.
Michigan	10% of total voters for all candidates at last gubernatorial election.	None specified.	Majority vote on amendment.
Mississippi	12% of total votes for all candidates for governor in last election.	No more than 20% from any one congressional district.	Majority vote on amendment and not less than 40% of total vote cast at election.
Missouri	8% of legal voters for all candidates for governor at last election.	The 8% must be in each of 2/3 of the congressional districts in the state.	Majority vote on amendment.
Montana	10% of qualified electors, the number of qualified voters to be determined by number of votes cast for governor in preceding election in each county and in the state.	The 10% to include at least 10% of qualified voters in one-half of the counties.	Majority vote on amendment.
Nebraska	10% of total votes for governor at last election.	The 10% must include 5% in each of 2/5 of the counties.	Majority vote on amendment which must be at least 35% of total vote at the election.
Nevada	10% of voters who voted in entire state in last general election.	10% of total voters who voted in each of 75% of the counties.	Majority vote on amendment in two consecutive general elections.
North Dakota	4% of population of the state.	None specified.	Majority vote on amendment.
Ohio	10% of total number of electors who voted for governor in last election.	At least 5% of qualified electors in each of 1/2 of counties in the state.	Majority vote on amendment.
Oklahoma	15% of legal voters for state office receiving highest number of voters at last general state election.	None specified.	Majority vote on amendment.
Oregon	8% of total votes for all candidates for governor at last election at which governor was elected for four-year term.	None specified.	Majority vote on amendment except for supermajority equal to supermajority voting require-ment contained in proposed amendment.
South Dakota	10% of total votes for governor in last election.	None specified.	Majority vote on amendment.
No. Mariana Islands	50% of qualified voters of commonwealth.	In addition, 25% of qualified voters in each senatorial district.	Majority vote on amendment if legislature approved it by majority vote; if not, at least 2/3 vote in each of two senatorial districts in addition to a majority vote.

Source: Survey conducted by Janice May, University of Texas at Austin and The Council of State Governments, January 2005.
Key:
(a) Only Article IV, the Legislature, may be amended by initiative petition.

(b) Before being submitted to the electorate for ratification, initiative mea-sures must be approved at two sessions of a successively elected legislature by not less than one-fourth of all members elected, sitting in joint session.

Table 1.4
PROCEDURES FOR CALLING CONSTITUTIONAL CONVENTIONS
Constitutional Provisions

State or other jurisdiction	Provision for convention	Legislative vote for submission of convention question (a)	Popular vote to authorize convention	Periodic submission of convention question required (b)	Popular vote required for ratification of convention proposals
Alabama	Yes	Majority	ME	No	Not specified
Alaska	Yes	No provision (c)(d)	(c)	10 years (c)	Not specified (c)
Arizona	Yes	Majority	(e)	No	MP
Arkansas	No	No			
California	Yes	2/3	MP	No	MP
Colorado	Yes	2/3	MP	No	ME
Connecticut	Yes	2/3	MP	20 years (f)	MP
Delaware	Yes	2/3	MP	No	No provision
Florida	Yes	(g)	MP	No	Not specified
Georgia	Yes	(d)	No	No	MP
Hawaii	Yes	Not specified	MP	9 years	MP (h)
Idaho	Yes	2/3	MP	No	Not specified
Illinois	Yes	3/4	(i)	20 years; 1988	MP
Indiana	No	No			
Iowa	Yes	Majority	MP	10 years; 1970	MP
Kansas	Yes	2/3	MP	No	MP
Kentucky	Yes	Majority (j)	MP (k)	No	No provision
Louisiana	Yes	(d)	No	No	MP
Maine	Yes	(d)	No	No	No provision
Maryland	Yes	Majority	ME	20 years; 1970	MP
Massachusetts	No		No	Not specified	
Michigan	Yes	Majority	MP	16 years; 1978	MP
Minnesota	Yes	2/3	ME	No	3/5 voting on proposal
Mississippi	No	No			
Missouri	Yes	Majority	MP	20 years; 1962	Not specified (l)
Montana	Yes (m)	2/3	MP	20 years	MP
Nebraska	Yes	3/4	MP (o)	No	MP
Nevada	Yes	2/3	ME	No	No provision
New Hampshire	Yes	Majority	MP	10 years	2/3 voting on proposal
New Jersey	No	No			
New Mexico	Yes	2/3	MP	No	Not specified
New York	Yes	Majority	MP	20 years; 1957	MP
North Carolina	Yes	2/3	MP	No	MP
North Dakota	No	No			
Ohio	Yes	2/3	MP	20 years; 1932	MP
Oklahoma	Yes	Majority	(e)	20 years	MP
Oregon	Yes	Majority	(e)	No	No provision
Pennsylvania	No	No			
Rhode Island	Yes	Majority	MP	10 years	MP
South Carolina	Yes	(d)	ME	No	No provision
South Dakota	Yes	(d)	(d)	No	(p)
Tennessee	Yes (q)	Majority	MP	No	MP
Texas	No	No			
Utah	Yes	2/3	ME	No	MP
Vermont	No	No			
Virginia	Yes	(d)	No	No	MP
Washington	Yes	2/3	ME	No	Not specified
West Virginia	Yes	Majority	MP	No	Not specified
Wisconsin	Yes	Majority	MP	No	No provision
Wyoming	Yes	2/3	ME	No	Not specified
American Samoa	Yes	(r)	No	No	ME (s)
No. Mariana Islands	Yes	Majority (t)	2/3	No (u)	MP and at least 2/3 in each of 2 senatorial districts
Puerto Rico	Yes	2/3	MP	No	MP

See footnotes at end of table.

PROCEDURES FOR CALLING CONSTITUTIONAL CONVENTIONS — Continued

Source: Survey conducted by Janice May, University of Texas at Austin and The Council of State Governments, January 2005.

Key:

MP—Majority voting on the proposal.

ME—Majority voting in the election.

(a) In all states not otherwise noted, the entries in this column refer to the proportion of members elected to each house required to submit to the electorate the question of calling a constitutional convention.

(b) The number listed is the interval between required submissions on the question of calling a constitutional convention; where given, the date is that of the first required submission of the convention question.

(c) Unless provided otherwise by law, convention calls are to conform as nearly as possible to the act calling the 1955 convention, which provided for a legislative vote of a majority of members elected to each house and ratification by a majority vote on the proposals. The legislature may call a constitutional convention at any time.

(d) In these states, the legislature may call a convention without submitting the question to the people. The legislative vote required is two-thirds of the members elected to each house in Georgia, Louisiana, South Carolina and Virginia; two-thirds concurrent vote of both branches in Maine; three-fourths of all members of each house in South Dakota; and not specified in Alaska, but bills require majority vote of membership in each house. In South Dakota, the question of calling a convention may be initiated by the people in the same manner as an amendment to the constitution (see Table 1.3) and requires a majority vote on the question for approval.

(e) The law calling a convention must be approved by the people.

(f) The legislature shall submit the question 20 years after the last convention, or 20 years after the last vote on the question of calling a convention, whichever date is last.

(g) The power to call a convention is reserved to the people by petition.

(h) The majority must be 50 percent of the total voted cast at a general election or at a special election, a majority of the votes tallied which must be at least 30 percent of the total number of registered voters.

(i) Majority voting in the election, or three-fifths voting on the question.

(j) Must be approved during two legislative sessions.

(k) Majority must equal one-fourth of qualified voters at last general election.

(l) Majority of those voting on the proposal is assumed.

(m) The question of calling a constitutional convention may be submitted either by the legislature or by initiative petition to the secretary of state in the same manner as provided for initiated amendments (see Table 1.3).

(n) Two-thirds of all members of the legislature.

(o) Majority must be 35 percent of total votes cast at the election.

(p) Convention proposals are submitted to the electorate at a special election in a manner to be determined by the convention. Ratification by a majority of votes cast.

(q) Conventions may not be held more often than once in six years.

(r) Five years after effective date of constitutions, governor shall call a constitutional convention to consider changes proposed by a constitutional committee appointed by the governor. Delegates to the convention are to be elected by their county councils. A convention was held in 1972.

(s) If proposed amendments are approved by the voters, they must be submitted to the U.S. Secretary of the Interior for approval.

(t) The initiative may also be used to place a referendum convention call on the ballot. The petition must be signed by 25 percent of the qualified voters or at least 75 percent in a senatorial district.

(u) The legislature was required to submit the referendum no later than seven years after the effective date of the constitution. The convention was held in 1985; 45 amendments were submitted to the voters.

Table 1.5
STATE CONSTITUTIONAL COMMISSIONS
(Operative during January 1, 2004 to January 1, 2005)

State	Name of commission	Method and date of creation and period of operation	Membership: number and type	Funding	Purpose of commission	Proposals and action
Utah	Utah Constitutional Revision Commission	Statutory: Ch. 89, *Laws of Utah*, 1969; amended by Ch. 107, Laws 1977, which made the commission permanent as of July 1 1977. (Codified as Ch. 54, Title 63, *Utah Code Annotated*, 1953.)	16: 1 ex officio, 9 appointed—by the speaker of the House (3), president of the Senate (3), and governor (3)—no more than 2 of each group to be from same party; and 6 additional members appointed by the 9 previously appointed members.	Appropriations through 1995 totaled $1,023,000. In recent years, annual appropriations have been $55,000. Currently, no funding for independent office or printed annual reports.	Study constitution and recommend desirable changes including proposed drafts.	Mandated to report recommendations at least 60 days before legislature convenes. Voter action on commission recommendations through 2000 include: approval of revised articles on legislature, executive, judiciary, elections and rights of suffrage, revenue and taxation, education, and corporations. At 2000 election voters approved an amendment to revise state and local government provisions recommended by the commission and referred by the legislature. Commission unanimously approved revision of impeachment provisions, approved by voters in 2004. Following completion of the study of the Revenue and Taxation article, the voters approved the revision in 2002.

Source: Janice May, University of Texas at Austin, January 2005.
Note: No constitutional conventions were held from January 1, 2000 through January 1, 2005.

Table 1.6
STATE CONSTITUTIONAL CHANGES BY CONSTITUTIONAL INITIATIVE: 2004

State	Number of proposals	Number of adoptions	Percentage adopted
Arizona	0	0	0.0%
Arkansas	1	1	100.0
California	7	1	14.3
Colorado	3	1	33.3
Florida	6	6	100.0
Illinois	0	0	0.0
Massachusetts	0	0	0.0
Michigan	2	2	100.0
Mississippi	0	0	0.0
Missouri	2	1	50.0
Montana	1	1	100.0
Nebraska	2	1	50.0
Nevada	3 (a)	0 (a)	0.0
North Dakota	1	1	100.0
Ohio	1	1	100.0
Oklahoma	0	0	0.0
Oregon	2	1	50.0
South Dakota	0	0	0.0
Total	31	17	54.8

Source: Janice May, University of Texas at Austin, January 2005.

(a) Five initiative proposals were on the ballot in 2004. Three were rejected and have been included in the table because action was final. Two were adopted in the first of two sucessive elections required for final adoption. They have been excluded from the table.

Chapter Two

FEDERALISM AND INTERGOVERNMENTAL RELATIONS

The New Politics of Federalism
By Paul E. Peterson

The maturation of the welfare state has altered partisan political and policy interests. Republicans are rediscovering the virtues of national power once celebrated by Alexander Hamilton, while Democrats are returning to their Jeffersonian roots.

Federalism is usually treated as a philosophical question. For the writers of *The Federalist Papers*—Alexander Hamilton, James Madison and John Jay—power was best divided between central and lower tiers of government so as to check each from threatening the liberties of individuals. But, in practice, political and economic interests often dictate the positions that are taken. Even the two principal writers of *The Federalist Papers,* Hamilton and Madison, entered into intense, bitter conflicts over the appropriate meaning of the U. S. Constitution. Hamilton, a New Yorker appreciative of the wealth passing through that rapidly growing port city, wanted a strong central state in order to promote commerce and international trade. Madison, together with his fellow Virginian, Thomas Jefferson, worried more about defending southern agrarian interests against northern speculators.

Jefferson is recognized as the spiritual father of the Democratic Party, while Hamilton is at times given comparable status among Republicans. But as political interests changed, so did the positions of the two political parties. Throughout most of the 20th century, it was the New Deal Democrats who celebrated an expansion of the national government in ways Hamilton might have blessed, while conservative Republicans defended states rights that Jefferson had extolled.

Today, the parties are returning to their historic roots. In the spring of 2005, the Republican leadership in Congress asked federal courts to assure jurisdiction in the Schiavo case, which raised issues long thought to be the preserve of state courts. Most Democrats opposed the move. Only weeks earlier, the Republican majority in Congress, at the behest of the president, had passed sweeping legislation that shifted class action suits that transcended state boundaries from state to federal courts, a nationalizing move that harkens back to the days of Hamilton and his close ally, Chief Justice John Marshall. Meanwhile, the vast majority of congressional Democrats fiercely defended the prerogatives of state trial courts—notwithstanding the party's deep-rooted preference of federal over state courts during the Great Society years.

Political and economic interests are dictating these changes in party position. Corporate interests closely associated with the Republican Party have long complained about venue-shopping by trial lawyers for courts in which plaintiffs can win large legal settlements. Meanwhile, those same trial lawyers have been one of the key financial pillars of the Democratic Party.

The changing partisan views of federalism are not limited to class action suits. Rather, they are rooted in broader societal changes, most importantly, the maturation of the welfare state. When the welfare state was in its expansive phase, Democrats supported national power as the agent of change. Through federal action, Social Security benefits increased, Medicare and Medicaid were adopted, welfare eligibility was expanded, school funding increased, and the federal government passed money to states and localities through a system of categorical and block grants.

Once the welfare state became as much of a burden as a blessing, politics began to change. With the election of Ronald Reagan, the politics of the welfare state shifted from growth to retrenchment. The age of retirement was lifted, some social security benefits were cut or eliminated, welfare was reformed, school reform was initiated, and new entitlements became impossible to enact. Reform no longer meant finding new ways to serve the putatively needy but rather testing ideas for making more effective use of tax dollars.

Political Trends

These changes were reinforced by political developments, both nationally and locally. It is too simple to say that parties like that level of government they happen to control at any specific moment. But if a party has little opportunity to win a particular bastion of power, they are unlikely to appreciate its virtues. When Republicans found themselves unable to capture undivided control of Congress for any more than four years out of over 60 between 1933 and 1968 and when control of the executive branch was in the hands of Democrats for all but eight of these same years, Republicans had few partisan incentives to support the expansion of federal power. For Democrats, the shoe was altogether on the other foot.

But as the South became solidly Republican instead of solidly Democratic, Republicans only had to approach parity elsewhere to capture national power, giving them an advantage in presidential and congressional elections. After decades in the wilderness, the Republicans now enjoy the opportunity to exercise unified power over the central government in the same way the Democrats once did. For the winners, it is hard not to become more interested in federal power; for the losers, it's easy to rediscover the value of state and local control.

Although change at the state and local level has been more gradual, the transformation has been no less dramatic. Traditionally, governments within the United States served conservative interests, such as banks, commercial firms, and manufacturing companies. Each community had to become an attractive place for business—low taxes, minimal regulations—or lose out to competing cities and towns with more supportive policies. Within state legislatures, agrarian interests were given preference over urban ones, in part because many state legislatures overrepresented voters in rural areas. Voting laws restricted access to the ballot of African Americans and other disadvantaged interests, especially in the South. State judges, key to court house rings, were usually beholden to conservative interests.

Beginning in the 1960s, a series of political and economic changes began to undermine the conservative bias of the lower tiers of the federalism system. In 1961, the Supreme Court required states to reapportion their state legislatures so that all representatives—in both the upper and lower chambers—would represent roughly equal numbers of residents. The 1966 voting rights legislation gave minority voters access to Southern politics, forcing candidates to find more balanced platforms upon which to campaign. An increasingly liberal Democratic party won sweeping majorities in many states, allowing them to elect and appoint state judges friendly to more liberal causes.

Economic forces were undermining business influence at the local level as well. With the globalization of the economy, and the amalgamation of firms into international corporations, corporate headquarters disappeared from middle-sized cities, leaving them without home-owned businesses with a vested stake in the town's economic fate. Most significantly, the hometown bank went the way of the spotted owl. Traditionally, it was the president of the leading bank in a community who organized business and commercial interests for political action. The bank's financial well-being was closely connected to that of the community as a whole. Local banks also were the traditional source of funding for local governments, when loans were needed to finance capital expenses and short-term deficits. As such, banks were natural community leaders. But tax reform in 1986 made it costly for banks to hold municipal loans, and the financial needs of local governments came to be supplied by an international investment community less engaged in the immediate affairs of any given community. Opportunities for local banks to shape local politics were reduced accordingly.

As economic elites lost the interest in and capacity to act in local affairs, their influence was replaced by policy professionals spawned by a maturing welfare state. As intergovernmental programs increased in number and size, so did the number of knowledgeable civil servants who had a stake in the programs they operated. These professionals became advocates for causes in which they believed and developed strong ties to groups dependent on the largess they distributed. The balance of power shifted from those with an interest in low taxes to those who wished to perpetuate a high level of welfare provision.

As just one sign of this transformation, growth in state and local government expenditure from their own fiscal resources grew almost as fast as federal domestic expenditure. As state and local governments expanded their activities, their workforce grew even when the size of the federal workforce hardly changed. Few realize that the federal civilian workforce numbered less than 3 million workers both in 1951 and, 50 years later, in 2001. Meanwhile, the size of the state workforce expanded from 1 million to 5 million, and local workers skyrocketed fourfold from 4 million to 12 million. The federal government may be paying half the cost of domestic public expenditure, but the state and local governments are doing most of the work.

Public Sector Unionism

In the early years of the 20th century, laws against public sector strikes had prevented government workers from exercising the crudest form of political power, the power to withhold their services. When Gov. Calvin Coolidge was asked to respond to the Boston police strike of 1918, he won widespread public backing when he declared "there is no right to strike against the public safety by anybody, anywhere, any time." So popular was his stance, it propelled him from a little known governor to the vice-presidency and beyond. For decades to come, public-sector unionists were at risk if they went on strike.

All this began to change in 1961 when President John Kennedy authorized collective bargaining by unions representing federal workers. The practice quickly spread to lower tiers of government. With the right to bargain well in hand by the mid-1970s, public sector unions were able to boost their membership rapidly. The percentage of public-sector employees unionized jumped from about 13 percent in the 1960s to around 40 percent in the mid-1970s, where it has since remained.

This expansion occurred at the same time that unions were losing ground in the private sector. Having peaked at about 38 percent of the private labor sector in 1952, it had fallen to 8.5 percent by 2002. As private-sector unions lost membership, the Democratic Party's most reliable base of support was eroding away beneath its feet. Fortunately for the party, public-sector unions filled the breach, as the membership in these unions became nearly one half of all union workers by 2002. Were it not for public-sector growth, the Democratic Party of the 21st century would bear little resemblance to the party that wrote New Deal and Great Society legislation.

By far, the most important of the public-sector unions are two teacher organizations, the National Education Association and the American Federation of Teachers. During the early 1970s, they conducted successful strikes in numerous cities, opening the floodgate to collective bargaining rights across the country. Teachers, spread as they are across the political landscape, located in every political constituency, trained in the arts of writing and speaking, are effective campaign workers and able policy advocates. Ever since the days of Jimmy Carter's endorsement of a national Department of Education, teacher unions have committed all but a small fraction of these resources to the service of Democratic Party candidates.

Significantly, teacher unions have more influence in state and local politics than at the national level. In Washington, teacher unions are challenged by a network of think tanks, cause organizations and policy professionals. In state and local politics, unions seldom face as well-defined an opposition. In Washington, presidents are able to use their rhetorical powers to control the political agenda. Interest groups must work within the constraints the agenda setter creates. At the state and local level, these same issues become matters of implementation, something that well-organized insiders can control.

What is true in education applies to other government employees as well. Public-sector unionism carries greater weight in state and local elections than in national ones, simply because, at the local level, elections have low visibility, with few voters and obfuscated issues. As V. O. Key noted long ago, it is in such contexts that the well organized have the most clout. According to some estimates, public sector employees out-vote the ordinary citizen in local politics by a ratio of anywhere between 2:1 and 6:1.

Partisanship and the Health of a Federal System

Nothing in this analysis should leave the reader convinced that Republicans will in short order become aggressive Hamiltonians. Especially within the judiciary, one should expect a sentimental attachment to past Republican federalism clichés. The quaint revival of a faded version of dual sovereignty theory by a bare majority of Supreme Court justices, all of them Republican appointees, is particularly out of step with the times. But one should not give too much weight to the Rehnquist court's rediscovery of dual sovereignty. Thus far, the Supreme Court decisions in which the concept has been invoked have been of minor significance.

Outside the courts, the pressures for a resurgent Hamiltonianism within the Republican Party seem stronger than ever. A security agenda requires a strong national government. Containing the welfare state will require the exercise of national control. State professionals can be expected to resist the new reform agenda to which many Republicans are committed. Public-sector unionism, one of the most powerful sources of resistance to Republican objectives, is more entrenched locally than nationally. Inasmuch as Republicans control all the power centers of the national government, they have little reason to trumpet the rights of states, many of which remain in Democratic hands.

Conversely, the Democratic Party must either win the presidency or find solace in the gubernatorial chairs it holds and the state legislators it has elected. Much of the time, it is fighting a rearguard action, one better fought in the hinterland than in the capital city. The street-level bureaucrat is now, more than ever, a major source of its political strength.

One should not expect either party to give up nominal commitment to the ideals they have each long expressed. But neither should one expect either party to act assiduously to protect them. Party interests have changed. So must their principles. We call attention to this fact not to lament it but to underline the durability—and value—of American federalism. Institutions need to have strengths beyond the interests of particular groups and parties. As Madison pointed out, federalism safeguards liberty by protecting minorities. As Brandeis observed, it provides places for experimentation. Its place in the American political system needs to be more deeply embedded than in the faith system of any one particular party. At the same time, Hamilton's view of the value of central authority cannot be gainsaid. Without a strong central government, a nation's economic prosperity is endangered. The United States needs to search for the appropriate balance as much today as it has in centuries in past. Shifts in partisan attachments may be one way of finding it.

Editor's Note

This article is drawn from a longer, more documented piece that will appear in Scott L. Greer, ed., *Rethinking Territorial Politics: Decentralization, Federalism, Democracy and the Welfare State* (Palgrave, forthcoming).

About the Author

Paul E. Peterson is the Henry Lee Shattuck Professor of Government at Harvard University.

State-Federal Relations: Defense, Demography, Debt, and Deconstruction as Destiny

By John Kincaid

Coercive federalism has shown great continuity since the late 1960s, as characterized by a shift of federal aid from places to persons, policy conditions and earmarks attached to federal aid, preemptions, federal encroachments on state taxation, federalization of state criminal law, defunct intergovernmental institutions, reduced federal-state cooperation within major intergovernmental programs, and federal court litigation. However, unfunded federal mandates and federal court orders mandating major state institutional change have become less prevalent. State policy activism remains vigorous, but the U.S. Supreme Court's state-friendly federalism jurisprudence has stalled since 2002.

State-federal relations reflect both long-term trends initiated in the late 1960s and shorter term trends triggered by the current president and by the terrorist attacks of September 11, 2001. The long-term trends are those of coercive or regulatory federalism. These trends continue largely unabated because Congress and the president feel politically and constitutionally uninhibited about displacing state powers.[1] The U.S. Supreme Court, which became more state-friendly in the 1990s, has again become less willing to restrain federal power. The shorter term trends are ones of fiscal constraint induced by the economic downturn of 2001-2003 but now being prolonged by the costs of national defense and homeland security, social welfare for senior citizens and long-term federal deficits.[2] Although state revenue collections have improved significantly since FY 2003, states face rising costs for major programs such as Medicaid, as well as a need to replenish rainy-day funds. Caught between increasing social welfare costs, reduced federal domestic spending, and voter resistance to tax increases, the watchwords for state officials are budget constraints and fiscal discipline.

A federalism bell that did not ring in 2004 was Electoral College reform. George W. Bush's victory in the popular and Electoral College votes quelled revival of this issue. Another federalism bell that stopped ringing is voting reform. Although implementation of the Help America Vote Act continues, the absence of a major voting scandal in the 2004 presidential election pushed voting reform off center stage.

4-D Destiny

The fiscal lifeblood of federalism will be defined for the foreseeable future by compelling costs associated with national defense, the demography of aging, long-term deficits, and deconstruction of federal fiscal roles in many domestic programs.

Defense and Homeland Security

The end of the Cold War in 1989 delivered a peace dividend, which, combined with a booming economy during much of the 1990s, enhanced domestic spending. This dividend expired with President Bush's declaration of a war on terrorism following the terrorist attacks of 2001. High and rising costs for defense, homeland security, veterans' benefits and international relations—all of which will consume nearly a quarter of federal spending in FY 2006—will be a long-term feature of the federal budget. Consequently, fewer federal dollars will be available for state and local governments. Furthermore, if all discretionary defense, domestic and international spending is capped, there will be tough defense-versus-domestic competition for money. Overall, reductions in federal domestic discretionary-spending (about a third of which is for grants-in-aid) are likely for the foreseeable future.

At the same time, the heavy reliance placed on National Guard units to prosecute the wars in Afghanistan and Iraq has left many states short-handed for responding to domestic emergencies. If recruitment for the National Guard declines as well, many states will lack sufficient military personnel to manage sizable emergencies. Additionally, there are likely to be reductions in federal aid for police and fire services. In an era marked by increased devastation from natural disasters, plus threats of catastrophic terrorism, state and local preparedness is crucial, but that preparedness will require more state and local own-source funding.

Generally, the Department of Homeland Security has established cooperative relationships with state and local agencies, and complaints about the slow flow of funds to states, and especially to cities, became less prevalent by late 2004, particularly when money for the country's 50 largest cities began to flow directly to them rather than through the governors' offices. Instead, concerns are now being expressed about secrecy surrounding how states are spending counterterrorism money. Nevertheless, the flow of federal money for homeland security will not be commensurate with the costs of state and local security responsibilities; hence, homeland security will be a long-running competitor for state and local tax dollars.

Demography

Social Security, Medicare and other health spending will consume about 46 percent of the FY 2006 federal budget. This can be compared to the categories of agriculture, commerce, community development, education, energy, environment, housing, job training, natural resources, social services, and transportation, which together, will consume only about 10 percent of the FY 2006 federal budget, and to interest payments on the national debt, which will absorb some 8 percent. The new Medicare prescription-drug benefit, which might cost $700 billion over the next 10 years, will add another huge component to federal social welfare spending.

The aging of the U.S. population is the states' single largest and most refractory fiscal challenge, one that will soon become a relentless feature of state budgeting and other policy-making. Federal aid will be constrained because the federal budget will face the same challenge. At the same time, senior citizens, living mostly on fixed and time-limited incomes, are likely to resist tax increases.

Debt

Increased defense and entitlement spending, along with tax reductions, which produced a $413 billion deficit in FY 2004, will put increasing downward pressure on federal spending on discretionary domestic programs, especially grants for states and local governments. For example, Congress failed to reauthorize surface transportation—the Safe, Accountable, Flexible, and Efficient Transportation Equity Act (SAFETEA)—in 2004 because President Bush insisted on a less costly bill of $256 billion compared to the House's $275 billion bill and Senate's $318 billion bill.

The projected federal deficit for FY 2005 is $427 billion, with the deficit still running at about $207 billion in 2010. Reductions in federal spending are expected, for example, for K-12 education, Medicaid, Community Development Block Grants, Section 8 housing rental assistance, low-income housing tax credit, low-income home-energy assistance, food stamps, some child-care assistance, Clean Water State Revolving Fund, public health, and bioterrorism, as well as the elimination of such programs as HOPE VI (public housing), the Community Services Block Grant and AMTRAK subsidies.

Deconstruction

Federal fiscal reductions and withdrawals from a variety of domestic programs have been evident in recent years and will become more so. Yet federal officials are reluctant to relinquish regulations. Consequently, state and local governments will be expected to pick up more of the costs of domestic services while also, in many instances, being expected to comply with federal regulations.

In response to this trend, the National Conference of State Legislatures recently revived its *Mandate Monitor*, estimating that the costs to states of carrying out federally mandated programs will be more than $29 billion in FY 2004 and over $35 billion in FY 2005. Strictly speaking, few if any of these costs stem from mandates. Instead, the costs stem from such things as conditions attached to federal aid, federal failures to release funds, substantive changes to entitlement programs, reduced funding for administration, unfunded increases in administrative rules, increased sanctions, and changes in federal tax policies.

Onward Coercive Federalism

Although the federal system remains cooperative in many respects, especially in most intergovernmental-administration arenas, the predominant political, fiscal, statutory, regulatory, and judicial trends have entailed impositions of federal dictates on state and local governments.

Grants-in-Aid

Although President Bush proposed a modest increase to $435.7 billion in federal aid for states and localities in FY 2006 (about 17 percent of the budget), federal aid has taken on three significant characteristics in this era of coercive federalism. First, aid has shifted substantially from places to persons; that is, almost two-thirds of federal aid is now dedicated for payments to individuals (i.e., social welfare).[3] Among the long-term consequences of this shift is that place-oriented aid for such functions as infrastructure, economic development and education has declined steeply, and the increased aid for social welfare has locked state budgets into programs ripe for escalating federal regulation and matching state costs.

Medicaid, which alone accounts for almost 45 percent of all federal aid and serves nearly 52 million people, is the leading example of this shift. Combined federal and state spending on Medicaid has increased 63 percent during the last five years. The federal government provides 57 percent of the nearly $300 billion of total Medicaid funding. President Bush has proposed $45 billion in Medicaid reductions over 10 years, a proposal strongly resisted by the governors. In turn, Bush wants to give states more flexibility and to reduce or eliminate the current process by which states must apply for waivers from federal rules. However, even with state cutbacks in services, Medicaid continues to display a voracious appetite for state dollars.

A second characteristic has been increased use of conditions of aid to achieve federal objectives that lie beyond Congress's constitutionally enumerated powers and to extract higher levels of spending on federal objectives from state and local governments. Conditions of aid, which are now often mistakenly called "mandates," are a powerful tool for federal policy-makers.[4] The 670-page No Child Left Behind Act (NCLB) of 2002 is the states' current *cause célebre* because of the costly testing and performance requirements established by the NCLB. Even the governor and legislature of Utah, the state that voted the most strongly for Bush in 2004, have demanded more freedom from the NCLB's "mandates."[5] Recent research seems to confirm state officials' complaints that the NCLB's compliance costs substantially exceed the law's grant-in-aid funding.[6] Although the U.S. Department of Education has recently taken a more flexible approach to enforcing the NCLB, President Bush wants to extend the NCLB's requirements beyond the eighth grade to all public high schools.

After a two-year battle, Congress reauthorized the Individuals with Disabilities Education Act (IDEA) and even authorized the federal government to pay by 2011 nearly 40 percent of the states' annual excess costs of educating the nation's 6.5 million children with disabilities. This 40 percent had been promised when IDEA was enacted in 1975, but it never exceeded 19 percent. However, IDEA funding remains discretionary, and the reauthorized IDEA imposes new regulations on the states while also providing relief from some previous rules.

Several other education programs, including Head Start, the Higher Education Act and the Workforce Investment Act, were not reauthorized by the 108th Congress. For the second time, Congress also failed to reauthorize the 1996 welfare reform law, which expired in 2002. Congress did revive the E-Rate program that provides grants to schools and libraries to connect to the Internet. The law also authorizes $250 million a year in grants to states over five years to improve the ability of 911 systems to track the location of cell phone callers.

Congress passed the Innocence Protection Act, which, among other things, provides grants to states to help expedite the processing of biological crime-scene evidence, preserve DNA evidence, defray the costs of post-conviction DNA testing, and represent defendants as well as victims in state capital cases. Congress also authorized the U.S. Department of Health and Human Services to give preference for its asthma-prevention grants to states that allow students with asthma or other life-endangering allergies to medicate themselves at school.

The third notable change affecting the delivery of aid to places has been a significant increase in congressional earmarking (i.e., pork-barreling). The number of earmarks increased from under 2,000 in 1998 to 9,362 by 2003. For example, the 2004 SAFETEA bill contained some 2,881 earmarks compared to 538 in the 1991 act and 1,800 in the 1998 law.[7] The Fund for the Improvement of Postsecondary Education even cancelled its FY 2005 competition for grants because 89 percent of the appropriation was already consumed by 419 earmarked grants (compared to two earmarks accounting for 18 percent of the appropriation in FY 1998). Earmarking advocates argue that members of Congress, as elected officials, are better qualified than "bureaucrats" to make funding allocations.

Mandates

Mandates have been another characteristic of coercive federalism; however, mandating plateaued with enactment of the Unfunded Mandates Reform Act (UMRA) of 1995. UMRA cut new mandate enactments sharply, but did not eliminate standing mandates. Currently, one sizable mandate looms on the horizon—a bill to standardize drivers' licenses, the Real ID Act, which could cost states hundreds of millions. States could opt out, but then their licenses would not be accepted for any federal-government purpose, including boarding an airplane, purchasing a firearm, and entering a federal building. The bill calls for a year and a half of implementation consultation among state and federal officials and others.

Preemptions

The historically unprecedented level of federal preemption of state powers characteristic of coercive federalism was well symbolized by enactment of the Class Action Fairness Act of 2005, which prohibits state courts from hearing most class-action suits that involve more than 100 plaintiffs and $5 million in potential damages. Such suits must be heard by federal courts. This is a major change in tort law and, thus, a major derogation of an historic state power. The act, however, is only the first of what President Bush and many members of Congress foresee as much broader preempting of state tort powers.

In March 2004, the U.S. Office of the Comptroller of the Currency issued a final rule preempting a range of state laws previously applicable to national banks. Federal preemption is not a new idea," said Comptroller John D. Hawke, "Its roots lie in the Supremacy Clause of the Constitution, and the courts have repeatedly held that the states cannot restrict the federally authorized activities of national banks."[8] Insurance regulation, long a state responsibility, will likely come under increased congressional scrutiny, especially with insurance companies pressing for federal intervention. As U.S. Sen. Richard C. Shelby's office put it, "If the state regulators are not up to the task of regulating the insurance industry, we may have to look at alternatives."[9]

Preemption is frequently upheld by the U.S. Supreme Court. In fact, the "Federalism Five" justices who ordinarily vote for the states in federalism cases often vote against the states in preemption cases. In a pair of 2004 cases, for example, the Court unanimously held that patients' rights laws in 10 states that allowed patients to sue their health plans over decisions to withhold coverage were preempted by the 1974 Employee Retirement Income Security Act .[10]

Taxation

Another characteristic of coercive federalism has been federal constraints on state taxation and borrowing, beginning especially with the enactment of limits on tax-exempt private-activity bonds in 1984. Federal judicial and statutory prohibitions of state taxation of Internet services and sales are among the most prominent, current constraints. In November 2004, Congress extended its Internet tax ban (i.e., the Internet Tax Non-Discrimination Act) to November 2007. Congress did revive the federal income-tax deduction for state and local sales taxes (which had been eliminated in 1986) for 2004 and 2005, primarily to benefit taxpayers who live in states lacking an income tax (e.g., Florida, South Dakota, Texas and Washington). However, itemizing taxpayers can only deduct their state and local income taxes or sales taxes, not both.

Talk in Congress and the White House about possibly repealing the estate tax permanently, limiting or eliminating the deductibility of all state and local taxes, providing new federal-tax deductions, and offering new tax incentives for saving and charitable giving could lead, directly and indirectly, to reductions in state and local revenues. Even more ominous for state-local revenue systems is the quietly growing discussion of enacting a federal sales tax or value added tax.

A potential time bomb for state and local economic-development efforts is a 2004 ruling by a three-judge panel of the U.S. Court of Appeals for the Sixth Circuit that a 1998 tax break awarded to DaimlerChrysler AG by Toledo and Ohio violated the U.S. Constitution's commerce clause. Business organizations, such as the Council on State Taxation, have joined with state and local officials in a vigorous effort to overturn this ruling and preserve states' rights.

Federalization of State Criminal Law

Another feature of coercive federalism has been the federalization of state criminal law, to the point where there are now some 3,500 federal criminal offenses, nearly half of which have been enacted since the mid-1960s. The number of federal prisoners has increased from about 20,000 in 1981 to nearly 175,000 today, and the number of federal prosecutors jumped from 1,500 in 1981 to more than 7,000 now. Generally, federal criminal laws are tougher than comparable state laws and make prosecutions and convictions easier than under state laws.

Demise of Intergovernmental Institutions

Coercive federalism has been marked, as well, by the demise of executive and congressional intergovernmental institutions established during the era of cooperative federalism to enhance cooperation. Most notable was the death of the U.S. Advisory Commission on Intergovernmental Relations in 1996 after 37 years of operation.

Decline of Political Cooperation

There also has been a decline in federal-state cooperation in major grant programs such as Medicaid and surface transportation, with Congress earmarking and altering programs more in response to national and regional interest groups than to elected state and local officials, who themselves are viewed as little more than interest groups.

Federal Court Litigation

Coercive federalism also has been marked by unprecedented numbers of federal court orders and a quantum leap in the number of times state and local governments are sued in federal courts. Although federal court orders dictating major and costly changes in such institutions as schools, prisons and mental health facilities have declined since the early 1990s, state and local governments are subject to high levels of litigation in federal courts, with various interests often trying to block major state policy initiatives through litigation. The U.S. Supreme Court resurrected the 11th Amendment in the 1990s to restrain some types of such litigation, but the reach of the Court's decisions has been quite limited.

U.S. Supreme Court's Stalled Federalism Revolution

Indeed, since 2002, the Supreme Court has exhibited a reluctance to continue its state-friendly federalism rulings initiated in 1991. In fact, in the major federalism case of 2003-2004, the Court, voting 5-4, held that states have no 11th Amendment immunity under Title II of the Americans with Disabilities Act against citizen lawsuits over gaining physical access to courts.[11] The justices also upheld unanimously a 1984 federal law that makes it a federal crime to bribe a state or local official whose agency receives more than $10,000 in federal grants or contracts.[12] The Court then generated turmoil in about a dozen state criminal-justice systems, plus the federal justice system, by overturning a Washington law that allowed judges to independently increase a convicted defendant's sentence beyond the usual length for the crime.[13]

The Court even sustained one of the key structural supports for coercive federalism, namely, partisan gerrymandering, which creates so many safe U.S. House seats and fosters ideological polarization in Congress. By a 5-4 vote, the Court rejected a Democrat challenge to post-2000 census partisan gerrymandering in Pennsylvania.[14]

Federalism and the Culture Wars

For the general public, federalism became salient in 2004 because of debates associated with the so-called culture wars of recent decades. Rulings by the Massachusetts Supreme Judicial Court in 2003 and 2004 upholding gay marriage triggered intense national controversy. President Bush endorsed a federal constitutional amendment to ban gay marriage nationwide; Democratic presidential candidate John Kerry wanted to leave gay marriage to the states. Bush also asked the federal courts to strike down Oregon's Death With Dignity Act, which permits physician-assisted suicide. Meanwhile, the U.S. Court of Appeals for the Ninth Circuit rejected again an administration effort to neuter California's medicinal marijuana law. As a result of such Bush initiatives, many liberals, historically hostile to states' rights, are now warming to states' rights.[15]

However, there also is growing pressure to allow more state regulation of abortion and for the Supreme Court to set aside its 1973 abortion ruling so as to restore state authority over abortion. Here, the tables are turned, with conservatives supporting states' rights and liberals opposing states' rights.

State Activism

Another, seemingly contradictory characteristic of coercive federalism has been state policy activism, especially since the early 1980s. However, this activism has been both a response to coercive federalism as states have bucked federal policies and filled federal policy voids and a stimulant of coercive federalism as interest groups have sought federal intervention to tranquilize hyperactive states.

State attorneys general, treasurers, pension-fund heads and others have pursued aggressive litigation and regulation in many policy areas. For example, eight states have joined in a federal lawsuit against utilities to reduce carbon dioxide emissions. The California Air Resources Board (CARB) shocked the automobile industry in 2004 by adopting regulations to reduce automobile and light-truck emissions of carbon dioxide and other greenhouse gases by 30 percent within 11 years. A leading justification for such state activism was expressed by CARB's chairman: "Absent federal leadership, it's important for California to demonstrate that there is a way to address global warming."[16] Nine automakers filed suit to overturn the regulation, but Republican Gov. Arnold Schwarzenegger vowed "to fight the expected court challenges."[17]

Highly publicized in 2004 were efforts by nearly half the states to explore mechanisms, such as state Web sites listing prescreened foreign pharmacies, to help citizens import cheaper pharmaceuticals from Canada in defiance of the U.S. Food and Drug Administration. Several states have approved and supported stem-cell research in defiance of President Bush's policy. Consequently, state activism has brought some intergovernmental policy competition into the federal system.

Conclusion

Although state activism will generate a kind of competitive state-federal federalism, coercive federalism will be the system's dominant motif and will be exacerbated by the fiscal pressures generated by defense, demography, debt, and deconstruction.

Notes

[1] See, John Kincaid, "Trend in Federalism: Continuity, Change and Polarization," *The Book of the States 2004*, (Lexington, KY: The Council of State Governments, 2004), 21-7; John Kincaid, "State-Federal Relations: Continuing Regulatory Federalism," *The Book of the States 2002*, (Lexington, KY: The Council of State Governments, 2002) 25–32; John Kincaid, "From Cooperation to Coercion in American Federalism: Housing, Fragmentation, and Preemption, 1780-1992," *Journal of Law and Politics* 9 (Winter 1993): 333-433.

[2] See, John Kincaid, "Trends in Federalism: Is Fiscal Federalism Fizzling?" *The Book of the States 2003*, (Lexington, KY: The Council of State Governments, 2003), 26-31.

[3] For explication, see John Kincaid, "The State of U.S. Federalism, 2000-2001," *Publius: The Journal of Federalism* 31 (Summer 2001): 1-69.

[4] See, for example, Karl Kronebusch, "Matching Rates and Mandates: Federalism and Children's Medicaid Enrollment," *Policy Studies Journal* 32:3 (2004): 317-37.

[5] Sam Dillon, "Strongly G.O.P. Utah House Challenges Bush's Signature Education Law," *New York Times*, February 16, 2005, A14; Associated Press, "States rebelling over new rules on education," *Express-Times* (Easton), February 18, 2004, A-8.

[6] Jennifer Imazeki and Andrew Reschovsky, "Is No Child Left Behind an Un (or Under) funded Federal Mandate? Evidence from Texas," *National Tax Journal* 57 (September 2004): 571-79.

[7] Brian Friel, "Defending Pork," *National Journal* 36 (May 8, 2004): 1405.

[8] Statement of the Comptroller of the Currency at *http://www.occ.treas.gov/2004-3aComprollersstatement.pdf*, accessed March 30, 2004.

[9] Quoted in Joseph B. Treaster, *"States vs. U.S.*: Who Will Police Insurance Firms?" *New York Times*, December 31, 2004, C3.

[10] *Aetna Health Care Inc.* v. *Davila* and *Cigna HealthCare of Texas Inc.* v. *Calad*, 124 S. Ct. 2488 (2004).

[11] *Tennessee* v. *Lane*, 124 S. Ct. 1978 (2004).

[12] *Sabri* v. *United States*, 124 S. Ct. 1941 (2004).

[13] *Blakely* v. *Washington*, 124 S. Ct. 2531 (2004).

[14] *Vieth* v. *Jubelirer*, 541 U.S. 267 (2004).

[15] See, for example, Jim Holt, "A States' Rights Left?" *New York Times Magazine*, November 21, 2004, 27-28; Jonah Goldberg, "Federalism vs. states' rights," *Express-Times* (Easton), December 2, 2004, A-10.

[16] Quoted in Stuart F. Brown, "California rocks the auto industry," *Fortune* 150 (November 1, 2004): 154.

[17] Quoted in Dan Hakim, "Automakers Sue to Block Emissions Law In California," *New York Times*, December 8, 2004, C1.

About the Author

John Kincaid is the Robert B. and Helen S. Meyner Professor of Government and Public Service and director of the Meyner Center for the Study of State and Local Government at Lafayette College in Easton, Penn. He is also editor of *Publius: The Journal of Federalism* and former executive director of the U.S. Advisory Commission on Intergovernmental Relations.

Reflections on Intergovernmental Re-Balancing: Back to the Future

By Carl W. Stenberg

The intergovernmental balance has shifted to the national government. Federal deficits, debt service, defense spending, and entitlement pressures will reduce discretionary spending, and could rekindle interest in decentralization and devolution. State leaders need to network horizontally and vertically to rebalance the federal system.

In the 1984–1985 edition of *The Book of the States* I contributed an article that attempted to sort out the reality from the rhetoric of the federalism debate taking place in Washington, DC, state capitols, county court houses and city halls. The debate focused on reallocation of functional and fiscal responsibilities, spurred by President Ronald Reagan's "Big Swap" proposal for the national government to take over the states' share of Medicaid in exchange for state assumption of full funding responsibility for welfare and food stamps. Other concerns were federal budget build-ups in defense and entitlements, elimination of grant-in-aid programs, and growing regulatory burdens and unfunded mandates. These developments contributed to tension and uncertainty at all governmental levels.

As then executive director of The Council of State Governments (CSG), I observed that "rebalancing" of intergovernmental relations had shifted the pendulum toward more state- and local-oriented federalism. I called upon states to capitalize on their increased institutional capacity and commit to pursue their historic roles as "laboratories of democracy," to formulate innovative approaches to domestic challenges and forge productive partnerships with the national government and their local governments.

Two decades later, the resiliency and dynamism of the federal system are both apparent. States and localities are still key program "rowers" in delivering important services and implementing national programs and regulations.[1] The national government is still the big borrower and big spender in the federal system, while "big government," in terms of personnel payrolls and range of functional responsibilities, resides at the state and local levels. State and local representatives still complain about unfunded mandates, under-funded federal programs, and unwarranted preemptions.

Re-balancing has continued and produced a shift toward national-oriented federalism. The president,

Congress and federal agencies have assumed significant policy "steering" roles, with the concurrence of the Supreme Court. Globalization, the New Economy, and the Information Age have raised important questions about matters on which the United States should speak with one or 50 voices.

This article comments on factors contributing to this latest intergovernmental power balance shift, and suggests steps state leaders could take to move the pendulum in a more sub-national direction.

Looking Upward

The changing relationship between the states and the national government can be captured in seven "d" words: deficit, debt, defense, demographics, discretion, deregulation and decentralization.

Deficits and Debt. Fiscal factors have been prominent determinants of intergovernmental balance. Although states enjoyed budget surpluses during most of the 1990s and the national government achieved a budget surplus during the Clinton administration, a current concern is the widening federal budget deficit, estimated at $413 billion by the Congressional Budget Office in FY 2004. States are recovering from severe budget crises accompanying the recent recession, and most must comply with constitutional balanced budget requirements. Tax cuts, coupled with politician's promises to not raise taxes, reduce deficit reduction options of national and state policymakers. Accompanying mounting federal budget deficits is national debt growth, estimated by the Government Accountability Office (GAO) at $6.8 trillion, or about $24,000 gross debt per person. Interest payments for debt service will limit future spending options for the president and Congress.[2]

Defense. The war against terror is the latest contributor to the defense build-up that began during the Reagan administration. Although the defense share of total 2004 federal spending is about 20 percent, compared with 27 percent in 1984, heightened security concerns at home and abroad will call for greater defense investments.

Demographics. Americans are benefiting from health care advances and living longer, more productive lives. They will draw down Social Security and other retirement accounts and depend more on Medicaid and Medicare to help cover rapidly rising health care expenses. Medicaid's growth over the past two decades produced a shift in major beneficiaries of federal grants-in-aid, from places to people, and there are no indications of slowdown; Medicaid now accounts for approximately 45 percent of total federal aid, and its share of state budgets has about doubled over the past 10 years.[3]

Discretion. The above factors reveal a sizable and expanding portion of the federal budget as non-discretionary. Debt service, entitlement payments for income support and health care, and defense spending will put much of the federal budget on "autopilot." In times of budget pressure, the discretionary portion—mainly grants-in-aid, amounting to $412 billion in 2003—will be looked to as a revenue source for on-going commitments and new national priorities.[4]

Deregulation. Deregulation has been a powerful force in the New Economy and Information Age, affecting markets, production processes, communications and skill requirements. Like businesses, governments have been compelled to become more nimble, entrepreneurial, performance-based, and customer-oriented. While deregulation has been a key component of private sector economic activity, the intergovernmental record has been mixed. Three examples follow.

1. The Unfunded Mandate Reform Act of 1995 (UMRA) was initially a major victory for state and local government representatives. UMRA sought to discourage Congress from imposing mandates and to ensure that compliance costs of bills containing federal mandates would be brought to the attention of congressional committees and, if enacted, would be accompanied by compensatory funds. But these hopes have not been realized. Coverage exemptions—such as Social Security, voting rights, grant conditions, national emergencies, program reauthorizations, and preemptions—"grandfathering" of all pre-1995 mandates, focus on fiscal impacts of individual bills instead of on cumulative federalism assessments, and underestimation of state and local compliance costs by federal agencies have limited UMRA's impact.[5]

2. Eligible states have received waivers of administrative requirements in Medicaid, environmental and other programs. Yet, over the past 20 years traditional instruments of regulatory federalism—cross-cutting requirements accompanying federal aid, crossover sanctions, full and partial preemptions, and direct orders - have become more popular with Congresses and presidents.

3. Two important Federalism Executive Orders have been issued, E.O. 12612 in 1987 by President Reagan and E.O. 13132 in 1999 by President Clinton. Together they contained "Fundamental Federalism Principles" and "Federalism Policy Criteria," which sought to constrain preemptions and grant conditions, broaden intergovernmental consultation on regulation, streamline waiver processes, and promote states' integrity and discretion. However, GAO found that federal agencies rarely identified federalism impacts in their administrative rulemaking.[6]

Decentralization. Observers called the 1990s the "devolution revolution" decade, featuring proposals to encourage states to play leadership roles as policy innovation "laboratories" and to shift significant federal program responsibilities to the states via administrative decentralization, rather than devolution of federal powers. K–12 education reform, environmental initiatives such as smart growth and anti-sprawl programs, and economic development incentives were examples of the former.[7] The Clinton administration's welfare reform initiative was the prime decentralization example. The Temporary Assistance to Needy Families (TANF) block grant, which replaced the Aid to Families with Dependent Children program established during the New Deal, gave states considerable latitude in setting priorities, determining eligibility, integrating state programs, re-engineering delivery systems, creating workfare programs, and engaging private and non-profit organizations in case management and service delivery. At the same time, the national government retained major roles in funding, although capped at the 1996 level, and standard-setting, such as limiting aid to five years, requiring welfare recipients to find work within two years, and curbing benefits for legal and illegal immigrants.

The number of block grants has reached record levels (from 18 to 25, depending on definitions, compared with 12 in 1983), and three (TANF, community development, and social services) are among the 20 largest grant programs. Yet, Congress continues to do business with states and localities chiefly through narrowly focused categorical instruments and to limit broad-based assistance (to less than 20 percent of total aid).[8] The Bush administration has proposed giving states greater authority and discretion by converting Medicaid, low-income housing vouchers, Head Start, job-training and child welfare programs into block grants. From the states' standpoint, the troubling trade-off with block grants is when, compared with the categorical programs they replace, more flexibility is exchanged for fewer federal dollars.

In summary, the seven "d's" have been powerful forces in determining state-federal power balances. They suggest re-appearance of a three-pronged scenario from the 1980s on the intergovernmental scene—sorting out and shifting of functions, decentralization of responsibilities through block grants, and disinvestment in categorical programs—leaving it to states and localities to shoulder increased responsibilities, pass along cuts, or eliminate programs. The functional turn-back or devolution of powers record has been sparse, administrative decentralization has been limited to a few block grants, and categorical grants have proven resilient (as underscored by the rebounding of categorical programs from the historic 25 percent reduction achieved by the Reagan administration and Congress, from 539 in 1980 to 404 in 1984, to over 660 programs 20 years later). But the budget pressures outlined above could well re-open the devolution debate.

Looking Outward

If re-balancing is to occur, state leaders will need to work together more strategically and build effective horizontal and vertical networks. This need is underscored by the advent of the New Economy, featuring globalization of commerce, communications and technology. Globalization has posed a serious question: on what matters should the United States speak with 50 voices, or with one voice? Business representatives, environmental and consumer groups, organized labor, and others engaged in interstate and international commerce often prefer a single, stable policy or standard—not a patchwork of 50—which clashes with the states' role as "laboratories." Congress has enacted 518 federal statutory preemptions since 1790, with 68 passed between 1995 and 2004.[9] Some of these have been partial, featuring a national minimum standard that states may exceed, while others fully preempt a field or impose maximum federal standards. In recent years states have lost authority to regulate nationally traded securities, pesticides and local telecommunications. Federal preemptions are under consideration in a wide range of areas, such as electronics recycling, greenhouse gas emissions, prescription drugs, lawn mower and leaf blower emissions, appliance energy consumption and biotechnology. There is no clear line between the states' police powers in enforcement and consumer protection, for example, and the demands of interstate commerce and global markets. But the common approach by the Congress and White House has been preemption.

In light of these national and international trends, what can state leaders do? One response has been efforts by state attorneys general to confront national authorities when they were acting too slowly or contrary to state interests. The state-led tobacco settlement, in which major tobacco companies agreed to make $250 billion in compensatory payments for costs of treating tobacco-related illnesses under state Medicaid programs, was a major breakthrough. As implementers of environmental policy, states have challenged administration efforts to weaken air quality regulations, criticized the Environmental Protection Agency's (EPA) reluctance to regulate interstate emissions from coal-fired power plants, and sued the EPA for failure to regulate carbon dioxide emissions. This activism indicates states can be on the frontlines when Congress and the administration are at stalemate on important national policy issues or unwilling to ensure appropriate levels of regulation to protect the public and enhance the quality of life.

A second trend is steady increase in formal and informal interstate cooperation, marked by growth in the number of compacts to more than 200. The Streamlined State Sales and Use Tax Agreement, signed by over 40 states, is an example of what can be done even in a complex, confusing and controversial area as tax policy. Although the effort was unsuccessful in preventing approval of the Internet Tax Nondiscrimination Act, which imposed a moratorium prohibiting states and local governments from levying taxes on Internet access, interstate cooperation could be an alternative to federal preemption in other areas. CSG and other organizations of state officials play vital roles in helping states network together regionally and nationally to find solutions to domestic problems. The establishment of CSG's National Center for Interstate Compacts to promote use of these instruments to address national and state priorities underscores their potential in facilitating state collaboration.[10] Continued development of model state legislation by CSG to share "best practices" and issuance of uniform laws by the National Conference of Commissioners of Uniform State Laws also could boost interstate relations, or "horizontal federalism," as a viable strategy for reducing pressures for national preemption and mandates.[11]

Looking Downward

States and localities are key "rowers" in the intergovernmental system. While national initiatives such as No Child Left Behind, Homeland Security, Elections Administration, and Community-Oriented Policing receive media attention, their success is dependent on effective implementation by sub-national units. Similarly, a productive partnership between state and local governments is essential for delivery of major state-assisted programs such as elementary and secondary education. To the extent state and local officials can successfully develop solutions to public problems, Congress may be less willing to play the roles of city council, county commission, or state legislature.

Generalizations about the "state of state-local relations" are difficult to make across 50 different systems and are often subject to the "Miles Law" factor—where you stand depends on where you sit. Just as in state-federal relations, friction points exist in state-local relations, such as financial aid cutbacks, unfunded mandates, and preemptions of authority.

State leaders could use at least six indicators to assess current conditions and remedial actions. These are extent to which states: (1) give localities greater discretionary authority over their forms of government, personnel policy, services and especially revenues; (2) provide financial aid to replace lost federal dollars and state recession budget cuts, and resist further cutbacks in local assistance payments; (3) work with localities to make their tax systems more progressive and fair; (4) assume greater financial and administrative responsibility for functions that are costly, ignore local boundaries, have negative spillovers, require inter-jurisdictional equity, or of regional or statewide impact—such as social welfare, courts, mental health, education, corrections and transportation; (5) exercise restraint in imposing state mandates on local governments, and demonstrate willingness to compensate for compliance costs or allow local implementation flexibility; and (6) provide inter-local and regional collaboration incentives.

These steps could go a long way toward building a more positive and productive state-local relationship. But they are difficult to sell. It is tempting for state officials to merely pass along aid cuts, unfunded mandates, and intrusive administrative conditions; there is not much local units as state "subdivisions" can do constitutionally or politically to stop such actions. But from the standpoint of effective implementation at the local level—which public opinion polls have found to be the most trustworthy and capable of delivering the most for their money—states should consider pursuing a "second-order devolution" approach outlined above.

Looking Ahead

Forecasting the future is a difficult and daunting task, particularly in a complex, dynamic federal system. Power balances between the states and the nation and states and their localities are affected by a variety of forces, such as international commerce, security, information technology, finances and demographics. For state leaders, the bad news during the past 20 years is that these and other factors have produced centralizing pressures that strengthened the role of the national government and supported "one size fits all" domestic and international approaches. But the good news is that while the deficit, debt, defense and demographic demands on the federal budget will put pressure on discretionary spending, which could lead to program cutbacks, more decentralization and even devolution initiatives could be on the horizon. And the states will remain on the frontlines as chief implementers of national programs and regulatory policy and innovation "laboratories."

Capitalizing on these trends and moving the pendulum in a more sub-national direction will require states to work together and with their local governments in more sustained and strategic ways than has been customary. Forging effective networks among state leaders on interstate issues and between state and local officials on state and sub-state issues that leads to effective collective action on common problems will be key to demonstrating their capacity and commitment to partnership federalism and to reducing centralizing pressures.

Notes

[1]David Osborne and Ted Gaebler, *Reinventing Government*, (Reading, MA: Addison-Wesley Publishing Co., 1992).

[2]John Kincaid, "Trends in Federalism: Continuity, Change and Polarization," *The Book of the States 2004* (Lexington, KY: The Council of State Governments, 2004), 22–23.

[3]*The Book of the States 2004* (Lexington, KY: The Council of State Governments, 2004), 41.

[4]National Academy of Public Administration, "Fiscal Future Positioning Committee Report," November 19, 2004.

[5]U.S. General Accounting Office, "Unfunded Mandates: Analysis of Reform Act Coverage," (Washington, DC: U.S. General Accounting Office, May 2004).

[6]Timothy Conlan, *From New Federalism to Devolution: Twenty-Five Years of Intergovernmental Reform* (Washington, DC: The Brookings Institution 1998); L. Nye Stevens, "Implementation of Executive Order 12612 in the Rulemaking Process, Testimony before the Committee on Governmental Affairs, U.S. Senate, May 5, 1999; "Comments on S. 1214—The Federalism Accountability Act of 1999," July 14, 1999.

[7]Parris N. Glendening, "The Devolution Conflict," *State Government News* (February 2003), 12–13; Richard P. Nathan, "The Devolution Revolution: An Overview," Rockefeller Institute Bulletin (Albany: The Nelson A. Rockefeller Institute of Government, 1996).

[8]David B. Walker, *The Rebirth of Federalism: Slouching toward Washington* (New York: Chatham House Publishers, 2000), 6–7; David R. Beam and Timothy J. Conlan, "Grants," in Lester M. Salamon, The Tools of Government (New York: Oxford University Press, 2002), 347–353.

[9]Joseph F. Zimmerman, "The United States Federal System: A Kaleidoscopic View," Paper presented at a research seminar, Rothermere American Institute, Oxford University, November 23, 2004; "Congressional Preemption: Regulatory Federalism," Paper presented at the annual conference of the American Political Science Association, September 4, 2004.

[10]John J. Mountjoy, "National Center for Interstate Compacts: A New Initiative," *Spectrum* (Fall 2004), 8–11.

[11]Joseph F. Zimmerman, *Interstate Relations: The Neglected Dimension of Federalism* (Westport, CN: Praeger, 1996; "Trends in Interstate Relations," Spectrum (Fall 2004), 5–7, 11.

About the Author

Carl W. Stenberg is a professor of public administration and government at the School of Government, University of North Carolina at Chapel Hill. He served previously as assistant director of the U.S. Advisory Commission on Intergovernmental Relations and executive director of The Council of State Governments.

Interstate Relations Trends

By Joseph F. Zimmerman

This article notes the importance of the United States Constitution's full faith and credit clause relative to sister state recognition of same sex marriages in Massachusetts, interstate commerce clause in removing barriers to trade, and interstate compact clause in promoting interstate cooperation, and summarizes developments involving interstate administrative cooperation and controversies.

Five most important interstate clauses—full faith and credit, interstate commerce, interstate compacts, privileges and immunities, and rendition—were incorporated in the U.S. Constitution by its drafters to make perfect the economic and political union.

Full Faith and Credit

Section 1 of Article IV contains a mandate: "Full Faith and Credit shall be given in each State to the public acts, records, and judicial proceedings of every other State" and grants Congress authority to "prescribe the manner in which such acts, records, and proceedings shall be proved, and the effect thereof." This authority was exercised in 1790, 1804, 1980, 1994, 1996 and 1999. The 1996 clarification was prompted by the Hawaiian Supreme Court's 1993 decision in *Baehr v. Miike* (852 P.2d 44 at 57-72) opining the statutory denial of the issuance of a marriage license to same sex couples violated equal protection provision and equal rights amendment to the state constitution and remanding the case for a trial. Trial judge Kevin S.C. Chang on December 3, 1996, ruled same sex couples had the constitutional right to marry. The decision's implementation was delayed until the state legislature had an opportunity to act. It proposed and voters ratified on November 3, 1998, a constitutional amendment (Art. I, §23) reversing the Supreme Court's decision by granting the legislature "the power to reserve marriage to opposite sex couples."

The Hawaiian Supreme Court's decision prompted a response from Congress in the form of the Defense of Marriage Act of 1996 (110 Stat. 2419, 1 U.S.C. §1) defining a marriage as "a legal union between one man and one woman as husband and a wife" and the term "spouse" as "a person of the opposite sex who is husband or a wife" and authorizing states to deny "full faith and credit to a marriage certificate of two persons of the same sex." On August 17, 2004, U.S. Bankruptcy Court Judge Paul B. Snyder in Tacoma, Washington, issued the first decision on the constitutionality of the act and ruled it does not vio-late the equal protection of the laws clause of the U.S. Constitution.

Currently, 39 states have enacted a state defense of marriage act, and Maryland, New Hampshire, Wisconsin and Wyoming have statutes or court decisions banning same sex marriages. Missouri voters on August 3, 2004, and Louisiana voters on September 18, 2004, ratified a defense of marriage constitutional amendment defining a marriage as between a man and a woman, and voters in 11 states approved a similar proposition on November 2, 2004. Four of the latter amendments—in Montana, Mississippi, Missouri and Oregon—also preclude civil unions.

The controversy over same sex marriages was reignited on November 18, 2003, by the 4 to 3 decision of the Massachusetts Supreme Judicial Court in *Goodridge v. Department of Health* (440 Mass. 309, 798 N.E.2d 941) holding unconstitutional a statute denying "the protections, benefits, and obligations conferred by civil marriage to two individuals of the same sex who wish to marry." The decision immediately raised an important legal question: Are same sex nonresidents eligible to marry in the Commonwealth? The answer is no for some nonresidents, since a 1913 Massachusetts statute disqualifies individuals from marrying if they are ineligible to marry in their home state.[1] The constitutionality of this law was upheld on August 18, 2004, by state Superior Court Judge Carol S. Ball.

The Massachusetts Senate requested an advisory opinion from the court whether a civil union statute would comply with the court's decision. The court's 4 to 3 majority on February 4, 2004, answered the question in the negative (440 Mass. 1201, 802 N.E.2d 565), but indicated the General Court (state legislature) had the option of not calling a same sex civil union a marriage if the term was drop for heterosexual marriages. Justice Martha B. Sosman, one of three dissenters, wrote "it is beyond the ability of the Legislature—and even beyond the ability of this court, no matter how activist it becomes in support of this cause—to confer a package of benefits and obligations on same-sex 'married' couples that would be truly identical to the entire package of benefits and obligations that being 'married' confers on opposite-sex couples" (440 Mass 1201 at 1213, 802 N.E.2d 565 at 574).

The General Court in 2004 proposed a constitutional amendment reversing the Supreme Judicial Court's decision. This proposal will not appear on the referendum ballot unless the General Court approves the proposal for a second time in 2005. Should the proposition appear on the 2006 ballot and voters approve it, same sex couples who married between May 17, 2004, and November 7, 2006, will be in a legal limbo as they were legally married, but their marriage will be illegal after adoption of the constitutional amendment.

In related developments, the California Supreme Court on August 12, 2004, unanimously invalidated more than 4,000 same sex marriages authorized by San Francisco Mayor Gavin Newsom, and California Attorney General William Lockyer on October 8, 2004, issued an opinion declaring a law barring same sex marriage does not violate the state constitution. New York State Comptroller Alan G. Hevesi on October 8, 2004, ruled the state pension system would treat same sex couples, involving a state employee, who legally marry in a Canadian province in the same manner as married couples of the opposite sex. He explained the congressional Defense of Marriage Act of 1996 applies only to same sex marriages in other states.

Courts in sister states commenced to be faced with petitions for dissolutions from persons united in a civil union in Vermont since July 2000. To be eligible for dissolution of a civil union in Vermont, one party must be a resident of the state for one year. Courts in other states have to wrestle with the question whether they have authority to dissolve a union. A Connecticut judge in 2002 dismissed a petition for dissolution on the ground the state does not recognized a civil union, but a Sioux City, Iowa, judge in 2003 granted a dissolution petition. On March 24, 2004, Essex County Probate and Family Court Judge John Cronin granted a petition for dissolution of a Vermont civil union, the first such dissolution granted in Massachusetts.

The complex problems caused by Vermont's civil union statute are illustrated by two Virginia women who decided to move to Vermont to enter a union. Frederick County Circuit Judge John R. Prosser in Virginia on August 24, 2004, voided the visitation rights order issue by a Vermont judge for Janet Miller-Jenkins, a current resident of Vermont, who entered into a civil union with Lisa Miller-Jenkins and Janet later became pregnant through in-vitro fertilization. Lisa filed a petition in a Vermont court to dissolve the civil union and establish parental rights. The Virginia ruling was based on the ground Virginia law supersedes Vermont law because Lisa and her daughter reside in Virginia.

Interstate Compacts

Section 10 of Article I of the U.S. Constitution authorizes a state to enter into a compact with one or more sister states with the consent of Congress. In 1893, the U.S. Supreme Court (148 U.S. 503 at 520) opined the consent requirement applies only to political compacts encroaching upon the powers of the national government. A compact may be bilateral, multilateral, section, or national in membership, and may be classified as advisory, facility, flood control and water apportionment, federal-state, promotional, service provision or regulatory. There are 26 functional types of compacts administered by a commission or by regular departments and agencies of party states.[2]

Recent developments include congressional consent (116 Stat. 2981) for an amendment to the New Hampshire-Vermont Interstate School Compact stipulating debts to finance capital projects may be incurred when approved by a majority vote at an annual or special district meeting of voters conducted by a secret ballot. The newly drafted Interstate Compact for Juveniles was enacted first by the North Dakota Legislative Assembly on March 13, 2003, and its lead has been followed by 20 additional state legislatures in 2003 and 2004. Enactment by 35 state legislatures is required for activation. Arkansas is dissatisfied with the Interstate Compact on the Placement of Children because each of the 50 member states has individual laws pertaining to participation in the compact, thereby causing bureaucratic delays.

The Registered Nurses and Licensed Practical or Vocational Nurses Interstate Compact dates to 1998 when Utah Gov. Michael O. Leavitt signed Senate Bill 149 enacting the compact subsequently enacted by 20 additional state legislatures. The National Council of State Boards of Nursing on August 16, 2002, approved an Advanced Practice Registered Nurses Interstate Compact. The Utah Legislature on March 15, 2004, became the first state to enact this compact.

State legislatures regulated the business of insurance until 1944 when the U.S. Supreme Court (322 U.S. 533, 64 S.Ct. 1162) opined the business was interstate commerce. Congress, reacting to pressure from states, enacted the McCarran-Ferguson Act of 1945 (59 Stat. 33, 15 U.S.C. §1011) overturning the court's decision by devolving authority to states to regulate the insurance industry. Unhappy with the continuation of nonharmonious state regulation of the industry, insurance companies lobbied Congress to preempt specific areas of state insurance regulatory authority. The Gramm-Leach-Bliley Financial Modernization Act of 1999 (113 Stat. 1353, 15 U.S.C. §6751) preempted 13 specific areas of state insurance regulation and threatened to establish a federal system of licensing insurance agents if 26 states did not establish a uniform licensing system by November 12, 2002. This threat was averted when 35 states were certified as having such a system on September 10, 2002. Recognizing the continuing threat of preemption, the National Association of State Insurance Commissioners drafted the Interstate Insurance Product Regulation Compact creating a commission with regulatory authority and the Utah State Legislature in 2003 enacted the compact and its lead has been followed by eight other state legislatures. Forty-nine state legislatures enacted the Producer Licensing Model Act and 39 states implemented state licensing reciprocity.

A deadlock on the Republican River Interstate Compact Administration led to the U.S. Supreme Court on May 19, 2003, settling an original jurisdiction dispute—*Kansas v. Nebraska and Colorado* (538 U.S. 720, 123 S.Ct. 1898)—involving the failure of Nebraska to deliver water to Kansas by issuing a decree approving the final settlement stipulation executed by the parties and filed with the special master on December 16, 2002. It provides "all claims, counterclaims, and cross-claims for which leave to file was or could have been sought…prior to December 15, 2002, are hereby dismissed with prejudice…" Kansas anticipated the court would order Nebraska to pay up to $100 million in damages.

Other developments relating to the interstate compact device include continuing pressure for restoration of the Northeast Dairy Compact that became inactive on October 1, 2001, when Congress refused to extend its consent for the compact.

A number of prominent certified public accountants are advocating a CPA interstate licensing compact and the Section on Administrative Law of the American Bar Association in 2003 established a committee to draft an administrative procedure act compact for interstate compact commissions.

The California, Delaware, District of Columbia, Idaho, Indiana, Mississippi, Montana, Nebraska, North Dakota, South Dakota, Texas and West Virginia state legislatures enacted the Interstate Enforcement of Domestic Violence Protection Orders Act drafted by the National Conference of Commissioners on Uniform State Laws (NCCUSL). South Caro-

lina in 2004 amended the NCCUSL's Uniform Electronic Transaction Act to grant U.S. Postal Service's electronic postmark the same legal validity and enforceability as certified or registered mail. Forty-six states, the District of Columbia and the U.S. Virgin Islands have enacted the uniform act. NCCUSL's Uniform Trust Code was enacted by 10 states and the District of Columbia, but the Arizona Legislature repealed the code because of complaints it endangers estate plans, favors creditors, and invades the privacy of families. The Colorado and Oklahoma state legislatures in 2004 rejected the code. Twenty-three state legislatures, however, enacted the Streamlined Sales and Use Tax Interstate Agreement.

Interstate Administrative Agreements

State legislatures have delegated broad discretionary authority to department heads to enter into administrative agreements with their counterparts in sister states. Numerous such agreements, formal written and verbal, are in effect, but it is impossible to determine the precise number.

The 39 states operating lotteries became aware the larger the jackpot the larger the ticket sales. Twenty-eight states participate in the Multi-State Powerball Lottery formed by an administrative agreement between the states, the District of Columbia and the U.S. Virgin Islands; 11 states participate in the Mega Millions Lottery; seven states operate the Big Game Lottery; three states participate in the Tri-State Megabucks Lottery; and three states are members of Lotto South. Recent developments include the 2003 decision by the Texas Lottery Commission to become a member of Mega Millions Lottery, the 2004 decisions of Maine and Tennessee to join the Powerball Lottery, and the newly established Tennessee Lottery Board in 2003 terminating negotiations with the Georgia Lottery Corporation to form a joint operation because of fears lawsuits would reduce the amount of money available for scholarships.

Attorneys general continue to form cooperative administrative partnerships to conduct investigations and file lawsuits against companies. Their greatest success in terms of a settlement was the recovery of $246 billion in Medicaid costs from five tobacco companies. The settlement does not require manufacturers of other brands, often sold at a major discount from regular brands, to contribute to the escrow account in each state. In consequence, 35 states by 2004 established directories of brands approved for sale.

Other developments include legal actions in May 2004 by the attorneys general of Connecticut, New

Jersey and New York, and the Pennsylvania secretary of environmental protection against Allegheny Energy, Inc., based in Pennsylvania, for emitting air pollution causing smog, acid rain, and respiratory problems in Pennsylvania and the other suing states. Eight states and the city of New York in 2004 filed suit against several electric energy companies operating 174 fossil fuel plants emitting annually an estimated 640 tons of carbon dioxide, the first suit targeting and seeking to reduce such emissions.

Joint actions by attorneys general in 2004 also resulted in Medco agreeing to pay $29.3 million to settle complaints by 20 states the company violated consumer protection and mail fraud statutes by switching patients to more expensive drugs and a group of rare stamp dealers agreeing to create a $680,000 restitution fund to settle a lawsuit brought by California, Maryland and New York charging them with a 20-year conspiracy to rig stamp auctions.

Seven states—Illinois, Michigan, Minnesota, New York, Ohio, Pennsylvania and Wisconsin—in 2004 joined as *amici curiae* a lawsuit filed in December 2003 by a number of environmental groups seeking to force EPA to initiate actions to prevent foreign fish and plant species from invading the Great Lakes. The EPA responded that it is working with the U.S. Coast Guard to implement the National Invasive Species Act to prevent introduction of exotic species through ballast water discharge.

The New England Compact Assessment Program was established by New Hampshire, Vermont and Rhode Island in 2004 as a common system for measuring student achievement and save money. The U.S. Department of Health and Human Services in 2004 approved plans by five states—Alaska, Michigan, Nevada, New Hampshire and Vermont—to pool their purchasing powers in order to obtain larger discount on prescription drugs for their Medicaid recipients. Illinois, Indiana, Maine, New Hampshire and Virginia have joined the E-Zpass consortia, an electronic toll network for motor vehicles extending from the Canadian border to the Mid-Atlantic States and the Midwest. Arizona and New Mexico signed the first interstate homeland security agreement. And the governors of Montana, Oklahoma, Oregon and Washington launched a multi-state AMBER alert web portal designed to distribute to law enforcement officers and others information about an abducted child and the suspected perpetrator(s).

In 1991, the Pacific Northwest Economic Region (PNWER) was established by the state legislatures of Alaska, Idaho, Montana, Oregon and Washington, provincial legislatures of Alberta and British Columbia, and legislature of the Yukon Territory. PNWER created in 2001 the Partnership for Regional Infrastructure Security that launched several initiatives to improve the security of all types of infrastructure.

The Multistate Anti-Terrorism Information Exchange (MATRIX), an interstate administrative agreement, appears to be dissolving. Utah on March 25, 2004, became the eighth state to drop out of the agreement. Florida, Michigan, Ohio and Pennsylvania remain as members. MATRIX promoters were convinced the computer-driven program would integrate data and information from criminal records, driver's licenses, vehicle registrations, etc. Concerns over privacy were expressed by the American Civil Liberties Union, Electronic Privacy Information Center, and Electronic Frontier Foundation.

Taxation Developments

Many interstate controversies involve taxation and the courts are called upon to resolve them because of the failure of Congress to initiate remedial legislation.[3] Resource rich states levy severance taxes that are passed along to consumers in sister states. The differential in the excise tax rates for cigarettes and alcohol has led to significant tax revenue loss by high tax states whose residents make purchases in neighboring states. So-called jock taxes levied by states on professional athletes are increasing in number and affect interstate relations. And Congress's decision to phase out its inheritance tax is encouraging wealthy citizens to establish residence in tax friendly states.

The Excise Tax Problem

Recent sharp state excise tax increases for cigarettes in a number of states offered new incentives for buttleggers and are responsible for the dramatic increase in the number of domestic and foreign online sellers of cigarettes who are required by law to report sales to state tax officials, but who seldom do so and cite the Internet Nondiscrimination Act of 2001 (115 Stat. 703, 47 U.S.C. §151) which expired in 2003. Congress, however, enacted the Internet Tax Freedom Act of 2004 (118 Stat. 2615, 47 U.S.C. §809). Cigarette sales and excise tax revenues in Delaware and New Hampshire increased dramatically as nonresidents made additional purchases in these states to avoid high excise taxes in their home states levied to discourage smoking.

Congress enacted the Jenkins Act of 1949 (63 Stat. 844, 15 U.S.C. §375) prohibiting use of the postal service to evade excise tax payments, but a violation is a misdemeanor. U.S. attorneys prefer to prosecute violators under the Mail Fraud Act of 1909 (35 Stat.

1088, 18 U.S.C. §1341) as a violation is a felony. In 2004, the U.S. Bureau of Immigration and Customs Enforcement (ICE) arrested 10 persons and charged them with trafficking in a multi-billion dollar black market in counterfeit major brands of tobacco products made in Asia. ICE and the U.S. Bureau of Alcohol, Tobacco, Firearms, and Explosives (ATF) have stepped up their enforcement efforts as reflected in the seizure of 79,277 cartons of counterfeit and genuine cigarettes in fiscal year 1998 and 225,981 cartons in fiscal year 2003.

Jock Taxes

These taxes date to 1991 when the California Legislature extended its income tax to the Chicago Bulls basketball team members and the Illinois General Assembly retaliated by levying a jock tax on nonresident professional athletes who are residents of a state levying a similar tax. Twenty states, Puerto Rico, Alberta and six cities impose such a tax on professional athletes. The nature of the tax varies with New York levying its personal income tax on a nonresident athlete based upon his income and the number of games played in the state in contrast to other states which based their respective income tax on the basis of the athlete's income and the number or preseason training days, practice days, and game days.

Estate Taxes

Congress enacted the Federal Revenue Act of 1926 (44 Stat. 9) providing taxpayers an 80 percent credit against the federal inheritance and estate tax for a similar tax paid to a state. The purpose of the act was to encourage state legislatures to enact a uniform tax based upon the national tax.

In revising the internal revenue code in 2001, Congress increased the exemption from the federal estate tax and reduced the tax credit to 75 percent in 2002, 50 percent in 2003, 25 percent in 2004, and 0 percent in 2005. Nineteen states levy an estate tax with exemptions ranging from $675,000 in Rhode Island and Wisconsin to $3,100,000 in Ohio. Congress' decision encourages wealthy individuals to establish residence in the 25 states not levying an estate tax and/or make gifts prior to their deaths.

Intangible Holding Companies

The 1992 U.S. Supreme Court in *Quill Corporation v. North Dakota* (504 U.S. 298, 112 S.Ct. 1904) ruled a state may not tax a corporation lacking a substantial nexus (physical presence) in a state. This decision encouraged certain national retail corporations to create intangible holding companies (passive in-

vestment companies) in states, particularly Delaware, not taxing royalty income. Such a corporation assigns its trademarks to its intangible holding company and it leases the trademarks to retailers who pay a fee to the company. Where allowed, the retailer takes advantage of a deduction of the fee, thereby reducing its gross corporate income subject to tax and state tax revenues. In 2004, Louisiana filed suits against Toys "R" Us Incorporated and Wal-Mart Stores Incorporated seeking corporation income taxes avoided by means of the intangible holding company.

Sixteen states have responded by enacting statutes establishing a combined income reporting system utilizing a formula to determine the in-state taxable income of a corporation. Eight other states enacted more limited statutes forbidding a corporation to deduct payments made to an intangible holding company in a sister state or include payments to the intangible holding company in the total taxable income of a corporation. Corporations with intangible holding companies have lobbied state legislatures not to enact statutes designed to prevent tax avoidance and governors to veto such bills. In 2003, the governor of Maryland vetoed such a bill.

Interstate Commerce

Disputes between states over interstate commerce trade barriers date to the Articles of Confederation and Perpetual Union which failed to provide a mechanism for resolving the disputes. The drafters of the U.S. Constitution decided it was essential to grant Congress plenary power to regulate interstate commerce (Art. I, §8) in order to make more perfect the economic and political union. The assumption apparently was made that Congress would enact a statute, backed by the Supreme Law of the Land clause (Art. VI), invalidating any interstate trade barrier established by a state statute or a regulation based upon a state's police, proprietary, and taxation powers. Congress, however, did not enact a major statute based upon its interstate commerce power until Congress enacted An Act to Regulate Commerce (24 Stat. 379, 49 U.S.C. §1) in 1887. References often were made to the silence of Congress during the 19th century and even today Congress has not exercised fully its power to regulate commerce between sister states. In consequence, heavy reliance historically has been placed upon courts to remove barriers not susceptible to removal by negotiations between party states.

Congress since 1965 has exercised its power of preemption to remove completely or partially regulatory authority from states. Republican control of Congress, commencing in 1995, slowed only slightly the pace of enactment of preemption statutes: 33 were enacted between 1995 and 1999 and 41 were enacted between 2000 and 2004. Recent statutes designed to remove or prevent erection of trade barriers include the Internet Nondiscrimination Act of 2001 (115 Stat. 703, 47 U.S.C. §1151), Public Company Accounting Reform and Corporate Responsibility Act of 2002 (116 Stat. 746, 15 U.S.C. §7201), Real Interstate Driver Equity Act of 2002 (116 Stat. 2342, 49 U.S.C. §10101), and Fair and Accurate Credit Transactions Act of 2003 (117 Stat. 108, 15 U.S.C. §1601).

A major dispute involves the direct interstate shipment of wine to consumers and raises the question whether the dormant interstate commerce clause supersedes the grant of authority to states to regulate the sale and consumption of alcoholic beverages by the 21st Amendment to the U.S. Constitution. The U.S. Court of Appeals for the 6th Circuit in 2003 in *Heald v. Engler* (342 F.3d 517 at 524) reversed the decision of the U.S. District Court for the Eastern District of Michigan granting summary judgment in favor of Michigan's scheme regulating the sale of wines by holding the state regulation is a constitutionally benign product of the state's three-tier regulatory system and consequently a valid exercise by the state of its 21st Amendment authority. The appeals court specifically ruled the Michigan "regulatory scheme treats out-of-state and in-state wineries differently, with the effect of benefiting the in-state wineries and burdening those from out-of-state."

A New York state law requiring wineries to sell their products through New York state wholesalers was challenged; 25 other states have similar laws or regulations. Judge Richard M. Berman of the U.S. District Court for the Southern District (232 F.Supp.2d 135 at 144) on November 12, 2002, held the New York law to be an unconstitutional barrier to interstate commerce because the exceptions for New York wineries allowed them to avoid wholesalers, and thereby allowed them to sell wines at a lower price. On February 13, 2004, the U.S. Court of Appeals for the 2nd Circuit (358 F.3d 228) reversed Judge Berman's decision and opined New York's regulatory scheme "is within the ambit of the powers granted to States by the 21st Amendment. New York's regulatory scheme allows licensed wineries, whether in state or out of state, direct access to a market of sophisticated oenophiles" and hence "(t)he scheme does so in a nondiscriminatory manner, while targeting valid state interests in controlling the importation and transportation of alcohol." Challenges based upon the Privileges and Immunities Clause and the First Amendment also were rejected. The U.S. Supreme Court in October 2004 agreed to hear appeals of the two Circuit Court decisions.

Summary and Conclusions

The Massachusetts Supreme Court's decision legalizing same sex marriages and the Vermont General Assembly's enactment of a same sex civil union statute will continue to result in controversies in sister states lacking a defense of marriage act relative to enactment of such an act and to raise questions whether courts in these states possess authority to dissolve a Massachusetts same sex marriage or a Vermont same sex civil union.

In general, interstate cooperation continues to be excellent as additional states enact interstate compacts and enter into interstate administrative agreements on a wide variety of subjects. Compacts, agreements and enactment of harmonious regulatory laws have been promoted as means to discourage Congress from exercising its powers of preemption removing regulatory authority completely or partially in specified fields from states. Nevertheless, we conclude disparate state regulatory statutes and regulations, increasing globalization of the domestic economy, international trade treaties, lobbying by interest groups, and technological developments will result in Congress enacting preemption statutes in addition to the 522 enacted since 1790.

Notes

[1]Massachusetts Laws of 1913, Chapter 360, Section 2, and Massachusetts General Laws, Chapter 207, Section 11.

[2]Joseph F. Zimmerman, *Interstate Cooperation: Compacts and Administrative Agreements*, (Westport, CT: Praeger Publishers, 2002) and Ann O'M. Bowman, "Trends and Issues in Interstate Cooperation," *The Book of the States 2004*, (Lexington, KY: The Council of State Governments, 2004), 34-40.

[3]Consult Joseph F. Zimmerman, *Interstate Economic Relations* (Albany, NY: State University of New York Press, 2004).

About the Author

Joseph F. Zimmerman is a professor of political science at Rockefeller College of the State University of New York at Albany. He is the author of numerous books including *Federal Preemption: The Silent Revolution* (1991), *Contemporary American Federalism: The Growth of National Power* (1992), *State-Local Relations* (1995), *Interstate Relations: The Neglected Dimension of Federalism* (1996), *Interstate Cooperation: Compacts and Administrative Agreements* (2002) and *Interstate Economic Relations* (2004).

Interstate Compacts: Trends and Issues
By John Mountjoy and Melissa Bell

Interstate compacts are a uniquely American invention, allowing multistate problem-solving in the face of complex public policy and federal intervention. This article provides a brief history of compacts, examines a 2004 survey of interstate compact administrators and briefly looks at new and emerging policy areas in which interstate compacts may play an important role. Finally, it describes The Council of State Governments' new service developed as a result of this work—the National Center for Interstate Compacts.

Despite their legal and structural differences, states share many common problems in a world in which economic and political issues are often discussed in global terms. As we become more integrated socially, culturally and economically, the volume of these issues will only increase and interstate compacts may be the perfect mechanism for developing state-based solutions to supra-state problems.[1] The last two decades have seen a resurgence in the development of new interstate compacts and the revision of existing compacts. Interstate compacts can provide states the means to address state problems with state solutions, thus avoiding federal intervention and preemption.

Interstate Compacts: Brief History

Interstate compacts are powerful, durable and adaptive tools for promoting and ensuring cooperative action among the states. Unlike federally imposed mandates, interstate compacts provide state-developed solutions to complex public policy problems.

Interstate compacts are contracts between states that carry the force and effect of statutory law and allow states to perform a certain action, observe a certain standard or cooperate in a critical policy area. Generally speaking, interstate compacts:

- establish a formal, legal relationship among states to address common problems or promote a common agenda;
- create independent, multistate governmental authorities (e.g., commissions) that can address issues more effectively than a state agency acting independently, or when no state has the authority to act unilaterally;
- establish uniform guidelines, standards or procedures for agencies in the compact's member states;
- create economies of scale to reduce administrative costs;
- respond to national priorities in consultation or in partnership with the federal government;

- retain state sovereignty in matters traditionally reserved for the states; and/or
- settle interstate disputes.[2]

Between 1783 and 1920, states approved 36 compacts, most of which were used to settle boundary disputes. But in the last 75 years, more than 150 compacts have been created, most since the end of World War II. They apply to a range of subject areas from conservation and resource management to civil defense, education, emergency management, energy, law enforcement, probation and parole, transportation and taxes.[3]

While the theory and purpose behind interstate compacts have changed little over the last 229 years, modern compacts differ greatly from their earlier and simpler cousins, tackling broader public policy issues and forging state partnerships for problem-solving and cooperation. What also differs is the way in which compacts are structured. Unlike federal actions that generally impose unilateral and rigid mandates, compacts afford states the opportunity to develop dynamic, self-regulatory systems, of which the member states can maintain control through a coordinated legislative and administrative process.

Compacts also enable the states to develop adaptive structures that can evolve to meet new and increased challenges that naturally arise over time. In short, through the compact device, states acting jointly cannot only control the solution to a problem but can also shape the future response as the problems to be addressed change. Modern compacts are a reinvigoration of our federalist system in which states may only be able to preserve their sovereign authority over interstate problems to the extent that they share their sovereignty and work together cooperatively through interstate compacts.[4]

Interstate Compact Survey: Findings

In February 2004, The Council of State Governments (CSG) conducted a 50-state survey of interstate compacts. This in-depth survey sought detailed information on compact administrators' interstate compact experiences, the experiences of their state in regards to compacts and their assessment of current needs in the compact field. Compact administrators handle the day-to-day operations of more than 200 interstate agreements. The purpose of this survey was to learn more about this group and the services they may need.

Individual compacts and their compact administrators were identified using CSG's *Interstate Compacts & Agencies 2003* directory.[5] From an initial sample size of 479 administrators representing 47 different compacts, 226 surveys were returned for a response rate of 51 percent.[6] All states and the District of Columbia were represented in these responses.

The vast majority (97.3 percent) of the administrators in the sample are full-time employees of their compacts. Most of them (75.7 percent) have at least one additional employee who works with them on compact administration. Most of the compact administrators in this study (76.6 percent) have not been involved with any other compact, so their current

involvement in their respective compacts is the only compact-related experience they have.

Interstate compacts can be viewed as a four-stage process. All compacts go through the stages of development, enactment, implementation and administration. Each of these stages presents their own set of challenges and obstacles.

Compact Development

The first stage is compact development. During this stage, compact proponents identify stakeholders, analyze the needs of the states involved, determine the purpose of the compact and decide on the components of the compact. The compact's language is drafted in this phase, and proponents must determine if congressional consent is needed.[7] To get a sense of the difficulty that administrators face in compact development, respondents were asked about the obstacles encountered during this stage. These are illustrated in Figure A.

- The most common obstacle cited was educating legislators and other state officials about compacts; 42.2 percent of respondents thought

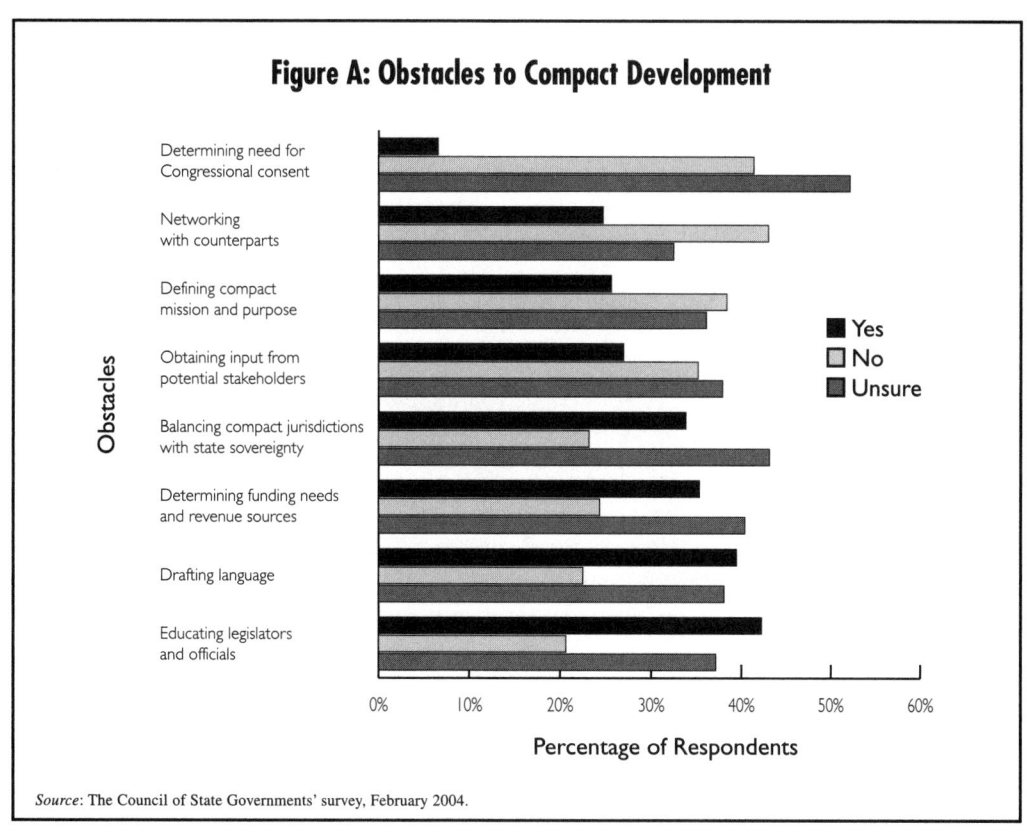

Figure A: Obstacles to Compact Development

Obstacles

- Determining need for Congressional consent
- Networking with counterparts
- Defining compact mission and purpose
- Obtaining input from potential stakeholders
- Balancing compact jurisdictions with state sovereignty
- Determining funding needs and revenue sources
- Drafting language
- Educating legislators and officials

Yes / No / Unsure

Percentage of Respondents

Source: The Council of State Governments' survey, February 2004.

this was an impediment in their compact's development phase.

- Another obstacle cited by 39.5 percent of respondents was the difficulty in drafting the language of the compact.
- Other common obstacles were determining funding needs and revenue sources as well as balancing the compact's jurisdiction with member state sovereignty, identified respectively by 35.3 percent and 33.8 percent of the respondents.

Compact Enactment

The second stage of the interstate compacts process is compact enactment. When one state, typically by statute, adopts the terms of a compact requiring approval by one or more states in order to take effect, this is considered an offer. When other states adopt identical compact language, this is considered acceptance. When the required number of states adopts the compact, the contract is deemed valid. During the compact enactment stage, proponents take

steps to make sure the compact becomes law in their respective states so that the contract is validated.

Respondents were asked about obstacles faced during this phase. These are highlighted in Figure B.

- As with compact development, more than 40 percent of respondents thought educating state legislators and other state officials about compacts was an obstacle.
- More than a third felt that promoting the compact within their respective states for enactment was problematic.
- And almost a third of respondents felt that determining funding needs and obtaining support from organizations that might be affected by the compact were obstacles during this phase of the interstate compacts process.

Compact Implementation

The third stage of the interstate compacts process is compact implementation. After the compact becomes law, proponents must establish the structures

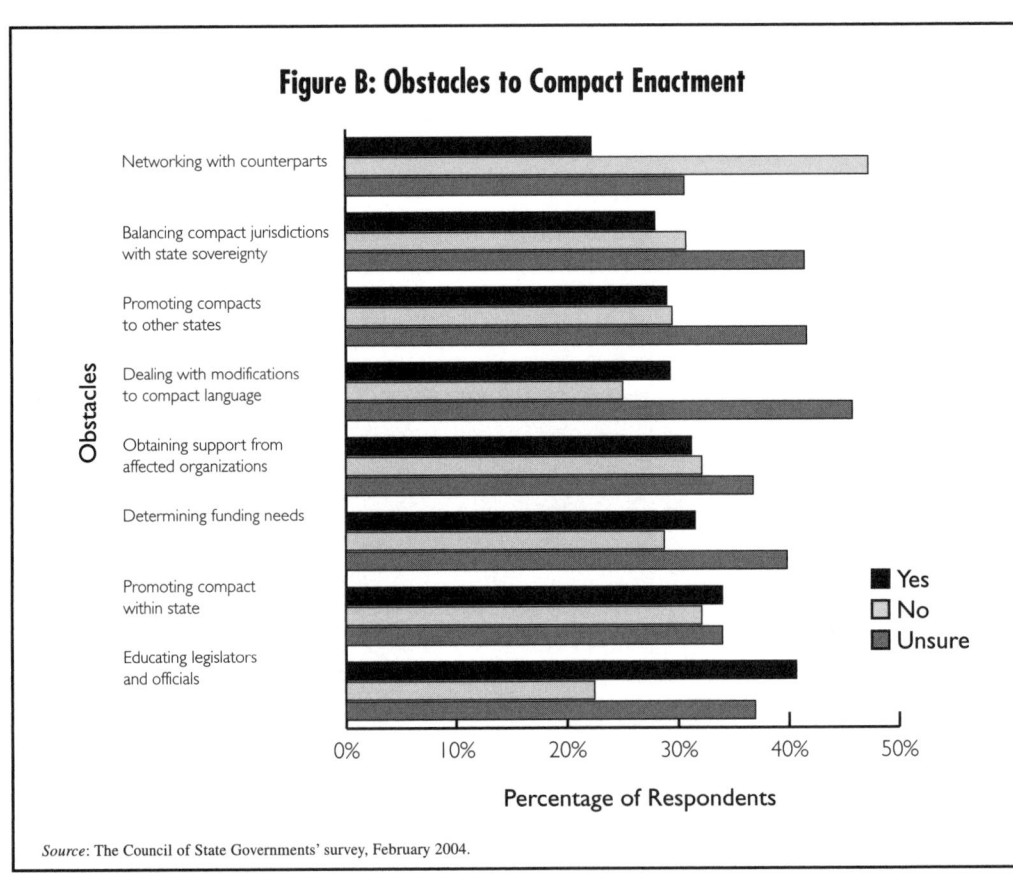

Figure B: Obstacles to Compact Enactment

Obstacles (y-axis):
- Networking with counterparts
- Balancing compact jurisdictions with state sovereignty
- Promoting compacts to other states
- Dealing with modifications to compact language
- Obtaining support from affected organizations
- Determining funding needs
- Promoting compact within state
- Educating legislators and officials

Legend: ■ Yes □ No ▨ Unsure

Percentage of Respondents (x-axis): 0%, 10%, 20%, 30%, 40%, 50%

Source: The Council of State Governments' survey, February 2004.

and procedures to administer the compact. This phase involves a great deal of logistical work.

Administrators were asked about obstacles to compact implementation (see Figure C). Unlike the other two stages of the interstate compacts process, there was only one obstacle in the third stage that was cited by more than 30 percent of the respondents.

- Almost a third of respondents felt that determining staffing needs was problematic.

Compact Administration

Compact administration is the final stage of the process in which compact administrators oversee the daily operations of the compact and execute the compact provisions. Obstacles to this stage are highlighted in Figure D.

- More than half of administrators believed that dealing with enforcement and compliance of the compact's terms are obstacles in the compact administration stage.
- As in the development and enactment stages,

educating legislators and state officials was once again one of the top-cited obstacles. It was identified as an obstacle by 39.8 percent of the administrators.

- And 37.8 percent of the administrators felt that promoting their compacts within their own states was problematic at this stage.

Types of Support to Aid the Interstate Compacts Process

The administrators were also asked to think about the needs of their current compacts and what types of support would be helpful to them. Their responses to potential kinds of support are outlined in Table A.

Although networking with counterparts in other states was not considered a major obstacle in any of the four stages of the interstate compact process, the most popular type of support among administrators was the desire for an outside organization to help provide networking opportunities for administrators. Compact administrators typically do not communi-

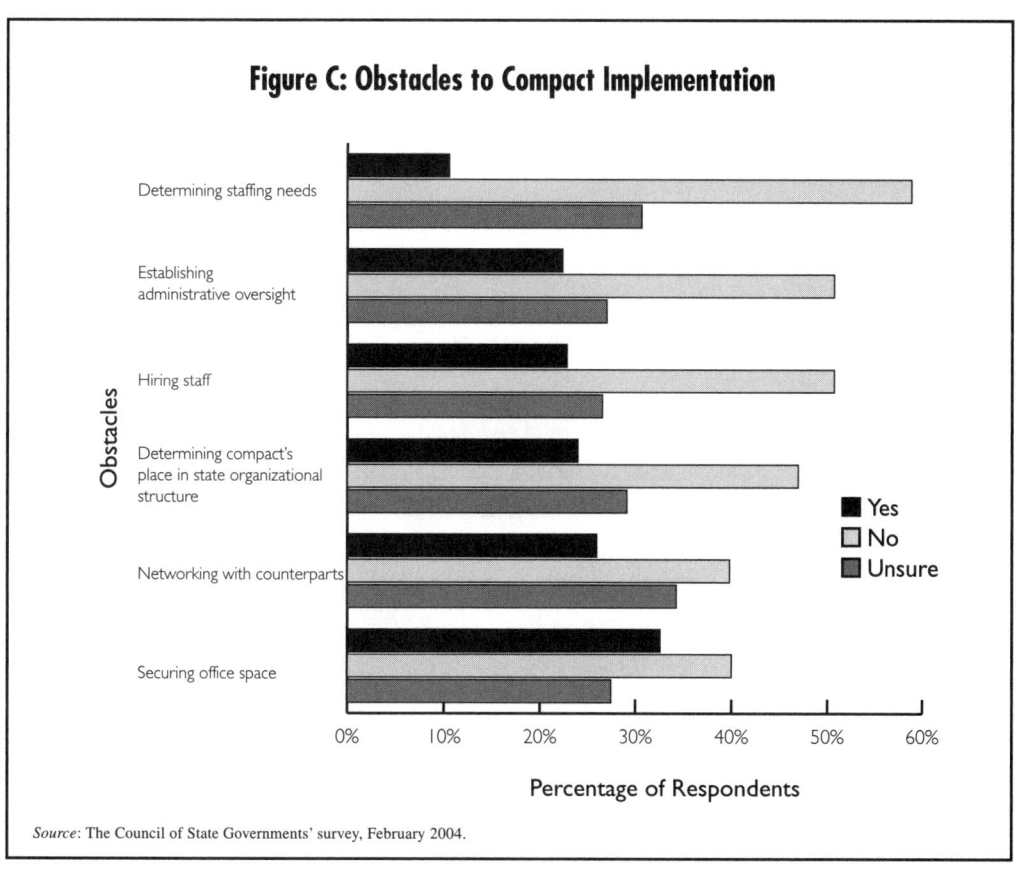

Figure C: Obstacles to Compact Implementation

Source: The Council of State Governments' survey, February 2004.

cate with their colleagues who administer other interstate compacts, usually limiting their networking to the close-knit circle of experts who administer their particular compact in other states. Perhaps administrators want to expand their networking opportunities outside their own compact.

The majority of compact administrators also identified the need for assistance in the legal interpretation of compact requirements with more than half wanting non-technical explanations of compact requirements. This response stems directly from the facts that compact administrators typically are not attorneys and that few states offer comprehensive and timely legal assistance to compact administrators.

Many of the administrators expressed a need for common tools for use during the compact process, including administrative functions and structures, compact performance evaluation and new technological tools for sharing information across state lines. Further, by examining and sharing best practices in

the field of compact administration, states could be able to streamline compact functions, eliminating redundancy and promoting some standardization in operations for a state's many compacts.

Administrators also liked the idea of a third party to help build coalitions to promote and support compacts and the concept of a clearinghouse of information related to compacts. They also thought it would be useful to have information on the impact that legislative and regulatory activity at the federal level would have on their compacts. In addition, they want help with determining the costs associated with their compacts as many compact offices operate on shoestring budgets and may not be able to meet the demands of the compact.

More than 40 percent of the respondents want help with revising their existing compact. When asked directly "Is there need to make changes to your existing compact?" 46.2 percent of them said yes. This is significant in that it indicates that the body of ex-

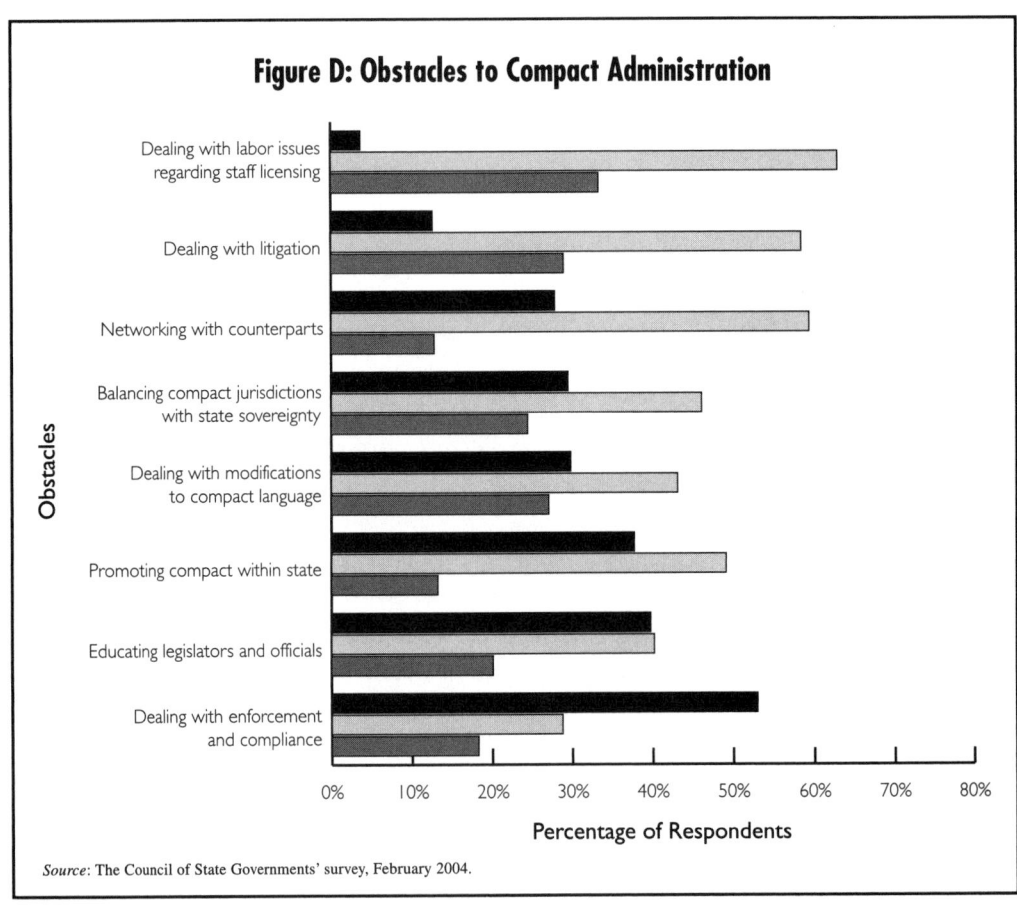

Figure D: Obstacles to Compact Administration

Obstacles (y-axis):
- Dealing with labor issues regarding staff licensing
- Dealing with litigation
- Networking with counterparts
- Balancing compact jurisdictions with state sovereignty
- Dealing with modifications to compact language
- Promoting compact within state
- Educating legislators and officials
- Dealing with enforcement and compliance

Percentage of Respondents

Source: The Council of State Governments' survey, February 2004.

Table A:
Most Popular Types of Compact-Related Support

Type of support	Percentage who thought it would be useful
Networking opportunities for administrators	72.7%
Legal interpretation of compact requirements	71.5
Common tools for use during compact process	65.0
Coalitions to promote and support compacts	61.0
Information clearinghouse about compacts	61.0
Non-technical explanations of compact requirements	52.3
Monitoring/evaluation of federal activities' impacts on compacts	52.1
Help with determining all costs associated with compacts	47.5
Help with revising existing compact	43.7

Source: The Council of State Governments' survey, February 2004.

isting compact law is outdated or in need of an overhaul. While a majority of regulatory compacts were developed in the 1950s, 1960s and 1970s, the world has evolved at a much faster pace since then. As such, CSG has seen firsthand the need to revise agreements whose purposes are quite relevant, but whose internal mechanisms require modification and modernization. Further, aged interstate compacts often require updates to their purpose and policies. What was taken as sound policy in the 1950s may or may not be relevant today, and issues that we take for granted today were not considered in previously.

Interstate Compacts: On the Horizon

As current policy areas evolve and new ones emerge, interstate compacts will likely play a significant role in the future of multistate problem-solving. With the federalism dynamic in flux, responsibilities are shifting both to and from the states. Interstate compacts offer a flexible solution to these issues, giving states the ability to solve problems regionally and nationally.

Emerging areas ripe for interstate cooperation include:

■ *Intelligence/Criminal Justice Information Sharing*—While efforts such as the Global Justice Information Sharing Initiative sponsored by the U.S. Department of Justice seek to establish standards and mutual understanding of the information sharing process, no true interstate mechanism currently exists to allow multi-jurisdictional access to criminal justice information. This issue becomes much more significant when one considers the role states and locali-

ties play in homeland security efforts.

■ *Emergency Medical Assistance*—Prior to the Sept. 11 terrorist attacks, states had already made great headway in adopting interstate agreements such as the Emergency Management Assistance Compact (EMAC) to cope quickly with natural and other disasters. States have now realized the need for more than just the sharing of equipment and resources for physical clean-up, which EMAC provides. They now see the dramatic need for interstate cooperation for medical assistance. States currently have no mechanism to facilitate nonfederal interstate emergency medical assistance in the event of a nuclear, biological or chemical attack.

■ *Elder Guardianship*—A July 2004 GAO report indicated an emerging need to protect incapacitated elderly adults.[8] The report highlighted specific breakdowns in collaboration between states and federal programs that jeopardized the safety of seniors, specifically in the areas of state court operation, accountability and consistency; state jurisdictional fluctuations; a lack of systematic information- sharing between and among varying agencies and levels of government; and a lack of adequate tracking of elder guardianship statistics.

■ *Metropolitan-Border Area Compacts*—Massive urban growth in the last several decades now requires states to work together, as never before, on behalf of cities and sprawling bi- or tri-state metropolitan areas. Issues such as education, economic development and tourism, and homeland security/public safety have evolved beyond the traditional borders of the city and state and now encompass multiple states as a single metro area on a wider basis. Examples include the Cincinnati/Northern Kentucky/Eastern Indiana area, Chicago/Northwestern Indiana, St. Louis/Southwestern Illinois, and Portland/Southern Washington areas. While the interstate compact has been used sparingly in this area, notably the Washington Area Metro Transit system and the New York/New Jersey Port Authority, emerging and changing policy issues may require states to work on behalf of cities in the creation of new or expanded interstate agreements.

- *Bioterrorism Preparedness*—Regional cooperation for bioterrorism preparedness is on the minds of many state officials. Mass casualty events, multistate training and prearranged payment provisions, chain-of-command issues and identified roles for key players are critical to an effective response. While other agreements may tackle broader cooperation issues, specific agreements might be crafted to promote independent regional responses based on a region's unique needs.

- *State Professional Licensing*—Currently, 46 professions are licensed at the state level, and these professions are evolving due to cultural and technological changes as well as increased mobility. With this in mind, states may need to cooperate further on consolidating state licensing standards and procedures. A recent analogous example is the Interstate Insurance Product Regulation Compact that was developed to streamline the introduction of new insurance products into states. Rather than dealing with separate state laws regulating insurance products, the new compact makes it much easier and quicker for products to come to market and meet the stringent demands of states. As of the end of 2004, the new insurance compact had been adopted in nine states.

- *National Animal ID*—With the growing concern about mad cow disease, both state and federal government officials are looking at new challenges to the traditional means of tagging and tracking livestock. While tracking an individual animal is currently feasible, it takes far too long and in the event of an outbreak, it would limit the ability of officials to quickly and accurately find an animal's point of origin. An interstate compact developed by states with input from relevant federal agencies may be a viable solution to the collection and sharing of vital information in a timely fashion.

- *Voter Registration Information*—The Help America Vote Act of 2002 specifically details what and how voter registration information is to be collected and stored. However, it makes no reference to sharing and coordinating such data between states to ensure that a citizen votes only once and in the appropriate jurisdiction. This issue is particularly relevant when one considers that between 1995 and 2000, more than 11 million people moved between states.[9] An interstate compact could al-

low member states to share voter registration information quickly and accurately.

Conclusion

In response to the needs of the interstate compact community (as partly identified by the survey) and the need to aid states in the formulation of solutions to emerging policy issues, CSG has created the National Center for Interstate Compacts. An information clearinghouse, training and technical assistance provider and primary facilitator in helping states manage the compact process, the center promotes the use of interstate compacts as an ideal tool to meet the demand for cooperative state action, to develop and enforce stringent standards, and to provide an adaptive structure for states that can evolve to meet new and changing demands over time.

The goals of the National Center for Interstate Compacts are to:

- educate stakeholder groups, compact staff, and state and local officials on the background, history, legality, structure, mechanics and use of interstate compacts;

- provide technical assistance to states in determining the need for new interstate compacts and to examine and, where appropriate, revise existing interstate agreements; and

- assist states in streamlining administrative structures and procedures, promoting the use of technology in compact activities, gaining federal support for their compact efforts, and creating standards for compact operations and rules and regulation development and publishing.

For more information on interstate compacts and the National Center for Interstate Compacts, please visit: www.csg.org (keyword: interstate compacts).

Notes

[1]Michael L. Buenger and Richard L. Masters, "The Interstate Compact for Adult Offender Supervision: Using Old Tools to Solve New Problems," *The Roger Williams University Law Review*, 1, 9 (Fall 2003).

[2]Michael H. McCabe, *Interstate Compacts: Background and History*, (Lexington, KY: The Council of State Governments, 1997).

[3]William K. Voit, *Interstate Compacts and Agencies*, 1998, (The Council of State Governments, 2000).

[4]See note 1 above.

[5]William Kevin Voit, Nancy J. Vickers and Thomas L. Gavenois, *Interstate Compacts & Agencies 2003*, (Lexington, KY: The Council of State Governments, 2003). Much

of the contact information was found and/or verified using Internet searches.

[6]The sample excluded compacts that are administered by separate interstate commissions, boundary compacts and compacts that have not been signed onto by more than one state; 35 were deemed ineligible.

[7]Today, it is well established that only those compacts that affect a power delegated to the federal government or alter the political balance within the federal system, require the consent of Congress.

[8]*Guardianships: Collaboration Needed to Protect Incapacitated Elderly People*, GAO-04-655, July 2004.

[9]*Census 2000 Special Reports: Domestic Migration Across Regions, Divisions and States—1995 to 2000*, Censr-7, (U.S. Census Bureau, U.S. Department of Commerce, August 2003).

About the Authors

John Mountjoy is the director of CSG's National Center for Interstate Compacts. He managed CSG's national effort on the Interstate Compact for Adult Offender Supervision and currently oversees the revision of the Interstate Compact for Juveniles and the Interstate Compact for the Placement of Children. He holds a Masters in Public Administration and a B.A. in Communications from Western Kentucky University.

Melissa Bell is the associate director of research for CSG. She is the author of several Trends Alerts on various topics, including immigration, fiscal affairs and medical malpractice. She has a Ph.D. in public policy from the University of Kentucky.

The Geographic Distribution of Federal Funds

By Edward N. Trevelyan

The U.S. Census Bureau's Consolidated Federal Funds Report *is a key source of government spending data, including not only agency and program detail, but also the geographic distribution of funds. This article provides details and insights into the make-up and significance of this flow of federal funds on state and local areas.*

Introduction

With domestic expenditures of $2.06 trillion in federal fiscal year 2003, the United States government spent nearly as much as the combined outlays of the 90,000 state and local governments in the United States.[1] As the president's FY 2006 budget begins its journey through the congressional review process, there is renewed interest in the relative merits of countless federal funding programs.

egory are three highly visible, and often politically charged programs. Social Security, Medicare and Medicaid accounted for $955 billion, or 46 percent of all U.S. government domestic spending.

Debate over budget items is informed by substantive policy details, including the degree to which federal dollars are perceived to affect local economies. The Census Bureau provides an important window into this geographic distribution of federal funds through its annual *Consolidated Federal Funds Report* (CFFR). This report covers most domestic spending by the federal government, tracked to recipients at the state, county, and in some cases, local levels. The largest item not covered is the interest payment on the federal debt, which cannot be meaningfully assigned by geographic area. The balance of this article will provide details and insights into the make-up and significance of these flows of federal funds.

CFFR Report Coverage

The *Consolidated Federal Funds Report* covers federal government expenditures or obligations for the categories listed below. For FY 2003, amounts reported totaled $2.1 trillion for the direct expenditure or obligation categories (items 1 thorough 5, below) and $966 billion for other federal assistance (items 6 through 8):

1. Retirement and disability ($636 billion)
2. Other direct payments ($446 billion)
3. Grants ($441 billion)
4. Procurement contracts ($327 billion)
5. Salaries and wages ($211 billion)
6. Direct loans ($34 billion)
7. Guaranteed or insured loans ($227 billion)
8. Insurance ($705 billion)

Table A

TOP 10 FEDERAL PROGRAMS, EXCLUDING LOANS AND INSURANCE

(Sorted by descending amount)

Code	Program	Amount
96.002	Social Security Retirement Insurance	$305,159,678,337
PC.100	Procurement Contracts—Department of Defense	201,229,509,585
93.778	Medical Assistance Program	167,790,232,644
93.773	Medicare—Hospital Insurance	152,257,430,553
93.774	Medicare—Supplementary Medical Insurance	121,796,655,308
PC.200	Procurement Contracts—All Federal Government Agencies other than Defense and USPS	112,525,535,206
96.004	Social Security Survivors Insurance	93,304,326,390
96.001	Social Security Disability Insurance	77,146,762,769
SW.500	Salaries and Wages—All Federal Government Civilian Employees except Defense and USPS	76,829,390,816
DO.200	Unemployment Compensation Benefit Payments	51,146,482,437

Source: U.S. Census Bureau.

The effects on the economy of this annual outflow of federal funds go well beyond the nearly $441 billion in grants, primarily to state and local governments. The $327 billion in defense and non-defense procurement contracts have equally profound impacts upon economic indicators nationwide, as do the $211 billion in salaries and wages paid to military and civilian employees. It is, however, the over $1 trillion in direct payments to individuals and others that has come to really drive federal spending and ultimately its effect on the national economy. In FY 2003, over 50 percent of the entire federal domestic budget was distributed under these "direct" programs. Dominating this cat-

Dollar amounts reported under these categories can represent either actual expenditures or obligations. As a general guide, the grants and procurement data in this report represent obligated funds, while direct payments, salaries and wages represent actual expenditures (outlays). Data on loan and insurance programs (categories 6 through 8) generally represent the contingent liability of the federal government. Because the latter categories represent available funds or "coverage," they are excluded in calculations of "total direct expenditure or obligation" (the $2.1 trillion referred to above).

Amounts Excluded From CFFR Coverage

Federal expenditures excluded conceptually are those that cannot be geographically distributed, all international transactions and foreign payments, and federal outlay categories not covered by any of the reporting systems that served as data sources for the CFFR. The largest item was net interest on federal government debt, which was estimated to be $153 billion in FY 2003. The fiscal year 2003 total outlays for the international affairs function in the federal budget were estimated at $21 billion.

For some agencies, data for selected object categories could not be obtained. These include the procurement actions of the judicial and legislative sectors of the federal government. Expenditures other than salaries and wages are not available for the Federal Deposit Insurance Corporation, National Credit Union Administration, and Federal Saving and Loans Insurance Corporation. Expenditures for the Central Intelligence Agency, the Defense Intelligence Agency, and the National Security Agency also are excluded from coverage, or otherwise not separately identifiable.

The federal budget outlays estimated for FY 2003 totaled $2.0 trillion. However, comparison of the federal budget amount with data reported in the CFFR can be misleading, since the federal budget amounts differ from CFFR in accounting concepts and the treatment of intragovernmental transfers. For example, outlays for many programs in the federal budget are reported on a net basis, whereas the CFFR reports gross outlays or obligations to nonfederal recipients.

Summary of Methodology

This is a consolidated report, developed by bringing together available statistics on federal government expenditures or obligations. The first phase of the CFFR program is to identify the available data sources. The following reporting systems and agencies are used as primary data sources:

- Federal Assistance Award Data System
- Department of Defense
- General Services Administration—Federal Procurement Data System
- Office of Personnel Management
- U.S. Postal Service

In addition to these primary sources, several other federal agencies are requested to provide data, usually for selected programs. Most of these are agencies that do not report under the requirements of the Federal Assistance Award Data System.

Relationship to Federal Assistance Award Data System

The Federal Assistance Award Data System (FAADS) is a quarterly report of financial assistance awards made by each federal agency. Coverage includes most (but not all) grants, direct payments to individuals and others, loans, and insurance coverage. Data submitted by federal agencies for the FAADS serve as the primary source for most of the statistics in the CFFR. The FAADS does not provide information on either salaries and wages or procurement contracts. All

Table B
TOP 10 FEDERAL RETIREMENT AND DISABILITY PROGRAMS
(Sorted by descending amount)

Code	Program	Amount
96.002	Social Security Retirement Insurance	$305,159,678,337
96.004	Social Security Survivors Insurance	93,304,326,390
96.001	Social Security Disability Insurance	77,146,762,763
DR.200	Federal Retirement and Disability Payments—Civilian	49,602,931,073
DR.100	Federal Retirement and Disability Payments—Military	33,428,532,000
96.006	Supplemental Security Income	32,494,880,366
64.109	Veterans Compensation for Service-Connected Disability	20,622,188,731
57.001	Social Insurance for Railroad Workers	8,836,027,975
64.110	Veterans Dependency and Indemnity Compensation for SVC-Connected Death	3,773,936,752
64.104	Pension for Non-Service-Connected Disability for Veterans	2,489,932,193

Source: U.S. Census Bureau.

Table C
TOP 10 FEDERAL OTHER DIRECT PAYMENT PROGRAMS
(Sorted by descending amount)

Code	Program	Amount
93.773	Medicare—Hospital Insurance	$152,257,430,553
93.774	Medicare—Supplementary Medical Insurance	121,796,655,308
DO.200	Unemployment Compensation Benefit Payments	51,146,482,437
DO.300	Federal Government Payments for Excess Earned Income Tax Credits	33,210,791,000
10.551	Food Stamps	21,421,437,521
DX.200	Federal Employee Life/Health Insurance Premium Payments—Employer Share	17,177,036,989
84.063	Federal Pell Grant Program	12,079,460,332
10.450	Crop Insurance	5,922,366,683
DX.550	Temporary State Fiscal Relief Fund	4,999,999,000
10.055	Production Flexibility Payments for Contract Commodities	4,232,389,246

Source: U.S. Census Bureau.

Table Descriptions and Data Sources

Total Expenditure: $2.1 trillion

All amounts in Table 2.3 are aggregates from the data included in Tables 2.4-2.9. These are national and state area summaries of the federal expenditure object categories (1 through 5) identified above under "CFFR Report Coverage." The "Total Expenditure" amount does not include data on contingent liabilities (loans and insurance, from categories 6 through 8), which are separately listed in Table 2.9.

CFFR data not obtained through the FAADS are otherwise obtained from federal agencies.

Data on financial assistance awards are submitted quarterly by federal government agencies. The Census Bureau collects these data and combines them to form a single quarterly database on federal government financial assistance awards. Each quarterly database is distributed to the Congress and to state governments. In addition to grant awards, the FAADS program covers direct payments to individuals (such as retirement benefits), direct payments for specified use (such as food stamp awards), direct loans, guaranteed loans and insurance coverage of the federal government. All financial assistance awards covered in the FAADS are identified by a Catalog of Federal Domestic Assistance (CFDA) program number (or a pseudo code, if a CFDA number is unavailable).

For grants, the FAADS data represent the federal obligation incurred at the time the grant is awarded. The amounts reported do not represent actual expenditures, since obligations in one time period may not result in outlays during the same time period. Moreover, initial amounts obligated may be adjusted at a later date, either through enhancements or de-obligations. These de-obligations may appear in the CFFR data as negative amounts. Users should be aware of what these amounts represent and use care in interpreting such data.

For FY 2003, the CFFR derived data from the FAADS by summing the four quarterly reports that covered financial assistance awarded between October 1, 2002, and September 30, 2003. All program awards identified in FAADS are reported by state, county, and (in certain cases) city of recipient. Submitting federal agencies use either FIPS codes for states, counties and places, or General Services Administration location codes.

Retirement and Disability: $636 billion

In the CFFR, data covering federal government direct payments are separated into two object categories: direct payments for retirement and disability benefits (Table 2.4), and all other direct payments (Table 2.5). Retirement and disability programs include federal employee retirement and disability benefits, Social Security payments of all types, selected Veterans Administration programs, and selected other federal programs.

Except as indicated below, data in Table 2.4, are compiled from amounts reported by the federal agencies for the FAADS. The following retirement and disability direct payment programs are not available from the FAADS, but are obtained from other data sources.

- Military retirement benefits data are supplied by the Department of Defense.

- Coast Guard retirement benefits data are obtained from the U.S. Coast Guard (now a unit of the Department of Homeland Security) and the Office of Personnel Management (OPM).

- Federal civilian employee retirement and disability payment data are obtained from the Compensation Group, OPM.

- Pension plan termination insurance payment data are provided by the Pension Benefit Guaranty Corporation (PBGC).

- Public Health Service (PHS), Commissioned Corps retirement data are reported by the PHS.

- National Oceanic and Atmospheric Administration (NOAA) Commissioned Corps data are provided by the U.S. Coast Guard, Pay and Personnel Center.

- Foreign Service Officers retirement data are provided by the State Department.

- The Tennessee Valley Authority (TVA) retirement data are reported by the TVA.

Other Direct Payments: $446 billion

Amounts shown in Table 2.5 come from the FAADS, except for those programs listed below. Direct payments for individuals are reported by state and county area only. The following other direct payment programs are not available from the FAADS, but are obtained from other data sources.

- Excess earned income tax credit data are reported by the Department of the Treasury, Internal Revenue Service, Statistics of Income Division.

- Crop Insurance data on the amount of indemnity payments (claims) and premium subsidies are provided by the Agriculture Department.

- The Federal Emergency Management Agency provides data for payments under the National Flood Insurance program.

- Legal Services Corporation provides annualized grant and contract payment data.

- U.S. Postal Service expenditures for current operations, other than procurement and salaries and wages, are provided by the Postal Service as part of that agency's total submission for CFFR.

- Data for the federal government (employer) share of premiums on federal employee life and health insurance are provided by the OPM, Compensation Group.

- The Education Department reports payments under the Federal Family Education Loan program.

- Statistics on federal expenditures for unemployment compensation are compiled from information obtained from the Department of Labor.

- The Office of Justice Programs provides data for payments under the Public Safety Officers' Benefit Program of the Department of Justice.

Grants: $441 billion

The principal source of the grants data in the CFFR (about 98 percent of all grants reported) is the information submitted quarterly for the FAADS. These

Table D
TOP 10 FEDERAL GRANT PROGRAMS
(Sorted by descending amount)

Code	Program	Amount
93.778	Medical Assistance Program	$167,790,232,644
20.205	Highway Planning and Construction	36,005,167,720
14.871	Section 8 Housing Choice Vouchers	20,947,329,022
93.558	Temporary Assistance for Needy Families	17,367,393,624
84.027	Special Education—Grants to States	8,848,672,262
84.010	Title I Grants to Local Education Agencies	8,384,322,863
10.555	Natonal School Lunch Program	7,035,861,276
93.600	Head Start	6,526,419,518
83.516	Disaster Assistance	5,555,554,783
93.767	State Children's Insurance Program (CHIP)	5,383,757,064

Source: U.S. Census Bureau.

data represent the federal obligation incurred at the time the grant is awarded.

Procurement: $327 billion

Statistics in Table 2.7 are provided by the U.S. Postal Service (USPS) for Postal Service procurement and by the Federal Procurement Data Center (FPDC) within the General Services Administration for procurement actions of nearly all other federal agencies, including the Defense Department.

The FPDC collects procurement statistics on a quarterly basis from most federal government departments and agencies, and provides these data according to the place of performance rather than the location of the prime contractor. Excluded from the procurement totals reported are the amounts for the judicial and legislative branches of government and most intergovernmental transfers of funds. Also excluded from the totals are amounts for procurement in foreign countries.

Procurement data awarded by the USPS include all outlays made under formal contractual agreements. The FPDC data include contractual actions for construction, purchases of equipment, and other purchases of tangible items by the federal government. Also included with the FPDC data are contractual actions for services often not generally associated with procurement, such as the purchase of utilities, building leases, and other services entered into via contractual agreement.

Salaries and Wages: $211 billion

Amounts reported for federal government salaries and wages are from four sources: the Department of Defense, the OPM, the USPS, and the U.S. Coast Guard (within the Department of Homeland Security).

Amounts reported include salaries and wages, housing allowances, and in general all other person-

Table E
FEDERAL PROCUREMENT PROGRAMS
(Sorted by descending amount)

Code	Program	Amount
PC.100	Procurement Contracts—Department of Defense	$201,229,509,585
PC.200	Procurement Contracts - All Federal Government Agencies other than Defense and USPS	112,525,535,206
PC.300	Procurement Contracts—U.S. Postal Service	13,658,031,503

Source: U.S. Census Bureau

nel compensation, except retired military pay, which is included in the CFFR's Retirement and Disability Category. Amounts for military personnel stationed overseas are also excluded from totals.

Direct Loans, Guaranteed Loans, and Insurance: $823 billion

All data on loans and insurance programs of the federal government, with the exception of data on flood insurance and student loan programs, come from the FAADS. Flood insurance data are provided by Federal Emergency Management Agency, a unit of the Homeland Security Department. Student loan data are provided by the Department of Education.

Loan and insurance program amounts in Table 2.9 reflect the volume of loan or insurance activities. These amounts represent either direct loans made to certain categories of borrowers, or the federal government contingent liability for loans guaranteed and direct insurance against loss. Loans and insurance data do not represent actual expenditures associated with the loan or insurance programs. Any actual outlays under these programs, such as insurance claims paid by the federal government, appear in the direct payments categories in the CFFR. Federal government contingent liability can vary by program, and caution should be used in comparing one federal loan or insurance program to another, or in interpreting the data presented to reflect actual federal outlays over time.

Statistical Calculations

Per capita federal expenditure amounts in Table 2.10 are computed using resident populations as of July 1, 2003. Percentage distributions of federal expenditures in Table 2.11 are computed based on U.S. expenditure totals in each object category.

The Defense Department and other agency expenditure amounts in Table 2.12 are computed from data in Tables 2.4 through 2.9. Figures for all Department of Defense agencies are tallied to arrive at a total for Department of Defense expenditures. This total is then netted from the grand total of federal government expenditures, and the residual categorized as nondefense expenditures. This procedure is followed for each state and outlying area. The defense/nondefense totals are then used to compute per capita and percent distribution amounts, using the procedure described above for Tables 2.10 and 2.11.

Data in Table 2.12 in the column on Energy Department defense-related activities are from the Department of Energy, Office of the Assistant Secretary for Defense programs. These data represent defense-related atomic energy activities, and are presented on an exhibit basis only. Since the data are for the Department of Energy, they are included in the columns for "All other federal agencies," rather than Department of Defense.

Per capita state rankings in Table 2.13 are derived from per-capita figures shown in Table 2.10. The District of Columbia and the outlying areas are excluded from the rankings.

Geographic Coverage and Presentation

The CFFR report presents data by state and county area. The District of Columbia and the Outlying Areas of American Samoa, Federated States of Micronesia, Guam, Republic of the Marshall Islands, Commonwealth of the Northern Mariana Islands, Republic of Palau, Commonwealth of Puerto Rico, and the U.S. Virgin Islands are included. In addition to county areas, municipal governments that are independent of any organized county are included in the CFFR as county equivalent areas.

It is important to note that the CFFR covers federal government payments to all types of recipients, both government and other, located in the geographic areas over which these governments have jurisdiction. For example, the federal payments to the New York City area could represent monies allocated to the city government, a private company located in the city, or a private citizen residing in the city. No attempt is made in the CFFR to provide information on the recipients (individually or by type) of federal money. For most programs, information on recipients and recipient types (and other details) can be found in the FAADS.

Estimates for Substate Grant Distributions

Many federal grant programs involve a direct payment to state governments, which are then responsible for program administration. Examples include: grants that are "passed through" to local governments (such as block grant programs); grants in which the financial impact of federal funds is spread out over all areas of the state, such as those for highway construction; and grants or assistance programs such as Low Income Home Energy Assistance, which the state can administer but for which the ultimate beneficiaries are found throughout the state.

The CFFR contains data on the substate allocation of funds for a selection of major grant programs of this "passed through" variety. Substate geographic distributions are obtained through a periodic survey conducted by the Census Bureau. To the extent possible, these data are allocated by county or county-equivalent area. Substate allocation figures for these programs are available for some, but not all, of the states and outlying areas.

More is not Always Better

All things being equal (which they rarely are), the receipt of a relatively high level of federal funds to a state or local area is desirable. In the competition for federal dollars and the perceived attainment of "receiving a fair share" of these funds, one must be mindful of the bases for "qualifying" for many assistance programs. If federal funds are received for purposes such as improving the health and quality of life of our children or seniors, or providing for national de-

fense and homeland security, these are generally recognized as positive outcomes. Similarly, if the funds received are to provide educational opportunities, improved housing, or a cleaner environment, that too would be welcomed by most citizens.

On the other hand, if federal funds are awarded to a geographic area due to "undesirable" circumstances, then these receipts might actually have negative connotations. Some examples of situations where the qualification for federal funds would be undesirable include: high crime rate; low student achievement; deteriorating infrastructure (roads, bridges, water and sewer systems, etc.); homelessness; low income or poverty; high unemployment; polluted land, water and air; crop failures; or disasters. If an area is receiving federal funds for these latter reasons, then clearly, more is not better.

While taxpayers are naturally curious about the degree to which taxes are "returned" to their geographic area (whether it be region, state, county, city or congressional district), it is important that they are mindful of this distinction between positive and negative "triggers" for federal funding. Similarly, economists, policy analysts, and other researchers must carefully weight their "balance of payment" models to account for these distinctions. Otherwise, such models have little intrinsic value, and can lead to misperceptions about the impact of taxation and federal assistance.

Furthermore, technical and statistical limitations must be carefully considered when CFFR data are used to bolster arguments about the impact of federal funds. While CFFR's geographic orientation can be enormously useful in identifying broad regional trends, it can produce misleading conclusions at the "micro" level unless the limitations are kept in mind. Among these limitations are the following:

- CFFR data represent expenditures or obligations to government and non-government recipients in state, county and county-equivalent areas. These data cannot, in any consistent and meaningful way,

Table F
FEDERAL SALARY AND WAGE PROGRAMS
(Sorted by descending amount)

Code	Program	Amount
SW.500	Salaries and Wages - All Federal Government Civilian Employees Except Defense and USPS	$76,829,390,816
SW.600	Salaries and Wages—U.S. Postal Service	50,428,120,500
SW.100	Salaries and Wages—Department of Defense (Active Military Employees)	46,908,385,000
SW.400	Salaries and Wages—Department of Defense (Civilian Employees)	27,336,125,000
SW.200	Salaries and Wages—Department of Defense (Inactive Military Employees)	7,445,634,000
SW.700	Salaries and Wages—U.S. Coast Guard (Uniformed Employees)	1,729,656,933

Source: U.S. Census Bureau

Table G
TOP 10 FEDERAL LOAN AND INSURANCE PROGRAMS
(Sorted by descending amount)

Code	Program	Amount
97.002	Flood Insurance	$661,793,028,787
14.117	Mortgage Insurance Homes	147,385,534,704
10.450	Crop Insurance	40,064,741,244
84.032	Federal Family Education Loans	28,132,568,336
84.268	Federal Direct Student Loans	22,072,946,267
64.114	Veterans Housing Guaranteed and Insured Loans	13,970,795,714
14.133	Mortgage Insurance Purchase of Units in Condominiums	10,661,965,649
59.012	Small Business Loans	8,110,128,255
10.051	Commodity Loans and Loan Deficiency Payments	7,424,473,761
10.410	Very Low to Moderate Income Housing Loans	4,165,519,838

Source: U.S. Census Bureau

be generalized to congressional district geographies. While there is a handful of instances in which the boundaries of counties (and even entire states and outlying areas) coincide with congressional district boundaries, the predominant relationship is one of "cross-cutting" boundaries. Because most data are reported to the county level of geography, they are of little value in determining district-level expenditures. Such precision might be possible, but only with more precise reporting.

- While every effort is made in the CFFR to portray an accurate and meaningful geographic distribution of federal funds, there are notable instances in which the geographic coding of federal funds may not match the true "place of performance." This problem is dealt with effectively by the careful data collection processes of several CFFR "feeder" agencies, such as the OPM, the FPDC and the USPS. However, current resource limitations prevent universal application of such processes (or the alternative of highly detailed postcollection editing). Perhaps the most recognizable outgrowth of this limitation is a tendency for grant coding to reflect corporate or "headquarters" addresses, to the detriment of more meaningful distribution data.

Looking to the Future

As we enter the 21st century, what are the dynamics, priorities and realities that will determine the demographic and economic future of the United States? In contrast to the "exuberance" of the 1990s, the economic climate is far more cautious, if not "guardedly optimistic." In this era of federal belt-tightening, states face growing pressure to shoulder a higher proportion of government services. Prescription drugs and other health care costs continue to outpace the rate of inflation and the traditional revenues that once supported them. Medicaid cost increases alone threaten to outpace state revenues. Retiring workers of the baby boom generation will soon impose new pressures on the solvency of the Social Security system.

Adding to these challenges are the fiscal pressures emanating directly or indirectly from the September 11, 2001 terrorist attacks. Many of the resources needed to address the resultant homeland security concerns must originate at the state and local levels. Areas of significant concern include training and equipping police, fire and emergency medical first-responders; security for borders, ports and waterways, airports, and communications networks; food and water safety; and vaccinations against biological and chemical agents.

Against this backdrop of economic and security concerns, as well as new budgetary limitations imposed by federal tax cuts and defense-related spending increases, the level and focus of federal assistance to state and local governments will be closely watched. As competing economic and fiscal agendas and budget priorities are debated, the Census Bureau's CFFR data will continue to provide a valuable research and reference resource.

Notes

[1]U.S. Census Bureau, *Consolidated Federal Funds Report, FY 2003*, http://www.census.gov/govs/www/cffr03.html; U.S. Census Bureau, *Survey of State and Local Government Finances, FY 2001-2002*, http://www.census.gov/govs/estimate/9299ussl_1.html; U.S. Census Bureau, *2002 Census of Governments*, http://www.census.gov/govs/www/gid2002.html.

About the Author

Edward N. Trevelyan is a survey statistician with the Federal Programs Branch, Governments Division, Bureau of the Census, U.S. Department of Commerce. Acting as the executive agent of the U.S. Office of Management and Budget, this office is responsible for several projects and studies on the geographic distribution of federal funds, and also serves as the Federal Audit Clearinghouse for collecting and disseminating audits and related data on the use of federal awards.

Table 2.1
TOTAL FEDERAL GRANTS TO STATE AND LOCAL GOVERNMENTS BY STATE AND REGION: 1995–2003
(In millions of dollars)

State or other jurisdiction	2003	2002	2001	2000	1999	1998	1997	1996	1995
United States	$441,038	$412,371	$338,977	$308,530	$294,469	$269,128	$229,778	$227,542	$228,936
Eastern Region									
Connecticut	$5,376	$5,279	$4,364	$4,033	$3,846	$3,653	$2,905	$3,080	$3,195
Delaware	1,181	1,121	892	838	825	678	629	600	560
Maine	2,610	2,270	1,905	1,770	1,664	1,602	1,378	1,389	1,315
Massachusetts	13,328	12,339	9,718	9,070	8,838	8,019	6,365	6,813	6,829
New Hampshire	1,865	1,632	1,288	1,238	1,120	1,042	842	890	866
New Jersey	11,481	10,822	8,478	7,876	7,262	7,108	6,602	6,506	6,639
New York	47,575	42,461	32,897	31,564	28,870	28,066	24,384	24,560	24,348
Pennsylvania	18,624	18,017	14,487	13,940	13,141	12,381	10,268	10,117	10,354
Rhode Island	2,234	2,094	1,607	1,574	1,411	1,368	1,144	1,176	1,276
Vermont	1,331	1,281	1,069	929	883	803	601	641	625
Regional Total	105,605	97,316	76,705	72,832	67,860	64,720	55,118	55,772	56,007
Midwestern Region									
Illinois	$15,720	$14,975	$11,883	$11,228	$10,586	$10,156	$9,296	$9,229	$9,487
Indiana	7,313	6,969	5,850	5,108	4,706	4,152	3,539	3,657	3,546
Iowa	3,877	4,060	3,079	2,714	2,595	2,424	1,977	2,030	2,074
Kansas	3,415	3,272	2,721	2,323	2,183	1,934	1,620	1,700	1,649
Michigan	12,970	13,279	10,887	10,107	9,764	8,618	7,237	7,194	7,589
Minnesota	6,914	6,492	5,260	4,753	4,499	4,199	3,952	3,535	3,685
Nebraska	2,512	2,342	2,054	1,720	1,651	1,511	1,227	1,232	1,440
North Dakota	1,537	1,425	1,284	1,101	1,009	1,067	1,074	734	768
Ohio	15,687	14,844	11,762	10,665	10,254	9,733	8,327	8,776	9,115
South Dakota	1,698	1,506	1,254	1,088	1,056	1,007	982	867	813
Wisconsin	7,544	7,255	5,843	5,254	4,842	4,697	3,617	3,679	3,729
Regional Total	79,187	76,419	61,877	56,061	53,145	49,498	42,848	42,633	43,895
Southern Region									
Alabama	$6,649	$6,344	$5,298	$4,833	$4,632	$4,161	$3,483	$3,325	$3,419
Arkansas	4,541	4,047	3,448	2,778	2,614	2,440	2,283	2,131	2,019
Florida	17,463	16,350	13,666	12,149	11,191	10,320	8,504	8,442	9,078
Georgia	10,561	10,500	7,929	7,520	6,752	6,233	5,469	5,359	5,461
Kentucky	6,634	6,346	5,100	4,687	4,395	4,236	3,702	3,355	3,437
Louisiana	7,820	7,437	6,173	5,300	5,228	4,708	4,457	4,734	5,291
Maryland	8,632	6,312	7,586	6,911	5,744	5,022	3,950	3,544	3,594
Mississippi	5,318	5,046	4,246	3,517	3,387	3,025	2,626	2,754	2,738
Missouri	8,655	8,429	6,868	5,939	5,478	5,065	4,231	4,091	4,159
North Carolina	11,613	10,939	9,122	8,158	7,608	7,133	6,284	5,227	5,487
Oklahoma	5,136	5,108	4,119	3,583	3,231	3,059	2,510	2,435	2,472
South Carolina	5,969	5,592	4,730	4,163	3,879	3,525	2,987	3,032	3,027
Tennessee	9,057	8,658	7,027	6,372	5,900	5,510	4,555	4,476	4,531
Texas	28,423	24,858	21,675	18,346	18,370	15,809	13,184	13,287	13,338
Virginia	7,886	7,714	5,908	5,163	4,749	4,423	3,518	3,403	3,504
West Virginia	3,562	3,298	2,971	2,729	2,490	2,480	2,100	2,088	2,074
Regional Total	147,919	136,978	115,866	102,148	95,648	87,149	73,843	71,683	73,629
Western Region									
Alaska	$3,022	$3,127	$2,314	$2,174	$1,929	$1,427	$1,303	$1,051	$1,125
Arizona	7,235	6,664	5,190	4,704	4,537	4,147	3,355	3,095	3,150
California	51,329	48,084	39,797	36,080	36,370	32,090	27,014	26,413	26,934
Colorado	6,014	4,740	3,916	3,591	3,446	3,048	2,444	2,410	2,391
Hawaii	1,911	1,835	1,514	1,348	1,335	1,190	1,184	1,126	1,162
Idaho	1,858	1,837	1,505	1,270	1,177	1,055	936	887	849
Montana	1,938	1,912	1,665	1,474	1,399	1,139	991	964	933
Nevada	1,955	1,840	1,442	1,340	1,249	1,081	983	876	882
New Mexico	4,322	3,954	3,586	3,032	2,750	2,547	2,152	1,942	1,866
Oregon	5,103	4,814	4,308	3,684	3,518	3,275	2,853	2,797	2,763
Utah	2,845	2,697	2,244	2,065	1,994	1,727	1,355	1,446	1,318
Washington	8,881	8,296	6,794	6,345	5,720	5,422	4,496	4,152	4,351
Wyoming	1,616	1,234	1,213	1,022	933	850	762	708	748
Regional Total	98,029	91,034	75,488	68,129	66,357	58,998	49,828	47,867	48,472
Regional total without California	46,700	42,950	35,691	32,049	29,987	26,908	22,814	21,454	21,538
Dist. of Columbia	4,310	4,832	4,020	4,675	5,293	4,101	2,740	2,578	2,238
American Samoa	110	93	58	59	131	91	121	71	73
Fed. States of Micronesia	136	126	94	...	...	...	...	...	...
Guam	400	251	176	138	188	266	125	134	162
Marshall Islands	66	58	48	...	...	...	...	...	...
No. Mariana Islands	89	66	60	47	54	39	35	31	41
Palau	51	41	35	...	...	...	...	...	...
Puerto Rico	4,808	4,828	3,899	3,842	5,284	3,895	3,719	3,387	3,535
U.S. Virgin Islands	282	266	111	195	216	256	371	373	217
Undistributed	43	65	183	10	248	116	1,032	3,009	592

Source: U.S. Department of Commerce, Bureau of the Census. *Consolidated Federal Funds Report for Fiscal Year 2003*, issued September 2004.

Key:
. . .—No data available.

Table 2.2
FEDERAL AID TO STATE AND LOCAL GOVERNMENTS, SELECTED PROGRAMS BY STATE: FISCAL YEAR 2003
(In millions of dollars)

State and outlying area	Total	USDA Total	Agricultural Marketing Service	Department of Agriculture — Cooperative State Research and Extension Service — Total	Extension activities	Research and education activities	Farm Service Agency	Food and Safety Inspection Service
United States, total	$385,693,169	$22,101,978	$506,272	$998,125	$429,069	$569,056	$3,330	$45,601
Alabama	5,895,622	377,373	6,507	31,472	16,415	15,057	128	1,347
Alaska	2,407,114	105,757	1,194	8,270	2,948	5,322	0	0
Arizona	7,028,362	394,608	12,950	11,418	3,714	7,704	109	687
Arkansas	3,850,593	242,986	8,017	20,064	8,451	11,613	94	153
California	46,210,746	2,753,094	57,618	43,690	12,823	30,867	47	102
Colorado	4,232,375	231,744	7,715	19,561	5,674	13,887	97	54
Connecticut	4,482,708	155,264	3,232	8,936	3,630	5,306	0	0
Delaware	1,024,668	57,134	1,095	7,564	2,847	4,717	0	376
Florida	17,256,091	972,874	19,700	27,832	10,756	17,076	40	0
Georgia	8,949,450	692,081	9,118	31,758	12,556	19,202	0	3,063
Hawaii	1,515,334	110,286	1,776	17,692	2,207	15,485	0	0
Idaho	1,651,106	108,887	2,440	7,645	2,185	5,460	3	0
Illinois	13,999,628	770,178	16,669	20,893	8,929	11,964	63	4,069
Indiana	6,282,796	324,709	6,480	21,648	10,565	11,083	71	1,716
Iowa	3,382,945	199,256	2,867	29,175	12,102	17,073	327	1,197
Kansas	2,758,845	181,968	5,499	15,982	7,861	8,121	410	1,883
Kentucky	5,968,259	338,472	8,228	24,247	13,464	10,783	0	163
Louisiana	6,486,491	451,640	19,458	18,278	8,800	9,478	0	1,855
Maine	2,404,349	84,457	2,441	9,418	4,160	5,258	0	71
Maryland	6,329,819	271,002	4,534	19,563	10,502	9,061	32	0
Massachusetts	9,840,765	290,876	4,925	13,377	4,155	9,2å22	26	0
Michigan	11,513,627	565,171	24,065	29,340	12,784	16,556	33	0
Minnesota	5,710,257	341,397	6,909	25,500	13,148	12,352	332	627
Mississippi	4,926,928	359,216	6,081	26,526	11,413	15,113	0	977
Missouri	7,139,839	383,951	10,098	27,397	12,476	14,921	94	411
Montana	1,434,638	101,827	3,597	14,422	4,814	9,608	0	522
Nebraska	2,079,263	134,766	3,350	16,841	7,526	9,315	245	20
Nevada	1,911,493	98,485	2,216	4,809	1,796	3,013	14	0
New Hampshire	1,424,871	53,376	2,885	5,342	1,959	3,383	0	0
New Jersey	10,169,482	400,199	7,440	11,241	4,700	6,541	0	385
New Mexico	3,765,693	209,342	7,308	9,751	3,799	5,952	63	555
New York	43,463,311	1,410,386	30,982	38,295	14,600	23,695	0	329
North Carolina	10,066,509	617,469	10,592	40,835	18,913	21,922	0	3,137
North Dakota	1,203,215	69,293	3,544	11,497	4,944	6,553	299	169
Ohio	13,232,799	627,633	15,508	29,353	11,650	17,703	0	5,374
Oklahoma	4,726,105	337,490	20,175	18,369	9,259	9,110	293	1,567
Oregon	4,715,818	404,706	7,435	16,838	6,104	10,734	0	0
Pennsylvania	16,654,854	664,758	13,053	26,618	13,949	12,669	0	59
Rhode Island	1,854,940	61,359	1,571	4,274	2,592	1,682	0	0
South Carolina	4,913,647	330,058	4,904	16,860	9,601	7,259	0	1,459
South Dakota	1,376,298	82,888	6,567	9,957	4,624	5,333	96	746
Tennessee	8,152,838	413,154	9,867	23,409	13,081	10,328	0	0
Texas	24,352,768	1,876,613	34,465	48,220	23,299	24,921	61	4,778
Utah	2,337,320	164,391	2,291	11,071	4,220	6,851	14	1,094
Vermont	1,184,613	58,988	1,973	7,915	2,470	5,445	0	434
Virginia	6,200,198	280,043	9,558	23,504	11,546	11,958	0	1,361
Washington	7,474,125	428,393	11,182	20,051	6,249	13,802	68	0
West Virginia	3,301,375	159,598	4,378	13,226	6,918	6,308	0	670
Wisconsin	6,772,649	315,929	7,838	28,307	11,863	16,444	253	3,519
Wyoming	1,420,298	41,527	951	5,783	1,647	4,136	18	295
District of Columbia	3,633,268	54,122	2,280	2,286	1,004	1,282	0	254
American Samoa	130,776	21,926	54	1,151	549	602	0	0
Fed. States of Micronesia	122,159	1,912	0	1,725	1,097	628	0	0
Guam	230,096	18,973	166	2,118	762	1,356	0	0
Marshall Islands	58,401	17	0	0	0	0	0	0
Northern Marianas	87,299	14,243	23	1,055	647	408	0	49
Palau	46,676	137	0	0	0	0	0	0
Puerto Rico	4,695,055	1,744,421	6,548	12,806	7,013	5,793	0	74
Virgin Islands	344,986	115,116	49	2,950	1,309	1,641	0	0
Undistributed	906,616	24,059	23,906	0	0	0	0	0

See footnotes at end of table

FEDERAL AID TO STATE AND LOCAL GOVERNMENTS, SELECTED PROGRAMS BY STATE: FISCAL YEAR 2003 — Continued

| | Department of Agriculture—Continued | | | | | | | | | |
| | Food and nutrition service | | | | | Forest service | | | | |
State and outlying area	Nutrition service total	Child nutrition programs	Commodity assistance programs	Food stamp program (a)	Needy family program	Special supplemental food program (WIC)	Forest Service total	Payments to states and counties	State and private forestry	National Forest Service	Other
United States, total	$19,245,996	$10,424,165	$165,055	$4,013,337	$96,045	$4,547,394	$559,888	$358,546	$185,771	$4,365	$11,206
Alabama	317,087	202,683	3,366	33,573	1,329	76,136	3,443	2,015	1,428	0	0
Alaska	57,600	29,740	293	7,742	333	19,492	17,705	8,875	7,859	0	971
Arizona	344,206	212,968	3,932	32,532	1,407	93,367	10,731	7,057	3,229	0	445
Arkansas	194,386	122,716	1,481	22,989	1,021	46,179	8,243	5,988	2,219	0	36
California	2,527,276	1,329,573	14,946	347,047	8,220	827,490	74,972	62,163	6,062	2,284	4,463
Colorado	171,786	95,214	2,535	26,856	646	46,535	12,501	5,433	6,915	21	132
Connecticut	136,161	75,639	1,320	26,388	728	32,086	0	868	0	0	0
Delaware	45,953	27,332	616	8,077	251	9,677	332	0	332	0	0
Florida	886,813	587,708	5,251	88,333	3,574	201,947	5,864	2,366	3,498	0	0
Georgia	625,034	403,338	3,850	74,269	1,838	141,739	4,681	1,231	3,449	0	1
Hawaii	82,871	42,283	913	12,966	229	26,480	1,471	0	1,471	0	0
Idaho	70,608	42,636	658	8,962	329	18,023	24,189	20,022	4,167	0	0
Illinois	693,593	412,816	7,073	94,181	2,961	176,562	4,403	287	1,932	46	2,138
Indiana	279,789	172,577	2,892	40,914	1,680	61,726	1,974	123	1,851	0	0
Iowa	145,807	88,756	2,263	19,788	789	34,211	1,101	0	876	217	8
Kansas	149,679	103,489	836	13,620	1,131	30,603	1,940	0	1,926	0	14
Kentucky	279,705	178,145	3,245	30,781	1,286	66,248	3,363	391	2,972	0	0
Louisiana	394,761	252,461	7,549	48,132	1,934	84,685	6,497	3,518	2,979	0	0
Maine	57,540	35,851	1,511	8,477	300	11,401	8,047	39	8,008	0	0
Maryland	238,359	142,339	1,885	36,086	1,895	56,154	2,682	0	2,682	0	0
Massachusetts	264,780	166,067	2,318	31,642	1,934	62,819	1,368	0	1,173	195	0
Michigan	486,937	262,820	9,427	89,394	3,681	121,615	5,186	2,725	2,090	279	92
Minnesota	284,518	161,107	2,934	56,594	1,895	61,988	8,673	3,886	2,502	329	1,956
Mississippi	280,969	179,435	2,246	34,164	1,064	64,060	10,566	7,311	3,255	0	0
Missouri	312,319	191,281	3,083	48,492	2,037	67,426	4,556	2,504	1,610	268	174
Montana	58,207	31,526	1,228	11,785	555	13,113	21,957	12,464	9,493	0	0
Nebraska	105,024	66,138	1,811	14,925	721	21,429	2,311	40	2,271	0	0
Nevada	86,020	49,274	621	11,150	227	24,748	3,849	428	3,326	95	0
New Hampshire	36,971	20,215	911	5,377	558	9,910	1,273	220	1,013	0	40
New Jersey	376,223	198,279	3,000	93,803	3,903	77,238	2,586	0	2,586	0	0
New Mexico	172,839	114,574	1,891	18,471	1,606	36,297	7,341	2,022	4,992	0	327
New York	1,311,174	724,661	12,455	264,580	14,319	295,159	6,793	8	6,677	0	108
North Carolina	529,630	333,520	3,793	74,988	1,548	115,781	14,185	964	13,186	11	24
North Dakota	43,799	24,721	768	7,809	464	10,037	1,544	0	1,544	0	0
Ohio	566,630	299,737	6,347	121,992	2,155	136,399	1,649	62	1,583	0	4
Oklahoma	277,386	168,616	2,210	45,367	1,379	59,814	4,186	1,214	2,972	0	0
Oregon	214,906	108,321	2,499	45,220	1,143	57,723	146,931	140,987	5,923	0	21
Pennsylvania	594,346	300,484	6,991	160,545	6,576	119,750	6,576	3,665	2,863	14	34
Rhode Island	53,383	31,131	332	7,389	301	14,230	1,631	0	1,631	0	0
South Carolina	281,239	188,862	2,795	32,232	769	56,581	9,084	3,104	5,980	0	0
South Dakota	56,701	30,563	928	10,888	611	13,711	4,621	3,699	920	0	2
Tennessee	355,065	219,022	4,885	39,163	1,440	90,555	4,256	529	3,727	0	0
Texas	1,755,111	1,102,541	8,759	190,187	5,085	448,539	10,552	4,435	6,055	0	62
Utah	133,704	80,407	906	19,542	1,376	31,473	9,813	1,913	7,900	0	0
Vermont	41,465	18,125	843	11,534	280	10,683	2,970	708	2,085	177	0
Virginia	218,202	141,834	1,486	4,460	1,313	69,109	5,786	293	5,301	51	141
Washington	332,121	189,878	2,244	40,114	1,257	98,628	46,100	40,191	5,909	0	0
West Virginia	117,733	74,385	1,818	11,634	783	29,113	3,743	1,869	1,866	0	8
Wisconsin	246,531	138,801	2,681	45,512	1,982	57,555	8,651	1,596	7,025	30	0
Wyoming	29,034	15,352	224	6,159	424	6,875	2,436	2,193	40	203	0
District of Columbia ...	47,860	24,764	968	10,190	475	11,463	1,442	0	1,292	145	5
American Samoa	20,441	8,916	22	5,529	1	5,973	280	0	280	0	0
Fed. States of Micronesia	0	0	0	0	0	0	187	0	187	0	0
Guam	15,511	5,960	45	2,611	349	6,546	102	0	102	0	0
Marshall Islands	0	0	0	0	0	0	17	0	17	0	0
Northern Marianas	12,857	4,429	9	8,296	123	0	259	0	259	0	0
Palau	0	0	0	0	0	0	137	0	137	0	0
Puerto Rico	1,715,850	176,088	3,387	1,359,583	1,633	175,159	675	8	667	0	0
Virgin Islands	111,496	14,067	1,775	90,303	197	5,154	609	0	609	0	0
Undistributed	0	0	0	0	0	0	0	0	0	0	0

See footnotes at end of table

FEDERAL AID TO STATE AND LOCAL GOVERNMENTS, SELECTED PROGRAMS BY STATE: FISCAL YEAR 2003 — Continued

| | | Department of Agriculture—Continued | | | | | | |
| | | Rural development activites | | | | | | |
State and outlying area	National Resources Conservation Service	Rural Develop. activities total	Community facilities grants	Rural regional, and cooperative development programs	Housing preservation grants	Water systems and waste disposal systems systems grants	Other	Appalachian Regional Commission
United States, total	$125,231	$617,535	$24,901	$38,630	$5,690	$438,957	$109,357	$35,974
Alabama	919	16,470	379	899	50	14,851	291	4,153
Alaska	2,575	18,413	3,724	681	38	13,899	71	8
Arizona	2,670	11,837	147	913	59	9,172	1,546	0
Arkansas	3,050	8,979	255	476	104	8,055	89	0
California	2,934	46,455	487	1,494	134	18,329	26,011	0
Colorado	856	19,174	112	46	55	915	18,046	2
Connecticut	0	6,067	50	53	0	5,964	0	0
Delaware	758	1,056	34	42	30	950	0	0
Florida	3,994	28,631	172	929	75	9,855	17,600	0
Georgia	1,511	16,916	579	961	292	13,189	1,895	2,588
Hawaii	4,064	2,412	250	19	79	1,366	698	0
Idaho	308	3,694	362	338	0	2,981	13	0
Illinois	9,327	21,161	404	3,344	268	16,035	1,110	77
Indiana	862	12,169	55	328	186	11,599	1	0
Iowa	8,609	10,173	1,278	633	0	8,226	36	0
Kansas	2,285	4,290	57	85	106	3,904	138	0
Kentucky	1,307	21,459	370	1,421	288	14,480	4,900	3,437
Louisiana	2,894	7,897	618	442	270	5,798	769	0
Maine	430	6,510	122	443	113	5,470	362	0
Maryland	1,462	4,370	107	952	90	2,368	853	723
Massachusetts	185	6,215	90	414	73	5,638	0	34
Michigan	606	19,004	666	1,021	239	17,078	0	0
Minnesota	1,143	13,695	535	2,232	83	8,442	2,403	36
Mississippi	13,845	20,252	1,581	616	44	16,817	1,194	3,569
Missouri	10,535	18,541	532	1,556	0	16,424	29	0
Montana	589	2,533	302	474	32	1,569	156	0
Nebraska	2,127	4,848	180	274	64	3,630	700	27
Nevada	0	1,577	50	263	0	903	361	0
New Hampshire	0	6,905	31	69	37	6,768	0	0
New Jersey	0	2,324	347	197	20	1,760	0	1
New Mexico	5,648	5,837	240	311	70	5,216	0	0
New York	1,540	21,273	264	2,857	251	17,488	413	2,000
North Carolina	841	18,249	3,543	1,345	391	11,424	1,546	2,504
North Dakota	2,423	6,018	633	740	30	4,501	114	0
Ohio	33	9,086	264	623	183	7,594	422	2,126
Oklahoma	4,522	10,992	416	1,680	227	5,833	2,836	1
Oregon	135	18,461	377	1,027	92	8,737	8,228	0
Pennsylvania	4,181	19,925	268	713	55	18,879	10	4,885
Rhode Island	0	500	22	115	0	363	0	0
South Carolina	643	15,869	202	1,466	323	13,793	85	817
South Dakota	981	3,219	331	784	4	2,098	2	0
Tennessee	2,276	18,281	501	1,161	206	16,042	371	4,728
Texas	7,211	16,215	154	684	303	9,528	5,546	66
Utah	709	5,695	323	173	0	4,564	635	0
Vermont	969	3,262	119	455	89	2,599	0	0
Virginia	2,311	19,321	1,304	593	237	16,463	724	1,010
Washington	1,947	16,924	48	1,122	0	9,780	5,974	0
West Virginia	6,058	13,790	263	346	56	10,222	2,903	2,899
Wisconsin	220	20,610	1,594	843	84	17,954	135	7
Wyoming	1,656	1,354	42	49	25	1,221	17	0
District of Columbia	0	0	0	0	0	0	0	276
American Samoa	0	0	0	0	0	0	0	0
Fed. States of Micronesia	0	0	0	0	0	0	0	0
Guam	1,076	0	0	0	0	0	0	0
Marshall Islands	0	0	0	0	0	0	0	0
Northern Marianas	0	0	0	0	0	0	0	0
Palau	0	0	0	0	0	0	0	0
Puerto Rico	6	8,462	0	-81	196	8,223	124	0
Virgin Islands	0	12	0	0	12	0	0	0
Undistributed	0	153	117	9	27	0	0	0

See footnotes at end of table

FEDERAL AID TO STATE AND LOCAL GOVERNMENTS, SELECTED PROGRAMS BY STATE: FISCAL YEAR 2003 — Continued

State and outlying area	Department of Commerce						Department of Defense		
	Dept. of Commerce total	Economic Development Aministration	National Oceanic and Atmospheric Administration	National Telecommunications and Information Administration	Corporation for National and Community Service	Corporation for Public Broadcasting	Dept. of Defense total	U.S. Army Corps of Engineers civilian construction program	U.S. Army National Guard construction
United States, total	$934,399	$434,480	$418,365	$81,554	$146,763	$368,206	$281,448	$8,529	$272,919
Alabama	23,300	14,457	5,866	2,977	211	2,525	6,608	17	6,591
Alaska	56,928	13,541	43,051	336	1,889	6,482	6	1	5
Arizona	7,096	4,143	2,197	756	3,378	4,796	5	0	5
Arkansas	7,589	6,939	0	650	3,106	1,676	493	493	0
California	70,771	46,697	20,568	3,506	32,635	35,957	10,802	384	10,418
Colorado	11,899	2,782	8,812	305	3,738	3,976	3,482	0	3,482
Connecticut	10,086	3,243	6,540	303	2,572	2,270	10	10	0
Delaware	2,039	0	2,039	0	1,693	0	2,774	0	2,774
Florida	24,205	10,981	11,004	2,220	2,835	12,811	289	11	278
Georgia	16,398	12,326	3,751	321	1,031	5,443	1,295	1,295	0
Hawaii	22,404	3,471	18,242	691	761	2,140	3,608	0	3,608
Idaho	10,561	9,139	1,375	47	2,282	1,356	4,757	3	4,754
Illinois	14,367	11,329	837	2,201	816	11,296	1,039	382	657
Indiana	8,352	7,340	83	929	315	6,153	8,971	3	8,968
Iowa	3,393	1,690	836	867	205	3,439	1,877	423	1,454
Kansas	6,210	3,459	0	2,751	3,060	2,813	958	267	691
Kentucky	13,694	12,982	20	692	4,239	4,357	868	796	72
Louisiana	27,074	5,411	19,333	2,330	0	3,219	1,891	8	1,883
Maine	13,693	4,137	7,966	1,590	2,172	1,577	7,193	0	7,193
Maryland	17,399	668	15,971	760	4,980	4,382	25	25	0
Massachusetts	18,543	3,663	13,399	1,481	0	12,003	1,566	24	1,542
Michigan	22,268	13,817	3,772	4,679	6,972	7,729	6,090	5	6,085
Minnesota	14,323	12,652	12	1,659	0	10,567	2,843	7	2,836
Mississippi	33,432	8,590	23,125	1,717	6,829	1,932	16,368	283	16,085
Missouri	8,758	6,993	167	1,598	0	4,799	4,378	1,051	3,327
Montana	5,046	3,915	0	1,131	2,915	1,472	4,866	33	4,833
Nebraska	5,990	1,939	0	4,051	0	5,286	982	124	858
Nevada	4,150	1,701	1,810	639	97	2,866	3,047	0	3,047
New Hampshire	9,255	771	6,878	1,606	0	1,351	12,195	9	12,186
New Jersey	8,956	6,736	2,120	100	4,820	3,324	1,201	0	1,201
New Mexico	13,635	10,546	44	3,045	3,766	3,005	-5	1	-6
New York	31,086	17,867	6,164	7,055	20,846	31,140	13,629	3	13,626
North Carolina	38,946	16,629	20,301	2,016	558	69,959	1	1	0
North Dakota	5,050	3,380	97	1,573	472	1,367	2,470	85	2,385
Ohio	17,294	12,613	3,189	1,492	7,794	10,319	37	37	0
Oklahoma	17,852	7,202	8,889	1,761	426	2,390	5,597	459	5,138
Oregon	50,327	10,284	37,873	2,170	279	4,249	2,853	21	2,832
Pennsylvania	21,245	17,222	1,883	2,140	816	10,441	5,487	162	5,325
Rhode Island	11,163	3,842	7,146	175	313	702	0	0	0
South Carolina	31,060	14,440	14,913	1,707	0	3,514	4,710	91	4,619
South Dakota	5,342	3,042	21	2,279	113	1,484	7,876	87	7,789
Tennessee	11,389	10,466	0	923	3,865	4,707	6,762	474	6,288
Texas	38,472	23,245	11,832	3,395	214	12,328	8,330	1,311	7,019
Utah	4,574	4,405	0	169	2,594	5,160	0	0	0
Vermont	3,320	2,833	267	220	1,034	1,351	695	0	695
Virginia	16,966	8,702	5,907	2,357	0	12,310	204	45	159
Washington	71,426	7,265	62,627	1,534	1,433	5,874	3,178	27	3,151
West Virginia	10,615	9,650	97	868	141	1,318	12,410	23	12,387
Wisconsin	13,083	4,433	6,607	2,043	5,581	7,187	4,872	42	4,830
Wyoming	935	922	8	5	0	857	-148	0	-148
District of Columbia ...	3,373	1,722	58	1,593	1,575	6,447	6	6	0
American Samoa	1,687	0	1,646	41	814	556	0	0	0
Fed. States of Micronesia	0	0	0	0	0	0	0	0	0
Guam	1,088	440	648	0	0	696	1,242	0	1,242
Marshall Islands	0	0	0	0	0	0	0	0	0
Northern Marianas	1,127	0	1,127	0	96	0	0	0	0
Palau	0	0	0	0	0	0	0	0	0
Puerto Rico	11,447	5,782	5,565	100	366	3,317	0	0	0
Virgin Islands	2,391	994	1,397	0	116	585	0	0	0
Undistributed	1,327	1,042	285	0	0	-1,054	90,755	0	90,755

See footnotes at end of table

FEDERAL AID TO STATE AND LOCAL GOVERNMENTS, SELECTED PROGRAMS BY STATE: FISCAL YEAR 2003 — Continued

| | | | | Department of Education | | | | | |
| | | | | Office of Special Education and Rehabilitative Services | | | Office of Vocational and Adult Education | | |
State and outlying area	Total	Office of English Language Acquisition (b)	Office of Educational Research and Improvement (b)	Total	Rehabilitation services and disability research programs (b) (c)	Office of Special Education programs (b)	Total	Vocational technical education programs (b)	Adult education and literacy programs (b)
United States, total	$29,194,683	$502,690	$389,600	$8,710,173	$1,779,478	$6,930,695	$1,527,074	$1,039,778	$487,296
Alabama	468,013	1,291	2,364	124,049	878	123,171	26,187	24,080	2,107
Alaska	141,213	2,465	7,487	1,429	976	4530	0	0	
Arizona	696,348	13,083	7,418	182,388	42,790	139,598	33,404	25,605	7,799
Arkansas	321,920	1,371	1,066	85,030	5,696	79,334	253	203	50
California	4,310,597	166,829	43,586	951,227	243,995	707,232	260,734	164,390	96,344
Colorado	422,615	13,909	5,868	134,107	27,416	106,691	20,217	14,238	5,979
Connecticut	325,959	7,103	8,296	94,502	266	94,236	16,310	9,957	6,353
Delaware	105,051	382	117	34,646	10,598	24,048	6,338	4,821	1,517
Florida	1,646,297	31,326	16,582	614,449	136,457	477,992	93,252	63,644	29,608
Georgia	88,952	339	2,814	3,661	1,335	2,326	15,782	536	15,246
Hawaii	178,407	3,432	353	45,763	11,982	33,781	8,314	6,272	2,042
Idaho	146,466	2,428	3,442	40,603	190	40,413	10,217	8,268	1,949
Illinois	1,391,052	25,330	15,161	478,262	102,974	375,288	71,601	45,640	25,961
Indiana	510,069	5,260	1,360	189,906	189	189,717	10,569	393	10,176
Iowa	308,195	2,653	19,441	121,125	27,075	94,050	18,844	14,817	4,027
Kansas	124,757	4,715	5,507	40,449	26,636	13,813	4,390	454	3,936
Kentucky	507,721	1,281	4,048	172,940	44,241	128,699	30,373	21,064	9,309
Louisiana	41,633	750	3,336	779	220	559	80	80	0
Maine	168,407	2,116	1,588	59,518	16,300	43,218	9,176	6,266	2,910
Maryland	528,117	5,100	8,775	181,548	37,384	144,164	16,694	10,706	5,988
Massachusetts	770,452	11,337	8,144	312,010	44,891	267,119	35,045	21,210	13,835
Michigan	1,161,549	4,316	9,377	364,267	77,837	286,430	66,628	47,341	19,287
Minnesota	100,745	2,935	4,358	7,299	1,512	5,787	23,886	23,504	382
Mississippi	402,512	701	3,311	88,707	1,848	86,859	23,568	16,775	6,793
Missouri	89,367	487	2,743	11,236	9,573	1,663	709	533	176
Montana	187,208	2,526	4,254	42,765	12,962	29,803	7,587	6,124	1,463
Nebraska	202,436	3,108	1,584	87,235	11,839	75,396	8,849	6,875	1,974
Nevada	154,801	3,698	2,311	46,970	188	46,782	10,597	7,269	3,328
New Hampshire	119,567	500	1,467	47,353	10,742	36,611	8,114	6,107	2,007
New Jersey	849,817	12,543	3,152	315,221	54,141	261,080	42,261	29,007	13,254
New Mexico	356,341	10,928	5,995	96,565	24,469	72,096	9,136	8,088	1,048
New York	2,576,151	30,128	23,906	749,216	137,862	611,354	97,802	58,259	39,543
North Carolina	816,402	5,910	14,311	288,827	70,985	217,842	52,689	33,575	19,114
North Dakota	133,045	542	1,979	28,305	8,690	19,615	6,153	4,770	1,383
Ohio	96,613	708	11,259	5,836	1,895	3,941	2,321	2,060	261
Oklahoma	513,956	12,080	6,690	146,522	37,616	108,906	26,921	19,849	7,072
Oregon	358,983	7,566	3,563	133,365	35,099	98,266	18,986	13,504	5,482
Pennsylvania	1,239,720	4,711	29,897	340,157	399	339,758	79,892	54,884	25,008
Rhode Island	19,815	123	1,979	1,077	561	516	1,621	1,487	134
South Carolina	109,336	72	6,736	52,596	47,308	5,288	295	119	176
South Dakota	70,648	2,034	1,229	9,860	9,246	614	1,799	0	1,799
Tennessee	548,358	2,017	706	234,826	62,055	172,771	31,669	30,817	852
Texas	2,685,207	65,581	15,648	786,763	187,893	598,870	151,452	107,864	43,588
Utah	247,075	5,022	4,402	95,780	22,241	73,539	13,372	11,241	2,131
Vermont	119,159	677	3,952	35,771	12,552	23,219	6,697	5,278	1,419
Virginia	679,007	3,835	34,307	236,654	61,891	174,763	42,189	29,245	12,944
Washington	529,234	6,810	9,525	148,825	5,057	143,768	1,982	1,822	160
West Virginia	217,435	551	1,633	56,901	1,114	55,787	12,653	8,557	4,096
Wisconsin	620,267	5,920	10,084	218,580	62,253	156,327	35,138	26,788	8,350
Wyoming	104,070	1,220	1,088	28,376	8,176	20,200	5,363	4,427	936
District of Columbia .	111,899	813	1,246	32,917	14,148	18,769	7,020	4,569	2,451
American Samoa	19,079	0	0	6,017	999	5,018	262	0	262
Fed. States of Micronesia	7,769	90	0	4,155	0	4,15587	0	87	
Guam	33,825	367	0	15,603	930	14,673	779	442	337
Marshall Islands	3,156	273	0	1,030	0	1,030	66	0	66
Northern Marianas ..	16,399	0	0	4,574	159	4,415	489	0	489
Palau	3,272	187	0	1,189	0	1,189	105	0	105
Puerto Rico	483,539	1,211	155	67,643	0	67,643	40,157	25,954	14,203
Virgin Islands	4,680	0	0	2,799	2,749	500	0	0	
Undistributed	0	0	0	0	0	00	0	0	

See footnotes at end of table

FEDERAL AID TO STATE AND LOCAL GOVERNMENTS, SELECTED PROGRAMS BY STATE: FISCAL YEAR 2003 — Continued

		Department of Education—continued									
		Office of Elementary and Secondary Education						*Office of Postsecondary Education*			
		Programs for the disadvantaged						*Higher education programs*			
State and outlying area	*Total*	*Migrants (b)*	*Others (b)*	*Impact aid (b)*	*No Child Left Behind Act (b)*	*Title I program*	*Other (b)*	*Total*	*Int'l education prog. (b)*	*Other (b)*	*Office of Student Financial Asstnce. (b) (c)*
United States, total	$15,949,551	$379,769	$618,340	$940,294	$3,628,503	$8,469,238	$1,913,407	$1,217,181	$54,417	$1,162,764	$898,414
Alabama	255,855	2,960	13,517	3,203	67,135	146,634	22,406	42,010	90	41,920	16,257
Alaska	117,239	0	0	77,815	12,826	0	5,534	26,598	0	10,876	1,717
Arizona	415,121	7,054	13,167	105,480	76,038	163,118	50,264	25,233	1,253	23,980	19,701
Arkansas	205,976	5,350	14,251	785	64,326	102,330	18,934	17,800	154	17,646	10,424
California	2,628,065	134,185	121,199	83,867	559,533	1,413,360	315,921	142,938	7,968	134,970	117,218
Colorado	206,057	7,920	7,705	18,878	47,823	95,327	28,404	24,614	454	24,160	17,843
Connecticut	188,936	3,252	5,289	6,275	48,762	101,534	23,824	6,767	548	6,219	4,045
Delaware	53,661	492	2,329	60	15,752	27,545	7,483	6,344	0	6,344	3,563
Florida	821,522	24,451	33,620	10,971	193,714	473,255	85,511	38,963	1,964	36,999	30,203
Georgia	39,352	734	0	19,765	14,503	0	4,350	15,377	330	15,047	11,627
Hawaii	101,169	1,385	2,480	43,671	10,261	26,543	16,829	15,708	1,741	13,967	3,668
Idaho	76,480	6,076	2,837	7,147	20,804	32,189	7,427	7,977	17	7,960	5,319
Illinois	716,043	3,030	51,152	11,110	183,624	398,654	68,473	48,682	2,744	45,938	35,973
Indiana	264,931	4,541	12,497	1,163	56,701	159,966	30,063	20,239	2,829	17,410	17,804
Iowa	124,185	1,672	7,992	349	49,606	53,661	10,905	11,224	639	10,585	10,723
Kansas	35,430	1,094	282	10,670	19,948	0	3,436	23,873	2,152	21,721	10,393
Kentucky	253,631	8,823	7,366	701	65,736	142,466	28,539	29,823	378	29,445	15,625
Louisiana	19,305	0	0	6,757	8,803	0	3,745	11,026	102	10,924	6,357
Maine	73,766	4,162	2,582	462	22,958	37,762	5,840	10,862	336	10,526	11,381
Maryland	268,485	703	7,535	7,484	53,729	172,580	26,454	31,575	853	30,722	15,940
Massachusetts	371,500	1,819	22,640	563	95,259	228,114	23,105	14,711	33	14,678	17,705
Michigan	649,427	10,072	30,285	4,158	141,413	376,376	87,123	32,971	5,359	27,612	34,563
Minnesota	31,189	0	0	11,644	10,968	0	8,577	14,333	835	13,498	16,745
Mississippi	252,111	1,791	7,495	3,504	66,941	137,339	35,041	20,233	51	20,182	13,881
Missouri	39,235	409	0	21,358	16,279	0	1,189	19,202	171	19,031	15,755
Montana	115,757	1,084	2,070	35,976	29,700	33,836	13,091	9,257	175	9,082	5,062
Nebraska	88,414	4,934	1,455	19,261	14,971	37,048	10,745	8,075	0	8,075	5,171
Nevada	88,310	271	2,326	3,690	20,552	40,137	21,334	2,696	0	2,696	219
New Hampshire	51,587	235	1,736	0	13,307	25,766	10,543	3,793	54	3,739	6,753
New Jersey	438,452	1,953	12,804	21,380	100,797	272,630	28,888	18,270	221	18,049	19,918
New Mexico	204,653	2,174	5,327	50,925	38,638	81,734	25,855	19,019	588	18,431	10,045
New York	1,550,427	10,258	57,371	8,131	290,886	991,038	192,743	50,793	880	49,913	73,879
North Carolina	400,650	7,145	11,233	13,846	109,739	206,143	52,544	38,003	2,104	35,899	16,012
North Dakota	83,946	332	1,732	27,475	21,072	25,022	8,313	6,164	64	6,100	5,956
Ohio	24,845	90	0	3,893	17,896	0	2,966	25,697	2,349	23,348	25,947
Oklahoma	275,764	2,495	3,570	37,108	66,405	117,605	48,581	32,134	0	32,134	13,845
Oregon	168,860	12,251	4,164	3,808	53,230	76,309	19,098	14,523	111	14,412	12,120
Pennsylvania	727,886	10,999	42,158	2,194	160,124	435,638	76,773	24,516	2,133	22,383	32,661
Rhode Island	4,381	0	0	1,243	1,768	0	1,370	6,061	0	6,061	4,573
South Carolina	34,385	431	338	3,559	26,253	0	3,804	10,703	493	10,210	4,549
South Dakota	45,720	0	0	39,197	2,923	0	3,600	4,510	147	4,363	5,496
Tennessee	241,899	979	7,605	3,049	59,364	139,287	31,615	22,611	20	22,591	14,630
Texas	1,496,740	65,355	42,240	80,891	307,066	831,366	169,822	105,143	4,209	100,934	63,880
Utah	104,548	1,467	2,835	10,485	34,069	41,420	14,272	12,004	825	11,179	11,947
Vermont	56,588	652	1,669	271	21,690	25,144	7,162	7,365	0	7,365	8,109
Virginia	307,790	731	8,483	41,612	48,832	153,328	54,804	35,002	1,473	33,529	19,230
Washington	316,106	15,420	9,681	51,997	83,002	123,317	32,689	29,113	3,609	25,504	16,873
West Virginia	119,240	376	4,468	11	25,765	83,030	5,590	19,692	69	19,623	6,765
Wisconsin	291,965	657	9,500	11,626	81,005	146,973	40,204	29,974	3,877	26,097	28,606
Wyoming	61,535	316	2,010	7,758	21,535	23,257	6,659	5,096	15	5,081	1,392
District of Columbia	66,011	318	2,185	1,329	15,758	34,596	11,825	2,815	0	2,815	1,077
American Samoa	11,976	0	127	0	810	0	11,039	737	0	737	87
Fed. States of Micronesia	2,889	0	0	0	1,389	0	1,500	548	0	548	0
Guam	14,705	0	0	61	970	0	13,674	1,664	0	1,664	707
Marshall Islands	1,363	0	0	0	772	0	591	374	0	374	50
Northern Marianas	9,050	0	0	0	30	0	9,020	2,231	0	2,231	55
Palau	840	0	0	0	140	0	770	770	0	770	181
Puerto Rico	333,593	6,871	15,033	1,678	34,603	235,861	39,547	22,810	0	22,810	17,970
Virgin Islands	5	0	0	0	0	0	5	1,657	0	1,657	219
Undistributed	0	0	0	0	0	0	0	0	0	0	0

See footnotes at end of table

FEDERAL AID TO STATE AND LOCAL GOVERNMENTS, SELECTED PROGRAMS BY STATE: FISCAL YEAR 2003 — Continued

State and outlying area	Election Assistance Commission	Department of Energy					Environmental Protection Agency			Equal Employment Opportunity Commission
		Total	Environ. and other defense programs	Energy conservation programs	Energy research and development programs	Other programs	Total	Hazardous substance response (Superfund) and L.U.S.T.	Other	
United States, total	$664,500	$643,648	$84,441	$408,335	$89,140	$61,732	$4,092,280	$208,389	$3,883,891	$30,852
Alabama	5,041	6,222	0	3,915	2,307	0	36,642	2,766	33,876	0
Alaska	5,000	2,997	675	1,779	539	4	77,714	1,143	76,571	192
Arizona	7,016	8,742	0	6,416	2,326	0	40,334	3,889	36,445	427
Arkansas	6,163	1,966	0	1,808	73	85	33,191	1,938	31,253	0
California	84,664	23,383	859	13,913	8,090	521	251,252	13,481	237,771	3,075
Colorado	7,037	11,418	2,095	7,390	1,933	0	53,637	9,665	43,972	622
Connecticut	5,000	12,189	0	10,370	1,819	0	48,046	1,662	46,384	636
Delaware	5,000	2,753	0	1,403	1,350	0	17,466	2,600	14,866	99
Florida	26,029	10,950	1,153	6,659	3,058	80	135,156	4,133	131,023	1,275
Georgia	12,557	12,760	1,356	7,518	3,697	189	52,306	3,210	49,096	188
Hawaii	5,000	1,889	0	914	975	0	15,951	1,149	14,802	146
Idaho	5,000	5,852	2,287	2,443	761	361	33,005	2,761	30,244	346
Illinois	44,935	30,161	18	27,046	3,093	4	192,514	8,936	183,578	2,315
Indiana	15,753	15,729	0	14,787	942	0	47,011	4,254	42,757	524
Iowa	5,000	9,767	0	7,480	2,287	0	87,113	2,667	84,446	1,734
Kansas	5,000	4,761	0	3,611	1,150	0	41,147	2,879	38,268	315
Kentucky	5,168	6,807	0	6,783	24	0	51,568	1,694	49,874	162
Louisiana	12,263	2,891	0	2,891	0	0	43,394	2,274	41,120	0
Maine	5,000	6,262	146	3,721	2,395	0	46,107	1,255	44,852	257
Maryland	7,274	4,143	126	2,545	499	973	88,295	4,725	83,570	644
Massachusetts	8,110	28,919	0	19,647	1,316	7,956	145,767	5,919	139,848	1,341
Michigan	15,739	33,755	1,146	28,443	4,166	0	155,034	7,401	147,633	607
Minnesota	5,314	16,367	0	16,145	222	0	112,574	5,023	107,551	1,592
Mississippi	5,451	3,372	0	2,228	1,144	0	47,536	2,202	45,334	0
Missouri	17,348	11,590	157	9,913	1,520	0	132,036	5,400	126,636	693
Montana	5,000	3,924	0	3,081	843	0	54,799	3,578	51,221	237
Nebraska	5,000	3,790	0	3,279	511	0	21,353	1,885	19,468	946
Nevada	5,000	41,648	11,210	863	1,569	28,006	36,546	1,403	35,143	680
New Hampshire	5,000	2,960	0	2,415	545	0	39,690	3,972	35,718	107
New Jersey	16,837	39,251	27,833	10,351	1,067	0	136,898	9,289	127,609	261
New Mexico	5,000	35,634	8,584	4,681	3,215	19,154	60,904	3,571	57,333	286
New York	66,098	32,662	0	26,359	6,192	111	271,078	10,031	261,047	2,123
North Carolina	8,782	8,263	0	7,531	732	0	79,413	4,099	75,314	138
North Dakota	5,000	3,077	0	2,907	170	0	44,532	1,181	43,351	149
Ohio	41,053	29,645	3,864	23,825	1,956	0	122,664	5,064	117,600	1,809
Oklahoma	5,000	3,892	0	3,557	335	0	58,150	1,794	56,356	403
Oregon	6,027	8,039	1,617	3,721	2,701	0	56,579	6,627	49,952	596
Pennsylvania	34,240	37,502	0	32,194	4,898	410	154,340	1,788	152,552	1,510
Rhode Island	5,000	2,038	0	1,988	50	0	40,132	2,142	37,990	110
South Carolina	6,820	8,733	4,209	3,869	507	148	43,756	3,134	40,622	597
South Dakota	5,000	3,126	0	2,092	1,034	0	36,988	1,026	35,962	205
Tennessee	8,478	12,265	736	8,456	585	2,488	48,754	3,145	45,609	355
Texas	23,476	18,589	2,028	13,703	2,018	840	211,366	5,949	205,417	624
Utah	8,818	7,290	0	4,640	2,650	0	32,615	3,364	29,251	306
Vermont	5,000	2,118	0	1,482	636	0	26,224	1,293	24,931	65
Virginia	11,632	8,399	557	5,381	2,461	0	88,864	9,305	79,559	213
Washington	12,898	25,699	13,333	8,791	3,568	7	105,237	6,287	98,950	688
West Virginia	5,327	4,701	0	4,668	33	0	63,081	2,010	61,071	130
Wisconsin	7,003	10,942	0	9,010	1,932	0	135,578	7,537	128,041	728
Wyoming	5,000	1,764	0	1,564	200	0	30,304	395	29,909	72
District of Columbia	5,000	9,863	452	6,040	2,976	395	78,736	5,161	73,575	37
American Samoa	1,000	353	0	279	74	0	0	0	0	0
Fed. States of Micronesia	0	0	0	0	0	0	0	0	0	0
Guam	1,000	56	0	56	0	0	3,804	120	3,684	0
Marshall Islands	0	0	0	0	0	0	0	0	0	0
Northern Marianas	0	220	0	220	0	0	1,729	45	1,684	0
Palau	0	17	0	17	0	0	0	0	0	0
Puerto Rico	3,151	792	0	801	-9	0	16,780	154	16,626	287
Virgin Islands	1,000	751	0	746	5	0	6,589	1	6,588	0
Undistributed	15,000	0	0	0	0	0	1	13	-12	0

See footnotes at end of table

FEDERAL AID TO STATE AND LOCAL GOVERNMENTS, SELECTED PROGRAMS BY STATE: FISCAL YEAR 2003 — Continued

| | | Department of Health and Human Services | | | | | | | | | |
| | | Administration for Children and Families | | | | | | | | | |
State and outlying area	Total	Total	Child care and develop.	Child support enforce.	Children and Family Services (Head Start)	Safe and Stable Families	Foster care and adoption assistance	Refugee and entrant assistance	Social Services Block Grant	Temporary Assistance to Needy Families (TANF)	Other
United States, total .	$221,042,178	$45,911,674	$5,166,233	$2,915,081	$8,121,028	$336,265	$6,117,576	$443,999	$1,740,149	$19,136,671	$19,342,672
Alabama	3,331,648	469,888	66,841	36,117	131,349	9,353	34,070	439	27,439	149,294	14,986
Alaska	833,093	180,255	17,143	8,388	55,075	1,489	15,276	73	2,826	71,046	8,939
Arizona	4,230,467	782,309	124,281	31,618	171,162	9,223	70,564	8,847	31,524	324,081	11,009
Arkansas	2,253,911	249,933	42,347	27,360	85,316	2,590	36,604	61	17,142	26,707	11,806
California	26,779,816	7,953,714	498,856	547,642	987,676	37,737	1,420,813	58,927	181,761	4,131,074	89,228
Colorado	2,121,628	533,981	59,687	41,085	132,113	3,119	77,668	7,618	25,465	155,760	31,466
Connecticut	2,548,564	513,834	50,857	27,025	65,761	1,519	48,113	1,825	15,540	260,192	43,002
Delaware	530,437	95,443	13,725	13,196	16,341	923	11,033	75	4,283	29,672	6,195
Florida	9,968,790	1,816,472	260,859	135,489	320,047	19,647	152,584	86,401	98,700	717,748	24,997
Georgia	5,652,054	945,720	194,073	67,060	211,768	12,894	70,300	7,420	45,623	319,992	16,590
Hawaii	729,885	171,029	17,515	2,595	36,188	2,645	25,265	485	7,268	77,399	1,669
Idaho	826,243	142,248	21,317	11,177	39,782	1,404	9,575	2,789	6,792	37,782	11,630
Illinois	7,399,570	1,758,529	205,123	107,909	331,550	7,284	406,413	12,969	82,927	505,583	98,771
Indiana	3,708,537	645,891	120,584	18,768	119,585	7,350	74,443	378	38,802	215,415	50,566
Iowa	1,912,417	344,632	33,839	16,259	69,905	2,602	45,126	5,034	17,389	124,687	29,791
Kansas	1,576,703	321,228	43,088	23,508	83,187	2,775	37,858	686	13,925	97,447	18,754
Kentucky	3,553,203	562,057	98,680	25,145	145,252	5,830	78,589	4,274	24,940	152,586	26,761
Louisiana	4,221,648	700,192	105,581	23,400	166,098	8,972	66,863	1,145	27,060	283,245	17,828
Maine	1,519,069	206,349	17,522	218	41,027	1,384	39,030	1,276	5,088	76,653	24,151
Maryland	3,496,805	731,176	94,527	65,938	99,668	5,534	158,272	4,271	43,439	228,617	30,910
Massachusetts	5,578,773	1,051,756	124,446	41,335	150,656	4,461	115,981	13,309	41,460	483,754	76,354
Michigan	6,993,521	1,859,962	227,729	196,696	292,234	13,449	240,913	12,845	79,742	685,252	111,107
Minnesota	3,567,118	845,499	77,697	87,913	111,523	4,649	96,695	11,402	31,592	355,192	68,836
Mississippi	3,021,289	442,081	57,690	12,675	186,630	5,337	15,437	1,900	19,379	131,250	11,783
Missouri	4,520,997	673,524	93,861	47,251	152,386	6,531	82,713	6,071	33,217	212,377	39,117
Montana	675,453	156,834	16,131	5,313	44,356	1,302	18,348	169	6,722	51,620	12,873
Nebraska	1,159,802	208,527	26,207	21,844	49,143	1,859	27,080	2,622	10,589	52,769	16,414
Nevada	877,958	184,303	23,489	25,235	35,611	1,489	23,086	272	12,125	57,113	5,883
New Hampshire	714,943	131,106	22,306	7,446	20,931	646	17,450	528	7,653	41,112	13,034
New Jersey	5,710,568	1,166,146	133,844	94,282	160,444	9,080	83,524	4,716	52,220	543,657	84,379
New Mexico	2,003,773	298,062	34,689	15,380	80,834	3,880	26,191	2,039	16,350	104,434	14,265
New York	27,695,268	5,857,489	487,633	129,222	517,369	562	756,784	61,676	121,328	3,490,958	291,957
North Carolina	6,053,836	951,002	177,742	65,895	203,157	9,806	71,210	5,362	51,644	331,439	34,747
North Dakota	491,060	113,324	12,277	15,375	34,689	1,094	14,158	1,782	3,803	26,275	13,715
Ohio	8,872,309	1,997,140	155,441	195,257	304,139	10,449	377,952	5,743	50,740	804,919	192,500
Oklahoma	2,501,992	541,796	92,459	30,521	124,238	6,539	53,391	1,132	20,554	199,325	13,637
Oregon	2,430,821	516,982	71,568	29,455	107,592	7,128	59,327	6,397	39,326	173,941	22,248
Pennsylvania	10,046,226	2,070,903	186,835	125,224	281,809	8,659	394,359	11,945	88,115	837,387	136,530
Rhode Island	1,146,580	200,223	18,125	3,655	32,760	1,990	20,582	692	5,144	104,311	12,964
South Carolina	3,227,785	398,933	77,603	19,722	106,072	8,802	42,721	218	22,961	108,580	12,254
South Dakota	557,312	114,795	18,080	4,849	42,849	1,361	8,526	1,256	3,643	22,110	12,121
Tennessee	5,256,045	617,081	124,092	35,527	144,108	9,108	40,078	2,357	32,571	208,611	20,629
Texas	13,197,720	2,224,036	371,038	173,450	613,763	39,338	208,737	23,239	116,522	630,524	47,428
Utah	1,192,830	262,689	33,861	15,375	56,333	1,864	26,611	2,954	11,222	102,559	11,910
Vermont	654,918	126,705	10,279	7,286	24,253	676	18,525	793	3,921	50,107	10,865
Virginia	2,957,129	721,814	88,058	49,402	187,492	11,002	106,687	10,339	43,065	188,475	37,294
Washington	4,124,268	970,445	112,308	68,642	164,951	6,719	86,829	16,571	36,466	440,257	37,882
West Virginia	1,919,417	314,786	31,453	19,559	67,183	2,762	37,615	0	11,941	128,280	15,993
Wisconsin	4,071,998	880,967	89,792	91,861	127,063	3,983	95,616	8,395	32,065	363,760	68,432
Wyoming	328,327	79,565	8,801	5,657	23,860	466	3,413	0	3,457	29,393	4,518
Dist. of Columbia ...	1,456,064	439,509	67,951	31,321	98,546	5,763	68,578	22,282	12,058	121,713	11,297
American Samoa ...	14,904	6,963	2,443	0	4,215	158	0	0	37	0	110
Fed. States of Micronesia	1,231	0	0	0	0	0	0	0	0	0	0
Guam	28,941	11,686	1,450	1,215	4,294	575	0	0	241	3,842	69
Marshall Islands	275	0	0	0	0	0	0	0	0	0	0
Northern Marianas	6,214	767	0	0	483	37	0	0	0	0	247
Palau	45	0	0	0	0	0	0	0	0	0	0
Puerto Rico	735,443	323,455	0	17,746	239,700	112	0	0	0	63,750	2,147
Virgin Islands	43,162	21,332	2,410	3,622	11,913	355	0	0	303	2,645	84
Undistributed	11,376	4,599	0	0	4,599	0	0	0	0	0	0

See footnotes at end of table

FEDERAL AID TO STATE AND LOCAL GOVERNMENTS, SELECTED PROGRAMS BY STATE: FISCAL YEAR 2003 — Continued

State and outlying area	Department of Health and Human Services						
	Administration on Aging	Agency for Healthcare Research and Quality (b)	Centers for Disease Control and Prevention	Centers for Medicare and Medicaid Services	Health Resources and Services Administration	Indian Health Service (c)	Substance Abuse and Mental Health Services Administration
United States, total	$1,284,698	$14,641	$720,071	$164,297,410	$5,930,432	$95,858	$2,787,394
Alabama	18,884	132	11,672	2,681,561	112,868	0	36,643
Alaska	10,494	0	5,027	534,631	63,127	8,569	30,990
Arizona	24,277	0	7,304	3,258,165	91,440	17,883	49,089
Arkansas	14,465	0	8,271	1,903,462	60,007	0	17,773
California	126,744	2,835	57,208	17,643,061	610,642	6,892	378,720
Colorado	14,285	28	11,988	1,417,466	102,945	270	40,665
Connecticut	14,292	0	8,062	1,907,911	69,823	0	34,642
Delaware	5,568	0	2,017	401,225	18,003	0	8,181
Florida	97,350	911	25,606	7,475,492	392,389	0	160,570
Georgia	24,960	0	38,351	4,401,467	176,311	0	65,245
Hawaii	8,221	274	4,445	495,175	38,772	0	11,969
Idaho	6,465	0	4,919	634,802	26,327	858	10,624
Illinois	52,640	0	24,723	5,216,407	239,593	134	107,544
Indiana	24,004	23	15,951	2,922,931	60,637	0	39,100
Iowa	16,599	46	7,241	1,472,955	47,812	280	22,852
Kansas	12,702	0	7,398	1,184,205	33,713	53	17,404
Kentucky	16,790	190	5,892	2,857,157	77,052	0	34,065
Louisiana	17,121	190	16,492	3,344,370	105,738	0	37,545
Maine	6,888	0	6,442	1,258,622	25,390	0	15,378
Maryland	27,609	202	13,962	2,559,913	109,569	0	54,374
Massachusetts	26,867	0	20,902	4,221,558	178,347	70	79,273
Michigan	43,207	339	23,781	4,849,805	136,138	2,217	78,067
Minnesota	20,849	389	10,755	2,589,073	59,785	2,884	37,884
Mississippi	11,741	190	7,524	2,442,863	91,812	0	25,078
Missouri	26,695	0	13,592	3,644,753	116,198	0	46,235
Montana	7,872	328	2,005	458,681	32,986	4,852	11,895
Nebraska	8,618	0	5,292	892,075	33,028	1,716	10,546
Nevada	9,592	0	5,974	628,519	31,299	2,704	15,567
New Hampshire	6,805	0	4,679	541,949	17,823	0	12,581
New Jersey	50,494	216	15,034	4,228,347	180,960	0	69,371
New Mexico	8,260	210	5,846	1,598,988	68,101	5,434	18,872
New York	87,391	348	71,388	20,831,046	611,709	37	235,860
North Carolina	31,642	760	20,317	4,823,510	133,409	678	92,518
North Dakota	6,981	0	2,822	343,289	14,153	2,584	7,907
Ohio	50,047	0	20,068	6,550,682	149,689	0	104,683
Oklahoma	20,971	0	9,489	1,827,667	47,053	22,608	32,408
Oregon	12,843	377	7,378	1,807,986	54,843	1,517	28,895
Pennsylvania	57,360	388	21,820	7,560,738	232,074	0	102,943
Rhode Island	6,192	0	3,634	894,173	27,927	0	14,431
South Carolina	15,313	2,354	9,523	2,667,490	101,279	0	32,893
South Dakota	7,973	0	3,101	390,930	22,854	5,253	12,406
Tennessee	20,680	511	13,601	4,450,074	104,590	2,975	46,533
Texas	67,023	650	46,550	10,306,039	350,404	263	202,752
Utah	5,813	325	7,644	853,464	36,593	95	26,207
Vermont	6,809	116	3,068	495,358	16,126	0	6,736
Virginia	26,546	524	11,888	2,019,799	102,922	0	73,636
Washington	24,432	978	12,299	2,953,312	107,052	1,998	53,752
West Virginia	10,920	0	4,522	1,510,311	66,032	0	12,846
Wisconsin	24,511	286	10,465	3,032,341	76,730	2,285	44,413
Wyoming	5,191	0	2,679	222,709	7,650	749	9,784
District of Columbia	11,045	0	27,083	832,684	113,201	0	32,542
American Samoa	1,318	0	285	4,416	1,336	0	586
Fed. States of Micronesia	0	0	1,231	0	0	0	0
Guam	2,738	0	1,115	9,679	1,726	0	1,997
Marshall Islands	0	0	275	0	0	0	0
Northern Marianas	875	0	319	2,806	811	0	636
Palau	0	0	45	0	0	0	0
Puerto Rico	15,866	522	6,667	230,842	129,311	0	28,780
Virgin Islands	2,860	0	1,228	8,476	8,090	0	1,176
Undistributed	0	0	1,212	0	4,233	0	1,332

See footnotes at end of table

FEDERAL AID TO STATE AND LOCAL GOVERNMENTS, SELECTED PROGRAMS BY STATE: FISCAL YEAR 2003 — Continued

State and outlying area	Department of Homeland Security						Department of Housing and Urban Development				
			Federal Emergency Management Agency						Comm. planning and development		
	Total (c)	Coast Guard	Total	Disaster relief	Emergency management planning and assistance	Other	Total	Fair housing and equal opportunity	Comm. Dev. Block Grant	Empwermt. zones and other economic devlpmnt.	Emergency shelter and homeless assistance
United States, total	$4,763,411	$69,310	$4,609,101	$4,205,706	$243,113	$160,282	$39,379,286	$49,045	$5,574,695	$108,767	$1,121,624
Alabama	51,592	1,182	50,410	19,334	30,912	164	512,065	592	72,430	982	10,904
Alaska	5,280	65	5,215	3,817	1,393	5	211,612	0	19,415	407	3,662
Arizona	11,356	646	10,710	6,239	4,459	12	498,986	947	79,380	370	24,819
Arkansas	36,382	882	35,500	20,555	14,805	140	260,491	50	35,117	426	4,210
California	532,642	3,122	529,520	517,735	11,785	0	4,467,112	4,003	582,064	6,405	171,888
Colorado	15,862	421	15,441	10,077	5,187	177	475,679	1,116	51,036	95	13,276
Connecticut	9,854	590	9,264	6,751	2,513	0	665,334	684	51,785	4,147	14,785
Delaware	4,087	400	3,687	2,643	986	58	104,536	365	10,092	0	4,520
Florida	168,027	3,959	164,068	157,477	6,316	275	1,441,227	3,215	207,752	5,602	54,369
Georgia	24,763	1,748	23,015	18,395	4,479	141	915,556	843	118,918	301	19,378
Hawaii	4,288	1,062	3,226	1,702	1,524	0	182,860	247	27,048	31	5,211
Idaho	2,485	789	1,696	139	1,557	0	88,251	263	17,854	47	2,550
Illinois	937	934	3	0	3	0	2,009,285	1,473	199,483	2,506	60,142
Indiana	15,359	639	14,720	5,152	9,474	94	571,940	902	87,820	6,769	13,465
Iowa	12,406	149	12,257	8,985	3,209	63	242,740	1,096	50,734	367	7,741
Kansas	14,989	657	14,332	12,237	2,005	90	219,805	611	47,548	95	4,352
Kentucky	34,290	452	33,838	27,467	6,307	64	485,183	1,045	66,729	963	11,957
Louisiana	154,509	1,051	153,458	149,883	3,377	198	572,440	492	91,370	581	21,824
Maine	5,390	792	4,598	2,876	1,717	5	205,343	230	24,577	687	7,136
Maryland	22,090	1,917	20,173	15,406	4,686	81	772,013	818	80,274	7	27,234
Massachusetts	27,522	759	26,763	23,280	3,457	26	1,807,016	1,947	152,666	3,120	52,445
Michigan	12,490	2,983	9,507	5,329	3,984	194	952,128	939	157,697	143	44,484
Minnesota	36,602	1,673	34,929	32,213	2,571	145	620,670	611	79,061	3,968	21,094
Mississippi	25,728	1,269	24,459	22,248	2,060	151	308,381	129	60,801	418	3,633
Missouri	36,976	1,501	35,475	32,162	2,988	325	719,494	1,045	116,775	10,003	18,845
Montana	3,323	323	3,000	1,471	1,523	6	109,520	167	15,057	1,425	1,838
Nebraska	7,280	301	6,979	4,782	2,197	0	161,077	824	31,287	787	4,574
Nevada	2,629	652	1,977	399	1,523	55	184,811	90	21,981	324	4,530
New Hampshire	7,347	1,097	6,250	4,253	1,903	94	165,785	0	15,235	56	4,476
New Jersey	39,568	2,502	37,066	32,683	4,259	124	1,502,409	336	131,842	4,538	27,508
New Mexico	10,706	466	10,240	8,558	1,605	77	191,514	168	38,685	1,184	6,140
New York	2,444,369	1,177	2,443,192	2,437,550	3,822	1,820	5,391,938	2,531	1,155,238	2,443	123,995
North Carolina	116,909	1,219	115,690	107,902	5,555	2,233	791,806	1,602	81,661	1,651	11,642
North Dakota	15,428	370	15,058	13,470	1,583	5	88,810	236	12,368	121	593
Ohio	33,412	2,514	30,898	24,415	6,219	264	1,551,609	2,425	226,714	11,725	52,747
Oklahoma	34,748	992	33,756	30,467	3,044	245	462,906	196	50,897	688	5,469
Oregon	30,724	1,166	29,558	16,106	13,452	0	351,121	236	39,623	626	10,360
Pennsylvania	23,683	1,399	22,284	16,810	5,467	7	1,803,317	1,833	267,662	10,559	59,290
Rhode Island	4,740	488	4,252	1,978	2,234	40	294,865	234	27,516	1,025	6,052
South Carolina	10,571	1,486	9,085	6,438	2,481	166	367,733	273	50,684	4,485	6,628
South Dakota	6,818	587	6,231	4,850	1,307	74	124,224	0	23,764	1,256	1,050
Tennessee	13,746	1,167	12,579	10,524	1,984	71	613,716	1,475	59,405	1,781	12,844
Texas	229,982	1,989	227,993	214,076	13,917	0	1,821,049	3,375	305,653	3,741	50,324
Utah	7,298	0	7,298	233	7,009	56	132,470	406	25,116	31	5,241
Vermont	2,970	463	2,507	1,816	681	10	103,628	289	17,036	34	2,054
Virginia	17,013	1,024	15,989	9,816	6,089	84	682,555	2,352	77,962	5,036	16,413
Washington	31,268	1,111	30,157	24,001	6,156	0	687,213	1,316	66,277	2,727	34,415
West Virginia	21,230	308	20,922	18,300	2,586	36	221,639	481	50,416	3,759	3,086
Wisconsin	14,456	1,857	12,599	9,076	3,213	310	507,761	488	98,013	242	17,311
Wyoming	6,122	188	5,934	4,210	1,633	91	39,625	83	5,320	27	328
District of Columbia ..	3,843	610	3,233	2,198	1,035	0	738,534	3,966	56,768	0	18,238
American Samoa	309	309	0	0	0	0	789	0	605	0	0
Fed. States of Micronesia	6,295	0	6,295	6,295	0	0	0	0	0	0	0
Guam	27,817	206	27,611	27,059	552	0	37,394	0	3,066	0	376
Marshall Islands	0	0	0	0	0	0	0	0	0	0	0
Northern Marianas ...	2,291	66	2,225	1,585	640	0	1,761	0	0	0	9
Palau	0	0	0	0	0	0	0	0	0	0	0
Puerto Rico	140,444	410	55,034	53,598	1,436	0	653,857	0	127,640	56	9,801
Virgin Islands	9,816	483	9,333	8,604	729	0	50,613	0	2,778	0	367
Undistributed	170,350	12,738	157,612	81	5,525	152,006	233,090	0	0	0	1

See footnotes at end of table

FEDERAL AID TO STATE AND LOCAL GOVERNMENTS, SELECTED PROGRAMS BY STATE: FISCAL YEAR 2003 — Continued

	\multicolumn{9}{c}{*Department of Housing and Urban Development—Continued*}								
		\multicolumn{8}{c}{*Housing programs*}								
						\multicolumn{4}{c}{*Public housing programs*}				
State and outlying area	*College housing*	*Housing opportunities for persons with AIDS*	*Native American block grant*	*Housing for special populations*	*Low rent housing assistance*	*Neighborhood revitalization*	*Drug elimination*	*Housing certificate program*	*Capital programs*
United States, total	$9,433	$253,581	$722,691	$991,556	$3,461,203	$554,598	$221,950	$20,949,628	$3,653,885
Alabama	201	1,696	2,564	8,970	112,214	4,322	6,615	191,098	82,040
Alaska	0	446	129,879	5,599	7,607	0	1,524	34,389	4,899
Arizona	106	2,102	148,238	10,801	14,892	9,400	5,383	173,948	10,174
Arkansas	0	74	0	12,388	25,492	10	1,382	143,523	27,915
California	356	35,190	42,250	119,690	113,702	42,359	7,571	3,017,157	115,430
Colorado	310	2,015	2,578	9,877	13,839	4,747	1,417	342,308	13,077
Connecticut	60	3,789	474	15,818	54,831	5,510	3,216	439,923	47,164
Delaware	0	1,204	0	2,964	9,243	3,492	1,136	57,235	8,227
Florida	48	35,163	2,420	44,817	95,237	37,672	9,637	808,224	80,720
Georgia	0	7,063	-175	10,944	112,150	23,583	7,156	479,474	99,574
Hawaii	327	1,314	0	6,026	10,711	135	1,900	97,994	28,686
Idaho	136	276	4,949	2,321	1,076	0	50	51,507	1,125
Illinois	429	5,664	859	60,784	252,635	25,456	8,185	1,050,295	249,830
Indiana	162	1,545	0	8,797	39,890	2,692	3,393	339,362	34,661
Iowa	0	301	225	5,860	4,805	0	475	140,273	11,031
Kansas	6	47	2,008	5,881	13,744	135	1,358	113,037	17,813
Kentucky	23	1,752	0	12,010	45,812	8,008	2,077	252,306	59,508
Louisiana	0	4,675	288	21,521	63,176	9,057	4,070	252,726	84,803
Maine	0	857	5,705	7,405	8,406	0	165	132,087	9,229
Maryland	0	6,670	418	33,684	73,774	25,961	5,393	433,933	49,987
Massachusetts	844	6,153	366	43,640	99,724	11,595	6,897	1,289,001	88,177
Michigan	481	2,732	11,722	31,656	47,281	2,194	2,141	534,394	53,346
Minnesota	629	1,317	15,675	22,923	38,264	64	2,865	363,474	45,730
Mississippi	0	1,570	1,216	6,595	27,258	4,080	2,159	154,683	29,698
Missouri	0	3,113	198	29,753	39,449	9,975	3,073	323,000	132,102
Montana	0	412	26,670	4,487	3,755	0	1,141	45,020	4,488
Nebraska	0	0	4,609	5,526	10,242	0	890	79,588	13,063
Nevada	0	944	9,392	5,404	16,140	0	741	110,785	7,373
New Hampshire	0	443	0	4,724	6,135	0	851	123,885	6,927
New Jersey	1,467	13,053	0	36,226	154,815	47,619	7,089	913,002	127,289
New Mexico	0	777	13,448	10,703	9,231	0	930	89,715	10,580
New York	636	54,492	4,552	98,501	819,283	18,661	37,954	2,274,264	521,449
North Carolina	285	2,692	13,890	19,271	96,015	35,680	5,281	410,916	77,855
North Dakota	267	0	18,275	2,521	2,720	0	647	44,172	2,137
Ohio	84	2,075	0	43,939	156,540	28,215	10,499	816,104	128,942
Oklahoma	25	858	128,269	6,097	23,974	15,176	3,359	188,156	22,757
Oregon	0	1,397	7,941	14,795	14,933	7,571	1,321	220,830	13,837
Pennsylvania	176	6,523	12	42,065	243,848	53,528	9,975	818,495	224,866
Rhode Island	240	1,138	702	12,051	20,697	0	1,396	191,481	20,214
South Carolina	77	2,039	1,501	11,254	30,712	7,867	2,605	205,632	28,584
South Dakota	0	0	33,842	1,548	2,464	0	1,287	53,368	2,306
Tennessee	487	1,958	0	18,597	91,556	28,876	6,099	282,022	80,601
Texas	925	13,637	1,479	29,659	112,855	22,589	6,825	1,047,890	136,611
Utah	187	503	3,493	3,195	3,826	0	389	78,171	3,973
Vermont	194	468	0	6,731	2,824	0	163	65,680	2,937
Virginia	37	1,443	220	18,409	62,319	14,406	4,003	401,635	38,874
Washington	115	4,640	54,340	14,696	34,773	25,159	3,447	367,384	48,891
West Virginia	0	370	0	3,713	15,454	3,598	978	116,361	12,974
Wisconsin	98	1,405	19,926	17,948	16,556	2,269	1,509	277,709	23,176
Wyoming	15	0	5,027	822	1,175	0	115	23,224	941
District of Columbia	0	8,535	3,246	10,551	-91,384	19,652	3,545	185,602	500,559
American Samoa	0	0	0	0	0	0	0	0	0
Fed. States of Micronesia	0	0	0	0	0	0	0	0	0
Guam	0	0	0	0	3,150	0	45	28,318	1,827
Marshall Islands	0	0	0	0	0	0	0	0	0
Northern Marianas	0	0	0	0	0	0	0	1,752	0
Palau	0	0	0	0	0	0	0	0	0
Puerto Rico	0	7,051	0	6,621	95,338	-7,078	19,627	256,281	118,574
Virgin Islands	0	0	0	778	20,654	363	0	16,288	8,673
Undistributed	0	0	0	0	155,391	0	1	547	77,661

See footnotes at end of table

FEDERAL AID TO STATE AND LOCAL GOVERNMENTS, SELECTED PROGRAMS BY STATE: FISCAL YEAR 2003 — Continued

State and outlying area	Department of Housing and Urban Development—Continued Housing programs—Con't Home ownership assistance	Other	Institute for Museum and Library Services	Department of the Interior Total	Bureau of Indian Affairs	Bureau of Land Management Total	Payments in lieu of taxes	Shared revenues	Bureau of Reclamation
United States, total	$1,617,774	$88,856	$234,166	$3,746,651	$820,953	$402,101	$218,173	$183,928	$265,952
Alabama	16,914	523	4,083	30,943	3,007	389	389	0	0
Alaska	3,680	105	1,599	193,865	101,843	49,773	15,196	34,577	0
Arizona	17,058	1,368	3,847	222,798	152,671	18,304	18,045	259	38,350
Arkansas	9,904	0	1,626	19,485	0	2,834	2,834	0	0
California	201,960	7,087	22,756	213,331	46,595	19,529	19,246	283	76,834
Colorado	19,385	603	3,356	115,892	5,353	17,910	17,646	264	21,792
Connecticut	17,294	5,854	2,512	6,077	831	29	29	0	0
Delaware	5,190	868	781	5,065	0	3	3	0	5
Florida	56,351	0	11,535	28,891	8,188	2,754	2,754	0	0
Georgia	35,621	726	4,500	16,671	0	1,495	1,495	0	0
Hawaii	3,230	0	1,838	8,748	1	21	21	0	193
Idaho	6,097	0	1,436	40,941	11,243	15,254	15,017	237	892
Illinois	85,072	6,472	11,743	24,759	0	609	609	0	3
Indiana	32,482	0	3,304	21,134	0	361	361	0	0
Iowa	18,530	1,302	5,280	10,502	71	247	247	0	287
Kansas	13,081	89	1,621	19,085	2,879	618	618	0	891
Kentucky	22,339	654	2,444	41,201	0	1,524	1,524	0	0
Louisiana	17,857	0	3,167	44,308	2,847	312	312	0	0
Maine	7,840	1,019	1,969	17,495	10,724	197	197	0	0
Maryland	27,837	6,023	3,406	11,337	1,110	92	92	0	0
Massachusetts	43,260	7,181	8,208	8,370	1,984	67	67	0	0
Michigan	61,354	1,564	6,006	42,909	20,702	2,350	2,350	0	0
Minnesota	22,767	2,228	3,722	49,915	28,632	1,531	1,531	0	0
Mississippi	15,609	532	2,360	16,464	5,131	859	859	0	0
Missouri	29,307	2,856	6,200	17,980	679	2,134	2,134	0	0
Montana	4,804	256	1,132	119,675	46,607	17,612	16,874	738	7,366
Nebraska	8,960	727	1,381	18,553	7,486	640	639	1	928
Nevada	7,107	0	2,230	82,441	14,775	47,971	13,133	34,838	3,159
New Hampshire	3,021	32	1,480	7,163	0	970	970	0	0
New Jersey	35,866	1,759	6,986	8,356	0	66	66	0	0
New Mexico	9,953	0	1,855	402,347	60,952	22,198	21,398	800	9,035
New York	272,207	5,732	18,283	28,155	3,320	87	87	0	46
North Carolina	30,524	2,841	5,782	25,805	13,126	2,348	2,348	0	0
North Dakota	4,753	0	984	66,830	31,601	974	967	7	18,047
Ohio	61,999	9,601	9,846	26,860	0	523	523	0	0
Oklahoma	16,968	17	3,251	70,508	51,668	1,488	1,487	1	589
Oregon	17,266	385	3,054	143,873	10,933	116,779	6,010	110,769	2,029
Pennsylvania	63,868	617	12,907	52,544	0	347	347	0	0
Rhode Island	10,296	1,823	848	7,388	2,008	0	0	0	0
South Carolina	13,938	1,454	3,075	9,006	289	241	241	0	0
South Dakota	3,339	0	703	130,474	58,883	2,577	2,501	76	60,872
Tennessee	25,843	2,172	3,751	19,269	389	1,371	1,371	0	0
Texas	84,901	585	14,114	57,318	3,161	2,586	2,586	0	1,624
Utah	7,939	0	2,014	117,291	3,134	18,845	18,657	188	20,206
Vermont	3,722	1,496	742	5,825	0	496	496	0	0
Virginia	35,280	4,166	4,535	26,592	492	2,297	2,297	0	0
Washington	28,741	292	4,320	114,099	88,635	5,128	5,104	24	1,818
West Virginia	9,129	1,320	1,229	44,932	0	1,620	1,620	0	0
Wisconsin	28,765	2,346	3,861	43,732	24,689	484	484	0	0
Wyoming	2,548	0	803	519,242	2,011	15,172	14,306	866	986
District of Columbia	15,075	4,181	3,030	-3,972	-7,697	18	18	0	0
American Samoa	184	0	147	35,040	0	0	0	0	0
Fed. States of Micronesia	0	0	0	104,018	0	0	0	0	0
Guam	612	0	114	37,899	0	2	2	0	0
Marshall Islands	0	0	56	53,652	0	0	0	0	0
Northern Marianas	0	0	151	21,017	0	0	0	0	0
Palau	0	0	0	42,835	0	0	0	0	0
Puerto Rico	19,946	0	2,107	4,425	0	26	26	0	0
Virgin Islands	712	0	96	69,661	0	39	39	0	0
Undistributed	-511	0	0	5,632	0	0	0	0	0

See footnotes at end of table

FEDERAL AID TO STATE AND LOCAL GOVERNMENTS, SELECTED PROGRAMS BY STATE: FISCAL YEAR 2003 — Continued

| | Department of the Interior—Con't | | | | | | | | | |
| | Fish & Wildlife Service | | | | Minerals Management Service | | | National Park Service | | |
State and outlying area	Total	Wildlife conservation and restoration	Sport fish restoration	Other	Total	Minerals Leasing Act	Other	Total	Historic preservation	Other
United States, total	$576,583	$293,527	$272,617	$10,439	$1,019,981	$947,006	$72,975	$93,541	$41,428	$52,113
Alabama	8,011	4,224	3,583	204	13,731	262	13,469	1,799	738	1,061
Alaska	24,840	11,462	13,338	40	12,764	9,011	3,753	940	745	195
Arizona	11,478	6,043	5,435	0	121	121	0	1,874	804	1,070
Arkansas	10,172	4,382	5,730	60	4,109	2,216	1,893	854	500	354
California	39,845	21,356	17,451	1,038	25,463	21,773	3,690	4,945	1,492	3,453
Colorado	10,441	4,457	5,959	25	53,947	53,768	179	1,346	713	633
Connecticut	4,304	1,489	2,605	210	0	0	0	913	470	443
Delaware	4,226	998	3,136	92	0	0	0	831	555	276
Florida	15,444	8,263	5,751	1,430	370	369	1	2,135	818	1,317
Georgia	12,648	7,879	4,769	0	0	0	0	2,528	671	1,857
Hawaii	5,764	3,222	2,542	0	0	0	0	1,148	503	645
Idaho	10,081	4,507	5,217	357	1,793	1,788	5	1,678	795	883
Illinois	10,727	4,980	5,637	110	109	0	109	2,186	738	1,448
Indiana	10,580	4,505	5,946	129	6	6	0	2,422	859	1,563
Iowa	5,954	3,321	2,633	0	0	0	0	2,259	875	1,384
Kansas	9,058	4,325	4,701	32	1,823	1,821	2	1,643	728	915
Kentucky	8,657	3,880	4,655	122	50	0	50	1,524	618	906
Louisiana	7,938	4,057	3,851	30	30,746	939	29,807	2,229	553	1,676
Maine	5,443	2,793	2,289	361	0	0	0	1,131	548	583
Maryland	5,295	2,597	2,157	541	0	0	0	973	973	0
Massachusetts	3,928	860	2,253	815	0	0	0	2,391	890	1,501
Michigan	17,723	9,178	8,533	12	431	375	56	1,703	633	1,070
Minnesota	16,349	6,145	10,204	0	17	5	12	3,386	915	2,471
Mississippi	8,626	4,369	3,901	356	1,156	70	1,086	556	556	0
Missouri	11,310	5,851	5,180	279	332	0	332	2,081	1,134	947
Montana	16,827	10,499	6,328	0	25,536	25,517	19	930	427	503
Nebraska	7,696	4,096	3,600	0	13	13	0	1,790	585	1,205
Nevada	9,556	4,683	4,873	0	5,055	5,046	9	1,925	812	1,113
New Hampshire	4,890	2,398	2,431	61	0	0	0	1,303	666	637
New Jersey	6,692	3,185	2,567	940	0	0	0	1,598	1,317	281
New Mexico	8,323	3,808	4,515	0	297,905	297,740	165	1,457	585	872
New York	20,075	10,010	9,951	114	0	0	0	4,627	1,128	3,499
North Carolina	9,052	5,205	3,763	84	0	0	0	1,279	823	456
North Dakota	6,877	3,652	3,213	12	4,944	4,929	15	1,900	650	1,250
Ohio	12,822	5,704	7,002	116	281	1	280	3,048	1,001	2,047
Oklahoma	10,222	5,209	4,920	93	2,371	2,137	234	1,381	727	654
Oregon	12,116	4,680	5,984	1,452	33	32	1	1,983	699	1,284
Pennsylvania	17,593	7,319	10,244	30	20	0	20	878	613	265
Rhode Island	4,180	1,306	2,834	40	0	0	0	1,200	673	527
South Carolina	7,437	4,082	3,091	264	0	0	0	1,039	690	349
South Dakota	6,980	3,176	3,804	0	393	392	1	769	473	296
Tennessee	16,641	9,433	6,959	249	0	0	0	382	366	16
Texas	25,421	13,340	12,053	28	17,077	442	16,635	3,696	912	2,784
Utah	19,063	14,590	4,470	3	50,614	50,547	67	1,706	903	803
Vermont	4,410	1,448	2,704	258	0	0	0	919	436	483
Virginia	10,208	6,431	3,677	100	0	0	0	4,174	1,797	2,377
Washington	15,953	10,798	4,837	318	1,089	1,079	10	1,476	1,023	453
West Virginia	8,394	4,326	4,068	0	414	0	414	1,782	1,256	526
Wisconsin	16,827	8,845	7,951	31	0	0	0	1,732	691	1,041
Wyoming	7,684	4,808	2,876	0	467,266	466,606	660	1,548	700	848
District of Columbia ...	3,133	2,212	921	0	0	0	0	574	417	157
American Samoa	995	424	571	0	0	0	0	106	106	0
Fed. States of Micronesia	0	0	0	0	0	0	0	172	172	0
Guam	1,272	668	604	0	0	0	0	345	345	0
Marshall Islands	0	0	0	0	0	0	0	0	0	0
Northern Marianas	1,521	717	804	0	0	0	0	361	358	3
Palau	0	0	0	0	0	0	0	215	215	0
Puerto Rico	3,348	962	2,386	0	0	0	0	1,051	318	733
Virgin Islands	1,533	370	1,160	3	0	0	0	263	263	0
Undistributed	0	0	0	0	2	1	1	457	457	0

See footnotes at end of table

FEDERAL AID TO STATE AND LOCAL GOVERNMENTS, SELECTED PROGRAMS BY STATE: FISCAL YEAR 2003 — Continued

State and outlying area	Department of the Interior—Con't			Office of Insular Affairs	Department of Justice		
	Office of Surface Mining, Reclamation and Enforcement					Federal Prison System	Office of Asset Forfeiture
	Total	Abandoned mine reclamation	Other		Total		
United States, total	$202,448	$146,341	$56,107	$365,092	$4,170,559	$6,359	$210,518
Alabama	4,006	2,930	1,076	0	55,095	0	1,319
Alaska	3,705	3,543	162	0	27,442	0	697
Arizona	0	0	0	0	78,482	225	1,693
Arkansas	1,516	1,388	128	0	32,529	0	448
California	0	0	0	120	496,241	0	23,261
Colorado	4,227	2,205	2,022	876	61,764	78	1,071
Connecticut	0	0	0	0	42,723	459	956
Delaware	0	0	0	0	12,829	0	0
Florida	0	0	0	0	238,375	170	28,671
Georgia	0	0	0	0	171,621	0	9,087
Hawaii	0	0	0	1,621	16,422	0	2,082
Idaho	0	0	0	0	18,447	0	152
Illinois	11,125	8,030	3,095	0	142,991	0	9,949
Indiana	7,765	6,573	1,192	0	77,295	0	2,442
Iowa	1,684	1,584	100	0	36,102	0	3,747
Kansas	2,173	2,080	93	0	41,353	0	2,023
Kentucky	29,446	17,792	11,654	0	59,875	260	1,510
Louisiana	236	75	161	0	56,140	0	2,024
Maine	0	0	0	0	20,320	0	473
Maryland	3,863	3,288	575	4	126,938	643	9,235
Massachusetts	0	0	0	0	91,821	909	2,177
Michigan	0	0	0	0	113,167	0	5,095
Minnesota	0	0	0	0	55,279	0	1,110
Mississippi	136	0	136	0	45,380	0	1,149
Missouri	1,444	1,098	346	0	71,318	0	4,069
Montana	4,797	3,807	990	0	33,716	0	529
Nebraska	0	0	0	0	27,507	0	3,898
Nevada	0	0	0	0	39,128	0	1,474
New Hampshire	0	0	0	0	40,246	0	1,063
New Jersey	0	0	0	0	107,548	1,591	3,802
New Mexico	2,477	1,762	715	0	55,906	0	2,493
New York	0	0	0	0	304,035	20	21,029
North Carolina	0	0	0	0	101,239	0	7,721
North Dakota	2,487	1,944	543	0	14,569	0	15
Ohio	10,186	8,294	1,892	0	95,665	257	9,495
Oklahoma	2,789	1,801	988	0	52,673	353	6,425
Oregon	0	0	0	0	46,707	120	627
Pennsylvania	33,706	24,435	9,271	0	131,147	0	3,414
Rhode Island	0	0	0	0	17,821	0	866
South Carolina	0	0	0	0	62,800	0	3,610
South Dakota	0	0	0	0	33,205	0	109
Tennessee	486	0	486	0	69,988	39	3,163
Texas	3,753	2,388	1,365	0	219,893	0	14,341
Utah	3,723	2,024	1,699	0	29,230	0	0
Vermont	0	0	0	0	20,460	0	1,032
Virginia	9,421	6,283	3,138	0	169,460	169	1,949
Washington	0	0	0	0	83,979	476	940
West Virginia	32,722	20,455	12,267	0	43,136	0	629
Wisconsin	0	0	0	0	61,042	0	2,997
Wyoming	24,575	22,562	2,013	0	13,677	0	206
District of Columbia ...	0	0	0	0	54,464	590	615
American Samoa	0	0	0	33,939	2,374	0	0
Fed. States of Micronesia	0	0	0	103,846	0	0	0
Guam	0	0	0	36,280	8,526	0	62
Marshall Islands	0	0	0	53,652	0	0	0
Northern Marianas	0	0	0	19,135	2,300	0	0
Palau	0	0	0	42,620	0	0	0
Puerto Rico	0	0	0	0	31,025	0	3,574
Virgin Islands	0	0	0	67,826	6,890	0	0
Undistributed	0	0	0	5,173	254	0	0

See footnotes at end of table

FEDERAL AID TO STATE AND LOCAL GOVERNMENTS, SELECTED PROGRAMS BY STATE: FISCAL YEAR 2003 — Continued

State and outlying area	Total	Department of Justice—Con't Office of Justice Programs Corrections, probation & payroll	Crime victims programs	Domestic preparedness & anti-terrorism programs	Education research, & statistics programs	Juvenile justice programs	Law Enforcement Assistance	Substance abuse programs	Other
United States, total	$3,953,682	$359,867	$495,210	$118,842	$176,458	$428,398	$2,374,907	$840,474	$95,196
Alabama	53,776	2,058	7,547	337	1,877	6,017	35,940	13,005	1,489
Alaska	26,745	740	2,816	0	1,735	4,012	17,442	5,711	580
Arizona	76,564	6,775	8,412	870	6,365	7,808	46,334	17,732	2,521
Arkansas	32,081	1,657	3,449	1,174	1,354	2,893	31,554	7,282	605
California	472,980	28,345	92,916	12,286	20,906	45,702	272,825	92,454	6,671
Colorado	60,615	5,857	8,039	1,666	3,604	9,181	32,268	13,481	2,169
Connecticut	41,308	1,471	4,443	19	3,162	3,485	28,728	10,767	194
Delaware	12,829	2,506	1,561	0	555	2,880	5,327	2,415	379
Florida	209,534	22,049	29,553	7,514	9,646	10,342	130,430	39,343	4,239
Georgia	162,534	26,290	12,099	1,504	1,696	11,645	109,300	18,924	1,897
Hawaii	14,340	62	2,858	195	316	3,761	7,148	3,166	577
Idaho	18,295	850	2,203	0	416	3,104	11,722	5,110	345
Illinois	133,042	8,223	25,733	7,282	2,750	13,551	75,503	21,473	1,676
Indiana	74,853	19,258	7,829	986	2,386	7,803	36,591	10,889	2,172
Iowa	32,355	378	5,964	1,421	932	4,491	19,169	9,114	439
Kansas	39,330	5,425	5,159	1,779	625	4,688	21,564	10,195	126
Kentucky	58,105	4,073	4,841	735	3,458	5,016	39,982	19,916	1,288
Louisiana	54,116	7,145	6,436	2,135	426	5,995	31,979	8,843	1,748
Maine	19,847	821	2,176	1,701	682	2,771	11,696	3,654	166
Maryland	117,060	8,229	8,596	2,342	5,445	12,885	79,563	23,218	1,689
Massachusetts	88,735	8,406	9,906	5,681	10,333	9,973	44,436	14,011	1,689
Michigan	108,072	23,698	11,818	3,320	1,876	10,522	56,838	21,670	1,755
Minnesota	54,169	4,518	5,733	1,109	2,312	6,126	34,371	9,207	978
Mississippi	44,231	12,932	3,791	152	1,417	1,538	24,401	9,069	416
Missouri	67,249	1,349	8,477	1,498	7,075	7,149	41,701	14,799	2,351
Montana	33,187	6,196	2,067	984	2,835	3,286	17,819	3,647	1,041
Nebraska	23,609	0	3,446	230	1,227	3,881	14,825	5,671	917
Nevada	37,654	1,023	2,922	145	905	7,080	25,579	11,356	2,135
New Hampshire	39,183	1,201	2,205	7,703	3,517	3,112	21,445	9,051	76
New Jersey	102,155	26,473	10,445	335	697	5,411	58,794	16,704	8,012
New Mexico	53,413	2,100	3,458	7,260	1,459	3,292	35,844	16,089	2,609
New York	282,986	30,603	25,826	8,413	5,000	25,748	187,396	70,544	5,405
North Carolina	93,518	13,382	12,863	767	10,223	7,928	48,355	19,106	862
North Dakota	14,554	1,932	1,720	504	399	2,633	7,366	2,816	704
Ohio	85,913	1,576	16,274	2,762	2,641	6,784	55,876	22,750	2,542
Oklahoma	45,895	532	5,958	7,595	78	5,528	26,204	8,128	1,105
Oregon	45,960	2,448	4,709	23	2,145	8,687	27,948	8,892	2,446
Pennsylvania	127,733	7,979	21,227	822	9,354	19,811	68,540	30,941	2,214
Rhode Island	16,955	509	2,634	1,123	1,605	2,684	8,400	2,567	379
South Carolina	59,190	5,860	7,118	3,101	7,609	5,713	29,789	10,907	753
South Dakota	33,096	10,264	1,971	220	2,703	3,284	14,654	3,624	705
Tennessee	66,786	1,922	12,951	1,096	5,259	6,843	38,715	13,222	1,352
Texas	205,552	11,535	27,570	4,965	770	24,637	136,075	61,051	-452
Utah	29,230	5,016	3,984	356	1,169	2,861	15,844	6,087	642
Vermont	19,428	294	1,987	718	426	2,784	13,219	2,818	160
Virginia	167,342	17,449	10,082	6,169	5,176	32,395	96,071	48,953	7,203
Washington	82,563	4,054	11,126	3,938	3,005	7,154	53,286	13,162	889
West Virginia	42,507	2,840	3,074	1,930	5,978	4,695	23,990	7,333	10,269
Wisconsin	58,045	362	7,181	1,063	2,524	9,594	37,321	14,491	734
Wyoming	13,471	986	1,175	0	784	3,309	7,217	3,269	851
District of Columbia ...	53,259	0	1,999	460	6,924	6,336	37,540	10,030	2,726
American Samoa	2,374	0	242	0	256	538	1,338	1,053	0
Fed. States of Micronesia	0	0	0	0	0	0	0	0	0
Guam	8,464	-100	342	287	175	2,768	4,992	1,690	546
Marshall Islands	0	0	0	0	0	0	0	0	0
Northern Marianas	2,300	0	423	0	79	668	1,130	914	0
Palau	0	0	0	0	0	0	0	0	0
Puerto Rico	27,451	66	5,146	0	7	4,127	18,105	7,005	99
Virgin Islands	6,890	250	730	167	180	1,489	4,074	1,155	113
Undistributed	254	0	0	0	0	0	254	0	0

See footnotes at end of table

FEDERAL AID TO STATE AND LOCAL GOVERNMENTS, SELECTED PROGRAMS BY STATE: FISCAL YEAR 2003 — Continued

State and outlying area	Total (c)	Bureau of Labor Statistics	Total	State Unemplmnt. Ins. and Emplmnt Svc. (b)	Workforce Investment (b)	Other (b)	Mine Health and Safety Admin.	Occpn'l Health and Safety Admin.	Vet. Emplmnt. and Training Admin.	Nat'l Fndn. on the Arts and the Hum.	Nbrhd. Reinvestment Corp.
United States, total ..	$8,017,978	$90,805	$7,585,018	$2,709,148	$3,416,538 #	$1,459,332	$8,223	$141,670	$192,262	$35,887	$69,861
Alabama	123,645	1,385	117,828	33,557	63,552	20,719	184	1,458	2,790	691	143
Alaska	66,443	919	61,924	23,928	26,680	11,316	43	1,895	1,662	746	416
Arizona	118,463	1,260	112,322	34,060	54,766	23,496	283	2,231	2,367	671	892
Arkansas	71,901	934	68,029	23,528	31,899	12,602	102	1,141	1,695	1,006	628
California	1,125,810	8,718	1,064,062	390,230	571,707	102,125	525	30,650	21,855	1,065	14,228
Colorado	89,292	1,608	82,682	42,471	27,114	13,097	154	961	3,887	772	1,491
Connecticut	96,903	1,756	89,320	51,039	27,055	11,226	39	1,638	4,150	1,309	1,165
Delaware	20,335	666	18,648	8,799	7,985	1,864	0	414	607	378	30
Florida	245,011	3,210	231,674	77,977	118,995	34,702	224	1,789	8,114	710	2,433
Georgia	157,545	1,873	150,855	48,132	84,579	18,144	204	1,394	3,219	504	843
Hawaii	51,256	777	47,596	14,776	18,081	14,739	0	2,128	755	591	127
Idaho	39,845	740	37,616	20,045	9,562	8,009	91	462	936	681	1,750
Illinois	348,325	2,963	333,577	130,348	171,518	31,711	211	1,509	10,065	739	909
Indiana	99,093	1,368	90,648	37,905	37,051	15,692	130	2,971	3,976	730	889
Iowa	57,744	2,070	50,268	24,056	12,037	14,175	152	2,245	3,009	588	268
Kansas	55,103	1,083	51,899	18,572	16,649	16,678	58	669	1,394	386	525
Kentucky	104,873	1,155	97,967	27,437	43,468	27,062	603	3,212	1,936	758	448
Louisiana	120,154	1,475	116,368	29,380	77,516	9,472	0	747	1,564	597	465
Maine	42,147	1,286	38,148	14,335	13,151	10,662	71	750	1,892	550	138
Maryland	191,700	1,425	181,021	55,820	55,326	69,875	0	3,918	5,336	593	1,894
Massachusetts	155,033	2,167	145,813	81,580	45,491	18,742	60	1,345	5,648	768	3,093
Michigan	278,282	2,908	257,003	106,295	109,409	41,299	198	10,474	7,699	751	490
Minnesota	112,854	1,976	101,598	47,653	31,265	22,680	262	4,804	4,214	653	949
Mississippi	81,200	701	78,681	19,264	49,928	9,489	73	523	1,222	730	92
Missouri	109,625	1,042	103,635	37,633	45,141	20,861	87	823	4,038	497	722
Montana	28,187	923	25,087	9,301	11,803	3,983	125	417	1,635	685	334
Nebraska	24,838	952	22,314	11,917	5,925	4,472	61	547	964	660	214
Nevada	47,764	855	43,674	25,756	14,857	3,061	173	1,823	1,239	665	148
New Hampshire	27,967	753	25,232	13,977	9,064	2,191	19	411	1,552	610	1,627
New Jersey	157,884	2,719	148,572	100,680	37,779	10,113	46	2,972	3,575	783	295
New Mexico	63,962	993	60,779	16,358	31,544	12,877	214	869	1,107	845	789
New York	561,316	4,827	536,783	165,061	236,466	135,256	303	6,837	12,566	677	7,524
North Carolina	193,282	2,429	180,447	67,985	45,596	66,866	101	6,321	3,984	730	2,061
North Dakota	18,698	670	17,162	6,934	8,626	1,602	63	197	606	594	473
Ohio	286,305	5,132	269,986	88,768	148,615	32,603	227	1,438	9,522	626	3,933
Oklahoma	72,267	1,161	66,841	20,565	33,253	13,023	97	1,218	2,950	643	1,015
Oregon	125,451	1,529	115,511	42,094	55,621	17,796	147	4,737	3,527	291	666
Pennsylvania	348,230	3,110	334,809	136,946	132,784	65,079	509	1,598	8,204	515	739
Rhode Island	32,847	823	30,777	16,433	11,005	3,339	0	605	642	506	1,155
South Carolina	89,889	1,309	83,794	31,613	37,349	14,832	72	2,388	2,326	955	0
South Dakota	29,377	669	27,730	6,474	10,909	10,347	48	403	527	824	277
Tennessee	135,868	1,348	126,711	35,537	62,189	28,985	158	4,127	3,524	604	1,503
Texas	464,653	4,145	447,949	122,250	248,372	77,327	651	2,435	9,473	768	4,494
Utah	54,730	1,337	50,683	30,839	10,968	8,876	160	1,569	981	589	392
Vermont	23,433	616	20,735	7,585	9,123	4,027	0	868	1,214	556	1,811
Virginia	257,262	1,850	247,959	37,130	50,096	160,733	259	3,729	3,465	912	1,767
Washington	247,514	1,721	232,625	80,753	116,442	35,430	129	7,864	5,175	793	640
West Virginia	60,187	1,025	57,163	15,092	37,842	4,229	490	491	1,018	641	784
Wisconsin	146,526	1,944	137,015	64,605	39,530	32,880	220	3,660	3,687	559	1,417
Wyoming	19,115	759	16,775	6,554	9,140	1,081	149	938	494	489	0
District of Columbia	274,757	764	271,979	129,123	27,395	115,461	0	463	1,551	557	170
American Samoa	1,196	0	1,196	0	323	873	0	0	0	169	0
Fed. States of Micronesia	934	0	934	0	934	0	0	0	0	0	0
Guam	2,677	74	2,396	10	1,435	951	0	207	0	198	0
Marshall Islands	1,245	0	1,245	0	1,245	0	0	0	0	0	0
Northern Marianas	1,894	0	1,873	20	253	1,600	0	21	0	436	0
Palau	362	0	362	0	362	0	0	0	0	8	0
Puerto Rico	246,603	663	243,481	18,346	217,310	7,825	0	2,091	368	295	429
Virgin Islands	5,817	240	5,257	1,622	2,458	1,177	0	275	45	240	0
Undistributed	2,359	0	0	0	0	0	48	0	2,311	0	176

See footnotes at end of table

FEDERAL AID TO STATE AND LOCAL GOVERNMENTS, SELECTED PROGRAMS BY STATE: FISCAL YEAR 2003 — Continued

State and outlying area	Social Security Administration supplemental security income	State Justice Institute	TVA payments in lieu of taxes	Department of Transportation Total	Federal Aviation Administration	Federal Highway Administration Total	Demonstration projects	Highway Trust Fund	Other	Federal Motor Carrier Safety Admin.
United States, total	$30,722	$2,033	$329,367	$38,913,822	$2,680,905	$29,650,561	$318,281	$28,613,682	$718,598	$168,703
Alabama	434	10	77,524	692,803	57,465	586,431	57	529,746	56,628	2,045
Alaska	174	1	0	642,987	152,845	447,843	34,927	381,394	31,522	934
Arizona	266	15	0	604,191	72,357	482,108	708	468,797	12,603	3,087
Arkansas	128	2	0	506,278	34,165	441,238	43,439	391,788	6,011	1,934
California	5,023	2	0	4,350,494	208,646	2,793,752	1,706	2,727,031	65,015	10,209
Colorado	261	26	0	510,824	55,649	409,324	1,354	400,956	7,014	1,928
Connecticut	314	0	0	481,507	6,742	386,823	1	386,786	36	1,016
Delaware	66	0	0	127,070	2,478	104,933	7,124	96,980	829	406
Florida	1,253	2	0	2,030,052	159,686	1,657,738	4,723	1,650,418	2,597	2,712
Georgia	1,430	2	5,161	961,716	46,298	781,141	305	777,787	3,049	5,743
Hawaii	29	13	0	153,680	23,816	122,322	6,704	114,678	940	230
Idaho	84	5	0	276,132	29,541	235,964	3,439	208,782	23,743	1,305
Illinois	1,592	45	331	1,367,459	71,351	871,025	1,989	868,749	287	4,271
Indiana	267	1	0	736,055	45,472	616,328	1,374	614,831	123	3,560
Iowa	359	1	0	420,786	36,079	353,387	7,934	345,345	108	2,974
Kansas	466	1	0	400,542	21,822	358,362	146	357,609	607	2,479
Kentucky	923	1	26,389	642,316	64,457	528,692	12,166	509,171	7,355	4,854
Louisiana	794	0	0	644,798	43,650	518,438	13	513,949	4,476	2,110
Maine	147	6	0	213,492	17,446	181,955	173	180,641	1,141	265
Maryland	937	64	0	677,553	22,052	494,626	4,768	425,455	64,403	603
Massachusetts	484	15	0	738,935	63,398	497,799	261	497,086	452	2,130
Michigan	1,767	216	0	949,827	80,803	791,419	7,877	776,453	7,089	4,614
Minnesota	548	6	0	557,575	56,567	378,485	1,129	366,821	10,535	3,119
Mississippi	141	45	18,130	466,473	29,126	405,451	29,488	364,200	11,763	2,590
Missouri	240	1	0	885,553	57,351	737,094	9,472	724,730	2,892	3,148
Montana	109	8	0	65,977	32,957	16,836	416	1,211	15,209	1,211
Nebraska	78	0	0	257,112	18,677	224,610	513	222,197	1,900	2,222
Nevada	124	1	0	286,035	55,297	200,888	17,337	180,236	3,315	1,457
New Hampshire	13	0	0	185,332	33,735	142,542	1,929	140,393	220	1,118
New Jersey	379	26	0	977,799	28,273	726,626	6,802	719,824	0	2,866
New Mexico	211	94	0	310,994	16,670	270,533	880	261,460	8,193	2,222
New York	1,317	168	0	2,198,722	117,963	1,261,038	5,381	1,250,255	5,402	9,922
North Carolina	1,004	0	1,557	988,058	72,424	826,519	713	815,108	10,698	3,839
North Dakota	1	0	0	212,989	14,864	184,921	2,086	182,491	344	1,578
Ohio	2,324	0	0	1,185,831	66,078	924,166	5,799	918,055	312	7,349
Oklahoma	424	0	0	492,900	33,032	431,925	-67	398,477	33,515	3,230
Oregon	26	2	0	628,351	33,355	526,037	817	378,464	146,756	2,341
Pennsylvania	2,331	1	0	1,824,190	108,430	1,367,694	2,750	1,346,714	18,230	5,768
Rhode Island	41	18	0	175,232	13,209	143,597	1,508	141,507	582	437
South Carolina	585	0	0	507,731	21,665	443,890	1,435	438,470	3,985	2,605
South Dakota	196	13	0	252,308	16,194	224,054	15,846	203,606	4,602	615
Tennessee	371	529	200,171	671,814	60,014	540,535	3,429	532,061	5,045	3,533
Texas	1,531	3	0	3,075,609	153,786	2,611,565	10,062	2,595,257	6,246	16,915
Utah	189	0	0	287,079	23,851	218,621	1,000	215,206	2,415	1,364
Vermont	210	24	0	124,100	2,222	107,999	52	107,664	283	756
Virginia	503	497	104	850,244	43,502	706,523	6,629	696,769	3,125	3,471
Washington	207	1	0	853,864	51,302	611,369	4,043	554,249	53,077	3,049
West Virginia	200	69	0	462,017	23,437	405,606	24,343	328,223	53,040	1,133
Wisconsin	105	0	0	686,008	46,410	587,380	1,709	579,126	6,545	3,834
Wyoming	35	0	0	281,520	20,345	248,647	10,095	232,874	5,678	716
District of Columbia ...	81	99	0	406,863	430	156,687	0	151,808	4,879	467
American Samoa	0	0	0	25,433	18,177	6,075	0	6,075	0	278
Fed. States of Micronesia	0	0	0	0	0	0	0	0	0	0
Guam	0	0	0	20,846	5,709	13,937	0	13,937	0	156
Marshall Islands	0	0	0	0	0	0	0	0	0	0
Northern Marianas	0	0	0	12,421	9,834	1,573	0	1,573	0	317
Palau	0	0	0	0	0	0	0	0	0	0
Puerto Rico	0	0	0	191,591	7,134	58,702	0	58,607	95	105
Virgin Islands	0	0	0	22,463	8,615	12,310	0	12,310	0	115
Undistributed	0	0	0	353,291	64,052	264,478	11,497	249,292	3,689	15,448

See footnotes at end of table

FEDERAL AID TO STATE AND LOCAL GOVERNMENTS, SELECTED PROGRAMS BY STATE: FISCAL YEAR 2003 — Continued

State and outlying area	Federal Railroad Administration	Department of Transportation			Department of the Treasury			Department of Veterans Affairs (b)	Payments to Dist. of Columbia and Metro System (WMATA (d))
		Federal Transit Administration	National Highway Traffice Safety Administration	Research and Special Projects Administration	Total	Dept. of the Treasurey Asset Forfeiture Fund	Other (d)		
United States, total ...	$6,462	$5,841,403	$419,473	$146,315	$5,412,773	$54,190	$5,358,583	$648,439	$401,306
Alabama	88	38,619	6,202	1,953	76,393	781	75,612	8,466	0
Alaska	0	34,962	6,334	69	25,052	52	25,000	218	0
Arizona	3	41,225	3,256	2,155	90,463	3,229	87,234	4,715	0
Arkansas	0	21,727	5,761	1,453	45,596	129	45,467	1,540	0
California	45	1,275,777	54,881	7,184	579,394	3,488	575,906	46,602	0
Colorado	0	38,323	4,415	1,185	73,298	164	73,134	12,060	0
Connecticut	0	80,217	6,018	691	57,984	81	57,903	6,430	0
Delaware	44	16,098	3,044	67	25,013	13	25,000	32	0
Florida	0	199,090	9,186	1,640	278,106	6,364	271,742	8,958	0
Georgia	0	112,995	14,265	1,274	139,932	740	139,192	11,553	0
Hawaii	0	5,824	1,418	70	25,005	5	25,000	0	0
Idaho	0	6,619	1,572	1,131	25,045	45	25,000	11,249	0
Illinois	58	405,554	7,962	7,238	213,214	2,054	211,160	18,980	0
Indiana	0	53,475	15,960	1,260	103,848	402	103,446	6,759	0
Iowa	404	20,562	4,933	2,447	49,923	168	49,755	13,850	0
Kansas	0	13,386	3,096	1,397	45,968	258	45,710	11,309	0
Kentucky	0	38,602	4,756	955	68,990	264	68,726	10,872	0
Louisiana	0	71,359	7,847	1,394	76,152	166	75,986	7,314	0
Maine	0	12,738	783	305	25,035	35	25,000	18,123	0
Maryland	0	146,661	12,685	926	92,585	2,378	90,207	4,920	0
Massachusetts	0	163,826	9,159	2,623	109,266	1,107	108,159	33,850	0
Michigan	0	64,881	6,953	1,157	169,904	925	168,979	17,255	0
Minnesota	1,000	105,270	7,689	5,445	83,681	37	83,644	14,928	0
Mississippi	48	21,896	6,661	701	48,583	216	48,367	11,715	0
Missouri	163	75,018	11,036	1,743	95,443	310	95,133	21,873	0
Montana	136	6,575	6,851	1,411	25,109	109	25,000	4,116	0
Nebraska	501	8,047	2,700	355	29,793	697	29,096	10,392	0
Nevada	0	25,570	2,467	356	34,315	339	33,976	5,924	0
New Hampshire	0	6,186	1,187	564	25,043	43	25,000	3,814	0
New Jersey	0	211,533	6,957	1,544	145,535	2,410	143,125	49,781	0
New Mexico	0	16,299	4,790	480	31,231	266	30,965	3,558	0
New York	0	787,286	18,003	4,510	333,576	10,678	322,898	20,764	0
North Carolina	0	79,377	3,955	1,944	138,103	1,244	136,859	3,903	0
North Dakota	0	6,168	3,750	1,708	25,002	1	25,001	3,322	0
Ohio	0	171,143	15,483	1,612	193,366	333	193,033	13,726	0
Oklahoma	0	19,759	3,487	1,467	58,763	54	58,709	28,858	0
Oregon	3,518	55,381	7,183	536	59,633	1,460	58,173	2,461	0
Pennsylvania	95	329,352	10,200	2,651	209,373	521	208,852	24,707	0
Rhode Island	0	12,569	3,728	1,692	25,076	64	25,012	7,191	0
South Carolina	97	29,049	9,704	721	69,170	955	68,215	24,946	0
South Dakota	0	4,390	6,600	455	25,007	0	25,007	1,890	0
Tennessee	0	53,015	12,457	2,260	97,238	311	96,927	5,409	0
Texas	0	264,431	22,354	6,558	361,966	7,431	354,535	28,382	0
Utah	242	39,020	2,979	1,002	38,049	15	38,034	2,337	0
Vermont	0	10,757	2,028	338	25,030	19	25,011	2,952	0
Virginia	0	82,704	11,376	2,668	121,683	1,330	120,353	11,293	0
Washington	0	178,791	7,753	1,600	100,828	521	100,307	41,071	0
West Virginia	20	23,110	5,919	2,792	30,813	66	30,747	17,426	0
Wisconsin	0	42,262	4,734	1,388	91,205	6	91,199	22,802	0
Wyoming	0	3,317	8,102	393	25,006	6	25,000	1,956	0
District of Columbia	0	189,027	1,835	58,417	25,216	195	25,021	922	401,306
American Samoa	0	259	512	132	5,000	0	5,000	0	0
Fed. States of Micronesia	0	0	0	0	0	0	0	0	0
Guam	0	476	568	0	5,000	0	5,000	0	0
Marshall Islands	0	0	0	0	0	0	0	0	0
Northern Marianas ..	0	174	472	51	5,000	0	5,000	0	0
Palau	0	0	0	0	0	0	0	0	0
Puerto Rico	0	120,054	5,400	196	423,771	1,705	422,066	965	0
Virgin Islands	0	609	763	51	5,000	0	5,000	0	0
Undistributed	0	9	9,304	0	0	0	0	0	0

See footnotes at end of table

FEDERAL AID TO STATE AND LOCAL GOVERNMENTS, SELECTED PROGRAMS BY STATE: FISCAL YEAR 2003 — Continued

Source: U.S. Department of Commerce, Bureau of the Census, Federal Aid to States for Fiscal Year 2003, September 2004.

Note: Negative amounts (-) are refunds (from the recipients) of advances from a prior year, or represent reductions in the amount of funds originally obligated to the recipients for the particular program or program category during the fiscal year. All amounts unless otherwise footnoted, represent actual expenditures of the federal government during the indicated (FY 2003) fiscal year.

Key:

(a) For Puerto Rico, amount shown is for the nutritional assistance grant program. All other amounts are grant payments for food stamp administration.

(b) The data were extracted from the FY 2000 quarterly data files submitted to the Federal Assistance Award System, since FY 2003 FAS data were not available at the time of publication.

(c) Column data will not add to total due to supplemental data for Puerto Rico extracted from the FY 2005 Budget of the U.S. Government. FY 2003 FAS data were not available at the time of publication.

(d) The data were extracted from the Appendix, FY 2005 Budget of the U.S. Government, since FY 2003 FAS data were not available at time of publication.

Table 2.3
SUMMARY OF FEDERAL GOVERNMENT EXPENDITURE, BY STATE AND OUTLYING AREA:
FISCAL YEAR 2003
(In millions of dollars)

State and outlying area	Total	Retirement and disability	Other direct payments	Grants	Procurement	Salaries and wages
United States	$2,061,486	$636,239	$446,119	$441,038	$327,413	$210,677
Alabama	36,871	12,232	7,698	6,649	7,067	3,224
Alaska	7,944	1,041	584	3,022	1,680	1,617
Arizona	37,801	12,022	6,653	7,235	8,557	3,335
Arkansas	18,340	7,038	4,558	4,541	864	1,339
California	219,706	61,236	49,480	51,329	37,050	20,611
Colorado	28,874	8,375	5,014	6,014	5,142	4,329
Connecticut	28,595	7,549	5,669	5,376	8,484	1,516
Delaware	5,061	1,945	1,201	1,181	245	489
Florida	113,341	45,192	30,041	17,463	10,899	9,746
Georgia	51,910	16,666	11,426	10,561	5,243	8,015
Hawaii	11,269	3,014	1,502	1,911	1,978	2,864
Idaho	8,654	2,865	1,566	1,858	1,531	834
Illinois	73,020	24,786	20,232	15,720	5,729	6,553
Indiana	35,525	13,394	9,178	7,313	3,302	2,338
Iowa	17,550	6,780	4,654	3,877	1,109	1,129
Kansas	18,208	6,196	4,469	3,415	2,020	2,108
Kentucky	31,153	10,169	6,119	6,634	5,119	3,112
Louisiana	31,646	9,559	8,424	7,820	3,195	2,648
Maine	9,966	3,403	1,753	2,610	1,312	888
Maryland	57,646	13,306	9,161	8,632	16,216	10,331
Massachusetts	51,265	13,794	12,339	13,328	8,357	3,446
Michigan	57,870	22,042	15,556	12,970	3,884	3,418
Minnesota	27,580	9,627	6,514	6,914	2,406	2,120
Mississippi	21,741	6,923	4,904	5,318	2,626	1,970
Missouri	43,874	13,509	9,887	8,655	7,992	3,832
Montana	7,092	2,315	1,497	1,938	497	845
Nebraska	11,000	3,956	2,732	2,512	608	1,192
Nevada	11,637	4,708	2,280	1,955	1,472	1,222
New Hampshire	7,349	2,838	1,336	1,865	738	571
New Jersey	53,679	18,388	14,190	11,481	5,461	4,159
New Mexico	18,736	4,388	2,281	4,322	5,819	1,926
New York	137,898	40,506	33,524	47,575	7,758	8,535
North Carolina	51,766	18,806	11,012	11,613	3,794	6,541
North Dakota	5,726	1,447	1,627	1,537	398	717
Ohio	69,902	25,348	16,957	15,687	6,548	5,362
Oklahoma	25,254	8,772	5,505	5,136	2,488	3,353
Oregon	21,253	8,024	5,147	5,103	1198	1,781
Pennsylvania	90,350	32,072	25,156	18,624	8,137	6,363
Rhode Island	8,036	2,535	1,791	2,234	659	817
South Carolina	28,038	10,106	5,486	5,969	3,614	2,863
South Dakota	6,202	1,809	1,641	1,698	381	673
Tennessee	42,602	13,744	8,922	9,057	7,522	3,357
Texas	140,451	39,149	29,117	28,423	29,823	13,939
Utah	13,500	3,892	2,051	2,845	2,665	2,047
Vermont	4,443	1,358	828	1,331	566	360
Virginia	82,454	19,553	9,420	7,886	30,839	14,756
Washington	43,368	13,587	8,513	8,881	6,629	5,758
West Virginia	14,226	5,663	3,048	3,562	665	1,289
Wisconsin	30,237	11,618	7,282	7,544	2,008	1,785
Wyoming	4,226	1,152	602	1,616	346	510
Dist. of Columbia	34,750	1,934	2,370	4,310	11,376	14,760
American Samoa	198	41	12	110	28	7
Fed. States of Micronesia .	145	0	7	136	1	0
Guam	1,539	207	92	400	526	315
Marshall Islands	182	1	0	66	115	0
No. Mariana Islands	141	22	15	90	8	6
Palau	53	0	1	51	1	0
Puerto Rico	14,661	5,477	2,847	4,808	561	968
Virgin Islands	615	146	107	282	26	55
Undistributed	34,366	14	141	43	32,133	2,035

Source: U.S. Department of Commerce, Bureau of the Census, September 2004.

Table 2.4
FEDERAL GOVERNMENT EXPENDITURE FOR DIRECT PAYMENTS FOR INDIVIDUALS FOR RETIREMENT AND DISABILITY, FOR SELECTED PROGRAMS, BY STATE AND OUTLYING AREA: FISCAL YEAR 2003
(In thousands of dollars)

| State and outlying area | Total | Social Security payments | | | Supplemental security income payments | Federal retirement and disability benefits | | Veteran benefits | | Other |
		Retirement insurance payments	Survivors insurance payments	Disability insurance payments		Civilian	Military	Payments for service connected disability	Other benefit payments	
United States	$636,238,733	$305,159,678	$93,304,326	$77,597,267	$32,494,880	$51,339,395	$33,428,532	$20,622,189	$6,956,813	$15,335,652
Alabama	12,232,032	4,727,454	1,821,795	1,880,893	756,410	1,259,667	857,350	439,198	220,098	269,167
Alaska	1,040,560	349,955	119,511	113,113	44,193	165,627	129,654	94,458	8,671	15,379
Arizona	12,021,799	5,862,970	1,511,898	1,353,461	464,694	1,022,979	938,866	498,963	132,534	235,434
Arkansas	7,038,393	2,964,026	1,023,813	1,115,684	376,005	485,563	389,649	341,940	123,716	197,996
California	61,235,997	29,608,935	8,358,408	6,976,636	4,907,257	4,678,750	3,455,792	1,705,756	556,491	976,972
Colorado	8,374,763	3,612,370	1,064,106	865,674	259,319	934,855	928,742	379,797	94,505	215,394
Connecticut	7,549,272	4,580,976	1,098,042	835,455	261,708	312,280	170,933	1,533,766	38,122	97,990
Delaware	1,945,047	992,545	271,898	236,256	64,028	152,482	118,109	54,483	15,483	39,526
Florida	45,191,664	23,066,580	578,984	4,516,207	1,993,325	3,498,369	3,518,148	1,545,179	494,080	800,792
Georgia	16,665,866	6,835,052	2,337,539	2,312,349	909,435	1,585,812	1,382,658	659,365	259,808	383,846
Hawaii	3,014,060	1,396,138	303,241	232,869	108,907	527,747	276,463	112,991	25,215	30,489
Idaho	2,864,526	1,355,160	393,787	319,213	95,544	257,202	184,503	125,692	30,469	102,956
Illinois	24,785,986	13,158,553	4,153,128	2,839,466	1,389,421	1,330,115	527,213	425,528	164,916	797,646
Indiana	13,393,781	7,141,750	2,246,429	1,693,822	473,696	704,828	316,060	312,302	96,359	408,536
Iowa	6,780,030	3,761,442	1,157,681	702,455	189,990	402,475	142,535	154,023	59,749	209,680
Kansas	6,195,937	3,094,855	937,197	614,598	180,836	485,447	334,161	181,092	63,164	304,588
Kentucky	10,168,614	3,931,319	1,602,809	1,909,855	863,478	656,624	361,195	341,866	134,042	367,425
Louisiana	9,559,415	3,732,585	1,909,986	1,466,456	800,162	536,115	428,179	332,438	170,961	182,532
Maine	3,402,746	1,518,318	447,471	487,971	142,935	293,535	178,319	216,656	49,225	68,315
Maryland	13,306,464	5,122,027	1,578,364	1,111,141	475,075	3,363,094	905,608	345,425	106,623	299,106
Massachusetts	13,793,808	7,234,895	1,935,032	1,858,583	760,329	916,061	298,002	456,777	119,350	214,780
Michigan	22,042,243	11,793,064	3,795,476	3,186,292	1,125,688	822,949	359,399	423,056	1,555,818	380,501
Minnesota	9,627,064	5,249,256	1,504,768	1,025,392	342,623	524,720	221,529	326,919	88,845	343,011
Mississippi	69,222,911	2,689,967	1,051,070	1,221,518	568,947	498,259	392,504	243,498	119,172	137,976
Missouri	13,508,667	6,492,508	2,061,769	1,830,403	544,554	1,057,772	531,357	388,531	153,518	448,255
Montana	2,315,005	1,028,927	326,217	247,725	68,070	241,601	118,321	110,221	26,728	147,196
Nebraska	3,956,001	1,935,110	588,309	366,366	102,204	262,755	220,627	180,477	47,983	252,172
Nevada	4,707,666	2,249,780	534,109	515,343	146,136	444,248	478,199	194,037	53,491	92,323
New Hampshire	2,837,972	1,464,553	354,821	355,563	62,070	249,195	170,598	119,796	27,025	34,351
New Jersey	18,388,407	10,653,417	2,739,321	2,061,764	710,312	1,149,977	316,373	369,670	103,925	283,649

FEDERAL GOVERNMENT EXPENDITURE FOR DIRECT PAYMENTS FOR INDIVIDUALS FOR RETIREMENT AND DISABILITY, FOR SELECTED PROGRAMS, BY STATE AND OUTLYING AREA: FISCAL YEAR 2003 — Continued

State and outlying area	Total	Social Security payments			Supplemental security income payments	Federal retirement and disability benefits		Veteran benefits		Other
		Retirement insurance payments	Survivors insurance payments	Disability insurance payments		Civilian	Military	Payments for service connected disability	Other benefit payments	
New Mexico	4,387,915	1,715,423	558,516	488,559	236,692	546,938	385,260	273,359	66,272	117,896
New York	40,505,751	21,749,984	5,828,090	5,384,359	3,043,360	1,911,051	469,657	823,095	280,702	1,015,453
North Carolina	18,805,741	8,848,486	2,451,600	2,763,871	844,294	1,299,938	1,275,163	808,095	252,880	261,414
North Dakota	1,447,202	695,024	263,402	125,166	33,259	122,475	56,573	51,868	15,107	84,329
Ohio	25,347,613	12,735,916	4,604,530	2,879,580	1,285,158	1,505,683	646,125	606,850	240,276	843,496
Oklahoma	8,772,478	3,737,576	1,283,374	985,089	350,857	991,094	517,465	512,612	186,981	207,430
Oregon	8,024,109	4,117,016	1,111,958	879,823	284,516	655,374	340,823	348,643	101,510	184,445
Pennsylvania	32,072,141	16,613,040	5,236,240	3,613,259	1,543,661	2,152,148	708,269	727,652	279,847	1,198,026
Rhode Island	2,534,589	1,325,569	311,799	337,697	131,892	191,188	102,032	88,392	25,109	20,910
South Carolina	10,105,743	4,381,256	1,330,217	1,519,426	479,137	823,066	883,264	382,951	155,286	151,141
South Dakota	1,808,942	850,803	277,641	163,610	55,689	184,220	90,797	80,065	27,601	78,516
Tennessee	13,744,487	6,109,114	2,066,520	2,040,487	740,140	1,073,024	736,293	473,048	193,114	312,747
Texas	39,148,877	17,006,775	6,302,423	4,098,860	1,997,670	3,208,066	3,244,053	1,792,057	604,430	894,544
Utah	3,891,861	1,740,730	498,349	332,436	105,303	725,383	217,129	112,226	26,841	133,464
Vermont	1,357,693	707,786	198,231	174,124	53,160	82,655	51,541	49,884	13,531	26,781
Virginia	19,553,290	6,821,366	2,119,130	1,960,462	616,469	3,460,011	3,213,879	650,028	208,751	503,193
Washington	13,587,099	6,260,669	1,695,878	1,404,787	568,401	1,328,170	1,207,877	689,217	150,634	281,465
West Virginia	5,663,150	2,170,265	973,619	1,109,408	375,390	332,370	138,073	225,301	82,459	256,284
Wisconsin	11,618,327	6,600,824	1,842,939	1,294,386	424,290	510,598	235,451	345,508	97,243	267,088
Wyoming	1,151,875	532,867	156,523	112,839	26,406	117,057	71,801	46,132	10,130	78,119
Dist. of Columbia	1,934,244	411,453	131,698	135,605	107,055	1,006,157	55,580	38,538	19,150	28,108
American Samoa	40,988	10,571	10,579	9,833	0	1,619	3,276	3,970	886	75
Fed. States of Micronesia	471	151	42	19	0	169	0	85	5	0
Guam	206,531	65,600	27,637	14,284	0	58,215	28,450	9,518	1,911	914
Marshall Islands	992	585	265	96	0	20	0	8	17	0
No. Mariana Islands	22,320	5,324	4,405	1,206	3,831	5,551	1,400	516	71	15
Palau	455	152	126	7	0	135	0	8	27	0
Puerto Rico	5,477,373	2,237,235	988,982	1,498,242	0	210,870	81,673	246,926	176,320	37,124
Virgin Islands	145,757	83,630	22,451	17,230	0	14,942	4,582	1,498	632	792
Undistributed	14,008	0	0	0	0	106	0	0	0	13,902

Source: U.S. Department of Commerce, Bureau of the Census, September 2004.

Table 2.5
FEDERAL GOVERNMENT EXPENDITURE FOR DIRECT PAYMENTS OTHER THAN FOR RETIREMENT AND DISABILITY, FOR SELECTED PROGRAMS, BY STATE AND OUTLYING AREA: FISCAL YEAR 2003
(In thousands of dollars)

State and outlying area	Total	Medicare benefits		Excess earned income tax credits	Unemployment compensation	Food stamp payments	Housing assistance	Agricultural assistance	Federal employees life and health insurance	Other
		Hospital insurance	Supplementary medical insurance							
United States	$446,119,217	$152,257,431	$121,796,655	$33,210,791	$51,146,482	$21,421,438	$4,331,165	$16,575,381	$17,177,037	$28,202,838
Alabama	7,698,399	2,852,086	1,980,767	860,614	372,690	466,124	120,093	324,401	300,220	421,404
Alaska	584,358	127,242	84,892	46,702	162,558	65,728	11,874	9,665	2,199	73,497
Arizona	6,652,753	2,197,806	1,979,853	610,809	417,638	25,837	25,837	80,121	218,503	624,944
Arkansas	4,557,886	1,521,311	1,115,207	463,347	364,976	304,340	29,763	395,741	102,271	260,931
California	49,480,339	16,664,500	15,027,966	3,699,038	7,413,498	1,808,412	189,565	636,526	1,232,622	2,809,214
Colorado	5,014,286	1,520,367	1,247,380	348,390	712,278	203,312	16,259	336,642	222,952	406,706
Connecticut	5,669,246	2,208,250	1,737,929	220,508	899,723	164,854	75,546	19,711	129,828	212,896
Delaware	1,201,123	387,419	310,849	85,156	144,072	47,791	11,139	25,781	37,766	151,149
Florida	30,041,135	11,500,750	11,272,865	2,327,127	1,447,107	987,926	115,682	246,874	793,904	1,348,900
Georgia	11,426,056	3,548,055	2,667,286	1,394,750	971,854	782,411	123,362	864,138	396,492	677,710
Hawaii	1,502,162	450,819	423,292	113,640	148,654	156,191	14,993	5,168	109,242	80,163
Idaho	1,566,125	438,684	350,348	143,135	203,316	76,580	2,203	169,126	51,658	131,075
Illinois	20,232,121	6,923,359	5,068,300	1,271,205	2,920,617	1,052,739	292,073	1,248,489	431,679	1,023,660
Indiana	9,177,938	3,106,280	2,267,768	621,070	751,983	483,697	44,995	439,337	210,728	1,252,079
Iowa	4,653,881	1,338,251	1,220,975	228,054	429,789	149,244	6,784	832,746	140,393	307,645
Kansas	4,468,647	1,335,039	1,141,003	249,665	437,057	140,387	16,837	838,006	92,725	217,928
Kentucky	6,118,924	2,204,916	1,583,113	503,658	563,854	486,231	51,676	148,151	160,865	416,459
Louisiana	8,424,174	3,235,135	2,017,915	984,835	340,861	685,267	82,853	351,635	160,756	564,917
Maine	1,752,855	634,685	479,611	111,699	145,978	124,070	9,944	45,712	65,999	135,157
Maryland	9,160,528	2,755,753	2,300,714	498,987	585,681	256,924	88,703	88,980	2,233,462	351,322
Massachusetts	12,338,842	4,938,698	3,202,728	383,172	2,423,590	253,771	126,723	24,170	302,005	683,985
Michigan	15,556,063	5,448,958	4,743,578	937,786	2,341,564	783,076	68,823	258,729	235,031	738,518
Minnesota	6,513,625	1,996,019	1,541,519	324,123	987,962	227,113	67,201	734,178	188,585	446,926
Mississippi	4,903,648	1,683,343	1,119,165	699,398	231,240	335,074	32,296	310,070	127,002	366,060
Missouri	9,886,700	3,325,927	2,526,733	643,286	694,558	567,586	63,298	480,715	1,078,007	506,591
Montana	1,497,132	384,085	313,748	102,316	83,929	68,951	4,275	359,606	54,489	125,733
Nebraska	2,731,805	698,390	598,448	154,411	151,580	89,302	11,610	768,320	78,879	180,866
Nevada	2,280,445	717,072	635,267	226,739	357,438	112,673	17,995	17,019	65,138	131,103
New Hampshire	1,336,404	522,289	376,023	75,130	123,240	39,887	8,882	12,033	76,339	102,582
New Jersey	14,189,929	5,063,458	4,274,332	705,856	2,647,862	338,821	216,405	14,632	355,561	573,001
New Mexico	2,280,773	633,650	556,879	312,940	152,919	183,505	14,161	86,784	113,753	226,182
New York	33,524,096	12,142,500	9,825,117	2,148,032	3,833,165	1,676,509	1,044,722	228,160	595,615	2,030,275
North Carolina	11,012,283	3,591,235	2,639,175	1,181,077	1,415,478	645,418	109,298	485,684	242,746	702,172
North Dakota	1,626,756	305,489	253,532	53,967	45,738	36,703	2,043	778,153	33,424	117,707
Ohio	16,957,123	6,373,496	5,009,228	1,150,361	1,711,892	880,175	206,024	454,891	350,395	820,661

FEDERAL GOVERNMENT EXPENDITURE FOR DIRECT PAYMENTS OTHER THAN FOR RETIREMENT AND DISABILITY, FOR SELECTED PROGRAMS, BY STATE AND OUTLYING AREA: FISCAL YEAR 2003 — Continued

State or other jurisdiction	Total	Medicare benefits		Excess earned income tax credits	Unemployment compensation	Food stamp payments	Housing assistance	Agricultural assistance	Federal employees life and health insurance	Other
		Hospital insurance	Supplementary medical insurance							
Oklahoma	5,505,357	2,036,611	1,329,325	483,257	342,231	362,458	28,868	290,983	260,715	370,910
Oregon	5,147,050	1,388,207	1,215,750	307,410	1,247,969	380,967	21,972	140,645	149,514	294,596
Pennsylvania	25,155,606	9,542,247	7,260,372	1,078,379	3,452,275	785,459	277,290	285,411	1,185,040	1,289,134
Rhode Island	1,790,977	691,340	491,851	92,808	249,382	68,801	24,782	6,088	42,587	123,337
South Carolina	5,486,356	1,755,239	1,369,360	696,803	507,008	443,356	35,312	155,835	154,534	368,910
South Dakota	1,640,858	335,667	268,683	77,351	31,444	50,515	5,473	653,926	21,368	196,431
Tennessee	8,921,671	3,516,172	2,141,843	836,654	719,854	721,795	104,548	159,696	187,931	533,178
Texas	29,116,948	9,580,312	6,702,239	3,555,844	2,746,180	1,880,852	131,009	1,451,790	1,033,239	2,035,485
Utah	2,051,372	599,026	441,391	196,329	275,547	102,205	7,269	39,931	133,017	256,656
Vermont	827,907	271,780	188,127	45,204	117,316	37,629	4,196	47,026	18,869	97,760
Virginia	9,420,394	2,799,634	2,267,647	737,000	797,241	366,234	74,843	236,233	1,385,540	756,023
Washington	8,513,362	2,239,920	1,932,925	484,174	2,231,437	394,383	44,320	275,210	381,606	529,386
West Virginia	3,047,545	1,188,887	887,751	214,989	202,009	216,065	16,611	22,888	93,326	206,020
Wisconsin	7,281,930	2,334,670	1,904,546	392,921	1,099,803	233,463	24,865	567,586	155,647	568,428
Wyoming	602,193	198,193	146,692	46,941	51,612	24,054	1,506	42,170	30,464	60,560
Dist. of Columbia	2,369,503	423,154	347,535	80,571	125,151	90,114	63,793	55,589	885,149	298,447
American Samoa	12,216	0	0	0	0	5604	0	0	0	6,612
Fed. States of Micronesia	7,442	0	0	0	0	0	0	0	0	7,442
Guam	91,511	807	609	0	0	53,437	3,195	140	18,444	14,878
Marshall Islands	49	0	0	0	0	0	0	0	0	49
No. Mariana Islands	14,507	0	0	0	0	7,103	0	13	0	7,391
Palau	1361	0	0	0	0	0	0	0	0	1361
Puerto Rico	2,846,715	566,063	995,566	3,173	287,006	0	115,686	19,440	49,815	809,966
Virgin Islands	106,793	1,490	10,937	0	28,071	18,494	21,693	4,687	0	8,720
Undistributed	141,036	0	0	0	0	0	0	0	0	141,036

Source: U.S. Department of Commerce, Bureau of the Census, September 2004.

Table 2.6
FEDERAL GOVERNMENT EXPENDITURE FOR GRANTS, BY AGENCY, BY STATE AND OUTLYING AREA: FISCAL YEAR 2003
(In thousands of dollars)

State and outlying area	Total	Department of Agriculture	Appalachian Regional Commission	Department of Commerce	Corporation for National and Community Service	Corporation for Public Broadcasting	Department of Defense	Department of Education
United States	$441,037,633	$24,920,393	$72,207	$1,666,347	$589,103	$368,206	$3,158,563	$37,761,108
Alabama	6,649,139	404,008	9,084	19,193	9,877	2,525	35,389	596,547
Alaska	3,022,268	128,539	0	90,349	3,314	6,482	20,910	307,358
Arizona	7,235,149	403,476	0	7,814	9,973	4,796	94,421	776,700
Arkansas	4,540,905	300,771	0	8,159	6,212	1,676	38,570	373,659
California	51,328,805	2,857,399	0	149,013	43,576	35,957	441,865	4,555,646
Colorado	6,014,437	277,631	0	72,109	7,778	3,976	33,771	449,956
Connecticut	5,376,059	164,394	33	15,777	8,487	2,270	38,551	388,739
Delaware	1,180,764	61,486	0	10,183	2,707	0	20,274	114,626
Florida	17,463,096	1,018,568	0	67,190	24,107	12,811	181,545	1,704,092
Georgia	10,561,235	773,549	2,716	24,924	29,387	5,443	52,187	1,031,167
Hawaii	1,910,963	105,078	0	51,173	5,759	2,140	46,029	236,293
Idaho	1,858,248	106,352	0	9,245	2,659	1,358	20,355	175,568
Illinois	15,720,026	801,509	0	30,995	18,843	11,296	79,450	1,461,879
Indiana	7,312,967	366,556	0	11,740	8,446	6,153	54,435	627,370
Iowa	3,877,274	255,803	0	9,714	4,553	3,439	25,847	338,565
Kansas	3,414,998	341,678	0	4,908	4,977	2,813	31,012	394,542
Kentucky	6,634,063	348,568	10,723	24,540	7,269	4,357	31,585	567,087
Louisiana	7,820,264	480,671	0	46,786	10,548	3,219	77,939	693,664
Maine	2,609,839	91,078	0	20,244	7,175	1,577	29,167	181,346
Maryland	8,632,085	289,473	2,678	46,351	14,181	4,382	215,052	583,155
Massachusetts	13,328,309	370,061	25	65,355	22,578	12,003	141,160	816,697
Michigan	12,969,959	611,453	0	29,453	15,229	7,729	53,662	1,193,350
Minnesota	6,913,535	395,736	40	22,269	9,696	10,567	61,245	542,457
Mississippi	5,318,478	375,624	5,768	47,987	17,028	1,932	14,195	474,189
Missouri	8,655,054	416,443	0	9,102	11,577	4,799	35,671	683,989
Montana	1,938,455	148,851	0	8,002	5,460	1,472	22,754	216,921
Nebraska	2,511,906	253,536	0	5,613	5,867	5,286	37,350	236,676
Nevada	1,954,975	108,374	0	5,192	3,430	2,866	24,159	207,264
New Hampshire	1,865,264	65,971	33	72,610	4,877	1,351	20,023	133,395
New Jersey	11,480,921	412,689	0	35,612	9,893	3,324	61,307	892,836
New Mexico	4,322,271	239,707	40	11,423	6,390	3,005	33,876	519,668
New York	47,574,675	1,422,470	3,139	66,720	30,460	31,140	140,743	2,772,630
North Carolina	11,613,214	683,796	3,735	38,970	11,530	69,959	66,316	986,947
North Dakota	1,537,080	187,552	0	1,917	3,241	1,367	23,972	157,867
Ohio	15,687,468	683,296	6,467	33,514	20,787	10,319	50,431	1,268,842
Oklahoma	5,135,642	412,722	0	16,595	7,666	2,390	26,613	570,017
Oregon	5,103,224	255,641	0	59,095	10,059	4,249	13,167	444,579
Pennsylvania	18,623,502	689,167	6,492	32,081	21,870	10,441	195,200	1,272,285
Rhode Island	2,234,355	67,143	0	15,184	5,399	702	17,718	147,423
South Carolina	5,968,807	346,718	1,216	66,194	4,967	3,514	47,859	564,394
South Dakota	1,697,605	245,621	0	2,810	2,290	1,484	20,820	181,939
Tennessee	9,057,023	428,023	5,187	11,903	11,286	4,707	31,787	659,144
Texas	28,422,544	3,020,560	15	58,761	29,341	12,328	119,997	3,108,563
Utah	2,844,897	177,958	0	4,031	7,313	5,160	21,247	293,219
Vermont	1,331,302	60,115	0	2,958	4,984	1,351	23,524	115,812
Virginia	7,885,964	406,321	4,405	55,506	9,670	12,310	62,296	813,027
Washington	8,880,811	385,059	0	89,944	15,785	5,874	59,381	715,357
West Virginia	3,561,882	172,932	10,207	9,321	6,854	1,318	26,427	283,147
Wisconsin	7,543,720	329,960	0	25,935	15,318	7,187	54,545	635,654
Wyoming	1,616,214	50,381	0	630	2,432	857	28685	118,777
Dist. of Columbia	4,310,169	68,326	204	20,462	18,425	6,447	31,864	316,155
American Samoa	110,243	7,544	0	2,044	0	556	0	10,651
Fed. States of Micronesia	136,328	2,783	0	36	0	0	0	11,741
Guam	400,329	16,271	0	2,310	0	696	176	22,014
Marshall Islands	65,850	650	0	0	0	0	0	4733
No. Mariana Islands	89,503	4,118	0	2,913	0	0	0	8,809
Palau	50,711	19	0	34	-15	0	0	3,011
Puerto Rico	4,807,666	1,796,308	0	11,382	7,345	3,317	19,701	712,753
Virgin Islands	281,660	18,009	0	2,163	227	585	2,337	60,643
Undistributed	43,349	5,899	0	0	0	-1,054	0	25,575

Source: U.S. Department of Commerce, Bureau of the Census, September 2004.

FEDERAL GOVERNMENT EXPENDITURE FOR GRANTS, BY AGENCY, BY STATE AND OUTLYING AREA: FISCAL YEAR 2003 — Continued

State and outlying area	Election Assistance Commission	Department of Energy	Environmental Protection Agency	Equal Employment Opportunity Commission	Department of Health and Human Services	Department of Homeland Security	Department of Housing and Urban Development	Institute of Museum and Library Services	Department of the Interior
United States	$649,500	$1,667,066	$3,996,749	$32,089	$253,240,716	$6,914,008	$32,054,913	$234,161	$3,428,083
Alabama	5,041	37,820	48,658	0	3,698,481	123,813	362,723	4,082	31,599
Alaska	5,000	19,870	87,086	163	1,285,580	16,755	127,321	1,599	109,980
Arizona	7,016	16,585	53,361	505	4,366,333	8,787	366,961	3,846	67,977
Arkansas	6,163	3,050	22,453	0	2,479,210	87,049	217,155	1,626	21,553
California	84,664	196,509	340,020	3,148	31,494,895	87,257	4,037,656	22,756	265,644
Colorado	7,037	55,881	52,504	431	2,560,643	27,254	429,603	3,356	111,672
Connecticut	5,000	41,183	39,778	756	3,178,309	20,577	573,007	2,511	6,340
Delaware	5,000	6,574	21,713	261	574,942	11,942	84,336	781	4,910
Florida	26,029	33,813	123,753	1,557	10,038,395	62,734	1,201,691	11,554	32,898
Georgia	12,557	46,591	73,687	177	6,009,198	29,366	740,321	4,500	20,105
Hawaii	5,000	5,385	28,341	139	853,200	3,933	158,943	1,839	23,650
Idaho	5,000	13,474	51,085	317	885,948	8,520	77,348	1,436	52,659
Illinois	44,935	73,926	154,123	1,595	8,916,589	59,461	1,626,957	11,742	19,137
Indiana	15,753	44,298	74,604	566	4,279,953	60,672	505,268	3,303	13,821
Iowa	5,000	-59,462	76,735	883	2,208,551	26,270	225,021	5,280	14,479
Kansas	5,000	13,010	37,294	352	1,748,174	28,759	193,634	1,621	20,139
Kentucky	5,168	19,057	44,535	222	3,814,152	92,700	402,831	2,445	46,628
Louisiana	12,263	10,655	70,881	18	4,669,054	259,727	459,139	3,167	46,581
Maine	5,000	5,890	40,783	216	1,662,066	13,717	177,204	1,969	9,565
Maryland	7,274	28,803	100,713	584	5,158,878	70,210	615,921	3,407	13,561
Massachusetts	8,110	108,544	135,951	1,651	8,342,865	53,569	1,607,360	8,209	9,205
Michigan	15,739	78,249	147,258	740	7,976,281	41,140	838,762	6,006	33,334
Minnesota	5,314	45,849	83,607	623	4,138,779	56,776	530,079	3,723	23,502
Mississippi	5,451	17,261	64,039	0	3,170,434	86,918	260,631	2,360	17,539
Missouri	17,348	19,380	87,186	771	5,327,120	63,690	609,269	6,199	17,943
Montana	5,000	8,447	29,188	230	815,539	15,395	86,191	1,132	86,646
Nebraska	5,000	6,075	31,930	532	1,301,877	15,038	135,059	1,380	15,580
Nevada	5,000	42,385	31,990	684	939,110	13,099	151,606	2,232	78,913
New Hampshire	5,000	7,332	37,640	107	936,563	20,587	148,857	1,480	9,255
New Jersey	16,837	36,940	88,364	591	6,035,176	49,396	1,254,945	6,986	9,977
New Mexico	5,000	77,283	40,346	248	2,208,578	11,480	149,291	1,855	354,406
New York	66,098	148,357	124,927	2,952	30,577,039	3,863,892	3,612,178	18,283	60,109
North Carolina	8,782	24,486	85,574	153	7,252,644	145,091	605,237	5,783	18,001
North Dakota	5,000	11,657	16,445	194	534,553	9,820	65,197	984	47,694
Ohio	41,053	52,419	1,170,525	1,895	9,890,042	130,142	1,253,270	9,845	30,320
Oklahoma	5,000	12,192	57,505	383	2,756,334	50,991	346,978	3,252	25,743
Oregon	6,027	15,732	62,239	537	2,849,298	40,464	303,404	3,052	157,700
Pennsylvania	34,240	8,745	139,724	2,000	11,559,081	80,574	1,425,325	12,906	78,750
Rhode Island	5,000	5,242	32,868	176	1,312,470	10,553	248,756	847	7,050
South Carolina	6,820	18,321	44,243	802	3,516,650	24,353	305,716	3,074	11,866
South Dakota	5,000	3,403	25,877	165	585,747	14,900	93,665	703	98,759
Tennessee	8,478	21,842	64,344	350	5,941,863	103,005	457,746	3,750	27,733
Texas	23,476	69,384	302,301	1,015	14,859,122	368,172	1,625,539	14,114	61,355
Utah	8,818	18,195	40,288	337	1,387,184	18,574	117,521	2,013	146,603
Vermont	5,000	4,662	27,758	55	741,667	6,391	86,263	742	7,340
Virginia	11,632	48,950	94,426	260	3,708,655	73,806	565,013	4,536	21,781
Washington	12,898	42,101	117,287	729	5,128,671	56,347	574,346	4,321	70,686
West Virginia	5,327	14,121	58,183	228	1,967,450	46,696	176,254	1,229	12,265
Wisconsin	7,003	43,275	85,540	1,193	4,571,344	30,222	438,405	3,861	27,981
Wyoming	5,000	7,754	22,926	120	370,458	8,105	34,370	803	533,589
Dist. of Columbia	5,000	33,559	80,730	88	1,655,609	10,390	766,993	3,030	18,763
American Samoa	1,000	37	900	0	18,200	15,302	1,142	147	35,040
Fed. States of Micronesia	0	0	0	0	4,360	9,320	0	0	104,018
Guam	1,000	494	4,288	0	37,150	180,318	34,357	114	37,929
Marshall Islands	0	0	0	0	5,937	38	0	56	53,652
No. Mariana Islands	0	3	76	0	12,060	10,409	566	151	21,014
Palau	0	0	0	0	4,522	-17	0	0	42,880
Puerto Rico	3,151	1,215	14,894	383	865,042	79,267	532,959	2,107	4,944
Virgin Islands	1,000	260	3,274	11	52,692	643	28,623	96	69,687
Undistributed	0	0	0	0	0	0	0	0	5,632

FEDERAL GOVERNMENT EXPENDITURE FOR GRANTS, BY AGENCY, BY STATE AND OUTLYING AREA: FISCAL YEAR 2003 — Continued

State and outlying area	Department of Justice	Department of Labor	National Aeronautics and Space Administration	National Archives and Records Administration	National Endowment for the Arts	National Endowment for the Humanities	National Science Foundation	Small Business Administration
United States	$6,980,342	$9,165,139	$1,086,371	$6,400	$96,910	$97,349	$4,780,864	$64,448
Alabama	83,318	123,297	52,482	0	895	798	40,041	1,370
Alaska	50,536	64,042	2,134	0	789	1567	29,630	116
Arizona	128,106	142,798	18,346	85	1,079	1,389	92,351	955
Arkansas	61,956	81,013	1672	0	584	693	10,336	14
California	750,126	1,036,076	191,574	808	9,230	9,290	737,954	3,579
Colorado	107,550	108,934	38,168	0	2,274	1,231	247,438	256
Connecticut	96,317	115,612	9,198	161	1,147	1,003	43,260	300
Delaware	35,304	23,034	1,704	0	610	683	25,412	0
Florida	368,406	298,735	33,211	232	1,415	1,317	143,743	1,258
Georgia	210,310	168,984	17,446	114	2,446	1,183	106,160	384
Hawaii	51,267	58,149	17,144	40	1,123	719	32,261	81
Idaho	38,520	55,074	3,621	18	700	472	13,709	497
Illinois	243,025	437,049	13,784	169	3,425	5,262	236,290	1,044
Indiana	97,773	124,667	5,292	20	846	1,413	65,501	255
Iowa	69,244	75,209	10,769	44	663	709	32,535	2,702
Kansas	59,809	78,978	2,856	0	686	1,123	27,048	639
Kentucky	113,227	135,609	6,284	163	1,337	574	25,309	861
Louisiana	131,723	135,998	14,348	10	1,173	1,446	35,146	100
Maine	43,625	62,901	1,979	20	1,084	1,674	21,338	1,821
Maryland	158,090	228,762	92,862	276	2,440	2,291	117,966	641
Massachusetts	126,299	201,475	52,296	286	3,359	5,342	371,202	592
Michigan	153,672	340,384	12,094	63	1,665	1,899	172,568	1,010
Minnesota	100,166	138,511	5,914	0	5,597	1,309	69,581	803
Mississippi	73,844	96,583	18,936	0	755	608	18,043	1,967
Missouri	127,556	151,414	12,656	43	2,313	1,546	52,434	2,445
Montana	52,061	40,595	7,576	9	816	463	31,954	163
Nebraska	56,136	37,571	2,707	0	863	1,323	26,296	153
Nevada	82,258	62,876	3,281	0	667	754	15,527	424
New Hampshire	66,052	33,994	13,324	12	746	924	17,118	111
New Jersey	168,418	216,631	15,163	324	1,207	2,329	116,958	1,783
New Mexico	78,645	74,136	6,846	20	1,010	738	33,264	1,186
New York	525,413	691,704	39,950	299	15,952	11,262	412,218	5,858
North Carolina	135,720	270,971	9,398	426	1,318	2,011	117,098	854
North Dakota	34,647	27,973	4,845	17	664	774	13,132	242
Ohio	187,819	313,830	43,062	20	1,650	2,868	81,033	4,337
Oklahoma	103,629	87,186	20,512	5	786	715	26,936	2,877
Oregon	81,846	156,304	4,797	9	1,134	1,812	58,876	2,892
Pennsylvania	213,521	440,141	17,229	165	2,804	3,540	206,300	4,488
Rhode Island	41,859	32,273	9,431	84	886	1,004	23,951	366
South Carolina	110,785	124,535	14,569	247	1,207	1,057	32,180	874
South Dakota	45,700	32,854	1186	15	641	460	14,133	2,672
Tennessee	112,841	150,579	8,307	199	925	1,319	48,300	857
Texas	425,380	542,199	73,103	89	2,684	3,068	171,972	815
Utah	55,022	76,764	5,336	0	1,021	688	34,231	120
Vermont	36,529	29,677	1,058	0	1,036	666	10,477	290
Virginia	206,915	265,118	57,439	525	1,486	5,100	147,992	5,595
Washington	168,519	312,213	8,144	44	2,006	942	119,556	551
West Virginia	67,793	59,659	40,288	0	644	656	10,084	1,590
Wisconsin	110,204	194,061	10,711	384	1,054	3,048	110,322	1,192
Wyoming	29,029	21,488	1103	30	627	453	8,076	0
Dist. of Columbia	196,754	124,630	18,847	928	3,701	1,977	97,592	279
American Samoa	7,676	1,042	0	0	247	211	0	150
Fed. States of Micronesia	0	4,071	0	0	0	0	0	0
Guam	11,284	25,276	0	0	244	268	188	0
Marshall Islands	0	784	0	0	0	0	0	0
No. Mariana Islands	7,285	2,189	0	0	351	259	0	0
Palau	0	261	0	0	0	0	0	0
Puerto Rico	64,131	219,585	4,477	0	629	832	27,346	0
Virgin Islands	16,342	8,686	0	0	270	267	769	0
Undistributed	0	0	0	0	0	0	0	0

FEDERAL GOVERNMENT EXPENDITURE FOR GRANTS, BY AGENCY, BY STATE AND OUTLYING AREA: FISCAL YEAR 2003 — Continued

State and outlying area	Social Security Administration	Department of State	State Justice Institute	Tennessee Valley Authority (a)	Department of Transportation	Department of the Treasury (b)	Department of Veterans Affairs	Other
United States	$9,902	$211,224	$2,033	$329,367	$45,935,691	$802,527	$633,699	$82,155
Alabama	0	1,053	10	77,524	870,005	899	8,466	143
Alaska	0	500	1	0	661,885	124	218	419
Arizona	0	3,949	15	0	648,492	3,326	4,715	991
Arkansas	0	822	2	0	814,125	214	1,540	628
California	566	24,269	2	0	3,883,572	4,119	46,603	15,034
Colorado	0	3,825	26	0	1,397,297	214	12,061	1,559
Connecticut	0	2,451	0	0	613,045	251	6,429	1,172
Delaware	0	618	0	0	173,890	57	32	32
Florida	0	5,015	2	0	2,050,900	6,701	8,927	2,514
Georgia	3,985	2	5,161	1,176,012	929	11,192	1052	
Hawaii	0	1165	13	0	221,412	91	0	241
Idaho	0	844	5	0	320,332	130	11,248	1,755
Illinois	6,347	9,600	45	331	1,428,946	2,280	18,980	1,013
Indiana	0	3,530	1	0	933,456	558	5,612	1,107
Iowa	0	2,818	1	0	529,384	254	11,996	268
Kansas	0	2,053	1	0	400,183	344	12,806	560
Kentucky	0	1,436	1	26,389	889,595	362	10,872	448
Louisiana	0	2,472	0	0	645,427	326	7,314	471
Maine	0	1,897	6	0	208,115	121	18,123	138
Maryland	0	6,420	64	0	858,299	2,473	4,753	2,126
Massachusetts	0	11,934	15	0	809,027	1,269	31,463	3,406
Michigan	301	5,282	216	0	1,217,385	1,004	13,377	654
Minnesota	0	3,499	6	0	640,696	182	15,993	1,018
Mississippi	0	874	45	18,130	515,248	264	11,715	92
Missouri	0	3,909	1	0	968,599	510	20,376	764
Montana	0	2,402	8	0	346,597	133	14,117	334
Nebraska	0	1,070	0	0	317,650	730	10,393	214
Nevada	0	548	1	0	165,852	410	5,924	148
New Hampshire	0	839	0	0	261,526	65	3,814	1657
New Jersey	0	2,613	26	0	1,987,675	2,657	49,781	482
New Mexico	0	1,854	94	0	457,204	331	3,558	789
New York	1,209	21,755	168	0	2,867,255	11,531	20,764	8,198
North Carolina	0	4,518	0	1,557	1,054,977	1,330	3,903	2,131
North Dakota	0	353	0	0	383,314	30	3,156	473
Ohio	0	6,319	0	0	1,376,562	604	12,168	4,028
Oklahoma	0	1,723	0	0	566,868	148	28,858	1,021
Oregon	0	3,602	2	0	562,035	1,547	2,461	666
Pennsylvania	0	9,144	1	0	2,132,196	806	23,467	820
Rhode Island	0	752	18	0	238,634	180	7,191	1,175
South Carolina	0	3,109	0	0	687,721	1,041	24,946	9
South Dakota	0	457	13	0	314,244	48	1,722	279
Tennessee	0	1,473	529	200,171	743,066	396	5,409	1,503
Texas	0	9,996	3	0	3,478,708	7,686	28,382	4,506
Utah	0	1,194	0	0	419,272	63	2,337	392
Vermont	446	794	24	0	156,865	19	2,953	1,846
Virginia	0	3,787	497	104	1,284,302	1,535	11,143	1,923
Washington	0	5,034	1	0	942,580	655	41,072	710
West Virginia	0	323	69	0	570,494	87	17,426	810
Wisconsin	579	3,305	22	0	809,712	154	20,102	1,471
Wyoming	0	121	0	0	368,440	6	1,956	0
Dist. of Columbia	455	19,651	99	0	422,396	384,632 (c)	922	1,243
American Samoa	0	0	0	0	8,356	0	0	0
Fed. States of Micronesia	0	0	0	0	0	0	0	0
Guam	0	0	0	0	25,952	0	0	0
Marshall Islands	0	0	0	0	0	0	0	0
No. Mariana Islands	0	0	0	0	19,303	0	0	0
Palau	0	0	0	0	0	0	0	0
Puerto Rico	0	242	0	0	75,555	358,705	966	429
Virgin Islands	0	26	0	0	15,050	0	0	0
Undistributed	0	0	0	0	3	0	0	7,294

Source: U.S. Department of Commerce, Bureau of the Census, September 2004.

(a) Payments in lieu of taxes have been categorized as "grants".

(b) Includes distributions to state and local governments of seized cash and other assets.

(c) Also includes Treasury payments to recipients that are separate from the government of the District of Columbia and Washington Metropolitan Transit Authority (WMATA).

Table 2.7
FEDERAL GOVERNMENT EXPENDITURE FOR PROCUREMENT CONTRACTS, BY AGENCY, BY STATE AND OUTLYING AREA: FISCAL YEAR 2003
(In thousands of dollars)

| State and outlying area | Total | Department of Defense | | | | | | Nondefense agencies | | |
		Total	Army	Navy	Air Force	Army Corps of Engineers	Other defense	Total	Department of Agriculture	Department of Commerce
United States	$327,413,076	$201,229,510	$50,272,843	$51,762,828	$54,293,150	$3,496,299	$41,404,390	$126,183,567	$4,656,951	$1,475,976
Alabama	7,067,435	5,510,444	2,311,201	304,057	404,808	99,161	2,391,217	1,556,991	35,212	3,271
Alaska	1,680,115	1,236,673	611,746	76,486	418,210	13,074	117,156	443,443	46,063	24,948
Arizona	8,556,995	7,564,129	2,801,557	1,800,541	1,233,586	21,460	1,706,985	992,866	53,953	9,191
Arkansas	864,051	577,668	217,883	22,863	179,603	75,378	81,941	286,383	32,812	30
California	37,049,547	26,078,513	3,718,533	6,325,069	12,608,835	282,167	3,143,909	10,971,034	508,018	24,244
Colorado	5,141,688	2,471,002	718,022	84,849	1,258,623	16,170	393,339	2,670,685	148,786	31,767
Connecticut	8,484,307	7,894,812	1,421,670	3,953,048	2,136,470	6,265	377,360	589,495	4,428	954
Delaware	244,804	164,300	55,986	7,629	61,605	6,269	32,810	80,504	3,849	670
Florida	10,898,964	7,998,672	1,935,114	2,269,277	2,982,907	163,925	647,450	2,900,312	47,177	17,207
Georgia	5,242,532	3,323,844	1,011,648	358,273	1,661,423	80,515	211,984	1,918,687	57,470	2,980
Hawaii	1,978,401	1,750,209	372,361	674,317	251,294	6,253	445,984	228,192	21,561	11,451
Idaho	1,531,332	207,157	73,879	14,814	83,379	13,453	21,632	1,324,176	93,349	222
Illinois	5,728,862	2,513,729	909,369	323,311	573,847	137,433	569,768	3,215,133	105,359	3,823
Indiana	3,301,567	2,566,740	1,226,966	458,237	190,740	42,017	648,760	734,826	27,370	4,392
Iowa	1,109,249	658,236	189,190	143,823	264,392	12,079	48,750	451,013	54,903	542
Kansas	2,020,127	1,219,202	435,053	61,244	633,109	11,233	78,564	800,925	97,980	675
Kentucky	5,119,069	3,223,397	518,436	308,396	153,958	74,003	2,168,603	1,895,672	16,880	471
Louisiana	3,194,691	1,951,317	316,363	1,070,027	65,106	253,353	246,468	1,243,373	200,913	11,085
Maine	1,311,784	1,175,637	112,525	919,251	12,535	12,354	118,997	136,147	2,796	1,249
Maryland	16,215,876	7,171,165	2,271,715	2,686,472	978,644	53,365	1,180,968	9,044,711	73,828	350,494
Massachusetts	8,357,478	6,364,760	2,012,160	2,314,462	1,609,067	64,495	364,576	1,992,718	6,785	32,983
Michigan	3,884,004	2,494,162	1,842,338	140,474	165,175	28,695	317,481	1,389,842	94,289	4,066
Minnesota	2,405,899	1,541,939	715,100	478,084	126,629	29,927	192,199	863,960	155,280	2,664
Mississippi	2,625,647	2,126,372	114,565	1,543,480	262,034	106,588	99,705	499,275	32,511	23,374
Missouri	7,991,663	6,243,784	715,969	3,337,122	1,785,015	162,379	243,298	1,747,879	220,983	5,909
Montana	497,284	189,961	46,878	1,839	104,127	14,311	22,806	307,323	104,236	270
Nebraska	608,205	312,153	77,867	6,094	194,642	22,059	11,491	296,052	72,344	2,199
Nevada	1,472,258	386,682	104,652	76,816	156,651	30,425	18,138	1,085,576	11,265	1,244
New Hampshire	738,325	531,084	101,371	135,024	217,002	4,502	73,185	207,241	2,825	6,969
New Jersey	5,460,981	3,873,075	1,279,535	1,520,112	210,271	272,028	591,130	1,587,906	9,651	6,972
New Mexico	5,818,972	955,369	421,447	56,038	368,229	56,724	52,931	4,863,603	32,119	1,229
New York	7,758,292	4,252,848	1,210,678	1,527,962	722,612	130,203	661,392	3,505,444	37,365	6,172
North Carolina	3,794,455	1,988,214	835,000	498,944	267,131	73,036	313,603	1,806,240	52,772	23,896
North Dakota	397,542	262,126	53,110	3017	134,817	42,055	29,127	135,415	21,670	174
Ohio	6,547,578	4,271,188	987,191	533,560	1,690,489	63,523	996,425	2,276,390	62,571	5,208
Oklahoma	2,487,848	1,470,524	434,628	97,278	686,739	37,550	214,329	1,017,323	10,268	13,070
Oregon	1,198,111	474,353	259,515	55,257	25,434	88,477	45,670	723,758	181,040	17,922
Pennsylvania	8,136,659	5,606,604	2,320,422	1,731,010	296,908	101,357	1,156,907	2,530,056	80,283	43,798
Rhode Island	659,084	498,783	24,318	431,056	1,916	20,057	21,436	160,301	19	6,301
South Carolina	3,614,372	1,486,512	408,689	623,916	167,049	43,308	243,549	2,127,861	8,305	12,675
South Dakota	380,964	196,303	55,934	18,134	49,832	7,597	64,806	184,661	17,563	879
Tennessee	7,521,940	2,160,985	396,132	49,889	1,337,322	61,881	315,761	5,360,954	78,918	595
Texas	29,823,365	20,820,951	4,392,132	3,645,721	10,015,943	221,876	2,545,280	9,001,414	471,753	35,699
Utah	2,664,844	1,871,074	255,571	166,799	1,264,625	5,614	178,465	793,770	34,180	222
Vermont	566,070	454,931	344,560	43,404	9,728	7,878	49,361	111,139	1420	2,800
Virginia	30,838,710	19,493,045	4,561,069	6,650,151	2,866,077	119,928	5,295,819	11,345,665	99,074	377,897
Washington	6,628,532	3,196,024	543,333	825,691	1,323,888	125,529	377,582	3,432,508	129,306	30,452
West Virginia	664,915	184,828	36,219	21,076	12,256	79,681	35,596	480,087	24,958	233
Wisconsin	2,007,637	1,243,698	707,299	225,023	47,426	18,941	245,008	763,939	113,691	3,649
Wyoming	345,985	71,775	7,219	184	35,833	2609	25,930	274,210	14,399	122
Dist. of Columbia	11,375,903	1,753,101	408,820	858,670	79,779	24,674	381,158	9,622,802	243,264	64,227
American Samoa	27,687	8113	603	0	84	1597	5829	19,575	19,087	0
Fed. States of Micronesia ...	1,022	0	0	0	0	0	0	1,022	6	878
Guam	525,782	509,121	574	351,410	118,348	21492	17,297	16,661	72	322
Marshall Islands	114,768	114,439	110,274	4164	0	0	0	329	0	329
No. Mariana Islands	8,425	7,351	6,373	972	0	0	6	1,074	0	0
Palau	658	658	0	0	0	658	0	0	0	0
Puerto Rico	561,295	402,964	47,220	92,235	3,664	24,705	253,140	158,331	4,712	267
Virgin Islands	25,742	4,091	699	56	0	11	3,324	21,652	73	79
Undistributed (a)	32,132,759	18,148,718	3,203,645	1,835,739	1,783,331	0	11,326,003	13,984,041	574,826	240,564

Source: U.S. Department of Commerce, Bureau of the Census, September 2004.

FEDERAL GOVERNMENT EXPENDITURE FOR PROCUREMENT CONTRACTS, BY AGENCY, BY STATE AND OUTLYING AREA: FISCAL YEAR 2003 — Continued

State and outlying area	Department of Education	Department of Energy	Environmental Protection Agency	General Services Administration	Department of Health and Human Services	Department of Homeland Security	Department of Housing and Urban Develop.	Department of the Interior	Department of Justice	Department of Labor
					Nondefense agencies					
United States	$1,020,944	$21,226,221	$1,011,180	15,525,853	7,057,404	$5,435,637	$977,316	$4,268,665	$4,240,018	$1,545,139
Alabama	95	1,139	1,553	205,154	63,794	41,817	5,896	18,934	42,190	22,891
Alaska	131	2	0	42,801	31,303	48,998	33	73,601	688	12,048
Arizona	4,011	78,902	376	76,089	49,352	90,704	1,265	129,390	104,221	17,694
Arkansas	83	1,742	70	14,367	39,642	139	1,022	6,055	4,662	6,979
California	52,002	2,307,060	34,466	1,038,599	272,259	215,455	126,432	243,449	192,575	119,132
Colorado	5476	1,060,956	34,431	369,571	23,299	27,910	81,100	194,156	9,849	7,431
Connecticut	32,623	1,380	1,853	51,131	17,522	47,024	4,082	6,493	6,574	16,300
Delaware	86	0	11,525	9,672	304	268	76	2,069	1,041	1,351
Florida	617	13,230	5,023	387,314	27,122	65,349	2,874	52,280	59,644	34,525
Georgia	30,630	11,718	25,524	500,753	489,713	74,914	69,454	23,249	14,731	50,632
Hawaii	9,950	0	0	39,908	7,760	21,358	222	30,023	2,213	13,722
Idaho	93	977,189	40	27,167	3,082	19,486	1,112	45,221	3,474	963
Illinois	18,862	862,084	13,441	311,485	88,313	12,297	96,588	10,025	37,916	23,014
Indiana	-188	4,719	3,322	50,788	56,208	7,716	-17,952	6,843	53,619	16,617
Iowa	38,493	24,385	99	35,534	69,167	13,504	100	3,642	812	12,369
Kansas	113	194	15,015	63,283	5,331	9,242	964	11,467	11,851	6,765
Kentucky	198	76,022	14,279	75,708	5,507	7,335	555	19,195	18,223	38,341
Louisiana	9	167,228	377	94,457	9,327	27,086	6,392	28,365	105,026	19,911
Maine	158	266	602	9,540	11,665	5,622	94	10,948	217	11,659
Maryland	242,340	180,043	83,302	1,152,410	2,798,531	254,293	74,500	198,807	246,343	86,409
Massachusetts	11,608	2,632	90,055	272,670	74,293	33,569	4,535	36,782	17,642	34,406
Michigan	383	3465	36,711	471,064	55,175	25,269	2,752	9,176	35,174	22,091
Minnesota	59,118	3,230	2,688	70,435	61,916	7,180	627	16,948	19,286	7,007
Mississippi	0	0	452	53,561	7,857	68,126	1,665	8,131	1,992	29,724
Missouri	959	484,289	18,908	287,944	64,076	3,555	-6,835	17,509	17,037	31,139
Montana	137	16,738	165	17,517	23,422	2,049	483	59,500	2,870	9,369
Nebraska	292	473	123	22,077	15,042	88	968	6,065	678	1,059
Nevada	93	794,526	3,858	20,951	8,925	711	1,239	52,679	1,117	43,764
New Hampshire	2,675	75	1,445	62,772	3,892	4,303	441	3,387	9,828	0
New Jersey	2,314	109,123	35,507	214,482	49,799	33,666	844	43,752	40,125	14,603
New Mexico	87	4,229,723	984	30,633	39,202	16,285	421	115,027	156,727	14,446
New York	28,263	722,685	20,209	582,062	146,003	80,278	31,863	181,061	73,849	73,009
North Carolina	36,876	147,569	60,236	124,221	280,313	35,307	1,400	15,706	131,989	14,738
North Dakota	98	10,973	472	10,604	6,468	3,934	3,442	10,602	10,539	5,074
Ohio	5,389	543,879	96,689	321,294	82,436	57,099	-2,704	14,996	20,936	29,486
Oklahoma	2,310	5,162	6,478	478,932	8,257	1,362	2,718	44,162	38,410	32,078
Oregon	4,254	2,049	4,522	142,876	11,055	10,362	438	79,868	5,200	18,113
Pennsylvania	17,329	474,656	82,508	234,678	72,851	20,558	102,199	72,377	49,593	43,993
Rhode Island	5,807	1,195	7,049	13,111	8,092	1,546	77	10,405	1,511	1,373
South Carolina	478	1,590,464	663	49,376	34,026	13,178	386	5,759	12,286	3,206
South Dakota	5,449	6,607	225	13,022	33,442	428	99	51,414	3,481	540
Tennessee	74	2,451,542	141	86,224	45,784	23,961	2,355	11,429	63,973	5,236
Texas	33,367	347,475	10,800	1,342,145	133,522	864,525	16,022	52,624	111,250	131,365
Utah	86	21,114	334	77,801	22,218	3,014	1,721	66,500	4,880	26,898
Vermont	27	2,167	807	20,221	927	2,225	0	2,406	655	5,323
Virginia	121,265	835,705	195,609	3,152,596	373,233	1,434,208	35,085	843,673	366,880	136,952
Washington	4,957	2,382,441	9,486	216,895	75,977	104,459	-1,281	67,038	5,665	11,789
West Virginia	2,112	50,017	1	37,110	6,193	7,451	14,876	13,970	97,248	18,322
Wisconsin	1,991	4,086	13,203	62,419	48,192	18,123	528	18,733	57,295	5,171
Wyoming	0	6,094	0	5,812	2,274	1,880	146	36,591	737	0
Dist. of Columbia	221,047	41,109	32,684	2,248,022	293,726	1,293,943	285,901	328,471	866,850	191,258
American Samoa	12	0	0	210	0	0	0	71	0	0
Fed. States of Micronesia	0	0	0	0	0	0	0	1	0	0
Guam	8	0	0	6,372	196	1,541	0	794	100	0
Marshall Islands	0	0	0	0	0	0	0	0	0	0
No. Mariana Islands	0	0	0	637	0	27	0	112	0	0
Palau	0	0	0	0	0	0	0	0	0	0
Puerto Rico	132	0	0	22,496	3,360	19,172	231	1,317	1,407	20,925
Virgin Islands	14	0	0	3,248	0	0	0	7,410	101	9
Undistributed (a)	16,151	166,695	32,875	193,631	896,060	251,740	7,267	848,005	1,096,836	44,188

See footnotes at end of table.

FEDERAL GOVERNMENT EXPENDITURE FOR PROCUREMENT CONTRACTS, BY AGENCY, BY STATE AND OUTLYING AREA: FISCAL YEAR 2003 — Continued

State and outlying area	NASA	National Archives and Records Admin.	National Science Foundation	Postal Service	Small Bus. Admin.	Social Security Admin.	Dept. of State	Dept. of Transportation	Dept. of the Treasury	Dept. of Veterans Affairs	Other nondefense (b)
								Nondefense agencies—continued			
United States	$11,799,660	$112,499	$62,280	$13,658,032	$47,950	$668,247	$2,456,575	$5,623,172	$2,483,251	$13,832,633	$7,037,966
Alabama	478,397	0	0	168,501	0	3,993	51,221	25,250	1,882	72,779	312,931
Alaska	10,091	374	0	34,084	0	634	55,664	46,865	141	14,680	293
Arizona	65,560	0	0	212,767	221	391	2,275	34,042	645	58,176	3,641
Arkansas	0	0	0	110,086	29	0	29	1,793	890	65,808	144
California	3,102,994	1,118	830	1,467,896	452	26,841	19,979	362,624	337,999	484,587	32,023
Colorado	212,638	0	7,340	242,057	213	5,129	23,775	43,511	16,224	63,909	61,158
Connecticut	101,785	0	39	187,229	0	309	2,039	9,222	1,018	94,564	2,926
Delaware	1,197	0	0	38,381	0	80	331	0	215	8,859	527
Florida	765,756	0	0	707,013	0	408	154,651	195,702	15,770	316,254	32,394
Georgia	13,995	21,906	0	370,358	47	3,743	6,532	26,667	11,654	72,531	39,487
Hawaii	1,448	0	0	44,233	0	537	60	4,243	17	19,311	174
Idaho	327	0	0	48,762	0	276	0	6,042	40,061	55,972	1340
Illinois	4,780	144	4,483	698,104	1,139	10,812	18,455	213,534	28,422	577,896	74,158
Indiana	24,950	0	0	261,760	0	692	1,516	50,165	2,961	154,851	24,477
Iowa	980	579	0	157,393	0	342	1,487	12,445	6,360	17,701	176
Kansas	398	3,140	4	147,062	0	0	39	36,087	7,100	383,581	634
Kentucky	871	0	0	167,311	0	2,226	6,216	3,364	6,866	244,118	1,191,986
Louisiana	309,222	0	0	176,071	0	258	1,550	29,682	372	46,136	9,909
Maine	0	0	0	73,953	65	0	5	1,042	0	6,009	257
Maryland	1,046,010	33,965	1,584	292,786	1,378	334,372	179,960	960,161	211,752	171,199	70,604
Massachusetts	134,751	4,423	962	386,904	0	3,244	14,143	384,350	137,205	298,081	10,695
Michigan	5,245	2,046	0	488,610	1000	5,987	661	7,857	42,873	73,119	2,828
Minnesota	7,341	0	0	278,207	35	250	2312	59,160	1,401	83,949	24,927
Mississippi	121,808	0	0	95,937	0	222	0	14,780	0	32,116	7,021
Missouri	3,684	3,867	43	324,324	100	14,920	4218	25,564	4,385	219,686	1,615
Montana	1,601	0	0	45,985	39	157	468	11,721	35	10,329	231
Nebraska	149	0	0	97,507	0	0	31	16,384	0	49,123	11,450
Nevada	534	0	0	81,639	0	62	84	38,295	779	23,564	248
New Hampshire	12,622	0	0	71,060	0	2,887	13,594	1,935	320	5,809	401
New Jersey	41,674	0	41	542,000	0	6,622	6,265	290,484	24,064	89,196	26,724
New Mexico	74,213	0	0	68,366	260	600	413	27,071	92	55,160	548
New York	23,121	2,369	0	1,033,568	0	10,522	6,633	151,332	51,730	220,217	23,133
North Carolina	19,582	0	63	346,622	96	1,387	126,909	54,384	1,676	74,713	243,186
North Dakota	0	0	0	37,224	307	1,390	85	1,467	4,262	6,360	270
Ohio	198,369	416	0	556,298	-20	1,442	2,584	40,221	8,073	215,605	16,123
Oklahoma	1,930	0	0	147,211	0	934	366	171,772	3,489	42,668	5,384
Oregon	6,132	0	0	140,467	53	19	3,570	40,338	174	54,671	637
Pennsylvania	22,381	1,211	69	672,467	0	16,007	897	67,514	32,969	261,913	159,806
Rhode Island	1069	0	0	57,440	0	27	-244	636	30,406	14,274	207
South Carolina	1400	0	0	138,963	0	573	135,685	54,145	8	45,328	20,957
South Dakota	117	0	0	40,200	0	58	447	611	49	7,729	2,300
Tennessee	13,794	0	0	257,380	0	211	12,931	43,173	529,914	1,718,950	1,718,578
Texas	3,718,251	3,824	182	882,308	-3	6,695	291,872	138,937	62,658	299,272	47,873
Utah	418,304	0	0	88,548	0	138	96	5,644	8,195	29,686	-15,810
Vermont	554	0	0	37,555	0	14	95	25,644	0	7,961	338
Virginia	520,598	5,895	8,328	353,184	518	45,403	384,844	843,750	509,108	406,579	295,282
Washington	5,340	883	0	252,272	249	1,830	993	52,330	4,012	71,941	5,473
West Virginia	21,007	0	0	87,821	0	441	1027	4,166	51,327	29,980	11,825
Wisconsin	11,144	0	2019	249,346	0	618	571	9,505	1,242	131,764	10,648
Wyoming	225	0	0	23,174	0	14	0	26,516	7,937	7,549	140,739
Dist. of Columbia	77,177	9,984	28,525	102,053	31,943	20,049	454,206	492,291	530,745	253,572	1,511,756
American Samoa	0	0	0	165	0	0	0	0	0	30	0
Fed. States of Micronesia	0	0	0	0	0	0	137	0	0	0	0
Guam	0	0	0	2,132	0	3	0	4,997	0	125	0
Marshall Islands	0	0	0	0	0	0	0	0	0	0	0
No. Mariana Islands	0	0	0	198	0	0	0	0	0	0	100
Palau	0	0	0	0	0	0	0	0	0	0	0
Puerto Rico	198	0	0	60,762	0	141	38	1,051	19	21,693	447
Virgin Islands	0	0	0	4,331	0	0	0	6,337	0	37	12
Undistributed (a)	173,944	16,354	7,765	0	9,829	134,338	464,901	446,369	239,300	7,229,999	892,404

Source: U.S. Department of Commerce, Bureau of the Census, September 2004.

(a) For all agencies, this line includes contract awards under $25,000 and procurement purchases made using government-issued purchase cards.

(b) Includes Fiscal Year 2000 procurement data for the Tennessee Valley Authority, which did not provide Fiscal Year 2003 procurement data.

(c) Data shown for U.S. Postal Service represent actual outlays for contractual commitments, while all other amounts shown represent the value of contract actions, and do not reflect federal government expenditures. Nonpostal data generally involve only current year contract actions; however multiple-year obligations may be reflected for contract actions of less than 3 years duration. Negative amounts represent the deobligation of prior year contracts.

Table 2.8
FEDERAL GOVERNMENT EXPENDITURE FOR SALARIES AND WAGES, BY AGENCY, BY STATE AND OUTLYING AREA: FISCAL YEAR 2003
(In thousands of dollars)

State and outlying area	Total	Nondefense civilian (a)	Department of Defense Total	Other defense civilian (b)	Military services Total	Active military	Inactive military	Civilian	Army Total	Active military
United States	$210,677,312	$128,987,168	$81,690,144	$4,685,214	$77,004,930	$46,908,385	$7,445,634	$22,650,911	$26,495,515	$14,854,048
Alabama	3,223,864	1,719,815	1,504,049	69,988	1,434,061	498,341	225,193	710,527	1,006,277	228,684
Alaska	1,616,563	696,309	920,254	12,704	907,550	704,441	38,444	164,665	340,966	240,426
Arizona	3,334,607	2,046,790	1,287,817	50,919	1,236,898	906,305	47,304	283,289	358,802	209,912
Arkansas	1,339,120	900,000	439,120	3,896	435,224	208,689	120,764	105,771	170,134	13,870
California	20,611,019	11,358,683	9,252,336	393,332	8,859,004	6,022,465	427,102	2,409,437	780,584	309,510
Colorado	4,329,051	2,578,677	1,750,374	145,855	1,604,519	1,175,498	120,072	308,949	754,940	625,898
Connecticut	1,516,299	1,075,432	440,867	44,632	396,235	267,750	59,413	69,072	57,528	1,786
Delaware	489,112	227,879	261,233	2,315	258,918	155,480	50,905	52,533	21,360	76
Florida	9,745,937	5,475,321	4,270,616	135,351	4,135,265	2,820,796	271,596	1,042,873	387,482	132,430
Georgia	8,014,506	3,769,827	4,244,679	100,250	4,144,429	2,778,047	285,047	1,081,325	2,471,507	1,992,112
Hawaii	2,863,720	451,926	2,411,794	40,549	2,371,245	1,641,229	90,861	639,155	781,478	607,430
Idaho	834,221	593,327	240,894	1,600	239,294	161,792	33,369	44,133	46,237	1,558
Illinois	6,552,599	4,735,374	1,817,225	76,263	1,740,962	1,091,846	197,920	451,196	398,970	24,890
Indiana	2,338,400	1,625,452	712,948	159,545	553,403	54,852	249,000	249,551	238,581	19,988
Iowa	1,129,283	948,011	181,272	2,856	178,416	25,235	107,077	46,104	102,784	9,690
Kansas	2,108,436	1,172,918	935,518	14,464	921,054	645,807	108,773	166,474	695,232	504,032
Kentucky	3,112,416	1,439,196	1,673,220	42,423	1,630,797	1,340,534	131,267	158,996	1,556,227	1,314,268
Louisiana	2,647,755	1,500,520	1,147,235	18,017	1,129,218	700,111	188,182	240,925	585,573	362,710
Maine	888,479	458,198	430,281	13,663	416,618	129,171	36,186	251,261	38,064	9,310
Maryland	10,331,302	7,211,521	3,119,781	116,172	3,003,609	1,347,423	207,465	1,448,721	886,549	271,244
Massachusetts	3,446,374	2,828,609	617,765	77,102	540,663	142,442	167,658	230,563	191,778	9,196
Michigan	3,417,861	2,862,717	555,144	99,578	455,566	66,157	128,865	260,544	304,823	16,796
Minnesota	2,119,854	1,824,740	295,114	15,424	279,690	37,150	167,017	75,523	144,897	10,374
Mississippi	1,969,926	858,688	1,111,238	11,385	1,099,853	623,491	137,479	338,883	219,526	15,010
Missouri	3,831,586	2,651,681	1,179,905	107,008	1,072,897	594,538	252,281	226,078	702,922	355,604
Montana	844,555	619,112	225,443	1,606	223,837	126,564	54,901	42,372	44,616	950
Nebraska	1,191,971	663,459	528,512	14,005	514,507	336,338	51,643	126,526	80,439	4,598
Nevada	1,222,032	742,585	479,447	5,835	473,612	367,871	28,716	77,025	34,873	4,332
New Hampshire	571,199	465,860	105,339	10,669	94,670	42,776	22,259	29,259	34,385	418
New Jersey	4,158,589	3,079,122	1,079,467	49,834	1,029,633	310,622	140,687	578,324	546,308	42,902
New Mexico	1,925,949	1,142,627	783,322	20,965	762,357	447,699	49,935	264,723	139,744	9,424
New York	8,535,231	7,112,671	1,422,560	86,197	1,336,363	724,114	281,706	330,543	885,951	521,170
North Carolina	6,540,669	2,362,775	4,177,894	75,715	4,102,179	3,423,535	184,264	494,380	1,923,012	1,622,638
North Dakota	717,096	348,246	368,850	2,754	366,096	256,094	50,958	59,044	39,731	798
Ohio	5,361,854	3,552,132	1,809,722	464,447	1,345,275	324,637	268,822	751,816	188,383	17,594
Oklahoma	3,352,613	1,381,121	1,971,492	59,056	1,912,436	941,437	138,224	832,775	684,254	486,438
Oregon	1,780,924	1,512,121	268,803	1,990	266,813	47,626	108,071	111,116	142,859	8,360
Pennsylvania	6,362,506	4,818,552	1,543,954	375,999	1,167,955	160,219	303,675	704,061	470,148	42,598
Rhode Island	816,835	355,789	461,046	4,118	456,928	164,637	54,316	237,975	33,608	3,116
South Carolina	2,862,699	1,023,057	1,839,642	52,419	1,787,223	1,351,581	128,601	307,041	572,147	396,302
South Dakota	673,239	479,991	193,248	1,780	191,468	122,951	28,677	39,840	40,337	2,394
Tennessee	3,357,249	2,792,888	564,361	38,250	526,111	134,000	181,982	210,129	252,839	12,426
Texas	13,939,234	7,770,534	6,168,700	187,620	5,981,080	4,379,236	432,101	1,169,743	3,197,301	2,426,718
Utah	2,046,807	1,054,269	992,538	48,059	944,479	219,790	136,150	588,539	178,556	11,552
Vermont	360,045	279,744	80,301	2,385	77,916	7,589	53,694	16,633	32,738	418
Virginia	14,755,627	4,841,084	9,914,543	1,340,273	8,574,270	5,748,496	224,620	2,601,154	1,896,677	976,904
Washington	5,758,246	2,518,586	3,239,660	44,234	3,195,426	2,069,947	212,151	913,328	1,043,179	762,698
West Virginia	1,288,892	1,128,610	160,282	1,088	159,194	30,341	72,743	56,110	106,175	7,828
Wisconsin	1,785,055	1,513,750	271,305	5,482	265,823	37,737	145,547	82,539	136,291	10,640
Wyoming	510,231	308,179	202,052	1,247	200,805	127,186	36,780	36,839	20,772	228
Dist. of Columbia	14,760,002	13,279,708	1,480,294	19,801	1,460,493	571,045	65,355	824,093	375,728	180,652
American Samoa	6,954	4,942	2,012	0	2,012	0	1,966	46	2,012	0
Micronesia	0	0	0	0	0	0	0	0	0	0
Guam	314,526	35,616	278,910	4,668	274,242	205,366	19,103	49,773	9,789	1,520
Marshall Islands	0	0	0	0	0	0	0	0	0	0
No. Mariana Islands	5,898	5,699	199	0	199	0	199	0	199	0
Palau	0	0	0	0	0	0	0	0	0	0
Puerto Rico	968,180	701,282	266,898	9,427	257,471	87,917	112,769	56,785	132,654	11,400
Virgin Islands	55,119	46,450	8,669	0	8,669	1,444	5,393	1,832	6,639	228
Undistributed	2,034,995	2,034,995	0	0	0	0	0	0	0	0

See footnotes at end of table.

FEDERAL GOVERNMENT EXPENDITURE FOR SALARIES AND WAGES, BY AGENCY, BY STATE AND OUTLYING AREA: FISCAL YEAR 2003 — Continued

	Department of Defense—continued									
	Military services—continued									
	Army—continued		Navy				Air Force			
State and outlying area	Inactive military	Civilian	Total	Active military	Inactive military	Civilian	Total	Active military	Inactive military	Civilian
United States	$4,739,067	$6,902,400	$27,928,356	$18,720,609	$582,308	$8,625,439	$22,581,059	$13,333,728	$2,124,259	$7,123,072
Alabama	180,441	597,152	38,171	28,924	7,959	1,288	389,613	240,733	36,793	112,087
Alaska	23,611	76,929	7,123	5,451	927	745	559,461	458,564	13,906	86,991
Arizona	25,902	122,988	210,911	184,582	7,684	18,645	667,185	511,811	13,718	141,656
Arkansas	81,733	74,531	5,859	3,805	1,753	301	259,231	191,014	37,278	30,939
California	250,774	220,300	6,602,340	4,842,388	78,410	1,681,542	1,476,080	870,567	507,595	501,557
Colorado	54,777	74,265	54,694	42,697	9,639	2,358	794,885	506,903	55,656	232,326
Connecticut	44,352	11,390	311,137	258,994	4,385	47,758	27,570	6,970	10,676	9,924
Delaware	14,535	6,749	2,635	1,618	1,017	0	234,923	153,786	35,353	45,784
Florida	158,671	96,381	2,154,677	1,579,606	41,928	533,143	1,593,106	1,108,760	70,997	413,349
Georgia	168,443	310,952	507,563	328,944	22,988	155,631	1,165,359	456,991	93,626	614,742
Hawaii	46,345	127,703	1,199,257	779,570	4,682	415,005	390,510	254,229	39,834	96,447
Idaho	28,524	16,155	8,126	3,366	1,941	2,819	184,931	156,868	2,904	25,159
Illinois	150,457	223,623	843,420	752,775	22,205	68,440	498,572	314,181	25,258	159,133
Indiana	172,885	45,708	185,384	19,513	6,057	159,814	129,438	15,351	70,058	44,029
Iowa	69,428	23,666	10,165	6,097	3,909	159	65,467	9,448	33,740	22,279
Kansas	71,289	119,911	8,081	6,439	1,618	24	217,741	135,336	35,866	46,539
Kentucky	99,451	142,508	26,177	11,249	4,044	10,884	48,393	15,017	27,772	5,604
Louisiana	106,608	116,255	161,893	89,882	17,095	54,916	381,752	247,519	64,479	69,754
Maine	20,733	8,021	350,968	111,040	7,893	232,035	27,586	8,621	7,560	11,205
Maryland	142,132	473,173	1,516,714	637,187	4,701	874,826	600,346	438,992	60,632	100,722
Massachusetts	101,399	81,183	45,064	27,754	3,438	13,872	303,821	105,492	62,821	135,508
Michigan	84,038	203,989	34,601	27,494	6,201	906	116,142	21,867	38,626	55,649
Minnesota	92,617	41,906	21,653	12,156	8,832	665	113,140	14,620	65,568	32,952
Mississippi	96,982	107,534	420,652	301,592	4,706	114,354	459,675	306,889	35,791	116,995
Missouri	184,232	163,086	119,060	82,799	26,562	9,699	250,915	156,135	41,487	53,293
Montana	30,407	13,259	1,812	794	1,018	0	177,409	124,820	23,476	29,113
Nebraska	29,020	46,821	31,851	28,277	2,983	591	402,217	303,463	19,640	79,114
Nevada	21,100	9,441	61,256	46,365	2,700	12,191	377,483	317,174	4,916	55,393
New Hampshire	17,222	16,745	36,098	32,242	1,343	2,513	24,187	10,116	4,070	10,001
New Jersey	104,068	399,338	174,124	58,182	3,712	112,230	309,201	209,538	32,907	66,756
New Mexico	29,131	101,189	14,852	10,002	2,842	2,008	607,761	428,273	17,962	161,526
New York	159,712	205,069	156,342	128,822	21,016	6,504	294,070	74,122	100,978	118,970
North Carolina	136,727	163,647	1,721,437	1,427,420	11,627	282,390	457,730	373,477	35,910	48,343
North Dakota	27,614	11,319	1,551	732	722	97	324,814	254,564	22,622	47,628
Ohio	132,627	38,162	46,642	26,332	17,267	3,043	1,110,250	280,711	118,928	710,611
Oklahoma	79,373	118,443	89,490	79,537	5,934	4,019	1,138,692	375,462	52,917	710,313
Oregon	60,711	73,788	25,536	18,809	5,990	737	98,418	20,457	41,370	36,591
Pennsylvania	198,456	229,094	519,270	84,219	24,870	410,181	178,537	33,402	80,349	64,786
Rhode Island	24,132	6,360	377,207	149,949	5,388	221,870	46,113	11,572	24,796	9,745
South Carolina	104,413	71,432	759,969	585,592	8,410	165,967	455,107	369,687	15,778	69,642
South Dakota	25,846	12,097	1,023	283	709	31	150,108	120,274	2,122	27,712
Tennessee	117,184	123,299	147,912	92,811	11,984	43,117	125,360	28,763	52,814	43,783
Texas	284,986	485,597	498,014	400,086	39,569	58,359	2,285,765	1,552,432	107,546	625,787
Utah	101,987	65,017	13,807	9,356	3,066	1,385	752,116	198,882	31,097	522,137
Vermont	24,611	7,709	1,552	1,257	236	59	43,626	5,914	28,847	8,865
Virginia	151,356	768,417	5,578,503	3,971,178	34,370	1,572,955	1,099,090	800,414	38,894	259,782
Washington	110,345	170,136	1,703,414	1,018,873	22,492	662,049	448,833	288,376	79,314	81,143
West Virginia	62,790	35,557	17,507	12,657	2,149	2,701	35,512	9,856	7,804	17,852
Wisconsin	80,709	44,942	16,428	8,926	7,128	374	113,104	18,171	57,710	37,223
Wyoming	15,219	5,275	521	35	486	0	179,562	126,923	21,075	31,564
Dist. of Columbia	23,241	171,835	833,227	185,893	41,136	606,198	251,538	204,500	978	46,060
American Samoa	1,966	46	0	0	0	0	0	0	0	0
Micronesia	0	0	0	0	0	0	0	0	0	0
Guam	8,011	258	158,857	127,912	0	30,945	105,596	75,934	11,092	18,570
Marshall Islands	0	0	0	0	0	0	0	0	0	0
No. Mariana Islands ..	199	0	0	0	0	0	0	0	0	0
Palau	0	0	0	0	0	0	0	0	0	0
Puerto Rico	100,966	20,228	93,726	68,043	2,587	23,096	31,091	8,474	9,216	13,401
Virgin Islands	4,579	1,832	103	103	0	0	1,927	1,113	814	0
Undistributed	0	0	0	0	0	0	0	0	0	0

See footnotes at end of table.

FEDERAL GOVERNMENT EXPENDITURE FOR SALARIES AND WAGES, BY AGENCY, BY STATE AND OUTLYING AREA: FISCAL YEAR 2003 — Continued

State and outlying area	Total (a)	Nondefense agencies								
		Department of Agriculture	Department of Commerce	Department of Education	Department of Energy	Environmental Protection Agency	Federal Deposit Insurance Corporation	General Services Administration	Department of Health and Human Services	Department of Homeland Security
United States	$128,987,168	$5,567,267	$2,400,051	$357,078	$1,303,605	$1,424,863	$498,446	$948,612	$4,616,737	$4,611,354
Alabama	1,719,815	69,553	5,694	79	0	2,753	2,684	3,556	3,813	22,494
Alaska	696,309	53,866	29,973	0	96	2,200	0	3,065	34,435	23,827
Arizona	2,046,790	102,838	9,254	0	15,560	262	1,682	4,061	204,877	147,619
Arkansas	900,000	113,840	2,725	0	2,129	0	1,803	1,332	27,315	9,693
California	11,358,683	463,403	56,448	13,903	43,917	72,229	30,019	71,252	89,287	594,626
Colorado	2,578,677	193,756	87,486	5,154	60,111	56,035	2,628	23,664	33,575	64,029
Connecticut	1,075,432	10,144	3,502	0	145	619	2,238	937	1,939	24,147
Delaware	227,879	12,703	436	0	0	0	868	231	712	1,331
Florida	5,475,321	49,190	49,190	371	103	6,864	5,243	6,980	15,808	330,088
Georgia	3,769,827	156,539	12,667	15,223	6,542	84,635	16,198	47,292	491,474	151,263
Hawaii	451,926	26,991	15,456	0	302	538	0	3,766	1,273	46,788
Idaho	593,321	149,337	6,362	0	31,982	1,836	0	1,329	2,836	10,308
Illinois	4,735,374	96,915	12,850	13,852	28,340	95,662	24,228	50,760	56,327	138,789
Indiana	1,625,452	49,785	65,449	104	0	110	3,113	3,037	2,884	26,806
Iowa	948,011	117,560	3,981	66	787	385	5,518	1,257	1,340	8,049
Kansas	1,172,918	61,085	9,369	0	0	41,188	6,458	1,638	11,997	9,695
Kentucky	1,439,196	65,370	6,016	0	1,120	200	3,872	1,248	1,062	26,393
Louisiana	1,500,520	168,939	9,022	0	6,828	946	4,062	2,996	12,543	44,919
Maine	458,198	16,757	4,542	0	0	0	0	455	1,412	21,834
Maryland	7,211,521	242,809	751,052	0	132,758	7,027	2,267	14,548	2,478,296	106,453
Massachusetts	2,828,609	25,761	32,761	7,053	1,390	57,544	17,917	19,420	41,279	95,247
Michigan	2,862,717	73,211	16,433	0	0	25,795	3,096	6,250	8,811	90,854
Minnesota	1,824,740	110,406	7,161	337	62	6,466	4,665	3,059	24,033	46,194
Mississippi	858,688	110,223	12,989	0	0	2,133	2,277	993	1,350	10,142
Missouri	2,651,681	260,202	29,432	7,310	7,908	677	15,565	57,836	32,455	49,065
Montana	619,112	170,487	6,679	0	9,733	2,528	1,091	1,272	50,951	17,777
Nebraska	663,459	87,252	4,883	0	1,272	87	3,143	1,195	4,397	24,741
Nevada	742,585	24,489	6,500	0	32,799	12,283	0	1,892	3,715	40,348
New Hampshire	465,860	20,015	1,856	0	0	0	2,192	1,156	585	6,994
New Jersey	3,079,122	31,518	14,966	0	1,525	18,000	4,400	14,317	12,014	108,033
New Mexico	1,142,627	88,807	4,299	0	72,909	150	1,495	2,630	139,727	40,576
New York	7,112,671	64,561	21,176	6,664	12,792	58,391	17,296	47,773	67,309	302,384
North Carolina	2,362,751	112,326	27,856	0	0	95,818	3,633	3,275	69,739	66,400
North Dakota	348,246	48,984	3,720	0	4,068	0	2,721	1,007	22,191	12,030
Ohio	3,552,132	55,542	8,782	2,084	13,748	42,345	2,709	8,428	42,078	52,724
Oklahoma	1,381,121	58,502	19,253	0	9,134	4,195	3,975	2,889	71,322	15,674
Oregon	1,512,121	254,061	18,896	0	102,972	9,244	1,530	2,618	11,407	33,238
Pennsylvania	4,818,552	97,718	13,437	7,993	30,131	67,993	5,561	42,650	68,747	84,936
Rhode Island	355,789	2,719	2,892	0	0	5,846	0	670	628	16,372
South Carolina	1,023,057	54,986	16,256	0	37,856	0	1,682	1,717	1,424	23,025
South Dakota	479,991	51,799	5,193	0	12,085	67	2,064	980	59,105	4,107
Tennessee	2,792,888	70,900	7,368	174	52,523	495	11,783	2,769	7,488	30,390
Texas	7,770,534	213,608	34,584	9,286	12,899	67,339	69,364	69,553	53,186	692,368
Utah	1,054,269	101,107	7,739	0	1,442	129	3,373	1,800	2,932	23,474
Vermont	279,744	17,401	2,032	0	0	0	0	0	297	648	49,961
Virginia	4,841,084	142,655	564,402	0	1,432	106,208	742	119,940	3,211	186,863
Washington	2,518,586	128,793	79,858	5,521	169,648	41,012	3,918	31,758	50,771	106,618
West Virginia	1,128,610	43,663	2,593	0	21,836	2,027	1,114	2,124	29,404	10,446
Wisconsin	1,513,750	101,142	6,679	0	55	144	5,592	1,813	3,970	17,315
Wyoming	308,179	47,551	3,290	0	4,140	0	0	894	4,726	2,518
Dist. of Columbia	13,279,708	589,840	269,324	261,501	358,526	420,806	191,955	250,145	245,179	471,942
American Samoa	4,942	368	951	0	0	0	0	0	0	91
Micronesia	0	0	0	0	0	0	0	0	0	0
Guam	35,616	3,371	1,887	0	0	133	0	0	0	7,167
Marshall Islands	0	0	0	0	0	0	0	0	0	0
No. Mariana Islands ...	5,699	409	0	0	0	156	0	0	47	1,195
Palau	0	0	0	0	0	0	0	0	0	0
Puerto Rico	701,282	31,867	2,450	403	0	3,285	712	2,024	8,703	51,275
Virgin Islands	46,450	823	0	0	0	78	0	64	0	9,719
Undistributed	2,034,995	0	0	0	0	0	0	0	0	0

See footnotes at end of table.

FEDERAL GOVERNMENT EXPENDITURE FOR SALARIES AND WAGES, BY AGENCY, BY STATE AND OUTLYING AREA: FISCAL YEAR 2003 — Continued

				Nondefense agencies—continued					
State and outlying area	Department of Housing and Urban Development	Department of the Interior	Department of Justice (c)	Department of Labor	National Aeronautics and Space Administration	National Archives and Records Administration	National Science Foundation	United States Postal Service	Small Business Administration
United States	$783,920	$4,017,547	$8,380,544	$1,178,654	$1,575,282	$134,106	$108,563	$50,428,121	$264,956
Alabama	6,073	7,953	73,586	9,370	218,154	54	0	622,138	3,365
Alaska	2,641	137,156	12,125	907	0	176	123	125,844	1,108
Arizona	8,572	228,842	131,197	3,821	271	0	0	785,576	1,603
Arkansas	4,177	16,548	42,707	3,281	0	1,014	0	406,459	3,128
California	48,351	378,412	614,877	63,456	191,932	5,598	0	5,419,757	32,584
Colorado	26,249	456,373	141,219	28,738	786	1,872	0	893,721	9,101
Connecticut	4,909	3,133	51,969	4,896	81	0	0	691,285	1,896
Delaware	359	2,246	10,944	720	0	0	0	141,711	415
Florida	19,471	75,678	403,133	30,129	146,922	0	0	2,610,430	4,996
Georgia	31,474	61,521	188,139	36,996	0	3,822	1,367,435	11,902	12,879
Hawaii	1,727	25,361	28,408	1,716	0	0	0	163,316	1,436
Idaho	948	116,359	16,745	2,147	0	0	0	180,038	904
Illinois	35,507	13,755	229,022	54,900	79	1,834	151	2,577,535	5,347
Indiana	5,861	13,396	72,483	6,605	57	0	0	966,469	1,607
Iowa	2,493	6,879	19,838	2,081	0	837	0	581,126	1,891
Kansas	12,572	19,688	66,268	3,980	0	1,572	0	542,983	1,318
Kentucky	5,161	18,426	117,551	27,652	0	0	0	617,744	2,199
Louisiana	7,622	62,117	124,941	6,710	769	0	0	650,090	1,874
Maine	496	10,617	9,646	1,819	0	0	0	273,048	1,254
Maryland	9,250	43,970	289,024	6,363	255,381	55,802	0	1,081,022	2,236
Massachusetts	17,461	65,418	99,296	32,341	144	4,205	0	1,428,526	3,285
Michigan	12,640	24,241	115,618	7,165	110	1,202	0	1,804,043	2,774
Minnesota	7,294	43,261	93,446	3,975	0	0	0	1,027,194	1,938
Mississippi	3,962	23,416	45,373	3,065	22,966	0	0	354,217	1,099
Missouri	8,685	47,506	104,026	27,712	72	25,981	0	1,197,467	5,703
Montana	618	107,722	13,214	1,582	0	0	0	169,785	1,006
Nebraska	3,089	24,214	16,736	2,447	0	0	0	360,015	1,234
Nevada	2,183	104,292	39,441	2,061	0	0	0	301,426	1,503
New Hampshire	3,099	4,810	11,888	2,969	98	0	0	262,367	995
New Jersey	9,364	19,335	218,687	13,246	156	0	0	2,001,169	2,488
New Mexico	2,520	251,090	35,991	2,384	4,712	74	0	252,420	1,353
New York	40,171	50,979	383,431	49,092	2,605	1,905	0	3,816,136	17,057
North Carolina	8,282	31,515	119,585	5,321	0	0	0	1,279,796	2,131
North Dakota	483	42,597	6,883	1,194	0	0	0	137,439	1,251
Ohio	18,138	17,046	104,347	29,979	153,958	2,529	0	2,053,960	3,664
Oklahoma	10,092	53,407	86,210	3,483	0	0	0	543,532	1,395
Oregon	4,377	182,121	54,800	2,992	96	0	0	518,632	1,849
Pennsylvania	30,967	66,149	317,280	68,210	0	2,310	0	2,482,878	5,943
Rhode Island	2,118	3,303	10,105	1,684	0	0	0	212,079	1,182
South Carolina	5,695	10,742	77,793	2,895	0	0	0	513,078	1,517
South Dakota	437	71,909	18,232	841	0	0	0	148,425	878
Tennessee	11,115	34,802	81,646	7,071	0	0	0	950,296	1,772
Texas	43,916	59,338	595,907	53,163	260,384	5,062	0	3,257,652	23,493
Utah	1,800	105,962	29,699	8,312	679	0	0	326,937	1,611
Vermont	407	3,166	7,690	460	0	0	0	138,660	1,173
Virginia	7,468	266,993	740,024	35,668	203,424	0	108,289	1,304,025	2,209
Washington	15,761	135,678	75,932	19,122	0	1,429	0	931,438	3,957
West Virginia	2,001	42,191	212,892	32,292	2,286	0	0	324,252	1,429
Wisconsin	5,545	33,340	51,096	7,120	105	0	0	920,635	1,995
Wyoming	382	90,296	8,471	1,014	0	0	0	85,564	943
Dist. of Columbia ..	263,531	284,833	1,717,154	450,795	109,055	16,828	0	376,798	71,033
American Samoa ...	0	1,058	0	0	0	0	0	610	0
Micronesia	0	0	0	0	0	0	0	0	0
Guam	63	1,465	5,560	49	0	0	0	7,873	1,474
Marshall Islands ...	0	0	0	0	0	0	0	0	0
No. Mariana Islands	0	764	1,527	225	0	0	0	732	0
Palau	0	0	0	0	0	0	0	0	0
Puerto Rico	6,343	8,185	71,225	2,438	0	0	0	224,346	2,439

See footnotes at end of table.

FEDERAL GOVERNMENT EXPENDITURE FOR SALARIES AND WAGES, BY AGENCY, BY STATE AND OUTLYING AREA: FISCAL YEAR 2003 — Continued

State and outlying area	Social Security Administration	Department of State	Department of Transportation	Department of the Treasury	Department of Veterans Affairs	All other nondefense (d)
			Nondefense agencies—continued			
United States	$3,682,084	$970,644	$6,501,692	$7,652,362	$11,966,240	$7,884,784
Alabama	131,542	462	33,756	36,063	208,627	220,949
Alaska	2,613	59	130,177	8,303	22,555	898
Arizona	30,429	1,108	64,334	45,897	244,195	14,373
Arkansas	24,746	73	25,099	16,479	193,546	2,780
California	349,442	11,539	559,316	840,256	1,109,829	105,521
Colorado	38,523	344	157,576	113,447	149,196	33,701
Connecticut	22,093	1,038	26,716	50,993	117,925	4,349
Delaware	3,876	0	3,446	11,503	35,002	587
Florida	129,484	22,686	327,495	209,596	749,800	25,273
Georgia	90,063	943	284,475	350,627	291,940	55,902
Hawaii	5,725	1,179	41,674	12,456	29,716	3,050
Idaho	6,716	0	14,560	9,182	41,260	308
Illinois	186,283	4,016	274,270	200,314	491,309	135,569
Indiana	42,401	0	127,527	62,813	163,027	9,676
Iowa	18,283	0	24,093	18,432	128,884	1,541
Kansas	18,188	111	115,938	105,569	132,127	5,150
Kentucky	41,645	161	45,199	236,420	150,904	65,764
Louisiana	45,417	3,858	38,916	45,419	204,101	9,192
Maine	10,151	85	19,632	10,456	53,447	601
Maryland	771,280	2,886	60,521	428,475	183,327	251,895
Massachusetts	66,633	3,067	153,864	229,538	301,536	32,761
Michigan	74,009	615	88,582	153,663	290,393	13,533
Minnesota	26,216	198	125,411	60,319	217,816	9,765
Mississippi	32,075	122	19,124	17,439	165,682	19,249
Missouri	134,089	40	128,118	214,671	279,003	11,606
Montana	6,776	111	16,779	8,179	31,403	1,049
Nebraska	9,800	130	18,825	19,567	78,305	1,367
Nevada	10,187	0	42,655	24,583	89,681	1,829
New Hampshire	7,683	4,112	79,844	14,301	33,276	680
New Jersey	58,369	962	196,614	103,540	175,898	9,916
New Mexico	40,332	487	81,295	13,585	102,648	2,558
New York	251,207	20,602	327,755	582,749	840,838	84,169
North Carolina	56,693	3,273	58,298	63,696	280,536	13,066
North Dakota	5,747	0	14,816	6,814	35,941	360
Ohio	83,917	0	171,205	192,922	445,307	25,761
Oklahoma	26,306	130	284,617	42,008	139,584	2,459
Oregon	25,011	0	32,165	38,941	173,578	2,586
Pennsylvania	221,016	3,383	107,388	466,619	526,541	85,337
Rhode Island	8,982	717	11,491	12,324	47,298	923
South Carolina	32,119	10,102	30,935	19,347	149,025	3,914
South Dakota	5,338	0	9,065	6,461	82,310	696
Tennessee	54,236	0	132,035	265,360	322,511	741,781
Texas	157,825	15,437	486,882	623,524	837,713	63,145
Utah	10,564	0	82,962	258,640	81,975	2,932
Vermont	3,534	0	9,686	5,668	37,589	293
Virginia	116,378	5,868	270,303	126,372	249,915	93,131
Washington	76,680	2,964	220,396	83,874	258,115	14,264
West Virginia	25,465	0	17,476	176,196	173,107	2,871
Wisconsin	36,990	0	32,641	44,478	222,442	6,932
Wyoming	2,149	0	9,602	5,422	40,710	301
Dist. of Columbia	19,434	847,776	826,028	916,569	418,497	3,787,855
American Samoa	195	0	1,420	0	56	0
Micronesia	0	0	0	0	0	0
Guam	606	0	5,330	0	477	20
Marshall Islands	0	0	0	0	0	0
No. Mariana Islands	226	0	257	148	0	12
Palau	0	0	0	0	0	0
Puerto Rico	25,603	0	31,660	41,765	135,270	24,020
Virgin Islands	794	0	1,448	380	547	18
Undistributed	0	0	2,267	2,267	0	1,876,546

Source: U.S. Department of Commerce, Bureau of the Census, September 2004.

Note: Department of Defense data represent salaries, wages and compensation, such as housing allowances; distributions by state are based on duty station. State detail for all other federal government agencies are estimates, based on place of employment.

(a) The "undistributed" amount includes the salary and wages data for the Federal Bureau of Investigation and for the Federal Judiciary that could not be geographically allocated.

(b) The "undistributed" amount represents Defense Logistics Agency salaries and wages that could not be geographically allocated.

(c) The "undistributed" amount includes the salaries and wages of the Federal Bureau of Investigation that could not be geographically allocated.

(d) The "undistributed" amount includes the salaries and wages for the Federal Judiciary that could not be geographically allocated.

Table 2.9
FEDERAL GOVERNMENT INSURANCE AND LOAN PROGRAMS, BY STATE AND OUTLYING AREA: FISCAL YEAR 2003
(In thousands of dollars)

	Direct loans by volume of assistance provided					Guaranteed loans by volume of coverage provided-continued			
		Department of Agriculture							Veterans housing
State and outlying area	Total	Commodity loans— price supports	Other agriculture loans	Federal direct student loans	Other direct loans	Total	Mortgage insurance for homes	Federal Family Education Loan program	guaranteed and insured loans- VA home loans
United States	$35,561,844	$7,424,474	$3,693,221	$22,072,946	$1,371,203	$226,971,244	$148,635,920	$28,132,568	$13,970,796
Alabama	814,893	210,348	64,522	501,604	38,419	2,268,600	1,304,122	338,397	238,813
Alaska	28,556	0	10,086	11,169	7,301	956,583	580,258	20,033	116,541
Arizona	557,182	3,562	41,107	509,431	3,082	8,142,602	5,694,506	1,108,555	649,781
Arkansas	502,259	344,019	99,850	54,786	3,604	1,691,596	922,720	231,635	109,887
California	3,040,961	738,193	179,387	2,025,121	98,259	22,026,079	13,683,394	2,685,029	777,942
Colorado	571,813	129,898	48,190	375,753	17,972	11,042,703	8,265,739	454,331	539,051
Connecticut	130,100	0	15,873	100,508	13,718	2,278,092	1,350,065	342,422	47,957
Delaware	62,917	1,240	17,399	44,267	12	494,359	330,726	42,841	61,825
Florida	667,449	74,685	100,014	457,756	34,993	11,374,305	7,130,454	1,639,424	1,085,084
Georgia	1,119,692	76,611	108,561	914,310	20,209	8,498,424	6,164,994	651,466	572,185
Hawaii	16,982	0	15,583	668	731	532,553	173,292	79,167	39,807
Idaho	388,031	24,279	55,758	307,645	349	1,326,360	966,258	35,052	106,697
Illinois	1,540,228	197,597	96,028	1,230,438	16,165	10,548,520	7,384,714	1,104,335	353,554
Indiana	908,471	102,513	73,200	694,007	38,751	5,308,387	3,895,542	735,852	230,930
Iowa	1,577,021	678,747	98,209	798,339	1,725	1,279,497	487,324	265,606	73,129
Kansas	305,951	29,916	65,110	182,142	28,783	1,648,464	953,999	260,995	134,670
Kentucky	369,451	77,002	105,864	174,075	12,514	2,755,396	1,316,827	300,613	148,075
Louisiana	327,312	96,150	107,826	48,437	74,899	2,224,178	1,140,932	625,694	126,308
Maine	81,700	235	47,921	31,135	2,409	542,212	226,625	154,578	35,642
Maryland	496,445	4,598	22,331	459,153	10,363	10,194,402	8,010,181	350,953	645,790
Massachusetts	937,618	29	39,264	891,098	7,227	3,359,981	1,978,898	788,067	60,831
Michigan	2,298,559	146,048	104,472	2,044,682	3,357	6,059,314	4,456,011	475,679	232,832
Minnesota	1,275,958	625,792	90,230	551,654	8,282	3,933,153	2,035,015	532,881	147,394
Mississippi	1,635,426	1,439,923	98,045	48,557	48,901	1,780,123	871,509	299,524	114,926
Missouri	545,612	87,827	80,614	346,382	30,788	4,433,078	2,802,405	769,883	269,089
Montana	134,122	22,914	38,158	71,642	1,408	655,231	304,989	101,372	41,089
Nebraska	493,970	262,550	69,096	154,190	8,134	1,372,541	715,514	230,618	151,644
Nevada	145,086	0	15,855	123,996	5,235	3,483,275	2,752,213	56,936	340,317
New Hampshire	51,042	0	22,283	28,587	172	801,383	386,505	197,049	36,847
New Jersey	419,606	1,493	24,984	375,201	17,928	7,105,158	5,521,907	410,995	152,359
New Mexico	171,206	4,412	30,894	134,773	1,126	1,629,743	1,083,455	99,494	166,101
New York	2,261,796	15,203	95,326	1,765,762	385,506	8,037,240	4,588,514	2,453,473	121,713
North Carolina	813,259	267,656	153,240	386,117	6,246	6,076,858	4,081,969	626,199	709,329
North Dakota	191,399	129,928	58,882	0	2,589	763,874	184,459	128,893	32,008
Ohio	1,931,715	57,716	105,238	1,724,026	44,735	7,492,837	5,130,597	1,012,830	418,633
Oklahoma	228,663	11,171	105,298	95,129	17,065	2,259,713	1,178,590	424,912	173,229
Oregon	807,278	7,110	56,991	742,177	1,001	2,768,331	1,982,398	220,664	215,303
Pennsylvania	200,403	4,943	95,191	93,564	6,705	6,566,838	3,009,531	2,506,153	300,580
Rhode Island	160,104	0	7,204	150,658	2,242	806,905	500,393	204,948	14,996
South Carolina	335,958	9,222	80,831	241,182	4,723	1,904,262	829,158	355,452	199,854
South Dakota	186,856	113,930	63,805	3,310	5,811	621,218	196,561	142,908	39,305
Tennessee	459,651	65,322	94,092	240,279	59,959	4,656,184	3,212,642	590,352	327,754
Texas	1,417,147	848,950	258,656	244,949	64,592	19,066,300	13,645,985	1,914,234	1,322,029
Utah	404,125	354,273	43,837	4,523	1,492	5,979,980	4,913,712	223,926	173,724
Vermont	43,457	8	27,685	15,136	628	361,285	54,867	143,476	12,826
Virginia	1,071,611	13,289	79,030	965,394	13,898	8,213,473	5,521,634	398,142	1,131,455
Washington	793,967	39,284	82,859	659,327	12,498	6,375,787	4,288,115	397,453	702,671
West Virginia	564,520	1,287	84,921	468,827	9,485	450,454	228,462	60,775	36,585
Wisconsin	483,404	100,319	114,730	263,063	5,290	2,282,275	1,013,077	464,200	177,729
Wyoming	20,205	4,281	14,766	13	1,145	389,650	143,726	57,824	32,709
Dist. of Columbia	235,823	0	750	231,966	3,107	701,490	258,485	340,873	5,226
American Samoa	2,346	0	0	0	2,346	3,000	0	0	0
Fed. States of Micronesia	4,408	0	3,809	0	599	0	0	0	0
Guam	153,834	0	249	2,081	151,504	19,309	502	0	1,122
Marshall Islands	1,366	0	1,366	0	0	0	0	0	0
No. Mariana Islands	11,416	0	1,231	0	10,184	263	0	0	0
Palau	560	0	560	0	0	0	0	0	0
Puerto Rico	154,533	0	71,753	82,122	659	1,259,165	780,415	75,407	14,730
Virgin Islands	6,415	0	4,207	1,833	376	168,259	1,036	0	190
Undistributed	0	0	0	0	0	0	0	0	0

FEDERAL GOVERNMENT INSURANCE AND LOAN PROGRAMS, BY STATE AND OUTLYING AREA: FISCAL YEAR 2003—Continued

State and outlying area	Guaranteed loans by volume of coverage provided					Insurance programs by volume of coverage provided				
	Mortgage insurance— condominiums	U.S.D.A. guaranteed loans	Small business loans	Other guaranteed loans	Total	Flood insurance	Crop insurance	Foreign Investment Insurance	Life Insurance for Veterans	Other insurance
United States	$10,661,966	$11,921,282	$12,957,211	$691,501	$704,823,389	$661,793,029	$40,064,741	$612,228	$1,880,191	$473,200
Alabama	16,135	286,512	84,622	0	5,441,169	5,175,116	235,500	0	25,583	4,971
Alaska	87,620	132,548	19,582	0	373,126	363,242	592	0	2,560	6,732
Arizona	168,620	157,405	363,735	0	4,586,448	4,399,680	135,606	0	45,002	9,160
Arkansas	8,448	346,050	72,855	0	1,666,002	1,194,980	452,550	0	16,071	2,401
California	1,748,663	264,539	2,866,513	0	47,901,144	44,636,332	2,980,851	28,669	197,117	58,176
Colorado	1,036,765	405,042	341,775	0	3,104,579	2,478,078	568,785	0	30,137	27,578
Connecticut	224,387	36,475	276,786	0	5,017,234	4,912,159	71,809	0	30,300	2,967
Delaware	3,572	29,688	25,708	0	2,857,587	2,809,725	42,084	0	5,778	0
Florida	685,632	233,773	599,937	0	282,991,752	280,053,010	2,688,462	26,967	172,717	50,596
Georgia	156,828	610,918	342,034	0	12,139,219	11,398,805	665,365	0	41,860	33,190
Hawaii	171,031	34,613	34,644	0	6,100,973	5,983,948	99,603	0	16,026	1,396
Idaho	6,276	128,323	83,754	0	1,342,278	872,913	459,081	0	8,085	2,199
Illinois	846,838	370,231	488,849	0	8,151,621	4,691,118	3,075,260	21,803	78,717	14,723
Indiana	76,428	201,959	167,677	0	4,218,900	2,604,801	1,583,266	0	28,315	2,518
Iowa	24,352	302,763	126,322	0	4,976,932	943,063	4,010,556	35	23,169	109
Kansas	6,690	205,416	86,693	0	2,858,927	999,309	1,823,253	5,991	18,601	11,774
Kentucky	52,397	872,287	65,196	0	2,236,148	1,832,922	381,234	0	18,378	3,613
Louisiana	14,609	224,927	91,707	0	48,683,570	48,253,477	384,370	0	22,139	23,583
Maine	7,235	59,676	58,456	0	1,036,882	970,345	56,661	0	9,876	0
Maryland	909,221	86,089	192,168	0	6,847,729	6,630,624	158,596	8,489	40,226	9,795
Massachusetts	181,032	36,847	314,307	0	6,612,392	6,473,289	42,334	44,100	51,090	1,579
Michigan	229,870	368,402	296,519	0	3,753,254	2,940,821	750,424	5,400	51,455	5,153
Minnesota	322,648	528,792	366,424	0	4,126,333	1,057,007	3,028,058	0	38,350	2,917
Mississippi	927	388,190	105,046	0	5,201,064	4,760,984	421,569	743	13,509	4,260
Missouri	64,152	346,872	180,676	0	3,339,904	2,422,787	865,114	0	36,088	15,914
Montana	7,671	141,135	58,976	0	948,768	345,272	581,491	0	7,560	14,445
Nebraska	1,589	199,665	73,512	0	3,897,600	1,330,670	2,550,462	0	13,828	2,640
Nevada	199,999	20,214	113,595	0	2,524,937	2,496,785	13,703	0	13,003	1,446
New Hampshire	70,333	20,383	90,266	0	700,358	678,625	11,367	0	9,861	505
New Jersey	549,992	16,238	453,666	1	29,450,339	29,308,877	63,175	3,000	65,568	9,719
New Mexico	16,442	194,853	69,399	0	1,344,509	1,256,394	70,945	0	13,604	3,566
New York	50,077	125,939	611,024	86,500	16,208,628	15,611,646	205,435	263,918	124,688	2,941
North Carolina	133,806	337,841	187,715	0	17,991,952	16,939,791	993,648	0	46,714	11,798
North Dakota	4,517	372,033	41,964	0	2,636,742	667,499	1,962,715	0	4,851	1,677
Ohio	198,988	414,471	317,318	0	4,657,826	3,503,525	1,070,189	0	70,401	13,711
Oklahoma	12,540	366,898	103,546	0	1,869,212	1,450,623	405,841	0	20,872	1,877
Oregon	62,610	137,534	149,822	0	4,594,312	4,045,769	516,584	4,500	23,806	3,654
Pennsylvania	99,569	173,008	477,998	0	7,509,568	7,149,724	251,432	0	98,172	10,240
Rhode Island	18,600	10,869	57,099	0	1,840,973	1,830,425	1,272	0	7,894	1,382
South Carolina	11,364	413,447	94,986	0	25,729,938	25,407,092	286,186	3,600	25,750	7,310
South Dakota	1,272	208,534	32,638	0	1,885,989	329,772	1,548,828	0	6,015	1,373
Tennessee	73,318	310,858	141,260	0	2,809,530	2,204,262	571,835	0	27,987	5,446
Texas	116,933	493,198	1,018,921	555,000	76,590,363	74,252,598	2,021,862	175,960	106,738	33,204
Utah	431,264	79,862	157,492	0	420,902	384,223	11,159	0	11,661	13,858
Vermont	8,601	51,381	90,135	0	352,016	333,732	13,876	0	4,409	0
Virginia	774,151	193,920	194,172	0	12,328,015	11,957,272	302,056	2,239	55,217	11,230
Washington	482,419	135,267	319,862	50,000	4,965,866	4,070,350	845,660	30,146	41,350	8,506
West Virginia	220	93,834	30,578	0	1,597,508	1,572,414	12,982	0	10,299	1,813
Wisconsin	27,742	373,642	225,885	0	2,111,150	1,355,260	709,386	4,500	40,117	1,886
Wyoming	686	123,113	31,592	0	341,727	267,769	61,671	0	3,590	8,697
Dist. of Columbia ...	30,910	0	65,997	0	95,720	78,179	0	12,314	3,543	1,684
American Samoa	0	3,000	0	0	435	435	0	0	0	0
Fed. States of Micronesia	0	0	0	0	0	0	0	0	0	0
Guam	0	14,871	2,813	0	32,121	31,091	0	0	0	1,030
Marshall Islands	0	0	0	0	0	0	0	0	0	0
No. Mariana Islands	0	0	263	0	273	273	0	0	0	0
Palau	0	0	0	0	0	0	0	0	0	0
Puerto Rico	225,720	72,255	90,638	0	3,542,609	3,538,449	0	0	4,160	0
Virgin Islands	260	164,681	2,093	0	268,338	265,698	0	0	384	2,256
Undistributed	0	0	0	0	0	0	0	0	0	0

Source: U.S. Department of Commerce, Bureau of the Census, February 2004.

Note: Amounts represent dollar volume of direct loans made during the fiscal year.

Table 2.10
PER CAPITA AMOUNTS OF FEDERAL GOVERNMENT EXPENDITURE, BY MAJOR OBJECT CATEGORY, BY STATE AND OUTLYING AREA: FISCAL YEAR 2003
(In dollars)

State and outlying area	United States resident population— July 1, 2003 (a)	Total	Retirement and disability	Other direct payments	Grants	Procurement	Salaries and wages
United States	290,809,777	$6,910.31	$2,167.50	$1,522.98	$1,496.00	$1,011.02	$712.81
Alabama	4,500,752	8,192.16	2,717.78	1,710.47	1,477.34	1,570.28	716.29
Alaska	648,818	12,243.59	1,603.78	900.65	4,658.11	2,589.50	2,491.55
Arizona	5,580,811	6,773.44	2,154.13	1,192.08	1,296.43	1,533.29	597.51
Arkansas	2,725,714	6,728.64	2,582.22	1,672.18	1,665.95	317.00	491.29
California	35,484,453	6,191.60	1,725.71	1,394.42	1,446.52	1044.11	580.85
Colorado	4,550,688	6,345.02	1,840.33	1,101.87	1,321.65	1,129.87	951.30
Connecticut	3,483,372	8,209.05	2,167.23	1,627.52	1,543.35	2,435.66	435.30
Delaware	817,491	6,190.71	2,379.29	1,469.28	1,444.38	299.46	598.31
Florida	17,019,068	6,659.64	2,655.35	1,765.15	1026.09	640.40	572.65
Georgia	8,684,715	5,977.19	1,918.99	1,315.65	1,216.07	603.65	922.83
Hawaii	1,257,608	8,960.91	2,396.66	1,194.46	1,519.52	1,573.15	2,277.12
Idaho	1,366,332	6,334.08	2,096.51	1,146.23	1,360.03	1,120.76	610.56
Illinois	12,653,544	5,770.68	1,958.82	1,598.93	1,242.34	452.75	517.85
Indiana	6,195,643	5,733.81	2,161.81	1,481.35	1,180.34	532.89	377.43
Iowa	2,944,062	5,961.06	2,302.95	1,580.77	1,316.98	376.78	383.58
Kansas	2,723,507	6,685.55	2,274.98	1,640.77	1,253.90	741.74	774.16
Kentucky	4,117,827	7,565.42	2,469.41	1,485.96	1,611.06	1243.15	755.84
Louisiana	4,496,334	7,038.24	2,126.05	1,873.57	1,739.25	710.51	588.87
Maine	1,305,728	7,632.30	2,606.01	1,342.43	1,998.76	1004.64	680.45
Maryland	5,508,909	10,464.19	2,415.44	1,662.86	1,566.93	2,943.57	1,875.38
Massachusetts	6,433,422	7,968.51	2,144.09	1,917.93	2,071.73	1,299.07	535.70
Michigan	10,079,985	5,741.09	2,186.73	1,543.26	1,286.70	385.32	339.07
Minnesota	5,059,375	5,451.26	1,902.82	1,287.44	1,366.48	475.53	419.00
Mississippi	2,881,281	7,545.47	2,402.72	1,701.90	1,845.87	911.28	683.70
Missouri	5,704,484	7,691.08	2,368.08	1,733.15	1,517.24	1,400.94	671.68
Montana	917,621	7,729.15	2,522.83	1,631.54	2,112.48	541.93	920.38
Nebraska	1,739,291	6,324.35	2,274.49	1,570.64	1,444.21	349.69	685.32
Nevada	2,241,154	5,192.58	2,100.55	1017.53	872.31	656.92	545.27
New Hampshire	1,287,687	5,707.26	2,203.93	1037.83	1,448.54	573.37	443.59
New Jersey	8,638,396	6,213.98	2,128.68	1,642.66	1,329.06	632.18	481.41
New Mexico	1,874,614	9,994.53	2,340.70	1,216.66	2,305.69	3,104.09	1027.38
New York	19,190,115	7,185.89	2,110.76	1,746.95	2,479.12	404.29	444.77
North Carolina	8,320,146	6,157.35	2,236.85	1,309.86	1,381.33	451.33	777.98
North Dakota	8,407,248	9,033.36	2,283.24	2,566.52	2,425.04	627.20	1,131.36
Ohio	11,435,798	6,112.53	2,216.51	1,482.81	1,371.79	572.55	468.87
Oklahoma	3,511,532	7,191.72	2,498.19	1,567.79	1,462.51	708.48	954.74
Oregon	3,559,596	5,970.74	2,254.22	1,445.96	1,433.65	336.59	500.32
Pennsylvania	12,365,455	7,306.68	2,593.69	2,034.35	1,506.09	658.02	514.54
Rhode Island	1,076,164	7,467.11	2,355.21	1,664.22	2,076.22	612.44	759.02
South Carolina	4,147,152	6,760.82	2,436.79	1,322.92	1,439.30	871.53	690.28
South Dakota	764,309	8,114.01	2,366.77	2,146.85	2,221.00	498.44	880.85
Tennessee	5,841,748	7,292.74	2,352.80	1,527.23	1,550.40	1,287.62	574.70
Texas	22,118,509	6,349.93	1,769.96	1,316.41	1,285.01	1348.34	630.21
Utah	2,351,467	5,741.00	1,655.08	872.38	1,209.84	1133.27	870.44
Vermont	619,107	7,176.49	2,192.99	1,337.26	2,150.36	914.33	581.55
Virginia	7,386,330	11,163.05	2,647.23	1,275.38	1,067.64	4,175.11	1,997.69
Washington	6,131,445	7,073.06	2,215.97	1,388.48	1,448.40	1081.07	939.13
West Virginia	1,810,354	7,858.35	3,128.21	1,683.40	1,967.51	367.28	711.96
Wisconsin	5,472,299	5,525.40	2,123.12	1,330.69	1,378.53	366.87	326.20
Wyoming	501,242	8,432.05	2,298.04	1,201.40	3,224.42	690.26	1017.93
District of Columbia	563,384	61,680.52	3,433.26	4,205.84	7,650.50	20,192.09	26,198.83
American Samoa	57,844	3,424.52	708.59	211.18	1,905.87	478.66	120.22
Fed States of Micronesia	108,143	1,343.26	4.36	68.81	1,260.63	9.45	0.00
Guam	163,593	9,405.53	1,262.47	559.38	2,447.10	3,213.96	1,922.61
Marshall Islands	56,429	3,219.24	17.57	0.87	1,166.95	2,033.84	0.00
Northern Marianas	76,129	1,847.56	293.18	190.56	1175.68	110.67	77.47
Palau	19,717	2,697.44	23.07	69.05	2,571.93	33.39	0.00
Puerto Rico	38,778,532	3,780.10	1,412.23	733.97	1,239.56	144.72	249.63
Virgin Islands	108,814	5,652.50	1,339.50	981.42	2,588.45	236.57	506.54

Source: U.S. Department of Commerce, Bureau of the Census, September 2004.

Note: U.S. total population and per capita figures in the top row include only the 50 states and the District of Columbia, the U.S. Outlying Areas represented at the bottom of the table are excluded from this figure.

(a) All population figures represent resident population as of July 1, 2003.

Table 2.11
PERCENT DISTRIBUTION OF FEDERAL GOVERNMENT EXPENDITURE, BY MAJOR OBJECT CATEGORY, BY STATE AND OUTLYING AREA: FISCAL YEAR 2003
(In dollars)

State and outlying area	Percent distribution of United States resident population— July 1, 2003 (a)	Total	Retirement and disability	Other direct payments	Grants	Procurement	Salaries and wages
United States	100%	100%	100%	100%	100%	100%	100%
Alabama	1.5	1.8	1.9	1.7	1.5	2.2	1.5
Alaska	0.2	0.4	0.2	0.1	0.7	0.5	0.8
Arizona	1.9	1.8	1.9	1.5	1.6	2.6	1.6
Arkansas	0.9	0.9	1.1	1.0	1.0	0.3	0.6
California	12.0	10.7	9.6	11.1	11.6	11.3	9.8
Colorado	1.5	1.4	1.3	1.1	1.4	1.6	2.1
Connecticut	1.2	1.4	1.2	1.3	1.2	2.6	0.7
Delaware	0.3	0.2	0.3	0.3	0.3	0.1	0.2
Florida	5.8	5.5	7.1	6.7	4.0	3.3	4.6
Georgia	2.9	2.5	2.6	2.6	2.4	1.6	3.8
Hawaii	0.4	0.5	0.5	0.3	0.4	0.6	1.4
Idaho	0.5	0.4	0.5	0.4	0.4	0.5	0.4
Illinois	4.3	3.5	3.9	4.5	3.6	1.7	3.1
Indiana	2.1	1.7	2.1	2.1	1.7	1.0	1.1
Iowa	1.0	0.9	1.1	1.0	0.9	0.3	0.5
Kansas	0.9	0.9	1.0	1.0	0.8	0.6	1.0
Kentucky	1.4	1.5	1.6	1.4	1.5	1.6	1.5
Louisiana	1.5	1.5	1.5	1.9	1.8	1.0	1.3
Maine	0.4	0.5	0.5	0.4	0.6	0.4	0.4
Maryland	1.9	2.8	2.1	2.1	2.0	5.0	4.9
Massachusetts	2.2	2.5	2.2	2.8	3.0	2.6	1.6
Michigan	3.4	2.8	3.5	3.5	2.9	1.2	1.6
Minnesota	1.7	1.3	1.5	1.5	1.6	0.7	1.0
Mississippi	1.0	1.1	1.1	1.1	1.2	0.8	0.9
Missouri	1.9	2.1	2.1	2.2	2.0	2.4	1.8
Montana	0.3	0.3	0.4	0.3	0.4	0.2	0.4
Nebraska	0.6	0.5	0.6	0.6	0.6	0.2	0.6
Nevada	0.8	0.6	0.7	0.5	0.4	0.4	0.6
New Hampshire	0.4	0.4	0.4	0.3	0.4	0.2	0.3
New Jersey	2.9	2.6	2.9	3.2	2.6	1.7	2.0
New Mexico	0.6	0.9	0.7	0.5	1.0	1.8	0.9
New York	6.5	6.7	6.4	7.5	10.8	2.4	4.1
North Carolina	2.8	2.5	3.0	2.5	2.6	1.2	3.1
North Dakota	0.2	0.3	0.2	0.4	0.3	0.1	0.3
Ohio	3.9	3.4	4.0	3.8	3.6	2.0	2.5
Oklahoma	1.2	1.2	1.4	1.2	1.2	0.8	1.6
Oregon	1.2	1.0	1.3	1.2	1.2	0.4	0.8
Pennsylvania	4.2	4.4	5.0	5.6	4.2	2.5	3.0
Rhode Island	0.4	0.4	0.4	0.4	0.5	0.2	0.4
South Carolina	1.4	1.4	1.6	1.2	1.4	1.1	1.4
South Dakota	0.3	0.3	0.3	0.4	0.4	0.1	0.3
Tennessee	2.0	2.1	2.2	2.0	2.1	2.3	1.6
Texas	7.5	6.8	6.2	6.5	6.4	9.1	6.6
Utah	0.8	0.7	0.6	0.5	0.6	0.8	1.0
Vermont	0.2	0.2	0.2	0.2	0.3	0.2	0.2
Virginia	2.5	4.0	3.1	2.1	1.8	9.4	7.0
Washington	2.1	2.1	2.1	1.9	2.0	2.0	2.7
West Virginia	0.6	0.7	0.9	0.7	0.8	0.2	0.6
Wisconsin	1.9	1.5	1.8	1.6	1.7	0.6	0.8
Wyoming	0.2	0.2	0.2	0.1	0.4	0.1	0.2
Dist. of Columbia	0.2	1.7	0.3	0.5	1.0	3.5	7.0
American Samoa	0.0	0.0	0.0	0.0	0.0	0.0	0.0
Fed. States of Micronesia	0.0	0.0	0.0	0.0	0.0	0.0	0.0
Guam	0.1	0.1	0.0	0.0	0.1	0.2	0.1
Marshall Islands	0.0	0.0	0.0	0.0	0.0	0.0	0.0
No. Mariana Islands	0.0	0.0	0.0	0.0	0.0	0.0	0.0
Palau	0.0	0.0	0.0	0.0	0.0	0.0	0.0
Puerto Rico	1.3	0.7	0.9	0.6	1.1	0.2	0.5
Virgin Islands	0.0	0.0	0.0	0.0	0.1	0.0	0.0
Undistributed	0.0	1.7	0.0	0.0	0.0	9.8	1.0

Source: U.S. Department of Commerce, Bureau of the Census, September 2004.

Note: Values for the 50 states, the District of Columbia and the U.S. outlying areas were used in calculating these distributions.

(a) All population figures represent resident population as of July 1, 2003.

Table 2.12
FEDERAL GOVERNMENT EXPENDITURE FOR DEFENSE DEPARTMENT AND ALL OTHER AGENCIES, BY STATE AND OUTLYING AREA: FISCAL YEAR 2003

State and outlying area	Federal expenditure (millions of dollars)		Per capita federal expenditure (dollars) (a)		Percent distribution of federal expenditure		Department of Energy, defense related activities (millions of dollars) (b)
	Department of Defense	All other federal agencies	Department of Defense	All other federal agencies	Department of Defense	All other federal agencies	
United States	$319,506	$1,741,978	$1,030	$5,880	$100	$100	$15,555
Alabama	7,907	5,636	1,756.87	6,435.29	2.5	1.7	22
Alaska	2,307	27,916	3,556.45	8,687.14	0.7	0.3	3
Arizona	90,885	16,895	1,771.29	5,002.15	3.1	1.6	0
Arkansas	1,445	180,466	530.14	6,198.50	0.5	1.0	0
California	39,240	23,690	1105.82	5,085.78	12.3	10.4	1,248
Colorado	5,184	23,690	1,139.14	5,205.88	1.6	1.4	719
Connecticut	8,545	20,050	2,453.13	5,755.92	2.7	1.2	0
Delaware	564	4,497	689.81	5,500.90	0.2	0.3	0
Florida	15,969	97,372	938.3	5,721.34	5.0	5.6	8
Georgia	9,003	42,907	1,036.69	4,940.50	2.8	2.5	0
Hawaii	4,484	6,785	3,565.89	5,395.01	1.4	0.4	0
Idaho	653	8,002	477.86	5,856.22	0.2	0.5	758
Illinois	4,938	68,082	390.22	5,380.47	1.5	3.9	253
Indiana	3,650	31,874	589.15	5,144.66	1.1	1.8	0
Iowa	1008	16,542	342.35	5,618.71	0.3	0.9	0
Kansas	2,520	15,688	925.24	5,760.31	0.8	0.9	0
Kentucky	5,289	25,864	1284.51	6,280.91	1.7	1.5	15
Louisiana	3,605	28,042	801.69	6,236.55	1.1	1.6	0
Maine	1,813	8,152	1,388.81	6,243.49	0.6	0.5	0
Maryland	11,412	46,235	2,071.48	8,392.71	3.6	2.7	190
Massachusetts	7,422	43,843	1153.61	6,814.90	2.3	2.5	0
Michigan	3,462	54,408	343.49	5,297.60	1.1	3.1	0
Minnesota	2,120	25,460	418.99	5,032.27	0.7	1.5	0
Mississippi	3,644	18,096	1,264.82	6,280.64	1.1	1.0	1
Missouri	7,991	35,883	1,400.78	6,290.31	2.5	2.1	391
Montana	556	6,536	606.44	7,122.71	0.2	0.4	0
Nebraska	1,099	9,901	631.66	5,692.69	0.3	0.6	0
Nevada	1,368	10,269	610.62	4,581.97	0.4	0.6	716
New Hampshire	827	6,522	642.27	5,064.99	0.3	0.4	0
New Jersey	5,330	48,349	617.04	5,596.94	1.7	2.8	0
New Mexico	2,158	16,578	1,151.08	8,843.45	0.7	1.0	3,469
New York	6,286	131,612	327.55	6,858.33	2.0	7.6	349
North Carolina	7,508	44,259	892.99	5,264.36	2.3	2.5	0
North Dakota	712	5,014	1122.56	7,910.10	0.2	0.3	0
Ohio	6,777	63,124	592.65	5,519.87	2.1	3.6	508
Oklahoma	3,986	21,268	1,135.14	6,056.57	1.2	1.2	0
Oregon	1,097	20,156	308.22	5,662.52	0.3	1.2	0
Pennsylvania	8,054	82,296	651.33	6,655.35	2.5	4.7	359
Rhode Island	1080	6,956	1003.17	6,463.94	0.3	0.4	0
South Carolina	4,257	22,871	1026.55	5,734.27	1.3	1.4	1,640
South Dakota	501	5,700	655.71	7,458.29	0.2	0.3	0
Tennessee	3,493	239,109	598.01	6,694.73	1.1	2.2	1,200
Texas	30,354	110,097	1,372.32	4,977.61	9.5	6.3	428
Utah	3,102	10,398	1,319.17	4,421.83	1.0	0.6	0
Vermont	610	3,833	985.77	6,190.72	0.2	0.2	0
Virginia	32,684	49,770	4,424.90	6,738.15	10.2	2.9	0
Washington	7,703	35,665	1,256.30	5,816.75	2.4	2.0	2,115
West Virginia	510	13,717	281.5	7,576.86	0.2	0.8	18
Wisconsin	1,805	28,432	329.84	5,195.56	0.6	1.6	0
Wyoming	374	3,852	746.77	7,685.28	0.1	0.2	8
Dist. of Columbia	3,321	31,429	5,894.45	55,786.07	1.0	1.8	1,136
American Samoa	13	185	231.67	319,286.00	0.0	0.0	0
Fed. States of Micronesia ...	0	145	0	1,343.26	0.0	0.0	0
Guam	817	722	4,992.00	4,413.52	0.3	0.0	0
Marshall Islands	114	67	2,028.01	1,191.23	0.0	0.0	0
No. Mariana Islands	9	132	117.56	1,729.99	0.0	0.0	0
Palau	1	53	33.39	2,664.04	0.0	0.0	0
Puerto Rico	771	13,890	198.85	3,581.25	0.2	0.8	0
Virgin Islands	20	595	180.85	5,471.65	0.0	0.0	0
Undistributed	18,149	16,217	0	0	5.7	0.9	3

Source: U.S. Department of Commerce, Bureau of the Census, September 2004.
(a) All population figures represent resident population as of July 1, 2003.
(b) These data are presented for illustrative purposes only. They were compiled from preiminary FY 2005 state budget allocation tables that were prepared for submission to Congress and that were found on the Department of Energy Web site.

Table 2.13
STATE RANKINGS FOR PER CAPITA AMOUNTS
OF FEDERAL GOVERNMENT EXPENDITURE: FISCAL YEAR 2003

State	Total	Retirement and disability	Other direct payments	Grants	Procurement	Salaries and wages
Alabama	9	2	9	23	7	19
Alaska	1	50	49	1	4	1
Arizona	26	35	44	40	8	28
Arkansas	28	7	12	15	49	40
California	36	48	30	27	18	32
Colorado	32	46	46	38	15	9
Connecticut	8	33	18	19	5	45
Delaware	37	15	28	29	50	29
Florida	30	3	6	49	29	34
Georgia	40	44	36	45	33	11
Hawaii	6	14	43	20	6	2
Idaho	33	42	45	36	16	27
Illinois	43	43	19	44	40	37
Indiana	46	34	27	47	37	48
Iowa	42	21	20	39	44	47
Kansas	29	24	16	43	23	16
Kentucky	16	10	25	16	13	18
Louisiana	25	38	5	14	24	30
Maine	15	5	32	11	19	24
Maryland	3	12	14	17	3	4
Massachusetts	11	36	4	10	11	36
Michigan	44	32	23	41	43	49
Minnesota	49	45	39	35	39	46
Mississippi	17	13	10	13	21	23
Missouri	14	16	8	21	9	25
Montana	13	8	17	8	36	12
Nebraska	34	25	21	28	47	22
Nevada	50	41	48	50	28	35
New Hampshire	47	30	47	25	34	44
New Jersey	35	37	15	37	30	41
New Mexico	4	20	41	5	2	6
New York	22	40	7	3	42	43
North Carolina	38	27	38	32	41	15
North Dakota	5	23	1	4	31	5
Ohio	39	28	26	34	35	42
Oklahoma	21	9	22	24	25	8
Oregon	41	26	29	31	48	39
Pennsylvania	19	6	3	22	27	38
Rhode Island	18	18	13	9	32	17
South Carolina	27	11	35	30	22	21
South Dakota	10	17	2	6	38	13
Tennessee	20	19	24	18	12	33
Texas	31	47	37	42	10	26
Utah	45	49	50	46	14	14
Vermont	23	31	33	7	20	31
Virginia	2	4	40	48	1	3
Washington	24	29	31	26	17	10
West Virginia	12	1	11	12	45	20
Wisconsin	48	39	34	33	46	50
Wyoming	7	22	42	2	26	7

Source: U.S. Department of Commerce, Bureau of Census, September 2004.
Note: States are ranked from largest per capita amount of federal funds (1) to smallest per capita amount of federal funds (50). Rankings are based upon per capita amounts shown in Table 2.10. Federal funds for loans and insurance coverage are excluded from consideration in this table. Also excluded are per capita amounts from the District of Columbia and the U.S. Outlying Areas.

Chapter Three

STATE LEGISLATIVE BRANCH

The "Good" Legislature
By Alan Rosenthal

This article, based on the author's book, Heavy Lifting: The Job of the American Legislature *(CQ Press, 2004), explores the factors that indicate whether a legislature is "good" or not. Neither a legislature's appearance, structure, nor it's product ought to be considered indicative. A legislature's performance of its principal functions is what counts. Legislatures do best at representing constituencies and constituents, next best at lawmaking, and least well at balancing the power of the executive. Critical to legislative performance of the latter two functions are leadership and standing committee systems.*

Any student of state legislatures at some time or another has been asked whether the legislature in a particular state is a good one, not so good, or even bad. Just how good or how bad? This is a difficult question to answer intelligently, but that hardly means that an answer is not given by academics and others. Often the media furnishes its own answer, at least to whether the legislature in its state is good or bad. The media usually tilts negatively, as is exemplified by the *New York Times* which characterizes the New York Legislature as the most dysfunctional in the nation.

What Standards Should We Use?

How a legislature is rated depends greatly on the standards applied to the assessment. Three of the most frequently used standards are appearance, product and structure.

The public, in general, goes by the standard of *appearance*. In most states the people do not like what they would see, if they were looking (which they aren't). The legislature is disheveled at best, ragged at worst. It is unpredictable and frustratingly elusive. Actually, it is a wonderful example of democratic politics. But while most Americans applaud democracy in principle, not many appreciate the nitty-gritty of democracy in practice. Add to the unappealing appearance of the legislature and the legislative process, the picture conveyed by a media that stresses the negative, conflictual and scandalous. The result is low marks for the legislature by the public in the states.

Product is an obvious standard. Most people care more about what comes out of the legislature than what goes on inside it. Political interest groups do not have much trouble assessing a legislature. A business organization, teachers association, or environmental group—any such entity judges a legislature in terms of what it does for or against its interests. Given this standard, one group's "good" legislature is another group's "bad" legislature. It is probably not possible to agree on product requisite for a

legislature's goodness, except in the most general sense. In any case, product as a standard rests on the assumption that the legislature is a means to an end, the end being what it produces. However, the legislature is not only or primarily a means to an end; rather, it is an end in itself. That is because the institution and the process allow for a democratic means of reaching settlements among the different values, interests and priorities that people have.

Structure as a standard came into prominence during the legislative reform movement of the late 1960s, the 1970s, and the early 1980s. A major assessment of the 50 state legislatures was conducted by the Citizens Conference on State Legislatures as part of the campaign for legislative reform. State legislatures were ranked from 1 to 50, depending on many factors, nearly all of which had to do with structure or capacity. Legislatures were awarded points if they had, among other things, deadlines for filing bills, superior offices for leaders, fewer than eighty members in the house, and so forth. The ranking that resulted from the evaluation—with California, New York and Illinois at the top—made as much sense as assessing a professional football team by the condition of its uniforms, the size of its locker rooms, and the cost of its training facilities rather than its performance on the field or the number of games it won and lost.

What matters is neither appearance, product, nor structure, but how the legislature functions, how it does its job. In short, what matters most is legislative performance.

The legislature's job is essentially threefold: representing, lawmaking, and balancing the power of the executive. The three components overlap, but they can be considered separately.

Representing constituencies and constituents entails legislators serving their districts' interests and expressing their constituencies' views. The former involves offering access to individuals and doing case work for them and bringing home the bacon, in the form of funding formulas and projects, to the district as a whole. The latter involves expressing the dominant policy positions of the constituency, that is first, if constituents care about an issue and second, if they generally agree as to what should be done about it.

Lawmaking involves the processes by which settlements are reached (or not reached) among contending values, interests, preferences and priorities which exist in the population and its organized groups and are represented and promoted in the legislature. In order to enact laws, including the most important one—the budget for the state, participants in the process engage in study, deliberation, strategizing, negotiation, compromise and attempts to build successive majorities.

Balancing the power of the executive. In a system of separated powers, such as ours, the legislature is obliged to check and balance the executive. Earlier in the nation's history, the legislature was the more powerful branch, but today the advantage is with the executive. Because the executive is one and the legislators are many (individuals who are also divided into contending parties and chambers), governors have the upper hand, should they choose to raise their arm. Unlike legislatures, chief executives can decide without having to build consensus. They can prioritize and focus their resources far more easily than can legislatures. And they have the bully pulpit—that is, access to the media—which allows them to build support among the public and indirectly within the legislature. To balance a strong executive, a legislature must be able to review seriously the governor's budgetary and programmatic priorities, ensuring that they are consonant with the legislature's. It must be able to initiate major items on its own, without depending upon the governor always to set the agenda.

How Well Do Legislatures Perform?

If representation were their only job, legislatures would deserve high ratings—on average an A or an A-. The "good" legislature would be practically ubiquitous. Different legislatures do it differently, as would have to be expected. Representing a district of nearly 850,000 people, as is the job of a California senator, is not at all the same as representing a district of 16,459 people, as is the job of a Wyoming senator. Either way, legislators offer constituents a connection to the political and governmental world–that is, if constituents want to take advantage of such a connection.

There is no question that most lawmakers take constituent service seriously and spend much of their time (and/or staff time) doing it. Serving the interests of constituents and constituency is a relatively simple matter and legislators, no matter what the nature of their constituencies, can be expected to try to help people out.

Expressing the views of constituents and constituency is more problematic, in particular because on most issues with which the legislature deals no views exist. On a few issues, however, a substantial proportion of the constituency does care (at least somewhat), as does the representative. Most often the views of the dominant constituency groups and those of the representative coincide. Only infrequently do they clash. At these times, depending on the issue, representatives will either take a Burkean position, voting according to their conscience or judgment, or a politically prudential position, going along with the dominant views of the constituency.

It may be argued, of course, that not everyone in the state is represented equally by legislatures. Shouldn't there be more women, minorities, blue-collar laborers, and younger people in legislatures? What about Republicans who live in Democratic dominated districts and vice versa? Are these political minorities fairly represented? Despite the fact that the legislature does not mirror the population of the state in demographic characteristics and despite the predominance of single-member districts in which minority party voters are shut out, the representational system works well. This is partly because the views of constituents are represented not only by the legislators they elect to office, but also by political parties and interest groups to which constituents belong or with whom they agree.

Lawmaking is even more variable than representation. What should we expect by way of legislating in bodies that work to resolve conflict and achieve settlements, and that have to deal with difficult problems facing the state and its people? What, in short, makes for good lawmaking? Two important elements are study and deliberation. The fact is that both study and deliberation play substantial roles—indeed, the largest roles—in lawmaking processes, even though attention usually focuses more on political gamesmanship. Other important elements are strategy and negotiations. Whatever a bill's substantive merits may be, it is necessary to put together and keep together the support required to get it enacted into law. Most members of what constitutes a majority have made a decision on the substantive and political merits of the case. Relatively few have to be won over through negotiations and bargaining. Still, disagreements—among members, between chambers, and with the governor—often have to be worked out.

So, what constitutes better legislative performance at lawmaking? Each legislature engages in lawmaking in somewhat different fashion depending on the situation, circumstances, and personalities involved. The lawmaking process varies among legislatures, nor is it the same from issue to issue or day to day in the same legislature. Just as there are various ways to skin a cat, so there are various ways to make law. Good lawmaking requires a nice combination of ingredients, with substantial amounts of study and deliberation included. In this process, the role of standing committees is extremely important. It is here that measures are reviewed, shaped, and agreed on and where study and deliberation are mainly brought to bear. Standing committees are said to be the workhorses of the legislature. Indeed, they have to be the workhorses, if the legislature is to be "good." This is not to minimize the importance of political considerations—that is, how a policy proposal plays in the state and what the public thinks of it.

Overall, legislatures do reasonably well at lawmaking, but not as well as they do representing. Here, they would receive a grade of B+ or B. In any particular state it is easy to second-guess the legislature and the process. Who can say if there is a better way to pass a bill, or defeat one? A legislature probably always can do better in the study and deliberation department, but perhaps at the risk of slighting political aspects. But the process is not really manageable, depending as it does on contingencies of all kinds. As long as there is disagreement among members, interest groups to deal with, another house to worry about limited time, or a governor who wants a piece of the action, the process can take just about any course. As long as study and deliberation play a substantial part, different positions are expressed, and majorities have their way, legislatures essentially are making law the way it ought to be made.

Performing the job of balancing the power of the executive overlaps that of lawmaking to a considerable extent. Balancing, however, requires more—that the legislature share with the governor the capacity to participate as equals in setting the priorities and policies for the state. Here is where legislatures are at the greatest disadvantage and where they perform least well. On average, they would receive no higher than a B or B- for this part of their job.

When it comes to balancing variation from legislature to legislature is easier to specify. In a few states legislatures appear to hold a predominant position, because they are accorded power to draft the state budget or because they have traditionally shaped the budget and the executive has acquiesced. In most

states, however, legislatures have to assert themselves if they want to balance their governor, let alone their budget. Some of these legislatures have managed a spirit of independence, even with an executive controlled by the same party as that which commanded a majority in each house of the legislature. They have proven to be coequal branches of government. Other legislatures have chosen not to challenge their governor, either because party was too strong a bond or because they lacked the will to assert themselves.

The balance of executive-legislative power depends partly on constitutional provisions, although constitutions can be changed. It depends also on what have become customary ways of doing things in a state. Finally, it depends on the personalities and politics at the time. At the very least, what is necessary for the legislature to do its balancing job is recognition that it ought to do it and that it have the will to try to do it.

What Conditions Have to Exist for a Legislature to be "Good"?

What appears vital to the legislature's performance are the following:

1. A connection by legislators to their constituencies and a responsiveness to constituency views where they exist.

2. A balance between the deliberative aspects of lawmaking on the one hand and the political aspects on the other, ensuring that the process takes into account arguments as to the merits of a measure. This ordinarily means that a legislative chamber delegates a major role to its standing committees, which have policy expertise, some continuity of membership, and the respect of the larger body.

3. Effective legislative leadership. Although leadership matters relatively little with regard to representation, it is hard to imagine the lawmaking process working without committee, party and chamber leadership. Among the many responsibilities of leadership are finding common ground, facilitating compromise, forging consensus, and enabling a legislative majority to find and work its will. It is even harder to imagine that the power of the executive could be balanced without effective leadership. Legislative leaders have to represent the senate and the house to the governor and then negotiate the best deal possible from their chamber's point of view.

What Will Make Legislatures Better?

It is easier to identify what will make legislatures worse than what will make them better. Term limits, for example, clearly will make them worse. The effects of their adoption in the 1990s are beginning to be felt. These effects vary from state to state, but overall term limits are impeding the legislature's job performance. This is demonstrated in a large-scale study conducted by the National Conference of State Legislatures, The Council of State Governments, the State Legislative Leaders Foundation, and a number of political scientists. Leaders generally are weakened, committees are more frequently bypassed, and governors are advantaged vis-a-vis the legislature. Although the results of investigation in a number of term-limited states are inconclusive on the point, a survey of the nation's legislators indicates that representation also suffers. Legislators in term-limited states reported spending less time than legislators in non-term-limited states keeping in touch with constituents, engaging in constituent service, securing state funds and projects for their districts, and being responsive to the demands and views of their constituents.

The first rule for physicians is "do no harm." That rule might well be applicable to the efforts of those who are critical of and want to bring substantial change to state legislatures. State legislatures are far from perfect, but they seem to be doing what they were intended to do. Ways in which their job performance can be improved and in which legislatures can become better probably do exist, but they are difficult to identify and even more difficult to implement effectively. Mechanistic reforms are not the answer, if institutional improvement is the objective. Rather, leaders and members have to want to build and/or refashion their institutions, have to be around long enough for changes they institute to take hold, and have to be succeeded by colleagues who are also committed to maintaining their legislatures as effective institutions. No single agenda for legislative improvement makes sense everywhere; no formulas exist that will work no matter what or where the problem. Making the legislature "good" is work that must be continually in progress and work that must be specific to each of the nation's states.

About the Author

Alan Rosenthal is a professor of public policy at the Eagleton Institute of Politics, Rutgers University. He has worked with legislatures throughout the nation and participated in programs of the National Conference of State Legislatures and The Council of State Governments. His latest book, from which this article is drawn, is *Heavy Lifting: The Job of the American Legislature* (CQ Press, 2004).

2004 Legislative Elections
By Tim Storey

Before launching into the analysis of the 2004 state legislative elections, it is instructive to go back two years to the last major legislative elections. The year 2002 was a banner year for the Republican Party in legislatures; they seized eight legislative chambers and claimed bragging rights by taking the majority of legislative seats nationwide for the first time in 50 years.

When it comes to state legislatures, Democrats bounced back big in 2004 despite their defeat at the top of the ticket where George Bush extended his stay in the White House by defeating John Kerry by a relatively close 35 electoral vote margin. The Democrats took control of seven legislative chambers and had a quasi-victory by gaining ties in both the Iowa Senate and Montana House—both controlled by the GOP before the election. The Democrats also regained the title of holding the most seats although their margin is a tiny fraction of 1 percent—a mere one seat at press time.

Republicans were not without victories in 2004 and some of them were historic. Helped in part by President Bush's coattails, they won four legislative chambers. Republicans still control more legislatures than the Democrats, but it's as close as possible without being tied. As 2005 sessions were gaveled to order, Republicans controlled 20 legislatures, Democrats held 19, and 10 were split with neither party having both legislative chambers. Nebraska is not only a unicameral legislature but also nonpartisan. Before the election, the breakdown was 21 Republican legislatures, 17 Democratic and 11 split.

The number of chambers controlled by each party also ended up very close after the election. Democrats hold 47 chambers—only two less than the 49 legislative bodies where Republicans have the majority. Two legislative chambers are tied in 2005—the Iowa Senate now deadlocked at 25–25, and the Montana House knotted at 50–50.

There were regular legislative elections in 85 chambers in 2004. All states except Alabama, Louisiana, Maryland, Mississippi, New Jersey and Virginia had seats up in 2004. In Michigan and Minnesota, just the House of Representatives were up for election—not the Senates. Overall, 79 percent, or 5,809, of the nation's legislative seats held scheduled elections. In 35 percent of those races, a major party candidate did not have opposition from the opposite party but may have had an opponent from a third party.

Control of Legislative Seats

Perhaps the parity in state legislatures is best understood by looking at the total number of seats held by each party. There are 7,382 total legislative seats in the 50 states. Of those, 7,316 are held by partisans from the two major political parties. Third party legislators hold 16 seats, and Nebraska voters choose the 49 senators there in a non-partisan election. As of mid-January 2005, the difference between the two major parties was a miniscule one seat, with the advantage going to the Democrats. That means that the Democrats have a .00014 percent edge over Republicans in the total number of seats held—almost exact parity. Heading into 2004 elections, Republicans had an advantage of just under 1 percent or 65 seats. Democrats closed the gap in November. The Democrats success came despite losing the race for the White House. This was only the sixth time since 1940 that the party winning the White House actually lost seats in state legislatures. The last time that happened was in 1992 when Bill Clinton won the presidency but Democrats lost well over 100 seats in legislatures.

Altered States

In every two-year election cycle, an average of 12 legislative chambers sees a shift in majority control. Democrats began the election cycle on a good note by taking control of the previously tied New Jersey Senate in the 2003 election. Last November, 13 legislative chambers switched party control bringing the total number of switches in this round to 14.

Republicans won control of four chambers previously held by Democrats including three Southern legislative chambers long held by Democrats. In the Oklahoma House, Republicans gained nine seats to take control for the first time in 82 years. In 2004, Oklahoma became the 12th state where term limits have taken effect, and the first-year impact definitely helped make Oklahoma House Democrats vulnerable to a takeover. There are 15 states with term limits for legislators on the books.

Another big Southern victory for Republicans was in Georgia where the House went Republican for the first time since 1870. A court-drawn redistricting map in use for the first time in the November election left Democrats open to a sweep by Republican challengers. Including several post-election party switches by Democrats changing to Republican, the GOP picked up a stunning 25 seats in the Georgia House to establish a comfortable majority of 99–81.

Like Georgia, the Tennessee Senate went Republican for the first time since the 1870s. The Republican advantage there is only one seat and that narrow margin led to a coalition vote electing Democratic Senator John Wilder as leader. Wilder is the longest serving legislative leader in the United States having assumed his post in 1971. Republicans also seized the Indiana House, a chamber that has swapped hands 14 times since 1938. The Montana House and Connecticut Senate have switched party control 15 times

since 1938 earning them the top spot in terms of the highest number of shifts in majority party.

Another chamber that has gone back and forth between the two parties is the Washington Senate taken back in this election by the Democrats. That marks the fourth time in the last 10 years that the Washington Senate has changed hands—the most volatile chamber in that regard over the past decade due partially to a competitive redistricting plan drawn by a commission following the 2000 census.

Other Democratic gains were largely in the West, where the party saw five legislative bodies go to their column. The Washington Senate, Oregon Senate, Montana Senate, Colorado Senate and Colorado House all switched to Democratic majorities. The Oregon Senate was tied entering the election. Democrats have not controlled both chambers of the Colorado legislature since 1960.

In addition to the Western gains, Democrats lone

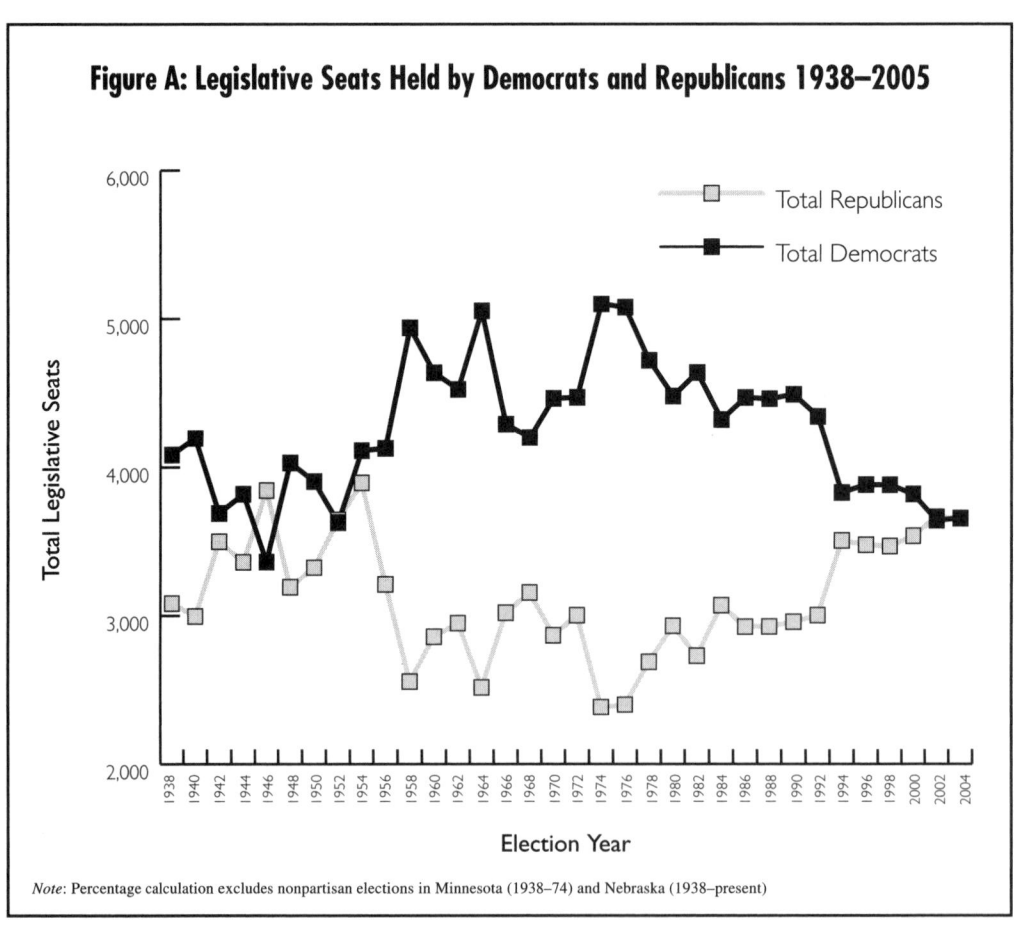

Figure A: Legislative Seats Held by Democrats and Republicans 1938–2005

Note: Percentage calculation excludes nonpartisan elections in Minnesota (1938–74) and Nebraska (1938–present)

bright spot in the South was in North Carolina where the House of Representatives moved back to the Democrats after two years of unsettled control that saw a tied chamber due to a legislator switching parties operate under a power sharing arrangement.

The only state in the Northeast where party control shifted was Vermont. Democrats took control of the Vermont House by picking up 14 seats to give them a comfortable working majority of 23 seats over the Republicans in 2005.

One Vote Does Count

The 2004 race for governor of Washington was one of the closest gubernatorial elections in American history. But a legislative race in Montana perhaps offered the best lesson for voters on why one vote really matters. After votes were tallied on election night, Constitution Party candidate Rick Jore appeared the victor by a mere two votes in

Montana House district 12 over the nearest challenger, Democrat Jeanne Windham. The Republican candidate received a few hundred votes less in the three-way race. Election officials conducted a recount that left the race exactly tied with 1,559 votes each. Under Montana law, if a legislative race ends in a tie, the sitting governor gets to select the person to serve. Outgoing Montana Gov. Judy Martz chose Jore saying that he better reflected the conservative views of the district. However, the Montana Supreme Court invalidated a handful of ballots counted for Jore and awarded the seat to Windham.

What makes this an even more cautionary tale is that the partisan composition of the Montana House ended up at 50 Republicans, 50 Democrats. The tied race proved critical in determining control of the Montana House. Voters should know that there are close races in every election, and sometimes, one vote decides the winner.

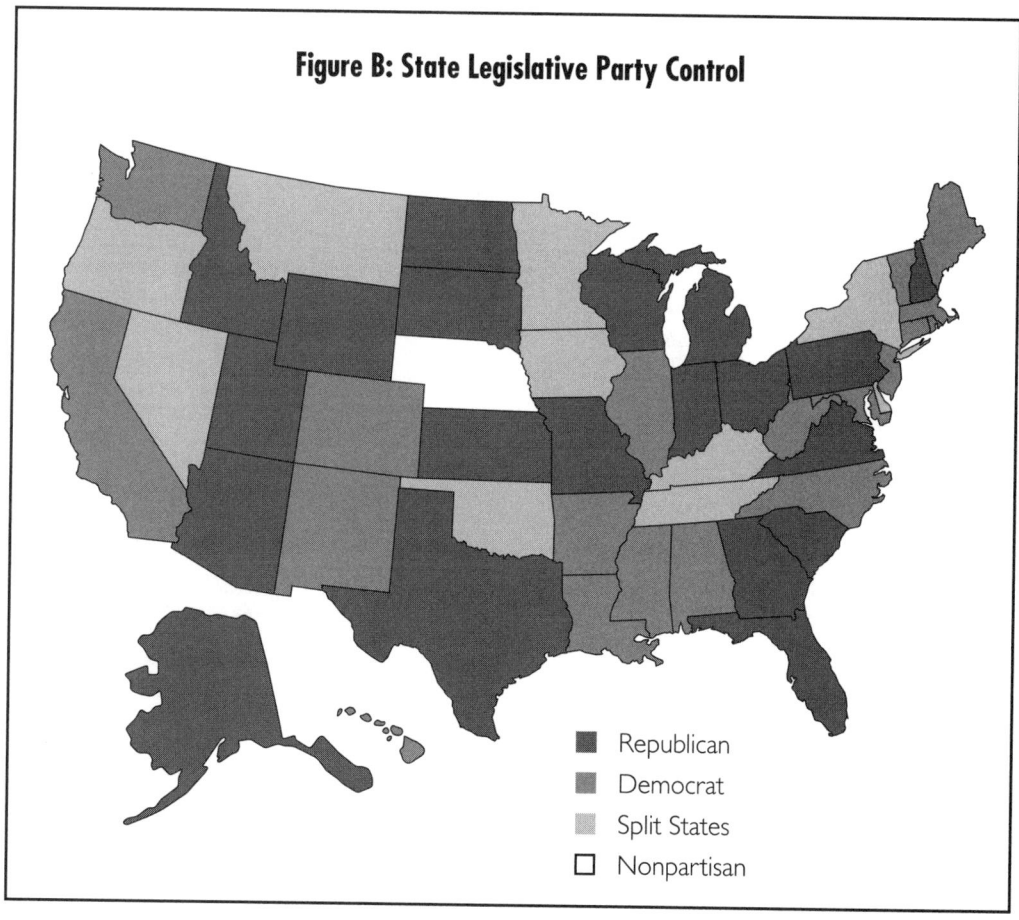

Figure B: State Legislative Party Control

- Republican
- Democrat
- Split States
- Nonpartisan

Regional Analysis

Democrats once again lost ground in the South, showing a net loss of 70 seats since the 2002 election. Republicans controlled not a single legislative chamber in the South until the 1994 election. In the 10 years since, they have made remarkable strides and now control half of the chambers in the region. The Democrats still have more seats in the South holding 53 percent of all Southern legislative seats down from 94 percent in 1960.

The strongest region for the GOP continues to be the Midwest, where they control 58 percent of all seats and only saw a net loss of one seat from 2002 to 2004. The Democrats made their largest gains in the East, picking up 58 seats during the last two years and in the West, where they netted 27 seats.

Divided Government

After factoring the winners in this year's 11 gubernatorial contests, the number of states with divided partisan control of government will once again be near a record high at 29—that is two less than the high mark of 31 last seen following the 1998 election. Democrats control all of state government in only eight states while Republicans claim both the legislature and governor in 12 states.

Turnover

Legislative turnover returned to normal levels in the 2004 election after spiking up in the post-redistricting election of 2002. Overall, 19.6 percent of the legislators will be new to their chambers in 2005. Some of those "freshmen" are actually moving from one chamber to the other or served previously in the legislature. That figure is considerably lower than the 26.3 percent turnover two years ago. Not surprisingly, the highest turnover was in the term limited states. The Maine Senate topped the list with just over 45 percent turnover. The Oklahoma House, where term limits took effect for the first time, saw 39.6 percent turnover in this election. Term limits prevented a total of 257 legislators in 12 states from running for reelection in the 2004 elections.

Demographics of Legislators

Since 1969, the number of women serving in legislatures has increased substantially from several hundred to 1,659 in 2005—or 22.5 percent. After three decades of growth, the number of women in legislatures has held steady in recent years. Colorado and Maryland currently have the highest percentages of women legislators, at 34 percent.

The 2000 census showed the percentage of Americans reporting Hispanic heritage was roughly equal to the percentage of African-Americans, at about 12.5 percent each. That equality is not evident in state legislatures, where just over 8 percent of legislators are black and only 3 percent are Latino. There are now 231 Hispanic state legislators according to a count by the National Association of Latino Elected Officials which is up 13 from 2003.

The average age of a state legislator is 53 years old. Lawyers remain the top occupational category but are only 16 percent of state legislators.

Conclusion

Only the Virginia House of Delegates and New Jersey Assembly stand for regular elections in 2005, so most legislators will get a break from campaigning. Several trends continued in 2004 legislative elections. The partisan competition for control of legislatures and state governments continued to grow in intensity resulting in near stalemate on Election Day. The costs of legislative campaigns continued to skyrocket in swing districts, and the sophistication of those campaigns continued to grow. The big question for 2006 is whether either party can break away and establish itself as the dominant party of legislatures.

About the Author

Tim Storey is a senior fellow in the Legislative Management Program of the National Conference of State Legislatures (NCSL) in Denver, Colo. He specializes in the areas of elections and redistricting as well as legislative staff organization and management. He has staffed NCSL's Redistricting Task Force since 1990 and authored many articles on the redistricting and elections process. Every two years, Storey leads NCSL's elections project tracking and analyzing the outcome of state legislative races and statewide ballot questions. He received his undergraduate degree from Mars Hill College and his master's degree from the Graduate School of Public Affairs of the University of Colorado.

The Effects of Legislative Term Limits
By Jennifer Drage Bowser

The following is a summary of the research conducted over the past three years by Joint Project on Term Limits. The project is a cooperative effort by the National Conference of State Legislatures, the Council of State Governments, the State Legislative Leaders Foundation and a group of legislative scholars.

The term limits movement of the 1990s may have run out of steam on the ballot, but the limits enacted between 1990 and 2000 certainly continue to have an impact in legislatures around the country. The first states to vote on implementing term limits were California, Colorado and Oklahoma in 1990, and the most recent state was Nebraska in 2000. In all, voters in 21 states approved legislative term limits. However, the limits have either been repealed by legislatures (in Idaho and Utah) or thrown out by state courts (in Massachusetts, Oregon, Washington and Wyoming) in six states, leaving 15 with term limits currently on the books. Twelve state legislatures presently operate under term limits, and limits in the remaining three will kick in between 2006 and 2010.

The Joint Project on Term Limits

The Joint Project on Term Limits (JPTL) was formed in 2000 in recognition of the fundamental changes term limits were expected to produce in state legislatures. Legislatures play a critical role in shaping and delivering state budgets and policies, and therefore an understanding of how term limits would reshape the legislative landscape is critical in maintaining the effectiveness the institution. The JPTL is a unique coalition of organizations and academics, comprised of the National Conference of State Legislatures, The Council of State Governments, the State Legislative Leaders Foundation, and a group of distin-

guished legislative scholars from various universities around the country.

The goal of the JPTL has been to identify the effects, both positive and negative, that term limits have on state legislatures, and to share ideas for adapting to the changes limits bring. It has sought to achieve this goal through a variety of methods, including case studies, data collection and survey work. Between 2001 and 2003, in-depth case studies were conducted in six states with term limits: Arizona, Arkansas, California, Colorado, Maine and Ohio. These states represent a range of types of legislatures, including part-time citizen legislatures, full-time professionalized legislatures and hybrid bodies. In 2003, case studies of three legislatures without term limits—Kansas, Illinois and Indiana—were conducted to form a control group, enabling researchers to iden-

Table A
STATES WITH LEGISLATIVE TERM LIMITS

State	Year enacted	House Limit	House First impact	Senate Limit	Senate First impact	Lifetime or consecutive
Arizona	1992	8	2000	8	2000	Consecutive
Arkansas	1992	6	1998	8	2000	Lifetime
California	1990	6	1996	8	1998	Lifetime
Colorado	1990	8	1998	8	1998	Consecutive
Florida	1992	8	2000	8	2000	Consecutive
Louisiana	1995	12	2007	12	2007	Consecutive
Maine	1993	8	1996	8	1996	Consecutive
Michigan	1992	6	1998	8	2002	Lifetime
Missouri (a)	1992	8	2002	8	2002	Lifetime
Montana	1992	8	2000	8	2000	Consecutive
Nebraska	2000	N.A.	N.A.	8	2006	Consecutive
Nevada	1996	12	2010	12	2010	Lifetime
Ohio	1992	8	2000	8	2000	Consecutive
Oklahoma (b)	1990	12	2004	12	2004	Lifetime
South Dakota	1992	8	2000	8	2000	Consecutive

Source: National Conference of State Legislatures.
Key:
N.A.—Not applicable
(a) Because of special elections in Missouri, eight House members were termed out in 2000 and one senator was termed out in 1998.
(b) Oklahoma's limits are not chamber-specific. Members are limited to a total of 12 years in the Legislature, which may be served in either chamber.

Table B
TURNOVER IN HOUSE CHAMBERS IN SELECT TERM LIMIT STATES (percent)

State	Average 1981–1990	Election years							
		1990	1992	1994	1996	1998	2000	2002	2004
Arizona	25%	25%	48%	35%	32%	25%	45% (a)	58%	33%
Arkansas	14	17	19	31	20	57 (a)	34	32	39
California	16	20	40	41	46 (a)	35	39	43	30
Colorado	30	22	35	28	34	35 (a)	37	29	28
Maine	25	25	34	48	42	30	31	48	38
Ohio	17	14	21	21	14	20	55 (a)	29	16

Sources: Data for 1981-2002: Gary Moncrief, Richard G. Niemi and Lynda W. Powell, "Time, Term Limits, and Turnover," *Legislative Studies Quarterly* XXIX (August 2004): 357-81. Data for 2004: National Conference of State Legislatures.
Key:
(a) Year of term limits' first impact.

tify which changes may be attributable to term limits and which may reflect broader institutional changes. In each case study, numerous interviews were conducted with legislators, legislative leaders, legislative staff, lobbyists, journalists and other observers of the legislature, and a wide array of data was collected.

In addition to the case studies, the JPTL has conducted two surveys. The first was a national survey of all legislators, conducted in 2002. It questioned legislators on their background, including occupations and prior elected offices held, and their attitudes and approaches to legislative work. The second survey was conducted in the nine case study states in 2003. It was sent to selected legislative observers, including senior legislative staff, experienced lobbyists and journalists, executive branch officials, and other individuals who had spent at least 10 years involved in or observing the legislature in one way or another. It asked questions about how the legislature had or had not changed in the past 10 years.

In all, the JPTL has collected the largest body of data ever gathered about the effects of term limits in multiple states.

The First Lesson: Results Vary

The first lesson to heed when studying term limits is that it is very difficult to generalize across states about their effects. What happens in Arkansas, a smaller population state with a citizen legislature, does not necessarily happen in Ohio, a large population state with a highly professionalized legislature. Results vary according to the type of limits too—states with shorter limits, such as Michigan's lifetime limit of six years in the House and eight in the Senate, are likely to see more dramatic effects than states with more generous limits, like Arizona's limit of no more than eight consecutive years per cham-

ber. What follows is a round-up of results of the JPTL to date.

Turnover

The most obvious effect of term limits is an increase in turnover. The increase is particularly dramatic in the first year of term limits' impact, when it is not uncommon for over half of a chamber to be ineligible to run for reelection. Over time, the turnover rates under term limits will likely level out. The immediate effect has been to increase turnover in the 10 house chambers where term limits had taken effect by 2000 by an average of 11.5 percent in the decade of 1991-2000 compared to 1981-1990.[1] In the 2004 elections, eight of the 10 highest turnover house chambers had term limits. The average turnover for all house chambers in 2004 was 20.6 percent, compared to 37.1 percent in term-limited house chambers.

High turnover is not necessarily a problem; in fact, many of the term limits states historically have high levels of turnover in their legislatures. The difference is that before term limits took hold, these legislatures generally had a handful of members who served for many years, and their leadership and expertise were a valuable resource to the institution. Term limits have removed these long-serving members, and the effects of that are proving to be profound.

Who Gets Elected

One of the term limits proponents' promises that was most appealing to voters was that term limits would bring more diversity to state legislatures. By and large, that has not happened. With a few exceptions, the numbers of female and minority legislators have not changed. Latinos have made gains in Arizona and California, but this is more likely attributable to the changing demographics of these states' populations than to term limits. The number

Table C
FEMALE LEGISLATORS IN SELECT TERM LIMIT STATES
(percent of total membership)

State	1993–1994	1995–1996	1997–1998	1999–2000	2001–2002	2003–2004	2005
Arizona	36%	30%	37%	36%	34%	27%	33%
Arkansas	10	13	17	15	13	16	16
California	24	20	22	26	28	30	31
Colorado	34	31	35	34	34	33	34
Maine	32	26	26	28	30	27	24
Ohio	22	24	22	21	22	20	20

Sources: 2005 election results and all data for California and Maine are from the Center for Women and Politics, Rutgers University. All other data from the Joint Project on Term Limits.

of women in the California legislature has grown dramatically, but JPTL analysts attribute this to factors other than term limits. For instance, the national women's group EMILY's List became more active in California during the 1990s, and Democrats made big gains during that period, leading to increases in both female and minority representation. The only state among the six JPTL case studies where an increase in female membership in the legislature may be attributable to term limits is Arkansas.

In most states, the average age of legislators has changed little. It has decreased by two years in Ohio, and in Arizona the Senate is becoming older in relation to the House, due to the house-to-senate migration that is becoming so common in term-limited legislatures.

One change that is certainly a result of term limits is that the legislature has become a rung on the career ladder for many elected officials. An increasing number of new legislators come to office with local or county legislative experience, and more choose to seek other elective office when their terms expire, rather than retiring from politics.

While one hears and reads much about the inexperience of new members in term limited legislatures, it is certainly not true that today's new members are less experienced or knowledgeable than the new members of the pre-term limits era. The problem is instead that there are so many more new members each session under term limits, and they have less time to learn.

Adaptations

States have responded to the huge influxes of new members with a remarkable array of new training programs. Dramatic improvements in new member orientations are universal in term limited legislatures. These sessions are often conducted in cooperation

with a university, include faculty pulled from legislative staff, state agencies, universities, think tanks and former legislators, and rely on a variety of training methods such as mock committee hearings and floor sessions. Curriculum includes instruction on legislative rules and procedures, policy issues, the budget process, computer systems, the roles of legislative staff, and in some legislatures, even bus tours of the state to make members familiar with the issues facing various regions. Other ideas include assigning veteran members to serve as mentors for new members, with a goal of providing continuous on-the-job training by helping the new members understand legislative procedures, conveying norms of legislative behavior, and passing on historical information about past legislative actions. Staff has reached out to new members with more summary documents, and an increased reliance on the web and electronic communications with members.

Legislative Leaders

Perhaps the most noticeable changes in many term limited legislatures have to do with leadership. Leaders rise to the top more quickly than before, but stay for a briefer period and wield less influence than in the past. Before term limits, leadership positions were often held by long-serving members whose tenure in leadership lasted for many years. Under term limits, the tenure of most presiding officers does not exceed two years, and they enter leadership with less legislative experience than in the past.

The path to leadership is evolving in many states. A near universal sentiment among those interviewed for the JPTL was that new members have to begin jockeying for leadership during their first term. In many states, a ladder has evolved, with presiding officers first serving as whip then majority leader before becoming speaker or president. The criteria for selecting leaders has changed in many states too—whereas leaders used to come to power through committee chairmanships or seniority, now many members look for leaders with campaign and fundraising skills.

The "lame duck" factor plays a critical role in the declining influence of party leaders in term limited legislatures. Since most leaders assume their leadership position during the last legislative session before they are termed out, members know their time is limited. They see less value in cooperating with a leader whose days are numbered, and leaders are less able to sanction members who challenge them. In short, members know that they can outwait a leader, and they do. What all of this adds up to is less procedural orderliness and diminished party discipline.

The role of leaders has changed under term limits too. They now have more responsibility than ever to educate inexperienced new members about basic procedures, processes and policies, and to explain the role of the legislature and pass on the norms of behavior for their chamber. This task becomes more difficult as leaders take on their position with limited legislative experience themselves. Leaders are also playing a greater role in fundraising and campaigns in many term limited states. This is particularly true in Ohio, where leadership has developed a highly organized system for aiding candidates in fundraising and campaigning through the caucuses. This has strengthened the leadership's role in the caucus in Ohio to the extent that the Ohio Legislature has not experienced the decline in leadership influence that other term-limited legislatures have.

A positive aspect of term limits is that it affords more members the opportunity to serve in leadership positions.

Adaptations

The Arkansas House increased their number of speakers pro tem from one to four, one from each congressional district, thus widening the speaker's leadership circle. They also established formal floor leader positions to help maintain party unity. In Colorado, staff has prepared leadership notebooks with calendar deadlines, procedural rules, and sketches of common floor situations, problems and reactions.

Committees

Most interviewees reported that committees are weaker and less collegial and courteous under term limits, due to the high turnover in committee chairs and the reduced legislative and policy experience of

members. Research in California indicates that committee gatekeeping has declined significantly. It is difficult for inexperienced legislators to identify problematic legislation, so fewer bills are killed in committee. The situation in Colorado is similar, where bills are less well-crafted when passed to the floor. In Maine, interview-ees report that members give less deference to the work of committees, and committee reports are more likely to be challenged on the floor than in the past, even if they were adopted unanimously or with large majorities.

Adaptations

Arizona reduced the number of committees to make up for the shortage of qualified chairs. In Arizona and Colorado, new members serve as vice-chair on committees, and this is viewed as a training position for an eventual move to chair. In Arkansas, each of the 10 House standing committees now has three permanent subcommittees, each with a chair and a vice-chair, giving many people committee responsibility and experience. In Maine, committee staff maintains files including bills considered, testimony received and amendments offered for several sessions before they are transferred to state archives.

Staff

The importance, and in some cases, the influence of legislative staff has grown under term limits. Legislators rely more than ever on nonpartisan staff for roles they have traditionally filled—providing procedural advice, policy history, and revenue and budgetary analysis. Interviewees in all case studies states, however, reported that non-partisan staff organizations have made significant efforts to remain nonpartisan and avoid providing policy advice. As a result, partisan staff has increased in both number and influence in many term limited states.

In all of the case studies states, staff report an increased workload under term limits. In addition to their traditional roles, they are called upon now to provide historical information on how past legislatures dealt with issues and to explain basic principles about issues. They explain legislative rules and procedures, and script the phrases used to make motions and move legislative actions. In many ways, legislative staff now represent the key repository of institutional memory in the legislature.

Adaptations

In many term limited legislatures, the number of staff, particularly partisan staff, has increased as workloads have increased. Many legislatures also offer more training opportunities to staff. Non-partisan staff organizations have carefully sought to maintain their non-partisan reputations.

Balance of Power

The JPTL has yielded mixed results on the questions of whether and how power has shifted under term limits. In half the states, interviewees felt that the legislature had lost power to the governor and executive branch. In the other half, however, there is little evidence to indicate that this has happened.

In California, Colorado and to a lesser extent Maine, the executive branch appears to have gained influence due to term limits. The governor and agency heads have greater expertise on issues, maintain institutional knowledge of issues, and can wait out the legislature as needed. Legislators may lack the policy-specific experience to effectively question departmental heads in committee hearings. Legislators may also avoid conflict with a governor who have influence over their futures—hoping for an executive appointment or help in running for another office.

In Arkansas and Ohio, it appears that the legislature may have gained influence due to term limits. Term limited legislators in Arkansas may feel that they have nothing to lose in not supporting the governor. Whereas they may have been more cooperative in the past as they looked toward a long legislative career, now they feel free to assert their independence, particularly in their last term. In Ohio, a particularly strong House speaker has consolidated the power of his caucus and the House leadership.

The results on the influence of lobbyists under term limits are mixed. On the one hand, they are a valuable resource for policy information and history. On the other, lobbyists face a challenge in forming relationships with a constantly changing membership, and new members are often suspicious of lobbyists. It does appear that the playing field has leveled for lobbyists—newer lobbyists can compete more evenly with veterans for influence, because the veterans have lost their old cultivated relationships. While it is clear that lobbyists' role has changed under term limits, it is not clear that they have gained or lost power as a result.

Adaptations

In Maine, a new oversight agency was established within the legislature. The Office of Program Evaluation and Governmental Accountability was modeled after similar agencies in other states. It has a professional, nonpartisan staff, and represents Maine's most ambitious attempt to address the effects of term limits. Colorado formed a joint task force to review ethics rules for lobbyists and make recommendations for changes.

Looking to the Future

It is clear that term limits have brought many changes to the legislatures where they are in effect. Term limited legislatures report more general chaos, a decline in civility, reduced influence of legislative leaders and committees, and in some states, a shift in power relationships. However, the bottom line is that legislatures are resilient and highly adaptive institutions, and they continue to function efficiently under term limits. Many of the problems experienced by term limited legislatures are the same problems faced by all legislatures; term limits simply tend to amplify and accelerate them. As term limits continue to tighten their hold, and as veteran members continue to cycle out, the term limited legislatures will continue to evolve. As they do, they will provide valuable ideas that all legislatures, term limited or not, can adopt to improve their institutions.

Notes

[1] Gary Moncrief, Richard G. Niemi and Lynda W. Powell, "Time, Term Limits, and Turnover," *Legislative Studies Quarterly* XXIX (August 2004): 357-81.

About the Author

Jennifer Drage Bowser is a program principal in the Legislative Management Program at the National Conference of State Legislatures. Her work focuses on the areas of term limits, elections, initiatives and referenda, and campaign finance reform. She is the project manager for the Joint Project on Term Limits.

State Legislative Redistricting in 2003–2004: Emerging Trends and Issues in Reapportionment

By Ronald E. Weber

Whereas the redistricting round of the 1990s can be described as the round of racial and ethnic predominance, the 2000 round showed a growing emergence of partisanship as the predominant pattern of conflict. The experience of state legislatures in the latest round should provide an overall pattern for state legislative redistricting agencies to weather the terrain and successfully create plans in the future. The future political and legal terrain will continue to be complex and multifaceted.

Introduction

This article assesses the progress of the states in redrawing state legislative district lines for the elections of the remainder of the decade as several states had to complete or revise their districting after the elections of 2002. It also describes the final emerging trends this decade and highlights the experience of several states during 2003–2004 in dealing with both old and new issues in redistricting. Whereas the redistricting round of the 1990s can be described as the round of racial and ethnic predominance, the 2000 round showed a growing emergence of partisanship as the predominant pattern of conflict. The state legislatures were able to take into account race or ethnicity in drawing lines as had been the emphasis in the previous decade; however, since political partisanship of voters correlates highly with the racial and ethnic makeup of populations, the use of race and ethnicity was subordinated to the use of partisan criteria with the 2000 decade proving to be a round of either partisan gerrymandering or bi-partisan protection of incumbent state legislators (see McDonald, 2004).

Supreme Court cases of the 1990s and early 2000s ultimately sanctioned the use of partisanship as a predominant factor in redistricting, even though the court in *Miller v. Johnson* (515 U.S. 900) in 1995 argued for the use of a set of race-neutral, objective criteria such as compactness, contiguity, respect for political subdivisions and respect for communities of interest. The first controlling case is *Easley v. Cromartie* (532 U.S. 234, 2001), where the court upheld North Carolina's use of partisanship when it redrew its unconstitutional congressional districting plan, despite the plaintiffs' contention that the plan relied predominantly on race. This decision opened the door to the unbridled use of partisanship as the

predominant factor in redistricting in the current decade. The second controlling case is *Vieth v. Jubelirer* (541 U.S. 267, 2004), where the court upheld Pennsylvania's use of partisanship when the state legislature created its congressional districting plan in 2002. A plurality of the Supreme Court along with one concurring justice held that the plaintiffs had been unable to prove a partisan gerrymander by the Pennsylvania state legislature under the current judicial standards of *Davis v. Bandemer* (478 U.S. 109, 1986) and hence upheld the Pennsylvania congressional districting plan. However, the plurality opinion of the Supreme Court signaled that four justices desire to overturn *Davis v. Bandemer* and rule partisan claims non-justiciable.

Partisanship Triumphs

Legislative redistricting is among the most partisan of policy activities undertaken by state legislatures. In essence, the legislature takes the position that political districting is a matter of preserving self-interest: the spoils of politics belong to the strongest and district line-drawing can be manipulated to improve the political position of the party which controls each chamber. A large number of states operate under the norm that each chamber is the primary arbiter of the lines for its chamber so that the house defers to the wishes of the senate and vice versa. Furthermore, many state legislators take the position that it is not the governor's job to intrude on the turf of the legislature when it comes to drawing districting lines for the state senate or house. Of course, some districting schemes require a degree of cooperation between the two chambers, such as "nesting" house districts within state senate districts. This cooperation gets a little dicey when one chamber is controlled by the Democrats and the other by the Republicans.

How each political party seeks to advance its political interests varies. The issue is to determine the best way to waste the vote of the partisans of the other party. To do so requires a great deal of information about past turnout patterns and levels of political support given by party followers. For example, Democrats are well aware that Republican supporters typically turn out at higher levels than Democratic followers. Democrats thus can "waste" Republican votes by using election history information to identify areas with proven records of Republican voting patterns along with higher than average levels of voter turnout. This has created the cul-de-sac theory of districting where Democrats concentrate all the neighborhoods with gated communities and cul-de-sac street patterns in Republican districts. This approach was refined to the nth degree in Texas redistricting in the 1990s and was followed again this decade as the Texas Legislature worked unsuccessfully on state legislative districts.

Republicans, on the other hand, find the use of racial and ethnic data most useful in locating potential Democratic voters. Here the approach is to pack potentially as many African-American or Hispanic minority voters into legislative districts so as to minimize the number of seats that the Democratic Party can win, while then spreading Republican supporters over the remaining districts. This approach was used effectively in the 1990s in Ohio where the Republican-dominated apportionment board drew state legislative districts by concentrating African-American populations at the highest possible levels in Democratic districts. Thus, the Republicans minimized the number of Democratic-leaning districts and produced a decade of Republican control of both chambers in Ohio. The Ohio Republicans also spent the decade fending off legal challenges by the Democrats to this approach of wasting minority Democratic voters (see the *Quilter v. Voinovich* cases of the 1990s). Since this approach was validated largely by the federal courts in the 1990s, state legislatures learned it might be legal to "waste" minority votes to achieve political gerrymandering. With the exception of Ohio, the state Democratic parties of the 1990s were more interested in cooperating with minority office holders who wanted potentially safe electoral districts than in fighting Republican efforts to pack minority populations in Democrat districts. But this all changed in the 2000 round of redistricting.

During the 1990s, a number of political scientists explored the question of what level of minority population is necessary to equalize the opportunity of minority voters to elect candidates of choice to congressional and state legislative office. Invariably, this research determined that a combination of cohesive minority group support along with white or "Anglo" voters would enable Democratic candidates to win congressional or state legislative office. And with regularity, the researchers determined that the appropriate minority population percentage was less than 50 percent and usually closer to 40 percent. This research gave ammunition to Democrats who argued that anything above those minority percentage levels constituted "packing" of minority populations and thus would minimize the opportunity of Democratic voters to elect Democrats. The author's work for plaintiff interests in the Shaw type of cases in the 1990s demonstrated that Democratic candidates could count on various levels of white or "Anglo" cross-over votes and that these votes had to be taken into account in determining whether plans were narrowly tailored to advance compelling state interests. Thus, the Democrats learned that they had been mistaken in the 1990s to attempt to maximize minority populations in state legislative districts as the minority office-holders often argued should be the case. Of course, the Republican sweep in the 1994 elections, particularly in the South, brought home to the Democratic Party the consequences of minority population maximization as the Republicans scored big gains in state legislative elections.

The two tables following this article have summarized the state conditions, litigation and final outcomes of the state senate and house redistrictings in 2001–2004 (see Tables A and B). These tables report whether there was any change in the number of seats after redistricting, whether the political conditions for redistricting was split or unified partisan control, whether the state adopted a plan that ended up being determined as valid, whether a suit was filed in state and/or federal courts, and if there was litigation, what the litigation's outcome was. The data from these two tables are employed throughout the remainder of this article to exemplify trends and issues in the 2001–2004 state legislative redistricting.

In this latest round of state legislative redistricting, the Democrats reversed their approach because of the lessons learned during the 1990s. Now the lines of the partisan battle are quite clear. Democrats want an optimum percentage of minority populations in state legislative districts. Their goal is neither to waste too many Democratic votes nor to have so few Democrats that the districts might not elect Democrats. Thus, this optimum percentage had to be determined in each state before beginning the state legislative districting.

In addition to the discussion of the partisan interests at play in the redistricting of New Jersey, South Carolina, Virginia and Wisconsin discussed in the author's article in the *The Book of the States 2003*, further evidence on the prevalence of partisanship is provided in McDonald (2004). In that article, McDonald categorizes the outcome of state legislative districting in the 50 states in terms of whether Democratic or Republican gerrymanders were achieved, whether the plan adopted was a bi-partisan incumbent protection plan, or whether the plan adopted had a neutral outcome. He found that in 27 states the plans adopted were either Democratic or Republican gerrymanders and in 17 of the other 23 states the outcomes were bi-partisan incumbent protection plans. Neutral outcomes were observed in only six states (McDonald, 2004: 386–388).

Is Retrogression a Problem Anymore?

In the 16 states covered wholly or in part under Section 5 of the U.S. Voting Rights Act of 1965 (as amended in 1982), the state legislature had to keep in mind the opportunity of minority voters to elect candidates of choice when redrawing state legislative district lines. The legal standard under the *Reno v. Bossier Parish School Board* (528 U.S. 320, 1999) case is that the minority group must not be deprived of the opportunity to elect candidates of choice when the previous plan permitted the group's voters to elect candidates of choice. This interpretation means that the percentage of the minority group population in a proposed district can be reduced only if the reduction does not make the group's voters unable to elect their preferred candidate. The exact parameters of the Section 5 standard of retrogression is determined by the Voting Section of the Department of Justice (DOJ) unless the state elects to seek pre-clearance from the U.S. District Court of the District of Columbia. The evidence on DOJ interpretation of the retrogression standard during this round shows that most of the state legislative plans adopted in the 16 covered jurisdictions received pre-clearance. DOJ only objected to the Florida House plan, the Georgia Senate plan, and the Texas House plan. In the case of the Louisiana House plan, the DOJ voting section fought an attempt by the Louisiana House to gain pre-clearance from the District Court of the District of Columbia. After one adverse federal court decision, the Louisiana House settled with the DOJ by redrawing several districts in the New Orleans area. The revised plan then received pre-clearance under Section 5. Thus, the 16 states were largely able to meet the legal requirements of Section 5 under *Reno v. Bossier Parish School Board* without much diffi-

culty. This left the battle over advancing minority voting rights to private plaintiffs that brought Section 2 lawsuits in several states seeking to enhance minority voting rights.

Final Trends in the 2000 Redistricting Round

Whereas the plans of the 1990s increased the representation of racial and ethnic minority interests within state legislatures, little evidence was found of similar gains in this redistricting round. There are several reasons for this conclusion. First, in the 16 states covered wholly or in part by Section 5 of the U.S. Voting Rights Act (VRA), the concept of retrogression limited further gains in minority representation. The result of such efforts was a preservation of the status quo in racial or ethnic representation in those states. Second, the main plaintiffs in Section 2 litigation against state legislative plans this round came from Latino interests not African-American interests. The burden of proof for Latino interests was difficult because high percentages of non-citizen population had to be taken into account in assessing Latino plaintiff claims. The experience in the two challenges already brought to the Texas Senate and House plans illustrated how difficult it was for Latino interests to gain additional districts that were not created by the state legislative plans. Third, in states with significant numbers of both African-American and Latino populations, the continuing desire for African-American and Latino interests to gain separate places at the table of representation limited the number of occasions which existed to create combined majority-minority districts. Since these two groups seem to vote together in general elections, those who wished to create combined majority-minority districts had to demonstrate that the two groups also supported the same candidates in primary elections. Here the evidence continued to be very mixed in the parts of the country where these conditions exist. Thus, there were few gains in racial and ethnic diversity in the state legislatures of the 2000s.

A major exception to the trend just elaborated occurred in the Massachusetts House districting and the South Dakota Senate and House districting. In Massachusetts, the Democratic Party majorities in the Senate and House were sufficient to permit the legislature to devise its own plans without any gubernatorial involvement. The plan proposed by a joint committee on redistricting and reapportionment proposed the creation of one additional House district with an African-American voting age population majority; however, a floor amendment undid the creation of the African-American majority district and the plan finally adopted was a status quo plan in terms of minority group representation. Both African-American and Latino voters brought separate actions in federal court challenging the adopted House plan on the basis of each minority group being "cracked" between and "packed" within several districts in the Boston area. Both African-American and Latino interests sought to get the court to order additional House districts with effective African-American and Latino population majorities. The court found African-American voters to be under represented in the 2001 House plan and ordered the state legislature to redraw the districts in the Boston area to provide additional African-American representation. On the other hand, the court did not find under representation of Latino voters in the 2001 House plan and upheld the plan in terms of Latino representation. Thus, the redrawn plan for the Massachusetts House enhances African-American representation while keeping Latino representation the same as in adopted plan of 2001.

In South Dakota, the state legislature in 2001 was in the hands of a Republican majority in both chambers with a Republican governor. South Dakota House districts from which two members are elected at-large are usually the same as the Senate districts, with the exception of one Senate district that has been divided into two single-member districts to enhance the chances of Native American representation in the House. The plan adopted by the state in late 2001 maintained the status quo in Native American representation and Native American voter interests then sued in federal court alleging a need for Section 5 pre-clearance under the VRA and that the plan violated Section 2 of the VRA for under representing Native American voters. Initially, the Federal court found that submission of the state legislative redistricting plan was required under Section 5 of the VRA and ordered the state legislature to submit it to the DOJ. The DOJ approved the plan concluding that the plan did not result in the retrogression of Native American voter interests. In the Section 2 lawsuit, the plaintiffs alleged that the state legislature packed Native American persons of voting age into one Senate and three House districts and that alternatively the Legislature could have adopted a plan that enhanced Native American representation in both the Senate and the House. The federal court in September 2004 agreed with the Native American plaintiff allegations and ordered the state legislature to redraw the Senate and House districts with an eye toward enhancing Native American representation in the South Dakota Legislature.

If this round displayed less consciousness of race and ethnicity in districting, does this mean that the states have ended the practice of constructing non-compact and bizarrely shaped legislative districts? No evidence exists that the plans adopted in this round are any less bizarre in shape than the plans that are being replaced. In this round, however, the bizarrely shaped districts have more to do with partisan considerations than with racial and ethnic considerations. The technology of redistricting now makes it easy to construct districts based on the partisan predispositions of the voters and a number of states have invested in the technology to enable them to do so. Since the courts now typically hold that an absence of geographic compactness may be evidence of impermissible race consciousness in districting, the states simply have to respond that they followed partisan preferences when drawing bizarrely shaped districts, not racial factors. The legal challenges of the 2000 round to partisan gerrymandering have fallen mostly on deaf ears from the state and/or federal courts.

The most prominent legal development of this decade has been the resurgence of challenges in state rather than in federal courts. Overall, this decade witnessed fewer court challenges in all with a total of 23 senate and 24 house plans challenged (contrast this experience with that of the previous decade when a total of 27 senate and 30 house plans were challenged, see Weber 1995). In this decade a majority of the plaintiffs sought relief in state courts because the federal courts must now defer to the state courts if the parties wish to be in state court (see *Growe v. Emison*, 507 U.S. 25, 1993). The need to litigate in state court did not usually delay the final resolution of the disputes at a time when the states were racing to meet candidate qualification deadlines for primary and general elections. The author had expected delays and competition between litigants to find the most favorable forum to hear their disputes. The only prominent exception to the general trend occurred in Texas, where the state court process yielded no state plans at all for the state Senate and House, leaving the final resolution to be handled by a three-judge panel of the federal court. In the end, state legislative districting plans were reviewed by federal courts in Alabama, California, Florida, Georgia, Illinois, Massachusetts, New Jersey, New York, Rhode Island, South Carolina, South Dakota, Texas, West Virginia and Wisconsin, with either state senate or house plans being invalidated or drawn by the courts in Florida, Georgia, Massachusetts, Rhode Island, South Carolina, South Dakota, Texas and Wisconsin. On the other hand, state courts were involved in reviewing state legislative plans in Alaska, Arizona, Colorado, Florida, Idaho, Illinois, Kansas, Maine, Maryland, Minnesota, Montana, New Hampshire, New Mexico, North Carolina, Oregon, Pennsylvania, Texas and Virginia. In 11 of those 18 states, the state court invalidated, ordered the redrawing, or redrew state senate or house plans. In the final analysis, legal challenges were found in the current round to be less successful than in the previous decade as the state legislatures more effectively justified the decisions they made in redrawing district lines.

One of the new trends opened up in state court review of adopted or proposed state legislative plans involved the potential electoral competitiveness of the districts. This issue took on prominence in the consideration and adoption of plans by state courts in Arizona and Minnesota. In Arizona, the redistricting process for state legislative districts had been turned over to the Arizona Independent Redistricting Commission (AIRC) as a result of voter adoption an initiative, Proposition 106, in the 2000 general election. After development and adoption of the state legislative plan in 2001, the initial plan was challenged in state court by Latino and Native American plaintiffs. The plaintiffs sought to revise the plan to create more politically competitive districts while continuing to protect the voting rights of minority persons. Initially, the state court deferred trial on the merits of the case until after the 2002 general elections and permitted the AIRC plan to be used in those elections. After trial, a Superior Court Judge in Maricopa County in mid January 2004 found for the plaintiffs and ordered the AIRC to revise the state legislative districts in time for the 2004 elections. The court ruled the plan violated the state's constitution by not giving enough consideration to the creation of electorally competitive districts. The AIRC then took action about one month later to revise the district map to create additional electorally competitive districts and the state court approved the revised plan in April 2004. However, a state appeals court stayed the order of the lower court and approved the plan employed in 2002 for use in the 2004 elections. Thus, a combination of having an independent commission create the map along with a lower state court that was willing to enforce state constitutional criteria regarding electoral competitiveness kept in play a plan that heightened the extent of electoral competitiveness when compared to the plan it replaced.

A second state where the process put a renewed emphasis on the electoral competitiveness of state legislative districts was Minnesota. There the state legislature, due to partisan differences between the two chambers, was unable to pass a state legislative plan by the statutory deadline of March 19, 2002. In anticipation of a partisan impasse, the Minnesota Supreme Court appointed a five-judge special redistricting panel and ordered them to release a redistricting plan only in the event a legislative redistricting plan was not adopted in a timely manner. When the deadline for legislative action expired, the special redistricting panel promulgated a plan for state Senate and House districts. Although the adopted plan was not governed by any explicit goal of fostering electoral competition, the employment of strict technical criteria related to population equality, contiguity, compactness, and the splitting of political sub-divisions resulted in a plan that created a larger number of districts without incumbents or paired incumbents. Thus, a larger number of open seat elections in electorally competitive districts occurred as a result of the Minnesota court-ordered plan devised by experts.

Next, there is the decades old problem of meeting the one-person, one-vote equal protection standard and other state constitutional criteria in state legislative districting. Several states were challenged in this round as they attempted to deal with meeting the one-person, one-vote equal protection standard and other criteria. And, for the most part state plans were not invalidated upon court review in terms of one-person, one-vote or other technical criteria challenges. Only in Alaska, Colorado, Georgia, Idaho, Maryland and North Carolina were plans invalidated on population or technical criteria with the courts ordering the redrawing or drawing of the plans themselves.

The most interesting case comes from Georgia (*Larios v. Cox*, 300 F. Supp. 2d 1320 (ND Ga. 2004)) where a three-judge federal court panel invalidated the state Senate and House plans on the basis of a one-person, one-vote challenge. The state legislature in formulating and revising the plans in 2001 and 2002 had assumed that a plus or minus 5 percent overall population deviation was a safe harbor in meeting the spirit of one-person, one-vote. However, plaintiffs attacked the plan and proved that state legislature had adopted "a deliberate and systematic policy of favoring rural and inner city interests at the expense of suburban areas north, east, and west of Atlanta." (300 F. Supp. 2d 1320, 1327 (ND Ga. 2004)). Furthermore, the court found that the state showed "an intentional effort to allow incumbent Democrats to maintain or increase their delegation, primarily by systematically underpopulating the districts held by incumbent Democrats, by overpopulating those of Republicans, and by deliberately pairing numerous Republican incumbents against one another." (*Larios v. Cox*, at 1329). The court held that these actions violated the principle of one-person, one-vote because while each district deviation was within a permissible range (9.98 percent), there were no legitimate policies offered to justify these deviations. The U.S. Supreme Court affirmed the lower court decision and after the state legislature was unable to draw new lines, court-appointed experts drew new maps that the court approved. The Georgia example shows that if state legislatures believe that plus or minus 5 percent overall population deviation is a safe harbor, they will have to be more careful than the Georgia legislature in justifying the reasons for the population deviations. Other state legislatures did so during this past round; however, given the precision of current computer technology and the availability of block level population data, population deviations beyond minimum levels are going to be subject to continued challenges based on the experience of Georgia in 2004.

This article also assesses the overall success of state reapportionment boards and commissions in shaping state legislative districting plans. A total of 12 states employed either a partisan or non-partisan board or commission in the development and adoption of state legislative plans, with five other states employing boards or commissions if the state legislature was unable to adopt a plan. Most of these commissions are set up to have members of both political parties represented, but the process of choosing a commission chair or tie-breaker creates a partisan advantage for one or the other party. Several of the state commissions were more likely to produce bipartisan plans as they require a super-majority of the commission to adopt plans, along with state supreme court validation and/or super-majorities of the legislature to approve the plans. Thus, most of the plans adopted by state reapportionment boards or commissions do show partisan outcomes. Only a few states such as Arizona, Hawaii, Iowa, Maine and Washington seem to be operating the most neutral processes for drawing state legislative districts at the present time.

Finally, the partisanship surrounding state legislative districting processes of the current round has spurred a renewed interest in citizen initiatives to create less partisan reapportionment boards and commissions in states without them at the present time. As of this writing, there are uncoordinated campaigns to reform state legislative districting processes in at least eight states, including California, Colorado, Florida, Georgia, Maryland, Massachusetts, Pennsylvania and Rhode Island. What proponents of change are suggesting is that states adopt board or commission forms such as that currently employed in Arizona or something akin to the neutral process employed by Iowa. This campaign for change has taken on new emphasis with the proposal coming from Governor Arnold Schwarzenegger of California to replace the state legislature of that state as the redistricting body with a panel of retired judges. The governor is planning to push this idea in a voter initiative geared to getting a new process and state legislative plans in place by the elections of 2006 (see Nagourney, *The New York Times*, February 7, 2005 and Frank, *Time Magazine*, January 6, 2005). In those states with the citizen initiative a possible fire-storm beginning in California may lead to fundamental reforms in the redistricting processes of other states in an attempt to dampen the partisanship of the state processes.

Thus, the future political and legal terrain faced by state legislative redistricters will continue to be complex and multi-faceted. One would expect that occasionally in the future legislatively adopted plans can be successfully attacked. However, the experience of state legislatures in the latest round should provide an overall pattern for state legislative redistricters to weather the terrain and successfully create plans in the future.

References

Butler, David and Bruce Cain. *Congressional Redistricting: Comparative and Theoretical Perspectives*. New York: Macmillan, 1992.

Cunningham, Maurice T. 2001. *Maximization, Whatever the Cost: Race, Redistricting, and the Department of Justice*. Westport, CT: Praeger.

Frank, Mitch. "*Arnold vs. the Gerrymanders*." *Time Magazine*. January 6, 2005.

Griffith, Benjamin E. March 1999. "Redistricting in the Post-Shaw World," National Conference of State Legislatures Redistricting Seminar, Denver, Colorado.

Lublin, David and D. Stephen Voss. "Racial Redistricting and Realignment in Southern State Legislatures." *American Journal of Political Science* 44: October 2000, 792–810.

McDonald, Michael P. "A Comparative Analysis of Redistricting Institutions in the United States, 2001–02." *State Politics and Policy Quarterly* 4: Winter 2004, 371–395.

Nagourney, Adam. February 7, 2005. "States See Growing Campaign to Change Redistricting Laws," *New York Times*.

Table A: State Conditions and Litigation Affecting State Senate Redistricting in the 2000s (n = 50)

State	Seat change	Split control	Valid plan	Suit(s) filed	Litigation outcome	Comment
Alaska	0	Y	Y	N	U	State court automatically approved and upheld plan.
Arizona	0	Y	Y	Y	O	State court disapproved 2001 plan and ordered state commission to re-draw plan. Redrawn plan approved by state court.
Arkansas	0	Y	Y	N	N	
California	0	N	Y	Y	U	State-adopted plan upheld by federal court against Hispanic challenge.
Colorado	0	N	N	N	O	State court disapproved original plan and approved revised plan.
Connecticut	0	Y	Y	N	N	
Delaware	0	Y	Y	N	N	
Florida	0	N	Y	Y	U	State court automatically reviewed and upheld plan.
Georgia	0	N	N	Y	O	After DOJ objected, state revised plan. Federal court disapproved revised plan on "one-person, one-vote" grounds and court redrew plan.
Hawaii	0	N	Y	N	N	
Idaho	0	N	N	Y	O	State court twice rejected commission plan, ordered new plan to be drawn up.
Illinois	0	Y	Y	Y	U	State court upheld compactness challenge; federal court upheld state plan from minority challenge.
Indiana	0	Y	Y	N	N	
Iowa	0	Y	Y	N	N	
Kansas	0	N	Y	N	U	State court automatically reviewed and upheld plan.
Kentucky	0	Y	Y	N	N	
Louisiana	0	Y	Y	N	N	
Maine	0	N	N	N	CP	State court drew plan after state commission failed to draw plan.
Maryland	0	N	N	Y	CP	State court declared plan unconstitutional; drew and adopted own plan.
Massachusetts	0	Y	Y	N	N	
Michigan	0	N	Y	N	N	
Minnesota	0	Y	N	Y	CP	State court imposed own plan due to inability of legislature to agree on a plan.
Mississippi	0	N	Y	Y	P	African-American challenge based on racial gerrymandering pending in federal court.
Missouri	0	Y	Y	N	N	
Montana	0	N	Y	Y	U	State court upheld plan in challenge brought by secretary of state.
Nebraska	0	Y	Y	N	N	
Nevada	0	Y	Y	N	N	
New Hampshire	0	Y	N	N	CP	State court imposed own plan because legislature failed to enact plan by deadline.
New Jersey	0	N	Y	Y	U	Minority challenge resulted in federal court upholding plan.
New Mexico	0	Y	N	Y	CP	State court imposed own plan because of gubernatorial veto of legislative plan.
New York	+1	Y	Y	Y	U	Hispanic challenge based on packing and cracking of miority voters dismissed by federal court.
North Carolina	0	N	N	Y	O	State court disapproved plan and ordered state legislature to redraw. DOJ and court approved new districts.
North Dakota	-2	N	Y	N	N	
Ohio	0	N	Y	N	N	
Oklahoma	0	Y	Y	N	N	
Oregon	0	Y	N	Y	CP	State court imposed corrected plan because state plan used incorrect census data.
Pennsylvania	0	N	Y	Y	U	State adopted plan upheld by state court against "one-person, one-vote" and compactness challenges.
Rhode Island	-12	Y	Y	Y	S	African-American challenge in federal court resulted in redrawn districts to settle challenge.
South Carolina	0	Y	N	Y	CP	Federal court imposed plan after governor vetoed state plan.
South Dakota	0	N	Y	Y	O	Federal court disapproved plan due to Native American challenge and ordered state legisature to redraw districts.
Tennessee	0	Y	Y	N	N	
Texas	0	Y	N	Y	U	Minority challenge resulted in federal court upholding plan.
Utah	0	N	Y	N	N	
Vermont	0	N	Y	N	N	
Virginia	0	Y	Y	Y	U	State Supreme Court upheld plan rejected by lower court for racial and partisan gerrymandering
Washington	0	N	Y	N	N	
West Virginia	0	N	Y	Y	D	Federal court dismissed complaint from members of legislature claiming violation of equal protection clause of the 14th Amendment.
Wisconsin	0	Y	N	Y	CP	Senate challenge resulted in federal court-drawn plan.
Wyoming	0	N	Y	N	N	

Source: Ronald E. Weber
Key:
Y—Yes

D—Court dismissed suit.
N—No
S—Suit settled.

O—Court overturned plan.
CP—Court imposed its own plan.
U—Court upheld plan.

Table B: State Conditions and Litigation Affecting State House Redistricting in the 2000s (*n* = 49)

State	Seat change	Split control	Valid plan	Suit(s) filed	Litigation outcome	Comment
Alabama	0	N	Y	Y	D	After DOJ preclearance, challenge of racial gerrymandering dismissed by federal court.
Alaska	0	Y	N	Y	O	Challenge to partisan gerrymandering upheld by state court which ordered a revised plan; revised plan upheld by state supreme court.
Arizona	0	Y	Y	Y	O	State court disapproved 2001 plan and ordered state commission to redraw plan. Redrawn plan approved by state court.
Arkansas	0	Y	Y	N	N	
California	0	N	Y	N	N	
Colorado	0	N	Y	N	U	State court automatically reviewed and upheld plan.
Connecticut	0	Y	Y	N	N	
Delaware	0	Y	Y	N	N	
Florida	0	N	Y	Y	CP	State court automatically reviewed and upheld plan; federal court approved minor adjustments to state plan due to DOJ objection.
Georgia	0	N	Y	Y	O	After federal court granted preclearance, "one-person, one-vote" challenge upheld by federal court. Federal court redrew plan.
Hawaii	0	N	Y	N	N	
Idaho	0	N	N	Y	O	State court twice rejected commission plan, ordered new plan to be drawn up.
Illinois	0	Y	Y	Y	U	State court upheld compactness challenge; federal court upheld state plan from minority challenge.
Indiana	0	Y	Y	N	N	
Iowa	0	Y	Y	N	N	
Kansas	0	N	Y	N	U	State court automatically reviewed and upheld plan.
Kentucky	0	Y	Y	N	N	
Louisiana	0	Y	Y	Y	S	Preclearance suit settled with state altering plan.
Maine	0	N	Y	Y	U	State court upheld plan against compactness and contiguity challenges.
Maryland	0	N	N	Y	CP	State court declared plan unconstitutional; drew and adopted own plan.
Massachusetts	0	Y	Y	Y	O	Federal court disapproved plan based on African-American challenge. State altered plan and federal court approved.
Michigan	0	N	Y	N	N	
Minnesota	0	Y	N	Y	CP	State court imposed plan due to inability of legislature to agree on a plan.
Mississippi	0	N	Y	N	N	
Missouri	0	Y	Y	N	N	
Montana	0	N	Y	Y	U	State court upheld plan in challenge brought by secretary of state.
Nebraska						
Nevada	0	Y	Y	N	N	
New Hampshire	0	Y	N	N	CP	State court imposed own plan because legislature failed to enact plan by deadline.
New Jersey	0	N	Y	Y	U	Minority challenge resulted in federal court decision to uphold plan.
New Mexico	0	Y	N	Y	CP	State court imposed own plan because of gubernatorial veto of legislative plan.
New York	0	Y	Y	N	N	
North Carolina	0	N	N	Y	O	State court disapproved plan and ordered state legislature to redraw. DOJ and court approved new districts.
North Dakota	-4	N	Y	N	N	
Ohio	0	N	Y	N	N	
Oklahoma	0	Y	Y	N	N	
Oregon	0	Y	N	Y	CP	State court imposed corrected plan because state plan used incorrect census data.
Pennsylvania	0	N	Y	Y	U	State adopted plan upheld by state court against "one-person, one-vote" and compactness challenges.
Rhode Island	-25	Y	N	N	N	
South Carolina	0	Y	N	Y	CP	Federal court imposed plan after governor vetoed state plan.
South Dakota	0	N	Y	Y	O	Federal court disapproved plan due to Native American challenge and ordered state legisature to redraw districts.
Tennessee	0	Y	Y	N	N	
Texas	0	Y	N	Y	O	Minority challenge caused federal court to make minor adjustments to state plan due to DOJ objection.
Utah	0	N	Y	N	N	
Vermont	0	N	Y	N	N	
Virginia	0	Y	Y	Y	U	State Supreme Court upheld plan rejected by lower court for racial and partisan gerrymandering
Washington	0	N	Y	N	N	
West Virginia	0	N	Y	Y	D	Federal court dismissed complaint from members of legislature claiming violation of equal protection clause of the 14th Amendment.
Wisconsin	0	Y	N	Y	CP	Senate challenge resulted in federal court-drawn plan.
Wyoming	0	Y	Y	N	N	

Source: Ronald E. Weber
Key:
Y—Yes
D—Court dismissed suit.
N—No
S—Suit settled.
O—Court overnturned plan.
CP—Court imposed its own plan.
U—Court upheld plan.

Table 3.1
NAMES OF STATE LEGISLATIVE BODIES AND CONVENING PLACES

State or other jurisdiction	Both bodies	Upper house	Lower house	Convening place
Alabama	Legislature	Senate	House of Representatives	State House
Alaska	Legislature	Senate	House of Representatives	State Capitol
Arizona	Legislature	Senate	House of Representatives	State Capitol
Arkansas	General Assembly	Senate	House of Representatives	State Capitol
California	Legislature	Senate	Assembly	State Capitol
Colorado	General Assembly	Senate	House of Representatives	State Capitol
Connecticut	General Assembly	Senate	House of Representatives	State Capitol
Delaware	General Assembly	Senate	House of Representatives	Legislative Hall
Florida	Legislature	Senate	House of Representatives	The Capitol
Georgia	General Assembly	Senate	House of Representatives	State Capitol
Hawaii	Legislature	Senate	House of Representatives	State Capitol
Idaho	Legislature	Senate	House of Representatives	State Capitol
Illinois	General Assembly	Senate	House of Representatives	State House
Indiana	General Assembly	Senate	House of Representatives	State House
Iowa	General Assembly	Senate	House of Representatives	State Capitol
Kansas	Legislature	Senate	House of Representatives	State Capitol
Kentucky	General Assembly	Senate	House of Representatives	State Capitol
Louisiana	Legislature	Senate	House of Representatives	State Capitol
Maine	Legislature	Senate	House of Representatives	State House
Maryland	General Assembly	Senate	House of Delegates	State House
Massachusetts	General Court	Senate	House of Representatives	State House
Michigan	Legislature	Senate	House of Representatives	State Capitol
Minnesota	Legislature	Senate	House of Representatives	State Capitol
Mississippi	Legislature	Senate	House of Representatives	State Capitol
Missouri	General Assembly	Senate	House of Representatives	State Capitol
Montana	Legislature	Senate	House of Representatives	State Capitol
Nebraska	Legislature	(a)		State Capitol
Nevada	Legislature	Senate	Assembly	Legislative Building
New Hampshire	General Court	Senate	House of Representatives	State House
New Jersey	Legislature	Senate	General Assembly	State House
New Mexico	Legislature	Senate	House of Representatives	State Capitol
New York	Legislature	Senate	Assembly	State Capitol
North Carolina	General Assembly	Senate	House of Representatives	State Legislative Building
North Dakota	Legislative Assembly	Senate	House of Representatives	State Capitol
Ohio	General Assembly	Senate	House of Representatives	State House
Oklahoma	Legislature	Senate	House of Representatives	State Capitol
Oregon	Legislative Assembly	Senate	House of Representatives	State Capitol
Pennsylvania	General Assembly	Senate	House of Representatives	Main Capitol Building
Rhode Island	General Assembly	Senate	House of Representatives	State House
South Carolina	General Assembly	Senate	House of Representatives	State House
South Dakota	Legislature	Senate	House of Representatives	State Capitol
Tennessee	General Assembly	Senate	House of Representatives	State Capitol
Texas	Legislature	Senate	House of Representatives	State Capitol
Utah	Legislature	Senate	House of Representatives	State Capitol
Vermont	General Assembly	Senate	House of Representatives	State House
Virginia	General Assembly	Senate	House of Delegates	State Capitol
Washington	Legislature	Senate	House of Representatives	State Capitol
West Virginia	Legislature	Senate	House of Delegates	State Capitol
Wisconsin	Legislature	Senate	Assembly (b)	State Capitol
Wyoming	Legislature	Senate	House of Representatives	State Capitol
Dist. of Columbia	Council of the District of Columbia	(a)		Council Chamber
American Samoa	Legislature	Senate	House of Representatives	Maota Fono
Guam	Legislature	(a)		Congress Building
No. Mariana Islands	Legislature	Senate	House of Representatives	Civic Center Building
Puerto Rico	Legislative Assembly	Senate	House of Representatives	The Capitol
U.S. Virgin Islands	Legislature	(a)		Capitol Building

Source: The Council of State Governments, *Directory I—Elective Officials 2005.*

(a) Unicameral legislature. Except in Dist. of Columbia, members go by the title Senator.

(b) Members of the lower house go by the title Representative.

Table 3.2
LEGISLATIVE SESSIONS: LEGAL PROVISIONS

State or other jurisdiction	Regular sessions				Special sessions		
	Legislature convenes			Limitation on length of session (a)	Legislature may call	Legislature may determine subject	Limitation on length of session
	Year	Month	Day				
Alabama	Annual	Jan. Mar. Feb.	2nd Tues. (b) 1st Tues. (c)(d) 1st Tues. (e)	30 L in 105 C	No	Yes (f)	12 L in 30 C
Alaska	Annual	Jan.	2nd Mon.	121 C	By petition, 2/3 members, each house	Yes	30 C
Arizona	Annual	Jan.	2nd Mon.	(i)	By petition, 2/3 members, each house	Yes	None
Arkansas	Biennial-odd year	Jan.	2nd Mon.	60 C (h)	No	No (j)	None
California	(l)	Jan.	1st Mon. (d)	None	No	No	None
Colorado	Annual	Jan.	No later than 2nd Wed.	120 C	By petition, 2/3 members, each house	Yes (g)	None
Connecticut	Annual	Jan. Feb.	Wed. after 1st Mon. (n) Wed. after 1st Mon. (o)	(p)	By petition, 2/3 members, each house (q) Joint call, presiding officers, both houses	Yes	None
Delaware	Annual	Jan.	2nd Tues.	June 30	Joint call, presiding officers, both houses	Yes	None
Florida	Annual	Mar.	1st Tues. after 1st Mon.	60 C (h)	Joint call, presiding officers, both houses or	Yes	20 C (h)
Georgia	Annual	Jan.	2nd Mon.	40 L	By petition, 3/5 members, each house	No	40 L
Hawaii	Annual	Jan.	3rd Wed.	60 L (h)	By petition, 2/3 members, each house	Yes	30 L (h)
Idaho	Annual	Jan.	Mon. on or nearest 9th day	None	No	No	20 C
Illinois	Annual	Jan.	2nd Wed.	None	Joint call, presiding officers, both houses	Yes (g)	None
Indiana	Annual	Jan.	2nd Mon. (d)(t)	odd-61 C or Apr. 29; even-30 C or Mar. 14	No	Yes	30 L or 40 C
Iowa	Annual	Jan.	2nd Mon.	odd-110 C even—100 C	By petition, 2/3 members, each house	Yes	None
Kansas	Annual	Jan.	2nd Mon.	odd-None; even-90 C (h)	Petition to governor of 2/3 members, each house	Yes	None
Kentucky	Annual	Jan.	1st Tues after 1st Mon.	odd-30 L even-60 L	No	No	None
Louisiana	Annual	Mar. (o) Apr. (n)	last Mon. (o) last Mon. (n)	even-60 L in 85 C; odd-45 L in 60 C	By petition, majority, each house	Yes	30 C
Maine	(l)(m)	Dec. Jan.	1st Wed. (b) Wed. after 1st Tues. (o)	3rd Wed. of June 3rd Wed. of April	By petition, majority, each house	Yes	None
Maryland	Annual	Jan.	2nd Wed.	90 C	By petition, majority, each house	Yes	30 C
Massachusetts	Biennial	Jan.	1st Wed.	(w)	By petition (x)	Yes	None
Michigan	Annual	Jan.	2nd Wed.	None	No	No	None
Minnesota	(y)	Jan.	Tues. after 1st Mon. (n)	120 L or 1st Mon. after 3rd Sat. in May (y)	No	Yes	None

See footnotes at end of table.

LEGISLATIVE SESSIONS: LEGAL PROVISIONS — Continued

State or other jurisdiction	Regular sessions				Special sessions		
	Year	Legislature convenes Month	Legislature convenes Day	Limitation on length of session (a)	Legislature may call	Legislature may determine subject	Limitation on length of session
Mississippi	Annual	Jan.	Tues. after 1st Mon.	125 C (z); 90C (z)	No	No	None
Missouri	Annual	Jan.	Wed. after 1st Mon.	May 30	By petition, 3/4 members, each house	Yes (g)	None
Montana	Biennial-odd year	Jan.	1st Mon.	90 L	By petition, majority, each house	Yes	30 C (aa)
Nebraska	Annual	Jan.	Wed. after 1st Mon.	odd-90 L; even-60 L	By petition, 2/3 members	Yes	None
Nevada	Biennial-odd year	Feb.	1st Mon.	120 C	No	No	None (k)
New Hampshire	Annual	Jan.	Wed. after 1st Tues.	45 L	By petition, 2/3 members, each house	Yes	15 L (r)
New Jersey	Annual	Jan.	2nd Tues.	None	By petition, majority, each house	Yes	None
New Mexico	Annual	Jan.	3rd Tues.	odd-60 C; even-30 C	By petition, 3/5 members, each house	Yes (g)	30 C
New York	Annual	Jan. (kk)	Wed. after 1st Mon.	None	By petition, 2/3 members, each house	Yes (g)	None
North Carolina	(y)	Jan.	3rd Wed. after 2nd Mon. (n)	None	By petition, 3/5 members, each house	Yes	None
North Dakota	Biennial-odd year	Jan.	Tues. after Jan. 3, but not later than Jan. 11	80 L	Yes (ff)	Yes	None
Ohio	(s)	Jan. (n)	1st Mon. (ee)	None	Joint call, presiding officers, both houses	Yes	None
Oklahoma	Annual	Feb.	1st Mon.	last Fri. in May	By vote, 2/3 members, each house	Yes (g)	None
Oregon	Biennial-odd year	Jan.	2nd Mon.	None	By petition, majority, each house	Yes	None
Pennsylvania	(dd)	Jan.	1st Tues.	None	By petition, majority each house	No	None
Rhode Island	Annual	Jan.	1st. Tues.	None	Joint call, presiding officers, both house	Yes	None
South Carolina	Biennial	Jan.	2nd Tues.	None	By vote, 2/3 members, each house	Yes	None
South Dakota	Annual	Jan.	2nd Tues.	odd-40 L; even-35 L	By petition, 2/3 members, each house	Yes	None
Tennessee	Annual	Jan.	(bb)	90 L (u)	By petition, 2/3 members, each house	Yes	30 L (u)
Texas	Biennial—odd year	Jan.	2nd Tues.	140 C	No	No	30 C
Utah	Annual	Jan.	3rd. Mon.	45 C	(cc)	No	None
Vermont	Annual	Jan.	Wed. after 1st Mon.	None	No	Yes	None
Virginia	Annual	Jan.	2nd Wed.	odd—30 C (h); even—60 C (h)	By petition, 2/3 members, each house	Yes	None
Washington	Annual	Jan.	2nd Mon.	odd—105 C; even—60 C	By vote, 2/3 members, each house	Yes	30 C
West Virginia	Annual	Jan.	2nd Wed.	60 C (h)	By petition, 3/5 members, each house	Yes (g)	None
Wisconsin	Annual (gg)	Jan.	1st Mon. (n)	None	By petition, majority members each house	No	None

See footnotes at end of table.

LEGISLATIVE SESSIONS: LEGAL PROVISIONS — Continued

State or other jurisdiction	Regular sessions			Limitation on length of session (a)	Special sessions		
	Legislature convenes				Legislature may call	Legislature may determine subject	Limitation on length of session
	Year	Month	Day				
Wyoming	Annual	Feb.	2nd Tues. (n)	odd—40 L; even—20 L; biennium—60 L	By petition, majority members each house	Yes	20 L
Dist. of Columbia	(hh)	Jan.	2nd day	None	No	No	None
American Samoa	Annual	Jan.; July	2nd Mon.	45 L	No	No	None
Guam	Annual	Jan.	2nd Mon. (ii)	None	Upon request of presiding officers, both houses	Yes (g)	10 C
No. Mariana Islands	Annual	(jj)	(jj)	90 L (jj)	No	No	20 C
Puerto Rico	Annual (v)	Jan.; Aug.	2nd Mon.; 3rd Mon.	5 mo.; 4 mo.	No	No	None
U.S. Virgin Islands	Annual	Jan.	2nd Mon.	None	No	No	None

Source: The Council of State Governments' survey, October 2003 and October 2004.

Note: Some legislatures will also reconvene after normal session to consider bills vetoed by governor. Connecticut—if governor vetoes any bill, secretary of state must reconvene General Assembly on second Monday after the last day on which governor is either authorized to transmit or has transmitted every bill with his objections, whichever occurs first: General Assembly must adjourn sine die not later than three days after its reconvening. Hawaii—legislature may reconvene on 45th day after adjournment sine die, in special session, without call. Louisiana—legislature meets in a maximum five-day veto session on the 40th day after final adjournment. Missouri—if governor returns any bill on or after the fifth day before the last day on which legislature may consider bills (in even-numbered years), legislature automatically reconvenes on first Wednesday following the second Monday in September for a maximum 10 C sessions. New Jersey—legislature meets in special session (without call or petition) to act on bills returned by governor on 45th day after sine die adjournment of the regular session; if the second year expires before the 45th day, the day preceding the end of the legislative year. Utah—if 2/3 of the members of each house favor reconvening to consider vetoed bills, a maximum five-day session is set by the presiding officers. Virginia—legislature reconvenes on sixth Wednesday after adjournment for a maximum three-day session (may be extended to seven days upon vote of majority of members elected to each house). Washington—upon petition of 2/3 of the members of each house, legislature meets 45 days after adjournment for a maximum five-day session.

Key:
C—Calendar day
L—Legislative day (in some states called a session day or workday; definition may vary slightly, however, generally refers to any day on which either house of legislature is in session).
(a) Applies to each year unless otherwise indicated.
(b) General election year (quadrennial election year).
(c) Year after quadrennial election.
(d) Legal provision for organizational session prior to stated convening date. Alabama—in the year after quadrennial election, second Tuesday in January for 10 C. California—in the even-numbered general election year, first Monday in December for an organizational session, recess until the first Monday in January of the odd-numbered year. Indiana—third Tuesday after first Monday in November. No. Mariana Islands—in year after general election, second Monday in January.
(e) Other years.
(f) By 2/3 vote each house.
(g) Only if legislature convenes itself. Special sessions called by the legislature are unlimited in scope in New Mexico.

(h) Session may be extended by vote of members in both houses. Arkansas—2/3 vote. Florida—3/5 vote, session may be extended by vote of members in each house. Hawaii—petition of 2/3 membership for maximum 15-day extension. Kansas—2/3 vote. Virginia—2/3 vote for 30 C extension. West Virginia—may be extended by the governor.
(i) No constitutional or statutory provision; however, legislative rules require that regular sessions adjourn no later than Saturday of the week during which the 100th day of the session falls.
(j) After governor's business has been disposed of, members may remain in session up to 15 C by a 2/3 vote of both houses.
(k) No limit, however legislators are only paid up to 20 calendar days during a special session.
(l) Regular sessions begin after general election, in December of even-numbered year. In California, legislature meets in December for an organizational session, recesses until the first Monday in January of the odd-numbered year and continues in session until Nov. 30 of next even-numbered year. In Maine, session which begins in December of general election year runs into the following year (odd-numbered); second session begins in next even-numbered year.
(m) Second session limited to consideration of specific types of legislation. Maine—budgetary matters; legislation in the governor's call; emergency legislation; legislation referred to committees for study.
(n) Odd-numbered years.
(o) Even-numbered years.
(p) Odd-numbered years—not later than Wednesday after first Monday in June; even-numbered—years not later than Wednesday after first Monday in May.
(q) Notice sent to secretary of state.
(r) Limitation is on payment of legislative pay and mileage.
(s) General Assembly meets during a two-year biennium that is divided into two annual regular sessions.
(t) Legislators may reconvene at any time after organizational meeting; however, second Monday in January is the final date by which regular session must be in process.
(u) Tennessee—Odd year, first half general assembly 45 legislative days; even year, second half general assembly 45 legislative days.
(v) Legislature meets twice a year. During general election years, the legislature only convenes on the January session.
(w) Legislative rules say formal business must be concluded by Nov. 15th of the 1st session in the biennium, or by July 31st of the 2nd session for the biennium.
(x) Joint rules provide for the submission of a written statement requesting special session by a specified number of members of each chamber.

LEGISLATIVE SESSIONS: LEGAL PROVISIONS — Continued

(y) Legal provision for session in odd-numbered year; however, legislature may divide, and in practice has divided, to meet in even-numbered years as well.

(z) 90 C sessions every year, except the first year of a gubernatorial administration during which the legislative session runs for 125 C.

(aa) 30 C if called by legislature; 60 C if called by governor.

(bb) Commencement of regular session depends on concluding date of organizational session. Legislature meets, in odd-numbered year, on second Tuesday in January for a maximum 15 C organizational session, then returns on the Tuesday following the conclusion of the organizational session.

(cc) Legislature may call itself into a veto override session.

(dd) Sessions are two years and begin on the 1st Tuesday of January of the odd numbered year. Session ends on November 30 of the even numbered year. Each calendar year receives its own legislative number.

(ee) Unless Monday is a legal holiday; in second year, the General Assembly convenes on the same date.

(ff) Legislative Council may reconvene the Legislature assembly. However, a reconvened session may not exceed the number of days available (80) but not used by the last regular session.

(gg) The legislature, by joint resolution, establishes the session schedule of activity for the remainder of the biennium at the beginning of the odd-numbered year.

(hh) Each Council period begins on January 2 of each odd-numbered year and ends on January 1 of the following odd-numbered year.

(ii) Legislature meets on the first Monday of each month following its initial session in January.

(jj) 60 L before April 1 and 30 L after July 31.

(kk) Session officially begins on the first Wednesday following the first Monday of the new legislative term (commencing the first of the year), and lasts until the legislature completes its business and adjourns sine die. However, over the past several years, both houses have adopted the tactic of declaring a recess at the call of the leaders, in order to facilitate easy recall of the legislature to override vetoes, etc. Over time the custom has become to formally adjourn both houses just before the new session opens; in the case of 2005, on January 7th. This leads to the rather interesting convention that when the governor calls the legislature into session, it is considered special or executive, even though the regular session is ongoing.

Table 3.3
THE LEGISLATORS: NUMBERS, TERMS, AND PARTY AFFILIATIONS: 2005

State or other jurisdiction	Senate Democrats	Republicans	Other	Vacancies	Total	Term	House/Assembly Democrats	Republicans	Other	Vacancies	Total	Term	Senate and House/Assembly totals
State and territory totals	1,001	982	13	5	2,069*	...	2,672	2,708	24	9	5,501*	...	7,570*
State totals	951	963	3	5	1,971*	...	2,638	2,683	14	9	5,411*	...	7,382*
Alabama	25	10	...	...	35	4	62	40	...	3	105	4	140
Alaska	8	12	...	...	20	4	14	26	...	...	40	2	60
Arizona	12	18	...	...	30	2	22	38	...	...	60	2	90
Arkansas	27	8	...	...	35	4	72	28	...	...	100	2	135
California	25	15	...	...	40	4	48	32	...	...	80	2	120
Colorado	18	17	...	...	35	4	35	30	...	...	65	2	100
Connecticut	24	12	...	...	36	2	99	52	...	...	151	2	187
Delaware	13	8	...	...	21	4	15	25	1 (a)	...	41	2	62
Florida	14	26	...	...	40	4	36	84	...	...	120	2	160
Georgia	22	34	...	...	56	2	80	99	1 (a)	...	180	2	236
Hawaii	20	5	...	...	25	4	41	10	...	...	51	2	76
Idaho	7	28	...	...	35	2	13	57	...	...	70	2	105
Illinois	31	27	1 (a)	...	59	(b)	65	53	...	...	118	2	177
Indiana	17	33	...	...	50	4	48	52	...	...	100	2	150
Iowa	25	25	...	...	50	4	49	51	...	...	100	2	150
Kansas	10	30	...	...	40	4	42	83	...	...	125	2	165
Kentucky	15	22	1 (a)	...	38	4	57	43	...	...	100	2	138
Louisiana	24	15	...	...	39	4	67	37	1 (a)	...	105	4	144
Maine	19	16	...	...	35	2	76	73	2 (d)	...	151	2	186
Maryland	33	14	...	...	47	4	98	43	...	...	141	4	188
Massachusetts	34	6	...	...	40	2	136	21	...	3	160	2	200
Michigan	16	22	...	...	38	4	52	58	...	...	110	2	148
Minnesota	35 (c)	31	1 (a)	...	67	4	66 (c)	68	...	...	134	2	201
Mississippi	28	24	...	...	52	4	75	47	...	...	122	4	174
Missouri	10	22	...	2	34	4	66	97	...	...	163	2	197
Montana	27	23	...	...	50	4	49	50	1 (o)	...	99	2	149
Nebraska	--------Nonpartisan election------				49	4	--------------------Unicameral----------------------						49
Nevada	9	12	...	...	21	4	26	16	...	...	42	2	63
New Hampshire	8	16	...	...	24	2	147	250	...	3	400	2	424
New Jersey	22	18	...	...	40	4 (e)	47	33	...	...	80	2	120
New Mexico	24	18	...	...	42	4	42	28	...	...	70	2	112
New York	28	34	...	...	62	2	104	46	...	...	150	2	212
North Carolina	29	21	...	...	50	2	63	57	...	...	120	2	170
North Dakota	15	32	...	...	47	4	27	67	...	...	94	4	141
Ohio	11	22	...	...	33	4	40	59	...	...	99	2	132
Oklahoma	26	22	...	...	48	4	44	57	...	...	101	2	149
Oregon	18	12	...	...	30	4	27	33	...	...	60	2	90
Pennsylvania	18	29	...	3	50	4	93	110	...	...	203	2	253
Rhode Island	33	5	...	...	38	2	60	15	...	...	75	2	113
South Carolina	20	26	...	...	46	4	50	74	...	...	124	2	170
South Dakota	10	25	...	...	35	2	19	51	...	...	70	2	105
Tennessee	16	17	...	...	33	4	53	46	...	...	99	2	132
Texas	12	19	...	...	31	4	63	87	...	...	150	2	181
Utah	8	21	...	...	29	4	19	56	...	...	75	2	104
Vermont	21	9	...	...	30	2	83	60	7 (f)	...	150	2	180
Virginia	16	24	...	...	40	4	38	60	2 (a)	...	100	2	140
Washington	26	23	...	...	49	4	55	43	...	...	98	2	147
West Virginia	21	13	...	...	34	4	68	32	...	...	100	2	134
Wisconsin	14	19	...	...	33	4	39	60	...	...	99	2	132
Wyoming	7	23	...	...	30	4	14	46	...	...	60	2	90
Dist. of Columbia (g)	11	1	1 (a)	...	13	4	----------------------Unicameral----------------------						13
American Samoa	--------Nonpartisan election------				18	4	--------Nonpartisan election-------				21 (l)	2	39
Guam	9	6	...	...	15	2	----------------------Unicameral----------------------						15
No. Mariana Islands	1	4	4 (m)	...	9	4	2	7	9 (n)	...	18	2	27
Puerto Rico	18(h)	8 (i)	1 (j)	...	28	4	32 (h)	18 (i)	1 (j)	...	51	4	79
U.S. Virgin Islands	11	...	4 (k)	...	15	2	----------------------Unicameral----------------------						15

See footnotes at end of table.

THE LEGISLATORS: NUMBERS, TERMS, AND PARTY AFFILIATIONS — Continued

Source: The Council of State Governments, March 2005.

* *Note:* Senate and combined body (Senate and House/Assembly) totals include Unicameral legislatures.

Key:

. . . - Does not apply

(a) Independent

(b) The entire Senate is up for election every 10 years, beginning in 1972. Senate districts are divided into three groups. One group elects senators for terms of four years, four years and two years; the second group for terms of four years, two years and four years; the third group for terms of two years, four years, and four years.

(c) Democratic-Farmer-Labor.

(d) Unenrolled (1); Green Independent Party (1),

(e) The first senatorial term at the beginning of each decade is two years.

(f) Independent (1); Progressive (6).

(g) Council of the District of Columbia.

(h) New Progressive Party.

(i) Popular Democratic Party.

(j) Puerto Rico Independent Party.

(k) Independent (2); Independent Citizens Movement (2).

(l) 21 seats; 20 are elected by popular vote and one is an appointed, non-voting delegate from Swains Island.

(m) Independent (1); Covenant (3).

(n) Covenant (8); Independent (1).

(o) Constitution.

Table 3.3A
THE LEGISLATORS: NUMBERS, TERMS, AND PARTY AFFILIATIONS BY REGION: 2005

State	Senate Democrats	Republicans	Other	Vacancies	Total	Term	House/Assembly Democrats	Republicans	Other	Vacancies	Total	Term	Senate and House/Assembly totals
State totals	951	963	3	5	1,971*	...	2,638	2,683	14	9	5,411*	...	7,382*
Eastern Region													
Connecticut	24	12	...	...	36	2	99	52	...	...	151	2	187
Delaware	13	8	...	...	21	4	15	25	1 (a)	...	41	2	62
Maine	19	16	...	...	35	2	76	73	2 (d)	...	151	2	186
Massachusetts	34	6	...	...	40	2	136	21	...	3	160	2	200
New Hampshire .	8	16	...	...	24	2	147	250	...	3	400	2	424
New Jersey	22	18	...	...	40	4 (e)	47	33	...	...	80	2	120
New York	28	34	...	...	62	2	104	46	...	...	150	2	21
Pennsylvania	18	29	...	3	50	4	93	110	...		203	2	253
Rhode Island	33	5	...	...	38	2	60	15	...	...	75	2	113
Vermont	21	9	...	...	30	2	83	60	7 (f)	...	150	2	180
Regional total	220	165	0	3	376	...	818	729	10	6	1,561	...	1,937
Midwestern Region													
Illinois	31	27	1 (a)	...	59	(b)	65	53	...	...	118	2	177
Indiana	17	33	...	...	50	4	48	52	...	...	100	2	150
Iowa	25	25	...	...	50	4	49	51	...	...	100	2	150
Kansas	10	30	...	...	40	4	42	83	...	...	125	2	165
Michigan	16	22	...	...	38	4	52	58	...	...	110	2	148
Minnesota	35 (c)	31	1 (a)	...	67	4	66 (c)	68	...	...	134	2	201
Nebraska	———Nonpartisan election———				49	4	———Unicameral———						49
North Dakota	15	32	...	...	47	4	27	67	...	...	94	4	141
Ohio	11	22	...	...	33	4	40	59	...	...	99	2	132
South Dakota	10	25	...	...	35	2	19	51	...	...	70	2	105
Wisconsin	14	19	...	...	33	4	39	60	...	...	99	2	132
Region total	184	266	2	...	501	...	447	602	0	0	1,049	...	1,550
Southern Region													
Alabama	25	10	...	...	35	4	62	40	...	3	105	4	140
Arkansas	27	8	...	...	35	4	72	28	...	...	100	2	135
Florida	14	26	...	...	40	4	36	84	...	...	120	2	160
Georgia	22	34	...	...	56	2	80	99	1 (a)	...	180	2	236
Kentucky	15	22	1 (a)	...	38	4	57	43	...	...	100	2	138
Louisiana	24	15	...	...	39	4	67	37	1 (a)	...	105	4	144
Maryland	33	14	...	...	47	4	98	43	...	...	141	4	188
Mississippi	28	24	...	...	52	4	75	47	...	...	122	4	174
Missouri	10	22	...	2	34	4	66	97	...	...	163	2	197
North Carolina ...	29	21	...	...	50	2	63	57	...	...	120	2	170
Oklahoma	26	22	...	...	48	4	44	57	...	...	101	2	149
South Carolina ...	20	26	...	...	46	4	50	74	...	...	124	2	170
Tennessee	16	17	...	...	33	4	53	46	...	...	99	2	132
Texas	12	19	...	...	31	4	63	87	...	...	150	2	181
Virginia	16	24	...	...	40	4	38	60	2 (a)	...	100	2	140
West Virginia	21	13	...	...	34	4	68	32	...	...	100	2	134
Region total	338	295	1	2	658	...	992	931	4	3	1,930	...	2,588
Western Region													
Alaska	8	12	...	...	20	4	14	26	...	...	40	2	60
Arizona	12	18	...	...	30	2	22	38	...	...	60	2	90
California	25	15	...	...	40	4	48	32	...	...	80	2	120
Colorado	18	17	...	...	35	4	35	30	...	...	65	2	100
Hawaii	20	5	...	...	25	4	41	10	...	...	51	2	76
Idaho	7	28	...	...	35	2	13	57	...	...	70	2	105
Montana	27	23	...	...	50	4	49	50	1 (g)	...	99	2	149
Nevada	9	12	...	...	21	4	26	16	...	...	42	2	63
New Mexico	24	18	...	...	42	4	42	28	...	...	70	2	112
Oregon	18	12	...	...	30	4	27	33	...	...	60	2	90
Utah	8	21	...	...	29	4	19	56	...	...	75	2	104
Washington	26	23	...	...	49	4	55	43	...	...	98	2	147
Wyoming	7	23	...	...	30	4	14	46	...	...	60	2	90
Regional total	209	227	...	...	436	...	405	465	1	0	870	...	1,306

Source: The Council of State Governments, March 2005.

* *Note:* Senate and combined body (Senate and House) totals include Nebraska's unicameral legislature.

Key:

... - Does not apply

(a) Independent.

(b) The entire Senate is up for election every 10 years, beginning in 1972. Senate districts are divided into three groups. One group elects senators for terms of four years, four years and two years; the second group for terms of four years, two years and four years; the third group for terms of two years, four years, and four years.

(c) Democratic-Farmer-Labor.

(d) Unenrolled (3); Green Independent Party (1).

(e) The first senatorial term at the beginning of each decade is two years.

(f) Independent (3); Progressive (4).

(g) Constitution.

Table 3.4
MEMBERSHIP TURNOVER IN THE LEGISLATURES: 2004

State or other jurisdiction	Senate Total number of members	Senate Number of membership changes	Senate Percentage change of total	House/Assembly Total number of members	House/Assembly Number of membership changes	House/Assembly Percentage change of total
Alabama	35	1	3%	105	4	4%
Alaska	20	2	10	40	10	25
Arizona	30	8	27	60	20	33
Arkansas	35	1	3	100	40	40
California	40	9	23	80	24	30
Colorado	35	6	17	65	18	28
Connecticut	36	4	11	151	16	11
Delaware	21	0	0	41	6	15
Florida	40	2	5	120	19	16
Georgia	56	20	36	180	45	25
Hawaii	25	2	8	51	9	18
Idaho	35	7	20	70	15	21
Illinois	59	4	7	118	12	10
Indiana	50	5	10	100	11	11
Iowa	50	9	18	100	11	11
Kansas	40	15	38	125	30	24
Kentucky	38	7	18	100	13	13
Louisiana	39	1	3	105	2	2
Maine	35	19	54	151	61	40
Maryland	47	0	0	141	4	3
Massachusetts	40	6	15	160	12	8
Michigan	38	0	0	110	35	32
Minnesota	67	1	1	134	26	19
Mississippi	52	3	6	122	1	1
Missouri	34	11	32	163	39	24
Montana	50	16	32	100	38	38
Nebraska	49	8	16	Unicameral		
Nevada	21	4	19	42	12	29
New Hampshire	24	6	25	400	135	34
New Jersey	40	0	0	80	0	0
New Mexico	42	6	14	70	10	14
New York	62	4	6	150	17	11
North Carolina	50	12	24	120	24	20
North Dakota	47	2	4	94	11	12
Ohio	33	6	21	99	18	18
Oklahoma	48	22	46	101	43	43
Oregon	30	6	20	60	19	32
Pennsylvania	50	2	4	203	13	6
Rhode Island	38	3	8	75	14	19
South Carolina	46	8	17	124	17	14
South Dakota	35	14	40	70	23	33
Tennessee	33	4	12	99	14	14
Texas	31	2	6	150	17	11
Utah	29	3	10	75	16	21
Vermont	30	5	17	150	32	21
Virginia	40	0	0	100	1	1
Washington	49	8	16	98	20	20
West Virginia	34	4	12	100	17	17
Wisconsin	33	5	15	99	20	20
Wyoming	30	7	23	60	14	23
Dist. of Columbia	13	3	23	Unicameral		
American Samoa	18	3	17	21	1	5
Guam	15	0	0	Unicameral		
No. Mariana Islands	9	4	44	18	9	50
Puerto Rico	28	17	11	51	22	43
U.S. Virgin Islands	15	0	0	Unicameral		

Source: The Council of State Governments, March 2005.
Note: Turnover calculated after 2004 legislative elections.

Table 3.5
THE LEGISLATORS: QUALIFICATIONS FOR ELECTION

State or other jurisdiction	House/Assembly					Senate				
	Minimum age	U.S. citizen (years) (a)	State resident (years) (b)	District resident (years)	Qualified voter (years)	Minimum age	U.S. citizen (years) (a)	State resident (years) (b)	District resident (years)	Qualified voter (years)
Alabama	21	:	3 (c)	1	:	25	:	3 (c)	1	:
Alaska	21	★	3	1	★	25	★	3	1	★
Arizona	25	★	3	1	:	25	★	3	1	:
Arkansas	21	★	2	1	★	25	★	2	1	★
California	18	3	3 (c)	1	★	18	3	3 (c)	1	★
Colorado	25	★	1	1	★	25	★	1	1	★
Connecticut	18	★	★	★	★	18	★	★	★	★
Delaware	24	:	3	1	:	27	:	3	1	:
Florida	21	:	2	2	:	21	:	2	2	:
Georgia	21	★	2 (c)	1	★	25	:	2 (c)	1	★
Hawaii	18	★	3	(d)	★	18	★	3	(d)	★
Idaho	21	★	:	1	★	21	★	:	1	★
Illinois	21	★	★	2 (e)	★	21	★	★	2 (e)	★
Indiana	21	★	2	1	★	25	★	2	1	★
Iowa	21	★	1	60 days	:	25	★	1	60 days	:
Kansas	18	★	★ (c)	★	★	18	★	★ (c)	★	★
Kentucky	24	:	2 (c)	1	★	30	:	6 (c)	1	★
Louisiana	18	★	2	3 mo.	★	18	:	2	3 mo.	★
Maine	21	5	1	6 mo. (f)	★	25	5	1	6 mo. (f)	★
Maryland	21	:	1 (c)	6 mo. (f)	:	25	:	1 (c)	6 mo. (f)	:
Massachusetts	18	:	:	1	★	18	:	5	★	★
Michigan	21	★	★	(d)	★	21	★	★	(d)	★
Minnesota	18	★	1	6 mo.	★	21	★	1	6 mo.	★
Mississippi	21	:	4 (c)	2	★	25	★	4 (c)	2	4
Missouri	24	★	★	1	2	30	★	★	1	3
Montana	18	:	1	6 mo. (g)	U	18	:	1	6 mo. (g)	:
Nebraska	U	U	U	U	U	21	★	1	★	★
Nevada	21	★	1 (c)	30 days (l)	★	21	★	1 (c)	30 days (l)	★
New Hampshire	18	:	2 (c)	1	★	30	:	7 (c)	1	★
New Jersey	21	★	2 (c)	1	★	30	★	4 (c)	1	★
New Mexico	21	★	★	★	★	25	★	★	★	★
New York	18	★	5	1 (h)	★	18	★	5	1 (h)	★
North Carolina	21	:	:	1	:	25	:	2	1	:
North Dakota	18	★	1	★	★	18	★	1	★	★
Ohio	18	★	30 days	1	:	18	★	30 days	1	★
Oklahoma	21	★	★	1	★	25	★	★	1	★
Oregon	21	★	:	1	★	21	★	:	1	:
Pennsylvania	21	:	4 (c)	1	:	25	★	4 (c)	1	★
Rhode Island	18	★	30 days	30 days	★	18	:	30 days	30 days	★
South Carolina	21	:	:	★	:	25	:	:	★	:

See footnotes at end of table.

THE LEGISLATORS: QUALIFICATIONS FOR ELECTION — Continued

State or other jurisdiction	House/Assembly					Senate				
	Minimum age	U.S. citizen (years) (a)	State resident (years) (b)	District resident (years)	Qualified voter (years)	Minimum age	U.S. citizen (years) (a)	State resident (years) (b)	District resident (years)	Qualified voter (years)
South Dakota	21	★	2	★	★	21	★	★	★	★
Tennessee	21	★	3 (c)	1	★	30	★	3	1	★
Texas	21	★	2	1	★	26	★	5	1	★
Utah	25	★	3 (c)	6 mo.	★	25	★	3 (c)	6 mo.	★
Vermont	18	★	2	1	...	18	★	2	1	...
Virginia	21	★	1	★	★	21	★	1	★	★
Washington	18	1	★	(d)	★	18	1	1	(d)	★
West Virginia	18	1	1 (c)	1	★	25	5	5 (c)	1	★
Wisconsin	18	★	1	(d)	★	18	★	1	(d)	★
Wyoming	21	★	★(c)	1	★	25	★	★(c)	1	★
Dist. of Columbia	U	U	U	U	U	18	...	1	★	...
American Samoa	25	★(i)	5	1	...	30 (j)	★(i)	5	1	★
Guam	U	U	U	U	U	25	★	5	...	...
No. Mariana Islands	21	...	3	(d)	★	25	...	5	(d)	★
Puerto Rico	25	...	2	1 (k)	...	30	...	2	1 (k)	...
U.S. Virgin Islands	21	★	...	3	...	21	★	...	3	★

Source: The Council of State Governments survey, October 2003 and October 2004.

Note: Many state constitutions have additional provisions disqualifying persons from holding office if they are convicted of a felony, bribery, perjury or other infamous crimes.

Key:

U— Unicameral legislature; members are called senators, except in District of Columbia.

★—Formal provision; number of years not specified.

...—No formal provision.

(a) In some states candidate must be a U.S. citizen to be an elector, and must be an elector to run.

(b) In some states candidate must be a state resident to be an elector, and must be an elector to run.

(c) State citizenship requirement.

(d) Must be a qualified voter of the district; number of years not specified.

(e) Following redistricting, a candidate may be elected from any district that contains a part of the district in which (s)he resided at the time of redistricting, and reelected if a resident of the new district he represents for 18 months prior to reelection.

(f) If the district was established for less than six months, residency is length of establishment of district.

(g) Shall be a resident of the county if it contains one or more districts or of the district if it contains all or parts of more than one county.

(h) After redistricting, must have been a resident of the county in which the district is contained for one year immediately preceding election.

(i) Or U.S. national.

(j) Must be registered matai.

(k) The district legislator must live in the municipality he/she represents.

(l) 30 days prior to close of filing for declaration of candidacy.

Table 3.6
SENATE LEADERSHIP POSITIONS: METHODS OF SELECTION

State or other jurisdiction	President	President pro tem	Majority leader	Assistant majority leader	Majority floor leader	Assistant majority floor leader	Majority whip	Majority caucus chair	Minority leader	Assistant minority leader	Minority floor leader	Assistant minority floor leader	Minority whip	Minority caucus chair
Alabama	(a)	ES	AT						EC				EC	EC
Alaska	ES	AP	EC						EC				EC	
Arizona	ES	ES	EC						EC				EC	EC
Arkansas	(a)	ES	EC		EC		EC	EC	EC	EC	EC		EC	EC
California	(a)	ES							EC					EC
Colorado	ES (bb)	ES (bb)	EC	EC	AP	AP	AP	EC	EC	EC			EC	EC
Connecticut (b)	(a)	ES	AP	AP	AP	AP	AP	AP	EC	AL	AL	AL	AL	AL
Delaware	EC/ES	AP	AP	AL	AP or AL	AP or AL	AP or AL	AP or AL	EC	AL	AL	AL	AL	AL
Florida	(a)	ES	EC		AP or AL		EC	EC	EC				EC	EC
Georgia	(a)		EC					EC (cc)	EC		EC			EC
Hawaii	ES	ES (f)	EC	EC	EC		EC (e)	(e)	EC	EC			EC	EC
Idaho	(a)	ES	EC				EC	EC	EC	AL/5	AL		AL	AL
Illinois			AP (c)	AP/6				AP	EC	AL	AL		AL	EC
Indiana	(a)	ES	EC	AL	EC		AL	EC	EC	EC			EC	EC
Iowa	ES	ES	EC	EC	EC		EC	EC	EC	EC	(bb)		EC	EC
Kansas	ES	ES (f)	EC	EC (d)	EC		EC (e)	(e)	EC	EC			EC	EC
Kentucky	ES	ES	EC		EC		EC	EC	EC	EC	EC		EC	EC
Louisiana	ES	AP	EC	EC	EC	EC	EC	EC	EC	EC	EC		EC	EC
Maine	ES	ES	EC	EC	EC (n)	EC	AP (bb)	EC	EC (bb)	EC	(bb)		EC	EC
Maryland	ES	ES	AP (n)	EC	EC	(n)			EC	EC				
Massachusetts	EC	ES	AP	AP	EC		EC	(p)	EC	EC			EC	(p)
Michigan (aa)	(a)	ES (i)	EC	AT/2	EC		AL	EC	EC	EC				EC
Minnesota	(a)	ES	EC	EC	ES		EC	EC	EC	ES			ES	EC
Mississippi	(a)	ES												EC
Missouri	ES	ES			ES		ES	EC		ES	ES			EC
Montana	ES	ES			ES				EC					EC
Nebraska (U)	(a)	ES (g)												
Nevada	(a)	ES	AP		EC		EC	EC	EC	AL			AL	AL
New Hampshire	ES	AP	EC	EC/3			EC	EC	EC	EC/3			EC	EC
New Jersey (h)	ES	ES	EC				EC	EC	EC		EC (u)		AL	EC
New Mexico	(a)	ES	EC (u)		EC (u)		EC	EC	EC (u)	AL/3			EC	EC
New York (v)	(a)	ES (i)	(i)	AT/2	AP		AT	AT (j)	EC				AL	AL (j)
North Carolina	(a)	ES	EC	EC			EC	EC	EC	EC			EC	EC
North Dakota	(a)	ES	EC	EC			EC	EC	ES (p)	ES			ES	(p)
Ohio (l)	ES (p)	ES	EC		EC		EC	EC	EC	EC/1			EC/1	(p)
Oklahoma	ES	ES	EC	EC	EC		EC	EC	EC	EC/2	EC		EC	EC
Oregon	ES	ES	EC	AL/3	EC		EC (p)	(p)	EC (p)	EC			EC	(p)
Pennsylvania	(a)	ES	EC	EC	EC		AP	EC	EC	AP/2 (o)			AP	EC
Rhode Island (k)	(a)	ES	EC	AL/6 (o)					EC					
South Carolina	(a)	ES	EC						EC					

See footnotes at end of table.

SENATE LEADERSHIP POSITIONS: METHODS OF SELECTION — Continued

State or other jurisdiction	President	President pro tem	Majority leader	Assistant majority leader	Majority floor leader	Assistant majority floor leader	Majority whip	Majority caucus chair	Minority leader	Assistant minority leader	Minority floor leader	Assistant minority floor leader	Minority whip	Minority caucus chair
South Dakota	(a)	ES	EC	EC	…	EC	EC	EC	EC	EC	…	…	EC	EC
Tennessee	ES	AP (m)	EC (m)	…	…	…	EC	EC (m)	EC (m)	EC	…	…	…	EC (m)
Texas	(a)	ES	ES	…	…	…	EC	EC (r)	EC	EC	…	…	EC	EC (r)
Utah (q)	ES	…	EC	EC	EC (r)	EC (r)	EC (r)	EC (r)	EC (t)	EC	EC	EC (r)	EC (r)	EC (t)
Vermont	(a)	ES	EC	EC	EC (r)	EC (r)	EC (r)	EC (r)	EC (t)	EC	EC	EC (r)	EC (r)	EC (t)
Virginia	(a)	ES	EC	EC	EC	EC	EC	EC	EC	EC	EC	EC	EC	…
Washington (s)	(a)	ES	EC	…	EC	EC	EC	EC	EC (t)	EC	EC (t)	EC (t)	AL	EC (t)
West Virginia	ES	AP	AP	…	EC	EC	AP	EC	EC	EC	EC	EC	EC	EC
Wisconsin	ES	ES	EC	EC	EC	EC	EC	EC	EC	EC	EC	EC	EC	EC
Wyoming	ES	ES (f)	…	…	EC	EC	EC	EC	…	…	EC	EC	EC	EC
Dist. of Columbia (U)	(w)	(x)	…	…	…	…	…	…	…	…	…	…	…	…
American Samoa	ES	ES	…	…	…	…	EC	…	EC	EC	…	…	EC	…
Guam (U)	ES (g)	ES (f)	EC	EC	…	…	…	…	EC	EC	…	…	…	EC
No. Mariana Islands	ES (ee)	AS	(ee)	…	…	…	…	…	…	…	…	…	…	…
Puerto Rico	ES (p)	ES (f)	AS	…	ES (y)	…	(dd)	(dd)	EC (p)	…	EC (z)	EC (t)	…	(p)
U.S. Virgin Islands (U)	ES	ES (f)	EC (z)	…	EC (z)	…	(n)	(n)	…	…	…	…	…	…

Source: The Council of State Governments' survey, October 2003 and October 2004.

Note: In some states, the leadership positions in the Senate are not empowered by the law or by the rules of the chamber, but rather by the party members themselves. Entry following slash indicates number of individuals holding specified position.

Key:
ES—Elected or confirmed by all members of the Senate.
EC—Elected by party caucus.
AP—Appointed by president.
AT—Appointed by president pro tempore.
AL—Appointed by party leader.
(U)—Unicameral legislative body.
…—Position does not exist or is not selected on a regular basis.
(a) Lieutenant governor is president of the Senate by virtue of the office.
(b) Position titles are as follows: chief deputy president pro tem, two deputy presidents pro tem, a chief assistant president pro tem, three assistant presidents pro tem, three deputy majority leaders (AP); a minority leader pro tem, two chief deputy minority leaders, a deputy minority leader-at-large, and three deputy minority leaders (AL).
(c) The president can, at his or her discretion, serve as majority leader and usually does.
(d) Assistant majority leader also serves as majority party caucus chairperson.
(e) Official title is assistant majority leader/whip.
(f) Official title is vice president. In Guam, vice speaker.
(g) Official title is speaker. In Tennessee, official also has the statutory title of lieutenant governor.
(h) Additional positions include deputy majority leader (EC), two deputy assistant minority leaders (EC), and minority leader pro tem (EC).
(i) President pro tempore is also majority leader.
(j) Majority caucus chair: official title is majority conference chair. Minority caucus chair: official title is minority conference chair.
(k) Additional positions include deputy president pro tempore.
(l) Additional positions include assistant president pro tempore (ES) and assistant minority whip (ES).
(m) President pro tem: official title is speaker pro tem. Official titles of majority party leaders: Democratic; official titles of minority party leaders: Republican.

(n) Majority leader also serves as majority floor leader; deputy majority leader is official title and serves as assistant majority floor leader. there is also an assistant deputy majority leader; there is also a deputy majority whip and assistant deputy majority whips; minority leader also serves as minority floor leader.
(o) Assistant majority leader: official title is deputy majority leader. Assistant minority leader: official title is deputy minority leader.
(p) President and minority floor leader are also caucus chairs. In Ohio and Puerto Rico, president and minority leader. In Oregon, majority leader and minority leader.
(q) Additional positions include assistant majority whip (EC) assistant majority whip (EC), minority whip (EC), assistant minority whip (EC) and minority caucus leader (EC).
(r) Majority leader serves as majority floor leader and majority caucus chair. Assistant majority leader serves as assistant majority floor leader and majority whip. Minority leader serves as minority floor leader and minority caucus chair. Assistant minority leader serves as assistant minority floor leader and minority whip.
(s) Additional positions include vice president pro tem (ES), majority assistant whip (EC), and Republican assistant whip (EC).
(t) Customary title of minority party leaders is the party designation (Republican).
(u) Majority leader also serves as majority floor leader. Minority leader also serves as minority floor leader.
(v) Additional positions include vice president pro tem (AT), deputy majority leader for legislative operations (AT), majority program development chair (AT), deputy minority leader (AL), senior assistant majority leader (AT), majority conference vice chair (AT), minority conference vice chair (AL), majority conference secretary (AT), deputy majority whip (AT), majority steering committee chair (AT), minority conference secretary (AL), assistant majority whip (AT), and assistant minority whip (AL).
(w) Chair of the Council, which is an elected position.
(x) Appointed by the chair; official title is chair pro tem.
(y) Official title is floor leader.
(z) Office title is alternate floor leader.
(aa) Additional positions include assistant president, associate president pro tempore, assistant majority caucus chair, assistant minority caucus chair.
(bb) Selected informally by majority caucus shortly after November election.
(cc) Official title is majority caucus leader.
(dd) Official title is caucus chairman.
(ee) Speaker also serves as majority leader.

Table 3.7
HOUSE LEADERSHIP POSITIONS: METHODS OF SELECTION

State or other jurisdiction	Speaker	Speaker pro tem	Majority leader	Assistant majority leader	Majority floor leader	Assistant majority floor leader	Majority whip	Majority caucus chair	Minority leader	Assistant minority leader	Minority floor leader	Assistant minority floor leader	Minority whip	Minority caucus chair
Alabama	EH	EH	EC						EC					
Alaska	EH	AS	EC				EC	EC	EC				EC	EC
Arizona	EH	AS	EC				EC		EC				EC	
Arkansas	EH	AS	AS	AS			EC	EC	EC				EC	
California	EH	AS			AS		AS		EC		EC		EC	EC
Colorado	EH(x)	AS	EC	EC			EC	EC	EC	EC			EC	EC
Connecticut	EH	AS/4(b)	EC	EC/4(b)		AS(b)	AS(b)	AS(b)	EC	AL(b)	AL(b)	AL(b)	AL(b)	AL(b)
Delaware	EC/EH	EH	EC				AS	AS	EC	AL	AL	AL	EC	AL
Florida	EH	EH	AS	AS	AS	AS	AS	EC	EC	AL	AL	AL	AL	EC
Georgia	EH	EH	EC				EC	EC	EC				EC	
Hawaii	EH	EH(a)	EC		EC		EC		EC	EC	EC	EC	EC	EC
Idaho	EH		EC	EC				EC	EC	EC	AL/2(c)		AL	AL(c)
Illinois	EH	AL	AS	AS/6	AS/2(c)			AS(c)	EC	AL/6	EC		AL	AL
Indiana	EH	AL	EC	AL	AL	AL	AL	AL	EC	AL	AL	AL	AL	AL
Iowa	EH	EH	EC	EC					EC	EC			EC	EC
Kansas	EC	EH	EC	EC	EC		EC	EC	EC		EC		EC	EC
Kentucky	EH	EH	EC				EC	EC	EC				EC	EC
Louisiana	EH	EH			EC				EC	AL			AL	AL
Maine	EH	AS(d)	EC(j)	EC(j)	(j)	(j)	(j)		EC(j)	EC(j)			(j)	(g)
Maryland	EH	EH	AS(e)	AS(e)	(e)	AS	AS	(g)	EC	EC	EC	EC	EC	(g)
Massachusetts	EC	EH	AS	AS				(h)	EC(h)	AL	EC	EC	(h)	(h)
Michigan	EH	EH	EC	EC	EC	EC	EC	EC	EC	EC	EC	EC	EC	EC
Minnesota	EH	AS	EC	EC					EC	AL				
Mississippi	EH	EH							EC	AL	EC		EC	EC
Missouri	EH	EH			EC	EC	EC	EC		EC	EC	EC	EC	EC
Montana	EH	EH	EH		EH		EH(i)				EH		EH	
Nebraska														
Nevada	EH	EH	AS	AS	EC	EC	AS(k)	AS	AS(k)	AL(k)	EC	EC	EC	EC
New Hampshire	EH	AS(a)	EC	EC/3			EC	EC(m)	EC	EC/4	EC		EC	EC(m)
New Jersey	EH	EH												
New Mexico	EH		EC		EC(h)		EC	EC	EC	AL/2	EC(h)	EC	EC	EC
New York	EH	AS	AS	AS		AS	AS	AS(o)	EC	AL	EC		AL	AL(o)
North Carolina	EH	AS	EC				EC	EC	EC	EC			EC	EC
North Dakota	EH	EH	EC	EC			EC	EC	EC	EC			EC	EC
Ohio	EH(g)	EH			EH	EH	EH	(g)	EH(g)		EH		EH	(g)
Oklahoma	EH	EH	AS	AS	AS	AS	AS	AS	EC	EC	EC	EC	EC	EC
Oregon	EH	EH	EC(q)	AL/7		EC	EC	(q)	EC(q)	AL/5			EC/3	(q)
Pennsylvania	EH	EH	EC	EC	EC	EC	EC	EC	EC	EC	EC	EC	EC	EC
Rhode Island	EH	AS	EC	EC/11(f)	EC		AL	EC	EC	AL/3(r)			AL	EC
South Carolina	EH	EH	EC						EC					

See footnotes at end of table.

HOUSE LEADERSHIP POSITIONS — METHODS OF SELECTION — Continued

State or other jurisdiction	Speaker	Speaker pro tem	Majority leader	Assistant majority leader	Majority floor leader	Assistant majority floor leader	Majority whip	Majority caucus chair	Minority leader	Assistant minority leader	Minority floor leader	Assistant minority floor leader	Minority whip	Minority caucus chair
South Dakota	EH	EH	EC	EC	...	...	EC	...	EC	EC	...	...	EC	...
Tennessee	EH	EH	EC	EC	EC	EC	EC	...	EC	EC	...	...	EC	EC
Texas	EH	AS	...	...	...	...	...	...	...	...	...	...	...	...
Utah	EH	AS	EC	EC	EC (s)	EC (s)	EC	...	EC (s)	EC (s)	...	...	EC (s)	EC (s)
Vermont	EH	...	EC	EC	(j)	(j)	(j)	(j)	EC	EC	(j)	(j)	(j)	(j)
Virginia	EH	...	EC (h)	...	(h)	...	EC	EC	EC (h)	EC (s)	(h)	EC	EC (h)	EC
Washington (o)	EH	EH	EC	EC	...	EC/2	EC	EC (t)	EC	...	EC	EC/2	(EC	EC
West Virginia	EH	AS	AS	AS	...	...	AS	AS	EC	...	EC	...	...	...
Wisconsin	EH	EH	EC	EC	EC	EC	EC	EC	EC	EC	EC	EC	EC	EC
Wyoming	EH	EH	...	...	EC	EC	EC	EC	...	...	EC	...	EC	EC
Dist. of Columbia	(i)													
American Samoa	EH	EH (a)	...	...	...	...	...	...	...	...	...	...	...	...
Guam	...	...	...	...	...	...	(i)							
No. Mariana Islands	EH (u)	...	(u)	...	EH (v)	...	...	...	EC	...	EC (w)	...	...	(g)
Puerto Rico	EH (g)	EH (a)	EC	...	EC (w)	...	...	...	EC (g)	...	EC (w)	...	...	...
U.S. Virgin Islands	...	...	...	...	...	...	(i)							

Source: The Council of State Governments' survey, October 2003 and October 2004.

Note: In some states, the leadership positions in the house are not empowered by the law or by the rules of the chamber, but rather by the party members themselves. Entry following slash indicates number of individuals holding specified position.

Key:

EH—Elected or confirmed by all members of the house.
EC—Elected by party caucus.
AS—Appointed by speaker.
AL—Appointed by party leader.
...—Position does not exist or is not selected on a regular basis.

(a) Official title is deputy speaker. In Hawaii, American Samoa and Puerto Rico, vice speaker.
(b) Official titles: speaker pro tem - deputy speaker; assistant majority leader - deputy majority leader.
(c) Official titles: majority floor leader is deputy majority leader, majority caucus chair is majority conference chair; minority floor leader is deputy minority leader, and minority caucus chair is minority conference chair.
(d) Each occurance.
(e) Majority leader also serves as majority floor leader. Official title of assistant majority leader is deputy majority leader.
(f) Official title is deputy majority leader.
(g) Speaker and minority leader are also caucus chair.
(h) Majority leader also serves as majority floor leader; minority leader also serves as minority floor leader.
(i) Unicameral legislature; see entries in Table 3.6, Senate Leadership Positions—Methods of Selection.
(j) Majority leader also serves as majority floor leader; assistant majority leader also serves as assistant majority floor leader and majority whip; minority leader also serves as minority floor leader; assistant minority leader also serves as assistant minority floor leader and minority whip.

(k) Official titles: assistant majority leader is deputy majority leader, majority whip is deputy majority whip, minority leader is deputy majority whip, minority leader is Democratic leader and assistant minority leader is deputy minority leader.
(l) Additional positions include four deputy speakers (EC), three assistant majority whips (EC), majority budget officer (EC), minority leader pro tem (EC), and three deputy minority leaders (EC).
(m) Official titles: majority caucus chair is majority conference leader and minority caucus chair is conference chair.
(n) Additional positions: deputy speaker (AS), assistant speaker (AS), assistant speaker pro tem (AS), minority leader pro tem (AL), assistant minority leader pro tem (AL), deputy majority leader (AL), deputy minority leader (AL), deputy majority whip (AS), deputy minority whip (AL), assistant majority whip (AL), assistant minority whip (AL), majority conference vice-chair (AS), minority conference vice-chair (AL), majority conference secretary (AS), minority conference secretary (AL), majority steering committee chair (AS), majority steering committee vice-chair (AS), minority steering committee chair (AL), minority steering committee vice-chair (AL), majority program committee chair (AS) and minority program committee chair (AL).
(o) Official titles: majority caucus chair is majority conference chair; minority caucus chair is minority conference chair.
(p) Additional positions include assistant majority whip (EH) and assistant minority whip (EH).
(q) Majority leader also serves as majority caucus chair; minority leader also serves as minority caucus chair.
(r) Official title is deputy minority leader.
(s) Assistant majority floor leader known as assistant majority whip, assistant minority floor leader known as assistant minority whip, minority caucus chair known as minority caucus manager.
(t) Additional position is caucus vice chair (EC).
(u) Speaker also serves as majority leader.
(v) Official title is floor leader.
(w) Official title is alternate floor leader.
(x) Selected informally by majority caucus shortly after November election.

Table 3.8
METHOD OF SETTING LEGISLATIVE COMPENSATION

State or other jurisdiction	Constitution	Statute	Compensation commission	Legislators' salaries tied or related to state employees' salaries
Alabama	★	. . .	. . .	. . .
Alaska	. . .	★	★	. . .
Arizona	. . .	. . .	★ (a)	. . .
Arkansas	★	★	. . .	. . .
California	★	. . .	★	. . .
Colorado	. . .	★	. . .	. . .
Connecticut	. . .	. . .	★ (b)	. . .
Delaware	. . .	★	★ (c)	. . .
Florida	. . .	★	. . .	Statute provides members same percentage increase as state employees.
Georgia	. . .	★	. . .	. . .
Hawaii	. . .	. . .	★ (d)	. . .
Idaho	. . .	. . .	★	. . .
Illinois	. . .	★	★	Salaries are tied to employment cost index, wages and salaries for state and local government workers.
Indiana	. . .	★	. . .	. . .
Iowa	. . .	★	★	. . .
Kansas	. . .	★	. . .	. . .
Kentucky	. . .	. . .	★ (e)	. . .
Louisiana	. . .	★	. . .	. . .
Maine	★	★ (f)	★	. . .
Maryland	. . .	. . .	★ (g)	. . .
Massachusetts	. . .	★ (h)	. . .	. . .
Michigan	. . .	. . .	★ (i)	. . .
Minnesota	. . .	★	★ (j)	. . .
Mississippi	. . .	★	. . .	. . .
Missouri	★	★ (k)	. . .	. . .
Montana	. . .	★	. . .	Tied to executive branch pay matrix.
Nebraska	★	★	. . .	. . .
Nevada	. . .	★	. . .	. . .
New Hampshire	★	. . .	. . .	. . .
New Jersey	★	★	★	. . .
New Mexico	★	★	. . .	. . .
New York	★	★	. . .	. . .
North Carolina	. . .	★	. . .	. . .
North Dakota	. . .	★	★	. . .
Ohio	★	★	. . .	. . .
Oklahoma	. . .	★	★	. . .
Oregon	. . .	★	. . .	. . .
Pennsylvania	. . .	★ (l)	. . .	. . .
Rhode Island	★	. . .	. . .	. . .
South Carolina	. . .	★	. . .	. . .
South Dakota	★	★	. . .	. . .
Tennessee	★	★	. . .	. . .
Texas	★ (m)	. . .	. . .	. . .
Utah	. . .	. . .	★	. . .
Vermont	. . .	★	. . .	. . .
Virginia	★	★ (n)	. . .	. . .
Washington	★	★	★	. . .
West Virginia	. . .	. . .	★ (o)	. . .
Wisconsin	. . .	★	. . .	The Commission plan is approved by Joint Committee on Employment Relations and the governor. It is tied to state employer compensation.
Wyoming	. . .	★	. . .	. . .
Dist. of Columbia	. . .	★	. . .	. . .

See footnotes at end of table.

METHOD OF SETTING LEGISLATIVE COMPENSATION — Continued

Source: National Conference of State Legislatures, 2003.
Key:
★— Method used to set compensation.
. . . — Method not used to set compensation.
(a) Arizona commission recommendations are put on ballot for a vote of the people.
(b) The Connecticut General Assembly takes independent action pursuant to recommendations of a Compensation Committee.
(c) Are implemented automatically if not rejected by resolution.
(d) Commission recommendations take effect unless rejected by concurrent resolution or the Governor. Any change in salary that becomes effective does not apply to the legislature to which the recommendation was submitted.
(e) The Kentucky committee has not met since 1995. The most recent pay raise was initiated and passed by the General Assembly.
(f) Presented to the Legislature in the form of legislation, the legislature must enact and the Governor must sign into law.
(g) Maryland commission meets before each four-year term of office and presents recommendations to General Assembly for its action. Recommendations may be reduced or rejected, not increased.
(h) In 1998 , the voters passed a legislative referendum starting with the 2001 session, members will receive an automatic increase or decrease according to the median household income for the commonwealth for the preceding 2 year period.
(i) If resolution is offered, it is put to legislative vote; if legislature does not vote recommendations down, the new salaries take effect January 1 of the new year.
(j) By May 1 in odd numbered years the Council submits salary recommendations to the presiding officers.
(k) Recommendations are adjusted by legislature or governor if necessary.
(l) Each chamber receives a cost of living increase that is tied to the Consumer Price Index.
(m) In 1991 a constitutional amendment was approved by voters to allow the Ethics Commission to recommend the salaries of members. Any recommendations must be approved by voters to be effective. This provision has yet to be used.
(n) In 1998 the Joint Rules Committee created a Legislative Compensation Commission. It was composed of two former governors and citizens that made recommendations regarding salary, per diem and office expenses.
(o) Submits, by resolution and must be concurred by at least four members of the commission. The Legislature must enact the resolution into law and may reduce, but shall not increase, any item established in such resolution.

Table 3.9
LEGISLATIVE COMPENSATION: REGULAR SESSIONS

State or other jurisdiction	Salaries			Per diem living expenses
	Regular sessions			
	Per diem salary (a)	Limit on days	Annual salary	
Alabama	$10 C	...	...	$2,280/m plus $50/d for three days each week that the legislature actually meets during any session (U).
Alaska	...	...	$24,012	$204/day (U) tied to federal rate. Legislators who reside in the capitol area receive 75% of federal rate.
Arizona	...	...	$24,000	$35/d for the 1st 120 days of regular session and for special session and $10/d thereafter; members residing outside Maricopa County receive an additional $25/d for the 1st 120 days of regular session and for special session and an additional $10/d thereafter (V). Set by statute.
Arkansas*	...	...	$13,751	$111/d (V) plus mileage tied to federal rate.
California	...	...	$99,000	$140/d (V) by roll call. Maximum allowable per diem is paid regardless of actual expenses.
Colorado	...	...	$30,000	$45/d for members living in the Denver metro area. $99/d for members living outside Denver (V). Per diem is determined by the legislature.
Connecticut	...	...	$28,000	No per diem is paid.
Delaware	...	...	$36,500	No per diem is paid.
Florida	...	...	$29,916	$103/d (V) tied to the federal rate. Earned based on the number of days in session. Travel vouchers are filed to substantiate.
Georgia	...	...	$16,200	$128/d (U) set by the legislature.
Hawaii	...	...	$32,000	$80 for members living outside Oahu; $10/d for members living on Oahu (V) set by the legislature.
Idaho	...	...	$15,646	$99/d for members establishing second residence in Boise; $38/day if no second residence is established and up to $25/d travel (U) set by Compensation Commission.
Illinois	...	...	$55,788	$85 (U) tied to federal rate.
Indiana	...	...	$11,600	$132 (U) tied to federal rate.
Iowa	...	...	$21,380.54	$86/d (U). $65/d for Polk County legislators (U) set by the legislature. State mileage rates apply.
Kansas	$78.75 C	...	...	$86/d (U) tied to federal rate.
Kentucky	$166.34 C	...	...	$94.60/d (U) tied to federal rate. (110% federal per diem rate).
Louisiana	...	...	$16,800	$113/d (U) tied to federal rate. Additional $6,000/yr (U) expense allowance.
Maine	...	...	$11,384–1st $8,302–2nd	$38/d housing or reimbursement for mileage in lieu of housing at the rate of .32/mile up to $38/d. $32/d meals (V) set by the legislature.
Maryland	...	...	$31,509	Lodging $96/d; meals $32/d (V) tied to federal rate and compensation commission.
Massachusetts	...	...	$53,379.93	From $10/d-$100/d, depending on distance from State House (V) set by the legislature.
Michigan	...	...	$79,650	$12,000 yearly expense allowance for session and interim (V) set by compensation commission.
Minnesota	...	...	$31,140	Senators receive $66/d and Representatives receive $56/L (U) set by the legislature.
Mississippi	...	...	$10,000	$86/d (U) tied to federal rate.
Missouri	...	...	$31,351	$76/d tied to federal rate. Verification of per diem is by roll call. Mileage is 34.5 cents per mile.
Montana	$76.80 L	...	...	$90.31/d (U).
Nebraska	...	...	$12,000	$86/d outside 50-mile radius from Capitol; $31/d if member resides within 50 miles of Capitol (V) tied to federal rate.
Nevada	$130	60	...	Federal rate for Capitol area (V). Legislators who live more than 50 miles from the capitol, if requiring lodging, will be paid Hud single room rate for Carson City area for each month of session.
New Hampshire	...	2 yr. term	$200	No per diem is paid.
New Jersey	...	...	$49,000	No per diem is paid.

See footnotes at end of table.

LEGISLATIVE COMPENSATION: REGULAR SESSIONS — Continued

State or other jurisdiction	Salaries Regular sessions Per diem salary (a)	Limit on days	Annual salary	Per diem living expenses
New Mexico	...	...	...	$146/d (V) tied to federal rate and the constitution.
New York	...	...	$79,500	Varies (V) tied to federal rate.
North Carolina	...	...	$13,951	$104/d (U) set by statute. $559/m expense allowance.
North Dakota	$125 C	...	...	Lodging reimbursement up to $650/m (V). $250/m additional compensation by statute.
Ohio	...		$54,942	No per diem is paid.
Oklahoma	...	...	$38,400	$110/d (U) tied to federal rate.
Oregon*	...	...	$15,396	$86/d (U) tied to federal rate.
Pennsylvania	...	...	$66,203.55	$125/d (V) tied to federal rate. Can receive actual expenses or per diem.
Rhode Island	...	...	$12,285.53	No per diem is paid.
South Carolina	...	...	$10,400	$95/d for meals and housing, for each statewide session day and cmte. meeting (V) tied to federal rate.
South Dakota	...	2 yr. term	$12,000	$110/L (U) set by the legislature.
Tennessee	...	...	$16,500	$129/L (U).
Texas*	...	...	$7,200	$125/d (U) set by Ethics Commission.
Utah	$120 C	...	...	$80/d (U) lodging allotment for each calendar day, tied to federal rate. $39/d (U) meals.
Vermont	...	...	$589/week during session	$50/d for lodging and $37/d for meals for non-commuters; commuters receive $32/d for meals (U) set by legislature.
Virginia	...	...	Senate- $18,000 House- $17,640	$115 (U) tied to federal rate.
Washington	...	...	$34,227	$82/d (U) tied to federal rate (85% Olympia area).
West Virginia	...	...	$15,000	$115/d (U) during session set by compensation commission. $150 per diem salary for special sessions.
Wisconsin	...	...	$45,569	$88/d maximum (U) set by compensation commission (90% of federal rate).
Wyoming	$125 L	...	...	$80/d (V) set by the legislature, includes travel days for those outside of Cheyenne.
Dist. of Columbia	...	...	$92,500	No per diem is paid.
Guam	...	...	N.R.	N.R.
Puerto Rico	...	...	$60,000	$122/d within 50 kilometers of capitol; $132 if outside 50 kilometers (U).
U.S. Virgin Islands	...	...	$65,000	$30/d (U) set by the legislature.

Source: National Conference of State Legislatures, 2004.
*—Biennial session. In Arkansas, Oregon and Texas, legislators receive an annual salary.
Key:
C—Calendar day
L—Legislative day
(U)—Unvouchered
(V)—Vouchered
d—day
w—week
m—month
y—year
. . . —Not applicable
N.R.—Not reported
(a) Legislators paid on a per diem basis receive the same rate during a special session.

Table 3.10
LEGISLATIVE COMPENSATION: INTERIM PAYMENTS AND OTHER DIRECT PAYMENTS

State or other jurisdiction	Per diem compensation and living expenses for committee or official business during interim (2002)	Other direct payments or services to legislators (2002)
Alabama	$2,280/m (U); $50/d for committee meetings and $75/d attendance other legislative business. Not restricted to meals and lodging.	None.
Alaska	$65/d (V)	Senators received $10,000/y and Representatives receive $8,000/y for postage, stationery and other legislative expenses. Staffing allowance determined by rules and presiding officers, depending on time of year.
Arizona	$35/d with prior approval of presiding officer (V) set by statute.	None.
Arkansas	$95/d with mileage (V) tied to federal rate.	Legislators are entitled to receive a maximum reimbursement of $9,600/y for legislative expenses.
California	$121/d (V) tied to federal rate.	Senators are allowed staff according to the size of their districts. Assemblymen receive $260,000/y to cover non-specified salary expenses, travel costs, publications, printing, postage, etc.
Colorado	$99/d per diem plus actual expenses (V).	$3,355/y
Connecticut	None.	Senators receive $5,500/y and Representatives receive $4,500/y (U) expense allowance.
Delaware	None.	$6,728/y for office expenses.
Florida	$50/d per diem or actual hotel plus $3 breakfast; $6 lunch; $12 dinner for authorized travel during committee weeks (V) set by Florida statutes.	$1,650/m for office expenses.
Georgia	$128/d (V) set by the Legislature. A committee roster is submitted with the members who attended the meeting. Those that did not attend do not get paid.	$7,000/y reimbursable expense account. If the member requests and provides receipts, the member is reimbursed for personal services, office equipment, rent, supplies, transportation, telecommunications, etc.
Hawaii	$10/d for official business on island of legal residence; $80/d for business on another island (V) set by the legislature.	House $4,500/m for Jan.-April staffing. Senate varies between $350-500/d for staffing allowance.
Idaho	Members are reimbursed for actual expenses (V).	$1,700/y for unvouchered constituent expense. No staffing allowance.
Illinois		Senators receive $67,000/y and Representatives $57,000/y for office expenses, including district offices and staffing.
Indiana	$112/d (V) tied to federal rate.	$25/d, 7 days a week during interim only. No staffing allowance.
Iowa	$86/d (U) set by the legislature. In addition, legislators may request reimbursement for meals, hotel/motel and air fare. State mileage rates apply.	$200/m to cover district constituency postage, travel, telephone and other expenses. No staffing allowance.
Kansas	During interim committee meetings, members receive $85/d tied to federal rate, plus round trip tolls and mileage reimbursement at 33¢. All legislators receive $270 (U) for 20 pay periods ($5,400) considered taxable income.	$5,400/y which is taxable income to the legislators. Staffing allowances vary for leadership who have their own budget Legislators provided with secretaries during the session only..
Kentucky	$163.56 for committee meetings (U). Legislators are reimbursed for actual expenses.	$1,503.19 for district expenses.
Louisiana	$116/d (U) tied to federal rate.	$500/m. Representatives receive an additional $1,500 supplemental allowance for vouchered office expenses,rent, travel mileage in district. Senators and Representatives staff allowance $2,000/m starting salary up to $3,000 with annual increases paid directly to staff person.
Maine	Actual attendance reimbursed at: $55 per diem; actual meals and mileage/housing expense. Chair of committee or presiding officer has to review and approve.	None.
Maryland	$96/d lodging; $30/d meals related to official business (V) tied to federal rate and compensation commission.	Members, $18,265/y for normal expenses of an office with limits on postage, telephone and publications. Members must document expenses. Legislators must use $5,800 for clerical services. Senators receive one administrative assistant & session secretary. Delegates receive one benefited employee and a session secretary.

LEGISLATIVE COMPENSATION: INTERIM PAYMENTS AND OTHER DIRECT PAYMENTS — Continued

State or other jurisdiction	Per diem compensation and living expenses for committee or official business during interim (2002)	Other direct payments or services to legislators (2002)
Massachusetts	None.	$7,200/y for office expenses.
Michigan	None.	$30,900/y for printing, mailings, travel, furniture and district offices. Senate Majority party receives $233,918; Senate Minority party receives $136,536 for staffing.
Minnesota	Senators receive $66/d and Representatives receive $56/d per approval of committee chair or leadership (U) set by the legislature.	None.
Mississippi	$85/d for committee meetings (U) tied to federal rate. $1,500 allowance (U).	None.
Missouri	None.	$1,000/m to cover all reasonable and necessary business expenses.
Montana	In state rate for meals, receipt not required . In state rate for lodging and mileage receipt required (V). Claim form required.	None.
Nebraska	None. Actual expense reimbursed with expense vouchers provided.	No allowance; however, each member is provided with two full-time capitol staff year-round.
Nevada	Statutory amount (V) maximum allowable per diem is paid regardless of actual expenses.	None.
New Hampshire	None.	None.
New Jersey	None.	$750 for supplies, equipment and furnishings supplied through a district office program. $100,000/y for district office personnel.
New Mexico	$145/d (V) tied to federal rate.	None.
New York	Varies (V) tied to federal rate.	Staff allowance set by majority leader for majority members and by minority leader for minority members. Staff allowance covers both district and capitol; geographic location; seniority and leadership responsibilities will cause variations.
North Carolina	$104/d (V) set by statute.	Non-leaders receive $6,708/y for any legislative expenses not otherwise provided. Full-time secretarial assistance is provided during session.
North Dakota	During interim committee meetings, members receive $100/d, $20/d meals (U); $45 plus tax/d lodging (V) plus round trip mileage reimbursement at 31¢. All members receive a $250/m allowance for expenses during their term in office.	None.
Ohio	None.	None.
Oklahoma	$25/d (U) set by the legislature.	$350/y for unvouchered office supplies plus seven rolls of stamps.
Oregon	$85/d committee and task force meetings (U) tied to federal rate.	$2,635/session; interim allowance is $400-550/m depending on geographic size of district. Staffing allowance of $3,908/m during session; $1,846/m during interim.
Pennsylvania	$124 (V) tied to federal rate. Can receive actual expenses or per diem.	Staffing is determined by the Senate Floor Leader.
Rhode Island	None.	None.
South Carolina	Member attending official meetings is eligible for $95/d subsistence and $35/d per diem (V) tied to the federal rate.	Senate $3,400/y for postage, stationery and telephone. House $1,800/y for telephone and $1,100/y for postage.Legislators also receive $1,000/m for in district expenses that is treated as income.

See footnotes at end of table.

LEGISLATIVE COMPENSATION: INTERIM PAYMENTS AND OTHER DIRECT PAYMENTS — Continued

State or other jurisdiction	Per diem compensation and living expenses for committee or official business during interim (2002)	Other direct payments or services to legislators (2002)
South Dakota	$110 per diem for each day of a committee meeting (U). Meals and lodging expenses are paid at state rate.	None.
Tennessee	$114/d (U) tied to federal rate.	$525/m for expenses in district and staff intrastate travel (U).
Texas	Senators receive $124/d for legislative business in Travis County, not to exceed 10 d/m (V). Representatives receive $124/d in Travis County, not to exceed 12 d/m (V). Per diem amount is determined by the Ethics Commission, number of days determined by Senate Caucus and the Committee on House Administration.	Senate: $25,000/m for staff salaries. House $10,750/m for staff salaries, supplies stationery, postage, district office rental, telephone expense, etc.
Utah	$42/d meals (U); up to $75/d for lodging (V).	None.
Vermont	Actual cost plus mileage (U) set by the legislature.	None.
Virginia	$200/d additional compensation for committee meeting attendance. No per diem is paid.	Legislators receive $1,250/m; leadership receives $1,750/m office expense allowance. Legislators receive a staffing allowance of $31,844/y; leadership receives $47,765/y.
Washington	$82/d (V) tied to federal rate (85% Olympia area). Maximum allowable per diem is paid regardless of actual expenses.	$1,350/quarter for legislative expenses, for which the legislator has not been otherwise entitled to reimbursement. No staffing allowance.
West Virginia	$85/d (U) set by compensation commission.	None.
Wisconsin	Per diem is paid year round up to $88/d (U) set by compensation commission (90% of federal rate)	Senate receives $66,000/two-year session plus a mailing for the district each year. Covers district mileage, copying and special documents; capitol expenses include printing, postage, subscriptions, phone etc.Senators receive $186,000/two-year session for staffing. Assembly members receive $12,500 plus an allowance for district size–min. $870, max. $2,900 that covers printing and postage. Staff salary paid by state.
Wyoming	$80/d (V) set by the legislature. Includes travel for those where meetings are not in "hometown."	Up to $450 per quarter.
Dist. of Columbia	None.	None.
Guam	N.R.	None.
Puerto Rico	$93/d within 35 miles of the capitol; $103/d beyond the 35 miles limit (U) tied to CPI.	Senate receives $10,833/m for staffing. House members receive $17,000/m for staffing.
U.S. Virgin Islands	None.	Senators receive an allowance that covers day-to-day operations. Staffing allowances vary with staffing requests.

Source: National Conference of State Legislatures, March 2002.
Notes:
(i) For more information on legislative compensation, see the Chapter 3 table entitled "Legislative Compensation: Regular Sessions."
(ii) Although the official definition of "per diem" is daily expense allowance, it is also used in some states to refer to an interim salary that is taxed and reported as separate income from the annual salary.
Key:
(U) —Unvouchered.
(V)—Vouchered.
d—day.
m—month.
w—week.
y—year.
N.R.—not reported.

Table 3.11
ADDITIONAL COMPENSATION FOR SENATE LEADERS

State or other jurisdiction	Presiding officer	Majority leader	Minority leader	Other leaders
Alabama	$2/day plus $1,500/mo	None	None	None
Alaska	$500	None	None	None
Arizona	None	None	None	None
Arkansas	None	None	None	None
California	Base plus $14,850	Base plus $7,425	Base plus $14,850	Second ranking minority leader; base plus $7,425.
Colorado	All leaders receive $99/day salary during interim when in attendance at committee or leadership meetings and committee meetings.			
Connecticut	$10,689	$8,835	$8,835	Deputy min. and maj. ldrs., $6,446 year; asst. maj. and min. ldrs. and maj. and min. whips $4,241/yr
Delaware	$16,600	$9,913	$9,913	Maj. and min. whips $6,243
Florida	$10,800	None	None	None
Georgia	$6,694.68/mo	$200/mo	$200/mo	President pro tem, $400/mo; admin. flr. ldr., $100/mo; asst. admin. flr. ldr., $100/mo
Hawaii	$37,000	None	None	None
Idaho	$3,000	None	None	None
Illinois	$22,641	None	$22,641	Asst. maj. and min. ldr., $16,979; maj. and min. caucus chair, $16,979
Indiana	$6,500	$5,000	$5,500	Asst. pres. pro tem $2,500; asst. maj. flr. ldr. and maj. caucus chair, $1,000; maj. caucus chair, $5,000; min. asst. flr. ldr. and min. caucus chair, $4,500; maj. and min. whips, $1,500; asst. min. caucus chair, $500
Iowa	$11,593	$11,593	$11,593	Pres. Pro Tem $1,243
Kansas	$12,103.78/yr	$10,919.74/yr	$10,919.74/yr	Asst. maj., min. ldrs., vice pres., $6,177.86/yr
Kentucky	$38.90/day	$31.43/day	$31.43/day	Maj., min. caucus chairs and whips, $24.09/day
Louisiana	$32,000	None	None	Pres. Pro Tem $24,500
Maine	150% of base salary	125% of base salary	112.5% of base salary	Pres. Pro Tem., 100% of base salary
Maryland	$10,000/yr.	None	None	None
Massachusetts	$35,000	$22,500	$22,500	Asst. maj. and min. ldr., $15,000
Michigan	$5,513	$26,000	$22,000	Maj. flr. ldr., $12,000; min. flr. ldr., $10,000
Minnesota	None	$43,596 (a)	$43,596 (a)	Asst. maj. ldr., $35,291 (a)
Mississippi	None	None	None	Pro tem resolution, $15,000/yr
Missouri	None	None	None	None
Montana	$5/day during session	None	None	None
Nebraska	None	None	None	None
Nevada	$900	$900	$900	Pres. Pro Tem, $900
New Hampshire	$50/two-yr term	None	None	None
New Jersey	1/3 above annual salary	None	None	None
New Mexico	None	None	None	None
New York	$41,500	None	$34,500	22 other leaders with compensation ranging from $13,000 to $34,000
North Carolina	$38,151 (a) and $16,956 expense allowance	$17,048 (a) and $7,992 expense allowance	$17,048 (a) and $7,992 expense allowance	Dep. pro tem: $21,739 (a) and $10,032 expense allowance
North Dakota (b)	None	$10/day	$10/day	Asst. ldrs., $5/day

See footnotes at end of table.

ADDITIONAL COMPENSATION FOR SENATE LEADERS — Continued

State or other jurisdiction	Presiding officer	Majority leader	Minority leader	Other leaders
Ohio	$80,549 base salary	President pro tem $73,493	$73,493 salary	Asst. pres. pro tem, $69,227; maj. whip, $64,967; maj.whip, $64,967; asst. min. ldr., $67,099; min. whip, $60,706; asst. min. whip, $54,060
Oklahoma	$17,932	$12,364	$12,364	None
Oregon	$1,283/mo.	None	None	None
Pennsylvania	$34,724.08	$27,780.58	$27,780.58	Maj. and min. whip, $21,083; maj. and min. caucus chair, $13,145; maj. and min. policy chairs, maj. and min. caucus admin., $8,681
Rhode Island	None	None	None	None
South Carolina	Lt. gov. holds this position	None	None	President pro tem, $11,000
South Dakota	None	None	None	None
Tennessee	$49,500 (a) plus $5,700 home office allowance. Add'l $750/yr of ex officio duties	None	None	None
Texas	None	None	None	None
Utah	$2,500	$1,500	$1,500	Maj. whip, asst. maj. whip, min. whip and asst. min. whip, $1,500
Vermont	$593/week during session. No add'l salary	None	None	None
Virginia	None	None	None	None
Washington	Lt. gov. holds this position	$36,064	$36,064	None
West Virginia	$50/day during session	$25/day during session	$25/day during session	Up to 4 add'l people named by pre siding officer receive $100 for a maximum of 30 days.
Wisconsin	None	None	None	None
Wyoming	$3/day	None	None	None
Dist. of Columbia	$10,000 (council chair)	Not applicable	Not applicable	Not applicable
Guam	None	None	None	None
Puerto Rico	$90,000/yr	$69,000/yr	$69,000/yr	President Pro Tem, $69,000
U.S. Virgin Islands	$10,000	None	None	None

Source: National Conference of State Legislatures, 2003.
(a) Total annual salary for this leadership position.
(b) House and Senate majority and minority leaders each receive additional compensation of $250.00 per month during their term of office, pursu-
ant to NDCC Section 54-03-20, in addition to other compensation amounts provided by law during legislative sessions.

Table 3.12
ADDITIONAL COMPENSATION FOR HOUSE LEADERS

State or other jurisdiction	Presiding officer	Majority leader	Minority leader	Other leaders
Alabama	$2/day plus $1,500/mo. expense allowance	None	None	None
Alaska	$500	None	None	None
Arizona	None	None	None	None
Arkansas	None	None	None	$2,400 Spkr. designate
California	Base plus $14,850	Base plus $7,425	Base plus $14,850	Second ranking minority ldr., $7,425
Colorado	All leaders receive $99/day salary during interim when in attendance at committee or leadership matters.			
Connecticut	$10,689	$8,835	$8,835	Dep. spkr., dep. maj. and min. ldrs., $6,446/yr; asst. maj. and min. ldrs.; maj. and min whips,$4,241/yr
Delaware	$16,600	$9,913	$9,913	Maj. and min. whips, $6,243
Florida	$10,800	None	None	None
Georgia	$6,094.68/mo.	$200/mo.	$200/mo.	Governor's flr. ldr., $200/mo; asst. flr. ldr.,$100/mo.; spkr. pro tem, $400/mo.
Hawaii	$37,000	None	None	None
Idaho	$3,000	None	None	None
Illinois	$22,641	$19,101	$22,641	Dpty. maj. and min., $16,273; asst. maj. and asst. min., $14,856; maj. and min. conference chair, $14,856
Indiana	$6,500	$5,000	$5,500	Speaker pro tem, $5,000; maj. caucus chair, $5,000; min. caucus chair, $4,500; asst. min. flr. leader, $3,500; asst. maj. flr. ldr., $1,000; maj. whip, $3,500; min. whip, $1,500
Iowa	$11,593	$11,593	$11,593	Speaker pro tem, $1,243
Kansas	$12,103.78/yr.	$10,919.74/yr.	$10,919.74/yr.	Asst. maj. and min. ldrs., spkr. pro tem, $6,177.68/yr.
Kentucky	$39.80/day	$31.43/day	$31.43/day	Maj. and min. caucus chairs & whips, $24.09/day
Louisiana	$32,000 (a)	None	None	Speaker pro tem, $24,500 (a)
Maine	150% of base salary	125% of base salary	112.5% of base salary	None
Maryland	$10,000/year	None	None	None
Massachusetts	$35,000	$22,500	$22,500	Asst. maj. and min. ldr., $15,000
Michigan	$27,000	None	$22,000	Spkr. pro tem, $5,513; min. flr. ldr., $10,000;maj. flr. ldr., $12,000
Minnesota	$43,596 (a)	$43,596 (a)	$43,596 (a)	None
Mississippi	None	None	None	None
Missouri	$208.33/mo.	$125/mo.	$125/mo.	None
Montana	$5/day during session	None	None	None
Nebraska	None	None	None	None
Nevada	$900	$900	$900	Speaker pro tem, $900
New Hampshire	$50/two-year term	None	None	None
New Jersey	1/3 above annual salary	None	None	None
New Mexico	None	None	None	None
New York	$41,500	$34,500	$34,500	31 leaders with compensation ranging from $9,000 to $25,000
North Carolina	$38,151 (a) and $16,956 expense allowance	$17,048 (a) and $7,992 expense allowance	$17,048 (a) and $7,992 expense allowance	Speaker pro tem, $21,739 and $10,032 expense allowance
North Dakota (b)	$10/day	$10/day	$10/day	Asst. ldrs., $5/day

See footnotes at end of table.

ADDITIONAL COMPENSATION FOR HOUSE LEADERS — Continued

State or other jurisdiction	Presiding officer	Majority leader	Minority leader	Other leaders
Ohio	$80,549 base salary	$69,227 base salary	$73,493 base salary	Spkr. pro tem, $73,493; asst. maj. ldr., $64,967; asst. min. ldr., $67,099; maj. whip, $60,706; min. whip, $60,706; asst. maj. whip, $56,443; asst. min. whip, $54,060
Oklahoma	$17,932	$12,364	$12,364	Speaker pro tem, $12,364
Oregon	$1,283/month	None	None	None
Pennsylvania	$34,724.08	$27,780.58	$27,780.59	Maj. and min. whips, $21,083; maj. and min. caucus chairs, $13,145; maj. and min. policy chairs, $8,681; maj. and min. caucus admin.,$8,681, maj. and min. caucus secretaries, $8,681
Rhode Island	None	None	None	None
South Carolina	$11,000/yr	None	None	Speaker pro tem, $3,600/yr
South Dakota	None	None	None	None
Tennessee	$49,500 (a) plus $5,700/yr home office for allowance. Add'l $750/yr. for ex-officio duties	None	None	None
Texas	None	None	None	None
Utah	$2,500	$1,500	$1,500	Whips and asst. whips, $1,500
Vermont	$593/week during session plus an additional $9,172 in salary	None	None	None
Virginia	$18,681	None	None	None
Washington	$40,064 (a)	None	$36,064(a)	None
West Virginia	$50/day during session	$25/day during session	$25/day during session	Up to four add'l people named by presiding officer receive $100 for a maximum of 30 days
Wisconsin	None	None	None	None
Wyoming	$3/day	None	None	None
District of Columbia	$10,000 (chair of council)	Not applicable	Not applicable	Not applicable
Puerto Rico	$90,000/yr.	$69,000/yr.	$69,000/yr.	Speaker pro tem, $69,000
Guam	None	None	None	None
U.S. Virgin Islands	None	None	None	None

Source: National Conference of State Legislatures, 2003.
(a) Total annual salary for this leadership position.
(b) House and Senate majority and minority leaders each receive additional compensation of $250/mo. during their term of office, pursuant to NDCC Section 54-03-20, in addition to other compensation amounts provided by law during legislative sessions.

Table 3.13
STATE LEGISLATIVE RETIREMENT BENEFITS

State or other jurisdiction	Participation	Plan name	Requirements for regular retirement	Employee contribution rate	Benefit formula
Alabama	None available.				
Alaska	Optional	Public Employees Retirement System	Age 60 with 10 yrs.	Employee 6.75%;	2% (first 10 yrs.); or 2.25% (second 10 yrs.); or 2.5% over 20 x average over 5 highest consecutive yrs. x yrs. of service
Arizona	Mandatory - except that officials subject to term limits may opt out for a term of office.	Elected Officials Retirement System	Age 65, 5+ yrs. service; or age 62, 10+ yrs. service; or 20 yrs. service; earlier retirement with an actuarial reduction of benefits. Vesting at 5 yrs.	Employee 7%	4% x years of credited service x highest 3 yr. average in the past 10 yrs. The benefit is capped at 80% of FAS. An elected official may purchase service credit in the plan for service earned in a non-elected position by buying it at an actuarially determined amount.
Arkansas	Optional. Those elected before 7/1/99 may have service covered as a regular state employee but must have 5 years of regular service to do so.	Arkansas Public Employees Retirement System	Age 65, 10 yrs. service; or age 55, 12 yrs. service; or any age, 28 yrs. service; any age if serving in the General Assembly on 7/1/79; any age if in elected office on 7/1/79 with 17 and 1/2 yrs. of service. As a regular employee, age 65, 5 yrs. service, or any age and 28 yrs.	Non-contributory	For service that began after 7/1/99: 2.07% x FAS x years of service. FAS based on three highest consecutive years or service. For service that began after July 1, 1991, $35 x years of service equals monthly benefit.
California	Legislators elected after 1990 are not eligible for retirement benefits for legislative service.				
Colorado	Mandatory	Either Public Employees' Retirement Association of State Defined Contribution Plan. A choice is not irrevocable.	PERA: age 65, 5 yrs. service; age 50, 30yrs. service; when age + service equals 80 or more (min. age of 55). DCP: no age requirement & vested immediately	Employee: 8%	PERA: 2.5% x FAS x yrs. of service, capped at 100% of FAS. DCP benefit depends upon contributions and investment returns.
Connecticut	Mandatory	State Employees Retirement System Tier IIA	Age 60, 25 yrs. credited service; age 62, 10 -25 yrs. credited service; age 62, 5 yrs. actual state service. Reduced benefit available with earlier retirement ages.	2%	(.0133 x avg. annual salary) + (.005 x avg. annual salary in excess of "breakpoint" x credited service up to 35 years. 2003 - $36,400 2004 - $38,600 2005 - $40,900 2006 - $43,400 2007 - $ 46,000 2008 - $48,800 2009 - $51,700 After 2009 - increase breakpoint by 6% per year rounded to nearest $100.
Delaware	Mandatory	State Employees Pension Plan	Age 60, 5 yrs. credited service	3% of total monthly compensation in excess of $6,000	2% times FAS times years of service before 1997 + 1.85% times FAS times years of service from 1997 on . FAS= average of highest 3 years.

See footnotes at end of table.

STATE LEGISLATIVE RETIREMENT BENEFITS — Continued

State or other jurisdiction	Participation	Plan name	Requirements for regular retirement	Employee contribution rate	Benefit formula
Florida	Optional. Elected officials may opt out and may choose between DB and DC plans.	Florida Retirement System	Vesting in DB plan, 6 years: in DC plan, 1 year. DB plan: Age 62 with 6 years; 30 years at any age. DC plan: any age	No employee contribution. Employer contribution for 2003-2004 for legislators is 11.28% of salary.	DB plan: 3% x years of creditable service x average final compensation (average of highest 5 yrs). DC plan: Dependent upon investment experience.
Georgia	Optional: Choice when first elected.	Georgia Legislative Retirement System	Vested after 8 yrs.; age 62, with 8 yrs. of service; age 60 with reduction for early retirement.	Employee rate 3.75% + $7 month	$32 month for each year of service.
Hawaii	Mandatory	Public Employees Retirement System; elected officials' plan	Age 55 with 5 years of service, any age with 10 years service. Vesting at 5 years.	Main plan is non-contributory; 7.8% for elected officials' plan for annuity.	3.5 x yrs. of service as elected official x highest average salary plus annuity based on contributions as an elected official. Highest average salary = average of 3 highest 12- month periods as elected official.
Idaho	Mandatory	Public Employees Retirement System	5 yrs. service minimum; age 65 unreduced; age 55 reduced	6.97%	Avg. monthly salary for highest 42 consecutive months x 2% x months of credited service.
Illinois	Optional	General Assembly Retirement System	Age 55, 8 yrs. service; or age 62, 4 yrs. service	8.5% for retirement; 2% for survivors; 1% for automatic increases; 11.5% total	3% of each of 1st 4 yrs.; 3.5% for each of next 2 yrs.; 4% for each of next 2 yrs.; 4.5% for each of the next 4 yrs.; 5% for each yr. above 12
Indiana	DB plan is optional for those serving on April 30, Defined contribution plan optional for those serving on April 30, 1989 and mandatory for those elected or appointed since April 30, 1989.	Legislator's Retirement System and Defined Benefit (DB) Plan and Defined Contribution Plan (DC).	DB plan: Vesting at 10 yrs. Age 65 with 10 yrs. Of legislative service; or if no longer in the legislature, these options apply: at least 10 yrs. Service; no state salary; at age 55+ Rule of 85 applies; or age 60 with 15 yrs. Of service. Early retirement with reduced benefit. Immediate vesting in the DC plan,	DC plan: 5% employee, 20% state (of taxable income), DB plan and employer contributions funded by appropriation.	DB benefit plan monthly benefit: Lesser of (a) $40 x years of General Assembly service completed before November 8, 1989 or (b) 1/12 of the average of the three highest consecutive years of General Assembly service salary. DC plan: numerous options for withdrawing accumulations in accord with IRS regulations. Loans are available. A participant in both plans may receive a benefit from both plans.
Iowa	Optional	Public Employees Retirement System	Age 65;age 62 with 20 yrs. service Rule of 88; reduced benefit at 55 with at least 4 years of service.	3.7% individual;	2% times FAS x years of service for first 30 years, + 1% times FAS times years in excess of 30 but no more than 5 in excess of 30. FAS is average of 3 highest years.
Kansas	Optional	Public Employees Retirement System	Age 65, age 62 with 10 yrs. of service or age plus yrs. of service equals 85 pts.	4% of salary, (4% annualized salary for Legislators).	3 highest yrs. x 1.75% x yrs. service divided by 12.
Kentucky	Optional. Those who opt out are covered by the state employees' plan	Kentucky Legislator's Retirement Plan	Age 65 with five years of service; any age with 30 years of service, and intermediate provisions. Early retirement with reduced benefits.	5% of creditable compensation, set by law at $27,500: not the same as actual salary.	2.75% of FAS (based on creditable compensation) x years of service. FAS is the average monthly earnings for the 60 months preceding retirement.
Louisiana	None available				

See footnotes at end of table.

STATE LEGISLATIVE RETIREMENT BENEFITS — Continued

State or other jurisdiction	Participation	Plan name	Requirements for regular retirement	Employee contribution rate	Benefit formula
Maine	Mandatory	Maine State Retirement Plan	Age 60 (if 10 yrs. of service on 7/1/93) and age 62 (if less than 10 yrs. of service on 7/1/93). Reduced benefit available for earlier retirement.	7.65% legislators; employer contribution is actuarially determined.	2% of average final compensation (the average of the 3 high salary years) times years of service.
Maryland	Optional	State Legislator's Pension Plan	Age 60, with 8 yrs.; age 50, 8+yrs creditable service (early reduced retirement)	5% of annual salary	3% of legislative salary for each yr of service up to a max. of 22 yrs. 3 months. Benefits are recalculated when legislative salaries are changed.
Massachusetts	Optional after each election or re-election to the General Court.	State Retirement System legislator's plan	Age 55 with 6 years Service; unreduced benefit at 65. Vesting at 6 years. Reduced benefits for retirement before age 65.	9%. Some legislators are grandfathered at lower rates.	2.5 times years of service times FAS. FAS = average of highest 36 months. Service credit is allowed for membership in other Massachusetts retirement plans.
Michigan	Optional	Legislative Retirement System (DB) for legislators elected before 3/31/97. Others may join the state defined contribution plan.	Age 55, 5 yrs. or age plus service equals 70	7%-13% For the DC plan, the state contributes 4% of salary. Members may contribute up to 3% of salary. The state will match the member's contribution in addition to the state 4% contribution.	For DB plans, various provisions, depending on when service started. For the DC plan, benefits depend upon contributions and earnings.
Minnesota	Mandatory	Legislators Retirement Plan before 7/1/97; Defined Contribution Plan (DCP) since then.	LRP: Age 62, 6 yrs. service and fully vested. DCP: age 55 and vested immediately. LRP members do not have Social Security coverage. DCP members have Social Security coverage.	LRP: 9% DCP: 4% from member, 6% from state.	2.7% x high 5 yr. avg. salary x length of service (yrs.) DCP benefit depends upon contributions and investment return.
Mississippi	Mandatory	Legislators' plan within the Public Employees' Retirement System	Age 60 with 4 or more years of service, or 25 years of service.	Regular: 7.25% state 9.75% to 10.75 effective July 1, 2005 Supplement for legislative service: 3%/6.33%	Legislators who qualify for regular state retirement benefits also automatically qualify for the legislators' supplemental benefits. Regular: 2% times FAS times years of service up to and including 25 years of service + 2.5% times FAS times service in excess of 25 years FAS is based on the high 4 years. Supplement: 1% times FAS times years of legislative service through 25 years, + 1.25% times FAS times years of service in excess of 25.
Missouri	Mandatory	Missouri State Employee Retirement System	Age 55; three full biennial assemblies (6 years) or Rule of 80. Vesting at 6 years of service.	Non-contributory	Monthly pay divided by 24 x years of creditable service, capped at 100% of salary. Benefit is adjusted by the percentage increase in pay for an active legislator.

See footnotes at end of table.

STATE LEGISLATIVE RETIREMENT BENEFITS — Continued

State or other jurisdiction	Participation	Plan name	Requirements for regular retirement	Employee contribution rate	Benefit formula
Montana	Optional	Public Employees Retirement System. Either a DB or a DC plan is available.	Vesting at 5 years Age 60 with at least 5 years service; age 65 regardless of years of service; or 30 years of service regardless of age	6.9% for DB plan. Employer contribution of 4.19% plus employee contribution of 6.9 % for DC plan.	DB plan: 1/56 times years of service times FAS. Early retirement with reduced benefits is available. DC plan: Employee contributions and earnings are immediately vested. Employer contributions and earnings are vested after 5 years.
Nebraska	None available				
Nevada	Mandatory		Age 60, 10 yrs. service	15% of session salary	Number of years x $25 = monthly allowance
New Hampshire	None available				
New Jersey	Mandatory	Public Employees' Retirement System	Age 60; no minimum service requirement. Early retirement with no benefit reduction with 25 years of service. Vesting at 8 years.	5% of salary	3% x Final Average Salary x years of service. FAS = higher of three highest years or three final years. Benefit is capped at 2/3 of FAS. Other formulas apply if a legislator also has other service covered by the Public Employee Retirement System.
New Mexico	Optional	Legislative Retirement Plan	Plans 1A and 1B: Age 65 with 5 years of service; 64/8; 63/11; 60/12; or any age with 14 years of service. Plan 2: 65 with five years of service or at any age with 10 years of service.	Plan 1A: $100 per year for service after 1959 Plan 1B: $200 per year (now closed to new enrollments). Plan 2: $500/year	Plan 1A: $250 per year of service. Plan 1B: $500 per year of service after 1959. Plan 2: 11 percent of the IRS per diem rate in effect on December 31st of the year a legislator retires x 60 x the years of credited service. For a legislator who retired in 2003 the benefit would be $957 per year of credited service. Annual 3% COLA.
New York	Mandatory	New York State and Local Retirement System	Age 62 with 5 years of service; 55 with 30 years; reduced benefit available at 55/5. Vesting at 5 years.	3% for first 10 years of membership (Tier 4 provisions).	Tier 4: 2% x final average salary (average of 3 highest consecutive years) x years of service to 30 years; multiplier of 1.5% after 30 years For members who retire with fewer than 20 years of service, the multiplier is 1.67.
North Carolina	Mandatory	Legislative Retirement System	Age 65 with 5 years of service; reduced benefit available at earlier ages.	7%	Highest annual compensation x 4.02% x years of service.
North Dakota	None available.				
Ohio	Optional	Public Employees Retirement System	Age 60 with 5 years service or 55 with 25 years service or at any age with 30 years service	8.5% of gross salary. A 10% contribution rate for legislators will be phased in over three years starting in 2006.	2.2% of final average salary times years of service up to and through 30 years of service. 2.5% starting with the 31st year of service and every year thereafter.
Oklahoma	Legislators may retain membership as regular public employees if they have that status when elected; one time option to join Elected Officials' Plan.	Public Employee Retirement System, as regular member or elected official member. [Information here is for the Elected Officials' Plan.]	Elected Officials' Plan: Age 60 with 6 years service vesting at 6 years.	Optional contribution of 4.5%, 6%, 7.5%, 8.5%, 9%, or 10% of total compensation.	Optional contribution of Avg. participating salary x length of service x computation factor depending on optional contributions ranging from 1.9% for a 4.5% contribution to 4% for a 10% contribution.

See footnotes at end of table.

STATE LEGISLATIVE RETIREMENT BENEFITS — Continued

State or other jurisdiction	Participation	Plan name	Requirements for regular retirement	Employee contribution rate	Benefit formula
Oregon	Optional	Public Employee Retirement System legislator plan	Age 55, 30+ yrs. Service, 5 years vesting.	16.317% of subject wages	1.67% x yrs. service and final avg. monthly salary
Pennsylvania	Optional	State Employees' Retirement System	Age 50, 3 yrs. service, any age with 35 years of service; early retirement with reduced benefit.	7.5%	3% x final avg. salary x credited yrs. of service (x withdrawal factor if under regular retirement age —50 for legislators).
Rhode Island	Legislators elected after January 1995 are ineligible for retirement benefits based on legislative service. (a)				
South Carolina	Mandatory, but members may opt out six months after being sworn into office.	South Carolina Retirement System	Age 60, 8 yrs. service; 30 yrs. of service regardless of age	10%	4.82% of annual compensation x yrs. service
South Dakota	None available.				
Tennessee	Optional	Employee Retirement System: Elected Class Members	Age 55, 4 yrs. service	5.43%	$70 per month x yrs. service with a $1,375 monthly cap
Texas	Optional	Employee Retirement System: Elected Class Members	Age 60, 8 yrs. service; age 50, 12 yrs. service. Vesting at 8 years.	8%	2.3% x district judge's salary x length of service, with the monthly benefit capped at the level of a district judge's salary, and adjusted when such salaries are increased. Various annuity options are available. Military service credit may be purchased to add to elective class service membership.
Utah	Mandatory	Governors' and Legislators' Retirement Plan	Age 62 with 10 years and an actuarial reduction; age 65 with 4 years of service for full benefits.	Non-contributory	$24.80/month (as of July 2004) x years of service; adjusted semi-annually according to consumer price index up to a maximum increase of 2%.
Vermont	None available. Deferred compensation plan available.				
Virginia	Mandatory		Age 50, 30 yrs. service (unreduced); age 55, 5 yrs. service; age 50, 10 yrs. service (reduced)	8.91% of creditable compensation	1.7% of average final compensation x yrs. of service
Washington	Optional. If before an election the legislator belonged to a state public retirement plan, he or she may continue in that by making contributions. Otherwise the new legislator may join PERS Plan 2 or Plan 3.	See column to left. PERS plan 2 is a DB plan. PERS plan 3 is a hybrid DB/DC plan.	PERS plan 2: Age 65 with 5 years of service credit. Plan 3: Age 65 with 10 years of service credit for the DB side of the plan; immediate benefits (subject to federal restrictions) on the DC side of the plan. The member may choose various options for investment of contributions to the DC plan.	PERS plan 2: Employee contribution of 2.43% for 2002. Estimated at 2005-2007. 3.33% for Plan 3: No required member contribution for the DB component. The member may contribute from 5% to 15% of salary to the DC component.	PERS plan 2: 2% x years of service credit x average final compensation. Plan 3: DB is 1% x service credit years x average final compensation. DC benefit depends upon the value of accumulations.
West Virginia	Optional		Age 55, if yrs. of service+age equal 80	4.5% gross income	2% of final avg. salary x yrs. Service. Final avg. salary is based on 3 highest yrs. out of last 10 yrs.

See footnotes at end of table.

STATE LEGISLATIVE RETIREMENT BENEFITS — Continued

Wisconsin	Mandatory	Age 62 normal; age 57 with 30 years of service.	2.6% of salary in 2003: adjusted annually	Higher benefit of formula (2.165% x years of service x salary for service before 2000; 2% x years of service x salary for service 2000 and after) or money-purchase calculation.
Wyoming	None available			
Dist. of Columbia	Mandatory	Age 62, 5 yrs. service; age 55, 30 yrs. service; age 60, 20 yrs. service	Before 10/1/87, 7%; after 10/1/87, 5%	Multiply high 3 yrs. average pay by indicator under applicable yrs. months of service.
Puerto Rico	Optional	After 1990, age 65 with 30 years of service.	8.28%	1.5% of average earnings multiplied by the number of years of accredited service.
		Retirement System of the Employees of the Government of Puerto Rico		
Guam	Optional	Age 60, 30 yrs. service; age 55, 15 yrs. service	5% or 8.5%	An amount equal to 2% of avg. annual salary for each of the first 10 yrs. of credited service and 2.5% of avg. annual salary for each yr. or part thereof of credited service over 10 yrs.
U.S. Virgin Islands	Optional	Age 60, 10 yrs. service	8%	At age 60 with at least 10 yrs. of service, at 2.5% for each

Source: National Conference of State Legislatures. November 2004.
Note: The following states do not have legislative retirement benefits: Alabama, Nebraska, New Hampshire, North Dakota, South Dakota, Vermont and Wyoming.
Key:
N.A.—Not available
(a) Constitution has been amended effective 1/95. Any legislator elected after this date is not eligible to join the State Retirement System, but will be compensated for $10,000/yr. with cost of living increases to be adjusted annually.

Table 3.14
BILL PRE-FILING, REFERENCE AND CARRYOVER

State or other jurisdiction	Pre-filing of bills allowed (b)	Bills referred to committee by: Senate	Bills referred to committee by: House/Assembly	Bill referral restricted by rule (a) Senate	Bill referral restricted by rule (a) House/Assembly	Bill carryover allowed (c)
Alabama	★(d)	(e) (f)	Speaker	L	L	...
Alaska	★	President	Speaker	L, M	L, M	★
Arizona	★	President	Speaker	L	L	...
Arkansas	★	President	Speaker	L	L	...
California	★	Rules Cmte.	Rules Cmte.	L	...	★(h)
Colorado	★	President	Speaker	L, M (i)	L (i)	...
Connecticut	★	Pres. Pro Tempore	Speaker	M	M	...
Delaware	★	Pres. Pro Tempore	Speaker	...	...	...
Florida	★	President	Speaker	L, M	M	...
Georgia	★	President (f)	Speaker	...	...	★
Hawaii	(j)	President	Speaker	...	...	★
Idaho	...	President (e)	Speaker	L	L	...
Illinois	★	Rules Cmte.	Rules Cmte.	...	...	★
Indiana	★(o)	Pres. Pro Tempore	Speaker	...	...	...
Iowa	★	President	Speaker	M	M	★
Kansas	★	President	Speaker	L	L	★
Kentucky	★	Cmte. on Cmtes.	Cmte. on Cmtes.	L	L	...
Louisiana	★	President (l)	Speaker (l)	L	L	...
Maine	★	Secy. of Senate and Clerk of House (n)		L	L	★
Maryland	★	President	Speaker	L	L	...
Massachusetts	★	Clerk	Clerk	M	M	★
Michigan	...	Majority Ldr.	Speaker	...	...	★
Minnesota	...	President	Speaker	L, M	L, M	★
Mississippi	★	President (e)	Speaker	L	L	...
Missouri	★	Pres. Pro Tempore	Speaker	L	L	...
Montana	★	President	Speaker	...	...	...
Nebraska	★	Reference Cmte.	U	L	U	★(p)
Nevada	★	(q)	(q)	L (t)	...	...
New Hampshire	★	President	Speaker	M	L, M	★
New Jersey	★(m)	President	Speaker	...	...	★
New Mexico	★(k)	(r)	Speaker	L, M	M	...
New York	★	Pres. Pro Tempore (s)	Speaker	M	M	★
North Carolina	...	Rules Chairman	Speaker	M	M	★
North Dakota	★	President (e)	Speaker	M	M	...
Ohio	★	Reference Cmte.	Rules & Reference Cmte.	L	L	★
Oklahoma	★	Majority Leader	Speaker	L	...	★
Oregon	★	President	Speaker	L	H	...
Pennsylvania	★	President Pro Tempore	Speaker	L	M	...
Rhode Island	★	President	Speaker	M	M	★
South Carolina	★	President	Speaker	M	M	★
South Dakota	★	President	Speaker	...	...	...
Tennessee	★	Speaker	Speaker	...	...	★
Texas	★	President	Speaker	L	L	...
Utah	★	President	Speaker	...	...	...
Vermont	(g)	President	Speaker	M	M	★
Virginia	★	Clerk	Clerk (u)	L	L	★
Washington	★	(v)	(v)	...	...	★
West Virginia	★	President	Speaker	L, M	L, M	★(j)
Wisconsin	...	President	Speaker	...	...	★(p)
Wyoming	★	President	Speaker	M	M	...
Puerto Rico	...	President	Secretary	M	M	...

See footnotes at end of table.

BILL PRE-FILING, REFERENCE AND CARRYOVER — Continued

Source: The Council of State Governments' survey, October 2003 and October 2004.

Key:

★— Yes

. . . —No

L—Rules generally require all bills be referred to the appropriate committee of jurisdiction.

M — Rules require specific types of bills be referred to specific committees (e.g., appropriations, local bills).

U—Unicameral legislature.

(a) Legislative rules specify all or certain bills go to committees of jurisdiction.

(b) Unless otherwise indicated by footnote, bills may be introduced prior to convening each session of the legislature. In this column only: ★ —pre-filing is allowed in both chambers (or in the case of Nebraska, in the unicameral legislature); . . . — pre-filing is not allowed in either chamber.

(c) Bills carry over from the first year of the legislature to the second (does not apply in Alabama, Arkansas, Montana, Nevada, North Dakota, Oregon and Texas, where legislatures meet biennially). Bills generally do not carry over after an intervening legislative election.

(d) Except between the end of the last regular session of the legislature in any quadrennium and the organizational session following the general election and special session.

(e) Lieutenant governor is the president of the Senate.

(f) Senate bills by president with concurrence of president pro tem, if no concurrence by rules committee. House bills by president pro tem with concurrence of president, if no concurrence, by rules committee.

(g) Bills are drafted prior to session but released starting first day of session.

(h) Bills introduced in the first year of the regular session and passed by the house of origin on or before the January 31st constitutional deadline a r e carryover bills.

(i) In either house, state law requires any bill which affects the sentencing of criminal offenders and which would result in a net increase of imprisonment in state correctional facilities must be assigned to the appropriations committee of the house in which it was introduced. In the Senate, a bill must be referred to the Appropriations Committee if it contains an appropriation from the state treasury or the increase of any salary. Each bill which provides that any state revenue be devoted to any purpose other than that to which is devoted under existing law must be referred to the Finance Committee.

(j) House only in even-numbered years.

(k) In the House only.

(l) Subject to approval or disapproval. Louisiana–majority members present.

(m) Prior to convening of first regular session only.

(n) For the joint standing committee system. Secretary of the Senate and clerk of House, after conferring, suggest an appropriate committee reference for every bill, resolve and petition offered in either house. If they are unable to agree, the question of reference is referred to a conference of the president of the Senate and speaker of the House. If the presiding officers cannot agree, the question is resolved by the Legislative Council.

(o) Only in the Senate.

(p) Any bill, joint resolution on which final action has not been taken at the conclusion of the last general-business floor period in the odd-numbered year shall be carried forward to the even-numbered year.

(q) Motion for referral can be made by any member.

(r) Senator introducing the bill endorses the name of the committee to which the bill is referred. If an objection is made, the Senate determines the committee to which the bill is referred.

(s) Also serves as majority leader.

(t) Suspension of rule - Majority of elected members.

(u) Under the direction of the speaker.

(v) By the membership of the chamber.

Table 3.15
TIME LIMITS ON BILL INTRODUCTION

State or other jurisdiction	Time limit on introduction of bills	Procedures for granting exception to time limits
Alabama	House: no limit. Senate: 22nd day of regular session (a).	Unanimous vote to suspend rules.
Alaska	35th C day of 2nd regular session.	Introduction by committee or by suspension of operation of limiting rule.
Arizona	House: 29th day of regular session; 10th day of special session. Senate: 22nd day of regular session; 10th day of special session.	House: Permission of rules committee. Senate: Permission of President.
Arkansas	55th day of regular session (50th day for appropriations bills).	2/3 vote of membership of each house.
California	Deadlines established by rules committee	Approval of rules committee and 2/3 vote of membership.
Colorado	House: 22nd C day of regular session. Senate: 17th C day of regular session (b).	House and Senate: Committees on delayed bills may extend deadline.
Connecticut	10 days into session in odd-numbered years, 3 days into session in even-numbered years (c).	2/3 vote of members present.
Delaware	House: no limit. Senate: no limit.	
Florida	House: noon of the first day of regular session. Senate: noon first day of regular session (b)(e).	Existence of an emergency reasonably compelling consideration notwithstanding the deadline.
Georgia	Only for specific types of bills	
Hawaii	Actual dates established during session.	Majority vote of membership.
Idaho	House: 20th day of session (d); 36th day of session (f). Senate: 12th day of session (d); 36th day of session (f).	House and Senate: Speaker/President Pro Tempore may designate any standing committee to serve as a privileged committee temporarily.
Illinois	House: determined by speaker (b)(d). Senate: determined by president.	House: rules governing limitations may not be suspended except for bills determined by a majority of members of the Rules Comm. to be an emergency bill, & appropriations bills implementing the budget. Senate: Rules may be suspended by a majority vote of members.
Indiana	House and Senate: mid-January.	House: 2/3 vote.
Iowa	House: Friday of 6th week of 1st regular session (d)(g)(i); Friday of 2nd week of 2nd regular session (d)(g)(h). Senate: Friday of 7th week of 1st regular session (d)(g); Friday of 2nd week of 2nd regular session (d)(g).	Constitutional majority.
Kansas	Actual dates established suring session	Resolution adopted by majority of members of either house may make specific exceptions to deadlines.
Kentucky	House: After 14th L day of odd-year session, during last 22 L days of even-year session Senate: After 14th L day of odd-year session, during last 20 L days of even-year session	Majority vote of membership of each house.
Louisiana	30th C day of odd-year session; 10th C day of even-year session.	2/3 vote of elected members of each house.
Maine	1st Wednesday in December of 1st regular session; deadlines for 2nd regular session established by Legislative Council.	Approval of majority of members of Legislative Council.
Maryland	No introductions during last 35 C days of regular session.	2/3 vote of elected members of each house.
Massachusetts	1st Wednesday in December even-numbered years, 1st Wednesday in November odd-numbered years.	2/3 vote of members present and voting.
Michigan	No limit.	
Minnesota	No limit	Must follow committee deadline process.
Mississippi	14th C day in 90 day session; 49th C day in 125 day session (o).	2/3 vote of members present and voting.
Missouri	House: 60th L day of regular session. Senate: March 1.	Majority vote of elected members each house; governor's request for consideration of bill by special message.
Montana	General bills & resolutions: 10th L day; revenue bills: 17th L day; committee bills and resolutions: 36th L day; committee bills implementing provisions of a general appropriation act: 75th L day; committee revenue bills: 62nd L day interim study resolutions: 75th L day (b)(i).	2/3 vote of members.
Nebraska	10th L day of any session (b).	3/5 vote of elected membership.
Nevada	Actual dates established at start of session.	Waiver granted by Senate Majority Floor Leader or Assembly Speaker.
New Hampshire	Actual dates established during session.	2/3 vote of members present.
New Jersey	Assembly: No limit. Senate: no limit.	Majority vote of members.

See footnotes at end of table.

TIME LIMITS ON BILL INTRODUCTION — Continued

State or other jurisdiction	Time limit on introduction of bills	Procedures for granting exception to time limits
New Mexico	30th L day of odd-year session (j); 15th L day of even-year session (j).	None.
New York	Assembly: for unlimited introduction of bills, 1st Tuesday in March; for introduction of 10 or fewer bills, last Tuesday in March (k)(l). Senate: 1st Tuesday in March (l)(m).	Unanimous vote.
North Carolina	Actual dates established during session.	Senate: 2/3 vote of membership present and voting shall be required.
North Dakota	House: 10th L day. Senate: 15th L day.	2/3 vote or approval of majority of Committee on Delayed Bills.
Ohio	No limit.	
Oklahoma	Time limit set in rules.	2/3 vote of membership.
Oregon	House: 36th C day of session (k). Senate: 36th C day of session.	2/3 vote of membership.
Pennsylvania	No limit.	
Rhode Island	2nd Tuesday in February.	Simple majority vote.
South Carolina	House: Prior to April 15 of the 2nd yr. of a two-yr. legislative session; May 1 for bills first introduced in Senate. Senate: May 1 of regular session for bills originating in House.	House: 2/3 vote of members present and voting. Senate: 2/3 vote of membership.
South Dakota	40-day session: 15th L day; committee bills and joint resolutions, 16th L day. 35-day session: 10th L day; committee bills and joint resolutions, 11th L day.	2/3 vote of membership.
Tennessee	House: general bills, 10th L day of regular session (m). Senate: general bills, 10th L day or regular session; resolutions, 40th L day (m).	Unanimous consent of Committee on Delayed Bills, or upon motion approved by 2/3 vote of members present.
Texas	60th C day of regular session.	4/5 vote of members present and voting.
Utah	12:00 p.m. on 11th day of general session.	Motion for request must be approved by 2/3 vote of members.
Vermont	House: 1st session - last day of February; 2nd session. last day of January. Senate: 1st session - 53 C day; 2nd session - 25 C days before start of session.	Approval by Rules Committee.
Virginia	Deadlines may be set during session.	
Washington	(Constitutional limit) No introductions during final 10 days of regular session (n).	2/3 vote of elected members of each house.
West Virginia	House: 45th C day. Senate: 41st C day.	2/3 vote of members present.
Wisconsin	No limit.	
Wyoming	House: 15th L day of session. Senate: 12th L day of session	2/3 vote of elected members.
Puerto Rico	1st session - within first 125 days; 2nd session - within first 60 days.	None.

Source: The Council of State Governments' survey, October 2003 and October 2004.

Key:
C — Calendar
L — Legislative
(a) Not applicable to local bills, advertised or otherwise.
(b) Not applicable to appropriations bills. In West Virginia, supplementary appropriations bills or budget bills.
(c) Not applicable to (1) bills providing for current government expenditures; (2) bills the presiding officers certify are of an emergency nature; (3) bills the governor requests because of emergency or necessity; and (4) the legislative commissioners' revisor's bills and omnibus validating act.
(d) Not applicable to standing committee bills.
(e) Not applicable to local bills and joint resolutions. Florida: Not applicable to local bills (which have no deadline) or claim bills (deadline is August 1 of the year preceding consideration or within 60 days of a senator's election).
(f) Not applicable to House State Affairs, Appropriations, Education, Revenue and Taxation, or Ways and Means committees, nor to Senate State Affairs, Finance, or Judiciary and Rules committees.
(g) Unless written request for drafting bill has been filed before deadline.

(h) Not applicable to bills co-sponsored by majority and minority floor leaders.
(i) Only certain measures may be considered in the Short Session- primarily those relating to appropriations, finance, pensions and retirement and localities; certain legislation from the 2001 Session; and legislation proposed by study commissions.
(j) Final date for consideration on floor in house of origin during first session. Bills introduced after date are not placed on calendar for consideration until second session.
(k) Not applicable to measures approved by Committee on Legislative Rules and Reorganization or by speaker; appropriation or fiscal measures sponsored by committees on Appropriations; true substitute measures sponsored by standing, special or joint committees; or measures drafted by legislative counsel.
(l) Resolutions fixing the last day for introduction of bills in the House are referred to the Rules Committee before consideration by the full House.
(m) Not applicable to certain local bills.
(n) Not applicable to substitute bills reported by standing committees for bills pending before such committees.
(o) Not applicable to Revenue & Appropriations and Local & Private bills. Time limits for those bills are: 51st calendar day (90-day session) and 86th calendar day (125-day session).

Table 3.16
ENACTING LEGISLATION: VETO, VETO OVERRIDE AND EFFECTIVE DATE

State or other jurisdiction	Governor may item veto appropriation bills		Days allowed governor to consider bill (a)			Votes required in each house to pass bills or items over veto (c)	Effective date of enacted legislation (d)
	Amount	Other (b)	During session: Bill becomes law unless vetoed	After session: Bill becomes law unless vetoed	Bill dies unless signed		
Alabama	...	...	6 (e)		10A	Majority elected	Date signed by governor
Alaska	★	...	15P	20P		2/3 elected (g)	90 days after enactment
Arizona	★	★	5	10A		2/3 elected	90 days after adjournment
Arkansas	★	...	5	20A		Majority elected	91st day after adjournment
California	(hh)	...	12	30A		2/3 elected	(j)
Colorado	★ (ff)	...	10 (h)	30A (h)		2/3 elected	90 days after adjournment (k)
Connecticut	★	...	5	15P		2/3 elected	(gg)
Delaware	★	...	10P	10P	30A	3/5 elected	Immediately
Florida	★	★	7 (h)(p)	15P (h)		2/3 present	60 days after adjournment
Georgia	★	★	6	40A		2/3 elected	July 1 for generals, date signed by governor for locals
Hawaii (l)	★ (f)	...	10 (o)(p)	45A (o)(p)	(p)	2/3 elected	Immediately
Idaho	★	★	5	10A		2/3 present	July 1
Illinois	★ (f)	...	60 (h)	60P (h)		3/5 elected (g)	(n)
Indiana	...	★	7	7P		Majority elected	(q)
Iowa	★	...	3	(r)	(r)	2/3 elected	July 1 (n)
Kansas	★	★	10 (h)	10P		2/3 membership	Upon publication
Kentucky	(hh)	★	10	90A	110P	Majority elected	90 days after adjournment
Louisiana (l)	★	★	10 (h)	20P (h)		2/3 elected	Aug. 15
Maine	(hh)	...	10	10P		2/3 present	90 days after adjournment
Maryland	★	★	6	30P (m)		3/5 elected	June 1 (s)
Massachusetts	★	★	10	10P	10A	2/3 present	90 days after enactment
Michigan	★	(hh)	14 (h)		14P (h)	2/3 elected and serving	90 days after adjournment
Minnesota	★	★	3	14A, 3P	3A, 14P	2/3 elected	Aug. 1 (t)
Mississippi	★	★	5	15P (m)		2/3 elected	July 1
Missouri	★	★	15	45A		2/3 elected	August 28 (u)
Montana (l)	★	...	10 (h)	25A (h)		2/3 present	Oct. 1 (t)
Nebraska	★ (v)	...	5	5A, 5P		3/5 elected	90 days following adjournment
Nevada	...	...	5	10A		2/3 elected	Oct. 1
New Hampshire	...	...	5	5P		2/3 present	60 days after enactment
New Jersey	★ (f)	...	45 (h)(w)	45A	(w)	2/3 elected	July 4; other dates usually specified
New Mexico	★	★	3 (ee)	(kk)	20A	2/3 present	90 days after adjournment
New York	★	...	10	30A	30A	2/3 elected	20 days after enactment
North Carolina	...	...	10	30A		3/5 elected	60 days after adjournment
North Dakota	★	★	3	15A		2/3 elected	60 days after adjournment
Ohio	★	★	10	10A	10A	3/5 elected (ii)	91st day after filing with secretary of state
Oklahoma	★	★	5	15A	15A	2/3 elected (g)	90 days after adjournment
Oregon	★	★	5 (o)	30A (o)		2/3 present	January 1st of following year. (jj)
Pennsylvania	★	★	10	30A, 10P	(i)	2/3 elected	60 days after signed by governor
Rhode Island	★	...	6	10A		3/5 present	Immediately
South Carolina	...	...	5	(m)		2/3 elected	Date of signature

See footnotes at end of table.

ENACTING LEGISLATION: VETO, VETO OVERRIDE AND EFFECTIVE DATE — Continued

State or other jurisdiction	Governor may item veto appropriation bills		Days allowed governor to consider bill (a)			Votes required in each house to pass bills or items over veto (c)	Effective date of enacted legislation (d)
			During session	After session			
	Amount	Other (b)	Bill becomes law unless vetoed	Bill becomes law unless vetoed	Bill dies unless signed		
South Dakota	★	★	5	15P		2/3 elected	July 1
Tennessee	★ (f)	...	10	10A		Majority elected	40 days after enactment
Texas	★	...	10P	20A		2/3 elected	90 days after adjournment
Utah	★	...	5P	60A (h)		2/3 elected	60 days after adjournment
Vermont	...	...	5P		3A	2/3 present	July 1
Virginia	★	★	7 (h)		30A (h)	2/3 present (y)	July 1 (z)
Washington	★	★	5	20A		2/3 present	90 days after adjournment
West Virginia	...	(hh)	5P	15A (aa)		Majority elected	90 days after enactment
Wisconsin	★	★	6P	6P		2/3 present	Day after publication date unless otherwise specified
Wyoming	★	★	3	15A		2/3 elected	Specified in act
American Samoa	★	★	10		30A	2/3 elected	60 days after adjournment (bb)
Guam	★	...	10		30P	2/3 elected	Immediately (cc)
No. Mariana Islands	★	...	40 (h)(dd)			2/3 elected	Immediately
Puerto Rico	★	...	10		30P	2/3 elected	Specified in act
U.S. Virgin Islands	★	★	10		30P (h)	2/3 elected	Immediately

See footnotes at end of table.

ENACTING LEGISLATION: VETO, VETO OVERRIDE AND EFFECTIVE DATE — Continued

Source: The Council of State Governments' surveys, October 2003 and October 2004.

Note: Some legislatures reconvene after normal session to consider bills vetoed by governor. Connecticut–if governor vetoes any bill, secretary of state must reconvene General Assembly on second Monday after the last day on which governor is either authorized to transmit or has transmitted every bill with his objections, which-ever occurs first; General Assembly must adjourn sine die not later than three days after its adjournment. Ha-waii–legislature may reconvene on 45th day after adjournment sine die, in special session, without call. Louisi-ana–legislature meets in a maximum five-day veto session on the 40th day after final adjournment. Missouri–if governor returns any bill on or after the fifth day before the last day on which legislature may consider bills (in even-numbered years), legislature automatically reconvenes on first Wednesday following the second Monday in September for a maximum 10-calendar day session. New Jersey–legislature meets in special session (without call or petition) to act on bills returned by governor on 45th day after sine die adjournment of the regular session: if the second year expires before the 45th day, the day preceding the end of the legislative year. Utah–if two-thirds of the members of each house favor reconvening to consider vetoed bills, a maximum five-day session is set by the presiding officers. Virginia–legislature reconvenes on sixth Wednesday after adjourn-ment for a maximum three-day session (may be extended to seven days upon vote of majority of members elected to each house). Washington–upon petition of two-thirds of the members of each house, legislature meets 45 days after adjournment for a maximum five-day session.

Key:

★—Yes

. . .—No

A—Days after adjournment of legislature.

P—Days after presentation to governor.

(a) Sundays excluded, unless otherwise indicated.

(b) Includes language in appropriations bill.

(c) Bill returned to house of origin with governor's objections.

(d) Effective date may be established by the law itself or may be otherwise changed by vote of the legislature. Special or emergency acts are usually effective immediately.

(e) Except bills presented within five days of final adjournment.

(f) Governor can also reduce amounts in appropriations bills. In Hawaii, governor can reduce items in execu-tive appropriations measures, but cannot reduce nor item veto amounts appropriated for the judicial or legisla-tive branches.

(g) Different number of votes required for revenue and appropriations bills. Alaska–three-fourths elected. Illinois–appropriations reductions, majority elected. Oklahoma–emergency bills, three-fourths vote.

(h) Sundays included.

(i) Last day of two year session.

(j) For legislation enacted in regular sessions: January of the following year. For legislation enacted in spe-cial sessions: Immediately upon chaptering by Secretary of State.

(k) An act takes effect on the date stated in the act, or if no date is stated in the act, then on its passage.

(l) Constitution withholds right to veto constitutional amendments.

(m) Bills vetoed after adjournment are returned to the legislature for reconsideration. Maryland–reconsid-ered at the next meeting of the same General Assembly. Mississippi–returned within three days after the begin-ning of the next session. South Carolina–within two days after the next meeting.

(n) Effective date for bills which become law on or after July 1. Illinois–a bill passed after May 31 cannot

take effect before June 1 of the next calendar year unless legislature by a three-fifths vote in each house, the bill provides for an earlier effective date. Iowa–if governor signs bill after July 1, bill becomes law on Aug. 15; for special sessions, 90 days after adjournment.

(o) Except Sundays and legal holidays. In Hawaii, except Saturdays, Sundays, holidays and any days in which the legislature is in recess prior to its adjournment. In Oregon, except Saturdays and Sundays.

(p) The governor must notify the legislature 10 days before the 45th day of his intent to veto a measure on that day. The legislature may convene on the 45th day after adjournment to consider the vetoed measures. If the legislature fails to reconvene, the bill does not become law. If the legislature reconvenes, it may pass the mea-sure over the governor's veto or it may amend the law to meet the governor's objections. If the law is amended, the governor must sign the bill within 10 days after it is presented to him in order for it to become law.

(q) Varies with date of the veto.

(r) Any bill presented to the governor within the last three days of a session must be acted on within 30 days after adjournment.

(s) Bills passed over governor's veto take effect 30 days after veto override or on date specified in bill, whichever is later.

(t) Different date for fiscal legislation. Minnesota, Montana–July 1.

(u) If bill has an emergency clause, it becomes effective upon governor's signature.

(v) No appropriation can be made in excess of the recommendations contained in the governor's budget except by a three-fifths vote. The excess is subject to veto by the governor.

(w) On the 45th day after the date of presentation, a bill becomes law unless the governor returns it with his objections, except that (1) if the legislature is in adjournment sine die on the 45th day, a special session is convened (without petition or call) for the sole purpose of acting upon bills returned by the governor; (2) any bill passed between the 45th day and the 10th day preceding the end of the second legislative year must be returned by the governor by the day preceding the end of the second legislative year; (3) any bill passed or reenacted within 10 days preceding the expiration of the second legislative year becomes law if signed prior to the seventh day following such expiration, or the governor returns it to the house of origin and two-thirds elected members agree to pass the bill prior to such expiration.

(x) August 1 after filing with the secretary of state. Appropriations and tax bills July 1 after filing with secretary of state, or date set in legislation by Legislative Assembly, or by date established by emergency clause.

(y) Must include majority of elected members.

(z) Special sessions–first day of fourth month after adjournment.

(aa) Five days for supplemental appropriation bills.

(bb) Laws required to be approved only by the governor. An act required to be approved by the U.S. Secretary of the Interior only after it is vetoed by the governor and so approved takes effect 40 days after it is returned to the governor by the secretary.

(cc) U.S. Congress may annul.

(dd) Twenty days for appropriations bills.

(ee) Except bills going up in the last three days of session, for which the governor has 20 days.

(ff) Must veto entire amount of any item; an item is an indivisible sum of money dedicated to a stated pur-pose.

(gg) No set date. Each section of each bill has an effective date determined by bill sponsor or sponsors.

(hh) Line item veto.

(ii) Except for bills needing 2/3 majority for original passage.

(jj) Unless emergency declared or date specific in text of measure.

(kk) Following adjournment of the legislature, the governor has 30 days to sign or veto bills delivered to him. If no action is taken, the bill does not become law (pocket veto).

Table 3.17
LEGISLATIVE APPROPRIATIONS PROCESS: BUDGET DOCUMENTS AND BILLS

Column groups: *Budget document submission* covers "Legal source of deadline" (Constitutional, Statutory) and "Submission date relative to convening" (Prior to session, Within one week, Within two weeks, Within one month, Over one month). *Budget bill introduction* covers "Same time as budget document," "Another time," and "Not until committee review of budget document."

State or other jurisdiction	Constitutional	Statutory	Prior to session	Within one week	Within two weeks	Within one month	Over one month	Same time as budget document	Another time	Not until committee review of budget document
Alabama	★	★		★				★		
Alaska	★	★	Dec. 15	(a)				★		
Arizona		★	★							★
Arkansas		★	★					★		
California	★									
Colorado		★	★(b)						76th day by rule	
Connecticut		★				(a)		★		
Delaware										★
Florida	★	★	★					★		
Georgia	★			(a)				★		
Hawaii		★	30 days						★	
Idaho		★		★					★	
Illinois		★					★		★	
Indiana		★				(a)				★(c)
Iowa		★							★	
Kansas		★			★(e)				★	
Kentucky		★			(a)			(g)		
Louisiana		★	(f)	(f)				★		
Maine		★		(a)				★(h)		
Maryland	★			★(e)				★		
Massachusetts		★				★		★		
Michigan		★				★(e)		★		
Minnesota		★				★			★	
Mississippi		★	★							★
Missouri	★					★			★	
Montana		★	★					★(c)		
Nebraska		★	★							★
Nevada	★		(a)					★		
New Hampshire		★				(a)				★(k)
New Jersey		★				★(e)			★	
New Mexico		★					(l)	★(m)		
New York	★				★(e)			★		
North Carolina										★
North Dakota		★	(n)					★		
Ohio		★					★(e)	★		
Oklahoma		★	★	★				★		
Oregon		★	Dec. 1 (e)						★(a)	
Pennsylvania	★						★	★		
Rhode Island		★					★			★
South Carolina		★		★					★	
South Dakota		★					★	★		
Tennessee		★			★(a)(e)	★(a)(e)		★		
Texas		★		6th day					★(t)	
Utah		★	(q)	★(r)					★(s)	
Vermont			(k)						(a)	
Virginia		★	Dec. 20					★	(i)	
Washington		★	Dec. 20 (d)					★		
West Virginia	★			★				★		
Wisconsin		★				★(j)				★
Wyoming		★	Dec. 1						(j)	
No. Mariana Islands		★	(a)							★
Puerto Rico		★				★				(u)
U.S. Virgin Islands		★	May 30			★(o)		★		

See footnotes at end of table.

LEGISLATIVE APPROPRIATIONS PROCESS: BUDGET DOCUMENTS AND BILLS — Continued

Source: The Council of State Governments' survey, October 2003 and October 2004. *Key:*

★—Yes

. . .—No

(a) Specific time limitations: Alaska—4th legislative day; Connecticut—not later than the first session day following the third day in February, in each odd numbered year; Georgia—first five days of session; Iowa—no later than February 1; Kentucky—10th legislative day; Maine—by Friday following the first Monday in January; Nevada—no later than 14 days before commencement of regular session; New Hampshire—by February 15; Oregon—Dec. 15 in even-numbered years; Tennessee—on or before February 1; No. Mariana Islands—no later than 6 months before the beginning of the fiscal year.

(b) Presented by November 1 to the Joint Budget Committee.

(c) Executive budget bill is introduced and used as a working tool for committee. Nebraska—Governor must submit his/her budget by January 15th each biennium of odd numbered years.

(d) For fiscal period other than biennium, 20 days prior to first day of session.

(e) Later for first session of a new governor; Kansas—21 days; Maryland—10 days after convening; Michigan—within 60 days; New Jersey—February 15; New York—February 1; Ohio—by March 15; Oregon—February 1; Tennessee—March 1.

(f) The governor shall submit his executive budget to the Joint Legislative Committee on the budget no later than 45 days prior to each regular session; except that in the first year of each term, the executive budget shall be submitted no later than 30 days prior to the regular session. Copies shall be made available to the entire legislature on the first day of each regular session.

(g) Bills appropriating monies for the general operating budget and ancillary appropriations, bills appropriating funds for the expenses of the legislature and the judiciary must be submitted to the legislature for introduction no later than 45 days prior to each regular session, except that in the first year of each term, such appropriation bills shall be submitted no later than 30 days prior to the regular session.

(h) Appropriations bill other than the budget bill (supplementary) may be introduced at any time. They must provide their own tax source and may not be enacted until the budget bill is enacted.

(i) Even-numbered years.

(j) Last Tuesday in January. A later submission date may be requested by the governor.

(k) No official submission dates. Occurs by custom early in the session.

(l) January 1.

(m) Governor has 30 days to amend or supplement the budget; he may submit any amendments to any bills or submit supplemental bills.

(n) For whole legislature. Legislative Council's Budget Section receives budget during legislature's December organizational session.

(o) By enacting annual appropriations legislation.

(p) No later than the 16th legislative day by rule.

(q) Governor must submit budget to Legislative Fiscal Analyst 34 days before official submission to legislature.

(r) Must submit to the legislature no later than 3 days after session begins.

(s) Legislative rules require budget bills to be introduced by the 43rd day of the session, three days prior to the constitutionally mandated end of the session.

(t) Within first 30 days of session.

(u) Prior to September 30.

Table 3.18
FISCAL NOTES: CONTENT AND DISTRIBUTION

State or other jurisdiction	Intent or purpose of bill	Cost involved	Projected future cost	Proposed source of revenue	Fiscal impact on local government	Other	All	Available on request	Bill sponsor	Appropriations committee — Members	Appropriations committee — Chair only	Fiscal staff	Executive budget staff
Alabama	★	★	...	★	★	★ (a)	...	★	★	...	...	...	...
Alaska	...	★	★	★	...	...	(d)	...	...	...	...	...	...
Arizona	★	★	★	★	★	★	★	★	★	★	...	★	★
Arkansas (f)	...	★	★	...	★	★	★	...	...	...	...	...	...
California	★	★	★	★	★	...	★	★	★	...	...	★	★
Colorado	★	★	★	★	★	★	★	...	...	...	...	...	...
Connecticut	★	★	★	★	★	...	(i)	...	...	...	...	...	...
Delaware	...	★	★	...	...	...	★	...	...	...	...	★	★
Florida	★	★	★	★	★	★	★	...	...	...	...	★	...
Georgia	...	★	★	...	★	...	★	★	...	...	...	...	...
Hawaii	...	...	...	...	...	★	...	...	...	...	★	★	★
Idaho	★	★	★	...	★	★	★	...	...	...	...	...	...
Illinois	...	★	★	★	★	...	★ (l)	★ (l)	...	...	...	★	★
Indiana	★	★	★	★	★	...	★	...	...	...	...	★	★
Iowa	...	★	★	★	★	★	....................(b).....................						
Kansas	★	★	★	★	★	...	...	★	★	...	★ (m)	★	★
Kentucky	★	★	★	★	★	★	...	★	★	★	...	★	...
Louisiana	...	★	★	...	★	...	★	★	...	...	★ (o)	...	...
Maine	...	★	★	...	★	...	...	...	★	★	...	★	★
Maryland	...	★	★	★	★	★	...	★	★ (y)	...	...	...	...
Massachusetts	...	★ (q)	★	...	...	★	★	...	...	★	...	...	...
Michigan	★	★	★	★	★	★ (r)	★ (s)	★	...	...	...	★	★
Minnesota	★	★	★	★	★	★	★	★	★	★	★	★	★
Mississippi	...	★	★	★	...	...	...	...	★ (y)	...	...	...	...
Missouri	★	★	★	★	★	...	...	★	★	...	...	...	★
Montana	...	★	★	...	★	★ (k)	★	...	...	...	...	★	★
Nebraska	...	★	★	★	★	...	★	...	...	...	...	★	...
Nevada	...	★	★	★	★	★	★	...	...	...	...	...	...
New Hampshire	★	★	★	★	★	...	...	★	...	...	...	★	★
New Jersey	★	★	★	★	★	★ (r)	★	...	...	...	...	...	...
New Mexico	★	★	★	★	(t)	★	...	★	★	★	...	(v)	(v)
New York	...	★	★	...	★	★ (n)	...	★	★	★	...	★	...
North Carolina	...	★	★	...	★	★	(c)	...	...	...	...	...	...
North Dakota (w)	...	★	★ (x)	★	★	★ (n)	...	★	...	...	...	★ (z)	★
Ohio	★	★	★	★	★	...	(aa)	...	...	...	...	...	...
Oklahoma	★	★	★	★	...	...	...	★	★	...	★	★	...
Oregon	★	★	★	★	★	★ (e)	★	...	...	...	★	★	★
Pennsylvania	★	★	★	★	★	...	★	...	★	★	★	★	★
Rhode Island	...	★	★	...	★	...	...	★	...	...	★	...	...
South Carolina	★	★	★	★	★	...	...	★	...	...	★ (j)	★	...
South Dakota	...	★	...	...	★	...	...	★	...	...	...	...	...
Tennessee	★	★	★	★	★	★	★	★	★	★	...	★	★
Texas	...	★	★	★	★	★ (g)	★	★	★	...	...	...	★
Utah	...	★	★	★	★	★ (u)	★	★	★	...	...	★	★
Vermont	..........(h)..........						...	★	...	...	★	...	...
Virginia	★	★	★	★ (bb)	★	★	...	★	★	★	...	...	...
Washington	★	★	★	★	★	...	...	★	★ (m)	...	★	★ (cc)	...
West Virginia	...	★	★	★	★	...	...	★	...	★	...	...	...
Wisconsin	★	★	★	★	★	★	★	...	...	...	...	★	★
Wyoming	...	★	★	★	...	...	(dd)	...	...	...	...	...	...
No. Mariana Islands	★	★	★	★	★	★	...	...	...	...	★	★	★
Puerto Rico	..........(p)..........												
U.S. Virgin Islands	★	★	...	★	★	...	★	...	★	★	...	★	...

See footnotes at end of table.

FISCAL NOTES: CONTENT AND DISTRIBUTION — Continued

Source: The Council of State Governments' survey, October 2003 and October 2004.

Note: A fiscal note is a summary of the fiscal effects of a bill on government revenues, expenditures and liabilities.

Key:

★— Yes

. . .—No

(a) Fiscal notes are included in bills for final passage calendar.

(b) Fiscal notes are available to everyone.

(c) Fiscal notes are posted on the internet and available to all members.

(d) Fiscal notes are available online to anyone who wishes to review them. Formal copies go to the bill sponsor and each committee to which the bill is referred. A bill cannot be passed from committee without a fiscal note.

(e) Assumptions (methodology/explanation of fiscal figures).

(f) Only retirement, corrections and local government bills require fiscal notes.

(g) Equalized education funding impact statement and criminal justice policy impact statement.

(h) Fiscal notes are not mandatory and their content will vary.

(i) The fiscal notes are printed with the bills favorably reported by the committees.

(j) Fiscal impact statements on proposed legislation are prepared by the Office of State Budget and sent to the House or Senate standing committee that requested the impact. All fiscal impacts are posted on the OSB web page.

(k) Mechanical defects in bill.

(l) A summary of the fiscal note is attached to the summary of the relevant bill in the Legislative Synopsis and Digest. Fiscal notes are prepared for the sponsor of the bill and are attached to the bill on file in either the office of the Clerk of the House or the Secretary of the Senate.

(m) Or to the committee to which referred.

(n) Bill impacting workers compensation benefits or premiums must have actuarial impact statement. Bills proposing changes in states and local government retirement system also must have an actuarial note.

(o) Prepared by the Legislative Fiscal Office when a state agency is involved and prepared by Legislative Auditor's office when a local board or commission is involved; copies sent to House and Senate staff offices respectively.

(p) The Legislature of Puerto Rico does not prepare fiscal notes, but upon request the economics unit could prepare one. The Department of Treasury has the duty to analyze and prepare fiscal notes.

(q) Fiscal notes are prepared only if cost exceeds $100,000 or matter has not been acted upon by the Joint Committee on Ways and Means.

(r) Other relevant data.

(s) Analyses prepared by the Senate Fiscal Agency are distributed to Senate members only; Fiscal notes prepared by the House Fiscal Agency are prepared for bills being voted on in any standing committee and are distributed to the chairperson and all committee members.

(t) Occasionally.

(u) Fiscal notes are to include cost estimates on all proposed bills that anticipate direct expenditures by any Utah resident and the cost to the overall Utah resident population.

(v) Fiscal impact statements prepared by Legislative Finance Committee staff are available to anyone on request and on the legislature's web site.

(w) Notes required only if impact is $5,000 or more.

(x) A four-year projection.

(y) And to the committee to which referred.

(z) Only select fiscal staff.

(aa) Fiscal notes are prepared for bills before being voted on in any standing committee or floor session. Upon distribution to the legislators preparing to vote, the fiscal notes are made available to all other legislators and interested parties.

(bb) The Dept. of Planning and Budget and other relevant state agencies, including the Dept. of Taxation , prepare impact statements, The Joint Legislative Audit And Review Commission (JLARC) prepares review statements as requested by committee chairpersons.

(cc) Distributed to appropriate fiscal and policy staff.

(dd) Fiscal notes are included with the bill upon introduction.

Table 3.19
BILL AND RESOLUTION INTRODUCTIONS AND ENACTMENTS:
2004 REGULAR SESSIONS

State	Duration of session**	Introductions Bills	Introductions Resolutions	Enactments Bills	Enactments Resolutions	Measures vetoed by governor	Length of session
Alabama	Feb. 3–May 17, 2004	1,397	937	311	330	5 (a)	30L
Alaska	Jan. 12–May 12, 2004	391	79	181	37	0	122C
Arizona	Jan. 12–May 26, 2004	1,127	100	343	11	10 (c)	136C
Arkansas	No regular session in 2004						
California	Jan. 5–Nov. 30, 2004	2,169	259	950	247	20	(b)
Colorado	Jan. 7–May 5, 2004	726	44 (d)	424	2	9 (c)	120C
Connecticut	Feb. 4–May 5, 2004	1,324	250	267	154	1	92C
Delaware	Jan. 13–June 30, 2004	411	93	218	19	1	43L
Florida	Mar. 2–April 30, 2004	2,691	262 (f)	494	3 (h)	22	60C
Georgia	Jan. 12–April 7, 2004	1,031	1,735	394	1,549	19	40C
Hawaii	Jan. 21–May 6, 2004	2,537	844	274	289	37 (a)	60L
Idaho	Jan. 12–Mar. 20, 2004	619	76	395	47	6	69C
Illinois	Jan. 6–July 24, 2004 (m)	4,637	1,199	412	1045	32 (a)	(b)
Indiana	Nov. 18–Dec. 5, 2003; Jan. 6–Dec. 12, 2004	973	253	98	200	0 (a)	29L
Iowa	Jan. 12–Apr. 20, 2004	890	212	177	3	29	100C
Kansas	Jan. 12–May 27, 2004	755	49	185	1	24 (c)	90L
Kentucky	Jan. 6–Apr. 13, 2004	999	558	165	32	2	60L
Louisiana	Mar. 29–June 21, 2004	2,604	863	931	779	12	60L
Maine	Jan. 7–Jan. 30, 2004	202	15	7	0	0	12L
Maryland	Jan. 14–Apr. 12, 2004	2,482	21	557	1	154 (a)	90C
Massachusetts	Jan. 3, 2003–July 30, 2004	7,718	N.A.	680	N.A.	(r)	N.A.
Michigan	Jan. 14, 2004–Dec. 29, 2004	1,545	16 (d)	596	0	55	(b)
Minnesota	Jan. 2–May 16, 2004	3,051	146	159	29	6	(b)
Mississippi	N.A.	N.A.	N.A.	N.A.	N.A.	N.A.	N.A.
Missouri	Jan. 7–May 30, 2004	1,653	60	210	1	8	N.A.
Montana	No regular session in 2004						
Nebraska	Jan. 7–Apr. 15, 2004	446	10	132	3	2	60L
Nevada	No regular session in 2004						
New Hampshire	Jan. 7–June 17, 2004	713 (p)	36 (p)	260	15	4	17L
New Jersey	Jan. 13, 2004–Jan. 10, 2006 (q)	5,577	838	186	65	3	N.A.
New Mexico	Jan. 20–Feb. 19, 2004	1,174	34	140	14	14	30C
New York	Jan. 7, 2004–Jan. 5, 2005	17,214 (e)	(i)	729 (e)	4,945	78 (e)	365C
North Carolina	May 10–June 18, 2004	850	32 (d)	203	13 (d)	1	44L
North Dakota	No regular session in 2004						
Ohio	Jan. 5–Dec. 29, 2004 (g)(k)	341	37 (d)	132	20 (d)	0	(b)
Oklahoma	Feb. 2–May 28, 2004	1,698	67 (o)	557	7 (o)	10	70L
Oregon	No regular session in 2004						
Pennsylvania	Jan. 6–Nov. 30, 2004	4,292	1267	239	647	11	N.A.
Rhode Island	Jan. 6–July 30, 2004	2,955	N.A.	662	407	30 (a)	(b)
South Carolina	Jan. 13–June 3, 2004	844 (l)	714 (n)	255 (l)	680 (n)	18 (a)	63L
South Dakota	Jan. 13–Mar. 15, 2004	530	8	311	1	5	35L
Tennessee	Jan. 13–May 21, 2004	2,969	1,618	616	1,495	0	(b)
Texas	No regular session in 2004						
Utah	Jan. 19–Mar. 3, 2004	602	71	375	43	6 (a)	45C
Vermont	Jan. 8–May 30, 2003; Jan. 6–May 20, 2004 (j)	1,100	618	188	554	3	160C
Virginia	Jan. 14–Mar. 16, 2004	2,181	825	1,028	2	7	45L
Washington	Jan. 12–Mar. 11, 2004	1,567	80	281	11	4	60C
West Virginia	N.A.	N.A.	N.A.	N.A.	N.A.	N.A.	N.A.
Wisconsin	Jan. 20, 2004–Jan. 3, 2005	1,524	0	116	0	40	(b)
Wyoming	Feb. 9–Mar. 5, 2004	310	16	133	3	1	20L

See footnotes at end of table.

INTRODUCTIONS AND ENACTMENTS: REGULAR SESSIONS — Continued

Source: The Council of State Governments' survey of legislative agencies, January 2005.

**Actual adjournment dates are listed regardless of constitutional or statutory limitations. For more information on provisions, see Table 3.2, Legislative Sessions: Legal Provisions.

Key:

C—Calendar day.

L—Legislative day (in some states, called a session or workday; definition may vary slightly; however, it general refers to any day on which either chamber of the legislature is in session.)

N.A.—Not available.

(a) Number of vetoes overridden: Alabama-3; Hawaii-7; Illinois-9; Indiana -3; Maryland-5; Rhode Island-9; South Carolina-16; Utah-2.

(b) Length of session: California—Senate 59L and House 62L; Illinois—Senate 85L (15 were perfunctory) and House 94L (34 were perfunctory); Michigan—Senate 109L and House 93L; Minnesota—Senate 51L and House 52L; Ohio—Senate 116L and House 122L; Rhode Island—Senate 63L and House 70L; Tennessee—Senate 45L and House 47L; Wisconsin—Senate 89L and Assembly 82L.

(c) Line item or partial vetoes. Arizona—includes two line item vetoes; Colorado—includes three partially vetoed measures; Kansas—includes 16 line item vetoes.

(d) Numbers include concurrent and joint resolutions only. For Colorado, numbers only include concurrent resolutions. For Michigan and North Carolina, numbers only include joint resolutions.

(e) At the time this information was received, there were still 31 30-day bills pending.

(f) Includes one-chamber resolutions.

(g) Senate: Dec. 8, 2004 and House: Dec. 29, 2004

(h) Does not include one-chamber resolutions.

(i) There are no official statistics for resolution introductions.

(j) Two-year session.

(k) The second session of the 125th General Assembly.

(l) Numbers includes joint resolutions.

(m) House convened on Jan. 6 and Senate convened on Jan. 14.

(n) Numbers include Senate, House and concurrent resolutions.

(o) Joint resolutions. Does not include simple and concurrent resolutions.

(p) For bills, number includes 188 retained from 2003 session. For resolutions, number includes eight retained from 2003 session.

(q) New Jersey has a two-year legislative session. Information reflects 2004 numbers.

(r) Total number of vetoes unavailable, however there were 21 non-budget vetoes overridden by the governor in 2003 and 2004.

Table 3.20
BILL AND RESOLUTION INTRODUCTIONS AND ENACTMENTS:
2004 SPECIAL SESSIONS

State	Duration of session**	Introductions Bills	Introductions Resolutions	Enactments Bills	Enactments Resolutions	Measures vetoed by governor	Length of session
Alabama	Nov. 8–Nov. 16, 2004	69	69	19	41	0	5L
Alaska	June 22–June 24, 2004	10	4	1	1	0	3C
Arizona	No special session in 2004						
Arkansas	No special session in 2004						
California	Nov. 18, 2003–Nov. 30, 2004	21	7	1	2	0	(f)
	Jan. 18–Nov. 30, 2004 (g)	18	2	1	0	0	61L
Colorado	No special session in 2004						
Connecticut	Jan. 26, 2004 (c)	0	6	0	6	0	1L
	Jan. 26, 2004 (c)	0	6	0	6	0	1C
	May 11, 2004 (d)	0	1	0	1	0	N.A.
	May 11–June 28, 2004	5	5	5	5	0	2L
Delaware	No special session in 2004						
Florida	No special session in 2004						
Georgia	May 3–May 7, 2004	7	147	4	146	0	5L
Hawaii	No special session in 2004						
Idaho	No special session in 2004						
Illinois	June 24–July 24, 2004	9	91	0	85	0	(e)
Indiana	No special session in 2004						
Iowa	Sept. 7, 2004	4	3	2	1	0	1C
Kansas	No special session in 2004						
Kentucky	Oct. 5–Oct. 19, 2004	11	72	1	0	0	11L
Louisiana	Mar. 7–Mar. 17, 2004	62	63	14	59	0	11C
Maine	Feb. 3–Apr. 30, 2004	124	26	265	0	2	38L
Maryland	Dec. 28, 2004–Jan. 11, 2005	4	1	8	0	1 (q)	15C
Massachusetts	No special session in 2004						
Michigan	No special session in 2004						
Minnesota	No special session in 2004						
Mississippi	N.A.	N.A.	N.A.	N.A.	N.A.	N.A.	N.A.
Missouri	No special session in 2004						
Montana	No special session in 2004						
Nebraska	No special session in 2004						
Nevada	Nov. 10–Dec. 4, 2004	1	151		15	0	25C
New Hampshire	No special session in 2004						
New Jersey	No special session in 2004						
New Mexico	No special session in 2004						
New York	No special session in 2004						
North Carolina	Nov. 4, 2004	3	1 (a)	1	1 (a)	0	1L
North Dakota	No special session in 2004						
Ohio	Dec. 13–Dec. 29, 2004 (b)	4	0	1	0	0	(b)
Oklahoma	May 19–Sept. 27, 2004	0	6	0	6	0	3C
Oregon	No special session in 2004						
Pennsylvania	No special session in 2004						
Rhode Island	No special session in 2004						
South Carolina	No special session in 2004						
South Dakota	No special session in 2004						
Tennessee	No special session in 2004						
Texas	Apr. 20–May 17, 2004	104	601 (i)	0	551 (i)	0	8L
Utah	June 28, 2004	1	0	1	0	0	1C
	Sept. 15, 2004	4	0	4	0	0	1C
Vermont	June 16, 2004	0	0	0	0	0	1L
Virginia	Mar. 17–May 7, 2004	29	74	4	0	0	N.A.
	July 13, 2004	2	6	1	0	0	N.A.
Washington	No special session in 2004						
West Virginia	N.A.	N.A.	N.A.	N.A.	N.A.	N.A.	N.A.
Wisconsin	No special session in 2004						
Wyoming	July 12–July 17, 2004	11	4	5	1	0	6L

See footnotes at end of table.

INTRODUCTIONS AND ENACTMENTS: SPECIAL SESSIONS — Continued

Source: The Council of State Governments' survey of state legislative agencies, January 2005.

** Actual adjournment dates are listed regardless of constitutional or statutory limitations. For more information on provisions, see Table 3.2, Legislative Sessions: Legal Provisions.

Key:

N.A.—Not available

C—Calendar day.

L—Legislative day (in some states, called a session or workday; definition may vary slightly; however, it generally refers to any day on which either chamber of the legislature is in session).

(a) Joint resolutions only.

(b) The Senate adjourned on Dec. 29, 2004, however the House adjourned on Dec. 17, 2004. Length of session: Senate—8L and House—4L.

(c) Continuation of 2003 session.

(d) House has not adjourned sine die.

(e) Senate—22L and House—17L.

(f) Length of session: Senate—41L and Assembly 49L.

(g) Session for Senate only.

(h) Number of vetoes overridden: 8.

(i) Resolution introductions include: 33 concurrent resolutions, 24 joint resolutions, 544 resolutions. Resolution enactments include: 18 concurrent resolutions and 533 resolutions.

Table 3.21
STAFF FOR INDIVIDUAL LEGISLATORS

State or other jurisdiction	Senate Capitol Personal	Senate Capitol Shared	Senate District	House/Assembly Capitol Personal	House/Assembly Capitol Shared	House/Assembly District
Alabama	. . .	YR/2	(u)	. . .	YR/10	(u)
Alaska	SO	. . .	YR	SO	. . .	YR
Arizona	YR	. . .	. . .	. . .	YR (a)	. . .
Arkansas	. . .	YR	. . .	. . .	YR	. . .
California	YR	. . .	YR	YR	. . .	YR
Colorado (b)	YR/5, SO/35	YR/5, SO/2	. . .	YR/5, SO/65	YR/2, SO/2	. . .
Connecticut (d)	YR/36	. . .	. . .	. . .	YR/38	. . .
Delaware	---(v)---					
Florida	YR (e)	. . .	YR (e)	YR (e)	. . .	YR (e)
Georgia	. . .	YR/3, SO/68	. . .	. . .	YR/25, SO/113	. . .
Hawaii	YR	. . .	. . .	YR	. . .	. . .
Idaho	. . .	SO/1.2, YR/2	. . .	. . .	SO/.86, YR/3	. . .
Illinois	YR	YR/1 (f)	YR (g)	YR	YR/2 (f)	YR (g)
Indiana	. . .	YR	. . .	. . .	YR	. . .
Iowa	SO	. . .	. . .	SO	. . .	. . .
Kansas	SO	. . .	. . .	. . .	SO/3	. . .
Kentucky	. . .	YR (h)	. . .	. . .	YR (h)	. . .
Louisiana	(i)	YR (j)	YR (i)	(i)	YR (j)	YR (i)
Maine	YR/24, SO/8	. . .	. . .	. . .	(l)	. . .
Maryland	YR, SO (t)	. . .	YR	YR (t)	SO (t)	YR
Massachusetts	YR	. . .	. . .	YR	. . .	. . .
Michigan	. . .	YR	. . .	YR	. . .	. . .
Minnesota	YR	. . .	. . .	YR	. . .	. . .
Mississippi	. . .	YR	. . .	. . .	YR	. . .
Missouri	YR	YR	. . .	YR	YR	. . .
Montana	. . .	SO	. . .	. . .	SO	. . .
Nebraska	YR (m)	. . .	. . .	------------------Unicameral------------------		
Nevada	SO (c)	YR	. . .	SO (c)	YR	. . .
New Hampshire	. . .	SO	. . .	. . .	YR	. . .
New Jersey	YR (e)	. . .	(e)	YR (e)	. . .	. . .
New Mexico (k)	SO	. . .	. . .	. . .	SO	. . .
New York	YR	. . .	YR	YR	YR	. . .
North Carolina	YR (w)	YR	. . .	YR (w)	YR	. . .
North Dakota	. . .	SO (c)	. . .	. . .	SO (c)	. . .
Ohio	YR	YR	. . .	YR	YR	. . .
Oklahoma	YR	. . .	. . .	. . .	YR	. . .
Oregon	YR	. . .	. . .	YR	. . .	YR
Pennsylvania	YR	. . .	YR	YR	. . .	YR
Rhode Island	. . .	YR/8	. . .	. . .	YR/7	. . .
South Carolina	. . .	. . .	. . .	YR	. . .	. . .
South Dakota	. . .	SO	. . .	. . .	SO	. . .
Tennessee	YR	. . .	. . .	YR	. . .	YR
Texas	YR	. . .	YR	YR	. . .	YR
Utah	(o)	SO	. . .	(o)	SO	. . .
Vermont	YR/1 (n)	. . .	. . .	YR/1 (n)	. . .	. . .
Virginia	SO (e)	. . .	(e)	SO (e)	SO/2	(q)
Washington	YR (p)	. . .	(q)	YR	. . .	. . .
West Virginia	SO	. . .	. . .	. . .	SO/17	. . .
Wisconsin	YR (r)	YR (r)	(r)	YR	YR (r)	(r)
Wyoming	. . .	. . .	. . .	. . .	. . .	. . .
No. Mariana Islands	YR (s)	(s)	. . .	YR (s)	(s)	(r)
Puerto Rico	YR (s)	. . .	. . .	YR (s)	. . .	. . .
U.S. Virgin Islands	YR (s)	. . .	. . .	------------------Unicameral------------------		

See footnotes at end of table.

STAFF FOR INDIVIDUAL LEGISLATORS — Continued

Source: The Council of State Governments' survey, October 2003 and October 2004.

Note: For entries under column heading "Shared," figures after slash indicated approximate number of legislators per staff person, where available.

Key:

. . . — Staff not provided for individual legislators.

YR — Year-round.

SO — Session only.

IO — Interim only.

(a) Representatives share a secretary with another legislator, however House leadership and committee chairs usually have their own secretarial staff. All legislators share professional research staff within their house.

(b) The number of year round staff is comprised of leadership staff and caucus staff. Each caucus may also hire additional shared staff during the session. During the session, each legislator can hire an aide for a limited number of hours.

(c) Secretarial staff; in North Dakota, leadership only.

(d) The numbers are for staff assigned to specific legislators. There is additional staff working in the leadership offices that also suport the rank and file members.

(e) Personal and district staff are the same. In Florida, two out of the three district employees may travel to the capitol for sessions.

(f) Partisan offices provide staff year-round.

(g) District office expenses allocated per year from which staff may be hired.

(h) Leadership offices provide staff support year-round. Individual legislators have access to clerical support year-round, augmented during a session.

(i) Each legislator may hire as many assistants as desired, but pay from public funds ranges from $2,000 to $3,000 per month per legislator. Assistant(s) generally work in the district office but may also work at the capitol during the session.

(j) The six caucuses are assigned one full-time position each (potentially 24 legislators per one staff person).

(k) Speaker, pro tem and leadership have staff year round.

(l) The House members do not have individual staff. There are 20 people who work year round in the three partisan offices, 12 of whom are legislative aides who primarily work directly with legislators.

(m) Senators offices have 2 year round staff members. Committee chair offices have 3-4 staff members year round.

(n) No personal staff except one administrative assistant for the Speaker and one for the Sneate Pro Tempore.

(o) Legislators are provided student interns during session.

(p) Leadership, caucus chair, and Ways and Means Committee chair have two full-time staff each. All other legislators have one full-time staff year round and one additional staff session only.

(q) Full-time staff may move to the district office during interim period.

(r) Some of personal staff may work in the district office. Total of all staff salaries for each senator must be within limits established by the Senate.

(s) Individual staffing and staff pool arrangements are at the discretion of the individual legislator.

(t) Senators have one year round administrative aide and one session only secretary. Delegates have one part-time year round administrative aide and a shared session only secretary.

(u) Six counties have local delegation offices with shared staff.

(v) Staffers are a combination of full time, part time, shared, personal, etc. andtheir assignments change throughout the year.

(w) Part time during interim.

Table 3.22
STAFF FOR LEGISLATIVE STANDING COMMITTEES

| | Committee staff assistance | | | | Source of staff services** | | | | | | | |
| | Senate | | House/Assembly | | Joint central agency (a) | | Chamber agency (b) | | Caucus or leadership | | Committee or committee chair | |
State or other jurisdiction	Prof.	Cler.	Prof.	Cler.	Prof.	Cler.	Prof.	Cler.	Prof.	Cler.	Prof.	Cler.
Alabama	●	★	●	★	B	B	B	B	...	...	B	B
Alaska	★	●	★	●	B	B	...	...	B	B	...	...
Arizona	★	★	★	★	B	...	...	B	B	...	B	B
Arkansas	★	★	★	★	B	B	...	...	...	...	...	...
California	★	★	★	★	B	B	B	B	B	B	B	B
Colorado	★	...	★	...	B	...	B	B	B	B	...	...
Connecticut	...	★	...	★	B	B	...	...	...	B	...	B
Delaware	...	...	...	...	B	B	...	...	...	...	...	...
Florida	★	★	★	★	B	B	S, H	S, H	S, H	S, H	S, H	S, H
Georgia	●	★	●	★	B	B	B	B	B	B	B	...
Hawaii	●	★	★	★	B	B	B	B	B	B	B	B
Idaho	★	★	★	★	B	B	...	...	...	...	B	B
Illinois	★	★	★	★	...	...	B	B	B	B	...	...
Indiana	●	...	●	...	...	...	...	...	...	...	B	B
Iowa	★	...	★	...	B	...	B (d)	...	B	...	B	...
Kansas	★	★	★	★	B	B (e)	...	...	...	...	...	...
Kentucky	★	★	★	★	B	B	...	...	...	...	...	...
Louisiana	★ (m)	★	★ (m)	★	B	B	B	B	B	B	B (g)	B (g)
Maine	★ (c)	★ (c)	★ (c)	★ (c)	B	B	S, H	S, H	S, H	S, H	...	B
Maryland	★ (h)	★ (h)	★ (h)	★ (h)	B	B	...	...	...	...	...	...
Massachusetts	★	★	★	★	...	...	...	...	...	...	...	...
Michigan	★	★	★	★	B	...	...	H	B	...	B	S
Minnesota	★	★	★	★	...	...	B	...	H	H	B	B
Mississippi	●	★	●	★	...	...	B	B	...	...	B	B
Missouri	★	...	★	...	B	...	B, S, H	...	S	S	S, H	...
Montana	★	★	★	★	B	...	...	B	...	...	...	...
Nebraska	★	★	U	U	...	...	...	...	...	...	...	...
Nevada	★	★ (h)	★	★ (h)	B	...	...	B	...	...	...	...
New Hampshire	●	★	★	★	B	...	S, H	S, H	...	...	...	...
New Jersey	★	★	★	★	B	B	...	...	...	...	...	...
New Mexico	★	★	★	★	...	...	B (g)	B (g)	...	...	...	...
New York	★	★	★	★	B	B	B	B	B	B	B	B
North Carolina	★	★ (i)	★	★ (i)	B	...	...	...	...	...	...	B (i)
North Dakota	●(f)	★	●(f)	★	B	...	...	B	...	...	...	...
Ohio	★	★	★	★	B	...	...	...	...	...	B	B
Oklahoma	★	★	★	★	...	...	B	B	...	...	...	...
Oregon	★	★	★	★	B	B	...	...	...	...	B	B
Pennsylvania	★	★	★	★	B	B	B	B	B	B	B	B
Rhode Island	★	★	★	★	B	B	...	...	B	B	...	...
South Carolina	★	★	★	★	B	B	B	B	B	B	B	B
South Dakota	★	★	★	★	B (h)	...	...	...	...	...	...	...
Tennessee	★	★	★	★	B	...	...	B (j)	...	...	S	B
Texas	★	★	★	★	B	B	...	B	...	...	B	B
Utah	★	★	★	★	B	...	...	B	...	...	...	...
Vermont	★	●	★	●	B	B	...	...	...	...	...	...
Virginia	★	★	★	★	B	...	B	B	...	...	(g)	(g)
Washington	★	★	★	★	...	...	...	...	B	B	B (k)	B (k)
West Virginia	★	★	★	★	B	B	B	B	B	B	B	B
Wisconsin	★	★	★	★	B	B	...	...	...	...	B	B
Wyoming	★	★	★	★	B	...	...	B	...	B	...	B
No. Mariana Islands	★	★	★	★	B (l)	B (p)	(l)	B (l)	B (l)	B (l)	B (l)	B (l)
Puerto Rico	★	★	★	★	B (l)	B (l)	B (l)	B (l)	B (l)	B (l)	B (l)	B (l)
U.S. Virgin Islands	★	★	U	U	S (l)	S (l)	S (l)	S (l)	S (l)	S (l)	S (l)	S (l)

See footnotes at end of table.

STAFF FOR LEGISLATIVE STANDING COMMITTEES — Continued

Source: The Council of State Governments' survey, October 2003.and October 2004.

** — Multiple entries reflect a combination of organizations and location of services.

Key:

★ — All committees
● — Some committees
. . . — Services not provided
B — Both chambers
H — House
S — Senate
U — Unicameral

(a) Includes legislative council or service agency or central management agency.

(b) Includes chamber management agency, office of clerk or secretary and House or Senate research office.

(c) Standing committees are joint House and Senate committees.

(d) The Senate secretary and House clerk maintain supervision of committee clerks. During the session each committee selects its own clerk.

(e) Senators select their secretaries and notify the central administrative services agency; all administrative employee matters handled by the agency.

(f) House and Senate Appropriations Committees have Legislative Council fiscal staff at their hearings.

(g) Staff is assigned to each committee but work under the direction of the chair.

(h) Committees hire additional staff on a contractual basis during session only under direction of chair.

(i) Member's personal secretary serves as a clerk to the committee or subcommittee that the member chairs.

(j) Bill clerks during session only.

(k) Each chamber has a non-partisan research staff which provides support services to committees (including chair).

(l) In general, the legislative service agency provides legal and staff assistance for legislative meetings and provides associated materials. Individual legislators hire personal or committee staff as their budgets provide and at their own discretion.

(m) House Appropriations and Senate Finance Committees have Legislative Fiscal Office staff at their hearings.

Table 3.23
STANDING COMMITTEES: APPOINTMENT AND NUMBER

State or other jurisdiction	Committee members appointed by:		Committee chairpersons appointed by:		Number of standing committees during regular 2004 session (a)	
	Senate	House	Senate	House	Senate	House
Alabama	CC	S	CC	S	24	24
Alaska	CC	CC	CC	CC	9	9
Arizona	P	S	P	S	13	18
Arkansas	(bb)	(d)	(bb)	S	10	10
California	CR	S	CR	S	23	29
Colorado	MjL, MnL	S, MnL	MjL	S	10 (a)	11 (a)
Connecticut	PT	S	PT	S	(e)	(e)
Delaware	PT	S	PT	S	26	27
Florida	P	S	P	S	24	18
Georgia	CC	S	CC	S	25	34
Hawaii	P (f)	(g)	P (f)	(g)	15	19
Idaho	PT (h)	S	PT	S	10	14
Illinois	P, MnL	S, MnL	P	S	21	37
Indiana	PT	S	PT	S	19	20
Iowa	MjL, MnL (i)	S	MjL (i)	S	16	17
Kansas	(j)	S	(j)	S	14	21
Kentucky	CC	CC	CC	CC	14	19
Louisiana	P	S (k)	P	S	17	17
Maine	P	S	P	S	4 (e)	6 (e)
Maryland	P	S	P	S	8	9
Massachusetts	P	S, MnL	P	S	4(e)	8 (e)
Michigan	MjL	S	MjL	S	21 (c)	22 (c)
Minnesota	CR	S	MjL	S	14	26
Mississippi	P	S	P	S	39 (c)	45 (c)
Missouri	PT (l)	S	PT	S	35	35
Montana	CC	S	CC	S	17	17
Nebraska	CC	U	E	U	14	U
Nevada	MjL (m)	S (m)	MjL (m)	S (m)	9	10
New Hampshire	P (n)	S (o)	P (n)	S	16	21
New Jersey	P	S	P	S	15 (c)	24 (c)
New Mexico	CC	S	CC	S	9 (aa)	14 (aa)
New York	PT (p)	S	PT (p)	S	33	37
North Carolina	PT	S	PT	S	20 (z)	31 (z)
North Dakota	CC	CC	MjL	MjL	11	12
Ohio	P (q)	S (q)	P (q)	S (q)	14	19
Oklahoma	PT, MnL	S	PT	S	18	24
Oregon	P	S	P	S	9 (cc)	15 (cc)
Pennsylvania	PT	S	PT	S	22	26
Rhode Island	P	S	P	S	11	10
South Carolina	E	S	E	E	15	11
South Dakota	PT, MnL	S	PT	S	14	14
Tennessee	S	S	S	S	14	15
Texas	P	S (r)	P	S	15	42
Utah	P	S	P	S	11	15
Vermont	CC	S	CC	S	11	14
Virginia	E	S	(s)	S	11	14
Washington	P (b)(t)	S (u)	CC	S (v)	15	21
West Virginia	P	S	P	S	18	15
Wisconsin	(w)	S	(w)	S	14 (c)	45 (c)
Wyoming	P (x)	S (x)	P (x)	S (x)	12	12
Dist. of Columbia	(y)	U	(y)	U	9	U
No. Mariana Islands	P	S	P	S	8	7
Puerto Rico	P	S	P	S	22	32
U.S. Virgin Islands	P	U	P	U	9	U

See footnotes at end of table.

STANDING COMMITTEES: APPOINTMENT AND NUMBER — Continued

Source: The Council of State Governments' survey, October 2004 and March 2005.

Key:

CC — Committee on Committees
CR — Committee on Rules
E — Election
MjL — Majority Leader .
MnL — Minority Leader
P — President
PT — President pro tempore
S — Speaker
U — Unicameral Legislature
(a) Includes appropriations committee.
(b) Lieutenant governor is president of the senate.
(c) Also, joint standing committees. Colorado, 12; Michigan, 5; New Jersey, 4; Wisconsin, 9.
(d) Members of the standing committees shall be selected by House District Caucuses with each caucus selecting five members for each "A" standing committee and five members for each "B" standing committee.
(e) Substantive standing committees are joint committees. Connecticut, 18 (there are also three statutory and three select committees); Maine, 17 (also joint committee on rules and special committee on health care); Massachusetts, 26.
(f) President appoints committee members and chairs; minority members on committees are nominated by minority party caucus.
(g) By resolution, with members of majority party designating the chair, vice-chairs and majority party members of committees, and members of minority party designating minority party members.
(h) Committee members appointed by the senate leadership under the direction of the president pro tempore, by and with the senate's advice.
(i) Appointments made after consultation with the president.

(j) Committee on Organization, Calendar and Rules.
(k) Speaker appoints only 12 of the 19 members of the Committee on Appropriations.
(l) Senate minority committee members chosen by minority caucus, but appointed by president pro tempore.
(m) Committee composition and leadership usually determined by party caucus, with final decision by leader.
(n) Appointments made after consultation with the minority leader.
(o) Speaker appoints minority members with advice of the minority floor leader.
(p) President pro tempore is also majority leader.
(q) The minority leader may recommend for consideration minority party members for each committee.
(r) For each standing substantive committee of the house, except for the appropriations committee, a maximum of one-half of the membership, exclusive of chair and vice-chair, is determined by seniority; the remaining membership of the committee is determined by the speaker.
(s) Senior members of the majority part on the committee is the chair.
(t) Confirmed by the senate.
(u) By each party caucus.
(v) By majority caucus. .
(w) Majority leader as chairperson, Organization Committee.
(x) With the advice and consent of the Rules and Procedures Committee.
(y) Chair of the Council.
(z) Does not include select or subcommittees.
(aa) Senate: Includes eight substantive committees and one procedural committee. House: Includes 12 substantive committees and three procedural committees.
(bb) Selection process based on seniority.
(cc) Senate includes eight substantive committees and one procedural committee. House includes 12 substantive committees and three procedural committees.

Table 3.24
RULES ADOPTION AND STANDING COMMITTEES: PROCEDURE

State or other jurisdiction	Constitution permits each legislative body to determine its own rules	Committee meetings open to public* House/ Senate Assembly		Specific, advance notice provisions for committee meetings or hearings	Voting/roll call provisions to report a bill to floor
Alabama	★	★	★	Senate: 4 hours, if possible House: 24 hours, except Rules & Local Legislations committees For meetings, by 4:00 p.m. on the preceding Thurs.; for first hearings on bills, 5 days	Senate: final vote on a bill is recorded. House: recorded vote if requested by member of committee and sustained by one additional committee member. Roll call vote on any measure taken upon request by any member of either house.
Alaska	. . .	★	★		
Arizona	★	★	★	Senate: agenda submitted to secretary 5 days prior to meeting House: agenda distributed Wed. prior to Mon. meeting and Thurs. prior to all other meetings.	Senate: roll call vote taken upon request. House: roll call vote required for final action on any bill.
Arkansas	★	★	★	Senate: 2 days House: 24 hours	Senate: roll call votes are recorded. House: report of committee recommendation signed by committee chair.
California	★	★	★	Senate: none House: none	Senate: roll call. House: roll call.
Colorado	★	★	★	Senate: final action on a measure is prohibited unless notice is posted one calendar day prior to its consideration (f) House: none	Senate: final action by recorded roll call vote. House: final action by recorded roll call vote.
Connecticut	★	★	★	Senate: one day notice for meetings, five days notice for hearings. House: one day notice for meetings, five days notice for hearings.	Senate: roll call required. House: roll call required.
Delaware	★	★	★	Senate: agenda released the day before meetings House: agenda for meetings released on last legislative day of preceding week	Senate: results of any committee vote are recorded. House: results of any committee vote are recorded.
Florida	★	★	★	Senate: during session–3 hours notice for first 50 days, 4 hours thereafter House: two days.	Senate: vote on final passage is recorded. House: vote on final passage is recorded.
Georgia	★	★	★	Senate: a list of committee meetings shall be posted by 10:00 a.m. the preceding Friday House: none	Senate: recorded roll call taken if one-third members sustain the call for yeas and nays. House: recorded roll call taken if one-fifth members sustain the call for yeas and nays.
Hawaii	★	★ (a)	★ (a)	Senate: 72 hours before 1st referral committee meetings, 48 hours before subsequent referral committee meetings House: 48 hours	Senate: final vote is recorded. House: a record is made of a committee quorum and votes to report a bill out.
Idaho	★	★ (a)	★ (a)	Senate: none House: none	Senate: bills can be voted out by voice vote or roll call. House: bills can be voted out by voice vote or roll call.
Illinois	★	★ (a)	★ (a)	Senate: 6 days House: 6 days	Senate: votes on all legislative measures acted upon are recorded. House: votes on all legislative matters acted upon are recorded.
Indiana	★	★	★	Senate: 48 hours House: prior to adjournment or the meeting day next preceding the meeting or announced during session	Senate: majority of quorum; vote can be by roll call or consent. House: majority of quorum; vote can be by roll call or consent.
Iowa	★	★	★	Senate: none House: none	Senate: final action by roll call. House: committee reports include roll call on final disposition.
Kansas	★	★	★	Senate: none House: none	Senate: vote recorded upon request of member. House: he total for and against actions recorded.
Kentucky	★	★	★	Senate: none House: none	Senate: each member's vote recorded on each bill. House: each member's vote recorded on each bill.
Louisiana	★	★ (a)	★ (a)	Senate: no later than 1:00 p.m. the preceding day House: no later than 4:00 p.m. the preceding day	Senate: any motion to report an instrument is decided by a roll call vote. House: any motion to report an instrument is decided by a roll call vote.

See footnotes at end of table.

RULES ADOPTION AND STANDING COMMITTEES: PROCEDURE — Continued

State or other jurisdiction	Constitution permits each legislative body to determine its own rules	Committee meetings open to public*		Specific, advance notice provisions for committee meetings or hearings	Voting/roll call provisions to report a bill to floor
		Senate	House/Assembly		
Maine	★	★	★	Senate: must be advertised two weekends in advance. House: must be advertised two weekends in advance.	Senate: recorded vote is required to report a bill out of committee. House: recorded vote is required to report a bill out of committee.
Maryland	★	★	★	Senate: none House: none	Senate: the final vote on any bill is recorded. House: the final vote on any bill is recorded.
Massachusetts	★	★	★	Senate: 48 hours for public hearings House: 48 hours for public hearings	Senate: voice vote or recorded roll call vote at the request of 2 committee members. House: recorded vote upon request by a member.
Michigan	★	★	★	Senate: none House: none	Senate: committee reports include the vote of each member on any bill. House: the daily journal reports the roll call on all motions to report bills.
Minnesota	★	★	★	Senate: 3 days House: 3 days	Senate: recorded vote upon request of one member. Upon the request of 3 members, the record of a roll call vote and committee report are printed in the journal. House: recorded roll call vote upon request by a member.
Mississippi	★	★	★	Senate: none House: none	Senate: bills are reported out by voice vote or recorded roll call vote. House: bills are reported out by voice vote or recorded roll call vote.
Missouri	★	★	★	Senate: 24 hours House: 24 hours	Senate: yeas and nays are reported in journal. House: bills are reported out by a recorded roll call vote.
Montana	★	★	★	Senate: 3 legislative days House: none	Senate: every vote of each member is recorded and made public. House: every vote of each member is recorded and made public.
Nebraska	★	★	U	Seven calendar days notice before hearing a bill.	In executive session, majority of the committee must vote in favor of the motion made.
Nevada	★	★	★	Senate: by rule—adequate notice House: by rule—adequate notice	Senate: recorded vote is taken upon final committee action on bills. House: recorded vote is taken upon final committee action on bills.
New Hampshire	★	★	★	Senate: 5 days House: 4 days	Senate: committees may report a bill out by voice or recorded roll call vote. House: committees may report a bill out by voice or recorded roll call vote.
New Jersey	★	★	★ (a)	Senate: 5 days House: 5 days	Senate: the chair reports the vote of each member present on a motion to report a bill. House: the chair reports the vote of each member present on motions with respect to bills.
New Mexico	★	★	★	Senate: none House: none	Senate: vote on the final report of the committee taken by yeas and nays. Roll call vote upon request. House: vote on the final report of the committee taken by yeas and nays. Roll call vote upon request.
New York	(b)	★ (a)	★ (a)	Senate: 1 week House: 1 week	Senate: each report records the vote of each Senator. Voting may be by proxy. House: at the conclusion of a committee meeting a roll call vote is taken on each of the bills considered. No proxy votes allowed.
North Carolina	(c)	★	★	Senate: none (g) House: none (g)	Senate: no roll call vote may be taken in any committee. House: roll call vote taken on any question when requested by member & sustained by one-fifth of members present.
North Dakota	★	★	★	Senate: notice posted the preceding Wed. or Thurs., depending on the committee House: notice posted the preceding Wed. or Thurs., depending on the committee	Senate: minutes include recorded roll call vote on each bill referred out. House: minutes include recorded roll call vote on each bill referred out.
Ohio	★	★	★	Senate: 2 days House: 5 days	Senate: every member present shall vote unless excused by the committee. Bills are reported by recorded roll call vote. House: every member present must vote. Bills are reported by recorded roll call vote.
Oklahoma	★	★	★	Senate: none House: 3 days for hearings requested by author; 10 days during interim.	Senate: roll call vote. House: voice vote/show of hands, except that a committee member can obtain a roll call vote if requested prior to the vote.

RULES ADOPTION AND STANDING COMMITTEES: PROCEDURE — Continued

State or other jurisdiction	Constitution permits each legislative body to determine its own rules	Committee meetings open to public* House/ Senate Assembly		Specific, advance notice provisions for committee meetings or hearings	Voting/roll call provisions to report a bill to floor
Oregon	★	★	★	Senate: 24 hours House: 24 hours (d)	Senate: the vote on all official actions is recorded. House: motions on measures before a committee are by recorded roll call vote.
Pennsylvania	★	★	★	Senate: none House: none	Senate: a majority vote of committee members. House: all votes are recorded.
Rhode Island	★	★	★	Senate: 48 hours prior to meeting. House: 48 hours prior to meeting.	Senate: majority vote of the members present. House: majority vote of the members present.
South Carolina	★	★	★	Senate: 24 hours House: 24 hours	Senate: no bill may be polled out unless at least 2/3 of the members are polled. Poll results are certified and published in journal. House: favorable report out of committee (majority of committee members voting in favor).
South Dakota	★	★	★	Senate and House: at least one legislative day must intervene between the is needed for final disposition	Senate and House: a majority vote of the members-elect daytaken by roll call is needed for final disposition on a bill. This applies to both houses. committee agenda and the committee meeting.
Tennessee	★	★	★	Senate: 6 days House: 72 hours when House is recessed or adjourned	Senate: aye and no votes cast by name on each question are recorded. House: bills are reported out by recorded roll call vote.
Texas	★	★	★	Senate: 24 hours House: (e)	Senate: bills are reported by recorded roll call vote. House: committee reports include the record vote by which the report was adopted, including the vote of each member.
Utah	★	★	★	Senate: 24 hours House: 24 hours	Senate: each member present votes on every question and all votes are recorded. House: each member present votes on every question and all votes are recorded.
Vermont	★	★	★	Senate: none House: none	Senate: vote is recorded for each committee member for every bill considered. House: vote is recorded for each committee member for every bill considered.
Virginia	★	★ (a)	★	Senate: none House: none	Senate: generally, a recorded vote is taken for each measure. House: vote of each member is taken and recorded for each measure.
Washington	★	★	★	Senate: 5 days House: 5 days	Senate: bills reported from a committee carry a majority report which must be signed by a majority of the committee. House: every vote to report a bill out of committee is by yeas and nays; the names of the members voting are recorded in the report.
West Virginia	★	★	★	Senate: none House: none	Senate: majority of committee members voting. House: majority of committee members voting.
Wisconsin	★	★	★	Senate: a list of public hearings is filed Monday of the preceding week House: a list of public hearings is filed Monday of the preceding week	Senate: number of ayes and noes, and members absent or not voting are reported. House: number of ayes and noes are recorded.
Wyoming	★	★	★	Senate: by 3:00 p.m. of previous day House: by 3:00 p.m. of previous day	Senate: bills are reported out by recorded roll call vote. House: bills are reported out by recorded roll call vote.
Puerto Rico	★	★	★	Senate: Must be notified every Thurs., one week in advance.	Senate: bills reported from a committee carry a majority vote House: bills reported from a committee carry a majority vote by referendum House: 24 hours advanced notice, no later than or in an ordinary meeting. 4:00 p.m. previous day

Source: The Council of State Governments' survey, October 2003 and October 2004.

Key:

★— Yes

* — Notice of committee meetings may also be subject to state open meetings laws; in some cases, listed times may be subject to suspension or enforceable only to the extent "feasible or "whenever possible.

U — Unicameral.

(a) Certain matters may be discussed in executive session. (Other states permit meetings to be closed for various reasons,but their rules do not specifically mention "executive session.")

(b) Not referenced specifically, but each body publishes rules and there are joint rules.

(c) Not referenced specifically, but each body publishes rules.

(d) May go to one hour notice when president and speaker proclaim sine de imminent.

(e) The House requires five calendar days notice before a public hearing at which testimony will be taken, and two hours notice or an announcement from the floor before a formal meeting (testimony cannot be taken at a formal meeting).

(f) The prohibition does not apply if the action receives a majority vote of the committee.

(g) If public hearing, five calendar days.

Chapter Four

STATE
EXECUTIVE BRANCH

The State of the States in 2005: Facing Up to the Problem?
By Katherine Willoughby

State governors' loathing of tax increases is never more apparent than in this year's state of the state addresses. In 2005, most governors are promoting economic development through tax cuts and credits in order to be able to light up an "open for business" sign in their state. Many governors are also calling for spending reductions and/or agency and program reorientations or reorganizations in order to reach budget balance.

Introduction

Last year, governors' addresses to their citizens about state fiscal environments were somber, "less dire" than in 2003, but "no less worrisome." This year, governors are still hesitant to claim seeing more than some clouds parting to reveal a bit of blue in their fiscal skies.[1] In the words of Nebraska's governor, "the budget proposal before you reflects both optimism and caution." Idaho's governor is equally cautious, "even with a conservative spending plan, and the benefit of year-end surpluses, we may very well find ourselves with a shortfall in FY2007." The bulk of worry rests with ever increasing Medicaid costs. Thus, it is not surprising that a prominent theme of state government chief executives in 2005 is change. South Carolina's governor speaks for many regarding the future of the states, "to prosper and to thrive economically and academically, things have to change. That has to be our path." While these chief executives have laid out a profusion of tax and spend ideas to reach budget balance, focused attention seems directed mostly to the spending side of the state budget equation. That is, governors in 2005 are claiming out of control spending as the biggest fiscal varmint.

As expected, most state of the state addresses begin with a litany of successes and changes realized in fiscal 2004 for which governors are claiming credit. Many drum relevant statistics – that personal income is up, jobs are on the increase, wages are growing, and that tourism and/or housing starts

are on the rise. Still, there is hesitancy in declaring that state fiscal skies are clear. Common refrains include, "We should do more" or "We should do better." In the words of New Hampshire's governor, "I am not here to advocate for more government, but better government, and that starts with open, ethical, honest government." As noted above, a primary view of governors is that states have a spending problem and not a revenue problem. In Vermont, a state with a fairly diversified tax structure and one that is very inclusive of citizens in budgetary decisions, Gov. Jim Douglas declares that "it is important to acknowledge that we did not get in this situation because Vermonters are taxed too little; we're here because government has spent too much." Indiana's governor is even more direct, "state government is too

Table A
STATE TAX COLLECTIONS BY TYPE OF TAX, 1994 AND 2004, 3RD QUARTER
(in percent)

	1994	2004
General sales and gross receipts	34.6%	33.8%
Individual income tax	31.5	33.5
Motor fuel sales	7.1	5.8
Corporate net income	6.6	5.5
Motor vehicles	3.3	3.0
Other sales and gross receipts	2.3	2.1
Tobacco products	2.0	2.1
Insurance	2.0	2.0
All other taxes including: property tax, public utilities, pari-mutuels, amusements, beverage and other licenses, death, gift and severance taxes, taxes on document and stock transactions.	10.4	12.3

Source: Table 3: State Tax Collections by State and Type of Tax. Data available in excel files qtx043t3 and qtx943t3 at http://www.census.gov/govs/www.qtax.html. Accessed on March 4, 2005.

Table B
STATE REVENUE GENERATING STRATEGIES IN FISCAL YEARS 2003 AND 2004

Revenue generating strategy (a)	Fiscal year 2003	Fiscal year 2004
Use carry-forward balances in the general fund	41%	67%
Draw down other contingency funds	9	57
Use one-time/windfall revenue	74	54
Increase tax collection enforcement	63	54
Increase short-term borrowing	7	52
Change tax structure to generate revenue increase	39	43
Use additional debt financing	15	33
Use budget stabilization or rainy day fund	26	23
Increase and/or add fees/charge	54	17
Use non-routine transfers from other fund	57	15
Conduct debt refinancing	37	15
Conduct sale of assets	24	7

Source: Government Performance Project 2005 State Survey, *http://www.results.gpponline.org.*
Note: To balance budgets many states make changes to revenues, expenditures and debt. States indicated that the following revenue actions were used to realize a balanced budget at the end of each fiscal year noted (percent of states responding that action was used).
Key:
(a) The number of survey responses was 46 for all revenue generating strategies except for "use budget stabilization or rainy day fund" and "use non-routine transfers from other fund". Those netted 47 responses.

four common-sense fundamentals – economic revitalization, education, quality of life and governance. ...To that end, we need a tax policy that is not only friendly to our citizens, but also creates a competitive environment for business. Business as usual will leave us behind our neighboring states."

Tax Collections and Changes, Then and Now

Table A illustrates a comparison of state tax proportions in 1994 and 2004. Subtle change in proportions over time indicates that states now depend equally on general sales and personal income taxes. The category "All other taxes" comprises a larger share of total tax proportion in the states than 10 years ago. Continued chipping away at business-related taxes in the last decade is most clearly evidenced in the decline of the corporate income tax as a significant state tax resource.

In truth, 2004 actual revenues bested 2004 estimates in most states. Still, following passage of fiscal 2005 budgets, virtually half (24) of the states instituted tax and fee changes expected to yield $3.5 billion more in revenues. The breakdown of revenue changes to realize this $3.5 billion includes:

■ 25 percent from changes to cigarette/tobacco taxes

■ 20 percent from changes to sales taxes

■ 20 percent from additions or changes to other taxes[2]

■ 14 percent from changes to or institution of new fees

■ 12 percent from changes to personal income taxes

■ 8 percent from changes to corporate income taxes

■ <1 percent each from changes to taxes on motor fuels and alcohol[3]

As illustrated above, collectively the states have relied most heavily on "sin" taxes for added revenue —the greatest proportion of new revenue in 2005 is expected from tax and fee increases related to cigarettes and tobacco products. Also, "collections of sales,

expensive, too antique in its practices, too indifferent to real, provable results, and in place after place after place, too slow....overhanging all our difficulties is the simple, brute fact that our state's public finances are in ruin. We have outspent our income year after year." Minnesota's Gov. Tim Pawlenty concurs that "[s]ome will argue that we should raise taxes rather than slow the growth in these programs. That is simply unrealistic. Income tax revenues would have to double every eight years to pay for these programs at their current rate of growth. We must restrain the growth in these programs to sustainable levels by wisely and humanely changing them so they are comparable to surrounding states, and more focused on those with the fewest resources and the greatest needs."

There are a few exceptions to the focus on spending. South Dakota's Gov. Mike Rounds points out that "some people have falsely claimed that the structural deficit [in this state] was caused because past legislatures just wanted to spend more money. The truth is that the structural deficit was caused by the repeal of the inheritance tax, the loss of gold mining taxes and the repeal of the transportation tax. All that added up to $39 million less in ongoing taxes collected every year." Some governors are emphasizing both sides of the budget equation as problematic. Perhaps Utah's governor sums the up general tenor of addresses this year. "My administration's policy priorities focus on

personal income, and corporate income taxes are projected to increase by 7.1 percent over prior year tax collections in fiscal 2005, based on enacted budgets" (NASBO, ix). After two years of real decline in state general funds in 2002 and 2003, and no growth in 2004, the real increase of 1.8 percent in 2005 is heartening (NASBO, p. 4). On the other hand, 2005 state expenditures have increased by 4.5 percent above prior years. And total year-end balances as a percent of expenditures are expected to remain below those in 2004; in 2005, this ratio is expected to be 3.4 percent, compared to 4.8 percent in 2004.

State Budget Balancing Measures

The 2005 Government Performance Project (GPP)[4] examined states regarding their financial management capacities. The project's recent survey results confirm how difficult it has been for states to balance in the last few years. When asked about the actions taken to stay on budget in recent years, states responded to using a multitude of revenue and expenditure actions. Table B illustrates that in 2003 more than half of states used one-time revenue, increased tax collection enforcement, used non-routine transfers from other funds, and increased or added fees and charges to pump up revenues. By 2004, in addition to using windfall revenues and increasing tax collection enforcement, more than half of states also used carry-forward balances in the general fund, raided any contingency funds, and substantially increased their use of short-term borrowing to facilitate cash flow.

Other revenue generating strategies used in either 2003 or 2004 include changing tax structures, using additional debt financing or conducting debt refinancing, and tapping rainy day or budget stabilization funds. A number of states also indicate using different methods not listed on the survey to increase revenues in these two years. Such methods include:

- Initiating tax amnesty programs;

- Accelerating tax payments (specifically, withholding);

- Pausing tax rate reductions and setting rates to begin later in the year;

- Joining a multi-state lottery consortium;

- Adding new games to the state's lottery;

- Securitizing tobacco settlement proceeds;

- Diverting tobacco settlement proceeds to the general fund; and

- Suspending implementation of voter initiatives to divert general funds elsewhere.

States also engaged a multitude of measures to reduce spending in these years. As illustrated in Table C, the most common expenditure reduction strategy used is simply cutting spending—most likely in a targeted way, but across the board as well. A majority (60 percent) of states conducted a hiring freeze in 2003; just 38 percent of states claimed use of this measure in 2004. Many states, although not a majority, also conducted program reorganizations in both years to reduce costs. Cutting aid to local governments was a fairly popular method of reducing or delaying state expenditures in both years – over a quarter of states cut local aid in 2003 and 2004. Close to a quarter of states indicate initiating layoffs in 2003; down to 15 percent of states indicating layoffs by 2004. All of the other methods for reining in spending were used in both years, even if by just a few states. A number of states also indicate using methods not listed to reduce expenditures in these two years. Such methods include:

- Initiating early retirement program(s);

- Freezing merit raises of state employees; suspending annual employee cost of living adjustments;

- Terminating and/or amending state contracts;

- Eliminating funding to non-essential appropriations;

- Suspending transfers from the general fund;

- Delaying scheduled payments to K-12 schools and payments to counties for property tax relief;

- Lapsing unspent agency appropriations to the General Fund and not allowing appropriations to be carried forward;

- Requiring or increasing employee contributions to health care costs; placing HMO plans into cost/efficiency tiers; engaging a pharmacy-benefits manager;

- Establishing holidays on state payments for state employee sick leave conversion liability; and

- Implementing monthly agency spending targets.

Recurrent Themes

Recurrent themes throughout the 2005 gubernatorial addresses include increasing and/or creating state relief programs for the military—through tuition assistance, increased death benefit payments, and/or new programs and services specifically for veterans and their families. For example, the governor of Oklahoma proposes "Operation Homefront" to provide "a tax exemption for military pension income for all veterans and purchase a $250,000 life insurance policy for every Guardsman." Some state legislatures are beginning to respond accordingly by passing part or all of such initiatives. Governors also brought up the Indian Ocean tsunami disaster and either recognized their state's support thus far or pledged additional relief to this part of the world.

Most governors recognize the influence of the "global economy" on the direction of their state, many couching their initiatives as methods of engagement with this economy. Minnesota's governor explains, "We all need to grasp the importance of the Rochester model. They're a successful global competitor. Why? Because they have seamlessly integrated science, technology, infrastructure, entrepreneurship, a partnering role for government, and lots and lots of hard work. Global competitiveness is Minnesota's strategic objective. We have lots of work to do to get us there." This theme coincides with governors' concerns related to economic development, job growth and specifically the out-migration of their young citizens. Many are advertising their states as "open for business." Others seek to initiate and/or strengthen programs that make it attractive for native born citizens to settle in state and pursue productive work. For example, Maine's governor suggests an "aggressive telecommunications strategy" so that every Mainer can "plug into the global economy from their community." Iowa's governor talks of expansion of "Great Places" throughout the state by energizing a consortium of state agencies to work together to streamline application processes, better package resources, and target the most innovative communities in the state. In Illinois, the governor is asking for more financial incentives to draw in companies that make homeland security products, as well as support for building a new airport in Peotone to expand air travel into and through the state. New

Mexico's Gov. Bill Richardson offers tax exemptions for that state's aviation industry, and he seeks to create the New Mexico Spaceport Authority to further develop this industry. In general, recommended education programs, research and development and other initiatives mentioned are geared to stemming out-migration as well as advancing in-migration. New York's Gov. George Pataki wants New York to become first in in-sourcing jobs. "Let's focus not just on keeping jobs, but on attracting new jobs and new investments from around the world."

As noted earlier, governors are very cognizant of the continued mismatch between state revenues and expenditures—many consider that it is not taxes that are too low, but spending that is too high. This is a scenario that most recognize cannot continue without significant consequences to the wealth of states and well being of citizens. Minnesota's governor emphasizes that "keeping a lid on taxes is not just good for the taxpayer. It's a powerful way to force government to be more accountable, set priorities and spend smarter." Most point to Medicaid as the primary spending culprit. Arkansas Gov. Mike Huckabee paints a picture evidenced in most states —almost all (91 percent) of the state's general revenue funds Medicaid, education and prisons. Thus, many governors expressed worry about how to fulfill Medicaid commitments, both now and in the future. Vermont's governor characterizes this area of state budgets as "growing at an unsustainable rate." Gov. Mitch Daniels proposes big changes to Medicaid in Indiana. "We will slow this unsustainable growth rate by half. Over time,

Table C
STATE EXPENDITURE REDUCTION MEASURES IN FISCAL YEARS 2003 AND 2004

Expenditure strategy (a)	Fiscal year 2003	Fiscal year 2004
Make targeted spending cuts	77%	68%
Conduct across the board spending cuts	68	47
Initiate program reorganization	40	47
Freeze hiring	60	38
Cut local aid	28	26
Implement privatization initiatives	13	17
Initiate layoffs	23	15
Reduce contribution to pension funds	15	11
Delay payments for purchases	17	9

Source: Government Performance Project 2005 State Survey, *http://www.results.gpponline.org.*
Note: To balance budgets many state make changes to revenues, expenditures and debt. States indicated that the following expenditure actions were used to realize a balanced budget at the end of each fiscal year noted (percent of states responding that action was used).
Key:
(a) The number of survey responses for the expenditure strategies was 47.

we will rebuild a broken, antiquated system so that it delivers better care to those who cannot afford to care for themselves, while remembering that taxpayers deserve compassion too."

State chief executives continue to have management reform on their minds as well. Washington's governor proposes "legislation to establish a new government management accountability and performance approach to government —GMAP for short." In this state—already well known for doing an excellent job managing information, the mantra "We should do better" helps focus on holding state agencies accountable for achieving results effectively and efficiently. Similarly, Oregon's governor claims to have thrown out the old rulebook—"This is not a current services budget. It funds programs based on whether they produce measurable outcomes." This budget also boasts a spending limitation and rainy day fund. According to Gov. Ted Kulongoski, "in 2005, we need to think and act differently."

Governors from both Rhode Island and South Dakota propose a red tape reduction taskforce to help eliminate barriers to conducting business and streamline government operations. New Hampshire's governor has been busy "zero-basing every department budget," requiring justification to the penny. Michigan's Gov. Jennifer Granholm mentions state reorganization as well as the abolishment of numerous boards and commissions as paths to greater efficiency. New York's governor is also asking to eliminate or consolidate "hundreds of commissions, task forces, boards and authorities that have been established over the course of many decades." In addition, Gov. Pataki asks that the state pass its budget on time—an important component of public budgeting transparency. Interestingly, Rhode Island's governor is throwing "open the doors of the state to all citizens who want to participate" by asking Rhode Islanders to apply for appointments on numerous boards and commissions in that state.

Other efficiency efforts focus on specific management areas. Nebraska's governor suggests advancing technology and "striving to be a customer friendly, customer responsive government in everything we do, from issuing permits to answering telephones." Efficiency efforts promoted by Tennessee's chief executive run the gambit from revamping the issuance and renewal of driver's licenses to continuing the overhaul of Medicaid. Missouri's governor presents a budget that includes a reduction of more than 1,000 full time state positions. Illinois' governor wants the state's Finance Authority to "look at new ways to provide financing for wind farms."

Reorganization ideas abound as well. Delaware's governor proposes a significant reorganization, "centralizing the administrative and support functions of state government in one agency." West Virginia's Gov. Joe Manchin wants reorganization in that state "with the goal of being more accountable for our actions and more coordinated in our economic development efforts." This governor is also seeks pension reform to remedy the fact that the state is currently spending over 11 percent of its revenues annually on pension liabilities. Specifically, Gov. Manchin is asking citizens to support a referendum to establish "a fixed mortgage payment to pay off unfunded liabilities." Gov. Daniels is calling for dramatic reorganization of Indiana's bureaucracy and has appointed the state's first inspector general to ferret out government waste. New Jersey's governor is creating an inspector general too. Maine's Gov. John Baldacci seeks to "consolidate financial, information technology, payroll, human resources, and administrative hearings services" to save the state $11 million in the next two years.

Georgia's governor has appointed a state property officer to conduct a complete inventory of and better manage state property. This governor has also invested in a business approach to government through engagement of a Commission for New Georgia which he touts in his address. This group of business and policy leaders feeds ideas about good management practices to Gov. Perdue. As well, the governor has reorganized his office, with an eye toward a state government that is customer service oriented. Similarly, Wisconsin's governor is redesigning the way that state conducts business. "We're rebidding costly state contracts.... We're trimming the state's vehicle fleet back to its level a decade ago. ...For the first time, we're asking state employees to pay a portion of their health insurance.... We've cut discretionary pay bonuses by 92 percent. We've eliminated more than 1,500 cell phones and sold seven airplanes." In Montana, the governor has formed a performance review committee to ask citizens and state employees alike for their ideas on how to deliver state services more efficiently.

In the area of education, specifically, many different efficiency measures are being touted by governors. For example, more than a few mention developing "centers of excellence" in state university systems, possibly requiring increased tuition to do so. Colorado's example of funding students, rather than academic institutions is another way of thinking about changed funding and funding channels for education in states. Indiana's governor has called for a moratorium on school building to support "instruction before construction." In Michigan, the governor is asking the state's universities to institute credit amnesty – "accept old credits of adults who re-enroll within the next three years to finish their degrees." Governors also talked of support for student receipt of college credit in high school to more quickly advance students through educational systems and on to viable careers. In Arizona, the governor spoke of all day kindergarten, moving students beyond high school to enhanced career and technical education – highlighting a renewed interest in states about community and technical colleges —and commitment to funding a medical school collaborative.

Revenue Ideas

Budget worries have not stemmed gubernatorial ideas about cutting taxes. Idaho's Gov. Dirk Kempthorne outlines a very specific tax incentive package for businesses. If a company in this state makes certain investments within a given timeframe, the governor proposes:

- A doubling of the investment tax credit to six percent for a five-year period;

- Removing the 50 percent limit on the investment tax credit;

- An enhanced jobs tax credit;

- A new income tax credit for real property improvement;

- Property tax abatement on qualified new construction; and

- Sales tax abatement on construction materials.

This governor also recommends that the state consider increasing the level of bonding to support capital investment. Idaho traditionally maintains a very low debt level compared to other states. Maine's governor joins Idaho's in looking to increased use of debt, in Maine's case, to support biomedical research and collaboration.

South Carolina's governor is depending upon reduction of the income tax to make that state more competitive. Pennsylvania's Gov. Edward Rendell is focusing on reducing the corporate income tax rate and modernizing the business tax structure of the Commonwealth. Tax credits are being recommended in New York, despite the fact that as Gov. Pataki notes, "New Yorkers' tax burden is $15 billion less today because of the broad, sweeping, fundamental changes we made in our tax code beginning in 1995." The governor is also recommending acceleration of the phase-

out of the state's temporary personal income tax increase. And, his plan includes property tax relief. The governor of Texas has a "game-plan" to eliminate that state's corporate tax over the next few years, combined "with a short-term strategy on reducing the food tax and change income taxes." Washington's governor is calling for tax relief for small and start-up enterprises.

Some states are taking advantage of increased revenues expected this year. In Alaska, the governor has proposed gas and oil credits for new fields. This state is experiencing a significant windfall in revenues for fiscal 2005, given high oil prices. This governor proposes to use the windfall for education and non-recurring expenditures, expressing that the increase in revenues should be considered "temporary." Wyoming and Montana are other states that have flush revenues, comparatively speaking. According to Wyoming's Gov. Dave Freudenthal, "We have money. Our revenues are remarkable and our prospects are bright. Money should not, and must not, change our commitment to solving problems and building this state. ...The amount of money available changes the rate at which we can convert our values into action – it should not change our values." Hawaii's governor wants "to use some of the revenues generated by [the state's] recent prosperity to pay for a modest yet important $63 million tax cut over the next two years for individuals and families with low to moderate incomes." Gov. Linda Lingle calculates that this tax cut would mean that "27,000 people will not longer have to file state tax returns, and 78,000 more will see their taxes reduced." She is also proposing food and medical tax credits, credits to advance partnerships between the state university and business, a reduction in the unemployment insurance tax wage base, a tax credit for the purchase of long-term care insurance, and greater flexibility for the state's department of commerce to institute more cuts to fees and assessments.

New Mexico's Gov. Richardson seeks to make a difference through tax cuts that include sales tax holidays, income tax exemptions, and eliminating the single parent penalty. Mississippi's governor just asks to reform the unemployment tax formula – "Over the last 20 years, because of flaws in the formula used in our state, we have been collecting much, much more in unemployment taxes than is needed to pay unemployment benefits." Ohio's governor has a tax reform plan to "cut personal income tax rates by 21 percent over five years, eliminate state income tax for Ohioans making less than $10,000 a year, and phasing out the tax on equipment and inventory and corporate tax." This plan is expected to reduce state revenues by $800 million in the next two years. The governor is asking for "restrained spending and reduced Medicaid growth" to support this tax reform package. Rhode Island's governor has presented a five-year tax reduction plan that includes "new lottery revenues dedicated to direct property tax relief."

Kentucky's governor is asking for extensive tax modernization—suggesting an income tax rate reduction along with numerous tax credits—in construction, research and development, Brownfields, clean coal technology and other environmentally related areas —historic preservation credits, and tuition tax credits. Gov. Granholm recommended the Michigan Jobs and Investment Act which, if enacted, would mean that "three out of four business tax payers will pay significantly less." Maryland's governor is encouraging business growth, specifically filmmaking "by offering film companies a rebate on the first $25,000 of wages paid to production employees on locations in the state." New Mexico's governor also seeks an extension of that state's 15 percent refund on filming expenses. Maryland's chief executive is also promoting extension of the state's research and development tax credit as well as addition of an "entrepreneurial investment technology tax credit" to advance business in-migration to the state.

Governors are marking the property tax for reform too. Missouri's governor suggests that school districts be allowed to use a sales or income tax to alleviate heavy dependence on the property tax. Maine's governor addressed the citizens of that state after signing into law government and property tax reforms that establish spending caps and expand property tax relief. Wisconsin's governor proposes simplifying the form used for the homestead credit—from 17 to one page. Also, "instead of just giving incentives to achieve a target property tax increase, we will provide bonuses for municipalities and counties that hold their property taxes even lower." In Texas, the governor agrees with property tax relief, taking it further, "It is time to cut property taxes for hardworking people of Texas. In fact, let's not only give Texans property tax relief…let's give them appraisal relief too. …Let's cap appraisals at three percent." Gov. Rick Perry seeks new revenues by instituting a "broad-based business tax that is fairly distributed, assessed at a low rate and reflects our modern economy."

Iowa's governor is asking for a tax rollback as well as a cap on future property tax increases. This governor also seeks an increase in the cigarette and tobacco related taxes, to be earmarked for health care. Kentucky's governor has requested an increase in the cigarette tax as "a matter of fairness and sound public policy." Even North Carolina's governor Michael Easley states that "the time has come to significantly increase the cigarette tax and reduce teen smoking."

Other interesting revenue generating strategies mentioned include Gov. Daniels' call to "the most fortunate among us, those citizens earning over $100,000 per year, for one year, to pay an additional one percent on the income they receive" to help balance the budget. Maryland's governor is asking for "a fully phased in slots program" that could mean more than $800 million in new revenue to the state annually. California's governor is presently stumping for a referendum similar to the federal government's Gramm-Rudman-Hollings sequester law (Emergency Deficit Control Act of 1985). In a special legislative session, Gov. Arnold Schwarzenegger says, "I will submit to you legislation that cuts expenditures across the board when they grow above revenues. We must take back responsibility for the budget. We must have a new approach that overrides the formulas, overrides the special interests and overrides the forces that have turned some of you from legislators into clerks." The governor also characterized the state's pension system as "out of control," calling for movement from a defined benefit to a defined contribution system. Colorado's governor seeks fiscal redress through the "specific provisions of TABOR" to support the state's transportation infrastructure, higher education and public safety needs. "This plan also proposed tax relief for working families. We should take a common-sense step to prevent the government from collecting dollars it can't use. Let's roll the personal income tax rate back to 4.5 percent."

Conclusion

While governors' tax and other revenue generating strategies generate the most interest, many other areas of policy interest were mentioned in this year's addresses. Governors also talked about:

- Cost containment of prescription drugs;

- Reducing the opportunities to develop and deal methamphetamines;

- Changing funding relationships with local governments;

- Advancing protection of natural resources, the environment, development of renewable energy resources, and water conservation;

- Strengthening government ethics law;

- Initiating elections reform;

- Negotiating related to tribal gaming;

- Advancing homeland security and public safety; and

- Legislating tort reform.

The Cato Institute's most recent fiscal policy report card[5] on U.S. governors finds most to be performing at an average to below average level, given their measure of excellence as keeping tax rates low and constraining spending. More than half (27) of governors received a grade of C or lower according to the Institute's fiscal policy measurement. Only four governors, two "freshmen" and two "seniors," received an "A" for promoting low tax rates and spending growth—those from California, Colorado, Montana and New Hampshire.

Certainly we can see that tax reform and, in particular, lowering taxes remains on the minds of most governors. And, many, if not most states have tinkered with their tax structures in the last few years. Finally, most states have employed many different revenue generating methods in the last two years in attempts to keep pace with spending. Perhaps North Dakota illustrates the fine line that governors walk concerning the need to increase revenues, support economic development, and manage spending commitments. North Dakota's Gov. John Hoeven (who received a "B" from the Cato Institute Study) explains this state's present good fortune. "As a result of growing revenues and good fiscal management, we will close this biennium with an ending fund balance of nearly $130 million, the largest in 20 years. And our state's revenues are projected to be strong through the next biennium. We have achieved these results through aggressive economic development efforts and we have achieved them without a tax increase." Going forward, this governor is calling for "more venture capital and investment tax credits for small businesses, …doubling the Homestead Tax Credit and repealing the unemployment insurance offset to Social Security for working seniors."

In light of their typical abhorrence for tax increases, it is hopeful that governors' focus this year is on restraining spending and retooling state government. Clearly, states cannot continue down a road in which revenues are lost (through tax cuts and credits) while spending commitments grow. If governors are going to stick to holding the line on revenues and even to retrenching revenues, then they must look to either increased borrowing to support spending growth or cut spending and/or the commitments that grow spending. Governors seem to be alerting their citizens that they have picked up some fiscal shears and are ready to start using them.

Notes

[1] U.S. governors report annually or biennially to their legislatures regarding the fiscal condition of their state, commonwealth or territory. Governors may use their address to lay out their policy and budget agendas for their upcoming or continuing administration. The 2005 state of the state addresses were accessed from January through March 1, 2005 at the National Governors Association Web site: Just two states, Florida and Louisiana, did not have the 2005 state of the state addresses on this Web site during this time. All quotes and data presented here are from the addresses available on this website, unless otherwise noted.

[2] Other taxes include any taxes not falling into mentioned categories – examples include taxes on nursing homes, gas and oil production, real estate conveyance, live entertainment, research and development, and other activities, services, and items.

[3] NASBO, *The Fiscal Survey of the States*, (Washington, D.C.: NASBO, December 2004), Table 7: Enacted Fiscal 2005 Revenue Actions by Type of Revenue and Net Increase or Decrease, p. 10.

[4] The GPP mission is to provide states information that can advance government management to achieve public goals and objectives. The GPP conducts a 50 state survey every few years that assesses states' capacity in managing financial and human resources, information and technology, and physical infrastructure. In 2005, the GPP conducted its survey online and integrated work of both academics and journalists to determine grades for states in each of these four areas. Results from this survey are available at *www.results.gpponline.org*. The GPP is sponsored by a grant from the Pew Charitable Trusts.

[5] Stephen Moore and Stephen Slivinski, "Fiscal Policy Report Card on America's Governors: 2004," *Policy Analysis Report* No. 537, (Washington, D.C.: The Cato Institute, March 2005).

About the Author

Katherine Willoughby is professor of Public Administration and Urban Studies in the Andrew Young School of Policy Studies at Georgia State University in Atlanta. Her research concentrates on state and local government budgeting and financial management, public policy development and public organization theory. She has conducted extensive research in the area of state budgeting practices, with a concentration on performance measurement applicability at this level of government in the United States.

Governors: Elections, Campaign Costs and Powers
By Thad Beyle

The 2004 gubernatorial elections and resignations continued the recent trend of changes in the governorships across the states. In addition to the 11 gubernatorial races, two governors resigned before their terms were up. In 2005, 37 of the incumbent governors will be serving in their first term. As in the past, there was a great range in gubernatorial election costs. During the four and a half decades, the overall institutional powers of governors continued to increase, especially in their veto power.

The governors continue to be in the forefront of activity as we move into the 21st century. With Republican governors across the states serving as his major supporters and guides, Texas Gov. George W. Bush sought and won the presidency in the 2000 election. He became the fourth of the last five presidents who had served as governor just prior to seeking and winning the presidency.[1] When George H. W. Bush, a non-governor, won the 1988 presidential election, he beat a governor, Michael Dukakis (D–Mass., 1975-1979 and 1983-1991). Clearly, presidential politics in the three decades following the Watergate scandal finds governors as major actors.

Additionally, the demands on the governors to propose state budgets and then to keep them in balance during the two recessions of the early 1990s and now in the early 2000s has made that governor's chair a "hot seat" in more ways than one.[2] In the current downturn, governors have moved from the half-decade of economic boom of the late 1990s, in which they could propose tax cuts and program increases, to an economic downturn period in which there is increasing demand for program support while state tax revenues fell off significantly. Proposed and adopted budgets fell victim to severe revenue shortfalls in most all of the states. Easy times had switched to hard times again. Now as we enter 2005, there are signs of an upturn in the economy easing some of the budgetary problems that governors have been facing.

2004 Gubernatorial Politics

The 2004 gubernatorial elections and resignations continued the recent trend of changes in the governorships across the states. In addition to the 11 gubernatorial races, two governors resigned their positions and left office before their terms were up.

In the 2004 gubernatorial elections, all 11 incumbent governors were eligible to seek re-election. However, three of the incumbents decided not to seek another term—Judy Martz (R-Mont.), Gary Locke (D-Wash.) and Bob Wise (D-W. Va.). Locke was finishing up his second term as governor while Martz and Wise were in their first and only terms. While the reasons for not seeking re-election varied, one common factor was apparent. In state level polls, each of the three had low job approval ratings. Their most recent ratings in 2003 - Martz 20 percent positive, Locke 33 percent positive, Wise 39 percent positive – were well below the average positive ratings of 55 percent for the 40 other governors for whom ratings were available. This meant that there was a considerable majority of potential voters who had a negative view on how well they had been performing as governor—hardly the strength that many incumbent governors have on their side in seeking re-election.

The other eight incumbents did seek re-election to another term, but only four of them were successful—Ruth Ann Minner (D-Del.), Michael Easley (D-N.C.), John Hoeven (R-N.D.) and Jim Douglas (R-Vt.)—a 50 percent success rate. Two of the other incumbents seeking another term were defeated in their own party's nomination process. Bob Holden (D-Mo.) was defeated in the Democratic Primary by State Auditor Clair McCaskill. Olene Walker (R-Utah) failed to gain the Republican Party's convention authorization to be one of the two candidates to be on the party's primary ballot—she came in fourth on that pre-primary vote. As lieutenant governor, Walker became an "accidental governor" when Republican Gov. Mike Leavitt resigned to accept an appointment in the Bush Administration as head of the Environmental Protection Agency in November 2003.

Two other incumbents seeking re-election were defeated in the November general election—Craig Benson (R-N.H.) was defeated by a 2-point margin by Democrat John Lynch, and Joe Kernan (D-Ind.) was defeated by an 8-point margin by Republican Mitch Daniels. Kernan was the other "accidental governor" who sought to win the seat for a full term

Table A: Gubernatorial Elections: 1970-2004

| | | Democratic Winner | | Number of incumbent governors | | | | | | | | |
| | | | | Eligible to run | | Actually ran | | Won | | Lost | | | |
Year	Number of races	Number	Percent	Number	Percent	Number	Percent	Number	Percent	Number	Percent	In primary	In general election
1970	35	22	63%	29	83%	24	83%	16	64%	8	36%	1 (a)	7 (b)
1971	3	3	100	0	...	...	...	...	...	...	...	...	...
1972	18	11	61	15	83	11	73	7	64	4	36	2 (c)	2 (d)
1973	2	1	50	1	50	1	100	...	...	1	100	1 (e)	...
1974	35	27 (f)	77	29	83	22	76	17	77	5	24	1 (g)	4 (h)
1975	3	3	100	2	66	2	100	2	100	...	...	...	...
1976	14	9	64	12	86	8	67	5	63	3	33	1 (i)	2(j)
1977	2	1	50	1	50	1	100	1	100	...	...	...	...
1978	36	21	58	29	81	23	79	16	73	7	30	2 (k)	5 (l)
1979	3	2	67	0	...	...	...	...	...	...	...	...	...
1980	13	6	46	12	92	12	100	7	58	5	42	2 (m)	3 (n)
1981	2	1	50	0	...	...	...	...	...	...	...	...	...
1982	36	27	75	33	92	25	76	19	76	6	24	1 (o)	5 (p)
1983	3	3	100	1	33	1	100	...	...	1	100	1 (q)	...
1984	13	5	38	9	69	6	67	4	67	2	33	...	2 (r)
1985	2	1	50	1	50	1	100	1	100	...	...	...	...
1986	36	19	53	24	67	18	75	15	83	3	18	1 (s)	2 (t)
1987	3	3	100	2	67	1	50	...	...	1	100	1 (u)	...
1988	12	5	42	9	75	9	100	8	89	1	11	...	1 (v)
1989	2	2	100	0	...	...	...	...	...	...	...	...	...
1990	36	19 (w)	53	33	92	23	70	17	74	6	26	...	6 (x)
1991	3	2	67	2	67	2	100	...	...	2	100	1 (y)	1 (z)
1992	12	8	67	9	75	4	44	4	100	...	...	...	...
1993	2	0	0	1	50	1	100	...	...	1	100	...	1 (aa)
1994	36	11 (bb)	31	30	83	23	77	17	74	6	26	2 (cc)	4 (dd)
1995	3	1	33	2	67	1	50	1	100	...	...	...	...
1996	11	7	36	9	82	7	78	7	100	...	...	...	...
1997	2	0	0	1	50	1	100	1	100	...	...	...	...
1998	36	11 (ee)	31	27	75	25	93	23	92	2	8	...	2 (ff)
1999	3	2	67	2	67	2	100	2	100	...	...	...	...
2000	11	8	73	7	88	6	86	5	83	1	17	...	1 (gg)
2001	2	2	100	0	...	...	...	...	...	...	...	...	...
2002	36	14	39	22	61	16	73	12	75	4	25	...	4 (hh)
2003	4 (ii)	1	25	2	50	2	100	...	...	2	100	...	2 (jj)
2004	11	6	55	11	100	8	73	4	50	4	50	2 (kk)	2 (ll)
Totals:													
Number	481	264		367		286		211		75		19	56
Percent	100	54.9		76.3		77.9		73.8		26.2		25.3	74.7

Source: The Book of the States, 2004, (Lexington, KY: The Council of State Governments, 2004), 146, updated.

Key:

(a) Albert Brewer, D-Alabama.

(b) Keith Miller, R-Alaska; Winthrop Rockefeller, R-Ark.; Claude Kirk, R-Fla.; Don Samuelson, R-Idaho; Norbert Tieman, R-Neb.; Dewey Bartlett, R-Okla.; Frank Farrar, R-S.D.

(c) Walter Peterson, R-N.H.; Preston Smith, D-Texas.

(d) Russell Peterson, R-Del.; Richard Ogilvie, R-Ill.

(e) William Cahill, R-N.J.

(f) One independent candidate won: James Longley of Maine.

(g) David Hall, D-Okla.

(h) John Vanderhoof, R-Colo.; Francis Sargent, R-Mass.; Malcolm Wilson, R-N.Y.; John Gilligan, D-Ohio.

(i) Dan Walker, D-Ill.

(j) Sherman Tribbitt, D-Del.; Christopher 'Kit' Bond, R-Mo.

(k) Michael Dukakis, D-Mass., Dolph Briscoe, D-Texas.

(l) Robert F. Bennett, R-Kan.; Rudolph G. Perpich, D-Minn.; Meldrim Thompson, R-N.H.; Robert Straub, D-Oreg.; Martin J. Schreiber, D-Wis.

(m) Thomas L. Judge, D-Mont.; Dixy Lee Ray, D-Wash.

(n) Bill Clinton, D-Ark.; Joseph P. Teasdale, D-Mo.; Arthur A. Link, D-N.D.

(o) Edward J. King, D-Mass.

(p) Frank D. White, R-Ark.; Charles Thone, R-Neb.; Robert F. List, R-Nev.; Hugh J. Gallen, D-N.H.; William P. Clements, R-Texas.

(q) David Treen, R-La.

(r) Allen I. Olson, R-N.D.; John D. Spellman, R-Wash.

(s) Bill Sheffield, D-Alaska

(t) Mark White, D-Texas; Anthony S. Earl, D-Wis.

(u) Edwin Edwards, D-La.

(v) Arch A. Moore, R- W. Va.

(w) Two Independent candidates won: Walter Hickel (Alaska) and Lowell Weiker (Conn.). Both were former statewide Republican office holders.

(x) Bob Martinez, R-Fla.; Mike Hayden, R-Kan.; James Blanchard, D-Mich.; Rudy Perpich, DFL-Minn.; Kay Orr, R-Neb.; Edward DiPrete, R-R.I.

(y) Buddy Roemer, R-La.

(z) Ray Mabus, D-Miss.

(aa) James Florio, D-N.J.

(bb) One Independent candidate won: Angus King of Maine.

(cc) Bruce Sundlun, D-R.I.; Walter Dean Miller, R-S.D.

(dd) James E. Folsom, Jr., D-Ala.; Bruce King, D-N.M.; Mario Cuomo, D-N.Y.; Ann Richards, D-Texas.

(ee) Two Independent candidates won: Angus King of Maine and Jesse Ventura of Minnesota.

(ff) Fob James, R-Ala.; David Beasley, R-S.C.

(gg) Cecil Underwood, R-W. Va.

(hh) Don Siegelman, D-Ala.; Roy Barnes, D-Ga.; Jim Hodges, D-S.C.; and Scott McCallum, R-Wis.

(ii) The California recall election and replacement vote of 2003 is included in the 2003 election totals and as a general election for the last column.

(jj) Gray Davis, D-Calif., Ronnie Musgrove, D-Miss.

(kk) Bob Holden, D-Mo.; Olene Walker, R-Utah, lost in the pre-primary convention.

(ll) Joe Kernan, D-Ind.; Craig Benson, R-N.H.

but failed. As lieutenant governor, he became governor in September 2003 when incumbent Democratic Gov. Frank O'Bannon died.

Thus the results of the 2004 elections brought seven new governors into office. They were split between the two parties—four Democrats and three Republicans—leaving the Republicans holding a 28 to 22 edge among the governors of the 50 states.

The two governors who resigned their positions and left office in 2004 were John Rowland (R-Conn.) and Jim McGreevey (D-N.J.). Rowland was facing a potential impeachment process over some unethical if not criminal steps taken during his tenure in office and McGreevey admitted to being gay and having had an affair with another man while serving as governor. In a December 2004 plea bargain, Rowland pled guilty to a charge of corruption. Both were succeeded in office by a member of their own party. In Connecticut, Lt. Gov. M. Jodi Rell assumed the governorship on July 1st after Rowland had resigned on June 30th. In New Jersey, Senate President Richard Codey became acting governor on November 16th after McGreevey resigned on November 15th. In New Jersey's unique succession arrangement, Codey had to retain his Senate post in addition to becoming acting governor as that was the basis of his succeeding to the office of governor.

Gubernatorial Elections

As can be seen in Table A, in the 481 gubernatorial elections held between 1970 and 2004, incumbents were eligible to seek another term in 367 (76 percent) of the contests. Two hundred eighty-six eligible incumbents sought re-election (78 percent) and 211 of them succeeded (74 percent). Those who were defeated for re-election were more likely to lose in the general election than in their own party primary by a 2.9-to-1 ratio, although as noted two of the incumbent losses in 2004 were tied to party primaries. Not since 1994 had an incumbent governor been defeated in their own party's primary.

Democratic candidates held a winning edge in these elections held between 1970 and 2004 (55 percent). And in 195 races (41 percent) the results led to a party shift in which a candidate from a party other than the incumbent's party won. Yet these party shifts have evened out over the years so that neither of the two major parties has an edge in these party shifts. In three of the five party shifts in the 2004 elections, a Democrat won the seat for the first time since the 1980 elections (Montana), and two Republicans won the seat for the first time since the 1984 elections (Indiana and Missouri). But there have been some interesting patterns in these shifts over the past 35 years of gubernatorial elections.

Between 1970 and 1992, Democrats won 200 of the 324 races for governor (62 percent). Then beginning in 1993 to date, Republicans leveled the playing field by winning 94 of the 157 races for governor (60 percent). Despite this Republican trend, Democratic candidates did win eight of the 11 gubernatorial races in 2000, when Gov. Bush won the presidency in a very close race. But, since the 1994 elections there have been more Republicans than Democrats serving as governor each year.

Another factor in determining how many governors have served in the states is how many of the newly elected governors are truly new to the office and how many are returning after complying with constitutional term limits or holding other positions. Looking at the number of actual new governors taking office over a decade, the average number of new governors elected in the states dropped from 2.3 new governors per state in the 1950s to 1.9 in the 1970s and to 1.1 in the 1980s. In the 1990s, the rate began to move up a bit to 1.4 new governors per state.

As we move through the first decade of the 21st century, we continue to find new faces in the governors' offices. New governors were elected in 43 of 64 elections held between 2000 and 2004 (67 percent). And as noted, two other governors succeeded to the office during 2004. So, in 2005, 37 of the incumbent governors will be serving in their first term (74 percent). The beginning of the 21st century has certainly proved to be a time of change in the governors' offices across the 50 states.

The New Governors

Over the 2001-2004 cycle of gubernatorial elections and resignations, there were several different routes to the governor's chair by the 37 elected governors and the two governors who have succeeded to the office. First were the 10 new governors who had previously held statewide office. These include: four attorneys general—Janet Napolitano (D-Ariz.), Jennifer Granholm (D-Mich.), Christine Gregoire (D-Wash.) and Jim Doyle (R-Wis.); two secretaries of state—Matt Blunt (R-Mo.) and Joe Manchin (D-W.Va.); two lieutenant governors—M. Jodi Rell (R-Conn.) and Kathleen Blanco (D-La.); one state insurance commissioner—Kathleen Sebelius (D-Kan.) and one state treasurer—Jim Douglas (R-Vt.).

Second were the eight members or former members of Congress who returned to work within their state. These included U.S. Senator Frank Murkowski (R-Alaska) and U.S. Congressmen Bob Riley (R-

Table B: Total Costs of Gubernatorial Elections: 1977-2003
(in thousands of dollars)

Year	Number of races	Total campaign costs		Average cost per state (2004$)	Percent change in similar elections (b)
		Actual $	2004$ (a)		
1977	2	$12,312	$38,840	$19,420	N.A.
1978	36	102,342	300,125	8,337	N.A. (c)
1979	3	32,744	86,167	28,722	N.A.
1980	13	35,634	82,677	6,360	N.A.
1981	2	24,648	51,782	25,891	+33
1982	36	181,832	360,064	10,002	+20 (d)
1983	3	39,966	76,710	25,570	-11
1984	13	47,156	86,683	6,668	+5
1985	2	18,859	33,497	16,748	-35
1986	36	270,605	471,438	13,095	+31
1987	3	40,212	67,583	22,528	-12
1988	12 (e)	52,208	84,343	7,029	-3
1989	2	47,902	73,809	36,905	+120
1990	36	345,493	505,107	14,031	+7
1991	3	34,564	48,477	16,159	-28
1992	12	60,278	82,011	6,834	-3
1993	2	36,195	47,814	23,907	-35
1994	36	417,873	538,496	14,958	+7
1995	3	35,693	44,728	14,909	-8
1996	11 (f)	68,610	85,019	7,729	+4
1997	2	44,823	53,045	26,522	+11
1998	36	470,326	548,166	15,227	+2
1999	3	16,277	18,666	6,222	-58
2000	11	97,098	107,647	9,786	+27
2001	2	70,400	75,944	37,972	+43
2002	36	839,650	891,348	24,760	+63
2003	3	69,939	72,626	24,209	+289

Source: Thad Beyle.

(a) Developed from the Table, "Historical Consumer Price Index for All Urban Consumers (CPI-U)," Bureau of Labor Statistics, U.S. Department of Labor. Each year's actual expenditures are converted to the 2004$ value of the dollar to control for the effect of inflation over the period.

(b) This represents the percent increase or decrease in 2004$ over the last bank of similar elections, i.e., 1977 v. 1981, 1978 v. 1982, 1979 v. 1983, etc.

(c) The data for 1978 are a particular problem as the two sources compiling data on this year's elections did so in differing ways that excluded some candidates. The result is that the numbers for 1978 under-represent the actual costs of these elections by some unknown amount. The sources are: Rhodes Cook and Stacy West, "1978 Advantage," *CQ Weekly Report,*(1979): 1757-1758, and *The Great Louisiana Spendathon* (Baton Rouge: Public Affairs Research Council, March 1980).

(d) This particular comparison with 1978 is not what it would appear to be for the reasons given in note (c). The amount spent in 1978 was more than indicated here so the increase is really not as great as it appears.

(e) As of the 1986 election, Arkansas switched to a four-year term for the governor, hence the drop for 13 to 12 for this off-year.

(f) As of the 1994 election, Rhode Island switched to a four-year term for the governor, hence the drop from 12 to 11 for this off-year.

Ala.), Rod Blagojevich (D-Ill.), Ernie Fletcher (R-Ky.), John Baldacci (D-Maine), Robert Ehrlich (R-Md.), and Mark Sanford (R-S.C.). Former Congressman Bill Richardson (D-N.M.) had also served as an administrator in the Clinton administration.

Third were six from the business sector: Craig Benson (R-N.H.), John Lynch (D-N.H.), John Hoeven (R-N.D.), Don Carcieri (D-R.I.), Jon Huntsman, Jr. (R-Utah) and Mark Warner (D-Va.).

Fourth were the five legislators or former legislators who moved up from a district to a statewide office. These included Sonny Perdue (R-from the Ga. Senate),

Tim Pawlenty (R-from the Minn. House), Brad Henry (D-from the Okla. Senate), and Mike Rounds (R-from the S.D. Senate). Also, under New Jersey's unique succession law, the current Senate President Richard Codey-D is now serving as acting governor after incumbent Jim McGreevey's resignation.

Fifth were the four mayors or former mayors: Linda Lingle (R-Maui, Hawaii), Jim McGreevey (D-Woodbridge, N.J.), Ed Rendell (D-Philadelphia, Pa.) and Phil Bredesen (D-Nashville, Tenn.).

Finally, were the six new governors who followed a unique path compared to their counterparts: actor-

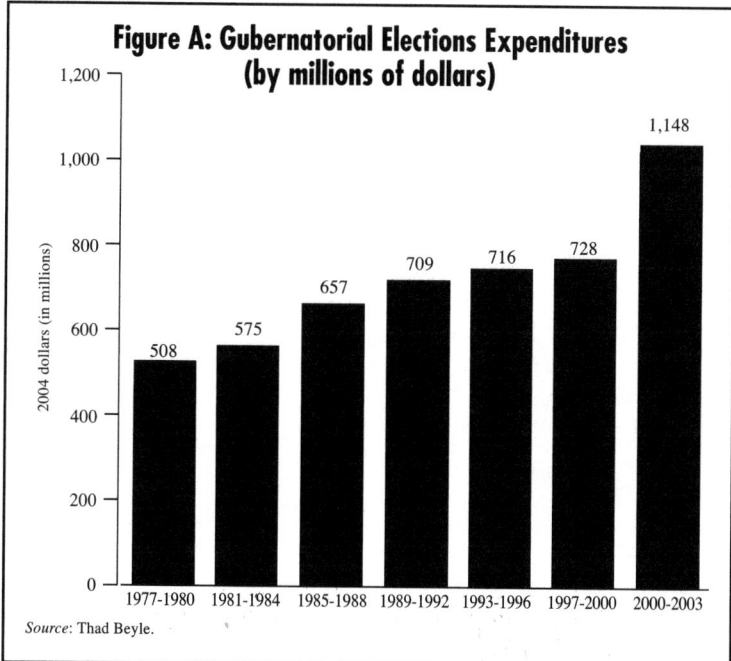

Figure A: Gubernatorial Elections Expenditures (by millions of dollars)

2004 dollars (in millions)

1977-1980: 508
1981-1984: 575
1985-1988: 657
1989-1992: 709
1993-1996: 716
1997-2000: 728
2000-2003: 1,148

Source: Thad Beyle.

(D-Wash.), and one is the "accidental governor" of Connecticut, M. Jodi Rell who became governor upon the resignation of Gov. John Rowland. While gubernatorial politics continues to be volatile, women are also continuing to hold their own in these races. In the 2001-2004 gubernatorial races, seven out of the 12 women running either as the incumbent or as the candidate of a major party won – a 58 percent success rate. There will be more soon.

Timing of Gubernatorial Elections

The election cycle for governors has settled into a regular pattern. Over the past few decades, many states have moved their elections to the off-presidential years in order to decouple the state and national level campaigns. Now, only 11 states hold their gubernatorial elections in the same year as a presidential election. Two of these states — New Hampshire and Vermont — still have two-year terms for their governor so their elections alternate between presidential and non-presidential years.

As can be seen in Table A, the year following a presidential election has only two states with gubernatorial elections.[3] Then in the even years between presidential elections, 36 states hold their gubernatorial elections, and in the year before a presidential election, three Southern states hold their gubernatorial elections.[4]

businessman Arnold Schwarzenegger (R-Calif.), former head of the Federal Office of Management and Budget Mitch Daniels (R-Ind.), former 2000 Winter Olympics Chairman Mitt Romney (R-Mass.), former Republican Party National Chairman Haley Barbour (R-Miss.), former State Supreme Court Justice Ted Kulongoski (D-Ore.) and former U.S. Attorney Dave Freudenthal (D-Wyo.).

In the 371 gubernatorial races between 1977 and 2004, among the candidates were 100 lieutenant governors (28 won), 83 attorneys general (21 won), 27 secretaries of state (seven won), 22 state treasurers (six won) and 14 state auditors, auditors general or comptrollers (three won). Looking at these numbers from a bettor's point of view, the odds of a lieutenant governor winning were 3.6-to-1, an attorney general 4.0-to-1, a secretary of state 3.9-to-1, a state treasurer 3.7-to-1 and a state auditor 4.7-to-1.

One other unique aspect about the current governors is that there will be eight women serving as governor in 2005 – one less than the nine women serving as governor in the last half of 2004 which was the all-time high for women serving at one time in the office. Seven are women were elected in their own right: Janet Napolitano (D-Ariz.), Ruth Ann Minner (D-Del.), Linda Lingle (R-Hawaii), Kathleen Sebelius (D-Kan.), Kathleen Blanco (D-La.), Jennifer Granholm (D-Mich.) and Christine Gregoire

Cost of Gubernatorial Elections

Table C presents data on the costs of the most recent elections. There is a great range in how much these races cost, from the all-time most expensive race recorded in New York in 2002 ($155.8 million in 2004 dollars) to the 2002 race in Nebraska ($1,697,424 in 2004 dollars). Both the New York and the Nebraska races saw an incumbent successfully win re-election.

But if we look at how much was spent by all the candidates per general election vote, a slightly different picture evolves. In 2003, the Louisiana

Table C: Costs of Gubernatorial Campaigns, Most Recent Elections 2000–2003

State	Year	Winner	Point margin	Total campaign expenditures All Candidates (2004$)	Cost Per Vote (2004$)	Winner Spent (2004$)	Winner Percent of all expenditures	Winner Vote percent
Alabama	2002	R★★★	+0.3	$33,512,464	24.51	$14,700,611	43.9	49.2
Alaska	2002	R#	+15	5,672,033	25.01	1,835,582	32.4	55.9
Arizona	2002	D#	+1	8,085,414	6.59	2,439,470	30.2	46.2
Arkansas	2002	R★	+6	4,790,362	5.94	2,898,362	60.5	53.0
California	2002	D★	+4.9	116,314,901	15.56	68,169,007	58.6	47.3
Colorado	2002	R★	+29	6,426,516	4.55	5,116,110	79.6	62.6
Connecticut	2002	R★	+12	8,353,753	8.17	6,493,702	77.7	56.1
Delaware	2000	D#	+19	3,437,090	10.62	1,483,384	43.2	59.2
Florida	2002	R#	+13	18,216,101	3.57	8,094,338	44.4	56.0
Georgia	2002	R★★★	+5	25,752,306	12.70	3,880,257	15.1	51.4
Hawaii	2002	R#	+4	10,041,642	26.28	5,741,536	57.2	51.1
Idaho	2002	R★	+14	2,374,205	5.77	1,181,847	49.8	56.3
Illinois	2002	D#	+8	51,768,316	14.63	23,789,347	46.0	52.2
Indiana	2000	D★	+14	20,017,471	9.19	10,707,268	53.5	56.6
Iowa	2002	D★	+8	13,958,685	13.61	6,424,202	46.0	52.7
Kansas	2002	D#	+8	16,201,626	19.39	4,631,042	28.6	52.9
Kentucky	2003	R#	+10	11,872,641	10.96	5,917,266	49.8	55.0
Louisiana	2003	D#	+3.8	40,427,109	28.72	6,871,733	17.0	51.9
Maine	2002	D#	+5.6	4,595,672	9.10	1,681,932	36.6	47.1
Maryland	2002	R#	+3.9	5,452,542	3.20	2,689,846	49.3	51.6
Massachusetts	2002	R#	+5	32,486,102	14.63	9,937,370	30.6	49.8
Michigan	2002	D★★★	+4	15,341,679	4.83	9,435,558	61.5	51.4
Minnesota	2002	R#	+8	6,334,174	2.81	2,681,285	42.3	44.4
Mississippi	2003	R★★★	+7	20,326,276	22.72	11,721,105	57.7	52.6
Missouri	2000	D#	+1	20,765,277	9.09	11,055,690	53.2	50.5
Montana	2000	R#	+4	5,109,476	12.46	1,069,605	20.9	51.0
Nebraska	2002	R★	+41	1,697,424	3.53	1,287,850	75.9	68.7
Nevada	2002	R★	+46	2,883,964	5.72	2,806,829	97.3	68.1
New Hampshire	2002	R#	+21	20,113,947	45.41	11,851,771	58.9	58.6
New Jersey	2001	D#	+15	39,452,688	17.71	16,414,420	41.6	56.4
New Mexico	2002	D#	+15	10,639,323	21.97	7,777,598	73.1	55.5
New York	2002	R★	+16	155,787,222	33.21	46,909,872	30.1	48.2
North Carolina	2000	D#	+6	31,241,242	10.62	12,217,327	39.1	52.0
North Dakota	2000	R#	+10	2,560,649	8.82	1,245,918	48.7	55.0
Ohio	2002	R★	+20	15,362,890	4.76	13,623,911	88.7	57.8
Oklahoma	2002	D#	+0.7	11,912,260	11.50	3,430,690	28.8	43.3
Oregon	2002	D#	+2.8	16,041,053	12.73	4,424,201	27.6	49.0
Pennsylvania	2002	D#	+9	69,151,599	19.31	41,574,906	60.1	53.4
Rhode Island	2002	R#	+10	7,350,029	22.15	2,592,029	35.3	54.8
South Carolina	2002	R★★★	+6	31,432,056	28.58	7,597,776	24.2	52.8
South Dakota	2002	R#	+15	9,833,246	29.39	1,724,149	17.5	56.8
Tennessee	2002	D#	+3	18,255,080	11.04	10,364,483	56.8	50.6
Texas	2002	R★	+18	112,055,236	24.61	29,617,542	26.4	57.8
Utah	2000	R★	+14	2,416,186	3.17	2,161,125	89.5	55.8
Vermont	2002	R#	+2.5	2,250,068	9.78	1,193,757	53.1	44.9
Virginia	2001	D#	+5	36,491,411	19.34	21,555,447	59.1	52.2
Washington	2000	D★	+19	7,277,630	2.95	4,194,591	57.6	58.4
West Virginia	2000	D★★★	+3	7,234,887	11.16	3,120,473	43.1	50.1
Wisconsin	2002	D★★★	+3.7	18,158,028	10.23	5,866,573	32.3	45.1
Wyoming	2002	D#	+2.1	2,735,552	14.75	781,845	29.0	50.0

Source: Thad Beyle.

Note: 2004$—Using the November 2004 CPI Index which was 1.910 of the 1982-84 Index = 1,000, the actual 2000 expenditures were based on a 1.722 value or .901 of the 2004$ index, the actual 2001 expenditures were based on a 1.771 index value or .927 of the 2004$ index, the actual 2002 expenditures were based on a 1.799 index value or .942 of the 2004$ index, and the 2003 expenditures were based on a 1.840 index value or .963 of the 2004$ index. Then the actual expenditures of each state's governor's race were divided by the .9 value for that year to get the equivalent 2004$ value of those expenditures.

Key:
★—Incumbent ran and won.
D—Democrat
★★—Incumbent ran and lost in party primary.
I—Independent
★★★—Incumbent ran and lost in general election.
R—Republican
#—Open seat.

Table D: Women Governors

Governor	State	Year elected or succeeded to office	How woman became governor	Tenure of service	Previous offices held	Last elected position held before governorship
Phase I - From initial statehood to adoption of the 19th Amendment to U.S. Constitution						
No women elected or served as governor						
Phase II - Wives of former governors elected governor, 1924-1966						
Nellie Tayloe Ross (D)	Wyoming	1924	E	1/1925-1/1927	F	...
Miriam "Ma" Ferguson (D)	Texas	1924	E	1/1925-1/1927 1/1933-1/1935	F	...
Lurleen Wallace (D)	Alabama	1966	E	1/1967-5/1968	F	...
Phase III - Women who became governor on their own merit, 1970 to date						
Ella Grasso (D)	Connecticut	1974	E	1/1975-12/1980	SH, SOS, (a)	(a)
Dixy Lee Ray (D)	Washington	1976	E	1/1977-1/1981	(b)	...
Vesta M. Roy (R)	New Hampshire	1982	S (c)	12/1982-1/1983	(d)	(d)
Martha Layne Collins (D)	Kentucky	1983	E	12/1983-12/1987	(e), LG	LG
Madeleine M. Kunin (D)	Vermont	1984	E	1/1985-1/1991	SH, LG	LG
Kay A. Orr (R)	Nebraska	1986	E	1/1987-1/1991	T	T
Rose Mofford (D)	Arizona	1988	S (f)	4/1988-1/1991	SOS	SOS
Joan Finney (D)	Kansas	1990	E	1/1991-1/1995	T	T
Barbara Roberts (D)	Oregon	1990	E	1/1991-1/1995	(g), C, SH, SOS	SOS
Ann Richards (D)	Texas	1990	E	1/1991-1/1995	C, T	T
Christy Whitman (R)	New Jersey	1993	E	1/1994-1/2001	(h)	(h)
Jeanne Shaheen (D)	New Hampshire	1996	E	1/1997-1/2003	(d)	(d)
Jane Dee Hull (R)	Arizona	1997	S (i)	9/1997-1/2003	(j), SOS	SOS
Nancy P. Hollister (R)	Ohio	1998	S (k)	12/1998-1/1999	LG	LG
Ruth Ann Minner (D)	Delaware	2000	E	1/2001-	SH, SS, LG	LG
Judy Martz (R)	Montana	2000	E	1/2001-1/2005	LG	LG
Sila Calderon (Pop D)	Puerto Rico	2000	E	1/2001-1/2005	M	M
Jane Swift (R)	Massachusetts	2001	S (l)	4/2001-1/2003	SS, LG	LG
Janet Napolitano (D)	Arizona	2002	E	1/2003-	(m), AG	AG
Linda Lingle (R)	Hawaii	2002	E	12/2002-	C, M (n)	M
Kathleen Sebelius (D)	Kansas	2002	E	1/2003-	SH, (o)	(o)
Jennifer Granholm (D)	Michigan	2002	E	1/2003-	(p), AG	AG
Olene Walker (R)	Utah	2003	S (q)	11/2003-1/2005	SH, LG	LG
Kathleen Blanco (D)	Louisiana	2003	E	1/2004-	SH, LG	LG
M. Jodi Rell (R)	Connecticut	2004	S (r)	7/2004-	SH, LG	LG
Christine Gregoire (D)	Washington	2004	E	1/2005-	AG	AG

Sources: National Governors Association Web site, www.nga.org, and individual state government Web sites.

Key:
S—Succeeded to office upon death, resignation or removal of the incumbent governor.
C—City council or county commission. SH—State house member.
E—Elected governor. SOS—Secretary of state
F—Former first lady. SS—State senate.
LG—Lieutenant governor. T—State treasurer.
M—Mayor.
(a) Congresswoman.
(b) Ray served on the U.S. Atomic Energy Commission from 1972-1975 and was chair of the AEC from 1973-1975.
(c) Roy as state senate president succeeded to office upon the death of Gov. Hugh Gallen.
(d) State senate president.
(e) State supreme court clerk.
(f) Mofford as secretary of state became acting governor in February 1988 and governor in April 1988 upon the impeachment and removal of Gov. Evan Mecham.

(g) Local school board member.
(h) Whitman was a former state utilities official.
(i) Hull as secretary of state became acting governor when Gov. Fife Symington resigned. Elected to full term in 1998.
(j) Speaker of the state house.
(k) Hollister as lieutenant governor became governor when Gov. George Voinovich stepped down to serve in the U.S. Senate.
(l) Swift as lieutenant governor succeeded Gov. Paul Celluci who resigned after being appointed ambassador to Canada. Was the first governor to give birth while serving in office.
(m) U.S. attorney.
(n) Lingle was mayor of Maui for two terms, elected in 1990 and 1996.
(o) Insurance commissioner.
(p) Federeal prosecutor.
(q) Walker as lieutenant governor succeeded to the governorship upon the resignation of Gov. Mike Leavitt in 2003, who had been appointed administrator of the U.S. Environmental Protection Agency.
(r) Rell as lieutenant governor succeeded to the governorship upon the resignation of Gov. John Rowland in 2004.

governor's race was the most expensive at $28.72 per vote, followed by the Mississippi race at $22.72 per vote, and the Kentucky race at $10.96 per vote. The Kentucky and Louisiana races were for an open seat, while the Mississippi race saw an incumbent governor defeated in his bid for reelection to a second term. The most expensive governor's race per vote in the 2000-2003 cycle was in the New Hampshire 2002 race when the candidates spent $45.41 per vote in 2004 dollars. The least expensive race during the same

cycle was in the Minnesota 2002 race when the candidates spent only $2.81 per vote.

In Figure A, by converting the actual dollars spent each year into the equivalent 2004 dollars, we see how the cost of these elections has increased over time. Since 1981, we have been able to compare the costs of each four-year cycle of elections with the previous cycle of elections.

In the 54 elections held between 1977 and 1980, the total expenditures were $507.8 million in

Table E: Impeachments and Removals of Governors

Name, party and state	Year	Process of impeachment and outcome		
Charles Robinson (R-Kan.)	1862	Impeached	Acquitted	
Harrison Reed (R-Fla.)	1868	Impeached	Acquitted	
William Holden (R-N.C.)	1870	Impeached	Convicted	Removed
Powell Clayton (R-Ark.)	1871	Impeached	Acquitted	
David Butler (R-Neb.)	1871	Impeached	Convicted	Removed
Henry Warmouth (R-La.)	1872	Impeached		Term ended
Harrison Reed (R-Fla.)	1872	Impeached	Acquitted	
Adelbert Ames (R-Miss.)	1876	Impeached		Resigned
William P. Kellogg (R-La.)	1876	Impeached	Acquitted	
Wiliam Sulzer (D-N.Y.)	1913	Impeached	Convicted	Removed
James "Pa" Ferguson (D-Texas)	1917	Impeached	Convicted	Resigned
John C. Walton (D-Okla.)	1923	Impeached	Convicted	Removed
Henry S. Johnston (D-Okla.)	1928	Impeached	Acquitted	
Henry S. Johnston (D-Okla.)	1929	Impeached	Convicted	Removed
Huey P. Long (D-La.)	1929	Impeached	Acquitted	
Henry Horton (D-Tenn.)	1931	Impeached	Acquitted	
Richard Leche (D-La.)	1939	Threatened		Resigned
Evan Mecham (R-Ariz.)	1988	Impeached	Convicted	Removed
John Rowland (R-Conn.)	2004	Threatened		Resigned

Other removals of incumbent governors

Name, party and state	Year	Process of impeachment and outcome
John A. Quitman (D-Miss.)	1851	Resigned after federal criminal indictment.
Lynn J. Frazier (R-N.D.)	1921	Recalled by voters during third term.
Warren T. McCray (R-Ind.)	1924	Resigned after federal criminal conviction.
William Langer (I-N.D.)	1934	Removed by North Dakota Supreme Court.
Thomas L. Moodie (D-N.D.)	1935	Removed by North Dakota Supreme Court.
J. Howard Pyle (R-Ariz.)	1955	Recall petition certified, but term ended before date set for recall election.
Marvin Mandel (D-Md.)	1977	Removed after federal criminal conviction.
Ray Blanton (D-Tenn.)	1979	Term shortened in bi-partisan agreement (a)
Evan Mecham (R-Ariz.)	1987	Recall petition certified, but impeached, convicted and removed from office before the date set for the recall election.
H. Guy Hunt (R-Ala.)	1993	Removed after state criminal conviction.
Jim Guy Tucker Jr. (D-Ark.)	1996	Resigned after federal criminal conviction.
J. Fife Symington (R-Ariz.)	1997	Resigned after federal criminal conviction.
Gray Davis (D-Calif.)	2003	Recalled by voters during second term.
James McGreevey (D-N.J.)	2004	Resigned due to personal reasons.

Sources: Thad Beyle and The Council of State Governments.
Key:
(a) See Lamar Alexander, *Steps Along the War: A Governor's Scrap-* *book* (Nashville, TN: Thomas Nelson, 1986), 21-9 for a discussion of this unique transition between governors.

equivalent 2004 dollars. In the 53 elections held between 2000 and 2003 — just over two decades later - the total expenditures were over $1,148 million in 2004 dollars, an increase of 126 percent. The greatest increases in expenditures were between the 1977-1980 and the 1987–1990 cycles, when there was a 43.9 percent increase, and between the 1992–1995 and the 2000–2003 cycles when there was a 60.9 percent increase.

These increases reflect the new style of campaigning for governor — with the candidates developing their own personal party by using outside consult-

ants, opinion polls, media ads and buys, and extensive fundraising efforts to pay for all of this. This style has now reached into most every state. Few states will be surprised by a high-price, high-tech campaign; they are commonplace now. The "air-war" campaigns have replaced the "ground-war" campaigns across the states.

Another factor has been the increasing number of candidates who are either wealthy or who have access to wealth and are willing to spend some of this money to become governor. For some, spending a lot of money leads to winning the governor's chair.

In 2002, Gov. Gray Davis spent $68.2 million in 2004 dollars in his successful bid for reelection in California, while Gov. George Pataki spent $46.9 million in 2004 dollars to win his third term. However, spending that amount of money and winning reelection did not deter those wanting to have Gov. Davis recalled from office less than a year later.

But spending a lot doesn't always lead to a win. For example, in the 2002 New York election, Thomas Golisano spent $81 million in 2004 dollars in his unsuccessful campaign for governor as an Independent candidate. And in Texas, Tony Sanchez also spent $81 million in 2004 dollars as the unsuccessful Democratic candidate. In California's 1998 gubernatorial election, three candidates spent $126 million in 2004 dollars in their campaigns. Two of these candidates won their party's nomination and faced off in November, with Gray Davis (D) at $43.9 million in 2004 dollars the winner over Republican candidate Dan Lundgren at $36.8 million in 2004 dollars. The largest spender at $45.4 million in 2004 dollars, Al Checci (D), wasn't even able to win the Democratic nomination.

A Shift Toward More Women Governors

As already noted, a unique aspect about the current governors is that there are eight women serving as governor in 2005. A little history helps to put this into perspective. There have been three phases in this history. In the first phase, which lasted until 1924, no woman was ever elected governor of any state. Remember, the 19th Amendment to the U.S. Constitution providing nationwide suffrage to women was only ratified in August 1920. (see Table D)

The second phase began in 1924, when the first two women were elected governors in the states of Texas and Wyoming—and both were the wives of former governors. Although both were elected on the same day, Wyoming's Nellie Tayloe Ross became the first woman governor to be sworn in—one week before "Ma" Ferguson in Texas took office. It wouldn't be until 1966 when outgoing Gov. George Wallace was instrumental in getting his wife Lurleen elected to succeed him that another woman was elected governor. The key to these wins was that they were wives of former and well-known governors.

The third phase began in the 1970s when women politicians began to move up the political ladder and win the governor's chair in their own right. This began with Ella Grasso of Connecticut (1974) as she moved up from serving several terms as secretary of state and then as a U.S. congresswoman. In effect, she was the first woman governor to win the office on her own merit. There was one other woman elected governor in the 1970s on her own merit – Dixy Lee Ray of Washington, then came three in the 1980s and four in the 1990s. Four other women became governor in the 1980–1999 period when as number two in the line of succession they succeeded to the office upon the death, resignation or removal of the incumbent governor.

In the first decade of the 21st century, we have seen 12 women become governor in the 50 states and Puerto Rico. In the 2000 elections, three women were elected governor—Ruth Ann Minner (D-Del.), Judy Martz (R-Mont.) and Sila Caldron (Pop. D-PR). In the 2002 elections, four women were elected governor—Janet Napolitano (D-Ariz.), Linda Lingle, (R-Hawaii), Kathleen Sebelius (D-Kan.) and Jennifer Granholm (D-Mich.). In the 2003 elections, Kathleen Blanco (D-La.) was elected governor and two other women moved up from lieutenant governor to governor when President Bush appointed their state's governor to a position in the Bush administration—Jane Swift (R-Mass.) in 2001 and Olene Walker (R-Utah) in 2003. In 2004, another woman Christine Gregoire (D-Washington) was elected governor and another woman lieutenant governor moved up to become governor upon the resignation of the incumbent governor—M. Jodi Rell (R-Conn.).

The last stepping stone to the governorship was as lieutenant governor for six of them, as attorney general for three others, mayor of a major city for two others, and as insurance commissioner for one other. And each had held other elected and appointed offices en route.

Gubernatorial Forced Exits

The California 2003 gubernatorial recall and replacement votes highlighted the fact that some elected governors faced situations in which they could lose their office without being beaten by a challenger at the ballot box, becoming ill or dying. (see Table E)

Between 1851 and 2004, 30 governors have faced the prospect of having to leave office through impeachment, removal or resignation due to a criminal conviction or actions that brought them into serious trouble. Sixteen governors have been impeached by the state house and while eight were acquitted of the charges by the state senate, seven were convicted by their state senates. Of these seven losers in the fight, six were then removed from office and one resigned upon his conviction.[5] Harrison Reed (R-Fla.) was impeached twice but acquitted both times in 1868 and 1873. Henry Johnson (D-Okla.) was also impeached twice and while he beat

Table F: Governors' Institutional Powers, 1960 v. 2005

Specific power	Scores		Percent change
	1960	2005	
Separately elected executive branch officials (SEP)	2.3	2.9	28%
Tenure potential (TP)	3.2	4.1	28
Appointment powers (AP)	2.9	3.1	7
Budget power (BP)	3.6	3.1	-14
Veto power (VP)	2.8	4.5	61
Gubernatorial party control (PC)	3.6	3.0	-17
Totals	18.4	20.7	12.5

Notes:

SEP - Separately elected executive branch officials: 5 = only governor or governor/lieutenant governor team elected; 4.5 = governor or governor/lieutenant governor team, with one other elected official; 4 = governor/lieutenant governor team with some process officials (attorney general, secretary of state, treasurer, auditor) elected; 3 = governor/lieutenant governor team with process officials, and some major and minor policy officials elected; 2.5 = governor (no team) with six or fewer officials elected, but none are major policy officials; 2 = governor (no team) with six or fewer officials elected, including one major policy official; 1.5 = governor (no team) with six or fewer officials elected, but two are major policy officials; 1 = governor (no team) with seven or more process and several major policy officials elected. [Source: CSG, *The Book of the States, 1960-1961* (1960): 124-125 and (2004): 175-180].

TP - Tenure potential of governors: 5 = 4-year term, no restraint on reelection; 4.5 = 4-year term, only three terms permitted; 4 = 4-year term, only two terms permitted; 3 = 4-year term, no consecutive election permitted; 2 = 2-year term, no restraint on reelection; 1 = 2-year term, only two terms permitted. [Source: Joseph A. Schlesinger, "The Politics of the Executive," in Politics in the American States, edited by Herbert Jacob and Kenneth N. Vines (Boston: Little, Brown, 1965) and CSG, *The Book of the States, 2004* (2004): 157-158].

AP - Governor's appointment powers in six major functional areas: corrections, K-12 education, health, highways/transportation, public utilities regulation, and welfare. The six individual office scores are totaled and then averaged and rounded to the nearest .5 for the state score. 5 = governor appoints, no other approval needed; 4 = governor appoints, a board, council or legislature approves; 3 = someone else appoints, governor approves or shares appointment; 2 = someone else appoints, governor and others approve; 1 = someone else appoints, no approval or confirmation needed. [Source: Schlesinger (1965), and CSG, *The Book of the States, 2004* (2004): 175-180].

BP - Governor's budget power: 5 = governor has full responsibility, legislature may not increase executive budget; 4 = governor has full responsibility, legislature can increase by special majority vote or subject to item veto; 3 = governor has full responsibility, legislature has unlimited power to change executive budget; 2 = governor shares responsibility, legislature has unlimited power to change executive budget; 1 = governor shares responsibility with other elected official, legislature has unlimited power to change executive budget. [Source: Schlesinger (1965) and CSG, *The Book of the States, 2004* (2004): 162-163 and NCSL, "Limits on Authority of Legislature to Change Budget" (1998).

VP - Governor's veto power: 5 = has item veto and a special majority vote of the legislature is needed to override a veto (3/5's of legislators elected or 2/3's of legislators present; 4 = has item veto with a majority of the legislators elected needed to override; 3 = has item veto with only a majority of the legislators present needed to override; 2 = no item veto, with a special legislative majority needed to override it; 1 = no item veto, only a simple legislative majority needed to override. (Source: Schlesinger (1965):, and CSG, *The Book of the States, 2004* (2004): 113-115, 162-163).

PC - Gubernatorial party control: 5 = has a substantial majority (75% or more) in both houses of the legislature; 4 = has a simple majority in both houses (less than 75%), or a substantial majority in one house and a simple majority in the other; 3 = split party control in the legislature or a nonpartisan legislature; 2 = has a substantial minority in both houses (25% or more), or a simple minority (25% or less) in one and a substantial minority in the other; 1 = has a simple minority in both houses. (Source: National Conference of State Legislatures web page, various dates).

Total - sum of the scores on the six individual indices. Score - total divided by six to keep 5-point scale.

peached governor resigned before there could be a trial by the senate.[7] And two other governors resigned in the face of a threatened impeachment effort.[8]

Thirteen governors faced other means of being forced to leave office. Five were convicted of criminal charges with three resigning after the conviction[9] and two being removed after their conviction.[10] One other governor resigned after a criminal indictment was made.[11] Two North Dakota governors were removed by the state Supreme Court as one was charged with conspiracy in raising money for his political party by trying to get 5 percent of the wages of the people he had appointed for a subscription to a new party newspaper—the court suspended him from office.[12] The other was disqualified from office as he had voted in Minnesota in 1930 which was within the last five years prior to his election as governor which was not allowed under the state's laws.[13] Four others have faced a recall initiative and while Gov. Lynn Frazier (R-N.D., 1921) and Gov. Gray Davis (D-Calif., 2003) were recalled by the voters, Gov. Evan Mecham (R-Ariz., 1988) was impeached, convicted and removed from office by the state legislature before the scheduled recall vote could be held, and Gov. Howard Pyle (R-Ariz., 1955) saw his term end before a recall vote could be held. In an interesting twist on how an incumbent's tenure was shortened, Gov. Ray Blanton (D-Tenn., 1979) found his term shortened and the locks to his gubernatorial office changed to keep him out in a bi-partisan agreement tied to illegal actions he was taking at the end of his term.[14]

Much of this gubernatorial turmoil occurred to 18 governors in nine different southern states. The leading individual states in experiencing the removal of the incumbent efforts were Arizona and Louisiana with four such actions each, North Dakota and Oklahoma with three such actions each, and Arkansas, Florida, Mississippi and Tennessee with two such actions each. With nearly one-third of these actions occurring within the last three decades, there is heightened awareness of these options of gaining a new governor.

the charges in the 1928 effort, he lost the fight and was removed in the 1929 effort. Another impeached governor escaped conviction as his term ended before the senate could take action[6] while another im-

Gubernatorial Powers

One way to view the changes that have been occurring in gubernatorial powers is to look at the *Index of Formal Powers of the Governorship* first developed by Joseph Schlesinger in the 1960s,[15]which this author has continued to update.[16] The index used here consists of six different indices of gubernatorial power as seen in 1960 and 2005. These indices include the number and importance of separately elected executive branch officials, the tenure potential of governors, the appointment powers of governors for administrative and board positions in the executive branch, the governor's budgetary power, the governor's veto power and the governor's party control in the legislature. Each of the individual indices is set in a five-point scale, with five being the most power and one being the least. (See Table F for details on how each of these indices and the overall index were developed.)

During the four and a half decades between 1960 and 2005, the overall institutional powers of the of the nation's governors increased by 12.5 percent. The greatest increase among the individual gubernatorial powers was in their veto power (plus 61 percent) as more governors gained an item veto, and in 1996 North Carolina voters were finally able to vote on a constitutional amendment giving their governor veto power. It was approved by a 3-to-1 ratio.

The indices measuring the governor's tenure potential (length of term and ability to seek an additional term or terms) and the number of separately elected executive branch officials showed identical 28 percent increases in favor of the governor. The governors' appointment power over specific functional area executive branch officials increased by only 7 percent. In addition, the states continue to hold to the concept of the multiple executive in terms of how many statewide elected officials there are. In 2004, there were 308 separately elected executive officials covering 12 major offices in the states.[17] This compares to 306 elected officials in 1972. Ten states also have multimember boards, commissions or councils with members selected by statewide or district election.

The gubernatorial budgetary power actually declined over the period (minus 14 percent). However, we must remember that during this same period, state legislatures were also undergoing considerable reform, and gaining more power to work on the governor's proposed budget was one of those reforms sought. Hence, the increased legislative budgetary power more than balanced out any increases in gubernatorial budgetary power.

There has also been a drop in the gubernatorial party control in the state legislatures over the period (mi-

nus 17 percent). Much of this can be attributed to the major partisan shifts occurring in the Southern states as the region has been moving from one-party dominance to a very competitive two-party system.[18] In 1960, 13 of the 14 governors were Democrats, and all 28 state legislative chambers were under Democratic control. In 2005, Republicans control eight governorships to the Democrats six, while the Democrats hold a 15-to-13 edge in control of the legislative chambers. Four Southern governors face a legislature completely controlled by the opposite party,[19] while three others face a legislature with split partisan control.[20]

Notes

[1] The former governors winning the presidency over the past three decades were Jimmy Carter (D-Ga., 1971-1975) in 1976, Ronald Reagan (R-Calif., 1967-1975) in 1980 and 1984, Bill Clinton (D-Ark., 1979-1981 and 1983-1992) in 1992 and 1996, and George W. Bush (R-Texas, 1995-2001) in 2000 and 2004.

[2] For an analysis of governors trying to handle the impact of the early 1990s economic downturn, see Thad Beyle, ed., *Governors in Hard Times* (Washington, D.C.: CQ Press, 1994).

[3] New Jersey and Virginia.

[4] Kentucky, Louisiana and Mississippi.

[5] James "Pa" Ferguson of Texas in 1917.

[6] Henry Warmouth (R-La.), 1872

[7] Adelbert Ames (R-Ms.), 1876.

[8] Richard Leche (D-La.), 1939 and John Rowland (R-Conn.), 2004.

[9] Warren McCray (R-Ind.), 1924, Jim Guy Tucker, Jr. (D-Ark.), 1993 and J. Fife Symington (R-Ariz.), 1997.

[10] Marvin Mandel (D-Md.), 1977 and H. Guy Hunt (R-Ala.), 1993.

[11] John A. Quitman (D-Miss.), 1851.

[12] William Langer (D-ND), 1934.

[13] Thomas Moodie (D-ND), 1935.

[14] See Lamar Alexander, *Steps Along the Way: A Governor's Scrapbook* (Nashville, TN: Thomas Nelson, 1986), 21-29 for a discussion of this unique transition between governors.

[15] Joseph A. Schlesinger, "The Politics of the Executive," *Politics in the American States*, 1st and 2nd ed, Herbert Jacob and Kenneth N. Vines, eds., (Boston: Little Brown, 1965 and 1971).

[16] Thad L. Beyle, "The Governors," *Politics in the American States* 8th ed., Virginia Gray and Russell L. Hanson, eds., (Washington, D.C.: CQ Press, 2003). Earlier versions of this index by the author appeared in the 4th edition (1983), the 5th edition (1990), the 6th edition (1996), and the 7th edition (1999).

[17] Kendra Hovey and Harold Hovey, "D-12 - Number of Statewide Elected Officials, 2004," *CQ's State Fact Finder, 2005* (Washington, D.C.: CQ Press, 2005): 113.

[18] The following states are included in this definition of the South: Alabama, Arkansas, Florida, Georgia, Kentucky,

Louisiana, Mississippi, North Carolina, Oklahoma, South Carolina, Tennessee, Texas, Virginia and West Virginia.

[19] Republicans Bob Riley in Ala., Mike Huckabee in Ark. and Haley Barbour in Miss., and Democrat Mark Warner in Va.

[20] Republican Ernie Fletcher in Ky., and Democrats Brad Henry in Okla. and Phil Bredesen in Tenn.

About the Author

Thad Beyle is Pearsall Professor of Political Science at the University of North Carolina at Chapel Hill. A Syracuse University AB and AM, he received his Ph.D. at the University of Illinois. He spent a year in the North Carolina governor's office in the mid-1960s and has worked with the National Governors Association in several capacities on gubernatorial transitions.

Staffing the Governor's Office: A Comparative Analysis

By Patrick Fisher and David Nice

The amount of staff support assigned to the governor's office varies considerably from state to state. Staffing levels tend to be higher in states where the scope and complexity of work facing state government is greater and in states where the Progressive Era reforms to foster direct democracy have not been adopted.

Introduction

A striking development in American politics since World War II is the growth of staff support for elected officials. Staff support for presidents, Congress, governors and state legislatures has increased dramatically, with gubernatorial staffing roughly quintupling from the mid-1950s to the mid-1990s.[1] The growth of staffing at the state level has been very uneven, however; the following analysis will seek to explain variations in gubernatorial staffing in the American states.

A variety of forces have contributed to the creation of large staff systems, including the growth and increasing complexity of governmental responsibilities, a belief that elected officials need the guidance of wise advisors, mistrust of the bureaucracy, public relations needs, officials' inclinations to keep together the team of people that have helped them in the past (in the last election campaign, for example), and officials' desire to have people who can serve as buffers and gatekeepers to absorb the anger of the public, regulate access to the officials, and take the blame for mistakes an failures.[2]

Large staff systems present a number of potential risks. Many critics have expressed concern over the prospect of unelected, largely invisible people exerting significant influence over public programs. An elected official may not be able to monitor the activities of a large staff very effectively, with the result that staffers pursue their own agendas. Staff members hired to help an elected official cope with a heavy workload may, by generating new proposals an added information, make the workload heavier. A large staff organization, created in part to compensate for the inadequacies of the bureaucracy, may come to display some of the same pathologies as the bureaucracy. Finally, in an era of limited resources and public cynicism about government, the cost of a large staff system may become a point of controversy, a consideration that contributed to reductions in congressional committee staffs in 1995 and reductions in and reluctance to expand legislative staffing in

some states.[3] A large staff, then, presents a number of significant risks and costs which must be weighed against the possible benefits.

In an era of increasing governmental responsibilities at the state level, gubernatorial staffs play an important role in many aspects of government. Governors' staffs are involved in public relations activities, legislative liaison, budgetary analysis, monitoring agency behavior and policy analysis.[4] Without adequate staff support, governors may be heavily dependent on information provided by interest groups, state agencies, and other outside sources whose interests may be very different for the governors'. Governors need staff assistance to draft proposals, analyze legislation that the governor may not have time to evaluate personally and assess programs being administered by state agencies.

The important role played by gubernatorial staffs implies that levels of staff support may have important implications for governors and for state policymaking. A governor with ample staff assistance is likely to be better equipped to face new demands and problems, while a limited staff may be overwhelmed by a rush of new concerns. Levels of staffing may also cast light on the political dynamics that encourage or discourage giving governors substantial staff assistance. We now turn to an examination of factors that influence gubernatorial staffing levels.

Possible Influences on Gubernatorial Staffing

A number of factors may help to shape whether a governor has abundant staff support or relatively limited staffing. Among the most likely influences on staffing are orientations toward government, the socioeconomic environment, the governor's formal power, and the task environment facing the governor's office. We will examine each of those factors in turn.

Orientations toward government influence many aspects of state politics.[5] Two different orientations affect gubernatorial staffing levels. First, ideology is likely to affect staffing. Generally speaking, liberals tend to be more supportive of governmental activism, and conservatives prefer more limited government.[6] A conservative ideological environment is likely to yield lower levels of staffing, both by providing a less supportive environment for new initiatives and by making revenue-raising more difficult. By contrast, a more liberal environment may yield more new initiatives, which will mean more work for staffers, an make revenue raising easier, which will make funding a large staff system easier.

A second aspect of orientations toward government is the Progressive tradition of direct democracy. In the late 1800s and early 1900s, many states adopted initiative and referendum provisions to enable citizens to bypass public officials and control policy directly. Those actions were prompted in part by mistrust of public officials and the belief that they would not respond to the needs or desires of ordinary citizens.[7] If those beliefs have persisted, then states that have adopted direct democracy provisions should, by virtue of a climate of mistrust of politicians, have lower levels of gubernatorial staffing.

The socioeconomic environment may also influence gubernatorial staffing, just as that environment affects many other aspects of state politics.[8] Two aspects of that environment, metropolitanization and affluence, are likely to be particularly relevant for staffing levels.

Historically speaking, metropolitan interests have often found governors to be more responsive than state legislatures to metropolitan concerns, although that tendency may be less pronounced since the reapportionment cases of the 1960s.[9] In addition, the greater complexity and diversity of metropolitan areas, coupled with the weaker social controls and impersonal encounters common in urban life, make metropolitan areas a source of many demands of government generally.[10] As a result, more metropolitan states are likely to produce added demands on the governor's office and a need for more staff support.

Affluence is another important aspect of the socioeconomic environment that is likely to affect gubernatorial staffing. In a relatively poor state, all available financial resources are likely to be consumed by what are regarded as vital services. Ample staffing for the governor's office is likely to seem a luxury that the state cannot afford in that context. By contrast, wealthier states can more readily generate financial resources for services and capabilities that go beyond the basic minimum.[11] Raising the needed funds for financing a large staff system will be considerably easier in more prosperous states, other things being equal.

The powers and responsibilities of governors are also likely to influence staffing levels. Just as the growth of the president's role in governing the country has helped fuel the growth of presidential staff support, the increasing powers and duties of governors have created a need for more gubernatorial staff.[12] Where governors play a larger role in the budget process, the legislative process, and in making personnel decisions, for example, they will need more staff support; clearly tasks of those types generate much of the staff work load.[13] Where governors have more extensive powers and responsibilities, then, we expect to find larger gubernatorial staffs.

Apart from a governor's formal powers, the workload placed on the governor's office is likely to affect the amount of staff support needed by the governor. Four significant aspects of that workload are likely to be federal aid, state-local spending, state population and the volume of legislation to be assessed.

A major responsibility of all governors in the modern era is intergovernmental relations. The governors' intergovernmental role takes many forms, from lobbying the federal government to participating in the administration of programs operated by more than one level of government to overseeing flows of intergovernmental grants.[14] Clearly the expansion of intergovernmental responsibilities has encouraged staff expansion.[15] States that receive proportionately more federal aid should, therefore, have a greater need for larger gubernatorial staffs.

In a related vein, the larger the state population the higher the levels of state and local government spending, meaning more funds to monitor and, because of the temptations that immense sums of money can cause, a greater need for monitoring. A larger state population will generate more mail, e-mail and telephone calls to the governor's office. Reaching out to a larger population will require more elaborate methods for managing public relations. A larger population, other things being equal, will include a greater variety of needs and viewpoints;[16] making sense of those various needs and viewpoints will be easier with staff assistance. Moreover, when some viewpoints cannot be reconciled, the staff can sometimes serve as a buffer between the chief executives and disappointed citizens.[17] Higher spending levels can also mean more agencies and programs to assess and analyze. Given that many governors have only modest interest or expertise in budgeting and fiscal administration, higher spending is likely to generate more work for the governor's staff and, consequently, create pressures for more staffing. Not surprisingly,

Table A
SIZE OF GOVERNOR'S STAFF
IN THE 50 STATES

State	Number of staff
Florida	310
Texas	266
New York	180
New Jersey	156
Lousiana	143
Illinois	130
Pennsylvania	90
California	86
Maryland	82
Georgia	77
North Carolina	76
Alaska	70
Massachusetts	70
Hawaii	67
Ohio	60
Michigan	56
West Virginia	56
Arkansas	55
Rhode Island	49
Minnesota	45
Kentucky	40
Wisconsin	40
Arizona	39
Colorado	39
Missouri	39
Tennessee	36
Washington	36
Indiana	34
Oklahoma	34
Virginia	34
Mississippi	33
Delaware	32
Connecticut	30
Oregon	29
New Mexico	27
Idaho	24
Kansas	24
New Hampshire	23
South Dakota	23
Alabama	22
South Carolina	22
Iowa	19
Maine	19
Montana	18
Utah	18
North Dakota	17
Vermont	14
New Hampshire	9
Wyoming	8
Nevada	N.A.

Source: The Book of the States
2004, 160.

then, states with larger populations are likely to have larger gubernatorial staffs.[18]

A third aspect of the workload is the volume of legislation introduced in a typical legislative session. Legislative proposals that originate in the governor's office need staff support in formulating the proposals and in selling them to the legislature. Proposals that originate elsewhere also add to the staff's workload, for the governor's policy agenda must be defended against conflicting proposals.[19] Where a larger volume of legislative proposals must be developed or assessed, a larger staff system will be needed.

Data and Methods

The staff in the 50 state governors' offices ranges from a high of 310 in Florida to eight in Wyoming (see Table A). There are five other states with staffs in triple figures–Texas, New York, Louisiana and Illinois–and one other state with a staff in the single digits–Nebraska. A majority of the states (35) fall into the range of 19 to 77 staff in the governor's office with the average being 57 staffers. It is important to note that the definitions as to who are staff vary considerably across the states and that the figures for the states are the number of staffers as defined by the respective states. Because staffing levels are distributed in a relatively skewed manner, a $\log_{10}$ transformation was used to correct for skewing.

Table B
STATE CHARACTERISTICS AND GUBERNATORIAL
STAFFING: ZERO-ORDER CORRELATIONS

	Number of gubernatorial staffers
Electoral conservatism	.20
Progressivism	-.28 (a)
Percent metropolitan, 2000	.52 (b)
Per capita income, 2000	.25
Governor's formal powers	.03
Federal aid per capita, 2000	-.25
State population, 2000	.72 (c)
Bills introduced, 2003	.68 (c)

Source: Patrick Fisher and David Nice.
Key:
(a) .05 significance.
(b) .01 significance.
(c) .001 significance.

In order to measure ideology, we utilized the findings of Erikson, Wright and McIver which are based on public opinion survey data. It is the most direct measure available of how citizens regard themselves ideologically. The measure is also related to many state policy decisions.[20]

Progressivism is measured by a Guttman scale, with each state given one point for having some sort of initiative provision (whether direct or indirect) and one point for having some sort of referendum provision.[21] The scale's coefficient of reproducibility is .98.

Data on metropolitanization, affluence, as measured by per capita income, and population are from Census sources. A square root transformation was used to correct for skewness in state population.

The measure of the governor's formal powers is based on the governor's tenure potential, appointment powers, budgeting powers, legislative budget changing powers, veto powers, and political strength in the legislature.[22] Data on federal grants per capita to each state and its localities and the volume of legislation introduced are from *The Book of the States*.[23]

Analysis

The zero-order correlations between gubernatorial staffing levels and various state characteristics are consistent with some of the preceding hypotheses, but others receive little or no support (see Table B). We expected that states with more conservative electorates, as measured by Erikson, Wright and McIver would have smaller gubernatorial staffs, but this is not the case. In fact, more conservative states tend to have larger gubernatorial staffs, though this is not statistically significant. On the other hand, states with a strong Progressive legacy, as measured by the presence of initiative and referendum provisions, tend to

Table C
REGRESSION ANALYSIS OF GUBERNATORIAL STAFFING

	b	beta	t
Electoral conservatism	-.013	-.036	-.318
Progressivism	-.078	-.211	-2.515(a)
Percent metropolitan, 2000	.007	.302	2.24 (a)
Per capita income, 2000	.001	-.226	-1.67
Governor's formal powers	.043	.054	.574
Federal aid per capita, 2000	.040	.084	.874
State population, 2000	.005	.487	4.34 (b)
Bills introduced, 2003	.357	.352	3.33 (c)

Source: Patrick Fisher and David Nice.
Note: r^2 = .76   F = 15.23 (b)
Key:
(a) .05 significance.
(b) .001 significance.
(c) .01 significance.

have relatively small staffs for governor, as we hypothesized.

The socioeconomic environment proves to be more consistent in its relationship with gubernatorial staffing. Staffs tend to be larger in more metropolitan states and in more affluent states, with the former tendency being particularly strong. By contrast, the formal powers of the governor are virtually unrelated to staffing levels.

Finally, two of the three workload measures are strongly related to the size of the governor's staff, with staffs tending to be larger in states with larger populations and more legislative activity. Federal aid per capita, however, actually displays a weak, negative relationship to staff levels.

Regression analysis of gubernatorial staffing levels supports the contention that the greater the size and complexity of the workload facing state government, the larger the governor's staff will tend to be (see Table C). Governors in states with large populations, high levels of metropolitization, and high levels of legislative activity are likely to confront a wide range of problems, issues, and demands on a recurring basis and are likely to need substantial staffs.

The analysis also indicates that states where the Progressive movement left a more lasting imprint, as indicated by the presence of initiative and referendum provisions, tend to have smaller gubernatorial staffs, other things being equal. This is consistent with what we expected–states that have large staffs for governors were less receptive to Progressive reforms and their attendant suspicion of politicians.

Despite our original expectations that states with relatively liberal climates of opinion, high per capita incomes, larger levels of federal aid, and governors with strong formal powers would also have larger gubernatorial staffs, these factors appear to be unrelated to gubernatorial staffing levels. As was the case with the zero-order correlations, ideology, affluence, federal aid and governor power were found to be essentially unrelated to gubernatorial staffing levels in the regression analysis. Overall the model is able to account for three-fourths of the total variation in staffing levels from state to state.

Discussion

Critics of big government are inclined to depict government as expanding in a relatively mindless way, at least in the sense that expansion allegedly takes place without regard for the actual amount of work that needs to be done or public sentiments regarding what government needs to do. A large body of evidence indicates, however, that the scope of government is strongly influenced by the tasks facing government and public sentiment regarding what government should be doing.[24] The results of this analysis are broadly consistent with the second perspective. Specifically, where governors must contend with the many demands of a larger population and the more difficult task of managing communications with a larger population, where state and local spending in higher, where a larger share of the population is concentrated in metropolitan areas and where there is more legislative activity, the governor cannot cope effectively without considerable staff support.

A significant component of the Progressive movement was distrust of politicians, a sentiment that underlay proposals to create policy processes that could bypass politicians entirely. Reformers hoped that the initiative and referendum would enable citizens to make policy directly and without the meddling of party bosses and tools of special interest groups. Ironically, some of the reformers might be appalled by the role played by political consultants and interest groups in large-scale initiative and referendum campaigns in some states today. Where the Progressives' direct democracy reforms, with their implicit distrust of politicians, have taken root, a large staff system appears somewhat out of place.

The office of governor has changed dramatically in the last 100 years, with dramatic increases in the scope and complexity of gubernatorial responsibilities.[25] In a similar fashion, state governments have become substantially more involved in a wide range of issues and programs during this century. Moreover, the job of governor does not promise to become any less demanding for the foreseeable future; if anything, the job will become more demanding in light of the revenue problems of many localities, efforts to devolve power away from the federal government, and the federal government's seeming inability to make fundamental decisions on any number of issues. The result is likely to be even more demands on gubernatorial staff.

Notes

[1]John Hart, *The Presidential Branch* (New York: Pergamon, 1987); Alan Rosenthal, *Governors and Legislatures* (Washington, DC: CQ Press, 1990), 46; Larry Sabato, *Goodbye to Good-time Charlie* (Washington, DC: CQ Press), 85; Thad Beyle, "Governors' Offices: Variations on Common Themes," in *Being Governor*, editors Thad Beyle and Lynn Muchmore (Durham, NC: Duke University Press, 1983), 158-73.

[2]Thomas Cronin, *The State of the Presidency*, 2nd edition (Boston: Little, Brown, 1980), 244-46; William Mullen and Paul Hagner, "The American Presidency," in *Chief Executives*, editors Taketsugu Tsurutani and Jack Gabbert (Pullman, WA: Washington State University Press, 1992), 1-59; Hart (1987), 45-47.

[3]Cronin (1980), 243-44; Edward H. Flentje, "Clarifying Purpose and Achieving Balance in Gubernatorial Administration," *Journal of State Government* 62: 161-167; Alan Rosenthal, "The Legislature: Unraveling of Institutional Fabric," in *The State of the States*, 3rd edition (Washington, DC: CQ Press, 1996), 134-37.

[4]Donald Sprengel, "Trends in Staffing the Governor's Office," *Comparative State Politics Newsletter* 9: 11.

[5]David Nice, *Policy Innovation in State Government* (Ames: Iowa State University Press, 1994); Robert Erikson, Gerald Wright and John McIver, *Statehouse Democracy* (New York: Cambridge, 1993).

[6]Lyman Sargent, *Contemporary Political Ideologies*, 12th edition (Belmont, CA: Wadsworth, 2002).

[7]Daniel Grant and Lloyd Omadahl, *State and Local Government in America*, 6th edition (Madison, WI: Brown and Benchmark, 1993); Thomas Cronin, *Direct Democracy* (Cambridge, MA: Harvard University Press, 1989); Alpheus Mason and Gordon Baker, *Free Government in the Making*, 4th edition (New York: Oxford, 1985).

[8]Thomas Dye, *Politics in States and Communities* (Englewood Cliffs, NJ: Prentice-Hall, 1996).

[9]Charles Adrian and Michael Fine, *State and Local Politics* (Chicago: Lyceum Books/Nelson-Hall, 1991), 247.

[10]John Bardo and John Hartman, *Urban Sociology* (Itasca, IL: Peacock, 1982), 101-102 and 129-30; Nice (1994), 26.

[11]Nice (1994).

[12]Cronin (1980), 244-46; Hart (1987), 45-6, and Beyle (1983), 162.

[13]Adrian and Fine (1991), 250-51.

[14]Thad Beyle, "Governors," in *Politics in the American States*, 7th edition, editors Virginia Gray, Russell Hanson, and Herbert Jacob (Washington, DC: CQ Press, 1999), 235-38; Adrian and Fine (1991), 255.

[15]Beyle (1983), 162.

[16]James Madison, "The Federalist Paper No. 10," in *The Federalist Papers*, by Alexander Hamilton, James Madison, and John Jay (New York: Bantam, 1982).

[17]Mullen and Hagner (1992), 31.

[18]Coleman Ransone, *The American Governorship* (Westport, CT: Greenwood, 1982), 110; Beyle (1983), 161.

[19]Adrian and Fine (1991), 250-51; Ransone (1982), 132.

[20]Erikson, Wright and McIver (1993); Nice (1994).

[21]Raw data are from *The Book of the States 2004* (Lexington, KY: The Council of State Governments, 2004), 329.

[22]Beyle (1999), 218,

[23]*The Book of the States* (2004), 42.

[24]Thomas Dye, *Understanding Public Policy* (Englewood Cliffs, NJ: Prentice-Hall, 2004); Alan Rosenthal, John R. Hibbing, Burdett A. Loomis, Karl T. Kurtz, and John Hibbing (Washington, DC: CQ Press, 2002); Aaron Wildavsky and Namoi Caiden, *The New Politics of the Budgetary Process*, 4th edition (New York: Longman, 2001); Nice (1994); Erikson, Wright and McIver (1993).

[25]Sabato (1983).

About the Authors

Patrick Fisher received his Ph.D. in political science from Washington State University and is currently an assistant professor of political science at Seton Hall University. He is the author of *Congressional Budgeting: A Representational Perspective* and has had articles published in the *Social Science Journal*, *Publius*, *Party Politics*, *Transportation Quarterly* and *White House Studies*.

David Nice is a professor of political science at Washington State University. Books written by Nice include *Public Budgeting*, *Policy Innovation in State Government*, *Amtrak*, *The Politics of Intergovernmental Relations* and *The Presidency*.

Gubernatorial Incapacity and Succession Provisions
By Brian J. Gaines and Brian D. Roberts

Very rarely are living governors replaced because of incapacity. The infrequency of such events is no excuse for ambiguous resolution mechanisms; yet, several states have gaps in their legal provisions. Clarity in the grounds and procedures for replacing a governor who can no longer perform the duties of office is difficult to achieve, but the alternative is to flirt with avertable crises. Below we highlight which states seem remiss, and we catalogue some pertinent issues, without endorsing any one model as the optimal approach to this knotty question.

In September 2003, Frank O'Bannon, the Democratic governor of Indiana, suffered a massive stroke. Early news stories reported that state officials had decided not to invoke the process for transferring authority to Lt. Gov. Joe Kernan (also a Democrat) until it became clear if there was any hope of O'Bannon recovering. The relevant language from Indiana's constitution is found in Article 5, sections 10(a) and (d):

(a) ...In case the Governor is unable to discharge the powers and duties of his office, the Lieutenant Governor shall discharge the powers and duties of the office as Acting Governor.

(d) Whenever the President pro tempore of the Senate and the Speaker of the House of Representatives file with the Supreme Court a written statement suggesting that the Governor is unable to discharge the powers and duties of his office, the Supreme Court shall meet within forty-eight hours to decide the question and such decision shall be final.

A day later, having consulted with the doctors treating O'Bannon, the Republican senate president pro tempore and Democratic house speaker wrote to the chief justice of the Indiana Supreme Court, and the court quickly ruled that Kernan should serve as acting governor, although O'Bannon would remain in office, entitled to salary and benefits. Five days later, O'Bannon passed away, and Kernan automatically succeeded him.

These unusual events, though traumatic for O'Bannon's family, did not constitute a political crisis. The transfer of authority was dignified, without any aura of legal ambiguity or partisan controversy. Gubernatorial successions arise in many ways, and Indiana's crisis was soon over-shadowed by the scandal-induced resignations of the governors of Connecticut and New Jersey. Every state except Hawaii has dealt with midterm gubernatorial vacancy, and succession at the apex of the executive branch is typically a smooth process, whether the precipitating event be a death, resignation under happy circumstance (e.g., following election or appointment to another office), forced resignation (e.g., following conviction of a crime or revelation of a scandal), or even impeachment, removal or recall. It is quite rare for a living governor to be too severely incapacitated to govern, but Indiana's experience is a reminder that rare events sometimes happen. Surprisingly, a number of states have lacunae in their legal frameworks for dealing with such gubernatorial incapacity, notwithstanding the fact that controversy and near-misses with constitutional crisis have arisen at the federal level and in several states. Here, we briefly review provisions for gubernatorial succession due to incapacity across all 50 states, in an effort to determine which are well-equipped to deal with such events, and which are vulnerable to crisis.

Recognition of the frailty of officials is longstanding: the federal constitution juxtaposes "inability to discharge the Powers and Duties of [the presidency]" with death, resignation and removal when broaching the line of succession in Article II, Section 1. However, nearly two centuries passed before the 25th Amendment filled out procedures for establishing "inability," the only inherently subjective condition of these four. The solution—also popular with states—was procedural rather than substantive. In lieu of any enumeration of conditions that constitute disability, most states (and the United States) specify procedures for replacement in the event of disability, thereby delegating discretion to individual decision-makers on a case-by-case basis. There are potential hazards in such discretion, particularly where natural partisan conflict can find its way into a determination of disability. Far more hazardous, though, is an absence of legal procedures for determining disability.

Table A lays out some key aspects of how the 50 states deal with incapacity in the governor. The first column lists constitutional provisions pertaining specifically to disability, and reveals that literally every state has at least some such language in its constitution. The word counts give a fairly crude indication of the level of detail in each state's provisions: sometimes a large number of words is deceptive insofar as the provisions are wordy, but not very detailed, or the section in question actually includes discussion of some aspect of succession other than disability (where possible, we provide a second disability-specific count in such cases). By contrast, low word counts reliably signal lack of specificity. For instance, the 53 words in Article III, Section 12 of the Alaska Constitution read simply:

> Whenever for a period of six months, a governor has been continuously absent from office or has been unable to discharge the duties of his office by reason of mental or physical disability, the office shall be deemed vacant. The procedure for determining absence and disability shall be prescribed by law.

The second column of the table lists statutory provisions that elaborate on the constitutional language about gubernatorial disability, and Alaska's cell is empty. The state Legislative Affairs Agency explains:

> To avoid a tedious recitation of procedures similar to those found in the 25th Amendment to the U.S. Constitution, the drafters of the constitution assigned to the legislature responsibility for specifying how the office of governor could be declared vacant. The legislature has not yet done so, which may be unfortunate if the task became complicated by the circumstances of a particular situation warranting the use of this section.[1]

"Unfortunate" seems an understatement, and Alaska is not alone; as Table A shows, by our count, about a third of the states similarly suffer from having "unclear" legal provisions on determination of gubernatorial disability.[2] Illinois is a surprising member of this club, since it has already weathered one political crisis stemming from the prolonged ill-health of a governor, and has dodged a bullet in recent memory. Gov. Henry Horner suffered a heart attack in November 1938, but clung to office through an extended convalescence rather than allow Lt. Gov. John Stelle, a fellow Democrat but also a hated rival, to take power. Unable to work for more than a few hours per day, Horner relied on a regency of unelected advisors, even as his foes launched an array of challenges.[3] In 1994, the possibility of a sudden gubernatorial transition again loomed. Just days after Lt. Gov. Bob Kustra had announced plans to resign, Gov. Jim Edgar underwent unscheduled, emergency heart surgery. Kustra then acted as

Edgar's proxy in budget negotiations, though, happily, the governor recovered quickly enough to sign the final spending bill from his hospital bed. Had Kustra resigned before chest pains seized Edgar, according to Article V, Section 6(a), that vacancy in the lieutenant governorship would have placed Democratic Attorney General Roland Burris first in the line of succession. In that event, a less speedy recovery by the governor might have precipitated a messy tussle for control.

A catalogue of all crises and near misses for all states would be very long indeed. At the dramatic end of the spectrum, in 1900, Kentucky saw William Goebel, the Democratic candidate for governor in a disputed election, shot, declared elected by the legislature, and then sworn in while hospitalized, only to pass away days later. In a more recent and more mundane case, Massachusetts Gov. Jane Swift—who had succeeded to the governorship when Paul Cellucci resigned to become ambassador to Canada—came under scrutiny while bedridden, awaiting the arrival of twins. Swift, a Republican, had to fend off allegations from Democrats serving on the Governor's Council that her physical absence from council meetings rendered her incapable of performing her constitutional duties.[4]

Given the many borderline or contested disability cases that did not result in succession, and many more near misses, determination of whether a chief executive is genuinely unable to perform duties is the crux of the matter, and the key column in Table A is the middle one, which identifies what actors take part in such determination. At a glance, one notes much variety. Indeed, this brief schematic cannot do justice to the diversity of procedures found across the nation. A few aspects seem particularly important.

How Many Actors (and Which ones) are Involved?

In most states, governors may designate themselves unfit to govern (presumably in anticipation of an expected medical crisis, or in the midst of a rapidly worsening condition). When others must make the declaration, one of the main protections against controversy is involvement of many actors, often representing all three branches of state government. Supreme courts are frequently included, more often as arbiters (as in Indiana) than as precipitators. South Dakota's constitution, though, provides its supreme court with "original and exclusive jurisdiction" to determine the question of disability. In justifying the designation of the supreme court as the body to "ascertain the truth" about any allegation of inability "unsound(ness of) mind," the drafters of Alabama's 1901 constitution explained, "The Committee can conceive of no safer body, no more august body, no body less liable to temptation to use the power for political gain or any other improper motive, than the Supreme Court of Alabama."[5]

Must the Designation be Bi-partisan?

In addition to being multi-member, supreme courts often (but not always) enjoy the appearance of non-partisanship. An alternative to ceding determination power to non-partisan actors is to ensure that the procedure used to determine disability involves a bipartisan group of actors. Requiring the involvement of a large array of actors has the effect of making it more likely that both major parties will take part, though numbers alone provide no guarantee of bi-partisanship. In Pennsylvania, state statute stipulates that the lieutenant governor and a majority of the governor's 26-member (as of 2004) cabinet make a determination of disability, but the cabinet is comprised of individuals appointed by the governor and confirmed by the state senate. The legislature enters the picture only in the event of a dispute about the governor's capacity to resume the power and duties of the office.

Can Succession Following from Disability Result in Partisan Changeover?

Almost all state lines of succession allow for party changeover at some depth. Although this is not a point inherently about disability, the prospect of a partisan turnover surely complicates consideration of an incumbent governor's fitness to stay on, given a dispute over disability. Accordingly, Table A includes a column showing the line of succession (and whether it is constitutionally or statutorily determined). The final column indicates how far down the line of succession party changeover can occur, and also provides examples in those states that have seen such party-switching successions. (To be clear, these cases did not necessarily involve disability, and all Civil War/Reconstruction switches were ignored). Indiana is unusual in the degree to which its laws mitigate *against* a change in gubernatorial party. First, the governor and lieutenant governor are elected on a common ticket. That is an increasingly common arrangement, and a clear insulation against partisan changeover, except in unusual circumstance. Furthermore, in the event of dual vacancies, Indiana requires the legislature to elect a replacement of the same party as the incumbent. It is only brand new changes in the constitution as of 2004—which broach

a line of succession for an interim governor while the legislature makes this choice—that permit a very temporary change of gubernatorial party stemming from disability.

In Pennsylvania, where the lieutenant governor also serves as president pro tempore of the senate, the potential for change in partisan control of the governorship has become more salient as two of the last three governors have either resigned (Tom Ridge) or temporarily relinquished their power (Bob Casey). The question of separation of powers is also raised, since the constitution requires the lieutenant governor to vote in the event of a tie vote in the Senate.[6] Concern over potential partisan shifts even further down the line of succession has recently prompted the Massachusetts legislature to consider a proposed constitutional amendment that would allow a governor who succeeded to the post from the office of lieutenant governor the capacity to appoint a new lieutenant governor subject to the confirmation of both legislative chambers.[7] In short, the shadow of partisan switches complicates every aspects of succession, including what mechanism for assessing gubernatorial incapacity is optimal.

Does the Successor Play a Role?

Section four of the 25th Amendment to the U.S. Constitution provides a role for the president's immediate successor, the vice president, in the determination of disability. Several states follow a similar practice. In Delaware, the immediate successor, while not in a position to make the determination unilaterally, could be a member of the opposite political party. There would appear to be some merit in excluding immediate successors from this process, so as to decrease the possibility of cabal. Alabama, for one, deliberately excludes the individual next in line to become governor from playing any part in rendering judgment on the fitness of the incumbent, a decision that the constitutional convention viewed as a "safeguard."

Is There Medical Involvement?

Another notable distinction among those states having clear provisions for the determination of disability is whether they require the involvement of individuals with medical expertise. States in this category include Georgia, Iowa, Nebraska and Oregon. As an example, Nebraska statutes designate the dean of the College of Medicine of the University of Nebraska and the chairperson of the Department of Psychiatry at the University of Nebraska Medical center as members of a three-person team who examine the governor and determine the issue of disability—a decision that requires unanimity among the examiners.[8] Iowa similarly lodges power to evaluate a seemingly disabled governor in a three-member body including "the person who is chief justice, the person who is director of mental health, and the person who is the dean of medicine at the state university of Iowa" and even elaborates, "Provided, if either the director or dean is not a physician…the director or dean may assign a member of the director's or dean's staff so licensed to assist and advise on the conference."[9]

Acting or Actual?

In Table A, for brevity, we finesse the discrepancy between an "acting" (where powers and duties, but not the office devolve) and "actual" governor (where both the powers and the office devolve). In many cases the distinction is far from trivial; and it can be an especially important consideration in the event of disability insofar as a living, but incapacitated governor might require health benefits. In Utah, a state that has a rather detailed process for determining disability, but very limited experience with midterm succession, considerable ambiguity on the acting-versus-actual point surrounded the transition from Gov. Mike Leavitt to Lt. Gov. Olene Walker upon Leavitt's acceptance of the office of administrator of the federal EPA in 2003. As of late 2004, the state's Constitutional Revision Commission was considering recommendations to clarify succession procedures.[10]

Conclusion

As we write, late in 2004, New Jersey's unusual gubernatorial succession law is making news. By most accounts the governor of New Jersey is among the strongest of the nation's chief executives. Excluding U.S. senators, the governor is the only statewide elected official. Vast appointment power allows the governor to select heads of executive departments, members of state and certain county commissions, judges and prosecutors. The reaches of power extend even into the legislative arena, where the governor is endowed not only with veto authority that requires a two-thirds majority in both chambers to counteract, but the capacity to request legislation for executive action in a manner that is favorable to pocket vetoes.[11] The extensive powers of the New Jersey governor are compounded by the state's succession laws. One of eight states without a separate lieutenant governor, New Jersey flouts traditional separation of powers principles by allowing (in the event of the absence, death or disability of the governor) the power of the governor to devolve upon

the president of the Senate *without* requiring this individual to relinquish his legislative post.[12] This scenario played out in 2001, as Senate President Donald DiFrancesco became acting governor following Gov. Christine Todd Whitman's departure to the Bush administration. The transition from DiFrancesco's acting governorship to the swearing-in of governor-elect Jim McGreevey in 2002 saw a week with an unprecedented four acting governors, including a farcical six-day stretch with both Republican and Democrat acting governors.[13] In the summer of 2004, McGreevey, in the midst of a scandal, precipitated another chaotic transition by announcing his resignation, but delaying it to prevent a special election for his successor. We would quickly concur that New Jersey's laws can use an overhaul; but, to give credit where due, it is not especially remiss in detailing how a stricken governor be evaluated. By contrast, many states simply have not dealt seriously with the issue.

Finally, we note that a special case of gubernatorial disability might occur in the course of a large-scale emergency wherein many other state officials are also afflicted. Since September 11, 2001, there has been renewed discussion of how American governments (federal and state) would cope with an attack or other disaster that disabled numerous officials simultaneously. Many states already have fairly specific provisions to allow continuity in the operations of state government in the event of some catastrophic event (terrorist attack, natural disaster, etc.). Most statutes of this nature have their origins in the cold war era, but a few states have enacted new statutes since the 9/11 attacks. Nevada offers one example,[14] and post-9/11 concern played a direct role when Virginia voters recently overwhelmingly supported a constitutional amendment adding an additional 14 potential successors to a line previously containing only three.[15] As officials and scholars revisit the question of how to handle the unthinkable in many states, they would do well also to re-examine their rules for handling an isolated emergency.

Inability, whether strictly medical or understood more broadly, is ambiguous and subjective in a way that death, resignation and removal are not, so clear provisions controlling how to determine when a governor should not retain office are critical. Those states that do have rules have, in many cases, passed a few trials. But the number of empirical data points is small, and it is not difficult to identify bothersome or problematic scenarios even in the states with detailed, modern constitutional and statutory provisions. Though rare, gubernatorial inability merits close attention.

Notes

[1] Gordon Harrison. *Alaska's Constitution: A Citizen's Guide*. 4th ed.(Juneau, AK: Alaska Legislative Affairs Agency, 2002), 80.

[2] We assembled Table A using LexisNexis and hardcopies of state codes and constitutions as well as interviews with officials in a number of states. Since constitutions and codes are constantly changing, we may have missed some provisions even with this multi-stage screening.

[3] Thomas B. Littlewood, *Horner of Illinois* (Evanston, IL: Northwestern University Press, 1969).

[4] *Boston Herald*, "Pregnant Pause Needed – Dems Remiss in Handling of Gov. Mom," 13 May 2001, Op.Ed., 23.

[5] *Official Proceedings of the Constitutional Convention of the State of Alabama, May 21st, 1901 to September 3rd, 1901*. Volume I (Wetumpka, AL: Wetumpka Printing Co., 1940), 482.

[6] George Strawley, "Senate's Top Republican Proposes New Rules for Lt. Governor," *Associated Press State and Local Wire*, 24 December 2002.

[7] *Boston Globe*, "Constitutional Questions," 11 February 2004, A22.

[8] R.R.S. Neb. § 84-127.

[9] Iowa Code 7.14.

[10] Nicole Warburton, "Guv's Succession May be Clarified," *Salt Lake Tribune*, 9 July 2004, B5. A determination was made that Walker assumed the full control of the power and responsibilities of the office.

[11] "Perspective: The Evolution of New Jersey's Gubernatorial Power," 25 *Seton Hall Legis. J.* 1 (2001): 5-6.

[12] Julia Nienaber Hurst, "Lieutenant Governors: Powerful in Two Branches," *The Book of the States* 2004 (Lexington, Ky: The Council of State Governments, 2004): 189.

[13] Mike Kelly, "Just Make us Proud; We're Longing for Return to Normalcy," *The Record* (Bergen County, NJ), 14 November 2004.

[14] Neb. Rev. St. § 239C.260.

[15] Michael Hardy, "Changes Secure Approval; Virginia Voters Back Two Amendments to State's Constitution," *Richmond Times-Dispatch*, 3 November 2004, A25. The previous list included only the lieutenant governor, attorney general and the speaker of the House. The amendment added the chairmen of the 14 standing committees in the Virginia House of Delegates.

About the Authors

Brian J. Gaines is an associate professor in the Department of Political Science and the Institute of Government and Public Affairs at the University of Illinois, Urbana-Champaign. He has served as a consultant for two Canadian Royal Commissions and for Polimetrix, Inc.

Brian D. Roberts is an assistant professor of Political Science and the director of the Cox School of Government at Principia College. From 1991 to 1994, he served as the director of research for the Texas Public Policy Foundation.

Table A
PROVISIONS FOR DISABILITY-BASED GUBERNATORIAL SUCCESSION IN THE 50 STATES

State	Constitutional article, section (total words)(a)	Statutory elaboration on disability	Actors involved in disability designation	Line of succession	Depth in line of succession for possible party switch
Alabama	V, 128 (297)	...	Any 2 in line of succession except successor, SC	LG, 6 more (C)	1 (1993)
Alaska	III, 12 (53)	...	Unclear	LG, apt. (C, S)	2 (unlikely) (none)
Arizona	V, 6 (206*)	...	Unclear	SS, 3 more (C)	1 (1988)
Arkansas	CA 6, 4 (96*)	21-1-304 (159)	Unclear	LG, 5(b) (C, S)	1 (1996)
California	V, 10 (105,* 62)	12070-12076 (259)	5-member commission, SC	LG, 6 more (C, S)	1 (1917)
Colorado	IV, 13[6] (137)	...	G; legislature, SC	LG, 4 more (C)	2 (unlikely) (none)
Connecticut	CA XXII, IV, 18c-h (869)	Vol. 1, 3, 31, 3-1a (370)	G; LG, 9-member council, SC, legislature	LG, PPT (C, S)	2 (1946)
Delaware	III, 20b (368)	...	G; 3-member board (incl LG), legislature	LG, 4 more (C)	1 (1895)(c)
Florida	IV, 3b (129)	...	G; 4 cabinet members, G, legislature, SC	LG, 6 more (C, S)	2 (none)
Georgia	V, IV (265)	...	Any 4 elected exec., SC, at least 3 physicians	LG, SH(b) (C)	1 (none)
Hawaii	V, 4 (147,* 43)	...	Unclear	LG, 7 more (C, S)	2 (none)
Idaho	IV, 12 (75,* 37)	67-805A[2] (43)	Unclear	LG, PPT, SH (C)	1 (none)
Illinois	V, 6c-d (136)	15 ILCS 5/0.01 (224*)	G; otherwise unclear	LG, 6 more (C, S)	2 (none)
Indiana	5, 10c-d (216)	...	G; PPT, SH, SC	LG, 6(b), leg-el (C)	2(b), no (none)
Iowa	IV, 17, 19 (248)	7.14 (362)	CJ, next in line of succession, 3-member board, G	LG, PPT, SH leg-el (C)	2 (none)
Kansas	I, 11 (167)	75-126 (147)	Unclear	LG, PPT, SH (C, S)	2 (none)
Kentucky	84 (286)	...	G; AG, SC	LG, PS (C)	2 (1834)(c)
Louisiana	IV, 17-18 (447)	...	G; 5/9 stwd elec. exec., G, legislature, SC	LG, 5 more (C)	1 (none)
Maine	V, 1, 14-15 (839,* 445)	...	G; legislature, SC; SS, SC	PPT, SH	1 (1959)
Maryland	II, 6 (851)	...	G; legislature, SC	LG, PS, leg. picks (C)	2 (1969)(c)
Massachusetts	XCI (459)	...	G; SC (or other body)	LG, 4 more (C)	2 (none)
Michigan	V, 26 (211,* 116)	...	G; PPT, SH, SC	LG, 2 more (C)	2 (none)
Minnesota	V, 5 (157)	4.06, c-e (383)	G, 3/4-member board, G, legislature	LG, 5 more (C, S)	2 (1915)(c)
Mississippi	V, 131 (319)	...	SS, SC	LG, PPT, SH (C)	1 (1876)
Missouri	IV, 11a-b (574)	...	G; 9-member board (LG), SC	LG, 6 more (C)	1 (none)
Montana	VI, 14[2-5] (235)	...	G; LG & AG, legislature	LG, PS, SH (C)	2 (none)
Nebraska	IV, 16 (197*)	84-127, 128 (353)	LG & 3-member board of medical and psych. experts	LG, SH (C)	2 (1960)
Nevada	V, 17-18 (230*)	223.080 (184*)	Unclear	LG, 3 more (C, S)	1 (none)
New Hampshire	II, 49-a (504)	...	G; AG & 5-member elected council, SC	PS, 3 more(b) (C)	1 (none)
New Jersey	V, 1[7-8] (284*)	...	G; legislature, SC	PS, 3 more (C, S)	1 (2001)
New Mexico	V, 7 (305*)	...	Unclear	LG, 7 more (C, S)	2 (1917)(c)
New York	V, 5-6 (455*)	...	Unclear	LG, 2 more (C)	2 (1829)(c)
North Carolina	III, 3 (329*, 197)	...	G; AG, legislature	LG, 10 more (C, S)	1 (none)
North Dakota	V, 11 (65*)	...	Unclear	LG, 4 more (C, S)	2 (1935)(c)
Ohio	III, 15, 22 (449*, 212)	...	G; legislature, SC	LG 6 more (C, S)	2 (1957)

See Footnotes at end of table

PROVISIONS FOR DISABILITY-BASED GUBERNATORIAL SUCCESSION IN THE 50 STATES — Continued

State	Constitutional article, section (total words)(a)	Statutory elaboration on disability	Actors involved in disability designation	Line of succession	Depth in line of succession for possible party switch
Oklahoma	VI, 15-16 (235*)	74, 8 (593)	G; PPT, SH, 6-member committee, legislature, SC	LG, PPT, SH (C, S)	1 (none)
Oregon	V, 8a (264*)	176.040, 176.050 (318)	G; SS,CJof SC, 2 medical experts	SS, 3 more (C)	1 (1909)
Pennsylvania	IV, 13 (65*)	71, 784.1-784.3 (333)	G; LG, Gov.'s Cabinet, legislature	LG, PPT, SH (C, S)	2 (1848)(c)
Rhode Island	IX, 9-10 (107*)	. . .	SC	LG, 4 more (C, S)	1 (none)
South Carolina	IV, 11-12 (431*, 334)	. . .	G; PPT & SH, AG, SS, Compt. Gen., legislature	LG, 5 more (C, S)	1 (none)
South Dakota	IV, 6 (188*)	. . .	SC	LG, 10 more (C, S)	2 (none)
Tennessee	III, 12 (70*)	8-1-109[b,1-2] (101)	G (to authorize power of atty,), otherwise unclear	LG, 4 more (C, S)	1 (none)
Texas	IV, 3a (249*)	. . .	Unclear	LG, 3 more (+ order of 14 ct. of appearls CJs) (C, S)	1 (none)
Utah	VII, 11 (538*, 167)	. . .	G; PS, SH, SC	LG, 5 more (C, S)	2 (none)
Vermont	II, 24 (161*)	. . .	Unclear	LG, 4 more (C, S)	1 (1991)
Virginia	V, 16 (559*, 341)	24.2-211 (341)	G; PPT, SH, AG, legislature	LG, 6 more (C, S)	1 (none)
Washington	III, 10 (378*)	. . .	Unclear	LG, 6 more (C)	1 (1919)
West Virginia	VII, 16 (133*)	. . .	Unclear	PS, 3 more	1 (none)
Wisconsin	V, 7-8 (222*)	17.025 (751)	7 member diasbility board that includes G (see 14.015 of statutes)	LG, 5 more (C, S)	2 (none)
Wyoming	IV, 6 (51*)	. . .	Unclear	SS, 7 more	1 (1949)

Source: Compiled by the authors from relevant constitutions, statutes and reference sources, 2004.

Key:
C—Constitutional provisions
CJ—Chief Justice
G—Governor
LG—Lieutenant Governor
PPT—President (Pro Tempore) of the Senate
PS—President of the Senate
S—Statute

SC—Supreme Court
SH—Speaker of the House
SS—Secretary of State
apt.—individual appointed into line of sucession by the governor, subject to legislative confirmation .
leg-el— individual elected by the legislature
(a) For those numbers followed by an asterick, the word count covers section with other details (e.g. succession in case of death).
(b) Successor takes power only on an interim or acting basis, pending special election.
(c) Occurred under a previous constitutional or statutory regime.

Table 4.1
THE GOVERNORS, 2005

State or other jurisdiction	Name and party	Length of regular term in years	Date of first service	Present term ends	Number of previous terms	Maximum consecutive terms allowed by constitution	Joint election of governor and lieutenant governor (a)	Official who succeeds governor	Birthdate	Birthplace
Alabama	Bob Riley (R)	4	1/03	1/07	…	2 (d)	No	LG	10/3/44	AL
Alaska	Frank H. Murkowski (R)	4	12/02	12/06	…	2	Yes	LG	3/28/33	WA
Arizona	Janet Napolitano (D)	4	1/03	1/07	…	2	(k)	SS	11/29/57	NY
Arkansas	Mike Huckabee (R)	4	7/96 (b)	1/07	1	2 (b)	No	LG	8/24/55	AR
California	Arnold Schwarzenegger (R)	4	11/03 (c)	1/07	…	2	No	LG	7/30/47	Aus.
Colorado	Bill Owens (R)	4	1/99	1/07	1	2	Yes	LG	10/22/50	TX
Connecticut	M. Jodi Rell (R)	4	7/04 (o)	1/07	…	…	Yes	LG	6/16/46	VA
Delaware	Ruth Ann Minner (D)	4	1/01	1/09	1	…	No	LG	1/17/35	DE
Florida	Jeb Bush (R)	4	1/99	1/07	1	2 (d)	Yes	LG	2/11/53	TX
Georgia	Sonny Perdue (R)	4	1/03	1/07	…	2	No	LG	12/20/46	GA
Hawaii	Linda Lingle (R)	4	12/02	12/06	…	2	Yes	LG	6/4/53	MO
Idaho	Dirk Kempthorne (R)	4	1/99	1/07	1	…	No	LG	10/29/51	CA
Illinois	Rod R. Blagojevich (D)	4	1/03	1/07	…	…	Yes	LG	12/10/56	IL
Indiana	Mitch Daniels (R)	4	1/05	1/09	…	2 (f)	Yes	LG	4/7/49	PA
Iowa	Thomas J. Vilsack (D)	4	1/99	1/07	1	…	Yes	LG	12/13/50	PA
Kansas	Kathleen Sebelius (D)	4	1/03	1/07	…	2	Yes	LG	5/15/48	OH
Kentucky	Ernie Fletcher (R)	4	12/03	12/07	…	2	Yes	LG	11/12/52	KY
Louisiana	Kathleen Babineaux Blanco (D)	4	1/04	1/08	…	2	No	PS	12/15/42	LA
Maine	John Baldacci (D)	4	1/03	1/07	…	2	(k)	PS	1/30/55	ME
Maryland	Robert L. Ehrlich Jr. (R)	4	1/03	1/07	…	2	Yes	LG	11/25/57	MD
Massachusetts	Mitt Romney (R)	4	1/03	1/07	…	…	Yes	LG	3/12/47	MI
Michigan	Jennifer Granholm (D)	4	1/03	1/07	…	2	Yes	LG	2/5/59	BC
Minnesota	Tim Pawlenty (R)	4	1/03	1/07	…	…	Yes	LG	11/27/60	MN
Mississippi	Haley Barbour (R)	4	1/04	1/08	…	2	No	LG	10/22/47	MS
Missouri	Matt Blunt (R)	4	1/05	1/09	…	2	No	LG	11/20/70	MO
Montana	Brian Schweitzer (D)	4	1/05 (e)	1/09	…	2 (g)	Yes	LG	9/4/55	MT
Nebraska	Dave Heineman (R)	4	1/05	1/07	…	2	Yes	LG	5/12/48	NE
Nevada	Kenny Guinn (R)	4	1/99	1/07	1	2	No	LG	8/24/36	AR
New Hampshire	John Lynch (D)	2	1/05	1/07	…	…	(k)	PS	11/25/52	MA
New Jersey	Richard Codey (D)	4	11/04 (i)	1/06	…	2	(k)	PS	11/27/46	NJ
New Mexico	Bill Richardson (D)	4	1/03	1/07	…	2	Yes	LG	11/15/47	CA
New York	George E. Pataki (R)	4	1/95	1/07	2	…	Yes	LG	6/24/45	NY
North Carolina	Michael F. Easley (D)	4	1/01	1/09	1	2 (f)	No	LG	3/23/50	NC
North Dakota	John Hoeven (R)	4	12/00	12/08	1	…	Yes	LG	3/13/57	ND
Ohio	Bob Taft (R)	4	1/99	1/07	1	2 (f)	Yes	LG	1/8/42	OH
Oklahoma	Brad Henry (D)	4	1/03	1/07	…	2	No	LG	6/10/63	OK
Oregon	Ted Kulongoski (D)	4	1/03	1/07	…	2	(k)	SS	11/5/40	MO
Pennsylvania	Edward G. Rendell (D)	4	1/03	1/07	…	2	Yes	LG	1/5/44	NY
Rhode Island	Don Carcieri (R)	4	1/03	1/07	…	2	No	LG	12/16/42	RI
South Carolina	Mark Sanford (R)	4	1/03	1/07	…	2	No	LG	5/28/60	FL

See footnotes at end of table.

THE GOVERNORS, 2005 — Continued

State or other jurisdiction	Name and party	Length of regular term in years	Date of first service	Present term ends	Number of previous terms	Maximum consecutive terms allowed by constitution	Joint election of governor and lieutenant governor (a)	Official who succeeds governor	Birthdate	Birthplace
South Dakota	Mike Rounds (R)	4	1/03	1/07	...	2	Yes	LG	10/24/54	SD
Tennessee	Phil Bredesen (D)	4	1/03	1/07	...	2	No	SpS (l)	11/21/43	NJ
Texas	Rick Perry (R)	4	12/00 (h)	1/07	1	...	No	LG	3/4/50	TX
Utah	Jon M. Huntsman Jr. (R)	4	1/05	1/09	...	...	Yes	LG	3/26/60	CA
Vermont	Jim Douglas (R)	2	1/03	1/07	1	...	No	LG	6/21/51	MA
Virginia	Mark R. Warner (D)	4	1/02	1/06	...	(j)	No	LG	12/14/54	IN
Washington	Christine Gregoire (D)	4	1/05	1/09	...	...	No	LG	3/24/57	WA
West Virginia	Joe Manchin III (D)	4	1/05	1/09	...	2	(k)	PS	8/24/47	WV
Wisconsin	Jim Doyle (D)	4	1/03	1/07	...	...	Yes	LG	11/23/45	D.C.
Wyoming	Dave Freudenthal (D)	4	1/03	1/07	...	2 (g)	(k)	SS	10/12/50	WY
American Samoa	Togiola Tulafono (D)	4	4/03 (m)	1/09	1	2	Yes	LG	2/28/47	AS
Guam	Felix P. Camacho (R)	4	1/03	1/07	...	2	Yes	LG	10/30/57	GU
No. Mariana Islands	Juan N. Babauta (R)	4	1/02	1/06	...	2 (n)	Yes	LG	9/7/53	CNMI
Puerto Rico	Anibal Acevedo-Vila (PDP)	4	1/05	1/09	...	...	(k)	SS	2/13/63	PR
U.S. Virgin Islands	Charles W. Turnbull (D)	4	1/99	1/07	1	(f)	Yes	LG	2/5/35	VI

Sources: The Council of State Governments survey, December 2004.

Key:

D — Democrat

PDP — Popular Democratic Party

R — Republican

LG — Lieutenant Governor

SS — Secretary of the Senate

PS — President of the Senate

SpS — Speaker of the Senate

. . . — Not applicable

(a) The following also choose candidates for governor and lieutenant governor through a joint nomination process: Florida, Kansas, Maryland, Minnesota, Montana, North Dakota, Ohio, Utah, American Samoa, Guam, No. Mariana Islands and U.S. Virgin Islands.

(b) Governor Huckabee, as lieutenant governor, became Governor in July 1996 after Governor Jim Guy Tucker resigned. He was elected to a full four-year term in November 1998.

(c) Governor Schwarzenegger was sworn in on November 17, 2003 after defeating Governor Gray Davis in a recall election.

(d) Limited to 8 consecutive years in office.

(e) Governor Heineman, as lieutenant governor, was sworn-in as Nebraska's governor on Friday, January 21, 2005 after Governor Johanns resigned on January 20, 2005 upon being confirmed as the United States Secretary of Agriculture.

(f) After two consecutive terms as Governor, the candidate must wait four years before becoming eligible to run again.

(g) Absolute limit of eight years of service out of every 16 years.

(h) Lt. Gov. Perry was sworn in on December 21, 2000 to complete President George W. Bush's term as governor of Texas.

(i) As Senate President Governor Codey took over the additional role of acting governor when Governor James E. McGreevey resigned from office on November 15, 2004. Codey previously served as acting governor from January 12, 2002 until January 15, 2002, when he shared the acting governor responsibilities with Senate Co-President, John Bennett, during the time between the expiration of Senate President Donald T. DiFrancesco's term (when he was also serving as acting governor) and the swearing in of the newly elected governor, James E. McGreevey.

(j) Governor cannot serve immediate successive terms.

(k) No lieutenant governor.

(l) Official bears the additional title of " lieutenant governor."

(m) Governor Tulafono, as lieutenant governor, became Governor in April 2003 after Governor Sunia's death.

(n) Absolute two-term limitation, but terms need not be consecutive.

(o) Lieutenant Governor Rell was sworn in as governor on July 1, 2004 after Governor John Rowland resigned.

Table 4.2
THE GOVERNORS: QUALIFICATIONS FOR OFFICE

State or other jurisdiction	Minimum age	State citizen (years)	U.S. citizen (years) (a)	State resident (years) (b)	Qualified voter (years)
Alabama	30	7	10	. . .	★
Alaska	30	7	7	7	★
Arizona	25	5	10	. . .	. . .
Arkansas	30	★	★	7	. . .
California	18	. . .	5	5	★
Colorado	30	. . .	★	2	. . .
Connecticut	30	. . .	★	★	★
Delaware	30	. . .	12	6	. . .
Florida	30	. . .	★	7	★
Georgia	30	. . .	15	6	★
Hawaii	30	. . .	. . .	5	★
Idaho	30	. . .	★	2	. . .
Illinois	25	3	★	3	★
Indiana	30	. . .	5	5	★
Iowa	30	. . .	2	2	. . .
Kansas	. . .	. . .	. . .	. . .	. . .
Kentucky	30	6	. . .	6	. . .
Louisiana	25	5	5	5	★
Maine	30	. . .	15	5	. . .
Maryland	30	. . .	(c)	5	5
Massachusetts	. . .	. . .	. . .	7	. . .
Michigan	30	. . .	★	★	4
Minnesota	25	. . .	★	1	★
Mississippi	30	. . .	20	5	★
Missouri	30	. . .	15	10	. . .
Montana	25	★	★	★	. . .
Nebraska	30	5	5	5	. . .
Nevada	25	2	2	2	★
New Hampshire	30	. . .	. . .	7	. . .
New Jersey	30	. . .	20	7	. . .
New Mexico	30	. . .	★	5	★
New York	25	★	★	1	. . .
North Carolina	30	. . .	5	2	★
North Dakota	30	. . .	★	5	★
Ohio	18	. . .	★	★	★
Oklahoma	31	. . .	. . .	. . .	★
Oregon	30	. . .	★	3	★
Pennsylvania	30	. . .	★	7	. . .
Rhode Island	18	30 days	★	30 days	★
South Carolina	30	5	5	5	. . .
South Dakota	21	★	★	2	. . .
Tennessee	30	7	★	. . .	. . .
Texas	30	. . .	★	5	. . .
Utah	30	5	★	5	★
Vermont	18	1	. . .	4	★
Virginia	30	. . .	★	5	5
Washington	18	. . .	★	★	★
West Virginia	30	5	★	1	★
Wisconsin	18	. . .	★	★	★
Wyoming	30	★	★	5	. . .
American Samoa	35	. . .	★	5	. . .
Guam	30	. . .	5	5	★
No. Mariana Islands	35	. . .	★	10	★
Puerto Rico	35	5	5	5	. . .
U.S. Virgin Islands	30	. . .	5	5	★

Sources: The Council of State Governments' survey of governor's offices, December 2004.

Key:

★— Formal provision; number of years not specified.

. . .— No formal provision.

(a) In some states you must be a U.S. citizen to be an elector, and must be an elector to run.

(b) In some states you must be a state resident to be an elector, and must be an elector to run.

(c) *Crosse v. Board of Supervisors of Elections* 243 Md. 555, 221A.2d431 (1966)—opinion rendered indicated that U.S. citizenship was, by necessity, a requirement for office.

Table 4.3
THE GOVERNORS: COMPENSATION, STAFF, TRAVEL AND RESIDENCE

State or other jurisdiction	Salary	Governor's office staff (a)	Access to state transportation			Travel allowance	Official residence
			Automobile	Airplane	Helicopter		
Alabama	$96,361	43	★	★	★	(b)	★
Alaska	85,766	70	★	★	...	(k)	★
Arizona	95,000	39	★	★	...	(b)	...
Arkansas	75,296	55	★	★	★	★	★
California	175,000	86	★	...	...	(c)	(d)
Colorado	90,000	39	★	★	...	(e)	★
Connecticut	150,000	30	★	★	★	(e)	★
Delaware	132,500	32	★	...	...	...	★
Florida	120,171	310	★	★	...	(b)	★
Georgia	127,303	87	★	★	★	(e)	★
Hawaii	94,780	67	★	★	★	★	★
Idaho	98,500	24	★	★	...	★(e)	...
Illinois	150,691	130	★	★	★	(b)	★
Indiana	95,000	34	★	★	★	(b)	★
Iowa	107,482	19	★	...	...	(b)	★
Kansas	98,331	24	★	★	...	(b)	★
Kentucky	127,146	80	★	★	★	(b)	★
Louisiana	94,532	117 (l)	★	★	★	(b)	★
Maine	70,000	19	★	★	★	(b)	★
Maryland	135,000	84	★	★	★	(e)	★
Massachusetts	135,000 (j)	78	★	...	★	(b)	...
Michigan	177,000	56	★	★	...	(e)	★
Minnesota	120,311	45	★	★	★	(e)	★
Mississippi	122,160	29	★	★	★	(e)	★
Missouri	120,087	38	★	★	...	(c)	★
Montana	93,089	18	★	★	★	(b)	★
Nebraska	85,000	9	★	★	...	(b)	★
Nevada	117,000	(g)	★	★	...	(c)	★
New Hampshire	96,060	23	★	...	...	(e)	★ (f)
New Jersey	157,000	156	★	...	★	$61,000	★
New Mexico	110,000	27	★	★	★	$79,200 (c)	★
New York	179,000	180	★	★	★	(b)	★
North Carolina	121,391	76	★	★	★	$11,500	★
North Dakota	85,506	17	★	★	...	(b)	★
Ohio	126,485	60	★	★	★	(f)	★
Oklahoma	110,298	34	★	★	...	(b)	★
Oregon	93,600	29	★	...	...	(e)	★
Pennsylvania	155,753	68	★	★	...	(b)	★
Rhode Island	105,194	49	★	...	...	N.A.	...
South Carolina	106,078	22	★	★	...	(b)	★
South Dakota	103,222	22.5	★	★	...	(b)	(m)
Tennessee	85,000	36	★	★	★	(e)	★
Texas	115,345	266	★	★	★	(b)	★
Utah	101,600	16.5	★	★	★	$76,000	★
Vermont	133,162	14	★	...	...	★	...
Virginia	124,855	43	★	★	★	(b)	★
Washington	139,087	36	★	★	...	(e)	★
West Virginia	90,000	56	★	★	★	(h)	★
Wisconsin	131,768 (n)	39.75	★	★	...	(e)	★
Wyoming	130,000	8	★	★	...	(b)	★
American Samoa	50,000	23	★	...	...	$105,000 (c)	★
Guam	90,000	42	★	...	...	$218/day	★
No. Mariana Islands	70,000	16	★	...	...	(e)(i)	★
Puerto Rico	70,000	352	★	...	...	...	★
U.S. Virgin Islands	80,000	86	★	...	...	(b)	★

See footnotes at end of table.

THE GOVERNORS: COMPENSATION, STAFF, TRAVEL AND RESIDENCE— Continued

Sources: The Council of State Governments' survey, December 2004.
Key:
★—Yes
. . .—No
N.A.—Not available.
(a) Definitions of "governor's office staff vary across the states–from general office support to staffing for various operations within the executive office.
(b) Reimbursed for travel expenses. Alabama–reimbursed for travel expenses. Arizona–receives up to $38/day for meals based on location; receives per diem for lodging out-of-state; default $28/day for meals and $50/day lodging in-state. Florida–reimbursed at same rate as other state officials: in state, choice between $50 per diem or actual expenses; out of state, actual expenses. Indiana–Statute allows $12,000 but due to budget cuts the amount has been reduced to $9,800 and reimbursed for actual expenses for travel/lodging. Illinois–no set allowance. Iowa –limit set in annual office budget. Kentucky–mileage at same rate as other state officials. Kansas- reimbursed for actual expenses. Louisiana–reimbursed for actual expenses. Massachusetts–As necessary. Montana–reimbursed for actual and necessary expenses. Nebraska–reimbursed for travel expenses. New York–reimbursed for actual and necessary expenses. North Dakota–reimbursed at state rate. Oklahoma–reimbursed for actual expenses. Pennsylvania–reimbursed for reasonable expenses. Texas

–full reimbursement. Virginia–reimbursed for travel related to the duties of office. Wyoming–$85/day or actual. U.S. Virgin Islands–reimbursed 100 percent.
(c) Amount includes travel allowance for entire staff. Missouri amount not available. California–$145,000 in state; $36,000 out of state. Nevada– these figures include travel expenses for governor and staff, $30,308 in state; $21,576 out of state. New Mexico–$79,200 (in state $45,600, out of state $33,600).
(d) In California–provided by Governor's Residence Foundation, a non-profit organization which provides a residence for the governor of California. No rent is charged; maintenance and operational costs are provided by California Department of General Services.
(e) Travel allowance included in office budget.
(f) Set administratively.
(g) Sixteen active and 21 authorized staff.
(h) Included in general expense account.
(i) Governor has a "contingency account" that can be used for travel expenses and expenses in other departments or other projects.
(j) Governor Romney waives his salary.
(k) Travel allowance- Alaska-$42/day per diem plus actual lodging expenses.
(l) Figure does not include 37 part time employees.
(m) Governor's residence is under construction.
(n) Governor Doyle remits a portion of his salary to the state.

Table 4.4
THE GOVERNORS: POWERS

State or other jurisdiction	Budget making power		Item veto power					Authorization for reorganization through executive order (a)
	Full responsibility	Shares responsibility	Governor has item veto power on all bills	Governor has item veto power on appropriations only	Governor has no item veto power	Item veto—2/3 legislators present or 3/5 elected to override	Item veto—majority legislators elected to override	
Alabama	...	...			★ (m)		★	★
Alaska	★ (b)	...				★		★ ★
Arizona	...	★	★			★		★ ★
Arkansas	... (b)	...	★			★		...
California	★ (b)	...	★			★		★ ★
Colorado	★	...	★			★		...
Connecticut	... (b)	★	★ ★			★		...
Delaware	★ (b)	...	★ ★			★		★
Florida	★	...		★ (d)		★		...
Georgia	...	★		★ ★		★		★
Hawaii	★	...	★		★			...
Idaho	★	...	★			★		...
Illinois	...	★	★		★			...
Indiana	★	...			★			★ ★ (f)
Iowa	...	★		★		★		★ ★
Kansas	★	...	★			★ ★		★ ★ (l)
Kentucky	★ (b)	...		★		★ (k)		★ ★
Louisiana	...	★		★ ★		★		★ ★
Maine	★	...	★			★	★	★ ★
Maryland	★	...	★			★		★ ★
Massachusetts	★	...	★			★ (k)		★ (g)
Michigan	★ (b)	★		★		★ (k)		★ ★
Minnesota	... (b)	★		★		★ (k)		★ ★
Missouri	★ (b)	...	★ ★	★		★		★
Montana	★	...	(j)		★ ★	★		(e)
Nebraska	★	...	★ ★	★ ★		★		...
Nevada	★	...			★		★	...
New Hampshire	★ (b)	...	★			★		...
New Jersey	★	...	★			★		...
New Mexico	★	...	★			★		...
New York	...	★	★ ★			★		...
North Carolina	★ (b)	...			★	★		★ ★
North Dakota	★	...		★		★		★
Ohio	★	...		★ ★		★		★ ★
Oklahoma	...	★			★		★	...
Oregon	★ (b)	...		★		★ ★		...
Pennsylvania	★	...		★		★ ★		★ ★
Rhode Island	★ (b)	...			★			★
South Carolina	...	★		★		★		...

See footnotes at end of table.

THE GOVERNORS: POWERS — Continued

State or other jurisdiction	Budget making power		Item veto power					Authorization for reorganization through executive order (a)
	Full responsibility	Shares responsibility	Governor has item veto power on all bills	Governor has item veto power on appropriations only	Governor has no item veto power	Item veto—2/3 legislators present or 3/5 elected to override	Item veto—majority legislators elected to override	
South Dakota	...	★	...	★		★	...	★
Tennessee	...	★	...	★		...	★	★
Texas	...	★	...	★		★	...	★
Utah	★	...	...	★		★	...	...
Vermont	★	...	...	...	★	...	...	★
Virginia	★	...	...	★		★	...	★
Washington	★	...	★ (h)	★		★	...	...
West Virginia	★ (b)	...	...	★		★	...	...
Wisconsin	...	★	...	★ (i)		★	...	...
Wyoming	...	★	★	...		...	...	...
American Samoa	★	...	...	...	...	...	...	★
Guam	...	...	...	...	...	...	...	★
No. Mariana Islands	★	★	...	★		★	...	★
Puerto Rico	★ (b)	...	...	...	★	...	...	...
U.S. Virgin Islands	★	...	...	★		★	...	★

Sources: The Council of State Governments' survey of governor's offices, December 2004.

Key:
★—Yes; provision for.
...—No; not applicable.

(a) For additional information on executive orders, see Table 4.5.
(b) Full responsibility to propose; legislature adopts or revises and governor signs or vetoes.
(c) Includes only executive branch officials who are popularly elected either on a constitutional or statutory basis (elected members of state boards of education, public utilities commissions, university regents, or other state boards or commissions are also included); the number of agencies involving theses officials is also listed.
(d) Governor may only veto a specific appropriation within a general appropriation bill or an entire bill. 2/3 of both houses can override.

(e) Statutory.
(f) Limited. Sole authority to grant clemency after recomendation of Iowa Board of Parole.
(g) Authorization for reorganization provided for in state constitution.
(h) Governor has veto power of selections for nonappropriations and item veto in appropriations.
(i) In Wisconsin, governor has "partial" veto over appropriation bills. The partial veto is broader than item veto.
(j) Amendatory veto while legislature is in session.
(k) 2/3 of elected legislators of each house to override.
(l) Only for agencies and office within the Governor's Office.
(m) Governor may amend one or more provisions of any bill, but legislature may override by a majority vote.

Table 4.5
GUBERNATORIAL EXECUTIVE ORDERS: AUTHORIZATION, PROVISIONS, PROCEDURES

State or other jurisdiction	Authorization for executive orders	Procedures								Provisions		
		Civil defense disasters, public emergencies	Energy emergencies and conservation	Other emergencies	Executive branch reorganization plans and agency creation	Create advisory, coordinating, study or investigative committees/commissions	Respond to federal programs and requirements	State personnel administration	Other administration	Filing and publication procedures	Subject to administrative procedure act	Subject to legislative review
Alabama	S,I (b)	★	★	★		★	★	★	★	(pp)		
Alaska	C	★(a)	★(a)	★(a)	★	★				★(c)		★
Arizona	I	★(a)	★(a)	★(a)	★	★	★		★	★	★	
Arkansas	C	★	★		★	★	★	★	★	★		
California	S		★		★	★	★	★	★	★		
Colorado	S,I	★	★	★(f)	★	★	★	★	★ (gg)	★		
Connecticut	S	★	★	★	★	★	★	★	★	★(c)		
Delaware	C	★	★	★(h)	★	★	★	★	★ (ii)(jj)(ll)	★		
Florida	C,S	★(mm)	★	★	★	★	★	★ (mm)	★			
Georgia	S,I (qq)	★	★	★	★	★	★	★	★	★		
Hawaii	S	★	★	★	★	★	★	★	★	★		
Idaho	S		I	I		I	I		(rr)	★		
Illinois	C,S	★	★	★	★	I	I	★	★	★		★
Indiana	C,S, Case Law	★	★		(limited)	★	★	★	★	★		
Iowa	S (ss)		★		★	★	★	★				
Kansas	C,S	★	★	★(m)	★	★	★	★	★ (n)(o)(p)	★(c)	★	(ee)
Kentucky	C,S	★	★	★	★	★	★	★	★	★(l)	★	★
Louisiana	C,S (g)	★	★	★	★	★		★	★	★		
Maine	(u)	★	★			(s)			★(v)	★		
Maryland	C,S	★	★	★	★	★	★	★	★	★		
Massachusetts	C,S	★	★	★	★	★	★	★	★	★		
Michigan	C	★	★		★	★	★	★	★ (y)	★	★	
Minnesota	S	★	★	I	★	★	★	★	I	★ (c)(l)	★	★(w)
Mississippi	C	★	★		★	★	★	★	★	★	★	★(w)
Missouri	C,S,Common Law	★	★	★(cc)	(dd)	★	★	★	★ (w)	★(w)		★(w)(bb)
Montana	S	★	★	★	★	★	★	★	★	★(c)		
Nebraska	C,S	★	★	★		★	★		★	★		
Nevada	S	★	S	I		★			I			
New Hampshire	S	★	★	★		★	★		★(o)	★		
New Jersey	C,S,I	★	★(a)	★(cc)		★			★ (aa)	★		
New Mexico	C	★	★	★	★	★	★		★			★(w)
New York	C,S	S	S	S	S	★	S	S	I	★	★	★
North Carolina	S,I	S	S	S	S,C	I	S	S	S,C	S		★
North Dakota	S,I	★	★	★		★			(j)(p)(q)(r)(y)(aa)	★		
Ohio	S,I (z)	★	★	★	★	★	★			★		

See footnotes at end of table.

GUBERNATORIAL EXECUTIVE ORDERS: AUTHORIZATION, PROVISIONS, PROCEDURES — Continued

State or other jurisdiction	Authorization for executive orders	Procedures								Provisions		
		Civil defense disasters, public emergencies	Energy emergencies and conservation	Other emergencies	Executive branch reorganization plans and agency creation	Create advisory, coordinating, study or investigative committees/commissions	Respond to federal programs and requirements	State personnel administration	Other administration	Filing and publication procedures	Subject to administrative procedure act	Subject to legislative review
Oklahoma	C	★	★	…	★	★	★	★	★	★	…	…
Oregon	C,S	★	★	★	★	★	★	…	…	★ (c)	…	…
Pennsylvania	C,S	★	★ (a)	★ (l)(t)(v)(ff)	★	★	…	★ (k)	★ (ff)	★ (c,l)	…	…
Rhode Island	S (a)	★	★ (a)	★	★ (a)	★	…	…	★	★	…	…
South Carolina	S	★	★	★	…	★	…	…	★	★	…	★
South Dakota	C	★	★	★	★	★	★	★	…	★ (c)	…	…
Tennessee	S	★	★	★	★	★	★	★	★	★ (c)	…	…
Texas	I	★	★	★	★	★	★	★	…	…	…	…
Utah	S	★	★	…	★ (ii)	★	★	★	★	…	…	…
Vermont	S,I	★	…	★	…	★	★	★	…	…	…	★(jj)
Virginia	S,I	★	★	★ (g)	★ (kk)	★	…	★	…	…	…	…
Washington	S	★	★	…	…	★	★	★	…	…	…	…
West Virginia	C,S	★	★	★	…	★	★	…	★ (o)(aa)(dd)	★ (c)	…	…
Wisconsin	C,S	★	…	★	…	…	★	★	★	…	…	…
Wyoming	(e)	…	…	★	★	★	★	★	★	★	…	…
American Samoa	C,S	★	★	★	★ (hh)	★	★	★	★	★ (oo)	★ (oo)	…
Guam	C	★	★	…	(hh)	★	S	★	★	★	I	…
No. Mariana Islands	C	★	I	★	C	S,I	S	★	★	S	…	…
Puerto Rico	I	★	★	★	C	★	★	★	★	★	…	…
U.S. Virgin Islands	C	★	★	★	★	★	★	★	★	★	…	★

See footnotes at end of table.

GUBERNATORIAL EXECUTIVE ORDERS: AUTHORIZATION, PROVISIONS, PROCEDURES — Continued

Sources: The Council of State Governments' survey, December 2004.

Key:

C—Constitutional
S—Statutory
I—Implied
★—Formal provision.
. . .—No formal provision.
(a) Broad interpretation of gubernatorial authority.
(b) Authorization for executive orders granted by constitution, statute, case law, common law, and implied.
(c) Executive orders must be filed with secretary of state or other designated officer. In Idaho, must also be published in state general circulation newspaper.
(d) Governor required to keep record in office. In Maine, also sends copy to Legislative Counsel, State Law Library, and all county law libraries in state.
(e) No specific authorization granted, general authority only.
(f) To regulate distribution of necessities during shortages.
(g) Broad grant of authority.
(h) Local financial emergency, shore erosion, polluted discharge and energy shortage.
(i) To reassign state attorneys and public defenders.
(j) To suspend certain officials and/or other civil actions.
(k) To transfer allocated funds.
(l) Filing.
(m) To give immediate effect to state regulation in emergencies.
(n) To control administration of state contracts and procedures.
(o) To impound or freeze certain state matching funds.
(p) To reduce state expenditures in revenue shortfall.
(q) To designate game and wildlife areas or other public areas.
(r) Appointive powers.
(s) Executive Orders generally may issue with respect to both emergent and non-emergent matters falling within the Executive Branch.
(t) For fire emergencies.

(u) Authority implied statutorily and by course of practice.
(v) To control procedures for dealing with public.
(w) Reorganization plans and agency creation.
(x) If an energy emergency is declared by the state's Executive Council or legislature.
(y) To assign duties to lieutenant governor, issue writ of special election.
(z) Executive authority implied except for emergencies which are established by statute.
(aa) To administer and govern the armed forces of the state.
(bb) Reorganization plans ans agency creation and for meeting federal program requirements.
(cc) To declare air pollution emergencies.
(dd) Relating to local governments.
(ee) Only for ERO's.
(ff) To transfer funds in an emergency.
(gg) Matters relating to the enforcement and administration of Connecticut law
(hh) Can reorganize, but not create.
(ii) Subject to legislative approval.
(jj) Only if reorganization order filed with the legislature.
(kk) To shift agencies between secretarial offices; all other reorganizations require legislative approval.
(ll) By executive order, governor may also suspend collection of fines and forfeitures, grant reprieves not exceeding 60 days and with approval of 3 cabinet members, grant full or conditional pardons, restore civil rights, commute punishment and remit fines and forfeiture for offenses.
(mm) Governor may also delineate an interjurisdictional area to prepare, plan, mitigate or respond to emergency.
(nn) Governor may also declare an office vacant.
(oo) If executive order fits definition of rule.
(pp) The Secretary of State also signs. Notices are sent to both houses of the legislature and a number of other state officials.
(qq) Governor customarily exercises powers via executive order; authorization implied via selected statutes.
(rr) Some implied.
(ss) Authorization for executive orders granted by statute, case law, common law and implied.

Table 4.6
STATE CABINET SYSTEMS

State or other jurisdiction	Authorization for cabinet system				Criteria for membership			Number of members in cabinet (including governor)	Frequency of cabinet meetings	Open cabinet meetings
	State statute	State constitution	Governor created	Tradition in state	Appointed to specific office (a)	Elected to specified office (a)	Gubernatorial appointment regardless of office			
Alabama	★	...	...	...	...	...	★	29	Monthly	★
Alaska	...	...	★	...	★	...	...	18	Gov.'s discretion	★ (b)
Arizona	...	...	★	...	★	...	★	38	Monthly	...
Arkansas	...	...	...	★	★	...	...	46	Monthly	...
California	★	...	★	...	★	...	★	13	Every two weeks	...
Colorado	...	★	...	...	★	...	...	21	Gov.'s discretion	★
Connecticut	...	★	...	...	★	...	...	27	Gov.'s discretion	...
Delaware	★	...	...	...	★	...	★	19	Gov.'s discretion	...
Florida	...	★	...	...	...	★	...	7	Every two weeks	★
Georgia	---------- (d) ----------									
Hawaii	★	★	...	...	★	...	★	25	Monthly	...
Idaho	---------- (d) ----------							22	Gov.'s discretion	...
Illinois	★	...	...	...	...	...	★	18	N.A.	...
Indiana	...	...	★	...	...	...	★	16	Bi-monthly	...
Iowa	★	...	...	...	★	...	...	32	Quarterly	...
Kansas	★	...	...	...	...	...	★	14	Bi-weekly	...
Kentucky	★	...	★	...	★	...	★	10	Weekly	...
Louisiana	★	...	★	★	★	...	...	14	Monthly	...
Maine	...	...	...	(i)	...	...	★	21	Weekly	...
Maryland	★	...	...	...	★	...	...	28	Every other week	...
Massachusetts	★	...	...	...	★	...	...	10	Bi-weekly	...
Michigan	...	...	★	★	★	...	★	24	Monthly	...
Minnesota	...	...	★	...	★	...	...	25	Regularly	...
Mississippi	---------- (d) ----------									
Missouri	...	★	...	★	★	...	...	17	Gov.'s discretion	...
Montana	★	...	★	...	★	...	...	17	Gov.'s discretion	★
Nebraska	...	...	★	★	★	...	★	29	Monthly	...
Nevada	---------- (d) ----------							22	At call of the governor	...
New Hampshire	---------- (d) ----------									
New Jersey	★	★	...	...	★	...	...	19	Gov.'s discretion	...
New Mexico	★	...	...	★	★	...	...	17	Weekly	...
New York	...	...	...	★	...	...	★	75	Gov.'s discretion	...
North Carolina (f)	★	★	★	...	...	...	★	10	Monthly	...
North Dakota	...	...	★	...	...	...	★	18	Monthly	★
Ohio	★	...	...	...	★	...	...	24	Gov.'s discretion	★
Oklahoma	★	...	...	...	...	...	★	10–15	Monthly	...
Oregon	---------- (d) ----------									
Pennsylvania	★	...	...	...	★ (c)	...	...	19	Gov.'s discretion	★
Rhode Island	---------- (d) ----------							14	Gov.'s discretion	Gov.'s discretion
South Carolina	★	...	...	...	★ (c)	...	...	15	Monthly	★
South Dakota	★	★	...	...	★	...	...	19	Monthly	★
Tennessee	★	...	...	...	★	...	...	28	Monthly	...
Texas	---------- (d) ----------									
Utah	★	...	★	(h)	★	...	...	31	Monthly	...
Vermont	★	...	...	...	★	...	...	7	Gov.'s discretion	...
Virginia	★	...	...	...	★	...	...	13	Weekly	...
Washington	...	...	★	...	★	...	...	28	Bi-weekly, weekly during legislative session	...
West Virginia	...	...	★	★	★	...	...	10	Weekly	...
Wisconsin	★	...	...	...	★	...	...	16	Gov.'s discretion	★
Wyoming	★	...	...	...	...	...	★	20	Monthly	...
American Samoa	★	★	...	...	★	...	★	16	Gov.'s discretion	...
Guam	...	...	★	...	★	...	...	55	Bi-monthly	...
No. Mariana Islands	...	★	...	...	★	...	...	16	Gov.'s discretion	★
Puerto Rico	★	★	...	...	★	...	★	(j)	Monthly	...
U.S. Virgin Islands	...	★	...	...	★	...	...	21	Monthly	★

See footnotes at end of table.

STATE CABINET SYSTEMS — Continued

Sources: The Council of State Governments' survey, December 2004.
Key:
★—Yes
. . . —No
N.A.—Not available
(a) Individual is a member by virtue of election or appointment to a cabinet-level position.
(b) Except when in executive session.
(c) With the consent of the senate.
(d) No formal cabinet system. In Idaho, however, sub-cabinets have been formed, by executive order; the chairs report to the governor.
(e) Sub-cabinets meet quarterly.
(f) Constitution provides for a Council of State made up of elective state administrative officials, which makes policy decisions for the state while the cabinet acts more in an advisory capacity.
(g) Cabinet consists of agencies, created by legislation; directors of agencies appointed by the governor.
(h) In Utah, department heads serve as cabinet; meets at discretion of governor, but when first appointed, department heads also require advice and consent of Senate.
(i) Authority implied statutorily and by course of practice.Some of those department heads along with other officials compose the Governor's Cabinet.
(j) 81 executive agencies, 11 government support agencies of the executive and 48 public corporations.
(k) No legal authorization, informal governor tradition. Members are appointed at the governor's discretion.

Table 4.7
THE GOVERNORS: PROVISIONS AND PROCEDURES FOR TRANSITION

State or other jurisdiction	Legislation pertaining to gubernatorial transition	Appropriation available to gov-elect ($)	Provision for:					
			Gov-elect's participation in state budget for coming fiscal year	Gov-elect to hire staff to assist during transition	State personnel to be made available to assist gov-elect	Office space in buildings to be made available to gov-elect	Acquainting gov-elect staff with office procedures and routing office functions	Transfer of information (files records, etc.)
Alabama	...	...	★	●	●	●	●	●
Alaska	●	★ (l)	...	●	●	●	●	★
Arizona	...	...	★	...	●	●	●	●
Arkansas	●	30,000	...	●	...	●	●	●
California	★	450,000	★	★	★	★	●	●
Colorado	★	10,000	...	★	★	★	★	★
Connecticut	★	0	...	★	...	★	●	★
Delaware	★	30,000	●	★	●	●	●	●
Florida	...	300,000	★	★	●	★	●	●
Georgia	★	50,000	★	★	★	★	★	★
Hawaii	★	50,000	★	★	★	★	●	●
Idaho	★	15,000	★	★	★	★	★	★
Illinois	...	...	...	★	...	★	★	★
Indiana	★	40,000	...	...	...	★	★	★
Iowa	★ (d)	10,000	★	★	(i)	●	●	★
Kansas	★	150,000 (g)	★	★	★	★	★	★
Kentucky	★	200,000	★	★	★	★	★	★
Louisiana	★	65,000	★	★	★ (f)	★ (h)	...	(c)
Maine	●	5,000	...	●	●	★	●	●
Maryland	★	●	...	★	★	★	★	★
Massachusetts	●	●	●	...	●	●	●	★
Michigan	...	1,200,000	...	★	...	...	★	★
Minnesota	★	0	★	...	★	★	●	★
Mississippi	★	60,000	★	★	★	★	★	★
Missouri	★	100,000	★	★	●	★	●	(i)
Montana	★	50,000	★	★	★	★	★	★
Nebraska	★	60,879	★	★	★	★	★	★
Nevada	★	Reasonable amount	★	●	●	●	●	★ (d)
New Hampshire	★	75,000	★	★	★	★	★	...
New Jersey	★	Unspecified	★	★	★	★	●	★
New Mexico	★	(b)	★	★	●	★	●	●
New York	...	...	...	...	★	★	★	★
North Carolina	★	80,000 (j)	(k)	★	★	★	●	●
North Dakota	●	10,000	(m)	(a)	●	...	●	★
Ohio	★	Unspecified (e)	●	★	●	...	●	★
Oklahoma	...	30,000	★	...	...	...	...	●
Oregon	★	...	★	★	★	★	★	★
Pennsylvania	★	100,000	...	★	●	●	●	...
Rhode Island	...	●	●	· (a)	●	●	●	●
South Carolina	...	●	●	●	●	●	●	●
South Dakota	●	●	●	●	●	●	●	●
Tennessee	★	★	●	★	★	★	●	●
Texas	●	●	●	●	●	●	●	●
Utah	...	(varies)	●	●	●	●	●	●
Vermont	...	(p)	★	●	●	●	●	...
Virginia	...	●	●	●	★ (i)	★ (i)	●	★
Washington	★	★	●	★	★	★	●	●
West Virginia	...	●	...	●	...	●	●	●
Wisconsin	★	Unspecified	★	★	★	★	★	★
Wyoming	...	●	...	●	●	●	●	●
American Samoa	...	Unspecified	★ (n)	★	●	●	★	●
Guam	★	(o)	...	...	★	★	★	...
No. Mariana Islands	★	Unspecified	...	★	★	★	★	★
Puerto Rico	...	250,000 (j)	...	●	●	●	●	●
U.S. Virgin Islands	★	100,000	...	★	★	★	★	★

See footnotes at end of table.

THE GOVERNORS: PROVISIONS AND PROCEDURES FOR TRANSITION — Continued

Sources: The Council of State Governments' survey, December 2004.

Key:

. . .—No provisions or procedures.

★—Formal provisions or procedures.

—No formal provisions, occurs informally.

N.A.—Not applicable.

(a) Governor usually hires several incoming key staff during transition.

(b) Legislature required to make appropriation; no dollar amount stated in legislation.

(c) In Louisiana—Statute directs the records and associated historical records of any governor to be transferred to the custody of the state archivist.

(d) Pertains only to funds.

(e) Determined in budget.

(f) No unclassified employees are made available; however, a list of civil service employees is made available within 60 days.

(g) Transition funds are used by both the incoming and outgoing administrations.

(h) The $65,000 may be used to rent space.

(i) Activity is traditional and routine, although there is no specific statutory provision.

(j) Inaugural expenses are paid from this amount.

(k) New governor can submit supplemental budget.

(l) Varies.

(m) Responsible for submitting budget for coming biennium.

(n) Can submit reprogramming or supplemental appropriation measure for current fiscal year.

(o) Appropriations given upon the request of governor-elect.

(p) Governor-elect entitled to 70% of Governor's salary.

Table 4.8
IMPEACHMENT PROVISIONS IN THE STATES

State or other jurisdiction	Governor and other state executive and judicial officers subject to impeachment	Legislative body which holds power of impeachment	Vote required for impeachment	Legislative body which conducts impeachment trial	Chief justice presides at impeachment trial (a)	Vote required for conviction	Official who serves as acting governor if governor impeached (b)	Legislature may call special session for impeachment
Alabama	★	H	maj. mbrs.	S	...	Majority of elected mbrs.	LG	★
Alaska	★	S	2/3 mbrs.	H	(c)	2/3 mbrs.	LG	★
Arizona	★ (d)	H	maj. mbrs.	S	★ (e)	2/3 mbrs.	SS	★
Arkansas	★	H	maj. mbrs.	S	★	2/3 mbrs.	LG	...
California	★	H	...	S	...	2/3 mbrs.	LG	...
Colorado	★	H	maj. mbrs.	S	★	2/3 mbrs.	LG	...
Connecticut	★	H	...	S	★	2/3 mbrs.	LG	...
Delaware	★	H	2/3 mbrs.	S	★ (f)	2/3 mbrs.	LG	...
Florida	★	H	2/3 mbrs.	S	★ (f)	2/3 mbrs.	LG	★
Georgia	★	H	...	S	★ (e)	2/3 mbrs.	LG	★ (g)
Hawaii	★	H	maj. mbrs.	S	...	2/3 mbrs.	LG	...
Idaho	★	H	2/3 mbrs.	S	★	2/3 mbrs.	LG	...
Illinois	★	H	2/3 mbrs.	S	...	2/3 mbrs.	LG	★
Indiana	★ (u)	H	2/3 mbrs.	S	...	2/3 mbrs.	LG	...
Iowa	★	H	...	S	...	2/3 mbrs.	LG	...
Kansas	★	H	... (m)	S	...	2/3 mbrs.	LG	...
Kentucky	★	H	maj. mbrs.	S	★	2/3 mbrs. present	LG	...
Louisiana	★	H	2/3 mbrs. elected	S	★	2/3 mbrs. elected	LG	★ (h)
Maine	★	H	...	S	★	2/3 mbrs. present	PS	...
Maryland	★	H	maj. mbrs.	S	...	2/3 mbrs.	LG	...
Massachusetts	★	H	maj. mbrs.	S	★	...	LG	★
Michigan	★	H	maj. mbrs.	S (i)	★	2/3 mbrs.	LG	...
Minnesota	★	H	maj. mbrs.	S	...	2/3 mbrs. present	LG	...
Mississippi	★	H	2/3 mbrs. present	S	★	2/3 mbrs. present	LG	...
Missouri	★	H	...	S (j)	(j)	(j)	LG	...
Montana	★	H	2/3 mbrs.	S	★	2/3 mbrs.	LG	★
Nebraska	★ (d)	S (k)	maj. mbrs.	(l)	(l)	2/3 mbrs. of sup.court	LG	...
Nevada	★	H	maj. mbrs.	S	★	2/3 mbrs.	LG	...
New Hampshire	★	H	...	S	★	...	PS	...
New Jersey	★	H	maj. mbrs.	S	★	2/3 mbrs.	PS	★
New Mexico	★	H	maj. mbrs.	S	★	2/3 mbrs.	LG	★
New York	★	H	maj. mbrs.	S	★	2/3 mbrs. present	LG	★
North Carolina	★	H	...	S	★	2/3 mbrs. present	LG	★
North Dakota	★ (d)	H	maj. mbrs.	S	★	2/3 mbrs.	LG	...
Ohio	★	H	maj. mbrs.	S	★	2/3 mbrs. present	LG	...
Oklahoma	★ (n)	H	...	S	★	2/3 mbrs. present	SS	★
Oregon	...		...	(o)	...	...	LG	...
Pennsylvania	★	H	maj. mbrs.	S	...	2/3 mbrs. present	LG	★
Rhode Island	★	H	1/4 mbrs. (p)	S	★	2/3 mbrs. present	LG	...
South Carolina	★	H	2/3 mbrs.	S	★	2/3 mbrs.	LG	...

See footnotes at end of table.

IMPEACHMENT PROVISIONS IN THE STATES — Continued

State or other jurisdiction	Governor and other state executive and judicial officers subject to impeachment	Legislative body which holds power of impeachment	Vote required for impeachment	Legislative body which conducts impeachment trial	Chief justice presides at impeachment trial (a)	Vote required for conviction	Official who serves as acting governor if governor impeached (b)	Legislature may call special session for impeachment
South Dakota	★ (d)	H	maj. mbrs.	S	★	2/3 mbrs.	LG	★
Tennessee	★	H	maj. mbrs.	S	★	2/3 mbrs. (q)	PS	★
Texas	★ (d)	H	maj. mbrs.	S	...	2/3 mbrs. present	LG	...
Utah	★ (d)	H	2/3 mbrs.	S	★	2/3 mbrs.	LG	★
Vermont	★	H	2/3 mbrs.	S	...	2/3 mbrs. present	LG	...
Virginia	★	H	...	S	...	2/3 mbrs. present	LG	★
Washington	★ (d)	H	maj. mbrs.	S	★	2/3 mbrs.	LG	★
West Virginia	★	H	...	S	★	2/3 mbrs.	PS	★
Wisconsin	★	H	maj. mbrs.	S	...	2/3 mbrs.	LG	...
Wyoming	★	H	2/3 mbrs.	S	★	2/3 mbrs.	SS	...
Dist. of Columbia	...	(r)	...	(r)	...	...	...	...
American Samoa	★ (s)	H	2/3 mbrs.	S	★	2/3 mbrs.	...	...
Guam	...	(r)	...	(r)	...	...	...	...
No. Mariana Islands	★ (t)	H	2/3 mbrs.	S	...		LG	★
Puerto Rico	★ (t)	H	2/3 mbrs.	S	★	3/4 mbrs.	SS	★
U.S. Virgin Islands	...	(r)	...	(r)	...	...	...	...

Sources: The Council of State Governments' survey December 2004.

Key:

★—Yes; provision for.

...—Not specified, or no provision for.

H—House or Assembly (lower chamber).

S—Senate.

LG—Lieutenant Governor

PS—President or Speaker of the Senate

SS—Secretary of state.

(a) Presiding justice of state court of last resort. In many states, provision indicates that chief justice presides only on occasion of impeachment of governor.

(b) For provisions on official next in line on succession if governor is convicted and removed from office, refer to Chapter 4, "The Governors."

(c) An appointed Supreme Court justice presides.

(d) With exception of certain judicial officers. In Arizona and Washington - justices of courts not of record. In Nevada and Utah - justices of the peace. In North Dakota and South Dakota - county judges, justices of the peace, and judicial magistrates. In Oklahoma - all judicial officers not serving on the Supreme Court.

(e) Should the Chief Justice be on trial, or otherwise disqualified, the Senate shall elect a judge of the Supreme Court to preside.

(f) Except in a trial of the chief justice, in which case the governor shall preside.

(g) Special sessions of the General Assembly shall be limited to a period of 40 days unless extended by 3/5 vote of each house and approved by the Governor or unless at the expiration of such period an impeachment trial

of some officer of state government is pending, in which event the House shall adjourn and the Senate shall remain in session until such trial is completed.

(h) In Louisiana - not specified; both the governor and the legislature appear to have authority to call a special session for impeachment.

(i) House elects three members to prosecute impeachment.

(j) All impeachments are tried before the state Supreme Court, except that the governor or a member of the Supreme Court is tried by a special commission of seven eminent jurists to be elected by the Senate. A vote of 5/7 of the court of special commission is necessary to convict.

(k) Unicameral legislature; members use the title "senator".

(l) Court of impeachment is composed of chief justice and supreme court. A vote of 2/3 of the court is necessary to convict.

(m) No statute, simple majority is the assumption.

(n) Includes justices of Supreme Court. Other judicial officers not subject to impeachment. seven eminent jurists to be elected by the Senate. A vote of 5/7 of the court of special commission is necessary to convict.

(o) No provision for impeachment. Public officers may be tried for incompetence, corruption, malfeasance, or delinquency in office in same manner as criminal offenses.

(p) Vote of 2/3 members required for an impeachment of the governor.

(q) Vote of 2/3 of members sworn to try the officer impeached.

(r) Removal of elected officials by recall procedure only.

(s) Governor, lieutenant governor.

(t) Governor and Supreme Court justices.

(u) Judges not included.

Table 4.9
CONSTITUTIONAL AND STATUTORY PROVISIONS FOR
NUMBER OF CONSECUTIVE TERMS OF ELECTED STATE OFFICIALS
(All terms last four years unless otherwise noted)

State or other jurisdiction	Governor	Lt. Governor	Secretary of state	Attorney general	Treasurer	Auditor	Comptroller	Education	Agriculture	Labor	Insurance
Alabama	2	2	2	2	2	...	...	...	2	...	...
Alaska	2 (a)	2	(b)	...	(w)	...	...	...	...	...	...
Arizona	2 (a)	(e)	2 (a)	2 (a)	2 (a)	...	...	2 (a)	...	...	...
Arkansas	2	2	2	2	2	...	...	...	...	...	...
California	2	2	2	2	2	...	2	2	...	...	...
Colorado	2	2	2	2	2	...	...	...	...	...	...
Connecticut	N	N	N	N	N	...	N	...	...	...	...
Delaware	2 (f)	2	...	N	N	N	...	...	...	...	N
Florida	2	2	...	2	N (g)	...	2	N	N	...	(g)
Georgia	2 (a)	N	N	N	...	...	...	N	N	N	N
Hawaii	2	2	(b)	...	...	...	...	...	...	...	...
Idaho	N	N	N	N	2	...	N	N	...	...	...
Illinois	N	N	N	N	N	...	N	...	...	...	...
Indiana	(h)	2	2	...	(h)	...	2 (i)	...	...	...	...
Iowa	N	N	N	N	N	N	...	...	...	...	...
Kansas	2	N	N	N	...	...	...	...	...	...	...
Kentucky	2	2	2	2	2	2	...	...	2	2	...
Louisiana	2 (a)	N	N	N	N	...	...	N	N	...	N
Maine	2 (a)	(k)	...	(j)	...	...	...	...	...	...	...
Maryland	2 (a)	2	...	N	...	...	N	...	...	...	...
Massachusetts	N	N	N	2	N	N	...	...	...	...	...
Michigan	2	2	2	2	...	...	...	...	...	...	...
Minnesota	N	N	N	N	(l)	N	...	...	...	...	(m)
Mississippi	2 (f)	2 (a)	N	N	N	N	...	...	...	...	...
Missouri	2 (f)	N	N	N	2 (f)	N	...	...	...	...	...
Montana	2 (n)	2 (n)	2 (n)	2 (n)	...	N	...	2 (n)	...	...	...
Nebraska	2 (a)	2 (a)	N	N	2 (a)	2 (a)	...	...	...	...	...
Nevada	2	2	2	2	2	...	2	...	...	...	...
New Hampshire	(o)	(k)	...	...	...	...	...	...	...	...	...
New Jersey	2 (a)	(k)	...	...	...	...	...	...	...	...	...
New Mexico	2 (a)	2 (a)	2 (a)	2 (a)	2 (a)	2 (a)	...	...	...	...	...
New York	N	N	...	N	...	N (c)	N	...	...	...	...
North Carolina	2 (a)	(b)	N	N	N	N	...	N	N	N	N
North Dakota	N	N	N (q)	N (q)	N	N	...	N	N (q)(r)	N (q)	N
Ohio	2 (a)	2	2	2	2	2	2	...	...	...	...
Oklahoma	2 (a)	N	...	N	2 (a)	N	...	2 (a)	...	2 (a)	N
Oregon	(h)	(d)	(h)	N	(h)	...	...	...	...	...	...
Pennsylvania	2	2	...	2 (a)	2 (s)	2 (a)	...	...	...	...	...
Rhode Island	2	2 (a)	2 (a)	2 (a)	2 (a)	...	...	...	...	...	...
South Carolina	2 (a)	2	N	N	N	...	N	N	N	...	...
South Dakota	2 (a)	2 (a)	2 (a)	2 (a)	2 (a)	...	2	2 (a)	...	...	...
Tennessee	2 (a)	(k)	...	(y)	...	...	...	...	...	...	...
Texas	N	N	...	N	(c)	...	N	...	...	...	...
Utah	N	N	(b)	N	N	N	...	...	...	...	...
Vermont	(o)	(o)	(o)	(o)	(o)	(o)	...	...	...	...	...
Virginia	(t)	(u)	...	(u)	...	...	...	...	...	...	...
Washington	N	N	N	N	N	N	...	N	...	...	...
West Virginia	2	N (k)	N	N	N	...	N	...	N	...	...
Wisconsin	N	N	N	N	N	...	...	N	...	...	...
Wyoming	N (n)	(d)	N	...	N	...	2	N	...	...	...
Dist. of Columbia	N (v)	2	...	...	...	...	...	...	...	...	...
American Samoa	2	2	(b)	...	...	...	(p)	...	...	...	...
Guam	2 (a)	2	(b)	...	...	...	(x)	...	...	...	...
No. Mariana Islands	(h)	N	...	...	...	...	(p)	...	...	...	(m)
Puerto Rico	N	(e)	...	...	...	...	...	...	...	...	...
U.S. Virgin Islands	2 (a)	N	(c)	...	(e)	...	(e)	...	...	...	(b)

See footnotes at end of table.

CONSTITUTIONAL AND STATUTORY PROVISIONS FOR
NUMBER OF CONSECUTIVE TERMS OF ELECTED STATE OFFICIALS — Continued

Source: The Council of State Governments surveys October and December 2004 and State constitutions and statutes, October 2002.

Note: All terms last four years unless otherwise noted. Footnotes specify if a position's functions are performed by an appointed official under a different title.

Key:

N—No provision specifying number of terms allowed.

. . . — Position is appointed or elected by governmental entity (not chosen by the electorate).

(a) After two consecutive terms, must wait four years and/or one full term before being eligible again.

(b) Lieutenant Governor performs this function.

(c) Comptroller performs this function.

(d) Secretary of State is next in line to the governorship.

(e) Finance Administrator performs function.

(f) Absolute two-term limitation, but not necessarily consecutive.

(g) Chief Financial Officer performs this function as of January 2003 and there is no limit to the number of terms.

(h) Eligible for eight out of any period of twelve years.

(i) State auditor performs this function.

(j) Serves 2 year term and is eligible to serve 4 terms.

(k) President or Speaker of the Senate is next in line of succession to the governorship. In Tennessee, Speaker of the Senate has the statutory title " Lieutenant Governor."

(l) Office of the State Treasurer was abolished on the first Monday in January 2003.

(m) Commerce administrator performs this function.

(n) Eligible for eight out of sixteen years.

(o) Serves two-year term, no provision specifying the number of terms allowed.

(p) State treasurer performs this function.

(q) The terms of the office of the elected officials are four years, except that in 2004 the agricultural commissioner, attorney general, secretary of state and the tax commissioner are elected to a term of two years.

(r) Constitution provides for a secretary of agriculture and labor. However, the legislature was given constitutional authority to provide for (and has provided for) a department of labor distinct from agriculture, and a commissioner of labor distinct from the commissioner of agriculture.

(s) Treasurer must wait four years before being eligible to the office of auditor general.

(t) Cannot serve consecutive terms, but after 4 year respite can seek re-election.

(u) Provision specifying individual may hold office for an unlimited number of terms.

(v) Mayor.

(w) Deputy Commissioner of Department of Revenue performs function.

(x) General services administrator performs function.

(y) Term is for eight years and official is appointed by judges of the State Supreme Court.

Table 4.10
SELECTED STATE ADMINISTRATIVE OFFICIALS: METHODS OF SELECTION

State or other jurisdiction	Governor	Lieutenant governor	Secretary of state	Attorney general	Treasurer	Adjutant general	Administration	Agriculture	Auditor	Banking
Alabama	CE	CE	CE	CE	CE	GS	G	SE	CE	GS
Alaska	CE	CE	(a-1)	GB	AG	GB	GB	AG	L	AG
Arizona	CE	(a-2)	CE	CE	CE	GS	GS	GS	L	GS
Arkansas	CE	CE	CE	CE	CE	G	G	G	CE	GS
California	CE	CE	CE	CE	CE	GS	. . .	G	GB	GS
Colorado	CE	CE	CE	CE	CE	GS	GS	GS	L	CS
Connecticut	CE	CE	CE	CE	CE	GE	GE	GE	L	GE
Delaware	CE	CE	GS	CE	CE	GS	GS	GS	CE	GS
Florida	CE	CE	GS	CE	CE (dd)	G	GS	CE	L	CE
Georgia	CE	CE	CE	CE	G	G	G	CE	(i)	G
Hawaii	CE	CE	(a-1)	GS	GS	GS	(x)	GS	CL	AG
Idaho	CE	CE	CE	CE	CE	GS	GS	GS	LS	GS
Illinois	CE	CE	CE	CE	CE	GS	GS	GS	SL	B
Indiana	CE	CE	CE	SE	CE	G	G	LG	G	G
Iowa	CE	CE	CE	CE	CE	GS	GS	CE	CE	GS
Kansas	CE	CE	CE	CE	SE	GS	GS	GS	LS	GS
Kentucky	CE	CE	CE	CE	CE	G	CG	CE	CE	G
Louisiana	CE	CE	CE	CE	CE	GS	GS	CE	L	GLS
Maine	CE	(o)	CL	CL	CL	G	G	G	N.A.	G
Maryland	CE	CE	GS	CE	CL	G	GS (a-16)	GS	LS	AG
Massachusetts	CE	CE	CE	CE	CE	G	G	CG	CE	G
Michigan	CE	CE	CE	CE	GS	GS	GS	B	CL	GS
Minnesota	CE	CE	CE	CE	(mm)	GS	GS	GS	CE	A
Mississippi	CE	CE	CE	CE	CE	GE	GS	SE	CE	GS
Missouri	CE	CE	CE	CE	CE	G	GS	GS	CE	AGS
Montana	CE	CE	CE	CE	GS	GS	GS	G	CE	A
Nebraska	CE	CE	CE	CE	CE	GS	GS	GS	CE	GS
Nevada	CE	CE	CE	CE	CE	G	G	BA	LS	A
New Hampshire	CE	(o)	CL	GC	CL	GC	GC	GC	N.A.	GC
New Jersey	CE	(o)	GS	GS	GS	GS	N.A.	BG	L	GS
New Mexico	CE	CE	CE	CE	CE	G	GS (a-16)	B	CE	G
New York	CE	CE	GS	CE	A	G	. . .	GS	CE (a-9)	GS
North Carolina	CE	CE	SE	CE	CE	A	G	CE	CE	G
North Dakota	CE	CE	CE	CE	CE	G	. . .	CE	CE	GS
Ohio	CE	CE	CE	CE	CE	CE	GS	GS	CE	(a-7)
Oklahoma	CE	CE	A	CE	CE	GS	. . .	GS	CE	GS
Oregon	CE	(a-2)	CE	SE	CE	G	GS	GS	SS	. . .
Pennsylvania	CE	CE	GS	CE	CE	GS	G	GS	CE	CS
Rhode Island	SE	SE	CE	SE	SE	GB	GB	CS	LS	CS
South Carolina	CE	CE	CE	CE	CE	CE	B	CE	BA	CE
South Dakota	CE	CE	CE	CE	CE	GS	GS	GS	L	CG
Tennessee	CE	(o) (y)	CL	CT	CL	G	G (a-16)	G	SL (a-9)	G
Texas	CE	CE	G	CE	CE (a-9)	G	A	SE	L	B
Utah	CE	CE	CE (a-1)	CE	CE	G	GS	GS	CE	GS
Vermont	CE	CE	CE	CE	CE	CL	G	G	CE	G
Virginia	CE	CE	GB	CE	GB	GB	GB	GB	SL	GB
Washington	CE	CE	CE	CE	CE	GS	GS	GS	CE	GS
West Virginia	CE	(o)	CE	CE	CE	GS	GS	CE	CE	GS
Wisconsin	CE	CE	CE	CE	CE	G	GS	GS	LS	A
Wyoming	CE	(a-2)	CE	G	CE	G	GS	GS	CE	A
American Samoa	CE	CE	(a-1)	GB	GB	N.A.	GB	GB	N.A.	N.A.
Guam	CE	CE	. . .	CE	CS	GS	GS	GS	N.A.	GS
No. Mariana Islands	CE	CE	. . .	GS	CS	. . .	G	. . .	GB	C
U.S. Virgin Islands	SE	SE	SE (a-1)	GS	GS	GS	GS	GS	GS	LG

Sources: The Council of State Governments' survey of state personnel agencies, January 2004 and January 2005.

Note: The chief administrative officials responsible for each function were determined from information given by the states for the same function as listed in *State Administrative Officials Classified by Function*, 2003, published by The Council of State Governments.

Key:
N.A.—Not available.
. . . — No specific chief administrative official or agency in charge of function.
CE—Constitutional, elected by public.
CL—Constitutional, elected by legislature.
SE—Statutory, elected by public.
SL—Statutory, elected by legislature.
L—Selected by legislature or one of its organs.
CT—Constitutional, elected by state court of last resort.
CP—Competitve process.

Appointed by:
G—Governor
GS—Governor
GB—Governor
GE—Governor
GC—Governor
GD—Governor
GLS— Governor
GOC—Governor & Council or cabinet
LG—Lieutenant Governor
LGS—Lieutenant Governor
AT—Attorney General
SS— Secretary of State
C—Cabinet Secretary
CG—Cabinet Secretary

Approved by:
Senate (in Nebraska, unicameral legislature)
Both houses
Either house
Council
Departmental board
Appropriate legislative committee & Senate

Senate

Governor

SELECTED STATE ADMINISTRATIVE OFFICIALS: METHODS OF SELECTION — Continued

State or other jurisdiction	Budget	Civil rights	Commerce	Community affairs	Comptroller	Consumer affairs	Corrections	Economic development	Education	Election administration
Alabama	CS	...	G	G	CS	CS	G	G (a-8)	B	CS
Alaska	G	GB	GB	GB	AG	...	GB	AG	GD	AG
Arizona	L	AT	GS	GS (a-7)	A	AT	GS	GS (a-7)	CE	CE (a-2)
Arkansas	A	...	GS	GS	G	A	B	GS	BG	CE (a-2)
California	G	...	...	GS	CE	G	GS	...	CE	CE
Colorado	G	CS	G	GS	C	CE	GS	G	AB	CS
Connecticut	CS	GE	GE	GE	CE	GE	GE	GE	BG	CS
Delaware	GS	CG	GS (a-2)	...	CG	AT	GS	GS	GS	GS
Florida	G	AB	N.A.	GS	CE (dd)	A	GS	(a-28)	GS	A
Georgia	G	G	BG	BG	CE	G	GD	N.A.	CE	A
Hawaii	GS	B	GS	N.A.	GS	A	GS	GS	B	CL
Idaho	GS	GS	GS	A	CE	CE (a-3)	B	A	CE	CE
Illinois	G	GS	GS	GS (a-7)	CE	CE (a-3)	GS	GS (a-7)	B	B
Indiana	G	G	LG	G	CE	AT	G	LG	CE	(k)
Iowa	GS	GS	...	GS	...	A	GS	GS	GS	A
Kansas	G	GS	GS	A	C	AT	GS	(m)	B	(n)
Kentucky	G	B	GC	G	CG	CE (a-3)	G	GC	B	B
Louisiana	A	A	GS	A	GS	AG	GS	GS	BG	CE
Maine	C	BA	G (a-11)	...	C	C	G	G	G	SS
Maryland	GS	G	GS	A	CE	A	AGS	GS	B	B
Massachusetts	CG	G	G	G	G	G	CG	G	B	SS (e)
Michigan	GS	GS	GS	N.A.	CS	N.A.	GS	N.A.	B	(s)
Minnesota	(mm)	GS	GS	GS (a-11)	(mm)	A	GS	GS	GS	CE (a-2)
Mississippi	GS	...	SE	A	GS	A	GS	GS	BS	A (nn)
Missouri	AGS	AGS	GS (a-11)	(d)	A	CE (a-3)	GS	GS	BG	SS
Montana	G	CP	GS	CP	CP	CP	GS	G	CE	SS
Nebraska	A	B	GS (a-11)	A	A	CE (a-3)	GS	GS	B	A
Nevada	(a-5)	G	G	...	CE	A	G	GD	B	(z)
New Hampshire	GC	CS	GC	G	AGC	AGC	GC	AGC	B	CL (a-2)
New Jersey	GS	A	GS	GS	(a-6)	A	GS	G	GS	A
New Mexico	G	G	GS (a-11)	G	...	G	GS	GS	B	G
New York	G	GS	GS	GS (a-2)	CE	GS	GS	GS	B	B
North Carolina	G	A	G	A	G	(d)	G	A	CE	G
North Dakota	(r)	G	G	CE	(r)	AT	G	G (a-7)	CE	SS
Ohio	GS	GS	GS	...	CE	(a-7)	GS	GS	B	GB
Oklahoma	A	A	G	G	A	GS	GS	GS	SE	A
Oregon	A	A	GS	G	A	GS	GS	GS	SE	A
Pennsylvania	G	B	GS	AG	G	AT	GS	GS	GS	C
Rhode Island	AG	B	G (a-11)	CS	CS	SE (a-3)	GB	G	B	F
South Carolina	A	B	GS	N.A.	CE	B	GS	GS (a-7)	CE	B
South Dakota	GS (a-15)	A	GS	GS (a-11)	CE (a-23)	A	GS	GS	GS	SS
Tennessee	A	G	G (a-11)	G (a-11)	SL	A	G	G	G	N.A.
Texas	G	B	G	G	CE	CE (a-3)	B	G (a-7)	B	(cc)
Utah	G	A	GS	GS	A	A	GS	A	B	A
Vermont	G (a-15)	A	G	G	G (a-15)	A	G	G	G	CE (a-2)
Virginia	B	GB	GB	GB	GB	GB	GB	GB	GB	GB
Washington	GS	B	GS	G	CE (a-4)	AT	GS	GS	CE	A
West Virginia	CS	GS	GS	B	CE (a-31)	AT	GS	B (a-8)	(ee)	CE (a-2)
Wisconsin	A	A	GS	A	A	A	GS	CS	CE	B
Wyoming	A	A	G	G	CE	G	GS	G	CE	A
American Samoa	GB	N.A.	GB	(a-7)	(a-4)	(a-3)	A	(a-7)	GB	G
Guam	GS	...	GS	...	CS	CS	GS	B	B	GS
No. Mariana Islands	G	A	GS	GS	C	GS	C	C	B	B
U.S. Virgin Islands	GS	GS	GS	GS	GS (a-15)	GS	GS	GS	GS	B

Appointed by:
A—Agency head
AB—Agency head
AG— Agency head
AGC—Agency head
AGS Agency head
ALS—Agency head
ASH—Agency head
B—Board or commission
BG—Board
BGS—Board
BS—Board or commission
BA—Board or commission
CS—Civil Service
LS—Legislative Committee
(a) Chief administrative official or agency in charge of function:
(a-1) Lieutenant Governor

Approved by:

Board
Governor
Governor & Council

Appropriate legislative committee
Senate president & House speaker

Governor
Governor & Senate
Senate
Agency head

Senate

(a-2) Secretary of state
(a-3) Attorney general
(a-4) Treasurer
(a-5) Administration
(a-6) Budget
(a-7) Commerce
(a-8) Community affairs
(a-9) Comptroller
(a-10) Consumer affairs
(a-11) Economic development
(a-12) Education (chief state school officer)
(a-13) Energy
(a-14) Environmental protection
(a-15) Finance
(a-16) General services
(a-17) Highways

SELECTED STATE ADMINISTRATIVE OFFICIALS: METHODS OF SELECTION — Continued

State or other jurisdiction	Emergency management	Employment services	Energy	Environmental protection	Finance	Fish & wildlife	General services	Health	Higher education	Highways
Alabama	G	CS	CS	B	G	CS	CS	B	B	G (a-29)
Alaska	AG	AG	...	GB	AG	GB	AG	AG	B	GB
Arizona	G	A	...	GS	A	B	A	GS	B	A
Arkansas	GS	G	A	BG/BS	G	(d)	A	BG	BG	BS (a-29)
California	GS	GS	G	GS	G	G	GS	GS	B	GS
Colorado	CS	GS	G	CS	CS	AB	GS	GS	GS	GS (a-29)
Connecticut	GE	A	A	GE	GE	CS (bb)	GE	GE	BG	GE (a-29)
Delaware	CG	CG	A	GS (a-19)	GS	CG	GS (a-5)	CG	B	GS (a-29)
Florida	A	GS	A	GS	CE (dd)	GS	GS	GS	N.A.	GOC
Georgia	G	A	G	B	G	A	A	A	B	B (a-29)
Hawaii	A	CS	CS	G	GS	CS	(a-9)	GS	B	CS
Idaho	A	GS	A	GS	GS	B	...	GS	B	B (a-29)
Illinois	GS	GS	GS (a-7)	GS	G (a-6)	GS (a-19)	GS (a-5)	GS	B	GS (a-29)
Indiana	G	G	LG	G	G (a-6)	A	G (a-5)	G	G	G (a-29)
Iowa	GS	GS	...	A	A	A	A	GS	...	A
Kansas	CS	GS	B	C	...	CS	GS	C	B	GS (a-29)
Kentucky	AG	AG	AG	G	G	B	CG (a-5)	CG	B	AG
Louisiana	A	A	GS	GS	GS	GS	GS	GS	B	GS (a-29)
Maine	C	N.A.	G	G	G (a-5)	G	C	G	B	G (a-29)
Maryland	AG	A	G	GS	GS	A	GS	GS	G	AG
Massachusetts	C	CG	CG	CG	G (a-5)	CG	G (a-5)	CG	B	G
Michigan	CS	GS	...	GS	GS (a-6)	GS	N.A.	GS	CS	GS (a-29)
Minnesota	GS	A	A	A	GS	A	GS (a-5)	GS	A	CE (u)
Mississippi	GS	BS	A	GS	GS	GS	N.A.	BS	BS	B (a-29)
Missouri	A	A	...	A	AGS	(w)	A	GS	B	B (a-29)
Montana	CP	CP	CP	GS	CP	GS	CP	GS	CP	GS (a-29)
Nebraska	A	A	A	GS	(ff)	(gg)	A	GS	B	GS (a-29)
Nevada	A	A	A	A	...	A	...	AG	B	...
New Hampshire	G	GC	G	GC	GC (a-5)	BGC	GC	AGC	B	GC (a-29)
New Jersey	GS	A	A	GS	A	B	(oo)	GS	B	A
New Mexico	G	GS (a-18)	GS	GS	GS	G	GS	GS	B	GS (a-29)
New York	G	GS (a-18)	B	GS	CE (a-9)	GS	G	GS	B (a-12)	GS (a-29)
North Carolina	G	G	A	G	G	G	G	G	B	A
North Dakota	A	G	...	A	A	G	G	G	B	G (a-29)
Ohio	A	GS	(a-11)	GS	GS	(a-19)	(a-5)	GS	B	(a-29)
Oklahoma	GS	B	GS	B	GS	B	GS (a-5)	(d)	(d)	B (a-29)
Oregon	G	GS	G	B	CE (a-4)	B	GS (a-5)	A	B	A
Pennsylvania	G	AG	AG	AG	G	B	GS	GS	AG	AG
Rhode Island	G	G	CS	GB	AG (a-6)	GB (bb)	GB	GB	B	GB (a-29)
South Carolina	A	B	A	B	B	B	A	GS	B	B (a-29)
South Dakota	CG	CG	A	GS	GS	CG	GS (a-5)	GS	B	GS (a-29)
Tennessee	A	G	A	G	G	B	G	G	B	G (a-29)
Texas	A	B	B	B	CE (a-9)	B	B	BG	B	B (a-29)
Utah	A	GS	A	GS	A	A	A	GS	B	GS (a-29)
Vermont	A	G	G	G	G	G	G	G	N.A.	G (a-29)
Virginia	GB	GB	GB	GB	GB	B	GB	GB	B	GB
Washington	A	A	A	GS	GS	B	GS (a-5)	GS	B	B (a-29)
West Virginia	GS	GS	GS	GS (a-13)	GS (a-5)	CS	C	GS	B	GS (a-29)
Wisconsin	A	A	A	A	A	A	GS (a-5)	A	N.A.	A
Wyoming	G	GS	A	GS	CE	CS	A	GS	B	GS (a-29)
American Samoa	G	A	GB	GB	(a-4)	GB	G	GB	(a-12)	GB (a-29)
Guam	GS	GS	G	GS	GS	GS	CS	GS	B	GS
No. Mariana Islands	G	C	C	G	GS	C	GS	GS	B	C
U.S. Virgin Islands	GS	GS	GS	GS	GS	GS	GS	GS	GS	GS

(a-18) Labor
(a-19) Natural Resources
(a-20) Parks and recreation
(a-21) Personnel
(a-22) Post-audit
(a-23) Pre-audit
(a-24) Public utility regulation
(a-25) Purchasing
(a-26) Revenue
(a-27) Social services
(a-28) Tourism
(a-29) Transportation
(a-30) Welfare
(a-31) Auditor
    (b) Responsibilities shared between Commissioner of Mental Health (GE) and Commissioner of Retardation (GE).

(c) Responsibilities shared between Section Manager -Central Account Service Manager (A) and Team Leader Audit Services (CS).
    (d) Method not specified.
    (e) The Director of Elections (SS) post is vacant, Secretary of State William Galvin (CE) is acting director.
    (f) Responsibilities shared between Director, Division of Substance Abuse and Mental Health (CG); and Director , Division of Developmental Disabilities Services (CG).
    (g) Responsibilities shared between Secretary of Health and Social Services (GS) ; and Secretary , Department of Services for Children, Youth and their families (GS).
    (h) Responsibilities shared between Director, Division of Licensing, Department of State (SS); and Secretary, Department of Professional Regulation (N.A.).
    (i) The State Auditor is appointed by the House and approved by the Senate.
    (j) Responsibilities shared between Deputy Director of Mental Health (G) and Deputy Director of Retardation (G).

SELECTED STATE ADMINISTRATIVE OFFICIALS: METHODS OF SELECTION — Continued

State or other jurisdiction	Information systems	Insurance	Labor	Licensing	Mental health & retardation	Natural resources	Parks & recreation	Personnel	Planning	Post audit
Alabama	G	G	G	...	G	G	CS	B	G (a-8)	LS
Alaska	AG	AG	GB	AG	AG	GB	AG	AG	...	B
Arizona	A	GS	B	...	A	GS	B	A	L (a-6)	(d)
Arkansas	GS	GS	GS	...	A	A	GS	A	...	L
California	...	CE	AG	G	GS	GS	GS	GS	...	(d)
Colorado	G	GS	GS	GS	GS	GS	C	GS	G	L
Connecticut	GE	GE	GE	CS	GE (b)	CS	CS	GE	A	(a-31)
Delaware	GS	CE	GS	CG	CG (f)	GS	CG	GS	CG	CE (a-31)
Florida	G	CE (dd)	N.A.	(h)	A	(a-14)	(a-14)	A	GS	CE
Georgia	CE	CE	CE	A	A	B	A	GS	G	(i)
Hawaii	CS	AG	GS	CS	(j)	GS	CS	GS	CS	CS
Idaho	GS (a-5)	GS	GS	A	N.A.	GS	B	GS	GS	CE (a-9)
Illinois	GS (a-5)	GS	GS	GS	GS (a-27)	GS	GS (a-19)	GS (a-5)	...	SL
Indiana	A	G	G	(l)	A	G	A	G	A	G
Iowa	A	GS	GS	GS	A	GS	A	A	...	...
Kansas	C	SE	GS	B	C	GS	CS	C	BG	L
Kentucky	AG	G	G	AG	CG	G	G	G	G	CE
Louisiana	A	CE	GS	A	GS	GS	LGS	B	A	CL
Maine	C	G	G	C	G	G	C	C	G	CL
Maryland	A	GS	GS	A	A (p)	GS	A	A	GS	N.A.
Massachusetts	C	G	G	G	CG (q)	CG	C	CG	...	G
Michigan	CS	GS	GS (a-7)	CS	(t)	GS	CS	CS	...	CL
Minnesota	A	GS (a-7)	GS	A	GS (a-27)	GS	A	GS	N.A	CE (a-31)
Mississippi	BS	SE	...	...	B	GS (a-14)	GS	B	A	CE (a-31)
Missouri	A	GS	GS	A	A	GS	A	G	N.A	CE (a-31)
Montana	A	GS	GS	CP	CP	GS	CP	CP	G	L
Nebraska	A	GS	GS	A	A	GS	B	A	GS	CE (a-31)
Nevada	G	A	G	...	GD	G	A	G	...	ALS
New Hampshire	GC (a-5)	GC	GC	...	AGC	GC	AGC	AGC	G	AGC (a-9)
New Jersey	A	GS	GS	A	A (pp)	A	A	GS	A	L (a-31)
New Mexico	G	G	GS	G	G	GS	G	G	...	CE (a-31)
New York	G	GS	GS	(jj)	(kk)	GS (a-14)	GS	GS	GS (a-11)	CE (a-9)
North Carolina	G	CE	CE	...	A	G	A	G	G	CE (a-31)
North Dakota	G	CE	G	CE (a-2)	A	A	G	A	...	...
Ohio	GS	GS	(a-5)	...	GS	GS	(a-19)	(a-5)	...	...
Oklahoma	A	CE	CE	...	B	B (a-28)	B (a-28)	GS	...	...
Oregon	A	GS	SE	GS	A	GOC	B	A	...	SS
Pennsylvania	G	GS	GS	G	AG	GS	A	G	G	CE (a-31)
Rhode Island	CS	CS	AGS	CS	GB	GB (a-14)	CS	CS	CS	CS
South Carolina	A	GS	GS	GS (a-18)	B (rr)	B	GS	A	AB	B (ss)
South Dakota	GS	GS	GS	CG	GS	GS	CG	GS	(a-15)	L
Tennessee	A	G	G	A	G	G	A	G	A	SL (a-9)
Texas	B	G	B	B	B	B	B	A	G (a-6)	L
Utah	A	GS	A	AG	AB	GS	AG	GS	G	CE (a-31)
Vermont	G	G	G	A	G	G	G	G	...	CE
Virginia	GB	SL	GB	GB	GB	GB	GB	GB	B (a-6)	SL (a-31)
Washington	GS	CE	GS	GS	A	CE	B	GS	GS (a-15)	CE
West Virginia	C	GS	GS	...	GS	GS	GS	C	GS (a-5)	LS
Wisconsin	A	GS	GS	GS	A	GS	A	GS	(a-6)	CE (a-31)
Wyoming	A	G	A	GS	A	G	GS	A	G	CE
American Samoa	(a-29)	G	N.A.	N.A.	(a-27)	AG	GB	A	(a-7)	G
Guam	GS	GS	GS	GS	GS (qq)	GS	GS	GS	GS	CE
No. Mariana Islands	C	CS	C	B	C	GS	C	GS	G	GS
U.S. Virgin Islands	G	SE	GS	GS	GS	GS	GS	GS	G	L

(k) Responsibilities shared between Co-Directors in Election Commission (G); appointed by the Governor, subject to approval by the Chairs of the State Republican/Democratic parties.

(l) Responsibilities shared between Executive Director, Health Professions Bureau; and Executive Director, Professional Licensing Agency (G).

(m) Responsibilities shared between Lieutenant Governor (CE), Director Business Development Division (C) and President Kansas Inc.(BG).

(n) Responsibilities shared between Secretary of the State (CE); and Deputy Assistant for Elections (SS).

(o) In Maine, New Hampshire, New Jersey, Tennessee and West Virginia, the Presidents (or Speakers) of the Senate are next in line of succession to the Governorship. In Tennessee, the Speaker of the Senate bears the statutory title of Lieutenant Governor.

(p) Responsibilities shared between Director, Mental Hygiene Administration (A); and Director, Developmental Disabilities Administration, Department of Health and Mental Hygiene (A).

(q) Responsibilities shared between Commissioner, Department of Mental Retardation (CG); and Commissioner, Department of Mental Health, Executive Office of Human Services (CG).

(r) Responsibilities shared between Assistant Executive Budget Analyst and Director or Management and Budget.

(s) Responsibilities shared between Secretary of State (CE); and Director, Bureau of Elections (CS).

(t) Responsibilities shared between Director, Department of Community Health (CS); and Deputy Director, Mental Health and Substance Abuse (CS), same department.

(u) The Lieutenant Governor currently serves as the agency head of the Department of Transportation.

(v) Responsibilities shared between the five Public Utility Commissioners (G).

(w) Responsibilities shared between Administrator, Division of Fisheries, Department of Conservation; Administrator, Division of Wildlife, same department (AB).

SELECTED STATE ADMINISTRATIVE OFFICIALS: METHODS OF SELECTION — Continued

State or other jurisdiction	Pre-audit	Public library development	Public utility regulation	Purchasing	Revenue	Social services	Solid waste management	State police	Tourism	Transportation	Welfare
Alabama	CS (a-9)	B	SE	CS	G	B	CS	G	G	G (a-17)	B (a-27)
Alaska	...	AG	GB	AG	GB	GB	CS	AG	G	AG	AG
Arizona	A (a-9)	B	B	A	GS	A	A	GS	AG	GB	AG
Arkansas	A	B	A	A	A	GS	A	G	GS	GS	A
California	CE (a-9)	GS	GS	GS	BS	GS	G	GS	N.A.	GS	AG
Colorado	C (a-9)	A	CS	CS	GS	GS	CS	CS	CS	GS (a-17)	CS
Connecticut	CE (a-9)	CS	GB	CS	GE	GE	CS	GE	GE	GE (a-17)	GE
Delaware	CE (a-31)	CG	CG	CG	CG	GS (g)	B	CG	CG	GS (a-17)	CG
Florida	CE	A	L	A	GOC	GS	A	A	G	GS	A
Georgia	(i)	AB	CE	A	G	GD	A	B	A	B (a-17)	A
Hawaii	CS	B	GS	GS	GS	GS	CS	...	B	GS	CS
Idaho	CE (a-9)	A	GS	A	GS	CE	...	GS	A	B (a-17)	A
Illinois	CE (a-9)	SS	GS	GS (a-5)	GS	GS	GS (a-14)	GS	GS (a-7)	GS (a-17)	GS
Indiana	CE	G	G	A	G	N.A.	A	G	LG	G (a-17)	A
Iowa	...	A	GS	A	GS	GS	A	A	A	GS	...
Kansas	(c)	GS	GS	C	GS	GS	C	GS	A	GS (a-17)	C
Kentucky	G (a-15)	G	G	CG (a-5)	G	CG	A	CG	G (a-7)	G	CG
Louisiana	A	BGS	BS	A	GS	GS	GS	GS	LGS	GS (a-17)	GS
Maine	C	B	G	CS	C	G	CS	G	C	G (a-17)	C
Maryland	A	A	GS	A	A	GS	A	GS	A	GS	GS (a-27)
Massachusetts	G (a-9)	B	G	CG	CG	CG	CG	CG	CG	G	CG
Michigan	CL	CL	GS	CS	CS	CS	CS	GS	(d)	GS (a-17)	GS (a-27)
Minnesota	CE (a-31)	N.A.	G (v)	A	GS	GS	GS	A	A	CE (u)	GS (a-27)
Mississippi	CE (a-31)	B	GS	A	GS	GS	A	GS	A	B (a-17)	GS
Missouri	A	B	GS	A	GS	GS	A	GS	A	B (a-17)	A
Montana	L	B	CE	CP	GS	GS	GS	A	CP	GS (a-17)	GS
Nebraska	A	B	B	A	GS	GS	A	GS	A	GS (a-17)	GS
Nevada	...	G	G	A	G	G	G	A	GD	BG	AG
New Hampshire	AGC (a-9)	AGC	GC	CS	GC	GC	AGC	AGC	AGC	GC (a-17)	AGC
New Jersey	...	...	GS	GS	A	GS	A	GS	A	GS	A
New Mexico	G		CE	CE	GS	...	...	GS	GS	GS (a-17)	GS
New York	CE (a-9)	B (a-12)	GS	G (a-16)	GS	GS	GS (a-14)	G	GS (a-11)	GS (a-17)	GS (a-27)
North Carolina	CE (a-31)	A	G	A	G	A	A	G	A	G	A
North Dakota	A	A	CE	A	CE	G	A	G	G	G (a-17)	G
Ohio	...	B	GS	(a-16)	(a-4)	G	(a-14)	A	(a-11)	GS (a-17)	GS
Oklahoma	A (a-9)	B	(hh)	A	GS	GS	A	GS	B	B (a-17)	GS
Oregon	A (a-6)	B	GS	A	GS	GS	B	GS	A	GS	GS
Pennsylvania	CE (a-4)	A	GS	A	GS	AG	A	GS	A	GS	GS
Rhode Island	CS (a-9)	G	(ll)	CS	CS	CS	CS	GB	A	GB (a-17)	CS
South Carolina	CE (a-9)	B	B	A	GS	GS	A	GS	GS	B (a-17)	GS
South Dakota	CE	CG	CE	CG	GS	G	CG	CG	GS	GS (a-17)	GS (a-27)
Tennessee	A	A	SE	A	G	G	A	G	G	G (a-17)	G
Texas	CE (a-9)	A	B	B	CE (a-9)	G	N.A.	B	A	B (a-17)	G
Utah	A	A	A	A	BS	GS	A	A	A	GS (a-17)	GS
Vermont	G (a-15)	G	G	A	G	G	A	A	G	G (a-17)	GS
Virginia	GB (a-9)	GB	SL	GB (a-16)	GB	GB	GB (a-14)	GB	CS	GB	GB (a-27)
Washington	CE (a-4)	B	GS	A	GS	GS	A	GS	A	B (a-17)	GS (a-27)
West Virginia	GS (a-5)	B	GS	CS	GS	C	B	GS	GS	GS (a-17)	GS
Wisconsin	A	A	GS	A	GS	A	A	A	GS	GS	A
Wyoming	CE	A	G	A	G	GS	A	A	A	GS	GS
American Samoa	(a-4)	(a-12)	N.A.	A	(a-4)	GB	GB	GB	(a-7)	GB (a-17)	N.A.
Guam	GS	(d)	(ii)	GS	GS	GS	GS	GS	B	GS	GS
No. Mariana Islands	G	B	B	C	C	C	A	GS	GB	CS	A
U.S. Virgin Islands	GS	GS	GS	GS	GS	G	GS	GS	GS	GS	GS

(x) Responsibilities shared between Director of Budget and Finance, (GS): Director of Human Resources, (GS) and the Comptroller, (GS).

(y) Elected to the Senate by the public and elected Lieutenant Governor by the Senate (CL).

(z) Responsibilities shared between Secretary of State (CE); Deputy Secretary of State for Elections, Office of Secretary of State (SS); and Chief Deputy Secretary of State, same office (A).

(aa) Responsibilities shared between Director of Budget and Finance (GS) and Comptroller (GS).

(bb) Responsibilities shared between Director of Wildlife, Director of Inland Fisheries and Director of Marine Fisheries.

(cc) Responsibilities shared between Secretary of State (G); and Division Director of Elections, Elections Division, Secretary of State (A).

(dd) Effective Jan. 1, 2003 the positions of Commissioner & Treasurer and Comptroller will merge into one Chief Financial Officer.

(ee) Responsibilities shared between Cabinet Secretary, Department of Education and the Arts (GS); and State School Superintendent, Department of Education (B).

(ff) Responsibilities shared between State Tax Commissioner, Department of Revenue (GS); Administrator, Budget Division (A) and the Auditor of Public Accounts (CE).

(gg) Responsibilities shared between Director, Game and Parks Commission (B), Division Administrator, Wildlife Division, Game & Parks Commission (A) and Assistant Director of Fish and Wildlife (A).

(hh) Responsibilities shared between Director, Public Utility Division, Corporation Commission (A); and 3 Commissioners, Corporation Commission (CE).

(ii) Responsibilities shared between Public Utility Regulation (GS) and Chair, Consolidated Commission on Utilities (GS).

(jj) Responsibilities shared between Secretary of State (GS) and Commissioner of State Education Department (B).

SELECTED STATE ADMINISTRATIVE OFFICIALS: METHODS OF SELECTION — Continued

(kk) Responsibilities shared between Commissioner, Office of Mental Health, and Commissioner, Office of Mental Retardation and Developmental Disabilities, both (GS).

(ll) Responsibilities shared between Administrator Thomas Ahearn (G) and Chairman Elia Germani (B).

(mm) Effective January 6, 2003 the offices of State Treasurer, State Budget Director and Commerce will be abolished and the duties will be transferred to the Commissioner of Finance, (GS), in the Department of Finance.

(nn) Responsibilities shared between the Assistant Secretary of State (A) and the Senior Counsel for Elections (A).

(oo) Responsibilities shared between Director, Division of Purchasing, Dept. of Treasury (GS), and Director, Division of Property and Management, Dept. of the Treasury (A).

(pp) Responsibilities shared between Director, Division of Mental Health Services, Dept of Human Services (A) and Director, Division of Developmental Disabilities, Dept. of Human Services (A).

(qq) Responsibilities shared between Director, Mental Health and Substance Abuse (GS) and Director, Department of Integrated Services for Individuals with Disabilities (GS).

(rr) Responsibilities shared between Director Stan Butkus (B) and State Director George Gintoli (B).

(ss) Responsibilities shared between Director George Schroeder (B) and State Auditor Thomas Wagner (B).

Table 4.11
SELECTED STATE ADMINISTRATIVE OFFICIALS: ANNUAL SALARIES BY REGION

State or other jurisdiction	Governor	Lieutenant governor	Secretary of state	Attorney general	Treasurer	Adjutant general	Administration	Agriculture	Auditor	Banking
Eastern Region										
Connecticut	$150,000	$110,000	$110,000	$110,000	$110,000	$148,816	$140,000	$117,669	(mm)	$117,669
Delaware (h)	132,500	64,900	109,800	120,800	97,400	95,200	102,400	102,400	93,200	99,200
Maine	70,000	(s)	N.A.	78,062	71,032	91,208	91,208	87,692	84,302	85,758
Massachusetts	135,000 (jj)	120,000 (jj)	120,000	122,500	120,000	127,624	150,000	99,617	120,000	108,105
New Hampshire	102,704	(s)	89,128	99,317	89,128	89,128	99,317	84,232	N.A.	89,128
New Jersey	175,000	(s)	141,000	141,000	141,000	141,000	N.A.	141,000	127,500	141,000
New York	179,000	151,500	120,800	151,500	109,190	120,800	120,800	120,800	151,500	127,000
Pennsylvania	144,416	121,309	103,980	120,154	120,154	103,980	125,000	103,980	120,154	103,980
Rhode Island	105,194	88,584	88,584	94,121	88,584	85,067	110,321	54,864	137,418	77,867
Vermont	133,162	56,514	84,427	101,067	84,427	78,250	120,536	102,190	84,448	89,960
Regional average	132,698	71,281	96,772	113,852	103,092	108,107	105,958	101,444	110,634	103,967
Midwestern Region										
Illinois	154,800	118,400	136,600	136,600	118,400	100,900	124,200	116,300	115,600	118,900
Indiana	95,000	76,000	66,000	79,400	66,000	98,046	89,962	74,431	83,070	87,126
Iowa	107,482	76,698	87,990	105,430	87,990	105,576	123,053	87,990	87,990	80,000
Kansas	98,331	111,523	76,389	76,389	76,389	91,232	91,350	91,362	96,804	80,185
Michigan	177,000	123,900	124,900	124,900	167,504	123,204	124,848	124,848	135,500	114,444
Minnesota	120,303	78,197	90,227	114,288	108,388 (v)	132,108	108,388	108,388	102,257	103,627
Nebraska	85,000	60,000	65,000	75,000	60,000	81,243	86,844	89,086	60,000	84,999
North Dakota	85,506	66,380	68,018	74,668	64,236	120,300	. . .	69,874	68,016	74,004
Ohio	126,485	73,715 (b)	90,725	93,434	93,434	101,670	73,715 (b)	66,851 (b)	97,501	54,974 (b)
South Dakota	95,389	12,635 (ee)	64,812	80,995	64,813	92,248	89,918	89,918	76,787	84,302
Wisconsin	131,768	69,579	62,549	127,868	62,549	93,486	129,617	108,914	109,948	94,275
Regional average	116,097	78,821	84,837	98,997	88,155	103,638	104,190	93,451	93,952	88,803
Southern Region										
Alabama	96,361	45,360	71,500	163,429	71,500	76,336	76,336	71,003	71,500	132,000
Arkansas	77,028	37,229	48,182	64,189	48,182	93,223	124,402	80,091	48,182	110,730
Florida	124,575	119,390	118,400	123,331	123,331	127,624	74,462	123,331	131,832	(a-4)
Georgia	127,303	83,148	112,776	125,871	117,893	123,069	117,892	110,247	125,000	117,893
Kentucky	125,130	91,075	91,075	91,075	91,075	125,000	109,907	91,075	91,075	N.A.
Louisiana	94,532	85,000	85,000	85,000	85,000	129,130	171,724	85,000	114,518	85,400
Maryland	145,000	120,833	84,583	120,833	120,833	92,972 (b)	100,131 (b)	100,131 (b)	N.A.	52,449 (b)
Mississippi	122,160	60,000	90,000	108,960	90,000	111,400	106,800	90,000	90,000	127,179
Missouri	120,087	77,184	96,455	104,332	96,455	81,672	112,356	97,044	96,455	. . .
North Carolina	121,391	107,136	107,136	107,136	107,136	90,143	104,672	107,136	107,136	107,136
Oklahoma	110,298	85,500	90,000	103,109	87,875	109,162	. . .	76,000	87,876	110,000
South Carolina	106,078	46,545	92,007	92,007	92,007	92,007	148,000	92,007	101,794	(a-4)
Tennessee	85,000	49,500 (s)	135,060	126,528	131,060	95,148	135,060	95,148	135,060	95,148
Texas	115,345	7,200	117,546	92,217	(a-9)	94,832	115,000	92,217	96,200	118,427
Virginia	124,855	36,321	135,311	110,667	118,644	103,285	135,311	95,130	141,612	136,796
West Virginia	95,000	(s)	70,000	85,000	75,000	75,000	75,000	75,000	75,000	60,000
Regional average	111,884	65,714	96,564	106,480	96,763	101,802	108,714	92,535	94,578	91,781
Western Region										
Alaska	85,776	80,040	(a-1)	91,200	91,200	91,200	91,200	68,796	. . .	87,852
Arizona	95,000	(a-2)	70,000	90,000	70,000	101,450	150,000	96,000	118,073	109,000
California	175,000	131,250	131,250	148,750	140,000	167,978	. . .	131,412	131,412	123,255
Colorado	90,000	68,500	68,500	80,000	68,500	129,684	130,896	130,896	126,996	102,816
Hawaii	94,780	90,041	(a-1)	105,000	(a-6)	166,488	. . .	90,000	85,302	78,388
Idaho	98,500	26,750	82,500	91,500	82,500	102,440	82,098	85,072	. . .	84,178
Montana	93,089	66,724	72,085	82,233	83,932	77,563	(a-4)	83,932	72,285	79,679
Nevada	117,000	50,000	80,000	110,000	80,000	93,130	109,582	87,464	95,885	82,109
New Mexico	110,000	85,000	85,000	95,000	85,000	96,000	94,451	131,560	85,000	79,564
Oregon	93,600	(a-2)	72,000	77,200	72,000	N.A.	123,756	101,844	101,844	N.A.
Utah	100,600	78,200	(a-1)	84,600	78,200	86,736	99,702	86,736	80,700	86,736
Washington	145,132	75,865	101,702	131,938	101,702	115,000	115,000	115,000	101,702	115,000
Wyoming	105,000	(a-2)	92,000	97,843	92,000	99,424	89,094	75,766	92,000	73,484
Regional Average	107,960	74,531	84,871	98,866	88,089	102,084	97,476	98,806	83,938	84,774
Regional Average without California	107,960	69,375	81,006	94,710	83,753	96,593	106,337	96,089	79,982	81,567
Guam	90,000	85,000	. . .	90,000	58,199	68,152	74,096	60,850	82,025	74,096
No. Mariana Islands	70,000	65,000	. . .	80,000	40,800 (b)	. . .	54,000	40,800 (b)	80000	40,800 (b)
U.S. Virgin Islands	80,000	75,000	(a-1)	76,500	76,500	85,000	76,500	76,500	76,500	75,000

Sources: The Council of State Governments' survey of state personnel agencies, January 2005 and January 2004.

Note: The chief administrative officials responsible for each function were determined from information given by the states for the same function as listed in State Administrative Officials Classified by Function, 2002, published by The Council of State Governments.

Key:
N.A.—Not available.
. . . — No specific chief administrative official or agency in charge of function.
(a) Chief administrative official or agency in charge of function:
(a-1) Lieutenant governor.
(a-2) Secretary of state.
(a-3) Attorney general.

SELECTED OFFICIALS: ANNUAL SALARIES — Continued

State or other jurisdiction	Budget	Civil rights	Commerce	Community affairs	Comptroller	Consumer affairs	Corrections	Economic development	Education	Election administration
Eastern Region										
Connecticut	$149,307	$114,000	$131,511	$150,000	$110,000	$117,668	$148,816	$131,511	$144,199	$113,464
Delaware (h)	117,400	65,700	(a-2)	. . .	138,532	96,094	117,400	109,800	138,200	71,800
Maine	80,267	61,672	(a-11)	N.A.	80,267	75,171	91,208	91,208	91,208	67,330
Massachusetts	110,000	91,598	(a-11)	108,000	137,500	108,000	132,667	108,000	164,767	(a-2)
New Hampshire	99,317	61,913	96,461	69,322	75,806	82,504	99,317	77,255	85,753	(a-2)
New Jersey	123,480	110,505	141,000	141,000	(a-6)	120,380	141,000	155,000	141,000	108,421
New York	165,998	109,800	120,800	120,800	151,500	101,600	136,000	120,800	170,165	109,800
Pennsylvania	134,000	107,541	109,756	85,379	123,032	91,619	115,533	109,756	115,533	64,763
Rhode Island	106,679	N.A.	N.A.	N.A.	95,874	(a-3)	118,914	N.A.	135,516	N.A.
Vermont	(a-15)	82,763	95,243	74,090	(a-15)	82,763	92,061	79,373	112,840	(a-2)
Regional average	116,994	80,549	100,378	74,859	111,948	96,992	119,292	98,270	129,918	82,913
Midwestern Region										
Illinois	121,000	100,900	124,200	(a-7)	115,235	(a-3)	127,576	(a-7)	225,000	115,128
Indiana	93,561	69,147	79,950	77,083	(a-23)	70,000	96,193	73,125	79,400	(m)
Iowa	126,175	78,000	. . .	83,930	. . .	105,781	105,000	126,125	118,000	70,242
Kansas	86,528	39,354	(a-1)	64,349	79,590	70,410	93,887	(o)	137,280	(p)
Michigan	130,050	N.A.	121,500	N.A.	104,199	N.A.	130,050	. . .	159,885	(e)
Minnesota	108,388 (v)	108,388	108,388	(a-11)	108,388 (v)	79,636	108,388	108,388	108,388	(a-2)
Nebraska	102,710	N.A.	(a-11)	80,594	94,869	(a-3)	(a-3)	91,865	141,977	64,099
North Dakota	(tt)	60,000	117,312	69,874	(kk)	71,340	76,404	74,988	77,436	26,460
Ohio	73,715 (b)	60,611 (b)	73,715 (b)	82,326	(a-4)	124,779	73,715 (b)	N.A.	190,008	45,198 (b)
South Dakota	(a-15)	N.A.	84,760	(a-11)	(a-23)	44,643	81,619	77,250	92,248	51,188
Wisconsin	107,776	87,151	105,000	N.A.	99,621	74,442	116,158	83,081	107,432	103,504
Regional average	100,605	54,868	92,565	69,818	85,102	77,512	100,876	86,984	130,641	61,980
Southern Region										
Alabama	144,979	. . .	130,000	76,336	118,921	110,404	95,000	(a-8)	170,754	53,775
Arkansas	102,168	. . .	(a-11)	(a-27)	124,402	80,767	118,700	111,172	122,295	53,218
Florida	130,000	119,284	. . .	115,000	(a-4)	85,450	115,000	(a-28)	198,000	100,500
Georgia	120,000	N.A.	141,755	135,000	N.A.	102,648	N.A.	(a-7)	112,777	81,000
Kentucky	125,000	99,446	125,000	110,000	94,533	(a-3)	91,660	162,270	191,075	N.A.
Louisiana	113,484	65,707	(a-11)	N.A.	(a-5)	78,000	102,003	135,200	180,000	N.A.
Maryland	116,208 (b)	80,210 (b)	116,208 (b)	N.A.	120,833	72,704 (b)	86,346 (b)	116,208 (b)	165,000	74,529 (b)
Mississippi	106,800	. . .	90,000	59,328	106,800	72,000	108,400	5,000 (j)	234,000	(q)
Missouri	90,000	68,268	97,032	77,103	86,364	(a-3)	97,044	97,032	149,124	59,088
North Carolina	(a-15)	N.A.	104,672	82,939	133,330	N.A.	104,672	N.A.	107,136	92,892
Oklahoma	90,000	59,220	105,660	N.A.	77,000	56,316	110,000	N.A.	95,898	73,957
South Carolina	105,168	85,000	(c)	N.A.	92,007	N.A.	124,698	(a-7)(c)	92,007	78,000
Tennessee	97,572	76,248	101,268	(a-11)	135,060	63,864	95,148	101,268	101,268	N.A.
Texas	100,000	56,958	112,352	112,352	92,217	(a-3)	150,000	(a-7)	164,748	(ff)
Virginia	123,197	76,240	135,311	104,867	110,469	95,130	130,466	198,284	150,931	76,355
West Virginia	87,648	45,000	90,000	85,008	75,000	98,506	75,000	(a-8)	146,100	70,000
Regional average	111,942	51,974	99,178	74,226	103,874	75,213	100,259	96,952	148,820	63,760
Western Region										
Alaska	105,732	98,124	91,200	91,200	106,508	. . .	91,200	78,828	91,200	76,248
Arizona	99,000	115,000	123,000	(a-7)	98,000	106,270	136,000	(a-7)	85,000	(a-2)
California	((a-15)	. . .	. . .	108,753	140,000	123,255	131,412	. . .	148,750	(a-2)
Colorado	121,200	102,384	149,688	130,896	108,000	80,000	127,260	149,688	166,050	89,028
Hawaii	(a-9)	86,041	100,000	N,A,	100,000	78,388	90,000	95,000	150,000	77,966
Idaho	88,500	55,075	83,932	65,638	65,546	54,912	83,932	93,088	80,425	48,000
Montana	80,704	52,039	83,932	65,577	68,839	50,232	83,932	98,800	80,425	44,701
Nevada	(a-5)	72,140	109,582	. . .	80,000	74,460	109,582	96,791	109,582	(oo)
New Mexico	79,135	75,641	100,818	74,158	. . .	83,389	95,594	100,818	126,071	65,000
Oregon	92,436	72,576	112,272	101,844	101,844	112,272	123,756	112,272	72,000	101,844
Utah	101,769	68,612	86,736	93,542	(a-15)	78,571	101,769	93,542	138,361	44,454
Washington	90,000	100,000	115,000	106,128	(a-4)	131,938	135,000	115,000	103,785	101,702
Wyoming	82,400	59,207	142,320	142,320	92,000	142,320	111,240	142,320	92,000	60,000
Regional average	98,605	73,603	99,883	84,850	89,872	85,847	109,283	99,934	111,050	77,197
Regional average without California	95,871	79,737	108,207	82,859	85,695	82,729	107,439	108,262	107,908	73,336
Guam	88,915	. . .	75,208	. . .	68,152	46,596	67,150	82,025	98,430	61,939
No. Mariana Islands	54,000	49,000	52,000	52,000	40,800 (b)	52,000	40,800 (b)	45,000	80,000	53,000
U.S. Virgin Islands	76,500	60,000	76,500	(hh)	76,500	76,500	76,500	85,000	76,500	76,500

(a-4) Treasurer.
(a-5) Administration.
(a-6) Budget.
(a-7) Commerce.
(a-8) Community affairs.
(a-9) Comptroller.
(a-10) Consumer affairs.

(a-11) Economic development.
(a-12) Education (chief state school officer).
(a-13) Energy.
(a-14) Environmental protection.
(a-15) Finance.
(a-16) General services.
(a-17) Highways.

SELECTED OFFICIALS: ANNUAL SALARIES — Continued

State or other jurisdiction	Emergency management	Employment services	Energy	Environmental protection	Finance	Fish & wildlife	General services	Health	Higher education	Highway
Eastern Region										
Connecticut	$120,000	$117,669	$107,635	$127,250	$150,000	(rr)	$140,000	$144,481	$150,000	$148,816
Delaware (h)	72,600	84,900	49,924	(a-19)	117,400	87,400 (a-5)	102400	146,500	74,700	(a-29)
Maine	64,667	N.A.	80,267	91,208	(a-5)	91,208	80,267	91,208	N.A.	(a-29)
Massachusetts	86,063	103,212	99,162	117,678	(a-5)	106,358	(a-5)	123,563	180,000	110,410
New Hampshire	71,482	89,162	70,005	96,461	(a-5)	84,232	99,317	77,255	66,779	(a-29)
New Jersey	126,000	116,270	92,610	141,000	118,190	97,755	(pp)	141,000	121,900	116,277
New York	124,705	(a-18)	120,800	(ss)	(a-9)	(ss)	136,000	136,000	170,165	(a-29)
Pennsylvania	115,000	105,000	102,944	102,690	134,000	107,541	109,756	115,533	87,355	118,300
Rhode Island	68,311	108,460	77867	108,460	(a-6)	108,460	N.A.	110,321	134,639	(a-29)
Vermont	N.A,	95,243	89,960	79,373	83,491	74,090	87,006	112,287	. . .	(a-29)
Regional average	84,883	946,888	89,117	110,992	120,179	102,369	103,007	119,815	98,554	114,246
Midwestern Region										
Illinois	100,900	124,200	(a-7)	116,300	(a-6)	(a-19)	(a-5)	131,100	198,500	(a-29)
Indiana	90,480	84,766	51,831	90,090	(a-6)	74,919	(a-5)	111,286	136,000	(a-29)
Iowa	70,246	113,580	. . .	106,122	101,088	106,122	100,339	122,720	. . .	135,595
Kansas	57,948	92,086	47,789	86,525	. . .	46,509	(a-5)	80,000	149,025	(a-29)
Michigan	95,788	104,040	. . .	135,050	(a-6)	(w)	N.A.	130,050	95,789	(a-29)
Minnesota	108,388	94,106	104,671	81,620	108,388 (v)	98,324	(a-5)	108,388	261,494	(a-1)
Nebraska	71,431	79,132	67,549	98,465	(z)	(aa)	75,972	102,511	121,551	99,954
North Dakota	82,800	72,498	. . .	72,108	84,000	72,600	94,000	132,600	N.A.	(a-29)
Ohio	54,974 (b)	73,715 (b)	49,941 (b)	73,715 (b)	(a-6)	54,974 (b)	54,974 (b)	73,715 (b)	190,445	(a-29)
South Dakota	59,987	68,390	38,396	(a-19)	96,445	68,390	(a-5)	89,918	157,869	97,240
Wisconsin	90,734	90,000	89,000	122,021	107,776	112,021	129,617	116,158	320,000	112,021
Regional average	80,334	90,592	52,125	97,449	89,559	86,702	85,683	108,950	148,243	103,800
Southern Region										
Alabama	125,000	81,999	77,997	120,942	76,336	95,178	65,686	186,036	146,380	76,336
Arkansas	75,000	117,219	95,110	103,526	(a-9)	105,531	110,224	176,077	125,679	(a-29)
Florida	103,728	114,400	59,072	115,000	(a-4)	121,294	74,462	157,200	N.A.	130,044
Georgia	119,156	73,518	106,103	N.A.	120,000	76,213	90,663	162,289	272,950	(a-29)
Kentucky	51,496 (b)	N.A.	51,496 (b)	97,572	125,000	105,823	109,906	101,568 (b)	233,000	62,312 (b)
Louisiana	81,058	42,827 (b)	N.A.	N.A.	(a-5)	96,795	(a-5)	123,136	202,238	(a-29)
Maryland	74,529 (b)	59,740 (b)	68,087 (b)	107,858 (b)	116,208 (b)	N.A.	(a-5)	116208 (b)	107,858 (b)	150,000
Mississippi	83,000	104,150	85,951	122,250	106,800	104,000	. . .	188,057	260,000	137,635
Missouri	73,872	89,592	. . .	(t)	82,968	(y)	81,396	112,356	135,000	130,008
North Carolina	80,568	106,849	80,568	89,659	124,471	100,749	104,672	142,027	312,504	135,452
Oklahoma	70,000	83,000	N.A.	82,000	90,000	87,000	74,520	180,000	N.A.	(a-29)
South Carolina	80,730	112,500	90,132	132,000	148,000	111,127	126,632	116,199	N.A.	(a-29)
Tennessee	82,896	112,560	95,148	93,720	135,060	95,148	95,148	140,508	160,416	95,148
Texas	75,504	120,000	81,120	132,000	(a-9)	115,000	115,000	112,352	115,000	(a-29)
Virginia	92,269	110,469	117,297	134,280	118,644	111,865	122,801	155,636	134,310	155,636
West Virginia	45,000	81,720	85,000	(a-13)	(a-5)	73,404	70,224	90,000	252,500	(a-29)
Regional average	82,113	88,159	68,318	93,346	114,385	92,633	94,574	141,228	153,615	121,814
Western Region										
Alaska	87,852	76,248	. . .	91,200	87,852	91,200	88,032	87,852	114,160	91,200
Arizona	57,501 (b)	103,390	. . .	125,500	71,558 (b)	121,000	114,000	130,000	160,000	120,000
California	114,191	123,255	123,000	131,412	131,412	129,418	129,418	123,255	(gg)	(a-29)
Colorado	103,320	127,260	130,896	113,304	109,296	123,072	130,896	130,896	130,896	130,896
Hawaii	92,000	66,312 (b)	72,2480 (b)	66,312 (b)	(vv)	66,312	(a-9)	100,000	325,008	72,480
Idaho	78,333	86,278	70,054	86,528	84,178	99,091	. . .	99,029	104,998	(a-29)
Montana	68,947	71,708	77,776	83,932	65,546	83,928	71,847	83,932	144,500	83,932
Nevada	74,248	90,225	97,103	107,116	(a-9)	109,582	N.A.	90,224	23,600 (nn)	(a-29)
New Mexico	94,451	91,839	95,573	94,451	107,494	89,302	94,451	106,999	102,000	98,001
Oregon	101,844	112,272	92,436	101,844	(a-4)	101,844	(a-5)	112,272	219,504	83,952
Utah	80,743	107,908	68,612	101,769	105,903	89,993	89,993	110,873	N.A.	(a-29)
Washington	89,352	135,000	86,000	135,000	115,000	115,000	(a-5)	135,000	128,942	(a-29)
Wyoming	61,800	87,549	60,273	92,705	92,000	95,790	68,000	88,999	87,500	(a-29)
Regional average	84,968	98,403	124,939	102,390	94,445	101,195	86,569	107,641	132,614	106,511
Regional average without California	82,533	96,332	125,100	99,972	91,602	98,843	82,998	106,340	132,815	105,116
Guam	68,152	73,020	55,303	60,850	88,915	60,850	47,918	74,096	160,000	88,915
No. Mariana Islands	45,000	40,800 (b)	45,000	58,000	54,000	40,800 (b)	54,000	80,000	80,000	40,800 (b)
U.S. Virgin Islands	71,250	76,500	69,350	76,500	76,500	76,500	76,500	76,500	76,500	65,000

(a-18) Labor.
(a-19) Natural resources.
(a-20) Parks and recreation.
(a-21) Personnel.
(a-22) Post audit.
(a-23) Pre-audit.
(a-24) Public utility regulation.

(a-25) Purchasing.
(a-26) Revenue.
(a-27) Social services.
(a-28) Tourism.
(a-29) Transportation.
(a-30) Welfare.
(a-31) Auditor

SELECTED OFFICIALS: ANNUAL SALARIES — Continued

State or other jurisdiction	Information systems	Insurance	Labor	Licensing	Mental health & retardation	Natural resources	Parks & recreation	Personnel	Planning	Post audit
Eastern Region										
Connecticut	$145,000	$117,669	$131,511	$93,248	(d)	$122,719	$113,464	$140,000	$107,635	(a-31)
Delaware (h)	138,200	93,200	102,400	78,500	(f)	109,800	88,200	109,800	84,666	(a-31)
Maine	82,451	91,208	91,208	75,171	91,208	91,208	40,134	80,267	80,267	82,659
Massachusetts	129,708	114,147	108,000	102,599	(u)	(a-14)	115,595	115,307	N.A.	N.A.
New Hampshire	95,000	84,670	80,213	...	81,191	96,461	64,036	75,806	69,322	(a-9)
New Jersey	120,393	141,000	141,000	120,380	(qq)	116,277	108,045	141,000	90,000	127,500
New York	143,500	127,000	127,000	(bb)	(ii)	(a-14)	127,000	120,800	(a-11)	(a-9)
Pennsylvania	119,042	103,980	115,533	85,000	105,000	115,533	107,541	119,042	90,000	120,154
Rhode Island	85,067	N.A.	N.A.	N.A.	N.A.	108,460	68,311	95,874	68,311	N.A.
Vermont	76,001	89,960	74,089	79,456	112,278	95,243	74,090	83,491	...	84,448
Regional average	113,436	96,283	97,095	84,120	117,861	110,938	90,642	108,139	71,100	93,974
Midwestern Region										
Illinois	(a-5)	118,900	108,300	118,900	(a-27)	116,300	(a-19)	(a-5)	...	(a-31)
Indiana	81,971	79,852	88,505	(n)	83,187	90,090	74,802	84,142	...	83,070
Iowa	126,175	103,618	89,958	N.A.	116,563	105,781	84,885	101,088	...	...
Kansas	96,425	76,389	92,086	63,665	N.A.	94,311	51,272	72,100	N.A.	98,254
Michigan	146,017	112,199	104,900	104,900	(x)	124,848	97,223	136,578	...	135,500
Minnesota	125,990	(a-7)	108,388	94,106	108,388	108,388	96,424	108,388	N.A.	(a-31)
Nebraska	93,910	83,294	80,068	85,946	95,000	116,361	93,714	85,301	86,844	(a-31)
North Dakota	110,160	68,018	60,000	(a-2)	62,400	68,784	69,501	68,400	...	...
Ohio	60,611 (b)	66,851 (b)	101,442	54,974 (b)	73,715 (b)	73,715 (b)	54,974 (b)	73,715 (b)	(a-6)	93,434
South Dakota	107,682	84,760	79,602	43,493	80,000	89,918	65,124	82,451	(a-15)	76,889
Wisconsin	95,455	95,455	85,952	(uu)	99,940	112,021	74,960	93,384	(a-6)	109,948
Regional average	106,236	90,702	92,346	68,778	91,195	100,047	79,925	93,613	33,162	79,541
Southern Region										
Alabama	134,565	76,336	76,336	...	134,566	76,366	70,686	137,498	(a-8)	152,305
Arkansas	112,371	103,989	102,396	...	89,348	88,484	97,007	87,862	...	127,238
Florida	115,000	(a-4)	111,718	97,400	(i)	(a-14)	(a-14)	96,000	115,000	1 (a-4)
Georgia	N.A.	110,234	110,260	86,415	N.A.	117,464	92,996	117,918	(a-6)	(a-31)
Kentucky	N.A.	N.A	N.A.	51,495 (b)	N.A.	95,593	N.A.	125,000	125,000	91,075
Louisiana	114,275	85,000	102,752	58,240 (b)	98,196	91,866	N.A.	64,272 (b)	52,458 (b)	123,735
Maryland	100,131 (b)	100,131 (b)	100,131 (b)	86,346 (b)	100,131 (b)	107,858 (b)	63,772 (b)	92,972 (b)	101,131 (b)	N.A.
Mississippi	140,000	90,000	...	...	142,561	122,250	104,000	94,800	77,385	90,000
Missouri	109,344	97,104	97,044	67,200	94,128	97,044	84,876	86,364	...	(a-31)
North Carolina	133,250	107,136	104,523	...	117,438	104,672	81,149	104,672	N.A.	(a-31)
Oklahoma	89,000	98,875	80,749	...	125,000	74,000	74,000	75,000	...	N.A.
South Carolina	107,000	100,074	104,423	(a-18)	(dd)	111,127	103,000	98,476	85,214	88,496
Tennessee	123,600	95,148	112,560	90,696	101,268	95,148	93,720	95,148	N.A.	(a-9)
Texas	120,000	163,800	125,000	76,000	140,000	132,000	115,000	85,968	(a-6)	96,200
Virginia	128,479	(ll)	111,371	94,166	155,636	135,311	113,359	122,171	(a-6)	141,612
West Virginia	83,772	60,000	60,000	...	90,000	70,000	74,568	81,732	(a-5)	80,400
Regional average	100,674	94,077	87,454	50,774	101,646	102,136	80,196	97,866	66,296	98,628
Western Region										
Alaska	87,852	87,852	91,200	87,852	87,852	91,200	81,744	81,744	...	87,852
Arizona	98,000	109,650	121,000	...	N.A.	109,450	120,996	108,000	(a-6)	N.A.
California	...	140,000	131,412	123,255	123,255	131,412	123,255	123,255	...	N.A.
Colorado	124,836	106,356	127,260	121,200	102,156	129,684	123,072	130,896	121,200	126,996
Hawaii	66,312 (b)	78,388	95,000	63,156 (b)	(k)	95,000	66,312 (b)	90,000	70,368 (b)	66,312
Idaho	82,098	78,250	86,278	55,994	N.A.	86,507	75,005	82,098	N.A.	82,500
Montana	98,520	72,285	83,932	73,015	82,389	83,932	66,355	66,520	93,088	108,908
Nevada	109,582	96,900	109,582	...	106,901	109,582	89,533	93,840	...	...
New Mexico	90,878	89,922	91,839	92,350	80,000	95,573	83,139	84,000	...	85,000
Oregon	136,416	112,272	72,000	72,576	106,992	101,844	101,844	92,436	...	101,844
Utah	105,903	86,736	86,736	78,571	87,592	97,635	97,635	99,702	(a-6)	80,700
Washington	135,000	101,702	135,000	135,000	135,000	135,000	104,520	135,000	(a-15)	131,244
Wyoming	79,100	79,795	67,909	59,333	132,033	33,399	72,000	74,650	62,000	92,000
Regional average	93,423	95,393	99,934	74,023	87,726	100,017	92,724	97,088	52,205	74,104
Regional average without California	101,208	91,676	97,311	69,921	84,993	97,401	90,180	94,907	56,556	80,280
Guam	74,096	74,096	73,020	74,096	67,150	60,850	60,850	74,096	75,208	82,025
No. Mariana Islands	45000	40,800 (b)	45,000	45,360	40,800 (b)	52,000	40,800 (b)	76,500	45,000	80,000
U.S. Virgin Islands	71,250	75,000	76,500	76,500	70,000	76,500	76,500	76,500	76,500	55,000

(b) Salary ranges and top figure in ranges follow: Arizona: Emergency Management, $93,918: Finance, $121,000. Hawaii: Employment Services, $98,112; Energy, $107,196; Environmental Protection, $98,112; fish and Wildlife, $98,112; Highways, $107,196; Information Systems, $98,112; Licensing, $93,432;Parks and Recreation,$98,112;Planning,$104,088; Post-Audit, $98,112; Pre-Audit, $98,112; Solid Waste Management, $93432;Welfare, $98,112. Kentucky: Minimum figure in range: top of range follows: Election administration $84,950; Emergency management,$84,950; Energy, $84,950; Health, $162,504; Highways, $102,794;Licensing, $ 84,950; Solid waste management, $70,209. Louisiana: Minimum figure in range: top of range follows :Employment services,$79,622; Historic preservation, $69,555; Licensing:, $103,355; Personnel, $119,496 Planning, $97,552; Pre-audit, $97,522;Welfare, $104,374. Maryland: Minimum figure in range: top of range follows: Adjutant general, $124,671; Administration, $134,290; Agriculture, $134,290; Banking, $81,322 Budget, $155,893; Civil rights, $107,521; Commerce, $155,893; Consumer affairs, $113,206; Corrections, $115,766;

SELECTED OFFICIALS: ANNUAL SALARIES — Continued

State or other jurisdiction	Pre-audit	Public library development	Public utility regulation	Purchasing	Revenue	Social services	Solid waste management	State police	Tourism	Transportation	Welfare
Eastern Region											
Connecticut	(a-9)	$99,290	$144,958	$86,667	$148,816	$148,816	$103,564	$145,000	$118,450	$148,816	148,816
Delaware (h)	(a-31)	73,297	80,900	78,500	110,700	(g)	13,800	135,200	72,352	109,800	102,000
Maine	(a-9)	77,438	101,420	69,326	85,758	91,208	58,573	80,267	69,326	91,208	73,590
Massachusetts	(a-9)	94,266	107,500	117,472	132,026	128,555	(a-14)	127,596	100,883	130,000	124,970
New Hampshire	(a-9)	77,255	94,024	53,586	99,317	102,704	75,806	89,128	77,255	99,317	89,321
New Jersey	...	...	141,000	118,335	105,987	141,000	83,350	126,000	92,600	141,000	113,566
New York	(a-9)	(a-12)	127,000	(a-16)	127,000	136,000	(a-14)	127,000	(a-11)	136,000	136,000
Pennsylvania	(a-4)	90,172	112,256	80,783	109,756	100,695	102,944	109,756	56,763	115,533	115,533
Rhode Island	(a-9)	85,067	106,679	99,471	110,278	110,321	68,311	124,114	N.A.	117,337	...
Vermont	(a-15)	79,913	109,013	87,006	83,574	108,992	79,372	95,243	68,785	94,993	108,992
Regional average	94,779	84,686	112,475	92,715	111,321	117,772	80,191	115,930	86,357	118,400	101,279
Midwestern Region											
Illinois	(a-9)	104,316	117,000	(a-5)	124,200	131,100	(a-14)	115,700	(a-7)	131,100	124,200
Indiana	66,000	74,802	88,120	55,246	88,120	82,000	74,724	111,118	74,802	90,636	78,448
Iowa	...	101,816	104,497	90,418	126,175	126,175	92,227	111,238	90,397	126,173	...
Kansas	(r)	77,557	81,200	80,000	91,350	94,856	75,795	82,215	60,900	91,350	72,000
Michigan	N.A.	122,400	109,242	96,820	103,000	130,050	108,428	124,848	N.A.	135,000	(a-27)
Minnesota	(a-31)	N.A.	(l)	94,106	108,388	108,388	108,388	99,911	104,671	(a-1)	108,388
Nebraska	94,869	80,850	96,025	75,972	92,335	102,509	57,591	82,923	54,380	99,954	102,509
North Dakota	84,000	66,300	69,874	52,824	73,821	106,560	58,812	66,000	70,368	96,996	106,560
Ohio	(a-22)	60,611 (b)	73,715 (b)	54,974	73,715 (b)	106,683	58,968 (b)	73,715 (b)	69,805	73,715 (b)	73,715 (b)
South Dakota	64,813	53,518	75,587	49,587	79,602	89,585	58,444	75,026	84,760	97,240	95,035
Wisconsin	109,948	100,347	114,303	74,594	112,021	116,158	97,526	91,312	89,000	112,021	88,208
Regional average	71,841	76,592	91,454	77,158	97,521	108,551	82,473	94,001	74,844	102,944	89,010
Southern Region											
Alabama	(a-9)	82,750	86,801	110,404	76,336	139,310	82,000	76,336	76,336	(a-17)	(a-27)
Arkansas	59,596	86,941	96,577	87,862	94,110	128,417	51,153	94,260	97,007	130,290	(a-27)
Florida	(a-4)	93,400	124,137	91,400	124,070	130000	93,731	121,603	112,400	121,400	62,052
Georgia	(a-31)	119,887	106,103	91,731	117,000	N.A.	88,686	120,957	117,800	153,595	114,920
Kentucky	(a-15)	94,077	106,433	(a-5)	N.A.	N.A.	42,559 (b)	N.A.	125,000	125,000	N.A.
Louisiana	52,458 (b)	113,544	78,000	83,241	104,042	87,734	93,242	87,740	75,920	131,425	56,139 (b)
Maryland	80,210 (b)	80,210 (b)	115,152	74,529 (b)	86,346 (b)	107,858 (b)	80,210 (b)	107,858 (b)	86,346 (b)	116,208 (b)	107,858 (b)
Mississippi	90,000	80,500	107,350	70,116	118,935	126,500	64,253	110,660	87,062	137,635	126,500
Missouri	86,364	76,200	N.A.	81,396	103,224	99,204	N.A.	80,040	74,200	130,008	88,188
North Carolina	(a-31)	88,442	119,315	92,757	104,672	101,914	87,832	100,134	88,442	104,672	N.A.
Oklahoma	(a-9)	72,000	(cc)	71,200	85,000	125,000	77,697	85,000	74,000	110,000	125,000
South Carolina	(a-9)	79,403	N.A.	82,281	123,874	129,484	132,000	80,295	103,000	129,780	129,484
Tennessee	96,624	127,056	95,148	N.A.	95,148	95,148	93,720	95,148	95,148	95,148	95,148
Texas	(a-9)	85,000	92,000	115,000	(a-9)	150,000	N.A.	102,000	112,352	155,000	150,000
Virginia	(a-9)	117,686	136796 (ll)	(a-16)	125,031	139,019	(a-14)	129,107	150,000	135,311	(a-27)
West Virginia	(a-31)	66,996	75,000	93,936	75,000	85,008	73,884	75,000	70,000	90,000	90,000
Regional average	94,458	91,506	87,924	86,160	95,313	102,787	74,703	91,630	96,563	121,363	97,002
Western Region											
Alaska	...	N.A.	78,828	88,032	91,200	91,200	N.A.	84,816	78,828	91,200	91,200
Arizona	(a-9)	113,025	98,450	85,000	131,674	135,000	87,450	126,450	109,000	121,450	105,747
California	133,333	108,744	117,818	...	123,255	123,255	117,818	131,412	N.A.	123,255	131,412
Colorado	(a-9)	108,905	126,552	94,416	130,896	130,896	103,308	125,244	62,000	130,896	N.A.
Hawaii	66,312 (b)	110,000	77,966	87,000	100,000	85,302	63,156 (b)	N.A.	252,000	100,000	66,312 (b)
Idaho	(a-9)	56,742	81,120	67,434	70,304	15,646	...	83,075	63,898	130,000	81,182
Montana	108,908	66,009	63,686	52,124	83,932	83,932	83,932	76,700	65,410	83,932	83,932
Nevada	98,052	92,052	101,528	82,810	109,582	110,050	...	104,567	96,791	109,582	103,257
New Mexico	87,210	65,557	N.A.	79,498	95,525	N.A.	...	94,451	90,821	(a-17)	108,178
Oregon	(a-6)	92,436	106,932	79,908	112,272	123,756	101,844	117,888	N.A.	123,504	123,756
Utah	(a-15)	78,571	N.A.	89,993	93,542	110,873	92,418	89,993	73,915	110,873	107,908
Washington	(a-4)	89,004	115,000	82,192	115,000	150,000	85,296	135,000	115,000	153,472	(a-27)
Wyoming	(a-9)	73,439	85,800	64,087	86,520	87,550	80,412	74,760	87,000	77,002	(a-27)
Regional average	90,335	81,114	81,052	73,269	103,362	95,958	62,741	95,720	84,205	111,782	91,257
Regional average without California	86,752	78,812	77,989	79,375	101,704	93,684	58,151	92,745	91,222	110,826	87,607
Guam	74,096	55,303	12,000	74,096	74,096	74,096	88,915	74,096	74,000	74,096	74,096
No. Mariana Islands ..	54,000	45,000	80,000	40,800 (b)	45,000	40,800 (b)	54,000	54,000	70,000	40,800 (b)	52,000
U.S. Virgin Islands	76,500	53,350	54,500	76,500	76,500	76,500	76,500	76,500	76,500	65,000	76,500

Economic development, $155,893; Election administration, $99,888; Emergency management, $99,888; Employment services, $92,801; Energy, $105,935; Environmental protection, $144,674; Finance, $155,893; General Services, $134,290; Health, $155,893; Higher education, $144,674; Information systems, $134,290; Insurance, $134,290; Labor, $134290; Licensing, $115,766; Natural resources, $144,674; Parks and recreation, $99,148; Personnel, $124,671; Planning, $134,290; Pre Audit, $107,521; Public library development, $107,521; Purchasing, $99,888; Revenue, $115,766; Social services, $144,674; Solid waste management, $107,521; Police, $144,674; Tourism, $115,766; Transportation, $155,893; Welfare, $144,674. New Mexico: Minimum figure in range: top of range follows:134,060.Ohio: Minimum figure in range: top of range follows: Lieutenant Governor, $132,350; Administration, $132,350; Agriculture, $122,574; Banking, $102,918; Budget, $132,350; Civil Rights, $112,320; Commerce, $132,350; Corrections,

SELECTED OFFICIALS: ANNUAL SALARIES — Continued

$132,350; Economic development, $132,350; Elections administration, $86,258; Emergency Management, $ 102,918; Employment services, $132,350; Energy, $94,182; Environmental protection, $132,350; Fish and Wildlife, $102,918; General services, $102,918; Health, $132,350; Information systems, $112,320; Insurance, $122,574; Licensing, $102,918; Mental health and retardation, $132,350; Natural resources, $132,350; Parks and recreation, $102,918; Personnel, $102,918; Public library development, $112,320; Public utility regulation, $132,350; Purchasing, $102, 918; Revenue, $132,350; Solid waste management, $81,598; State police, $132,350; Transportation, $132,350; Welfare, $132,350 Utah: Minimum figure in range: top of range follows: Administration, $102,600; Agriculture, $87,500; Banking, $87,500; Budget, $102,600; Civil rights, $80,433; Commerce, $87,500; Community affairs, $94,300; Consumer affairs, $76,190; Corrections, $102,600; Elections administration, $41,433; Emergency management, $94,723; Employment services, $111,800; Energy, $64,750; Environmental protection, $102,600; Finance, $102,670; Fish & wildlife, $94,723; General services, $97,260; Health, $111,800; Higher education, $160,000; Highways, $111,800; Historic preservation, $80,433; Information systems, $105,500; Insurance, $87,500;Labor, $87,500; Licensing, $82,640; Mental health & retardation, $94,723; Natural resources, $102,600; Parks & recreation, $94,723; Personnel, $102,600; Planning, $102,600; Pre-audit, $102,670; Public library development, $80,433; Public utility regulation, $94,300; Purchasing, $97,260; Revenue, $94,300; Social services, $111,800; Solid waste management, $124,155; State police, $94,723; Transportation, $111,800; Welfare, $111,800 Northern Mariana Islands: $49,266 top of range applies to the following positions: Treasurer, Banking, Comptroller, Corrections, , Employment Services, Fish and Wildlife, Highways, Insurance, Mental Health and Retardation, Parks and Recreation, Purchasing, Social/Human Services, Transportation.

(c) The present Secretary of Commerce forgoes regular salary and receives $1 in compensation.

(d) Responsibilities shared between Commissioner Thomas Kirk, Mental Health: $148,816 and Commissioner Peter O'Meara, Retardation: $148,816.

(e) Responsibilities shared between Secretary of State, $124,900 and Bureau Director, $102,143.

(f) Responsibilities shared between Director, Division of Substance Abuse and Mental Health, Department of Health and Social Services, $121,100; and Director, Division of Developmental Disabilities Service, same department, $101,900.

(g) Function split between two cabinet positions: Secretary, Dept. of Health and Social Services : $117,400 (if incumbent holds a medical license, amount is increased by $12,000) and Secretary, Dept. of Svcs. for Children, Youth and their Families, $109,800 ; if a Board-certified physician , a supplement of $3,000 is added.

(h) Salaries represent those reflected for the position in section 10a of FY2004 Budget Act effective 7/21/2003.

(i) Responsibilities shared between, Director of Mental Health, Department of Children and Family Services, $83,890; and Director, Substance Abuse, same department, $77,738.

(j) Maximum salary available is $183,240; incumbent has requested reduces salary.

(k) Responsibilities shared between Deputy Director of Mental Health, $92,000 and Deputy Director of Retardation, $92,000.

(l) Responsibilities shared between five commissioner's with salaries of $88,448 each.

(m) Responsibilities shared between Co-Directors, Election Commission, $50,500.

(n) Responsibilities shared between Executive Director, Health Professions Bureau, $54,274; and Executive Director, Professional Licensing Agency, $61,915.

(o) Responsibilities shared between Lieutenant Governor , $111,523; Director, Business Development Division, same department, $86,275; and President, Kansas Inc., salary unavailable.

(p) Responsibilities shared between Secretary of State, $76,389 and Deputy Secretary of State, $62,301.

(q) Responsibilities shared between Assistant Secretary of State, $80,000 and Senior Counsel for Elections, $50,000.

(r) Responsibilities shared between Central Account Service Manager, Division of Accounts & Reports, Department of Administration, $70,428; and

Team Leader, Audit Services, same division and department, $57,948.

(s) In Maine, New Hampshire, New Jersey, Tennessee and West Virginia, the presidents (or speakers) of the Senate are next in line of succession to the governorship. In Tennessee. the speaker of the Senate bears the statutory title of lieutenant governor.

(t) Responsibilities shared between Directors, $84,876 and $86,2000.

(u) Responsibilities shared between Commissioner, Department of Mental Retardation, $182,831; and Commissioner, Department of Mental Health, $126,871.

(v) State Treasurer Position was abolished in January 2003. Functions now served by The Department of Finance, Commissioner.

(w) Responsibilities shared between Director, Dept. of Natural Resources, $124,848 and Chief, Fish, $102,142 and Chief, Wildlife, $91,045.

(x) Responsibilities shared between Director, Dept. pf Community Health, $130,050 and Chief Deputy Director , Mental Health and Substance Abuse Services, $114,000.

(y) Responsibilities shared between Administrator, Department of Conservation, $82,800; Administration, Division of Protection, same department, $92,832.

(z) Responsibilities shared between, State Auditor-$60,000; Director of Revenue-$92,335; Budget Administrator-$102,710 .

(aa) Responsibilities shared between Game & Parks Director-$93,714; Game & Parks Asst Dir-Fish & Wildlife-$72,292; Wildlife Division Administrator-$66,323.

(bb) Responsibilities shared between Commissioner, State Education Department, $170,165; Secretary of State, Department of State, $120,800.

(cc) Responsibilities shared between Commissioners, Corporations Commission, varying salary levels for four commissioners, $72,000; $84,000; $87,875; and $87,875.

(dd) Responsibilities shared between Director for Mental Retardation , $138,396 and Director of Mental Health, $140,000.

(ee) Annual salary for duties as presiding officer of the Senate.

(ff) Responsibilities shared between Secretary of State, $117,546; and Division Director, $86,811.

(gg) Responsibilities shared between Chancellor of California Community Colleges, $185,484 and California Post Secondary Education Commission $130,000.

(hh) Responsibilities for St. Thomas, $74,400; St. Croix, $76,500; St. John, $74,400.

(ii) Responsibilities shared between Commissioner of Mental Health, $136,000 and Commissioner of Mental Retardation, $136,000.

(jj) Governor Romney and Lieutenant Governor Healey waive their salaries.

(kk) Responsibilities shared between Director of Fiscal Management, $84,000 and Director of Management and Budget, $94,000.

(ll) Banking has this responsibility.

(mm) Responsibilities shared between Kevin Johnston, $149,226 and Robert Jaekle, $149,226.

(nn) James Rogers, the Interim Chancellor only accepts the minimum amount of pay permitted through FLSA.

(oo) Responsibilities shared between Secretary of State, $80,000; Deputy Secretary of State for Elections, $79,885 and Chief Deputy Secretary of State, $87,876.

(pp) Responsibilities shared between Director, Division of Purchasing, Dept. of the Treasury, $118,335 and Director, Division of Property and Management, Dept. of the Treasury,$110,000.

(qq) Responsibilities shared between Director, Division of Mental Health Services, Dept. of Human Services, $113,566 and Director, Division of Developmental Disabilities, Dept. of Human Services, $101,498.

(rr) Responsibilities shared between Director of Wildlife, David May, Director of Inland Fisheries, Bill Hyatt and Director of Marine Fisheries, Eric Smith.

(ss) This is the statutory salary. The current incumbent's salary is less than this amount.

(tt) Responsibilities shared between Assistant Executive Budget Analyst, $66,912 and Director of Management and Budget, $94,000.

(uu) Position vacant, authorized pay range $68280 - $105,834.

(vv) Responsibilities shared between Director of Budget, $99,996 and Comptroller, $100,000.

2004 Lieutenant Governors' Elections

By Julia Nienaber Hurst

Lieutenant governors lead today and prepare for tomorrow. Most have significant state leadership roles and all are first in line of succession to become governor. The 2004 election factors and results indicate this office is continuing to grow in influence and that lieutenant governors will further impact state legislative trends and governments.

The results of the 2004 elections indicate the office of lieutenant governor continues to be on the rise in notoriety and influence. In this election cycle, the following four factors point to the significant and growing impact these officeholders will have on state government: 1) the rate of re-election of incumbents, 2) the vast government background and experience of those who ran for the office, 3) the outcome of ballot questions related to the office of lieutenant governor, and 4) ongoing consideration of the creation of the office in several states. These indicators were present in a total of 13 states covering every region of the country reinforcing the fact the growing influence of this office appears to be a consistent national trend, not an anomaly.

In 2004, 14 states prominently considered questions related to the office of lieutenant governor and gubernatorial succession. In nine states, lieutenant governors faced election. Five of the six incumbent lieutenant governors won re-election while the four new officeholders have significant government backgrounds. Several of the newly elected lieutenant governors have been given more powers in the office of lieutenant governor than in history. In addition, three states' voters approved ballot measures to deepen gubernatorial succession lines or retain powers in the office. Two more states are likely to create the office of lieutenant governor in the next 12–24 months. These factors warrant a deeper look at the growing importance and power of the office of lieutenant governor.

Lieutenant Governor Elections

For the purposes of this article, a lieutenant governor is defined as the officeholder in a state or territory first in line for succession to governor. Forty-two states and four territories have the office of lieutenant governor as successor; five states have the Senate presiding officer as successor; and three states and one territory have the secretary of state as successor. Twenty-four states and four territories elect the governor and lieutenant governor as a team in the general election. The remaining 18 states with a lieutenant governor elect that office separately in the

general election from the governor.

Five of the six incumbent lieutenant governors running for reelection in 2004 won. The Indiana lieutenant governor, who is elected as a team with the governor, was defeated. The lieutenant governor had not previously held elected office and had assumed the office through appointment when the governor succeeded to the office in 2003. In addition, of the states with a senate president first in line of gubernatorial succession, Maine alone elected a new senate president since the sitting president was term limited out of office.

In January of 2005, 18 of the 54 sitting lieutenant governors (33 percent) were expected to be women (New Jersey will have a vacancy). This is substantially identical to the 19 women of 55 officeholders serving after the 2002 elections. As of this writing, Republicans continue to hold more offices of lieutenant governor than Democrats with 30 being Republican, 23 being Democrat, and one being from the Popular Democratic Party.

Between September 2003 and November 2004, four gubernatorial successions occurred, three due to gubernatorial resignations (Utah, Connecticut and New Jersey) and one due to death (Indiana). In January 2005, the Nebraska lieutenant governor became governor through succession when the previous governor was tapped for a presidential Cabinet post. By April of 2005, seven of the sitting governors had once held the position of lieutenant governor (or first in line of gubernatorial succession). These are the governors of Arkansas, Connecticut, Delaware, Louisiana, Nebraska, New Jersey and Texas.

Lieutenant governors have more power in 2005 than perhaps ever in history. In July 2004, South Carolina statutorily moved the Office of Elder Affairs under the direct supervision and authority of the lieutenant governor. Likewise, Utah's Lt. Gov. Gary Herbert has a greatly expanded role being named the state's head of homeland security and liaison for water, rural and infrastructure affairs. These duties are in addition to the state required role of chief elections officer. In Indiana, the newly created

Department of Agriculture reports to the lieutenant governor, as do the Departments of Commerce and Tourism. She is also the head of state Homeland Security and Rural Affairs.

Experienced Candidates

Perhaps the growing powers of the office of lieutenant governor helped to draw the experienced field of candidates running for the office in 2004. The four new lieutenant governors have significant government experience, three as state senate leaders and one as a long-serving county commissioner. The experience of the lieutenant governor candidates who ran and won in open seats, and defeated one incumbent, is notably higher than the candidates in 2002.

In Indiana, Lt. Gov. Becky Skillman has been a state senator since 1992. She previously served as county recorder and county clerk since 1977. She was the first woman elected to Senate Republican leadership and served as majority caucus chairman. Missouri Lt. Gov. Peter Kinder had been in the state Senate since 1992 and he served as president pro tem since 2001. He also served as a U.S. congressional staffer for three years in the 1980s.

Montana Lt. Gov. John Bohlinger served three terms in the Montana House of Representatives and was in his second term in the state Senate when elected. On an interesting note, Bohlinger is a Republican who was elected to office on a team ticket with a Democrat governor. Lt. Gov. Gary Herbert was Utah County's longest serving county commissioner, with 14 years of public service under his belt.

Ballot Questions

In both Indiana and Virginia, voters approved Constitutional amendments that deepen and clarify the lines of gubernatorial succession. In both states, the reason noted for addressing the issue of succession was the realization, after September 11, 2001, of the importance of having established clear gubernatorial succession (*Munster Times, Virginia Times Dispatch*). Succession establishes which officeholder becomes governor if both the governor and lieutenant governor are unable to discharge the duties.

In Indiana, the speaker of the Indiana House and the Senate president pro tem will be next in line of gubernatorial succession, after the lieutenant governor, until the General Assembly can meet and select a new governor. Virginia's measure identifies additional elected officials who will succeed the governor in cases of "an emergency or enemy attack and until the House of Delegates is able to meet to elect a governor." Two years ago, the Secure Virginia Panel

recommended this action. The succession line begins with lieutenant governor, then attorney general, speaker of the house, the chairmen of the 14 standing committees of the House of Delegates, then the Senate president pro tem, and finally the Senate majority leader.

A Nebraska ballot question further indicated that voters are backing power in the office of lieutenant governor. By a margin on 61 percent to 39 percent, Nebraskans defeated an effort to remove the power to preside over the Senate from the lieutenant governor.

More Lieutenant Governors

The gubernatorial successor in New Jersey has potentially more power than any other lieutenant governor or governor in the country. On November 15, 2004, New Jersey Senate President Richard Codey became governor through succession upon the resignation of the previous governor (New Jersey has no lieutenant governor so the Senate president is first in line of succession). Unlike any other state, Codey retains all his power as Senate president and acquires all power of the governor.

This unusual "power" situation and the frequency with which successions have occurred in New Jersey led the legislature to put the question of creating the office of lieutenant governor before the voters in November 2005. It would be only the second statewide elected office in the state, the other being office of governor. Polls in April 2005 show public support for the move and one state senator called the impending creation of the office "a seismic shift in state government."

A similar amendment may be placed before voters in Arizona in the next 24 months. In the 2004 legislative session, Arizona House Concurrent Resolution 2003 was considered. The resolution, if passed and subsequently approved by voters, would have changed the title of the state's secretary of state, the office holder first in line of gubernatorial succession, to 'lieutenant governor.' The resolution passed the House but was narrowly defeated in a Senate committee. Press reports indicated the measure died only due to debate over when the title change would become effective if passed. Some said an immediate title change might give a greater advantage to the sitting secretary of state if she chose to run for governor.

Future Trends

The constitutional and legislative power of the office, coupled with the initiative taken by the lieutenant governor and the duties given by the governor, may have bearing on lieutenant governors successes in future elections, both in re-election efforts and in runs for higher office. Certainly states will continue to refine the role of lieutenant governor, in some cases creating the office, in others deepening the gubernatorial succession lines, and in still others adding duties and powers to the office. The growing power and influence of the office may also continue the trend of drawing more experienced candidates to the office. Some would argue, as well, that the understanding and attention of the both the press and the electorate in a given state will affect the future of the office. Those who realize that this officeholder can become governor at a moment's notice may give more attention to the office and the accomplishments of the person holding it.

About the Author

Julia Nienaber Hurst is executive director of the National Lieutenant Governors Association (*www.nlga.us*). Hurst's nearly 15 years of state government experience includes time as chief operating officer of The Council of State Governments, four sessions as a legislative chief of staff, and time as a multi-state lobbyist.

Table 4.12
THE LIEUTENANT GOVERNORS, 2005

State or other jurisdiction	Name and party	Method of selection	Length of regular term in years	Date of first service	Present term ends	Number of previous terms	Maximum consecutive terms allowed by constitution
Alabama	Lucy Baxley (D)	CE	4	1/03	1/07	. . .	2
Alaska	Loren Leman (R)	CE	4	12/02	12/06	. . .	2
Arizona	. . . . (a)						
Arkansas	Winthrop Rockefeller (R)	CE	4	1/96 (b)	1/07	1.5 (b)	2
California	Cruz Bustamante (D)	CE	4	1/98	1/06	1	2
Colorado	Jane E. Norton (R)	CE	4	1/03	1/07	. . .	2
Connecticut	Kevin Sullivan (D)	CE	4	1/04 (g)	1/07	. . .	. . .
Delaware	John Carney (D)	CE	4	1/01	1/05	. . .	2
Florida	Toni Jennings (R)	CE	4	3/03	1/07	. . .	2
Georgia	Mark Taylor (D)	CE	4	1/99	1/07	1	. . .
Hawaii	James Aiona (R)	CE	4	12/02	12/06	. . .	2
Idaho	Jim Risch (R)	CE	4	1/03	1/07	. . .	. . .
Illinois	Patrick Quinn (D)	CE	4	1/03	1/07	. . .	. . .
Indiana	Becky Skillman (R)	CE	4	1/05	1/09	. . .	2
Iowa	Sally Pederson (D)	CE	4	1/99	1/07	1	. . .
Kansas	John E. Moore (D)	CE	4	1/03	1/07	. . .	. . .
Kentucky	Stephen Pence (R)	CE	4	12/03	12/07	. . .	2
Louisiana	Mitch Landrieu (D)	CE	4	1/04	1/08	. . .	. . .
Maine	. . . . (a)						
Maryland	Michael Steele (R)	CE	4	1/03	1/07	. . .	2
Massachusetts	Kerry Healey (R)	CE	4	1/03	1/07	. . .	. . .
Michigan	John D. Cherry (D)	CE	4	1/03	1/07	. . .	2
Minnesota	Carol Molnau (R)	CE	4	1/03	1/07	. . .	. . .
Mississippi	Amy Tuck (R)	CE	4	1/00	1/08	1	2
Missouri	Peter Kinder (R)	CE	4	1/05	1/09	. . .	. . .
Montana	John Bohlinger (R)	CE	4	1/01	1/09	. . .	2 (c)
Nebraska	Rick Sheehy (R)	CE	4	1/05 (e)	1/07	. . .	2
Nevada	Lorraine Hunt (R)	CE	4	1/99	1/07	1	2
New Hampshire	. . . . (a)						
New Jersey	. . . . (a)						
New Mexico	Diane Denish (D)	CE	4	1/03	1/07	. . .	2
New York	Mary Donohue (R)	CE	4	1/99	1/07	1	. . .
North Carolina	Beverly Purdue (D)	CE	4	1/01	1/09	1	2
North Dakota	Jack Dalrymple (R)	CE	4	12/00	12/08	. . .	. . .
Ohio	Bruce Johnson (R)	SE	4	1/03	1/07	. . .	2
Oklahoma	Mary Fallin (R)	CE	4	1/95	1/07	2	. . .
Oregon	. . . . (a)						
Pennsylvania	Catherine Baker Knoll (D)	CE	4	1/03	1/07	. . .	2
Rhode Island	Charles J. Fogarty (D)	SE	4	1/99	1/07	1	2
South Carolina	R. Andre Bauer (R)	CE	4	1/03	1/07	. . .	2
South Dakota	Dennis Daugaard (R)	CE	4	1/03	1/07	. . .	2
Tennessee	. . . . (a)						
Texas	David Dewhurst (R)	CE	4	1/03	1/07	. . .	. . .
Utah	Gary Herbert (R)	CE	4	1/05	1/09	. . .	. . .
Vermont	Brian Dubie (R)	CE	2	1/03	1/07	1	. . .
Virginia	Tim Kaine (D)	CE	4	1/02	1/06	. . .	. . .
Washington	Brad Owen (D)	CE	4	1/97	1/09	2	. . .
West Virginia (d)	Earl Ray Tomblin (D)	(d)	2	1/95	1/07	6	. . .
Wisconsin	Barbara Lawton (D)	CE	4	1/03	1/07	. . .	. . .
Wyoming	. . . . (a)						
American Samoa	Ipulasi Aitofele Sunia (D)	CE	4	4/03 (f)	1/09	(f)	2
Guam	Kaleo Moylan (R)	CE	4	1/03	1/07	. . .	2
No. Mariana Islands	Diego T. Benavente (R)	CE	4	1/02	1/06	. . .	. . .
Puerto Rico	. . . . (a)						
U.S. Virgin Islands	Vargrave Richards (D)	SE	4	1/03	1/07	. . .	2

Source: The Council of State Governments and the National Lieutenant Governors Association, January 2005.

Key:
CE—Constitutional, elected by public.
SE—Statutory, elected by public.
. . . —Not applicable.
(a) No lieutenant governor. In Tennessee, the speaker of the Senate, elected from Senate membership, has statutory title of "lieutenant governor."
(b) Elected in November 1996 in a special election when Mike Huckabee assumed the office of governor after Governor Jim Guy Tucker's resignation on July 15, 1996.
(c) Eligible for eight out of 16 years.

(d) In West Virginia, the President of the Senate and the Lieutenant Governor are one in the same. The legislature provided in statute the title of Lieutenant Governor upon the Senate President. The Senate President serves 2 year terms, elected by the Senate on the first day of the first session of each two year legislative term.
(e) Lt. Governor Sheehy was appointed to the position of Lieutenant Governor January 24, 2005 by Governor Heineman.
(f) Lt. Governor Sunia was appointed to the position of Lieutenant Governor in April 2003 by Governor Togiola Tulafono.
(g) Senate President pro Tempore Sullivan took office after Lieutenant Governor Rell was sworn in as governor on July 1, 2004 after Governor John Rowland resigned.

Table 4.13
LIEUTENANT GOVERNORS: QUALIFICATIONS AND TERMS

State or other jurisdiction	Minimum age	State citizen (years)	U.S. citizen (years) (a)	State resident (years) (b)	Qualified voter (years)	Length of term (years)	Maximum consecutive terms allowed
Alabama	30	7	10	7	★	4	2
Alaska	30	...	7	7	★	4	2
Arizona	............................(c)............................
Arkansas	30	7	★	7	...	4	2
California	18	★	★	5	★	4	2
Colorado	30	...	★	2	★	4	2
Connecticut	...	★	★	★	★	4	...
Delaware	30	★	12	16	★	4	2
Florida	30	★	★	7	★	4	2
Georgia	30	★	15	6	★	4	...
Hawaii	30	5	★	5	★	4	2
Idaho	30	...	★	2	...	4	...
Illinois	25	...	★	3	...	4	...
Indiana	30	5	5	5	...	4	2
Iowa	30	...	2	2	...	4	...
Kansas	...	...	...	...	...	4	...
Kentucky	30	6	...	6	...	4	2
Louisiana	25	5	5	5	...	4	...
Maine	............................(c)............................
Maryland	30	...	(d)	5	5	4	2
Massachusetts	...	★	★	★	★	4	...
Michigan	30	(h)	(h)	4	4	4	2
Minnesota	25	★	★	1	...	4	...
Mississippi	30	★	20	5	★	4	2
Missouri	30	...	15	10	★	4	...
Montana	25	2	★	2	★	4	2 (e)
Nebraska	30	5	5	5	...	4	2
Nevada	25	2	★	2	★	4	2
New Hampshire	............................(c)............................
New Jersey	............................(c)............................
New Mexico	30	★	★	5	★	4	2
New York	30	★	★	5	★	4	...
North Carolina	30	...	5	2	★	4	2
North Dakota	30	...	★	5	★	4	...
Ohio	18	...	★	★	★	4	2
Oklahoma	31	★	★	★	10	4	...
Oregon	............................(c)............................
Pennsylvania	30	★	★	7	★	4	2
Rhode Island	18	★	★	★	30 days	4	2
South Carolina	30	5	5	5	★	4	2
South Dakota	21	2	★	2	...	4	2
Tennessee	............................(c)............................
Texas	30	...	★	5	...	4	...
Utah	30	5	★	5	★	4	...
Vermont	...	...	...	4	...	2	...
Virginia	30	...	★	5	5	4	...
Washington	18	★	★	★	★	4	...
West Virginia (f)	25	1	1	1	★	2	...
Wisconsin	18	★	★	★	★	4	...
Wyoming	............................(c)............................
American Samoa	35	(g)	★	5	★	4	2
Guam	30	...	5	5	★	4	2
No. Mariana Islands	35	...	★	10	★	4	...
Puerto Rico	............................(c)............................
U.S. Virgin Islands	30	...	5	5	5	4	2

Sources: The Council of State Government's survey, December 2004 and state constitutions, statutes and secretaries of state web sites, January 2005.
Note: This table includes constitutional and statutory qualifications.
   Key:
   ★— Formal provision; number of years not specified.
   . . . — No formal provision.
   (a) In some states you must be a U.S. citizen to be an elector, and must be an elector to run.
   (b) In some states you must be a state resident to be an elector, and must be an elector to run.
   (c) No lieutenant governor. In Tennessee, the speaker of the Senate, elected from Senate membership, has statutory title of "lieutenant governor."

   (d) *Crosse v. Board of Supervisors of Elections* 243 Md. 555, 221 A.2d431 (1966)–opinion rendered indicated that U.S. citizenship was, by necessity, a requirement for office.
   (e) Eligible for eight out of 16 years.
   (f) In West Virginia, the President of the Senate and the Lieutenant Governor are one in the same. The legislature provided in statute the title of Lieutenant Governor upon the Senate President. The Senate President serves 2 year terms, elected by the Senate on the first day of the first session of each two year legislative term.
   (g) Must be a U.S. national.
   (h) In order to be a qualified voter in the state (which is a requirement for office) one must be a U.S. Citizen and a resident of the State of Michigan.

Table 4.14
LIEUTENANT GOVERNORS: POWERS AND DUTIES

State or other jurisdiction	Presides over Senate	Appoints committees	Breaks roll-call ties	Assigns bills	Authority for governor to assign duties	Member of governor's cabinet or advisory body	Serves as acting governor when governor out of state
Alabama	★	★(p)	★	★(p)	...	...	...
Alaska (q)	...	...	...	...	★	★	...
Arizona	....................................(b)...................................						
Arkansas	★	...	★	...	...	...	★
California	...	...	★	...	...	...	★
Colorado	...	...	...	...	★	★	★
Connecticut	★	...	★	...	★	★	★
Delaware	★	...	★	...	...	...	★
Florida	...	...	...	...	★	...	★
Georgia	★	...	...	...	★	...	...
Hawaii (r)	...	...	...	...	★	...	★
Idaho	★	...	★	★	★	...	★
Illinois	...	...	...	...	★	★	...
Indiana	★	...	★	...	...	★	...
Iowa	...	(a)	...	...	★	(g)	(f)
Kansas	...	...	...	...	...	★	...
Kentucky	...	...	...	...	★	★	...
Louisiana	...	...	...	...	★	★	★
Maine	....................................(c)...................................						
Maryland	...	...	...	...	★	★	★
Massachusetts	...	★	★	...	★	★	★
Michigan	★	...	★	...	★	★	★
Minnesota	...	...	...	...	★	★	★
Mississippi	★	★	★	★	...	...	★
Missouri	★	...	★	...	★	★	★
Montana	...	...	...	...	★	★	★
Nebraska	★(d)	...	★	...	★	...	★
Nevada	★	...	★(e)	...	...	...	★
New Hampshire	....................................(c)...................................						
New Jersey	....................................(c)...................................						
New Mexico	★	...	★	...	...	★	★
New York	★	...	★(o)	...	★	★	★
North Carolina	★	...	★	...	...	...	★
North Dakota	★	...	★	...	...	★	★
Ohio	...	...	...	...	★	★	...
Oklahoma	★(n)	...	★	...	★	★	★
Oregon	....................................(b)...................................						
Pennsylvania	★	...	★	...	...	...	...
Rhode Island (j)	...	...	...	...	...	...	...
South Carolina	★	...	★	★	★	...	(i)
South Dakota	★	(h)	★	★	★	(m)	...
Tennessee	....................................(c)...................................						
Texas	★	★	★	★	...	...	★
Utah	...	...	...	...	★	★	...
Vermont	★	★ (a)	★	...	...	...	★
Virginia	★	...	★	...	...	...	...
Washington	★	★	★	...	...	...	★
West Virginia (l)	★	★	...	★	...	...	...
Wisconsin	...	...	...	...	★	...	...
Wyoming	....................................(b)...................................						
American Samoa	...	...	...	...	...	...	★
Guam	(d)	...	...	...	★	★	★
No. Mariana Islands	...	...	...	...	★	(k)	★
Puerto Rico	....................................(b)...................................						
U.S. Virgin Islands	...	...	...	...	★ (g)	★	★

See footnotes at end of table.

LIEUTENANT GOVERNORS: POWERS AND DUTIES — Continued

Sources: The Council of State Governments' survey, December 2004 and state constitutions and statutes.

Key:

★— Provision for responsibility.

. . . — No provision for responsibility.

(a) Appoints all standing committees. Iowa - appoints some special committees; Vermont–appoints all committees as one of three members of Senate Committee on Committees.

(b) No lieutenant governor; secretary of state is next in line of succession to governorship.

(c) No lieutenant governor; senate president or speaker is next in line of succession to governorship. In Tennessee, speaker of the senate bears the additional statutory title of "lieutenant governor."

(d) Unicameral legislative body. In Guam, that body elects own presiding officer.

(e) Except on final passage of bills and joint resolutions.

(f) Only in emergency situations.

(g) Presides over cabinet meetings in absence of governor.

(h) Conference committees.

(i) As directed by the governor.

(j) Under state law responsible for overseeing a number or policy areas in state government through councils and committees, which he chairs.

(k) The Lieutenant Governor is an automatic member of the Governor's cabinet.

(l) In West Virginia, the President of the Senate and the Lieutenant Governor are one in the same. The legislature provided in statute the title of Lieutenant Governor upon the Senate President. The Senate President serves 2 year terms, elected by the Senate on the first day of the first session of each two year legislative term.

(m) If assigned.

(n) Only for joint sessions.

(o) With respect to procedural matters, not legislation.

(p) The Lieutenant Governor serves on the Assignment Committee (five members) and in such capacity has input in the appointment of committees and assigning of bills.

(q) The Lieutenant Governor oversees the Division of Elections; signs and files administrative regulations; publishes Administrative Code and Online Public Notice System; Regulates use of State Seal; Presides during the organization of first session of each legislature; certify ballot measures and writes ballot summaries; authenticate supplements to Alaska Statutes; chairs the Alaska Historical Commission; serves on the Alaska Workforce Board; distributes legislative joint resolutions.

(r) Serves as Secretary of State.

Secretaries of State and Election Reform in the States
By Meredith B. Imwalle

The U.S. Congress passed landmark legislation in 2002 that was intended to improve the administration of elections in this country. The nation's chief state election officials are working now to implement those reforms, despite the fact that much-anticipated federal guidance is late and promised federal funds may never arrive.

Introduction

The most striking thing about November 2, 2004 is what didn't happen. There were no media reports of widespread voter disenfranchisement, and only scattered reports of voting equipment glitches and poll worker mistakes. Election Day was not without its challenges, such as long lines at polling places and large numbers of provisional ballots cast, but media reports on November 3 reflected a positive outcome: the elections ran smoothly overall.

In fact, elections for local, state and federal offices this year operated much the way Congress intended when it passed the Help America Vote Act of 2002 (HAVA), election reform legislation drafted after the 2000 election to improve voting system technology and election administration procedures. The states met the law's 2004 deadlines, and some states have completed reforms they could have postponed until 2006. But the states' work is far from finished. The law gives states only until January 1, 2006 to implement statewide voter registration databases and to provide updated voting equipment that is accessible to the disabled.

The secretaries of state, the chief state election officials in 39 states, are focused now on meeting the deadlines HAVA imposed and continuing to improve the elections process overall. Between now and the 2008 elections, voters can expect to see significant and positive changes in many key areas of election reform.

It is likely that the states will concentrate on four areas of election reform in the coming months: statewide voter registration databases, voting equipment, voter education and poll worker training programs. This article will not speculate about what the end results might be. Abraham Lincoln once said, "With high hope for the future, no prediction is ventured.[1]" In keeping with that cautiously optimistic spirit, I will describe work in progress that is clearly headed in the right direction.

Statewide Voter Registration Databases

HAVA gives each state until January 1, 2006 to implement a statewide voter registration database that includes the name and registration information for every voter in the state, and assigns a unique identifier to each one.[2] The states have indicated that the development of these databases will be a priority over the next few months. Since the passage of HAVA, Congress has appropriated $3 billion in election reform money to the states. According to a survey conducted by the National Association of Secretaries of State (NASS),[3] the states will spend most of that money on the statewide voter registration databases. More than half of the survey's respondents said their state will spend up to 40 percent of its HAVA funds developing, implementing and maintaining its database, and one in five states will spend as much as 70 percent.

The databases promise to streamline election administration—every state and local election official will be able to immediately access the information from anywhere in the state—and reduce the need for provisional ballots, but the states have been precluded from moving ahead as quickly as many had hoped. Even though HAVA was enacted in 2002, the states did not receive federal funding for the required databases until June 2004. Guidance expected from the U.S. Election Assistance Commission (EAC), which was created by HAVA to help the states implement the law, has still not been received. And a requisite Social Security Administration system intended to enable the states to verify the validity of voter registrations was not completed until September 2004.

Despite these obstacles, the states are making progress. Fifteen states actually used the databases in November 2004, and as many as 10 more states have systems in place and are simply fine-tuning them.[4] Almost every state has at least started the acquisition process.

Voting Equipment

Voters in the United States used six different types of voting systems on November 2, 2004. Before Election Day, experts predicted that more than 55 million voters would use optical scan systems; more than 50 million would use direct response electronic voting machines (DREs); 32 million would vote on punch cards, 22 million would vote on lever machines and the remainder would use paper ballots or some combination of systems.[5] Updating voting equipment is another one of the states' priorities. In fact, voters in most states can expect to see at least one piece of new equipment in their polling places in 2006.

Under HAVA, states have until January 1, 2006 to implement a voting system that meets the following requirements[6]:

- Notifies a voter if he/she over-votes, or selects more than one candidate for the same race, and gives him or her the opportunity to correct the ballot;

- Produces a permanent paper record with a manual audit capacity;

- Provides levels of access, privacy and independence to disabled voters that are equal to those available to other voters; and

- Provides alternative language accessibility in accordance with the requirements of the Voting Rights Act.[7]

If spending amounts are any indication, the states will be very focused on voting equipment in the near future. Close to 40 percent of the NASS survey participants reported that their state will spend 50 percent or more of its election reform money on voting equipment. Seventy-five percent of the respondents said their state will spend at least one-quarter of its HAVA money on equipment.

Some of the states have already started replacing their old systems. More than 324 jurisdictions throughout the country have switched voting systems since HAVA passed. Georgia and Nevada established uniform voting systems statewide, and both states used them in the 2004 election. Maryland will implement a uniform system in 2006.[8]

Many of the states that have not yet introduced HAVA-compliant voting systems have been waiting for the federal government to release updated voting equipment guidelines. The EAC, in cooperation with the National Institute for Standards and Technology, is required by HAVA to issue the voluntary guidelines. The first discussion draft will be available in April 2005, and it is still unclear when the final draft will be completed. In order to meet HAVA's deadline for revamping their voting systems, the states will have to proceed now with selecting and installing new equipment.

Voter Education

In 2004, the secretaries of state reached out to voters in unprecedented ways. This was due in large part to the fact that, for the first time, the states had federal dollars to spend on these efforts.

Sixty-three percent of the states NASS surveyed will spend up to 10 percent of their HAVA funds on voter education. Seventy-five percent of the states used HAVA funds on extensive voter education efforts during 2004, including:

- Mock elections;

- Distribution of sample ballots;

- Presentations to community organizations and schools; and

- Easy-to-read instructional guides for voters.

The Arkansas secretary of state's staff worked with the Martin Luther King Commission to conduct a mock election during a national youth conference. Iowa's secretary of state sent voter guides to every household in the state. North Dakota's secretary of state used HAVA money to fund $56,000 in grants to Native American tribal organizations in order to help educate voters in that minority community. Minnesota and Michigan offered polling place locators on their Web sites.

The states hope to continue these efforts, but they may be forced to scale back due to lack of funding. Congress failed to appropriate $800 million in authorized HAVA funds for fiscal year 2005—money the states were counting on to help pay for future voter education campaigns.

Poll Worker Training

States launched more comprehensive poll worker training programs this year than ever before. Poll worker training programs are typically conducted at the county level, but an overwhelming majority of chief state election officials report that they have taken a more active role since HAVA passed. Forty-four percent of the states NASS surveyed will spend up to 10 percent of their HAVA money on poll worker training efforts including:

- Producing training materials;

- Establishing training standards; and

• Conducting specialized workshops.

Connecticut's secretary of state conducts many training sessions personally, and reviews and certifies any training sessions conducted by other staff members. Georgia provides printed training materials and videos to local jurisdictions. Indiana was one of several states that issued guidebooks this year with step-by-step instructions for poll workers. And before this year's election, Oregon conducted public meetings with the disability community and produced a brochure for election officials entitled, "How to Assist Voters with Disabilities."

Efforts in these states and others have made a significant impact on the quality of poll worker training programs, and have helped lend some level of uniformity to poll worker training statewide. The states intend to continue and expand these programs, but may struggle to finance them if HAVA is not fully funded.

Conclusion

These reforms are just part of the comprehensive plans the states developed for implementing HAVA's federally mandated election reforms. The budgets the states included in their plans were largely based on the amount of money Congress promised when it passed the HAVA in 2002.

Seventy-four percent of the states NASS surveyed used federally authorized amounts when calculating their budgets for fiscal year 2003. Sixty-three percent of the respondents based their FY 2004 budgets on authorized amounts and 65 percent used authorized amounts to develop their FY 2005 budgets.

Only half of the survey participants will be able to fulfill all of the elements of their plans if HAVA is not fully funded. Unfortunately, soft expenditures like voter education initiatives and poll worker training programs will likely be the areas that suffer most. The states may be forced to rely on outside groups like NASS and other nonprofit, nonpartisan organizations to continue these efforts. In the absence of federal funds, financing for the work will have to come from philanthropic groups and other appropriate grant programs.

The states will use the money they have on more tangible expenditures, specifically voting equipment and voter registration databases. While many states have already purchased new voting equipment and started the process of acquiring voter registration databases, they will still look to the EAC for guidance. The secretaries of state will continue to urge the EAC to develop and publish updated voluntary voting system guidelines in time for the states to meet the January 1, 2006 HAVA deadline for implementing the equipment. And the secretaries will look to the EAC to develop and publish recommended guidelines for statewide voter registration databases well in advance of HAVA's January 1, 2006 implementation deadline.

The secretaries of state achieved significant reforms in 2004. They will continue to improve the elections process, even if promised federal guidance is delayed and approved federal funds are not received. Between now and 2006, the nation's chief state election officials will work toward their ultimate goal—a positive voting experience for every American who votes.

Notes

[1] Abraham Lincoln, Second Inaugural Address, (Washington, D.C.: March 4, 1865).

[2] United States Congress, Help America Vote Act of 2002: Title III, Subtitle A, Section 303

[3] The National Association of Secretaries of State, How States are Spending Federal Election Reform Dollars. (The National Association of Secretaries of State, November 15, 2004). *http://www.nass.org/Survey%20Summary%20 HAVA.pdf.*

[4] Electionline, "The 2004 Election," (December 2004). *http://www.electionline.org/site/docs/pdf/ERIP%20Brief 9%20Final.pdf.*

[5] Election Data Services, "New Study Shows 50 Million Voters will use Electronic Voting Systems, 32 Million Still with Punch Cards in 2004," (February 12, 2004). *http:// www.electiondataservices.com/EDSInc_VEstudy2004.pdf.*

[6] Help America Vote Act of 2002: Title III, Subtitle A, Section 303.

[7] United States Congress, Voting Rights Act of 1965: Section 203.

[8] Election Data Services.

About the Author

Meredith B. Imwalle is the director of communications for the National Association of Secretaries of State. She served as a delegate-at-large to the second annual Congressional Conference on Civic Education and she is a member of the steering committee of the Council for Excellence in Government's Campaign for the Civic Mission of Schools. Imwalle is a member of the Public Relations Society of America.

Table 4.15
THE SECRETARIES OF STATE, 2005

State or other jurisdiction	Name and party	Method of selection	Length of regular term in years	Date of first service	Present term ends	Number of previous terms	Maximum consecutive terms allowed by constitution
Alabama	Nancy Worley (D)	E	4	1/03	1/07	0	2
Alaska	-- (a) --						
Arizona	Jan Brewer (R)	E	4	1/03	1/07	0	2
Arkansas	Charlie Daniels (D)	E	4	1/03	1/07	0	2
California	Bruce McPherson (R)	E (i)	4	3/05 (i)	1/07	0	2
Colorado	Donetta Davidson (R)	E	4	7/99 (b)	1/07	1 (b)	2
Connecticut	Susan Bysiewicz (D)	E	4	1/99	1/07	1	. . .
Delaware	Harriet Smith Windsor (D)	A	. . .	1/01	. . .	0	. . .
Florida	Glenda Hood (R)	A	. . .	2/03	. . .	0	. . .
Georgia	Cathy Cox (D)	E	4	1/99	1/07	1	. . .
Hawaii	-- (a) --						
Idaho	Ben Ysursa (R)	E	4	1/03	1/07	0	. . .
Illinois	Jesse White (D)	E	4	1/99	1/07	1	. . .
Indiana	Todd Rokita (R)	E	4	1/03	1/07	0	2
Iowa	Chet Culver (D)	E	4	1/99	1/07	1	. . .
Kansas	Ron Thornburgh (R)	E	4	1/95	1/07	2	. . .
Kentucky	Trey Grayson (R)	E	4	12/03	12/07	0	2
Louisiana	W. Fox McKeithen (R)	E	4	1/88	1/08	4	. . .
Maine	Matthew Dunlap (D)	L	2	1/05	1/07	0	. . .
Maryland	R. Karl Aumann (R)	A	. . .	1/03	. . .	0	. . .
Massachusetts	William Francis Galvin (D)	E	4	1/95	1/07	2	. . .
Michigan	Terri Lynn Land (R)	E	4	1/03	1/07	0	2
Minnesota	Mary Kiffmeyer (R)	E	4	1/99	1/07	1	. . .
Mississippi	Eric Clark (D)	E	4	1/96	1/08	2	. . .
Missouri	Robin Carnahan (D)	E	4	1/05	1/09	0	. . .
Montana	Brad Johnson (R)	E	4	1/05	1/09	0	(c)
Nebraska	John Gale (R)	E	4	12/00 (d)	1/07	(d)	. . .
Nevada	Dean Heller (R)	E	4	1/95	1/07	2	2 (f)
New Hampshire	William Gardner (D)	L	2	12/76	12/06	14	. . .
New Jersey	Regena Thomas (D)	A	. . .	1/02	1/06	0	. . .
New Mexico	Rebecca Vigil-Giron (D)	E	4	1/87 (g)	1/07	2	2
New York	Randy Daniels (R)	A	. . .	4/01	. . .	0	. . .
North Carolina	Elaine Marshall (D)	E	4	1/97	1/09	2	. . .
North Dakota	Alvin Jaeger (R)	E	4 (h)	1/93	1/07 (h)	2	. . .
Ohio	J. Kenneth Blackwell (R)	E	4	1/99	1/07	1	2
Oklahoma	M. Susan Savage (D)	A	4	1/03	1/07	0	. . .
Oregon	Bill Bradbury (D)	E	4	1/99 (e)	1/09	(e)	2
Pennsylvania	Pedro A. Cortes (D)	A	. . .	5/03	. . .	0	. . .
Rhode Island	Matthew Brown (D)	E	4	1/03	1/07	0	2
South Carolina	Mark Hammond (R)	E	4	1/03	1/07	0	. . .
South Dakota	Chris Nelson (R)	E	4	1/03	1/07	0	2
Tennessee	Riley Darnell (D)	L	4	1/93	1/09	3	. . .
Texas	Roger Williams (R)	A	. . .	2/05	. . .	0	. . .
Utah	-- (a) --						
Vermont	Deb Markowitz (D)	E	2	1/99	1/07	3	. . .
Virginia	Anita Rimler (D)	A	. . .	1/02	. . .	0	. . .
Washington	Sam Reed (R)	E	4	1/01	1/09	1	. . .
West Virginia	Betty Ireland (R)	E	4	1/05	1/09	0	. . .
Wisconsin	Douglas LaFollette (D)	E	4	1/99	1/07	1	. . .
Wyoming	Joe Meyer (R)	E	4	1/99	1/07	1	. . .
American Samoa	-- (a) --						
Guam	-- (a) --						
No. Mariana Islands	-- (a) --						
Puerto Rico	Marisara Pont Marchese	A	. . .	NA	. . .	. . .	. . .
U.S. Virgin Islands	(a)						

See footnotes at end of table.

THE SECRETARIES OF STATE, 2005 — Continued

Sources: The Council of State Governments' survey October 2004 and state Web sites, January 2005.

Key:

E—Elected by voters

A—Appointed by governor.

L—Elected by legislature.

. . .—No provision for.

(a) No secretary of state.

(b) Secretary Davidson was appointed by Gov. Bill Owens in July 1999 upon the death of Secretary Vikki Buckley. She was elected to finish out the remaining two-year term in November 2000, and then was re-elected to a full four-year term in November 2002.

(c) Eligible for eight out of 16 years.

(d) Secretary Gale was appointed by Gov. Mike Johanns in December 2000 upon the resignation of Scott Moore. He was elected to a full four-year term in November 2002.

(e) Secretary Bradbury was appointed Secretary of State in November 1999 and was elected to a four-year term in November 2000 and 2004.

(f) Term limits were not effective until Secretary Heller's second term in office. His second term counts as his first.

(g) Secretary Vigil-Giron served from 1987–1991. She was elected again in 1998 and in 2002.

(h) Because of a constitutional change approved by voters in 2000, the term for the secretary elected in 2004 will be only two years. It will revert to a four year term in 2007.

(i) Appointed in March 2005 upon the resignation of Kevin Shelley.

Table 4.16
SECRETARIES OF STATE: QUALIFICATIONS FOR OFFICE

State or other jurisdiction	Minimum age	U.S. citizen (years) (a)	State resident (years) (b)	Qualified voter (years)	Method of selection to office
Alabama	25	7	5	★	E
Alaska	....................(c)....................				
Arizona	25	10	5	. . .	E
Arkansas	18	★	★	★	E
California	18	★	★	★	E
Colorado	25	★	2	. . .	E
Connecticut	18	★	★	★	E
Delaware	. . .	. . .	★	. . .	A
Florida	....................(f)....................				
Georgia	25	10	4	★	E
Hawaii	....................(c)....................				
Idaho	25	★	2	★	E
Illinois	25	★	3	. . .	E
Indiana	. . .	. . .	★	. . .	E
Iowa	18	. . .	. . .	. . .	E
Kansas	. . .	. . .	. . .	. . .	E
Kentucky	30	★	★	. . .	E
Louisiana	25	5	5	★	E
Maine	. . .	. . .	. . .	★	(e)
Maryland	. . .	. . .	. . .	. . .	A
Massachusetts	18	★	5	★	E
Michigan	18	★	★	★	E
Minnesota	21	★	★	★	E
Mississippi	25	★	5 (d)	★	E
Missouri	. . .	★	★	2	E
Montana	25	★	2	★	E
Nebraska	. . .	★	★	★	E
Nevada	25	2	2	. . .	E
New Hampshire	18	★	★	★	(e)
New Jersey	18	★	★	★	A
New Mexico	30	★	5	★	E
New York	18	★	★	. . .	A
North Carolina	21	. . .	. . .	★	E
North Dakota	25	★	5	★	E
Ohio	18	★	★	★	E
Oklahoma	31	★	10	★	A
Oregon	18	. . .	★	★	E
Pennsylvania	. . .	. . .	. . .	. . .	A
Rhode Island	18	★	30 days	. . .	E
South Carolina	18	★	★	★	E
South Dakota	. . .	. . .	. . .	. . .	E
Tennessee	. . .	. . .	. . .	. . .	(e)
Texas	18	★	. . .	. . .	A
Utah	. . .	. . .	. . .	. . .	A
Vermont	....................(c)....................	★	★	★	E
Virginia	. . .	. . .	. . .	. . .	A
Washington	18	★	★	★	E
West Virginia	. . .	★	★	★	E
Wisconsin	18	★	★	★	E
Wyoming	25	★	1	★	E
American Samoa	....................(c)....................				
Guam	....................(c)....................				
No. Mariana Islands	....................(c)....................				
Puerto Rico	....................(c)....................				
U.S. Virgin Islands	. . .	5	5	. . .	A

Source: The Council of State Governments' survey of secretaries of state, October 2004.

Key:

★—Formal provision; number of years not specified.

. . .—No formal provision.

A—Appointed by governor.

E—Elected by voters.

(a) In some states you must be a U.S. citizen to be an elector, and must be an elector to run.

(b) In some states you must be a state resident to be an elector, and must be an elector to run.

(c) No secretary of state.

(d) State citizenship requirement.

(e) Chosen by joint ballot of state senators and representatives. In Maine and New Hampshire, every two years. In Tennessee, every four years.

(f) As of January 1, 2003, the office of Secretary of State shall be an appointed position (appointed by the governor). It will no longer be a cabinet position, but an agency head and the Department of State shall be an agency under the governor's office.

Table 4.17
SECRETARIES OF STATE: ELECTION AND REGISTRATION DUTIES

State or other jurisdiction	Chief election officer	Determines ballot eligibility of political parties	Receives initiative and/or referendum petition	Files certificate of nomination or election	Supplies election ballots or materials to local officials	Files candidates' expense papers	Files other campaign reports	Conducts voter education programs	Registers charitable organizations	Registers corporations (a)	Processes and/or commissions notaries public	Registers securities	Registers trade names/marks
	Election								*Registration*				
Alabama	★	★	...	★	★	★	★	★	★	★	★	...	★
Alaska (b)	★	★	★	★	★	...	...	★	...	...	★	...	...
Arizona	★	★	★	★	...	★	★	★	★	...	★	...	★
Arkansas	★	★	★	★	...	★	★	★	★	★	★	...	★
California	★	★	★	★	...	★	★	★	...	★	★	...	★
Colorado	★	★	★	★	...	★	★	★	★	★	★	...	★
Connecticut	★	★	...	★	★	★	★	★	★	★	★	...	★
Delaware	...	...	...	(c)	...	★	(d)	...	★ (e)	★	★	...	★
Florida	★	★	★	★	...	★	★	...	...	★	...	...	★
Georgia	★	★	...	★	★	★	★	★	★	★	...	★	★
Hawaii (b)	...	...	...	★	...	★	★	...	...	★	★	...	...
Idaho	★	★	★	★	★	★	★	★	...	★	★	...	...
Illinois	...	...	★	(h)	...	...	...	...	...	★	★	★	★
Indiana	★	★	...	★	★	★	★	★	★	★	★	...	★
Iowa	★	★	...	★	...	...	...	★	...	★	★	...	★
Kansas	★	★	...	★	...	★	★	★	★	★	★	...	★
Kentucky	★	★	...	★	...	...	...	★	★	★	★	...	★
Louisiana	★	...	...	...	★	...	...	★	★	★	★	★	★
Maine	★	★	★	★	★	...	...	★	...	★	★	...	★
Maryland	...	★	★	...	...	...	...	...	★	★	★	...	★
Massachusetts	★	★	★	★	★	(d)	(d)	★	...	★	★	★	★
Michigan	★	★	★	★	...	★	★	★	...	★	★	...	...
Minnesota	★	★	★	★	...	...	...	★	★	★	★	...	★
Mississippi	★	★	★	★	★	★	★	★	★	★	★	★	★
Missouri	★	★	★	★	...	...	...	★	★	★	★	★	★
Montana	★	★	★	★	★	...	...	★	★	★	★	...	★
Nebraska	★	★	★	★	★	...	...	★	...	★	★	...	★
Nevada	★	★	★	★	★	★	★	★	...	★	★	★	★
New Hampshire	★	★	...	★	★	★	★	★	★	★	★	...	★
New Jersey	...	...	...	...	...	...	...	...	...	...	...	...	...
New Mexico	★	★	★	★	...	★	★	★	...	★	★	...	★
New York	...	...	...	...	...	...	...	...	★	★	★	★	★
North Carolina	...	...	...	...	...	...	...	...	★	★	★	★	★
North Dakota	★	★	★	★	★	★	★	...	★	★	★	...	★
Ohio	★	★	★	★	★	★	...	★	...	★	★	...	...
Oklahoma	...	...	★	★ (f)	...	★	...	...	★	★	★	...	★
Oregon	★	★	★	★	★	★	★	★	★	★	★	★	★
Pennsylvania	★	★	...	★	...	...	★	★	★	★	★	...	★
Rhode Island	★	★	...	★	★	...	...	★	...	★	★	...	★
South Carolina	...	...	...	...	...	...	...	...	★	★	★	...	★
South Dakota	★	★	★	★	...	★	★	★	...	★	★	...	★
Tennessee	...	★	...	★	★	...	...	★	★	★	★	...	★
Texas	★	★	...	★	★	...	...	★	★	★	★	...	★
Utah (b)	★	★	★	★	★	★	★	★	...	★	★	...	...
Vermont	★	★	...	★	★	★	★	★	...	★	★	...	★
Virginia	...	...	...	★	...	...	...	★	★	★	...	★	★
Washington	★	★	★	★	...	...	...	★	★	★	...	★	★
West Virginia	★	★	...	★	...	★	★	★	★	★	...	...	★
Wisconsin	...	...	...	...	...	...	...	...	...	...	★	...	★
Wyoming	★	★	★	★	(i)	★	★	★	★	★	★	★	★
American Samoa (b)	...	...	...	★	...	★	★	★	★	★	★	...	...
Guam (b)	...	...	...	...	...	...	...	...	...	...	...	...	...
Puerto Rico	...	...	...	...	...	...	...	...	★	★	★	★	★
U.S. Virgin Islands (b)	...	...	...	...	...	...	...	...	★	★ (g)	★	...	★

See footnotes at end of table.

SECRETARIES OF STATE: ELECTION AND REGISTRATION DUTIES — Continued

Source: The Council of State Governments' survey of secretaries of state, October 2004.

Key:

★—Responsible for activity.

. . .—Not responsible for activity.

(a) Unless otherwise indicated, office registers domestic, foreign and non-profit corporations.

(b) No secretary of state. Duties indicated are performed by lieutenant governor. In Hawaii, election related responsibilities have been transferred to an independent Chief Election Officer.

(c) Files certificates of election for publication purposes only; does not file certificates of nomination.

(d) Federal candidates only.

(e) Incorporated organizations only.

(f) Files certificates of congressional and judicial retention elections only; does not file certificates of nomination.

(g) Both domestic and foreign profit; but only domestic non-profit.

(h) Office issues document, but does not receive it.

(i) Materials not ballots.

Table 4.18
SECRETARIES OF STATE: CUSTODIAL, PUBLICATION AND LEGISLATIVE DUTIES

State or other jurisdiction	Custodial			Publication					Legislative				
	Archives state records and regulations	Files state agency rules and regulations	Administers uniform commercial code provisions	Files other corporate documents	State manual or directory	Session laws	State constitution	Statutes	Administrative rules and regulations	Opens legislative sessions (a)	Enrolls or engrosses bills	Retains copies of bills	Registers lobbyists
Alabama	...	...	★	★	...	★	★	★	...	...	★	★	...
Alaska (b)	...	★	...	...	...	...	★	...	★	★	...	★	...
Arizona	★	★	★	...	...	...	★	...	★	...	...	★	★
Arkansas	★	★	★	★	...	★	★	...	★	...	...	★	★
California	★	...	★	★	...	...	★	...	...	...	...	...	★
Colorado	...	★	★	★	...	...	★	...	★	...	...	★	★
Connecticut	★(c)	★	★	★	★	...	...	...	...	S	...	★	...
Delaware	★	★	★	★	...	...	...	...	★	...	...	...	...
Florida	★	★	...	★	...	★	★	★	★	...	...	...	...
Georgia	★	★	...	...	★	...	★	...	★	...	...	...	...
Hawaii (b)	...	★	...	...	...	★	★	★	★	...	...	★	...
Idaho	...	...	★	...	★	★	★	...	...	...	...	★	★
Illinois	★	★	★	★	★	★	★	★	★	H	...	★	★
Indiana	★	★	★	★	...	...	...	...	...	...	...	★	...
Iowa	★	...	★	★	...	...	★	...	...	...	...	★	...
Kansas	...	★	★	★	...	★	...	...	★	★	...	★	★
Kentucky	★	...	★	★	...	...	...	...	...	...	★	★	...
Louisiana	★	...	★	★	★	...	...	★	...	...	...	★	...
Maine	★	★	★	★	...	...	★	★	★	...	...	...	...
Maryland	...	...	...	...	...	...	...	...	(d)	...	...	...	...
Massachusetts	★	★	★	★	★	★	★	★	★	...	...	★	★
Michigan	★	★	★	...	...	★	★	★	★	...	...	...	★
Minnesota	★	★	★	★	★	★	★	★	...	H	...	★	...
Mississippi	★	★	★	★	★	★	...	★	★	H	★	★	★
Missouri	★	★	★	★	★	...	★	...	★	H	★	★	...
Montana	★	★	★	★	...	...	★	...	★	H	★	★	...
Nebraska	★	★	★	★	...	...	...	...	...	...	...	★	...
Nevada	★	★	★	★	...	...	...	...	...	...	...	★	...
New Hampshire	★	...	★	★	★	...	★	...	...	...	★	★	★
New Jersey	★	...	...	...	...	...	★	...	...	...	...	★	...
New Mexico	...	...	★	...	★	★	★	★	...	H	...	★	★
New York	...	★	★	...	★	★	★	...	★	...	...	★	...
North Carolina	★	★	★	★	★	★	★	...	...	...	...	...	★
North Dakota	...	...	★	★	...	...	...	...	...	...	★	★	★
Ohio	...	★	★	★	★	★	★	...	...	...	★	★	...
Oklahoma	...	★	...	★	...	...	★	★	★	...	...	★	...
Oregon	★	★	★	★	★	...	★	...	★	...	...	★	★
Pennsylvania	...	...	★	★	...	...	...	...	...	...	★	★	...
Rhode Island	★	★	★	★	★	...	★	...	...	...	...	★	★
South Carolina	...	...	★	★	...	...	★	...	...	...	...	★	...
South Dakota	★	★	★	★	★	...	★	...	...	H	...	★	★
Tennessee	★	★	★	★	★	★	★	...	★	...	...	★	...
Texas	★	★	★	★	...	★	...	...	★	...	...	★	★
Utah (b)	...	...	...	...	...	...	★	...	...	...	...	★	★
Vermont	★	★	★	★	★	★	★	...	★	H	...	★	★
Virginia	...	...	...	...	...	...	...	...	...	...	...	...	...
Washington	★	...	...	★	★	...	...	...	...	...	...	★	...
West Virginia	★	★	★	★	...	...	★	...	★	...	...	★	...
Wisconsin	...	...	...	...	...	...	...	...	...	...	...	...	...
Wyoming	★	★	★	★	★	...	★	...	...	H	...	★	★
American Samoa (b)	...	★	...	★	...	★	★	★	★	...	...	...	...
Guam (b)	...	...	...	...	...	...	...	...	...	...	...	...	...
Puerto Rico	...	★	★	★	...	★	★	★	★	...	...	...	...
U.S. Virgin Islands (b)	...	★	★	★	...	...	...	★	...	...	★	★	...

Sources: The Council of State Governments survey of secretaries of state, October 2004.

Key:
★—Responsible for activity.
...—Not responsible for activity.
(a) In this column only: Both houses; H—House; S—Senate.

(b) No secretary of state. Duties indicated are performed by lieutenant governor.
(c) The secretary of state is keeper of public records, but the state archives is a department of the Connecticut State Library.
(d) Code of Maryland regulations.

Attorneys General: Emerging Trends and Issues
By Angelita Plemmer

As the state's chief state legal officer, the attorney general commonly serves as the most visible and influential state official in the fight against crime. In recent years, multistate efforts by attorneys general have increased their visibility, power, influence and success in enforcement efforts in a number of complex legal areas impacting all areas of public life.

Antitrust

State attorneys general have been characterized as "the guardians of the gates of effective antitrust enforcement." During the past quarter century, state attorneys general have played an increasingly significant role in ensuring the operation of the free market. Even before the 1890 passage of the Sherman Act, the key federal antitrust law, the majority of states had some form of state law prohibiting price-fixing. State attorneys general are authorized to enforce both federal and state laws that address both vertical and horizontal price fixing, tying of a less popular item to a desired item, and anticompetitive mergers. This unique ability to pursue violations in both federal and state court has resulted in many multistate cases that are national in scope, in addition to local bid-rigging and price fixing cases. The goal of state attorneys general in antitrust enforcement now, as always, is competition, and accordingly, lower prices, to provide higher quality and a greater variety of innovative new products for citizens of their states.

During the past decade, the trend in state antitrust enforcement has been toward multistate litigation filed by a number of the attorneys general on cases with national impact. Multistate litigation typically includes cost sharing arrangements among the attorneys general and may also include deputization of staff attorneys from one state to act as assistant attorneys general in other states for investigation and litigation purposes. Some examples of successful multistate coordination in antitrust cases include vertical price fixing cases in the agricultural chemical, shoe and music industries. Recently, attorneys general have concentrated on the pharmaceutical industry, challenging tying arrangements and attempted monopolization, as well as anticompetitive activities designed to delay entry into the market by generic competitors.

Although federal law bars recovery for antitrust violations by indirect purchasers, nearly half the states have statutes that specifically permit indirect purchasers to recover damages for state antitrust law violations. This ability of some attorneys general to pursue claims on behalf of indirect purchasers has led to a novel multistate litigation technique in which suits brought in various state courts are resolved by a single settlement. For example, 23 attorneys general entered into a settlement with vitamin manufacturers to resolve indirect purchaser claims resulting from a 10-year price fixing conspiracy.

State attorneys general also use federal and state antitrust laws to challenge anticompetitive activity within a single state. For example, the attorney general of New York successfully challenged an arrangement between two hospitals through which they negotiated jointly with third-party payers and allocated services among themselves. The California attorney general reached a settlement with a ferry company accused of forcing customers to purchase tickets for other cruises in order to obtain tickets to its most popular destination, Alcatraz Island.

As the enforcers of state and federal antitrust laws and as the chief legal officers of their respective states, attorneys general have a substantial interest in ensuring that antitrust laws are applied in a manner that is consistent with underlying congressional policy and judicial precedent. Accordingly, attorneys general communicate their views on antitrust and competition policy through amicus briefs, comments on proposed federal regulations, legislative advocacy and National Association of Attorneys General (NAAG) resolutions.

The education of state and local government officials on the fundamentals of antitrust laws is an important function performed by many attorneys general. Many attorneys general review state contracts, professional licensing board regulations and proposed business practices for anticompetitive effects. In some states, the attorney general reviews the regulations of state boards and agencies to determine whether they unnecessarily limit competition. The regulations of professional licensing boards concerning advertising, solicitation of business and the location of offices are typical regulations reviewed by the attorneys general.

Bankruptcy

Bankruptcy laws impact attorney general activities in numerous ways. Bankruptcy is a federal law and attorneys general may be responsible for collecting a vast array of types of debts owed to the states, ranging from traditional contracts with private parties, to student loans, to enforcing domestic support obligations owed to dependent spouses and children. Whenever one of those debtors files bankruptcy, the state must carefully evaluate how and whether it can continue to collect its debt so as not to violate the limitations imposed by the bankruptcy laws.

Recent trends show that bankruptcy issues, in connection with the regulatory activities of attorneys general, are impacting a number of legal areas, rather than simply traditional debt collection activities. Whenever states seek to collect restitution for amounts owed to victims in consumer protection and antitrust cases, or to require cleanup of environmentally contaminated facilities, or to order a party to cease and desist from unlawful activities, they may find that the defendant will file bankruptcy in order to resist those enforcement efforts. The Bankruptcy Code allows many, but not all, of the states' enforcement activities to continue, despite the bankruptcy filing, and also limits the state's ability to deny licenses, grants and permits to those who have filed bankruptcy. Thus, it is critical for states to thread their way through the web of special rights and responsibilities created by the code. Bankruptcies have a national scope, so states have frequently chosen to work together, often with the assistance of NAAG, to present a common front in the bankruptcy case to resolve common issues. In doing so, they attempt to ensure that the rights of not only the states as such, but also the rights of their citizens, are protected to the greatest degree allowed by the Code.

In the recent MCI/Worldcom bankruptcy case, for instance, about 15 states jointly audited the debtor's tax filings and have argued that the company engaged in an elaborate tax avoidance scheme that may have diverted hundreds of millions of dollars from state tax coffers. In the First Alliance case, six lead states worked with the Federal Trade Commission and private class counsel to obtain remedies for some 20,000 consumers in about 20 states who had been victimized by a predatory mortgage lending scheme, eventually obtaining tens of millions of dollars in restitution from the debtor, even after it filed bankruptcy.

Civil Rights

Attorneys general have civil rights enforcement responsibilities either as counsel to state civil rights agencies or pursuant to their own independent authority. In addition, many states have passed legislation that has enhanced their enforcement ability. States' civil rights enforcement efforts include working with the public, law enforcement entities, state, federal and local government agencies to ensure nondiscrimination. The areas of enforcement are varied, but more recent trends include actions in fair employment, housing discrimination, disability rights, mortgage lending, and bias-related crimes. Many of the civil rights issues and trends are also addressed through education, training programs, litigation and outreach. Towards this end, a number of attorneys general have established sections of their offices committed to such efforts known as, for example, the Civil Rights Enforcement Section, Disability Rights Project or the Office of Civil Rights.

Consumer Protection

Attorneys general continue to lead the nation in protecting their states' consumers. Attorneys general protect citizens from online scams, such as phishing, fraudulent auctions and spam; price gouging and charities fraud in the wake of disasters; telephone and mail fraud and home repair scams, which target elderly consumers disproportionately; subprime lending abuses, such as payday lending and illegal debt-counseling operations; and the improper marketing of prescription drugs.

The consumer protection programs administered by attorneys general are multifaceted. Attorneys general have primary responsibility in their states for the enforcement of state consumer protection laws. Every state has a consumer protection statute prohibiting deceptive acts and practices. These broad general statutes are supplemented in all jurisdictions by laws that target specific industries or practices found to be particularly problematic. Among the areas addressed in these statutes are auto repair, telemarketing and do-not-call, identity theft, spam, price gouging and enhanced penalties for victimizing the elderly. Attorneys general have varied tools and authority to address abuses and illegalities in the marketplace. These include civil and criminal litigation, mediation, public education, creating and commenting on state and federal legislative proposals, and cooperative enforcement ventures with state, local and federal enforcement agencies.

A continued trend among attorneys general is that they continue to supplement their state-specific enforcement efforts with multistate investigatory and litigation efforts. This sharing and leveraging of sometimes-scant resources and collective action on issues that transcend state borders have produced successful results in efforts to stop consumer frauds involving misleading telecommunications advertising, the deceptive off-label marketing of prescription drugs and illegal overcharging of consumers for their leased vehicles.

Perennial areas of investigation and enforcement include: retail sales, automobile rental, home repair, telemarketing and telecommunications. Areas of more recent concern include Internet-based marketing schemes; privacy, including identity theft, spam, the failure of both brick-and-mortar and online businesses to comply with required or self-imposed privacy policies; and the misleading advertising of prescription drugs and dietary supplements.

Criminal Law

As the state's chief law enforcement official, the attorney general commonly serves as the most visible and influential state official in the fight against crime. While the constitutional and statutory authority of attorneys general in the area of criminal law varies by jurisdiction, the attorney general, typically is a critical component in the successful investigation and prosecution of criminal activity, as well as upholding criminal convictions that are challenged through direct appeal and collateral proceedings in state and federal courts. In recent years, attorneys general have emerged as leaders in the legal and policy discussions taking place in the law enforcement community.

The ability of the attorney general to take an active role in criminal investigations and prosecutions depends on statutory or constitutional authority. While some attorneys general are responsible for the prosecution of all violations of state law, as is the case in Alaska, Delaware and Rhode Island, other attorneys general have almost no criminal authority in their jurisdiction. In Connecticut, for example, all criminal prosecutions are conducted under the Office of the Chief State's Attorney rather than through the Office of the Attorney General.

In many jurisdictions, the attorney general's office has its own criminal investigative unit with authority to conduct investigations statewide. For example, the Office of the Attorney General of Kentucky recently announced the creation of the Kentucky Bureau of Investigation, the first investigative unit of its kind in the commonwealth. In a number of jurisdictions, the statewide investigative bureau is directly under the attorney general's supervision and authority. In Wis-

consin, for instance, the attorney general is the head of the state Department of Justice, which houses the Division of Criminal Investigation, the statewide investigation entity. Similarly, in New Jersey and Rhode Island, among other jurisdictions, the attorney general exercises supervisory control over the state police, which conduct statewide criminal investigations. In still other jurisdictions, the criminal investigative authority of the attorney general is limited to particular issues. For example, in Florida, the only criminal investigative section within the Office of the Attorney General is the Medicaid Fraud Control Unit.

In addition to direct investigative involvement, attorneys general, in most jurisdictions, provide important training services to peace officers and local prosecutors, ranging from manuals and newsletters, to seminars and training academies. For instance, through the California attorney general's Advanced Training Center, California law enforcement officers from across the state receive specialized training from recognized experts in the field.

Although attorneys general are continuing their law enforcement efforts in traditional areas such as organized crime, white collar crime and Medicaid fraud, emerging trends in criminal justice matters are demanding more attention, including issues related to gang violence, victims' rights, and prescription drug abuse and diversion. Still other growing areas of concern have led to an organized effort on the part of the attorneys general, including coordination through working groups and task forces within NAAG, related to interstate movement of registered sex offenders, manufacturing of methamphetamine using common pre-cursor chemicals found in over-the-counter products, and issues of legal preparedness in the context of homeland security and a potential terrorist attack.

Cybercrime

As the states' top law enforcers, attorneys general are facing an increasing number of crimes occurring using computers and the Internet. Today's technology-driven world provides a new arena for criminals and other unscrupulous actors as perpetrators are becoming more adept at using computers and the Internet to commit fraud, identity theft, stalking and online exploitation of children through online luring and exposure to child pornography. In response, many attorneys general have established task forces, either entirely within their offices or in collaboration with other state law enforcement entities, to investigate and prosecute online child exploitation. In Texas, the cyber crime unit has arrested more than 200 predators since its inception.

In addition to an increasing number of cases involving identity theft using the computer, as well as cyberstalking, a traditional sex crime with a high tech component, attorneys general are addressing a sharp rise in crimes involving online commerce, particularly in the sale of illegal merchandise. For example, Massachusetts recently sought and obtained a court order barring Internet merchants from selling illegal weapons, such as stun guns and switchblades, in the state. As Americans become more proficient in using the Internet for their shopping needs, attorneys general have seen a sharp increase in the number of cases of fraud perpetuated by sellers on Internet auction sites, especially by the seller failing to deliver the merchandise after receiving payment or by the seller using shills to bid up the price. As an example, Oklahoma recently charged an online auction seller with failing to deliver $30,000 worth of trailers that he sold on eBay.

Attorneys general are also involved in addressing the proliferation of computer intrusion-related crimes, such as hacking, denial of service attacks, computer viruses and worms, all of which demonstrate that the critical elements of our infrastructure remain vulnerable to cyber attacks. In May 2004, 50 prosecutors from attorney general offices attended an intensive training on investigating and prosecuting criminals who perpetrate these types of crimes.

A recent issue addressed by the attorneys general is the growth of peer-to-peer (P2P) networks that allow the free sharing of digital files. The P2P software has often been hijacked by criminals who use it for illegal purposes, such as trading in child pornography and piracy of movies and music. In response, more than 40 attorneys general sent a letter to the networks warning them that they may face enforcement actions if they do not take steps to stem illegal activity. The attorneys general also asked the networks to stop adding encryption features that prevent law enforcement agencies from policing the networks to determine whether they are aiding illegal activity.

End of Life

In 2002, Oklahoma Attorney General and NAAG President Drew Edmondson launched an initiative to explore how attorneys general could help improve end-of-life health care for the citizens of their states. Attorneys general in each state are charged with protecting constituents in matters affecting the public interest, including consumer protection of those who are dying. A report resulting from the initiative, "Im-proving End of Life Care: The Role of Attorneys General," identified three areas of concern in which attorneys general can play a major role:

- Ensuring competent end-of-life care;

- Removing barriers to effective pain management; and

- Acknowledgement and respect for the wishes of those who are dying.

Since the report was issued, a number of attorneys general have sought to improve end-of-life health care in their states. NAAG began an End of Life Health Care Project in 2004 to enhance the ability of attorneys general to assist constituents as they plan for how they want to live at the end of their lives. How much and what type of curative treatment is desired and under what circumstances? Where would they like to live while they are dying? Is avoiding or minimizing pain more important than the number of days one can stay alive or should every effort be made to keep them alive as long as possible? Who should make health care decisions for them if they become unable to do so? These are very personal questions and answers vary among individuals and according to circumstances. Fourteen attorneys general, through their work on the NAAG End of Life Health Care Working Group, provide leadership on how attorneys general and their staffs can help citizens address these issues. In addition, attorneys general from most states have designated staff to be involved in end-of-life health care activities.

At the state level, a number of attorneys general have created their own state task forces or are otherwise working in conjunction with physicians and other health care providers, consumers, legislators, grassroots coalitions and advocacy groups to improve end of life care. Some have focused on the places in which people die—hospices, nursing homes, hospitals and homes, to ensure quality care and to prevent other considerations from creating barriers to that care. Ensuring access to pain management to alleviate suffering at the end of life is an important and challenging counterbalance to the need for law enforcement to prevent drug diversion. Legislation and legal issues in the area of decision-making are also important to end of life care. A number of attorneys general have simplified advance directive requirements and procedures through leadership or participation on state end-of-life commissions, legislative proposals brochures and Web sites for citizens of their states, and advisory opinions.

Environment

The state attorney general is the primary enforcer of laws protecting the environment and natural resources. As a general rule, attorneys general have responsibility for enforcing federal environmental statutes when enforcement of those laws devolves to the states, as well as responsibility for state-specific environmental protection laws. In some cases, local prosecutors share criminal enforcement authority with the attorney general. Similarly, attorneys general sometimes work with the U.S. Department of Justice and the U.S. Environmental Protection Agency on joint environmental enforcement cases, allowing both groups to leverage their limited resources.

As environmental enforcement practice has matured, many attorneys general have integrated air, water and waste disposal issues into largely standardized initiatives. New practice areas have tended to focus on three emerging sets of issues. 1. Regional or geographically linked questions including water issues in the West, downwind air pollution questions and coastal issues such as cruise ship pollution, invasive species and coastal zone management; 2. Cleanup statutes and broad principles of tort law, including natural resource damage claims that are the conclusion of long-standing cleanup efforts; and 3. Litigation of the limits of federal environmental authority in a variety of contexts. Issues touching on the relationship between state and federal powers include the scope of federal review over state permitting programs, the definition of "waters of the United States," and the discretionary—or ministerial—responsibility of the federal government to promulgate regulations on specific subjects, to mention only a few.

Legislation

NAAG's role in the federal legislative process is clearly defined by the association. NAAG takes positions on federal legislation in several ways. NAAG policies are created either by members voting on resolutions at full-member conferences or by signing onto letters as a group. Generally, resolutions and sign-on letters are limited to those matters that diminish or office of attorneys general or preempt state law.

Frequently, attorneys general across the country are asked by Congress, media, business organizations and constituents for their views on bills pending in Congress that affect the powers and duties of attorneys general. Often, such legislation seeks to preempt state law in the areas of consumer protection, environment, antitrust, bankruptcy, securities, criminal law and many other areas within the jurisdiction of attorneys general.

During the 108th Congress, attorneys general from around the country came to Capitol Hill to testify before both House and Senate committees on issues affecting the states. State attorneys general testified often on behalf of consumers regarding fair credit, on-line pharmaceuticals, identity theft, banking issues and predatory lending. In addition, during the 108th Congress, attorneys general testified on environmental bills, securities and many other issues. Many of the following issues on which attorneys general have taken policy positions, testified or monitored actively, will be in consideration again in the 109th Congress beginning in January of 2005:

Antitrust

- Medicare Prescription Drug, Improvement, and Modernization Act of 2003
- Drug Price Competition
- Prescription Drug Importation
- Patient Access to Health Care
- Antitrust Exemption for Insurance Industry
- Antitrust Enforcement
- Retail Gas Prices

Bankruptcy

- Bankruptcy Overhaul

Consumer Protection

- Identity Theft
- "Do Not Call"
- SPAM
- Household Goods Movers
- Fair Credit Reporting Act
- Cell Phone Bill of Rights
- Online Pharmaceuticals
- OCC Preemption of State Authority over OCC Chartered Banks
- Privacy
- Rent to Own
- Jurisdictional Certainty Over Digital Commerce Act
- Debt Counseling, Debt Consolidation and Debt Settlement
- Predatory Lending
- Anti-Pyramid Scheme Legislation

- Drug Price Disclosure
- Internet File Sharing
- Protecting Older Americans from Fraud
- Flu Vaccine Price Gouging

Criminal

- Crime Victims Bill of Rights
- Gangs
- DNA and the Innocence Protection Act
- Hate Crimes
- Homeland Security/USA Patriot Act/ Immigration
- Firearms
- Sex Offender Registry
- Youth
- Witness Protection
- Voice-Over-Internet-Protocol

Cybercrime

- E-Checks
- Database Protection
- Identification Database
- Spyware

End-of-life Health Care

- Pain Management
- Advance Directives
- Palliative Care Improvements

Environmental

- Exemptions from Environmental Laws for Department of Defense
- State role in Hydropower Licensing

Tobacco

- Attorneys' Fees
- PACT Act/Delivery Sales of Cigarettes
- FDA Regulation of Tobacco

Violence Against Women

- Children in Domestic Violence Settings
- Sexual Assault in Prisons

State Solicitors and Appellate Chiefs

One notable development in the management of attorney general offices is the increasing use of state solicitors to oversee the offices' respective appellate practices. On the criminal law side, most attorney general offices engage exclusively in (or almost exclusively) appellate work. The head of the criminal section is usually a de facto state solicitor for that portion of the office's work. On the civil side, however, most attorney general offices traditionally had no single hand guiding their respective appellate practices. The various civil sections (e.g., environmental, consumer protection, civil rights and civil defense) would independently oversee their sections' appellate briefs and arguments. Over the past decade, this has started to change. More than half the states now have a state solicitor (or a person with a different title who serves that role), whose responsibility is to oversee the office's civil appellate work to ensure high quality and consistency of positions.

The role of the state solicitor and his or her team of deputies and assistants varies from office to office. Most state solicitor units do not take over the bulk of their respective offices' civil appeals. Rather, they provide editorial assistance and general advice to various other attorneys scattered throughout the office. Among the exceptions are the state solicitor units in New York and Oregon, and the Civil Appeals unit in Illinois, which handle most of their respective offices' civil appeals. State Solicitors improve the quality of an office's briefs and oral arguments and ensure consistent positions are taken by the attorney general throughout the office.

Tobacco

In 1994, states sued the four largest tobacco companies[1] in the United States for health care costs imposed on the states by consumers' consumption of cigarettes. In 1998, the attorneys general of 46 states and six U.S. territories signed the Tobacco Master Settlement Agreement (MSA) with these companies to settle state suits to recover costs associated with treating smoking-related illnesses.[2] According to the MSA, tobacco companies agree to make payments to the states in perpetuity with a present value of $206 billion. In return, the states agreed to release the Participating Manufacturers from specified claims that the states (but not individuals) had and might have in the future for costs arising out of tobacco-related illnesses.

Since 1998, almost 50 tobacco manufacturing companies (known as Subsequent Participating

Manufacturers under the agreement) have joined the MSA. Most recently, in 2004, the nation's largest non-participating tobacco manufacturer, General Tobacco, joined the MSA. Attorneys general hope that other tobacco companies that have not joined the agreement will join to make the coverage of the MSA close to universal. The MSA, enforced by attorneys general, contains a number of public health provisions designed to reduce youth smoking. It prohibits tobacco companies from targeting youth in advertising, promotions or marketing. It also bans industry actions aimed at initiating, maintaining or increasing youth smoking. Other provisions of the agreement are: bans on all outdoor advertising, including billboards, signs and placards in arenas, stadiums, shopping malls and video game arcades; limits on advertising outside retail establishments to a size of 14 square feet; and bans on transit advertising of tobacco products.

Tobacco companies are also prohibited from attempting to suppress research that may limit information about the health hazards from the use of their products, into smoking and health, or into the marketing or development of new products; and they are prohibited from making any material misrepresentations regarding the health consequence of smoking.

As the chief legal officers of their respective jurisdictions, attorneys general have played a critical role in ensuring MSA compliance by tobacco companies. A number of states have been successful in recent actions to enforce a number of the MSA's key public health provisions. Courts have ruled in favor of attorneys general who have sought penalties for enforcement violations surrounding advertising programs that violate the Agreement's youth targeting provisions; initiated investigations of flavored cigarettes; pursued retailers that allow the illegal sale of tobacco products to minors; and questioned claims by tobacco manufacturers that they are producing less harmful products.

As a result of the work of the attorneys general and the public health community, U.S. consumption of tobacco products is down nearly 20 percent and youth smoking has been reduced by more than 25 percent. Total payments to date made under MSA equal $35.3 billion, some of which state legislatures are designating for public health and tobacco control programs.

One of the most recent successes for attorneys general was the passage of changes to the Allocable Share Provision of the Model Escrow Statute in 39 states. This legislation is also under consideration in other states. The changes were enacted to ensure that settling states would receive the benefits of the MSA and that companies that refused to enter into the MSA would not be able to profit unfairly by their non-participation. In addition, states are seeing the benefits of the passage of complementary NPM enforcement legislation, which enhanced the ability of the MSA settling states to ensure a non-participating manufacturer's compliance with escrow regulations in current state statutes.

Conclusion

Cooperation and coordination by attorneys general have become an invaluable means of supplementing state-specific litigation, investigation and enforcement activities in a variety of legal areas. States continue to face increasing caseloads and diminishing resources, stemming from decreased state funding. Cross-border cooperation acknowledges that crime knows no borders, particularly as crimes become more high-tech. These cooperative ventures extend to local and federal enforcement agencies as well, and have resulted in countless successes in uncovering abuses and illegalities in the marketplace, and ensuring the health and welfare of citizens across the country.

Notes

[1] Philip Morris, RJR, Brown and Williamson and Lorillard.

[2] Florida, Minnesota, Texas and Mississippi settled their tobacco cases separately from the MSA states in 1997.

About the Author

This article was edited and compiled by **Angelita Plemmer**, director of communications for the National Association of Attorneys General. A former print journalist, Plemmer joined the association staff in 2001. She formerly worked as the public information office for the city of Roanoke and as the assistant city manager for public information for the city of Alexandria, Va. She holds a master's degree in journalism from Columbia University and a bachelor of arts degree from the University of Virginia.

Table 4.19
THE ATTORNEYS GENERAL, 2005

State or other jurisdiction	Name and party	Method of selection	Length of regular term in years	Date of first service	Present term ends	Number of previous terms	Maximum consecutive terms allowed
Alabama	Troy King (R)	E	4	3/04 (i)	1/07	0	2
Alaska	Scott Nordstrand (Acting)	A	. . .	2/05	. . .	0	. . .
Arizona	Terry Goddard (D)	E	4	1/03	1/07	0	2 (a)
Arkansas	Mike Beebe (D)	E	4	1/03	1/07	0	2
California	Bill Lockyer (D)	E	4	1/99	1/07	1	2
Colorado	John W. Suthers (R)	E	4	1/05 (n)	1/07	0	2
Connecticut	Richard Blumenthal (D)	E	4	1/91	1/07	3	★
Delaware	M. Jane Brady (R)	E	4	1/95	1/07	2	★
Florida	Charlie Crist (R)	E	4	1/03	1/07	0	2
Georgia	Thurbert E. Baker (D)	E	4	6/97 (j)	1/07	1 (j)	★
Hawaii	Mark J. Bennett (R)	A	4 (l)	12/02	12/06	0	. . .
Idaho	Lawrence Wasden (R)	E	4	1/03	1/07	0	★
Illinois	Lisa Madigan (D)	E	4	1/03	1/07	0	★
Indiana	Steve Carter (R)	E	4	1/01	1/09	1	. . .
Iowa	Tom Miller (D)	E	4	1/79	1/07	4	★
Kansas	Phill Kline (R)	E	4	1/03	1/07	0	★
Kentucky	Greg Stumbo (D)	E	4	1/04	1/08	0	2
Louisiana	Charles C. Foti Jr. (D)	E	4	1/04	1/08	0	★
Maine	G. Steven Rowe (D)	(b)	2	1/01	1/05	0	4
Maryland	J. Joseph Curran Jr. (D)	E	4	1/87	1/07	4	★
Massachusetts	Tom Reilly (D)	E	4	1/99	1/07	1	2
Michigan	Mike Cox (R)	E	4	1/03	1/07	0	2
Minnesota	Mike Hatch (D)	E	4	1/99	1/07	1	★
Mississippi	Jim Hood (D)	E	4	1/04	1/08	. . .	★
Missouri	Jeremiah W. Nixon (D)	E	4	1/93	1/09	3	★
Montana	Mike McGrath (D)	E	4	1/01	1/09	1	2 (c)
Nebraska	Jon Bruning (R)	E	4	1/03	1/07	0	★
Nevada	Brian Sandoval (R)	E	4	1/03	1/07	0	2
New Hampshire	Kelly Ayotte	A	. . .	7/04	. . .	0	. . .
New Jersey	Peter C. Harvey (D)	A	. . .	3/03	. . .	0	. . .
New Mexico	Patricia A. Madrid (D)	E	4	1/99	1/07	1	2 (a)
New York	Eliot Sptizer (D)	E	4	1/99	1/07	1	★
North Carolina	Roy Cooper (D)	E	4	1/01	1/05	1	★
North Dakota	Wayne Stenehjem (R)	E	4 (d)	12/00	12/06	1	★ (d)
Ohio	Jim Petro (R)	E	4	1/03	1/07	0	2
Oklahoma	W. A. Drew Edmondson (D)	E	4	1/95	1/07	2	★
Oregon	Hardy Myers (D)	E	4	1/97	1/09	2	★
Pennsylvania	Tom Corbett (R)	E	4	1/05	1/09	0	2 (a)
Rhode Island	Patrick Lynch (D)	E	4	1/03	1/07	0	2 (a)
South Carolina	Henry McMaster (R)	E	4	1/03	1/07	0	★
South Dakota	Larry Long (R)	E	4	1/03	1/07	0	2 (a)
Tennessee	Paul G. Summers (D)	(f)	8	1/99	1/07	0	. . .
Texas	Greg Abbott (R)	E	4	1/03	1/07	0	★
Utah	Mark Shurtleff (R)	E	4	1/01	1/09	1	★
Vermont	William H. Sorrell (D)	E	2	5/97 (e)	1/07	3 (e)	★
Virginia	Judith W. Jagdmann (R)	E	4	2/05 (o)	1/06	0	(g)
Washington	Rob McKenna (R)	E	4	1/05	1/09	0	★
West Virginia	Darrell Vivian McGraw Jr. (D)	E	4	1/93	1/09	3	★
Wisconsin	Peg Lautenschlager (D)	E	4	1/03	1/07	0	★
Wyoming	Pat Crank (D)	A (h)	. . .	1/03	1/07	0	. . .
Dist. of Columbia	Robert Spanoletti (D)	A	. . .	6/03	. . .	0	. . .
American Samoa	Fiti Sunia	A	4	N.A.	N.A.	N.A.	. . .
Guam	Douglas Moylan	E	4	1/03	1/07	0	. . .
No. Mariana Islands	Pamela Brown	A	4	2003	N.A.	N.A.	. . .
Puerto Rico	Roberto J. Sanchez-Ramos	A	4	N.A.	. . .	0	. . .
U.S. Virgin Islands	Alva Swan	A	4	N.A.	. . .	0	. . .

Sources: The Council of State Governments' survey of attorneys general, November 2004 and state Web sites.

★—No provision specifying number of terms allowed.

. . .—No formal provision, position is appointed or elected by governmental entity (not chosen by the electorate).

A—Appointed by the governor.

E—Elected by the voters.

L—Elected by the legislature.

(a) After two consecutive terms , must wait four years and/or one full term before being eligible again.

(b) Chosen biennially by joint ballot of state senators and representatives.

(c) Eligible for eight out of 16 years.

(d) The term of the office of the elected official is four years, except that in 2004 the attorney general was elected for a term of two years.

(e) Appointed to fill unexpired term in May 1997. Elected in 1998 to full term.

(f) Appointed by judges of state Supreme Court.

(g) May hold office for an unlimited number of terms.

(h) Must be confirmed by the Senate.

(i) Appointed to fill unexpired term in March 2004.

(j) Appointed to fill unexpired term in June 1997. Elected in 1998 to a full term.

(l) Appointed to fill unexpired term in February 2004.

(m) Appointed to fill unexpired term in February 2004.

(n) Appointed to fill unexpired term in January 2005.

(o) Appointed to fill unexpired term in February 2005.

Table 4.20
ATTORNEYS GENERAL: QUALIFICATIONS FOR OFFICE

State or other jurisdiction	Minimum age	U.S. citizen (years) (a)	State resident (years) (b)	Qualified voter (years)	Licensed attorney (years)	Membership in the state bar (years)	Method of selection to office
Alabama	25	7	5	★	...	...	E
Alaska	...	★	...	...	...	...	A
Arizona	25	10	5	...	5	5	E
Arkansas	...	...	★	★	...	...	E
California	18	★	★	★	(c)	(c)	E
Colorado	25	★	2	...	★	(d)	E
Connecticut	18	★	★	★	10	10	E
Delaware	...	...	...	...	...	...	E
Florida	30	★	7	★	★	5	E
Georgia	25	10	4	★	★	7	E
Hawaii	...	1	1	...	★	(e)	A
Idaho	30	★	2	...	★	★	E
Illinois	25	★	3	★	★	...	E
Indiana	...	2	2	★	5	...	E
Iowa	18	★	★	...	...	...	E
Kansas	...	...	...	...	...	...	E
Kentucky	30	...	2 (f)	...	8	2	E
Louisiana	25	5	5 (f)	★	5	5	E
Maine	...	...	...	...	...	...	(g)
Maryland	...	★(h)	★	★	★	10	E
Massachusetts	18	...	5	★	...	★	E
Michigan	18	★	★	...	★	★	E
Minnesota	21	★	30 days	★	...	...	E
Mississippi	26	★	5	★	5	★	E
Missouri	...	★	1	...	...	...	E
Montana	25	★	2	...	5	★	E
Nebraska	...	...	...	...	...	...	E
Nevada	25	★	2 (f)	★	...	...	E
New Hampshire	18	...	...	★	★	★	A
New Jersey	18	...	★	...	...	...	A
New Mexico	30	★	5	★	★	...	E
New York	30	★	5	...	(i)	...	E
North Carolina	21	★	★	★	★	(i)	E
North Dakota	25	★	5	★	★	★	E
Ohio	18	★	★	★	...	...	E
Oklahoma	31	★	10	10	...	...	E
Oregon	18	★	★	★	...	...	E
Pennsylvania	30	★	7	...	★	★	E
Rhode Island	18	★	30 days (f)	★	...	...	E
South Carolina	...	★	30 days	★	...	...	E
South Dakota	18	★	★	★	(i)	(i)	E
Tennessee	...	...	...	...	...	...	(j)
Texas	...	...	★	...	(i)	(i)	E
Utah	25	★	5 (f)	★	★	★	E
Vermont	18	★	★	★	...	...	E
Virginia	30	★	1 (k)	★	...	5 (k)	E
Washington	18	★	★	★	★	★	E
West Virginia	25	...	5	★	...	...	E
Wisconsin	...	★	★	...	...	...	E
Wyoming	...	★	★	★	4	4	A (l)
Dist. of Columbia	...	...	★	...	★	★	A
American Samoa	...	...	(c)	...	(i)	(i)	A
Guam	...	...	...	...	...	...	A
No. Mariana Islands	...	...	3	...	5	...	A
Puerto Rico	...	★	...	...	★	★	A
U.S. Virgin Islands	...	...	★	★	★	★	A

Sources: The Council of State Governments' survey of attorneys general, October 2004 and state constitutions and statutes, February 2005.

Key:
★ — Formal provision; number of years not specified.
. . . . — No formal provision.
A—Appointed by governor.
E—Elected by voters.
(a) In some states you must be a U.S. citizen to be an elector, and must be an elector to run.
(b) In some states you must be a state resident to be an elector, and must be an elector to run.
(c) No statute specifically requires this, but the State Bar Act can be interpreted as making this a qualification.

(d) Licensed attorneys are not required to belong to the bar association.
(e) No period specified, all licensed attorneys are members of the state bar.
(f) State citizenship requirement.
(g) Chosen biennially by joint ballot of state senators and representatives.
(h) Crosse v. Board of Supervisors of Elections 243 Md. 555, 2221A.2d431 (1966)—opinion rendered indicated that U.S. citizenship was, by necessity, a requirement for office.
(i) Implied.
(j) Appointed by judges of state Supreme Court.
(k) Same as qualifications of a judge of a court of record.
(l) Must be confirmed by the Senate.

Table 4.21
ATTORNEYS GENERAL: PROSECUTORIAL AND ADVISORY DUTIES

State or other jurisdiction	Authority in local prosecutions:				Issues advisory opinions:				Reviews legislation:	
	Authority to initiate local prosecution	May intervene in local prosecutions	May assist local prosecutor	May supersede local prosecutor	To state executive officials	To legislators	To local prosecutors	On the constitutionality of bills or ordinances	Prior to passage	Before signing
Alabama	A	A,D	A,D	A	★	★	★	...	★	...
Alaska	(a)	(a)	(a)	(a)	★	★	...	★	★	★
Arizona	A,B,C,D,F	B,D	B,D	B	★	★	★	...	...	...
Arkansas	...	...	D	...	★	★	★	★	...	...
California	A,B,C,D,E	A,B,C,D,E	A,B,C,D,E	A,B,C,D,E	★	★	★	...	...	...
Colorado	B,F	B	D,F (b)	B	★	★	★	★	★	★
Connecticut	...	...	...	...	★	(c)	...	★	(e)	(e)
Delaware	A (j)	(j)	(j)	(j)	★	★	...	★	★(o)	★(o)
Florida	F	...	D	...	★	★	★	...	...	...
Georgia	B,D,E,F,G	B,D,G	A,B,D,E,F,G	...	★	★	★	...	...	...
Hawaii	A,B,C,D,E	A,B,C,D,E	A,B,C,D,E	A,B,C,D,E	★	★	...	★(k)	★	★
Idaho	B,D,F	...	D	...	★	★	★	★	★	★
Illinois	D,F	D,G	D	G	★	★	★	...	...	...
Indiana	F	...	D	...	★	★	★	★	...	...
Iowa	D,F	D,F	D,F	D,E,F	★	★	★	...	(p)	(p)
Kansas	A,B,C,D,F	A,D	D	A,F	★	★	★	★	...	(g)
Kentucky	D,F,G	B,D,G	D	B	★	★	★	★	...	...
Louisiana	A,D,G	A,D,G	D	G	★	★	★	★	★	★
Maine	A	A	A	A	★	★	...	★	★	★
Maryland	B,F	D	D	...	★	★	★	★	★	★
Massachusetts	A	A	A,D	A	★	★(h)	★	★	(g)	(g)
Michigan	A	A	D	(b)	★	★	★	★	...	...
Minnesota	B,F	B,D,G	A,B,D,G	B	★	★(h)	★	...	...	(g)
Mississippi	A,D,F	D,F	A,D,F	D,F	★	★	★	...	...	...
Missouri	F,G	...	B,F	G	★	★	★	...	(g)	(g)
Montana	D,F	A,B,D	A,B,D	A	★	★(i)	★	...	...	...
Nebraska	A	A	A	A	★	★	★	★	(t)	...
Nevada	D,F,G	D	...	...	★	...	★	★	...	...
New Hampshire	A	A	A	A	★	★	★	...	(q)	(q)
New Jersey	A	A,B,D,G	A,D	A,B,D,G	★	★	★	★	★	★
New Mexico	B,D,E,F	D,E,F	A,B,D,E,F	D,E,F,G	★	★	★	★	★	★
New York	B,F	B,D,F	D	B	★	★(h)	★	★	★	★
North Carolina	...	D	D	...	★	★	★	★	★	...
North Dakota	A,D,E,F,G	A,D,G	A,B,D,E,F,G	A,G	★	★	★	...	(f)	(g)
Ohio	F	D	D	F	★	(i)	★	...	...	...
Oklahoma	A,B,C,E,F	A,B,C,E,F	A,B,C,E	E	★	★	★	...	(r)	(r)
Oregon	B,D,F	B,D	B,D	...	★	★	★	...	...	★
Pennsylvania	D,F,G	...	...	G	★	★	...	★	...	...
Rhode Island	A	A	...	...	★	★	...	...	★	...
South Carolina	A,D,E,F (b)	A,B,C,D,E,F	A,D	A,E	★	(l)	★	★	★(m)	★(g)
South Dakota	A,B,D,E,F (b)	D,G (b)	A,B,D,E	D,F	★	★	★	...	★	...
Tennessee	D,F,G (b)	D,G (b)	D	...	★	★	★	★	...	...
Texas	F	...	D	...	★(d)	★(d)	★(d)	★(d)	(n)	(n)
Utah	A,B,D,E,F,G	E,G	D,E	E	★	★(l)	★	★	★(g)	★(g)
Vermont	A	A	A	G	★	★	★	★	★	★
Virginia	B,F	B,D,F	B,D,F	B	★	★	★	★	★	★
Washington	B,D	D	D	...	★	★	★	...	(g)	(g)
West Virginia	...	...	...	...	★	★	★	★	...	...
Wisconsin	B,C,F	B,C,D	D	B	★	★	★	★(k)	(e)	(e)
Wyoming	B,D,F	B,D	B,D	G	★	★	★	★(k)	★	★
Dist. of Columbia	F	D	D	F	★	★	(s)	★	★	★
American Samoa	A (j)	(j)	(j)	(j)	★	...	(j)	(e)	(g)	(g)
Guam	A	A	A	A	★	★	★	★	(g)	B
No. Mariana Islands	A (j)	(j)	(j)	(j)	★	★	...	★	...	...
Puerto Rico	A	(j)	(j)	(j)	★	★	...	...	★	★
U.S. Virgin Islands	A (j)	(j)	(j)	(j)	★	...	...	★	★	★

See footnotes at end of table.

ATTORNEYS GENERAL: PROSECUTORIAL AND ADVISORY DUTIES — Continued

Source: The Council of State Governments' survey of attorneys general, October 2004.

Key:

A—On own initiative.
B—On request of governor.
C—On request of legislature.
D—On request of local prosecutor.
E—When in state's interest.
F—Under certain statutes for specific crimes.
G—On authorization of court or other body.
★—Has authority in area.
. . .—Does not have authority in area.
(a) Local prosecutors serve at pleasure of attorney general.
(b) Certain statutes provide for concurrent jurisdiction with local prosecutors.
(c) To legislative leadership.
(d) Only upon request by a statutorily authorized requestor.
(e) Informally reviews bills or does so upon request.
(f) Opinion may be issued to officers of either branch of General Assembly or to chairman or minority spokesman of committees or commissions thereof.

(g) Only when requested by governor or legislature.
(h) To legislature as a whole not individual legislators.
(i) To either house of legislature, not individual legislators.
(j) The attorney general functions as the local prosecutor.
(k) Bills, not ordinances.
(l) Only when requested by legislature.
(m) Has concurrent jurisdiction with states' attorneys.
(n) Official opinions, when requested, regarding proper construction or constitutionality of proposed or enacted legislation.
(o) Also at the request of agency or legislature.
(p) No requirements for review.
(q) When legislation impacts the office or upon request.
(r) If required by legislature; may assist in drafting.
(s) The office of attorney general prosecutes local crimes to an extent. The office's Legal Counsel Division may issue legal advice to the office's prosecutorial arm. Otherwise, the office does not usually advise the OUSA, the district's other local prosecutor.
(t) If requested by a legislator.

Table 4.22
ATTORNEYS GENERAL: CONSUMER PROTECTION ACTIVITIES, SUBPOENA POWERS AND ANTITRUST DUTIES

State or other jurisdiction	May commence civil proceedings	May commence criminal proceedings	Represents the state before regulatory agencies (a)	Administers consumer protection programs	Handles consumer complaints	Subpoena powers (b)	Antitrust duties
Alabama	★	★	★	★	★	●	A,B,C
Alaska	★	★	★	★	★	★	A,B,C
Arizona	★	...	...	★	★	(n)	A,B,C,D
Arkansas	★	...	★	★	★	●	A,B
California	★	★	...	★	★	★	A,B,C
Colorado	★	★	★	★	★	★	A,B,C,D
Connecticut	★	(l)	★	★	★	●	A,B,D
Delaware	★	★	★	★	★	★	A,B,D
Florida	★	...	...	★	★	★	A,B,C,D
Georgia	★	★	★	...	...	●	...
Hawaii	★	★	...	★	★	●	A,B,C,D
Idaho	★	...	★	★	★	★	A,B,D
Illinois	★	★ (n)	★	★	★	●	A,B,C
Indiana	★	...	★	★	★	★	A,B
Iowa	★	★	★	★	★	★	B,C
Kansas	★	★	★	★	★	★	A,B
Kentucky	★	★	★	★	★	★	A,B,C,D
Louisiana	★	★	★	★	★	★	A,B,D
Maine	★	★	★	★	★	★	A,B,C
Maryland	★	★ (f)	...	★	★	★	B,C,D
Massachusetts	★	★	★	★	★	★	A,B,C,D
Michigan	★	★	★	★	★	★	A,B,C
Minnesota	★	...	★	★	★	●	A,B,C
Mississippi	★	★	...	★	★	★	A,B,C,D
Missouri	★	★	★	★	★	★	A,B,C
Montana (h)	...	...	...	...	...	...	A,B
Nebraska	★	★	★	★	★	★	A,B,C,D
Nevada	★	★	★	★	★ (m)	★	A,B,C,D
New Hampshire	★	★	★	★	★	★	A,B,C
New Jersey	★	★	★	★	★	★	A,B,C,D
New Mexico	★	★	★	★	★	★	A,B,C (p)
New York	★	★	★	★	★	★	A,B,C,D
North Carolina	★	★(e)	★	★	★	★	A,B,C,D
North Dakota	★	...	★	★	★	★	A,B,D
Ohio	★	★	★	★	★	★	A,B,C,D
Oklahoma	★	★	★	★	★	★	A,B,C,D
Oregon	★	★(e)	★	★	★	★	A,B,C
Pennsylvania	★	★	...	★	★	★	A,B,C,D
Rhode Island	★	★	...	★	★	●	B,C
South Carolina	★(a)	★(c)	★	...	★(m)	●	A,B,C,D
South Dakota	★	★	★	★	★	★	A,B,C
Tennessee	★	(e)(f)	(e)	...	...	★	B,C,D
Texas	★	★(j)	★	★	★	●	A,B,D
Utah	★(d)	★	★(d)	...	★(g)	●	A (i),B,C,D (i)
Vermont	★	★	★	★	★	★	A,B,C,D
Virginia	★	(e)	★	★(g)	★(g)	●	A,B,C,D
Washington	★	...	(k)	★	★	★	A,B,D
West Virginia	★	...	★	★	★	★	A,B,D
Wisconsin	★	★	★	★	★	●	A,B,C (p)
Wyoming	★	...	★	★	★	●	A,B
Dist. of Columbia	★	★ (o)	★	★	★	★	A,B,C,D
American Samoa	★	★	★	★	★	★	...
Guam	★	★	★	★	★	●	A,B,C,D
No. Mariana Islands	★	★	★	★	★	★	A,B
Puerto Rico	★	★	...	...	...	★	A,B,C,D
U.S. Virgin Islands	★	★	★	★	★	●	A

See footnotes at end of table.

ATTORNEYS GENERAL: CONSUMER PROTECTION ACTIVITIES, SUBPOENA POWERS AND ANTITRUST DUTIES — Continued

Source: The Council of State Governments' survey of attorneys general, October 2004.

Key:

A—Has parens patriae authority to commence suits on behalf of consumers in state antitrust damage actions in state courts.

B—May initiate damage actions on behalf of state in state courts.

C—May commence criminal proceedings.

D—May represent cities, counties and other governmental entities in recovering civil damages under federal or state law.

★—Has authority in area.

. . . — Does not have authority in area.

(a) May represent state on behalf of: the "people of the state; an agency of the state; or the state before a federal regulatory   agency.

(b) In this column only: ★ broad powers and ● limited powers.

(c) When permitted to intervene.

(d) Attorney general has exclusive authority.

(e) To a limited extent.

(f) May commence criminal proceedings with local district attorney.

(g) Attorney general handles legal matters only with no administrative handling of complaints.

(h) Exercise consumer protection authority only in cooperation with the state department of administration.

(i) Opinion only, since there are no controlling precedents.

(j) Under specific statutes for specific crimes.

(k) The Public Counsel Unit appears and represents the public before the Utilities & Transportation Commission.

(l) In certain cases only.

(m) On a limited basis because the state has a separate consumer affairs department.

(n) Antitrust only.

(o) In antitrust not criminal proceedings.

(p) May represent other governmental entities in recovering civil damages under federal or state law.

Table 4.23
ATTORNEYS GENERAL: DUTIES TO ADMINISTRATIVE AGENCIES AND OTHER RESPONSIBILITIES

State or other jurisdiction	Serves as counsel for state	Appears for state in criminal appeals	Duties to administrative agencies							
			Issues official advice	Interprets statutes or regulations	Conducts litigation: On behalf of agency	Conducts litigation: Against agency	Prepares or reviews legal documents	Represents the public before the agency	Involved in rule-making	Reviews rules for legality
Alabama	A,B,C	★(a)	★	★	★	★	★	(b)	(b)	★
Alaska	A,B,C	★	★	★	★	...	★	...	★	★
Arizona	A,B,C	★	★	★	★	...	★	★	...	...
Arkansas	A,B,C	★	★	★	★	...	★	...	...	...
California	A,B,C	★	★	★	★	...	★	...	...	...
Colorado	A,B,C	★(a)	★	★	★	★	★	(e)	★	★
Connecticut	A,B,C	(b)	★	★	★	★(i)	★	★	★	★
Delaware	A,B,C	★	★	★	★	...	★	...	...	★
Florida	A,B,C	★	★	★	★	...	★	...	...	...
Georgia	A,B,C	★	★	★	★	★	★	...	...	...
Hawaii	A,B,C	★	★	★	★	★	★	★	★	★
Idaho	A,B,C	★(a)	★	★	★	★	★	...	...	...
Illinois	A,B,C	★	...	★	★	...	★	...	★	★
Indiana	A,B,C	★	★	★	★	...	★	★	★	★
Iowa	A,B,C	★	★	★	★	...	★	...	★	★
Kansas	A,B,C	★	★	★	★	★	★	...	★	★
Kentucky	A,B,C	★	★	★	★	...	...	★	★	...
Louisiana	A,B,C	(h)	★	★	★	...	★	...	...	★
Maine	A,B,C	★	★	★	★	...	★	...	★	★
Maryland	A,B,C	★	★	★	★	(b)	★	...	★	★
Massachusetts	A,B,C	(b)(c)(d)	★	★	★	★	★	★	★	★
Michigan	A,B,C	★	★	★	★	★	★	★	★	★
Minnesota	A,B,C	(c)(d)	★	★	(a)	★	★	...	...	...
Mississippi	A,B,C	...	★	★	★	...	★	★	★	...
Missouri	A,B,C	★	★	★	★	...	★	...	...	...
Montana	A,B,C	★	★	★	★	...	★	...	★	★
Nebraska	A,B,C	★	★	★	★	★	★	...	★	★
Nevada	A,B,C	★	★	★	★	...	★	...	...	...
New Hampshire	A,B,C	★	★	★	★	★	★	★	(f)	(f)
New Jersey	A,B,C	★	★	★	★	★	★	...	★	★
New Mexico	A,B,C	★	★	★	★	★	★	(b)	...	...
New York	A,B,C	(b)	...	★	★	★	(b)	(b)	★	★
North Carolina	A,B,C	★	★	★	★	★	★	...	★	★
North Dakota	A,B,C	(b)	★	★	★	...	★	...	...	...
Ohio	A,B,C	★	★	...	★	...	★	...	...	...
Oklahoma	A,B,C	★	★	★	★	★	★	★	★	★
Oregon	A,B	★	★	★	★	...	★	...	★	★
Pennsylvania	A,B	...	★	★	★	...	★	...	...	...
Rhode Island	A,B,C	★	★	★	★	★	★	...	★	★
South Carolina	A,B,C	★(d)	(a)	★	★	(b)	★	...	...	★
South Dakota	A,B,C	★	★	★	★	★	★	...	(e)	...
Tennessee	A,B,C	★(a)	★	★	★	...	★	(e)	(e)	★
Texas	A,B,C	★(g)	★	★	★	★	★	...	★	...
Utah	A,B,C	★(a)	★	★	★	★	★	(b)	★	★
Vermont	A,B,C	★	★	★	★	★	★	★	★	★
Virginia	A,B,C	★	★	★	★	★	★	★	★	★
Washington	A,B	★	★	★	★	★	★	...	...	...
West Virginia	A,B,C	★	★	★	★	★	(b)	(b)	(b)	(b)
Wisconsin	A,B,C	★	★	★	★	★	★	...	★	★
Wyoming	A,B,C	★	★	★	★	★	★	...	★	...
Dist. of Columbia	A,B	★(j)	★	★	★	...	★	...	★	★
American Samoa	A,B,C	★(a)	★	★	★	...	★	...	★	★
Guam	A,B,C	★	★	★	(d)	★	★	(b)	★	★
No. Mariana Islands	A,B,C	★	★	★	★	★	★	...	★	★
Puerto Rico	A,B,C	★	★	★	★	★	★	★	...	★
U.S. Virgin Islands	A,B	★	★	★	★	★	★	★	...	★

Source: The Council of State Governments' survey of attorneys general, October 2004.

Key:
A—Defend state law when challenged on federal constitutional grounds.
B—Conduct litigation on behalf of state in federal and other states' courts.
C—Prosecute actions against another state in U.S. Supreme Court.
★—Has authority in area.
. . .—Does not have authority in area.
(a) Attorney general has exclusive jurisdiction.
(b) In certain cases only.

(c) When assisting local prosecutor in the appeal.
(d) Can appear on own discretion.
(e) Consumer Advocate Division represents the public in utility rate making hearings and rule making proceedings.
(f) Limited.
(g) Primarily federal habeas corpus appeals only.
(h) Upon DA recusal.
(i) Rarely.
(j) However, OUSA handles felony cases and most major misdemeanors.

State Treasurers: Guardians of the Public's Purse
By The National Association of State Treasurers

State treasurers are the chief financial officers of the states who assume the duties of assuring the absolute safety of all taxpayer dollars as well as guaranteeing the prudent use of public resources that fund vital government programs. In several states, treasurers also improve the financial security of our citizens by providing college savings opportunities, financial education and returning unclaimed property.

From management of state investments in a time of profound budgetary grief to taking an active and central role in defining what is greater corporate governance, state treasurers are vital players in the healthy management of not only state budgets, but federal policy on a multitude of issues that impact citizens in each and every state of the union.

State treasurers also play a unique role in policy setting at both the state and federal levels. On issues ranging from corporate governance to accounting standards, state treasurers are at the forefront of policy discussions and initiatives that attempt to safeguard investments made by and on behalf of the residents of their states.

Through this fiscal oversight and policy setting, state treasurers work daily to protect and benefit their individual states and the nation as a whole.

Selection and Term of Service

State treasurers are elected by the people in 37 states, elected by the legislature in four states and appointed by the governor in nine states. Forty state treasurers serve four-year terms in office, while the state treasurers of Maine, New Hampshire, Tennessee and Vermont serve two-year terms. The remaining state treasurers serve at the discretion and pleasure of the state official making the appointment.

Responsibilities of State Treasurers

All state treasurers are responsible for cash management, a fundamental duty of the states' chief financial officers. All but three state treasurers are responsible for banking services and in 37 states, state treasurers are responsible for some aspect of debt management—issuance, service or both. Thirty-two state treasurers are administrators of unclaimed property programs and 29 invest retirement or trust funds for their respective state. Several examples—though certainly not an exhaustive listing—are given below and touch on the wide array of responsibilities held by state treasurers.

Managing State Budgets

During the tight budget restrictions facing states over the past three years, even the squandering of a dime can raise constituent concerns. Therefore, it is especially important for treasurers in every state to make due with what they have. Managing shortfalls in state budgets, while largely viewed by the public as an issue for their state's governor and state legislature, also relies heavily on the guidance of the state's treasurer. Today's treasurers must learn to stretch every dollar and adopt an "out of the box" approach to financing.

While the task of investing available state funds may seem fairly straightforward to the public, the process is quite complex and requires specialized knowledge and skill. Treasurers must invest using the safest, most efficient methods available while earning the highest possible return. State treasurers' performance and record of investment income critically affects the bottom line of the states' fiscal fitness, which in turn can have a measurable impact on the well being of the states' budgetary status in any given year.

State treasurers, in particular, have fiduciary responsibility not only for pension plans and general state funds, but also for other investment vehicles, such as state college savings plans. The state treasurers, who collectively have fiduciary responsibility for more than one trillion dollars in public funds, contend that greater corporate responsibility is vital, since the business practices of U.S. corporations have a profound effect on public monies ranging from pension funds to state tax revenue investments.

Corporate Governance Reform

The management and oversight of state investments are key functions of the state treasurers. Based on their unique investment role, the state treasurers also are among the most powerful entities speaking out and taking action to promote the development and implementation of corporate standards and practices designed to restore and maintain investor confidence in the capital markets and protect shareholder rights. This will ultimately preserve, protect and grow the public fund assets under the management and custody of state treasurers across the nation.

Since 2001, the state treasurers have undertaken a broad review of investment management and policy issues surrounding corporate governance in the U.S. equity markets. Through the National Association of State Treasurers (NAST) Committee on Corporate Governance, the state treasurers have developed innovative policies to enhance and improve corporate governance. In addition, many treasurers have taken an active role in improving corporate governance and financial reporting practices, calling upon corporations they do business with to verify that their accounting procedures are sound and that the money the state invests on behalf of its residents is safe.

An example of one improvement is the development of the "Investor Protection Principles" for investments made with public funds. The principles set out the following obligations, among others:

- Investment banks shall sever the link between compensation for analysts and investment banking;

- Investment banks shall prohibit investment banking input into analyst compensation;

- Money management firms shall disclose client relationships, including management of corporate 401(k) plans, where the money management firm could invest state or pension fund monies in the securities of a client;

- Money management firms shall, in making investment decisions, consider the quality and integrity of a company's accounting and financial data, as well as whether the company's outside auditors also provide consulting or other services to the company; and

- Money management firms shall, in deciding whether to invest state or pension fund monies in a company, consider the corporate governance policies and practices of the company.

The principles have been adopted by many state and national organizations as a prime way to hold businesses accountable to the shareholders and other investors who have a stake in their companies.

In 2003, NAST adopted a set of major policy objectives designed to enhance general corporate governance structures. The policies established minimum standards corporations should follow to enhance corporate performance, including standards relating to corporate board structure and performance, access

to the proxy process which allows shareholders to meaningfully engage in improving corporate performance, and improved director qualification requirements to increase board member independence and diversity, and new director compensations measures.

Recently, NAST approved a policy resolution designed to make mutual funds disclose more information to shareholders. The resolution calls upon institutional investors, including all state and local public fund investors, to adopt into their investment practices and procedures the Mutual Fund Protection Principles.

The policy resolution calls for reforms to mutual fund business practices including higher standards of disclosure directed at fund holdings, trading costs and soft dollar practices. The principles require enhanced disclosure of portfolio manager compensation, fund ownership and holding period requirements. Mutual fund board reform measures include requirements that approval of fund management fees only be conducted by independent directors; require that at least three-quarters of the mutual fund board and the chairman shall be independent; and assurances that the independent directors meet at least annually with the chief compliance officer of the fund as well as the independent auditor without management present.

Treasurers and other public investors are also encouraged to give significant weight to mutual fund managers who embrace the principles and to encourage other defined benefit, deferred contribution and other savings plans to adopt them into their investment management practices.

College Savings Plans

One of the greatest financial worries of many American families is, "How will I be able to afford a college education for my children?" All 50 states°and the District of Columbia have created innovative college savings programs designed to meet the savings needs of their citizens.

In 44 states and the District of Columbia, the state treasurer plays a vital role in the administration of the program, including oversight of all program operations, serving as the board chair or board member, and investment manager or committee member.

The mission of the state plans is to increase access to higher education by offering families a simple, safe, affordable and dedicated way to save for college tuition. Section 529 plans come in two forms, prepaid tuition programs and savings plans. The prepaid tuition program offers families a method to prepay tuition based on current college tuition rates and provides a guarantee to keep pace with tuition inflation. The savings plans offer dedicated qualified state college savings accounts, which provide families a variable rate of return in a tax advantaged college savings account.

To date, more than 7 million children across the country have been enrolled in state college tuition or savings plan. These programs seek to make saving for college easier for the average family. These programs represent positive, productive and affordable options that can ensure the education of our most precious resources: the children of America. State sponsored savings plans promote:

- Planning for education expenses;

- Saving for education expenses instead of relying on debt;

- Reliance on family resources instead of total reliance on government aid programs; and

- State-level planning designed to meet the differing needs in each state instead of a "one size fits all" national approach.

Parents and other individuals have saved more than $64 billion to help their children and loved ones pay for future college costs. More importantly, in excess of 750,000 students have used more than $5.6 billion from these plans to fund their college education.

Participants in both types of programs receive a federal tax exemption on the investment earnings of the accounts, when the funds are used to pay for qualified higher education expenses, which include tuition, room and board, books and fees, and any other expenses that students are required to pay to attend any accredited college or university in the United States.

In 2004, state treasurers led a review of Section 529 plan disclosure documents in order to develop a set of disclosure principles that would allow consumers to make objective comparisons of fees and expenses for qualified tuition programs. By the end of 2004, all 50 states and the District of Columbia were implementing these disclosure principles in Section 529 college savings plans. The disclosure principles include tables and charts that provide a clear, concise and consistent description of fees and expenses. Additionally, the principles specify information that should be prominently stated for each program, such as the risk involved in investing in the plan, the need to consider state tax treatment and other benefits, and the availability of other state 529 programs.

State treasurers are committed to the goal of providing opportunities for families to save to send their children to college and will continue to strive to make Section 529 plans the most effective way for families to meet their college savings goals. NAST will monitor the implementation of the disclosure principles and will make revisions to the principles as necessary to improve the information available to participants and the public.

Unclaimed Property

State treasurers are responsible for the administration of unclaimed property programs in 32 states and the District of Columbia. Unclaimed property (sometimes referred to as abandoned property) refers to accounts in financial institutions and companies that have had no activity generated or contact with the owner for one year or a longer period. Common forms of unclaimed property include savings or checking accounts, stocks, uncashed dividends or payroll checks, refunds, traveler's checks, trust distributions, unredeemed money orders or gift certificates, insurance payments and life insurance policies, annuities, certificates of deposit, customer overpayments, utility security deposits, mineral royalty payments and contents of safe deposit boxes.

Acting in the best interest of consumers, each state has enacted an unclaimed property statute that protects funds from reverting back to the company if it has lost contact with the owner. These laws instruct companies to turn forgotten funds over to a state official who will then make a diligent effort to find owners or their heirs. Most states hold lost funds until owners are found, returning them at no cost or for a nominal handling fee upon filing a claim form and verification of your identity. Since it is impossible to store and maintain all of the contents that are turned over from safe deposit boxes, most states hold periodic auctions and hold the funds obtained from the sale of the items for the owner. Some states also sell stocks and bonds and return the proceeds to the owner in the same manner.

In order to return this money to owners, state unclaimed property programs publish names of owners in newspapers, set up displays at state fairs, malls, and other public events, work with other public officials such as legislators and local librarians, and make searchable databases available via the Internet including www.missingmoney.com. Each year through these activities hundreds of millions of lost dollars are returned to owners.

State treasurers remain active in advocating improvements in unclaimed property statutes and regulations that further protect and return Americans' forgotten assets. Recent developments in this arena have included lowering dormancy periods for funds to be reported from demutualized insurance companies and eliminating dormancy fees and expiration dates for gift certificates and prepaid gift cards. Treasurers are also trending toward stricter enforcement of unclaimed property laws by employing more auditors and levying interest and penalties for overdue funds that are discovered.

Financial Literacy Initiatives

State treasurers are viewed as trusted and credible sources of sound financial advice and have long recognized the need for responsible fiscal decision-making for the management of both public funds and personal finances. Over the past few decades, state treasurers have taken an active role in promoting financial literacy to the residents of their state.

State treasurers operate financial education programs for the benefit of the citizens of the states, drawing upon their substantial expertise in the financial management of both personal and public funds to provide opportunities to educate the citizens of the states on savings, from birth to retirement.

Thirty-five state treasurers presently offer some type of program ranging from "Bank at School" programs designed to teach students basic monetary concepts to women's conferences that help adults gain control of their personal finances.

Under the leadership of the state treasurer's office, Delaware has been a pioneer in improving "financial literacy" since the late 1990s. *The Delaware Money School* was established to bring community based financial education to participants in a stress free setting. More than 400 *Money School* classes have reached close to 5,200 participants. Taught by volunteer analysts, financial planners, economists and other financial professionals, this program continues to be conducted with assistance from corporate sponsorships. *Money School* topics range from homeown-ership, debt management and investments to estate planning. Several states have adopted Delaware's program molding it to fit their individual needs, with great success.

Conclusion

The roles and responsibilities of state treasurers are countless and critically important to the fiscal well being of their respective states. Sound and profitable investments made by state treasurers make it possible for budgets to be balanced, for taxpayer-supported programs to be maintained and grown, and for a positive and equitable level of investment growth for public funds to be achieved.

About the Author

The National Association of State Treasurers, an organization of state financial leaders, encourages the highest ethical standards, promotes education and the exchange of ideas, builds professional relationships, develops standards of excellence and influences public policy for the benefit of the citizens of the states. NAST is composed of all state treasurers, or state financial officials with comparable responsibilities from the United States, its commonwealths, territories and the District of Columbia.

Table 4.24
THE TREASURERS, 2005

State or other jurisdiction	Name and party	Method of selection	Length of regular term in years	Date of first service	Present term ends	Number of previous terms	Maximum consecutive terms allowed by constitution
Alabama	Kay Ivey (R)	E	4	1/03	1/07	0	2
Alaska (a)	Tom Boutin	A	4	2/05	N.A.	1	...
Arizona	David Petersen (R)	E	4	1/03	1/07	0	2 (b)
Arkansas	Gus Wingfield (D)	E	4	1/03	1/07	0	2
California	Philip Angelides (D)	E	4	1/99	1/07	1	2
Colorado	Mike Coffman (R)	E	4	1/99	1/07	1	2
Connecticut	Denise Nappier (D)	E	4	1/99	1/07	1	«
Delaware	Jack Markell (D)	E	4	1/99	1/07	1	«
Florida (c)	Tom Gallagher (R)	E	4	1/88	1/07	2	...
Georgia	W. Daniel Ebersole	A	Pleasure of the Board	11/97	N.A.	0	...
Hawaii (d)	Georgina Kawamura	A	4	12/02	N.A.	0	...
Idaho	Ron Crane (R)	E	4	1/99	1/07	1	2
Illinois	Judy Baar Topinka (R)	E	4	1/95	1/07	2	★
Indiana	Tim Berry (R)	E	4	2/99	1/07	1	(e)
Iowa	Michael Fitzgerald (D)	E	4	1/83	1/07	4	★
Kansas	Lynn Jenkins (R)	E	4	1/03	1/07	0	...
Kentucky	Jonathan Miller (D)	E	4	1/00	12/07	1	2
Louisiana	John Kennedy (D)	E	4	1/00	1/08	1	★
Maine	David Lemoine (D)	L	2	1/05	1/07	0	...
Maryland	Nancy Kopp (D)	L (l)	4	2/02	1/07	0	...
Massachusetts	Timothy Cahill (D)	E	4	1/03	1/07	0	★
Michigan	Jay Rising	A	Governor's discretion	1/03	...	0	★
Minnesota (f)	Peggy Ingison	A	...	2/04	...	0	...
Mississippi	Tate Reeves (R)	E	4	1/04	1/08	0	★
Missouri	Sarah Steelman (R)	E	4	1/05	1/09	0	(g)
Montana	Janet Kelly	A	4	1/05	N.A.	0	2
Nebraska	Ron Ross	E (j)	4	12/03	1/07	0	2 (b)
Nevada	Brian Krolicki (R)	E	4	1/99	1/07	1	2
New Hampshire	Michael Ablowich	L	2	12/02	12/07	1	...
New Jersey	John McCormac	A	Governor's discretion	1/02	N.A.	0	...
New Mexico	Robert Vigil (D)	E	4	1/03	1/07	0	2 (b)
New York	Aida Brewer	A	Governor's discretion	2/02	N.A.	0	...
North Carolina	Richard Moore (D)	E	4	1/01	1/09	1	★
North Dakota	Kelly Schmidt (R)	E	4	1/05	1/09	0	★
Ohio	Jennette Bradley (R)	E (k)	4	1/05	1/06	0	2
Oklahoma	Robert Butkin (D)	E	4	1/95	1/07	2	2 (b)
Oregon	Randall Edwards (D)	E	4	1/01	1/09	1	(e)
Pennsylvania	Robert Casey Jr. (D)	E	4	1/05	1/09	0	2 (h)
Rhode Island	Paul Tavares (D)	E	4	1/99	1/07	1	2 (b)
South Carolina	Grady Patterson Jr. (D)	E	4	1/66	1/07	7	...
South Dakota	Vernon L. Larson (R)	E	4	1/03	1/07	0	2 (b)
Tennessee	Dale Sims	L	2	10/03	1/07	1	...
Texas (i)	Carole Keeton Strayhorn (R)	E	4	1/99	1/07	1	2 (b)
Utah	Edward Alter (R)	E	4	1/81	1/09	6	★
Vermont	Jeb Spaulding (D)	E	2	1/03	1/07	1	★
Virginia	Jody Wagner	A	Governor's discretion	1/02	N.A.	0	...
Washington	Michael Murphy (D)	E	4	1/97	1/09	2	★
West Virginia	John Perdue (D)	E	4	1/97	1/09	2	★
Wisconsin	Jack Voight (R)	E	4	1/95	1/07	2	★
Wyoming	Cynthia Lummis (R)	E	4	1/99	1/07	1	★
American Samoa	Francis Leasiolagi	A	4	N.A.	N.A.	N.A.	...
District of Columbia	N. Anthony Calhoun	A	Pleasure of CFO	1/01	N.A.	N.A.	...
Guam	Yasela Pereira	CS	...	10/96	...	...	...
No. Mariana Islands	Antoinette S. Calvo	A	4	N.A.	N.A.	N.A.	...
Puerto Rico	Juan Flores Galarza	N.A.	4	N.A.	N.A.	N.A.	...
U.S. Virgin Islands	Bernice A. Turnbull	A	4	N.A.	N.A.	N.A.	...

Source: National Association of State Treasurers, January 2005.

Key:

★— No provision specifying number of terms allowed.

. . . — No formal provision, position is appointed or elected by governmental entity (not chosen by the electorate).

N.A. — Not available.

A — Appointed by the governor. (In the District of Columbia, the Treasurer is appointed by the Chief Financial Officer. In Georgia, position is appointed by the State Depository Board.)

E — Elected by the voters.

L — Elected by the legislature.

CS — Civil Service.

(a) The Deputy Commissioner of Department of Revenue performs this function.

(b) After 2 consecutive terms, must wait four years and/or one full term before being eligible again.

(c) Effective January 2003, the official title of the office of state treasurer is Chief Financial Officer.

(d) The Director of Finance performs this function.

(e) Eligible for eight out of any period of twelve years.

(f) The Commissioner of Finance performs this function.

(g) Absolute two-term limitation, but not necessarily consecutive.

(h) Treasurer must wait four years before being eligible for the office of auditor general.

(i) The Comptroller of Public Accounts performs this function.

(j) Governor Johanns appointed Ron Ross in December 2003 to fill a vacancy in the Treasurer's office.

(k) Governor Taft appointed Jennette Bradley in December 2004 to fill a vacancy in the Treasurer's office.

(l) Elected in February 2002 and re-elected to a full four-year term in February 2003.

Table 4.25
TREASURERS: QUALIFICATIONS FOR OFFICE

State	Minimum age	U.S. citizen (years)	State resident (years)	Qualified voter (years)	Method of selection to office
Alabama	25	7	5	★	E
Alaska	. . .	. . .	. . .	. . .	A
Arizona	25	10	5	. . .	E
Arkansas	21	★	★	★	E
California	18	★	★	★	E
Colorado	25	★	2	. . .	E
Connecticut	18	★	★	★	E
Delaware	18	★	★	★	E
Florida	30	★	7	★	E
Georgia	. . .	. . .	. . .	. . .	A
Hawaii	. . .	★	★	. . .	E
Idaho	25	★	2	★	E
Illinois	25	★	3	. . .	E
Indiana	18	★	★	★	E
Iowa	18	★	★	★	E
Kansas	. . .	. . .	. . .	. . .	E
Kentucky	30	★	2	. . .	E
Louisiana	25	5	5	★	E
Maine	. . .	★	★	. . .	L
Maryland	18	. . .	. . .	. . .	L
Massachusetts	. . .	. . .	5	. . .	E
Michigan	. . .	. . .	. . .	. . .	A
Minnesota	21	★	★	★	E
Mississippi	25	★	5	★	E
Missouri	. . .	★	1	. . .	E
Montana	. . .	. . .	. . .	. . .	A
Nebraska	19	★	★	★	E
Nevada	25	★	2	★	E
New Hampshire	. . .	. . .	★	. . .	L
New Jersey	. . .	. . .	★	. . .	A
New Mexico	30	★	5	★	E
New York	. . .	★	★	. . .	A
North Carolina	21	★	★	★	E
North Dakota	25	★	5	★	E
Ohio	18	★	★	★	E
Oklahoma	31	★	10	★	E
Oregon	18	. . .	★	. . .	E
Pennsylvania	. . .	. . .	. . .	. . .	E
Rhode Island	18	★	30 days	★	E
South Carolina	. . .	★	★	★	E
South Dakota	. . .	. . .	. . .	. . .	E
Tennessee	. . .	. . .	. . .	. . .	L
Texas	18	★	★	. . .	E
Utah	25	★	5	★	E
Vermont	18	★	2	★	E
Virginia	. . .	. . .	. . .	★	A
Washington	18	★	★	★	E
West Virginia	18	★	5	★	E
Wisconsin	18	★	★	★	E
Wyoming	25	★	★	★	E

Source: National Association of State Treasurers, January 2005.

Key:

★—Formal provision; number of years not specified.

. . .—No formal provision.

A—Appointed by the governor.

E—Elected by the voters.

L—Elected by the legislature.

Table 4.26
TREASURERS: DUTIES OF OFFICE

State	Cash management	Investment of general funds	Investment of retirement and/or trust funds	Oversight of retirement funds	Oversight / management of debt issuance	Unclaimed property	Link deposit program	College Savings / Prepaid Tuition Programs
Alabama	★	★	★	★	★	★	★	★
Alaska	★	★	★	★	★	★	...	...
Arizona	★	★	★	★	N.A.	...	...	★
Arkansas	★	★	★	★	★	...	...	★
California	★	★	★	★	★	...	...	★
Colorado	★	★	★	★	★	★	...	★
Connecticut	★	★	★	★	★	★	...	★
Delaware	★	★	...	★	★	...	...	★
Florida	★	★	★	★	★	★	...	...
Georgia	★	★	★	★	★	...	...	★
Hawaii	★	★	★	★	★	★	...	★
Idaho	★	★	★	★	★	...	...	★
Illinois	★	★	★	★	...	★	★	★
Indiana	★	★	★	★	★	...	★	★
Iowa	★	★	★	★	★	★	★	★
Kansas	★	...	★	★	★	★	★	★
Kentucky	★	...	...	★	...	★	★	★
Louisiana	★	★	★	★	★	★	★	★
Maine	★	★	★	★	★	★	★	★
Maryland	★	★	★	★	★	...	★	★
Massachusetts	★	★	★	★	★	★	★	...
Michigan	★	★	★	★	★	★	...	★
Minnesota	★	★	...	★	★	...	...	★
Mississippi	★	★	★	★	★	★	...	★
Missouri	★	★	★	★	★	★	★	★
Montana	★	★	...	★	★	...	...	...
Nebraska	★	★	★	★	N.A.	★	...	★
Nevada	★	★	★	★	★	★	...	★
New Hampshire	★	★	★	★	★	★	...	★
New Jersey	★	★	★	★	★	★	...	★
New Mexico	★	★	★	★	★	...	...	...
New York	★	★	★	★	★	...	★	★
North Carolina	★	★	★	★	★	★	...	★
North Dakota	★	...	★	★	...	...	...	...
Ohio	★	★	★	★	★	...	★	★
Oklahoma	★	★	★	★	★	★	★	★
Oregon	★	★	★	★	★	...	...	★
Pennsylvania	★	★	★	★	★	★	★	★
Rhode Island	★	★	★	★	★	★	...	★
South Carolina	★	★	★	★	★	★	...	★
South Dakota	★	...	...	★	...	★	...	★
Tennessee	★	★	★	★	★	★	...	★
Texas (d)	★	★	★	★	★	★	★	★
Utah	★	★	★	★	★	★	...	★
Vermont	★	★	★	★	★	★	...	★
Virginia	★	★	★	...	★	★	...	★
Washington	★	★	★	★	★	...	★	★
West Virginia	★	★	★	★	★	★	...	★
Wisconsin	★	...	★	★	★	★	...	★
Wyoming	★	★	★	★	...	★	...	★

Source: National Association of State Treasurers, January 2005.
Note: For additional information on functions of the treasurers' offices, see Tables in Chapter 7 entitled Allowable Investments, Cash Management Programs and Services, and Demand Deposits.
Key:
★—Responsible for activity.
. . .—Not responsible for activity.
N.A.—Not applicable. State does not issue debt.

Trends in State Government Accounting, Auditing and Treasury

By W. Daniel Ebersole

State financial management leaders are working to offer increased services and transparency even as they contend with the need to accomplish more with limited resources. Government accountability, innovation in technology and strategic partnership initiatives will usher states into an exciting era of positive change.

Opportunities

Accounting and Financial Reporting

For several decades, state and local governments have looked to the Governmental Accounting Standards Board (GASB) for accounting and financial reporting standards. Without adequate funding, however, the independent standard-setting services provided by GASB cannot be sustained. In 2004, the National Association of State Auditors, Comptrollers and Treasurers (NASACT) worked successfully with the National Association of State Treasurers and the Government Finance Officers Association to implement a bond assessment fee to supplement GASB's budget. The assessment, which is being collected by The Bond Market Association, was expected to shore up any cracks in GASB's funding, allowing for the seamless continuation of the board's vital services to state and local governments. Although the system is currently in place, there is still much work to do to achieve the level of collections necessary for the funding of GASB. In addition, the concept of a "filing fee," which would be imposed on all governmental entities that prepare financial statements according to generally accepted accounting principles as promulgated by GASB, is being explored.

The issuance of timely financial statements and disclosures continues to be a topic that state governments address on a regular basis. Our research shows that 27 states issued their comprehensive annual financial reports in fewer days after year-end in fiscal year 2003 than in fiscal year 2002. Interim disclosure of financial-related information is also becoming a reality in some states. NASACT has worked with interested parties to discuss the mechanics of providing interim information and to develop a template for information that might be useful. Several states served as pilots in 2004 to implement the recommended template and have begun providing interim disclosures on their Web sites. The usefulness of the interim disclosures will be examined in the coming year as participating states begin to receive feedback.

Addressing current issues faced by state government finance officials is not enough—we must also work together to identify issues that will affect our profession in the future. In partnership with the Association of Government Accountants, NASACT will participate in a research project to ascertain the extent, if any, to which certain provisions of the Sarbanes-Oxley Act might be applicable and appropriate for state and local governments in the United States to implement. The development of a survey and the gathering of data for this project will occur over the next six to nine months. Additionally, state government officials will remain alert to the notion of a worldwide convergence of accounting principles, as conversations about the need for international accounting standards continue.

Corporate Governance and Accountability

While certainly not a new topic, corporate governance continues to be a priority for state finance officials. Corporate scandals that have plagued our nation have resulted in a number of reforms that attempt to restore investor confidence and re-establish the integrity of our nation's corporations and financial reporting practices. Better shareholder access through reforms being implemented as a result of the Sarbanes-Oxley Act is key among the issues being considered by financial officials as stewards of public monies.

A strong corporate governance structure can be linked to a healthy and stable economy. As investors in U.S. and foreign corporations, states are shareholders with a keen interest in making sure directors are doing their jobs to oversee the financial well-being of the companies in which they serve. Accountability has always been of utmost importance to financial officials in managing taxpayer dollars, and carrying out fiduciary duties through better shareholder participation only improves this notion. More democratic forms of corporate governance are necessary to assure that there is a proper structure in place for appropriate management of corporate affairs. State finance officials will continue to promote successful reforms so that the companies in which they invest seek greater transparency and better accountability.

Institutional investors often face public criticism for investing in companies that are operating in countries designated by the state department as sponsoring terrorism. This issue, however, is not a simple one. Public pension funds have the ability to identify financial risks associated with companies having operations that may expose states to countries listed by the federal government as sponsors of terrorism. Public pension funds do not, however, have the ability to determine which companies compromise national security through the business they conduct, and public pension funds are not in a position to determine foreign policy.

The issue is further clouded by the fact that institutional investors may or may not have information about which companies have businesses or subsidiaries operating in terrorism-sponsoring states. When registering on U.S. exchanges, a company is required to provide only information that the U.S. Securities and Exchange Commission considers to be "material." State finance officials are diligent about seeking information about the firms in which they invest and as part of their fiduciary duty will factor in any financial risk associated with business in these countries. However, the responsibility for national security lies with the federal government.

Technology and Innovation

The delivery of benefits in the states is an important task performed by finance officials, and thus the quest for efficient, cost-effective delivery systems remains an area of special interest. The electronic benefit transfer card has been a very effective means of delivering food stamp benefits; however, the number of programs that can be run on the card is limited. Although stored value cards have been around for some time, more and more states are now considering the use of stored value cards to deliver other types of benefit payments.

There are numerous advantages to using stored value cards as a method of payment. Originally offered as an alternative for paper checks and direct deposit, the use of stored value cards in the states

has expanded to include payments for payroll, child support and unemployment. Some benefits of using stored value cards include card acceptance wherever the credit card is accepted, cash withdrawal at ATMs worldwide, zero consumer fraud liability under credit card rules, and 24-hour customer service support. Payment flexibility is an important benefit for the recipient, and increased efficiency and administrative cost reduction add value for states.

The authentication of electronic credentials remains a technological challenge for both the public and private sector. Through the Electronic Authentication Partnership, a public-private partnership working to develop interoperability among public and private electronic authentication systems, state finance officials are working to find a solution to the problem. The partnership has recently developed its first board, which will set into motion initiatives to provide the public and private sectors with a straightforward means of relying on digital credentials issued by several different e-authentication systems.

State finance officials will also be keeping a close watch on the development of an initiative designed to facilitate common reporting—the emergence of eXtensible Business Reporting Language (XBRL). XBRL provides a common XML-based platform for critical business reporting processes and has the potential to improve the reliability and ease of communicating financial data among users.

In the wake of slightly improving budget situations for some states, enterprise resource planning (ERP) has once again become a viable topic of discussion. A survey of the states conducted in 2004 indicates that of 26 responding states, over two-thirds have completed implementation of new ERP systems, have started ERP implementation, or are in the planning stages for ERP. The business process re-engineering that typically precedes an ERP implementation is an important step toward greater efficiency. States report that other advantages ERP can bring include easier online processing, better system interfacing, easier data retrieval, improved reporting, faster posting of expenditures to federally funded programs and faster drawdown of federal funds.

Benchmarking, Best Practices and Partnering for Success

As state governments continue work to streamline operations and reach new levels of efficiency and innovation, benchmarking, the study of best practices and partnering to accomplish goals are logical starting points.

In order to improve, state governments must first

have some measure by which to examine performance. With that aim in mind, the National Association of State Comptrollers asked its Benchmarking Committee to investigate the feasibility of a national benchmarking project to collect performance metrics for the accounting and payroll functions in state government. The objective of the project was to build a database of state performance metrics and practices that participants can use to assess their own performance. In 2004, a pilot project by six states was undertaken to gather performance metrics on four comptroller functions. The results of the project were presented at the 2004 NASACT annual conference, and the group will be looking for ways to expand the project in 2005 to involve more states and cover other areas of financial management.

Cost recovery projects continue to be a vehicle for states looking to recover more fully their costs of administering federal programs. States are finding that recovery auditing offers a win-win scenario. Agencies do not need a budget to get started, and contingency fees are based upon a percentage of actual recovered dollars. Additionally, accounts payable firms contracted to perform recovery services use software developed specifically for the purpose of identifying overpayments—software that also provides benchmarking capabilities. Based upon recent audit recovery successes, more states will likely look to this method as a low-cost, high-yield investment of time and resources.

The receipt of credit card payments by both state and local governments is a topic that has also been scrutinized lately by state finance leaders. NASACT is currently gathering data about the receipt of payments via credit cards by states with a view toward creating a "government" rate for interchange fees that reflects the high volume and low risk that state and local governments present to the market. Once the survey data for this initiative is analyzed, those working on this project intend to negotiate with the major credit card vendors for lower interchange fees for government.

Challenges

One of the biggest challenges state governments are likely to face in coming years is the shortage of qualified, trained professionals to fill vacant positions in government financial management. With more and more government finance professionals retiring or migrating to the private sector and fewer students pursuing finance-oriented degrees and careers, labor shortages are on the horizon for many states.

NASACT recently expressed its support of a project called the Cooperative for Contemporary Curricula in Financial Management, or C3FM. This initiative will address the shortage of qualified individuals going into government finance by exploring the feasibility of a financial management education partnership in the Western region. We look forward to seeing results from the project, which is being spearheaded by the Hatfield School of Government at Portland State University, and to examining ways that the program might be expanded to the national level to address the same problem in other regions of the country.

As it does on a regular basis, GASB has promulgated some especially challenging new standards; of particular note are those standards on accounting and reporting of other postemployment benefits (OPEB), of which health care is the largest. The new standards will require for each OPEB plan a statement of plan net assets, a statement of changes in plan net assets, a schedule of funding progress and a schedule of employer contributions. Because many OPEB plans in the past have been funded on a pay-as-you-go basis and have not established trust funds to collect assets to meet long-term liabilities, states expect to be reporting large OPEB liabilities when the standard becomes effective in fiscal year 2007.

State finance officials remain keenly aware of ever-evolving security, privacy and information technology concerns. With the emergence of new technologies including wireless applications, state finance professionals find it increasingly important to become educated on advances that affect the security of equipment, data and entire systems.

Not investing in technology is not an option for states. E-commerce and e-government have become the norm, not the cutting-edge exception, and governments have made great progress toward utilizing technology to offer expanded and improved services to citizens. This is an exciting time for state finance officials who are now more familiar with the benefits—and the costs—involved with implementing new technologies.

Conclusions and Perspectives

State government financial management wears a different face today than in the past. State leaders are operating in an environment that grows increasingly complex with each new technological advance or political shift. And as citizens come to expect a certain level of service from government, state leaders will continue to be challenged to think strategically to address growing demands for efficient service, accountability and convenience.

Now more than ever, state finance leaders must work together across the divides between states, functions and agencies to develop integrated and innovative solutions to old problems. State budgets, although improving, will likely continue to slow the pace of investment in new technologies to improve state operations. Our task will be to think creatively to address the inevitable new challenges.

About the Author

W. Daniel Ebersole is director of the Georgia Office of Treasury and Fiscal Services and president of the National Association of State Auditors, Comptrollers and Treasurers. He is a past president of the National Association of State Treasurers and a current member of the Finance and Strategic Planning Committees of The Council of State Governments. Ebersole has been commissioner of the Georgia Merit System, senior executive assistant to Gov. Zell Miller, deputy director of the Office of Planning and Budget, and Senate research director.

AUDITORS AND COMPTROLLERS

Table 4.27
THE STATE AUDITORS, 2005

State or other jurisdiction	State Agency	Agency head	Title	Legal basis for office	Method of selection	Term of office	U.S. citizen	State resident	Maximum consecutive terms allowed
Alabama	Dept. of Examiners of Public Accounts	Ronald L. Jones	Chief Examiner	S	L	7 yrs.	★	★	None
Alaska	Division of Legislative Audit	Pat Davidson	Legislative Auditor	C, S	L	(a)	⋮	⋮	None
Arizona	Auditor General	Debra K. Davenport	Auditor General	S	LC	5 yrs.	⋮	⋮	None
Arkansas	Legislative Auditor	Charles L. Robinson	Legislative Auditor	N.A.	L	N.A.	★	⋮	None
California	Bureau of State Audits	Elaine Howle	State Auditor	S	G	4 yrs.	★	⋮	None
Colorado	State Auditor	Joanne Hill	State Auditor	C	L	5 yrs.	★	⋮	None
Connecticut	Auditors of Public Accounts	Kevin P. Johnston, Robert G. Jaekle	State Auditors	C	L	4 yrs.	⋮	⋮	None
Delaware	Auditor of Accounts	R. Thomas Wagner, Jr.	Auditor of Accounts	C, S	E	4 yrs.	★	★	None
Florida	Auditor General	William O. Monroe	Auditor General	C, S	L	(a)	⋮	⋮	None
Georgia	Dept. of Audits and Accounts	Russell W. Hinton	State Auditor	S	L	Indefinite	⋮	★	None
Hawaii	Office of the Auditor	Marion M. Higa	State Auditor	C, S	LC	8 yrs.	⋮	★	None
Idaho	Legislative Services Office —Legislative Audits	Raymond Ineck	Supervisor of Legislative Audits	S	LC	Indefinite	⋮	⋮	None
	Office of Performance Evaluations	Rakesh Mohan	Director	N.A	N.A	N.A	N.A	N.A	None
Illinois	Auditor General	William G. Holland	Auditor General	C, S	L	10 yrs.	★	★	None
Indiana	State Board of Accounts	Charles Johnson, III	State Examiner	S	G	4 yrs.	⋮	⋮	None
Iowa	Auditor of State	David A. Vaudt	Auditor of State	C, S	E	4 yrs.	★	★	None
Kansas	Legislative Division of Post Audit	Barbara J. Hinton	Legislative Post Auditor	S	LC	(b)	★	★	None
Kentucky	Auditor of Public Accounts	Crit Luallen	Auditor of Public Accounts	C, S	E	4 yrs.	★	★	2
Louisiana	Legislative Auditor	Steve J. Theriot	Legislative Auditor	C, S	L	(a)	★	★	None
Maine	State Auditor	Neria Douglas	State Auditor	S	ED	Indefinite	⋮	⋮	None
Maryland	Office of Legislative Audits	Bruce A. Myers	Legislative Auditor	S	E	4 yrs.	★	★	None
Massachusetts	State Auditor	A. Joseph DeNucci	Auditor of the Commonwealth	C, S	E	4 yrs.	⋮	★	None
Michigan	Auditor General	Thomas H. McTavish	Auditor General	C	L	8 yrs.	★	★	None
Minnesota	Legislative Auditor	James R. Nobles	Legislative Auditor	S	LC	6 yrs.	⋮	★	None
Mississippi	State Auditor	Patricia Anderson	State Auditor	C	E	4 yrs.	★	★	None
Missouri	State Auditor	Phil Bryant	State Auditor	C, S	E	4 yrs.	★	★	None
Montana	State Auditor	Claire McCaskill	State Auditor	C, S	E	4 yrs.	⋮	★	None
Nebraska	Legislative Audit Division, Legislative Branch	Scott A. Seacat	Legislative Auditor	C, S	LC	2 yrs.	★	★	None
Nevada	Auditor of Public Accounts	Kate Witek	Auditor of Public Accounts	C, S	E	4 yrs.	★	★	None
New Hampshire	Legislative Auditor	Paul Townsend	Legislative Auditor	S	LC	Indefinite	⋮	⋮	None
New Jersey	Legislative Budget Assistant	Michael L. Buckley	Legislative Budget Assistant	S	LC	2 yrs.	⋮	⋮	None
New Mexico	State Auditor	Richard L. Fair	State Auditor	C, S	L	5 yr. term and until successor is appointed	★	★	N.A.
New York	State Auditor	Domingo Martinez	State Auditor	C	E	4 yrs.	★	★	2
North Carolina	Office of the State Comptroller, State Audit Bureau	Alan G. Hevesi	Deputy Comptroller —State Services	C, S	E	4 yrs.	★	★	None
	State Auditor	Leslie W. Merritt, Jr.	State Auditor	C, S	E	4 yrs.	★	★	None

See footnotes at end of table.

THE STATE AUDITORS, 2004 — Continued

State or other jurisdiction	State Agency	Agency head	Title	Legal basis for office	Method of selection	Term of office	U.S. citizen	State resident	Maximum consecutive terms allowed
North Dakota	State Auditor	Robert R. Petersen	State Auditor	C, S	E	4 yrs.	…	★	None
Ohio	Auditor of State	Betty D. Montgomery	Auditor of State	C	E	4 yrs.	★	★	2
Oklahoma	State Auditor and Inspector	Jeff McMahan	State Auditor and Inspector	C, S	E	4 yrs.	★	★	None
Oregon	Secretary of State, Audits Division	Cathy Pollino	State Auditor	C	SS	(c)	…	…	N.A.
Pennsylvania	Auditor General	Jack Wagner	Auditor General	C	E	4 yrs.	★	…	2
	Legislative Finance and Budget	Philip R. Durgin	Executive Director	S	LC	(b)	…	…	None
Rhode Island	Auditor General	Ernest A. Almonte	Auditor General	S	LC	(b)	…	…	None
South Carolina	Legislative Audit Council	George L. Schroeder	Director	S	LC	4 yrs.	…	…	None
	State Auditor	Thomas L. Wagner, Jr.	State Auditor	S	SB	Indefinite	…	…	N.A.
South Dakota	Dept. of Legislative Audit	Martin L. Guindon	Auditor General	S	L	8 yrs.	★	…	None
Tennessee	Comptroller of the Treasury, Dept. of Audit	John G. Morgan	Comptroller of the Treasury	C, S	L	2 yrs.	★	…	No
Texas	State Auditor	John Keel, CPA	State Auditor	S	LC	(b)	★	★	None
Utah	State Auditor	Auston G. Johnson	State Auditor	C, S	E	4 yrs.	★	★	None
Vermont	State Auditor	Randy Brock	State Auditor	C, S	E	2 yrs.	★	★	None
Virginia	Auditor of Public Accounts	Walter J. Kucharski	Auditor of Public Accounts	C	L	4 yrs.	…	…	None
Washington	Office of the State Auditor	Brian Sonntag	State Auditor	C, S	E	4 yrs.	★	…	None
West Virginia	Legislative Auditor	Aaron Allred	Legislative Auditor		LC	Indefinite	…	…	None
Wisconsin	Legislative Audit Bureau	Janice Mueller	State Auditor	C, S	LC		…	…	None
Wyoming	Dept. of Audit	Michael Geesey	Director	S	GC	6 yrs.	…	★	None
Guam	Office of the Public Auditor	Doris Flores Brooks	Public Auditor		E	4 yrs.	★	★	2
Puerto Rico	Office of the Comptroller of Puerto Rico	Manuel Diaz Saldana	Comptroller of Puerto Rico	C, S	GL	10 yrs.	★	…	1

Source: Auditing in the States: A Summary, 2003 Edition, The National Association of Auditors, Comptrollers and Treasurers, January 2005.

Key:
E—Elected by the public.
L—Appointed by the legislature.
G—Appointed by the governor.
SS—Appointed by the secretary of state.
LC—selected by legislative committee, commission or council.
ED—appointed by the executive director of legislative services

GC—Appointed by governor, secretary of state and treasurer.
GL—Appointed by the governor and confirmed by both changers of the legislature
SB—Appointed by state budget and control board.
C—Constitutional
S—Statutory
N.A.—Not available.
(a) Serves at the pleasure of the legislature
(b) Serves at the pleasure of a legislative committee.
(c) Serves at the pleasure of the secretary of state.

Table 4.28
STATE AUDITORS: SCOPE OF AGENCY AUTHORITY

State or other jurisdiction	Authority to audit all state agencies	Authority to audit local governments	Authority to obtain information	Authority to issue subpoenas	Authority to specify accounting principles for local governments	Investigations Agency investigates fraud, waste abuse, and/or illegal acts	Agency operates a hotline
Alabama	★	★	★	★	★ (q)	★	. . .
Alaska	★	. . .	★	. . .	. . .	★	. . .
Arizona	★	★	★	. . .	★ (r)	★	. . .
Arkansas	N.A.	N.A.	N.A.	N.A.	N.A.	N.A.	N.A.
California	★	★	★	★	. . .	★	★
Colorado	★	★	★	★	★	★	. . .
Connecticut	★	. . .	★	. . .	. . .	★	★
Delaware	★	★	★	★	. . .	★	★
Florida	(a)	★	★	. . .	. . .	★	. . .
Georgia	★	(g)	★	★	★	★	. . .
Hawaii	(a)	★	★	★	. . .	★	. . .
Idaho	★	★	★	★	. . .	★	. . .
Illinois	★	★	★	★	. . .	★	. . .
Indiana	★	★	★	★	★	★	. . .
Iowa	★	★	★	★	. . .	★	. . .
Kansas	★	★	★	★	. . .	★	. . .
Kentucky	(b)	★	★	★	. . .	★	★
Louisiana	★	(h)	★	★	★	★	. . .
Maine	N.A.	N.A.	N.A.	N.A.	N.A.	N.A.	N.A.
Maryland	(a)	★	★	★	. . .	★	★
Massachusetts	★	★	★	. . .	. . .	★	★
Michigan	★	. . .	★	★	. . .	★	. . .
Minnesota							
Legislative Auditor	★	(i)	★	★	. . .	★	. . .
State Auditor	(c)	★	★	★	★	★	. . .
Mississippi	★	★ (j)	★	. . .	★	★	★
Missouri	★	★	★	★	. . .	★	★
Montana	★	. . .	★	. . .	. . .	★	★
Nebraska	★	★	★	. . .	★	★	★
Nevada	★	. . .	★	. . .	. . .	★	. . .
New Hampshire	★	. . .	★	. . .	. . .	★	. . .
New Jersey	★	(k)	★	. . .	. . .	★	. . .
New Mexico	★ (d)	★	★	. . .	. . .	★	. . .
New York	★	★	★	★	★	★	. . .
North Carolina	★	. . .	★	★	. . .	★	★
North Dakota	★	★	★	. . .	★	★	. . .
Ohio	★	★	★	★	★	★	★
Oklahoma	★ (e)	(l)	★	★	. . .	★	. . .
Oregon	★	★	★	★	★	★	★
Pennsylvania							
Auditor General	(b)	. . .	★	★	. . .	★	★
Legislative Budget and Finance Cmte.	★	. . .	★	★	. . .	. . .	. . .
Rhode Island	★	(m)	★	★	★	★	. . .
South Carolina							
Legislative Audit Council	★	(n)	★	. . .	. . .	★	. . .
State Auditor	(s)	. . .	★	. . .	. . .	★	. . .
South Dakota	★	★	★	★	★	★	. . .
Tennessee	★	★	★	★	★	★	★
Texas	★	. . .	★	★	★ (o)	★	★
Utah							
Legislative Auditor	★	★	★	★	. . .	★	
State Auditor	(f)	★	★	★	★		
Vermont	★	. . .	★	★	★	★	. . .
Virginia	★	. . .	★	. . .	★	★	. . .
Washington	★	★	★	★	★	★	. . .
West Virginia	N.A.	N.A.	N.A.	N.A.	N.A.	N.A.	N.A.
Wisconsin	★	★	★	★	. . .	★	. . .
Wyoming	★	★	★	★	(p)	★	. . .
Guam	. . .	★	★	★	★	★	★
Puerto Rico	★	★	★	★	★	★	★

See footnotes at end of table.

STATE AUDITORS: SCOPE OF AGENCY AUTHORITY — Continued

Sources: *Auditing in the States*, 2003 Edition, The National Association of State Auditors, Comptrollers and Treasurers 2003.

Key:

★— Provision for responsibility.

. . .—No provision for responsibility.

N.A.—Not available.

(a) The legislature or legislative branch is excluded from audit authority.

(b) The legislative and judicial branches are excluded from audit authority.

(c) State agencies are audited by the Office of Legislative Auditor.

(d) The Gaming Commission, Mortgage Finance Authority, State Lottery Commission, Student Loan Guarantee Corporation are excluded from audit authority.

(e) Higher education and most public trusts are only audited upon request by various authorities. Commissioners of the Land Office are excluded since the State Auditor and Inspector serve on this commission.

(f) State Retirement and Worker's Compensation Fund are excluded from audit authority.

(g) All local governments are excluded from audit authority, except Public School Systems and Regional and Local libraries.

(h) Performs only investigative audits of local governments.

(i) Financial audits of local governments are excluded from audit authority.

(j) All local governments excluded but municipalities.

(k) Entities not receiving state aid or state grants and school districts receiving less than 80% funding from the state are excluded from audit authority.

(l) The State Auditor and Inspector have the authority to audit counties, Generally, cities, towns, school districts, fire protection districts, rural water districts can be audited upon request by citizen petition or various authorities.

(m) No local governments are specifically excluded, but the agency goes in on orders from the Joint Cmte. and Legislative Services.

(n) County, school districts, special purpose districts are excluded from audit authority.

(o) Comptroller prescribes guidelines but SAO has responsibility to review and comment.

(p) Set by statute.

(q) Municipalities not covered.

(r) Except for cities and towns, and certain special taxing districts.

(s) Ports Authority, Public Service Authority, Research Authority and 16 technical colleges are excluded from audit authority.

Table 4.29
STATE AUDITORS: TYPES OF AUDITS

State or other jurisdiction	Financial statement	Single audit	Financial related	Compliance only	Economy and efficiency	Program	Sunset	Performance measures	IT	Accounting and review sources	Agreed upon procedures	Other audits
Alabama	★	★	★		★	★	★	★				
Alaska	★	★	★	★	★	★	★	★	★			(a)
Arizona	N.A.	★	★		★	★	★	★	N.A.		N.A.	N.A.
Arkansas	N.A.	N.A.	N.A.	N.A.	N.A.	N.A.	N.A.	N.A.	N.A.	N.A.	N.A.	(b)
California	★	★	★	★	★	★	★	★	★			
Colorado	★	★	★	★	★	★	★	★	★	★	★	
Connecticut	★	★	★	★	★	★		★			★	
Delaware	★	★	★	★	★	★		★	★	★	★	(c)
Florida	★	★	★	★	★	★	★		★		★	
Georgia	★	★	★	★	★	★	★		★			
Hawaii					★	★		★	★			(b)
Idaho	★	★	★	★	★		★		★		★	(d)
Illinois	★	★	★	★	★	★			★		★	
Indiana	★	★		★					★		★	
Iowa	★	★	★						★			
Kansas	★	★				★		★	★		★	
Kentucky	★	★	★	★	★		★	★	★	★	★	
Louisiana	★	★	★	N.A.	★	★	★	★	★		★	
Maine	N.A.	N.A.	N.A.	N.A.	N.A.	N.A.	N.A.	N.A.	N.A.	N.A.	N.A.	(e)
Maryland	★		★	★	★				★			
Massachusetts	★	★	★	★	★	★	★	★	★	★	★	(f)
Michigan	★	★	★		★	★	★	★	★		★	
Minnesota Legislative Auditor		★	★			★						
State Auditor	★	★			★				★		★	(g)
Mississippi	★	★		★		★		★				(h)
Missouri	★	★	★	★	★	★			★			
Montana	★	★	★	★	★	★		★	★		★	
Nebraska	★	★	★	★		★			★	★	★	
Nevada				★	★	★			★			
New Hampshire	★				★			★				
New Jersey	★	★	★	★	★	★		★				
New Mexico	★	★			★			★	★		★	
New York	★		★	★	★	★		★	★		★	(i)
North Carolina	★	★	★		★	★			★	★	★	
North Dakota	★	★	★		★			★	★			
Ohio	★	★	★	★					★	★	★	

See footnotes at end of table.

STATE AUDITORS: TYPES OF AUDITS — Continued

State or other jurisdiction	Financial statement	Single audit	Financial related	Compliance only	Economy and efficiency	Program	Sunset	Performance measures	IT	Accounting and review sources	Agreed upon procedures	Other audits
Oklahoma	★	★	★	★	★	★	…	…	★	…	★	(j)
Oregon	★	★	★	★	★	★	…	…	★	★	★	(k)
Pennsylvania												
Auditor General	★	★	★	★	★	…	…	★	★	…	…	(l)
Legislative Budget and Finance Cmte.	…	…	…	…	…	…	…	…	…	…	…	…
Rhode Island	…	★	…	…	★	★	…	…	…	…	…	…
South Carolina												
Legislative Audit Council	…	…	…	…	★	★	…	…	…	…	★	…
State Auditor	★	★	…	…	…	…	…	…	…	…	…	…
South Dakota	★	★	★	…	★	…	…	…	…	…	★	…
Tennessee	★	★	★	★	★	★	★	…	★	★	★	(m)
Texas	★	★	★	★	★	…	…	★	★	★	★	(n)
Utah												
Legislative Auditor	…	…	…	…	★	★	★	★	…	…	…	(o)
State Auditor	★	★	★	★	★	★	…	★	★	★	★	…
Vermont	★	★	★	★	★	…	…	★	★	★	★	…
Virginia	★	★	★	…	…	…	…	★	★	…	★	…
Washington	N.A.	N.A.	N.A.	N.A.	N.A.	N.A.	N.A.	N.A.	N.A.	N.A.	N.A.	N.A.
West Virginia	★	★	★	★	★	…	…	★	★	…	★	…
Wisconsin	…	…	…	…	…	…	…	…	…	…	…	…
Wyoming	…	…	…	…	…	★	…	…	…	…	…	…
Guam	…	★	…	…	★	★	…	…	★	…	…	(b)
Puerto Rico	…	…	…	★	★	★	…	…	★	…	…	…

Sources: Auditing in the States: A Summary, 2003 edition. The National Association of State Auditors, Comptrollers and Treasurers.

Note: Government audits are divided into two types, financial and performance audits. Financial audits include financial statement audits and financial related audits. Performance audits include economy and efficiency audits and program audits. In addition, government auditors perform a number of other audit-related functions that do not fall into one of these categories. State audit agencies must make certain that audit coverage is broad enough to fulfill the needs of potential audit report users.

Key:
★—Provision for responsibility.
…—No provision for responsibility.
N.A.—Not available.
(a) Fraud, special audits, studies, and program evaluations.
(b) Investigations.

(c) Attestation engagements.
(d) Sunset analyses, mandatory health insurance analyses.
(e) Federal grant audits.
(f) Special requests and follow-up reviews.
(g) Special investigation reviews.
(h) Investigations and best practices reviews.
(i) Performance reviews.
(j) Internal control reviews: studies.
(k) Quality assurance reviews.
(l) Fraud investigations.
(m) Informational reports, including referrals or investigation or fraud.
(n) Special investigations.
(o) Internal controls review, investigative, management advisory, training and other educational services.
(p) Special projects, consulting, feasibility studies.

Table 4.30
THE STATE COMPTROLLERS, 2005

State	Agency or office	Name	Title	Legal basis for office	Method of selection	Approval or confirmation, if necessary	Date of first service	Present term ends	Consecutive time in office	Length of term	Elected comptrollers maximum consecutive terms	Civil services or merit system employee
Alabama	Office of the State Comptroller	Robert L. Childree	State Comptroller	S	(c)	AG	5/1987	(b)	18 yrs.	(b)	...	★
Alaska	Division of Finance	Kim J. Garnero	Director of Finance	S	(d)	AG	8/1999	(a)	5 yrs.	(a)	...	...
Arizona	Financial Services Division	D. Clark Partridge	State Comptroller	S	(d)	AG	4/2002	N.A.	3 yrs.	(g)	...	...
Arkansas	Dept. of Finance and Administration	Richard Weiss	Director	S	G	...	5/2002	(a)	3 yrs.	(a)	...	...
California	Office of the State Controller	Steve Westly (D)	State Controller	C	E	...	1/2003	1/2007	2 yrs.	4 yrs.	2 terms	...
Colorado	Office of the State Controller	Leslie Shenefelt	State Controller	S	CS	...	7/2004	(b)	1 yr.	(b)	...	★
Connecticut	Office of the Comptroller	Nancy Wyman (D)	Comptroller	C	E	...	1/1995	1/2007	10 yrs.	4 yrs.	unlimited	...
Delaware	Dept. of Finance	David W. Singleton	Secretary of Finance	S	G	AS	1/2005	(a)	6 mos.	(a)	...	...
Florida	Dept. of Financial Services	Tom Gallagher (R)	Chief Financial Officer	C	E	...	1/2003	12/2006	2 yrs.	4 yrs.	2 terms	...
Georgia	Office of Treasury and Fiscal Services	Lynn Vellinga	State Accounting Officer	S	SDB	SDB	10/2004	(b)	10 mos.	(b)	...	★
Hawaii	Dept. of Accounting and General Services	Russ K. Satio	State Comptroller	S	G	AS	12/2002	(a)	2 yrs.	(a)	...	...
Idaho	Office of State Controller	Keith Johnson (R)	State Controller	C,S	E	...	1/2003	12/2006	2 yrs.	4 yrs.	2 terms	...
Illinois	Office of the Comptroller	Daniel W. Hynes (D)	State Comptroller	C	E	...	11/1999	1/2007	6 yrs.	4 yrs.	unlimited	...
Indiana	Office of the Auditor of State	Connie Kay Nass (R)	Auditor of State	C	E	...	1/1999	12/2006	6 yrs.	4 yrs.	2 terms	...
Iowa	State Accounting Enterprise	Calvin McKelvogue	Chief Operating Officer	S	G	AS	7/2004	N.A.	1 yr.	(a)	...	...
Kansas	Division of Accounts and Reports	Dale Brunton	Director	S	(d)	...	10/2000	N.A.	4 yrs.	(b)	...	...
Kentucky	Office of the Controller	Edgar C. Ross	Controller	S	(f)	AG	6/1975	N.A.	30 yrs.	(i)	...	...
Louisiana	Division of Administration	Jerry Luke LeBlanc	Commissioner of Administration	S	G	AS	1/2004	1/2008	7 yrs.	(a)	...	...
Maine	Bureau of Accounts and Controls	Edward Karass	State Controller	S	(f)	AG	4/2003	1/2007	1 yr.	(i)	...	...
Maryland	Office of the Comptroller	William Donald Schaefer (D)	State Comptroller	C,S	E	...	1/1999	1/2007	6 yrs.	4 yrs.	unlimited	...
Massachusetts	Office of the Comptroller	Martin J. Benison	Comptroller	S	G	AG	1/1999	1/2007	6 yrs.	(j)	...	...
Michigan	Office of Financial Management	Michael J. Moody	Director	S	SBD	SBD	8/2002	8/2004	3 yrs.	(k)	...	★
Minnesota	Department of Finance	Peggy Ingison	Commissioner	S	G	AS	2/2004	1/2007	1 yr.	(a)	...	...
Mississippi	Department of Finance and Administration	J.K. Stringer Jr.	Executive Director	S	G	AS	1/2004	1/2008	1 yr.	(a)	...	...
Missouri	Division of Accounting	Thomas J. Sadowski	Director	C,S	(d)	...	2/2005	N.A.	6 mos.	(g)	...	...
Montana	Administrative Financial Services Division	Paul Christofferson	Administrator	S	G	...	6/2004	N.A.	1 yr.	4 yrs. (a)	...	...
Nebraska	Accounting Division	Paul Carlson	State Accounting Administrator	S	(d)	AG	11/2000	N.A.	4 yrs.	(g)	...	...
Nevada	Office of the State Controller	Kathy Augustine (R)	State Controller	C	E	...	1/1999	12/2006	6 yrs.	4 yrs.	2 terms	...
New Hampshire	Division of Accounting Services	Sheri Rockburn	Comptroller	S	G	...	8/2004	(b)	1yr.	4 yrs.	...	...

See footnotes at end of table.

THE STATE COMPTROLLERS, 2005 — Continued

State	Agency or office	Name	Title	Legal basis for office	Method of selection	Approval or confirmation, if necessary	Date of first service	Present term ends	Consecutive time in office	Length of term	Elected comptrollers maximum consecutive terms	Civil services or merit system employee
New Jersey	Office of Management and Budget	Charlene M. Holzbaur	Director/State Controller	S	G	AS	10/1999	(b)	5 yrs.	(a)	…	…
New Mexico	Department of Finance and Administration, Financial Control Division	Anthony I. Armijo	State Controller and Director	N.A.	G	N.A.	1/1991	(b)	14 yrs.	N.A.	N.A.	…
New York	Office of the State Comptroller	Alan G. Hevesi (D)	State Comptroller	C,S	E	…	1/2003	12/2006	2 yrs.	4 yrs.	unlimited	…
North Carolina	Office of the State Controller	Robert L. Powell	State Controller	S	G	GA	7/2001	7/2008	4 yrs.	7 yrs.	…	…
North Dakota	Office of Management and Budget	Pam Sharp	Director	S	G	…	1/2003	(a)	2 yrs.	(a)	…	…
Ohio	Office of Management and Budget	Thomas W. Johnson	Director	S	G	AS	1/1999	1/2007	6 yrs.	(a)	…	…
Oklahoma	Office of State Finance	Brenda Bolander	State Comptroller	S	(e)	…	12/2001	(b)	3 yrs.	(h)	…	…
Oregon	State Controller's Division	John J. Radford	State Controller	S	(d)	AG	11/1989	(b)	15 yrs.	(g)	…	…
Pennsylvania	Comptroller Operations	Harvey C. Eckert	Deputy Secretary for Comptroller	S	G	…	3/1983	(b)	22 yrs.	(a)	…	…
Rhode Island	Office of Accounts and Control	Lawrence C. Franklin Jr.	State Controller	S	(d)	…	8/1986	N.A.	18 yrs.	(b)	…	★
South Carolina	Office of the Comptroller General	Richard Eckstrom (R)	Comptroller General	C	E	…	1/2003	1/2007	2 yrs.	4 yrs.	unlimited	…
South Dakota	Office of the State Auditor	Richard L. Sattgast (R)	State Auditor	C	E	…	1/2003	1/2007	2 yrs.	4 yrs.	2 terms	…
Tennessee	Division of Accounts	Jan I. Sylvis	Chief of Accounts	S	(f)	…	12/1995	N.A.	9 yrs.	(b)	…	…
Texas	Office of the Comptroller of Public Accounts	Carole Keeton Strayhorn (R)	Comptroller of Public Accounts	C,S	E	…	1/1999	1/2007	6 yrs.	4 yrs.	unlimited	…
Utah	Division of Finance	Kim S. Oliver	Director	S	(d)	AG	4/1996	N.A.	8 yrs.	(g)	…	★
Vermont	Department of Finance	James Reardon	Commissioner	S	G	AS	2/2005	2/2009	6 mos.	(a)	…	…
Virginia	Department of Accounts	David A. Von Moll	Comptroller	S	G	GA	11/2001	(a)	3 yrs.	(a)	…	…
Washington	Office of Financial Management	Victor Moore	Director	C,S	G	…	1/2005	N.A.	7 mos.	(a)	…	…
West Virginia	Office of the State Auditor	Glen B. Gainier III (D)	State Auditor	C	E	…	1/1993	1/2005	13 yrs.	4 yrs.	unlimited	…
	Division of Finance, Office of the State Comptroller	Andrew J. Fizer	State Comptroller	S	(d)	AG	7/2002	N.A.	3 yrs.	(g)	…	…

Sources: Comptrollers: Technical Activities and Functions, 2003 Edition, National Association of State Auditors, Comptrollers and Treasurers, 2005.

Key:
…—No provision for.
C—Constitutional
S—Statutory
N.A.—Not applicable.
E—Elected by the public.
G—Appointed by the Governor.
CS—Civil Service.
AG—Approved by the governor.
AS—Approved/confirmed by the Senate.
SBD—Approved by State Budget Director.

GA—Confirmed by the General Assembly.
SDB—Confirmed by State Depository Board.
(a) Serves at the pleasure of the governor.
(b) Indefinite.
(c) Appointed by the Director of the Dept. of Finance (merit system position).
(d) Appointed by the head of the department of administration or administrative services.
(e) Appointed by the head of finance. department or agency.
(f) Appointed by the head of financial and administrative services.
(g) Serves at the pleasure of the head of the department of administration or administrative services.
(h) Serves at the pleasure of the head of the finance department or agency.
(i) Serves at the pleasure of the head of the financial and administrative services.
(j) Two full terms coterminous with the governor.
(k) Two-year renewable contractual term; classified executive service.

Table 4.31
STATE COMPTROLLERS: QUALIFICATIONS FOR OFFICE

State	Minimum age	U.S. citizen (years)	State resident (years) (b)	Education years or degree	Professional experience and years	Professional certification and years	Other qualifications	No specific qualifications for office
Alabama	★	★	★	★, B.S.	★, 6 yrs.	...	...	
Alaska	...	...	...	...	...	...	...	★
Arizona	...	★, 1 yr.	★, 1 yr.	★, B.S.	★, 7–10 yrs.	★(a)	...	
Arkansas	★	...	...	...	★	...	...	
California	★	...	...	...	...	...	(b)	
Colorado	...	...	★, 6 mos.	★(i)	★	★, CPA	...	
Connecticut	...	...	★	...	...	...	...	
Delaware	...	...	...	...	...	...	...	★
Florida	★	...	★, 7 yrs.	...	...	...	...	
Georgia	...	...	...	...	...	...	...	★
Hawaii	...	...	...	...	...	...	...	★
Idaho	★	★(j)	★, 2 yrs.	...	...	...	...	
Illinois	★	★	★, 3 yrs.	...	...	...	...	
Indiana	...	...	★(j)	...	...	...	,,,	
Iowa	...	...	...	...	...	...	...	★
Kansas	...	...	...	...	...	...	...	★
Kentucky	...	...	...	...	. ..	...	(c)	★
Louisiana	...	...	...	...	...	...	...	★
Maine	...	...	...	...	...	...	(d)	★
Maryland	...	...	...	...	...	...	...	★
Massachusetts	...	...	...	★(k)	★, 7 yrs.	...		
Michigan	...	...	...	★(l)	★, 7 yrs.	★, CPA	...	
Minnesota	...	...	...	...	★	...	...	
Mississippi	...	...	...	★(k)	★, 10 yrs.	★, CPA	(e)	...
Missouri	...	...	...	...	...	...	...	★
Montana	...	...	...	...	...	...	...	★
Nebraska	...	...	...	★(m)	★(n)	★, CPA	...	
Nevada	★	★	★	...	...	...	...	...
New Hampshire	...	...	...	...	...	...	(f)	★
New Jersey	...	...	...	...	...	...	...	★
New Mexico	30	★	5	N.A.	N.A.	N.A.	N.A.	N.A.
New York	★	★	★, 5 yrs.	...	...	...	...	...
North Carolina	...	★	★	★	★	...	(g)	...
North Dakota	...	...	...	...	...	...	...	★
Ohio								
Oklahoma	...	...	...	...	...	...	...	★
Oregon	...	...	...	...	...	...	...	★
Pennsylvania	...	...	...	...	...	...	...	★
Rhode Island	...	...	★	★(h)	★	★, CPA	...	...
South Carolina	★	★	★	...	...	...	...	...
South Dakota	★	★	★, 1 yr.	...	...	...	...	...
Tennessee	...	...	...	★	★, 7 yrs.	★, CPA	...	...
Texas	★	★ (j)	★, 1 yr.	...	...	...	...	...
Utah	...	...	...	★	★, 6 yrs.	★, CPA	...	...
Vermont	...	...	...	...	...	...	...	★
Virginia	...	...	...	...	...	...	...	★
Washington	★	★, Whole life	★	★ (o)	★	★, J.D.	...	...
West Virginia—								
Office of State Auditor	...	★	★	...	,,,	...	...	
Div. of Finance, Office of State Comptroller	...	★	★	★, B.S.B.A.	★, 7 yrs.	...	...	
Wisconsin	...	...	...	★ (p)	...	★, CPA	...	...
Wyoming	★	★	★	...	...	...	...	...

Sources: Comptrollers: Technical Activities and Functions, 2003 Edition, The National Association of State Auditors, Comptrollers and Treasurers, 2005.

Key:
★—Formal provision.
. . .—No formal provision.

(a) Any of those mentioned or CFE, CPM, etc
(b) 18 yrs. At time of election or appointment and a citizen of the state.
(c) The Kentucky Revised Statutes state that The state controller shall be a person qualified b education and experience for the position and held in high esteem in the accounting community.
(d) There are no educational or professional mandates, yet the appointed official is generally qualified by a combination of experience and education.
(e) At least 5 yrs. experience in high level management.
(f) Education and relevant experience.
(g) Qualified by education and experience for the position.
(h) Master's degree in accounting, finance or business management or public administration.
(i) 5 yrs. or college degree.
(j) Years not specified.
(k) Master's degree.
(l) 4 yrs. and bachelor's degree.
(m) 4 yrs. with major in accounting.
(n) 3 yrs. directing the work of others.
(o) 7 yrs. and law degree.
(p) Bachelor's degree in accounting.

Table 4.32
STATE COMPTROLLERS: DUTIES AND RESPONSIBILITIES

State	Appropriation control	Budgetary reporting	Comprehensive annual financial report (CAFR)	Disbursement of state funds	Maintenance of the general ledger and chart of accounts	Payroll processing	Pre-auditing of payments	Post-audit	Operation of statewide financial management system	Management of state travel policies
Alabama	★	★	★	★ (a)	★	★	★	...	★	★
Alaska	★	...	★	★	★	★	...	...	★	★
Arizona	★	...	★	★	★	★	★	★	★	★
Arkansas	★	★	★	...	...	...	★	★	...	...
California	★	★	★	★	★	★	★	★	★	...
Colorado	★	...	★	★	★	★	★	★	★	★
Connecticut	...	...	★	...	★	★	...	★	...	...
Delaware	★	...	★	★ (b)	★	★	★	★	★ (c)	★
Florida	★	...	★	★	★	★	★	★	★	★
Georgia	★	...	...	...	...	...	...	...	...	...
Hawaii	★ (e)	...	★	★	★	★	★ (d)	N.A.	★	★
Idaho	★	...	★	★ (f)	★	★	...	...	...	...
Illinois	★	★	★	★	★	★	★ (g)	★	★	★
Indiana	...	★	★	★	★	★	★	★	★	★
Iowa	★	...	★	★	★	★	...	★	★	★
Kansas	★	...	★	...	★	★	...	★	★	★
Kentucky	★	...	★	★	★	★	...	...	...	★
Louisiana	★	★	★	★	★	★	...	★ (i)	★	★
Maine	...	★	★	...	★	★	★ (h)	★ (j)	...	...
Maryland	★	...	★	★ (a)	★	★	★	...	★	★
Massachusetts	...	★	★	...	★	★	...	...	★	★
Michigan	★	★	★	★	★	★	★	★ (k)	★	★
Minnesota	★	★	★	★	★	★	★	★	★	★
Mississippi	★	...	★	★	★	★	★	...	★	★
Missouri	★	...	★	★	★	★	★	★	★	...
Montana	...	★	★	★	★	★	★	...	★	★
Nebraska	★ (l)	★ (l)	★	★	★	★	...	★	★	★
Nevada	★	★	★	★	★	★	★	...	★	★
New Hampshire	★	★	★	...	★	★	★	★	★	...
New Jersey	★	...	★	★	★	★	...	★	★	★
New Mexico	N.A.	N.A.	N.A.	N.A.	N.A.	N.A.	N.A.	N.A.	N.A.	N.A.
New York	★ (m)	...	★	★	★	★	★	★	...	★
North Carolina	★ (o)	★	★	★	★	★	★ (n)	★	★	...
North Dakota	★	★	★	...	★	★	...	...	...	★
Ohio	★	★	★	★	★	★	...	★	★	★
Oklahoma	★	...	★	★	★	★	★	★	★	★
Oregon	...	★ (p)	★	...	★	★	★ (a)	★	★	★
Pennsylvania	...	...	★	...	★	★	...	★	★	★
Rhode Island	★	...	★	...	★	★	★	...	★	★
South Carolina	★	★	★	★ (q)	★	...	★	...	...	★

See footnotes at end of table.

STATE COMPTROLLERS: DUTIES AND RESPONSIBILITIES — Continued

State	Appropriation control	Budgetary reporting	Comprehensive annual financial report (CAFR)	Disbursement of state funds	Maintenance of the general ledger and chart of accounts	Payroll processing	Pre-auditing of payments	Post-audit	Operation of statewide financial management system	Management of state travel policies
South Dakota	…	…	…	★	NA	★	★	…	…	★
Tennessee	…	…	★	★	★	★	★ (r)	★ (s)	…	★
Texas	★	★	★	★	★	★	★ (r)	★	★	…
Utah	★	…	★	★	★	★	★ (t)	★	★	★
Vermont	★	★	★	…	★	…	★	★	★	★
Virginia	★ (u)	…	★	★	★	★	★	★ (v)	★	★
Washington	★	★ (w)	★	…	★	…	…	…	★	★
West Virginia Office of State Auditor	★ (x)	★ (y)	…	★	…	★	★	…	…	…
Div. of Finance, Office of State Comptroller	★ (x)	…	★	…	★	…	★	…	★	★
Wisconsin	★	★	★	★	★	★	★ (z)	★	…	★
Wyoming	★	…	★	…	★	★	★	…	★	★

Sources: Comptrollers: Technical Activities and Functions, 2003 Edition, The National Association of State Auditors, Comptrollers and Treasurers 2005.

Key:
★—Formal provision; number of years not specified.
…—No formal provision.
A—Appointed by governor.
(a) Responsibilities shared between Comptroller and Treasury.
(b) Responsibilities shared between Department of Finance and State Treasurer's Office.
(c) Responsibilities shared between Department of Finance and the Auditor of Accounts.
(d) Except for various autonomous agencies.
(e) Responsibilities shared between Office of State Controller and the Division of Financial Management.
(f) Responsibilities shared between Office of the State Controller and the State Treasurer's Office.
(g) Responsibilities shared between state agencies and the Office of the State Comptroller.
(h) Responsibilities shared between agencies and the Office of the State Controller.
(i) Responsibilities shared between Office of the State Controller and the State Auditor.
(j) Responsibilities shared between Office of the State Comptroller and the Legislative Auditor.
(k) Responsibilities shared between Dept. of Finance and the Office of the Legislative Auditor.
(l) Responsibilities shared between Accounting Division and the Dept. of Administrative Services.

(m) Responsibilities shared between Comptroller and Budget Director.
(n) Responsibilities shared between office of the State Comptroller with delegation to state agencies and universities.
(o) Responsibilities shared between shared Comptroller and Office of State Budget and Management
(p) Responsibilities shared between State Controller and the Dept. of Administrative Services.
(q) Responsibilities shared, Comptroller General issues warrants, Treasurer issues checks, colleges maintain their own systems and write their own checks.
(r) Responsible for all departments that have not been authorized to do their own based own excellent performance.
(s) Responsibilities shared between Division of Audits and Department of Audit.
(t) Responsibilities shared between various agencies and the division of Finance.
(u) Responsibilities shared between Comptroller and Dept. of Planning and Budget.
(v) Responsibilities shared between Comptroller and Auditor
(w) Responsibilities shared between Office of Financial Management and all state agencies.
(x) Responsibilities shared between State Budget Office within the Office of the State Comptroller and the Office of the State Auditor.
(y) Responsibilities shared between State Budget Office and the Office of the State Auditor.
(z) Responsibilities delegated to state agencies by the State Controller's Office.

Chapter Five

STATE
JUDICIAL BRANCH

Trends in State Courts:
Rising Caseloads and Vanishing Trials
By David B. Rottman

During 2004, alarms sounded in many states both because of the conduct of the 2004 judicial elections and where improving state finances did not translate into adequate funding for the courts. The losers are the members of the public and businesses with disputes for which they cannot obtain resolution.

Introduction

Americans think about their judicial system the way they think about the water departments in their towns: the local water department is absolutely essential, but only comes to people's minds when something appears to malfunction: a water main explodes, water restrictions go into effect because of shortages, or reports of contamination set off alarms.[1]

The metaphor is apt. Several alarms sounded during 2004, triggered primarily by the manner in which candidates, interest groups and political parties campaigned in judicial races. The 2004 judicial elections continued trends first dramatically evident in 2000: heavy spending, heavy involvement by non-candidate groups[2], and campaign conduct—especially by outside groups—that included sharply negative attacks which might be ordinary in non-judicial elections but have with great care traditionally been barred from judicial races. While the 2004 elections signaled trouble ahead, they also provided some reassurance that the provisions built into the constitutions of all 39 states that elect judges to keep judicial races different from those held for the political branches of state government can be preserved (for an extended treatment of the 2004 elections, see the earlier article in this chapter, "2004 Judicial Elections").

During 2004 other alarms sounded in many states where improving state finances did not translate into adequate funding for the courts, interrupting the services the courts provide. The courts in most states have been left to accommodate the steady rise in their workload without securing a commensurate growth in resources. The losers are the members of the public with disputes for which they cannot obtain resolution.

As in previous election years, the state courts were asked to resolve disputes concerning elections for legislative and executive branch offices. Prominent examples from 2004 include court challenges to election outcomes concerning the party controlling the Montana Legislature, the mayoral race in San Diego, and the governorship of Washington (still a trial court, with a jury trial set for May 2005). Inevitably, such disputes place the judiciary in the middle of a partisan political controversy that might affect subsequent relationships between the two branches.[3]

Court reform continued along mainly familiar tracks, including the longstanding movement toward court systems that are more centralized, streamlined, and funded at the state rather than the local level. Still more imaginative ways were found to respond to the needs of the growing number of citizens that prefer to represent themselves in court. For example, California's network of support includes the provision of a family law facilitator in each county, family law information centers, five "pilot" models for self-help centers, and small claims advisors who assist litigants in these lawyer-free proceedings.[4]

Like water departments, courts need to anticipate changing demand for their service before alarms start to sound. Some signs that fundamental changes are taking place in the demand for court services were much discussed during 2004. Attention focused on the implications of what became known as "the vanishing trial" phenomenon, a sustained decline in the number of trials, both trials by jury and trials by judge, in the state courts.[5]

Trends in the Work of the State Courts

Throughout the year, the state courts conducted their essential but little noticed mission of responding to demand by adjudicating nearly one hundred million cases brought to them by the public, businesses and government. Courts like water departments must adjust their supply to accommodate increases and changes in the location of demand. There were signs in 2004 that trends in demand have been slowly reshaping the composition of disputes courts are asked to resolve and also the role of trials in to resolving those disputes.

Rising Demand. Demand for court action continues to grow at a more rapid rate than the increase in the size of the general population. In 2002 (the most recent year for which statistics are available), 96.2 million cases were filed in the state courts.

Traffic-related cases accounted for 60 percent of all cases filed, a proportion that has been steadily declining for some time as administrative agency proceedings replace court adjudication for many traffic offenses. There has also been a slow but steady shift in the nature of the demand on the courts. The proportion of civil cases (tort, contract, and real property) has increased at a slower rate than criminal and family-related cases (see Table A).

The number of appeals filed in appellate courts has not increased as rapidly as that in trial courts. Still, in 2002, 278,000 appeals were filed in state appellate courts, an increase of 9 percent since 1993.[6]

A gap between demand and supply. The number of judges has not been increasing in pace with the rising case volume. The state judiciary grew by 5 percent between 1993 and 2002.[7] Consequently, a gap is forming between the demand for court adjudication and the supply of judges to provide the adjudication. This gap is wider than might at first be assessed because the changes are replacing uncom-

Table A: Trends in State Trial Court Case Filings, 1993–2002

Civil cases	+12%
Criminal cases	+19
Domestic relations	+14
Juvenile cases	+16
Traffic cases	+2

plicated, quick to resolve traffic cases with more complicated and time intensive criminal, civil and domestic relations case.

Taking the long view. We need to step back still further in time to 1976, to gain sufficient perspective to join in the discussions, prevalent in 2004, of the future of the state courts.

Issues of comparability over time and among states give us an incomplete picture of what has taken place. Still, we know that between 1976 and 2002, the number of criminal cases doubled, as measured in the 23 states for which reliable and comparable caseload information is available for the full time period. The cases in question were heard in courts of general jurisdiction, which primarily adjudicate felony cases. Much of the increase was recorded prior to the late 1980s (see Figure A).

Civil cases increased at a slightly slower pace than

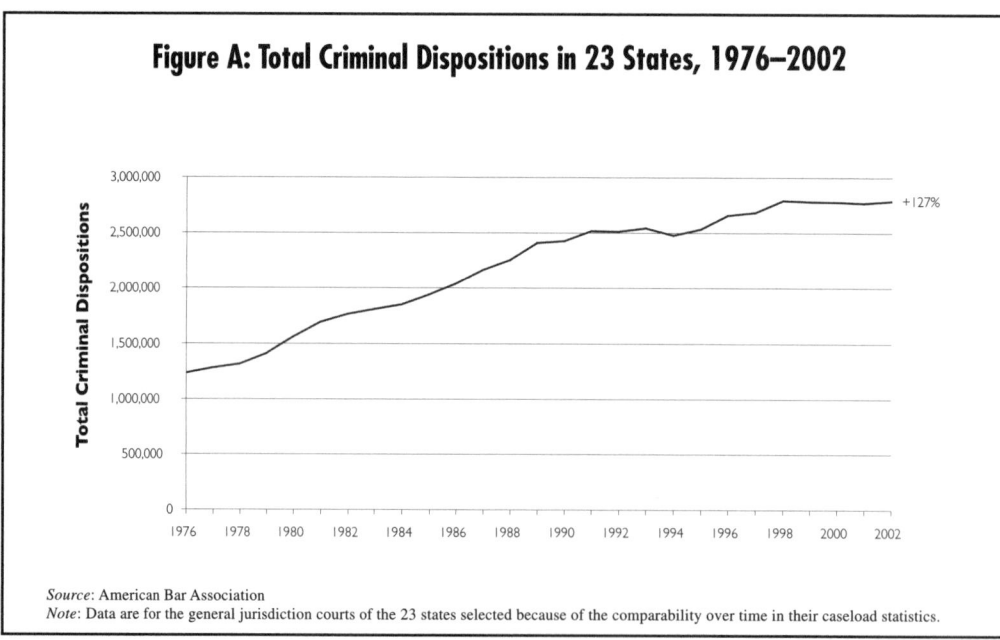

Figure A: Total Criminal Dispositions in 23 States, 1976–2002

Source: American Bar Association
Note: Data are for the general jurisdiction courts of the 23 states selected because of the comparability over time in their caseload statistics.

criminal cases over the 1976–2002 period. However, the trend was distinct, with sharp increases in the late 1970s and early 1980s, followed up a precipitous climb in the number of cases until 1992. Over the last 10 years, civil cases are becoming less common in state courts of general jurisdiction (see Figure B).

The "Vanishing Trial" Phenomenon. For reasons that remain uncertain, the number of jury trials (and bench trials as well in criminal cases) has declined since 1976 (see Figure C). There were 15 percent fewer jury trials in criminal cases in 2002 than in 1976 despite the just documented sharp increase in the number of such case being brought to the courts and a growing population. For most of the recent past, fewer and fewer criminal cases have been decided by a jury (or a judge) trial. The exception was the late 1980s and early 1990s when the number of jury trials increased, although not sufficiently to keep the proportion of criminal cases decided by a trial from declining.

The pattern for civil juries in trial courts of general jurisdiction (basically tort, contract and real property cases) is different. The number of trials in 1976 was never subsequently equaled. Rather, in the face of rising civil caseloads, the number of trials remained relatively constant until the end of the 1990s. Most of the 32 percent decline in jury trials was recorded during those years.

Reading the tealeaves. These trends outlining a diminished role for the jury in deciding cases, especially for civil cases, have been treated as tealeaves through which the future of the state courts (and the courts generally because of similar trends in the federal courts) can be divined. Observers differ on the causes of the reduction in the use of juries and on how profound are the implications of these trends.[8]

Jury trials now account for 2 percent of all civil and criminal case dispositions in the state courts. Their significance for the justice system vastly exceeds what their proportion of dispositions might indicate because jury decisions set the parameters within which negotiated settlements are reached in the vast majority of civil cases that settle between the parties and the vast majority of criminal cases resolved by a plea agreement. What is happening in jury trials? In one scenario, litigants, their lawyers, and judges are responding to changes in the practice of law, one that gives emphasis to settlements and the less costly and time draining judicial determination of a summary judgment. In another less benign scenario, the state courts are no longer responding well to the demand for dispute resolution. Potential litigants are turning to dispute resolution like private judges (hired by the parties to the dispute) and mediation. In those forums, the courts often have limited, if any, oversight. One possible future for the state courts sees them assuming an expanded role in ensuring that private dispute resolution is fair and the underlying legal analyses contribute to the im-

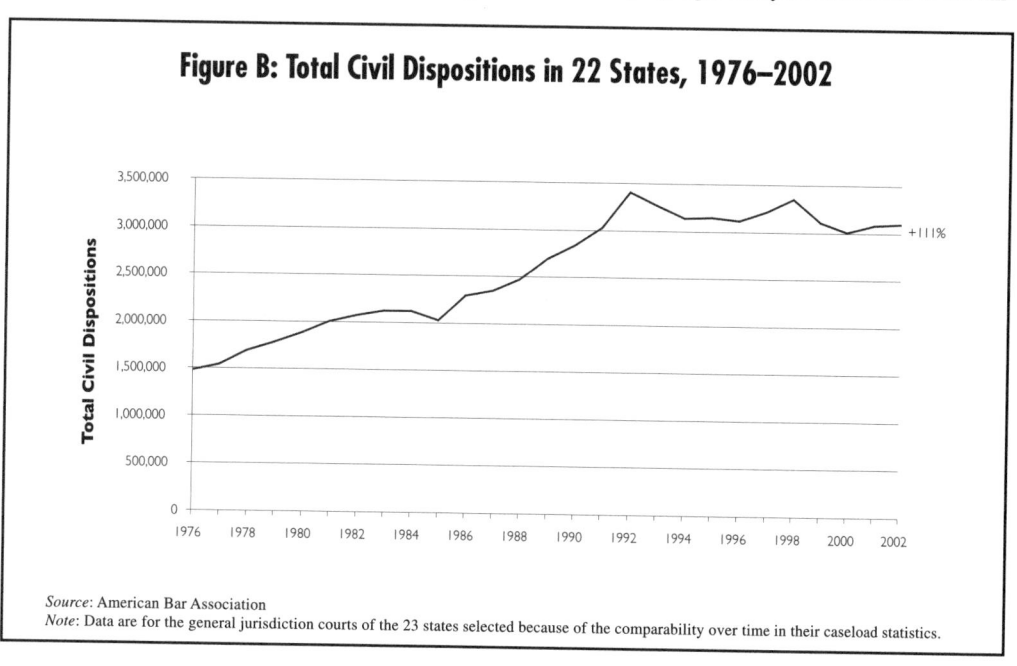

Figure B: Total Civil Dispositions in 22 States, 1976–2002

Source: American Bar Association

Note: Data are for the general jurisdiction courts of the 23 states selected because of the comparability over time in their caseload statistics.

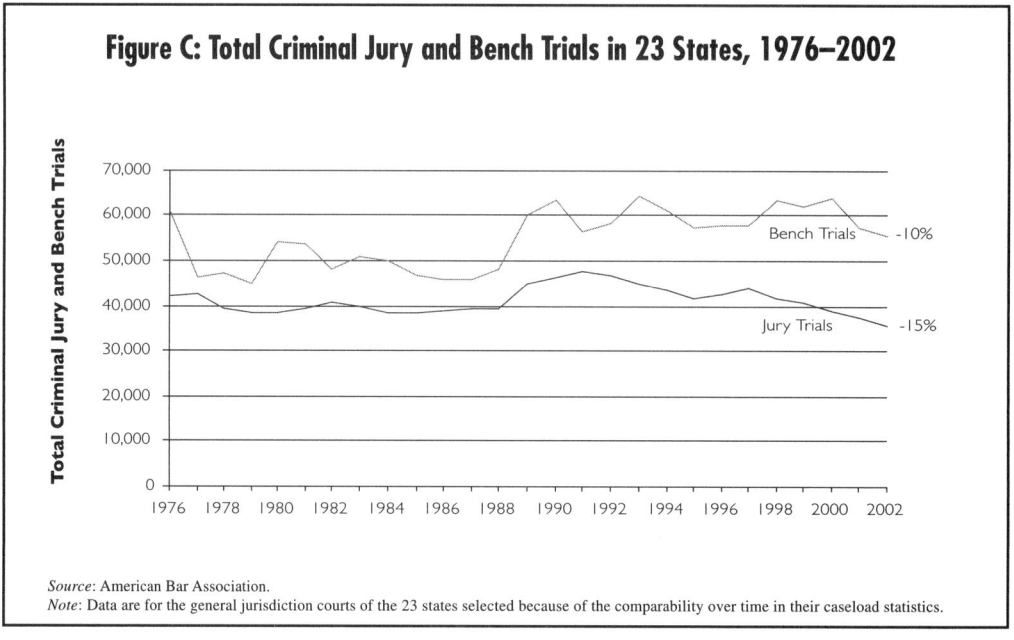

Figure C: Total Criminal Jury and Bench Trials in 23 States, 1976–2002

Source: American Bar Association.
Note: Data are for the general jurisdiction courts of the 23 states selected because of the comparability over time in their caseload statistics.

provement of American law.

The year of celebrity trials. Real jury trials may be on the decline but the public's exposure to them is on the rise due to a series of celebrity trials. The year 2004 was rich in such trials, notably the criminal cases against Kobe Bryant, Scott Peterson and Martha Stewart and the pre-trial maneuvers for the Michael Jackson and Robert Blake trials: "Aside from the war in Iraq, the most frequently reported story on broadcast TV morning news shows last year was the Peterson Case." In all, celebrity trial stories outnumbered those about the California gubernatorial recall by two to one.[9] Such pervasive coverage makes the jury more visible than ever before, but in a form so far from typical as to be aberrations. The typical jury trial begins and ends on the same day, typically including the time required for jury deliberations.[10]

The citizen juror. The continuing importance of juries also is evident in the growing proportion of Americans who have served as a member of a jury. The best evidence from the late 1970s indicates that about some 6 to 10 percent of all American adults had served as a juror (that is, been sworn in as a juror on a specific case) compared to the 25 to 30 percent who can claim such experience today. A 2004 national survey found that 62 percent of all adults reported receiving a summons for jury service, with 29 percent having served as a jury member.[11]

What underlies such a dramatic change? The catalyst that began the democratization process was the replacement in 1968 of the "key man" system in the federal courts, in which local jury commissioners handpicked the individuals who would be in the jury pool for each term of system. By 1973, all of the states had made the same change. Initially, the list of registered voters defined the jury pool. Over time, all but four states have expanded their source lists to include licensed drivers, utility customers, and state income tax payers. The jury also became more democratic as automatic exceptions from jury service, like that once given to all women and to members of various occupations were gradually greatly reduced or eliminated. The U.S. Supreme Court halted the practice through which lawyers would use their peremptory challenges (ones for which no reason had to be stated) to exclude African-Americans or other ethnic groups from a jury.[12] The diversification of the jury pool is one so that it increasingly resembles the public at large is one of the great accomplishments of the American courts in the past 50 years. It is a cause to rejoice.

Jury Democracy and Judicial Elections. A democratic jury is not to everyone's satisfaction, however: "As the diversity of our society and its jurors has increased to the point that litigants can expect jurors unlike themselves, the pressure has risen to restrict

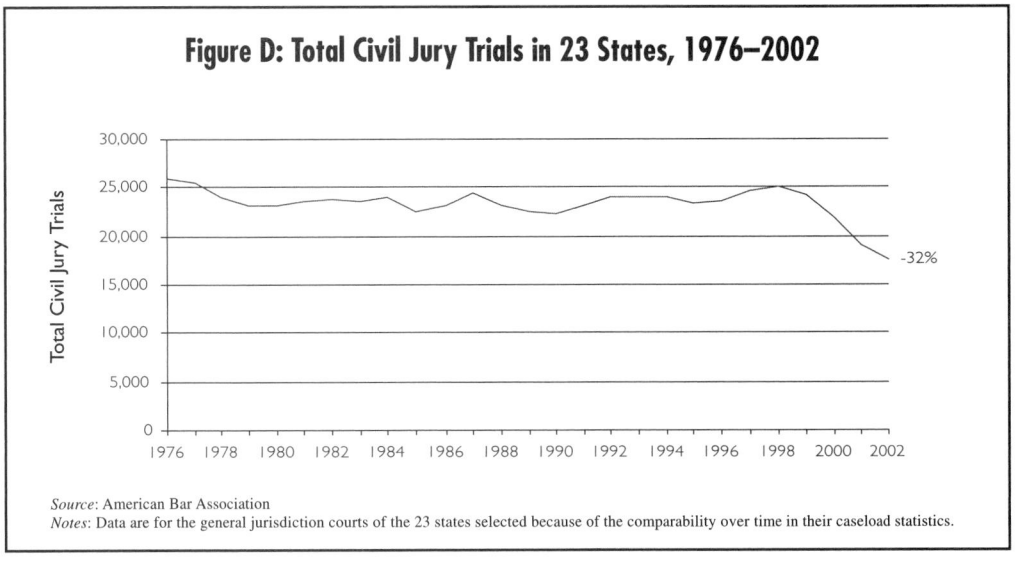

Figure D: Total Civil Jury Trials in 23 States, 1976–2002

Source: American Bar Association
Notes: Data are for the general jurisdiction courts of the 23 states selected because of the comparability over time in their caseload statistics.

the power of juries."[13] Indeed, the "hottest" 2004 judicial elections were fueled by claims that certain jurisdictions by virtue of their demographic makeup were inhospitable to corporate defendants, especially those from out-of-state. In some respects, the realization of the promise of a jury system in which all citizens participate has contributed to the animus with which judicial elections are being conducted today.

What Lies Ahead?

State court workloads are on the rise. Current trends, such as reduced number of trial proceedings are unlikely to offer much relief. The three branches of government need to work out approaches, such as that pioneered last year in California, to provide stable funding for the courts. The courts, in turn, need to present a compelling case for their budget needs and then to monitor the effectiveness and efficiency with which the money so allocated is spent. There have been significant advances in the methodologies through which the courts can measure their resource needs and monitor their performance. Judicial and court staff workload assessments provide objective assessments of the number of positions needed to handle caseloads and identify where judicial and staff resources are "being allocated and used prudently."[14] *CourTools* offers 10 practical measures of court outcomes, including access and fairness; time to disposition, trial date certainty, and cost per case.[15] There is ground for some optimism that such objective standards for establishing the need for court resources and accounting for the use of those resources

can be grounded in the demonstrable needs of the public and businesses for court resolution of disputes.

Notes

[1] John Russonelo, "Speak to Values: How to Promote the Courts and Blunt Attacks on the Judiciary," Court Review 41, 2, 2004.

[2] Emily Heller, "Chamber Scores Big in Judicial Elections," *National Law Journal* (November 8, 2004).

[3] These election law cases are important to the democratic process, concerning issues such as ballot access, accurate vote counts, and voter challenges; they often must be resolved with considerable haste. The William and Mary Law School and National Center for State Courts have established an Election Law Program to offer assistance to state judges who are called upon to resolve legal issues involving election law.

[4] Bonnie Hough, "Self-Represented Litigants in California: Court Programs Helping Litigants Represent Themselves", *Future Trends in State Courts 2004*. Williamsburg, VA: National Center for State Courts, 2004.

[5] The phenomenon was explored by the ABA Litigation Section's Vanishing Trial Project, which culminated in a symposium in December 2003.

[6] See *O'Neill v Coughlan*, Case No. 1:04CV1612 (N.D.OH 2004) (in which the court issued a temporary injunction to prevent the state from enforcing sanctions against a candidate for Ohio Supreme Court), 64. Available at *http://www.legalaffairs.org/howappealing/20040914ONeillinjunction.pdf*.

[7] Brian Ostrom, Neal Kauder, and Robert LaFountain, *Examining the Work of State Courts, 2003: A National Perspective from the Court Statistics Project*, Williamsburg

VA: National Center for State Courts, 2004, pp. 10–11.

[8]Brian Ostrom, Shauna Strickland, and Paula Hannaford-Agor, "Examining Trial Trends in State Courts: 1976–2002", *Journal of Empirical Legal Studies* Vol. 1, No. 1, pp. 755–72 (NB: The entire issue is devoted to "The Vanishing Trial" phenomenon).

[9]Glenn Garvin, "Jury is in: Celebrity Trials a Hit for TV", *The Miami Herald*, June 14, 2004. The article notes that these celebrity cases have "created a whole new class of TV journalists, nomadic bands that wander from courthouse to courthouse".

[10]The best estimate of jury trial length is 13:30 hours in civil cases and 11:07 hours in criminal cases. Jury deliberations account for 1:55 hours and 2:45 hours, respectively, of those proceedings. See Dale A. Sipes and Mary E. Oram, *On Trial: The Length of Civil and Criminal Trails*, (National Center for State Courts: Williamsburg, VA, 1988).

[11]Harris Interactive Market Research, *Jury Service: Is Fulfilling Your Civic Duty a Trial?* (A report prepared for the American Bar Association, August, 2004 (*http://www.abanews.org/releases/juryreport.pdf*)

[12]I am grateful to my colleague Paula Hannaford-Agor for this summary of factors underlying the post-1960s changes to the jury pool. U.S. Supreme Court decisions were the agents of much of the expansion in jury service: *Taylor v. Louisiana* (which ended automatic exemptions for women in 1975 and *Batson v. Kentucky* (prohibiting lawyers from creating all white juries) in 1986.

[13]Kenneth S. Klein, "Unpacking the Jury Box" 47 Hastings L.J. 1326.

[14]The state of the art of such assessments can be found in two studies conducted on behalf of the Minnesota State Court Administrator's Office by the National Center for State Courts. See Brian Ostrom et al., *Minnesota Judicial Workload Assessment 2002* Williamsburg, VA: National Center for State Courts, 2003 and Minnesota Court Staff Workload Assessment, 2004, Williamsburg, VA: National Center for State Courts, 2004.

[15]The measures are described at *http://www.ncsconline.org/D_Research/CourTools/tcpm_courttools.htm*.

About the Author

David B. Rottman is a principal court research consultant at the National Center for State Courts, where he has worked since 1987. His current interests include judicial selection, public opinion on the courts, the evolution of court structure, and the pros and cons of problem-solving courts. He is the author of books on modern Ireland, social class and community courts. Rottman has a doctorate in sociology from the University of Illinois at Urbana, and previously worked at the Economic and Social Institute in Dublin, Ireland.

2004 Judicial Elections

By David B. Rottman and Roy A. Schotland

Judicial elections in 2004 were in the spotlight again, mostly for the wrong reasons. Many campaigns were costly and negative in tone. A few candidates signaled how they would decide types of cases. Positive developments include new and active campaign oversight committees, and public funding for appellate candidates in North Carolina.

The Spotlight

In 2004, judicial elections again drew unprecedented attention. Notable coverage included a *Business Week* cover story on "The Battle Over The Courts: How Politics, ideology, and special interests are compromising the U.S. Justice System." The article dealt with "bitter polarization" in the process of appointing federal judges and in more and more of the 39 states in which judges face some type of elections: "This isn't a problem just in a few places where court elections have become circuses."[1] Even overseas, *The Economist* headlined a story "Guilty, Your Honour?" "This year's judicial elections may be worryingly free-speaking.... Judicial elections have grown more contentious, and so more costly, with business and lawyers' groups spending huge sums in contests where tort law is at stake."[2]

The 2004 Elections

These reports got it essentially right. The 2004 judicial elections were near the levels they leapt to in 2000 and continued in 2002: heavy spending, heavy involvement by non-candidate groups (like the Chamber of Commerce on one side—active in 15 races spread across 12 states in 2004—and plaintiffs' trial lawyers and unions on the other[3]), and campaign conduct—especially by the outside groups—that included sharply negative attacks which might be ordinary in non-judicial elections but are a dramatic departure from the era when these elections were "about as exciting as a game of checkers . . . played by mail."[4]

Several striking features were new in 2004. In perhaps the most heated election, in which a West Virginia Supreme Court incumbent was defeated, an all-time record was set for an individual contribution in a judicial race—by the CEO of a coal company active in West Virginia and with one lawsuit pending before the Supreme Court and another that may reach there. The CEO (not himself a West Virginian) gave at least $2,260,000 (some reports say

his total involvement in the race reached $3.5 million) to "And for the Sake of Kids," which attacked one 3–2 decision in which the incumbent had been in the majority.[5] (The previous record was $200,000 in a 1982 Texas primary.[6]) The race was "noted for money and malice."[7] The candidates themselves raised $2.8 million and "527" groups spent, in total, an additional $4.5 million.[8]

In a new high for spending by judicial candidates, two running for one open Illinois Supreme Court seat spent $9 million (all in the general election and all in one down-state district), spending almost identical amounts. Interest groups spent $1,201,000 and political parties spent another $3,284,000 to run television ads to help or harm one of the candidates (also, two groups spent $195,000 on TV ads attacking the state Supreme Court itself for allegedly upholding unjustifiably high awards and pushing businesses and doctors out of the state[9]). After the election, the winner reflected on the spending: "That's obscene for a judicial race. What does it gain people? How can people have faith in the system?"[10]

Overall, candidates alone spent more than $39 million on 44 contests waged in 20 states. When final spending is tallied, this figure will approach the $45 million spent in 2000 for 46 seats.[11] Four incumbent justices of the 28 running in contested races were defeated, two in primaries. Non-candidates' spending (parties and other groups) was approximately $10 million mainly in six states, compared to at least $16 million in five states in 2000.[12]

But the sky is not falling. Two positive steps taken toward keeping judicial elections different from other elections were notable: North Carolina became the second state granting public funds to judicial candidates, and 12 of the 16 candidates in appellate races participated, including four of the five winners.[13] (Wisconsin has had some public funding for Supreme Court candidates since 1979.) North Carolina also became the first state east of Colorado to mail voter guides to all voters, with information about candidates.[14] And in several states, new campaign conduct committees initiated by state or local bar associations made major moves to improve the "culture" of these campaigns. In Georgia, the Committee for Ethical Judicial Campaigns was established in April 2004 to monitor and comment on judicial campaigns; this unofficial, independent committee's members included lawyers, non-lawyers and leaders of diverse community groups. The committee sought to fill some of the gap created when the 11th Circuit Court of Appeals gutted Georgia's law regulating judicial campaign conduct.[15] The group intervened in a Court of Appeals race, rebuking a candidate for running misleading television ads. The rebuked candidate lost,[16] but of course many factors contributed to that.[17]

In Illinois, a statewide oversight committee was also established for the first time, prompted by early concerns about what promised to be a nasty, noisy, and costly race. The State Bar Association subsequently established a Committee on Supreme and Appellate Campaigns. Each candidate complained to the committee about the other's ad. The committee urged stopping both ads, but the ads went on.[18] Nevertheless, the presence of such committees is a major advance. In 2000 and 2002, Ohio had the "poster case" problematic ads run by non-candidates. In 2002, protests by the state's new monitoring committee and the candidates against ads on both sides drew much attention. In 2004, the races were hot enough that the candidates broke spending records—but there were no problematic ads.[19]

A closely watched question was how much candidates would, relying on a U.S. Supreme Court decision in 2002, campaign by announcing their views on disputed legal and social issues, or even appearing to promise a specific decision in certain types of cases.[20]

Some candidates indeed chose to speak freely, and by doing so won more press coverage-but so far, did not win more than that. The leading example involved a lower court judge who challenged an Ohio Supreme Court incumbent. His campaign included informing the voters of stands on various issues before the Supreme Court and of his political party affiliation. Although Ohio's judicial candidates run in partisan primaries, there is no party label on the general election ballots and an Ohio Canon limits partisanship in the general election. When the candidate's conduct led to a complaint filed with the official disciplinary body, the candidate won a federal-court injunction against any steps against him for the content of his campaign statements—and that won him substantial press coverage.[21] However, of the three contests for Ohio Supreme Court seats, this candidate lost by the widest margin, 60 percent–40 percent, although in another contest, the long time and highly regarded chief justice was challenged by a retired municipal court judge.[22]

Neither is the sky about to clear. In South Dakota, a proposed amendment to the state constitution would have ended contestable elections for trial court judges and made them subject, like the state's appellate judges, to a "merit" screening for initial appointments, with subsequent retention elections. The amendment, which the legislature had approved almost unanimously, was rejected by 62 percent of voters.[23]

Television ads, especially sponsored by non-candidates, were more pervasive in 2004. In 2000, TV ads ran in only four states' judicial elections. In 2004, 15 states featured TV ads (10 for the first time) in their judicial elections at an estimated cost of over $21 million. Such ads—especially those run by single-issue or single-interest groups—are problematic because they encourage the public to think that judges are just like other elective officials, although even the states in which judges face contestable elections have an array of constitutional provisions that make the judiciary unique (e.g., far longer terms than any other officials). Judges swear an oath to decide cases based on the applicable law and the specific facts; very few judges ever have decisional leeway like U.S. Supreme Court justices.

Targeting judges because of a single decision or issue continued in 2004, e.g. in five judges' retention elections.[24] A Kansas trial judge was targeted for defeat by a "Justice for Children Committee," spearheaded by the mother of a rape victim. Others in the jurisdiction vigorously defended the judge as a respected, even-handed judge who made the appropriate legal decision.[25] The judge was retained with 63 percent. An Iowa judge trial judge was targeted for defeat by a "Judicial Accountability Committee" for granting a "divorce" to two lesbians who had been joined in an out-of-state civil union. The judge was retained by 58 percent.[26] And two Arizona judges targeted by "No Bad Judges.com" because of decisions on abortion, were retained by 68 and 69 percent.[27] Also, a Missouri Supreme Court Justice whose retention was opposed by the "Missouri Family Network" because he had written "activist" opinions, was approved by 62 percent of the voters.[28]

What Lies Ahead?

The Economist story noted, "There remains the old question: should judges be elected at all, rather than appointed? Back in 1906 Roscoe Pound, a scholar at Harvard Law School, started a campaign to have judges appointed by saying: "Putting courts into politics, and compelling judges to become politicians, in many jurisdictions has almost destroyed the traditional respect for the bench." When he spoke, 8 in 10 American judges stood for election. Today, the figure is 87 percent. Americans are still reluctant to accept that politicians should be chosen by the people, but not judges."

There is some irony to this state of affairs. The public clings to their right to elect their judges, but is just as convinced that the electoral process, especially raising campaign funds, damages courts at least by appearing to influence the judges' decisions.[29] We have had a trend from partisan to nonpartisan (19 states have made this switch, most recently Arkansas, Mississippi and North Carolina). Merit selection and retention elections, the great hope of mid-20th century reformers, has hit a wall of public resistance to diminishing voters' role in selecting judges. New approaches relying on greater scrutiny of candidate qualifications as part of the nomination process has been recommended by the ABA and by New York's Commission to Promote Public Confidence in Judicial Elections, but such a step remains untested and may prove to be heavily burdened by elitist associations.

Notes

[1] Mike France and Lorraine Woellert, with (Brian Grow), *Business Week*, September 27, 2004, (Cover Story).

[2] *The Economist*, July 24, 2004, at 28–9. Forbes Magazine ran a cover story on judicial elections. See "The Secret War on Judges," *Forbes Magazine*, July 21, 2003 (cover story). The *Forbes* cover story was featured in a TV ad run on behalf of the incumbent in West Virginia. See *http://www.brennancenter.org/programs/buyingtime_2004/storyboard_2004_index.html* (third storyboard listed for West Virginia).

[3] Emily Heller, "Chamber Scores Big in Judicial Elections," *National Law Journal* (November 8, 2004).

[4] William C. Bayne, "Lynchard's Candidacy, Ads Putting Spice Into Justice Race," *Com. Appeal*, Oct. 29, 2000, available at 2000 WL 27939675.

[5] *Contributions from Individuals and 2 organizations affiliated with Massey Energy Co. to And for the Sake of Kids*, Center for Public Integrity, available at www.publicintegrity.org/527/. See also, Paul J Nyden, "Massey CEO's Political Donations Questioned," Charleston Gazette, 10\21\04. Because of that CEO's contributions and unrelated reasons, motions (by both plaintiffs and defendants) to disqualify several West Virginia Supreme Court Justices from the cases involving the CEO's company, are pending as we write. The company is involved in two cases: (1) In 2002, it was

found liable in a contract action for $50,000,000 (a judgment which, with interest, is now over $60,000,000); that may still be appealed to the Supreme Court. (2) The company is one of several defendants in an unrelated action for flood damages; although that matter has not yet gone to trial, the Supreme Court was asked to rule on an important pretrial issue and did so on Dec. 10, 2004, unanimously upholding plaintiffs' position on some issues and defendants' on other issues. The defeated incumbent did not participate because his son was a lawyer for plaintiffs.

[6] Roy Schotland, "Elective Judges' Campaign Financing: Are State Judges' Robes the Emperor's Clothes of American Democracy?," 2 J. *Law & Pol.* 57, 148 (1985).

[7] Heller, n. 3 above.

[8] The figures are not yet final. Also, $800,000 of the total was raised by a candidate who lost the primary to the same incumbent.

[9] *www.stateline.org*, Illinois report for October 21, 2004.

[10] See 2004 State Supreme Court Election Highs and Lows, available at *http://www.faircourts.org/files/SC04StateTrends.pdf*.

[11] For 2000 figures see Roy Schotland, *Financing Judicial Elections*, 2000: Change and Challenge, 2001 M.S.U.-D.C.L.L. Rev. 849, at note 6.

[12] Buying Time 2004: Television Advertising in State Supreme Court Elections by State and Sponsor, Brennan Center Publication available at *www.brennancenter.org*. See also Schotland, n. 11 above.

[13] The one successful, privately funded winner requested public funding but was deemed ineligible.

[14] Also in Ohio, an online voter guide was available about judicial candidates. In December 2000, 17 chief justices called for such steps. Call To Action, 34 Loy. (L.A.) L.Rev. 1353, 1357 (2001); on voter guides, see Peter Brien, "Voter Pamphlets: The Next Best Step in Election Reform," 28 *Notre Dame J.Legis.* 87 (2002).

[15] See *Weaver v. Bonner*, 309 F3d1312 (11th Cir.2002), rehearing and rehearing en banc denied, 57 Fed.Appx. 416 (11th Cir. 2003).

[16] According to some election day press interviews, some voters were "offended by the vast amount of money that [the losing candidate] had spent." Others were offended by his ads. Jonathan Ringlel, "Bernes Trumps Big-Spending Rival," *Fulton County Daily Report*, Nov. 29, 2004.

[17] That committee's intervention did raise an issue new for such groups: the need for recusal rules for oversight committee members. After the election, a reporter learned that one Committee member had been a leading supporter of a losing candidate who had opposed the primary winner, who in the general election was criticized by the Committee. Jonathan Ringel, "Ethics Group Hits Bumps in Monitoring Campaigns," *Fulton County Daily Report*, Nov. 12, 2004.

[18] Matt Adrian, *State Bar Says Court Attack Ads Misleading*, Ryan Keith, Associated Press, October 21, 2004.

[19] For the first election year since 1995, when Ohio adopted an expedited disciplinary process, there were no proceedings against any judicial candidates.

[20] In *Republican Party of Minnesota v. White*, 535 U.S. 765 (2002), the Court held unconstitutional Minnesota's obsolete provision limiting what judicial candidates could

"announce"; only eight States had such a provision, the others having repealed it after 1990, when the Model Code of Judicial Conduct recommended repeal. The Court was explicit that the decision did not touch a different provision limiting candidates' "pledg[ing] or promis[ing], and North Carolina has repealed such a provision, but naturally there are various views about the implication of what the Court did decide.

[21]*O'Neill Calls Supreme Court 'Dead Wrong' on School Funding*, Press release by the William O'Neill for Supreme Court Committee, September 21, 2004. The press release said that the Judge "broke with legal precedent yesterday and became the first judge in Ohio's history to exercise his constitutional right to speak out on an issue of controversy during a campaign."

[22]See *O'Neill v. Coughlan*, Case No.1:04CV1612 (N.D.OH 2004)(in which the court issued a temporary injunction to prevent the state from enforcing sanctions against a candidate for Ohio Supreme Court), available at *http://www.legalaffairs.org/howappealing/20040914ONeillinjunction.pdf.*

[23]South Dakota House Joint Resolution 1003 (HJR1003) passed 68–0 in the House and 27–7 in the Senate. In 2000, Florida voters rejected a similar ballot proposition, even more overwhelmingly.

[24]In addition, two Illinois intermediate appellate judges were defeated for retention: Gordon Maag and Clyde L. Kuehn. In Illinois, the only state that requires a 60 percent affirmative vote for a judge to be retained, defeats are not uncommon. Maag was running at the same time for a Supreme Court seat, but lost that too; and Kuehn was a recent appointee to fill a vacancy.

[25]A chronicle of the campaign itself, including articles and editorials, can be found at *http://www.ljworld.com/section/judgemartin.* Judge Martin had faced retention twice before, securing approval both times, by 82 percent in 1996 and 78 percent in 2000. (See generally, *http//www.ksos.org/elections/election_statistics.html* (for yearly general election results).)

[26]It was the Judge's first time before the electorate. The Judge enjoyed strong support from the State Bar Association, whose President after the election stated that he was "proud of voters" for "recogniz[ing] that our judges apply the rule of law and [do] not bend with the wind." Frank Santiago, "Embattled District Judge to Stay on Bench," *Des Moines Register*, November 3, 2004.

[27]Ruelas, "Judges an unexpected target," *Arizona Republic*, Nov. 1, 2004; and election results.

[28]"Voters retain Teitelman, all other state judges," *St. Louis Post-Dispatch*, Nov. 5, 2004.

[29]A 2001 national survey of American adults found that nearly identical proportions of the American public believe that judicial campaign contributions influenced judicial decisions, and also favor electing their judges. David B. Rottman, "The White Decision in the Court of Opinion: Views of Judges and the General Public," *Court Review* (Spring 2002), at 19.

About the Authors

David B. Rottman is a principal court research consultant at the National Center for State Courts, where he has worked since 1987. His current interests include judicial selection, public opinion on the courts, the evolution of court structure, and the pros and cons of problem-solving courts. He is the author of books on modern Ireland, social class, and community courts. Rottman has a Ph.D. in sociology from the University of Illinois at Urbana, and previously worked at the Economic and Social Institute in Dublin, Ireland.

Roy A. Schotland is a professor of law at Georgetown University Law Center and a senior advisor for the National Center for State Courts. He is a graduate of Columbia University and Harvard Law School and clerked for Justice William J. Brennan Jr. Schotland is the co-founder of the Chief Justices' 2000 Summit on Judicial Selection and 2001 Symposium on Judicial Campaign Conduct and the First Amendment. He is also the co-author of three amicus briefs for the Conference of Chief Justices.

Table 5.1
STATE COURTS OF LAST RESORT

State or other jurisdiction	Name of court	Justices chosen (a) At large	Justices chosen (a) By district	No. of judges (b)	Term (in years) (c)	Chief justice Method of selection	Term of office for chief justice
Alabama	S.C.	★		9	6	Popular election	6 years
Alaska	S.C.	★		5	10	By court	3 years (d)
Arizona	S.C.	★		5	6	By court	5 years
Arkansas	S.C.	★		7	8	Popular election	8 years
California	S.C.	★		7	12	Appointed by governor	12 years
Colorado	S.C.			7	10	By court	Indefinite
Connecticut	S.C.	★		7	8	Legislative appointment (e)	8 years
Delaware	S.C.	★		5	12	Appointed by governor, with consent of Senate	12 years
Florida	S.C.	(f)		7	6	By court	2 years
Georgia	S.C.	★		7	6	By court	4 years
Hawaii	S.C.	★		5	10	Appointed by governor, with consent of Senate (g)	10 years
Idaho	S.C.	★		5	6	By court	4 years
Illinois	S.C.		★	7	10	By court	3 years
Indiana	S.C.	★		5	10 (h)	Judicial nominating commission appointment	5 years
Iowa	S.C.	★		7	8	By court	8 years
Kansas	S.C.	★		7	6	Rotation by seniority	Indefinite
Kentucky	S.C.		★	7	8	By court	4 years
Louisiana	S.C.		★	7	10	By seniority of service	Duration of service
Maine	S.J.C.	★		7	7	Appointed by governor	7 years
Maryland	C.A.		★	7	10	Appointed by governor	Indefinite
Massachusetts	S.J.C.	★		7	To age 70	Appointed by governor (j)	To age 70
Michigan	S.C.	★		7	8	By court	2 years
Minnesota	S.C.	★		7	6	Popular election	6 years
Mississippi	S.C.		★	9	8	By seniority of service	Duration of service
Missouri	S.C.	★		7	12	By court (k)	2 years
Montana	S.C.	★		7	8	Popular election	8 years
Nebraska	S.C.		★ (l)	7	6 (m)	Appointed by governor from Judicial Nominating Commission	Duration of service
Nevada	S.C.	★		7	6	Rotation	2 years
New Hampshire	S.C.	★		5	To age 70	Appointed by governor with approval of elected executive council	To age 70
New Jersey	S.C.	★		7	7 (n)	Appointed by governor, with consent of Senate	Duration of service
New Mexico	S.C.	★		5	8	By court	2 years
New York	C.A.	★		7	14	Appointed by governor from Judicial Nomination Commission	14 years
North Carolina	S.C.	★		7	8	Popular election	8 years
North Dakota	S.C.	★		5 (o)	10	By Supreme and district court judges	5 years (p)
Ohio	S.C.	★		7	6	Popular election	6 years
Oklahoma	S.C.		★	9	6	By court	2 years
	C.C.A.		★	5	6	By court	2 years
Oregon	S.C.	★		7	6	By court	6 years
Pennsylvania	S.C.	★		7	10	Rotation by seniority	Duration of term
Rhode Island	S.C.	★		5	Life	Appointed by governor from Judicial Nominating Commission (i)	Life
South Carolina	S.C.	★		5	10	Legislative election	10 years

See footnotes at end of table.

STATE COURTS OF LAST RESORT — Continued

State or other jurisdiction	Justices chosen (a) At large	Justices chosen (a) By district	Name of court	No. of judges (b)	Term (in years) (c)	Chief justice Method of selection	Chief justice Term of office for chief justice
South Dakota		★(q)	S.C.	5	8	By court	4 years
Tennessee	★		S.C.	5	8	By court	4 years
Texas	★		S.C.	9	6	Partisan election	6 years
Texas	★		C.C.A.	9	6	Partisan election	6 years (r)
Utah	★		S.C.	5	10 (s)	By court	4 years
Vermont	★		S.C.	5	6	Appointed by governor from Judicial Nomination Commission, with consent of Senate	6 years
Virginia	★		S.C.	7	12	Seniority	Indefinite
Washington	★		S.C.	9	6	By court	4 years
West Virginia		★	S.C.A.	5	12	Rotation by seniority	1 year
Wisconsin	★		S.C.	7	10	Seniority	Until declined
Wyoming	★		S.C.	5	8	By court	4 years
Dist. of Columbia	★		C.A.	9	15	Judicial Nominating Commission appointment	4 years
Puerto Rico	★		S.C.	7	To age 70	Appointed by governor, with consent of Senate	To age 70

Sources: Number of judges from Court Statistics Project, *State Court Caseload Statistics*, 2003 (National Center for State Courts 2004). All other information from *State Court Organization* 1998 (National Center for State Courts); state constitutions, statutes and court administrative offices.

Key:
S.C.—Supreme Court
S.C.A.—Supreme Court of Appeals
S.J.C.—Supreme Judicial Court
C.A.—Court of Appeals
C.C.A.—Court of Criminal Appeals
H.C.—High Court

(a) See Chapter 5 table entitled, "Selection and Retention of Judges," for details.
(b) Number includes chief justice.
(c) The initial term may be shorter. See Chapter 5 table entitled, "Selection and Retention of Judges," for details.
(d) A justice may serve more than one term as chief justice, but may not serve consecutive terms in that position.
(e) Governor nominates from candidates submitted by Judicial Selection Commission.
(f) Regional (5), Statewide(2), Regional based on District of Appeal

(g) Judicial Selection Commission nominates.
(h) Initial two years; retention 10 years.
(i) With House and Senate confirmation.
(j) Chief Justices are appointed, until age 70, by the Governor with the advice and consent of the Executive (Governor's) Council.
(k) Selection is typically rotated among the judges.
(l) Chief justice chosen statewide; associate judges chosen by district.
(m) More than three years for first election and every six years thereafter.
(n) Followed by tenure.
(o) A temporary court of appeals was established July 1, 1987 to exercise appellate and original jurisdiction was delegated by the supreme court. This court does not sit, has no assigned judges, has heard no appeals and is currently unfunded.
(p) Or expiration of term, whichever is first.
(q) Initially chosen by district; retention determined statewide.
(r) Presiding judge of Court of Criminal Appeals.
(s) Initial three years; retention 10 years.

Table 5.2
STATE INTERMEDIATE APPELLATE COURTS AND GENERAL TRIAL COURTS: NUMBER OF JUDGES AND TERMS

State or other jurisdiction	Intermediate appellate court — Name of court	No. of judges	Term (years)	General trial court — Name of court	No. of judges	Term (years)
Alabama	Court of Criminal Appeals	5	6	Circuit Court	142	6
	Court of Civil Appeals	5	6			
Alaska	Court of Appeals	3	10	Superior Court	32 (a)	6
Arizona	Court of Appeals	22	6	Superior Court	159	4
Arkansas	Court of Appeals	12	8	Chancery/Probate Court and Circuit Court	115	(b)
California	Court of Appeals	105	12	Superior Court	1,498 (c)	6
Colorado	Court of Appeals	16	10	District Court	132 (d)	6
Connecticut	Appellate Court	9	8	Superior Court	180	8
Delaware	…	…	…	Superior Court	19	12
				Court of Chancery	(e)	12
Florida	District Courts of Appeals	62	6	Circuit Court	509	6
Georgia	Court of Appeals	12	6	Superior Court	188	4
Hawaii	Intermediate Court of Appeals	4	10	Circuit Court	30 (f)	10
Idaho	Court of Appeals	3	6	District Court	39 (g)	4
Illinois	Appellate Court	52 (h)	10	Circuit Court	492 (i)	6
Indiana	Court of Appeals	15 (k)	10 (l)	Superior Court, Probate Court and Circuit Court	296	6 (j)
Iowa	Court of Appeals	9	6	District Court	179 (m)	6
Kansas	Court of Appeals	10	4	District Court	234 (n)	4
Kentucky	Court of Appeals	14	8	Circuit Court	114 (dd)	8
Louisiana	Court of Appeals	53	10	District Court	230 (o)	6
Maine	…	…	…	Superior Court	16	7
Maryland	Court of Special Appeals	13	10	Circuit Court	146	15
Massachusetts	Appeals Court	25	(p)	Superior Court	82	(p)
Michigan	Court of Appeals	28	6	Circuit Court	210	6
Minnesota	Court of Appeals	16	6	District Court	263	6
Mississippi	Court of Appeals	10	8	Circuit Court	49	4
Missouri	Court of Appeals	32	12	Circuit Court	134 (q)	6
Montana	…	…	…	District Court	40 (r)	6
Nebraska	Court of Appeals	6	6 (s)	District Court	54	6
Nevada	…	…	…	District Court	56	6 (t)
New Hampshire	…	…	…	Superior Court	29 (u)	6
New Jersey	Appellate Division of Superior Court	34	7 (v)	Superior Court	415 (w)	(p)
New Mexico	Court of Appeals	10	8	District Court	72	7 (x)
New York	Appellate Division of Supreme Court	55	5 (y)	Supreme Court	346 (ii)	6
	Appellate Terms of Supreme Court	15	5 (y)	County Court	128	(z)
North Carolina	Court of Appeals	15	8	Superior Court	106 (aa)	8
North Dakota	…	…	…	District Court	42 (ll)	6
Ohio	Court of Appeals	68	6	Court of Common Pleas	376	6

See footnotes at end of table.

STATE INTERMEDIATE APPELLATE COURTS AND GENERAL TRIAL COURTS — Continued

State or other jurisdiction	Intermediate appellate court			General trial court		
	Name of court	No. of judges	Term (years)	Name of court	No. of judges	Term (years)
Oklahoma	Court of Appeals	12	6	District Court	228 (bb)	4
Oregon	Court of Appeals	10	6	Circuit Court	166	6
Pennsylvania	Superior Court	15	10	Tax Court	1 (jj)	6
	Commonwealth Court	9	10	Court of Common Pleas	409	10
Rhode Island	...	...	...	Superior Court	22 (kk)	Life
South Carolina	Court of Appeals	9	6	Circuit Court	48 (cc)	6
South Dakota	...	...	...	Circuit Court	38	8
Tennessee	Court of Appeals	12	8	Chancery Court	33	8
	Court of Criminal Appeals	12	8	Circuit Court	85	8
				Criminal Court	31	8
				Probate Court	2	(ee)
Texas	Court of Appeals	80	6	District Court	418	4
Utah	Court of Appeals	7	10 (ff)	District Court	70 (gg)	6
Vermont	...	...	...	Superior Court and District Court	34 (hh)	6
Virginia	Court of Appeals	11	8	Circuit Court	150	8
Washington	Court of Appeals	22	6	Superior Court	175	4
West Virginia	...	...	...	Circuit Court	65	8
Wisconsin	Court of Appeals	16	6	Circuit Court	241	6
Wyoming	...	...	...	District Court	17	6
Dist. of Columbia	...	...	...	Superior Court	58	15
Puerto Rico	Circuit Court of Appeals	33	16	Court of First Instance	328	12

Sources: National Center for State Courts, *State Court Caseload Statistics, 2003* and *State Court Organization, 1998.*

Key:

... —Court does not exist in jurisdiction or not applicable.
(a) Plus nine masters.
(b) Circuit court judges serve four-year terms. Chancery probate court judges serve six-year terms. (Some judges serve both circuit and chancery courts).
(c) Plus 414 commissioners and referees.
(d) Plus 11 Water Court judges.
(e) One chancellor and four vice-chancellors.
(f) Plus 19 family judges.
(g) Plus 83 full-time magistrate/judges.
(h) Plus 9 circuit court judges assigned to the appellate court.
(i) Plus 360 associate judges.
(j) Associate judges four years.
(k) Plus one tax court judge.
(l) Two years initial; 10 years retention.
(m) Plus 135 part-time magistrates, 12 associate juvenile judges, one associate probate judge, and six part-time alternate district associate judges.
(n) Includes 74 magistrates.
(o) Plus eleven commissioners.
(p) To age 70.

(q) Plus 175 associate circuit judges, 15 family court judges, 1 drug commissioner, 4 probate and 3 deputy probate commissioners.
(r) Plus five water judges and one worker's compensation judge.
(s) More than three years for first election and every six years thereafter.
(t) The initial term is for three years but not more than five years.
(u) Plus 10 full-time marital masters.
(v) Followed by tenure.
(w) 21 are surrogates that also serve as deputy superior court clerks.
(x) On reapportionment until age 70.
(y) Or duration.
(z) Fourteen years for Supreme Court; 10 years for county court.
(aa) Includes 13 special judges and there in addition 100 clerks who hear uncontested probate.
(bb) This includes 73 district, 77 associate district and 78 special judges.
(cc) Plus 22 masters-in-equity.
(dd) Plus 54 domestic relations commissioners.
(ee) Locally determined.
(ff) Three years initial; six years retention.
(gg) Plus seven domestic court commissioners.
(hh) Plus 15 magistrates for Family Court.
(ii) Plus 50 acting supreme court judges and 12 quasi-judicial staff.
(jj) Plus six magistrates.
(kk) Plus four magistrates.
(ll) Plus 7.5 judicial referees.

Table 5.3
QUALIFICATIONS OF JUDGES OF STATE APPELLATE COURTS AND GENERAL TRIAL COURTS

| State or other jurisdiction | Years of minimum residence | | | | Minimum age | | Legal credentials | |
| | In state | | In district | | | | | |
	A	T	A	T	A	T	A	T
Alabama	1	1	. . .	1	. . .	. . .	Licensed attorney	Licensed attorney
Alaska	5	5	. . .	. . .	. . .	. . .	8 years practice	5 years practice
Arizona	10 (a)	5	(b)	1	(ee)	30	(c)	(d)
Arkansas	2	2	(b)	. . .	30	28	8 years practice	6 years practice/bench
California	. . .	. . .	. . .	. . .	. . .	. . .	10 years state bar	10 years state bar
Colorado	★	★ (e)	. . .	★	. . .	. . .	5 years state bar	5 years state bar
Connecticut	★	★	(f)	(f)	. . .	. . .	10 years state bar	Member of the bar
Delaware	★	★	(f)	(g)	. . .	. . .	Learned in law	Learned in law
Florida	★ (h)	★	(i)	★ (j)	. . .	. . .	10 years state bar	5 years state bar
Georgia	★	3	. . .	. . .	. . .	30	7 years state bar	7 years state bar
Hawaii	★	★	. . .	. . .	. . .	. . .	10 years state bar	10 years state bar
Idaho	2	1	. . .	. . .	30	. . .	10 years state bar	10 years state bar
Illinois	★	★	★	★	. . .	. . .	Licensed attorney	. . .
Indiana	. . .	1	(b)	★	. . .	. . .	10 years state bar (k)	. . .
Iowa	. . .	. . .	. . .	★	. . .	. . .	Licensed attorney	. . .
Kansas	. . .	. . .	. . .	★	30	. . .	10 years active and continuous practice (l)	5 years state bar
Kentucky	2	2	2	2	. . .	. . .	8 years state bar and licensed attorney	8 years state bar
Louisiana	2	2	2	2	. . .	. . .	5 years state bar	5 years state bar
Maine	. . .	. . .	. . .	. . .	. . .	. . .	Learned in law	Learned in law
Maryland	5	5	6 mos.	6 mos.	30	30	State bar member	State bar member
Massachusetts	. . .	. . .	. . .	. . .	. . .	. . .	. . .	No law degree required
Michigan	. . .	. . .	(b)	. . .	. . .	. . .	State bar member (m)	State bar member
Minnesota	. . .	. . .	(n)	. . .	. . .	. . .	State bar member	State bar member
Mississippi	5	5	. . .	. . .	30	26	5 years state bar	5 years practice
Missouri	(o)	(o)	(b)	★	30	30	State bar member	State bar member
Montana	2	2	. . .	. . .	. . .	. . .	5 years state bar	5 years state bar
Nebraska	3 (p)	. . .	★	★	30	30	5 years practice	5 years practice
Nevada	2	2	. . .	. . .	25	25	State bar member	. . .
New Hampshire	. . .	. . .	. . .	. . .	. . .	. . .	. . .	. . .
New Jersey	. . .	(q)	. . .	(q)	. . .	. . .	Admitted to practice in state for at least 10 years	10 years practice of law
New Mexico	3	3	. . .	★	35	35	10 years active practice (r)	6 years active practice
New York	★	★	(s)	(s)	. . .	18	10 years state bar	10 years state bar
North Carolina	. . .	N.A.	. . .	★	. . .	. . .	State bar member	State bar member
North Dakota	★ (p)	★	. . .	★	. . .	. . .	License to practice law	State bar member
Ohio	★ (p)	★	(t)	★	. . .	. . .	6 years practice	6 years practice
Oklahoma	. . .	(u)	1	★	30	. . .	5 years state bar	(v)
Oregon	3	3	. . .	(w)	. . .	. . .	State bar member	State bar member
Pennsylvania	1	1	(f)	★	. . .	. . .	State bar member	State bar member
Rhode Island	. . .	. . .	. . .	. . .	21	. . .	License to practice law	State bar member
South Carolina	5	5	. . .	. . .	32	32	8 years state bar	8 years state bar
South Dakota	★	★	★	★	. . .	. . .	State bar member	State bar member
Tennessee	5	5	★ (x)	1	35	30	Qualified to practice law	Qualified to practice law
Texas	★	. . .	. . .	2	35	25	(y)	(z)
Utah	5 (aa)	3	. . .	★	30	25	State bar member	State bar member
Vermont	5	5	. . .	(bb)	. . .	. . .	5 years state bar	5 years state bar
Virginia	. . .	★	. . .	★	. . .	. . .	5 years state bar	5 years state bar
Washington	1	1	1	1	. . .	. . .	(cc)	State bar member
West Virginia	5	★	. . .	★	30	30	10 years state bar	5 years state bar
Wisconsin	10 days	10 days	10 days	10 days	. . .	. . .	5 years state bar	5 years state bar
Wyoming	3	2	. . .	. . .	30	28	9 years state bar	. . .
Dist. of Columbia	★	★	90 days	90 days	. . .	. . .	5 years state bar	5 years state bar (dd)
No. Mariana Islands	. . .	. . .	. . .	. . .	. . .	30	N.A.	N.A.
Puerto Rico	5	. . .	. . .	. . .	. . .	. . .	10 years state bar	7 years state bar

See footnotes at end of table.

QUALIFICATIONS OF JUDGES — Continued

Sources: National Center for State Courts, *State Court Organization*, 1998 and state web sites, November 2003.

Key:

A—Judges of courts of last resort and intermediate appellate courts.

T—Judges of general trial courts.

★—Provision; length of time not specified.

. . .—No specific provision.

N.A.— Not applicable

(a) For court of appeals, five years.

(b) No local residency requirement stated for Supreme Court. Local residency required for Court of Appeals.

(c) Supreme Court- ten years state bar, Court of Appeals - five years state bar.

(d) Admitted to the practice of law in Arizona for five years.

(e) State residency requirement for District Court, no residency requirement stated for Denver Probate Court, Denver Juvenile Court or Water Court.

(f) Local residency not required.

(g) Court of Chancery does not have residency requirement, Superior Court requires residency.

(h) For District Courts of Appeal must reside within the territorial jurisdiction of the court

(i) Initial appointment, must be resident of district at the time of original appointment.

(j) Circuit court judge must reside within the territorial jurisdiction of the court.

(k) In the Supreme Court and the Court of Appeals, five years service as a general jurisdiction judge may be substituted.

(l) Relevant legal experience, such as being a member of a law faculty or sitting as a judge, may qualify under the 10 year requirement.

(m) Supreme Court: state bar member and practice at least five years.

(n) No residency requirement stated for Supreme Court, Court of Appeals varies.

(o) At the appellate level must have been a state voter for nine years. At the general trial court level must have been a state voter for three years.

(p) No state residency requirement specified for Court of Appeals.

(q) For Superior court: out of a total of 427 authorized judgeships (including thirty-two in the appellate division), there are restricted superior court judgeships that require residence within the particular county of assignment at time of appointment and reappointment; there are 142 unrestricted judgeships for which assignment of county is made by the chief justice.

(r) Supreme Court and Court of Appeals: and/or judgeship in any court of the state.

(s) No local residency requirement stated for Court of Appeals, local residency requirement for presiding judge of Supreme Court, Appellate Divisions.

(t) No local residency requirement for Supreme Court, Court of Appeals requires district residency.

(u) Six months if elected.

(v) District Court: judges must be a state bar member for four years or a judge of court record. Associate judges must be a state bar member for two years or a judge of a court of record.

(w) Local residency requirement for Circuit Court, no residency requirement stated for Tax Court.

(x) Supreme Court: One justice from each of three divisions and two seats at large. Court of Appeals and Court of Criminal Appeals: Must reside in the grand division served.

(y) Ten years practicing law or a lawyer and judge of a court of record at least 10 years.

(z) District Court: judges must have been a practicing lawyer or a judge of a court in this state, or both combined, for four years.

(aa) Supreme Court is five; Court of Appeals is three.

(bb) No local residency requirement stated for Superior Court, District Court must reside in geographic unit.

(cc) Supreme Court: State bar member; Courts of Appeals: five years state bar.

(dd) Superior Court: Judge must also be an active member of the unified District of Columbia bar and have been engaged, during the five years immediately preceding the judicial nomination, in the active practice of law as an attorney by the United States, of District of Columbia government.

(ee) Court of Appeals minimum age is 30.

Table 5.4
COMPENSATION OF JUDGES OF APPELLATE COURTS AND GENERAL TRIAL COURTS

State or other jurisdiction	Court of last resort	Chief Justice salaries	Assoc. Justice salaries	Intermediate appellate court	Chief/Presiding salaries	Judges salaries	General trial courts	Salary
Alabama	Supreme Court	$153,000	(a)	Court of Criminal Appeals	(b)	(b)	Circuit courts	(c)
Alaska	Supreme Court	118,000	$118,000	Court of Appeals	$111,000	$111,000	Superior courts	(h)
Arizona	Supreme Court	129,000	127,000	Court of Appeals	124,000	124,000	Superior courts	$121,000
Arkansas	Supreme Court	136,000	126,000	Court of Appeals	124,000	122,000	Chancery courts	118,000
California	Supreme Court	191,000	176,000	Court of Appeals	171,000	165,000	Superior court	144,000
Colorado	Supreme Court	116,000	114,000	Court of Appeals	112,000	109,000	District courts	105,000
Connecticut	Supreme Court	150,000	138,000	Appellate Court	137,000	130,000	Superior courts	125,000
Delaware	Supreme Court	153,000	147,000		...	...	Superior courts	140,000
Florida	Supreme Court	155,000	155,000	District Court of Appeals	143,000	143,000	Circuit courts	135,000
Georgia	Supreme Court	153,000	153,000	Court of Appeals	152,000	152,000	Superior courts	(d)
Hawaii	Supreme Court	117,000	116,000	Intermediate Court	112,000	111,000	Circuit courts	107,000
Idaho	Supreme Court	104,000	102,000	Court of Appeals	101,000	101,000	District courts	96,000
Illinois	Supreme Court	169,000	169,000	Court of Appeals	159,000	159,000	Circuit courts	146,000
Indiana	Supreme Court	115,000	115,000	Court of Appeals	110,000	110,000	Circuit courts	90,000
Iowa	Supreme Court	127,000	123,000	Court of Appeals	122,000	112,000	District courts	112,000
Kansas	Supreme Court	118,000	115,000	Court of Appeals	114,000	111,000	District courts	100,000
Kentucky	Supreme Court	129,000	124,000	Court of Appeals	122,000	119,000	Circuit courts	114,000
Louisiana	Supreme Court	124,000	118,000	Court of Appeals	118,000	112,000	District courts	106,000
Maine	Supreme Judicial Court	121,000	105,000		...	...	Superior courts	103,000
Maryland	Court of Appeals	151,000	132,000	Court of Special Appeals	127,000	124,000	Circuit courts	120,000
Massachusetts	Supreme Judicial Court	132,000	127,000	Appellate Court	122,000	117,000	Superior courts	113,000
Michigan	Supreme Court	165,000	165,000	Court of Appeals	151,000	151,000	Circuit courts	140,000
Minnesota	Supreme Court	147,000	134,000	Court of Appeals	132,000	126,000	District courts	118,000
Mississippi	Supreme Court	115,000	113,000	Court of Appeals	108,000	105,000	Chancery courts	104,000
Missouri	Supreme Court	126,000	123,000	Court of Appeals	115,000	115,000	Circuit courts	108,000
Montana	Supreme Court	97,000	96,000		...	...	District courts	88,000
Nebraska	Supreme Court	119,000	119,000	Court of Appeals	113,000	113,000	District courts	110,000
Nevada	Supreme Court	(i)	(i)		...	...	District courts	(j)
New Hampshire	Supreme Court	117,000	113,000		...	...	Superior courts	106,000
New Jersey	Supreme Court	164,000	159,000	Appellate division of	150,000	...	Superior courts	141,000
New Mexico	Supreme Court	101,000	99,000	Court of Appeals	96,000	94,000	District courts	90,000
New York	Court of Appeals	156,000	151,000	Appellate divisions of	148,000	144,000	Supreme courts	137,000
North Carolina	Supreme Court	118,000	115,000	Court of Appeals	112,000	111,000	Superior courts	105,000
North Dakota	Supreme Court	102,000	99,000		...	...	District courts	91,000
Ohio	Supreme Court	137,000	128,000	Court of Appeals	120,000	120,000	Courts of common pleas	110,000
Oklahoma	Supreme Court	110,000	107,000	Court of Appeals	103,000	102,000	District courts	110,000
Oregon	Supreme Court	108,000	105,000	Court of Appeals	105,000	103,000	Circuit courts	96,000
Pennsylvania	Supreme Court	147,000	143,000	Superior Court	141,000	138,000	Courts of common pleas	96,000
Rhode Island	Supreme Court	146,000	133,000		...	...	Superior courts	124,000
South Carolina	Supreme Court	125,000	120,000	Court of Appeals	118,000	117,000	Circuit courts	120,000
								114,000

See footnotes at end of table.

Table 5.4
COMPENSATION OF JUDGES OF APPELLATE COURTS AND GENERAL TRIAL COURTS – CONTINUED

State or other jurisdiction	Court of last resort	Chief Justice salaries	Assoc. Justice salaries	Intermediate appellate court	Chief/Presiding salaries	Judges salaries	General trial courts	Salary
South Dakota	Supreme Court	$105,000	$103,000	...	...	...	Circuit courts	$96,000
Tennessee	Supreme Court	124,000	124,000	Court of Appeals	$118,000	...	Chancery courts	113,000
Texas	Supreme Court	115,000	113,000	Court of Appeals	(e)	(e)	District courts	(f)
Utah	Supreme Court	116,000	114,000	Court of Appeals	110,000	$109,000	District courts	104,000
Vermont	Supreme Court	115,000	110,000	...	...	...	Superior/District/Family	104,000
Virginia	Supreme Court	144,000 (g)	136,000 (g)	Court of Appeals	130,000 (g)	129,000 (g)	Circuit courts	126,000
Washington	Supreme Court	135,000	135,000	Court of Appeals	128,000	128,000	Superior courts	122,000
West Virginia	Supreme Court	95,000	95,000	...	...	...	Circuit courts	90,000
Wisconsin	Supreme Court	130,000	122,000	Court of Appeals	115,000	115,000	Circuit courts	109,000
Wyoming	Supreme Court	105,000	105,000	...	...	...	District courts	100,000
Dist. of Columbia	Court of Appeals	168,100	167,600	...	...	...	Superior courts	158,000
Guam	...	(k)	(l)	...	...	...	Superior courts	100,000
No. Mariana Islands	Commonwealth Supreme Court	130,000	126,000	...	...	...	Superior courts	120,000
Puerto Rico	Supreme Court	125,000	120,000	Appellate Court	90,000	90,000	Superior courts	80,000
U.S. Virgin Islands	...	145,000	135,000	...	...	...	Territorial courts	135,000

Source: National Center for State Courts, *Survey of Judicial Salaries* (April 2004).

Note: Compensation is shown according to most recent legislation, even though laws may not yet have taken effect.

There are other non-salary forms of judicial compensation that can be a significant part of a judge's compensation package. It should be noted that many of these can be important to judges or attorneys who might be interested in becoming judges or justices. These include retirement, disability, and death benefits, expense accounts, vacation, holiday, and sick leave and various forms of insurance coverage.

Key:

(a) Salary range is between $152,000 and $190,000.
(b) Salary range is between $151,000 and $189,000.
(c) Salary range is between $112,000 and $140,000.
(d) Salary range is between $110,000 and $143,000.
(e) Salary range is between $107,000 and $112,000, based on local supplements.
(f) Salary range is between $102,000 and $111,000, Masters between $76,000 and $90,000, Associates $80,000 and $83,000, based on local supplements.
(g) Plus $6,500 in lieu of travel, lodging and other expenses.
(h) Salary range is between $109,000 and $ 116,000, varies by location and cost of living.
(i) Salary range is between $140,000 and $171,000 and may include longevity pay.
(j) Salary range is between $100,000 and $159,000 and may include longevity pay and may be dependent on election clycle.
(k) Salary range is between $128,000 and $161,000.
(l) Salary range is between $126,000 and $154,000.

Table 5.5
SELECTED DATA ON COURT ADMINISTRATIVE OFFICES

State or other jurisdiction	Title	Established	Appointed by (a)	Salary
Alabama	Administrative Director of Courts	1971	CJ (b)	$105,000
Alaska	Administrative Director	1959	CJ (b)	116,000
Arizona	Administrative Director of Courts	1960	SC	(g)
Arkansas	Director, Administrative Office of the Courts	1965	CJ (c)	93,000
California	Administrative Director of the Courts	1960	JC	(h)
Colorado	State Court Administrator	1959	SC	112,000
Connecticut	Chief Court Administrator (d)	1965	CJ	144,000
Delaware	Director, Administrative Office of the Courts	1971	CJ	108,000
Florida	State Courts Administrator	1972	SC	126,000
Georgia	Director, Administrative Office of the Courts	1973	JC	117,000
Hawaii	Administrative Director of the Courts	1959	CJ (b)	90,000
Idaho	Administrative Director of the Courts	1967	SC	97,000
Illinois	Administrative Director of the Courts	1959	SC	159,000
Indiana	Executive Director, Division of State Court Administration	1975	CJ	99,000
Iowa	Court Administrator	1971	SC	121,000
Kansas	Judicial Administrator	1965	CJ	100,000
Kentucky	Administrative Director of the Courts	1976	CJ	114,000
Louisiana	Judicial Administrator	1954	SC	112,000
Maine	Court Administrator	1975	CJ	92,000
Maryland	State Court Administrator	1955	CJ (b)	119,000
Massachusetts	Chief Justice for Administration & Management	1978	SC	122,050
Michigan	State Court Administrator	1952	SC	130,000
Minnesota	State Court Administrator	1963	SC	118,000
Mississippi	Court Administrator	1974	SC	85,000
Missouri	State Courts Administrator	1970	SC	115,000
Montana	State Court Administrator	1975	SC	87,000
Nebraska	State Court Administrator	1972	CJ	103,000
Nevada	Director, Office of Court Administration	1971	SC	100,000
New Hampshire	Director of the Administrative Office of the Court	1980	SC	96,000
New Jersey	Administrative Director of the Courts	1948	CJ	150,000
New Mexico	Director, Administrative Office of the Courts	1959	SC	96,000
New York	Chief Administrator of the Courts	1978	CJ	148,000
North Carolina	Director, Administrative Office of the Courts	1965	CJ	108,000
North Dakota	Court Administrator (h)	1971	CJ	89,000
Ohio	Administrative Director of the Courts	1955	SC	115,000
Oklahoma	Administrative Director of the Courts	1967	SC	102,000
Oregon	Court Administrator	1971	SC	(i)
Pennsylvania	Court Administrator	1968	SC	140,000
Rhode Island	State Court Administrator	1969	CJ	107,000
South Carolina	Director of Court Administration	1973	CJ	99,000
South Dakota	State Court Administrator	1974	SC	92,000
Tennessee	Director	1963	SC	118,000
Texas	Administrative Director of the Courts (i)	1977	SC	98,000
Utah	Court Administrator	1973	SC	104,000
Vermont	Court Administrator	1967	SC	104,000
Virginia	Executive Secretary to the Supreme Court	1952	SC	128,000
Washington	Administrator for the Courts	1957	SC (e)	116,000
West Virginia	Administrative Director of the Supreme Court of Appeals	1975	SC	88,000
Wisconsin	Director of State Courts	1978	SC	115,000
Wyoming	Court Coordinator	1974	SC	87,000
Dist. of Columbia	Executive Officer, Courts of D.C.	1971	(f)	158,000
Guam	Administrative Director of Superior Court	N.A.	CJ (m)	90,000
No. Mariana Islands				70,000
Puerto Rico	Administrative Director of the Courts	1952	CJ	96,000
U.S. Virgin Islands	Court/Administrative Clerk	N.A.	N.A.	85,000

Source: Salary information was taken from National Center for State Courts, Survey of Judicial Salaries (April 2004). Other information from State Court Administrator web sites.

Key:
SC—State court of last resort.
CJ—Chief justice or chief judge of court of last resort.
JC—Judicial council.
N.A.—Not available.
(a) Term of office for all court administrators is at pleasure of appointing authority.
(b) With approval of Supreme Court.
(c) With approval of Judicial Council.
(d) Administrator is an associate judge of the Supreme Court.
(e) Appointed from list of five submitted by governor.
(f) Joint Committee on Judicial Administration.
(g) Salary range is between $101,000 and $163,000.
(h) Salary range is between $ 168,000 and $185,000.
(i) Salary range is between $87,000 and $117,000.

Table 5.6
SELECTION AND RETENTION OF JUDGES

State or other jurisdiction	Court	Methods of initial selection				Initial term of office (years)	Method of retention (c)
		Appointive systems		Elective systems			
		Merit (a)	Gubernatorial or Legislative (b)	Non-partisan	Partisan		
Alabama	Supreme Court	...	...	...	★	6	Re-election (6 yr. term)
	Court of Civil App.	...	...	...	★	6	Re-election (6 yr. term)
	Court of Crim. App.	...	...	...	★	6	Re-election (6 yr. term)
	Circuit Court	...	...	...	★	6	Re-election (6 yr. term)
Alaska	Supreme Court	★	...	...	...	3	Retention election (10 yr. term)
	Court of Appeals	★	...	...	...	3	Retention election (8 yr. term)
	Superior Court	★	...	...	...	3	Retention election (6 yr. term)
Arizona	Supreme Court	★	...	...	...	2	Retention election (6 yr. term)
	Court of Appeals	★	...	...	...	2	Retention election (6 yr. term)
	Superior Court— county pop. > 250,000	★	...	...	...	2	Retention election (4 yr. term)
	Superior Court— county pop. < 250,000	...	...	★	...	4	Re-election (4 yr. term)
Arkansas (d)	Supreme Court	...	...	★	...	8	Re-election for additional terms
	Court of Appeals	...	...	★	...	8	Re-election for additional terms
	Circuit Court	...	...	★	...	6	Re-election for additional terms
California	Supreme Court	...	G	...	...	12	Retention election (12 yr. term)
	Courts of Appeal	...	G	...	...	12	Retention election (12 yr. term)
	Superior Court (e)	...	...	★	...	6	Nonpartisan election (6 yr. term) (f)
Colorado	Supreme Court	★	...	...	...	2	Retention election (10 yr. term)
	Court of Appeals	★	...	...	...	2	Retention election (8 yr. term)
	District Court	★	...	...	...	2	Retention election (6 yr. term)
Connecticut	Supreme Court	★	...	...	...	8	(g)
	Appellate Court	★	...	...	...	8	(g)
	Superior Court	★	...	...	...	8	(g)
Delaware (h)	Supreme Court	★	...	...	...	12	(i)
	Court of Chancery	★	...	...	...	12	(i)
	Superior Court	★	...	...	...	12	(i)
Florida	Supreme Court	★	...	...	...	1	Retention election (6 yr. term)
	District Court of Appeal	★	...	...	...	1	Retention election (6 yr. term)
	Circuit Court	...	...	★	...	6	Re-election for additional terms
Georgia	Supreme Court	...	...	★	...	6	Re-election for additional terms
	Court of Appeals	...	...	★	...	6	Re-election for additional terms
	Superior Court	...	...	★	...	4	Re-election for additional terms
Hawaii	Supreme Court	★	...	...	...	10	Reappointed to subsequent term by Judicial Select. Com. (10 yr. term)
	Inter. Court of Appeals	★	...	...	...	10	Reappointed to subsequent term by Judicial Select. Com. (10 yr. term)
	Circuit and Fam. Courts	★	...	...	...	10	Reappointed to subsequent term by Judicial Select. Com. (10 yr. term)
Idaho	Supreme Court	...	...	★	...	6	Re-election for additional terms
	Court of Appeals	...	...	★	...	6	Re-election for additional terms
	District Court	...	...	★	...	4	Re-election for additional terms
Illinois	Supreme Court	...	...	...	★	10	Retention election (10 yr. term)
	Apellate Court	...	...	...	★	10	Retention election (10 yr. term)
	Circuit Court	...	...	...	★	6	Retention election (6 yr. term)
Indiana	Supreme Court	★	...	...	...	2	Retention election (10 yr. term)
	Court of Appeals	★	...	...	...	2	Retention election (10 yr. term)
	Circuit Court	...	...	...	★	6	Re-election for additional terms
	Circuit Court (Vanderburg Co.)	...	...	★	...	6	Re-election for additional terms
	Superior Court	...	...	...	★	6	Re-election for additional terms
	Superior Court (Allen Co.)	...	...	★	...	6	Re-election for additional terms
	Superior Court (Lake Co.)	★ (j)	...	...	...	2	Retention election (6 yr. term)
	Superior Court (St. Joseph Co.)	★	...	...	...	2	Retention election (6 yr. term)
	Superior Court (Vanderburg Co.)	...	...	★	...	6	Re-election for additional terms
Iowa	Supreme Court	★	...	...	...	1	Retention election (8 yr. term)
	Court of Appeals	★	...	...	...	1	Retention election (6 yr. term)
	District Court	★	...	...	...	1	Retention election (6 yr. term)
Kansas	Supreme Court	★	...	...	...	1	Retention election (6 yr. term)
	Court of Appeals	★	...	...	...	1	Retention election (4 yr. term)
	District Court (17 districts)	★	...	...	...	1	Retention election (4 yr. term)
	District Court (14 districts)	...	...	...	★	4	Re-election for additional terms

See footnotes at end of table.

SELECTION AND RETENTION OF JUDGES — Continued

State or other jurisdiction	Court	Methods of initial selection				Initial term of office (years)	Method of retention (c)
		Appointive systems		Elective systems			
		Merit (a)	Gubernatorial or Legislative (b)	Non-partisan	Partisan		
Kentucky	Supreme Court	. . .	. . .	★	. . .	8	Re-election for additional terms
	Court of Appeals	. . .	. . .	★	. . .	8	Re-election for additional terms
	Circuit Court	. . .	. . .	★	. . .	8	Re-election for additional terms
Louisiana	Supreme Court	. . .	. . .	. . .	★(k)	10	Re-election for additional terms
	Court of Appeals	. . .	. . .	. . .	★(k)	10	Re-election for additional terms
	District Court	. . .	. . .	. . .	★(k)	6	Re-election for additional terms
Maine	Supreme Judicial Court	. . .	G	. . .	. . .	7	Reappointment by gov. subject to legislative confirmation
	Superior Court	. . .	G	. . .	. . .	7	Reappointment by gov. subject to legislative confirmation
Maryland (h)	Court of Appeals	★	. . .	. . .	. . .	(l)	Retention election (10 yr. term)
	Court of Special Appeals	★	. . .	. . .	. . .	(l)	Retention election (10 yr. term)
	Circuit Court	★	. . .	. . .	. . .	(l)	Nonpartisan election (15 yr. term) (m)
Massachusetts (h)	Supreme Judicial Court	★	. . .	. . .	. . .	to age 70	. . .
	Appeals Court	★	. . .	. . .	. . .	to age 70	. . .
	Trial Court of Mass.	★	. . .	. . .	. . .	to age 70	. . .
Michigan	Supreme Court	. . .	. . .	. . .	★(n)	8	Re-election for additional terms
	Court of Appeals	. . .	. . .	★	. . .	6	Re-election for additional terms
	Dist. Court/Circuit Court	. . .	. . .	★	. . .	6	Re-election for additional terms
Minnesota	Supreme Court	. . .	. . .	★	. . .	6	Re-election for additional terms
	Court of Appeals	. . .	. . .	★	. . .	6	Re-election for additional terms
	District Court	. . .	. . .	★	. . .	6	Re-election for additional terms
Mississippi	Supreme Court	. . .	. . .	★	. . .	8	Re-election for additional terms
	Court of Appeals	. . .	. . .	★	. . .	8	Re-election for additional terms
	Chancery Court	. . .	. . .	★	. . .	4	Re-election for additional terms
	Circuit Court	. . .	. . .	★	. . .	4	Re-election for additional terms
Missouri	Supreme Court	★	. . .	. . .	. . .	1	Retention election (12 yr. term)
	Court of Appeals	★	. . .	. . .	. . .	1	Retention election (12 yr. term)
	Circuit Court	. . .	. . .	. . .	★	6	Re-election for additional terms
	Circuit Court (Jackson, Clay, Platte & Saint Louis Counties)	★	. . .	. . .	. . .	1	Retention election (6 yr. term)
Montana	Supreme Court	. . .	. . .	★	. . .	8	Re-election; unopposed judges run for retention
	District Court	. . .	. . .	★	. . .	6	Re-election; unopposed judges run for retention
Nebraska	Supreme Court	★	. . .	. . .	. . .	3	Retention election (6 yr. term)
	Court of Appeals	★	. . .	. . .	. . .	3	Retention election (6 yr. term)
	District Court	★	. . .	. . .	. . .	3	Retention election (6 yr. term)
Nevada	Supreme Court	. . .	. . .	★	. . .	6	Re-election for additional terms
	District Court	. . .	. . .	★	. . .	6	Re-election for additional terms
New Hampshire (h)	Supreme Court	★	. . .	. . .	. . .	to age 70	. . .
	Superior Court	★	. . .	. . .	. . .	to age 70	. . .
New Jersey	Supreme Court	. . .	G	. . .	. . .	7	Reappointed by gov. (to age 70) w/ advice & consent of the Senate
	Appellate Div. of Superior Court	. . .	G	. . .	. . .	7	Reappointed by gov. (to age 70) w/ advice & consent of the Senate
	Superior Court	. . .	G	. . .	. . .	7	Reappointed by gov. (to age 70) w/ advice & consent of the Senate
New Mexico	Supreme Court	★	. . .	. . .	. . .	(p)	(q)
	Court of Appeals	★	. . .	. . .	. . .	(p)	(q)
	District Court	★	. . .	. . .	. . .	(p)	(q)
New York	Court of Appeals	★	. . .	. . .	. . .	14	(i)
	Appellate Div. of Supreme Court	★	. . .	. . .	. . .	5	(r)
	Supreme Court	. . .	. . .	. . .	★	14	Re-election for additional terms
	County Court	. . .	. . .	. . .	★	10	Re-election for additional terms
North Carolina	Supreme Court	. . .	. . .	★(s)	. . .	8	Re-election for additional terms
	Court of Appeals	. . .	. . .	★(s)	. . .	8	Re-election for additional terms
	Superior Court	. . .	. . .	★(s)	. . .	8	Re-election for additional terms

See footnotes at end of table.

SELECTION AND RETENTION OF JUDGES — Continued

State or other jurisdiction	Court	Appointive systems Merit (a)	Gubernatorial or Legislative (b)	Elective systems Non-partisan	Partisan	Initial term of office (years)	Method of retention (c)
North Dakota	Supreme Court	. . .	. . .	★	. . .	10	Re-election for additional terms
	District Court	. . .	. . .	★	. . .	6	Re-election for additional terms
Ohio	Supreme Court	. . .	. . .	. . .	★(t)	6	Re-election for additional terms
	Court of Appeals	. . .	. . .	. . .	★(t)	6	Re-election for additional terms
	Court of Common Pleas	. . .	. . .	. . .	★(t)	6	Re-election for additional terms
Oklahoma	Supreme Court	★	. . .	. . .	. . .	1	Retention election (6 yr. term)
	Court of Criminal Appeals	★	. . .	. . .	. . .	1	Retention election (6 yr. term)
	Court of Appeals	★	. . .	. . .	. . .	1	Retention election (6 yr. term)
	District Court	. . .	. . .	★	. . .	4	Re-election for additional terms
Oregon	Supreme Court	. . .	. . .	★	. . .	6	Re-election for additional terms
	Court of Appeals	. . .	. . .	★	. . .	6	Re-election for additional terms
	Circuit Court	. . .	. . .	★	. . .	6	Re-election for additional terms
	Tax Court	. . .	. . .	★	. . .	6	Re-election for additional terms
Pennsylvania	Supreme Court	. . .	. . .	. . .	★	10	Retention election (10 yr. term)
	Superior Court	. . .	. . .	. . .	★	10	Retention election (10 yr. term)
	Commonwealth Court	. . .	. . .	. . .	★	10	Retention election (10 yr. term)
	Court of Common Pleas	. . .	. . .	. . .	★	10	Retention election (10 yr. term)
Rhode Island	Supreme Court	★	. . .	. . .	. . .	Life	. . .
	Superior Court	★	. . .	. . .	. . .	Life	. . .
	Worker's Compensation Court	★	. . .	. . .	. . .	Life	. . .
South Carolina	Supreme Court	. . .	L (u)	. . .	. . .	10	Reappointment by legislature
	Court of Appeals	. . .	L (u)	. . .	. . .	6	Reappointment by legislature
	Circuit Court	. . .	L (u)	. . .	. . .	6	Reappointment by legislature
South Dakota	Supreme Court	★	. . .	. . .	. . .	3	Retention election (8 yr. term)
	Circuit Court	. . .	. . .	★	. . .	8	Re-election for additional terms
Tennessee	Supreme Court	★	. . .	. . .	. . .	(v)	Retention election (8 yr. term)
	Court of Appeals	★	. . .	. . .	. . .	(v)	Retention election (8 yr. term)
	Court of Crim. Appeals	★	. . .	. . .	. . .	(v)	Retention election (8 yr. term)
	Chancery Court	. . .	. . .	. . .	★	8	Re-election for additional terms
	Criminal Court	. . .	. . .	. . .	★	8	Re-election for additional terms
	Circuit Court	. . .	. . .	. . .	★	8	Re-election for additional terms
Texas	Supreme Court	. . .	. . .	. . .	★	6	Re-election for additional terms
	Court of Criminal Appeals	. . .	. . .	. . .	★	6	Re-election for additional terms
	Court of Appeals	. . .	. . .	. . .	★	6	Re-election for additional terms
	District Court	. . .	. . .	. . .	★	4	Re-election for additional terms
Utah	Supreme Court	★	. . .	. . .	. . .		
	Supreme Court	★	. . .	. . .	. . .	(w)	Retention election (10 yr. term)
	Court of Appeals	★	. . .	. . .	. . .	(w)	Retention election (6 yr. term)
	District Court	★	. . .	. . .	. . .	(w)	Retention election (6 yr. term)
	Juvenile Court	★	. . .	. . .	. . .	(w)	Retention election (6 yr. term)
Vermont	Supreme Court	★	. . .	. . .	. . .	6	Retained by vote of Gen. Assembly (6 yr. term)
	Superior Court	★	. . .	. . .	. . .	6	Retained by vote of Gen. Assembly (6 yr. term)
	District Court	★	. . .	. . .	. . .	6	Retained by vote of Gen. Assembly (6 yr. term)
Virginia	Supreme Court	. . .	L	. . .	. . .	12	Reappointment by the legislature
	Court of Appeals	. . .	L	. . .	. . .	8	Reappointment by the legislature
	Circuit Court	. . .	L	. . .	. . .	8	Reappointment by the legislature
Washington	Supreme Court	. . .	. . .	★	. . .	6	Re-election for additional terms
	Court of Appeals	. . .	. . .	★	. . .	6	Re-election for additional terms
	Superior Court	. . .	. . .	★	. . .	4	Re-election for additional terms
West Virginia	Supreme Court	. . .	. . .	. . .	★	12	Re-election for additional terms
	Circuit Court	. . .	. . .	. . .	★	8	Re-election for additional terms
Wisconsin	Supreme Court	. . .	. . .	★	. . .	10	Re-election for additional terms
	Court of Appeals	. . .	. . .	★	. . .	6	Re-election for additional terms
	Circuit Court	. . .	. . .	★	. . .	6	Re-election for additional terms
Wyoming	Supreme Court	★	. . .	. . .	. . .	1	Retention election (8 yr. term)
	District Court	★	. . .	. . .	. . .	1	Retention election (6 yr. term)
Dist. of Columbia	Court of Appeals	★	. . .	. . .	. . .	15	Reappointment by judicial tenure commission (o)
	Superior Court	★	. . .	. . .	. . .	15	Reappointment by judicial tenure commission (o)

See footnotes at end of table.

SELECTION AND RETENTION OF JUDGES — Continued

Source: American Judicature Society's, *Judicial Selection in the States: Appellate and General Jurisdiction Courts*, March 2005.

Key:

★—Yes

. . .—No

(a) Merit selection through nominating commission.

(b) Gubernatorial (G) or legislative (L) appointment without nominating commission.

(c) In a retention election, judges run unopposed on the basis of their record.

(d) In November 2000, Arkansas voters passed an amendment to the Arkansas constitution shifting judicial elections to a nonpartisan system.

(e) The California constitution provides that local electors may choose gubernatorial appointments instead of nonpartisan election to select superior court judges. As of July 1999, no counties have chosen gubernatorial appointments.

(f) If the election is uncontested, the incumbent's name does not appear on the ballot.

(g) Commission reviews incumbent's performance on noncompetitive basis; governor re-nominates and legislature confirms.

(h) Merit selection established by executive order in Delaware, Maryland, Massachusetts and New Hampshire. In all other jurisdictions, merit selection established by constitutional or statutory provision.

(i) Incumbent reapplies to nominating commission and competes with other applicants for nomination to the governor. The governor may reappoint the incumbent or another nominee. The senate confirms the appointment.

(j) Three of the judges run in partisan elections for 6 years terms then have to be re-elected for additional terms.

(k) Louisiana judicial elections are partisan in as much as the candidates' party affiliations appear on the ballot. However, two factors lead a somewhat nonpartisan character to these elections: (I) primaries are open to all candidates; and (2) judicial candidates generally do not solicit party support for their campaigns.

(l) Until the first general election following the expiration of one year from the date of the occurrence of the vacancy.

(m) May be challenged by other candidates.

(n) Although party affiliations for Supreme Court candidates are not listed on the general election ballot, candidates are nominated at party conventions.

(o) Initial appointment is made by the President of the United States and is confirmed by the Senate. Six months prior to the expiration of the term of office, the judge's performance is reviewed by the tenure commission. Those found Well Qualified are automatically reappointed. If a judge is found to be qualified, the President may nominate the judge for an additional term (subject to Senate confirmation). If the President does not wish to re-appoint the judge, the District of Columbia Nominating Commission compiles a new list of candidates.

(p) Until next general election.

(q) Partisan election at next general election after appointment for eight-year term for appellate judges, six-year term for district. The winner thereafter runs in a retention election for subsequent terms.

(r) Commission reviews and recommends for or against reappointment by governor.

(s) Beginning in 2004, these elections are nonpartisan.

(t) Although party affiliations for judicial candidates are not listed on the general election ballot, candidates are nominated in partisan party elections.

(u) South Carolina has a 10 member Judicial Merit Selection Commission that screens judicial candidates and reports the findings to the state's General Assembly. Since 1997, the Assembly is restricted to voting only on those candidates found qualified by the Judicial Merit Selection Commission. However, the nominating commission itself is not far removed from the ultimate appointing body, and cannot be considered to be nonpartisan as control over member nominations is vested in majority party leadership. Although most nominating commissions contain members appointed by the governor or legislature, no other commission actually contain the governor or current legislators who have final approval over the candidate as voting members of the commission. In contrast, the Judicial Merit Selection Commission in South Carolina contains 6 current members of the General Assembly appointed by the Speaker or the House of Representatives, the Chairman of the Senate Judiciary Committee, and the President Pro Tempore of the Senate. State legislators also choose the remaining four members of the Commission who are selected from the general public.

(v) Until next biennial general election.

(w) First general election three years after appointment.

Table 5.7
REMOVAL OF JUDGES

		Methods of removal	
	Judicial conduct commissions, boards, councils	*Impeachment*	*Recall*	*Gubernatorial, Supreme Court and/or legislative*
Alabama	The Judicial Inquiry Commission investigates complaints against judges and files complaints with the Court of the Judiciary. The Court of the Judiciary may censure, suspend, or remove a judge. Decisions of the Court of the Judiciary may be appealed to the Supreme Court.	Judges may be impeached.	. . .	. . .
Alaska	Judges may be suspended, removed from office, retired, or censured by the Supreme Court upon the recommendation of the Commission on Judicial Conduct.	Judges may be impeached by two-thirds of the Senate and convicted by two-thirds of the House of Representatives.	. . .	. . .
Arizona	The Supreme Court may censure, suspend, remove, or retire a judge upon recommendation of the Commission on Judicial Content.	Judges may be impeached by a majority vote of the House of Representatives and convicted by a two-thirds vote of the Senate.	Judges are subject to recall election.	. . .
Arkansas	The Judicial Discipline and Disability Commission, which is responsible for enforcing the Arkansas Code of Judicial Conduct, has the authority to investigate, as well as to initiate, complaints concerning misconduct of judges. After notice and hearing, the Commission may, by majority vote of the membership, recommend to the Supreme Court that a judge be suspended or removed, and the Supreme Court sitting en banc may take such action.	Judges may be impeached by the House of Representatives and convicted by two-thirds of the Senate.	. . .	The Governor may remove judges for good cause upon the address of two-thirds of the members of both houses of the general assembly.
California	The Commission on Judicial Performance investigates complaints of judicial misconduct and incapacity and may privately admonish, suspend, censure, retire, or remove a judge. The Commission's decisions are subject to review by the Supreme Court.	Judges may be impeached by the Assembly and convicted by two-thirds of the Senate.	Judges are subject to recall election.	. . .
Colorado	On the recommendation of the Judicial Discipline Commission, the Supreme Court may remove, retire, suspend, censure, reprimand, or discipline a judge.	Judges may be impeached by a majority vote of the House of Representatives and convicted by a two-thirds vote of the Senate.	Judges are subject to recall election.	. . .
Connecticut	The Judicial Review Council investigates complaints of judicial misconduct. If the investigation indicated that there is probable cause that the judge is guilty of misconduct, the Council conducts a hearing and makes a recommendation to the Supremem Court. The Supreme Court may suspend or remove the judge.	Judges may be impeached by the House of Representatives and removed by two-thirds vote of the Senate.	. . .	Judges may be removed by the Governor on the address of two-thirds of the general assembly.
Delaware	Judges may be removed, retired, or disciplined by a two-thirds vote of the Court on the Judiciary.	Judges may be impeached by a majority of the House of Representatives and convicted by two-thirds of the Senate.	. . .	. . .
Florida	On the recommendation of the Judicial Qualifications Commission, the Supreme Court may discipline, retire, or remove a judge.	Judges may be impeached by a two-thirds vote of the House of Representatives and convicted by a two-thirds vote of the Senate.	. . .	. . .
Georgia	The Judicial Qualifications Commission may discipline, retire, or remove a judge. Removal and retirement decisions must be reviewed by the Supreme Court.	Judges may be impeached by the House of Representatives and convicted by a two-thirds vote of the Senate.	. . .	. . .

See footnotes at end of table.

REMOVAL OF JUDGES — Continued

State or other jurisdiction	Methods of removal			
	Judicial conduct commissions, boards, councils	Impeachment	Recall	Gubernatorial, Supreme Court and/or legislative
Hawaii	The Commission on Judicial Conduct has the authority to investigate and conduct hearings concerning allegations of judicial misconduct or disability and to recommend to the Supreme Court that a judge be reprimanded, disciplined, suspended, retired, or retired.	. . .	. . .	. . .
Idaho	The Idaho Judicial Council investigates complaints against Idaho judges and may recommend to the Supreme Court the discipline, removal, or retirement of judges. The Supreme Court may review the recommendation of the Judicial Council and take additional evidence. The court may then reject the recommendation of the Judicial Council, or order discipline, removal, of retirement of the judge.	Judges may be impeached by a majority vote of the House of Representatives and convicted by a two-thirds vote of the Senate.	. . .	. . .
Illinois	The Judicial Inquiry Board files complaints with the courts Commission. After notice and hearing, the Commission may reprimand, censure, suspend, retire, or remove a judge.	Judges may be impeached by a majority vote of the House of Representatives and removed by two-thirds vote of the Senate.	. . .	. . .
Indiana	On the recommendation of the Commission on Judicial Qualifications, the Supreme Court may discipline, suspend, retire, or remove a judge.	Judges may be impeached by the House of Representatives and convicted by the Senate.	. . .	Judges may be removed by joint resolution of the General Assembly, upon the agreement of two-thirds of each house.
Iowa	The Commission on Judicial Qualifications has the authority to investigate complaints of Judicial misconduct and recommend to the Supreme Court that it retire, discipline, or remove a judge.	Judges may be impeached by a majority of the House of Representatives and convicted by two-thirds of the Senate.	. . .	. . .
Kansas	Judges of the Court of Appeals and District Court may be removed by the Supreme Court on the recommendation of the Commission on Judicial Qualifications. The Commission on Judicial Qualifications is authorized to investigate allegations of misconduct and to recommend a formal hearing. If the charges are proven by clear and convincing evidence, the Commission may admonish the judge, issue a cease-and-decease order, or recommend to the Supreme Court public censure, suspension , removal or compulsory retirement.	Judges may be removed by impeachment and conviction, as prescribed in Article 2 of the Kansas Constitution.	. . .	Supreme Court justices are subject to retirement upon certification to the Governor (after a hearing by the Supreme Court Nominating Commission) that the justice is so incapacitated as to be unable to perform his duties.
Kentucky	After notice and hearing the Judicial Conduct Commission may admonish, reprimand, censure, suspend, retire, or remove a judge. The commission's decisions are subject to review by the Supreme Court.	Judges may be impeached by the House of Representatives and convicted by two-thirds vote of the Senate.	. . .	. . .
Louisiana	On recommendation of the Judiciary Commission, the Supreme Court may censure, suspend, remove, or retire-judges.	Judges may be impeached by the House of Representatives and removed by a two-thirds vote of the Senate.	. . .	. . .

See footnotes at end of table.

REMOVAL OF JUDGES — Continued

	Methods of removal			
	Judicial conduct commissions, boards, councils	Impeachment	Recall	Gubernatorial, Supreme Court and/or legislature
Maine	The Supreme Judicial Court may retire, remove, or discipline judges upon recommendation of the Committee on Judicial Responsibility and Disability.	Judges may be impeached by the House of Representatives and convicted by two-thirds vote of the Senate.	. . .	Judges may be removed upon the address by the Governor of both houses of the legislature.
Maryland	Judges may be removed or retired by the Court of Appeals on the recommendation of the Commission on Judicial Disabilities.	Judges may be impeached by a majority of the House of delegates and convicted by two-thirds of the Senate.	. . .	Judges may be removed by the Governor upon address of the General Assembly with the concurrence of two-thirds of the members of each House. Judges may also be retired by the General Assembly with a two thirds vote of each House and the Governor's concurrence.
Massachusetts	The Commission on Judicial Conduct investigates complaints of judicial misconduct. Following a formal hearing, the commission may recommend to the Supreme Judicial Court removal, retirement, or reprimand of a judge.	Judges may be impeached by the House of Representatives and convicted by the Senate.	. . .	The Governor, with consent of the Governor's Council, may remove judges upon the address of both Houses of the General Court. The Governor, with consent of the Governor's Council, may also retire judges because of advanced age or mental or physical disability.
Michigan	On the recommendation of the Judicial Tenure Commission, the Supreme Court may censure, suspend, retire, or remove a judge.	Judges may be impeached by a majority vote of the House of Representatives and convicted by a two-thirds vote of the Senate.	. . .	The Governor may remove a judge upon the concurrent resolution of two-thirds of the members of both Houses of the Legislature.
Minnesota	After a public hearing and on the recommendation of the Board on Judicial Standards, the Supreme Court may censure, retire, or remove a judge.	Judges may be impeached by a majority vote of the House of Representatives and convicted by a two-thirds vote of the Senate.	Judges are subject to recall election.	. . .
Mississippi	On the recommendation of the Commission on Judicial Performance, the Supreme Court may censure, remove, or retire a judge.	Judges may be impeached by two-thirds vote of the House of Representatives and removed by the Senate.	. . .	Judges may be removed by the Governor on the joint address of two-thirds of both Houses of the Legislature.
Missouri	On the recommendation of the Commission on Retirement, Removal, and Discipline, the Supreme Court may suspend, discipline, reprimand, retire, or remove a judge.	Judges may be impeached by the House of Representatives. Impeachments are tried by the Supreme court or by special commission in the case of impeachments of the Governor or a Supreme Court Justice. Convictions require the concurrence of five-sevenths of the court or commission.	. . .	. . .
Montana	On the recommendation of the Judicial Standards Commission, the Supreme Court may retire, censure, suspend, or remove a judge.	Judges may be impeached by a two-thirds vote of the House of Representatives and convicted by a two-thirds vote of the Senate.	. . .	. . .

See footnotes at end of table.

REMOVAL OF JUDGES — Continued

State or other jurisdiction	Methods of removal			
	Judicial conduct commissions, boards, councils	Impeachment	Recall	Gubernatorial, Supreme Court and/or legislature
Nebraska	Based on the recommendation of the judicial qualifications commission, the Supreme Court may reprimand, censure, discipline, suspend, retire, or remove a judge.	Judges may be impeached by majority vote of the legislature and removed with the concurrence of two thirds of the members of the court of impeachment. The Supreme Court sits as the court of impeachment, unless a supreme court justice has been impeached. In that case, seven district court judges are selected to try the impeachment.	...	Judges may be impeached by majority vote of the legislature and removed with the concurrence of two thirds of the members of the court of impeachment. The Supreme Court sits as the court of impeachment, unless a supreme court justice has been impeached. In that case, seven district court judges are selected to try the impeachment.
Nevada	The Commission on Judicial Discipline may discipline, censure, retire, or remove a judge. Commission decisions may be appealed to the Supreme Court.	Judges may be impeached by a majority vote of the Assembly and convicted by a two-thirds vote of the Senate.	Judges are subject to recall election	Judges may be removed by legislative resolution, passed by two-thirds of the members of both Houses.
New Hampshire	The Governor with the consent of the Executive Council, may remove judges for reasonable cause upon the joint address of both houses of the General Court.	Judges may be impeached by the House of Representatives and convicted by the Senate.	...	...
New Jersey	When the Supreme Court certifies to the Governor that a judge is so incapacitated that she/he cannot substantially perform his/her duties, a three-person commission is appointed to look into the matter. Upon the Commission's recommendation, the Governor may retire the judge from office.	Judges may be impeached by a majority vote of all members of the General Assembly and removed by a two-thirds vote of the Senate.	...	Removal proceedings may be instigated by a majority of either House, by the Governor filing a complaint with the Supreme Court, or by the Supreme Court on its own motion. The Supreme Court conduct composed of private citizens appointed by the Court. The committee reviews all allegations of misconduct and either dismisses the charges or recommends a formal hearing. Based upon the hearing, judges may be reprimanded, censured and suspended without pay, or removed from office.
New Mexico	On the recommendation of the Judicial Standards Commission, the Supreme Court may discipline, retire, or remove a judge.	Judges may be impeached by a majority vote of the House of Representatives and removed by a two-thirds vote of the Senate.	...	...
New York	Judges may be admonished, censured, retired, or removed from office by the Commission on Judicial Conduct. The Commission's disciplinary actions are subject to review by the Court of Appeals.	Judges may be impeached by a majority vote of the Assembly and removed by a two-thirds vote of the Court for the Trial of Impeachments. The Court consists of the President of the Senate, the Senators, and the judges of the Court of Appeals.	...	Judges of the Courts of Appeals and justices of the Supreme Court may be removed by two-thirds vote of both houses of the legislature. Other judges may be removed by a two-thirds vote of the senate on he recommendation of the Governor.
North Carolina	On the recommendation of the Judicial Standards Commission, the Supreme Court may censure or remove a judge.	Judges may be impeached by the House of Representatives and convicted by a two-thirds vote of the Senate.	...	Judges may be removed for mental or physical incapacity by joint resolution of two-thirds of the members of the General Assembly.

See footnotes at end of table.

REMOVAL OF JUDGES — Continued

State	Judicial conduct commissions, boards, councils	Methods of removal		
		Impeachment	Recall	Gubernatorial, Supreme Court and/or legislature
North Dakota	On the recommendation of the Commission on Judicial Conduct, the Supreme Court may discipline, censure, suspend, retire, or remove a judge.	Judges may be impeached by a majority vote of the House of Representatives and convicted by a two-thirds vote of the Senate.	Judges are subject to recall election.	. . .
Ohio	Complaints alleging judicial misconduct may be filed with the Disciplinary Council or with a certified grievance committee of the Board of Commissioners on Grievances and Discipline, both of which have the authority to investigate and file formal complaints with the Board. If two-thirds of the members of the board believe there is substantial credible evidence to support the complaint, the Supreme Court appoints a commission of five judges to determine whether retirement, removal, or suspension is warranted. The Commission's decision may be appealed to the Supreme court.	. . .	. . .	Judges may be removed by a concurrent resolution of two-thirds of both Houses of the general Assembly.
Oklahoma	Judges are subject to removal from office, or to compulsory retirement, by proceedings in the Court on the Judiciary.	Judges may be impeached by the House of Representatives and convicted by two-thirds of the Senate.	. . .	. . .
Oregon	On the recommendation of the Commission on Judicial Fitness and Disability, the Supreme Court may censure, suspend, retire, or remove a judge.	. . .	Judges are subject to recall election.	. . .
Pennsylvania	The Judicial Conduct Board investigates complaints regarding judicial conduct filed by individuals or initiated by the board. The board determines whether probable cause exists to file formal charges, and presents its case to the court of judicial discipline. The court has the authority to impose sanctions, ranging from a reprimand to removal from office, if the formal charges are sustained.	Judges may be impeached by the House of Representatives and convicted by a two -thirds vote of the Senate.	. . .	. . .
Rhode Island	The Commission on Judicial Tenure and Discipline reviews complaints against judges. Following a formal hearing, the Commission either dismisses the complaint or recommends to the Supreme Court that the judge be reprimanded, censured, suspended, removed, or retired. The Commission may also recommend the retirement of a judge for physical or mental disability.	Judges may be impeached by a majority of the House of Representatives and convicted by a two-thirds vote of the Senate.	. . .	. . .
South Carolina	The Commission on Judicial Conduct is authorized to investigate complaints of judicial misconduct and incapacity. Disciplinary counsel appointed by the Supreme Court evaluates each complaint and either dismisses the complaint or conducts a preliminary investigation. If evidence supports the complaint, a full investigation is authorized. If the investigation supports the filing of formal charges, a hearing is conducted, after which recommendation is made to the Supreme Court for sanctions, dismissal, transfer to inactive status, retirement, or removal.	Judges may be impeached by a two-thirds vote of the House of Representatives and convicted by a two-thirds vote of the Senate.	. . .	Judges may be removed by the Governor upon the address of two-thirds of each house of the General Assembly.

See footnotes at end of table.

REMOVAL OF JUDGES — Continued

State or other jurisdiction	Judicial conduct commissions, boards, councils	Methods of removal		Gubernatorial, Supreme Court and/or legislature
		Impeachment	Recall	
South Dakota	On the recommendation of the Judicial Qualifications Commission , the Supreme Court, after a hearing, may censure, remove, or retire a judge,	Judges may be impeached by a majority of the House of Representatives and convicted by two-thirds vote of the Senate.	...	...
Tennessee	Upon recommendation by the Court of the Judiciary, the General Assembly may remove judges by a two-thirds vote of both Houses, with each House voting separately.	Judges may be impeached by the House of Representatives and convicted by two-thirds vote of the Senate.	...	...
Texas	The State Commission on Judicial Conduct investigates, and if warranted, prosecutes allegations of misconduct. Upon a Commission recommendation of removal or retirement, the Supreme Court selects a review tribunal from among Court of Appeals judges to verify the findings and enter a judgment. Judges may appeal decisions of the review tribunal to the Supreme Court.	Judges may be impeached by the House of Representatives and removed by two-thirds vote of the Senate.	...	Judges may be removed by the Governor on address of two-thirds of the House and Senate. The Supreme Court may remove District Court judges from office.
Utah	The Judicial Conduct Commission may reprimand, censure, suspend, retire, or remove a judge. The Commission's decisions are subject to review by the Supreme Court.	Judges may be impeached by a two-thirds vote of the House of Representatives and convicted by a two-thirds vote of the Senate.	...	...
Vermont	The Judicial Conduct Board investigates complaints of judicial misconduct or disability and recommends any necessary action to the Supreme Court. Possible disciplinary actions include public reprimand of the judge, suspension for a part or the remainder of the judge's term of office, or retirement of the judge if physically or mentally disabled.	Judges may be impeached by a two-thirds vote of the House of Representatives and convicted by a two-thirds vote of the Senate.	...	...
Virginia	The Judicial Inquiry and Review Commission investigates complaints of judicial misconduct or serious mental or physical disability that interferes with a judges duties. The Commission may conduct hearings and gather evidence to determine whether the charges are substantial. If the Commission finds the charges to significant, a formal complaint is filed with the Supreme Court of West Virginia. The Supreme Court may dismiss the complaint or it may retire, censure, or remove the judge.	Judges may be impeached by the House of Delegates and removed by a two-thirds vote of the Senate.	...	...
Washington	The Commission on Judicial Conduct investigates complaints of judicial misconduct or disability and recommends to the Supreme Court that the judge be suspended, removed , or retired. The Supreme makes the final decision after reviewing the commission's record and hearing argument on the matter.	...	...	Judges may be removed from office by joint resolution of the legislature, in which three-fourths of the members of each house must concur.

See footnotes at end of table.

REMOVAL OF JUDGES — Continued

State or other jurisdiction	Methods of removal			
	Judicial conduct commissions, boards, councils	Impeachment	Recall	Gubernatorial, Supreme Cout and/or legislature
West Virginia	The Judicial Hearing Board investigates complaints against judges and makes recommendations to the Supreme Court regarding the disposition of those complaints. The Court has the authority to censure, suspend, and retire judges.	Judges may be impeached by the House of Delegates and removed by a two-thirds vote of the Senate.	. . .	. . .
Wisconsin	On the recommendation of the Judicial Commission and after review, the Supreme Court may reprimand, censure, suspend, or remove a judge.	Judges may be impeached by a majority vote of the Assembly and convicted by a two-thirds vote of the Senate.	Judges are subject to recall election	Judges may be removed by address of both Houses of the Legislature with the concurrence of two-thirds of the members of each House.
Wyoming	The Supreme Court, on its own motion or on the recommendation of the Commission on Judicial Conduct and Ethics, may censure, suspend, retire, or remove a judge.	Judges may be impeached by a majority of the House of Representatives and convicted by two-thirds of the Senate.	. . .	. . .
Dist. of Columbia	The Judicial Disabilities and Tenure Commission has the authority to suspend, involuntarily retire, or remove judges upon the filing of an order with the D.C. Court of Appeals.	. . .	. . .	. . .

Source: American Judicature Society, *Judicial Selection in the States*, March 2005. http://www.ajs.org

Key:
. . .—No provision for method.
N.A. - Not available.

Chapter Six

STATE POLITICAL PARTIES, ELECTIONS AND ETHICS

The Future of Political Parties in the States

By Sarah M. Morehouse and Malcolm E. Jewell

The increase in the level of two-party competition, particularly in the Southern states, has produced many parties which are cohesive and disciplined to capture public office and govern once that office has been attained. More parties are using preprimary endorsements to control nominations. They have become multimillion dollar organizations and contribute to their state candidates and rival the national parties in fundraising capability. Governors and their legislative parties are governing more effectively.

The Party as Coalition Building

A party is defined in terms of effort: collective effort directed toward capturing public office and governing once that office is attained. Most definitions of political parties as organizations assume the electoral and governing functions. Anthony Downs defined the party as "a team seeking to control the governing apparatus by gaining office in a duly constituted election," essentially the definition that is used here (Downs 1957). Party organization matters. It matters to the candidates for governor whether they can count on party resources to win the nomination and election. It matters whether legislators identify with the party and commit to the platform because they can be counted on to support it in the legislative session. These are minimal conditions for political parties to fulfill, and they are possible under our state systems, because state political parties are alive and well but they are different in important respects from the state parties of the 1950s and even the 1980s.

Fifty years ago, most state parties were poor and weak. The Progressive reformers of the early decades of the 20th century emasculated the 19th century state party machines, which controlled nominations, monopolized campaign resources and dominated the mobilization of voters. Because state political parties had been primarily labor-intensive organizations, dependent upon patronage for party workers and funds, they were slow to adapt to technologically-based campaigning. At first, they could not provide the services to candidates that have become standard in contemporary campaigns. Candidates had to buy these services elsewhere, and thus they became expert at raising money, organizing their candidacies and running for office. Since that time, increased party competition and large-scale fundraising combined to strengthen party organizations. Now most state parties are multimillion-dollar organizations with experienced directors and knowledgeable staffs. They now provide sophisticated services to candidates, including training, issue development, polling, media consulting and coordination of campaign assistance. With their greatly increased role in statewide, congressional, and state legislative campaigns, they supplement the candidates' own campaign organizations and resources.

The Growth in Two-Party Competition

The Civil War and Reconstruction had a massive and enduring effect on national and state politics, establishing Democratic domination in Southern states and Republican domination in most Northern states. From the end of Reconstruction until the start of the New Deal in 1933, most political developments had the effect of strengthening and reinforcing this one-party dominance in most of the states. The New Deal realignment in the 1930s destroyed the sectional base of American politics as well as Republican control over most Northern states. Under Franklin Roosevelt's leadership, a new Democratic coalition was built in most northern states that included not only Catholic and ethnic group voters but a large proportion of the lower and middle-income voters in urban and metropolitan areas. The Democratic coalition also included the Solid South and Roosevelt consistently won every Southern state plus the border states by large margins. The most important changes in the New Deal Coalition since 1944 have occurred in the South.

In the Southern states, the Republican Party was slow to take advantage of the success that Republican presidential candidates were enjoying. In 1952 Dwight Eisenhower carried four of the 11 Southern states and Republican presidential candidates won between three and five Southern states in the next four elections and in 1972, Richard Nixon carried all of the Southern states. But the Republicans did not elect a Southern governor until 1966, and it was not until the 1980 election that they held the governorship in more than two or three Southern states at the same time. During the period from 1952 to 1978, the Republicans did not have a majority in any Southern legislative chamber, and in most of these legislatures they were heavily outnumbered by Democrats.

In the 1980s and 1990s the most important changes in party alignments and competition were in Southern states. It has taken years to develop really competitive party systems in them. Republican parties had to get organized, enlist workers, raise money and recruit viable candidates. They had a head start in Tennessee, Florida, Virginia, and to some extent in North Carolina because of presidential campaigns and in both Tennessee and North Carolina because there had been pockets of traditional Republican strength in the mountain areas. These four states all elected Republican governors in the 1960s or 1970s, and all began to elect Republicans to about one-fourth of the legislative seats by the mid-1960s and 1970s.

Republican parties were slow starters in South Carolina, Texas and Georgia. In the 1960s they had virtually no strength in the legislature and elected no governors (with Georgia and South Carolina Republicans not even running a gubernatorial candidate in 1962). But in the 1980s and 1990s, Republicans held the governorship more than half the time in both South Carolina and Texas. In the 1990s Republicans averaged over 40 percent of the legislature in these two states, and following the 1996 and 1998 elections they held a narrow majority in one of the legislative chambers in each state. By the 1990s, Republicans in Georgia had won one-third of the legislature and in 2002 they elected a Republican governor.

In the remaining four deep Southern states—Alabama, Arkansas, Mississippi and Louisiana—the Republican Party lagged behind. They are less urban than most of the other Southern states. In all four states until the 1960s the Republicans generally ran no gubernatorial candidates or very weak ones. The first Republican governor in Arkansas was Winthrop Rockefeller, elected in 1966 and 1968, his victory resulted from his political skills and ample campaign funds. In Louisiana the Republicans did not elect a governor until 1979. The first Republican governor in Alabama was not elected until 1986 (and again in 1990). It was not until 1991 (and again in 1995) that the Mississippi Republicans elected a governor. Republicans in these four states were even less successful in electing members to the legislature. In 1958 there was not a single Republican in any of these four legislatures. In the 1980s and 1990s Republicans in these four states averaged control of the governorship 40 percent of the time, but all of these governors faced legislatures where the Democrats held at least two-thirds of the seats and often much more.

The pace of Republican progress in the South accelerated in the 1990s. During the eight year period beginning with the 1994 election, Republicans controlled the governorship some of the time in every state except North Carolina. They controlled the governorship all of the time or a majority of the time in eight of the Southern states. Even more dramatic progress was made in the legislature. Republicans controlled the house or senate or both for some time during this eight-year period in Florida, South Carolina, North Carolina, Texas and Virginia. This expanded control was brought about by the party running more candidates for southern legislative seats and targeting more realistically the seats they had some chance of winning. Another important factor is that incumbents have a big advantage over other candidates in legislative elections. In the years ahead, an increasing number of Southern legislatures are likely to have close two-party competition for control. By 2000 in most Southern states the Republican Party held at least one-third of the seats. And in another one-third of the seats the party was well enough organized, had learned how to recruit candidates, and had enough support from voters to be competitive for control of the legislature (Jewell and Morehouse 2001, 33–37).

Measuring Two-Party Competition. Measures of two-party competition differ depending on the offices that are included, the time period chosen and the method of aggregating the statistics that is used. We will concentrate on the partisan vote for governor and partisan strength in the state legislature to measure the breadth and depth of party strength. Austin Ranney designed a widely used and long-standing measure which includes those indicators of party competition for control of state government (1976, 59–60). His four components of inter-party competition are averaged over the time period:

1. The percentage of the vote for the governor's office.

2. The percentage of senate seats won.

3. The percentage of house seats won.

4. The percentage of years the party controlled the governorship, the senate and the house.

Ranney used these four components to calculate his index of interparty competition which have been updated for 1980–2000. The index is actually a measure of control of government, with a score of zero indicating complete Republican control and a score of 100 indicating absolute Democratic control. At its midpoint (50.00), control of government is evenly split between the two parties indicating a highly competitive state. In order to understand the current pattern of competition, we will look at data for the elections of 1980 through 2000 (which include five or six elections for governors who serve four-year terms and 11 elections for two-year legislative terms).

The first column of data in Table A measures which party had the most control, with the states having the highest numbers being the most Democratic and those with the lowest being the most Republican. The actual numbers range from 80.8 to 25.1. (Nebraska is omitted from the table because its legislature is nonpartisan.) The states with scores from 80.8 to 60.7 are classified as Democratic; those with scores from 59.5 to 51.5 are close states leaning Democratic; those from 48.3 to 40.9 are close states leaning Republican; and those from 37.9 to 25.1 are classified as Republican.

When we look at the first column in Table A the more obvious finding is that there are more Democratic states (19) than Republican states (only eight). The Democratic states include all but one of the 11 Southern states (Florida barely misses out). They also include several border states, such as West Virginia, Kentucky, Oklahoma and Missouri, and traditionally strong Northern states, such as Rhode Island and Massachusetts. The small number of states classified as Republican includes several Western and Southwestern (but not coastal) states, along with New Hampshire. The most competitive states include 12 that are leaning Democratic and 10 that are leaning Republican. In terms of geography, the 22 competitive states include a number of Northeastern, Midwestern and West Coast states, particularly those that are more urbanized.

This table shows that over the period from 1980 to 2000 there were considerably more Democratic than Republican states. This pattern is misleading, however, because it ignores changes that occurred during the period from 1980 through the 2000 elections—specifically the Republican growth that took place during the later years. If we compare party control for the 1980–1994 period with that of the 1996-2000 period, we discover that 40 of the states became more Republican during the last three of those elections, only six became more Democratic and three were essentially unchanged. John Bibby and Thomas Holbrook's classification which includes elections from 1999–2002, places only nine states in the Democratic category, and only three of them are

Table A: State Party Control and Two-Party Competition, 1980–2000		
State	Party control	Party competition
Democratic States		
Maryland	80.8	692
Arkansas	79.2	708
Hawaii	78.7	713
Georgia	77.7	723
Louisiana	76.5	735
Mississippi	75.8	742
West Virginia	75.4	746
Rhode Island	74.9	751
Massachusetts	73.4	766
Kentucky	72.9	771
Alabama	72.6	774
North Carolina	67.2	828
Oklahoma	66.4	836
South Carolina	62.6	874
Missouri	62.6	874
Virginia	62.2	878
New Mexico	62.1	879
Tennessee	61.6	884
Texas	60.7	893
Close States, Leaning Democratic		
California	59.5	905
Washington	59.4	906
Minnesota	59.2	908
Florida	57.7	923
Nevada	57.7	923
Connecticut	57.7	923
Maine	54.9	951
Oregon	54.2	958
Vermont	53.9	961
New York	52.3	977
Wisconsin	52.0	980
Delaware	51.5	985
Close States, Leaning Republican		
Illinois	48.3	983
Michigan	48.0	980
Iowa	46.9	969
Alaska	46.5	965
New Jersey	45.7	957
Indiana	44.2	942
Montana	44.1	941
Ohio	44.1	941
Pennsylvania	43.9	939
Colorado	40.9	940
Republican States		
North Dakota	37.9	879
Arizona	35.2	852
Wyoming	35.0	850
New Hampshire	33.5	835
Kansas	33.1	831
Idaho	30.8	808
South Dakota	27.2	772
Utah	25.1	751

Source: Calculated by the authors using the Ranney Index components.

Southern states: Arkansas, Mississippi and Alabama (all three of which now have Republican governors). They say that in their four year time period: "the relative strength of the parties is nearly perfectly balanced: the vast majority of the states are competitive two-party states, and the number of modified Republican states is nearly equal to the number of modified Democratic states." (Bibby and Holbrook, 2004, 87).

The second column of data in Table A measures how closely competitive each state was from 1980 through 2000. The same Ranney index data are used. But in this case those with the highest numbers had the closest two-party competition; those with the lowest numbers were most controlled by one party or the other. The scale can run from 1,000 for the most competitive to 500 for the least; the actual numbers run from 985 to 692. The stronger the control by one party, either Democratic or Republican, as shown in the first column, the less competitive the two parties will be and, thus, the lower the score for party competition as shown in the second column. The 22 most competitive states which have been labeled as close, have competition scores ranging from 905 to 985; the highest scores include Delaware, Illinois, Wisconsin, Michigan, New York and Iowa. As of the election of 2004, half of these states have Republican governors and half have Democratic governors.

Does the existence of competition really matter to the operation of the political parties? Does it affect the kind of policy that is produced? The thesis with regard to the beneficial effects of two-party competition declares that it brings about parties that are cohesive and disciplined to combat the traditional enemy. This cohesion shows itself in the ability of the party to control nominations, to present a united front in the election, and, thereafter, to discipline the legislators to uphold the governor's program to make a good record for the next election. It is generally considered that this type of competition-cohesion situation will benefit the have-nots in the political system because the political leaders would be more likely to act in their behalf than in a one-party situation in which their next election was assured. In a one-party situation in which the parties are not cohesive electoral units and are divided into one or more factions that do battle within the party, there is little responsibility. These claims will be investigated in this article, beginning with the ability to the parties to control nominations.

The Role of Parties in Nominations

In about 22 states, party leaders and officeholders are able to exert influence over nominations. They make preprimary endorsements as a way to increase party control over the nomination or to guide the primary voters toward choosing a party-endorsed candidate. States with strong parties are most likely to have preprimary endorsing procedures (Morehouse

and Jewell 2003, 55).

The growth of the direct primary movement early in the 20th century turned over to the voters one of the major functions of political parties: the nomination of candidates. Some of the stronger political party organizations were able to delay adoption of direct primary laws for many years in states such as New York, Connecticut and Rhode Island. In such states and a number of others, strong party organizations adopted procedures enabling them to endorse the candidates they preferred before the primaries in an effort to control, or at least influence, the nominating process. These endorsements were usually made either in meetings of a state committee or in the conventions of delegates elected in local caucuses.

Preprimary conventions have taken two forms. In some states, parties persuaded the legislature to establish a legal foundation for the endorsement process. Some of these laws provided that candidates must get a certain percentage of the convention vote to get on the primary ballot or get on the ballot automatically if two or more candidates receive a certain percentage of the vote (30 percent in Colorado, 25 percent in New York and 20 percent in New Mexico). In Utah, only the top two vote-getters in the convention can get on the primary ballot, and any candidate getting 70 percent of the convention vote is automatically nominated. At the present time there are seven states that by law provide for preprimary endorsements by party conventions (New York, Colorado, Connecticut, North Dakota, Utah, Rhode Island and New Mexico).

In the absence of legislative action, one or both parties in some states have adopted party rules providing for endorsement by the party. The endorsements made under party rules, like those based on state law, are usually made in conventions open to the public. Normally the candidates endorsed under party rules have no advantage of ballot access or position, but the courts have held that the Massachusetts parties can require candidates to receive a minimum percentage of the convention vote in order to get on the primary ballot. Endorsements are made under party rules by both parties in Massachusetts and Minnesota, and the Delaware Republicans. The California Democrats endorsed for governor in 1990, considered and rejected doing so in 1994 and have not done so since. There are a few other states where party leaders or organizations at the state or local level, usually meeting behind closed doors, sometimes endorse candidates. These include Illinois, Pennsylvania, Ohio and Michigan. In New Jersey, county party committees endorse gubernatorial candidates in an effort to control the entry and success of candidates. The Louisiana Republicans have endorsed for governor but the party is young and has not played a major role in gubernatorial politics. Both parties in Virginia have, from time to time, held conventions instead of primaries, in accordance with state laws, an option which also exists in South Carolina, Alabama and Georgia (Bibby and Holbrook 2004, 84).

There are a number of ways in which a political party might benefit from making preprimary endorsements:

1. Political parties have an obvious interest in nominating the strongest possible candidates, the ones who have the best chance of winning in the general election. It is not necessarily true that a plurality of voters who participate in a direct primary will choose the candidate most likely to win in the general election.

2. One important step the party can take in its effort to nominate the strongest possible candidate is to recruit candidates who have the potential for winning.

3. The party has an interest in fostering unity and minimizing the risk of bitter antagonisms that sometimes result from divisive primaries and can result in defeat in November elections. A party endorsement may lead activists and some voters to rally around the endorsee or even lead some unendorsed candidates to drop out of the primary.

4. Party leaders and political activists may believe that it is important to nominate a candidate whose views on issues and whose record of accomplishment in office are in the mainstream of the party. A mainstream candidate should also be more electable than someone holding extreme positions on issues.

5. A political party that plays a role in nominations may be a stronger, more vital institution. If party activists and local organizations have an opportunity to participate in preprimary endorsements, their interest in party organization and its activities may be enhanced.

6. Public officials who have been endorsed by the party before the primary and who win nomination and election may have greater political strength and be more effective in getting their programs passed in the legislature.

Table B sets out the relationship between party strength and nominating systems. The states are listed by party system strength over a 20-year period, 1982-2002. Party system strength can be estimated from the magnitude of the governor's vote in the primary. If the average primary vote for each state's governors over the time period is 80-100 percent, we predict that coalition-building for the nomination is not episodic—that there is a steady corps of party leaders within both parties who outlast individual gubernatorial candidates and can recruit and help each prospective candidate. If the average primary vote is between 60 and 79 percent, both parties may be making modest efforts to aid their candidates. The weakest category, 35–59 percent, indicates that there is no steady corps of party leaders in either party. Factions within the party battle it out in the primary, and there is no effort on the part of the party leaders to influence the nomination contest.

The matching of party system strength with strength of pre-primary endorsement provides striking proof that it is only in states that have strong or moderately strong party systems that preprimary endorsements occur. Ten of the 16 states with the strongest parties have preprimary endorsing procedures, and one additional state, Iowa, has a post-primary convention to endorse a candidate if no candidate receives a majority in the primary. Eleven of the 26 states with moderate party strength practice preprimary endorsements. In these 11 states, the party leaders have devised ways to influence the nominations. They may bargain among potential contenders. Bargaining might consist of agreements for appointments within the administration in exchange for support of the leading contender. It might consist of a promise of support in a future endorsement contest. In the last four years, Wisconsin, South Carolina, Alabama and Georgia have been added to the list of parties which endorse by party rule or practice.

Thus, there are several reasons why a potential candidate for governor wants the endorsement. The most important is the money and services, such as organizational assistance and personnel, the party provides. In Minnesota the state party organizations provide the endorsee with fund-raising assistance, computer facilities, phone banks, access to lists of voters and campaign workers. In most states, a candidate who wins the endorsement is likely to attract campaign workers and contributions. If all these resources are bestowed on an endorsee, it is likely that he or she will eliminate the other primary candidates. Rivals may be eliminated because they do not receive the required convention vote. Or they may drop out because they believe that a challenge would be

Table B:
Gubernatorial Nominations and Party System Strength

	Party nominations for governor		
Party system strength (1982–2002)	Strong: preprimary endorsements by law	Moderate: preparty endorsements by party rule or practice	Weak: primary only, no major competitive party endorsements
Strong (n=16)	New York Colorado Connecticut North Dakota	Ohio Delaware (R) Virginia a Michigan (D) Massachusetts Iowa (c) New Jersey	Vermont Indiana (pre-1976) (b) North Carolina Missouri Idaho(1963-1971) (b)
Moderate (n=26)	Utah Rhode Island New Mexico	South Carolina a California (D) (1990) Wisconsin (R) Alabama (a) Illinois Georgia (a) Pennsylvania Minnesota	Tennessee Maine Oregon Arkansas Texas Hawaii Nevada Florida Maryland South Dakota Montana New Hampshire Washington Wyoming Arizona
Weak (n=8)			Kansas Alaska Oklahoma West Virginia Nebraska Mississippi Kentucky Louisiana

Source: Calculated by the authors.

Note: Party system strength is measured by averaging the governors' percent of the primary votes in gubernatorial primaries 1982–2002. In states with strong party systems, the average primary vote received by governors-to-be was 80-100 percent. In moderately strong party systems, it was 60–79 percent. In weak party systems it was 35–59 percent. The five most recent elections were used with the following exceptions: Alaska, Connecticut, Minnesota, and Maine which went back to the 1982 elections and did not use elections in which independents won; and ten elections apiece were used for the states with two-year terms: New Hampshire and Vermont. Rhode Island (7) changed to a four-year term in 1995.

Key:
(a) State party officials may by law choose either the primary or the convention.
(b) Dates in parentheses indicate dates preprimary endorsements were used.
(c) There is a postprimary nominating convention if no candidate receives at least 35 percent.

futile in the face of the endorsee's resources. Endorsees need to eliminate potential primary rivals because their success rate when challenged in a primary has dropped in recent years to 53 percent. Their overall nomination success rate, however, stands at 76 percent. When governors run again and are endorsed (as they usually are), they win renomination over 95 percent of the time, and this figure has not significantly changed over time (Morehouse and Jewell 2003, 136–137). Thus the endorsement is worth working toward.

The Role of Parties in Elections

The Role of Party Organizations. One of the most important functions of political parties is to elect their candidates to political office. Traditionally, the job of the party organization had been to provide the workers who would mobilize the voters, getting them registered, keeping them informed, and getting them to the polls. Before the 1960s there was no technology by which a candidate could create a personal campaign organization. Campaigns were labor intensive, relying little on capital or technology. Now most candidates for statewide, congressional and legislative office organize their own campaigns. They spend much of their time personally raising money. They hire the campaign managers, media experts, pollsters and fund-raisers who can make a successful campaign possible.

What role is there for the political party to play in

a candidate-centered campaign? Political scientists talk about the service role of the party in campaigns. If the political party succeeds in raising substantial amounts of money, it can provide a number of resources to candidates, such as campaign funds, but equally important, it can provide expertise and technological assistance. In recent years, several Southern state Republican parties have developed sophisticated techniques for targeting legislative races, rather than contesting every district, and this strategy has helped these parties to make major gains.

What specific kinds of help from the state party are most valuable to its candidates? Voter registration and get-out-the-vote campaigns as well as provision of workers at polling places are important because they are collective activities that should benefit all of the party's candidates' state, district and local level. The party may run advertising, on television, in newspapers, or on billboards, supporting its entire ticket. Often the party can provide candidates with lists of donors who have frequently made financial contributions to the party's candidates. The state party can conduct polls and share the results with candidates. The party can conduct workshops and training programs on campaign techniques, ranging from how to prepare eye-catching brochures to how to stage events that will generate news coverage from state newspapers and television stations.

Electing Governors. In more than half of gubernatorial races there is an incumbent running in the general election. From 1970–2003, 78 percent of eligible gubernatorial incumbents ran for reelection and 75 percent of them succeeded (Beyle, 2004). There are two basic reasons why gubernatorial incumbents usually win. They have the advantage of visibility, records of accomplishment that they can run on, and usually considerable success in raising campaign funds. Voters who identify with a political party are somewhat less likely than in the past to vote consistently for the candidates of their party. Consequently, the reelection of an incumbent governor is becoming more of a personal victory than a partisan one in many states.

We can demonstrate this by looking at what happened when there is no incumbent in the race. One – fourth of incumbents lose, but the party in power loses the governorship more than half the time when no incumbent is running, and this proportion of losses has been growing in recent elections. As of 2005, there is a Republican 28 to 22 seat margin in governors' chairs.

The Cost of the Candidate-Centered Campaign. How much does it cost a candidate to run for gover-

nor? The answer depends on a number of factors: the size of the state electorate and the number of media markets in the state, whether candidates must face both primary and general election opposition, how close the elections are and how much money the candidates are able to raise. In 2002, the candidate cost of gubernatorial elections in the 36 states which had them was $839,650,000. This was a 63 percent increase over 1998 (Beyle, 2004). There is a great range in how much these races cost. New York's race was the all-time most expensive race recorded ($146.8 million) while the race in Wyoming cost $833,181. Both states saw an incumbent win election. If we use the measure of how much was spent by all candidates per election vote, a different picture emerges. In 2002, the New Hampshire governor's race was the most expensive at $42.77 per voter followed by New York at $31.28 per vote. These increases reflect candidate spending, not party spending, although parties give very generously to candidates in some states.

The increases reflect the new style of campaigning for governor with candidates developing their own campaigns. Beyle mentions that there is an increase in the number of candidates who are wealthy or have access to wealth and are willing to spend some of this money to become governor. In 2002, Gov. Gray Davis spent $674.2 million in his successful bid for reelection in California and Gov. George Pataki of New York spent $44.2 million to win his third term. In Texas, Tony Sanchez spent $76.3 million in his unsuccessful bid for governor (Beyle, 2004).

Generally speaking, candidates who spend the most money win elections, but this is not necessarily why they win. Many contributors and particularly PACs prefer to give to the candidate they consider most likely to win. A politically strong, experienced candidate, and particularly an incumbent, has the best opportunity to raise money, which enhances his or her already strong chance of winning.

State Parties and Campaign Funding

What candidates for governor spend is far from the total amount spent on the campaign. State parties do not abandon their gubernatorial candidates once they are nominated. Most of them are multi-million-dollar organizations with enlarged and more professional staffs and have expanded their activities in the areas of candidate support and party building. More than 80 percent of state parties contribute to gubernatorial, state constitutional, congressional and state legislative candidates (Aldrich 2000, 656). In addition to providing candidates with names of appropriate donors and the array of campaign services, including training, issue development, polling, and media consulting, state parties engage in labor-intensive voter mobilization programs and party building activities, including publishing newsletters, recruiting candidates, sharing mailing lists with local units, and joint county-state fund raisers and get-out-the-vote drives. The spectacular gains by Southern Republican candidates for congressional, state and local office in recent years are a product of much stronger Republican organization (Jewell and Morehouse 2001, 99). Party organization matters. With either party now capable of winning gubernatorial elections in each of the 50 states there are powerful incentives for state parties to build and maintain strong organizations.

State political parties in recent years have been playing a significant role in the funding of state legislative candidates. Some of this funding comes from the state party organization, some from local parties and some from campaign committees that are organized in most legislatures by the party caucuses. Parties are particularly likely to contribute to legislative candidates who are not incumbents, especially if they are in close races. One recent study of 11 states shows that seven of the 22 parties provide 10–20 percent of the total funds received from legislative candidates and nine others provide at least 5 percent (Gierzynski and Breaux 1996).

In recent years, almost half of the states have established programs to provide public funding to political party organizations, individual candidates or both. As of 2000, eight states (Alabama, California, Idaho, Iowa, New Mexico, Ohio, Vermont and Virginia) allocated funds to state and sometimes to local political parties, but not to candidates. Another nine states (Florida, Hawaii, Massachusetts, Maryland, Michigan, Nebraska, New Jersey, Vermont and Wisconsin) allocated funds only to political candidates. Six states (Arizona, Kentucky, Maine, Minnesota, North Carolina and Rhode Island) provided funding to both political parties and candidates. The number of states providing public funding has been changing in recent years because more states, sometimes using the voter initiative, have been adopting public funding programs for candidates (Malbin and Gais 1998, ch. 4). In theory, a program providing public funds for political parties should strengthen the party organizations. The more funding they have, the more functions they can perform, and the more effectively they can serve the needs of their candi-

dates. How much difference public funding makes depends on the size of that funding and the ability of the party to raise funds from other sources. There has been no comprehensive research on the impact of public funding on state parties.

State Parties and National Parties: The Money Relationship. Until the 1970s political scientists referred to the national parties as weak and dependent upon their state affiliates for money. The national committees have been transformed into large-scale and wealthy enterprises which can play a major role in providing services to candidates and to their state partners. This has produced an often uneasy partnership between the national and state party committees. The national committees are often seen as dominating their weaker partners in exchange for the money to function as effective organizations.

The Rules: Hard, Soft and State Money. The financial rules that apply to presidential and congressional candidates are not the same as those in effect for state gubernatorial and legislative elections, and likewise, national and state parties face different financial restrictions. Taken together, these rules define three kinds of money for state parties: federal "hard money," nonfederal "soft money," and "state money."

The national parties and their affiliates may raise and spend only hard money subject to federal contribution limits and source restrictions. It is the only money that can be used to directly support federal candidates (Malbin ed. 2003, 8–11). It can also be used to fund generic activities which benefit the whole ticket if matched with Levin Amendment funds or state money funds to be described below.

Up until the passage of the Bipartisan Campaign Reform Act of 2002, or BCRA, the national parties could raise and send unlimited amounts of money to their state partners to be used for "party building activities," or activities which benefited both national and state candidates and included voter registration and identification, campaign material, voter turnout programs and generic party advertising. These funds had to be raised and spent under state rules and via state parties. The size and sources of soft money as it was called were subject only to the laws of the state where it was spent. Beginning in 1980, the national parties became deeply involved in raising and disbursing soft money in cooperation with the state parties. In 1996 and 2000, both national parties spent a significant amount of soft money for the first time on issue advocacy ads. These ads were run in states and congressional districts as candidate-specific broadcast advertising with the obvious purpose of helping the presidential or congressional candidate. The FEC treated these as a form of generic party advertising. BCRA has banned the national parties from raising and sending this type of money to the states for party building activities. The Levin amendment to BCRA permits state parties to raise a form of soft money limited to $10,000 per source if such contributions are allowed under state law. There are 13 states where the law will not permit contributions of this size. Since the 2003–2004 electoral cycle was the first time these new regulations could take effect, their impact is being studied at this very moment.

Many state party executive directors speak of money that is raised and spent according to state laws as "state money" and we will use the term to distinguish it from nonfederal soft money. There are 24 states where contributions by individuals and PACs to political parties are limited, and several have stricter limits than the $10,000 per year Levin Amendment soft money provision. Table C shows what these contribution limits were for 2002. In these states the parties have to raise the money to pay for the nonfederal share of administrative and generic activities according to the dictates of state law. In addition, there are 24 states where parties are limited in what they may contribute to gubernatorial candidates. Twelve of the states without contribution limits to parties have limits on party spending for candidates. Since they cannot spend much money on their candidates, this situation offers an unusual opportunity for the national parties to send generous amounts of hard money to those states which, when matched with Levin money, could be used for voter registration and get-out-the-vote activities.

This discussion was intended to emphasize the fact that the rules under which each state operates are sovereign with respect to what the party may raise and spend for state candidates. The national committees may not give money to a state party unless it conforms to rules in that state. Likewise, federal rules are sovereign with respect to federal candidates. State parties may not support their congressional candidates with state money unless it is raised according to federal rules. Areas of overlap are the administrative and generic expenses to benefit the whole ticket, which are paid out of both federal and nonfederal (or state) money accounts according to a formula set by the Federal Elections Commission for each election cycle.

State Parties and National Parties: Financial Partners

The purpose of the following section is to examine the relationship between the national parties and state parties under the previous era of soft money to better predict their future relationship under BCRA. The financial reports of thirty state parties were examined during three election cycles, the 1996 presidential year, the 1998 midterm (gubernatorial) year, and the 2000 presidential year (Morehouse and Jewell, 2003). The party funds represent the total hard and soft money raised by state party committees, national party committees, and senatorial and congressional committees. In the presidential years of 1996 and 2000, the 30 state parties raised an average of over 60 percent of the hard money total (69 percent in 1996 and 62 percent in 2000). In the 1998 midterm cycle, they raised an average 82 percent of the total raised in hard money funds. Hard money funds from the national parties dropped dramatically from the presidential year of 1996 in which they contributed $47.5 million to state parties to 1998 when the combined total was $31.5 million.

Soft money was not as easily raised by the state parties for many reasons, among them state campaign finance regulations which limited fundraising (Table C). National party soft money increased dramatically from 1992 through the 2000 presidential cycle. The Democrats increased their soft money from $64,500 million in 1996 to $149,841 million in 2000, a 132 percent increase, and the Republicans raised their soft money from $50.2 million to $129.9 million, an increase of 159 percent. State parties did not raise soft money as avidly as hard money. For the state parties under study, the average percent contributed by the state parties to the soft money account in 1996 and 2000 was about 37 percent, and in 1998, the average was about 59 percent.

Most state party executive directors claimed that they were not dependent upon soft money, even in a presidential year. According to the executive director of the Georgia Republicans: "We are not addicted, but we take what we can get" (Joe King, 1998).

Overall it appears that state parties were not the financially dependent partners that many observers predicted. The state parties raised over 60 percent of the hard money and 37 percent of the soft money in presidential election years. When the noise of the presidential election subsided and the midterm cycles began, the parties foraged for an average 82 percent of the hard money and 59 percent of the soft money to keep the office open, pay for utilities, and pay for

Table C:
Contribution Limits to State Parties and From State Parties

State parties	Annual individual contributions to state parties	Annual PAC contributions to state parties	Contributions from state parties to candidates for governor
Alabama	---------------------- (a) ----------------------		
Alaska	$5,000	$1,000	$100,000
Arizona	None	None	75,610 (in 2000) (e)
Arkansas	None	None	2,500
California	25,000 (as of 11/6/02) (c)	25,000 (as of 11/6/02) (c)	Unlimited
Colorado	2,500	2,500	Unlimited
Connecticut	5,000	5,000	Unlimited
Delaware	20,000 (b)	20,000 (b)	Limited by office
Florida	None	None	50,000 for publicly funded
Georgia	None	None	5,000 election yr.; 1,000 nonelection yr.
Hawaii	50,000	50,000	50,000
Idaho	None	None	10,000 per primary or general election
Illinois	---------------------- (a) ----------------------		
Indiana	---------------------- (a) ----------------------		
Iowa	---------------------- (a) ----------------------		
Kansas	15,000	5,000	Unlimited in general election
Kentucky	2,500	2,500	1,000 per slate
Louisiana	100,000 (b)	100,000 (b)	Unlimited
Maine	None	None	5,000
Maryland	4,000 (c)	6,000 (c)	Unlimited
Massachusetts	5,000	5,000	3,000; in kind unlimited funding (d)
Michigan	None	None	68,000
Minnesota	None	None	20,000 election yr.; 5,000 nonelection yr.
Mississippi	---------------------- (a) ----------------------		
Missouri	None	None	10,000
Montana	None	None	15,000
Nebraska	None	None	825,000 for publicly funded (e)
Nevada	None	None	5,000 per primary or general election
New Hampshire	5,000	Unlimited	1,000; unlimited for public funding
New Jersey	37,000	37,000	2,600 per primary and general election
New Mexico	---------------------- (a) ----------------------		
New York	76,500 (c)	76,500 (c)	Primary prohibited; gen. elect. unlimited
North Carolina	---------------------- (a) ----------------------		
North Dakota	---------------------- (a) ----------------------		
Ohio	16,000	16,000	523,000 per primary or general election
Oklahoma	5,000	5,000	5,000
Oregon	---------------------- (a) ----------------------		
Pennsylvania	---------------------- (a) ----------------------		
Rhode Island	1,000 (limit 10,000)	1,000 (limit 10,000)	25,000; in kind unlimited (d)
South Carolina	3,500 (c)	3,500 (c)	50,000
South Dakota	3,000	Unlimited	Unlimited
Tennessee	---------------------- (a) ----------------------		
Texas	---------------------- (a) ----------------------		
Utah	---------------------- (a) ----------------------		
Vermont	2,000 (b)	2,000 (b)	Unlimited
Virginia	---------------------- (a) ----------------------		
Washington	Unlimited	3,200 (c)	0.64 per voter
West Virginia	1,000	1,000	1,000 per primary or general election
Wisconsin	10,000 (limit 10,000)	6,000	Unlimited
Wyoming	25,000 (b) (limited 25,000)	Unlimited	Primary prohibited; gen. elect. unlimited

Source: U.S. Federal Election Commission, 2002. Campaign Finance Law 2002, Contribution and Solicitation Limitations: Chart 2-A and Chart 2-B. www.fec.gov/pubrec/cfl/cfl02chart2a; or 2b.

Note: Corporations and labor unions are prohibited from contributing in Alaska, Arizona, Connecticut, Michigan, Minnesota, New Hampshire, North Carolina, North Dakota, Ohio, Pennsylvania, Rhode Island, South Dakota, Wisconsin and Wyoming. Corporations are prohibited from contributing in: Iowa, Kentucky, Massachusetts, Montana, Oklahoma, Tennessee and West Virginia. Corporations and labor unions are limited the same as PACs in: California, Colorado, Delaware, Hawaii, Louisiana, New Jersey, South Carolina, Vermont and Washington. Labor unions only in Iowa, New York, Oklahoma, Tennessee and West Virginia. In KA and Maryland, corporations and unions are limited the same as individuals. In Kentucky, labor is limited like individuals. In Alabama, Indiana, Massachusetts, Mississippi, New York and Texas, limits on corporate and labor contributing vary. Corporations and unions are unlimited in Florida, Georgia, Idaho, Maine, Missouri, Nebraska and Nevada.

Key:
(a) There are 14 states that do not limit individual or PAC contributions to, or contributions from, the parties: Alabama, Illinois, Indiana, Iowa, New Mexico, North Carolina, North Dakota, Oregon, Pennsylvania, Tennessee, Texas, Utah and Virginia.

(b) Delaware, Vermont and Wyoming contributions are for a two-year cycle, and in Louisiana and Maryland, contributions are for a four-year period.

(c) California, Maryland, New York, South Carolina, Texas and Washington limit monetary contributions for election purposes, but not contributions to overhead expenses, therefore allowing unlimited contributions to the party administrative and housekeeping account.

(d) In Massachusetts, and Rhode Island, cash contributions are limited but in-kind contributions are not. Therefore, they are treated as if they permit unlimited party contributions.

(e) In Arizona and Nebraska, total is from political party and all political organizations combined.

national party issue advertising. Also on their minds in 36 states is a gubernatorial campaign with an underticket and state legislators to keep or challenge and the need to raise state money to pay for it all.

State Parties and State Money. What portion of the total receipts in a presidential election year is state money to be spent on state activities? Overall, just about one-half of the total funds came from state money in the years we studied. For the Republicans, the percent of the total raised for state activities was 51 percent in the presidential cycle of 1996 and 49 percent for the presidential cycle of 2000. For the Democrats, the corresponding percentages were 47 percent for 1996 and 53 percent for 2000.

In midterm election years, the percentage of the state share of the total budget is larger, as one might expect given the gubernatorial races. In 1998, the Republican state accounts claimed 55 percent of the total state and federal accounts and for the Democrats the percentage was 63. In summary, state party accounts amount to 50 to 60 percent of the total state spending, indicating robust state fundraising.

Table D summarizes the state party finances for the 30 state parties under study and the proportion of total funds from all sources raised by the state parties themselves in 1996, 1998 and 2000. How much of the total funds did the state parties raise themselves? The answer is: a very high proportion. In the presidential years of 1996 and 2000, the state parties provided an average 76 percent of the total funds raised from all sources. In the gubernatorial year of 1998, the state contribution of the total funds raised averaged 89 percent. Overall, in 1998, the state parties contributed 82 percent of the hard money, 60 percent of the soft money, and, of course, 100 percent of the state money. This picture is hardly one of state dependency on national party largesse.

In view of this evidence, it is clear that state parties have maintained their autonomy and will not be seriously impacted by the Bipartisan Campaign Reform Act of 2002 and its ban on soft money. LaRaja (2003, 132–149) however, has found a strong relationship between party strength and the amount of soft money a state party spends, suggesting that a reduction of soft money may decrease the levels of

Table D: Party Funds from All Sources and Percentage Raised from State Party (in thousands)

State party	Raised in 1995–96		Raised in 1997–98		Raised in 1999–2000	
	Total	% from state party	Total	% from state party	Total	% from state party
California						
Democrat	$31,730	73%	$35,864	81%	$42,674	66%
Republican	25,386	62	24,300	83	50,790	74
Colorado						
Democrat	7,729	61	1,248	96	2,527	85
Republican	6,312	72	1,816	96	4,328	77
Connecticut						
Democrat	3,727	64	4,400	80	3,369	98
Republican	3,124	97	3,964	85	4,308	92
Florida						
Democrat	22,993	74	16,515	95	59,267	63
Republican	31,920	93	41,697	95	77,995	75
Georgia						
Democrat	12,505	84	17,952	96	17,110	87
Republican	30,876	90	8,901	90	13,272	82
Illinois						
Democrat	15,593	76	19,231	82	31,677	71
Republican	17,222	84	14,706	92	34,291	80
Kansas						
Democrat	2,510	73	1,811	93	2,631	96
Republican	1,198	80	1,177	89	2,148	91
Minnesota						
Democrat	11,560	75	15,483	94	16,530	72
Republican	11,585	95	16,647	93	23,603	83
New Jersey						
Democrat	9,788	94	12,730	98	16,124	96
Republican	21,582	97	19,605	97	17,635	94
New York						
Democrat	15,435	98	21,077	66	43,597	58
Republican	27,141	97	49,467	91	31,358	86
Oregon						
Democrat	4,293	40	2,988	81	13,770	55
Republican	2,100	66	1,874	90	11,187	62
Pennsylvania						
Democrat	15,762	60	5,463	86	46,730	57
Republican	16,044	79	12,661	97	42,438	68
Ohio						
Democrat	17,173	67	11,749	81	24,811	56
Republican	24,405	81	17,273	92	38,678	74
Tennessee						
Democrat	4,992	48	4,115	89	6,705	49
Republican	8,583	74	6,267	86	7,865	68
Texas						
Democrat	11,840	67	12,267	73	14,999	70
Republican	9,438	72	10,321	94	12,350	77
Total	768,976					

Sources: Federal Election Commission and campaign finance reports filed with secretaries of state and elections divisions.

state party activity and weaken them. He further suggests that BCRA will diminish the incentives for levels of party to work together and reduce the efforts of state and local parties on behalf of the entire party ticket. Instead they will focus on the state elections (LaRaja, 2003, 101–120).

Of interest is the likely impact of the Levin Amendment which allows soft money to be raised in amounts of up to $10,000. In general, state parties will have to work harder to raise the party-building money and there will be less of it to spend. They will have to raise their own matching hard money, but they have proved they are capable of doing so, having raised well over 60 percent of it in presidential election years and 82 percent in midterm years. The fact that there will be less soft money to spend will mean that state parties may be able to better control their operations. There is disagreement over the percentage of soft money that was actually spent on issue ads, but researchers agree that issue ads have been problematic for both candidates and state parties. Several party executive directors said they were not dependent upon soft money. It is clear that state parties are not decomposing, nor have they become dependent upon the national parties. Instead, they have been adapting to technologically driven politics, providing crucial services and financial resources to candidates. They have maintained their autonomy as they have become more sophisticated and professionalized.

The Role of Parties in Governing

The governor is at one time the head of the party and the head of the government. His or her success as a party leader is vital to success in electoral coalition building as well as legislative coalition building (Morehouse 1998, ch.7). Governors of strong party states such as New York are endorsed in conventions and legislative party cohesion is traditionally strong. In some states where the party is weak or divided, governors face legislatures in which sit remnants of the factions that opposed them in primary contests. Thus the ability of governors to get legislative approval for their programs presented in the state of the state address depends on party leadership developed over time by coalition building (Ehrenhalt 1998).

Surprisingly, very few political scientists have studied the relationship between the political efforts of party leaders and gubernatorial candidates to capture the nomination and their success when in office in passing the party programs. The recent research by Wright, Osborn and Winburn (2004), draws on a new data set and investigates the degree of policy representation across the state legislatures and at the same time identifies the importance of parties as intermediary institutions linking mass preferences and the policy behavior of elected representatives. They find that the highest level of representation occurs in strong party chambers. This means that in most cases of strong representation, constituencies are connected to their legislator's voting by party affiliation. In those systems, more conservative districts elect Republicans and more liberal districts elect Democrats, and strong party voting is the norm in these chambers. The researchers also found that party competition within the legislature has a marked relationship with legislative partisanship. Party voting clearly is stronger in the chambers where the parties approach numerical parity and falls off greatly where one party dominates the chamber. This research provides confirmation of our hypotheses that party competition brings party cohesion which brings policy leadership.

The Governor's Program. The governors of all states go into office with platforms that are the work of the candidates and their parties. A platform reflects enough of the governor's major priorities that it can be used as a basis for his or her legislative program. Each year the governor presents a state of the state address to a joint gathering of both legislative houses outlining the substance of the program he or she wants passed for the session. The governor's budget message follows shortly thereafter and other special messages on high priority programs are given throughout the legislative session. Through the power of initiation alone the governor's influence over the legislature is substantial. The governor sets the agenda for public decision making and largely determines what the business of the legislature will be in any one session.

The Governor and the Legislature. The governor works closely with the legislative leaders in his or her party as well as the leaders of the opposition party in the legislature when they are in the majority. When the governor has a majority in the chamber, this party leadership includes the speaker of the house, the presiding officer of the senate, majority leaders and chairs of committees who support the governor's program and see that bills within it are guided through the legislature. Governors head the ticket on which legislators campaign for election, and legislators hope that the governor's coattails will help them win. In strong party states, many of those who attend the party nominating convention are state legislators as well as local party leaders who benefit from the governor's power and have a stake in the governor's success. If governors have a strong interest in party coalition building, they will involve themselves in legislative elections.

When the governor's statewide party is weak, the legislative party is usually weak as well, and the chief executive must bargain with the leaders of the opposition party to try to get a portion of the program passed. In this case governors make modest demands which do not adequately represent the party's voters.

Governors in over half the states have minority parties in the legislature, and their strategies in these situations are different. In a divided government, the governor lacks many of the advantages that accrue to a governor who is backed by a majority. The leaders are members of the opposition party and are in a position to control the legislative timetable and agenda. The ability of the governor to get his or her program passed under conditions of divided government depends on the strength of the statewide party as well as the cohesion of the legislative party. Opposition leaders will recognize more heed to compromise if the governor is politically strong and has widespread public support.

Party Voting on the Governor's Program. We tested the assertion that the influence of the governor over the legislative party is based on his or her political leadership within the electoral party, the party outside the legislature. Our test was performed on 10 states; five were primary-only states where the parties do not use any endorsement process in gubernatorial primary elections (California, Kansas, Oregon, Tennessee and Texas), and five were endorsing states (Colorado, Connecticut, Illinois, Minnesota and New York), where the possibility of a strong coalition exists because gubernatorial candidates are endorsed in a convention or party gathering and party cohesion is strong. We tested legislative roll-call voting on the governor's program bills for each of the 10 states. The strongest finding was that political party is highly correlated with support for the governors' programs in endorsing states (0.754) and is weakly correlated in primary-only states (0.192). This contrast was caused by the exceedingly high correlation between party and support in Connecticut, Minnesota and New York .These findings strongly confirm the hypotheses that legislators from strong party/endorsing states would be more supportive of the governor than legislators from weak party/primary only states. Support from the governors' parties is higher in endorsing than in primary-only states. In primary-only states, there is much less partisan loyalty, parties are weaker,

and gubernatorial candidates must build their own electoral and governing organizations (Morehouse and Jewell 2003, 190–192).

Conclusions

There have been numerous changes in state political parties in the last 30 years. The most obvious is the increase in the level of two-party competition, particularly in Southern states, where the Republican Party in recent years has been able to elect more governors and has succeeded in winning a much larger share of legislative seats and even, in a few states a legislative majority. We can now say that there are no longer any states where one party holds a monopoly of power. From 1960 through 2002 every state in the union had at least one Democratic governor and one Republican governor. The 1994 election brought about a sharp decline in Democratic control of governorships and legislatures in a number of states, although this is not necessarily the beginning of a trend. The growing party competitiveness in many states can be explained partly by the decline in traditional party loyalties and the willingness of more voters to split their tickets in national and state elections.

The character of state party organizations has changed in the last 30 years. Fewer party workers are motivated by the expectation of receiving tangible benefits, and more are driven by a commitment to policy issues and to the candidates who espouse these issues. New campaign technologies have made it possible for candidates to organize their own campaigns and become more independent of party organizations. But these technologies, and particularly television, have made campaigns more expensive.

These changes have made party organizations less powerful but have not necessarily made them less useful to candidates. State and local parties have become primarily service organizations, offering candidate assistance in financing and running their campaigns. State party organizations have been able to obtain funds from individuals and interest groups, from national parties and in some states from public financing. This has made it possible for them to maintain larger state offices and staffs and to offer valuable resources to their candidates. In many states the governor maintains control of the state party through the state chair and works to strengthen its effectiveness.

One important organizational trend has been the growth of state legislative campaign committees, usually run by legislative leaders, supplementing the campaign efforts of state and local parties. These committees provide financing and services to legislative candidates, particularly to those who are non-incumbents and those in close races. The parties increasingly use sophisticated techniques to target those races, particularly in legislative districts where there is a realistic chance of winning, and thus a good prospect for recruiting candidates. There has also been an increase in the practice of state parties working closely with interest groups and PACs to channel funds toward candidates in targeted districts.

One of the greatest challenges facing state parties is to recruit and nominate the strongest possible candidates for statewide and legislative office. The parties' efforts to affect the nominating process are handicapped by the large number of primaries that are open to all or most voters. Candidates who have little or no experience in, or obligation to, the party can often win nomination if they have the financial resources to run expensive media campaigns.

Some political parties continue to make preprimary endorsements, under state law or party rule, in an effort to influence the choice of nominees. This system works best where parties are relatively vigorous and are strongly committed to the endorsement system. One would think that some of the state parties that have been losing elections would at least explore the possibility of experimenting with the endorsement process, which works—however imperfectly—in a number of states.

Many state parties' organizations are becoming stronger, not weaker. They have become service parties to their candidates and began the process of fundraising well before the infusion of money from their national committees. In fact, party development within the state parties paralleled the resurgence of national party organizations. In our sample of 30 state parties, they contributed the bulk of hard, soft and state money raised within their borders in presidential and midterm elections.

The governor is the chief policy maker in the American states and his or her ability to provide political leadership affects the quality and distribution of resources. We have examined the governor's influence over the political party, both outside and within the legislature. The major theme has been that the coalitions formed by the governor to get the party nomination affect his or her ability to see the program through the legislature. A strong governor with an electoral coalition can get support for his or her policies. States are moving to address many of the social problems that exist in our society, such as the growing disparity between the poor and the wealthy, the shrinking middle class, the disconnect between

education skills and job opportunities, and the spector of a bankrupt Medicaid system. The ability of the governor and the party to provide the leadership for these extensive commitments is the key to the continuation of our federal system.

Many state political parties are becoming stronger, not weaker. They have adapted to the new technology, and provide valuable services to state and national candidates. Far from the predicted decline, state parties have become parties in service. They provide services such as polling, campaign seminars, advertising and fundraising. State parties maintained their autonomy as they became more professionalized and more durable.

At any given time, the working relationship between the national party and a particular state party will depend upon the ability of the two sets of leaders to overcome the differences that arise because the two parties have somewhat different priorities and needs and because some disagreements over financing are inevitable. In the long run the relations between the national and state parties seem certain to become closer.

References

Aldrich, John H. 2000. "Southern Parties in State and Nation." *Journal of Politics* 62:643–70.

Beyle, Thad L. 2004. "Governors: Elections, Campaign Costs, Profiles, Forced Exits and Powers." In *The Book of The States*, 36th ed., ed. Keon S. Chi. Lexington, KY: Council of State Governments.

Bibby, John F. and Thomas M. Holbrook. 2004. " Parties and Elections." In *Politics in the American States*, 8th ed., eds. Virginia Gray and Russell Hanson. Washington, D.C.:62–99.

Downs, Anthony. 1957. *An Economic Theory of Democracy*. Harper and Row.

Ehrenhalt, Alan. 1998. "It Pays to Know Where The Bodies are Buried." *Governing* 11(9):5–6.

Gierzynski, Anthony, and David A. Breaux. 1996. "Financing State Legislative Elections: The Role of Political Parties." Paper presented at the Annual Meeting of the Western Political Science Association.

Jewell, Malcolm E., and Sarah M. Morehouse.2001. *Political Parties and Elections in American States*. Washington, D.C.: C.Q. Press.

La Raja, Raymond J. 2003. "State Parties and Soft Money: How Much Party Building?" In *The State of the Parties*. 4th ed. eds. John C. Green and Rick Farmer. Lanham, MD: Rowman and Littlefield.

2003. "State Political Parties After BCRA." In *Life After Reform*. ed. Michael J. Malbin. Lanham, MD: Rowman and Littlefield.

Malbin, Michael J., and Thomas L. Gais. 1998. *The Day After Reform*. Albany: Rockefeller Institute Press.

Morehouse, Sarah M. 1998. *The Governor as Party Leader: Campaigning and Governing*. Ann Arbor: University of Michigan Press.

Morehouse, Sarah M. and Malcolm E. Jewell. 2003. *State Politics, Parties and Policy*. Lanham, MD: Rowman and Littlefield.

Ranney, Austin. 1976. "Parties in State Politics." In *Politics in the American States*, 3rd. ed., eds. Herbert Jacob and Kenneth N. Vines. Boston: Little Brown. Gerald Wright, Tracy Osborn and Jonathan Winburn. 2004. "Parties and Representation in the American Legislatures." Paper presented at the Annual Meeting of the Midwest Political Science Association.

About the Authors

Sarah M. Morehouse is professor emerita of Political Science at the University of Connecticut. She is the author of *The Governor as Party Leader* (1998) and co-author with Malcolm Jewell of *Political Parties and Elections in American States* (2001) and *State Politics, Parties and Policy* 2nd ed. (2003).

Malcolm E. Jewell is a retired political science professor at the University of Kentucky, where he specialized in state politics and legislatures. In addition to books coauthored with Sarah Morehouse, he is coauthor of two books on Kentucky politics and the Kentucky legislature, and a book on legislative leadership.

2004 Election Success and State Initiatives

By R. Doug Lewis

States are in danger of losing federal HAVA funds unless action is taken in 2005. Despite a successful election in 2004, several issues face states to assure voter satisfaction and service. If states fail to act, Congress may do so.

What a difference four years makes. It is amazing how perspective changes when an election is not close. While Election 2000 was not as bad as its characterization, Election 2004 was a dramatic improvement—but nonetheless it demonstrated areas of needed improvements. Those in the elections profession still are concerned about administrative challenges discovered in 2004. With more than 11 million additional voters and dramatic increases in voter registration, due to the efforts of the campaigns and scores of political activist organizations, the administrative process was strained even greater than in Election 2000.

Election resources were stretched thin in many places due to the largest turnout of voters in more than 40 years. How did states manage such spectacular increases (e.g., Ky. had a 16 percent increase in voters between the 2000 and 2004 elections; Minn.—14 percent; Mich. up 13 percent; Ohio—16 percent; Md.—15 percent and an astounding increase for Utah up 20 percent, New Mexico up 26 percent, and Fla. up 27 percent)?

One of the reasons the states and the local jurisdictions were able to handle this incredible increase in voters was due directly to the statewide planning process done by states to comply with the federal Help America Vote Act (HAVA).

Attention to problems found (in 2000 and before) were identified and addressed by state and local election officials. Developing discussions throughout each state, local jurisdictions were able to get the political support from local leaders to make improvements to their own processes without any significant influx of federal or state funds because monies from HAVA had not been distributed in time to have major impact in 2004. The stress of "getting it right" with the national awareness and four years of constant criticism of the process contributed to heightened attention to details for all concerned. However, there are things we probably can and should do better, with changes by legislators.

Federal Issues Loom Immediately: Failure to Act can be Expensive

Some feel the decisions ought to begin with Congress, but most of the nation's elections administrators believe the real solutions to the challenges are more likely to be the responsibility of individual states—if there are to be effective solutions.

First, there is the need of the states to meet requirements of HAVA. At this writing, seven states had not yet completed the details necessary to receive their FY 2003 funds: Alaska, Hawaii, Ill., N.Y., Okla., S.D. and Utah, while most states are preparing to receive their FY 2004 funds. Most are in process and should be done by the time this article appears, but South Dakota and New York have larger hurdles to conquer. South Dakota needs its legislature to provide the 5 percent matching funds to qualify for federal HAVA funds. New York is mired in conflict within its own legislature about major portions of necessary legislation to make its state compliant with HAVA.

The risk for these states is they are playing Russian roulette with the U.S. Congress, which is now indicating that any undistributed funds available at appropriation time in the fall of 2005 are likely to be taken back by Congress. States not fully funded and in compliance by about July 2005 are likely to lose federal matching funds and still be responsible for compliance with state funds. That includes about 20 states who have not yet complied to qualify for FY 2004 funds. Some states have enough money to partially qualify for matching funds for FY 2004, but if they do not fully qualify quickly, there is a very real possibility the federal government will force them to repay all the distributed funds . . . and still comply with state funds. The seriousness of this amounts to millions of dollars each for many states; N.Y. alone is risking a $156 million loss of federal funds and then a necessity of producing a like amount from the state to meet its compliance requirements rather than simply a 5 percent match that gets them the $156 million.

Election 2004 Issues:
States Must Address Action Quickly

Let's review concerns expressed by political groups and media about Election 2004. Editorial limitations prevent a discussion of all concerns policy makers have heard. Rather this article focuses on those appearing to have greatest needs for decisions.

Voting Equipment and Standard—The great debate that raged on the effectiveness and security of voting equipment, and especially electronic equipment, appears to have been somewhat overblown in predictions of rampant fraud or ultimate and dire massive failures. Neither happened. While there were some examples of voting equipment foul-ups, so far the problems seem to be more of human failures rather than machine failures; i.e., if humans had done what they were supposed to have done, the equipment would have rendered votes accurately. It is important to remember that those criticizing voting equipment often ignore the imperfection of paper ballots. There are imperfections in all voting processes and almost always because humans—voters, or poll workers, or technicians or election officials—make mistakes. The presumption that paper ballots are perfect, and that voting equipment is mistake prone, is an erroneous judgment.

As this is being written, it appears states must proceed with purchasing voting equipment without the benefit of having national standards for disability compliance or for security standards. HAVA requires states to purchase at least one voting device per polling site that allows persons with disabilities, especially the blind and visually impaired, to vote independently and privately. To meet the 2006 deadline in HAVA, states will need to proceed with a full court press in 2005 to identify and purchase systems.

Those who wait until the deadline looms stand to have delivery problems, training problems and potential election disasters in 2006 because units are too new to both election officials and voters. State leaders are urging congressional leaders to revamp deadline dates for HAVA compliance, but there is a genuine reluctance by some members of both political parties to reopen the HAVA legislation. Since no one can accurately predict what will happen to the legislation if it is opened, it appears unlikely as of this writing that there is sufficient political will to reopen the legislation and change deadlines. That leaves states faced with immediate action at the state level.

It appears that standards from the federal government (the Election Assistance Commission and the National Institute of Standards and Technology) will come too late to meet the HAVA deadlines. Even if they complete standards by mid year 2005, the lag time for vendors to design and produce units to meet new standards are likely to take an additional year beyond the final published standards. Additionally, government purchasing processes take long lead times.

Long lines at the polls seem to be one of the major concerns in 2004, and yet the choices available to fix the problem are rarely heeded. The principal solution for this is a recognition that the longer the ballot is in a presidential election year, the longer it takes voters to vote. Keeping initiatives, referendum, and state Constitutional amendments to a minimum in a presidential election year is certainly one key solution but one that is rarely acceptable to policy-makers.

The second part of the problem is recognition that more voting equipment is needed for the increased numbers of voters that appear in a presidential year. Most states and local jurisdictions do not provide sufficient quantities of voting equipment needed for an off-presidential year election, let alone one where more voters show up than have appeared in any election in 40 years.

This becomes a matter of the "public will" to do what is necessary: buy enough voting equipment to provide enough machines for the voters who showed up in Election 2004 and elections professionals can probably whip this issue for the foreseeable future. That means buying not just enough equipment for the voters, but enough spares to replace the units that malfunction during the election.

Blaming election officials for long lines is not going to fix this problem without initially solving the first two problems: limiting the ballot size and buying enough voting machines to do the job. Election officials cannot run to the nearest electronics store and buy extra voting machines on the spur of the moment. Despite the election administrators request for more equipment, that decision is usually made at least one to two years in advance and it is a decision made by budget and political authorities who are not election officials.

Immediate Policy Concerns of the States

What are systemic problems that face policy-makers immediately? The following must receive attention of each and every state:

Voter Registration Issues

Voter Registration Deadlines: States that have less than a 30-day cutoff for voter registration imperil the ability of the election official to assure the voter is on the roll and not disenfranchised. Well intentioned legislators who have provided for shorter cutoff periods trying to enfranchise more voters have actually forced the unintended consequence of almost assuring that the records are not accurate. Two, and probably only two solutions, are available in this regard: establish 30-day cutoff of registration, or have same day registration (which creates additional administrative problems and may prove difficult in states with huge population centers or where a history of voter fraud has occurred). Clearly too short a period works to the disadvantage and possible disenfranchisement of voters and to the integrity of the process.

Voter Registration Groups: The importance of groups dedicated to voter registration efforts is certainly welcome within our democracy. Their efforts reward the process with more Americans eligible to participate. However, Election 2004 proved conclusively there is a major problem where some voter groups, special interest groups and candidate organizations engage in voter registration drives and then burden the process because of innocent or intentional manipulation of the process. States need to quickly address legal changes for necessary training of "deputy or outside registrars" and must set deadlines for turning in the registrations immediately upon soliciting them from voters. Allegations of (1) "bogus registrations" or (2) where voter groups accept registrations but then only turn in the ones they think are for their candidates, must not be allowed to damage the fundamental faith of voters in the process. States need to force all organizations to receive official training by election officials. Concurrently, give election administrators the ability to stop efforts of groups or individuals who can't seem to follow law and procedures. Voter registration (VR) applications need to be turned in within 48 hours of being completed by the voter.

This process must be fair to both the voter and the official election administration. If the VR groups are allowed to sit on applications for weeks or months at a time, voters can not check to see if the organization actually turned it in. They burden the process by turning in applications on the last day or two before registration cutoff. There has to be accountability built into the VR process. A valid name, address and phone number or some form of identification of the solicitor of the VR application is necessary to improving this process. Continual process abusers need to be prohibited from engaging in VR drives. Thousands of voters thought they had registered

through one of these groups only to discover that their applications never arrived or arrived too late to get on the official rolls. What is the difference? The difference is whether the voter votes an actual ballot or a provisional ballot that may not be qualified in a later decision. That is a significant difference. States need to provide for effective enforcement perhaps by giving the chief election official of each state the ability to use internal legal staff to prosecute.

Absentee and Early Voting Issues

Policy-makers must allow enough time to end early voting with sufficient time for local election officials to produce official poll books to be distributed to polling sites showing voters who voted early. There can be disagreement on how much time is necessary, but most election officials would recommend no less than four full days prior to election day. The process of identifying early voters on rolls is paramount to correctly serving voters as well as preventing double voting.

Absentee ballot applications, likewise, need to have a prior cutoff date so the elections office can receive the application and have ability to return the ballot by mail to the absentee voter. A cutoff date is likely to require at least seven days prior to election. Allowing voters to request absentee ballots up to the day before election almost guarantees that large numbers in urban areas will be ill served: because they have requested an absentee ballot the election official almost always has to deny the opportunity to vote in person to avoid duplicate voting. That is not fair to the voter or the election process.

Absentee ballots tend to be paper based and the trend is growing for states to lessen the restrictions on why a voter can vote by absentee ballot. California allows any voter to register as a permanent absentee voter; Texas allows voters 65 and older to register as absentee voters. All states need to consider allowing election officials to open and process absentee ballots prior to election day. Examples of states allowing officials to open the ballots prior to election are: Ark., Calif., Iowa, Idaho, Kan., Mass., Mo., Ohio, Tenn., Texas and Utah. Among the states allowing them to count the ballots (but not reveal results) prior to election day: Calif., Fla., Kan., Mo. and Texas.

Provisional Voting

Policy-makers need to address the short term issues in provisional voting. Long term, the numbers of provisional voters is likely to decrease to a much smaller, more manageable number because statewide voter databases will do a better job of keeping up address changes and eliminate need for voters to request a provisional ballot. Michigan, even in 2004, with extraordinary numbers of voters going to the polls, found their provisional ballots were an exceedingly small part of their election because of effective use of the statewide voter database. But until statewide databases are created, debugged and functional, there is an interim problem.

Multiple lawsuits were filed in a variety of states to force states to count the provisional ballot regardless of whether the voter was in the right polling site. So far, all final adjudications of this have indicated state law prevails as called for in HAVA. But those suits did not settle the issue of what races should be counted whenever a provisional ballot is cast. Most states have indicated the voter must go to the proper polling site to have any of the voter's votes counted. Some states (e.g., N.Y., Wash., Calif.) allow the voter to have votes counted for any wide jurisdictional race such as presidential and other federal races, statewide races, and countywide races, regardless of whether the voter is in the correct polling site. States need to decide, on a state-by-state basis, what is appropriate and fair to the voter.

Additionally, states need to review policies on how long election administrators have to qualify provisional ballots. If the spirit of offering provisional ballots is to assure that voters have some method of fail safe when they are inadvertently left off the official rolls, then states need to determine if the spirit

of the law can be met by providing less than two weeks to check and qualify those ballots.

Poll watchers—A Continuing Source of Problems

It is time for states to revisit the whole concept of poll watchers—distinct from the concerns about official poll workers. Voters often confuse the actions of poll watchers as being an election official who is challenging them. Legislators need to review and define when and how election officials can regulate the poll watcher process.

These are not the only concerns but are the major policy issues for states immediately and failure to act this year may lead to congressional action instead. The nation's elections administrators meet during the first quarter of 2005 to draw up recommendations for states and Congress about the best solutions for the most vexing of systemic problems. The Election Center's National Task Force on Election Reform 2004 will publish their findings to help policy-makers at all levels find appropriate solutions.

About the Author

R. Doug Lewis, CERA (Certified Election/Registration Administrator), is executive director of The Election Center, a nonpartisan, nonprofit organization representing the nation's election officials. He has been called upon by Congress, the federal agencies, state legislatures, and national and worldwide news media for solutions to voting issues.

Table 6.1
STATE EXECUTIVE BRANCH OFFICIALS TO BE ELECTED: 2005–2009

State or other jurisdiction	2005	2006	2007	2008	2009
Alabama	…	G,LG,AG,AR,A,SS,T	…	…	…
Alaska (a)	…	G,LG	…	…	…
Arizona	…	G,AG,SS,SP,T,(b)	…	…	…
Arkansas	…	G,LG,AG,A,SS,T,(g)	…	…	…
California (c)(h)	…	G,LG,AG,SS,SP,T (c)(h)	…	…	…
Colorado	…	G,LG,AG,SS,T	…	…	…
Connecticut	…	G,LG,AG,C,SS,T	…	…	…
Delaware	…	AG,A,T	…	G, LG, (d)	…
Florida	…	G,LG,AG,AR,CFO	…	…	…
Georgia	…	G,LG,AG,AR,SS,SP (e)(f)	…	…	…
Hawaii	…	G,LG	…	…	…
Idaho	…	G,LG,AG,SS,SP,T,(h)	…	…	…
Illinois	…	G,LG,AG,C,SS,T	…	…	…
Indiana (k)	…	A,SS,T	…	G, LG, AG, SP	…
Iowa	…	G,LG,AG,AR,A,SS,T	…	…	…
Kansas	…	G,LG,AG,SS,T,(i)	G,LG,AG,AR,A,SS,T	…	…
Kentucky	…		G,LG,AG,AR,SS,T (j)	…	…
Louisiana	…	(j)		(j)	…
Maine (k)	…	G			…
Maryland	…	G,LG,AG,C			…
Massachusetts	…	G,LG,AG,A,SS,T	…	…	…
Michigan	…	G,LG,AG,SS (l)		(l)	…
Minnesota	…	G,LG,AG,A,SS			…
Mississippi	…		G,LG,AG,AR,A,SS,T (m)		…
Missouri	…	A		G,LG,AG,SS,T	…
Montana	…	G,LG,AG,SS,T	…	G,LG,AG,A,SS,SP	…
Nebraska	…	G,LG,AG,SS,T,(h)	…	…	…
Nevada	…	G	…	G	…
New Hampshire	G		…	G	…
New Jersey	G		…	…	G
New Mexico	…	G,LG,AG,A,SP,T,(o)	…	…	…
New York	…	G,LG,AG,C	…	…	…
North Carolina	…	SS,AG,AR,(q),(n)	…	G,LG,AG,AR,A,SS,SP,T, (p)	…
North Dakota	…	G,LG,A,AG,SS,T	…	G,LG,A,T,(q)	…
Ohio	…		…	…	…
Oklahoma	…	G,LG,AG,A,SP,T,(r)	…	…	…
Oregon	…	G,SP	…	AG,SS,T	…
Pennsylvania	…	G,LG	…	AG,A,T	…
Rhode Island	…	G,LG,AG,SS,T	…	…	…
South Carolina	…	G,LG,AG,AR,C,SS,SP,T,(s)	…	…	…

See footnotes at end of table.

STATE EXECUTIVE BRANCH OFFICIALS TO BE ELECTED: 2005–2009—Continued

State or other jurisdiction	2005	2006	2007	2008	2009
South Dakota	...	G,LG,AG,A,SS,T,(t)	...	(t)	...
Tennessee	...	G	...		...
Texas	...	G,LG,AG,AR,C,(u)	...	(u)	...
Utah	...		...	G,LG,AG,A,T	...
Vermont	...	G,LG,AG,A,SS,T	...	G,LG,AG,A,SS,T	...
Virginia	G,LG,AG				G,LG,AG
Washington	...		...	G,LG,AG,A,SS,SP,T (f)	...
West Virginia	SP	G,LG,AG,SS,T	...	G,AG,AR,A,SS,T	SP
Wisconsin	...	G,A,SS,SP,T	...		SP
Wyoming	...	G,LG	...		...
American Samoa	...		...	G, LG	...
U.S. Virgin Islands	...	G,LG	...		...
Totals for year					
Governor	2	37	3	12	2
Lieutenant Governor	1	31	3	10	1
Attorney General	1	30	3	10	1
Agriculture	0	7	3	2	0
Auditor	0	15	2	8	0
Chief Financial Officer	0	1	0	0	0
Comptroller	0	6	0	0	0
Secretary of State	0	26	3	7	0
Supt. of Public Inst. (v)	1	8	0	4	1
Treasurer	0	24	3	9	0

Sources: The Council of State Governments' survey, October 2004 and state election administration offices and web sites, January 2005.

Note: This table shows the executive branch officials up for election in a given year. Footnotes indicate other offices (e.g., commissioners of labor, insurance, public service, etc.) also up for election in a given year. The data contained in this table reflect information available at press time.

Key:

... —No regularly scheduled elections   G —Governor
LG—Lieutenant Governor   AG—Attorney General
AR—Agriculture   A—Auditor
C—Comptroller   CFO—Chief Financial Officer
SS —Secretary of State   SP—Superintendent of public instruction (v)
T —Treasurer

(a) Election of school boards established to maintain system of state dependent public school systems established in areas of the unorganized borough and military reservations not served by other public school systems.
(b) Corporation commissioners (5)–6 year terms, 2004–4 (one due to resignation), 2006–2.
(c) Insurance commissioner and Board of Equalization.
(d) Insurance Commissioner.
(e) Public service commissioners (5)–6 year terms, 2004–1, 2006–2, 2008–2. Commissioner of labor–4 year term, 2006.
(f) Insurance commissioner, commissioner of public lands.
(g) Land commissioner.
(h) Controller.(i) Commissioner of insurance–2006; Board of education members (10)–4 year terms, 2004–5, 2006–5, 2008–5.
(j) Commissioner of elections–4 year term, 2007; commissioner of insurance–4 year term, 2007; board of elementary and secondary education (8)–4 year terms, 2007–4; public service commissioners (5)–6 year terms, 2004–2, 2006–1, 2008–2.

(k) In Maine the legislature elects constitutional officers (AG,SS,T) in even-numbered years for 2 year terms; the auditor will be elected by the legislature in 2004 and will serve a 4 year term.
(l) Michigan State University trustees (8)–8 year terms, 2004–2, 2006–2, 2008–2, 2010–2; University of Michigan regents (8)–8 year terms, 2004–2, 2006–2, 2008–2; Wayne State University governors (8)–8 year terms, 2004–2, 2006–2, 2008–2; State Board of Education (8)–8 year terms, 2004–2, 2006–2, 2008–2.
(m) Commissioner of insurance, transportation commissioners (3), public service commissioners (3).
(n) Tax Commissioner.
(o) Commissioner of public lands–4 year term, 2006; board of education (10)–6 year terms, 2004–5, 2008–5; corporation commissioners (3)–6 year terms, 2004.
(p) Commissioner of labor; commissioner of insurance.
(q) Public Service Commissioner (3)–6 year terms, 2004–1, 2006–1, 2008–1.
(r) Corporation commissioner (3)–6 year terms; commissioner of insurance–4 year term; commissioner of labor–4 year term.
(s) Adjutant general–4 year term.
(t) Commissioner of school and public lands, 2006; public utility commissioners (3)–6 year terms, 2004–1, 2006–1, 2008–1.
(u) Commissioner of general land office–4 year term, 2006; railroad commissioners (3)–6 year terms, 2004–1, 2006–1, 2008–1; board of education (15)–4 year terms, 2004–8, 2006–7, 2008–8, 2010–7.
(v) Superintendent of public instruction or commissioner of education.
(w) All of the positions will appear next on the ballot in 2004. However, the positions of secretary of state, attorney general, commissioner of agriculture and tax commissioner will only be elected to terms of two years. They will again appear on the ballot in 2006 and be elected to terms of four years and every four years thereafter. This one time ballot change is to establish a new four-year cycle as approved by the voters of North Dakota in June 2000. The remaining positions will appear on the ballot in the same four-year-cycle as the governor and president of the United States.

Table 6.2
STATE LEGISLATURES: MEMBERS TO BE ELECTED, 2005–2009

State or other jurisdiction	Total legislators		2005		2006		2007		2008		2009	
	Senate	House/Assembly	Senate	House	Senate	House	Senate	House	Senate	House	Senate	House
Alabama	35	105	…	…	35	105	…	…	…	…	…	…
Alaska	20	40	…	…	…	40	…	…	10	40	…	…
Arizona	30	60	…	…	30	60	…	…	30	60	…	…
Arkansas	35	100	…	…	17	100	…	…	18	100	…	…
California	40	80	…	…	20	80	…	…	20	80	…	…
Colorado	35	65	…	…	17	65	…	…	18	65	…	…
Connecticut	36	151	…	…	36	151	…	…	36	151	…	…
Delaware	21	41	…	…	…	…	…	…	11	41	…	…
Florida	40	120	…	…	20	120	…	…	20	120	…	…
Georgia	56	180	…	…	56	180	…	…	56	180	…	…
Hawaii	25	51	…	…	13	51	…	…	12	51	…	…
Idaho	35	70	…	…	35	70	…	…	35	70	…	…
Illinois	59 (a)	118	…	…	(b)	118	…	…	(b)	118	…	…
Indiana	50	100	…	…	25	100	…	…	25	100	…	…
Iowa	50	100	…	…	25 (d)	100	…	…	25 (c)	100	…	…
Kansas	40	125	…	…	…	125	…	…	40	125	…	…
Kentucky	38	100	…	…	19	100	…	…	19	100	…	…
Louisiana	39	105	…	…	…	…	39	105	…	…	…	…
Maine	35	151	…	…	35	151	…	…	35	151	…	…
Maryland	47	141	…	…	47	141	…	…	…	…	…	…
Massachusetts	40	160	…	…	40	160	…	…	40	160	…	…
Michigan	38	110	…	…	38	110	…	…	…	110	…	…
Minnesota	67	134	…	…	67	134	…	…	…	134	…	…
Mississippi	52	122	…	…	…	…	52	122	…	…	…	…
Missouri	34	163	…	…	17	163	…	…	17	163	…	…
Montana	50	100	…	…	25	100	…	…	25	100	…	…
Nebraska	49	U	…	…	24	U	…	…	25	U	…	…
Nevada	21	42	…	…	11	42	…	…	10	42	…	…
New Hampshire	24	400	…	…	24	400	…	…	24	400	…	…
New Jersey	40	80	…	80	…	…	40	80	…	…	…	80
New Mexico	42	70	…	…	…	70	…	…	42	70	…	…
New York	62	150	…	…	62	150	…	…	62	150	…	…
North Carolina	50	120	…	…	50	120	…	…	50	120	…	…
North Dakota	47	94	…	…	24	48	…	…	23	46	…	…
Ohio	33	99	…	…	17	99	…	…	16	99	…	…
Oklahoma	48	101	…	…	24	101	…	…	24	101	…	…
Oregon	30	60	…	…	15	60	…	…	15	60	…	…
Pennsylvania	50	203	…	…	25	203	…	…	25	203	…	…
Rhode Island	38	75	…	…	38	75	…	…	38	75	…	…
South Carolina	46	124	…	…	38	124	…	…	46	124	…	…

See footnotes at end of table.

Table 6.2
STATE LEGISLATURES: MEMBERS TO BE ELECTED, 2005–2009

State or other jurisdiction	Total legislators		2005		2006		2007		2008		2009	
	Senate	House/Assembly	Senate	House	Senate	House	Senate	House	Senate	House	Senate	House
South Dakota	35	70	...	...	35	70	...	...	35	70	...	...
Tennessee	33	99	...	...	17	99	...	...	16	99	...	...
Texas	31	150	...	...	16	150	...	...	15	150	...	...
Utah	29	75	...	...	15	75	...	...	14	75	...	...
Vermont	30	150	...	...	30	150	...	...	30	150	...	...
Virginia	40	100	...	100	...	...	40	100	...	...	...	100
Washington	49	98	...	...	24	98	...	...	25	98	...	...
West Virginia	34	100	...	...	17	100	...	...	17	100	...	...
Wisconsin	33	99	...	...	17	99	...	...	16	99	...	...
Wyoming	30	60	...	...	15	60	...	...	15	60	...	...
American Samoa	18	20	...	...	(e)	20	...	...	(e)	20	...	...
U.S. Virgin Islands	15	U	...	...	15	U	...	...	15	U	...	...
Totals	2,004	5,431	0	180	1,144	4,978	171	407	1,089	4,730	0	180

Sources: The Council of State Governments' survey, October 2004 and state election web sites, January 2005.

Note: This table shows the number of legislative seats up for election in a given year. As a result of redistricting, states may adjust some elections. The data contained in this table reflect information available at press time. See the Chapter 3 table entitled, "The Legislators: Numbers, Terms, and Party Affiliations," for specific information on legislative terms.

Key:

... —No regularly scheduled elections

U—Unicameral legislature

(a) The entire Senate is up for election every 10 years, beginning in 1972. Senate districts are divided into three groups. One group of senators is elected for terms of four years, four years and two years; two years, four years and four years; four years, two years and four years.

b) After redistricting there will be a lottery for which districts in the Senate will receive the set of terms.

(c) Even-numbered Senate districts.

(d) Odd-numbered Senate districts.

(e) In American Samoa, Senators are not elected by popular vote. They are selected by county councils of chiefs.

Table 6.3
METHODS OF NOMINATING CANDIDATES FOR STATE OFFICES

State or other jurisdiction	Method(s) of nominating candidates
Alabama	Primary election; however, the state executive committee or other governing body of any political party may choose instead to hold a state convention for the purpose of nominating candidates.
Alaska	Primary election.
Arizona	Petition.
Arkansas	Primary election.
California	Primary election or independent nomination procedure.
Colorado	Assembly/primary. Political parties hold state assemblies to nominate candidates for the primary ballot. A candidate is placed on the ballot if he/she receives 30 percent of the vote or, after two ballots, is one of the two candidates receiving the highest number of votes. Candidates (including those from major political parties) can also petition their name on the ballot. Each party's gubernatorial candidate selects a lieutenant governor candidate after the primary election.
Connecticut	Convention/primary election. Major political parties hold state conventions (convening not earlier than the 68th day and closing not later than the 50th day before the date of the primary) for the purpose of endorsing candidates. If no one challenges the endorsed candidate, no primary election is held. However, if anyone (who received at least 15 percent of the delegate vote on any roll call at the convention) challenges the endorsed candidate, a primary election is held to determine the party nominee for the general election.
Delaware	Primary election for Democrats and Primary election and Convention for Republicans..
Florida	Primary election.
Georgia	Primary election/convention.
Hawaii	Primary election.
Idaho	Primary election. New parties nominate candidates for general election after qualifying for ballot status.
Illinois	Primary election.
Indiana	Primary election held for the nomination of candidates for governor and U.S. senator; state party conventions held for the nomination of candidates for other state offices.
Iowa	Primary election; however, if there are more than two candidates for any nomination and none receives at least 35 percent of the primary vote, the primary is deemed inconclusive and the nomination is made by the party convention. (Applicable only for recognized political parties.)
Kansas	Primary election. Minor party candidates are nominated at their respective state conventions Independent candidates are nominated by petition.
Kentucky	Primary election. A slate of candidates for governor and lieutenant governor that receives the highest number of its party's votes but which number is less than 40 percent of the votes cast for all slates of candidates of that party, shall be required to participate in a runoff primary with the slate of candidates of the same party receiving the second highest number of votes.
Louisiana	Primary election.
Maine	Primary election.
Maryland	Primary election. Petition only for unaffiliated or non-recognized parties in general elections only.
Massachusetts	Primary election.
Michigan	Primary election held for governor, state senate and state house. State convention held to nominate candidates for lieutenant governor, secretary of state and attorney general.
Minnesota	Primary election. Candidates for minor parties or independent candidates are by petition. They must have the signatures of 2,000 people who will be eligible to vote in the next general election.
Mississippi	Primary election.
Missouri	Primary election.
Montana	Primary election.
Nebraska	Primary election.
Nevada	Primary election. Independent candidates are nominated by petition for the general election. Minor parties nominated by petition or by party.
New Hampshire	Primary election.
New Jersey	Primary election. Independent candidates are nominated by petition for the general election.
New Mexico	Statewide candidates petition to go to convention and are nominated in a primary election. District and legislative candidate petition for primary ballot access.
New York	Primary election/petition.
North Carolina	Primary election. New parties by convention.
North Dakota	Convention/primary election. Political parties hold state conventions for the purpose of endorsing candidates. Endorsed candidates are automatically placed on the primary election ballot, but other candidates may also petition their name on the ballot.
Ohio	Primary election.
Oklahoma	Primary election.
Oregon	Primary election, convention and petition.
Pennsylvania	Primary election, and nomination papers for minor political parties and political bodies.
Rhode Island	Primary election.
South Carolina	Primary election for Republicans and Democrats; party conventions held for five minor parties. Candidates can have name on ballot via petition.

See footnotes at end of table.

METHODS OF NOMINATING CANDIDATES FOR STATE OFFICES — Continued

State or other jurisdiction	Method(s) of nominating candidates
South Dakota	Primary election. Any candidate who receives a plurality of the primary vote becomes the nominee; however, if no individual receives at least 35 percent of the vote for the candidacy for the offices of governor, U.S. senator, or U.S. congressman, a runoff election is held two weeks later. Lt. governor, attorney general, secretary of state, auditor, treasurer, school and public lands commissioner, and public utilities commissioner are nominated by party convention.
Tennessee	Primary election/petition.
Texas	Primary election/convention. Minor parties without ballot access nominate candidates for the general election after qualifying for ballot access by petition.
Utah	Convention, primary election and petition. Parties generally nominate their candidates in a convention. If one candidate does not get a certain percentage of delegate votes, the top two candidates go to a primary. Candidates not affiliated with a party can gain ballot access by petition.
Vermont	Primary election. Major parties that fail to nominate by primary election and minor parties can nominate by filing of a statement to nomination by the state party committee. Independents can be nominated by petition.
Virginia	Primary election.
Washington	Primary election; minor parties hold convention for nomination and qualify at primary election.
West Virginia	Primary election for major parties. Convention is held for official parties that received less than 10 percent of the last gubernatorial vote total. Minor parties and independent candidates nominated by petition.
Wisconsin	Primary election/petition.
Wyoming	Primary election.
Dist. of Columbia	Primary election. Independent and minor party candidates file by nominating petition.
American Samoa	Individual files petition for candidacy with the chief election officer. Petition must be signed by statutorily-mandated number of qualified voters.
U.S. Virgin Islands	Primary election.

Sources: The Council of State Governments' survey of state election administration offices, October 2004 and state election websites, January 2005.

Note: The nominating methods described here are for state offices; procedures may vary for local candidates. Also, independent candidates may have to petition for nomination. ..

Table 6.4
ELECTION DATES FOR NATIONAL, STATE AND LOCAL ELECTIONS
(Formulas and dates of state elections)

State or other jurisdiction	National (a)			State (b)			Local		
	Primary	Runoff	General	Primary	Runoff	General	Primary	Runoff	General
Alabama	June, 1st T June 3, 2008	…	Nov., ★ Nov. 4, 2008	June, 1st T June 6, 2006	June, Last T June 27, 2006	Nat. Nov. 7, 2006	V	V	V
Alaska	Aug., 4th T Aug. 26, 2008	…	Nov., ★ Nov. 4, 2008	Nat.	Aug. 22, 2006	Nat.	Nov. 7, 2006	…	V
Arizona	Feb., 4th T Feb. 26, 2008	…	Nov., ★ Nov. 4, 2008	8th T Prior Sept. 19, 2008	…	Nat. Nov. 7, 2006	Mar., 2nd T	May 3rd T	8 T prior to Nat. or Nat.
Arkansas	3 wks. Prior to Runoff May 20, 2008	June, 2nd T June 10, 2008	Nov., ★ Nov. 4, 2008	Nat.	Nat. May 16, 2006	Nat. June 6, 2006	Nat. Nov. 7, 2006	Nat.	Nat.
California	(l) June. 3, 2008	…	Nov., ★ Nov. 4, 2008	Mar. ★	…	Nat.	…	…	Nat.
Colorado	(l) (m) Date not set at press time.	…	Nov., ★ Nov. 4, 2008	Aug., 2nd T	…	Nat.	V Nov. 7, 2006	…	V
Connecticut	Aug. 2nd T Mar. 4, 2008	…	Nov., ★ Nov. 4, 2008	Aug. 2nd T	Aug. 2006	Nat.	56th day preceding elect. … Nov. 7, 2006	…	Nat. or May, 1st M (c)
Delaware	(l) Feb. 2008	…	Nov., ★ Nov. 4, 2008	Sept., 1st S After 1st M	…	Nat.	… Nov. 4, 2008	…	(d)
Florida	Mar., 2nd T Mar. 14, 2008	…	Nov., ★ Nov. 4, 2008	9th T Prior	Sept. 5, 2006	Nat.	State Nov. 7, 2006	…	Nat.
Georgia	July, 3rd T July 15, 2008	21 days AP Aug. 5, 2008	Nov., ★ Nov. 4, 2008	Nat. July 19, 2006	Nat. Aug. 8, 2006	Nat.	Nat.	Nat.	Nat.
Hawaii	(l) (m) Date not set at press time.	…	Nov., ★ Nov. 4, 2008	Sept., 2nd Last S	Sept. 23, 2006	Nat. Nov. 7, 2006	State Nov. 7, 2006	…	Nat.
Idaho	May, 4th T May 27, 2008	…	Nov., ★ Nov. 4, 2008	Nat.	May 23, 2006	Nat.	Nat. Nov. 7, 2006	…	Nat.
Illinois	Mar., 3rd T Mar. 18, 2008	…	Nov., ★ Nov. 4, 2008	Nat.	March 14, 2006	Nat.	… Nov. 7, 2006	…	…
Indiana	May, ★ May 6, 2008	…	Nov., ★ Nov. 4, 2008	Nat.	May 2, 2006	Nat.	Nat. Nov. 4, 2008	…	Nat.
Iowa	(k) Date not set at press time.	…	Nov., ★ Nov. 4, 2008	June, ★	June 6, 2006	Nat.	State Nov. 7, 2006	…	Nat.
Kansas	(l) (m) Date not set at press time.	…	Nov., ★ Nov. 4, 2008	Aug., 1st T (d)	Aug. 1, 2006	Nat. (d)	5 wks. Prior Nov. 7, 2006	…	April 1st T
Kentucky	May, 1st T after 4th M May 28, 2008	…	Nov., ★ Nov. 4, 2008	Nat.	35 days after P May 15, 2008	Nat. June 19, 2008	Nat. Nov. 6, 2007	…	Nat.
Louisiana (f)	(l) Mar. 9, 2008	…	Nov., ★ Nov. 4, 2008	(l) (p) Oct. 20, 2007	(l) (p) Date not set at press time.	(p)	V Nov. 17, 2007	…	V

See footnotes at end of table.

ELECTION DATES FOR NATIONAL, STATE AND LOCAL ELECTIONS – CONTINUED

State or other jurisdiction	National (a)			State (b)			Local		
	Primary	Runoff	General	Primary	Runoff	General	Primary	Runoff	General
Maine	(l) (m) Date not set at press time.	...	Nov., ★ Nov. 4, 2008	June, 2nd T June 13, 2006	...	Nat. Nov. 7, 2006	...	...	V
Maryland	Mar., 1st T Mar. 4, 2008	...	Nov., ★ Nov. 4, 2008	Nat.	... Mar. 7, 2006	Nat.	Nat. Nov. 7, 2006	...	Nat.
Massachusetts	(l) Date not set at press time.	...	Nov., ★ Nov. 4, 2008	7th T Prior	... Sept. 19, 2006	Nat.	V Nov. 7, 2006	...	V
Michigan	Feb., 4th T Feb. 26, 2008	...	Nov., ★ Nov. 4, 2008		Aug., ★ Aug. 8, 2008	...Nat.	V Nov. 7, 2006	...	V
Minnesota	(l) (m) Date not set at press time.	...	Nov., ★ Nov. 4, 2008	Sept., 1st T after 2nd M	... Sept. 12, 2006	Nat.	State (d) Nov. 7, 2006	...	Nat. (d)
Mississippi	June, 1st T (g) June 3, 2008	...	Nov., ★ Nov. 4, 2008	Aug., ★(e)	3rd T AP Aug. 8, 2006	Nat. (d) Aug. 29, 2006	May, 1st T (d) Nov. 7, 2006	2nd T AP	June, ★ (d)
Missouri	Feb., ★ Feb. 5, 2008	...	Nov., ★ Nov. 4, 2008	Aug., ★	... Aug. 5, 2008	Nat.	State Nov. 4, 2008	...	Nat.
Montana	June, ★ June 3, 2008	...	Nov., ★ Nov. 4, 2008	Nat.	... June 3, 2008	Nat.	Nat. Nov. 4, 2008	...	Nat.
Nebraska	May, 1st T After 2nd M May 13, 2008	...	Nov., ★ Nov. 4, 2008	Nat.	... May 9, 2006	Nat.	Nat. Nov. 7, 2006	...	Nat.
Nevada	Sept., 1st T Sept. 2, 2008	...	Nov., ★ Nov. 4, 2008	Nat.	... Sept. 5, 2006	Nat.	V Nov. 7, 2006	...	V
New Hampshire	Sept., 2nd T Sept. 9, 2008	...	Nov., ★ Nov. 4, 2008	Nat.	... Sept. 12, 2006	Nat.	V Nov. 7, 2006	...	Nat.
New Jersey	June, ★ June 3, 2008	...	Nov., ★ Nov. 4, 2008	June, ★	... June 7, 2005	Nat.	June, ★ June 8, 2005	...	Nat.
New Mexico	June, 1st T June 3, 2008	...	Nov., ★ Nov. 4, 2008	Nat.	... June 6, 2006	Nat.	Nat. Nov. 7, 2006	...	Nat.
New York	Mar., 1st T Mar. 4, 2008	...	Nov., ★ Nov. 4, 2008	Sept., ★	... Sept. 5, 2006	Nat.	State Nov. 7, 2006	Sept., 2 wks	Nat. AP (d)
North Carolina	May, ★ May 6, 2008	4 wks. AP June 3, 2008	Nov., ★ Nov. 4, 2008	Nat.	4 wks. AP May 6, 2008	Nat. (d) June 3, 2008	Nat. Nov. 4, 2008	Nat.	Nat.
North Dakota	(n) Date not set at press time.	...	Nov., ★ Nov. 4, 2008	June, 2nd T	... June 10, 2008	Nat.	... Nov. 4, 2008	...	June, 2nd T (e)
Ohio	Mar., ★ Mar. 4, 2008	...	Nov., ★ Nov. 4, 2008	Nat.	... Mar. 7, 2006	Nat.	Nat. (d) Nov. 7, 2006	...	Nat. (d)
Oklahoma	July, last T (h)	...	Nov., ★ Nov. 4, 2008	Nat.	Aug., 4th T July 25, 2006	Nat. Aug. 22, 2006	Nat. Nov. 7, 2006	...	Nat.

See footnotes at end of table.

ELECTION DATES FOR NATIONAL, STATE AND LOCAL ELECTIONS – CONTINUED

State or other jurisdiction	National (a) Primary	National (a) Runoff	National (a) General	State (b) Primary	State (b) Runoff	State (b) General	Local Primary	Local Runoff	Local General
Oregon	May, 3rd T / May 20, 2008	...	Nov., ★ / Nov. 4, 2008	Nat.	...	Nat.	Nat. / Nov. 7, 2006	...	Nat.
Pennsylvania	April, 4th T / Apr. 22, 2008	...	Nov., ★ / Nov. 4, 2008	Nat.	May 8, 2006	Nat.	Nat. / Nov. 7, 2006	...	Nat.
Rhode Island	(l) / Date not set at press time.	...	Nov., ★ / Nov. 4, 2008	Sept., 2nd T after 1st M	Apr. 25, 2006	Nat.	State / Nov. 7, 2006	...	Nat.
South Carolina	(l) / June 1, 2008	2nd T AP / June 17, 2008	Nov., ★ / Nov. 4, 2008	June, 2nd T	Sept. 12, 2006	Nat. / June 27, 2006	State (d) / Nov. 7, 2006	State	Nat. (d)
South Dakota	June, 1st T / June 3, 2008	...	Nov., ★ / Nov. 4, 2008	Nat.	2nd T AP / June 13, 2006	Nat. / June 13, 2006	State / Nov. 7, 2006	...	Nat.
Tennessee	Feb., 2nd T / Feb. 12, 2008	...	Nov., ★ / Nov. 4, 2008	Aug., 1st T★ / Aug. 3, 2006	Nat. / June 6, 2006	Nat. / Nov. 7, 2006	Feb., 2nd T / May, 1st T	...	Aug 1st T★
Texas	Mar., 2nd T / Mar. 11, 2008	Apr., 2nd T / Apr. 8, 2008	Nov., ★ / Nov. 4, 2008	Nat.	Nat. / Mar. 7, 2006	Nat. / Apr. 11, 2006	Nat. / Nov. 7, 2006	Nat.	Nat.
Utah	(l) (m)	...	Nov., ★ / Nov. 4, 2008	June, 4th T	...	Nat.	State / Nov. 4, 2008	...	Nat.
Vermont (i)	(l) / Date not set at press time.	...	Nov., ★ / Nov. 4, 2008	Sept., 2nd T / Sept. 12, 2006	... / June 24, 2008	Nat. / Nov. 7, 2006	...	...	March, 1st T
Virginia	(l) / Date not set at press time.	...	Nov., ★ / Nov. 4, 2008	June, 2nd T	...	Nat.	State or Feb., last T / Nov. 8, 2005	...	Nat. or May, 1st T
Washington	(l) (m)	...	Nov., ★ / Nov. 4, 2008	Sept., 3rd T (o)	June 14, 2005	Nat.	State / Nov. 4, 2008	...	Nat.
West Virginia	May, 2nd T / May 13, 2008	...	Nov., ★ / Nov. 4, 2008	Nat.	... / Sept. 16, 2008	Nat.	Nat. / Nov. 4, 2008	...	Nat.
Wisconsin	Sept., 2nd T / Sept. 9, 2008	...	Nov., ★ / Nov. 4, 2008	Nat.	... / May 13, 2008	Nat.	Nat. / Nov. 7, 2006	...	Nat.
Wyoming	(l) (m)	...	Nov., ★ / Nov. 4, 2008	Aug., 1st T after 3rd M	... / Sept. 12, 2006	Nat.	State / Nov. 7, 2006	...	Nat.
Dist. of Columbia	(l) / Date not set at press time.	...	Nov., ★ / Nov. 4, 2008	...	Aug. 22, 2006	...	Sept, 1st T after 2nd M	...	Nov., ★
American Samoa	(j)	14 days after gen. / Nov. 21, 2008	Nov., / Nov. 4, 2008	(j)	14 days after gen.	Nov., ★ / Nov. 18, 2008	(j) / Nov. 4, 2008	...	(o)
U.S. Virgin Islands	...	...		Sept., 2nd S / Sept. 13, 2008	14 day AP / Sept. 27, 2008	Nov. 1st T / Nov. 4, 2008	Sept., 2nd S	14 days AP	Nov., 1st T

See footnotes at end of table.

ELECTION DATES FOR NATIONAL, STATE AND LOCAL ELECTIONS — Continued

Sources: The Council of State Governments' survey of state election offices, October 2004 and state web sites, February 2005.

Note: This table describes the basic formulas for determining when national, state and local elections will be held. For specific information on a particular state, the reader is advised to contact the specific state election administration office. All dates provided are based on the state election formula.

Key:

★—First Tuesday after first Monday.

. . .—No provision.

M—Monday.

T—Tuesday.

TH—Thursday.

S—Saturday.

Nat.—Same date as national elections.

State—Same date as state elections.

Prior—Prior to general election.

AP—After primary.

V—Varies.

(a) National refers to presidential elections.

(b) State refers to election in which a state executive official or U.S. senator is to be elected. See Table 6.2, State Officials to be Elected.

(c) Unless that date conflicts with Passover, then 1st Tuesday following last day of Passover.

(d) In Delaware, elections are determined by city charter. In Iowa, partisan election only. In Kansas, state and county elections. In Minnesota, county elections only. In Mississippi, state and county elections are held together; municipal elections are held in separate years. In Montana, municipalities only. In New York, runoff in New York City only. In Ohio, municipalities and towns in odd years and counties in even years. In South Carolina, school boards vary.

(e) Cities only.

(f) Louisiana has an open primary which requires all candidates, regardless of party affiliation, to appear on a single ballot. If a candidate receives over 50 percent of the vote in the primary, that candi-

date is elected to the office. If no candidate receives a majority vote, then a single election is held between the two candidates receiving the most votes. For national elections, the first vote is held on the first Saturday in October of even-numbered years with the general election held on the first Tuesday after the first Monday in November. For state elections, the election is held on the second to last Saturday in October with the runoff being held on the fourth Saturday after first election. Local elections vary depending on the location and the year.

(g) Except in presidential election year when congressional races correspond to Super Tuesday.

(h) The primary election is held on the 4th Tuesday in August in each even-numbered year, including presidential election years. The presidential preferential primary is held on the 1st Tuesday in February during presidential election years.

(i) In Vermont, if there is a tie in a primary or general election (and a recount does not resolve the tie) the appropriate superior could order a recessed election, among the tied candidates only, within three weeks of the recount. In state primary runoffs, the runoff election must be proclaimed within seven days after primary; after proclamation, election is held 15-22 days later. Local elections are held by annual town meetings which may vary depending on town charter.

(j) American Samoa does not conduct primary elections (In addition, elections are conducted for territory-wide offices. There are no local elections).

(k) Eight days before any other nomination process.

(l) Formula not available at press time.

(m) State did not hold a presidential primary in 2004.

(n) On one designated day, following presidential nominating contests in the states of Iowa and New Hampshire and prior to the first Wednesday in March in every presidential election year, every political party entitled to a separate column may conduct a presidential preference caucus. Before August 15 of the odd-numbered year immediately preceding the presidential election year, the secretary of state shall designate the day after consulting with and taking recommendations from the two political parties casting the greatest vote for president of the United States at the most recent general elections when the office of president appeared on the ballot.

(o) Must be held on the third Tuesday of the preceding September or on the seventh Tuesday immediately preceding such general election, whichever occurs first.

(p) In Louisiana, a Congressional primary election is not held.

Table 6.5
POLLING HOURS: GENERAL ELECTIONS

State or other jurisdiction	Polls open	Polls close	Notes on hours (a)
Alabama	No later than 8 a.m.	Between 6 and 8 p.m.	
Alaska	7 a.m.	8 p.m.	
Arizona	6 a.m.	7 p.m.	
Arkansas	7:30 a.m.	7:30 p.m.	
California	7 a.m.	8 p.m.	
Colorado	7 a.m.	7 p.m.	
Connecticut	6 a.m.	8 p.m.	
Delaware	7 a.m.	8 p.m.	
Florida	7 a.m.	7 p.m.	
Georgia	7 a.m.	7 p.m.	
Hawaii	7 a.m.	6 p.m.	
Idaho	8 a.m.	8 p.m.	Clerks have the option of opening polls at 7 a.m. Idaho is in two time zones—MST and PST.
Illinois	6 a.m.	7 p.m.	
Indiana	6 a.m.	6 p.m.	
Iowa	7 a.m.	9 p.m.	
Kansas	7 a.m.	7 p.m.	Counties may choose to open polls as early as 6 a.m. and close as late as 8 p.m.
Kentucky	6 a.m.	6 p.m.	
Louisiana	6 a.m.	8 p.m.	
Maine	Between 6 and 10 a.m.	8 p.m.	Applicable opening time depends on variables related to the size of the precinct.
Maryland	7 a.m.	8 p.m.	
Massachusetts	No later than 7 a.m.	8 p.m.	
Michigan	7 a.m.	8 p.m.	
Minnesota	7 a.m.	8 p.m.	Towns outside of the twin cities metro area with less than 500 inhabitants may have a later time for the polls to open as long as it is not later than 10 a.m.
Mississippi	7 a.m.	7 p.m.	
Missouri	6 a.m.	7 p.m.	
Montana	7 a.m.	8 p.m.	Polling places with fewer than 200 electors may open at noon.
Nebraska	7 a.m MST/8 a.m. CST	7 p.m. MST/8 p.m. CST	
Nevada	7 a.m.	7 p.m.	
New Hampshire	No later than 11 a.m.	No earlier than 7 p.m.	Polling hours vary from town to town. The hours of 11 a.m. to 7 p.m. are by statute.
New Jersey	6 a.m.	8 p.m.	
New Mexico	7 a.m.	7 p.m.	
New York	6 a.m.	9 p.m.	
North Carolina	6:30 a.m.	7:30 p.m.	
North Dakota	Between 7 and 9 a.m.	Between 7 and 9 p.m.	Counties must have polls open by 9 a.m., but can choose to open as early as 7 a.m. Polls must remain open until 7 p.m., but can be open as late as 9 p.m. The majority of polls in the state are open from 8 a.m. to 7 p.m. in their respective time zones (CST and MST).
Ohio	6:30 a.m.	7:30 p.m.	
Oklahoma	7 a.m.	7 p.m.	
Oregon	7 a.m.	8 p.m.	
Pennsylvania	7 a.m.	8 p.m.	
Rhode Island	7 a.m.	9 p.m.	
South Carolina	7 a.m.	7 p.m.	
South Dakota	7 a.m.	7 p.m.	
Tennessee	8 a.m.	7 p.m. CST/ 8 p.m. EST	Poll hours are set by each county election commission. Polling places shall be open a minimum of 10 hours but no more than 13 hours. All polling locations in the eastern time zone shall close at 8 p.m. and those in the central time zone shall close at 7 p.m.
Texas	7 a.m.	7 p.m.	
Utah	7 a.m.	8 p.m.	
Vermont	Between 5 and 10 a.m.	7 p.m.	The opening time for polls is set to by local boards of civil authority.
Virginia	6 a.m.	7 p.m.	
Washington	7 a.m.	8 p.m.	
West Virginia	6:30 a.m.	7:30 p.m.	
Wisconsin	7 a.m.	8 p.m.	Polls in fourth class cities, villages and towns open at 9 a.m.; extendable by the governing body to no earlier than 7 a.m.
Wyoming	7 a.m.	7 p.m.	
Dist. of Columbia	7 a.m.	8 p.m.	
Guam	8 a.m.	8 p.m.	
U.S. Virgin Islands	7 a.m.	7 p.m.	

Sources: The Council of State Governments survey, October 2003 and state election Web sites, January 2005.

Note: Hours for primary, municipal and special elections may differ from those noted.

(a) In all states, voters standing in line when the polls close are allowed to vote; however, provisions for handling those voters vary across jurisdictions.

Table 6.6
VOTER REGISTRATION INFORMATION

State or other jurisdiction	Closing date for registration before general election (days)	Persons eligible for absentee registration (a)	Cut-off for receiving absentee ballots	Absentee votes signed by witness or notary	Residency requirements	Registration in other places	Criminal status	Mental competency
Alabama	10	M/O	Close of polls	N or 2W	S, C (m)	. . .	★	★
Alaska	30	A	10 days after election	N or 2W	. . .	★	★	★
Arizona	29	A	7 p.m. Election Day	. . .	S, C, 29	. . .	★	★
Arkansas	30	A	7:30 p.m. Election Day	. . .	(n)	★	★	. . .
California	15	A	8 p.m. Election Day	. . .	S	. . .	★	★
Colorado	29	A	7 p.m. Election Day	. . .	S, 30	. . .	★	. . .
Connecticut	14	A	8 p.m. Election Day	. . .	S, T	. . .	★	. . .
Delaware	20	A	12 p.m. day before election	N or W	S (o)	. . .	★	★
Florida	29	A	7 p.m. Election Day	W	S, C	. . .	★	★
Georgia	(b)	A	Close of polls	W (x)	S, C	. . .	★	★
Hawaii	30	A	Close of polls	W (x)	S	. . .	★	★
Idaho	25	A	8 p.m. Election Day	. . .	S, C, 30	. . .	★	. . .
Illinois	28	M/O	Close of polls	. . .	S, P, 30	★	★	. . .
Indiana	29	C, D, E, M/O, O, P, T	Close of polls	. . .	S, P, 30	. . .	★	. . .
Iowa	10 (c)	A	Close of polls	. . .	S	★	★	★
Kansas	15	A	Close of polls	. . .	S	★	★	★
Kentucky	29	A	Close of polls	. . .	S, C, 28	★	★	★
Louisiana	30	A	12 a.m. day before election	N or 2W	S	. . .	★	★
Maine	Election day	A	Close of polls	N or 2W	S, M	. . .	. . .	★
Maryland	21	A	Friday after election	. . .	S, C	. . .	★	★
Massachusetts	20	A	10 days after election	. . .	S	. . .	★	★
Michigan	30	A	8 p.m. Election Day	W (x)	S, T, 30 (p)	. . .	★	. . .
Minnesota	Election day (d)	A	Election Day	N or W	S, 20	. . .	★	★
Mississippi	30	A	5 p.m. day before election	W	S, C, 30	. . .	★	★
Missouri	28	A	Close of polls	N	S	. . .	★	★
Montana	30	A	Close of polls	. . .	S, C, 30	. . .	★	★
Nebraska	(f)	A	10 a.m. 2 days after election	W	S	. . .	★	★
Nevada	(k)	M/O	Close of polls	. . .	S, C, 30; P, 10 (t)	. . .	★	★
New Hampshire	Election day (d)	B, D, E, R, S, T	5 p.m. day after election	. . .	S (w)	. . .	★	. . .
New Jersey	29	A	8 p.m. Election Day	W or N	S, C, 30 (q)	. . .	★	. . .
New Mexico	28	T	7 p.m. Election Day	. . .	S	. . .	★	★
New York	25	A	Postmarked day before election	W (x)	S, C, 30 (r)	★	★	★
North Carolina	25	A	5 p.m. day before election	2W	S, C,30	★	★	. . .
North Dakota	(e)	(e)	2 days after election	W (x)	(e)	(e)	(e)	(e)
Ohio	30	A	Close of polls	. . .	S, 30	. . .	★	★
Oklahoma	25	A	7 p.m. Election Day	N or W	S	. . .	★	★
Oregon	21	A	8 p.m. Election Day	. . .	S	. . .	★	. . .
Pennsylvania	30	B, D, M/O, O, P, R, S, T	5 p.m. Friday before election	W (x)	S, P, 30	. . .	★	. . .
Rhode Island	30	D	9 p.m. Election Day	N or 2W	S, 30	. . .	★	★
South Carolina	30	B, C, D, S (i)	Close of polls	W	S (v)	. . .	★	★
South Dakota	15	A	Close of polls	. . .	S	. . .	★	★
Tennessee	30	A	Close of polls	W (x)	S	. . .	★	★
Texas	30	A	Before close of polls	(y)	S, C	. . .	★	★
Utah	20	(g)	12 p.m. Monday after election	W (x)	S, 30	. . .	★	★
Vermont	(l)	(h)	Close of polls	. . .	S	. . .	. . .	. . .
Virginia	29	(j)	Close of polls	W	S, P	. . .	★	★
Washington	15 (c)	M/O	10 days after election	. . .	S, C, P, 30	. . .	★	★
West Virginia	20	A	Close of polls	. . .	S	. . .	★	★
Wisconsin	Election day (c)(u)	A	Close of polls	W	S, 10	. . .	★	★
Wyoming	Election day (d)	A	7 p.m. Election Day	. . .	S (s)	. . .	★	★
Dist. of Columbia	30	A	10 days after election	. . .	D, 30	★	★	★
American Samoa	30	M/O	N.A.	N.A.	N.A.	N.A.	N.A.	N.A.
Guam	10	A	N.A.	N.A.	N.A.	N.A.	N.A.	N.A.
Puerto Rico	50	A	N.A.	N.A.	N.A.	N.A.	N.A.	N.A.
U.S. Virgin Islands	30	M/O	N.A.	N.A.	N.A.	N.A.	N.A.	N.A.

See footnotes at end of table.

VOTER REGISTRATION INFORMATION — Continued

Sources: Federal Election Commission, http://www.fec.gov., December 2003 and Election Assistance Commission, March 2004

Key:

★—Column 6: State provision prohibiting registration or claiming the right to vote in another state or jurisdiction. Columns 7 and 8: State provision regarding criminal status or mental competency.

. . .—No state provision.

N.A.—Information not available.

Column 4: N—Notary, W—Witness. Numbers indicated the number of signatures required. Column 5: S—State, C—County, D—District, M—Municipality, P—Precinct, T—Town. Numbers represent the number of days before an election for which one must be a resident.

Note: Previous editions of this chart contained a column for Automatic cancellation of registration for failure to vote for ___ years. However, the National Voter Registration Act requires a confirmation notice prior to any cancellation and thus effectively bans any automatic cancellation of voter registration. In addition, all states and territories except Puerto Rico and the U.S. Virgin Islands allow mail-in registration.

(a) In this column: A—All of these; B—Absent on business; C—Senior citizen; D—Disabled persons; E—Not absent, but prevented by employment from registering; M/O—No absentee registration except military and oversees citizens as required by federal law; O—Out of state; P—Out of precinct (or municipality in PA); R—Absent for religious reasons; S—Students; T—Temporarily out of jurisdiction.

(b) The 5th Monday before a general primary, general election, or presidential preference primary; the 5th day after the date of the call for all other special primaries and special elections.

(c) By mail: Iowa 15 days; Washington 30 days; Wisconsin, 13 days.

(d) Minnesota—delivered 21 days before an election or election-day registration at polling precincts; New Hampshire– Received by city or town clerk 10 days before election or election-day registration at precincts; Wyoming– delivered 30 days before or election-day registration at polling precincts.

(e) No voter registration.

(f) Received by the 2nd Friday before election or postmarked by the 3rd Friday before the election.

(g) There are several criteria including religious reasons, disabled, etc., or if the voter otherwise expects to be absent from the precinct on election day.

(h) Anyone unable to register in person.

(i) In South Carolina, all the following are eligible for absentee registra-tion in addition to those categories already listed: electors with a death in the family within 3 days before the election; overseas military, Red Cross, U.S.O. government employees, and their dependents and spouses residing with them; persons on vacation; persons admitted to the hospital as emergency patients 4 days prior to election; persons confined to jail or pre-trial facility pending disposition of arrest/trial; and persons attending sick/disabled persons.

(j) In Virginia, the following temporarily out of jurisdiction persons are eligible for absentee registration: (1)uniformed services voters on active duty, merchant marine, and persons temporarily residing overseas by virtue of employment (and spouse/dependents of these persons residing with them), who are not normally absent from their locality, or have been absent and returned to reside within 28 days prior to an election, may register in person up to and including the day of the election; (2) members of uniformed services discharged from active duty during 60 days preceding election (and spouse/dependents) may register, if otherwise qualified, in person up to and including the day of the election.

(k) By 9 p.m. on the 5th Saturday preceding any primary or general election.

(l) Postmarked, submitted or accepted by noon on the 2nd Saturday before an election

(m) At the time of registration.

(n) Must live in Arkansas at the address in Box 2 of your voter application.

(o) Must be a permanent state resident.

(p) Must be a resident of the town or city at least 30 days before election day.

(q) Must be a resident of the state and county at your address for 30 days before election.

(r) Must be a resident of the county or the City of New York at least 30 days before election.

(s) Must be an actual and physically bona fide resident.

(t) Must have continuously resided in the state and county at least 30 days and in precinct at least 10 days before election. Must claim no other place as legal residence.

(u) Registration may be completed in the local voter registration office 1 day before the election.

(v) Must claim the address on the application as your only legal place of residence.

(w) Must have a permanent established domicile in the state.

(x) Only if assisted by another party

(y) If unable to sign.

Table 6.7
VOTING STATISTICS FOR GUBERNATORIAL ELECTIONS BY REGION: 2001–2004

State	Date of last election	Primary Republican	Primary Democrat	Primary Independent	Primary Other	Primary Total votes	General Republican	Percent	General Democrat	Percent	General Independent	Percent	General Other	Percent	General Total votes
Eastern Region															
Connecticut	2002	21,670	31,799	(b)	0	53,459	573,958	56.0%	448,984	44.0%	0	0.0%	0	0.0%	1,022,942
Delaware	2004	78,783	71,735 (d)	0	1,613	152,131	Results not available before this publication						46,903	9.3	505,190
Maine	2002	227,960 (d)	746,190	0	2,752	976,902	209,496	41.5	238,179	47.1	10,612	2.1	100,875	4.6	2,194,179
Massachusetts	2002	155,952	69,965	0	0	225,917	1,091,988	49.8	985,981	44.9	15,335	0.7	13,028	2.9	441,968
New Hampshire	2002	336,948	262,086	0	0	599,034	259,663	58.8	169,277	38.3	0	0.0	42,138	1.9	2,227,165
New Jersey	2001	20,936	633,078	18,598	0	672,612	928,174	41.7	1,256,853	56.4	0	0.0	128,743	2.8	4,579,078
New York (c)	2002	538,757 (d)	1,242,236	0	0	1,780,993	2,262,255	49.4	1,534,064	33.5	654,016	14.3	79,346	2.2	3,581,989
Pennsylvania	2002	26,824	122,535	0	399	149,758	1,589,408	44.4	1,913,235	53.4	0	0.0	0	0.0	332,056
Rhode Island	2002	27,462	31,143	0	2,171	60,776	181,827	54.8	150,229	45.2	22,922	10.1	3,446	1.5	227,369
Vermont	2002						103,436	45.5	97,565	42.9					
Regional total		1,435,292	3,210,767	18,598	6,935	4,671,582	7,200,205	47.6	6,794,367	44.9	702,885	4.6	414,479	2.7	15,111,936
Midwestern Region															
Illinois	2002	917,759	1,252,516	0	0	2,170,275	1,594,960	45.1	1,847,040	52.2	23,089	0.7	73,794	2.1	3,538,883
Indiana	2004	505,758	283,924	0	0	789,682	1,302,912	53.2	1,113,900	45.4	0	0.0	31,684	1.3	2,448,496
Iowa	2002	199,234	80,443 (d)	0	399	280,076	456,612	44.5	540,449	52.7	0	0.0	28,741	2.8	1,025,802
Kansas	2002	296,094	87,850 (d)	0	0	383,944	376,830	45.1	441,858	52.9	0	0.0	17,004	2.0	835,692
Michigan	2002	583,391	1,046,680	0	46,269	1,630,071	1,506,104	47.4	1,633,796	51.4	0	0.0	37,665	1.2	3,177,565
Minnesota	2002	195,099	224,238	0	36	465,606	999,473	44.4	821,268	36.5	9,698	0.4	422,034	18.7	2,252,473
Nebraska	2004	147,718	61,312	0	0	209,066	330,349	68.7	132,348	27.5	0	0.0	18,294	3.8	480,991
North Dakota	2004	42,135	35,597	0	0	77,732	220,803	71.3	84,877	27.4	4,193	1.3	0	0.0	309,873
Ohio	2002	658,700 (d)	585,615 (d)	0	121,438	1,365,753	1,865,007	57.7	1,236,924	38.3	0	0.0	127,061	4.0	3,228,992
South Dakota	2002	111,264	68,037	0	0	179,301	189,920	56.8	140,263	41.9	2,393	0.7	1,983	0.6	334,559
Wisconsin	2002	803,439	230,232	741	18,831	1,053,243	734,779	41.4	800,515	45.2	10,489	0.5	229,566	12.9	1,775,349
Regional total		4,460,591	3,788,151	741	186,973	8,604,749	9,577,749	49.3	8,793,238	45.3	49,862	0.2	987,826	5.0	19,408,675
Southern Region															
Alabama	2002	357,497	435,310	0	0	792,807	672,225	49.2	669,105	48.9	0	0.0	25,723	1.9	1,367,053
Arkansas	2002	92,237	279,097	0	0	371,334	427,082	53.0	378,250	46.9	0	0.0	210	0.0	805,542
Florida	2002	(d)	1,357,381	0	0	1,357,381	2,856,845	56.0	2,201,427	43.2	0	0.0	42,309	0.8	5,100,581
Georgia	2002	511,249	434,893 (d)	0	0	946,142	1,041,700	51.4	937,070	46.2	0	0.0	47,123	2.4	2,025,893
Kentucky	2003	160,050	298,082	0	0	458,341	596,284	55.0	487,159	45.0	0	0.0	0	0.0	1,083,443
Louisiana (a)	2003	(a)	(a)				676,484	48.0	731,358	52.0	0	0.0	0	0.0	1,407,842
Maryland	2002	256,486	581,885	2,953	71	841,395	561,884	32.7	979,740	57.1	169,244	9.9	6,200	0.3	1,717,068
Mississippi	2003	177,122	504,319	0	0	681,441	470,404	52.6	409,787	45.8	0	0.0	14,296	1.6	894,487
Missouri	2004	604,757	847,748	0	3,755	1,456,260	1,382,419	50.8	1,301,442	47.9	0	0.0	35,678	1.3	2,719,599
North Carolina	2004	364,420	444,559	0	0	808,979	1,495,021	42.8	1,939,154	55.6	0	0.0	52,513	1.5	3,486,688
Oklahoma	2002	205,876	350,389	0	0	556,265	441,277	42.6	448,143	43.3	146,200	14.1	0	0.0	1,035,620
South Carolina	2002	384,944	114,346	0	0	499,290	585,422	52.8	521,140	47.1	0	0.0	1,163	0.1	1,107,725
Tennessee	2002	534,824	539,018	0	809	1,074,651	786,803	47.6	837,284	50.6	28,704	1.7	376	0.0	1,653,167
Texas	2002	1,003,388 (d)	620,463 (d)	0	0	1,623,851	2,632,591	57.8	1,819,798	40.0	0	0.0	101,538	2.2	4,553,927
Virginia	2001	(b)					887,234	47.0	984,177	52.2	0	0.0	15,310	0.8	1,886,721
West Virginia	2004	26,041	149,362	0	0	175,403	253,131	34.0	472,758	63.5	0	0.0	18,544	0.2	744,433
Regional total		4,678,891	6,956,852	2,953	4,653	11,643,540	15,766,806	49.9	15,117,792	47.8	344,148	0.1	360,983	0.1	31,589,789

See footnotes at end of table.

VOTING STATISTICS FOR GUBERNATORIAL ELECTIONS BY REGION — Continued

State	Date of last election	Primary election					General election								
		Republican	Democrat	Independent	Other	Total votes	Republican	Percent	Democrat	Percent	Independent	Percent	Other	Percent	Total votes
Western Region															
Alaska	2002	72,248	32,547	0	2,723	107,518	129,279	55.8%	94,216	40.7%	0	0.0%	7,989	3.5%	231,484
Arizona	2002	320,090	234,084	0	3,263	557,437	554,465	45.2	566,284	46.2	84,947	6.9	20,415	1.7	1,226,111
California	2002	2,328,937	2,402,077	56,268	401,769	5,286,204	3,169,801	42.4	3,533,490	47.3	0	0.0	773,020	10.3	7,476,311
Colorado	2002	189,705	98,897	0	0	288,602	884,583	62.6	475,373	33.7	0	0.0	52,646	3.7	1,412,602
Hawaii	2002	79,871	188,781	0	1,463	270,115	197,009	51.1	179,647	46.6	0	0.0	8,801	2.3	385,457
Idaho	2002	145,549	38,083	0	1,106	184,738	231,566	56.3	171,711	41.7	13	0.0	8,187	2.0	411,477
Montana	2004	110,198	94,795	0	0	204,993	205,313	46.0	225,016	50.4	0	0.0	15,817	3.5	446,146
Nevada	2002	117,474	88,974	0	0	206,448	344,001	68.2	110,935	22.0	0	0.0	49,143	9.7	504,079
New Mexico	2002	98,320	168,496	0	0	266,816	189,074	39.0	268,693	55.5	0	0.0	26,466	5.5	484,233
Oregon	2002	357,764	374,246	109,905	16,610	858,525	517,243	40.1	530,708	41.0	213,657	16.5	32,153	2.4	1,293,761
Utah	2004		(b)				524,816	57.8	373,670	41.2	0	0.0	8,220	0.9	906,706
Washington	2004	521,889	768,066	0	13,069	1,303,024	1,373,232	48.8	1,373,361	48.8	0	0.0	63,465	2.2	2,810,058
Wyoming	2002	90,685	36,799	0	0	127,484	88,873	47.9	92,662	50.0	0	0.0	3,924	2.1	185,459
Regional total		4,432,730	4,525,845	166,173	440,003	9,661,904	8,409,255	47.3	7,995,766	44.9	298,617	1.6	1,070,246	6.0	17,773,884
Regional total without California		2,103,793	2,123,768	109,905	38,234	4,375,700	5,239,454	50.8	4,462,276	43.3	298,617	2.8	297,226	2.8	10,297,573

Sources: The Council of State Governments' survey of election administration offices, October 2003 and March 2005 and state elections web sites.

Key:

(a) Louisiana has an open primary which requires all candidates, regardless of party affiliation, to appear on a single ballot. If a candidate receives over 50 percent of the vote in the primary, he is elected to the office. If no candidate receives a majority vote, then a single election is held between the two candidates receiving the most votes.

(b) Candidate nominated by convention.

(c) Total includes the Conservative Party. Governor Pataki was the candidate for both parties.

(d) Candidate ran unopposed.

Table 6.8
VOTER TURNOUT FOR PRESIDENTIAL ELECTIONS BY REGION: 1996, 2000 AND 2004
(In thousands)

State or other jurisdiction	2004 Voting age population (a)	2004 Number registered	2004 Number voting (b)	2000 Voting age population (a)	2000 Number registered	2000 Number voting (b)	1996 Voting age population (a)	1996 Number registered	1996 Number voting (b)
U.S. Total	208,247	170,937	122,501	205,410	156,420	105,587	195,193	132,796	96,414
Eastern Region									
Connecticut	2,574	1,823	1,579	2,499	1,874	1,460	2,300	1,900	750
Delaware	594	554	376	582	505	328	547	(c)	271
Maine	1,042	957	741	968	882	652	934	1,001	606
Massachusetts	4,931	3,973	2,927	4,749	4,009	2,734	4,623	(c)	2,556
New Hampshire	991	690	678	911	857	569	860	755	514
New Jersey	6,669	5,009	3,612	6,245	4,711	3,187	6,124	(c)	3,076
New York	14,206	11,837	7,448	13,805	11,263	6,960	13,564	9,161	6,439
Pennsylvania	9,404	8,367	5,770	9,155	7,782	4,912	9,197	6,806	4,506
Rhode Island	803	709	437	753	655	409	751	603	390
Vermont	490	419	312	460	427	294	430	385	261
Regional total	41,700	34,338	23,879	40,127	32,965	21,505	39,330	20,611	19,369
Midwestern Region									
Illinois	9,423	8,594	5,274	8,983	7,129	4,742	11,431	6,663	4,418
Indiana	4,592	4,009	2,468	4,448	4,001	2,180	4,146	3,500	2,135
Iowa	2,152	2,107	1,522	2,165	1,841	1,314	2,138	1,776	1,252
Kansas	2,038	1,694	1,188	1,983	1,624	1072	1,823	1,257	1,129
Michigan	7,541	7,164	4,876	7,358	6,861	4,233	7,072	6,677	3,849
Minnesota	3,823	2,977	2,828	3,547	3,265	2,439	3,412	2,730	2,211
Nebraska	1,257	1,160	778	1,234	1085	697	1,208	1,015	677
North Dakota	487	(d)	316	477	(c)	288	437	(c)	272
Ohio	8,604	7,973	5,722	8,433	7,538	4,702	8,300	6,638	4,534
South Dakota	573	502	388	543	471	316	530	456	324
Wisconsin	4,119	(d)	2,997	3,930	(d)	2,599	3,786	(d)	2,196
Regional total	44,609	36,180	28,357	43,101	33,815	24,582	44,283	30,712	22,997
Southern Region									
Alabama	3,252	2,597	1,883	3,333	2,529	1,666	3,220	2,471	1,534
Arkansas	1,960	1,686	1,055	1,929	1,556	922	1,873	1,369	884
Florida	12,539	10,301	7,610	11,774	8,753	5,963	11,043	8,078	5,444
Georgia	6,080	4,968	3,302	5,893	3,860	2,583	5,396	3,811	2,299
Kentucky	3,012	2,819	1,796	2,993	2,557	1,544	2,928	2,391	1,388
Louisiana	3,092	2,806	1,943	3,255	2,730	1,766	3,137	(c)	1,784
Maryland	3,922	3,105	2,384	3,925	2,715	2,024	3,811	2,577	1,794
Mississippi	2,014	1,865	1,140	2,047	1,740	994	1,961	1,826	894
Missouri	4,297	4,194	2,731	4,105	3,861	2,360	3,902	3,343	2,158
North Carolina	5,978	5,537	3,501	5,797	5,122	2,915	5,800	4,300	2,515
Oklahoma	2,515	2,143	1,464	2,531	2,234	1,234	2,419	1,823	1,206
South Carolina	2,967	2,315	1,618	2,977	2,157	1,386	2,872	1,814	1,203
Tennessee	4,284	3,532	2,437	4,221	3,181	2,076	3,660	3,056	1,894
Texas	14,996	13,098	7,411	14,850	10,268	6,407	13,698	10,541	5,612
Virginia	5,194	4,528	3,195	5,263	3,770	2,790	5,089	3,323	2,417
West Virginia	1,406	1,169	756	1,416	1,068	648	1,414	(c)	636
Regional total	77,508	66,663	44,226	76,309	58,101	37,278	72,223	50,723	33,662
Western Region									
Alaska	460	472	313	436	474	286	410	415	245
Arizona	3,800	2,643	2,013	3,625	2,173	1,532	3,233	2,245	1,404
California	22,075	16,557	12,421	24,873	15,707	10,966	19,527	15,662	10,263
Colorado	3,246	2,890	2,130	3,067	2,274	1,741	2,843	2,285	1,551
Hawaii	873	647	432	909	637	368	882	545	370
Idaho	950	798	598	921	728	502	858	700	492
Montana	680	638	450	668	698	411	647	590	417
Nevada	1,580	1,094	830	1390	898	609	1,180	778	464
New Mexico	1,318	1,105	756	1,263	973	599	1,224	838	580
Oregon	2,665	2,120	1,837	2,530	1,944	1,534	2,344	1,962	1,399
Utah	1,522	1,278	928	1,465	1123	771	1,322	1,050	691
Washington	4,456	2,884	2,859	4,368	3,336	2,487	4,122	3,078	2,294
Wyoming	370	246	244	358	220	214	343	241	216
Regional total	43,995	33,372	25,811	45,873	31,185	22,020	38,935	30,389	20,386
Regional total without California	21,920	16,815	13,390	21,000	15,478	11,054	19,408	14,727	10,123
Dist. of Columbia	435	384	228	411	354	202	422	361	186

Sources: 1996 data provided by Committee for the Study of the American Electorate, with update by the state election administration offices. U.S. Congress, Clerk of the House, Statistics of the Presidential and Congressional Election, 2004, U.S. Census Bureau, Current Population Survey, November 2002, released July 2004. The Council of State Governments' survey of election officials, January 2002. 2000 data provided by the Federal Election Commission.

Key:
(a) Estimated population, 18 years old and over. Includes armed forces in each state, aliens, and institutional population.
(b) Number voting is number of ballots cast in presidential race.
(c) Information not available.
(d) No statewide registration required. Excluded from totals for persons registered.

Trends and Issues in State Ethics Agencies
By David E. Freel

States vary greatly in how they identify and define "ethics" in the public sector. Meaningful and accurate comparisons of remedial state ethics processes are therefore difficult to easily render. However, ethics governance that involves standards of conduct and protections against conflicts of interest within the states often shares common traits. These traits include the creation of boards designed with oversight independent of appointment authorities, often delegated a trio of educational, advisory, and enforcement authority, in order to administer uniform standards and financial disclosure for public officers. These bodies share a vital goal of securing increased protection to the broader public interest by recognizing and limiting the inherent or acquired personal and familial conflicts of interest of those public servants who make and implement public policy and expend public funds.

Trend issues in ethics involve a reexamination of state ethics boards and their processes, questions regarding what ethical standards apply to the privatization of public duties, continuing controversy over alleged improprieties attributed to gifts and gratuities and/or unique private sector and nonprofit interests acquired by those serving the public, and efforts to enhance traditional compliance models with values principles.

Introduction—Comparing the States

Drawing general comparisons aimed at readily classifying or categorizing processes designed to oversee standards of conduct or identifying noteworthy ethics developments throughout the states is often difficult. As this author has previously noted, when ethics comparisons or trends are summarized to generalizations, all too often they are misleading or incorrect.[1] Apart from differences in demographics, summaries often fail to explain legitimate regional, political or jurisdictional factors or variations that bring about change or reconsideration.

In addition, ethics oversight presents a unique number of core factors that compound attempts to simplify comparison. These include: how states define "ethics," (nearly all states regulate ethics and disclosure, but in varying degree and subject matter), the breadth of those governed (some states regulate only state executive officials; others, both state and local officials, and/or local public employees or those in the private sector interacting with public agencies), the extent of authority granted oversight agencies, and the nature and composition of those governing ethical conduct.[2] However, the majority of state boards and commissions share some common attributes.

State Ethics Boards and Commissions

The National Conference of State Legislatures identifies entities with ethics oversight authority in each of the states.[3] With respect to state executive officials, however, 11 states place ethics statutes or rule provisions and their regulative processes under the authority of a single officeholder, rather than within a board or commission.[4] Montana places responsibility with a commissioner.[5]

The Council on Governmental Ethics Laws (COGEL), composed in large part of ethics, campaign finance, lobbying and public records entities largely in the United States and Canada, lists 40 different state boards, committees, commissions and/or individual commissioners that govern ethical conflicts of interests, standards of conduct and disclosure. Some of these boards or commissions serve as legislative committees assigned specific ethics responsibility for their members.[6] This compilation also includes more than one ethics oversight body in a few states (such as Washington, Kentucky and Ohio) that separate ethics authority among the three branches of government.

A recent research report prepared in November of 2004 for the Connecticut General Assembly by its Office of Legislative Research examined ethics oversight throughout the country, and focused primarily upon the executive branch. This report concludes that there are 36 state boards and commissions that administer codes of ethics for state officials.[7] Underscoring the difficulties in comparative "ethics" analysis of state board authority highlighted at the outset of this article, this author tallies a total of 38 state boards and commissions (35 of which are listed in the research report) that have executive branch conflict of interest ethics responsibilities.[8]

Despite unique individual characteristics, these 38 state boards or commissions have many similarities. They often embody authority apart from those they govern, in an effort to operate as independent bodies, with membership configured in an odd rather than an even number, and delegated power to administer conflict of interest standards and personal disclosure requirements, usually through a trio of educational, advisory and investigative processes. Many of the 38 govern conflict of interest restraints on public officials that are described in similar language. Most have authority across branches of government and many have lobbying jurisdiction as an additional part of their "ethics" oversight. While challenges to the efficacy of their mission may occur, many of these bodies exhibit a volume of work in applying ethics statutes or rule provisions to those they govern.[9] Whether by statute or rule, these provisions are largely designed at reducing personal conflicts of interest in public decision-making process and the implementation of public policy on behalf of the broader public interest.

Independent Ethics Boards and Commissions

Challenges to the real or perceived independence of boards or commissions assigned the duty of ethics oversight may be a constant,[10] particularly due to the reality of their duties and/or their continuing evolution. Legislation creating the vast majority, 31 of the 38 state boards and commissions, established these entities to stand apart from and hold power over their appointing authorities, with many having separate budgets and staffing.[11] Historically, some boards have demonstrated this independence by taking actions against the interests of their appointing authority, even in the face of litigation or other challenges.[12] (Boards largely composed of cabinet appointees, however, or those perceived as failing to exercise independence from their appointing authority, continue to experience questions regarding their effectiveness, as discussed in ethics trends below.) To achieve autonomy, states are significantly split over whether the governor of the state serves as the sole appointing authority, or whether board appointments are divided among senior executive, legislative or judicial officers. Regardless, most states utilize balancing measures over board composition either through empowering separate appointing authorities or by generally subjecting appointments to legislative confirmation.

To further support the autonomy of ethics authority, most of these boards routinely have the power to hire their own staff and manage their own budget. In fact, nine of these boards and commissions, charged largely with combined ethics, disclosure and other duties, often with state and local oversight (Alabama, Florida, Massachusetts, Ohio and Pennsylvania serve as examples), retain annual budgets of $1 to 2 million, with staff size between 11 and 30.[13] The California Fair Practices Commission stands out as the largest, with a current budget of $6 million and a staff of 60.[14] While the ability to manage a budget supports board independence, securing adequate funding and resources for the authority of many of these agencies, especially for smaller boards, and particularly in times of across-the-board general revenue funding cuts, is often argued to be a fundamental factor of true board independence and effectiveness that remains an ongoing concern in many states, having seen double-digit budget cuts or reductions.[15]

Due to the role of ethics oversight, one vital key to the successful operation of these boards is that their actions be viewed as objective and impartial. While the experiences of the author and others indicate that this is ultimately most dependent upon the quality and integrity of individual board appointees, regardless of past expertise as a regulated public official, [16] many states attempt to instill impartiality and finality in board composition. They do so by not only varying appointing authorities or mandating legislative, judicial or non-partisan panel participation in their selection, but also by restricting the total number of board members from any one political party to less than a majority, and by establishing an odd, rather than even, number of board members, or by placing other limitations on terms.[17] (As an example, one of the seven state boards that stand in contrast to the majority, the Ohio Ethics Commission, established in 1974, has an even number of members, mandated by law in Ohio to be three Democrats and three Republicans.) Of note in other types of limitations upon board membership, although not included in the 38 ethics boards, is the membership limitation within the Arizona Citizens Elections Commission. The commission was created upon voter initiative in 1998 to address issues of campaign finance, and statute restricts its membership to no more than two of five members from any one county.[18] Considering the routine dominance of state board members from or around capital cities, this is an interesting control on board composition.

The Alabama Ethics Commission, now 30 years old, represents a classic example of public policy efforts to establish an independent state ethics board. It has partisanship limitations on its five members, who are individually appointed by executive and legislative leaders, all subject to Senate confirmation. Board members cannot otherwise be public officials, candidates or lobbyists. Less stereotypically, former commission employees also cannot be members.[19] In fact, statute in Alabama attempts to further dictate the ethical quality of commission appointees, stating "each of whom shall be a fair, equitable citizen of this state and of high moral character and ability."[20]

Delegated Powers

Most state ethics boards are delegated a trio of process responsibilities to implement ethics authority that include educational or training functions, the ability to render advice construing ethics statutes or rules as they apply to regulated populations, and some enforcement or investigative ability to examine or sanction the conduct of those regulated.[21]

In recent years, one trend has been to focus increasing attention to education as an integral part of ethics oversight. In many states, while compliance standards may have predominated initial concepts of reform, education is now a mandatory, rather than voluntary, requirement upon those in state executive positions, either as a matter of law or chief executive order.[22] While often described as compliance training, educational focus upon increasing awareness of public policy restraints governing the conduct of public servants and assisting in recognizing personal interests that conflict with public interest has also been supplemented with values-based presentations and discussions.[23]

While a few state boards rely upon the assistance of their state attorney general or other outside legal advisors to assist the board's role in rendering advisory opinions or providing investigative and/or enforcement services to the board, the authority of many boards provides for a specialized focus on ethics provisions to be accomplished by the staff of the board.[24] Some states provide that this ethics advice gives unique protection to the requester.

In Ohio, for example, a written opinion in response to prospective circumstances, if fully followed, provides immunity from criminal prosecution, civil suit, and removal from office based upon an alleged ethics law violation. In the recent dismissal of an appeal to a criminal conviction under that state's ethics-related statutes in late 2003, the chief justice of the Ohio Supreme Court took the opportunity of the dismissal to acknowledge and support this authority.[25]

Such a legislative delegation of authority provides protection to those with clear questions regarding the future application of ethics statutes. This protection serves not only to encourage questions before the public servant acts or the public interest is subjected to allegations of a competing conflict, but also enables requesters to receive reliable transparent advice that stands independent of their personal view of their own conflict.

Most state ethics boards also have a third companion process involving some level of separate investigative and/or enforcement capabilities.[26] The author has previously discussed differences in state ethics investigative and enforcement processes.[27] Regardless, while the breadth of this authority varies greatly across the states, the specialized expertise of these boards and their staffs to examine alleged misconduct is often not replicated in other governing authorities.

The power to participate in the enforcement of ethics protections remains a significant component of the implementation of a uniform standard of behavior and is part of the public expectation of some remedial response to unethical conduct. Whether the form of oversight chosen by an individual state is to empower a board with adequate resources to effectively investigate and refer misconduct to others for enforcement, or to delegate the imposition of civil or administrative sanctions, this responsibility is crucial to securing a more consistent adherence to ethics laws, not only to benefit the public, but also for fairness to those public servants who observe the standards.

With delegated powers of education, advice and investigation, most state boards and commissions oversee a similar regime of statutory or administrative rule provisions that apply to gifts and other tangible forms of value, family, or the outside business relationships of public officials. These restraints are designed to protect against either the appearance or reality of improper influence upon public policy. While most states bar things of value coming to public officials at certain dollar or floor levels of substance from those who do business and/or are regulated by the public officials or their agencies, states also generally impose limits upon the conduct of public officials while in their public role, and under "revolving door" provisions, for a period after they leave their public role. Comparisons of those standards can also be found in the ethics literature.[28] The breadth and limitations of these laws and standards involving governmental ethical conduct, and the processes used to implement them, however, continue to generate trend ethical issues throughout the country.

Trends—The Reassessment of Ethics Boards and Processes

During 2004, a critical analysis of the composition and processes of state boards and commissions having conflicts of interest and standards of conduct authority began in a number of states. Following the history of ethics reform, this reexamination of processes comes in the wake of public attention within several states that experienced alleged or evidenced ethical breaches at the highest levels of state government.

In Connecticut, a series of ethical lapses at the state level culminated with the former governor of Connecticut resigning in the summer of 2004, in the face of impeachment for the improper receipt of gifts from those doing business with the state. That state's ethics commission is currently undergoing intense scrutiny regarding their ability to independently investigate their appointing authority, their processes to do so, and the effectiveness of their staff, including the removal of their former director.[29] Ironically, this scrutiny of the Connecticut Ethics Commission comes after the commission and its former director secured an admission from their past governor that he had lied in a previous commission settlement of issues related to improper gifts, and follows the governor's recent guilty plea to federal corruption charges and pending criminal charges against other senior state officials in his administration.[30] Critics have suggested that the commission should be reconstituted with members outside of the appointment authority of the governor, such as former judges, or a greater proportion of public members.

In New Jersey, public attention to another series of state scandals, and questions regarding the role of the New Jersey Executive Commission on Ethical Standards in failing to identify or adequately respond to those allegations, lead the new governor in November of 2004 to the appointment of two "special ethics counsel" to conduct an audit of the effectiveness of that state's ethics commission.[31] These special ethics counsels have been charged with identifying "potential improvements in ethics laws, regulations, codes, training, compliance monitoring and enforcement" and are to return a report to the governor within 120 days.

New Jersey, unlike the majority of its state counterparts contrasted above, requires commission appointees to come from within the executive branch, appointed to the commission by their chief executive, with concurrent terms to his.[32] Seven must be either state officers or employees in the executive branch; two are public members. In January 2006, the makeup of the commission will change to four executive branch members and four public members. With critical review and recommendation to come shortly into 2005 from special ethics counsel, it will be interesting to observe what significant changes may be suggested to a board composition where independence may be less assured by the nature of appointees, or what other enhancements in duties and resources for ethics oversight are proposed.

At least two other states are reviewing or have overhauled the authority of their ethics board and their processes as 2004 concluded and 2005 begins. The Massachusetts Ethics Commission recently acquired rule-making powers it requested to augment authority. The enactment of this power has been described as allowing the commission to create "'safe harbors' for conduct that may be prohibited by the literal language of the law but that does not offend its purpose."[33] However, recently, the chairman and its members also voted to conduct an ethics "audit" of the agency and its performance in response to concerns about whether the commission has focused its authority on alleged serious rather than more routine misconduct.[34]

In 2004, the Illinois General Assembly passed new ethics legislation, including the creation of an Executive Ethics Commission. Illinois had an executive branch ethics board in earlier years under executive order, composed of executive branch officials, which had been discontinued. The new Illinois Executive Ethics Commission consists of nine commissioners appointed by state constitutional officers, with the attorney general serving as an advisor. The commission is to provide public information, receive complaints, conduct administrative hearings, issue subpoenas, and make rulings and recommendations in disciplinary cases. The Commission has jurisdiction over the employees and officers of the executive branch.[35]

These varied developments in ethics oversight in states have consistently followed attention to alleged or founded misconduct by senior state officials within their respective jurisdictions. Additional questions of alleged favoritism and conflicts of interest have brought another trend ethics issue to general attention, the question of what, if any ethical standards apply to privatization of public services and no-bid contracts for service provision.

Privatization and Ethical Standards

The privatization of traditional services provided by government has raised significant questions about what, if any, ethical standards apply in the award of public contracts to provide public services, as well as to whether those performing services must meet conflict of interest or other ethics restraints. Florida, Maryland, Connecticut, New Jersey and California have all faced recent challenges to alleged conflicts of interest in contracts, often not subjected to competitive bid processes, which have been granted to companies to perform various types of services to state citizens.[36] While some of these challenges have focused upon allegations of the improper influence of political contributions made by those who have secured public contracts, others have focused upon allegations of improper gift giving or political cronyism in the award of state business.

New Jersey's response has been the enactment of a so-called "play-to-pay" statute seen as far-reaching in its impact on restrictions upon the award of public contracts to campaign contributors.[37] Although often part of ethics reform initiatives, these limitations on un-bid contracts to campaign contributors are also viewed as a part of campaign finance or lobbying reform.[38] In some states, proposed remedies to questions of conflicts involving the award of contracts include increased disclosure by those soliciting contracts or those who will perform the contracted services.[39]

While a few states have addressed potential ethical conflicts created by the state transitioning existing public services to the private sector,[40] the question of what ethical standards, if any, apply to those in the private sector performing ongoing services to the public appears to be a question for future ethics attention. This attention is warranted if the notion of conflicts of interest and standards of conduct is to protect the public from the improper influences of personal or financial conflicts of interest in securing purchases or service provision. Particularly in light of recent ethics issues within the private sector, it is doubtful that alleged conflicts of interest in the acquisition of the best and most economical public services will be viewed by the public as alleviated solely because they are conducted by private sector providers.

Gifts and Gratuities and Other Unique Conflicts of Interest

Issues of gifts and gratuities continue to be a trend topic throughout the states in 2004, not only among state executive officials, but also in other sectors of public officials, such as the judicial community.[41] Reforms being considered in executive branch agencies discussed earlier in this article have largely emerged from state scandals involving gifts. Connecticut's consideration of reform comes in the wake of the resignation and criminal guilty plea to federal charges by the former governor that emanated from allegations of improper gift giving. The former Illinois governor's indictment by the United States Attorney's Office on criminal charges stemming from gifts and vacations given to him and members of his administration to steer state business, led to the creation of a new ethics oversight body in Illinois, as previously highlighted.

Scandals in Indiana have also led its governor to ban gifts to executive officials, as well as proposals by the speaker of the Indiana House of Representatives to increase lobbyist disclosure.[42] Prosecuting authorities and the Ethics Commission in Ohio continue to examine free trips, meals, lodging and entertainment paid by investment firms to members of public pension fund boards after the guilty plea to criminal ethics charges of one fund trustee.[43] The New Hampshire legislature is reviewing new gift restrictions upon its members, while proposals in the Louisiana legislature look to place tighter limits upon gifts given by lobbyists to the families of public officials.[44]

While the potential impropriety of what are seen as traditional conflicts of interest such as gifts from contractors and regulatees continues as an ethics issue throughout the states, new questions of the influence of different means of generosity by those doing business with government officials have arisen.

Questions involving private sector companies donating to charitable causes backed by public officials as a possible means of exerting influence have surfaced in Florida.[45] Insurance companies facing large losses and potential investigations into their practices in that state have been identified as large financial contributors to charities endorsed by executive and legislative branch leaders. While Florida ethics laws prohibit state employees from accepting large gifts, they do not address charitable giving to entities supported or backed by public officials and some see no questions of improper influence.

While not resolving the direct issue of donations made by a lobbyist or contractor, ethics commissions in Hawaii, Mississippi and Ohio have addressed issues involving conflicts of interest arising between nonprofits and public officials under their authority.[46] Ongoing ethical issues will likely continue related to the application or need for further conflict of interest restraints involving non-profits in their interaction with government.

Trends in ethics governance, however, are not limited to the examination or enactment of new compliance measures. They include the incorporation of new strategies of deterrence.

Supplementing Compliance with Values Identification

One trend in ethics oversight is the addition of values-based dialogue to ethics compliance measures. Ethicists have long challenged adherence to legal compliance measures alone that do not promote values discussions or considerations.[47] They argue that ethics restrictions in and of themselves do not reach fundamental motivations and behaviors, nor create incentives for those with self-interest to understand and act in accord with or in advancement of broader public interests. As a result, more educational trainings offered by state boards are incorporating values discussions. Increased attention to values has also led to the endorsement or adoption of model codes of ethical behavior by governors and ethics bodies that present ideal, rather than mandatory, statements of ethical conduct that are designed to compliment ethics laws or regulations.[48] The addition of values considerations to compliance understanding appears to be a natural outgrowth of ethics education, but the extent to which governmental institutions are empowered or even capable of addressing core ethical principles will itself likely be a topic of continuing discussion.

Interesting for its innovation and attention to ethical action beyond compliance measures, although not the product of one of the enumerated state ethics boards, is an initiative of the Miami-Dade Commission on Ethics and Public Trust. The commission has stepped beyond traditional notions of ethical compliance models and recently adopted a Model Student Ethics Commission program designed to teach and encourage students to apply good governance and ethical standards to their behavior and future actions.[49]

Additional Resources

While comparisons or trend ethics issues may be difficult to readily identify among the states, the author has identified those above, and there are resources for general assistance to those examining these questions in more depth.

COGEL conducts annual surveys in the topic areas of ethics, lobbying, campaign finance, public records and electronic filing. COGEL's membership includes those responsible for ethics administration in all three branches of government, at the national, state, provincial and local level in the United States and Canada, as well as a growing number of other countries. It also includes professionals, academics and individuals practicing or interested in these areas. The *2003 and 2004 COGEL Blue Book Ethics Update* and the 2004 tables have been extensively used here. These surveys summarize the authority and responsibility, as well as advisory, enforcement, litigative and legislative developments, of individual states and other jurisdictions. They are available on searchable CD, and include in the identification of the issue or development those issues that the ethics agency itself classifies as the year's most significant. Survey updates are available to members at a relatively modest cost through COGEL's Web site at *www.cogel.org*. Additional information is available through The Council of State Governments, the National Conference of State Legislatures, and the Ethics Resource Center, a small portion of which has been cited in this article.

Notes

[1]The author's previous ethics article for *The Book of States 2004* attempted to wrestle with differences often overlooked or underestimated in identifying "ethics" issues among the states, comparing those subject to oversight, and contrasting remedial processes and their staff and funding. The author continues to recommend that those seeking an accurate assessment of ethics agencies or trend concerns within the states, whether taken from this article or another summary, highlight the specific issue within targeted jurisdictions, and then contact more than one experienced resource to verify assessments within those jurisdictions. While comparisons drawn in this article come largely from summaries prepared by agencies or individual offices charged with ethics oversight, and are often, in the author's experience, the most accurate, an agency's description may be limited or their oversight alone may color the perception and description of the issue. For purposes of organizing this summary, the author's own identification of classifications or trends may also diverge from the manner in which others identify those identical questions.

[2]David Freel, "Comparing State Ethics Laws and Ethics Trends and Issues," *The Book of States 2004*, (Lexington, KY: The Council of State Governments, 2004).

[3]*http://ncsl.org/programs/ethics/comprehensive_list.htm*. This comprehensive index does not separately identify the Louisiana Board of Ethics (see http://www.ethics.state.la.us). It also does not list the Kentucky Executive Branch Ethics Commission (see http://ethics.ky.gov/) or the Tennessee Ethics Committee (see *http://www.state.tn.us/governor/newsroom/releases/Feb03/02-03-03%20ethics.htm*).

[4]Statutes in Arizona, Colorado, Idaho, New Hampshire,

New Mexico, North Dakota, South Dakota, Vermont and Wyoming vary in the breadth of their application to public officials, but are largely overseen by respective offices of secretary of state. (Vermont also subjects ethics oversight of executive branch officials to a cabinet secretary. See *http://www.vermont.gov/tools/whatsnew2/index.php? topic=ExecutiveOrders&id=248&v=Article*.) Utah and Virginia's ethics laws are directly regulated by their respective offices of the attorney general. (For reference, as well, a number of other states refer advisory or investigative matters before their ethics boards and commissions to their office of attorney general.) See generally, the *COGEL Blue Book: 2004 Ethics Update* published by the Council on Governmental Ethics Laws (COGEL), containing summary charts at the end of this article, and available through *www.cogel.org*.

[5]Montana does not have a board or commission; instead, a single commissioner of political practices, who is subject to Senate confirmation. See *http://www.state.mt.us/cpp*.

[6]The *COGEL Blue Book: 2004 Ethics Update* Charts at the end of this article notably do not include information from the South Carolina Ethics Commission (see *http://www.state.sc.us/ethics/*), the Tennessee Ethics Committee, referred to above, or the newly reconstituted Illinois Executive Ethics Commission (see *http://www.ag.state.il.us/government/ethics_commission.html*).

[7]*http://search.cga.state.ct.us/dl2004/rpt/doc/2004-R-0881.doc*. States listed are Alabama, Alaska, Arkansas, California, Connecticut, Delaware, Florida, Georgia, Hawaii, Indiana, Illinois, Iowa, Kansas, Kentucky, Louisiana, Maryland, Massachusetts, Michigan, Mississippi, Missouri, Montana, Nebraska, Nevada, New Jersey, New York, North Carolina, Ohio, Oklahoma, Oregon, Pennsylvania, Rhode Island, South Carolina, Texas, Washington, West Virginia and Wisconsin.

[8]Montana is listed in the Research Report; however, Montana does not have a board or commission, as indicated above. Researchers also noted, but chose not include the Maine Commission on Governmental Ethics and Elections Practice (see *http://www.state.me.us/ethics/About.htm*) and the Minnesota Campaign Finance and Public Disclosure Board (see *http://www.cfboard.state.mn.us/giftban.htm*), because their primary responsibilities are campaign finance and lobbying, yet both have ethics-related functions. (In contrast, in this regard, researchers chose to include the Texas Ethics Commission, although its primary responsibility is campaign finance and lobbying. See *http://www.ethics.state.tx.us/tec/statdty.htm*.) Also not included was the Tennessee Ethics Committee, referred to above. This author's reference to 38 states then includes those in the Research Report and listed above, plus Maine, Minnesota and Tennessee, but not Montana. For convenience, the author often uses the term "board" to refer to both boards and commissions, although he recognizes that states may define them distinctly.

[9]See *COGEL Blue Book: 2004 Ethics Update*, Ethics Agency Table on Advisory Opinions, Investigations and Training, at article's end.

[10]See *http://www.ct.gov/governorrell/cwp/view.asp? A=1793&Q=284936* and see Frederick M. Herrmann, "Empowering Governmental Ethics Agencies," *Spectrum: The Journal of State Government*, Summer 2004, Vol. 77, No. 3, 33.

[11]Alabama, Alaska, Arkansas, California, Connecticut, Delaware, Florida, Georgia, Hawaii, Iowa, Kansas, Louisiana, Maryland, Massachusetts, Michigan, Minnesota, Mississippi, Missouri, Nebraska, Nevada, New York, Ohio, Oklahoma, Oregon, Pennsylvania, Rhode Island, South Carolina, Texas, Washington, West Virginia, and Wisconsin. In contrast, in Illinois, Indiana, New Jersey, North Carolina, Tennessee, Vermont and Washington, appointments are made by the governor, without concurrence of the legislature, and membership often includes cabinet members or delegates.

[12]See note 2 above, 286.

[13]See *COGEL Blue Book: 2004 Ethics Update*, Ethics Agency General Information Table at end.

[14]See *COGEL Blue Book: 2004 Ethics Update*, Ethics Agency General Information Table at end. Note that even the California Political Fair Practices Commission absorbed a $500,000 budget reduction this past year, with reduced staffing resulting, though appropriations are statutorily mandated by the initiative that created the body. See, *COGEL Blue Book: 2004 Ethics Update* and note 2 above.

[15]See *COGEL Blue Book: 2003 and 2004 Ethics Updates*. Also see notes 2 and Herrmann, note 10 above.

[16]See Herrmann, note 10 above.

[17]See *COGEL Blue Book: 2004 Ethics Update* and the Connecticut Legislative research at *http://search.cga.state.ct.us/dl2004/rpt/doc/2004-R-0881.doc*.

[18]See *http://www.ccec.state.az.us/ccecscr/pub/pdf/ActRules.pdf* at Section 16-955.

[19] See *http://www.ethics.alalinc.net/news/history.pdf* for a description of the 30-year old Alabama Ethics Commission, widespread challenges to its authority, and some humorous insight into its creation, in what was referred to as a "game of chicken" between legislative chambers attempting to outdo one another with the "hope-and full expectation" that ethics reform would be killed by the legislature or governor.

[20]See *http://www.ethics.alalinc.net/news/history.pdf*.

[21]See *COGEL Blue Book: 2004 Ethics Update*, Ethics Agency Table on Advisory Opinions, Investigations, and Training, at article's end, and the Connecticut Legislative research at *http://search.cga.state.ct.us/dl2004/rpt/doc/2004-R-0881.doc*.

[22]See *COGEL Blue Book: 2004 Ethics Update*, and Ethics Agency Table on Advisory Opinions, Investigations, and Training, at article's end, and the Hawaii Ethics Commission as an example *http://www.state.hi.us/ethics/noindex/newleg.htm*.

[23] See *http://www.ncsl.org/programs/ethics/ethics_training.htm*.

[24]See *COGEL Blue Book: 2004 Ethics Update*, described above.

[25]See *http://www.ethics.ohio.gov/AdvisoryOpinion_Definition.html* and State v. Urbin, 100 Ohio St.3d 1207, 2003-Ohio-5549. It is noted, that while the opinion supported both the protection afforded the requester and the viability of Ethics Commission opinions interpreting statute, it also restated the general principle that the courts remain sovereign in the final construction of statute.

[26]See note 21 above.

[27]See note 2 above.

[28]See *COGEL Blue Book: 2003 and 2004 Ethics Updates*, note 2 above, *http://www.csg.org/CSG/StatesNews/default.htm* and *http://www.ncsl.org/programs/ethics/*.

[29]See *http://www.ct.gov/governorrell/cwp/view.asp?A=1793&Q=284936*, the *COGEL Blue Book: 2003 and 2004 Ethics Updates*, the Connecticut Legislative research at *http://search.cga.state.ct.us/dl2004/rpt/doc/2004-R-0881.doc* and numerous articles in the *New York Times* and Connecticut newspapers.

[30]*http://www.washingtonpost.com/wp-dyn/articles/A21937-2004Dec23.html*.

[31]*http://www.state.nj.us/infobank/circular/eoc3.htm*.

[32]*http://www.state.nj.us/lps/ethics*.

[33]*http://www.mass.gov/ethics/fall_04.pdf*.

[34]"Massachusetts Ethics Panel Hires Consultant," *Boston Globe*, December 14, 2004. *http://nl.newsbank.com/nl-search/we/Archives?p_action=list&p_topdoc=11*.

[35]*http://www.ag.state.il.us/government/ethics.html*.

[36]*http://www.governing.com/articles/12priv.htm* and *http://www.nj.com/statehouse/ledger/index.ssf?/base/news-1/1085466863193220.xml*.

[37]*http://www.njchamber.com/media/pay%20to%20play%20ny%20times.htm*, *http://www.eagleton.rutgers.edu/NJProject/Reedarticle08_22.html*, and Council on Governmental Ethics Laws, Guardian, Fall 2004.

[38]*http://www.citizen.org/congress/campaign/state_local/pay_to_play/articles.cfm?ID=10982*.

[39]*http://www.duluthsuperior.com/mld/duluthsuperior/news/politics/10476358.htm*.

[40]*http://www.ethics.ohio.gov/opinions/90-006.pdf*.

[41]*http://www.judicialaccountability.org/judgesrulesongifts.htm*.

[42]*http://www.indystar.com/articles/4/205299-6864-009.html*.

[43]*COGEL Blue Book: 2004 Ethics Update*

[44]*http://www.theadvertiser.com/apps/pbcs.dll/article?AID=/20041221/OPINION01/412210309/1014* and *http://www.latimes.com/news/local/la-me-lobby7nov07,0,7940218.story*.

[45]*http://www.theadvertiser.com/apps/pbcs.dll/article?AID=/20041221/OPINION01/412210309/1014*.

[46]See *http://www.state.hi.us/ethics/noindex/newsltr/2004-3.pdf*, *http://www.ethics.state.ms.us/ethics/ethics.nsf/webpage/A_news_director?OpenDocument* and *http://www.ethics.ohio.gov/PressReleases/12232003.html*.

[47]*http://www.ncsl.org/programs/ethics/ethics_training.htm* and *http://www.josephsoninstitute.org/seminars/etw_public-administration.htm*.

[48]*http://ethics.ky.gov/Model%20Code%20of%20Ethics.doc* and *http://www.ethics.ohio.gov/ModelEthicsCode_stateagencies.html*.

[49]*http://www.miamidade.gov/ethics/training.asp*.

About the Author

David E. Freel has been the executive director of the Ohio Ethics Commission since 1994. Before joining the Ethics Commission staff, he was a faculty member of the Ohio State University College of Law. Freel has written articles on Ohio's ethics law and given ethics presentations at seminars and conferences in the United States and Canada. He is a past president of the Council on Governmental Ethics Laws (COGEL) and was honored with the COGEL Service Award in 2002.

Table 6.9
ETHICS AGENCIES: JURISDICTION SUBJECT AREAS

State or other jurisdiction	Agency	Campaign finance	Conflict of interest	Elections administration	Ethics	Financial disclosure	Freedom of information	Gift restriction	Lobbying	Public records
Alabama	Ethics Comm.	Y	N	Y	N	N	Y	Y	Y	Y
Alaska	Legisltv. Ethics Cmte.	N	Y	N	Y	N	N	Y	N	N
	Public Ofcs. Comm.	Y	N	N	N	Y	N	Y	Y	Y
Arizona	Citizens Clean Elections Comm.	Y	N	N	N	Y	N	N	N	Y
Arkansas	Ethics Comm.	Y	Y	N	Y	Y	N	Y	Y	Y
California	Fair Political Practices Comm.;	Y	Y	N	Y	Y	N	Y	Y	N
	L.A. Co. Metro. Transit Authority;	N	Y	N	Y	Y	N	Y	Y	Y
	L.A. Ethics Comm.;	Y	Y	N	Y	Y	N	Y	Y	Y
	Oakland Public Ethics Comm.;	Y	N	Y	N	Y	Y	Y	N	Y
	San Diego Ethics Comm.;	Y	N	Y	Y	N	Y	Y	Y	Y
	San Francisco Ethics Comm.	Y	Y	N	Y	Y	N	Y	Y	N
Colorado	Denver Bd. of Ethics	N	Y	N	Y	N	N	Y	N	N
Connecticut	Freedom of Info. Comm.;	Y	N	N	N	Y	N	Y	N	Y
	State Ethics Comm.	N	Y	N	Y	Y	N	Y	Y	N
Delaware	Public Integrity Comm.	N	Y	N	Y	Y	N	Y	Y	N
Florida	City of Jacksonville;	Y	Y	N	Y	Y	N	Y	Y	Y
	Comm. on Ethics;	N	Y	N	Y	Y	N	Y	Y	N
	Elections Comm.	Y	N	N	N	N	N	N	N	N
Georgia	State Ethics Comm.	Y	N	N	N	Y	N	Y	Y	Y
Hawaii	Campaign Spending Comm.;	Y	N	N	N	N	N	N	N	N
	Honolulu Ethics Comm.	N	Y	N	Y	Y	N	Y	N	N
	State Ethics Comm.;	N	Y	N	Y	Y	N	Y	Y	N
Idaho	Secretary of State	Y	N	Y	N	N	N	N	Y	N
Illinois	Chicago Bd. of Ethics;	Y	Y	Y	Y	Y	Y	Y	Y	Y
	City of Champaign	Y	N	Y	N	Y	N	Y	N	N
Indiana	Public Access Counselor's Ofc.;	Y	N	N	Y	N	N	Y	N	N
	State Ethics Comm.	Y	N	N	N	N	Y	Y	Y	N
Iowa	Ethics & Campaign Discl. Bd.	Y	Y	N	Y	Y	N	Y	Y	N
Kansas	Govtl. Ethics Comm.	Y	Y	N	Y	Y	N	Y	Y	N
Kentucky	Exec. Branch Ethics Comm.;	N	Y	N	Y	Y	N	Y	Y	N
	Legisltv. Ethics Comm.	N	Y	N	Y	Y	N	Y	Y	N
Louisiana	Board of Ethics	Y	Y	N	Y	Y	N	Y	Y	N
	Ethics Admin.	Y	Y	N	Y	Y	N	Y	Y	N
Maine	Comm. on Govtl. Ethics & Election Practices	Y	N	Y	N	N	Y	Y	Y	Y
Maryland	House of Representatives	Y	N	Y	N	N	Y	Y	Y	Y
	Anne Arundel Co. Ethics Comm.;	N	Y	N	Y	Y	N	Y	Y	N
	Montgomery Co. Ethics Comm.;	N	Y	N	Y	Y	Y	Y	Y	Y
	State Ethics Comm.	N	Y	N	Y	Y	Y	Y	Y	Y
Massachusetts	Ethics Comm.	N	Y	N	Y	Y	N	Y	N	N
Michigan	Dept. of State	Y	N	Y	N	Y	Y	Y	Y	Y
	State Bd. of Ethics	N	N	N	Y	N	N	N	N	N
Minnesota	Camp. Finance & Public Discl. Bd.	Y	Y	N	N	Y	N	Y	Y	N
Mississippi	Ethics Comm.	Y	N	N	N	N	N	Y	N	N
Missouri	Ethics Comm.	Y	Y	N	N	Y	N	Y	Y	Y
Montana	Commr. of Political Practices	Y	N	N	Y	Y	N	N	Y	N
Nebraska	Accountability & Discl. Comm.	Y	Y	N	Y	Y	N	Y	Y	N
Nevada	Comm. on Ethics	N	Y	N	Y	Y	N	Y	N	N
New Hampshire	------------------------ N.A. ------------------------									
New Jersey	Exec. Comm. on Ethical Stds.	N	Y	N	Y	Y	N	N	N	N
New Mexico	Sec. of State, Bureau of Elections and Ethics Administration	Y	Y	N	Y	Y	N	Y	Y	Y
New York	Buffalo Bd. of Ethics;	Y	N	Y	N	N	Y	Y	Y	N
	Dept. of State Cmte. on Open Govt.;	Y	N	N	N	Y	N	Y	N	N
	NYC Conflicts of Interest Bd.;	N	Y	N	Y	Y	N	Y	N	N
	State Ethics Comm.;	N	Y	N	Y	Y	N	Y	N	N
	Suffolk Co. Camp. Finance Bd.;	Y	N	N	N	N	N	N	N	N
	Temp. State Comm. on Lobbying	N	N	N	N	N	N	Y	Y	Y
North Carolina	Bd. of Ethics	N	Y	N	Y	Y	N	N	N	N
North Dakota		Y	N	Y	N	N	N	N	Y	N
Ohio	Ethics Comm.;	N	Y	N	Y	Y	N	Y	Y	N
	Legisltv. Insp. Gen. Ofc.	N	Y	N	Y	Y	N	Y	Y	N

See footnotes at end of table.

ETHICS AGENCIES: JURISDICTION SUBJECT AREAS — Continued

State or other jurisdiction	Agency	Campaign finance	Conflict of interest	Elections administration	Ethics	Financial disclosure	Freedom of information	Gift restriction	Lobbying	Public records
Oklahoma	Ethics Comm.	Y	Y	Y	Y	Y	Y	Y	Y	Y
Oregon	Govt. Standards & Practices Comm.	N	Y	N	Y	Y	N	Y	Y	N
Pennsylvania	Ethics Comm.	N	Y	N	Y	Y	N	N	N	N
Rhode Island	Ethics Comm.	N	Y	N	Y	Y	N	Y	N	N
South Carolina	House Legisltv. Ethics Cmte.	Y	N	Y	N	N	Y	Y	Y	N
South Dakota	---------- N.A. ----------									
Tennessee	---------- N.A. ----------									
Texas	Ethics Comm.;	Y	N	Y	N	N	Y	Y	Y	Y
	San Antonio City Attorney's Ofc.	Y	Y	N	Y	Y	Y	Y	Y	Y
Utah	State Elections Ofc.	Y	N	N	Y	N	N	Y	Y	Y
Vermont	---------- N.A. ----------									
Virginia	State Bd. of Elections	Y	N	N	Y	N	N	Y	Y	N
Washington	King Co. Bd. of Ethics;	N	Y	N	Y	Y	N	Y	N	N
	King Co. Ofc. of Citizen Complaints;	Y	N	Y	N	Y	Y	Y	N	N
	State Comm. on Judcial Conduct;	Y	Y	N	N	N	Y	Y	N	N
	State Exec. Ethics Bd.;	Y	N	Y	N	N	Y	Y	N	N
	State Legisltv. Ethics Bd.;	N	Y	N	Y	N	N	Y	N	Y
	State Public Discl. Comm.	Y	N	N	N	Y	N	N	Y	N
West Virginia	Ethics Comm.	N	Y	N	Y	Y	N	Y	Y	N
Wisconsin	Ethics Bd.	N	Y	N	Y	Y	N	Y	Y	N
Wyoming	---------- N.A. ----------									
Guam	Ethics Comm.	Y	N	N	N	N	N	Y	N	N
Puerto Rico	Ofc. of Govt. Ethics	N	Y	N	Y	Y	N	Y	N	N
U.S. Virgin Islands	Dept. of Justice	Y	N	N	N	N	N	Y	N	N

Source: The Council on Governmental Ethics Laws, *2004 Ethics Update*.
Key:
Y—Yes
N—No
N.A.—Not available.

Table 6.10
ETHICS AGENCIES: JURISDICTION

State or other jurisdiction	Agency	Executive branch employees	Judges	Judicial employees	Legislative employees	Legislators	Lobbyists	Local appointed officials	Local elected officials	Local employees	Private sector/vendors	State appointed officials	State elected officials	State employees	State colleges & universities
Alabama	Ethics Comm.	Y	Y	Y	N	Y	Y	Y	Y	Y	Y	Y	N	Y	Y
Alaska	Legisltv. Ethics Cmte.;	N	N	N	N	Y	N	N	N	N	N	N	N	N	N
	Public Ofcs. Comm.	Y	Y	N	Y	Y	Y	Y	Y	Y	Y	Y	N	N	Y
Arizona	Citizens Clean Elections Comm.	N	N	N	N	N	Y	N	Y	N	Y	N	Y	N	N
Arkansas	Ethics Comm.	Y	Y	Y	Y	Y	Y	Y	Y	Y	N	Y	Y	Y	Y
California	Fair Political Practices Comm.;	Y	Y	Y	Y	Y	Y	Y	Y	Y	N	Y	Y	Y	Y
	L.A. Co. Metro. Transit Authority;	N	N	N	N	N	Y	Y	Y	Y	Y	N	N	N	N
	L.A. Ethics Comm.;	Y	N	Y	Y	Y	Y	Y	Y	Y	N	Y	N	N	N
	Oakland Public Ethics Comm.;	N	N	N	N	N	N	Y	N	Y	Y	N	N	Y	N
	San Diego Ethics Comm.;	N	N	N	N	N	Y	Y	N	Y	Y	N	N	Y	N
	San Francisco Ethics Comm.	N	N	N	N	N	Y	Y	Y	Y	Y	N	N	Y	N
Colorado	Denver Bd. of Ethics	N	N	N	N	N	N	Y	Y	Y	N	N	N	N	N
Connecticut	Freedom of Info. Comm.;	Y	Y	Y	Y	Y	Y	Y	Y	Y	Y	Y	Y	Y	Y
	State Ethics Comm.	Y	Y	Y	Y	Y	Y	N	N	N	Y	Y	Y	Y	Y
Delaware	Public Integrity Comm.	Y	Y	Y	Y	Y	Y	Y	Y	Y	N	Y	Y	Y	Y
Florida	City of Jacksonville;	Y	N	N	Y	N	Y	Y	Y	Y	Y	N	N	N	N
	Comm. on Ethics;	Y	Y	Y	Y	Y	Y	Y	Y	Y	N	Y	Y	Y	Y
	Elections Comm.	N	N	N	N	N	N	N	Y	N	N	N	N	Y	N
Georgia	State Ethics Comm.	N	Y	N	N	Y	N	N	Y	N	Y	Y	Y	N	N
Hawaii	Campaign Spending Comm.;	N	N	N	N	Y	N	N	Y	N	Y	N	Y	N	N
	Honolulu Ethics Comm.;	Y	N	N	N	N	N	Y	Y	Y	N	N	N	N	N
	State Ethics Comm.;	Y	Y	Y	Y	Y	Y	N	N	N	Y	Y	Y	Y	Y
Idaho	Secretary of State	N	Y	Y	N	Y	Y	Y	N	N	N	N	N	N	N
Illinois	Chicago Bd. of Ethics;	Y	N	N	Y	N	Y	Y	Y	Y	Y	N	N	N	N
	City of Champaign	N	N	N	N	N	N	Y	N	N	N	N	N	N	N
Indiana	Public Access Counselor's Ofc.;	Y	Y	Y	Y	N	Y	Y	Y	Y	Y	Y	Y	Y	Y
	State Ethics Comm.	N	N	N	N	Y	N	N	N	N	N	N	N	N	N
Iowa	Ethics & Campaign Discl. Bd.	Y	N	N	N	N	N	N	N	N	Y	N	Y	Y	Y
Kansas	Govtl. Ethics Comm.	Y	Y	Y	Y	Y	Y	N	Y	N	Y	Y	Y	Y	Y
Kentucky	Exec. Branch Ethics Comm.;	Y	N	N	N	N	Y	N	N	N	Y	Y	Y	Y	Y
	Legisltv. Ethics Comm.	N	N	N	N	Y	Y	Y	N	N	N	N	N	N	N
Louisiana	Ethics Admin.	Y	N	Y	Y	Y	Y	Y	Y	Y	Y	Y	Y	Y	Y
Maine	Comm. on Govtl. Ethics & Election Practices;	N	Y	Y	N	N	N	Y	N	N	Y	Y	N	N	N
	House of Representatives	N	Y	N	N	N	N	N	N	N	Y	N	N	N	N
Maryland	Anne Arundel Co. Ethics Comm.;	Y	N	N	Y	Y	Y	Y	Y	Y	N	N	N	N	N
	Montgomery Co. Ethics Comm.;	Y	N	N	Y	N	Y	Y	Y	Y	N	N	N	N	N
	State Ethics Comm.	Y	N	Y	N	N	Y	N	N	N	Y	Y	Y	Y	Y
Massachusetts	Ethics Comm.	Y	Y	Y	Y	Y	Y	Y	Y	Y	Y	Y	Y	Y	Y
Michigan	Dept. of State;	N	N	N	N	Y	Y	Y	N	N	Y	N	Y	Y	Y
	State Bd. of Ethics	Y	N	N	N	N	N	N	Y	N	Y	N	Y	N	N
Minnesota	Camp. Finance & Public Discl. Bd.	Y	Y	N	N	Y	Y	Y	Y	Y	N	N	N	N	N
Mississippi	Ethics Comm.	N	N	N	N	N	N	N	N	N	Y	N	N	N	N
Missouri	Ethics Comm.	Y	Y	Y	N	Y	Y	Y	Y	Y	N	Y	Y	Y	Y
Montana	Commr. of Political Practices	Y	Y	Y	Y	Y	Y	N	Y	N	N	Y	Y	Y	N
Nebraska	Accountability & Discl. Comm.	Y	N	N	Y	Y	Y	Y	Y	Y	Y	Y	Y	Y	Y
Nevada	Comm. on Ethics	Y	N	N	Y	Y	N	Y	Y	Y	N	Y	Y	Y	Y
New Hampshire	------------------------------ N.A. ------------------------------														
New Jersey	Exec. Comm. on Ethical Stds.	Y	N	N	N	N	N	N	N	N	N	N	N	N	N
New Mexico	Secretary of State, Bureau of Elections and Ethics Admin.	Y	Y	Y	Y	Y	Y	Y	N	N	N	Y	N	N	N
New York	Buffalo Bd. of Ethics;	N	N	N	N	N	N	Y	N	Y	Y	N	N	Y	N
	Dept. of State Cmte. on Open Govt.;	Y	Y	Y	Y	Y	Y	Y	N	Y	Y	N	N	Y	Y
	NYC Conflicts of Interest Bd.;	N	N	N	N	N	N	Y	Y	Y	N	N	N	N	N
	State Ethics Comm.;	Y	N	N	N	N	N	N	N	N	Y	Y	Y	N	N
	Suffolk Co. Camp. Finance Bd.;	N	N	N	N	Y	N	N	Y	N	N	N	N	N	N
	Temp. State Comm. on Lobbying	N	N	N	N	N	Y	N	N	N	Y	N	N	N	N
North Carolina	Bd. of Ethics	Y	N	N	N	N	N	N	N	N	N	N	N	N	N
North Dakota	------------------------------ N.A. ------------------------------														
Ohio	Ethics Comm.;	Y	N	N	N	N	N	Y	Y	Y	Y	Y	Y	Y	Y
	Legisltv. Insp. Gen. Ofc.	N	N	N	Y	Y	Y	N	N	N	N	N	N	N	N

See footnotes at end of table.

State or other jurisdiction	Agency	Executive branch employees	Judges	Judicial employees	Legislative employees	Legislators	Lobbyists	Local appointed officials	Local elected officials	Local employees	Private sector/vendors	State appointed officials	State elected officials	State employees	State colleges & universities
Oklahoma	Ethics Comm.	Y	Y	Y	N	Y	Y	N	N	Y	Y	Y	N	Y	Y
Oregon	Govt. Standards & Practices Comm.	Y	Y	Y	Y	Y	Y	Y	Y	Y	Y	Y	Y	Y	Y
Pennsylvania	Ethics Comm.	Y	N	N	Y	Y	N	Y	Y	Y	N	Y	Y	Y	Y
Rhode Island	Ethics Comm.	Y	Y	Y	Y	Y	N	Y	Y	Y	N	Y	Y	Y	Y
South Carolina	House Legisltv. Ethics Cmte.	N	N	N	N	N	N	N	N	N	Y	N	N	N	N
South Dakota	---------- N.A. ----------														
Tennessee	---------- N.A. ----------														
Texas	Ethics Comm.;	Y	Y	Y	N	Y	Y	N	N	N	Y	Y	N	N	Y
	San Antonio City Attorney's Ofc.	N	N	N	N	N	Y	Y	Y	Y	N	N	N	N	N
Utah	State Elections Ofc.	N	Y	Y	Y	Y	Y	N	N	N	Y	Y	N	N	N
Vermont															
Virginia	State Bd. of Elections	N	Y	N	N	Y	N	Y	N	N	Y	N	N	N	N
Washington	Seattle Ethics & Elections Comm.;	N	N	Y	N	N	N	N	Y	Y	Y	N	N	N	N
	King Co. Bd. of Ethics;	Y	N	N	Y	N	N	Y	Y	N	Y	N	N	N	N
	King Co. Ofc. of Citizen Complaints;	N	N	Y	Y	N	N	Y	N	Y	Y	N	N	Y	N
	State Comm. on Judicial Conduct;	N	Y	Y	N	N	N	N	Y	N	N	Y	N	N	N
	State Exec. Ethics Bd.;	Y	N	N	N	N	N	N	N	N	N	N	N	N	Y
	State Legisltv. Ethics Bd.;	N	N	N	Y	Y	N	N	N	N	N	N	N	N	N
	State Public Discl. Comm.	N	Y	N	N	Y	Y	N	Y	Y	N	Y	Y	N	Y
West Virginia	Ethics Comm.	Y	Y	Y	Y	Y	Y	Y	Y	Y	Y	Y	Y	Y	Y
Wisconsin	Ethics Bd.	Y	Y	N	N	Y	Y	N	N	N	N	Y	Y	N	Y
Wyoming	---------- N.A. ----------														
Guam	Ethics Comm.	N	N	N	N	N	N	N	N	N	Y	N	N	N	N
Puerto Rico	Ofc. of Govt. Ethics	Y	N	N	N	N	N	Y	Y	Y	N	Y	Y	Y	N
U.S. Virgin Islands	Dept. of Justice	N	N	N	N	N	N	N	N	N	Y	N	Y	N	N

Source: The Council on Governmental Ethics Laws, *2004 Ethics Update*.
Key:
Y—Yes
N—No
N.A.—Not available.

Table 6.11
ETHICS AGENCIES: ADVISORY OPINIONS, INVESTIGATIONS & TRAINING

State or other jurisdiction	Agency	Advisory opinions			Investigations					Training			
		Authority to issue	Binding on inquirer	Estimated number per year	Authority to investigate — On own initiative	Reimbursement	Anonymous complaints	Respond to complaint	Estimated number per year	Agency trains	Optional or required	Estimated number per year	Training methods
Alabama	State Ethics Comm.	Y	N	48	N	Y	Y	Y	329	Y	O	56	...
Alaska	Legisltv. Ethics Cmte.;	Y	Y	3-5	Y	N	Y	Y	4-6	Y	O	2	C
	Public Ofcs. Comm.	Y	Y	5-25	Y	Y	N	Y	5-10	Y	R	20-May	C, T, V, VT, CD, W
Arizona	Citizens Clean Elections Comm.	N	N	...	Y	Y	N	Y	22	Y	O	30	C, CD, W
Arkansas	Ethics Comm.	Y	N	7	Y	Y	N	Y	112	Y	R	13	C
California	Fair Political Practices Comm.;	Y	Y	300-400	Y	N	N	Y	892	Y	B	73	C
	L.A. Co. Metro. Trans. Authority;	Y	N	150	Y	N	Y	Y	150	Y	R	52+	C
	L.A. Ethics Comm.;	Y	N	N.A.	Y	Y	Y	Y	150	Y	B	35-40	...
	Oakland Public Ethics Comm.;	Y	N	1-2	N	Y	Y	Y	30-40	N	B	4	...
	San Diego Ethics Comm.;	Y	N	4	Y	Y	Y	Y	38	Y	R	N.A.	C, T, V, VT, CD, W
	San Francisco Ethics Comm.	Y	N	N.A.	Y	N	Y	Y	38	Y	O	20	...
Colorado	Denver Bd. of Ethics	N	N	50	N	Y	Y	Y	15 (a)	Y	R	5,000	...
Connecticut	Freedom of Info. Comm.;	Y	Y	700	Y	Y	Y	Y	N.A.	Y	O	70	C, T, V, VT, CD, W
	State Ethics Comm.	Y	Y	30	Y	Y	Y	Y	75	Y	B	35	...
Delaware	Public Integrity Comm.	Y	N	60	Y	Y	Y	Y	3-7	Y	B	15-20	C, VT
Florida	City of Jacksonville;	Y	Y	N.A.	N	N	N	N	N.A.	Y	R	10	C, T, VT, W
	Comm. on Ethics;	Y	Y	23 (b)	Y	Y	Y	Y	107 (b)	Y	O	30	C, W
Georgia	Elections Comm.	N	N	...	N	N	N	Y	300 (i)	N			...
	State Ethics Comm.	Y	N	1	Y	Y	N	Y	100	Y	O	44	C
Hawaii	Camp. Spending Comm.;	Y	Y	12	Y	N	Y	Y	20	Y	N.A.	5	C, T
	Honolulu Ethics Comm.;	Y	N	5-10	Y	N	Y	Y	20-30	Y	B	30	C, VT
	State Ethics Comm.	Y	Y	1-5	Y	Y	Y	Y	10-20	Y	B	30-60	C, V
Idaho	Secretary of State	N	N	...	Y	Y	N	Y	5 (c)	N			C, T, V, VT, CD, W
Illinois	Chicago Bd. of Ethics	Y	N	30	Y	N	N	Y	25	Y	B	60	C, VT, W
Indiana	Public Access Counselor's Ofc.;	Y	N	64	N	Y	Y	Y	N.A.	Y	O	29	C, T, VT, CD, W
	State Ethics Comm.	Y	N	5	Y	N	Y	Y	50	Y	O	35	C,T,VT,CD,W
Iowa	Ethics & Camp. Discl. Bd.	Y	N	10	Y	Y	Y	N	10	Y	N.A.	5	C,W
Kansas	Govtl. Ethics Comm.	Y	Y	25-30	Y	Y	Y	Y	3-5	Y	O	35-40	C
Kentucky	Exec. Branch Ethics Comm.;	Y	Y	50	Y	N	Y	Y	28	Y	O	27	C
	Legisltv. Ethics Comm.	Y	Y	5	N	N	N	Y	5-7	Y	B	2	C, VT
Louisiana	Board of Ethics	Y	N	N.A.	Y	N	N	Y	N.A.	Y	N.A.	N.A.	...
Maine	Ethics Admin.	Y	N	390	Y	Y	Y	Y	113	Y	N.A.	60	C
	Comm. on Govtl. Ethics & Election Practices;	Y	Y	<6	Y	Y	Y	Y	<10	Y	R	(d)	C,T,VT,CD,W
	House of Representatives	Y	Y	10+	Y	Y	Y	Y	4	N	O	N.A.	W
Maryland	Montgomery Co. Ethics Comm.;	Y	Y	10	Y	Y	Y	Y	N.A.	Y	R	15	C
	State Ethics Comm.	Y			Y				N.A.	Y			...

See footnotes at end of table.

ETHICS AGENCIES: ADVISORY OPINIONS, INVESTIGATIONS & TRAINING — Continued

State or other jurisdiction	Agency	Advisory opinions			Investigations					Training			
		Authority to issue	Binding on inquirer	Estimated number per year	Authority to investigate			Respond to complaint	Estimated number per year	Agency trains	Optional or required	Estimated number per year	Training methods
					On own initiative	Reimbursement	Anonymous complaints						
Massachusetts	State Ethics Comm.	Y	Y	8 (e)	Y	Y	Y	Y	60 (f)	Y	B	65 (f)	C,CD
Michigan	Dept. of State;	N	N	N.A.	N	N	N	N	N.A.	Y	O	6	…
	State Bd. of Ethics	Y	N	2	Y	N	N	N	0	N	N	N	…
Minnesota	Camp. Finance & Public Discl. Bd.	Y	N	10	Y	N	N	Y	2	N	N	…	…
Mississippi	Ethics Comm.	N	N	N.A.	N	N	Y	Y	N.A.	N	N	…	…
Missouri	Ethics Comm.	Y	N	15	Y	N	Y	Y	180	Y	N.A.	25	…
Montana	Commr. of Political Practices	Y	N	50	N	N	N	Y	15–20	Y	O	2	C
Nebraska	Accountability & Discl. Comm.	Y	N	9	Y	Y	N	Y	30	Y	O	8	C
Nevada	Comm. on Ethics	Y	Y	20	Y	Y	N	Y	100	Y	O	25	C,VT,CD
New Hampshire					N.A.								
New Jersey	Exec. Comm. on Ethical Stds.	Y	N	20	Y	N	Y	Y	35	Y	B	15	C, CD,W
New Mexico	Secretary of State, Bureau of Elections and Ethics Administration	N	N	N.A.	Y	N	N	Y	20	Y	N.A.	3	C,VT,W
New York	Buffalo Bd. of Ethics;	Y	N	0	Y	Y	Y	Y	1–2	N	…	0	…
	Dept. of State Cmte. on Open Govt.;	Y	N	800 (h)	N	Y	Y	Y	N.A.	Y	N.A.	50	C, T, VT, CD, W
	NYC Conflicts of Interest Bd.;	Y	Y	535 (g)	Y	Y	Y	Y	62 (g)	Y	O	(i)	C,VT,W
	State Ethics Comm.;	Y	N	5–10	Y	N	Y	Y	60+	N	O	65	C, VT, W
	Suffolk Co. Camp. Finance Bd.;	Y	N	0	Y	N	N	Y	0	N	O	2	N.A.
	Temp. State Comm. on Lobbying;	Y	Y	5	Y	N	N	Y	10	Y	N.A.	6	C, T,W
	Bd. of Ethics	Y	N	10–15	Y	N	N	Y	5–10	Y	O	100+	…
North Carolina					N.A.								
North Dakota					N.A.								
Ohio	Ethics Comm.;	Y	Y	145	Y	Y	Y	Y	87	Y	B	158	C
	Legisltv. Insp. Gen. Ofc.	Y	N	N.A.	Y	N	Y	Y	5	Y	N.A.	3	C
Oklahoma	Ethics Comm.	Y	N	5–7	Y	N	Y	N	over 10	Y	O	over 10	C,W
Oregon	Govt. Standards & Practices Comm.	Y	Y	40–50	Y	N	N	Y	50–100	Y	O	50–60	C
Pennsylvania	Ethics Comm.	Y	N	125–200	Y	Y	N	Y	100	Y	O	50	C, VT
Rhode Island	Ethics Comm.	Y	N	120	Y	Y	N	Y	30	Y	O	25	C, W
South Carolina	House Legisltv. Ethics Cmte.	Y	Y	2	N	Y	Y	Y	3	Y	N.A.	1	…
South Dakota					N.A.								
					N.A.								
Tennessee					N.A.								
Texas	Ethics Comm.;	Y	Y	10	Y	Y	Y	Y	76	Y	B	37	C
	San Antonio City Attorney's Ofc.	N	N	20	Y	N	Y	Y	1–3	Y	B	30	…
Utah	State Elections Ofc.	Y	N	3	Y	Y	Y	N	3	N	N.A.	N.A.	C, T, V, VT, CD, W
North Dakota	Ofc. of the Treasurer				N.A.								

See footnotes at end of table.

ETHICS AGENCIES: ADVISORY OPINIONS, INVESTIGATIONS & TRAINING — Continued

State or other jurisdiction	Agency	Advisory opinions			Investigations					Training			
					Authority to investigate								
		Authority to issue	Binding on inquirer	Estimated number per year	On own initiative	Reimbursement	Anonymous complaints	Respond to complaint	Estimated number per year	Agency trains	Optional or required	Estimated number per year	Training methods
Virginia	State Bd. of Elections	N	N	…	N	Y	Y	N	N.A.	Y	O	1-2 dozen	C, T, V, VT, CD, W
Washington	Seattle Ethics & Elections Comm.;	Y	N	30	Y	Y	Y	Y	75	Y	O	25	C
	King Co. Bd. of Ethics;	Y	N	Varies	Y	N	Y	Y	Varies	Y	B	64 (g)	C
	King Co. Ofc. Of Citizen Complaints;	N	N	…	Y	Y	Y	Y	10-20	N	N.A.	3-5	C, T, V, VT, CD, W
	State Comm. on Judicial Conduct;	N	N	…	Y	Y	Y	Y	360	Y	O	4	C, T, V, VT, CD, W
	State Exec. Ethics Bd.;	Y	N	10	Y	Y	Y	Y	100	Y	O	40	…
	State Legisltv. Ethics Bd.;	Y	N	8	Y	Y	N	Y	5-12	Y	B	3-10	…
	State Public Discl. Comm.	Y	Y	0-2	N	Y	N	Y	50-75	Y	O	59	…
West Virginia	Ethics Comm.	Y	Y	35-40	N	Y	N	Y	10-15	Y	O	15-20	C
Wisconsin	State Ethics Bd.	Y	N	40	Y	Y	Y	Y	10	Y	R	25	C
Wyoming							N.A.						
Guam	Ethics Comm.	N	N	…	N	Y	Y	N	N.A.	N	…	…	…
Puerto Rico	Ofc. of Govt. Ethics	Y	Y	1,738	Y	Y	Y	Y	500	Y	R	400	C,T,VT,CD
U.S. Virgin Islands	Dept. of Justice	N	N	N.A.	N	Y	Y	N	N.A.	N	…	…	…

Source: The Council on Governmental Ethics Laws, Ethics Update 2004.
Key:
Y—Yes
N—No
O—Optional
B—Both
R- Required
N.A.—Not available
C—Classroom
T—Teleconference
V—Videoconference
VT—Video tape

CD—CDRom
W—Web-based
(a) In 2002.
(b) Three year average.
(c) In elections years.
(d) One biennially for new Legislature.
(e) Formal advisory opinions.
(f) In Fiscal Year 2004.
(g) In 2003.
(h) Written opinions.
(i) Estimated.
(j) 182 in 2001 and 377 in 2003.

Table 6.12
ETHICS AGENCIES: PERSONAL FINANCIAL DISCLOSURE STATEMENTS

State or other jurisdiction	Agency	Agency heads	Board or commission members	Judges	Legislators	Candidates for legislature	State elected officials	Candidates for statewide office	Other	Number filed per year	File via web	File other electronic	FDS available electronically	Reviews or audits conducted	Reviews or audits available electronically
Alabama	Ethics Comm.	Y	Y	N	Y	Y	Y	Y	(a)(h)	30,946	N	N	Y	N	N
Alaska	Public Ofcs. Comm.	Y	Y	N	Y	Y	Y	Y		2,000	Y	Y	N	Y	N
Arizona	Citizens Clean Elections Comm.	N	N	N	Y	Y	Y	Y	(z)	6	N	Y	N	Y	N
Arkansas	Ethics Comm.				(f)					240 (f)	N	Y	Y	Y	N
California	Fair Political Practices Comm.;	Y	Y	Y	Y	Y	Y	N	(a)	21,000	N	Y	Y	Y	N
	L.A. Co. Metro. Trans. Authority;	Y	Y	N	N	N	N	N	(pp)	1,200	Y	Y	N	Y	N
	L.A. Ethics Comm.;	Y	Y	N	Y	Y	N	N	(c)(aa)	6,000	N	Y	Y	Y	N
	Oakland Public Ethics Comm.;	Y	Y	N	Y	Y	N	N	(c)(bb)	750	Y	Y	Y	Y	N
	San Diego Ethics Comm.;	Y	Y	N	N	N	N	N	(c)	350	N	Y	Y	Y	N
	San Francisco Ethics Comm.	Y	Y	N	N	N	N	N	(gg)(kk)	650	N	N	N	Y	N
Colorado					N.A.										
Connecticut	Freedom of Info. Comm.;	Y	N	N	N	N	N	N		N.A.	N	Y	Y	Y	N
	State Ethics Comm.	Y	Y	Y	Y	Y	Y	Y		1,500	N	Y	Y	Y	N
Delaware	Public Integrity Comm.	Y	Y	Y	Y	Y	Y	N	(i)	300+	N	N	N	Y	N
Florida	City of Jacksonville;	Y	Y	N	N	N	N	N	(j)	100	N	N	N	N	N
	Comm. on Ethics	Y	Y	N	N	N	Y	N	(k)	30,000	N	N	N	N	N
Georgia	State Ethics Comm.	Y	Y	N	Y	Y	Y	Y	(a)(au)	7,000	Y	Y	N	Y	N
Hawaii	Campaign Spending Comm.;	N	N	N	N	Y	N	N		N.A.	N	Y	Y	Y	N
	State Ethics Comm.;	Y	Y	N	Y	Y	Y	Y		2,000	Y	Y	N	Y	N
	Honolulu Ethics Comm.	N	N	N	N	N	Y	N		575	Y	Y	Y	Y	N
Idaho	Secretary of State	Y	Y	N	N	Y	Y	Y	(a)(v)	3,000 (mm)	Y	Y	N	Y	N
Illinois	Chicago Bd. of Ethics;	Y	Y	N	N	N	Y	N	(ll)	12,000	N	N	Y	Y	N
	City of Champaign	N	N	N	N	N	N	N	(c)(ll)	N.A.	N	Y	Y	Y	N
Indiana	Public Access Counselor's Ofc.;	Y	N	N	N	N	N	N		N.A.	Y	Y	Y	Y	Y
	State Ethics Comm.	Y	Y	N	N	N	Y	Y		400+	Y	Y	Y	Y	Y
Iowa	Ethics & Camp. Discl. Bd.	Y	Y	N	N	Y	Y	Y		600	Y	Y	Y	Y	N
Kansas	Govtl. Ethics Comm.	Y	Y	N	N	Y	Y	Y	(a)(cc)	6,000	N	Y	Y	Y	N
Kentucky	Exec. Branch Ethics Comm.;	Y	Y	N	N	N	Y	Y		1,300	N	Y	Y	Y	N
	Legisltv. Ethics Comm.;	N	N	N	Y	Y	N	N	(oo)	150	N	Y	N	Y	N
Louisiana	Ethics Admn.	N	N	N	Y	Y	N	N	(e)(qq)	7,339	Y	Y	N	Y	N
Maine	Comm. on Govtl. Ethics & Election Practices	N	N	N	Y	Y	N	N		<450	Y	Y	Y	N	N
Maryland	House of Representatives	N	N	N	Y	Y	N	N		<450	N	Y	Y	Y	N
	Anne Arundel Co. Ethics Comm.;	Y	Y	N	N	N	N	N	(b)(w)	200+	N	Y	Y	Y	N
	Montgomery Co. Ethics Comm.;	Y	Y	N	N	N	N	N		1,400	N	N	N	Y	N
	State Ethics Comm.	Y	Y	Y	Y	Y	Y	Y	(rr)	11,000	N	Y	N	Y	N
Massachusetts	State Ethics Comm.	Y	Y	Y	Y	Y	Y	Y	(b)(y)	4,711	N	N	N	Y	N
Michigan	Dept. of State	N	N	N	N	N	Y	Y		10,000	Y	Y	Y	Y	N
Minnesota	Camp. Finance & Public Discl. Bd.	Y	Y	Y	Y	Y	Y	Y		1,300	Y	N	N	N	N
Mississippi	Ethics Comm.	N	N	N	N	N	N	Y		N.A.	N	N	Y	N	N

See footnotes at end of table.

ETHICS AGENCIES: PERSONAL FINANCIAL DISCLOSURE STATEMENTS — Continued

State or other jurisdiction	Agency	Who must file with agency							Other	Number filed per year	File via web	File other electronic	FDS available electronically	Reviews or audits conducted	Reviews or audits available electronically
		Agency heads	Board or commission members	Judges	Legislators	Candidates for legislature	State elected officials	Candidates for statewide office							
Missouri	Ethics Comm.	Y	Y	N	Y	Y	Y	Y	(a)(m)	9,500	N	N	N	N	N
Montana	Commr. of Political Practices	Y	N	N	Y	Y	Y	N		190	N	N	N	N	N
Nebraska	Accountability & Discl. Comm.	Y	Y	N	Y	Y	Y	Y	(a)(n)	2,500	N	N	N	N	N
Nevada	Comm. on Ethics	Y	Y	N	N	N	N	N	(a)(ss)	300	N	N	N	N	N
New Hampshire							N.A									
New Jersey	Exec. Comm. on Ethical Stds.	Y	Y	N	N	N	N	N	(o)	2,000	N	Y	N	Y	N
New Mexico	Secretary of State, Bureau of Elections and Ethics Administration	Y	Y	Y	Y	Y	Y	Y		N.A	Y	Y	N	N	N
New York	Buffalo Bd. of Ethics;	Y	Y	N	N	N	N	N		550	Y	Y	N	Y	N
	Dept. of State Cmte. on Open Govt.;	N	N	N	N	N	N	N	(c)(dd)	N.A.	N	N	N	Y	N
	NYC Conflicts of Interest Bd.;	Y	Y	N	N	N	Y	Y	(p)	8,000	Y	Y	N	Y	N
	State Ethics Comm.;	Y	Y	N	N	N	Y	N		18,000	Y	Y	Y	Y	N
	Temp. State Comm. on Lobbying;	N	Y	N	Y	Y	N	N	(ee)	apx. 20,000	N	Y	Y	Y	N
	Suffolk Co. Camp. Finance Bd.	Y	Y	N	N	N	N	N	(b)(tt)	200	N	Y	N	Y	N
	Bd. of Ethics	Y	Y	N	Y	N	N	N	(q)	2500+	Y	Y	N	Y	N
North Carolina							N.A									
North Dakota							N.A									
Ohio	Ethics Comm.;	Y	Y	N	N	N	Y	Y	(a)(r)	10,500	N	Y	N	Y	N
	Legisltv. Insp. Gen. Ofc.	N	N	N	Y	Y	N	N	(s)	343	Y	Y	N	Y	N
Oklahoma	Ethics Comm.	Y	Y	Y	Y	Y	Y	Y	(b)(ff)	6,000	Y	Y	N	Y	N
Oregon	Govt. Standards & Practices Comm.	Y	Y	Y	Y	Y	Y	Y	(b)(d)(uu)	4,200	N	Y	N	Y	N
Pennsylvania	Ethics Comm.	Y	Y	N	Y	Y	Y	Y	(a)(hh)	150,000	Y	Y	N	Y	N
Rhode Island	Ethics Comm.	Y	Y	Y	Y	Y	Y	Y	(c)	6,500	N	Y	N	Y	N
South Carolina	Ethics Comm.	Y	Y	N	Y	Y	N	N		800	Y	Y	N	Y	N
	House Legisltv. Ethics Cmte.	N	N	N	Y	Y	N	N								
South Dakota							N.A									
Tennessee							N.A									
Texas	Ethics Comm.;	Y	Y	N	Y	Y	Y	Y	(ii)	2,500	Y	Y	N	N	N
	San Antonio City Attorney's Ofc.	Y	Y	Y	N	N	N	N	(c)(vv)	700	N	N	N	N	N
Utah	State Elections Ofc.	N	N	N	Y	Y	Y	Y	(jj)	3,500	Y	Y	N	Y	N
Vermont	Ofc. of the Treasurer	N	N	N	N	N	Y	N		N.A.	Y	Y	N	Y	N
Virginia	State Bd. of Elections	N	N	N	N	N	N	N		N.A.	N	Y	Y	N	N
Washington	Seattle Ethics & Elections Comm.;	N	Y	N	N	N	N	N	(c)(xx)	1,964	Y	Y	N	N	N
	King Co. Bd. of Ethics;	Y	Y	Y	N	N	N	N	(b)(t)	apx. 2,400	N	Y	N	Y	N
	King Co. Ofc. of Citizen Complaints;	N	N	N	N	N	N	N		N.A.	N	Y	N	N	N
	State Exec. Ethics Bd.;	N	N	N	N	N	N	N		N.A.	N	Y	Y	Y	N
	State Legisltv. Ethics Bd.;	N	Y	N	Y	Y	Y	Y		N.A.	N	Y	N	N	N
	State Public Discl. Bd.	Y	Y	Y	Y	Y	Y	Y	(g)	6,500-8,500	N	Y	N	Y	N
West Virginia	Ethics Comm.	Y	Y	Y	Y	N	Y	Y	(a)	2,600	N	N	N	Y	Y
Wisconsin	Ethics Comm.	Y	Y	N	Y	N	Y	Y	(b)	2,400	N	Y	N	N	N
Wyoming							N.A									
Guam	Ethics Comm.	N	N	N	N	N	N	N	(ww)	N.A.	N	N	Y	N	N
Puerto Rico	Ethics Comm.	Y	Y	Y	Y	Y	Y	Y	(d)(nm)	10,600	Y	Y	Y	Y	N
U.S. Virgin Islands	Dept. of Justice	N	N	N	N	N	N	N		N.A.	N	N	N	Y	N

See footnotes at end of table.

ETHICS AGENCIES: PERSONAL FINANCIAL DISCLOSURE STATEMENTS — Continued

Source: The Council on Governmental Ethics Laws, *2004 Ethics Update.*

Key:

Y—Yes

N—No

N.A.—Not available

(a) City and county elected officials and candidates.

(b) County elected officials and candidates.

(c) City elected officials and candidates.

(d) City elected officials.

(e) City and county office candidates.

(f) Disclosures are filed with Secretary of State. Ballot and legislative question committees make their filings with the commission.

(g) Financial statements to be filed with Public Disclosure Commission, not ethics board.

(h) Certain other employees.

(i) Senior employees; Quasi-Public Agency members and senior employees.

(j) Division directors and their equivalents.

(k) Local officers and employees file with the supervisor of elections of the county in which they reside. Candidates file with the officer before whom they qualify.

(l) Aldermen must file with the city clerk. All city employees whose annual compensation rate is at or above an amount specified by the Board each year must file with the Board.

(m) Some political subdivisions have established their own method of disclosing conflicts of interest and therefore their candidates for office are not required to file the disclosure statement.

(n) City elected officials and candidates for same file if city falls within a certain population category. Members of certain boards file if duties fall within statutory criteria.

(o) Executive branch employees from assistant division director up; casino and gaming employees.

(p) Certain political party chairs, candidates for statewide elected office.

(q) High level appointees and employees in the executive branch of state government, including gubernatorial appointees to non-advisory boards/commissions. By invitation, employees and appointees as designated by the nine elected heads of the Council of State agencies, the Board of Governors of the 16-campus University system, the president pro tempore of the Senate and the Speaker of the House of Representatives.

(r) School board treasurers, superintendents and business managers. High-ranking state employees. Public university and college presidents must file.

(s) High ranking legislative employees are also required to file. Also accept filings by other legislative employees as "voluntary filers."

(t) Local officials, candidates.

(u) State Board & Authority members, not Commission members. Do not file directly with agency; reports are filed with filing offices.

(v) City and county appointed officers and employees.

(w) County employees.

(y) Designated state and county employees in policy-making positions.

(z) Persons making independent expenditures exceeding $550.

(aa) Other employees designated in the agency Conflict of Interest Code.

(bb) Filings made with the city clerk.

(cc) Any state employee designated by an agency head who is in a major policy making position, responsible for contracting, purchasing or procurement, responsible for writing or drafting specifications for contracts, responsible for awarding grants, benefits or subsidies, or responsible for inspecting, licensing or regulating any person or entity.

(dd) Deputy and assistant agency heads, managers, annual salary over $83,500; employees involved in negotiating, authorizing or approving contracts, leases, franchises, revocable consents or land use applications; compensated board and commission members. Pursuant to legislative change, effective Jan. 1, 2004, salary threshold will be eliminated as a criterion for filing, replaced by "policymakers," and low level managers will no longer be required to file.

(ee) Lobbyists and clients.

(ff) Employees of state educational institutions who make policy or spending decisions.

(gg) City and county elected officials.

(hh) Disclosure requirements also apply to many local and state employees.

(ii) State political chairs.

(jj) Political action committees, political issues committees, political parties, corporations.

(kk) Employees who are designated in the Campaign and Governmental Conduct Code file Statements of Economic Interests with their department heads.

(ll) This is campaign disclosure, not personal financial disclosure. Reports are scanned upon receipt and available for viewing on the internet. The information is also entered into a database and available to review/search on the Internet. Desk audits are made on each report.

(mm) In an election year.

(nn) High level position public servants, purchase officials bid board members and public (government owned) Corporations Board.

(oo) Major management personnel of Legislative Research Commission.

(pp) Board members and employees who make financial decisions including persons who participate or procurement source selection teams and consultants.

(qq) Lobbyists, in accordance with La R.S. 24:50 et seq.

(rr) All state employees who are determined by the State Ethics Commission to be "public officials" or who have procurement responsibilities for contracts in excess of $10,000 per year must file financial disclosure statements.

(ss) The 2003 Legislature passed significant changes to the financial disclosure statutes. The changes include: the secretary of state is now responsible for accepting financial disclosure statement filings of elected public officers and candidates; the annual filing date is now Jan. 15; creation of a new sections within the Ethics in Government Law regarding new filing requirements for both appointed and elected public officers.

(tt) Political committees (including PACs) which support candidates for non-judicial county elected offices.

(uu) City and county chief executive officers; designated state agency directors and superintendents and business managers of pubic school districts.

(vv) Executive level employees also file financial disclosure, e.g. the city manager and the assistant city managers; assistant department heads; members of police and fire departments involved in procurements; the city clerk; all executive secretaries. Also, "specified employees," i.e. higher-level employees who are not on executive staff file a shorter financial disclosure form reporting gifts.

(ww) Key administrators of state agencies, including the technical college and university systems.

(xx) City employees that fit criteria for filing.

Table 6.13
LOBBYISTS: DEFINITIONS AND PROHIBITED ACTIVITIES

Columns grouped under "Definition of a lobbyist includes" (Legislative lobbying through Time standard) and "Prohibited activities involving lobbyists" (Making campaign contributions at any time through Other).

State or other jurisdiction	Legislative lobbying	Administrative agency lobbying	Elective officials as lobbyists	Public employees as lobbyists	Compensation standard	Expenditure standard	Time standard	Making campaign contributions at any time	Making campaign contributions during legislative sessions	Making expenditures in excess of $ per official per year	Solicitation by officials or employees for contributions or gifts	Contingent compensation	Other
Alabama	★	★	...	★	★	★	★	★	★	...	★	★	...
Alaska	★	★	(ee)	(ee)	★	...	★	(x)	★	$100	...	★	(bb)
Arizona	★	★	★	★	★	★	★	★	★	$10	★	★	...
Arkansas	★	★	★	★	★	★	★	...	...	...	...	...	(z)
California	★	★	...	...	★	...	★	...	...	$10/mo.	...	★	(a)
Colorado	★	...	...	★	★	...	...	...	★	...	★	★	...
Connecticut	★	★	...	...	★	★	★	...	★	$50	...	★	(d)
Delaware	★	★	...	...	★	★	...	...	...	...	...	★	★
Florida	★	★	...	...	★	...	★	...	...	$100 (dd)	★	★	...
Georgia	★	...	...	...	★	★	...	★	...	...	...	★ (b)	...
Hawaii	★	★	...	...	★	★	★	...	...	...	...	★	...
Idaho	★	...	★	★	★	...	...	...	...	...	★	★	...
Illinois	★	★	...	★	★	...	...	...	...	...	...	...	...
Indiana	★	...	...	...	★	★	...	★	...	...	★	★	(ff)
Iowa	★	★	★	★	★	...	...	★	...	★	★	★	...
Kansas	★	★	...	...	...	★	★	★	...	(c)	★	★	...
Kentucky	★	★ (j)	...	...	...	...	...	★	...	$100 (e)	★	★	...
Louisiana	★	...	...	...	★	★	★	...	★ (k)	...	...	...	...
Maine	★	(m)	...	...	★	★	...	...	★	...	...	★	...
Maryland	★	★	...	...	★	★	...	★	...	...	★	★	(n)
Massachusetts	★	★	...	★	★	★	★	...	...	...	★	★	(o)
Michigan (f)	★	★	...	★	★	★	★	...	...	(d)	(d)	★	(o)
Minnesota	★	★	...	★	★	★	...	...	★	...	...	★	...
Mississippi	★	★	...	★	★	★	★	...	...	...	...	★	...
Missouri	★	★	★	★	★	★	★	...	...	...	...	...	(p)
Montana	★	...	...	...	★	★	...	...	...	...	...	...	...
Nebraska	★	...	...	...	...	...	...	...	...	...	★ (q)	★	...
Nevada	★	★	...	★	...	...	...	...	★ (g)	...	★	★	...
New Hampshire	★	...	...	...	★	...	...	...	...	...	...	...	...
New Jersey	★	★	...	...	★	★	★	...	...	...	...	...	...
New Mexico	★	★	...	...	...	...	...	★	...	...	...	★	★
New York	★	★	...	...	★	★	...	...	...	$75	...	★	...
North Carolina	★	...	...	(r)	...	...	...	★	...	...	...	★	...
North Dakota	★	...	...	...	...	★	...	...	...	...	...	...	...
Ohio	★	★	...	★	★	...	...	...	...	$300	★ (h)	★	(t)
Oklahoma	★	(y)	...	...	...	...	...	...	...	...	...	★	...
Oregon	★	...	...	★	...	★	★	...	...	$100 (u)	...	★	...
Pennsylvania	★	★	...	...	★	...	...	...	...	...	...	★	★
Rhode Island	★	...	...	★	...	★	★	...	...	...	...	★	...
South Carolina	★	★	...	★	...	★	...	★	...	$0	★	★	...
South Dakota	★	...	★	★	...	...	...	...	...	...	...	...	(cc)
Tennessee	★	★	...	...	...	...	...	★	...	...	★	...	...
Texas	★	★	...	★	★	★	★	...	★	(v)	...	★	(w)
Utah	★	★	...	...	...	...	...	★	...	...	...	★	(aa)
Vermont	★	★	...	...	...	★	...	★	...	...	...	★	...
Virginia	★	(i)	...	★	...	...	★	...	...	...	★	★	...
Washington	★	★	...	★	...	...	...	★	...	...	...	★	★
West Virginia	★	★	...	...	...	...	...	...	...	$25	★	...	(l)
Wisconsin	★	★	...	★	★	★	★	...	★	$0	★	★	...
Wyoming	★	...	★	...	★	★	...	...	...	$100	...	...	(s)
Dist. of Columbia	★	★	...	...	★	★	★	...	...	$100	...	...	...

See footnotes at end of table.

LOBBYISTS: DEFINITIONS AND PROHIBITED ACTIVITIES — Continued

Sources: The Council of State Governments' survey, October 2003; The Council on Governmental Ethics Laws, *Lobbying: 2004 Update* and state statutes and rules books, February 2004.

Key:

★—Application exists.

. . .—Not applicable.

(a) Making campaign contributions if the lobbyist's firm/employer is registered to lobby the agency of the candidate/officeholder.

(b) Not specific to lobbyists.

(c) Gift limit is $40 per calendar year, recreation limit is $100 per calendar year and honoraria is a maximum of $200 per speech.

(d) Lobbyists making gifts in excess of the following thresholds to state officials: Connecticut, $10 for gifts per year, $50 for food and drink per year; Michigan, $49 per month per official. Food and beverage for immediate consumption is reportable but not limited.

(e) Food and beverages for legislator, spouse and immediate family.

(f) The Michigan Lobby Act uses the term lobbyist agent to define an individual or firm compensated more than $500.00 to lobby on behalf of clients or employers. The term lobbyist is defined under the act as the interest group or other person that makes expenditure in excess of $500.00 to lobby a single public official or in excess of $1,975.00 to lobby any number of public officials. These thresholds are for the 2004 calendar year.

(g) Also applies to one month prior to and one month after session.

(h) By regulatory agency which sets rates, charges, fees or prices.

(i) Administrative does not have to register or report as long as they are lobbying in an official capacity.

(j) Lobbying definition includes governor, lt. governor, constitutional officers, secretary of the cabinets and staff.

(k) No lobbyist on behalf of himself or his principal, shall offer or provide to a legislator or his principal campaign committee any campaign contribution or loan resulting from a fundraising event held during a legislative session unless written notice of the fundraising function was given to the Board of Ethics at least 30 days prior to the function.

(l) Food and beverage expenditures, no limit, not included in the $25 prohibition.

(m) Adoptions of regulations and executive orders.

(n) Lobbyist cannot solicit or transmit political contributions on behalf of members or candidates for the General Assembly or the four statewide Executive Offices.

(o) State senators or representatives may not lobby for balance of term when they resign from office. This prohibition does not apply to other public officials.

(p) Employment of non-registered lobbyists.

(q) Gifts valued at more than $50 in a calendar month.

(r) State government agency liaisons lobbying on issues concerning their agency (no fee).

(s) Must itemize items of $50.00 or more.

(t) Campaign contributions/expenditures are specifically exempted from Ohio's lobbying laws.

(u) No limit on food and beverage consumed in presence of purchaser or provider; entertainment, such as NBA games, etc, is $100 per occasion or $250 per calendar year.

(v) Expenditures in excess of $500 for entertainment, $500 for gifts and $500 for an award momento per year.

(w) False communications, admission to floor of legislature, offering a loan, a gift of cash or negotiable instrument, an expenditure for transportation and lodging except for fact finding trips and a conference in which the member renders service.

(x) Alaska law prohibits lobbyists from giving campaign contributions to candidates for the legislature other than to the candidate(s) that are campaigning to represent the district in which the lobbyist is registered to vote.

(y) The office of the Governor and the Corporation Commission are the only two executive branch agencies/offices included in the definition of lobbying.

(z) Covered in Senate and House Rules.

(aa) Making contributions to a governor or governor's PAC during a legislative session or during the period for veto overrides.

(bb) Entertainment Ban 41-1232.08.

(cc) All costs incurred for the purpose of influencing legislation. However personal expenses of the lobbyist spent on his own meals, travel, lodging or phone while in attendance as the legislative session not reported.

(dd) Amount is per occurrence

(ee) Specifically exempted.

(ff) Having a prior felony for unlawful lobbying.

Table 6.14
LOBBYISTS: REGISTRATION AND REPORTING

State or other jurisdiction	Agency which administers registration and reports requirements for lobbyists	Frequency	Legislation/administrative action seeking to influence	Expenditures benefiting public officials or employees	Compensation received [broken down by employer(s)]	Total compensations received	Categories of expenditures	Total expenditures	Contributions received from others for lobbying purposes	Other	Number of registered lobbyists
Alabama	Ethics Comm.	Quarterly	★	★	...	...	...	...	...	...	565
Alaska	Public Offices Comm.	Monthly (b)	★	★	★	★	★	★	...	★ (pp)	140
Arizona	Secretary of State	Quarterly and Semi-annually	★	★	★	★	★	★	★	...	4,629
Arkansas	Ethics Comm.	Quarterly and Annually (jj)	★	★	...	...	★	★	★	...	302
California	Fair Political Practices Comm. Secretary of State	Quarterly Reporting Bi-annual Registration	★	★	★	★	★	★	★	(e)	1,089
Colorado	Secretary of State	Monthly	★	★	★	★	★	★	★	...	493
Connecticut	State Ethics Comm.	Biennially, Monthly (b)	★	★	★	★	★	★	★ (d)	...	4,357
Delaware	Public Integrity Comm.	Quarterly	★	★	...	...	★	★	...	...	213
Florida	Lobbyist Registration Office, Legislative Info. Svcs. Div.	Semi-annually	...	★	...	...	★	★	...	...	2,029
Georgia	State Ethics Comm.	Annually and monthly (h)	★	★	...	...	...	...	...	(qq)	1,225
Hawaii	State Ethics Comm.	Jan., March, May (o)	★ (i)	★	★	★	★	★	★	...	287
Idaho	Secretary of State	Monthly (a) and annually	★	★	...	...	★	★	...	...	264
Illinois	Secretary of State	Semi-annually and annually	...	★	...	...	★	★	...	(j)	2,131
Indiana	Lobby Registration Comm.	Semi-annually	★	★	...	...	★	★	...	(k)	1,400
Iowa	Secretary of Senate, Clerk of House Ethics and Disclosure Board	Monthly (b) Quarterly	★	...	★	★	...	★	★	(p)	500
Kansas	Ethics Comm.	(m)	★	★	...	...	★	★	...	...	567
Kentucky	Legislative Ethics Comm.	(n)	★	★	★	★	★	★	★	...	632
Louisiana	Ethics Administration Program	Annually and semi-annually (u)	...	★	...	...	★	★	...	...	509
Maine	Comm. on Gov't'l. Ethics	Monthly (a) and after session	★	★	★	★	★	★	★	...	189
Maryland	Ethics Comm.	Semi-annually and annually	★	★	★	★	★	★	(q)	...	755
Massachusetts	Secretary of Commonwealth Public Records Division Lobbyist Section	Semi-annually	★	★	★	★	★	★	...	(w)	639
Michigan	Department of State Bureau of Elections	Semi-annually	★	★ (r)	...	...	★	★	...	(s)	1,250
Minnesota	Campaign Finance & Public Disclosure Board	Semi-annually	★	★ (t)	...	...	★	★	★	...	1,210
Mississippi	Secretary of State	Annually and 2 times per session	★	★	★	★	...	★	...	...	369
Missouri	Ethics Comm.	Semi-annually and annually (a)	★	★	...	...	★	★	...	(q)(v)	1,200
Montana	Commr. of Political Practices	Annually (non-session) Monthly (during session)	★	★	...	...	★	★	★	...	1,074
Nebraska	Clerk of Legislature	Quarterly	★	★	★	★	★	★	★	...	N.A.
Nevada	Legislative Counsel Bureau	(x)	...	★	...	...	★	★	...	...	842
New Hampshire	Secretary of State	Three reports per year	...	★ (ll)	★	★	...	★	...	(mm)	178
New Jersey	Election Law Enforcement Comm.	Annually and quarterly	★	★	★	★	★	★	...	...	577
New Mexico	Secretary of State	Before, during & after session	★	★	...	...	★	★	★	...	900
New York	NYTS Commission on Lobbying	Bi-monthly and semi-annually	★	★	★	★	★	★	...	...	5,800
North Carolina	Secretary of State	After session and year end	...	...	(y)	...	★	...	...	...	600
North Dakota	Secretary of State	Annually	...	...	...	...	...	...	...	...	688
Ohio	Office of the Legislative Inspector General	(kk)	★	★	...	...	★	★	...	...	1,506
Oklahoma	Ethics Comm.	Semi-annually	...	★	...	...	...	...	...	...	508
Oregon	Gov't Standards & Practices Comm.	(cc)	★ (i)	★	...	...	★	★	...	(oo)	416
Pennsylvania	State Ethics Comm.	Quarterly and upon termination	★	★	★ (ii)	★ (ii)	★ (jj)	★	...	★ (ee)	784
Rhode Island	Secretary of State	(dd)	★	★	★	★	★	★	...	...	815
South Carolina	Ethics Comm.	Semi-annually	★	...	★	★	...	★	...	...	347
South Dakota	Secretary of State	Annually	★	...	...	...	...	★	...	...	534
Tennessee	Registry of Election Finance	Semi-annually	...	...	...	...	...	...	...	★ (rr)	540
Texas	Ethics Comm.	Monthly and annually (z)	★	★	★	...	...	★	...	...	1,454
Utah	State Elections Office	Annually (ff)	★	★	...	...	★	★	...	...	521
Vermont	Secretary of State	3 times per year	...	★	★	★	...	★	★	...	300

See footnotes at end of table.

LOBBYISTS: REGISTRATION AND REPORTING — Continued

			Disclosures required in lobbyist reports							
State or other jurisdiction	Agency which administers registration and reports requirements for lobbyists	Frequency	Legislation/administrative action seeking to influence	Expenditures benefiting public officials or employees	Compensation received [broken down by employer(s)]	Total compensations received	Categories of expenditures	Total expenditures	Contributions received from others for lobbying purposes	Other	Number of registered lobbyists
Virginia	Secretary of Commonwealth	Annually	★	★	(aa)	★	★	★	. . .	★	946
Washington	Public Disclosure Comm.	Monthly (nn)	. . .	★	★	★	★	★	★	. . .	862
West Virginia	Ethics Comm.	Every two years	★	★	. . .	. . .	★	★	. . .	(bb)	521
Wisconsin	Ethics Board	Biennially and Semi-annually	★	(gg)	★	★	★	★	. . .	. . .	800
Wyoming	Secretary of State	Annually	. . .	. . .	. . .	. . .	★	★	. . .	. . .	N.A.
Dist. of Columbia	Office of Campaign Finance	Biennially	★	★	★	★	★	★	★	. . .	172

Sources: The Council of State Governments' survey, October 2003; The Council on Governmental Ethics Laws, *Lobbying: 2004 Update* and state statutes and rules books, February 2004.

Key:

★—Application exists.

. . .—Not applicable.

(a) During legislative session. In Missouri, filed with the secretary of Senate and clerk of the House.

(b) During legislative session, quarterly thereafter.

(c) Must make separate disclosure report.

(d) If formed primarily for lobbying.

(e) These answers apply to reporting requirements, not registration. When registering, firm lists lobbyists, employers, agencies to be lobbied, effective date and length of contract, lobbying interest of each employer. Employer lists each employee lobbyist, firm contracted with, general lobbying interests, agencies to be lobbied and nature and interest of lobbyist employer.

(f) Also, first, second and fourth quarters.

(g) In detail, if over $10 per person.

(h) Registration annually. Monthly reporting during session, end of July and end of December.

(i) Subject areas only.

(j) Required to declare general subject matter of lobbying activity.

(k) Compensation received per employer, and total compensations received along with contributions from other for lobbying purposes is required to disclose compensation paid to others but not compensation received from others.

(l) In the Senate, reports are required only if $15 or more is provided to senators or their staff on any one day.

(m) January, February, March, April, May and September.

(n) Initial registration covers a two-year period. Reporting is monthly January, February, March, April, May, then quarterly.

(o) Register within five days of becoming a lobbyist and renew every odd-numbered year. Reporting three times a year. Reports due January 31, March 31 and May 31.

(p) Campaign contributions to state office candidates.

(q) To a limited extent.

(r) Food and beverage expenditures for public officials with itemization required over $49.99 in a one-month period or $300 in a calendar year. Travel and lodging expenditures for public officials in excess of $650.00. Group food and beverage expenditures for public officials.

(s) Financial transactions with public officials, immediate family members or their businesses of $1,0000 or more. Name and address of employees - any person compensated or reimbursed for lobbying in excess of $20.00 during any 12 month period.

(t) Not political contributions.

(u) Register annually. Expenditure reports are filed semi-annually. First report is due on August 15th covering the period of January 1st through June 30th. The second report is due on February 15th and covers the period of July 1st through December 31st. The second report is cumulative.

(v) Business relationships with public officials, if over $50.

(w) Campaign contributions are reported.

(x) Every other year in odd-number years when legislature is in session.

(y) In North Carolina, the principal shall estimate and report the compensation paid or promised directly or indirectly, to all lobbyists based on estimated time, effort and expense in connection with lobbying activities on behalf of the principal. If a lobbyist is a full-time employee of the principal, or is compensated by means of an annual fee or retainer, the principal shall estimate and report the portion of all such lobbyists' salaries or retainers that compensate the lobbyists for lobbying.

(z) Annually if expenditures are not more than $1,000 during a calendar year.

(aa) In the Commonwealth of Virginia, the lobbyist registers and reports. The employer (principal does not register and/or report).

(bb) No compensation reporting. The registered lobbyist reports expenditures made by the lobbyist or the employer for the lobbying purposes. Principal (employer or organization) represented makes no reports to us.

(cc) Registration is biennially; reporting is twice during non-session years and three times during session years.

(dd) At specified times during legislative session and at end of legislative session.

(ee) Reports required from lobbyist's principal.

(ff) Ten days after the general session, seven days before a general election, and seven days after the end of a special session or veto override session. Registrations expire at the end of even-numbered years.

(gg) Such expenditures are prohibited.

(hh) New York's Lobbying Act of 2000 requires a description of the subject lobbied or expected to be lobbied, as well as listing the legislative bill number and the rule, regulation, and ratemaking number lobbied or expected to be lobbied.

(ii) Must report all contributions to a principal in excess of 10 percent of principals total resources.

(jj) Reports are filed monthly if the General Assembly is in session.

(kk) Registration for executive agency lobbyists is annual. Registration for legislative lobbyists is every two years coinciding with legislative session. All lobbyists and their employers report three times per calendar year.

(ll) Expenditures benefiting public officials over $50.00.

(mm) General topic for each registration, not specific bills.

(nn) Employer's of lobbyists are required to file an annual report due by February 28th for lobbying expenses incurred during the previous period.

(oo) Expenditures for legislative officials are itemized only if they exceed $70.00 on a single occasion.

(pp) If married to or spousal equivalent of public official or legislative employee, lobbyists may only make contributions to legislative candidates in their voting district. Those contributions must be reported within 30 days.

(qq) General business of party lobbied for, employment provided, members of public officials immediate family must be disclosed.

(rr) Contributions made to candidates.

2004 Initiatives and Referendums
By John G. Matsusaka

Ballot propositions continue to drive the policy agenda in the states, and 2004 spilled over into the presidential election. The most popular issue was marriage, with 13 states approving constitutional amendments defining marriage as between a man and a woman.

Ballot propositions have been driving the policy agenda in the states for some time now, and this year was no exception. Constitutional amendments defining marriage played a role in the presidential campaign, and wins by high profile propositions on illegal immigration, stem cell research, and clean energy are likely to trigger a wave of similar legislative activity across the country.

In all, 162 state-level measures went before the voters on November 2, 2004 with about two-thirds of them passing. The total number of measures was down by about 25 percent from November 2000, with much of the drop-off due to a decline in bond and revenue measures as states put their fiscal crises behind them. The 162 propositions were distributed across 34 states. California had the most-16-although this number was below the state's average of 18 for general elections, and well below the peak of 48 measures in 1914. Table A lists the number of propositions by state, and the highest profile issues in each state. The passage rate of 67 percent was up somewhat from 62 percent in 2002.

Of the 162 propositions, 101 were placed on the ballot by legislatures ("legislative measures") and 59 were "initiatives," qualified by citizen petition. There were also two petition referendums, measures that proposed to repeal laws passed by the legislature, and that qualify for the ballot by petition (Prop. 72 in California and R-55 in Washington).[1]

The number of initiatives was up from 53 in 2002, and brings the total for the last 10 years to more than 360. As Figure A shows, this is the highest 10-year total in history, and comes on the heels of big jumps in initiative activity in the preceding two decades. The initiative revolution that began with California's Prop. 13 in 1978, shows no sign of slowing, and in fact seems to be accelerating.

I&R and the Presidential Election

One of the most interesting developments this past year was the possibility that ballot propositions could influence the presidential election. Colorado's Amendment 36 proposed to allocate the state's nine presidential electors in proportion to the popular vote received by each candidate instead of giving them all to the state winner. The twist was that the measure was written to be retroactive: if approved, it would have applied to the presidential votes cast on the same day, in effect transferring four electoral votes from George Bush to John Kerry.

Leading up to the election, there was speculation that the electoral votes of the two candidates could be close enough so that the election would turn on the fate of Amendment 36. If so, the initiative would have promptly landed in court, requiring judges to determine the winner in a reprise of 2000.

As it turned out, the presidential election was not as close as expected, and Amendment 36 was soundly defeated, 34 percent to 66 percent. The measure was intended to jumpstart reform of the Electoral College, partly in response to dissatisfaction with the fact that the popular vote winner did not become president in 2000. The thrashing of Amendment 36, and the lack of controversy in the 2004 presidential race, will likely put a damper on reform efforts in the near future.

The other issue that played a role in the presidential campaign was marriage. Constitutional amendments to define marriage as solely the union of a man and a woman were on the ballot in 11 states, including the critical "battleground" states of Michigan and Ohio (the others were Arkansas, Georgia, Kentucky, Mississippi, Montana, North Dakota, Oklahoma, Oregon and Utah; and Louisiana and Missouri adopted earlier in 2004). These measures were responses to a Massachusetts Supreme Court ruling in February 2004 holding that the state's constitution contained a right to gay marriage. Legislatures and in some cases citizen groups placed these amendments on the ballot to prevent their own judges from finding a right to gay marriage in their constitutions. All of the amendments were approved by large margins.

There were several schools of thought of how the marriage amendments might matter. One view was that the amendments would mobilize religious conservative voters to go to the polls, and once there they would support the GOP. The other view was that gay marriage proponents would turn out disproportionately and this would help the Democrats. Yet another possibility was the amendments would bring out black voters—who register among the highest disapproval of gay marriage among major demographic groups—which would help the Democrats.

What actually happened is not clear at the time of writing. Exit polls noted a large fraction of voters who claimed to be motivated by "values' but what this means is unclear. Moreover, there is not yet any reliable evidence that the marriage amendments did in fact disproportionately boost turnout of any particular group. Even if they did not affect turnout, they may have crystallized the distinction between the two presidential candidates for voters with strong feelings about the issue.

Conservatives versus Liberals

The initiative and referendum processes have stubbornly refused to play ideological favorites. Direct democracy had its origins in the Progressive movement of the early 20th century, and progressives used the processes to advance a host of issues that would be called "liberal" under today's terminology, such as welfare, old age pensions, and women's suffrage.[2] Starting in the 1970s, conservatives began to score big wins as well, especially on tax measures, but also on social policies such as capital punishment, abortion, and affirmative action/racial preferences. 2004 was a fairly typical year in this regard. Conservatives won big on the 11 marriage amendments, a Florida amendment requiring parental notification of abortion, and a Colorado measure cutting off public services to illegal immigrants. Conservatives suffered a loss when a Maine initiative that would have capped property taxes was rejected. Liberals got their share with wins in Florida and Nevada on measures that increase the minimum wage, and a Colorado amendment that requires large utilities to generate a certain amount of power from clean energy sources such as solar, hydro, wind and biomass. Liberals were defeated in an attempt to legalize the use, production, and sale of marijuana in Alaska, and the repeal of California law that required large businesses to provide health

Table A: State-By-State Totals, 2004

State	Number of initiatives & referendums (a)	Number of legislative measures (a)	Notable issues
Alabama	0	8 (3)	Obsolete racial language
Alaska	3 (1)	1 (1)	Marijuana legalization
Arizona	1(1)	7 (3)	Illegal immigrants
Arkansas	1(1)	3 (1)	Marriage
California	12 (5)	4 (4)	Stem cell bonds, employer health care
Colorado	4 (2)	2 (1)	Presidential electors
Florida	6 (6)	2 (2)	Contingency fees, malpractice
Georgia	0	2 (2)	Marriage
Hawaii	0	4 (4)	Criminal procedures
Indiana	0	3 (3)	
Kentucky	0	1 (1)	Marriage
Louisiana	0	4 (4)	Right to hunt and trap
Maine	2 (0)	0	Property tax limit
Michigan	2 (2)	0	Marriage
Mississippi	0	1 (1)	Marriage
Missouri	1 (1)	0	
Montana	4 (3)	3 (2)	Marriage, mining with cyanide
Nebraska	4 (2)	4 (2)	Gambling
Nevada	6 (3)	2 (1)	Education spending
New Hampshire	0	1 (0)	
New Mexico	0	7 (7)	Four bond measures
North Carolina	0	3 (3)	
North Dakota	1 (1)	0	Marriage
Ohio	1 (1)	0	Marriage
Oklahoma	0	9 (9)	Marriage, lottery
Oregon	6 (2)	2 (2)	Marriage, logging
Rhode Island	0	14 (10)	12 bond measures
South Carolina	0	2 (1)	Minibottles
South Dakota	1 (0)	2 (0)	
Utah	1 (0)	3 (3)	Marriage, bonds for open space
Virginia	0	2 (2)	Apportionment
Washington	5 (2)	0	Sales tax for education
West Virginia	0	1 (1)	
Wyoming	0	4 (2)	Pain and suffering awards
Total	61 (33)	101 (75)	

Source: Data for elected officials are current as of January 2005 and have been provided by the Center for American Women and Politics, Eagleton Institute of Politics, Rutgers University.
Key:
★—Denotes that this position is filled through a statewide election.
W—Denotes that this position is filled through a statewide election and is held by a woman.
. . .—Denotes that this position is filled through methods other than a statewide election.

insurance to their workers.

The mixed results for liberals and conservatives reinforce that initiatives and referendums are ideologically neutral. They provide opportunities for groups of any ideology that are not given a fair hearing by the legislature.[3]

High Profile Issues

As usual, a wide variety of issues were considered this past year. Table B lists the number of various types of issues. Some of the more prominent issues are discussed in what follows:

Table B:
Subjects in 2004

Subject	Number of propositions
Abortion	1
Alcohol & marijuana	4
Apportionment	1
Bonds	21
Crime	6
Economic development	5
Education	7
Elections	7
Environment (includes animals)	10
Gambling	13
Government administration	6
Government powers	10
Health care	3
Initiative & referendum	5
Immigration	1
Insurance	1
Lawsuits	7
Marriage	11
Minimum wage	2
Miscellaneous	7
Officeholders, qualifications & salaries	4
Impeachment and succession	3
Taxes	22
Term limits	4
Transportation	1

Source: Initiative & Referendum Institute

Marijuana

The marijuana legalization movement appears to be losing steam. The most far-reaching proposition, Alaska's Measure 2 that would have entirely legalized marijuana for people over the age of 21, was decisively rejected 43-57. An attempt to establish state-run medical marijuana dispensaries in Oregon (Measure 33) was also rejected. The only success was in Montana, were voters approved a measure to allow limited use of marijuana for medical purposes (I-148). A total of 11 states now allow medical marijuana.[4]

Gambling

Gambling was one of the most popular topics in 2004, with 13 measures on the ballot in six states. These measures were among the most expensive, with over $90 million spent on two gambling initiatives in California alone. Voters were not particularly receptive to expansions in gambling, rejecting a California measure that would have allowed un-limited tribal gambling, a California measure that would have allowed nontribal gambling, and a Washington measure that would have allowed non-tribal gambling.

Nebraska voters faced five measures related to casinos, and rejected the three that would have authorized the casinos. The brightest spot for gambling was in Oklahoma, were voters approved two propositions establishing a state lottery and another that expanded Indian gaming. A measure in Florida that allowed slot machines in Miami-Dade and Broward counties narrowly passed.

Election Reform

The Electoral College was the most visible issue concerning elections, due to Colorado's Amendment 36, discussed above. Proposals to create runoff primary elections instead of closed primaries were rejected in California (Prop. 62) and approved in Washington (I-872). A measure to allow runoff primaries in local elections was rejected in New Mexico (Amendment 3).

Fiscal Measures

A total of 41 tax and bond measures went before the voters in November, down by about one-third from 2002. The bond measure involving the most money was Prop. 71 in California, an initiative that authorized a $3 billion bond issue to be used for stem cell research. The measure was approved 59 percent to 41 percent, attracting support from both conservatives and liberals. California voters also approved Prop. 61, which authorized a $750 million bond issue for children's hospitals. All told, the state's voters added an estimated $250 million to the state's annual debt service when all the bonds are issued, according to the state's nonpartisan Legislative Analyst. Arkansas voters approved $500 million bond issue for economic development. The largest bond issue to fail was Utah's Initiative 1 that would have authorized $150 million for open spaces, and increased the sales tax to service the debt.

The most expensive tax measure was Washington's I-884 that would have increased the state's sales tax by 1 percent (to a national high of 7.5 percent) with the money going to education. The tax increase was anticipated to generate about $1 billion per year.

Voters turned it down, 39 percent to 61 percent. California voters approved a 1 percent surtax on millionaires, with the proceeds dedicated to mental health services. Sin tax measures were approved in Colorado, Montana and Oklahoma, and rejected in Alabama.

Environment

Voters decided 10 environmental measures, endorsing the "green" position in four cases and the "brown" position in six cases. The most far-reaching was Colorado's Amendment 37, discussed above, that requires large utilities to use clean energy sources. Voters in four states expressed their support for hunting either by approving hunting rights (Louisiana and Montana) or rejecting limits on bear hunting (Alaska and Maine).

Heath Care Costs, Malpractice, and Lawsuits

The rising cost of health care featured prominently in the presidential campaigns and played out in the states with 10 measures. An alleged cause of rising costs is lawsuits, and trial lawyers were the target of several propositions. Measures to limit pain-and-suffering awards were approved in Nevada (Question 3) and rejected in Oregon (Measure 35) and Wyoming (Amendment D). Measures to limit attorney fees or require mediation were approved in Florida (Amendment 3) and Wyoming (Amendment C). Counter-initiatives sponsored by trial lawyers were rejected in Nevada (Questions 4, 5) and approved in Florida (Amendments 7, 8). California's Prop. 72 mandating employer-provided health insurance was rejected.

Money

Final totals are unavailable at the time of writing, but the amount of money involved was considerable. Estimates are that roughly $200 million was spent in California, over $30 million in Florida, and over $10 million in Colorado. To put these numbers in perspective, the presidential campaigns of George Bush and John Kerry were expected to spend in the vicinity of $300 million to $350 million. Despite concerns about the role of money in ballot proposition campaigns, however, it remains the case that money can't buy you law. Gambling interests spent upwards of $90 million on two initiatives in California yet only managed 16 percent and 24 percent of the votes in favor. Money allows groups to make proposals but does not determine the final outcome.[5]

Author's Note

This article uses referendums instead of referenda as the plural of referendum following the Oxford English Dictionary and common practice.

Notes

[1]For state-by-state descriptions of legal provisions, see Dane M. Waters, *The Initiative and Referendum Almanac*, (Carolina Academic Press, 2003), or *www.iandinstitute.org*.

[2]John G. Matsusaka, "Fiscal Effects of the Voter Initiative in the First Half of the Twentieth Century," Journal

[3]Ibid.

[4]See note 1 above.

[5]Elisabeth R. Gerber, The Populist Paradox: Interest *Group Influence and the Promise of Direct Legislation*, (Princeton University Press, 1999).

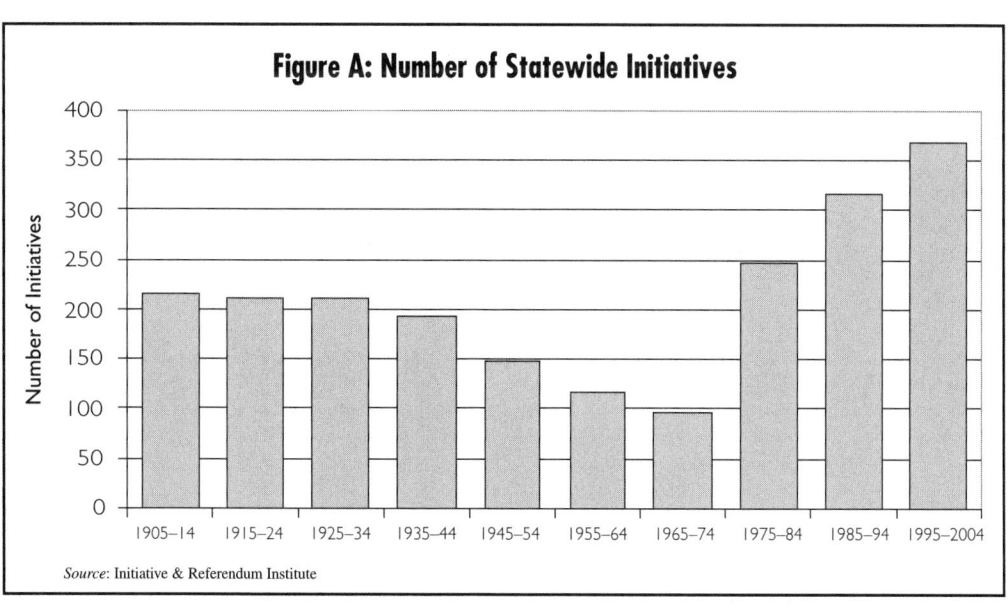

Figure A: Number of Statewide Initiatives

Source: Initiative & Referendum Institute

About the Author

John G. Matsusaka is a professor of business and law at the University of Southern California and president of the Initiative and Referendum Institute at USC. He is the author of *For the Many or the Few: The Initiative, Public Policy*, and *American Democracy* (University of Chicago Press, 2004).

Table 6.15
STATE INITIATIVES & REFERENDUMS, 2004

State	Measure	Type of election	Type	Topics addressed by measure		Pass	Fail
Alabama (a)	Amendment 1	General	LR	Economic Development	Commerce / State and Local Government	★	
	Amendment 2	General	LR	Constitutional Law	Civil Law / Obsolete Language		★
	Amendment 3	General	LR	Economic Development	Commerce / State and Local Government	★	
	Amendment 4	General	LR	Economic Development	Commerce / Agriculture	★	
	Amendment 5	General	LR	Education	Property Taxes / State and Local Government		★
	Amendment 6	General	LR	Judicial	State and Local Government / Salaries		★
	Amendment 7	General	LR	Taxes	State and Local Government / Budget		★
	Amendment 8	General	LR	Transportation	Taxes / Vehicles		★
Alaska	Measure 1	General	LR	Elections	Initiative Signatures	★	
	Measure 2	General	I	Criminal and Civil Justice	Marijuana / Health		★
	Measure 3	General	I	Natural Resources	Criminal and Civil Justice / Bear Baiting		★
	Measure 4	General	I	Elections	Senate Vacancies	★	
Arizona	Proposition 100	General	LR	Natural Resources	Environment / State and Local Government		★
	Proposition 101	General	LR	Initiatives and Referenda	Elections / Restrictions on Initiatives		★
	Proposition 102	General	LR	Education	Economic Development	★	
	Proposition 103	General	LR	Judicial	Justices of the Peace		★
	Proposition 104	General	LR	Initiatives and Referenda	Elections	★	
	Proposition 105	General	LR	Board of Education	Constitutional Law / Federal	★	
	Proposition 200	General	I	Constitutional Law	Elections / Illegal Immigration	★	
	Proposition 300	General	LR	Legislatures	Salaries		★
Arkansas	Amendment 1	General	LR	Elections	Legislatures / Term Limits	★	
	Amendment 2	General	LR	Economic Development	Taxes / Bond	★	
	Amendment 3	General	I	Constitutional Law	Civil Law / Marriage		★
	Referred Question 1	General	LR	Education	Property Taxes		★
California	Proposition 1A	General	LR	State and Local Government	Taxes / Social Services	★	
	Proposition 55	March 2, 2004 Primary	LR	Education	Bonds	★	
	Proposition 56	March 2, 2004 Primary	I	Budget	Taxes		★
	Proposition 57	March 2, 2004 Primary	LR	Budget	Bonds / Economy	★	
	Proposition 58	March 2, 2004 Primary	LR	Constitutional Law	Civil Law	★	
	Proposition 59	General	LR	Elections	Anti-runoff / State and Local Government	★	
	Proposition 60	General	LR	Revenue	State Property	★	
	Proposition 60A	General	LR	Health	Bond / Revenue	★	
	Proposition 61	General	I	Elections	Runoff Primary		★
	Proposition 62	General	I	Health	Taxes		★
	Proposition 63	General	I	Economic Development	Constitutional Law	★	
	Proposition 64	General	I	Taxes	Revenues / Civil Law	★	
	Proposition 65	General	I	Criminal and Civil Justice	Taxes / State and Local Government		★
	Proposition 66	General	I	Health	Taxes / Revenue		★
	Proposition 67	General	I	Gambling/Lotteries	Taxes		★
	Proposition 68	General	I	Criminal Justice	Law Enforcement / State and Tribal Government		★
	Proposition 69	General	I	Gambling/Lotteries	Taxes / DNA	★	
	Proposition 70	General	I	Health	Stem Cell Research / State and Tribal Government		★
	Proposition 71	General	I	Health	Stem Cell Research / Bond	★	
	Proposition 72	General	PR	Health	Insurance / Economic Development		★

See footnotes at end of table.

STATE INITIATIVES & REFERENDUMS, 2004—Continued

State	Measure	Type of election	Type	Topics addressed by measure	Pass	Fail
Colorado	Amendment 34	General	I	Economic Development; Constitutional and Civil Law; Contractor Liability		★
	Amendment 35	General	I	Taxes; Health; Tobacco	★	
	Amendment 36	General	I	Elections; Electoral Votes		★
	Amendment 37	General	I	Energy; Natural Resources	★	
	Referendum A	General	LR	Labor; State and Local Government; Civil Service	★	
	Referendum B	General	LR	Constitutional Law; Civil Law; Obsolete language	★	
Connecticut (a)				(b)		
Delaware (a)				(b)		
Florida	Amendment 1	General	LR	Constitutional Law; Health; Privacy	★	
	Amendment 2	General	LR	Elections; Constitutional Law; Filing Initiatives	★	
	Amendment 3	General	I	Judicial; Health; Attorney Contingency Fees	★	
	Amendment 4	General	I	Gambling/Lotteries; Taxes; Education	★	
	Amendment 5	General	I	Employment; Labor; Minimum Wage	★	
	Amendment 6	General	I	Transportation	★	
	Amendment 7	General	I	Health; Constitutional and Civil Law; Patient Rights	★	
	Amendment 8	General	I	Health; Constitutional and Civil Law; Medical License Revocation	★	
Georgia (a)	Amendment 1	General	LR	Constitutional Law; Civil Law; Marriage	★	
	Amendment 2	General	LR	Judicial; Jurisdiction	★	
Hawaii (a)	Amendment 1	General	LR	Criminal and Civil Justice; Law Enforcement; Sexual assault	★	
	Amendment 2	General	LR	Criminal and Civil Justice; Public Safety; Sex Offenders	★	
	Amendment 3	General	LR	Criminal and Civil Justice; Constitutional Law	★	
	Amendment 4	General	LR	Criminal and Civil Justice; Felony Charges		
Idaho				(b)		
Illinois (f)				(b)		
Indiana (a)	Public Question 1	General	LR	Property Taxes; Revenues; Economic Development	★	
	Public Question 2	General	LR	State and Local Government; Administrative; Term Limits	★	
	Public Question 3	General	LR	Gubernatorial Succession; State and Local Government	★	
Iowa (a)				(b)		
Kansas (a)				(b)		
Kentucky (a)	Amendment 1	General	LR	Constitutional Law; Civil Law; Marriage	★	
Louisiana (a)	Amendment 1	Sept. 18, 2004	LR	Constitutional Law; Civil Law; Marriage	★(c)	
	Amendment 1	Open Primary Election	LR	Natural Resources; Constitutional Law; Civil Law	★	
	Amendment 2	General	LR	Taxes; Revenues; Revenues	★	
	Amendment 3	General	LR	Labor; Government Administration; Veterans	★	
	Amendment 4	General	LR	Agriculture; Commerce; Economic Development	★	
Maine	Question 1	Carry-over Measure June 8, 2004	I	Education; Funding	★(d)	
	Question 1	General	I	Property Taxes; Revenues		★
	Question 2	General	I	Natural Resources; Criminal and Civil Justice		★

See footnotes at end of table.

STATE INITIATIVES & REFERENDUMS, 2004—Continued

State	Measure	Type of election	Type	Topics addressed by measure			Pass	Fail
Maryland (a)				(b)				
Massachusetts				(b)				
Michigan	Proposal 04-1	General Election	I	Gambling/Lotteries	Constitutional Law	Civil Law	★	
	Proposal 04-2	General Election	I	Marriage	Constitutional Law			★
Minnesota (a)				(b)				
Mississippi	Amendment 1	General Election	LR	Marriage	Constitutional Law	Civil Law	★	
Missouri	Amendment 1	August 3, 2004 Primary Election	I	Gambling			★	
	Amendment 2	August 3, 2004 Primary Election	LR	Marriage	Constitutional Law	Civil Law	★	
	Amendment 3	General Election	I	Transportation	Taxes	Revenue	★	
Montana	C-40	General Election	LR	Environment	Natural resources	Budget	★	
	C-41	General Election	LR	Environment	Natural resources	Constitutional and Civil Law	★	
	C-42	General Election	LR	Term limits	Elections	Legislature		★
	C-96	General Election	I	Marriage	Constitutional Law	Civil Law	★	
	I-147	General Election	I	Environment	Natural resources			★
	I-148	General Election	I	Health	Criminal justice	Medical Marijuana		★
	I-149	General Election	I	Tobacco	Health	Taxes	★	
Nebraska	Initiative Measure 417	General Election	I	Gambling/Lotteries	Taxes	Legislature	★	
	Initiative Measure 418	General Election	I	Initiatives	Elections		★	
	Initiative Measure 419	General Election	I	Gambling/Lotteries	Taxes	Taxes	★	
	Initiative Measure 420	General Election	I	Gambling/Lotteries	Local Government		★	
	Amendment 1	General Election	LR	Property Taxes	Historical Properties		★	
	Amendment 2	General Election	LR	Lieutenant Governor	Legislature		★	
	Amendment 3	General Election	LR	Gambling/Lotteries	Budget	Revenues		★
	Amendment 4	General Election	LR	Gambling/Lotteries	Budget			★
Nevada	Question 1	General Election	I	Education	Budget		★	
	Question 2	General Election	I	Education	Budget		★	
	Question 3	General Election	I	Judicial	Health	Attorney Contingency Fees	★	
	Question 4	General Election	I	Insurance Rates		Frivolous Lawsuits		★
	Question 5	General Election	I	Judicial	Legal			★
	Question 6	General Election	I	Labor	Employment	Minimum Wage	★	
	Question 7	General Election	LR	Elections	Constitutional and Civil Law		★	
	Question 8	General Election	LR	Taxes	Revenue	Obsolete language		★
New Hampshire (a)	Question 1	General Election	LR	Judicial	Legislature			★(e)
New Jersey (a)				(b)				
New Mexico (a)	Amendment 3	General Election	LR	Elections	State and Local Government	Runoff	★	
	Amendment 4	General Election	LR	Property Taxes	Revenue	Veterans	★	
	Amendment 5	General Election	LR	State and Local Government	Education	Handicapped	★	
	Bond Issue 1	General Election	LR	Taxes	Revenue	Bond	★	
	Bond Issue 2	General Election	LR	Health and Human Services	Taxes	Revenue	★	
	Bond Issue 3	General Election	LR	Taxes	Revenue	Bond	★	
	Bond Issue 4	General Election	LR	Education	Taxes	Bond	★	

See footnotes at end of table.

STATE INITIATIVES & REFERENDUMS, 2004 — Continued

State	Measure	Type of election	Type	Topics addressed by measure	Topics addressed by measure (b)	Pass	Fail
New York (a)							
North Carolina (a)	Amendment 1	General	LR	Taxes	Commerce	★	
	Amendment 2	General	LR	Education	Budget	★	
	Amendment 3	General	LR	Judicial	Election Reform	★	
North Dakota	Constitutional 1	General	I	Marriage	Constitutional and Civil Law	★	
Ohio	Amendment 1	General	I	Marriage	Constitutional and Civil Law	★	
Oklahoma	Question 705	General Election	LR	Lottery	Education	★	
	Question 706	General Election	LR	Lottery	Education	★	
	Question 707	General Election	LR	State Government	Local Government	★	
	Question 708	General Election	LR	Budget	Rainy Day Fund	★	
	Question 711	General Election	LR	Marriage	Constitutional Law	★	
	Question 712	General Election	LR	Gambling	Tribal Relations	★	
	Question 713	General Election	LR	Tobacco	Revenue	★	
	Question 714	General Election	LR	Property Taxes	Revenue	★	
	Question 715	General Election	LR	Property Taxes	Senior Citizens	★	
Oregon	Measure 30	Special Election February 3, 2004	LR	Taxes	Budgets		★
	Measure 31	General Election	LR	Elections	Legislature	★	
	Measure 32	General Election	LR	Taxes	Revenues	★	
	Measure 33	General Election	I	Health	Medical Marijuana		★
	Measure 34	General Election	I	Natural Resources	Economic Development		★
	Measure 35	General Election	I	Judicial	Limits Settlement Amounts		★
	Measure 36	General Election	I	Marriage	Civil Law	★	
	Measure 37	General Election	I	Constitutional Law	State and Local Government	★	
	Measure 38	General Election	I	Labor	State Accident Insurance Fund		★
Pennsylvania (a)	Question 1	2004 General Primary	LR	Water and Wastewater Infrastructure Grant		★	
Rhode Island (a)	Amendment 1	General Election	LR	Separation of Powers	Constitutional and Civil Law	★	
	Amendment 2	General Election	LR	Constitutional Law	Constitutional Convention		★
	Question 3	General Election	LR	Transportation	Revenue/Bonds	★	
	Question 4	General Election	LR	Education	Revenue/Bonds	★	
	Question 5	General Election	LR	Education	Revenue/Bonds	★	
	Question 6	General Election	LR	Cultural	Revenue/Bonds		★
	Question 7	General Election	LR	Natural Resources	Local Government	★	
	Question 8	General Election	LR	Environment	Natural Resources	★	
	Question 9	General Election	LR	Education	Revenue/Bonds	★	
	Question 10	General Election	LR	Education	Revenue/Bonds	★	
	Question 11	General Election	LR	Cultural	Revenue/Bonds		★
	Question 12	General Election	LR	State and Local Government	Revenue/Bonds		★
	Question 13	General Election	LR	Education	Revenue/Bonds	★	
	Question 14	General Election	LR	Commerce and Economic Development	Revenue/Bonds	★	
South Carolina (a)	Question 1	General Election	LR	Commerce and Economic Development		★	
	Question 2	General Election	LR	Agriculture	Revenue		★

See footnotes at end of table.

STATE INITIATIVES & REFERENDUMS, 2004 — Continued

State	Measure	Type of election	Type	Topics addressed by measure	Pass	Fail
South Dakota	Amendment A	General Election	LR	Judicial; Elections; Nominations		★
	Amendment B	General Election	LR	Education; Revenue		★
	Measure 1	General Election	I	Taxes; Exempts Food		★
Tennessee (a)				(b)		
Texas (a)				(b)		
Utah	Amendment 1	General Election	LR	Legislature; Constitutional Law; Impeachment	★	
	Amendment 2	General Election	LR	Education; Commerce; Economic Development	★	
	Amendment 3	General Election	LR	Marriage; Constitutional Law; Civil Law	★	
	Initiative 1	General Election	I	Taxes, Revenue/Bonds; Environment/Natural Resources; Cultural		★
Vermont (a)				(b)		
Virginia (a)	Amendment 1	General Election	LR	Elections; Redistricting/Apportionment	★	
	Amendment 2	General Election	LR	Gubernatorial Succession; State and Local Government; Emergency Preparedness	★	
Washington	Initiative 297	General Election	I	Environmental Protection	★	
	Initiative 872	General Election	I	Elections	★	
	Initiative 884	General Election	I	Education; Taxes; Revenue		★
	Initiative 892	General Election	I	Gambling; Taxes; Revenue		★
	Referendum 55	General Election	PR	Education; Charter Schools	★	
West Virginia (a)	Amendment 1	General Election	LR	Veterans; Bond	★	
Wisconsin (a)				(b)		
Wyoming	Amendment A	General Election	LR	State Government; Local Government; State and Local Government		★
	Amendment B	General Election	LR	Commerce; Economic Development	★	
	Amendment C	General Election	LR	Medical Malpractice; Judicial; Mediation before Lawsuits	★	
	Amendment D	General Election	LR	Pain and Suffering Awards; Judicial; Health		★

Source: The Council of State Governments' survey of election web sites, January 2005.

Key:
LR—Legislative referendum
I—Initiative
PR—Popular referendum
O—Other
(a) State does not have an initiative process.
(b) State had no ballot measures in November 2004.
(c) State District judge ruled that the amendment violated the state constitution.
(d) This citizen-initiated legislation was presented to the voters in November, 2003, along with a competing measure proposed by the Legislature. At the 2003 election, the citizen initiative received a greater number of votes than either the competing measure or the option to reject both measures. It received less than a majority but more than one third of the total votes cast on that question. Accordingly, the Maine Constitution requires that the citizen initiative be resubmitted by itself to the voters for their approval or rejection at the next statewide election.
(e) Requires 2/3 majority to pass.
(f) The state has an initiative process, but it is unusable.

Chapter Seven

STATE FINANCE AND DEMOGRAPHICS

State Budgets: Recent Trends and Outlook
By Donald J. Boyd

States are recovering from the recent fiscal crisis, but many will need to cut spending further or increase taxes to bring spending and revenue into line. In addition, states must confront fiscal pressures in Medicaid, elementary and secondary education, and other areas, and will face risks from actions to reduce the federal budget deficit.

The Fiscal Crisis and How States Have Responded

State tax revenue fell 10 percent between fiscal year 2000 and 2003, adjusted for inflation, population growth and legislated changes—far more than the relatively mild recession would have suggested, and nearly twice as much as in the crises of the early 1980s and early 1990s.

States were better prepared for this recession than the prior one. They buffered much of the initial revenue shock by drawing fund balances down from 10.4 percent of expenditures to 3.2 percent, a drop of 7.2 percentage points compared with only a 3.7 percent drop in the previous recession (when fund balances at the start were lower). States also garnered considerable nonrecurring revenue by issuing bonds that allowed them to convert annual tobacco settlement revenue into a few large payments. Drawing down balances and tapping nonrecurring revenue sources allowed states to push some of the problem off to future years.

Elected officials and the public in most states have had little appetite for tax and fee increases. Cumulative increases in response to this crisis have amounted to only 3.5 percent of own-source revenue, down sharply from the 9 percent increases in each of the prior two crises. Spending cuts have been more popular: states have cut real per-capita general fund spending by about 6.4 percent from its 2001 peak, similar to reductions in the 1980s crisis but far deeper than in the early 1990s when states hardly cut aggregate spending at all.

Tax revenue fell so far in this crisis that subsequent tax increases and economic growth have not been enough to raise revenue to its prior level. For the nation as a whole, state tax revenue in 2004 was still 6.7 percent below the 2000 pre-crisis peak, adjusted for inflation and population growth.[1] By contrast, four years after the last crisis hit real per-capita state tax revenue in 1994 was 6.8 percent above its 1990 pre-crisis peak (Figure A). Tax revenue has continued to recover in 2005, but assuming states hit their budgeted estimates they will still end the year

more than 4 percent below 2000.

The failure of state tax revenue to recover to pre-crisis levels despite tax increases and economic growth is widespread, as Figure B shows: 36 states had lower real per capita tax revenue in 2004 than in 2000, and the median for these "shortfall" states was 8.0 percent below 2000. States that are the furthest below 2000 generally rely heavily on income tax revenue or had economies that were hit disproportionately hard by the recession. Wyoming and several other states with large increases in revenue benefited from increases related to oil, natural gas and other natural resources that tend not to follow the national business cycle. Simply put, current state revenue structures cannot support as much spending as before the crisis.

To be sure, states have cut spending, although it is difficult to measure quite how much. The earliest available data on state expenditures come from reports state budget offices provide to the National Association of State Budget Officers (NASBO). Unfortunately, these data generally serve the needs of the annual budget process and are not always classified the same way from year to year (or from state to state). In each of the last two recessions, the NASBO data tended to show considerably deeper cuts in state budgets than the more comprehensive and consistent expenditure data reported by the Census Bureau two years later. NASBO data might overstate spending cuts in this crisis as well, but we won't know for nearly two years.

NASBO data show that total state general fund expenditures have declined by 3.3 percent between 2000 and 2004, adjusted for inflation and population growth.[2] However, this overstates cuts in recurring spending because it includes capital spending financed by the general fund as well as operating expenditures. States tend to scale general fund capital spending back sharply in crises, either deferring capital projects or financing them from other sources such as bonds and dedicated revenue. Although these cuts help to balance annual budgets, the spending can spring back sharply

Figure A: Real Per Capita State Government Tax Revenue Indexed to Pre-Crisis Peak, 2 Crises (actual revenue, not adjusted for legislation)

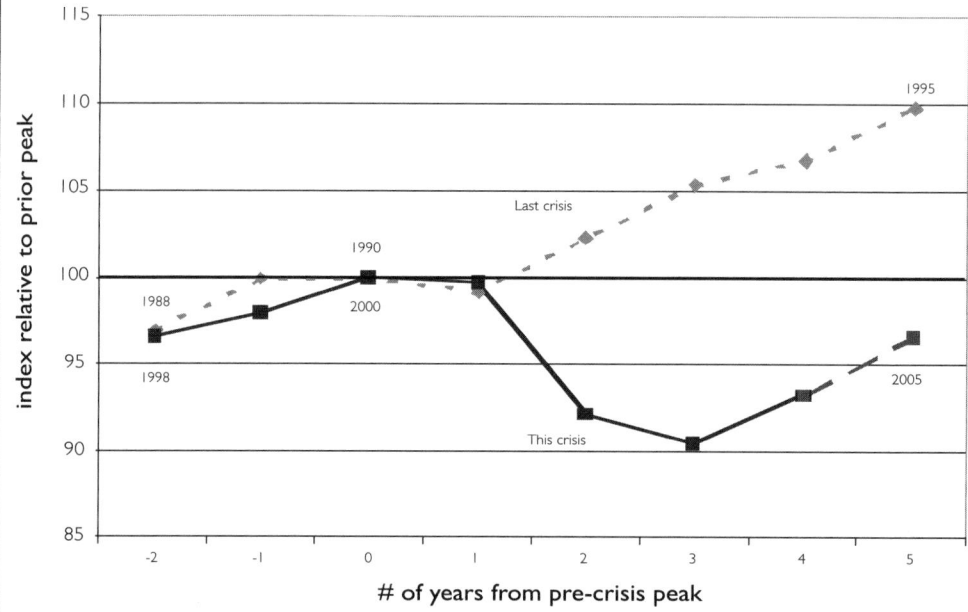

Sources:

Taxes:
  Through 2002, cenfin database (Rockefeller Institute database of Census Bureau data). For 2003, Census state tax collections from their website (2002 tax data from this Census source matches 2002 from other Census sources, giving comfort that the 2002 to 2003 growth rate is appropriate). For 2004, growth rate from Rockefeller Institute Revenue Report tax data (as collected by Nick Jenny) applied to 2003 Census tax data. For 2005: assume that state budget offices' forecasted growth rates (from NASBO's Fiscal Survey) for income, sales, and corporate taxes reflect what will happen to taxes as a whole (see below)

Population:
  Through 2002, cenfin database. For 2003, 2004, from same census pop source. For 2005, assumed to grow 1% based on recent prior history the population data were pieced together from various Census Bureau sources and are all on a July 1 (not April 1) basis.

Inflation:
  slgcwpi (state and local government chain-weighted price index)—BEA. For 2005 (cy 2004), assumed to be 3 percent based on my earlier analysis of how inflation was running for the year.

after the crisis ends. Between 2000 and 2004 state governments cut general fund capital spending by 48 percent in real per-capita terms—reductions that probably will not be sustained.

Table A removes general fund capital spending, showing just spending on operations. By this measure, spending fell by 2.9 percent between 2000 and 2004—well shy of the 6.7 percent tax revenue decline in the same period.[3] As the table shows, spending on Medicaid increased by 6.4 percent, while all other areas in aggregate were cut back. State support for higher education was cut particularly sharply, leading to double-digit tuition increases in many public universities.

In about half of the states general fund spending grew faster than tax revenue between 2000 and 2004, adjusted for inflation and population growth, and by at least 5 percentage points faster in more than a dozen states. The implication is that despite improving revenue collections, many states still will need to raise taxes or cut spending further to keep budgets balanced. This is consistent with reports that approximately half the states faced gaps for FY 2006 at the time governors were preparing proposed budgets.[4]

Spending Pressures

Medicaid: After a brief slowdown in the late 1990s, Medicaid returned for several years to double-digit

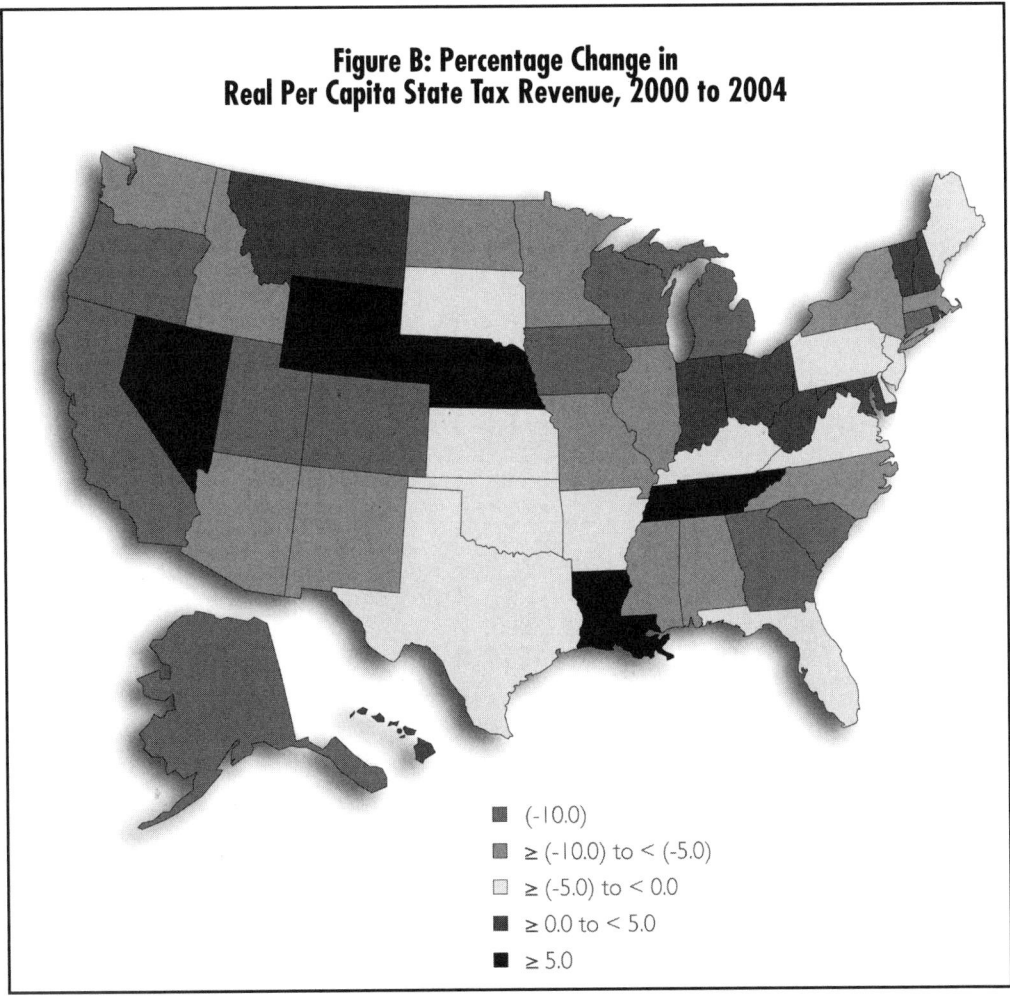

Figure B: Percentage Change in Real Per Capita State Tax Revenue, 2000 to 2004

■ (-10.0)
■ ≥ (-10.0) to < (-5.0)
☐ ≥ (-5.0) to < 0.0
■ ≥ 0.0 to < 5.0
■ ≥ 5.0

growth rates and now is the single-largest area of state government spending (including spending from state funds and federal funds), ahead of elementary and secondary education. The growth resulted from many factors that are difficult or impossible for states to control, including expensive and rapidly evolving technologies and drugs (which affect privately funded health care as well as public programs), and growth in enrollment of expensive-to-care-for disabled and "dual eligible" populations (individuals eligible both for Medicare and for Medicaid). In addition, state and federal policy choices to expand Medicaid to cover more low-income children and pregnant women and to reach out to potentially eligible populations and enroll them in Medicaid have contributed to spending increases.[5]

Many of these forces will continue to drive Med-icaid costs upward in coming years. In addition, the aging of the population will begin to have a significant impact. This is important because the average elderly Medicaid recipient costs more than seven times as much to care for as the average low-income adult or child. Economy.com forecasts the population aged 65 and over will grow by about 8.5 percent between 2005 and 2010, and growth will accelerate after that. By contrast, the under-65 population is expected to grow by 3.8 percent between 2005 and 2010. As the population ages, states may find it difficult to finance rapidly increasing demand for Medicaid-financed prescription drugs and expensive long-term care services. Many Southwestern and Mountain states are likely to feel this pressure soonest, with most facing growth in the next 10 years of 45 percent or more[6] (see Table B).

Table A:
Real Per Capita General Fund Operating Expenditures

	Amount per capita (2004 $)		
Programs	FY 2000	FY 2004	Percent change
Total	$1,821.2	$1,768.7	-2.9%
Elementary and secondary education	656.5	626.8	-4.5
Medicaid	275.1	292.8	6.4
Higher education	231.1	203.5	-11.9
All other	658.5	645.6	-1.9

Sources: National Association of State Budget Officers Expediture Report 2001 and 2003 (state expenditures), Bureau of Economic Analysis (state and local government chain-weighted price index), and Bureau of the Census (population).

Table B:
Projected Growth in Population Aged 65+: States Facing Fastest Growth, 2005 to 2010

State	2005 to 2010	2005 to 2015
United States median	8.5%	24.7%
Nevada	28.8	71.2
Arizona	22.5	57.9
Alaska	21.5	49.5
Colorado	21.0	52.4
Utah	20.5	52.2
Idaho	19.0	48.9
Georgia	18.4	48.4
Washington	18.1	46.7
Oregon	17.6	47.3
Texas	15.2	39.9

Source: Rockefeller Institute analysis of projections from economy.com.

and secondary education enrollment growth is slowing in most of the nation, although there will be pockets of rapid growth. Over the next five years, the number of children in the 5–19 age group is forecasted by Economy.com to decline in two-thirds of the states. Most of the significant exceptions are in the southwest or west—Nevada, Arizona, Alaska, California and Texas all will see population in this age group increase by 5 percent or more over the next five years.

However, the pressures to increase spending per pupil are larger than ever. Even before the No Child Left Behind Act (NCLB), states were raising graduation and learning standards, creating demand for updated textbooks and curricula, smaller class sizes, more highly qualified teachers, more academic intervention services, enhanced summer learning opportunities, and other supports, all of which cost money. NCLB will intensify these demands. In addition, almost every state has had its system of financing education challenged in court and about two-thirds of challenges in the past 15 years have been successful, creating additional pressure to spend more.

The costs of meeting higher standards and responding to court challenges cannot be estimated with any confidence, but it is clear they could be very large. One recent study estimated statistically the costs of bringing low-performing school districts in Texas up to the statewide average on certain exams, and concluded that it would take a doubling of state aid to school districts in Texas to accomplish this.[8] The court-appointed referees in a New York lawsuit recently issued a report estimating an increased need of $5.6 billion annually in New York City, a more-than-40 percent increase.[9] Cost studies associated with litigation in other states also have concluded that spending increases would need to be very large. Some researchers argue that higher spending will not lead systematically to higher student achievement, but in the context of the existing education system it seems clear that states, school districts, parents, and courts will seek considerably higher spending.

Higher education: Higher education is the third-largest spending category for the state-local sector. Public colleges and universities enroll more than 12 million students and account for more than 77 percent of all higher education enrollment. State

Analysts at the Centers for Medicare and Medicaid Services recently forecasted that state government Medicaid spending will continue to grow faster than the overall economy for the foreseeable future, rising at an average annual rate of 8.6 percent for the nation as a whole over the period from 2006 through 2014—3.6 percentage points faster annually than the economy is projected to grow, and 5.4 percentage points faster than population growth plus general price inflation.[7] Thus, even without major changes in federal participation Medicaid seems likely to strain state finances.

Elementary and secondary education: Elementary

expenditures on higher education as a share of gross domestic product have fallen almost continuously since 1976, in part reflecting graduation of baby boomers from the higher education system and in part reflecting lower priority for higher education than for other services. State contributions to public higher education institutions were battered in the recent fiscal crisis—real state appropriations for public higher education institutions fell by 7.8 percent between FY 2002 and FY 2004, and declined in 36 states, contributing to widespread double-digit increases in tuition.

Labor markets are demanding that workers have more higher education—the U.S. Department of Labor estimates that occupations in which three-quarters or more of workers have at least some college education will constitute 43 percent of the new jobs in the decade from 2002 to 2012, despite accounting for only 29 percent of current jobs.[10] This labor market demand is likely to lead to higher college participation rates among people in the labor force of all ages.

In addition, underlying demographic forces will drive up enrollment in some states, as baby boomers' children exit high school and enter college. For the nation as a whole, this should place only mild pressure on the higher education system, but in some states the population in the largest college-going age group, 20–24 year olds, will grow substantially. According to Economy.com, growth will be fastest in the Northeastern states and California and as a result these states may face additional pressure to finance higher education.

Other important areas of state and local finance: Medicaid, elementary and secondary education, and higher education are the three largest areas in the typical state budget and all face spending pressure. Some smaller areas will face pressure as well, while others may provide fiscal savings. One notable area that could cause difficulty for some governments is employee pensions: state and local government pension fund earnings more than doubled relative to state and local budgets between 1990 and 2000, allowing governments to scale back contributions (with a lag) by more than 30 percent despite rising pension obligations. That trend has since reversed and many state and local governments now face rapidly rising pension contributions that are sometimes quite significant relative to their budgets.

Federal Budget Cuts and Policy Changes

Federal deficit-reducing actions will affect states in several important ways, including cuts in grant programs and proposals to restructure the federal tax system. The discussion below is based on the president's proposed budget; the final budget could impose larger cuts than those discussed here, or smaller cuts, but is likely to include significant cuts in any event.

Federal grants to state and local governments were $423 billion in FY 2004, accounting for one quarter of the federal budget for domestic programs. Grants account for approximately 30 percent of all state government revenue and 4 percent of local government revenue.[11] Approximately one-third of federal grants are labeled "mandatory" and the rest are discretionary. Large well-known mandatory grant programs include Medicaid, Temporary Assistance to Needy Families and child nutrition programs. Large well-known discretionary programs include Title I education grants for the disabled, special education grants, and various public housing and community development grants.

Cuts in Federal Grants
Other than Medicaid

The president's budget proposes sharp cuts in grants to state and local governments. In FY 2006, discretionary grants would be cut by 9.2 percent in real per capita terms, and grants for mandatory programs other than Medicaid would be cut by 5.8 percent.[12] Combined, these cuts would be equivalent to about a 2.4 percent reduction in state government tax revenue.

The budget does not itemize cuts in grants beyond 2006, but it proposes caps on domestic discretionary spending that would lead to cuts between 2005 and 2010 of 16 percent, adjusted for inflation and population growth. If discretionary grants, which account for about one-third of domestic discretionary budget authority, share proportionately in these cuts and if cuts in non-Medicaid mandatory grants are proportionate to cuts in non-Medicaid mandatory entitlement programs, the recurring annual cut in these grants by 2010, in real per capita terms, would be the equivalent of about a 4 percent cut in state government tax revenue. Put in perspective, that would be a permanent drop in state government revenue that is almost as large as the cyclical tax revenue drop of the 1990s recession and a little less than half as large as the tax revenue decline in the recent fiscal crisis. These are large enough to get the attention of state governments, particularly since there would be no reason to expect grant revenue to bounce back in later years.

Medicaid Cuts and Restructuring[13]

The president has proposed $45 billion in net federal Medicaid savings over the next 10 years, reflecting $60 billion of cuts and $15 billion in new initiatives. Most of the federal savings would result in higher costs to states, but some would result in state savings, for a net cost to states of $34 billion over 10 years. The largest changes that would provide savings to states include reductions in payments Medicaid will make to pharmacies and provisions that would make it harder for people seeking to enter nursing homes to shield assets from Medicaid. The largest changes that would shift costs from the federal government to states include limits on intergovernmental transfers (IGTs can allow states to increase federal reimbursement without increasing expenditures), limits on administrative expenditures, and restrictions on case management expenditures. The president's budget also proposed to increase outreach to and coverage of children, increasing federal and state expenditures. All told, Medicaid changes appear likely to increase state Medicaid expenditures by about 2–3 percent over 10 years.

Federal Tax Reform

Perhaps the largest risk is the possibility that the federal government will enact a major overhaul of the federal tax system, adopting a retail sales tax, a consumption tax or a value-added tax. Whatever the merits of these changes for the federal tax system and the nation's economy, all of these choices could create major—and largely undiscussed—problems for state and local government finances. Depending on very important details, these proposals could (a) eliminate the deductibility of state and local income and property taxes, raising the effective cost of state and local services and having dramatically different impacts across states, (b) tread into the traditional state-local terrain of sales taxes, making it difficult for state and local governments to raise revenue from these taxes, (c) make it impractically expensive for states to have their own income taxes if federal tax changes are in place of the existing federal income tax, and/or (d) raise the costs to states of maintaining and improving infrastructure, if municipal bond interest is no longer tax-exempt.

Conclusions

The recent recession is behind states, and state revenue is recovering. However, tax revenue fell so sharply during the recent fiscal crisis that despite economic recovery and recent tax increases, real per capita revenue remains below its prior peak in 70 percent of the states.

States have raised taxes by far less in this crisis than in the prior one, and cut spending by more. They also drew down fund balances by more, and have relied heavily on tobacco bonds and other nonrecurring revenue. The net result is that many states still face budget gaps and are likely to need more spending cuts or tax increases to bring revenue and spending into balance.

As states continue to work their way out of this hole, they will confront spending pressures from their own citizens and economies, and fiscal risks from actions to reduce the federal deficit. Medicaid is now the largest state spending area, and restraining price and utilization of health care will remain difficult. In addition, the impending growth in the elderly population also will place pressure on Medicaid over the next decade, and sooner in many Southwestern and Mountain states. States will face pressure to raise spending on elementary and secondary education in an effort to achieve higher standards, and will face labor market and demographic demands for additional spending on higher education.

Federal budget cuts will add to fiscal pressures states face. The president's FY 2006 budget proposed cuts in discretionary grants and mandatory grants other than Medicaid that are the equivalent of about a 2.4 percentage point drop in tax revenue in 2006, and could grow to the equivalent of about a 4 percentage-point drop—almost as large as the tax revenue drop in the 1990 recession, but presumably permanent. The federal budget also would cut Medicaid, exacerbating fiscal pressure on the states.

Finally, if the federal government overhauls the federal tax system by moving toward a consumption-based tax, it could make it extremely difficult for state and local governments to raise revenue. Debates over federal tax policy have so far paid very little attention to tax reform's impact on state and local governments.

While the recovery in tax revenue is welcome news for state governments, they will need this revenue growth and more, or cuts in spending, to keep budgets in balance in coming years.

Notes

[1] For this purpose, I do not adjust for legislative changes because I am interested in how much states can spend – revenue states actually collect.

[2] General fund expenditures are a reasonably good indicator of spending supported by taxes and other revenue states raise from their own sources (excluding federal aid). Arguments can be made for alternative measures of state-

financed spending, but all have their flaws and I find this measure preferable for the purpose here.

[3] Operating expenditures actually increased by 14 percent in nominal terms, but that is not a good measure of underlying pressures because it does not take into account the fact that prices and population have increased since 2000. Real per capita expenditures is a better measure.

[4] See Elizabeth C. McNichol, "State Fiscal Crisis Lingers," Center on Budget and Policy Priorities, Revised February 15, 2005.

[5] For an analysis of recent Medicaid spending growth, see John Holahan and Ghosh Arunabh, "Understanding the Recent Growth in Medicaid Spending, 2000 to 2003," Health Affairs Web Exclusive, January 26, 2005.

[6] A more meaningful but less intuitive way to look at the data is to examine the change in the elderly population as a share of the total population. This does not alter in any significant way conclusions about which states will face pressures soonest, so I present the simpler approach.

[7] Stephen Heffler, Sheila Smith, Sean Keehan, Christine Borger, M. Kent Clemens and Christopher Truffer, "U.S. Health Spending Projections for 2004–14," *Health Affairs*—Web Exclusive, February 23, 2005.

[8] Andrew Reschovsky and Jennifer Imazeki, "Financing Education So That No Child Is Left Behind: Determining the Costs of Improving Student Performance," *Developments in School Finance 2003*, (National Center for Education Statistics, 2004).

[9] John D. Feerick, E. Leo Milonas and William C. Thompson, Report and Recommendations of the Judicial Referees, Supreme Court of the State of New York, *Campaign for Fiscal Equity, Inc., et al., vs. The State of New York et al.*, Index No. 111070/93, Honorable Leland DeGrasse,

November 30, 2004.

[10] Daniel E. Hecker, "Occupational Employment Projections to 2012," *Monthly Labor Review*, (U.S. Bureau of Labor Statistics, February 2004).

[11] Based on Census Bureau data for FY 2002.

[12] The Center on Budget and Policy Priorities has issued several reports on the impact of the federal budget on grants and on other domestic programs. This analysis is based on many of the same data sources as those analyses. There are two main reasons for differences in numbers between the analyses: I adjust for population growth, and I compare 2006 and later grants to grants in 2005 rather than to a projected baseline. Sources: Federal budget for FY 2006, unpublished OMB tables underlying federal budget, and Carlitz, Ruth, Domestic Discretionary Funding Levels for 2006 through 2010, Detailed Data, Center on Budget and Policy Priorities, February 28, 2005.

[13] This section draws heavily on Victoria Wachino, Andy Schneider and Leighton Ku, *Medicaid Budget Proposals Would Shift Costs To States And Be Likely To Cause Reductions In Health Coverage*, (Center on Budget and Policy Priorities, February 18, 2005).

About the Author

Donald J. Boyd is the director of fiscal studies at the Rockefeller Institute of Government of the State University of New York. His past positions include director of the economic and revenue staff for New York state's budget office, and director of the tax staff for New York's Assembly Ways and Means Committee. Boyd holds a Ph.D. in managerial economics for Rensselaer Polytechnic Institute.

State Budgets in 2004 and 2005:
The Long and Twisty Recovery
By Nick Samuels

In 2004, states turned an important corner on the road to fiscal recovery. Compared to previous years, revenue collections have recovered healthily, although they are not vastly surpassing budgeted estimates as they did in the late 1990s boom. The news isn't all good, however. Expenditure pressures remain immense. Pent-up demand for spending in areas that were cut during the fiscal crisis still exists, while K–12 education and Medicaid battle each other to consume ever larger pieces of the budget pie. Federal budget deficits and their inevitable effect on domestic spending also will wear heavily on states as grants-in-aid are reduced or eliminated.

Introduction

After three years of dangling from a budgetary precipice, states gained firmer footing in 2004, pulling themselves over the fiscal edge, but still finding themselves on slippery ground. Following a dramatic revenue slide that served as the catalyst for a lingering fiscal crisis, state tax collections finally have started a meaningful recovery. That revenue decline and the budget trauma that it caused required states to make substantial spending cuts. But not every category of state spending was subject to those cuts equally. For both policy and political reasons, K–12 education was largely spared the budget axe. While states took considerable action to contain the ever-rising costs of Medicaid, as an entitlement they were limited in how much they could do, and policy and politics play here, too. States now face a different, less stark, but equally difficult budget dilemma than they have dealt with for the past three years, one on the expenditure side. During the period of fiscal stress, all budget players understood why the answer was "no." Now, pent-up demand for spending in areas that suffered the brunt of cuts competes with requests for new spending, the desire to expand education spending, and with Medicaid and other health care costs. Furthermore, both the White House and Congress have put states on notice that, amid federal budget deficits and expensive policy priorities elsewhere, funds for states will decrease.

The Current State Fiscal Condition

Revenues in Fiscal 2004

The state revenue picture brightened substantially in 2004, by several different measures. From a bud-

getary perspective, revenues were healthy. In fiscal 2004,[1] collections of sales, personal income and corporate income taxes surpassed originally budgeted estimates in 35 states, were on target in 10 and failed to meet expectations in only five states.[2] In contrast, in fiscal 2002 at the depth of the state budget crisis, 42 states missed their revenue targets. While certainly good news, it should be noted that the 2004 revenue estimates had been tempered substantially compared to previous years when targets were missed continually. Indeed, while 2004 collections beat budgeted estimates, they didn't by much; sales taxes were 0.5 percent higher, personal income taxes were 1.7 percent higher, and corporate income taxes were 7.8 percent above estimates. Overall, 2004 revenue collections beat budgeted projections by 1.6 percent.

From the standpoint of final revenue collections in 2004, states finally had a year of substantial growth. According to the Nelson A. Rockefeller Institute of Government, state general fund tax revenue grew by 7.5 percent in fiscal 2004 in nominal terms, compared to the previous fiscal year.[3] When adjusted for both inflation and legislated tax changes, growth was 3.2 percent. Again, both figures contrast sharply with previous years. The Rockefeller Institute figures indicate that nominal tax growth was –5.7 percent in fiscal 2002, or –7.8 percent on an adjusted basis, and 1.8 percent in fiscal 2003, or an adjusted –3.5 percent. Looking at collections of individual taxes further underscores the extent of the recovery. Personal income taxes—the revenue source that fueled the late 1990s budgetary boom—decreased by 10.8 percent in fiscal 2002, according to the Rockefeller Institute, and by 2.0 percent in fiscal 2003, but in fiscal 2004 grew by 8.4 percent. In fiscal 2002 the corporate income tax declined by a whopping 18.2 percent, while growing by 11.7 percent and 11.2 percent in fiscal years 2003 and 2004, respectively. The sales tax, which had nearly flat growth of 0.2 percent in fiscal 2002, increased by 1.8 percent in fiscal 2003 and by 6.6 percent in fiscal 2004.

Revenues in Fiscal 2005

Since the fiscal crisis began in 2001, states have used tax and fee increases (in tandem with expenditure cuts and the use of reserve funds) to balance their budgets. The budgets states enacted for fiscal 2005 continued this trend. Twenty-four states increased taxes and fees for fiscal 2005 (and 11 decreased them), for a net change of $3.5 billion. Also as in recent years, most of the enacted increase ($888.4 million) comes from cigarette and other tobacco taxes. Those taxes, combined with increases in the sales tax ($710.6 million) and in the "other" tax category ($707.7 million) account for just less than two-thirds of the net fiscal 2005 enacted increase.[4]

In response to the fiscal downturn, states began increasing taxes in fiscal 2002, when they enacted a small $300 million increase. But in fiscal 2003 and 2004, enacted increases totaled $8.3 billion and $9.6 billion, respectively (the combined fiscal 2002–2005 enacted increase is $21.7 billion). This follows a pattern laid down during good or bad budget times. For example, during the economic slowdown in the late 1980s and early 1990s, states increased taxes by $43.6 billion (between fiscal 1988 and fiscal 1994). States gave most of that back as the economy turned around and through the late 1990s boom: between fiscal 1996 and fiscal 2001, states enacted $33.1 billion in tax decreases.

State Spending in 2004

Amid improved revenues and with some caution, state spending increased slightly in fiscal 2004, although they still face significant spending pressure. The fiscal year after the revenue slide began was perhaps the harshest for states: in 2002, 38 states made post-enactment budget cuts that totaled a net $13.7 billion. (In fiscal 2003, 40 states made budget cuts that totaled $11.8 billion.) By comparison, 15 states were forced to make cuts in their fiscal 2004 budgets, by $2.2 billion. Among the strategies that states used to balance their budgets were layoffs of state employees (in two states), furloughs (two states), and early retirement incentives (one state).

Six states made across-the-board percentage cuts to their budgets. The net result of these actions in fiscal 2004, in budgetary terms, was a 3.0 percent nominal increase in state general fund spending, a 0.3 percent increase when adjusted for inflation. The comparison to the previous fiscal year again is a bold one. In fiscal 2003, state general fund spending grew by 0.6 percent nominally, a 2.4 percent decrease in inflation-adjusted terms. In fiscal 2002, the nominal and real figures were 1.3 percent and –1.4 percent, respectively. Based on appropriations for fiscal 2005, state general fund spending will increase by 4.5 percent nominally and 1.8 percent in real terms. While spending shrank in nine states in fiscal 2004, only three states budgeted for less spending in fiscal 2005. Three states had spending growth of 10 percent or more in fiscal 2004 and appropriated budgets in eight states do in fiscal 2005.

Medicaid and Other Health Care

Medicaid continues to burden state budgets heavily. (It is the means-tested entitlement program that provides medical care for more than 50 million low-income individuals, and which is financed 57 percent by the federal government and 43 percent by the states.) In fact, Medicaid has grown so quickly that in fiscal 2004 it is estimated to have become the largest single functional category of state spending, accounting for 21.9 percent of the total (including general funds, other state funds, federal grants-in-aid, and bonds). The other categories of total state spending in fiscal 2004 are: elementary and secondary education (21.5 percent); higher education (10.5 percent); public assistance (2.1 percent); corrections (3.4 percent); transportation (7.9 percent); and all other (32.6 percent). Total estimated fiscal 2004 state spending from all sources is estimated to be $1.2 trillion.

Indeed, the effect of Medicaid's rapid growth is to crowd out other categories of states spending, forcing them to become smaller wedges of the state budget pie, even if spending on those functions (such as K–12 education) increases. Furthermore, in times of fiscal stress such as the one states are currently emerging from, the dominance and nature of Medicaid and K–12 education, the two largest state spending functions, magnify budget cuts in other areas. With cuts to K–12 education and Medicaid both difficult from a policy and political perspective, balancing the budget weighs more heavily on the remaining categories. The result is that 100 percent of the budget must be balanced on less than 100 percent of the total.

Overall, health care plays a major role in state budgets. Including Medicaid, health care accounts for approximately 31 percent of all state spending. For fiscal 2001 (the most recent year for which figures are available), Medicaid accounted for 69.2 percent of all state health spending. Other categories were: the State Children's Health Insurance Program (1.2 percent); state employee health care (8.3 percent); health care in the corrections system (1.3 percent); higher education health (2.0 percent); direct public health care (2.8 percent); community-based services (5.6 percent); state facility-based services (3.0 percent); population health expenditures (6.3 percent); and insurance and access expansion (0.4 percent).[6]

Other Indicators

The fiscal downturn also took a heavy toll on the state credit market. Between 2001 and 2003, negative changes in state credit ratings and negative outlook and review actions far outweighed positives ones. The improving fiscal situation in 2004 has changed that. According to Moody's Investors Service, of 19 state rating or outlook changes in 2004, all but two were positive, and included upgrades for four states.[7] But pressure still remains. "Despite signs of improvement, states have yet to return to the revenue expansion or fund-balance levels they experienced before the 2001 recession," says Moody's. "States must replace non-recurring measures used in recent years to balance their budgets."[8]

The Near Future

The near future for state budgets is brightening, but also will provide state leaders with many difficult decisions. After a lengthy period of scrambling with post-enactment budget cuts, significant pent-up demand exists to restore spending. Important and popular programs absorbed decreases in their budgets during the economic ebb and now want those funds restored, not to mention increased. However,

several factors will complicate this. Perhaps the most major is the certainty of less assistance from the federal government. With on-budget deficits of more than $400 billion projected each year through 2010,[9] and the president's proposed budget reflecting a 3 percent decrease in domestic discretionary spending, states can expect decreasing federal aid. Particularly worrisome to states are various Medicaid proposals, which may grant states more flexibility to manage their programs, but also may cost them more in the long-run as they absorb assorted costs. Additionally, states have unfunded pension obligations to confront, and courts in several states, hearing education equity lawsuits, may force states to make unplanned spending increases.

Notes

[1] The fiscal year in 46 states begins in July and ends in June. The exceptions are Alabama and Michigan, where the fiscal year runs October–September, New York, where it is April–March, and Texas, where the fiscal year runs September–August. Twenty states budget biennially.

[2] National Association of State Budget Officers, *The Fiscal Survey of States*, (NASBO, December 2004), 9.

[3] Nelson A. Rockefeller Institute of Government, *State Fiscal Brief*, (February 2005), 2.

[4] See note 2 above.

[5] National Association of State Budget Officers, *2003 State Expenditure Report*, (NASBO, September 2004), 8.

[6] National Association of State Budget Officers, *2000–2001 State Health Care Expenditure Report*, (NASBO, Fall 2003), 3.

[7] Moody's Investors Service, *2005 Outlook for State Ratings: Sector Revised to Stable from Negative*, (February 2005), 5.

[8] Ibid.

[9] Congressional Budget Office, *CBO's Current Budget Projections*, (March 2005).

About the Author

Nick Samuels is a senior fiscal analyst at the National Association of State Budget Officers.

State Tax Collections: Eroding Tax Bases

By William F. Fox and LeAnn Luna

Both a slow economy and tax policies contributed to the recent state fiscal crises. Tax rate increases and one time revenue sources can solve temporary budget deficits, but maintaining the integrity of income and sales tax bases is necessary to prevent structural deficits. Extending the sales tax to selected services, participating in the Streamlined Sales Tax Project, and requiring corporate combined reporting are among the potential solutions discussed by the authors.

Introduction

The recent state budget crises forced many states to take a fresh look at their entire fiscal structure. In numerous cases, the solution to the budgetary shortfalls amounted to little more than stopgap measures, including "temporary" sales tax increases and depleting rainy day funds to meet ordinary operating expenses and more exotic steps such as sale/leaseback agreements for public facilities.[1] Unfortunately the focus on short-term solutions may keep states from dealing with underlying structural deficits. Legislators, with a view towards long-term fiscal stability, need to better understand the fundamental attributes of their revenue sources, why some of their tax bases continue to erode, and some options for stemming the erosion.

Imposition of broad, non-discriminatory tax bases with low rates is a basic tenet of almost all good tax systems. A tax system with these attributes will often accomplish the related goals of fairness, administrative efficiency, economic neutrality and revenue sufficiency. Broad bases and low rates help ensure that business competition, and not taxes, determines winners and losers, reduce the incentives to structure business transactions to fit tax-advantaged exceptions written into the tax code, and increase the likelihood that the tax system provides sufficient revenues over the long term. Unfortunately, many recent state practices are inconsistent with these goals.

This article will begin with a review of the recent performance of state taxes. Next we will examine the extent and causes of declines in the corporate income and sales tax bases, followed by various state responses to the base declines. Finally, the essay will conclude with a discussion of federal legislation implications and tax policy recommendations.

Revenue Trends

State tax revenues in 2002 comprised the lowest share of personal income in more than 15 years (see Figure A), as revenues declined by 4.4 percent in 2001 (see Figure B). This is the only decline in nomi-

nal state tax revenue since at least 1970. Inflation-adjusted tax revenues have fallen in other years, but the real 2002 decline is also much greater than during any other year. State revenues rebounded only slightly in 2003, increasing by about 2.1 percent in nominal dollars. Much of the meager growth in 2003 is attributable to rate increases.

The personal and corporate income taxes declined in 2002 as the sales tax grew very slightly. The largest decline was in the corporate income tax (20.7 percent), followed by the personal income tax (10.7 percent). Such large declines certainly created difficulties for states, particularly since the degree to which tax revenues fell was unexpected in most states. Only the individual income tax continued to fall in 2003 (2.0 percent).

The declines were obviously due in part to economic conditions, but state tax structures also played a part. Economists term the rate of growth of tax revenues divided by the rate of growth of state personal income as revenue elasticity.[2] An elasticity greater than one means tax revenues grow faster than the economy, an elasticity of one means that revenues grow at the same rate as the economy, and an elasticity below one means that tax revenues grow more slowly than the economy. States can select certain low elasticity tax instruments as long as the necessary set of fast growing instruments is chosen as well. Tax revenues in the average state have grown more slowly than the economy during the past decade, as evidenced by elasticities lower than one for all taxes except the individual income tax (see Table A).

Declining Tax Bases

Corporate Income Tax Base Erosion

The corporate income tax base has been eroding for many years. The effective corporate income tax rate has fallen by about one-third since the late 1980s, even as the simple average nominal tax rate rose about 0.1 percent.[3] Thus, the effective tax rate decline must be substantially the result of an eroding

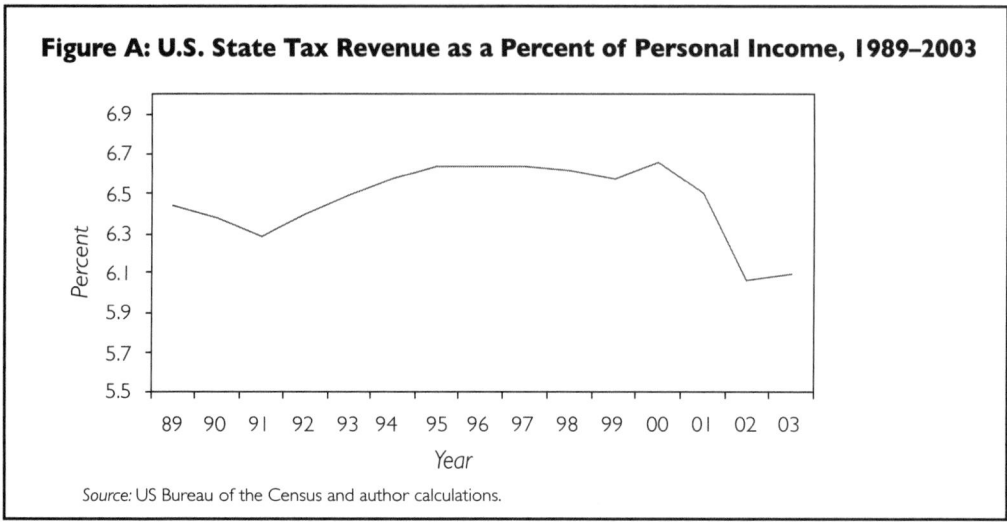

Figure A: U.S. State Tax Revenue as a Percent of Personal Income, 1989–2003

Source: US Bureau of the Census and author calculations.

taxable base relative to actual corporate profits. Three primary factors have contributed to this trend: legislated base changes, federal tax base shrinkage and tax planning.

The federal tax base decline accounts for as much as 30 percent of corporate tax erosion. The corporate tax structure in almost every state begins with the federal definition of profits so state tax bases move with the federal base. For example the bonus depreciation provisions enacted in 2002 and 2003 have had a dramatic impact on taxable income in those states that did not decouple from federal deprecation rules.[4] The deductibility of stock options for tax purposes has also reduced the corporate income tax base relative to book income, although those deductions should generally be offset by an increase in the personal income tax base.

Several types of legislated exemptions have narrowed the base. Tax competition among states for increasingly mobile businesses has resulted in a variety of state tax concessions. Tax breaks targeted at selected firms and concessions built into the tax code that are intended for all firms are granted in essentially every state.[5] For example, numerous states have reduced the corporate income tax liability of many firms that are intensive exporters out of state (such as many manufacturers), by altering the traditional three-factor apportionment formula to emphasize the sales factor. The traditional three-factor formula, which placed equal weight on property, payroll and sales, is now the exception rather than the rule, with over two-thirds of the states at least double weighing the sales factor. Thirteen states have sales factors that exceed 50 percent and nine states have a single sales factor apportionment formula for at least some taxpayers (Fox et al, 2005).

Many states also, perhaps unwittingly, allow tax planning to erode corporate income tax bases as they permit each firm to separately report their income tax liability. Separate reporting can allow related companies to shift income into low tax or no tax states through a variety of strategies. For example, many businesses exploit the passive investment company (PIC) loophole by forming a PIC in states, such as Delaware, that either exclude intangible income from taxation or levy low rates. The PIC imposes a fee on related operating entities that is allowable as a deduction in many separate reporting states (See Luna 2004). Companies can also manipulate transfer prices between related firms, or charge inter-company management fees and interest expense to move profits from one state to another.

Corporations have become more adept at exploiting differences in tax structures to minimize their taxes. Many exploit the protections provided by P.L. 86-272 and use multiple entities to avoid nexus in some market states. The emergence of limited liability companies (LLCs) as a viable entity for large businesses also provides tax avoidance opportunities.

Sales Tax Base Erosion

The sales tax base has been declining relative to personal income for decades. The base has fallen from about 51.4 percent of personal income in the average state in 1979 to 41.5 percent in 2001. The decline can be attributed to four basic causes: cross border shopping, technological changes, legislated exemptions and changing purchasing patterns.[6]

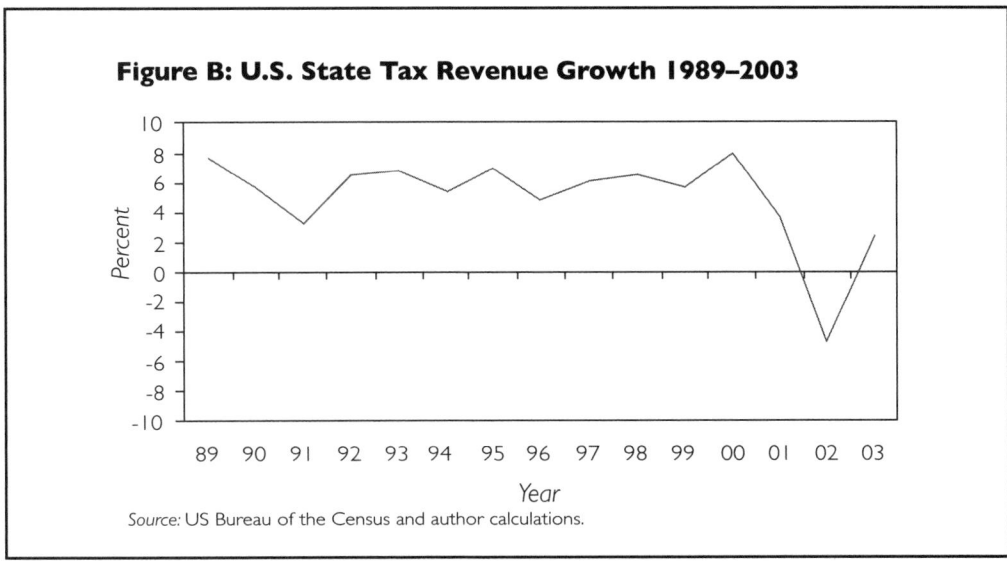

Figure B: U.S. State Tax Revenue Growth 1989–2003

Source: US Bureau of the Census and author calculations.

The recent dramatic growth in remote sales (e.g. mail order and electronic commerce) continues to cause erosion of the sales tax base. Although every sales taxing state has an equivalent use tax on remote purchases, the failure of the seller to collect the tax allows for rampant tax evasion. Bruce and Fox (2004) estimate that states lost $15.5 billion in 2003 from inability to collect tax on Internet sales, and the losses are growing rapidly. Perhaps surprisingly, even business customers commonly fail to remit use taxes owed. For example, the state of Washington (2003) found the use tax to have a 27.9 percent non-compliance rate for registered business taxpayers, by far the greatest of any tax. Interestingly, non-compliance was greatest for the largest firms, which are those with over $50 million in receipts. Compliance is nearly non-existent for individuals except for a few items like automobiles that must be registered with the state. Nineteen states have added a line item on their individual income tax returns for voluntary reporting of use taxes or have begun to provide compliance information with the return (Manzi, 2003), but compliance rates and collections are both negligible.

The Internet and other technological advances have affected the sales tax base beyond the facilitation of remote sales. The technologies have created a number of new services that are not contemplated in most sales tax statutes, such as on-line subscriptions, email, instant messaging and on-line gaming.

States have legislated many new exemptions in recent years, particularly in years when tax revenues were growing very rapidly. For example, Missouri and Georgia recently exempted food from the sales tax, bringing the number of exempting states to 30. Six states currently exempt some clothing from the sales tax, and an additional 12 states offer sales tax holidays (generally during the back-to-school season) on items such as clothing.[7] A variety of reasons have been used to justify the exemptions including equity, economic development and administrative convenience. A careful analysis of new exemptions would probably lead to the conclusion that some represent good tax policy and others do not, but the net effect is to narrow the base. For example, exemptions that exempt large classes of business to business transactions are likely to be good policy while those that exempt select categories of consumer purchases are likely to create adverse effects.

Finally, the consumption of services continues to grow rapidly, as evidenced by services increasing from 47.4 percent of consumption in 1979 to 58.8 percent in 2002. The relative transition from consumption of goods to services erodes the base since most goods are included in the tax base (with the notable exception of food for consumption at home) and most services, and particularly professional and construction services, are exempt. The effects of declining goods consumption have been less pronounced than they might otherwise have been because food for consumption at home accounts for about one-half of the reduction in goods, meaning one untaxed set of transactions has tended to replace another set in many states.

How are States Responding?

Many states have historically used higher rates, and particularly for the sales tax, to offset base erosion. The result is that the median state sales tax rate was 3.25 percent in 1970, 4.0 percent in 1980, and 5.0 percent in 1990. The number of sales tax rate increases has slowed, but there are now 20 states (out of 45 sales taxing states) with at least a 6.0 percent state sales tax rate. During recent years states have been less likely to increase rates on broad tax bases than in the past, though some have raised the sales or income tax and many have raised tobacco taxes.

Higher tax rates are generally not a good solution to eroding tax bases, though they may replace the revenue losses. Maintaining broad tax bases is a more effective state policy and many states have sought to limit eroding tax bases in two ways: general solutions to underlying problems and fixes for specific problems. Examples of more general solutions are combined reporting for the corporate income tax and the Streamlined Sales Tax Project (SSTP) for the sales tax. Fixes to specific problems include legislation that attacks particular avoidance techniques, such as anti-PIC legislation. Narrow solutions often permit other forms of tax planning.

Corporate Income Tax

Many states have enacted anti-PIC legislation to prevent the shifting of expenses to low tax or no tax states (Dennehy and Ehrlich, 2004). For example, 12 states deny deductions for royalties and interest paid by the "related" operating company to the holding company. However, the laws are written in different ways and are often very narrow, meaning the impacts of the add-back provisions on tax planning will differ across states and in some cases may achieve relatively little. For example, many states have different definitions of what constitutes a "related party," using ownership rules that range from 30 percent to 80 percent and vary depending on the type of entity that owns the stock (e.g., individual, partnership, or corporation).

Furthermore, many state statutes only require an add-back of royalty expense, allowing corporations to deduct other forms of payments, such as interest expense and management fees. In addition, Arkansas requires the add-back of "intangible expense" but does not define the term, leaving the definition open to interpretation. Also, North Carolina denies royalty payments for the use of trademarks, which permits related corporations to transfer any other intangible, such as a patent, copyright or trade name to the PIC, and create nowhere income on the intercompany payments. Tennessee's legislation only requires reporting of the related-firm transactions, leaving any add-back to the discretion of the Department of Revenue.

Some states have asserted that the presence of intangible assets in the operating entity's domicile creates taxable nexus for the PIC licensor. Others evaluate transactions between affiliated companies for a valid business purpose or argue that they lack economic substance. Several states also have powers similar to Internal Revenue Code Section 482, which authorizes the tax department to use its discretion to adjust income and deductions necessary to make a fair and reasonable determination of the amount of tax liability. While these solutions are more comprehensive than limited restrictions on specific inter-company transactions, they still place the burden on the revenue departments to not only find the abuse but interpret statutes. More involvement by the courts will be necessary to settle interpretation disputes.

State efforts to slow revenue losses caused by the increased use of LLCs are similarly varied. Unless the state imposes an entity-level or withholding tax on LLC profits, the profit passed through to corporate members may escape tax altogether, particularly if the corporate member is domiciled in a no-tax state or a state such as Delaware that does not tax income from intangible investments. Tax avoidance is possible because the law is currently unclear whether simply owning an interest in an LLC creates nexus for the member if that is its only presence in the state. Several states have passed LLC entity-level taxes or withholding taxes in response to this type of tax planning.

Currently, 23 states have adopted a throwback rule, in an attempt to lessen nowhere sales that result when the shipping entity has no nexus in the market state (e.g. because of PL 86-272 protection) or where the market state imposes no income tax. Throwback rules require that non-taxed sales be thrown back to the state of origin and included in both the numerator and denominator for apportionment purposes. The effect

---

Table A

SELECTED U.S. TAX ELASTICITIES, 1992 TO 2003

Tax	U.S. average
Total	0.91
General sales	0.96
Selective sales	0.83
Individual income	1.00
Corporate	0.48

Source: U.S. Bureau of the Census and author calculations.

---

is to make those otherwise nontaxable sales ("nowhere income") subject to tax in the home state at that state's rate. Throwback rules, however, have several policy shortcomings. First, the imposition of throwback rules by only a few states prevents use of the throwback state for tax planning but does not prevent planning from other states. In addition, the throwback rule imposes additional tax on corporations producing in the home state but selling out of state. Finally, the higher tax burden in the home (production) state encourages firms to move.

Combined reporting for related entities involved in a unitary business is a more comprehensive solution towards combating corporate income tax erosion. In general, combined reporting ignores the existence of separate entities and taxes the business on its combined income, regardless of corporate form. The advantage of combined reporting is that transfer prices and inter-company charges (e.g., management fees, royalties, and interest) are irrelevant in the tax calculation because the expenses are effectively eliminated in combination. The expectation is that combined reporting will increase overall state corporate income tax revenues, although a particular business could owe more or less, depending on the income and losses of the members of the unitary group (e.g. if one entity has a taxable loss, combining the operations of that entity with a profitable company allows for the immediate use of operating losses.)

Combined reporting is not a perfect solution because only worldwide combined reporting will prevent the use of non-U.S. PICs for tax planning. Further, there are uncertainties about what entities are part of a unitary operation. There are few bright-line tests other than ownership, and states can come to different conclusions regarding which entities must be included in the combined report. Also the courts in California and elsewhere have issued varying opinions on how to treat related entities without nexus in the home state.[8]

Sales Tax

States can prevent sales tax base erosion by broadening the base to include selected services, avoiding tax concessions and exemptions, and aggressively pursuing taxpayers with nexus in their state. Participation in the SSTP also offers great potential to stem the lost revenues on remote transactions.

Many states are aggressively pursuing out-of-state taxpayers regarding nexus compliance. States are forming revenue agency compacts to share information and to coordinate the collection and audit activities among states in a region. The Southeastern Association of Tax Administrators, with 12 member states and eight associate member states, is one of the largest compacts in the country. The Great Lakes region and Midwest have also formed compacts.

States are sending nexus questionnaires to registered businesses, and others are increasing state audit staff and the number of audits conducted. For example, North Carolina's Project Compliance added 39 audit positions and increased revenues from audits by $40 million during FY 2004. The project estimates 46 new positions for FY 2005 with $75 million additional revenue collections. South Carolina plans to add 100 new audit positions by the end of FY 2005.

Some states, such as Mississippi and Missouri, are enticing non-compliant taxpayers with amnesty programs. Others are publishing the names of non-compliant taxpayers on Web sites in an attempt to shame taxpayers to pay taxes. New Jersey and Pennsylvania have gone as far to have "nexus cops"—policemen placed on the highway to conduct roadside stops and interviews of truck drivers to try to identify business activities that would constitute nexus in their states.

Over the past several years, the states have undertaken the SSTP in cooperation with the business community in an effort to find a mechanism through which vendors can be required to collect the use tax on remote transactions. The SSTP offers great potential to simplify the sales tax and increase tax collections. The *Quill* case was decided on commerce clause grounds that the compliance costs for multi-state vendors exceed those for single state vendors. Therefore, the SSTP's intent is to simplify sales and use tax compliance to the point that compliance burdens for remote and local vendors are similar and any effects on interstate commerce are eliminated. The National Governors Association reports that 20 states have passed legislation in compliance with the Streamlined Sales Tax Agreement that grew out of the SSTP, though not all states may have fully complied with the agreement. Economists view the SSTP as an attempt to enforce a destination-based sales tax. The conventional wisdom has been that destination-based consumption taxes are less distorting than origin-based structures (which exist if remote sales cannot be taxed).

Federal Legislation

Future federal legislation has significant implications for state tax base erosion. On the sales tax front, legislation authorizing the SSTP agreement offers the greatest potential for allowing states to maintain their tax bases. Congress recently extended the Internet Tax Freedom Act for the second time and eroded the sales tax base further by broadening the moratorium to all forms of access to the Internet.

Federal legislation can also be important for corporate income taxation. For example, the just enacted Job Creation Act of 2004 includes a wide variety of tax breaks for business taxpayers along with the closing of some previously available "loopholes." P.L. 86-272 limits the ability of states to assert income tax nexus on companies selling tangible goods with only a marketing presence in their state. H.R. 3220 is a pending bill with significant congressional support that expands P.L. 86-272 protection to other activities, such as sales of intangibles and services, and essentially requires a physical presence standard for any state tax on income.

The U.S. Court of Appeals for the Sixth Circuit in *Cuno v. DaimlerChrysler Inc*. recently ruled that tax credits offered by the state of Ohio to encourage DaimlerChrysler to expand its operations in Toledo violated the Commerce Clause of the Constitution. If the decision withholds almost certain scrutiny by the U.S. Supreme Court, many seemingly routine tax incentives used by states could be ruled invalid. The prospect for federal legislation to permit such tax concessions has already been raised.

Conclusion

The fiscal crises recently suffered by many states were in part self-inflicted because of tax policy decisions that allowed sales and income tax bases to erode. The traditional response to a short term fiscal shortfall is often to raise rates and delay spending. A better long-term solution is to work towards broader income and sales tax bases that allow for both lower overall rates and for collections to grow with the economy.

Notes

[1] Careful execution of a strategy to place revenues in a rainy day fund during periods of high revenue growth and to spend them in lower growth time periods can be part of a sound fiscal policy.

[2] The growth in revenues not adjusted for rate changes is often termed buoyancy rather than elasticity.

[3] The effective tax rate is total state corporate income tax revenues divided by total corporate profits. Corporate profits are based on U.S. Department of Commerce national income accounts data.

[4] Approximately 34 states now do not follow federal depreciation rules.

[5] Some overlap exists between these two groups. In some cases, states build a discretionary concession into the code but describe the characteristics of qualifying firms so narrowly that only one or a very small number of firms could possibly obtain the concession.

[6] See Fox (1988, 2003) for further discussion of these points.

[7] See the Federation of Tax Administrators Web site at www.taxadmin.org.

[8] Under the Finnigan approach, the sales of all members of the unitary group are included in the numerator for apportionment purposes. Under the Joyce approach, the sales of related entities without nexus in the filing state are excluded from the numerator.

References

Bruce, Donald and William F. Fox. 2004. "State and Local Sales Tax Revenue and Losses from E-Commerce: Estimates as of July 2004," *State Tax Notes*,33(7): 511-518.

Dennehy, Edward K. and Stephen E. Ehrlich. 2004. "PICing Away at Passive Investment Companies: States Enact Legislation to Curtail Revenue Losses," *State Tax Notes*: 33(11): 777-783.

Fox, William F. 1998. "Can the Sales Tax Survive a Future Like its Past?" in *The Future of State Tax Policy*, edited by David Brunori, Urban Institute Press.

Fox William F. 2003. "History and Economic Impact of the Sales Tax," in *Sales Taxation*, Edited by Jerry Janata, Institute for Professionals in Taxation, forthcoming.

Fox, William F., LeAnn Luna, and Mathew N. Murray. 2005. "How Should a Tax on Multistate Business Be Structured?" *National Tax Journal*, LVII, No. 1, `139-159.

Luna, LeAnn. 2004. "Corporate Tax Avoidance Strategies and Solutions." *Journal of Multi-State Taxation and Incentives*, 14(2): 6-17, 46-48.

Manzi, Nina. 2003. "Use Tax Collection on Income Tax Returns in Other States." Policy Brief, Minnesota House of Representatives Research Department.

State of Washington. 2003 "Department of Revenue Compliance Study," Research Report #2003-1.

About the Authors

William F. Fox is William B. Stokely Distinguished Professor of Economics and director of the Center for Business and Economic Research at the University of Tennessee. He is past president and recipient of the Steven D. Gold Award from the National Tax Association.

LeAnn Luna is an assistant professor of Accounting and research assistant professor in the Center for Business and Economic Research at the University of Tennessee. Prior to receiving her PhD in accounting from the University of Tennessee, she worked as a tax consultant for an international public accounting firm.

Fundamental Federal Tax Reform and the States

By W. Bartley Hildreth

State and local governments face significant impacts from fundamental federal income tax reform, including new budget costs and the effective loss of revenue choices. It is hard to pin down the precise nature of these implications prior to congressional action. At the least, any discussion of federal tax reform legislation deserves careful scrutiny by state and local officials because there are significant fiscal federalism implications.

On January 7, 2005, President George W. Bush issued Executive Order 13369 establishing the President's Advisory Panel on Federal Tax Reform. This nine member panel, all appointed by the president, has the challenge of providing, by July 31, 2005, "revenue-neutral" policy options for reforming the Federal Internal Revenue Code. While major reforms such as a flat tax or a National Retail Sales Tax (NRST) are possibilities, the executive order requires that at least one option "should use the federal income tax as the base for its recommendation." The panel's proposals should simplify the tax laws, handle equity issues in "an appropriately progressive manner," and promote "long run economic growth and job creation." Interestingly, policy options should continue "recognizing the importance of homeownership and charity in American society." This last point emphasizes that tax reform, in whatever form, is unlikely to challenge the mortgage interest deduction and the deduction for charitable contributions. However, all other tax preferences, such as the state and local tax deductions, are not sacrosanct. Accordingly, this article explores the ramifications for state (and local) governments given the serious discussion for fundamental federal income tax reform during the 109th Congress.

The president's call for tax reform was not greeted with widespread public support.[1] Although public attitudes can shift and the details of any legislation can deviate from the basic forms, there are clues to how such reforms can impact states. As Table A outlines, states are likely to find that major federal tax reform weakens their current state tax structures, increases borrowing costs, and, if that was not enough, imposes a new budget cost—actual payment of a federal tax. Wrapped up in the debate over tax reform, moreover, is the ongoing question of the appropriate size of government at all levels. Therefore, it is in the interest of state (and local) officials to understand the basics of the tax reform discussion. Since there are many reform ideas under discussion, the follow-

ing sections sketch only the most basic elements of the reform proposals and their likely impact.[2]

Tax Reform Objectives

Tax reform proposals generally have three tax objectives: (1) to tax consumption instead of savings; (2) to achieve a lower and more uniform tax rate; (3) and to broaden the tax base. The task is to achieve these objectives while achieving a revenue-neutral result, meaning that the new tax system should generate the same amount of revenue as the tax system it replaces. Otherwise, reform advocates would have to explain how they would cut federal spending to accommodate lower revenues. While some reformers assert that tax reform could spur economic growth sufficient to offset any revenue loss, the emerging concern over federal deficits appears to mute that argument.

Basic alternatives to the current income tax system are either the flat tax or the NRST, although there are variations of each that will not be dealt with here. Both reforms are essentially consumption taxes. Conceptually, all productivity activity accrues income to someone. Income is either consumed or saved. Thus, the only difference between income and consumption is savings, as shown by the following formulas:

- Income = Consumption + Savings
- Consumption = Income – Savings

Both the flat tax and the NRST, as consumption taxes, explicitly remove savings from taxation. By exempting savings, the tax base is smaller than it would be under an income tax system that taxed consumption and some savings. Since reformers also desire low and uniform rates, the taxation of consumption has to be as broad as possible. Each exemption makes it more difficult to preserve the desired low tax rate.

Currently, the federal income tax system—as detailed in the Internal Revenue Code (IRC) that governs the IRS—is a hybrid of both an income tax and a consumption tax. The IRC defines taxable income,

Table A:
Impact of Fundamental Federal Income Tax Reforms on State and Local Government Budgets

	National retail sales tax	Flat tax
Expenditure		
Impose a federal tax on state & local government services	★	...
Impose a federal tax on state & local wages and salaries	★	...
Impose a federal tax on state & local non-cash compensation	...	★
Borrowing		
Eliminate tax exempt securities	★	★
Increase cost of borrowing	★	★
Increased interest cost changes the financial ability to do capital projects	★	★
Imperil debt covenants and pledged revenue security	★	★
Revenue: Income tax		
Loss of federal tax deduction	★	★
Loss of federal tax definitions upon which state income tax depends	★	★
Loss of federal-state sharing of tax information to promote tax compliance	★	★
Decline in public willingness to support state & local income tax	★	★
Revenue: Sales and use tax		
Loss of federal tax deduction	★	★
Sticker shock when consumer adds federal tax to state & local tax rates	★	...
Higher combined tax rates increase incentive for consumers to avoid and evade tax	★	...
Decline in public willingness to support state & local sales tax	★	★
Revenue: Property tax		
Loss of federal tax deduction	★	★
Decline in house prices (at least in the short run) which reduces the property tax base	★	★
Decline in public willingness to support state & local property tax	★	★

Source: W. Bartley Hildreth.
Key:
★—Yes
... —No

vate capital to invest in a market economy. Taking a political perspective, some reformers want to completely do away with the IRS as we know it; a new tax scheme is one way to accomplish that objective.

The National Retail Sales Tax

A national retail sales tax would operate similarly to current state sales tax systems. In fact, most reforms call for the states to administer the federal tax, thereby eliminating the IRS. Adopting a sales tax would reduce the number of tax returns from the 130 million individuals filing IRS Form 1040s in 2003, to a much smaller number because businesses (and government, as clarified later), rather than individuals, would have the responsibility to collect and remit the tax. This does not mean, however, that the economic burden would shift from individuals to business. Indeed, the economic burden would remain on individuals. Rather, the required tax remittance and reporting would shift to the business. In a positive view, individuals would be saved from the administrative cost of compliance. From a negative view, indirect taxes make it difficult for a taxpayer to estimate his or her true tax burden (termed a fiscal illusion).

While the same rate of taxation would apply to all consumption, the percentage of income that is consumed (and thus subject to taxation) varies greatly. Lower income households spend a greater percentage of their incomes on consumption than families with higher income, especially for the basic necessities of life. Higher income taxpayers have more discretionary income, and save more. Reform proposals recognize these realities by incorporating a rebate (or credit) based on the poverty level and processed by the Social Security Administration.

The Flat Tax on Consumption

Generally, proposals for a flat tax on consumption incorporate both a personal tax and a business cash-flow tax. For individuals, the personal tax is termed a wage tax. One wage tax proposal defines earned income as "paid in cash and which is received during the taxable year for services performed in the

including all or part of earned wages and salaries as well the taxable parts of so-called "unearned" income—e.g., interest, dividends and capital gains. However, the tax code permits some income to be tax-deferred (e.g., IRAs, 401(k) plans, and employer-provided pensions) or even tax-exempt altogether (e.g., the interest earned on tax-exempt state and local government securities).

Tax reform proposals go further by exempting savings. Why? From an economic perspective, the answer is to reward individual savings and to gain macroeconomic benefits derived from having more pri-

United States." This definition excludes interest, dividends, capital gains, stock options, and perhaps even bonuses, since such payments are received after year-end. Individuals, for example, would not pay federal tax on interest and dividends, because that money would already be taxed at its source. Individuals would get to reduce their earned income by the following: all savings (in most proposals); a personal exemption for each family member; and, a limited number of deductions. President Bush instructed his tax reform panel to respect the deductions for mortgage interest expenses and charitable contributions. This is another way of saying that political realities hinder pure base broadening. Every deduction or exemption, however, restricts the tax base and forces up the tax rate under a revenue-neutral goal.

A flat tax on all forms of business would replace the corporate income tax. Currently, non-corporate businesses (e.g., partnerships and limited liability companies) pass business income through the personal tax returns of the owners. By removing this preference for non-corporate businesses, all businesses would pay a flat tax on the value added after subtracting the following: the materials and services that are the inputs to the production process; the complete expensing of investments in the year made; wages paid in cash; and, employer-provided pensions. The calculation looks like this:

- Consumption = Sales – Inputs – Investments – Wages – Pension Benefits.

This form of tax structure is known as the subtraction form of the "value-added tax," as utilized by Canada, Japan and other countries. A business is allowed to subtract the cost of the inputs paid for property and services. Furthermore, the business would expense all investments in the year of purchase, thereby avoiding the current depreciation method. Because the business would not pay tax on cash wages paid, each wage recipient would owe the personal wage tax on those amounts. While flat tax proposals permit businesses to deduct payments for retirement contributions on behalf of employees (because doing so promotes the savings goal), proposals do not give the same tax advantage to employer-provided health care benefits (since health care is viewed as consumption). By this logic, both the business and the employee would have an incentive to minimize health care costs. Also, there is no deduction for property, income or payroll taxes paid.

Impact of Change

Prior to his appointment as the current director of

Table B:
What is the NRST Quoted Tax Rate?

Example	Tax-exclusive rate	Tax-inclusive rate
Retail price	$100	$100
Tax due based on a national retail sales tax rate of 30 percent	$30	$30
Cost to consumer	$130	$130
Quoted rate	30/100 (30%)	30/130 (23%)

Source: W. Bartley Hildreth

---

the Congressional Budget Office, economist Douglas Holtz-Eakin concluded: "In simple terms, federal tax reform is simultaneously the reform of each state and local government tax system."[3] Accordingly, there are more reform impacts than can be examined in this overview. Generally, both tax reform proposals would terminate the deduction for state and local property and income taxes (and, as provided in a 2004 law, the optional sales tax deduction). Reformers view these deductions as another form of consumption. The logical conclusion is that voters will exercise conservation. Specifically, high-tax taxpayers will have an incentive to move away from high-tax areas.

Under a NRST, governments (and nonprofits) are considered consumers, and therefore, taxed. In the case of a government enterprise that charges end-consumers, such as a water system, the NRST could be included on the bill and remitted to the federal government. For general government activities supported by general taxes, however, the government jurisdiction itself would be responsible for paying the tax on purchased items. In addition, as a "taxable employer," state and local governments would have to pay an equivalent tax on wages and salaries. These two features—a tax on purchases and a tax on wages—result in a new expenditure line-item in every state and local government budget: payment of national tax. Interestingly, there is an exemption for education expenditures in most proposals because education is considered an investment rather than current consumption.

The flat tax would impose a federal tax on the noncash compensation paid to public employees. There would not be any tax due on wages paid in cash or for retirement contributions, but all other forms of benefits, such as health care expenses by the employer, would be taxed as a form of consumption. Again, this would require a new line-

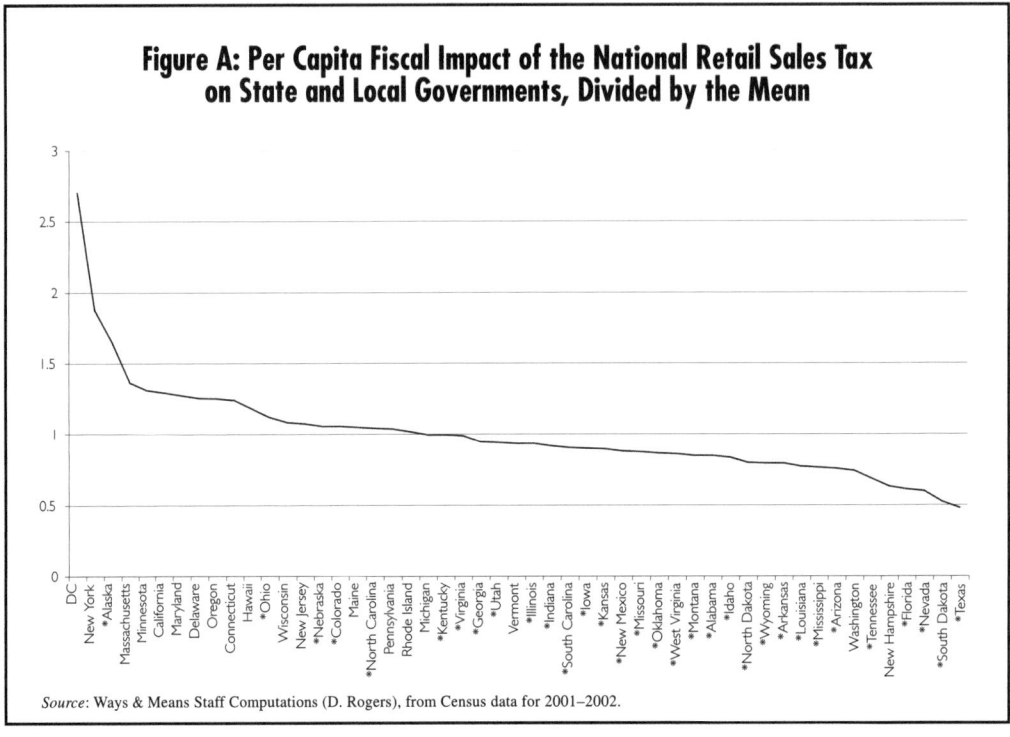

Figure A: Per Capita Fiscal Impact of the National Retail Sales Tax on State and Local Governments, Divided by the Mean

Source: Ways & Means Staff Computations (D. Rogers), from Census data for 2001–2002.

item in the public budget (at a rate of 19 percent by one proposal).

State sales (and use) taxes would face a significant impact from a NRST. To effectively serve as the tax administrator for the NRST, each state would need to adopt the national sales tax base definition as its own. Conceivably, this could expand the base to include remote sales (e.g., mail-order and internet activity) which currently escapes, for the most part, state tax nexus. Also, the national sales tax base would define as taxable many items that heretofore had been exempted from the income tax base, such as employer-provided health insurance, new house sales, and purchases by federal, state and local governments. While base-broadening is laudable, there is little, if any, evidence to suggest that national lawmakers are any less susceptible than their state counterparts to the insatiable demand to carve out tax exemptions. As exemptions proliferate, the NRST could become as complex (and narrow) as the current state systems.

What is the NRST rate that will achieve revenue neutrality? Offsetting only federal income tax collections would require a sales tax rate of 26.8 percent, based upon the assumptions used by Bill Gale of the Brookings Institution in 2004.[4] Offsetting all

federal taxes including the payroll tax would require a 60.7 percent tax. It gets more complicated because the rates can be quoted like the current retail sales tax (termed a tax-exclusive rate) or the income tax (the tax-inclusive rate), as demonstrated in Table B. Gale's estimates, but on a tax-inclusive rate, translate into a 21 percent rate to offset only the income tax and 37.8 percent for all federal taxes. For comparison, a prominent NRST legislative proposal in the past Congress (the "FairTax") asserted that a 23 percent tax-inclusive rate (the same as a 30 percent tax-exclusive rate) would offset all federal taxes.

Voter support for existing state taxes may decline after federal tax reform. Sticker-shock is likely when consumers have to pay a double-digit NRST rate on top of a combined state and local sales tax rate that itself can reach almost 10 percent. As a result, voters may rethink their support for state and local taxation, especially sales taxes. The flat tax carries its own negative impact because businesses would no longer be able to deduct, as a business expense, state and local tax payments, and, as a result, may be less likely to support state tax policy.

Voluntary compliance may be impacted. High combined sales tax rates may increase "off the book" sales. If this happens, states may face less

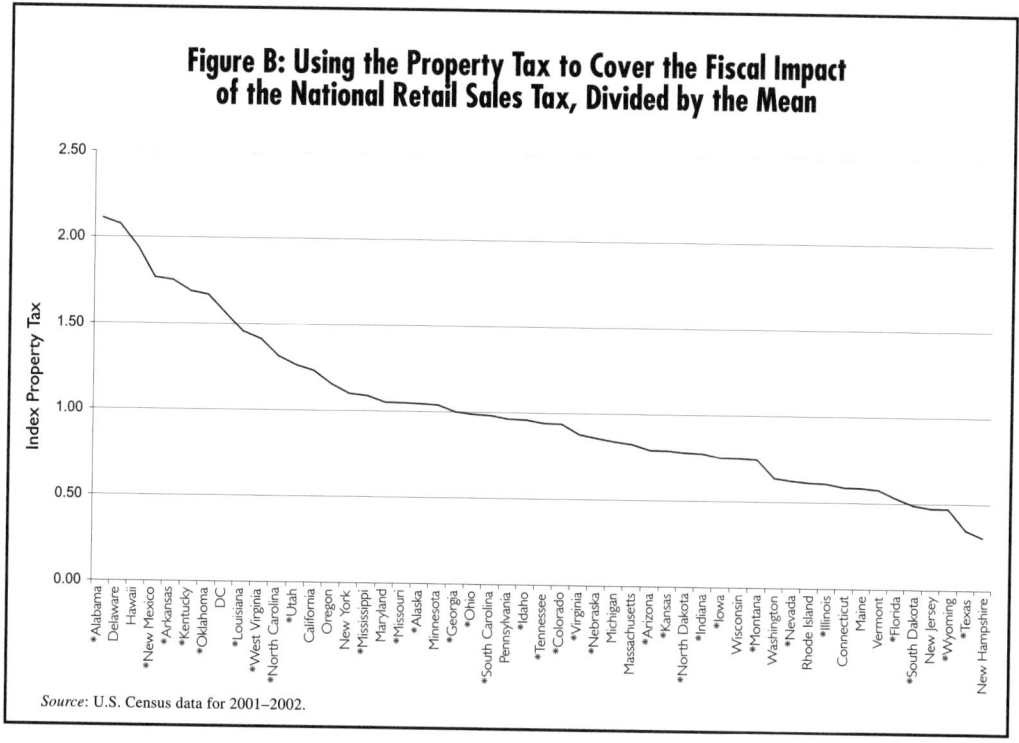

Figure B: Using the Property Tax to Cover the Fiscal Impact of the National Retail Sales Tax, Divided by the Mean

Source: U.S. Census data for 2001–2002.

reliable collections, thereby jeopardizing the balanced budget.

Although state sales taxes, for the most part, exempt business production inputs, the NRST would exempt all purchases made in furtherance of a bona fide business purpose to produce taxable activity. This broader exemption, while consistent with economic logic saying businesses do not bear the ultimate tax burden, reduces the tax base.

Specifically with regard to the property tax, property values are expected to decline due to the loss of the mortgage interest deduction and the deduction for real estate taxes. Moreover, the NRST is imposed on new home sales. An open question is whether interest rates will decline enough to offset the expected reduction in property values (of up to 20 percent).[5] Voter support for the property tax may decline as a result.

Adoption of a NRST would eliminate the federal income tax system and, therefore, make it difficult for states to continue their own income tax system. Most states rely heavily on the IRC to define taxable income, and enter into extensive data exchange with the IRS to promote tax compliance. Absent the federal income definitions, states would have to articulate their own definitions, and back it up with audit

protocols, to overcome the loss of the details from individual and business income tax records.

Under fundamental federal tax reform, all forms of investments, including bonds, would generate tax-exempt interest, thereby removing the preference given to the current municipal bond market. By losing their ability to borrow at a (tax-exempt) rate lower than U.S. Treasury (taxable) securities, state and local governments would end up borrowing at a higher rate than the U.S. Treasury. This result is the case in Canada where provincial and municipal governments face borrowing rates up to one full percentage point (100 basis points) higher than their federal government because they all borrow at taxable rates. Accordingly, states would pay more to borrow money after tax reform. Tax reform advocates, however, claim that an increase in aggregate personal savings will provide individuals with more money to invest, which, in turn, will drive down the overall cost of capital, therefore allowing state and local governments to borrow at lower rates than possible even with (the eliminated) tax-exempt bonds. This assumes, however, in part, that demand for state and local government securities does not weaken as the tax-advantages are removed. In terms of budget decisions, an increase in borrowing cost makes capital investments less attractive than labor-intensive services. Moreover, debt covenants may be imperiled, specifically in regards to pledged revenue security and coverage ratios.

Comparative Impacts

What are the state-by-state impacts of a 30 percent tax-exclusive NRST? One straight-forward estimate is to tally, by state, certain new costs and revenues losses.[6] Specifically, the NRST would impose a direct budget cost on all state and local end-consumer current operations and capital outlays, except for education services which would be exempt from taxation as a form of investment instead of consumption. Additionally, the NRST is expected to cause states to lose their ability to continue corporate and personal income taxes due to the loss of federal tax conformity. Adding together both of these new costs and revenue losses, and then adjusting each state's results by population, produces a per capita fiscal impact index that is normed by the mean of the series so that 1 equals the average index amount. As shown in Figure A, the less impacted states (at about half the average fiscal impact) are states without a personal income tax system while states at the other extreme (at over 1.5 times the average fiscal index) are states, and the District of Columbia, that rely extensively on the income tax. There are distinct differences, also, when viewed by the most recent presidential election (an asterisk denotes states where President Bush received a majority of the votes in 2004).

Moreover, if there is sticker-shock such that states are unable to turn to the sales tax to offset these new costs and income tax revenue losses, then, arguably, the pressure will fall to the property tax. Adding together both new costs and revenue losses, and dividing by the state's existing property tax reliance, yields a property tax impact index that is normed by the mean of the series so that 1 equals the average index amount. As shown in Figure B, the results are less striking when viewed by the last Presidential election because the highest affected states are those that currently place little reliance upon the property tax (at over 1.5 times the average state). These figures may be sobering, but they convey only a narrowly defined set of impacts of fundamental tax reform, leaving out, for instance, the increased cost of borrowing and other implications.

Summary

Presented almost as an afterthought in a review of the benefits of tax reform, the 2005 Economic Re-

port of the President makes the following disclosure:

> Finally, tax reform could impose large transition costs on state and local governments. Some tax reform proposals call for repeal of Federal income taxes. Since most state income taxes rely on the Federal tax as a starting point, states would either have to find another source of revenue or administer their income taxes on their own. Other proposals would impinge on the traditional state reliance on sales taxes by adding a Federal tax on this base.[7]

This statement is only the tip of the iceberg. State and local budgets (and debt) face significant impacts from fundamental federal income tax reform, including new budget costs and the effective loss of revenue choices. It is hard to pin down the precise nature of these implications prior to congressional action. At the least, any discussion of federal tax reform legislation deserves the careful scrutiny by state and local officials because there are significant fiscal federalism implications.

Notes

[1] For example, the mid-November, 2004, national poll by the New York Times and CBS News found that only a quarter of respondents favored a flat tax rate. Similarly, the NBC News/*Wall Street Journal* poll in December 2004 found the same results for a national consumption or sales tax, while a majority favored the existing tax system.

[2] Material consulted include: *The Economic Effects of Comprehensive Tax Reform* (Congressional Budget Office, 1997); *Comparing Income and Consumption Tax Bases* (Congressional Budget Office, 1997); *Impact on State and Local Governments and Tax-Exempt Organizations of Replacing the Federal Income Tax* (Joint Committee on Taxation, 1996); and, Robert Strauss, "Federal Consumption Taxes: Implications for the State and Local Sector," *State Tax Notes*, March 15, 1999. Various institutions and groups have material on the Web.

[3] Douglas Holtz-Eakin, "Fundamental Tax Reform and State and Local Governments," *National Tax Journal*, 49:3 (September 1996), 475–86.

[4] William G. Gale, "A Note on the Required Tax Rate in a National Retail Sales Tax: Preliminary Estimates for 2005–2014" (August 2004). Accessed: *http://www.brook. edu/views/papers/gale/20040812.htm.*

[5] Gravelle, Jane G. "Effects of Flat Taxes and Other Proposals on Housing," *Congressional Research Service Report for Congress* (June 1996); but see "Fundamental Tax Reform and Residential Housing Values," Donald Bruce and Douglas Holtz-Eakin, *Journal of Housing Economics*, 8:4 (1999), 249–71.

[6] Based on the suggestion of Diane L. Rogers of the U.S. House Ways and Means Committee staff, and using Cen-

sus data for 2001–02.

[7]*Economic Report of the President*. (Council of Economic Advisors, February 2005), 81.

References

Esenwein, Gregg A. and Jane G. Gravelle. "The Flat Tax, Value-Added Tax, and National Retail Sales Tax: Overview of the Issues," *Congressional Research Service Report for Congress* (September 24, 2004).

"Fundamental Tax Reform: Possibilities and Problems: A Symposium," *National Tax Journal*, 49:3 (September 1996), 317–500.

Hildreth, W. Bartley and James A. Richardson, eds. *Handbook on Taxation*. (New York: Marcel Dekker, Inc., 1999).

Huffman, Gregory W. and Evan F. Koenig, "The Dynamic Impact of Fundamental Tax Reform, Part 2: Extensions," *Economic and Financial Review* (Federal Reserve Bank of Dallas, Second Quarter 1998), 19–31.

Slemrod, Joel, with Jon Bakija. T*axing Ourselves: A Citizen's Guide to the Great Debate over Tax Reform*. (Cambridge, MA: MIT Press, 1996).

Slemrod, Joel. ed. *Tax Policy in the Real World*. (New York: Cambridge University Press, 1999).

Strauss, Robert P. "The Effects of a Flat Federal Consumption Tax on the States," *State Tax Notes*, February 26, 1996, 649–659.

Strauss. Robert P. Further Implications of a Federal Consumption Tax for State and local Tax Administration. *State Tax Notes*, October 14, 1996, 1085–94.

Viard, Alan D. "The Transition to Consumption Taxation, Part 2: The Impact on Existing Financial Assets," *Economic and Financial Review* (Federal Reserve Bank of Dallas, Second Quarter 2001), 20–31.

Zodrow, George R. and Peter Mieszkowski, *United States Tax Reform in the 21st Century*. (New York: Cambridge University Press, 2002).

About the Author

W. Bartley Hildreth is the Regents Distinguished Professor of Public Finance in the Hugo Wall School of Urban and Public Affairs and the W. Frank Barton School of Business at Wichita State University. He specializes in municipal securities and state and local finance. He has chaired the Governor's Tax Review Committee and has served on the board of the Kansas Development Finance Authority.

Trends in State Retirement Systems
By Frank T. Baumgardner

Systems are battling back utilizing new plan structures, alternative investments, and corporate activism to improve their fiscal positions. The recent recession and current demographic trends have had a serious impact on state-administered public employee retirement systems. This article will present information about the current condition of state-administered public employee retirement systems, the problems they face, and the solutions they are employing.

Introduction

State-administered public employee retirement systems are among the largest institutional investors in the world. There are currently 218 state systems in the United States with a total 21.2 million active and inactive members. They command a total of $1.8 trillion in retirement assets, making them major players in the financial markets.

Public employee retirement systems were founded as a means of social welfare, similar to Social Security, to provide public servants with sufficient retirement income. The recent recession and current demographic trends have had a serious impact on state systems. With systems seeing an erosion of their financial position, many are looking at alternative investments and increasing their role in corporate governance to help them return to a fiscal stability that will enable them to meet future obligations.

This article will present information about the current condition of state-administered public employee retirement systems, the problems they face and the solutions they are employing.

Overview

The number of state-defined benefit public employee retirement systems (218) has shown modest growth recently. Over the past decade, the number of state administered public employee retirement systems has grown by 28 from the 190 in fiscal year 1993. These new systems usually extended state retirement benefits to new classes of employees, such as local law enforcement personnel, legislators or judges.

Membership in a state-administered public employee retirement system is not limited to state employees; in fact, local governments employ more than two-thirds of the active employees covered by state systems. In 2003, local government employees were 69.5 percent, or 8.7 million, of the total 12.5 million state system active members.

State system assets totaled $1.8 trillion in fiscal year 2003, or just over 83.2 percent of the total $2.2 trillion held by all public employee retirement systems that year. These assets were distributed across several asset classes, but more than three-fifths were concentrated in corporate stocks or other securities:

- Corporate stocks were worth $665.6 billion (36.9 percent)
- Other securities, which include investments held in trust by other agencies, mutual funds, foreign and international securities, conditional sales contracts, and other securities classifications totaled $442.6 billion (24.6 percent)

The remaining $694.5 billion in assets (38.5 percent) were distributed across a variety of other investments including corporate bonds, federal government securities, mortgages, real estate holdings and savings deposits.

System Size

State-administered public employee retirement systems are very large organizations. Ninety of the 218 systems had membership greater than 25,000 in 2003. The six largest systems individually had membership greater than the population of Wyoming (507,000) and the combined membership of the 10 largest (7,800,000) exceeds the population of Virginia (7,500,000).[1] The 10 largest systems and their memberships were:

- California Public Employees Retirement System (CalPERS) (1,480 thousand)
- Texas Teachers Retirement System (1,080 thousand)
- New York Public Employees Pension and Retirement System (964 thousand)
- Florida State Management Services Retirement System (892 thousand)
- Ohio Public Employees Retirement System (797 thousand)
- California Teachers Retirement System (CalSTRS) (720 thousand)
- Virginia Employees Retirement System (505 thousand)
- Wisconsin Employees Retirement System (487 thousand)

Table A
Percent Distribution of Assets in State Public Employee Retirement Systems: Fiscal Years 1997, 2002 and 2003

Asset Class	2003	2002	1997
Corporate stocks	36.9%	36.9%	34.8%
Total other securities (a)	24.6	21.8	20.3
Corporate bonds	14.4	16.3	15.2
Federal governmental securities	10.1	10.2	18
Cash and short-term investments	4.4	5.1	4.7
Mortgages held directly	1.2	1.1	1
Total other investments (b)	8.5	8.6	6.1

Key:
(a) Total Other Securities includes: investments held in trust by other agencies, securities of state and local governments, foreign and international securities, shares held in mutual funds, conditional sales, contracts, direct loans, loans to members, etc.
(b) Total Other Investments includes: real property, venture capital, partnerships, real estate investment trusts, and leverage buy-outs.

- North Carolina Teachers and State Employees Retirement System (469 thousand)
- Michigan Public School Employees Retirement System (468 thousand)

In addition to their large membership, state systems administer an enormous wealth of funds. An annual compilation of retirement fund data by *Pensions & Investments* magazine shows state-administered public employee retirement systems hold 7 of the top 15 spots in the world when ranked in terms of total retirement asset holdings. The top six in membership cited above hold more retirement assets than major corporations such as GE, IBM, Boeing, Verizon, Ford, AT&T or Daimler Chrysler.[2]

Membership and assets are concentrated in the largest systems. The largest 21 of the 218 systems accounted for 56.4 percent of total membership of all state systems in fiscal year 2003. These same systems also control 58.1 percent or $1,047.7 billion of the total $1,802.7 billion state retirement system assets.

The concentration of such large asset holdings in these top systems has made them very important players in the corporate world. Over the last several years, many systems have shown an increasing interest in influencing the direction of corporate boards.

Membership

State-administered public employee retirement systems had 21.2 million members in 2003, a 3.1 percent increase from 2002. Total membership has grown by 6.0 million or 39.5 percent over the past decade, while active membership increased 2.3 million (22.6 percent) and inactive membership increased 1.8 million (127.2 percent) over that period. Of the current 21.2 million members, 12.5 million are active members, 5.4 million are current beneficiaries, and 3.3 million are inactive members. Active members are employees who currently contribute to the system while inactive members are former employees or employees on military or other extended leave who retain retirement credits in the system.

Receipts

State-administered public employee retirement systems are funded in three ways:
- Current active members of systems (employees) pay contributions.
- Governments (employers) also make contributions
- Fiduciaries invest the system assets and earn returns on investment.

Total receipts for fiscal year 2003 were $130.0 billion. Earnings on investment constituted 52.5 percent ($68.2 billion) of total receipts, government contributions made up 28.5 percent ($37.0 billion), and employee contributions the remaining 19.1 percent ($24.8 billion).

Fiscal year 2003 did see a turnaround on investment earnings, which were $68.2 billion compared with the prior fiscal year's net loss of $63.5 billion. Even so, the 2003 figure was far less than the pre-recession levels that routinely averaged in the hundreds of billions of dollars.

Employee and government contributions both increased in fiscal year 2003. Employee contributions grew 7.7 percent from $23.0 billion to $24.8 billion. Government contributions grew by a much larger margin, from $32.0 billion to $37.0 billion, or just over 15.4 percent, in the same period.

Payments and Other Outlays

Total state retirement expenditures, or outlays, for 2003 were $109.0 billion, an 11.1 percent increase from 2002 ($98.2 billion). There are three types of outlays: benefit payments, withdrawals, and administrative and miscellaneous payments.

The largest outlay, benefit payments, totaled $98.8 billion for fiscal year 2003, an 11.4 percent increase from the 2002 level ($88.7 billion). Benefit payments made up 90.6 percent of total outlays for the year. Withdrawals accounted for 3.9 percent of outlays, totaling $4.2 billion, and increased 29.6 percent from the prior year ($3.3 billion). Administrative and miscellaneous expenses constituted the remaining 5.5

percent of total outlays, totaling $6.0 billion, a decrease of 3.6 percent from 2002 ($6.3 billion).

Beneficiaries and Monthly Benefit Payments

There were a total 5.4 million beneficiaries of state-administered public employee retirement systems in fiscal year 2003. This is an increase of 4.6 percent over the prior year. Of those, 85.6 percent (4.6 million) were retired on account of age or service, 6.3 percent (342,000) were retired on account of a disability, and 8.0 percent (436,000) were survivors of deceased former active members. These numbers increased by 4.3 percent, 6.5 percent, and 7.3 percent respectively from the prior year.

Monthly benefit payments averaged $1,449 for 2003, an increase of 5.5 percent from the previous year. These payments varied widely across the country. Retirement systems in Connecticut averaged the highest ($2,112), followed by Wisconsin ($2,075) and Colorado ($2,055), while systems in Iowa ($846), Indiana ($827), and Kansas ($822) had the lowest. Many factors influence these numbers including cost of living, inflation, and the composition and number of beneficiaries. Average benefit payments have consistently exceeded inflation rates over the past decade putting increasing pressure on systems.

The ratio of annuitants to active members increased to 43.2 percent in 2003 from 41.8 percent in 2002. This number likely will continue growing as the baby boomers begin to retire. The increase of the annuitant-to-active-member ratio has far-reaching implications on funding.

Receipts Compared with Payments

Systems must increase their funding reserves each year to cover future liabilities. These liabilities grow along with membership and inflation, so systems work to ensure a net inflow of funds to meet their future financial commitments.

Receipts exceeded payments in fiscal year 2003 by $20.9 billion. This is in contrast to 2002 when funds showed a net outflow of $106.7 billion. Although the net outflow in fiscal year 2002 damaged the financial position of the systems, several prior years showed very large net inflows of funds averaging in the hundred billions of dollars. This is not to say that the large net outflow in 2002 was not significant: it was, however, it is important to remember that retirement system fiduciaries and actuaries plan for the cyclical nature of the business cycle and have built assumptions into their plans to buffer against it.

Investments and Assets

Total asset holdings of state-administered public employee retirement systems for fiscal year 2003 were $1,803 billion, up from $1,775 billion in 2002. These assets were distributed across several classes, as seen in Table A.

The distribution of assets in 2003 was largely unchanged from the prior year. The percentage of cash and short-term investments, corporate bonds, and total other investments decreased slightly while the percentage of total other securities increased proportionately.

Comparing 2003 to1997 highlights the redistribution of assets from traditional asset classes to other types of securities. Although the percentage distribution of most asset classes held relatively stable over the period, total other securities increased sharply while federal government securities decreased significantly.

The systems are investing larger proportions of their funds in alternative asset classes such as: investments held in trust by other agencies, securities of state and local governments, foreign and international securities, shares held in mutual funds, conditional sales, contracts, direct loans, loans to members and the like. There are several possible reasons fund managers are opting for some reallocation—low interest rates; the downturn in the stock market; emerging markets abroad; and opportunities in private equity offering growth opportunities.

Current Issues

Funding considerations dominate discussions concerning public employee retirement systems. System administrators must earn consistently high yields to keep up with their actuarial liabilities. Poor investment returns require systems to either increase employer contributions or limit benefits, both difficult measures.

The recent stock market decline, changing demographics, and the increasing costs of health care have placed considerable burden on retirement systems, making it difficult for some to keep up with their actuarial liabilities. As in the private sector, some state governments are considering switching retirement structures from defined benefit to defined contribution to minimize the government's exposure to market risk. Others are utilizing alternative investments and increasing their role in corporate governance to ensure they reap maximum returns on their investments. This section will address the funding problems now facing systems, the alternative benefit structures they are considering, and some of the alternative investment solutions they are employing.

Funding Levels

Most public pensions are pre-funded, meaning assets for retirement benefits accumulate during a participants pre-retirement years.[3] An actuarial funding level can be used to gauge a pre-funded plan's health. This is calculated by dividing the plans assets by its liabilities for accrued benefits. A fully funded pension plan has assets equal to its liabilities and a ratio of 100 percent. A system whose assets are less than its liabilities is underfunded. This does not mean that the system will not be able to meet its benefit obligations, but that it will need more funding to meet them in the long term.

The Public Fund Survey, conducted annually by the National Association of State Retirement Administrators (NASRA), showed a significant decrease recently in the actuarial funding level for the 125 state retirement systems included in the survey: 91.1 percent in 2003, down from 96.3 percent in 2002, and 100.9 percent in 2001.[4] The research director for NASRA cited two factors causing the drop in this ratio: the declining equity market and the generous benefit enhancements of the late 1990s.[5]

Other factors related to system funding issues are increasing life expectancy and underpayment by the government, especially during times of fiscal stress and rising health care costs. With many systems providing health care benefits to their retirees, this is becoming an important financial factor since healthcare costs are growing rapidly and are difficult to predict. In fact, *The Economist* magazine reports that the future burden of healthcare costs could easily be as great as the cost of pensions.[6]

Changing demographics exacerbate these problems. Systems have more retirees, who are in turn living longer, increasing the ratio of annuitants to active members. Annuitants typically require more service than active members, increasing administrative expenses and placing a strain on funding. More annuitants also require plans to be more liquid to be available to pay benefits, inevitably placing assets in less lucrative classes leading to smaller returns.[7]

Defined Benefit and Defined Contribution Plans

Due to the financial problems defined benefit plans are now facing, both public and private sector employers are examining alternative structures to relieve their pension burdens. These include defined contribution plans, such as 401(k)s, and hybrid systems.

In a defined benefit retirement plan, the payments an employee receives upon retirement are defined by an agreement between the employer and the employee. In a defined contribution plan, the contributions the employee and employer make are defined; however, the end retirement benefits depend upon the growth of the contributions rather than an agreed upon allotment.

Defined benefit plans have several advantages for employees. Primarily, they shift the market risk to the employer, which gives employees greater financial stability in retirement. In addition, many plans protect against inflation by earmarking benefit payments to some measure such as the Consumer Price Index. There are also disadvantages for the employees; since these systems are typically structured to reward longer service, the rules of defined benefit plans usually hinder a member's mobility.

Employers benefit by offering defined benefit retirement plans because their stability helps attract and retain a quality workforce and increase diversity.[8] This comes at a financial cost, however, since employers take on the market risk.

Defined contribution plans offer employees more career mobility and greater control over their retirement planning. Smart investing and saving could provide greater returns; however, because professional fiduciaries rather than individual members administer defined benefit plans, members in defined contribution plans typically earn lower rates of return.[9] Employees also shoulder the market risk so their benefits are not guaranteed.

Defined contribution plans effectively shift the market risk from the employer to the employee, a major advantage for employers. Since defined contribution plans are often not as appealing to perspective employees, in a competitive employment market this can make attracting and retaining employees more difficult.

Some private pension plans are developing hybrid systems, attempting to share the market risk between both the employer and the employee, which might be adapted by public systems in the future. GE, for example is developing a system that would allow defined contribution participants to invest their money in a fund which would mirror the GE defined benefit plan investment lineup and provide for a minimum 5 percent guaranteed return.[10]

Move to Alternative Asset Classes and Corporate Activism

In addition to examining alternative retirement offerings, pension funds are turning to alternative investments and corporate activism to ease their funding problems. Pensions and Investments magazine reported, "CalPERS moved approximately 17 billion to alternatives at the expense of traditional asset classes over the past three or four years."[11] This constitutes nearly 10.0 percent of its $170.7 billion in asset holdings. Other funds are considering similar moves into alternative investments. CalSTRS, for example, is considering hedging, emerging market bonds, and other non-traditional assets as a way to generate greater returns.[12]

State public employee retirement funds are also increasing their role in corporate governance to assure that businesses act in ways that best benefit the financial interests of the systems. This movement began in the early 80's when CalPERS began publishing "focus lists" of companies with bad corporate governance.[13]

Fiduciaries have continued to take a growing interest in utilizing their shareholder rights. NASRA has asked the Securities and Exchange Commission to allow proxy voting reforms that will help them, "exercise the rights of shareholder ownership in order to promote the best economic interests of plan members and beneficiaries."[14] NASRA says, "(their) best alternative is to address problematic situations by improving the boards to reflect an appropriate shareholder perspective."

Perhaps the best-known recent example of a pension fund using its proxy rights to influence the direction of a corporate board occurred this year when CalPERS led a campaign against the Disney Corporation chairman and succeeded in stripping him of his role.[15] With such large asset holdings, many of these systems control large portions of major corporations. It will be interesting to watch their influence on corporate governance over the next several years.

Author's Note

This article is released to inform interested parties of ongoing research and to encourage discussion of work in progress. The views expressed on technical issues are those of the author and not necessarily those of the U.S. Census Bureau.

Notes

[1]Table 1: Annual Estimates of the Population for the United States and States, and for Puerto Rico: April 1, 2000 to July 1, 2004 (NST-EST2004-01), Source: Population Division, U.S. Census Bureau, (Release Date: December 22, 2004).

[2]Vince Calio, "Mega Funds," Pensions & Investments, (September 20, 2004) P&I/Watson Wyatt World 300. Ranked by U.S. dollars, in millions. U.S. fund data is from the P&I 1000, published January 26; all other fund data as of December 31, unless otherwise noted.

[3]Keith Brainard, "Public Fund Survey Summary of Findings FY 2003," (September 2004).

[4]Rob Kozlowski, "Funding levels for Public Plans fall in FY03," Pensions & Investments, (November 1, 2004).

[5]See note 3 above.

[6]"Enough to live on," The Economist, (March 25, 2004).

[7]See note 3 above.

[8]Gary W. Anderson and Keith Brainard, "Profitable Prudence: The Case for Public Employer Defined Benefit Plans," (April 26, 2004).

[9]See note 2 above.

[10]Phyllis Feinberg, "DC offering linked to GE pension plan on the way," Pensions & Investments, (August 9, 2004).

[11]Christine Williamson, "CalPERS separates alpha, beta," Pensions & Investments, (November 15, 2004).

[12]Joel Chernoff, "CalSTRS joins hunt for alpha," Pensions & Investments, (July 12, 2004).

[13]"Profit huggers," The Economist, (April 1, 2004).

[14]Letter to Mr. Jonathan G. Katz, Secretary of Securities and Exchange Commission, from NASRA, December 22, 2003.

[15]Paul R. La Monica, "Eisner out as Disney chair," CNN Money, (March 4, 2004). http://money.cnn.com/2004/03/04/news/companies/disney/.

About the Author

Frank Baumgardner is a statistician with the U.S. Census Bureau. He received a B.S. from Miami University in economics and decision sciences. He began his career with the U.S. Census Bureau in 2003 with the Governments Division where he focuses on state and locally administered public employee retirement system statistics.

TABLE B
MEMBERSHIP AND BENEFIT OPERATIONS OF STATE-ADMINISTERED EMPLOYEE RETIREMENT SYSTEMS, LAST MONTH OF FISCAL YEAR: MARCH 2003

State	Total membership	Total active members	Total inactive members	Beneficiaries receiving periodic benefit payments				Periodic benefit payments for the month (dollars)				Average monthly benefit payment
				Total (a)	Retired by service	Retired on disability	Survivors	Total (a)	Retired by service	Retired on disability	Survivors	
United States	21,209,882	12,538,604	3,250,341	5,420,937	4,642,902	342,286	435,749	$7,852,487,401	$7,013,919,983	$462,604,657	$375,962,761	$1,449
Alabama	326,639	214,895	25,360	86,384	74,348	6,135	5,901	114,777,439	105,330,442	5,142,580	4,304,417	1,329
Alaska	94,676	46,526	20,924	27,226	24,479	558	2,189	46,841,362	43,770,450	933,249	2,137,663	1,720
Arizona	433,703	229,744	124,702	79,257	72,434	5,562	1,261	112,615,009	103,532,281	6,777,887	2,304,841	1,421
Arkansas	166,596	109,633	16,051	40,912	34,552	3,207	3,153	54,256,565	49,016,813	3,458,470	1,781,282	1,326
California	2,397,755	1,377,772	332,300	687,683	528,124	79,130	80,429	1,066,744,721	912,660,799	112,877,244	41,206,678	1,551
Colorado	357,275	191,332	99,681	66,262	56,126	7,966	2,170	136,173,243	109,171,966	15,952,577	11,048,700	2,055
Connecticut	190,727	119,381	9,819	61,527	53,602	3,519	4,406	129,964,827	119,701,392	5,738,667	4,524,768	2,112
Delaware	58,344	38,498	984	18,862	13,763	2,155	2,944	20,449,406	17,007,439	1,785,283	1,656,684	1,084
Florida	891,754	620,163	64,912	206,679	186,427	12,211	8,041	220,088,992	204,896,128	9,191,932	6,000,932	1,065
Georgia	602,377	357,142	142,530	102,705	82,871	8,957	10,877	185,005,535	158,841,854	11,945,269	14,218,412	1,801
Hawaii	97,831	62,292	4,150	31,389	28,546	1,184	1,659	47,593,000	45,176,000	909,000	1,508,000	1,516
Idaho	96,025	62,490	7,906	25,629	23,397	418	1,814	25,180,154	22,927,532	502,548	1,750,074	982
Illinois	932,817	463,965	236,088	232,764	194,008	3,343	35,413	360,750,666	336,019,694	4,561,654	20,169,318	1,550
Indiana	367,980	229,110	47,701	91,169	71,522	6,638	13,009	75,380,476	53,229,211	4,890,277	17,260,988	827
Iowa	281,651	163,971	39,444	78,236	76,145	1,086	1,005	66,220,845	62,970,043	2,269,380	981,422	846
Kansas	248,881	147,294	40,404	61,183	57,307	316	3,560	50,295,283	49,168,020	177,140	950,123	822
Kentucky	370,132	219,349	55,446	95,337	91,006	2,427	1,904	139,349,596	131,306,236	5,176,360	2,867,000	1,462
Louisiana	370,998	216,526	44,600	109,872	89,479	6,475	13,918	178,354,604	160,313,695	7,845,731	10,195,178	1,623
Maine	87,678	51,848	5,056	30,774	24,533	1,853	4,388	34,754,091	27,705,962	2,092,196	4,955,933	1,129
Maryland	330,647	192,836	45,990	91,821	75,235	5,585	11,001	103,350,670	84,682,451	6,286,145	12,382,074	1,126
Massachusetts	305,623	206,502	7,270	91,851	82,891	2,962	5,998	143,058,311	127,217,954	8,590,223	7,250,134	1,558
Michigan	623,561	395,379	27,625	200,557	169,774	9,360	21,423	294,835,479	252,938,921	12,599,222	29,297,336	1,470
Minnesota	586,357	280,450	185,835	120,072	108,171	4,178	7,723	189,722,058	173,952,630	5,606,590	10,162,838	1,580
Mississippi	328,419	155,590	112,698	60,131	48,277	3,986	7,868	57,145,106	49,405,763	3,436,235	4,303,108	950
Missouri	383,112	262,223	26,701	94,188	81,824	2,057	10,307	134,118,192	124,327,499	1,816,393	7,974,300	1,424
Montana	103,820	53,387	23,679	26,754	25,267	688	799	25,035,941	24,025,609	460,025	550,307	936
Nebraska	71,133	45,149	14,301	11,683	10,962	342	379	13,201,362	12,548,949	422,968	229,445	1,130
Nevada	112,623	77,610	7,701	27,312	23,814	1,329	2,169	50,592,674	47,083,208	1,077,436	2,432,030	1,852
New Hampshire	74,484	50,910	6,569	17,005	13,958	1,261	1,786	20,470,083	17,537,833	1,728,250	1,204,000	1,204
New Jersey	705,187	440,615	63,468	201,104	182,084		19,020	354,601,304	323,291,873	0	31,309,431	1,763
New Mexico	188,306	120,955	25,134	42,217	38,066	1,414	2,737	65,679,482	61,434,397	1,821,310	2,423,775	1,556
New York	1,333,418	782,538	118,976	431,904	376,664	24,722	30,518	652,158,001	603,229,096	29,267,349	19,661,556	1,510
North Carolina	697,775	454,249	80,793	162,733	135,947	12,589	14,197	206,107,171	178,339,106	16,170,337	11,597,728	1,267
North Dakota	43,447	27,207	5,567	10,673	9,327	387	959	9,896,905	9,045,937	195,360	655,608	927
Ohio	1,531,223	734,148	464,477	332,598	268,914	34,704	28,980	514,740,621	434,247,785	57,952,065	22,540,771	1,548
Oklahoma	224,470	143,008	10,080	71,382	60,716	5,955	4,711	87,072,882	77,088,894	5,247,228	4,736,760	1,220
Oregon	310,268	159,769	53,815	96,684	91,526	5,158	0	184,602,124	177,552,344	7,049,780	0	1,909
Pennsylvania	682,299	367,315	75,770	239,214	210,478	12,662	16,074	309,959,996	287,565,039	12,943,842	9,451,115	1,296
Rhode Island	51,818	28,505	3,965	19,348	16,737	1,569	1,042	36,015,082	31,154,871	2,920,594	1,939,617	1,861
South Carolina	442,717	219,006	130,720	92,991	74,958	10,559	7,474	120,156,232	104,728,432	9,726,378	5,701,422	1,292

See footnotes at end of table

TABLE B
MEMBERSHIP AND BENEFIT OPERATIONS OF STATE-ADMINISTERED EMPLOYEE RETIREMENT SYSTEMS, LAST MONTH OF FISCAL YEAR: MARCH 2003 – CONTINUED

State	Total membership	Total active members	Total inactive members	Beneficiaries receiving periodic benefit payments				Periodic benefit payments for the month (dollars)				Average monthly benefit payment
				Total (a)	Retired by service	Retired on disability	Survivors	Total (a)	Retired by service	Retired on disability	Survivors	
South Dakota	63,934	35,114	12,379	16,441	13,546	394	2,501	15,977,083	14,250,385	339,051	1,387,647	972
Tennessee	304,196	198,917	22,158	83,121	71,595	4,227	7,299	76,720,000	69,550,000	2,256,000	4,914,000	923
Texas	1,635,614	1,176,389	134,880	324,345	293,784	14,984	15,577	496,621,797	450,815,452	30,593,711	15,212,634	1,531
Utah	150,095	94,833	23,280	31,982	31,982	0	0	42,311,610	42,311,610	0	0	1,323
Vermont	41,035	23,837	7,683	9,515	8,193	623	699	8,847,449	7,982,581	436,569	428,299	930
Virginia	504,796	311,811	84,227	108,758	91,583	15,609	1,566	132,228,706	112,118,000	19,108,000	1,002,706	1,216
Washington	356,359	216,709	29,545	110,105	93,165	5,027	11,913	148,256,556	127,574,483	5,639,167	15,042,906	1,347
West Virginia	107,171	64,319	14,436	28,416	28,416	0	0	37,556,750	37,556,750	0	0	1,322
Wisconsin	486,819	263,500	107,032	116,287	108,292	6,572	1,423	241,267,880	223,631,200	16,357,961	1,278,719	2,075
Wyoming	55,317	33,893	5,529	15,895	14,087	243	1,565	15,384,080	13,984,974	329,024	1,070,082	968

Source: U. S. Department of Commerce, U. S. Census Bureau, December 2004.
Key:
(a) Detail may not add to totals due to rounding.

Table C
NUMBER, MEMBERSHIP AND MONTHLY BENEFIT PAYMENTS OF STATE-ADMINISTERED EMPLOYER RETIREMENT SYSTEMS: 1993–2003

State	2003	2002	2001	2000	1999	1998	1997	1996	1995	1994	1993
Number of systems	218	219	220	219	213	214	214	203	200	192	190
Membership last month of fiscal year:											
Total Membership	21,209,882	20,575,129	19,946,136	19,863,442	18,857,782	18,792,096	17,755,195	17,335,904	17,107,747	16,034,883	15,206,551
Active members	12,538,604	12,407,222	12,244,404	12,281,004	11,757,108	11,358,499	11,210,405	11,121,324	10,967,868	10,545,461	10,224,417
Inactive members	3,250,341	2,987,492	2,750,575	2,796,005	2,578,496	3,009,997	2,291,754	2,048,359	2,115,251	1,510,051	1,430,369
Percent distribution:	100.0	100.0	100.0	100.0	100.0	100.0	100.0	100.0	100.0	100.0	100.0
Active members	59.1	60.3	61.4	61.8	62.3	60.4	63.1	64.2	64.1	65.8	67.2
Other	40.9	39.7	38.6	38.2	37.7	39.6	36.9	35.8	35.9	34.2	32.8
Beneficiaries receiving periodic benefits:											
Total number retired or survivors	5,420,937	5,180,415	4,951,157	4,786,433	4,522,178	4,423,600	4,253,036	4,166,221	4,024,628	3,979,371	3,551,765
Former active members, retired service	4,642,902	4,453,077	4,282,245	4,086,451	3,872,834	3,798,600	3,661,670	3,599,888	3,483,053	3,484,001	3,099,491
Former active members, retired disability	342,286	321,346	277,493	271,902	264,360	254,718	241,303	225,521	220,309	213,802	187,795
Survivors of former active members	435,749	405,992	391,419	428,080	384,984	370,282	350,063	340,812	321,266	281,568	264,479
Percent distribution:	100.0	100.0	100.0	100.0	100.0	100.0	100.0	100.0	100.0	100.0	100.0
Percent former active members, retired service	85.6	86.0	86.5	85.4	85.6	85.9	86.1	86.4	86.5	87.6	87.3
Percent former active members, retired disability	6.3	6.2	5.6	5.7	5.8	5.8	5.7	5.4	5.5	5.4	5.3
Percent survivors of former active members	8.0	7.8	7.9	8.9	8.5	8.4	8.2	8.2	8.0	7.1	7.4
Recurrent benefit payments for last month of fiscal year:											
Total amount of benefit for retired/survivors	7,852,487,401	7,116,489,779	6,551,024,839	5,739,832,168	5,131,270,653	4,638,426,325	4,277,792,550	4,142,330,275	3,781,984,022	3,309,137,550	2,823,434,232
Amount former active members, retired service	7,013,919,983	6,351,351,225	5,857,036,896	5,099,631,979	4,568,694,980	4,167,810,596	3,853,280,996	3,751,445,046	3,412,094,819	2,990,611,108	2,525,531,815
Amount former active members, retired disability	462,604,657	435,866,540	359,326,850	316,997,005	280,965,382	257,442,309	220,712,545	209,156,037	193,334,198	171,342,146	161,872,085
Amount survivors of former active members	375,962,761	329,272,014	334,661,093	323,203,184	281,610,291	213,173,420	203,799,009	181,729,192	176,555,005	147,184,296	136,030,332
Percent distribution:	100.0	100.0	100.0	100.0	100.0	100.0	100.0	100.0	100.0	100.0	100.0
Percent former active members, retired service	89.3	89.2	89.4	88.8	89.0	89.9	90.1	90.6	90.2	90.4	89.4
Percent former active members, retired disability	5.9	6.1	5.5	5.5	5.5	5.6	5.2	5.0	5.1	5.2	5.7
Percent survivors of former active members	4.8	4.6	5.1	5.6	5.5	4.6	4.8	4.4	4.7	4.4	4.8
Average monthly payment for beneficiaries (in dollars):											
Average for all beneficiaries	1,449	1,374	1,323	1,199	1,135	1,049	1,006	994	940	832	795
For former active members, retired service	1,511	1,426	1,368	1,248	1,180	1,097	1,052	1,042	980	858	815
For former active members retired disability	1,352	1,356	1,295	1,166	1,063	1,011	915	927	878	801	862
For survivors of former active members	863	811	855	755	731	576	582	533	550	523	514

Source: U. S. Department of Commerce, U. S. Census Bureau, December 2004.
Note: Detail may not add to totals due to rounding.

Table D

NATIONAL SUMMARY OF FINANCES OF STATE-ADMINISTERED EMPLOYEE RETIREMENT SYSTEMS: 1993–2003
(in thousands)

Item	2002–2003	2001–2002	2000–2001	1999–2000	1998–1999	1997–1998	1996–1997	1995–1996	1994–1995	1993–1994	1992–1993
Receipts	$129,993,356	-$8,448,868	$95,532,600	$247,352,850	$219,670,158	$212,136,999	$188,018,445	$156,317,595	$123,296,177	$110,071,915	$103,101,915
Employee contributions	24,780,564	23,006,094	21,892,512	20,665,828	19,786,741	18,334,766	17,435,994	16,406,926	15,721,701	14,738,018	13,431,836
Government contributions	36,996,114	32,059,268	32,608,891	33,853,730	33,467,754	34,620,047	36,893,266	32,984,590	31,606,859	29,114,635	27,491,787
From state governments	19,190,046	16,795,329	17,124,394	17,180,666	16,878,613	17,619,625	20,170,257	16,894,307	16,228,399	15,519,680	14,819,274
From local governments	17,806,068	15,263,939	15,484,497	16,673,064	16,589,141	17,000,422	16,723,009	16,090,283	15,378,460	13,594,955	12,672,513
Earnings on investments	68,216,678	-63,514,230	41,031,197	192,833,292	166,415,663	159,182,186	133,689,185	106,926,079	75,967,617	66,219,262	62,178,292
Payments	109,087,129	98,225,642	90,181,285	79,457,536	70,741,261	65,481,683	58,957,458	55,299,915	49,523,895	45,320,754	40,402,413
Benefits	98,835,637	88,713,825	80,990,697	72,216,032	64,230,736	59,658,756	53,743,045	50,507,371	45,759,560	41,249,020	37,115,679
Withdrawals	4,220,641	3,257,640	3,465,317	3,754,613	3,118,299	3,222,767	2,840,955	2,644,613	2,191,399	2,573,775	2,080,625
Administration	6,030,851	6,254,177	5,725,271	3,486,891	3,392,226	2,600,160	2,373,458	2,147,931	1,572,936	1,497,959	1,206,109
Amount of cash and investment holdings at end of the fiscal year	1,802,682,364	1,774,662,873	1,784,734,059	1,797,953,426	1,581,779,624	1,426,403,895	1,220,527,088	1,044,650,139	913,929,489	811,742,778	741,741,645
Cash and deposits	79,762,295	90,565,875	93,834,423	98,327,876	81,416,739	72,354,184	57,325,477	49,367,394	54,163,156	41,274,783	48,855,709
Securities	1,570,340,383	1,531,401,377	1,540,661,766	1,544,764,421	1,393,773,838	1,265,801,454	1,089,349,314	927,183,387	804,714,178	722,382,594	621,901,004
Governmental	181,761,640	181,193,500	197,739,933	221,223,557	224,457,008	228,588,766	219,784,346	216,325,590	201,044,921	187,994,565	169,455,599
Federal Government	181,312,675	180,721,339	197,015,832	220,863,102	223,883,387	228,319,703	219,584,946	215,929,452	200,514,330	187,665,856	169,362,067
United States Treasury	139,453,009	124,273,164	137,331,033	161,312,021	165,903,963	169,033,658	164,944,185	167,050,802	160,717,959	158,533,221	137,916,240
Federal agency	41,859,666	56,448,175	59,684,799	59,551,081	57,979,424	59,286,045	54,640,761	48,878,650	39,796,372	29,132,635	31,445,827
State and local government	448,765	472,161	724,101	360,455	573,621	269,063	199,400	396,138	530,591	328,709	93,532
Nongovernmental	1,388,578,943	1,350,207,877	1,342,921,833	1,323,540,864	1,169,316,830	1,037,212,688	869,564,968	710,857,797	603,669,257	534,388,029	452,445,405
Corporate bonds	258,944,790	290,050,962	313,157,127	278,566,269	239,054,115	211,349,020	185,259,386	175,830,923	164,324,545	159,362,455	140,033,039
Corporate stocks	665,569,706	653,982,383	619,459,993	636,606,069	577,726,637	518,863,787	424,794,006	350,140,658	300,547,610	269,219,186	234,935,259
Mortgages	21,490,162	20,052,800	21,796,616	20,454,176	18,837,843	20,752,082	12,160,708	23,576,186	16,665,236	16,863,344	18,500,499
Foreign and international securities	225,134,367	216,166,650	230,458,313	246,904,776	195,411,813	167,440,243	130,681,334	0	0	0	0
Other nongovernmental securities	217,439,918	169,955,082	158,049,784	141,009,574	138,286,422	118,807,556	116,669,534	161,310,030	122,131,866	88,943,044	58,976,608
Other investments	152,579,686	152,695,621	150,237,870	154,861,129	106,589,047	88,248,257	73,852,297	68,099,358	55,052,154	48,085,401	60,262,351
Real property	32,711,410	34,818,209	35,566,610	42,222,968	31,008,159	29,347,473	28,538,000	26,783,244	24,510,964	22,254,420	21,332,066
Miscellaneous investments	119,868,276	117,877,412	114,671,260	112,638,161	75,580,888	58,900,784	45,314,297	41,316,114	30,541,190	25,830,981	38,930,285

See footnotes at end of table

Table D
NATIONAL SUMMARY OF FINANCES OF STATE-ADMINISTERED EMPLOYEE RETIREMENT SYSTEMS: 1993–2003 — CONTINUED (in thousands)

Item	2002–2003	2001–2002	2000–2001	1999–2000	1998–1999	1997–1998	1996–1997	1995–1996	1994–1995
Receipts	100.0%	100.0%	100.0%	100.0%	100.0%	100.0%	100.0%	100.0%	100.0%
Employee contributions	19.1	-272.3	22.9	8.4	9.0	8.6	9.3	10.5	12.8
Government contributions	28.5	-379.5	34.1	13.7	15.2	16.3	19.6	21.1	25.6
From state governments	14.8	-198.8	17.9	6.9	7.7	8.3	10.7	10.8	13.2
From local governments	13.7	-180.7	16.2	6.7	7.6	8.0	8.9	10.3	12.5
Earnings on investments	52.5	751.7	42.9	78.0	75.8	75.0	71.1	68.4	61.6
Payments	100.0	100.0	100.0	100.0	100.0	100.0	100.0	100.0	100.0
Benefits	90.6	90.3	89.8	90.9	90.8	91.1	91.2	91.3	92.4
Withdrawals	3.9	3.3	3.8	4.7	4.4	4.9	4.8	4.8	4.4
Administration	5.5	6.4	6.3	4.4	4.8	4.0	4.0	3.9	3.2
Amount of cash and investment holdings at end of the fiscal year	100.0	100.0	100.0	100.0	100.0	100.0	100.0	100.0	100.0
Cash and desposits	4.4	5.1	5.3	5.5	5.1	5.1	4.7	4.7	5.9
Securities	87.1	86.3	86.3	85.9	88.1	88.7	89.3	88.8	88.0
Governmental	10.1	10.2	11.1	12.3	14.2	16.0	18.0	20.7	22.0
Federal Government	10.1	10.2	11.0	12.3	14.2	16.0	18.0	20.7	21.9
United States Treasury	7.7	7.0	7.7	9.0	10.5	11.9	13.5	16.0	17.6
Federal agency	2.3	3.2	3.3	3.3	3.7	4.2	4.5	4.7	4.4
State and local government	0.0	0.0	0.0	0.0	0.0	0.0	0.0	0.0	0.1
Nongovernmental	77.0	76.1	75.2	73.6	73.9	72.7	71.2	68.0	66.1
Corporate bonds	14.4	16.3	17.5	15.5	15.1	14.8	15.2	16.8	18.0
Corporate stocks	36.9	36.9	34.7	35.4	36.5	36.4	34.8	33.5	32.9
Mortgages	1.2	1.1	1.2	1.1	1.2	1.5	1.0	2.3	1.8
Foreign and international securities	12.5	12.2	12.9	13.7	12.4	11.7	10.7	0.0	0.0
Other nongovernmental securities	12.1	9.6	8.9	7.8	8.7	8.3	9.6	15.4	13.4
Other investments	8.5	8.6	8.4	8.6	6.7	6.2	6.1	6.5	6.0
Real property	1.8	2.0	2.0	2.3	2.0	2.1	2.3	2.6	2.7
Miscellaneous investments	6.6	6.6	6.4	6.3	4.8	4.1	3.7	4.0	3.3

Source: U. S. Department of Commerce, U. S. Census Bureau, December 2004.
Note: Detail may not add to totals due to rounding.

Trends in Public Retirement Systems: Stresses in the System

By Sujit M. CanagaRetna

Severe weaknesses in the financial health of the nation's public retirement systems rank as yet another force currently buffeting state and local government finances. Further compounding the problems faced by these public retirement funds are the following developments: the precarious financial position of private sector pensions and the federal Pension Benefit Guaranty Corporation; the looming shortfalls expected in the Social Security and Medicare programs in coming decades; and the low personal savings rates of most Americans, coupled with the high rates of consumer and household debt. Given that the baby boomer generation is rapidly nearing retirement age and that America's senior population is growing faster than the number of younger workers needed to cover their retirement needs, policy-makers across the country are paying a great deal of attention to this unfortunate confluence of events.

For some years now, a variety of interest groups and concerned citizens have emphasized that policy-makers need to initiate concrete steps to prepare for the "graying" of America and the huge increase in the number of retirees. In fact, the number of people in the United States aged 65 and over is expected to nearly double by 2030; specifically, that age group is forecast to grow from about 13 percent of the total population in 2000, to 20 percent in 2030, and to remain above 20 percent for at least several decades thereafter.[1] In this context, there is growing concern that more attention needs to be directed toward retirement planning and developing a retirement infrastructure that has the capacity to absorb the retirement needs of all Americans.

Financial planners often recommend the three-legged stool concept in planning for retirement. Each leg of the stool represents a source of income in retirement, and the goal is to cumulatively attain a standard of living comparable to, if not slightly below, the one experienced prior to retirement. In this analysis, if the first leg of the stool is Social Security income, the other two legs of the stool refer to personal savings and retirement or pension system income. Alas, a close review of national financial and demographic trends reveals that all three legs of this metaphorical retirement stool remain rickety, a development that could seriously endanger the retirement plans of a majority of Americans.

Social Security payments remain critical for most retirees; these payouts make up about 40 percent of the total income of people 65 and over. In addition, about two-thirds of those people receive at least half of their income from Social Security, and one-third receives at least 90 percent.[2] In fact, in 2008, a scant

four years away, the first cohort of baby boomers will reach 62 and be eligible to claim Social Security benefits; a few years later in 2011, they will be eligible to claim Medicare benefits. However, the Social Security Trust Fund will start paying out more than it takes in by 2018 and be depleted by 2044, based on current projections, while Medicare will start running deficits in 2013 and run out of money in 2026 requiring remedial action from policy-makers.[3]

Unfortunately, alongside the tenuous long-term financial viability of Social Security, there are serious problems associated with the other two legs of the symbolic retirement stool. It is becoming increasingly clear that relying on personal savings to bolster retirement income is not a realistic option for most Americans. According to the federal government, during the past few decades, savings as a proportion of disposable income has declined steadily. Specifically, the nation's personal savings rate has plummeted from 11.2 percent of disposable income in 1982 (the highest level in the past three decades) to 1.7 percent in 2001, a precipitous decline indeed, before rising marginally to 2 percent in 2003.[4] Further compounding this rapidly shrinking personal savings rate is the mountain of debt accumulated by most American households in recent years. Since 1999, household debt has leapt from 70 percent, to nearly 83 percent of the current gross domestic product.[5] Moreover, consumers racked up $1.1 trillion in new mortgage and consumer debt between the end of 2001 and the third quarter of 2003, bringing the total of consumer and mortgage loans held by the Federal Deposit Insurance Corporation (FDIC) insured institutions to $2.6 trillion.[6]

Finally, the remaining leg of the figurative retirement stool, income flows from both public and private pension plans, is also wobbly. The asset base of both private and public sector pension plans experienced substantial erosion as a result of the bleak economic tide that enveloped the country in the initial years of this decade. For 10 years, between March 1991 and March 2001, the American economy experienced an unprecedented growth spurt and the positive flows of this expansion reflected very well on the asset base of both private and public sector retirement plans. However, in mid-2001, the U.S. economy began lurching to a stop, and the tragic events of September 11, 2001, pushed the already teetering economy into recession. Despite technically emerging from this recession after two quarters, the lingering effects of the economy continued for several years later with job creation, in particular, being very tepid. Compounding these economic trends were a number of additional problems that resulted in the equity markets taking a walloping for almost a three-year period, 2000 through 2002.

The Pension Benefit Guaranty Corporation (PBGC), the federal organization that protects the pensions of 44.3 million American workers, indicated earlier this year that it was running a deficit of $11.2 billion and warned about its ability to protect private pensions in the future.[7] Deficit forecasts for 2004 continue to be alarming with an increasing number of corporations seeking to be "trusteed" by the PBGC. Major corporations ranging from Bethlehem Steel to United Airlines to a host of others indicated their inability to meet their pension obligations to their retired employees and sought the protection of the PBGC in meeting these retirement expenditures.

At the public pension level, the scenario remains bleak too. These economic and stock market developments, alongside crushing unfunded liability growth, according to the National Association of State Retirement Administrators, resulted in the actuarial funding levels of public retirement plans plunging to lower levels in fiscal year 2002, compared to fiscal year 2001.[8] Specifically, between the fiscal years 2001 and 2002, the actuarial value of public retirement systems' assets increased by 3 percent, or $57 billion; in contrast, liabilities grew by $154 billion, or 8.1 percent. Also, studies released by Wilshire Associates in March 2003 and 2004 confirmed this trend, indicating that the funding ratio (the ratio of pension assets-to-liabilities) for all state pension plans combined declined from 106 percent in 2001, to 91 percent in 2002, to 82 percent in 2003; the median (50th percentile) state pension plan had

a funding ratio of 79 percent in the March 2004 survey.[9]

In the last few years, these public retirement funds have attracted a great deal of attention, sometimes because of their shrinking asset base and sometimes for a variety of other reasons.[10] From an 1857 retirement plan established in New York City to assist policemen injured in the line of duty, according to the latest federal data (June 30, 2002), the number of state and local government pension plans across the nation proliferated to 2,670, serving every stratum of state and local government. The importance of payments to beneficiaries from these state and local government retirement systems is a given, and the onus is on policy-makers to ensure the solvency and financial health of these plans. Notwithstanding the $2.2 trillion in cash and investment holdings in these retirement systems at the end of fiscal year 2002, more than 17.3 million total members and payments to over 6.2 million beneficiaries during this period, there is considerable interest in ensuring that this component of the U.S. retirement system remains on firm financial ground and continues to flourish in coming years.[11]

The stresses faced by state and local government retirement systems in the aftermath of what has been described as the worst fiscal crisis to sweep over states in more than six decades, and the continued sluggish performance of the economy, is illustrated by reviewing federal data over the most recent 10-year period. Specifically, total receipts plunged precipitously by 102 percent between June 1998 and June 2002 ($263.4 billion to–$6.1 billion), while they grew by 109 percent between June 1993 and June 1998 ($125.9 billion to $263.4 billion). Conversely, total payments by state and local government retirement systems more than doubled between June 1993 and June 2002 ($52.6 billion to $122 billion).

In addition to the information gleaned from the federal government, information obtained by means of a survey forwarded to 190 state and local government retirement plans in the 50 states and the District of Columbia remains useful here too. Of these 190 plans, 105 plans provided information for at least three of the five questions posed to them. Based on the survey responses, 36 of the 105 plans specifically had an asset base greater than $10 billion but less than $100 billion; two additional plans had an asset base greater than $100 billion. In terms of the number of annuitants (members or their family members receiving benefits) as a percentage of actives (members continuing to work and contribute), the survey indicated that a majority of the plans (70 plans) fell between 20 percent and 69.9 percent. The survey also revealed that in terms of actuarial funding ratios, i.e., the actuarial value of a pension plan's assets divided by its actuarial liabilities, only 25 of the 93 plans that provided information (of the 105 plans, 12 plans did not provide either the value of their actuarial assets or liabilities or both) were fully funded, with the remaining 68 plans underfunded to varying degrees.

State legislatures play a critical role in the administration of these retirement plans given the fact that they are responsible for some of the appointments to the boards of trustees, most often the administrative entity charged with the responsibility of managing and planning investments and benefit payouts. Hence, these trustees play a pivotal role in ensuring the continued growth of the retirement system funds taking into consideration a number of factors, such as the active-to-inactive member ratio, active participants to number of retirees receiving payments ratio, the overall investment climate (national and international) and ways to tweak an investment portfolio to diminish negative economic trends. One example where a legislature immersed itself in the activities of a state retirement system involves Maryland. After learning about their state pension fund's abysmal record, Maryland legislators and other state policymakers began a series of investigations and explorations into determining the reasons for this poor performance. In response to these queries and concerns, comprehensive reforms were introduced, both statutorily and organizationally, including a number of senior officials being relieved of their duties. In addition, federal authorities indicated that they had initiated a criminal investigation of a number of former employees, an investigation that eventually resulted in indictments, trials and convictions for several employees for fraud. A number of other legislatures also delved into the affairs of their public retirement systems either to buttress their finances through a bond issue (California, Illinois, Kansas) or to initiate reforms to enhance their efficiency and effectiveness (Louisiana).

Policy Options and Considerations

Ensuring both the short-term and long-term financial viability of the different elements in America's retirement systems, both private and public, remains of paramount importance. It is a challenge and responsibility that extends to policy-makers at every level of government—federal, state and local—and every American. In fact, first resuscitating and then sustaining the financial health of our different retire-

ment income flows provides the underpinnings for the foundation of the United States as an economic, political and military powerhouse in the global context. Consequently, it is imperative that policy-makers and citizens alike initiate efforts now to bolster the shaky pillars of America's current retirement system so that the costs of making these fundamental reforms in the future are minimized.

In reviewing and analyzing related data, it is quickly apparent that all three legs of the proverbial retirement stool are wobbly and require urgent attention. Research shows weaknesses in the Social Security and Medicare systems and the PBGC; the low savings rate in contemporary American society coupled with the crushing level of consumer debt; and, finally, the severe losses suffered by a majority of the public sector retirement plans in recent years due to the souring economy, the collapse of the equities markets and occasional lax oversight by plan administrators. The grim news percolating from these different retirement sources in recent years accentuates the importance for both citizens and policy-makers to be energized about initiating remedial action. The fact that in a short four years the first wave of baby boomers will begin retiring in sizable numbers, precipitating tremendous fiscal strains on these different retirement sources, further reinforces the urgency for these reforms.

In formulating comprehensive policy responses to this nascent crisis, it is important to consider the following issues.

• In order to overcome the severe disadvantages associated with an abysmally low savings rate, is it time for policy-makers—at all levels of government—to begin an assortment of educational and incentive programs to first, instill the importance of savings, and then increase savings rates? These programs could be introduced into the curriculum of schools throughout the country, possibly as early as the elementary level, building up in complexity as children proceed through the school system. At the other end, even greater incentives for individuals to save for retirement could also potentially be offered by the different levels of government. A quick comparison of household savings ratios among the world's three largest economic regions reinforces the fact that the United States lags significantly in this area, a statistic that should spur remedial action at every level of our society. According to a report released in June 2004, the household saving ratio in 2002 in the Euro area loomed at about 15 percent, ahead of the approximately 6.5 percent in Japan and significantly ahead of the United States' ratio of about 2 percent.[12] The United States has to improve its performance in this critical area and the sooner policy-makers initiate programs to do so, the better.

- In order to avoid a financial catastrophe related to Social Security, Medicare and the PBGC in the near future, is it time for policy-makers, primarily at the federal level, to engage the public in a substantive debate about fundamental reforms? The sooner this discussion is initiated the better because the potential for these federal programs to quickly convert from ticking time bombs to explosive issues looms large. While there has been some peripheral discussion about reforming the Social Security and Medicare systems, the PBGC's plight has largely been out of the public arena. The PBGC, which is mandated to protect the pensions of bankrupt and flailing corporations, remains severely underfunded and an ever increasing number of corporations, from small, relatively unknown ones to the more famous, established ones, have sought the protection of this federal agency. Bethlehem Steel, Consolidated Freightways, Acme Steel and the National Steel Pellet Company are a mere fraction of the companies covering more than 500,000 Americans that have failed in the past three years and been taken over by the federal government. The level of pension underfunding in the airline industry alone is estimated to be about $31 billion on a termination basis at the end of 2003, a staggering amount for just a single industry. Cumulatively, the level of pension underfunding for the companies seeking the protection of the federal government could be gargantuan, possibly eclipsing the magnitude of the federal government's bail out of the savings and loan industry in the 1980s. At a time when the fiscal demands being leveled at the federal government are increasing exponentially, and at a time when the federal government's budget situation is awash in a sea of red ink, the potential for these ticking fiscal time bombs (Social Security, Medicare and the PBGC) to explode remains a most alarming possibility.

- Finally, is it time for state policy-makers and citizens to closely and continuously monitor the performance of state and local government retirement funds so as to avoid the financial pitfalls faced by some entities with the introduction of features such as Deferred Retirement Option Plans, the

mismanagement of fund assets, the investment choices made by fund managers, the practice of deferring contributions to retirement funds during a time of budget shortfalls among other issues? Another important development related to these public sector retirement funds in these fiscally trying times involves the administrative entities of these plans whittling away at the benefits they offer to lower their expenditures. Will this emerging trend affect the ability of state and local governments to attract top-flight candidates to staff public sector positions? The case could be made that the ability of the public sector to attract high-caliber employees pivoted around the benefits offered in the public sector from the defined benefit retirement plan to healthcare coverage, both before and during retirement.

These policy considerations related to America's retirement systems remain of great importance as policy-makers and citizens deal with the onset of an aging population and a series of other, complex policy issues that will confront the nation in the next few decades. The sooner we begin the discussion about strengthening the shaky legs of our figurative retirement stool, the better.

Note: In October 2004, the Southern Legislative Conference (SLC), the southern office of The Council of State Governments, issued a 50-state Special Series Report entitled "America's Public Retirement Plans: Stresses in the System." This article is based on information and analysis carried out for this report.

Notes

[1]The Congress of the United States, Congressional Budget Office (CBO), Baby Boomers' Retirement Prospects: An Overview, November 2003.

[2]Ibid., 4.

[3]"Medicare and Social Security Challenges," *The New York Times*, March 2, 2004.

[4]U.S. Department of Commerce, Bureau of Economic Analysis, Personal Income and its Disposition, March 1, 2004.

[5]"Debt-Heavy Economy May Be Too Jittery About Rates," *The New York Times*, January 31, 2004.

[6]"Consumer Debt: How Much Is Too Much," EconSouth, Federal Reserve Bank of Atlanta, First Quarter 2004.

[7]"Pension Agency Deficit Mounts," *The Baltimore Sun*, January 16, 2004.

[8]National Association of State Retirement Administrators, Public Fund Survey: Summary of Findings, August 2003.

[9]Wilshire Associates, Inc., 2003 Wilshire Report on State Retirement Systems: Funding Levels and Asset Allocation,

March 12, 2003 and 2004 Wilshire Report on State Retirement Systems: Funding Levels and Asset Allocation, March 12, 2004.

[10]There has been a spate of articles in media outlets across the country probing the financial status of the nation's public retirement system. This reporting has been particularly pronounced in the aftermath of the 2000–2002 stock market declines when the shriveling asset base of these retirement funds prompted all sorts of inquiries and analysis by a range of different investigative bodies and interested parties.

[11]U.S. Department of Commerce, State and Local Government Employee Retirement Systems, *www.census.gov/ govs/www/retire.html.*

[12]"Comparison of Household Savings Ratios: Euro Area, Japan and United States," *Statistics Brief,* (Organization for Economic Co-operation and Development, June 8, 2004), No. 8.

About the Author

Sujit M. CanagaRetna is currently the senior fiscal analyst at The Council of State Governments' Southern Office, the Southern Legislative Conference (SLC), where he has been since March 1998. He is responsible for tracking fiscal, economic development and transportation trends for CSG and SLC. CanagaRetna has a bachelor's degree (BA) from Bennington College, Vermont and graduate degrees in International Affairs and Public Administration (MIA/MPA) from Columbia University. Prior to joining CSG/SLC, CanagaRetna worked for the New York City Comptroller's Office.

Table A
ACTUARIAL FUNDING RATIO

State or other jurisdiction	Plan name	Actuarial assets Value	Actuarial assets Date	Actuarial liabilities Value	Actuarial liabilities Date	Actuarial funding ratio percent
Washington	Judicial Retirement System (a)	$ 8,000,000	Sept. 2002	$ 95,000,000	Sept. 2002	8.4%
West Virginia	Teachers' Retirement System (Defined Benefit)	1,190,882,000	June 2003	6,243,834,000	June 2003	19.1
Illinois	General Assembly Retirement System	49,676,302	June 2003	196,510,067	June 2003	25.3
Illinois	Judges' Retirement System	330,053,560	June 2003	1,076,231,965	June 2003	30.7
Illinois	Teachers' Retirement System of Illinois (b)	23,124,823,000	June 2003	46,933,432,000	June 2003	49.3
Illinois	State Universities' Retirement System	9,714,500	June 2003	18,025,000	June 2003	53.9
Oklahoma	Teachers' Retirement System	6,436,852,137	June 2003	11,925,161,689	June 2003	54.0
Alaska	Teachers' Retirement System	3,752,285	June 2003	5,835,609	June 2003	64.3
Washington	Law Enforcement Officers' and Firefighters' Retirement System—Plan 2 (a)	2,646,000,000	Sept. 2002	4,042,000,000	Sept. 2002	65.5
Louisiana	State Employees' Retirement System	6,487,538,000	June 2003	9,796,306,000	June 2003	66.2
Louisiana	Teachers' Retirement System	11,828,900,000	June 2003	17,173,300,000	June 2003	68.9
Maine	Maine State Retirement System	5,900,000,000	June 2002	8,500,000,000	June 2002	69.4
Massachusetts	Massachusetts Teachers' Retirement System	17,074,650,000	Dec. 2003	24,519,059,000	Dec. 2003	69.6
Iowa	Iowa Public Employees' Retirement System	15,403,200,907	June 2003	22,108,936,178	June 2003	69.7
Louisiana	Firefighters' Retirement System of Louisiana	658,376,086	June 2003	944,688,430	June 2003	69.7
Alaska	Public Employees' Retirement Board	7,687,281	June 2003	10,561,563	June 2003	72.8
West Virginia	Public Employees' Retirement System	2,699,941,000	June 2003	3,691,001,000	June 2003	73.1
Indiana	Indiana State Teachers' Retirement Fund	6,100,000,000	June 2003	8,200,000,000	June 2003	74.4
Iowa	Judicial Retirement System	70,017,875	June 2003	93,561,000	June 2003	74.8
New Hampshire	New Hampshire Retirement System	3,500,000,000	June 2003	4,669,000,000	June 2003	75.0
Kansas	Public Employees' Retirement System	10,853,000,000	Dec. 2003	14,440,000,000	Dec. 2003	75.2
Ohio	State Teachers' Retirement System	51,696,919,000	June 2003	68,734,061,000	June 2003	75.2
Colorado	Public Employees' Retirement Association	30,600,000,000	Dec. 2003	40,500,000,000	Dec. 2003	75.6
Oklahoma	Public Employees' Retirement System	5,354,795,771	July 2003	6,974,583,356	July 2003	76.8
Connecticut	Teachers' Retirement Board	11,961,346,260	June 2002	15,253,882,989	June 2002	78.4
Mississippi	Public Employees' Retirement System of Mississippi	16,980,000	June 2003	21,486,000	June 2003	79.0
Ohio	State Highway Patrol Retirement System	527,604,456	Dec. 2002	663,069,805	Dec. 2002	79.6
Iowa	Iowa Dept of Public Safety Peace Officers' Retirement, Accident, and Disability System	246,443,600	June 2003	306,098,170	June 2003	80.5
Missouri	Public School Retirement System	20,048,000,000	June 2003	24,719,400,000	June 2003	81.1
Minnesota	Public Employees' Retirement Association	11,195,902,000	July 2003	13,776,198,000	July 2003	81.3
Nevada	Public Employees' Retirement System	15,900,000,000	June 2003	19,500,000,000	June 2003	81.5
Washington	Public Employees' Retirement System—Plans 2 & 3 (a)	10,701,000,000	Sept. 2002	13,093,000,000	Sept. 2002	81.7
Missouri	Public School Non-Teacher Employee Retirement System	1,677,800,000	June 2003	2,049,700,000	June 2003	81.9
Kentucky	Kentucky Retirement Systems	15,500,000,000	June 2003	18,890,000,000	June 2003	82.1
Texas	Municipal Retirement System	10,815,090,275	Dec. 2003	13,100,126,794	Dec. 2003	82.6
Ohio	Police and Fire Pension Fund (c)	8,682,703,560	Jan. 2003	10,508,366,996	Jan. 2003	82.6
South Carolina	South Carolina Retirement Systems (d)	22,860,101,000	June 2003	27,377,055,000	June 2003	83.5
Massachusetts	Massachusetts State Retirement System	15,930,753,000	Dec. 2003	18,996,053,000	Dec. 2003	83.9
Washington	School Employees' Retirement System—Plans 2 & 3 (a)	1,519,000,000	Sept. 2002	1,804,000,000	Sept. 2002	84.2
Oklahoma	Police Pension and Retirement System	1,392,043,000	July 2003	1,646,979,675	July 2003	84.5

See footnotes at end of table.

ACTUARIAL FUNDING RATIO—Continued

State or other jurisdiction	Plan name	Actuarial assets		Actuarial liabilities		Actuarial funding ratio percent
		Value	Date	Value	Date	
North Dakota	Teachers' Fund for Retirement	1,438,400,000	July 2003	1,690,300,000	July 2003	85.1
Washington	Public Employees' Retirement System—Plan 1 (a)	10,757,000,000	Sept. 2002	12,532,000,000	Sept. 2002	85.8
Washington	Teachers' Retirement System—Plans 2 & 3 (a)	3,800,000,000	Sept. 2002	4,422,000,000	Sept. 2002	85.9
New Jersey	Judicial Retirement System	372,800,000	June 2003	431,500,000	June 2003	86.4
Oregon	Public Employees' Retirement System	35,537,100,000	Dec. 2002	39,520,500,000	Dec. 2002	89.9
Texas	County and District Retirement System	9,788,900,000	Dec. 2003	10,813,500,000	Dec. 2003	90.5
Arkansas	Arkansas Local Police and Fire Retirement System	553,000,000	Dec. 2003	610,000,000	Dec. 2003	90.7
Missouri	State Employees' Retirement System	6,057,329,072	June 2003	6,662,291,406	June 2003	90.9
Nebraska	Nebraska Public Employees' Retirement Systems	5,259,423,944	June 2003	5,760,891,499	June 2003	91.3
Wyoming	Wyoming Retirement System (e)	4,657,898,000	Jan. 2004	5,077,443,000	Jan. 2004	91.7
Washington	Teachers' Retirement System—Plan 1 (a)	9,366,000,000	Sept. 2002	10,209,000,000	Sept. 2002	91.7
New Jersey	Teachers' Pension and Annuity Fund	34,600,000,000	June 2003	37,300,000,000	June 2003	92.8
Utah	State Retirement Systems	14,700,000,000	Dec. 2003	15,800,000,000	Dec. 2003	93.0
Alabama	Teachers' Retirement Systems of Alabama	18,100,000,000	June 2003	19,400,000,000	June 2003	93.3
Maryland	State Retirement and Pension System	32,631,465,000	June 2003	34,974,601,000	June 2003	93.3
Texas	Teachers' Retirement System	89,033,023,666	Aug 2003	94,263,027,542	Aug 2003	94.5
California	California Public Employees' Retirement System (f)	156,067,000,000	June 2002	163,961,000,000	June 2002	95.2
Alabama	Employees' Retirement System of Alabama	8,100,000,000	Sept. 2002	8,400,000,000	Sept. 2002	96.4
Montana	Public Employee Retirement Association (g)	3,679,960,000	June 2002	3,815,811,000	June 2002	96.4
Missouri	Missouri Local Government Employees Retirement System	2,604,000,000	June 2002	2,700,000,000	June 2002	96.4
South Dakota	South Dakota Retirement System	4,685,890,770	June 2003	4,818,943,695	June 2003	97.2
Pennsylvania	Public School Employees' Retirement System	52,900,000,000	June 2003	54,400,000,000	June 2003	97.2
New Mexico	Public Employees' Retirement Association	8,971,080,804	June 2003	9,215,945,484	June 2003	97.3
Illinois	Illinois Municipal Retirement Fund	17,529,890,818	Dec. 2003	17,966,103,485	Dec. 2003	97.6
Texas	Employees' Retirement System of Texas	19,478,554,993	Aug 2003	19,959,111,546	Aug 2003	97.6
New Jersey	Public Employees' Retirement System	27,400,000,000	June 2003	28,000,000,000	June 2003	97.9
Wisconsin	Wisconsin Retirement System	62,685,300,000	Dec. 2003	63,211,700,000	Dec. 2003	99.2
Tennessee	Consolidated Retirement System—State, Teachers & Higher Education Employees	22,099,000,000	July 2003	22,152,000,000	July 2003	99.8
Arizona	Arizona State Retirement System	24,303,639,447	June 2003	24,303,639,447	June 2003	100.0
Arizona	Public Safety Personnel Retirement System	8,600,000,000	June 2003	8,600,000,000	June 2003	100.0
Dist. of Columbia	District of Columbia Teachers' Retirement Fund	917,800,000	Sept. 2003	917,800,000	Sept. 2003	100.0
Dist. of Columbia	Police Officers' and Fire Fighters' Retirement Board	1,427,800,000	Sept. 2003	1,427,800,000	Sept. 2003	100.0
Delaware	State of Delaware Employees' Deferred Compensation Plan	209,343,469	April 2004	209,343,469	Apr. 2004	100.0
New York	Teachers' Retirement System	74,400,000,000	June 2002	74,400,000,000	June 2002	100.0
Tennessee	Consolidated Retirement System—Political Subdivision Pension Plan	3,606,000,000	July 2003	3,606,000,000	July 2003	100.0
Washington	Judges' Retirement System (a)	5,000,000	Sept. 2002	5,000,000	Sept. 2002	100.0
Washington	Washington State Patrol Retirement System (a)	689,000,000	Sept. 2002	686,000,000	Sept. 2002	100.4
Georgia	Employees' Retirement System (a)	12,124,414,000	June 2002	11,994,850,000	June 2002	101.1
Virginia	State Retirement System	38,957,000,000	June 2003	38,265,000,000	June 2003	101.8
New Jersey	State Police Retirement System	1,865,100	June 2003	1,815,700	June 2003	102.7

See footnotes at end of table.

ACTUARIAL FUNDING RATIO — Continued

State or other jurisdiction	Plan name	Actuarial assets		Actuarial liabilities		Actuarial funding ratio percent
		Value	Date	Value	Date	
New Jersey	Police and Fireman's Retirement System	18,400,000,000	June 2002	17,900,000,000	June 2002	102.8
Minnesota	Teachers' Retirement Association	17,384,179,000	June 2003	16,856,379,000	June 2003	103.1
Pennsylvania	State Employees' Retirement System	27,465,000,000	Dec. 2003	26,179,000,000	Dec. 2003	104.9
Washington	Volunteer Firefighters' and Reserve Officers' Relief and Pension Principal Fund (h)	124,000,000	Dec. 2002	118,000,000	Dec. 2002	105.1
North Carolina	North Carolina Retirement Systems (i)	55,183,599,877	Dec. 2002	51,877,037,007	Dec. 2002	106.4
Texas	Law Enforcement & Custodial Officer Supplemental Retirement Fund	666,588,289	Aug 2003	597,914,188	Aug 2003	111.5
Florida	Florida Retirement System (FRS) (j)	101,900,000,000	July 2002	89,300,000,000	July 2002	114.1
Georgia	Public School Employees' Retirement System	727,529,000	June 2002	630,295,000	June 2002	115.4
Texas	Judicial Retirement System—Plan II	129,425,907	Aug 2003	111,115,600	Aug 2003	116.5
Washington	Law Enforcement Officers' and Firefighters' Retirement System—Plan 1 (a)	5,095,000,000	Sept. 2002	4,338,000,000	Sept. 2002	117.5
Georgia	Legislative Retirement System	26,637,000	June 2002	21,779,000	June 2002	122.3
Georgia	Georgia Judicial Retirement System	228,417,000	June 2002	175,154,000	June 2002	130.1
Idaho	Public Employee Retirement System of Idaho	6,498,685,238	July 2003	534,638,594	July 2003	1215.5

Source: The Council of State Governments' Southern Office Survey (For additional details on the survey responses, please see, Sujit CanagaRetna, America's Public Retirement Plans: Stresses in the System, Special Series Report, Southern Legislative Conference, October 2004, www.slcatlanta.org/Publications.htm.)

Note: The survey was forwarded to 190 plans of which responses were received from 105 plans. Of these 105 plans, 12 plans did not provide information on their actuarial assets and/or actuarial liabilities. (See Table B, below, for these 12 plans). Hence, it was impossible to calculate an acturial funding ratio for these 12 plans. This lowered the number of plans for which information is presented in Table A above from 105 plans to 93 plans.

Key:

(a) For this Washington state plan's actuarial liability, the Present Value of Fully Projected Benefits (PVFPB) is presented.

(b) Illinois issued $10 billion in pension obligation bonds in June 2003. TRS' share of $4,330,374,000 was received after the close of the fiscal year and not included in asset figures.

(c) The market value of this plan is unaudited.

(d) Data for the SCRS includes South Carolina Retirement System (serving state employees, teachers and other government employees); Police Officers' Retirement System; General Assembly Retirement System; and

the Judges' and Solicitors' Retirement System.

(e) Data for the Wyoming Retirement System includes the Public Employee Retirement System; Wyoming Game & Fish Employees' Retirement System; Volunteer Firemen's Retirement System; Paid Firemen's System (Plan A and Plan B); Wyoming Law Enforcement System; and the Wyoming Judicial Retirement Plan.

(f) Data for CalPERS includes the California Public Employees' Retirement System; the Legislators' Retirement System; Judges' Retirement System I; Judges' Retirement System II; State Peace Officers' and Firefighters' Defined Contribution Program; and the Volunteer Firefighters' Length of Service Award System.

(g) Data for MPERA includes the Public Employees' Retirement System; Judges' Retirement System (JRS); Highway Patrol Officers' Retirement System (HPORS); Sheriffs' Retirement System (SRS); Game Wardens' & Peace Officers' Retirement System (GWPORS); and the Volunteer Firefighters' Compensation Act (VFCA).

(h) For the Volunteer Firefighters' and Reserve Officers' Relief and Pension Principal Fund, relief liabilities are not included; only pension liabilities.

(i) Data for the North Carolina Retirement System includes the Teachers' and State Employees' Retirement System; Local Government Employees' Retirement System; Consolidated Judicial Retirement System; and the Firemen and Rescue Squad Workers' Pension Fund.

(j) This is based on the market value as of March 25, 2004.

Table B
TWELVE PLANS THAT DID NOT PROVIDE EITHER ACTUARIAL ASSETS AND/OR ACTUARIAL LIABILITIES

State or other jurisdiction	Plan name	Actuarial assets		Actuarial liabilities	
		Value	*Date*	*Value*	*Date*
Alaska	Alaska State Pension Investment Board	Not provided	...	Not provided	...
Colorado	Colorado County Officials and Employees Retirement Association	Not provided	...	Not provided	...
Colorado	State of Colorado 457 Match Plan Plus	$246,972,207	March 2005	Not available	...
Dist. of Columbia	District of Columbia 457 Deferred Compensation Plan (DCPlus)	Not available	...	Not available	...
Florida	Deferred Compensation Plan	Not available	...	Not available	...
Florida	Municipal Police Officers' and Firefighters' Retirement Trust Funds Office	Unknown	...	Unknown	...
Maryland	Teachers and State Employees Supplemental Retirement Plans	Not applicable	...	Not applicable	...
New Mexico	State Deferred Compensation Plan	Not provided	...	Not provided	...
Nevada	457 Deferred Compensation Plan	$0	Dec. 2003	$0	Dec. 2003
Nevada	Deferred Compensation Plan	Not available	...	Not available	...
Texas	Judicial Retirement System—Plan 1	Not available	...	$19,959,111,546	Aug. 2003
Georgia	Georgia Military Pension Fund	Not applicable	June 2002	$8,322,000	June 2002

Source: The Council of State Governments' Southern Office Survey (For additional details on the survey responses, please see, Sujit CanagaRetna, America's Public Retirement Plans: Stresses in the System, Special Series Report, Southern Legislative Conference, October 2004, www.slcatlanta.org/Publications.htm.)

Note: The survey was forwarded to 190 plans of which responses were received from 105 plans. Of these 105 plans, 12 plans did not provide information on their actuarial assets and/or actuarial liabilities. (See Table B, below, for these 12 plans). Hence, it was impossible to calculate an acuarial funding ratio for these 12 plans. This lowered the number of plans for which information is presented in Table A above from 105 plans to 93 plans.

Table 7.1
STATE TAX AMNESTY PROGRAMS
1982–2005

State or other jurisdiction	Amnesty period	Legislative authorization	Major taxes covered	Accounts receivable included	Collections ($ millions) (a)	Installment arrangements permitted (b)
Alabama	1/20/84–4/1/84	No (c)	All	No	$3.2	No
Arizona	11/22/82–1/20/83	No (c)	All	No	6.0	Yes
	1/1/0–2/28/02	Yes	Individual income	No	N.A.	No
	9/1/03–10/31/03	Yes	All (t)	N.A.	73.0	Yes
Arkansas	9/1/87–11/30/87	Yes	All	No	1.7	Yes
California	12/10/84–3/15/85	Yes	Individual income	Yes	154.0	Yes
		Yes	Sales	No	43.0	Yes
	2/1/05–3/31/05	Yes	Income, Franchise, Sales	N.A.	N.A.	Yes
Colorado	9/16/85–11/15/85	Yes	All	No	6.4	Yes
	6/1/03–6/30/03	N.A.	All	N.A.	18.4	Yes
Connecticut	9/1/90–11/30/90	Yes	All	Yes	54.0	Yes
	9/1/95–11/30/95	Yes	All	Yes	46.2	Yes
	9/1/02-12/2/02	N.A.	All	N.A.	109	N.A.
Florida	1/1/87–6/30/87	Yes	Intangibles	No	13.0	No
	1/1/88–6/30/88	Yes (d)	All	No	8.4 (d)	No
	7/1/03–10/31/03	Yes	All	N.A.	80	N.A.
Georgia	10/1/92–12/5/92	Yes	All	Yes	51.3	No
Idaho	5/20/83–8/30/83	No (c)	Individual income	No	0.3	No
Illinois	10/1/84–11/30/84	Yes	All (u)	Yes	160.5	No
	10/1/03–11/17/03	Yes	All	N.A.	532	N.A.
Iowa	9/2/86–10/31/86	Yes	All	Yes	35.1	N.A.
Kansas	7/1/84–9/30/84	Yes	All	No	0.6	No
	10/1/03–11/30/03	Yes	All	Yes	53.7	N.A.
Kentucky	9/15/88–9/30/88	Yes (c)	All	No	100	No
	8/1/02–9/30/02	Yes (c)	All	No	100	No
Louisiana	10/1/85–12/31/85	Yes	All	No	1.2	Yes (f)
	10/1/87–12/15/87	Yes	All	No	0.3	Yes (f)
	10/1/98–12/31/98	Yes	All	No (q)	1.3	No
	9/1/01–10/30/01	Yes	All	Yes	173.1	No
Maine	11/1/90–12/31/90	Yes	All	Yes	29.0	Yes
	9/1/03–11/30/03	Yes	All	N.A.	34.7	N.A.
Maryland	9/1/87–11/2/87	Yes	All	Yes	34.6 (g)	No
	9/1/01–10/31/01	Yes	All	Yes	39.2	No
Massachusetts	10/17/83–1/17/84	Yes	All	Yes	86.5	Yes (h)
	10/1/02–11/30/02	Yes	All	Yes	96.1	Yes
	1/1/03–2/28/03	Yes	All	Yes	N.A.	N.A.
Michigan	5/12/86–6/30/86	Yes	All	Yes	109.8	No
	5/15/02–6/30/02	Yes	All	Yes	N.A.	N.A.
Minnesota	8/1/84–10/31/84	Yes	All	Yes	12.1	No
Mississippi	9/1/86–11/30/86	Yes	All	No	1.0	No
	9/1/04–12/31/04	Yes	All	No	7.9	No
Missouri	9/1/83–10/31/83	No (c)	All	No	0.9	No
	8/1/02–10/31/02	Yes	All	Yes	76.4	N.A.
	8/1/03–10/31/ 03	Yes	All	Yes	20	N.A.
Nebraska	8/1/04–10/31/04	Yes	All	No	7.5	No
Nevada	2/1/02–6/30/02	N.A.	All	N.A.	7.3	N.A.
New Hampshire	12/1/97–2/17/98	Yes	All	Yes	13.5	No
	12/1/01–2/15/02	Yes	All	Yes	13.5	N.A.
New Jersey	9/10/87–12/8/87	Yes	All	Yes	186.5	Yes
	3/15/96–6/1/96	Yes	All	Yes	359.0	No
	4/15/02–6/10/02	Yes	All	Yes	276.9	N.A.
New Mexico	8/15/85–11/13/85	Yes	All (i)	No	13.6	Yes
	8/16/99–11/12/99	Yes	All	Yes	45	Yes
New York	11/1/85–1/31/86	Yes	All (j)	Yes	401.3	Yes
	11/1/96–1/31/97	Yes	All	Yes	253.4	Yes (o)
	11/18/02–1/31/03	Yes	All	Yes	582.7	Yes (s)
North Carolina	9/1/89–12/1/89	Yes	All (k)	Yes	37.6	No

See footnotes at end of table.

STATE TAX AMNESTY PROGRAMS — Continued

State or other jurisdiction	Amnesty period	Legislative authorization	Major taxes covered	Accounts receivable included	Collections ($ millions) (a)	Installment arrangements permitted (b)
North Dakota	9/1/83–11/30/83	No (c)	All	No	0.2	Yes
	10/1/03–1/31/04	Yes	N.A.	N.A.	6.9	N.A.
Ohio	10/15/01–1/15/02	Yes	All	No	48.5	No
Oklahoma	7/1/84–12/31/84	Yes	Income, Sales	Yes	13.9	No (l)
	8/15/02–11/15/02	N.A.	All (r)	Yes	N.A.	N.A.
Pennsylvania	10/13/95–1/10/96	Yes	All	Yes	N.A.	No
Rhode Island	10/15/86–1/12/87	Yes	All	No	0.7	Yes
	4/15/96–6/28/96	Yes	All	Yes	7.9	Yes
South Carolina	9/1/85–11/30/85	Yes	All	Yes	7.1	Yes
	10/15/02–11/30/02	Yes	All	Yes	66.2	N.A.
South Dakota	4/1/99–5/15/99	Yes	All	Yes	0.5	N.A.
Texas	2/1/84–2/29/84	No (c)	No (c)	No	0.5	No
	3/11/04–3/31/04	No (c)	No (c)	No	N.A.	No
Vermont	5/15/90–6/25/90	Yes	All	Yes	1.0 (e)	No
Virginia	2/1/90–3/31/90	Yes	All	Yes	32.2	No
	9/2/03–11/3/03	Yes	All	Yes	98.3	N.A.
West Virginia	10/1/86–12/31/86	Yes	All	Yes	15.9	Yes
	9/1/04–10/31/04	Yes	All	N.A.	10.4	Yes
Wisconsin	9/15/85–11/22/85	Yes	All	Yes (n)	27.3	Yes
	6/15/98–8/14/98	Yes	All	Yes	30.9	N.A.
Dist. of Columbia	7/1/87–9/30/87	Yes	All	Yes	24.3	Yes
	7/10/95–8/31/95	Yes	All (p)	Yes	19.5	Yes

Source: The Federation of Tax Administrators, January 2005.

Key:

N.A.—Not available.

(a) Where applicable, figure indicates local portions of certain taxes collected under the state tax amnesty program.

(b) No indicates requirement of full payment by the expiration of the amnesty period. Yes indicates allowance of full payment after the expiration of the amnesty period.

(c) Authority for amnesty derived from pre-existing statutory powers permitting the waiver of tax penalties.

(d) Does not include intangibles tax and drug taxes. Gross collections totaled $22.1 million, with $13.7 million in penalties withdrawn.

(e) Preliminary figure.

(f) Amnesty taxpayers were billed for the interest owed, with payment due within 30 days of notification.

(g) Figure includes $1.1 million for the separate program conducted by the Department of Natural Resources for the boat excise tax.

(h) The amnesty statute was construed to extend the amnesty to those who applied to the department before the end of the amnesty period, and permitted them to file overdue returns and pay back taxes and interest at a later date.

(i) The severance taxes, including the six oil and gas severance taxes, the resources excise tax, the corporate franchise tax, and the special fuels tax were not subject to amnesty.

(j) Availability of amnesty for the corporation tax, the oil company taxes, the transporation and transmissions companies tax, the gross receipts oil tax and the unincorporated business tax restricted to entities with 500 or fewer employees in the United States on the date of application. In addition, a taxpayer principally engaged in aviation, or a utility subject to the supervision of the State Department of Public Service was also ineligible.

(k) Local taxes and real property taxes were not included.

(l) Full payment of tax liability required before the end of the amnesty period to avoid civil penalties.

(m) Texas does not impose a corporate or individual income tax. In practical effect, the amnesty was limited to the sales tax and other excises.

(n) Waiver terms varied depending upon the date the tax liability was assessed.

(o) Installment arrangements were permitted if applicant demonstrated that payment would present a severe financial hardship.

(p) Does not include real property taxes. All interest was waived on tax payments made before July 31, 1995. After this date, only 50% of the interest was waived.

(q) Exception for individuals who owed $500 or less.

(r) Except for property and motor fuel taxes.

(s) Multiple payments can be made so long as the required balance is paid in full no later than March 15, 2003.

(t) All taxes except property, estate and unclaimed property.

(u) Does not include the motor fuel use tax.

Table 7.2
STATE EXCISE TAX RATES
(As of January 1, 2005)

State or other jurisdiction	General sales and gross receipts tax (percent)	Cigarettes (cents per pack of 20)	Distilled spirits ($ per gallon)	Motor fuel (cents per gallon)		
				Gasoline	Diesel	Gasohol
Alabama	4.0%	42.5 (d)	(g)	18.0 (j) (v)	19.0 (j) (v)	18.0 (j) (v)
Alaska	. . .	160	$12.80 (i)	8.0	8.0	. . .
Arizona	5.6	118	3.00	18.0 (l)	18.0 (l)	18.0 l)
Arkansas	6	59 (e)	2.50 (i)	21.5	22.5	21.5
California	7.25 (b) (r)	87	3.30 (i)	18.0 (q)	18.0 (q)	18.0 (q)
Colorado	2.9	87	2.28	22.0	20.5	22.0
Connecticut	6.0	151	4.50 (i)	25.0	26.0	25.0
Delaware	. . .	55	3.75 (i)	23.0 (t)	22.0 (t)	23.0 (t)
Florida	6.0	33.9	6.50 (i)	14.5 (k) (q)	27.3 (k) (q)	14.5 (k) (q)
Georgia	4.0	37	3.79 (i)	7.5 (q)	7.5 (q)	7.5 (q)
Hawaii	4.0	140	5.98	16.0 (j) (q)	16.0 (j) (q)	16.0 (j) (q)
Idaho	6.0	57	(g)	25.0 (p) (q)	25.0 (p) (q)	22.5 (p) (q)
Illinois	6.25 (b)	98 (d)	4.50 (i)	20.1 (j) (l) (q)	21.5 (j) (l) (q)	20.1 (l) (q)
Indiana	6.0	55.5	2.68 (i)	18.0 (l) (q)	16.0 (l) (q)	18.0 (l) (q)
Iowa	5.0	36	(g)	20.5	22.5	19.0
Kansas	5.3	79	2.50 (i)	24.0	26.0	24.0
Kentucky	6.0	3 (e)	1.92 (h)(i)	17.4 (l) (m) (q)	14.4 (l) (m) (q)	17.4 (l) (m) (q)
Louisiana	4.0	36	2.50 (i)	20.0	20.0	20.0
Maine	5.0	100	(g)	25.2 (n)	26.3(n)	25.2 (n)
Maryland	5.0	100	1.50	23.5	24.25	23.5
Massachusetts	5.0	151	4.05 (h) (i)	21 .0	21.0	21.0
Michigan	6.0	200	(g)	19.0 (q)	15.0 (q)	19.0 (q)
Minnesota	6.5	48	5.03 (i)	20.0	20.0	20.0
Mississippi	7.0	18	(g)	18.4 (q)	18.4 (q)	18.4 (q)
Missouri	4.225	17 (d)	2.00	17.03 (q)	17.03 (q)	17.03 (q)
Montana	. . .	170	(g)	27.0	27.75	27.0
Nebraska	5.5	64	3.75	26.3 (i) (n)	26.3 (i) (n)	26.3 (i) (n)
Nevada	6.5	80	3.60 (i)	23.0 (j)	27.0 (j)	23.0 (j)
New Hampshire	. . .	52	(g)	19.5 (q)	19.5 (q)	19.5 (q)
New Jersey	6.0	240	4.40	14.5 (q)	17.5 (q)	14.5 (q)
New Mexico	5.0	91	6.06	18.9 (q)	22.9 (q)	18.9 (q)
New York	4.25	150 (d)	6.44 (i)	23.2 (q)	21.45 (q)	23.2 (q)
North Carolina	4.5 (u)	5	(g)(h)	26.85(m) (q)	26.85(m) (q)	26.85(m) (q)
North Dakota	5.0	44	2.50 (i)	21.0	21.0	21.0
Ohio	6.0	55	(g)	26.0 (a) (q)	26.0 (a) (q)	26.0 (a) (q)
Oklahoma	4.5	103	5.56 (i)	17.0 (q)	14.0 (q)	17.0 (q)
Oregon	. . .	118	(g)	24.0 (j)	24.0 (j)	24.0 (j)
Pennsylvania	6.0	135	(g)	30.0 (q)	36.4 (q)	30.0 (q)
Rhode Island	7.0	246	3.75	31.0 (q)	31.0 (q)	31.0 (q)
South Carolina	5.0	7	2.72 (i)	16.0	16.0	16.0
South Dakota	4.0	53	3.93 (i)	22.0 (j)	22.0 (j)	20.0 (j)
Tennessee	7.0	20 (d)(e)	4.40 (i)	21.4 (j) (q)	18.4 (j) (q)	21.4 (j) (q)
Texas	6.25	41	2.40 (i)	20.0	20.0	20.0
Utah	4.75	69.5	(g)	24.5	24.5	24.5
Vermont	6.0	119	(f) (g)	20.0 (q)	26.0 (q)	20.0 (q)
Virginia	5.0 (r)	20 (d) (s)	(g)	17.5 (j)(o)	16.0 (j)(o)	17.5 (j)(o)
Washington	6.5	142.5	(g) (h)	28.0 (q)	28.0 (q)	28.0 (q)
West Virginia	6.0	55	(g)	27.0 (q)	27.0 (q)	27.0 (q)
Wisconsin	5.0	77	3.25	29.1 (n)	29.1 (n)	29.128.5 (n)
Wyoming	4.0 (b)	60	(g)	14.0 (q)	14.0 (q)	14.0 (q)
Dist. of Columbia	5.75	100	1.50 (i)	22.5	22.5	22.5

See footnotes at end of table.

TAXES

STATE EXCISE TAX RATES — Continued

Source: Compiled by The Federation of Tax Administrators from various sources, January 2005.

Key:

... — Tax is not applicable.

(a) Effective July 1, 2004, tax rate is scheduled to invrease to 26 cents per gallon.

(b) Tax rate may be adjusted annually according to a formaula based on balances in the unappropriated general fund and the school foundation fund.

(c) The tax rates listed are fuel excise taxes collected by distributor/retailers in each state. Additional taxes may apply to motor carriers.

(d) Counties and cities may impose an additional tax on a pack of cigarettes in Alabama, 1-6 cents; Illinois, 10-15 cents; Missouri, 4-7 cents; New York City,$1.50; Tennessee, 1 cent; and Virginia, 2-15 cents.

(e) Dealers pay an additional enforcement and administrative fee of 0.1 cents per pack in Kentucky and 0.05 cents in Tennessee. In Arkansas, a fee of $1.25/1,000 cigarette fee is imposed.

(f) 10 percent on-premise sales tax.

(g) In 18 states, the government directly controls the sales of distilled spirits. Revenue in these states is generated from various taxes, fees and net liquor profits.

(h) Sales tax is applied to on-premise sales only.

(i) Other taxes in addition to excise taxes for the following states: Alaska, under 21 percent—$2.50/gallon; Arkansas, under 5 percent—$0.50/gallon, under 21 percent—$1.00/gallon, $0.20/case and 3 percent off—14 percent on-premise retail taxes; California, over 50 percent—$6.60/gallon; Connecticut, under 7 percent—$2.05/gallon; Delaware, under 25 percent— $2.50/gallon; Florida, under 17.259 percent—$2.25/gallon, over 55.780 percent—$9.53/gallon, 6.67 cents/ounce on-premise retail tax; Georgia, $0.83/gallon local tax; Illinois, under 20 percent—$0.73/gallon,$1.845/gallon in Chicago and $2.00/gallon in Cook County; Indiana, under 15 percent—$0.47/gallon; Kansas, 8 percent off- and 10 percent on-premise retail tax; Kentucky, under 6 percent—$0.25/gallon, $0.05/case and 9 percent wholesale tax; Louisiana, under 6 percent - $0.32/gallon; Massachusetts, under 15 percent—$1.10/gallon, over 50 percent alcohol—$4.05/proof gallon, 0.57 percent on private club sales; Minnesota, $0.01/bottle (except miniatures) and 9 percent sales tax; Nebraska, petroleum fee—Nevada, under 14 percent—$0.70/gallon and under 21 percent—$1.30/gallon; New York, under 24 percent—$2.54/gallon, $1.00/gallon New York City; North Dakota, 7 percent state sales tax; Oklahoma, 13.5 percent on-premise; South Carolina, $5.36/case and 9 percent surtax; South Dakota, under 14 percent— $0.93/gallon, 2 percent wholesale tax;

Tennessee, $0.15/case and 15 percent on-premise, under 7 percent—$1.21/gallon; Texas, 14 percent on-premise and $0.05/drink on airline sales; and District of Columbia, 8 percent off- and 10 percent on-premise sales tax.

(j) Tax rates do not include local option taxes. In Alabama, 1-3 cents and inspection fee; Hawaii, 8.8-18 cents; Illinois, 5 cents in Chicago and 6 cents in Cook County (gasoline only); Nevada 1.75 to 7.75 cents; Oregon, 1-3 cents; South Dakota, 1 cent; Tennessee, 1 cent; and Virginia, 2 percent.

(k) Local taxes for gasoline and gasohol vary from9.7 cents to 17.7 cents. Plus a 2.07 cents/gallon pollution tax.

(l) Carriers pay an additional surcharge equal to Arizona, 8 cents; Illinois, 6.3 cents (gasoline) and 6.0 cents (diesel); Indiana, 11 cents; Kentucky, 2 percent (gasoline) and 4.7 percent (diesel).

(m) Tax rate is based on the average wholesale price and is adjusted quarterly. The actual rates are: Kentucky, 9 percent; and North Carolina, 17.5 cents plus 7 percent.

(n) A portion of the rate is adjustable based on maintenance costs, sales volume, or cost of fuel to state government.

(o) Large trucks pay an additional 3.5 cents.

(p) Tax rate is reduced by the percentage of ethanol used in blending (reported rate assumes the maximum 10 percent ethanol).

(q) Other taxes and fees; California-sales tax applicable; Florida—sales tax applicable; Georgia—3 percent sales tax applicable; Hawaii—sales tax applicable; Idaho—clean water tax; Illinois—sales tax applicable and environmental fee; Indiana—sales tax applicable; Kentucky—environmental fee; Michigan— sales tax applicable; Mississippi—environmental fee; Missouri—inspection fee; Nebraska—petroleum fee; New Hampshire—oil discharge cleanup fee; New Jersey—petroleum fee; New Mexico—Petroleum loading fee; New York- sales tax applicable; North Carolina- Inspection tax; Ohio—plus 3 cents commercial; Oklahoma—environmental fee; Pennsylvania- oil franchise tax; Rhode Island—leaking underground storage tank tax (LUST);Tennessee—petroleum tax and environmental fee; Vermont—petroleum cleanup fee; Washington—$0.5 percent privilege tax; West Virginia—sales tax added to excise; Wyoming—license tax.

(r) Includes statewide local tax of 1.25 percent in California and 1.0 percent in Virginia.

(s) Tax rate is scheduled to increase ot 30 cents per pack on July 1, 2005.

(t) Plus 0.5 percent GRT.

(u) tax rate scheduled to decrease to 4 percent after June 30, 2005.

(v) Inspection fee.

Table 7.3
FOOD AND DRUG SALES TAX EXEMPTIONS
(As of January 1, 2005)

State or other jurisdiction	Tax rate (percentage)	Exemptions Food (a)	Prescription drugs	Nonprescription drugs
Alabama	4%	...	★	...
Alaska	none	...	...	...
Arizona	5.6	★	★	...
Arkansas	6	...	★	...
California (b)(c)	7.25	★	★	...
Colorado	2.9	★	★	...
Connecticut	6	★	★	★
Delaware	none	...	...	...
Florida	6	★	★	★
Georgia	4	★(d)	★	...
Hawaii	4	...	★	...
Idaho	6	...	★	...
Illinois	6.25	1 percent	1percent	1percent
Indiana	6	★	★	...
Iowa	5	★	★	...
Kansas	5.3	...	★	...
Kentucky	6	★	★	...
Louisiana	4	★ (d)	★	...
Maine	5	★	★	...
Maryland	5	★	★	★
Massachusetts	5	★	★	...
Michigan	6	★	★	...
Minnesota	6.5	★	★	★
Mississippi	7	...	★	...
Missouri	4.225	1.225	★	...
Montana	none	...	...	...
Nebraska	5.5	★	★	...
Nevada	6.5	★	★	...
New Hampshire	none	...	...	...
New Jersey	6	★	★	★
New Mexico	5	★	★	...
New York	4.25	★	★	★
North Carolina (f)	4.5	★ (d)	★	...
North Dakota	5	★	★	...
Ohio	6	★	★	...
Oklahoma	4.5	...	★	...
Oregon	none	...	...	...
Pennsylvania	6	★	★	★
Rhode Island	7	★	★	★
South Carolina	5	...	★	...
South Dakota	4	...	★	...
Tennessee	7	6 percent	★	...
Texas	6.25	★	★	★
Utah	4.75	...	★	...
Vermont	6	★	★	★
Virginia (b)	5.0	4 percent (e)	★	★
Washington	6.5	★	★	...
West Virginia	6	...	★	...
Wisconsin	5	★	★	...
Wyoming (c)	4	...	★	...
Dist. of Columbia	5.75		★	★

Source: The Federation of Tax Administrators, January 2005.
Key:
★— Yes, exempt from tax.
. . . — Subject to general sales tax,
(a) Some states tax food, but allow an (income) tax credit to compensate poor households. They are: Hawaii, Idaho, Kansas, South Dakota and Wyoming.
(b) Includes statewide local tax of 1.25 percent in California and 1 percent in Virginia.

(c) The tax rate may be adjusted annually according to a formula based on balances in the unappropriated general fund and the school foundation fund.
(d) Food sales are subject to local sales tax.
(e) Tax rate on food is scheduled to decrease to 3.5 percent on 1/1/05. Statewide local tax is included.
(f) Tax rate scheduled to decrease to 4 percent after 6/30/05.

Table 7.4
STATE INDIVIDUAL INCOME TAXES
(Tax rates for the tax year 2005—as of January 1, 2005)

State or other jurisdiction	Tax rate range (in percent) Low	High	Number of brackets	Income brackets ($) Low	High	Personal exemptions ($) Single	Married	Dependents	Federal income tax deductible
Alabama	2.0	5.0	3	500 (b)	3,000 (b)	1,500	3,000	300	★
Alaska				----------(x)----------					...
Arizona	2.87	5.04	5	10,000 (b)	150,000 (b)	2,100	4,200	2,300	...
Arkansas (a)	1.0	7.0 (e)	6	3,999	28,500	20 (c)	40 (c)	20 (c)	...
California (a)	1.0	9.3	6	6,147(b)	40,346 (b)	85 (c)	170 (c)	265 (c)	...
Colorado	4.63		1	--------- Flat rate ---------		---------- None ----------			...
Connecticut	3.0	5	2	10,000 (b)	10,000 (b)	12,750 (f)	24,500 (f)	0	...
Delaware	2.2	5.95	6	5,000	60,000	110 (c)	220 (c)	110 (c)	...
Florida				----------(x)----------					...
Georgia	1.0	6.0	6	750 (g)	7,000 (g)	2,700	5,400	2,700	...
Hawaii (a)	1.4	8.25	9	2,000 (b)	40,000 (b)	1,040	2,080	1,040	...
Idaho (a)	1.6	7.8	8	1,129 (h)	22,577 (h)	3,200 (d)	6,400 (d)	3,200 (d)	...
Illinois	3.0		1	--------- Flat rate ---------		2,000	4,000	2,000	...
Indiana	3.4		1	--------- Flat rate ---------		1,000	2,000	1,000	★
Iowa (a)	0.36	8.98	9	1,242	55,890	40 (c)	80 (c)	40 (c)	...
Kansas	3.5	6.45	3	15,000 (b)	30,000 (b)	2,250	4,500	2,250	...
Kentucky	2.0	6.0	5	3,000	8,000	20 (c)	40 (c)	20 (c)	★
Louisiana	2.0	6.0	3	12,500 (b)	25,000 (b)	4,500 (i)	9,000 (i)	1,000 (i)	...
Maine (a)	2.0	8.5	4	4,350 (b)	17,350 (b)	2,850	5,700	2,850	...
Maryland	2.0	4.75	4	1,000	3,000	2,400	4,800	2,400	...
Massachusetts	5.3		1	--------- Flat rate ---------		4,400	8,800	1,000	...
Michigan (a)	3.9		1	--------- Flat rate ---------		3,100	6,200	3,100	...
Minnesota (a)	5.35	7.85	3	19,010 (j)	62,440 (j)	3,100 (d)	6,200 (d)	3,100 (d)	...
Mississippi	3.0	5.0	3	5,000	10,000	6,000	12,000	1,500	★ (s)
Missouri	1.5	6.0	10	1,000	9,000	2,100	4,200	2,100	★
Montana (a)	2.0	6.9	7	2,300	13,900	1,900	3,800	1,900	...
Nebraska (a)	2.56	6.84	4	2,400 (k)	26,500 (k)	101 (c)	202 (c)	101 (c)	...
Nevada				----------(x)----------					...
New Hampshire				----------(y)----------					...
New Jersey	1.4	6.37	6	20,000 (l)	75,000 (l)	1,000	2,000	1,500	...
New Mexico	1.7	6	4	5,500 (m)	16,000 (m)	3,200 (d)	6,400 (d)	3,200 (d)	...
New York	4.0	7.7	7	8,000 (n)	500,000 (n)	0	0	1,000	...
North Carolina (o)	6.0	8.25	4	12,750 (o)	120,000 (o)	3,200 (d)	6,400 (d)	3,200 (d)	...
North Dakota	2.1	5.54 (p)	5	29,050 (p)	319,100 (p)	3,200 (d)	6,400 (d)	3,200 (d)	...
Ohio (a)	0.743	7.5	9	5,000	200,000	1,300 (q)	2,600 (q)	1,300 (q)	★ (r)
Oklahoma	0.5	6.65 (r)	8	1,000 (b)	10,000 (b)	1,000	2,000	1,000	★ (s)
Oregon (a)	5.0	9.0	3	2,650 (b)	6,550 (b)	154 (c)	308 (c)	154 (c)	...
Pennsylvania	3.07		1	--------- Flat rate ---------		---------- None ----------			...
Rhode Island				----------(t)----------					...
South Carolina (a)	2.5	7.0	6	2,460	12,300	3,200 (d)	6,400 (d)	3,200 (d)	...
South Dakota				----------(x)----------					...
Tennessee				----------(y)----------					...
Texas				----------(x)----------					★ (u)
Utah (a)	2.3	7.0	6	863 (b)	4,313 (b)	2,325 (d)	4,500 (d)	2,400 (d)	...
Vermont (a)	3.6	9.5	5	27,950 (v)	307,050 (v)	3,100 (d)	6,200 (d)	3,100 (d)	...
Virginia	2.0	5.75	4	3,000	17,000	800	1,600	800	...
Washington				----------(x)----------					...
West Virginia	3.0	6.5	5	10,000	60,000	2,000	4,000	2,000	...
Wisconsin	4.6	6.75	4	8,840 (w)	132,580 (w)	700	1,400	400	...
Wyoming				----------(x)----------					...
Dist. of Columbia	4.5	9 (z)	3	10,000	30,000	1,370	2,740	1,370	...

See footnotes at end of table.

STATE INDIVIDUAL INCOME TAXES — Continued

Source: The Federation of Tax Administrators from various sources, January 2005.

Key:

★—Yes

. . .—No

(a) Eight states have statutory provision for automatic adjustment of tax brackets, personal exemption or standard deductions to the rate of inflation. Michigan, Nebraska and Ohio indexes the personal exemption amounts only.

(b) For joint returns, the taxes are twice the tax imposed on half the income.

(c) Tax credits.

(d) These states allow personal exemption or standard deductions as provided in the Internal Revenue Code. Utah allows a personal exemption equal to three–fourths the federal exemptions.

(e) Plus a three percent surtax. A special tax table is available for low income taxpayers reducing their tax payments.

(f) Combined personal exemptions and standard deduction. An additional tax credit is allowed ranging from 75 percent to 0 percent based on state adjusted gross income. Exemption amounts are phased out for higher income taxpayers until they are eliminated for households earning over $54,500.

(g) The tax brackets reported are for single individuals. For married households filing separately, the same rates apply to income brackets ranging from $500 to $5,000; and the income brackets range from $1,000 to $10,000 for joint filers.

(h) For joint returns, the tax is twice the tax imposed on half of the income. A $10 filing tax is charged for each return and a $15 credit is allowed for each exemption.

(i) Combined personal exemption and standard deduction.

(j) The tax brackets reported are for single individual. For married couples filing jointly, the same rates apply for income under $27,780 to over $110,390.

(k) The tax brackets reported are for single individuals. For married couples filing jointly, the same rates apply for income under $4,000 to over $46,750.

(l) The tax brackets reported are for single individuals. For married individuals filing jointly, the same rates apply for income under $20,000 to over $150,000.

(m) The tax brackets reported are for single individuals. For married couples filing jointly, the same rates apply for income under $8,000 to over $40,000. Married households filing separately pay the tax imposed on half the income. Tax rate is scheduled to decrease in tax year 2005.

(n) The tax brackets reported are for single individuals. For married taxpayers, the same rates apply to income brackets ranging from $16,000 to $500,000.

(o) The tax brackets reported are for single individuals. For married taxpayers, the same rates apply to income brackets ranging from $200,000. Lower exemption amounts allowed for high income taxpayers. Tax rates scheduled to decrease after year 2003.

(p) The tax brackets reported are for single individuals. For married taxpayers, the same rates apply to income brackets ranging from $47,450 to $311,950. An additional $300 personal exemption is allowed for joint returns or unmarried heads of households.

(q) Plus an additional $20 per exemption tax credit.

(r) The rate range reported is for single persons not deducting federal income tax. For married persons filing jointly, the same rates apply to income brackets ranging from $2,000 to $21,000. Separate schedules, with rates ranging from 0.5 percent to 10 percent, apply to taxpayers deducting federal income taxes.

(s) Deduction is limited to $10,000 for joint returns and $5,000 for individuals in Missouri and to $5,000 in Oregon.

(t) Twenty–five percent federal tax liability. Federal income tax liability prior to the Economic Growth and Tax Relief Act of 2001.

(u) One half of the federal income taxes are deductible.

(v) The tax brackets reported are for single individuals. For married couples filing jointly, the same rates apply for income under $46,700 to over $307,050.

(w) The tax brackets reported are for single individuals. For married taxpayers, the same rates apply to income brackets ranging from $11,240 to $168,560. An additional $250 exemption is provided for each taxpayer or spouse age 65 or over.

(x) No state income tax.

(y) State income tax is limited to dividends and interest income only.

(z) Tax rate decreases are scheduled for tax year 2005.

Table 7.5
STATE PERSONAL INCOME TAXES: FEDERAL STARTING POINTS
(As of January 1, 2004)

State or other jurisdiction	Relation to Internal Revenue Code	Tax base
Alabama	. . .	. . .
Alaska	(a)	(a)
Arizona	1/1/04	Federal adjusted gross income
Arkansas	. . .	. . .
California	11/11/03	Federal adjusted gross income
Colorado	Current	Federal taxable income
Connecticut	Current	Federal adjusted gross income
Delaware	Current	Federal adjusted gross income
Florida	(a)	(a)
Georgia	1/1/04	Federal adjusted gross income
Hawaii	12/31/03	Federal taxable income
Idaho	1/1/04	Federal taxable income
Illinois	Current	Federal adjusted gross income
Indiana	1/1/03	Federal adjusted gross income
Iowa	1/1/04	Federal adjusted gross income
Kansas	Current	Federal adjusted gross income
Kentucky	12/31/01	Federal adjusted gross income
Louisiana	Current	Federal adjusted gross income
Maine	5/28/03	Federal adjusted gross income
Maryland	Current	Federal adjusted gross income
Massachusetts	Current	Federal adjusted gross income
Michigan	Current (b)	Federal adjusted gross income
Minnesota	6/15/03	Federal taxable income
Mississippi	. . .	. . .
Missouri	Current	Federal adjusted gross income
Montana	Current	Federal adjusted gross income
Nebraska	4/15/04	Federal adjusted gross income
Nevada	(a)	(a)
New Hampshire	(c)	(c)
New Jersey	. . .	. . .
New Mexico	Current	Federal adjusted gross income
New York	Current	Federal adjusted gross income
North Carolina	5/1/04	Federal taxable income
North Dakota	Current	Federal taxable income
Ohio	Current	Federal adjusted gross income
Oklahoma	Current	Federal adjusted gross income
Oregon	Current	Federal taxable income
Pennsylvania	. . .	. . .
Rhode Island	6/3/01	Federal adjusted gross income
South Carolina	12/31/02	Federal taxable income
South Dakota	(a)	(a)
Tennessee	(c)	(c)
Texas	(a)	(a)
Utah	Current	Federal taxable income
Vermont	1/1/02	Federal taxable income
Virginia	12/31/03	Federal adjusted gross income
Washington	(a)	(a)
West Virginia	1/1/04	Federal adjusted gross income
Wisconsin	12/31/02	Federal adjusted gross income
Wyoming	(a)	(a)
Dist. of Columbia	Current	Federal adjusted gross income

Source: Compiled by the Federation of Tax Administrators from various sources, January 2005.

Key:
. . .—State does not employ a federal starting point.
Current—Indicates state has adopted the Internal Revenue Code as currently in effect. Dates indicate state has adopted the IRC as amended to that date.
(a) No state income tax.
(b) Or 1/1/99, taxpayer's option.
(c) On interest and dividends only.

Table 7.6
RANGE OF STATE CORPORATE INCOME TAX RATES
(For tax year 2005—as of January 1, 2005)

State or other jurisdiction	Tax rate (percent)	Tax brackets Lowest	Tax brackets Highest	Number of brackets	Tax rate (a) (percent) financial institution	Federal income tax deductible
Alabama	6.5	------- Flat Rate -------		1	6.5	★
Alaska	1.0–9.4	10,000	90,000	10	1.0–9.4	. . .
Arizona	6.968 (b)	------- Flat Rate -------		1	6.968 (b)	. . .
Arkansas	1.0–6.5	3,000	100,000	6	1.0–6.5	. . .
California	8.84 (c)	------- Flat Rate -------		1	10.84 (c)	. . .
Colorado	4.63	------- Flat Rate -------		1	4.63	. . .
Connecticut	7.5 (d)	------- Flat Rate -------		1	7.5 (d)	. . .
Delaware	8.7	------- Flat Rate -------		1	8.7–1.7 (e)	. . .
Florida	5.5 (f)	------- Flat Rate -------		1	5.5 (f)	. . .
Georgia	6.0	------- Flat Rate -------		1	6.0	. . .
Hawaii	4.4–6.4 (g)	25,000	100,000	3	7.92 (g)	. . .
Idaho	7.6 (h)	------- Flat Rate -------		1	7.6 (h)	. . .
Illinois	7.3 (i)	------- Flat Rate -------		1	7.3 (i)	. . .
Indiana	8.5	------- Flat Rate -------		1	8.5	. . .
Iowa	6.0–12.0	25,000	250,000	4	5.0	★(k)
Kansas	4.0 (l)	------- Flat Rate -------		1	2.25 (l)	. . .
Kentucky	4.0–8.25	25,000	250,000	5	(a)	. . .
Louisiana	4.0–8.0	25,000	200,000	5	(a)	★
Maine	3.5–8.93 (m)	25,000	250,000	4	1.0	. . .
Maryland	7.0	------- Flat Rate -------		1	7.0	. . .
Massachusetts	9.5 (n)	------- Flat Rate -------		1	10.5 (n)	. . .
Michigan	------- See Note -------					
Minnesota	9.8 (o)	------- Flat Rate -------		1	9.8 (o)	. . .
Mississippi	3.0–5.0	5,000	10,000	3	3.0–5.0	. . .
Missouri	6.25	------- Flat Rate -------		1	7.0	★(k)
Montana	6.75 (p)	------- Flat Rate -------		1	6.75 (p)	. . .
Nebraska	5.58–7.81	50,000		2	(a)	. . .
Nevada	------- See Note -------					
New Hampshire	8.5 (q)	------- Flat Rate -------		1	8.5 (q)	. . .
New Jersey	9.0 (r)	------- Flat Rate -------		1	9.0 (r)	. . .
New Mexico	4.8–7.6	500,000	1 million	3	4.8–7.6	. . .
New York	7.5 (s)	------- Flat Rate -------		1	7.5 (s)	. . .
North Carolina	6.9 (t)	------- Flat Rate -------		1	6.9 (t)	. . .
North Dakota	2.6–7.0	3,000	30,000	5	7.0 (b)	★
Ohio	5.1–8.5 (u)		50,000	2	(u)	. . .
Oklahoma	6.0	------- Flat Rate -------		1	6.0	. . .
Oregon	6.6 (b)	------- Flat Rate -------		1	6.6 (b)	. . .
Pennsylvania	9.99	------- Flat Rate -------		1	(a)	. . .
Rhode Island	9.0 (b)	------- Flat Rate -------		1	9.0 (v)	. . .
South Carolina	5.0	------- Flat Rate -------		1	4.5 (w)	. . .
South Dakota	. . .	. . .		. . .	6.0–0.25 (b)	. . .
Tennessee	6.5	------- Flat Rate -------		1	6.5	. . .
Texas	------- See Note -------					
Utah	5.0 (b)	------- Flat Rate -------		. . .	5.0 (b)	. . .
Vermont	7.0–9.75 (b)	10,000	250,000	4	7.0–9.75 (b)	. . .
Virginia	6.0	------- Flat Rate -------		1	6.0 (x)	. . .
Washington	------- See Note -------					
West Virginia	9.0	------- Flat Rate -------		1	9.0	. . .
Wisconsin	7.9	------- Flat Rate -------		1	7.9	. . .
Wyoming	------- See Note -------					
Dist. of Columbia	9.975 (y)	------- Flat Rate -------		. . .	9.975 (y)	. . .

See footnotes at end of table.

RANGE OF STATE CORPORATE INCOME TAX RATES — Continued

Source: Compiled by the Federation of Tax Administrators from various sources, January 2005.

Key:

★—Yes

. . .—No

Note: Michigan imposes a single business tax (sometimes described as a business activities tax or value added tax) of 1.9% on the sum of federal taxable income of the business, compensation paid to employees, dividends, interest, royalties paid and other items. Similarly, Texas imposes a franchise tax of 4.5% of earned surplus or 2.5 mills of net worth. Nevada, Washington, and Wyoming do not have state corporate income taxes.

(a) Rates listed include the corporate tax rate applied to financial institutions or excise taxes based on income. Some states have other taxes based upon the value of deposits or shares.

(b) Minimum tax is $50 in Arizona, $50 in North Dakota (banks), $10 in Oregon, $250 in Rhode Island, $500 per location in South Dakota (banks), $100 in Utah, $250 in Vermont.

(c) Minimum tax is $800. The tax rate on S-Corporations is 1.5% (3.5% for banks).

(d) Or 3.1 mills per dollar of capital stock and surplus (maximum tax $1 million) or $250.

(e) The marginal rate decreases over 4 brackets ranging from $20 to $650 million in taxable income. Building and loan associations are taxed at a flat 8.7%.

(f) Or 3.3% Alternative Minimum Tax. An exemption of $5,000 is allowed.

(g) Capital gains are taxed at 4%. There is also an alternative tax of 0.5% of gross annual sales.

(h) Minimum tax is $20. An additional tax of $10 is imposed on each return.

(i) Includes a 2.5% personal property replacement tax.

(k) Fifty percent of the federal income tax is deductible.

(l) Plus a surtax of 3.35% (2.125% for banks) taxable income in excess of $50,000 ($25,000).

(m) Or, the Maine Alternative Minimum Tax.

(n) Rate includes a 14% surtax, as does the following: an additional tax of $7.00 per $1,000 on taxable tangible property (or net worth allocable to state, for intangible property corporations); minimum tax of $456.

(o) Plus a 5.8% tax on any Alternative Minimum Taxable Income over the base tax.

(p) A 7% tax on taxpayers using water's edge combination. Minimum tax is $50.

(q) Plus a 0.50 percent tax on the enterprise base (total compensation, interest and dividends paid). Business profits tax imposed on both corporations and unincorporated associations.

(r) The rate reported in the table is the corporation business franchise tax rate. The minimum tax is $500. An Alternative Minimum Assessment based on Gross Receipts applies if greater than corporate franchise tax. Corporations not subject to the franchise tax are subject to a 7.25% income tax. Banking and financial corporations are subject to the franchise tax. Corporations with net income under $100,000 are taxed at 6.5%. The tax on S corporations is being phased out through 2007. The tax rate on a New Jersey S corporation that has entire net income not subject to federal corporate income tax in excess of $100,000 will remain at 1.33% for privilege periods ending on or before June 30, 2006. The rate will be 0.67% for privilege periods ending on or after July 1, 2006, but on or before June 30, 2007; and there will be no tax imposed for privilege periods ending on or after July 1, 2007. The tax on S corporation with entire net income not subject to federal corporate income tax of $100,00 or less is eliminated for privilege periods ending on or after July 1, 2007.

(s) Or 1.78 mills per dollar of capital (up to $350,000); or a 2.5% alternative minimum tax; or a minimum tax of $10,000 to $100 depending on payroll size; if any of these is greater than the tax computed on net income. Small corporations with income under $290,000 are subject to lower rates of tax on net income. An additional tax of 0.9 mills per dollar of subsidiary capital is imposed on corporations. For banks, the alternative bases of tax are 3% of alternative net income; or up to 1/50th mill of taxable assets; or a minimum tax of $250.

(t) Financial institutions are also subject to a tax equal to $30 per one million in assets.

(u) Or 5.82 mills time the value of the taxpayer's issued and outstanding share of stock with a maximum payment of $150,000. An additional litter tax is imposed equal to 0.11% on the first $50,000 of taxable income, 0.22% on income over $50,000; or 0.14 mills on net worth. A $50 to $1,000 minimum tax applies, depending on worldwide gross receipts.

(v) For banks, the alternative tax is $2.50 per $10,000 of capital stock ($100 minimum).

(w) Savings and Loans are taxed at a 6% rate.

(x) State and national banks subject to the state's franchise tax on net capital is exempt from the income tax.

(y) Minimum tax is $100. Includes surtax.

Table 7.7
PROPERTY TAXES BY STATE AND REGION: 2002 AND 2003
(In thousands of dollars)

State or other jurisdiction	Year: 2003 Quarter: 1	Year: 2003 Quarter: 2	Year: 2003 Quarter: 3	Year: 2003 Quarter: 4	Year 2002 Quarter: 1	Year 2002 Quarter: 2	Year 2002 Quarter: 2	Year 2002 Quarter: 2
Eastern Region								
Connecticut	(c)	(c)	(c)	(c)	(c)	(c)	(c)	(c)
Delaware	(c)	(c)	(c)	(c)	(c)	(c)	(c)	(c)
Maine	368	29,711	16,694	-109	422	30,415 (a)	13,265	3,509
Massachusetts	48	21 (b)	2 (a)	10	53 (a)	20 (a)	2 (a)	10
New Hampshire	487,636 (a)	8,692	4,843	3,135	480,326 (a)	10,811 (a)	4,926	3,627
New Jersey	0	2 (a)	6	240 (a)	0 (a)	0 (a)	0	0
New York	(c)	(c)	(c)	(c)	(c)	(c)	(c)	(c)
Pennsylvania	4,033	50,332	9,321 (b)	8,288 (b)	2,971 (a)	41,546 (a)	9,359 (a)	7,970
Rhode Island	0	847 (a)	16	0 (a)	470 (a)	669 (a)	0	0
Vermont	131,342 (a)	103,929	103,929	103,929 (a)	91,654 (a)	114,232 (a)	91,467 (a)	92,263
Regional average	62,343	19,343	13,481	11,549	57,590	19,769	11,902	10,738
Midwestern Region								
Illinois	15,267	14,843	12,435 (a)	14,683 (a)	14,816	12,747 (a)	14,096	12,523
Indiana	1,427	314	1,484 (a)	1,518	1,550	2,204	1,139 (a)	1,627
Iowa	(c)	(c)	(c)	(c)	(c)	(c)	(c)	(c)
Kansas	23,173	5,676	17,537	9,773	22,115	7,755 (a)	16,459 (a)	9,480
Michigan	710,514	191,186	869,305 (a)	1,055,186	632,222 (a)	175,895 (a)	411,687 (a)	656,488
Minnesota	4,783	46	70 (a)	270,122 (a)	5,496 (a)	233 (a)	102 (a)	2,897
Nebraska	30	1,596	49	1,392	1,596 (a)	1,596 (a)	2,105	1,543
North Dakota	1,250	121	14	56	1,155	154	12	53
Ohio	270 (a)	36,176	2,500 (a)	376 (a)	1,264 (a)	14,896 (a)	2,083 (a)	206
South Dakota	(c)	(c)	(c)	(c)	(c)	(c)	(c)	(c)
Wisconsin	46,008 (a)	14,813	1,555 (a)	14,696	42,788 (a)	14,482 (a)	106 (b)	13,849 (b)
Regional average	72,975	24,070	82,268	124,346	65,727	20,906	40,708	63,515
Southern Region								
Alabama	111,398	12,454	9,927 (a)	78,244	109,815	12,308	9,639	70,755
Arkansas	10,654	124,240	56,029	30,372 (a)	18,766 (a)	115,200 (a)	60,899 (a)	273,162
Florida	184,176	128,132	22,710	20,100 (a)	190,749	177,042	21,980 (a)	35,793
Georgia	20,535	5,995	7,246	31,182	24,070	3,992 (a)	6,084	28,526
Kentucky	114,022	56,173	41,013	224,439	109,973	56,972 (a)	47,104	219,271
Louisiana	6,140	9,689 (a)	11,108	11,108	8,270	8,720 (a)	6,140 (a)	6,140
Maryland	3,823	7,847	371,546	102,796	30,684 (a)	14,328 (a)	233,706	43,513
Mississippi	26,724 (b)	247	513 (a)	9,080	25,527 (a)	232 (a)	484	14 (b)
Missouri	18,597 (b)	826	488 (a)	3,081	17,106 (a)	783 (a)	431	2,864 (b)
North Carolina	0	0	0	0	0	0	0	0
Oklahoma	(c)	(c)	(c)	(c)	(c)	(c)	(c)	(c)
South Carolina	4,346 (a)	858	30	1,178	6,358 (a)	2,604 (a)	595 (a)	3,199(b)
Tennessee	(c)	(c)	(c)	(c)	(c)	(c)	(c)	(c)
Texas	(c)	(c)	(c)	(c)	(c)	(c)	(c)	(c)
Virginia	-26	103,929 (a)	78	774	25	22,343 (a)	99	0
West Virginia	307	688	1,169	827	737	1,003 (a)	1,497 (a)	1,034
Regional average	31,294	28,192	32,616	32,074	24,156	25,964	9,115	34,674
Western Region								
Alaska	10	48,190 (a)	602	-37	-35	48,631	460	81
Arizona	82,929 (b)	82,929	82,929	82,929	82,311 (a)	82,311 (a)	82,928 (a)	82,928
California	551,180 (b)	585,420	505,011 (a)	419,565 (a)	526,487 (a)	550,965 (a)	532,860	498,648 (a)
Colorado	(c)	(c)	(c)	(c)	(c)	(c)	(c)	(c)
Hawaii	(c)	(c)	(c)	(c)	(c)	(c)	(c)	(c)
Idaho	(c)	(c)	(c)	(c)	(c)	(c)	(c)	(c)
Montana	40,562	78,777	14,640	63,977	41,481 (a)	75,183 (a)	12,546	51,922 (b)
Nevada	44,288	37,060	22,130 (a)	21,176	22,840 (a)	44,003 (a)	2,917	25,892
New Mexico	27,297	9,559	4,035	9,207	700 (b)	169 (b)	18 (b)	39,398 (b)
Oregon	5,628	6,811	7,110	3,289	5,059	6,788 (a)	6,788	6,958
Utah	(c)	(c)	(c)	(c)	(c)	(c)	(c)	(c)
Washington	467,362	403,472 (b)	417,025	293,613	428,883 (a)	382,334 (a)	400,114	315,465
Wyoming	25,993	50,797	10,292	65,321	21,399 (a)	50,936 (a)	6,095	67,096
Regional Average	95,788	100,232	81,829	73,772	86,856	95,486	86,553	85,108
Regional Average without California	57,839	59,800	46,564	44,956	50,220	57,530	45,979	47,513
Washington D.C.	248,823	159,020	412,873	4,113	189,972 (a)	157,905 (a)	355,823	24,319

Source: U.S. Department of Commerce, Bureau of the Census, October 2004.

Note: Property taxes as defined by the Census Bureau; refer to real property (e.g., land and structures) as well as personal property; either tangible (e.g., automobiles and boats) or intangible (e.g., bank accounts and bonds). For additional information consult http://www.census.gov/govs/www/class_ch7_tax.html.

Key:
(a)—Revised
(b)—Estimated
(c)—No tax in state

Table 7.8
FISCAL 2004 STATE GENERAL FUND, PRELIMINARY ACTUAL, BY REGION
(In millions of dollars)

State or other jurisdiction	Beginning balance	Revenues	Adjustments	Resources	Expenditures	Adjustments	Ending balance	Budget stabilization fund
Eastern Region								
Connecticut (g)	$0	$12,881	$0	$12,881	$12,678	0	202	$202
Delaware (a)	464	2,736	0	3,200	2,554	0	646	137
Maine	37	2,621	0	2,658	2,643	0	15	0
Massachusetts (a)	752	23,196	0	23,949	22,470	0	1,479	872
New Hampshire	0	1,321	0	1,321	1,305	0	16	0
New Jersey (a)	373	24,383	6	24,761	23,939	0	822	288
New York (a) (w)	815	42,327	-1,900	41,242	42,065	-1,900	1,077	794
Pennsylvania (aa)	209	21,813	130	22,152	21,926	150	77	260
Rhode Island (bb)	50	2,841	-58	2,834	2,790	0	44	87
Vermont (hh)	0	922	51	973	915	58	0	45
Regional totals	2,700	135,041	—	135,971	133,285	—	4,176	2,685
Midwestern Region								
Illinois (j)	317	23,081	3,598	26,996	22,632	4,182	182	276
Indiana (k)	442	10,684	409	11,535	11,244	0	291	242
Iowa (l)	0	4,513	0	4,513	4,561	-73	26	0
Kansas (m)	123	4,519	3	4,644	4,317	0	327	0
Michigan (q)	174	8,076	457	8,707	8,695	0	12	0
Minnesota (a) (r)	369	14,289	0	14,658	13,734	0	924	410
Nebraska (u)	3	2,720	30	2,752	2,576	0	177	87
North Dakota	15	956	0	971	894	0	77	9
Ohio (y)	52	24,031	0	24,083	23,839	87	157	181
South Dakota (dd)	0	852	40	892	889	3	0	158
Wisconsin (a) (kk)	-282	11,041	0	10,759	10,654	0	105	0
Regional totals	1,213	104,762	—	110,510	104,035	—	2,278	1,363
Southern Region								
Alabama (b)	113	5,560	120	5,792	5,491	40	261	104
Arkansas	0	3,526	0	3,526	3,526	0	0	0
Florida	682	23,170	0	23,852	21,542	0	2,310	966
Georgia (a) (h)	1,268	16,080	0	17,348	16,265	0	1,083	0
Kentucky (n)	163	7,087	371	7,620	7,294	77	250	51
Louisiana (o)	0	6,765	61	6,826	6,743	38	45	0
Maryland (p)	123	9,994	376	10,493	10,262	0	230	497
Mississippi (s)	41	3,582	-29	3,594	3,591	0	3	43
Missouri (t)	216	6,934	0	7,150	6,662	0	488	222
North Carolina (x)	251	14,691	246	15,187	14,704	195	287	267
Oklahoma (z)	34	5,124	-223	4,936	4,833	0	102	209
South Carolina (a) (cc)	46	5,116	0	5,162	4,865	243	55	25
Tennessee (ee)	64	8,688	15	8,767	8,357	61	349	217
Texas (ff)	88	29,465	234	29,787	29,434	-628	981	366
Virginia	328	12,333	0	12,660	12,387	0	274	0
West Virginia (jj)	196	3,083	40	3,319	3,019	10	291	54
Regional totals	3,613	161,198	—	166,019	158,975	—	7,009	3,021
Western Region								
Alaska (c)	0	2,023	278	2,301	2,301	0	0	2,109
Arizona (d)	192	6,467	225	6,884	6,517	0	368	14
California (a) (e)	1,607	76,582	2,571	80,760	77,634	0	3,127	0
Colorado (f)	217	6,045	-227	6,035	5,689	0	346	0
Hawaii	117	3,908	0	4,025	3,840	0	185	0
Idaho (i)	16	2,098	-26	2,087	1,987	0	100	0
Montana	43	1,376	0	1,419	1,287	0	132	0
Nevada (v)	108	2,305	49	2,461	2,320	0	141	1
New Mexico (a)	245	4,647	133	5,025	4,383	162	480	0
Oregon	93	4,908	0	5,001	5,479	0	-478	0
Utah (gg)	16	3,685	-33	3,668	3,569	46	53	67
Washington (ii)	405	11,345	208	11,958	11,452	0	506	0
Wyoming (ll)	4	790	-2	792	788	0	4	246
Regional totals	3,063	126,179	—	132,416	127,246	—	208	4,964
Regional totals without California	1,456	49,597	—	51,656	49,612	—	1,837	2,437

See footnotes at end of table.

FISCAL 2004 STATE GENERAL FUND, PRELIMINARY ACTUAL, BY REGION — Continued

Source: National Association of State Budget Officers, *Fiscal Survey of States,* December 2004.

Note: For all states, unless otherwise noted, transfers into budget stabilization funds are counted as expenditures and transfers from budget stabilization funds are counted as revenues.

Key:

N.A.—Not available.

(a) In these states, the ending balance includes the balance in the budget stabilization fund.

(b) Revenue adjustments reflect a $75.6 million transfer from the Federal Fiscal Relief Fund, $19.7 million of SWAP agreements, $14.5 million from the cigarette tax, $3.2 million from the removal of the contractor's sales tax exemption, and $6.9 million from civil court cost increases. Expenditure adjustments reflect $39.8 million from the Medicaid Supplemental State General Fund appropriation.

(c) Revenue adjustments reflect a constitutional budget reserve (CBR) draw.

(d) Revenue adjustments represent fund transfers, federal cash assistance, a judicial collections program, a tax amnesty program and settlement monies from a lawsuit.

(e) The revenue adjustment is a prior year revenue adjustment of $2,570.7 million.

(f) Revenue adjustments include diversions to the State Education Fund and the Older Coloradoans Program, as well as transfers to the General Fund to mitigate revenue declines. Ending balance is $122.7 million above the statutory reserve requirement. Current law requires monies in excess of the statutory reserve to be credited to the Highway User's Tax Fund and the Capital Construction Fund.

(g) A portion of the fiscal 2004 general fund surplus was transferred to balance the general fund in fiscal 2005. In fiscal 2004, the state ended the year with and ending balance of $202.2 million. This amount is included in the budget stabilization fund.

(h) The tobacco tax increase provided $180 million in additional revenue.

(i) Revenue adjustments include $0.4 million in transfers from other funds and $26.2 million in transfers to other funds.

(j) Revenue adjustments include $2,109 million transfers into general funds and $1,489 million of pension obligation reimbursements transfers-in. Expenditure adjustments include accounts payable pay-down of $673 million, $1,416 million to repay short-term borrowing that came due in fiscal year 2004, and transfers-out of $2,093 million.

(k) Revenue adjustments reflect one-time transfers from dedicated funds and the federal Jobs and Growth Tax Relief Reconciliation Act of 2003 and the Rainy Day Fund.

(l) In October 2003, Governor Vilsack initiated a 2.5 percent across-the-board cut in allotments, for a total reduction of $82.5 million, to bring the General Fund into balance after the October 10, 2003 Revenue Estimating Conference meeting. In June 2004, Governor Vilsack rescinded 10 percent of the cut, or $8.3 million, resulting in a net across-the-board cut of 2.25 percent, or $74.2 million, for fiscal 2004. A supplemental appropriation also was passed during the 2004 legislative session, totaling $1 million.

(m) Revenue adjustments reflect released encumbrances.

n) Revenue includes $109.5 million in Tobacco Settlement funds. Revenue adjustments include $102.2 million that represents appropriation balances carried over from the prior fiscal year. $199.9 from fund transfers into the General Fund, and $68.7 Federal Fiscal Relief funds. Expenditure adjustments represent appropriation balances forwarded to the next fiscal year.

(o) Revenue adjustments include $19.2 million in carry-forwards, $4 million in non-recurring funds, the use of $7.5 million of fund balances and $29 million from premiums generated on bond sales. Expenditure adjustments include $35.2 million in carry-forwards.

(p) Revenue adjustments reflect transfers from other funds.

(q) Fiscal 2004 revenue adjustments include federal and state tax law changes (-$209.6 million); unrestricted federal aid ($169 million); a revenue sharing freeze ($278.5 million); prior year work projects ($35.1 million); drivers license fees and fines ($50.1 million); escheats law change ($15 million); casino tax increase ($3.6 million); other revenue adjustments (-$34.5 million); deposits from state restricted funds ($84.2 million); and pending legislative action to repeal pharmaceutical tax credit ($10 million). The estimated ending balance will likely be expended by fiscal year end close.

(r) The ending balance includes budget reserve of $409.7 million.

(s) Revenue adjustments include a fiscal 2003 year-end transfer of $29.1 million to the Working Cash Stabilization Reserve Fund.

(t) Revenues are net of refunds. Refunds for Fiscal 2004 totaled $1,075.3 million. Revenues include the following: $229.9 million transferred to the General Revenue Fund. $84.7 million from bond proceeds for capital improvement projects, and $274.1 million of Federal Fiscal Relief pursuant to the Jobs and Growth Tax Relief Reconciliation Act of 2003.

(u) Revenue adjustments are transfers between the General Fund and other funds.

(v) The fiscal 2003 ending balance and fiscal 2004 beginning balance differ due to rounding. Fiscal 2004 figures reflect legislatively approved amounts.

(w) The ending balance includes $794 million in the tax stabilization reserve fund (rainy day fund), $262 million in the Community Projects Fund and $21 million in reserve funds for litigation risks. Revenue and expenditure adjust-

ments reflect $1.9 billion in deferred spending from fiscal 2002-2003 to fiscal 2003-2004 due to the timing of the state's tobacco securitization transaction.

(x) Revenue adjustments include $136.9 million of Federal Fiscal Relief and $108.8 million of funds originally appropriated for Hurricane Floyd recovery. Expenditure adjustments include $116.7 million transfer to the Rainy Day Fund and a $78.8 transfer to the Repair and Renovation Reserve.

(y) Federal reimbursements for Medicaid and other human services programs are included in the general revenue fund. Beginning balances are unreserved fund balances. The actual cash balances would be higher by the amount reserved for encumbrances and designated transfers from the general fund revenue fund. Expenditures for fiscal 2004 do not include encumbrances outstanding at the end of the year. Ohio reports expenditures based on disbursements for the general revenue fund. Expenditure adjustments reflect miscellaneous transfers-out of $55.3 million. These transfers-out are adjusted for an anticipated net change in encumbrances from fiscal 2003 levels of $31.4 million.

(z) Revenue adjustments reflect a rainy day fund deposit of $208.8 million and an increase to the General Revenue Fund cash-flow reserve of $14.2 million.

(aa) Revenue adjustments include $142.5 million in prior year lapses and a -$13 million adjustment to the beginning balance. total expenditures reflect the total amount appropriated plus supplemental appropriations. Expenditure adjustments reflect projected current-year disbursements and the statutory transfer of $190 million to the budget stabilization (rainy day) Fund.

(bb) Revenue adjustments reflect a contribution to budget stabilization fund.

(cc) Expenditure adjustments reflect funds applied to the fiscal 2003 and fiscal 2002 deficits.

(dd) Revenue adjustments reflect $22.8 million of one-time receipts, $16 million transferred from the Property Tax Reduction Fund to cover the budget shortfall, and $1.4 million obligated cash carried forward from fiscal 2003. Expenditure adjustments reflect $1.4 million transferred to the Budget Reserve Fund from the prior year's obligated cash and $1.2 million of obligated cash to the Budget Reserve Fund.

(ee) Tennessee's ending balance is committed to fund one-time appropriations in the next fiscal year. It is not an uncommitted balance. Revenue adjustments reflect $28 million transfer from the debt service fund reserve, a $25.5 million transfer from debt service fund unexpended appropriations, and a -$39 million transfer to the rainy day fund. Expenditure adjustments reflect a $21 million transfer to the Transportation Equity Fund, a $27 million transfer to the capital outlay projects fund, and $12.2 million for dedicated appropriations.

(ff) Revenue information is from the Comptroller's December 2003 certification revenue estimate, updated to reflect the Comptroller's April 2004 revised revenue estimate. Revenue adjustments reflect dedicated account balances. Total expenditures are 2004 appropriated as reported by the Legislative Budget Board. Total expenditures include $345 million held in reserve for transfer to the Rainy Day Fund and other adjustments to reconcile the actual ending balance reported by the Comptroller.

(gg) Revenue adjustments include: $35.6 million reserve from prior fiscal year, $14 million lapsing balances from agencies, $9.8 million transfer from tobacco settlement funds, $10.2 million transfers from various restricted accounts, $5.2 million industrial assistance fund reserve from previous fiscal year, $3.4 million from other miscellaneous sources, ($4.3 million) transfer to the Rainy Day Fund per statute, and ($107.2 million) reserve for following year. Year-end revenues were $94.5 million higher than estimated largely due to better anticipated sales and income tax receipts. $34.8 million of these surplus revenues were transferred to the rainy day fund per statute. The remaining $11.0 million of expenditure adjustments were various minor year-end closing entries.

(hh) Revenue adjustments reflect a $28.9 million 2003 Act 68 sales tax implementation, -$1.3 million Vermont Economic Development Authority debt forgiveness, $17.3 million direct applications and transfers in, $5.9 million additional property transfer tax to the general fund. Expenditure adjustments include $1.3 million (net) to the human services caseload reserve. $4.5 million to the transportation fund, $1.7 million to the general bond fund, $2 million to the health access trust fund, $10.5 million to internal service funds, $1 million to miscellaneous other funds, $20.9 million to the budget stabilization reserve, and $15.5 million to the general fund surplus reserve.

(ii) Revenue adjustments represent transfers from other accounts to the General Fund.

(jj) The beginning balance reflects $146.4 million of reappropriations, $8.3 million of surplus appropriations, and a $41.3 million unappropriated surplus balance. Revenue adjustments reflect a $39.8 million transfer from special revenue, and $0.1 million in prior year redeposits. Expenditures reflect $2,898.8 million of regular appropriations, $74 million of reappropriations, $14.7 million of surplus appropriations, and $30 million of 31-day (prior year) expenditures. Expenditure adjustments reflect a $9.8 million transfer to the rainy day fund.

(kk) The general fund balance improved by $387.4 million during fiscal 2004. The fiscal 2004 ending balance includes a required statutory balance of $35 million.

(ll) The state budgets on a biennial basis. To complete the survey using annual figures, certain assumptions and estimates were required. Caution is advised when making projections using this information.

Table 7.9
FISCAL 2005 STATE GENERAL FUND, APPROPRIATED, BY REGION
(In millions of dollars)

State or other jurisdiction	Beginning balance	Revenues	Adjustments	Resources	Expenditures	Adjustments	Ending balance	Budget stabilization fund
U.S. total	$18,201	$539,780	N.A.	$562,186	$562,297	N.A.	$11,728	$9,647
Eastern Region								
Connecticut (f)	0	13,310	0	13,310	13,226	0	84	286
Delaware (a)	646	2,777	0	3,423	2,846	0	578	148
Maine (n)	15	2,652	54	2,721	2,710	0	11	0
Massachusetts (a) (p)	1,479	23,521	0	25,000	24,351	0	649	624
New Hampshire	16	1,260	0	1,276	1,326	0	-50	17
New Jersey (a)	822	27,059	0	27,881	27,478	5	398	288
New York (a) (w)	1,077	42,655	0	43,732	43,039	-434	1,127	794
Pennsylvania (z)	77	22,806	0	22,883	22,876	2	5	267
Rhode Island (aa)	44	2,954	-60	2,938	2,938	0	1	90
Vermont (gg)	0	950	36	986	956	30	0	46
Regional totals	4,176	139,944	N.A.	144,150	141,746	N.A.	2,803	2,560
Midwestern Region								
Illinois (i)	182	23,217	2,385	25,784	23,004	2,598	182	276
Indiana (j)	291	11,093	286	11,669	11,378	0	291	46
Iowa (k)	0	4,603	-63	4,540	4,452	0	88	0
Kansas (k)	327	4,542	0	4,869	4,658	0	210	0
Michigan (q)	0	8,417	341	8,758	8,757	0	1	0
Minnesota (a) (r)	924	13,929	0	14,853	14,221	0	632	631
Nebraska (u)	177	2,776	-84	2,868	2,758	101	8	177
North Dakota	77	942	0	1,019	910	0	109	9
Ohio (x)	157	24,862	0	25,020	24,933	-33	120	181
South Dakota (cc)	0	953	27	980	980	0	0	139
Wisconsin (a) (jj)	105	11,650	0	11,755	11,745	0	11	0
Regional totals	2,240	106,984	N.A.	112,115	107,796	N.A.	1,652	1,459
Southern Region								
Alabama (b)	261	5,763	0	6,025	5,924	36	65	140
Arkansas	0	3,630	0	3,630	3,630	0	0	0
Florida	2,310	22,606	0	24,916	24,049	0	868	999
Georgia (a) (g)	1,145	16,376	0	17,521	16,376	0	1,145	0
Kentucky (l)	223	7,363	153	7,738	7,587	152	0	117
Louisiana (m)	0	6,820	42	6,861	6,861	0	0	0
Maryland (o)	230	10,542	475	11,247	11,159	0	87	520
Mississippi (s)	3	3,695	0	3,698	3,698	0	0	43
Missouri (s)	488	6,708	0	7,197	7,171	0	26	232
North Carolina (x)	287	15,645	0	15,933	15,916	0	16	267
Oklahoma (y)	102	4,906	-12	4,997	4,764	0	232	209
South Carolina (a) (bb)	55	5,223	0	5,277	5,073	55	149	75
Tennessee (dd)	349	8,922	-58	9,213	9,116	96	1	275
Texas (ee)	981	29,659	56	30,696	29,460	508	728	458
Virginia	274	13,159	0	13,433	13,402	0	31	0
West Virginia (ii)	291	3,072	0	3,362	3,320	32	11	85
Regional totals	6,999	164,089	N.A.	171,744	167,506	N.A.	3,359	3,420
Western Region								
Alaska (c)	0	1,927	361	2,333	2,333	0	0	2,059
Arizona (d)	368	6,877	238	7,483	7,474	0	8	25
California (a)	3,127	77,251	0	80,378	78,681	0	1,697	0
Colorado (e)	224	6,259	-266	6,217	5,971	0	246	0
Hawaii	185	4,220	0	4,405	4,112	0	292	0
Idaho (h)	100	2,085	-22	2,164	2,087	0	77	21
Montana (t)	132	1,335	0	1,466	1,326	0	140	0
Nevada (v)	141	2,505	58	2,704	2,545	0	160	0
New Mexico (a)	480	4,622	4	5,106	4,384	14	708	0
Oregon	-478	5,304	0	4,826	4,710	0	116	0
Utah (ff)	0	3,692	119	3,812	3,809	0	3	67
Washington (hh)	506	11,652	102	12,259	11,794	0	465	0
Wyoming (kk)	4	992	33	1,028	1,023	0	5	35
Regional totals	4,789	128,721	N.A.	134,181	130,249	N.A.	3,917	2,207
Regional totals without California	1,662	51,470	N.A.	53,803	51,568	N.A.	2,220	2,207

See footnotes at end of table.

FISCAL 2005 STATE GENERAL FUND, APPROPRIATED, BY REGION – CONTINUED
(In millions of dollars)

Source: National Association of State Budget Officers, *The Fiscal Survey of the States* (December 2004).

Note: For all states unless otherwise noted, transfers into budget stabilization funds are counted as expenditures and transfers from budget stabilization funds are counted as revenue.

Key:

N.A.—Data are not available.

(a) In these states, the ending balance includes the balance in the budget stabilization fund.

(b) Expenditure adjustments reflect a $36 million transfer to the Education Trust Fund Rainy Day Fund.

(c) Revenue adjustments reflect a constitutional budget reserve (CBR) draw.

(d) Revenue adjustments represent fund transfers, a withholding adjustment to compensate for federal withholding changes and a judicial collections program.

(e) Revenue adjustments include diversions to the State Education fund and the Older Coloradoan's Program, as well as transfers to the General Fund to mitigate revenue declines. Ending balance is projected to be $13.9 million above the statutory reserve requirement. Current law requires monies in excess of the statutory reserve to be credited to the Highway User's Tax Fund and the Capital Construction Fund.

(f) In fiscal 2005, the state projects ending the year with an ending balance of $86.7 million. This amount is included in the budget stabilization fund.

(g) The Federal Flexible Assistance grants provide an additional $278.4 million for expenditure.

(h) Revenue adjustments include $21.5 million in transfers to other funds. The largest of these transfers is $21million to the Budget Stabilization Fund.

(i) Revenue adjustments include $2,385 million on transfers into general funds. Expenditure adjustments include $495 million to repay pension obligation bond debt service, and transfers-out of $2,103 million.

(j) Revenue adjustments reflect one-time transfers from dedicated funds and the Rainy Day Fund.

(k) Revenue adjustments reflect a reduction of $63.4 million to restore the phase-out of the sales tax on residential utilities which was eliminated inadvertently through an unrelated item veto during the 2003 legislative session.

(l) Kentucky is operating in fiscal year 2004-2005 without an enacted executive branch appropriations bill. The Governor has issued an Executive Order to establish a quarterly Public Services Continuation Plan, and the Executive branch is operating under it the General Assembly enacted appropriations bills for the judicial and legislative branches. Revenue includes $108.8 million in Tobacco Settlement funds. Revenue adjustments include $85.1 million that represents appropriation balances carried over from the prior fiscal year, and $67.6 million from fund transfers into the General Fund. expenditure adjustments represent appropriation balances forwarded to the next fiscal year.

(m) Revenue adjustments include $17.3 million in non-recurring revenue from the fiscal 2003 surplus, the use of $2.7 million of fund balances and 421.7 million carried-forward.

(n) Revenue adjustments reflect $54 million in legislative and statutorily authorized transfers, which include repayment of a $-10 million Retiree Health Insurance Fund General Fund loan and a $39.6 million transfer from the Retiree Health Insurance Fund to the General fund by converting back to pay-as-you-go basis. $11.4 million from the Highway fund unallocated surplus, $3 million transferred from the Highway Fund. $3.5 million from lapsed funds, $3.3 million from hospital rate adjustments and various adjustments netting to $3.2 million.

(o) Revenue adjustments reflect transfers from other funds, including $91 million from the Rainy Day Fund. Expenditures include appropriations to the Rainy Day Fund of $103.7 million.

(p) The fiscal 2005 revenue figure is based on a tax estimate agreed upon by the executive office for Administration and Finance and the Legislature on January 14, 2004. this figure has not been adjusted to reflect actual tax collections exceeding benchmarks set in January.

(q) Fiscal 2005 revenue adjustments include anticipated federal and state law changes $-560.9 million); driver's license fees and fines ($98.1 million); casino tax increase ($42.9 million); increased tax audits (485.1 million); escheats law change ($15 million); deposits from state restricted funds ($7 million); suspension of county revenue sharing payments ($182.3 million); a revenue sharing freeze ($339.4 million); other revenue adjustments ($-11.7 million); a freeze on interfund borrowing rates ($20 million); and several pending actions including the sale of properties ($83.4 million); Repeal of the pharmaceutical tax credit ($10 million); tax law changes ($15 million); and deposits of restricted revenue sources to the general fund ($15.5 million).

(r) The ending balance includes budget reserve of $631.4 million.

(s) Revenues are net of refunds. Estimated refunds for Fiscal 2005 totaled $1,219.6 million. Revenues include $214.6 million transferred to the General Revenue Fund.

(t) Total appropriated expenditures include 46 million of anticipated supplemental appropriations.

(u) Revenue adjustments are transfers between the General Fund and other funds. Per Nebraska law, this includes a transfer to the Cash Reserve Fund (Rainy Day Fund) of the amount the prior year's net general Fund receipts exceeded the official forecast. expenditure adjustments are carryover appropriations from the prior fiscal year and a small amount reserved for supplemental/deficit appropriations.

(v) The fiscal 2004 ending balance and fiscal 2005 beginning balance differ due to rounding. Fiscal 2005 figures reflect legislatively approved amounts.

(w) The ending balance includes $794 million in the tax stabilization reserve fund (rainy day fund) and $312 million in the Community Projects Fund and $21 million in reserve funds for litigation risks.

(x) Federal reimbursements for Medicaid and other human services programs are included in the general revenue fund. Beginning balances are undesignated fund balances. The actual cash balances would be higher by the amount reserved for encumbrances and designated transfers from the general revenue fund. Expenditures for fiscal 2005 do not include encumbrances outstanding at the end of the year. Ohio reports expenditures based on disbursements for the general revenue fund. Expenditure adjustments reflect projected miscellaneous transfers-out of $17.6 million. These transfers-out are adjusted for an anticipated net change in encumbrances from fiscal 2004 levels of $-50.6 million. Ohio budgets on a biennial basis. The fiscal year 2005 budget was enacted in July 2003. The order reductions for 2005.

(y) Revenue adjustments reflect an increase to the General Revenue Fund cash-flow reserve of $12 million.

(z) Expenditure adjustments reflect a transfer of 25 percent of the ending balance to the budget stabilization (rainy day) fund.

(aa) Revenue adjustments reflect a contribution to budget stabilization fund.

(bb) Expenditure adjustments reflect agencies' carryforward dollars.

(cc) Revenue adjustments reflect $7.6 million from one-time receipts and $19.4 million transferred from the Property Tax Reduction Fund to cover the anticipated budget shortfall.

(dd) Tennessee's ending balance is committed to fund one-time appropriations in the next fiscal year. It is not an uncommitted balance. Revenue adjustments reflect a $-58.4 million transfer to the rainy day fund. Expenditure adjustments reflect a $21.6 million transfer to the Transportation Equity Fund, a $58.6 million transfer to the capital outlay projects fund, and $16.2 million for dedicated appropriations.

(ee) Revenue information is from the Comptroller's December 2003 certification revenue estimate, updated to reflect the Comptroller's April 2004 revised revenue estimate. Revenue adjustments reflect dedicated account balances. Total expenditures are 2005 appropriatedas reported by the Legislative Budget Board. Total expenditures include $258 million in appropriations from the Rainy Day Fund. Expenditure adjustments include $104 million held in reserve for transfer to the Rainy day Fund and other adjustments to reconcile the actual ending balance reported by the Comptroller.

(ff) Revenue adjustments include a $107.2 million reserve from the prior fiscal year, $7 million of increased accounts receivable collections, and $5.1 million of transfers from various restricted accounts. The beginning balance does not match the fiscal 2004 ending balance due to a surplus in fiscal 2004.

(gg) Revenue adjustments reflect a $12.5 million in direct applications and transfers in. $7.9 million increase in property transfer tax revenue estimate, and $15.6 million from general fund surplus reserve. Expenditure adjustments include $1.1 million to the budget stabilization reserve and $28.6 million to the general fund surplus reserve.

(hh) Revenue adjustments represent transfers from other accounts to the General Fund.

(ii) The beginning balance reflects $203.3 million of reappropriations, $21.2 million of surplus appropriations, and a $66 million unappropriated surplus balance. Expenditures reflect $3,071.8 million of regular appropriations, $203.3 million of reappropriations, $21.2 million of surplus appropriations, and $23.8 million of 31-day (prior year) expenditures. Expenditures adjustments reflect a $31.7 million transfer to the rainy day fund.

(jj) Although the fiscal 2004 balance increase was substantial, it was less than anticipated by final legislative action. Consequently this minor shortfall in fiscal 2004 lowers the expected fiscal 2005 ending balance below a required statutory balance for fiscal 2005 of $40 million. Because the projected fiscal 2005 ending balance remains positive, however, it is not deemed a budget gap requiring correction prior to the next biennial budget.

(kk) The state budgets on a biennial basis. To complete the survey using annual figures, certain assumptions ans estimates were required. Caution is advised when making projections using this information.

Table 7.10
ALLOWABLE STATE INVESTMENTS

State	CDs within state	CDs nationally	Other time deposits	Bankers' acceptances	Commercial paper	Corporate notes/bonds	Corporate stocks (foreign)	Corporate stocks (domestic)	Derivatives	Equities	Mortgage backed securities	Mutuals	State/local government obligations	U.S. Treasury obligations	U.S. agency obligations	Eurodollars—CDs or TDs	Real Estate	Repurchase agreements	Venture capital	Other
Alabama																		★		
Alaska	(a)	★	★	★	★	★					★	★	★	★	★					
Arizona	★		★	★	★	★	★	★		★	★	★	★	★	★			★		
Arkansas	★	★	★	★	★	★					★		★	★	★			★		
California	★		★	★	★	★	★	★		★	★	★	★	★	★			★		
Colorado	★			★	★	★							★	★	★			★		(b)
Connecticut																★				
Delaware	★			★	★	★			★		★	★	★	★	★			★		(c)
Florida	★			★	★	★					★		★	★	★			★		
Georgia	★			★	★						★		★	★	★			★		
Hawaii	★	★	★		★	★						★		★	★			★		(d)
Idaho	★												★					★		(e)
Illinois	★	★		★	★	★							★	★	★			★		(f)
Indiana	★												★	★	★			★		(f)
Iowa	★											★		★	★			★		
Kansas	★	★		★	★	★					★		★	★	★			★		
Kentucky	★		★	★	★	★					★		★	★	★			★		
Louisiana	★	★		★	★	★		★		★	★	★	★	★	★			★		(g)
Maine	★	★	★	★	★							★	★	★	★			★		
Maryland	★		★	★	★	★					★	★	★	★	★			★		
Massachusetts	★	★(h)	★	★	★			★		★		★	★	★	★			★		
Michigan	★	★	★	★	★	★	★	★	★	★	★		★	★	★	★		★		(i)
Minnesota				★	★	★					★		★	★	★			★		(j)
Mississippi	★			★		★								★	★			★		
Missouri	★			★	★								★	★	★			★		
Montana	★			★	★	★							★	★	★			★		
Nebraska	★	★	★	★	★	★						★		★	★		★	★		
Nevada	★	★		★	★	★		★	★		★		★	★	★	★		★		(k)
New Hampshire	★													★	★			★		(l)
New Jersey	★	★	★	★	★	★	★	★		★	★	★	★	★	★			★		
New Mexico	★			★	★	★	★	★		★	★		★	★	★			★		(m)
New York	★			★	★	★				★	★			★	★			★		
North Carolina	★	★		★	★	★	★	★		★			★	★	★			★		
North Dakota	★																			
Ohio	★			★	★	★					★	★	★	★	★			★		

See footnotes at end of table.

ALLOWABLE STATE INVESTMENTS—Continued

State	CDs within state	CDs nationally	Other time deposits	Bankers' acceptances	Commercial paper	Corporate notes/bonds	Corporate stocks (foreign)	Corporate stocks (domestic)	Derivatives	Equities	Mortgage backed securities	Mutuals	State/local government obligations	U.S. Treasury obligations	U.S. agency obligations	Eurodollars-CDs or TDs	Real Estate	Repurchase agreements	Venture capital	Other
Oklahoma	★	★	★	★	★	…	…	…	(n)	…	…	(o)	★	★	★	…	…	★	…	…
Oregon	★	…	…	★	★	★	…	…	…	…	★	…	★	★	★	…	…	★	…	(p)
Pennsylvania	★	★	★	★	★	…	…	…	…	…	★	…	…	★	★	…	…	★	…	…
Rhode Island	★	★	…	…	★	★	…	…	…	…	…	…	…	★	★	…	…	★	…	…
South Carolina	★	…	…	…	★	★	★	★	…	★	…	★	★	★	★	…	★	★	★	…
South Dakota	★	★	★	★	★	★	…	★	…	★	★	★	★	★	★	…	…	★	…	…
Tennessee	★	…	…	★	★	★	…	…	…	(o)	★	★	★	★	★	…	★	★	…	…
Texas	…	★	★	★	★	★	(q)	(q)	★	…	…	★	★	★	★	…	…	★	…	(r)
Utah	★	…	…	★	★	…	…	…	…	…	…	…	★	★	★	…	…	★	…	…
Vermont	…	…	…	★	★	★	…	…	…	…	…	★	★	★	★	★	★	★	…	…
Virginia	★	★	★	★	★	★	★	★	…	★	★	…	★	★	★	…	★	★	…	…
Washington	★	★	★	★	★	…	★	★	…	★	★	★	★	★	★	…	★	★	…	…
West Virginia	…	★	★	★	★	★	★	★	…	★	★	★	★	★	★	…	…	★	★	(s)
Wisconsin	…	…	…	…	★	★	…	…	…	…	…	…	★	★	★	…	…	★	…	…
Wyoming	★	★	★	★	★	★	…	★	★	…	…	★	★	★	★	…	…	★	…	…

Source: National Association of State Treasurers, January 2005.

Key:
★—Yes
…—No

(a) Nothing is restricted by Statute. Commission is subject to prudent investor rule. The Commissioner evaluated each fund's time horizon and risk.
(b) Asset back securities.
(c) Convertible corporate bonds.
(d) Student loans.
(e) Money market funds, SBAs.
(f) Money market mutual funds.
(g) Collateralized mortgage obligations, other mortgages, asset backed.

(h) Authorized to do business in Massachusetts.
(i) Massachusetts Municipal Depository Trust per statute.
(j) Emergency loans to municipalities within the state.
(k) Collateralized mortgage obligations.
(l) Does not include retirement mutual funds.
(m) All fixed income.
(n) Derivatives are permitted if they otherwise meet statutory definition of permissible investment.
(o) Money market mutual funds only.
(p) Certain trust funds can invest in equities.
(q) Trust funds only.
(r) Collateralized CDs.
(s) Private equity, emerging market securities, real estate mortgages and leverage buyout funds.

Table 7.11
CASH MANAGEMENT PROGRAMS AND SERVICES

| State | Reviews of cash management programs | | | | Agency preparing cash management services | | | | | |
| | Banking relations | | Investment practices | | | | | | | |
	Reviewing agency	Frequency of review	Reviewing agency	Frequency of review	Lock boxes	Wire transfers	Zero balance accounts	Information services	Account reconciliation systems	Automated clearinghouse
Alabama	…	…	SE	Annually	B	B	B	I	I	B
Alaska	SE	Annually	SE	N.A.	B	I	B	I	I	B
Arizona	SE	Quarterly	SE	Quarterly	B	I,B	B	I	I	I,B
Arkansas	SE	Quarterly	SE	Quarterly	NU	B	B	I,B	I,B	B
California	SE	Annually	SE	Monthly	B	I,B	I,B	I	I,B	B
Colorado	SE	Ongoing	OF	Ongoing	B	B	B	B	B	B
Connecticut	SE	Quarterly	OF	Weekly	B	I,B	B	I,B	I,B	I,B
Delaware	(a)	5–7 years	(a)	Annually	B	I,B	B	I,B	I	I,B
Florida	SE	(b)	SE (c)	Annually	I,B	NU	B	NU	B	B
Georgia	SE	Annually	SE	Quarterly	B	I	NU	NU	NU	NU
Hawaii	SE	(b)	SE	(d)	B	I	B	NU	I	B
Idaho	SE	Quarterly	SE	Daily	B	I,B	B	I,B	I	B
Illinois	SE	(d)	SE	Quarterly	B	I,B	B	I,B	NU	I,B
Indiana	SE	Annually	SE	Annually	B	I,B	I,B	NU	I	I,B
Iowa	SE	4 years	SE	Annually	B	I	B	I	I	I
Kansas	SE	Ongoing	N.A.	N.A.	B	I	I	NU	I	I,B
Kentucky	SE	2 years	SE	Quarterly, Annually (e)	NU	B (f)	B	I	I	B
Louisiana	SE	Annually	SE, OF	Annually	B	B	B	B	B	B
Maine	SE	3 years	SE, OF	Semi-Annually	NU	I,B	B	I,B	I,B	B
Maryland	SE	Annually	SE	Annually	B	I	B	I,B	I,B	I,B
Massachusetts	SE	Quarterly	SE	Quarterly	B	B	B	B	B	I,B
Michigan	SE	(d)	SE	(d)	B	I,B	B	NU	I,B	B
Minnesota	SE	3 years	SE, OF	…	B	I	I	I	I	I
Mississippi	…	…	…	…	B	NU	NU	NU	NU	B
Missouri	SE	Quarterly	SE	Monthly	I,B	I,B	B	I,B	I,B	I,B
Montana	SE	Monthly	SE	Monthly, Annually	NU	I,B	NU	I	NU	I,B
Nebraska	SE	Ongoing	SE	Ongoing	B	B	I,B	I,B	I	B
Nevada	SE	Ongoing	SE	Quarterly	B	I	B	I,B	I,B	B
New Hampshire	SE	Quarterly	SE	Quarterly	B	I	I	I	I	B
New Jersey	SE	Quarterly	OF	Annually	B	I,B	B	I	I,B	I
New Mexico	SE	(d)	SE, OF	Monthly	B	I,B	B	I	I,B	B
New York	SE	…	SE	…	B	I	I	I	I,B	B
North Carolina	…	…	…	…	B	I	B	NU	NU	NU
North Dakota	SE	…	SE	…	NU	B	NU	NU	NU	B
Ohio	SE	Quarterly	SE	Quarterly	I,B	I,B	NU	NU	NU	NU

See footnotes at end of table.

CASH MANAGEMENT PROGRAMS AND SERVICES — Continued

| | Reviews of cash management programs | | | | Agency preparing cash management services | | | | | |
| | Banking relations | | Investment practices | | | | | | | |
State	Reviewing agency	Frequency of review	Reviewing agency	Frequency of review	Lock boxes	Wire transfers	Zero balance accounts	Information services	Account reconciliation systems	Automated clearinghouse
Oklahoma	SE	Ongoing	SE	Ongoing	B	NU	B	I	NU	I,B
Oregon	SE	Ongoing	SE, OF	Ongoing	I,B	I	I,B	I	I,B	I
Pennsylvania	SE	As needed	SE, OF	Daily, Monthly	B	B	B	NU	I,B	B
Rhode Island	SE	Quarterly	SE	Quarterly	B	I,B	I,B	I,B	I,B	I,B
South Carolina	SE	Annually	SE	Annually	B	I,B	I	NU	I	B
South Dakota	SE	Annually	SE	Annually	I	B	B	NU	I	B
Tennessee	SE	Annually	SE	Annually	I	I,B	B	I	I	B
Texas	SE	Annually	SE	Annually	I,B	I	B	I	I	I,B
Utah	SE	Annually	SE	Quarterly	B	B	B	I	NU	I
Vermont	SE	2 years	SE	Ongoing	B	B	B	I,B	I	I,B
Virginia	SE	Annually	OF	Annually	B	I	B	B	I,B	I,B
Washington	SE	Semi-Annually	SE	Annually	B	B	B	I	I	I,B
West Virginia	SE	Quarterly	N.A.	N.A.	I	NU	NU	I	I,B	B
Wisconsin	SE	6 years	SE	N.A.	B	B	B	I,B	I,B	I
Wyoming	SE	Daily	SE, OF	Quarterly	NU	I,B	I	NU	I	I

Source: National Association of State Treasurers, January 2005.

Key:
SE—State employee
N.A.—Not applicable
OF—Outside firm
B—Performed by bank
I—Within treasurer's office

NU—Not utilized
(a) Cash Management Policy Board reviews and implements.
(b) Outside firm utilized occasionally.
(c) Reviewed when contract expires.
(d) No set period for review.
(e) Quarterly review by Investment Commission, annual review by State Auditor.
(f) Initiated in-house by electronic link to bank.

Table 7.12
DEMAND DEPOSITS

State	Method for selecting depository						Treasurer's approval	Selection of depository made by	Compensation of demand depositories	Collateral above federal level	Percentage requiring collateral
	Competitive bid	Application	Negotiation	Depositor's convenience	Compensating balances	Agency's convenience					
Alabama						★		Individual agencies	CMB	Yes	100
Alaska	★			★	★	★		Cash manager	CMB	Yes	105
Arizona	★		★	★	★	★	★	Treasurer	CMB	Yes	102
Arkansas			★	★	★		★	Treasurer	CMB, SF	Yes	105
California							★	Treasurer	CMB	Yes	110
Colorado	★			★		★	★	Treasurer, Controller	CMB, SF, MB	Yes	102
Connecticut	★		★	★		★	★	Treasurer	CMB, SF, MB	Yes	(a)
Delaware	★		★	★				Treasurer, Board	CMB, SF	No (b)	102 (c)
Florida	★							Treasurer	SF	Yes	100
Georgia		★				★	★	Individual agencies	SF	Yes	::
Hawaii	★			★			★	Treasurer	SF	Yes	100
Idaho		★				★	★	Treasurer	CMB, SF	No	::
Illinois	★		★				★	Treasurer	SF	Yes	100
Indiana							★	Treasurer	CMB	No	0
Iowa	★				★	★		Treasurer	CMB, SF	No	::
Kansas	★	★	★			★		Treasurer, Board	SF	Yes	100
Kentucky	★	★				★	★	(d)	CMB, SF (e)	Yes	100
Louisiana		★						Treasurer	SF	Yes	100
Maine				★		★	★★	Treasurer	CMB	Yes	10 (f)
Maryland	★	★		★		★	★★	Treasurer	(g)	Yes	100 (h)
Massachusetts	★	★	★			★	★★	Treasurer	CMB, SF	Yes	(i)
Michigan	★					★★	★★	Treasurer	CMB	Yes	25
Minnesota		★				★		Comm. of Finance	CMB, SF	Yes	110
Mississippi	★					★	★★	Treasurer, Finance Dept.	CMB, SF	Yes	105
Missouri	★	★		★	★	★	★★	Board (j)	CMB	Yes	100
Montana	★	★				★		Treasurer	SF	Yes	50
Nebraska	★	★			★	★★	★★	Treasurer	CMB	Yes	110
Nevada						★★	★★	Treasurer, Board	CMB, SF	No	102
New Hampshire					★	★	★		(k)	Yes	::
New Jersey	★			★		★	★	Treasurer	CMB, SF	Yes	100
New Mexico	★					★★	★★	Treasurer	SF	Yes	100
New York	★			★		★	★★	Treasurer (l)	SF	Yes	102
North Carolina							★★	Treasurer	(m)	Yes	100
North Dakota	(k)	(k)	(k)	(k)	(k)	(k)	(k)	State Constitution	SF	No	::
Ohio			★				★	Treasurer, Board (n)	CMB, SF	::	100

See footnotes at end of table.

DEMAND DEPOSITS—Continued

State	Method for selecting depository							Selection of depository made by	Compensation of demand depositories	Collateral above federal level	Percentage requiring collateral
	Competitive bid	Application	Negotiation	Depositor's convenience	Compensating balances	Agency's convenience	Treasurer's approval				
Oklahoma	...	...	...	★	...	...	★	Treasurer	CMB, SF	Yes	110
Oregon	...	...	...	...	...	...	★	Treasurer	CMB, SF	Yes	25
Pennsylvania	...	★	★	...	...	...	...	Board (n)	CMB	Yes	100
Rhode Island	...	...	★	★	...	★	★	Treasurer	SF	Yes	100
South Carolina	...	...	...	★	★	★	★	Treasurer	CMB	Yes	100 (o)
South Dakota	★	...	...	...	...	...	★	Treasurer	CMB, SF, MB	Yes	100
Tennessee	...	★	...	...	...	...	★	Treasurer	SF	Yes	105
Texas	★	★	...	...	...	★	★	Treasurer	CMB, SF	No	105
Utah	★	...	...	★	...	...	★	Treasurer	SF	Yes	...
Vermont	★	...	...	★	...	★	★	(p)	SF, MB	Yes	100
Virginia	...	...	...	★	...	★	★	(q)	CMB, SF	Yes	50-100 (r)
Washington	★	...	...	★	...	★	★	Treasurer	CMB, SF	Yes	10
West Virginia	...	...	...	...	...	★	★	Treasurer	CMB	Yes	65
Wisconsin	★	...	...	★	...	...	...	Treasurer, Board	CMB	No	N.A.
Wyoming	★	...	...	...	...	...	...	Treasurer	CMB, SF	Yes	102

Source: National Association of State Treasurers, January 2005.

Key:
★—Method utilized.
...—Method not utilized.
N.A.—Not available.
CMB—Compensating balances.
SF—Service fee.
MB—Minimum balance.
(a) Varies based upon bank's risk based capitol ratios.
(b) No requirements if a bank meets credit criteria.
(c) If a bank does not meet credit criteria.
(d) Treasurer, Finance Secretary and a selection committee are responsible for the selection of institutions.
(e) CMB for Imprest and receipt accounts, SF for primary depository.
(f) Demand deposits that exceed 25 percent of a bank's retained earnings must be collateralized.

(g) Combination of fees, CMB.
(h) Any public funds in excess of FDIC must be collateralized.
(i) No deposits meet collateral requirements. A contractual $100 million collateral exists with the central depository bank but is not required by law.
(j) Must be approved by State Treasurer, State Auditor, Governor.
(k) Determined by Treasurer.
(l) RFP issued, Treasury employee committee reviews.
(m) Transaction fee.
(n) Treasurer is chair of Board.
(o) 100 percent collateralization over $300,000.
(p) State Treasurer, State Auditor, & Governor are responsible.
(q) Cash and banking services manager.
(r) Banks are required to secure all deposits in excess of FDIC insurance by 50 percent. Savings and Loans required to secure all deposits by 100 percent.

The Population 65 Years and Older: Aging in America
By Karen Humes

The growth of the 65-and-older population in the United States impacts many facets of our society, challenging policy-makers to meet the needs of aging Americans. There are many basic characteristics of the 65-and-older population that are important components for understanding how to best meet their needs. This article describes the growth of this segment of the U.S. population, as well as discusses its geographic distribution and selected characteristics.

The growth of the older population, defined here as those 65 and older, greatly influences many aspects of our society, challenging national and state policy-makers, among others, to meet the needs of aging Americans.[1] The demographic, social, health and economic characteristics of the 65-and-older population are important components for understanding how to best meet their needs. This article will describe the past and projected growth of this segment of the U.S. population, as well as discuss its geographic distribution and selected characteristics.

Growth of the Older Population in the United States

Throughout the 20th century, the older population has increased dramatically (Figure A). Decennial census data show that the older population grew tenfold between 1900 and 2000, increasing from 3.1 million to 35 million, respectively. To put this increase in perspective, the U.S. population under age 65 grew threefold between 1900 and 2000 (rising from 76 million to 281.4 million). The older population also increased its proportion of the total U.S. population, growing from 4.1 percent in 1900 to 12.4 percent in 2000. The oldest-old population, those 85 and older, grew over thirty fold, from 122,000 in 1900 (representing 0.2 percent of the total U.S. population) to 4.2 million in 2000 (representing 1.5 percent of the total U.S. population).

The increase in the proportion of older people reflects sustained low fertility levels and relatively larger declines in mortality at older ages, especially in the latter third of the 20th century.[2] The U.S. began the 20th century experiencing relatively high levels of fertility and mortality, which resulted in a young population with a median age of 22.9 years in 1900.[3] In general, as fertility and mortality rates declined, the U.S. population aged, evident in a median age of 35.3 years in 2000.

Beyond 2000, the older population is projected to increase dramatically, particularly between 2010 and 2030. By 2030, the older population is expected to be twice as large as it was in 2000, growing from 35 million to 71.5 million, while the total U.S. population growth is projected to be slower (281.4 million in 2000 to 363.8 million in 2030). In 2030, the older population is projected to account for 19.6 percent (about 1 in 5) of the population.

The dramatic growth of the older population between 2010 and 2030 represents the effect of the "baby boom" generation. The baby boomers are the post-World War II generation born from 1946 to 1964, which will begin turning age 65 in 2011, creating a sharp rise in the older population. The magnitude of the baby boomers is reflected in the fact that 70 percent more people were born from 1946 to 1964 than during the preceding two decades.[4]

After 2030, the growth of the older population is expected to slow. At that time, the proportion of older people is projected to become fairly stable, even though the absolute number of older people is projected to continue to grow. The oldest-old population, however, is projected to increase rapidly after 2030, when the baby boomers start to move into this age group.[5]

Geographic Distribution of the Older Population in the United States

Figure B shows the proportion of older people in each state's population, as well as several prevalent patterns in 2003.[6] High proportions of older people are located in a band of states stretching from Montana and North Dakota southward to Oklahoma and Arkansas. Another band of high proportions of older people stretches from Maine and Rhode Island (except New Hampshire) southward to Tennessee and Alabama. Additionally, many of the states in the West have lower proportions of older people.[7] Age patterns are affected by a state's fertility and mortality levels, as well as by the migration of younger and older people to and from the state.[8]

Overall, 32 states had a proportion of older people

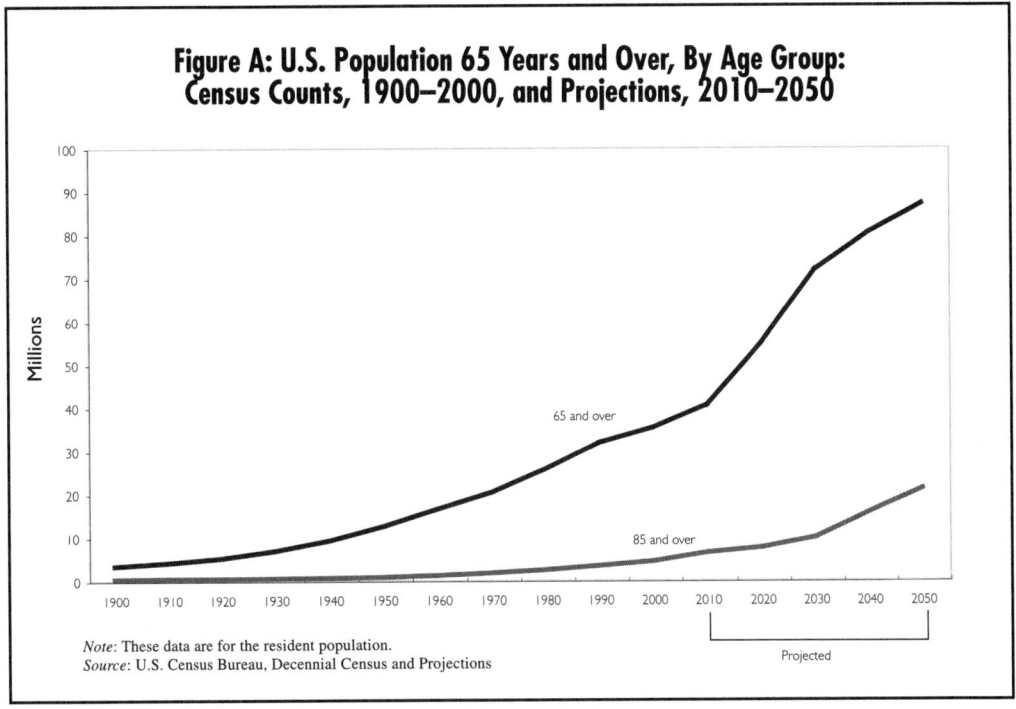

Figure A: U.S. Population 65 Years and Over, By Age Group: Census Counts, 1900–2000, and Projections, 2010–2050

Note: These data are for the resident population.
Source: U.S. Census Bureau, Decennial Census and Projections

that equaled or exceeded the national proportion of 12 percent. Florida had the highest proportion of older people (16.7 percent), followed by West Virginia and Pennsylvania (14.9 percent and 14.8 percent, respectively). Alaska had the lowest proportion of older people (6.3 percent).

Numerically, California had the largest older population (3.6 million). Florida and New York ranked second and third with 2.8 million and 2.3 million, respectively. Alaska had the smallest older population (39,600).

Demographic Composition

The sex ratio (the number of males per 100 females) is a basic indicator of sex composition. For the total U.S. population, there were 95.8 males for every 100 females in 2003. For the older population, there were 73.7 men for every 100 women. The lower sex ratio for the older population is generally driven by the fact that average life expectancy is greater for females than for males.

At the state level, 28 states had older-population sex ratios that equaled or exceeded the national sex ratio of 73.7. Of the 10 states with the highest older-population sex ratios in 2003, eight are in the West (Alaska, 97.8; Nevada, 87.2; Idaho, 84.1; Wyoming,

82.8; Montana, 82.6; Arizona, 82.5; Utah, 82.3; and New Mexico, 80.9), one is in the South (Florida, 79.1), and one is in the Northeast (New Hampshire, 78.8). The District of Columbia had the lowest older-population sex ratio (60.7).[9] Policy-makers in government and private-sector organizations face the challenge of planning for the needs of a fast-growing, older population where women outnumber men.

In 2003, the proportion of the older population that was minority was lower than the total U.S. proportion minority (18.0 percent compared with 32.2 percent).[10] Sixteen states had proportions of older people that were minority that equaled or exceeded the national proportion of 18 percent. Of the 10 states with the highest proportions minority among the older population, most are in the West (Hawaii, 78.1 percent; New Mexico, 39 percent; California, 33.1 percent; and Alaska, 27.5 percent) or South (the District of Columbia, 74.3 percent; Texas, 31.6 percent; Mississippi, 26.6 percent; Louisiana, 26.4 percent; and Maryland, 24.5 percent), and one is in the Northeast (New York, 23.8 percent). Maine had the lowest proportion minority among its older population (1.2 percent). As the older population grows larger in the coming decades, it is projected that the proportion minority will increase, particularly the proportion

Hispanic. Greater flexibility may be required in future programs and services to meet the needs of a more diverse older population.[11]

Social Characteristics

In 2003, being widowed was much more common among the older population than among the population 15 and older (31.1 percent compared with 6.2 percent). This was particularly true for older women, as they were three times as likely as older men to be widowed.[12] In 25 states, the proportions of older people who were widowed equaled or exceeded the national proportion of 31.1 percent. Rhode Island had the highest proportion (36.4 percent). The states ranking second through 10th are located in the South (Mississippi, 35.8 percent; Louisiana, 34.2 percent; Alabama, 34.1 percent; Kentucky and the District of Columbia, each with 33.6 percent; North Carolina, 33.5 percent; and Arkansas, 33.2 percent) and in the Northeast (Pennsylvania, 35 percent, and Massachusetts, 33.2 percent). Alaska had the lowest proportion of older people who were widowed (24.9 percent).

The older population was about three times as likely as the total U.S. population to live alone (29.8 percent compared with 10.3 percent) in 2003. Thirty-three states had proportions of older people who lived alone that equaled or exceeded the national proportion of 29.8 percent. All the U.S. regions were represented among the 10 states with the highest proportions of older people who lived alone (the District of Columbia, 42.9 percent; Nebraska, 35.3 percent; Rhode Island 34.7 percent; North Dakota, 34.6 percent; Montana, 33.1 percent; South Dakota and Massachusetts, each with 33 percent; Maine, 32.9 percent; Pennsylvania 32.8 percent; and Oklahoma, 32.7 percent). Among the states, Hawaii had the lowest proportion of older people who lived alone (21.9 percent). Being widowed and/or living alone are important indicators of the well-being of the older population because they are typically linked to income, health status and the availability of caregivers. For example, older people who lived alone were more likely than older people who lived with their spouses to be in poverty.[13] Thus, in the present and the future, these indicators can provide additional information for efforts to assess potential physical and social needs of the older population.

In 2003, a lower proportion of the older population (70.7 percent) than of the population 25 and older (83.6 percent) were high school graduates or had more education. In 29 states, the proportions of older people with a high school diploma or more educa-

tion equaled or exceeded the national proportion of 70.7 percent. Eight of the 10 states with the highest proportions of older people with a high school diploma or more education are located in the West (Utah, 84 percent; Wyoming, 82 percent; Washington, 82 percent; Montana, 80.5 percent; Colorado, 80.3 percent; Idaho, 79.9 percent; Oregon, 78.9 percent; and Nevada, 78.7 percent), and two are in the Midwest (Nebraska, 80.3 percent, and Iowa, 78.5 percent). The lowest proportion of older people with a high school diploma or more education was in Kentucky (55.8 percent). Educational attainment is another important indicator of the well-being of the older population. In general, higher levels of education are associated with higher incomes, higher standards of living, and above-average health.[14] Thus, educational attainment is a factor that policy-makers can monitor when planning specialized services and programs for the growing older population.

Disability

In 2003, the proportion of the older population reporting a disability (one or more) was 39.9 percent, compared with 14.3 percent of the population 5 and older.[15] Twenty-three states had proportions of older people who reported a disability that equaled or exceeded the national proportion of 39.9 percent. Eight of the 10 states with the highest proportions of older people who reported a disability are located in the South (Mississippi, 54.2 percent; Arkansas, 50.5 percent; West Virginia, 49.9 percent; Kentucky, 47.7 percent; Alabama, 47 percent; Louisiana, 46.7 percent; Georgia, 45.6 percent; and Tennessee, 44.6 percent), and two are in the West (New Mexico, 45.8 percent, and Alaska, 45.3 percent). Hawaii had the lowest proportion of older people who reported a disability (34.4 percent).

Income and Poverty

In 2003, the median income for all households was $43,564.[16] Households with an older householder had a much lower median income ($26,736), in part reflecting the fact that the vast majority of the older population was retired from full-time work. Nineteen states had median incomes for households with an older householder that equaled or exceeded the national level of $26,736. The 10 states with the highest median incomes for households with an older householder represent all U.S. regions except the Midwest (Hawaii, $39,378; Alaska, $37,540; Maryland, $33,203; Delaware, $32,850; Utah, $32,754; Connecticut, $32,306; New Jersey, $31,931; Washington, $31,882; Virginia, $31,863; and California,

Figure B: Percent of State Population 65 Years and Over: 2003

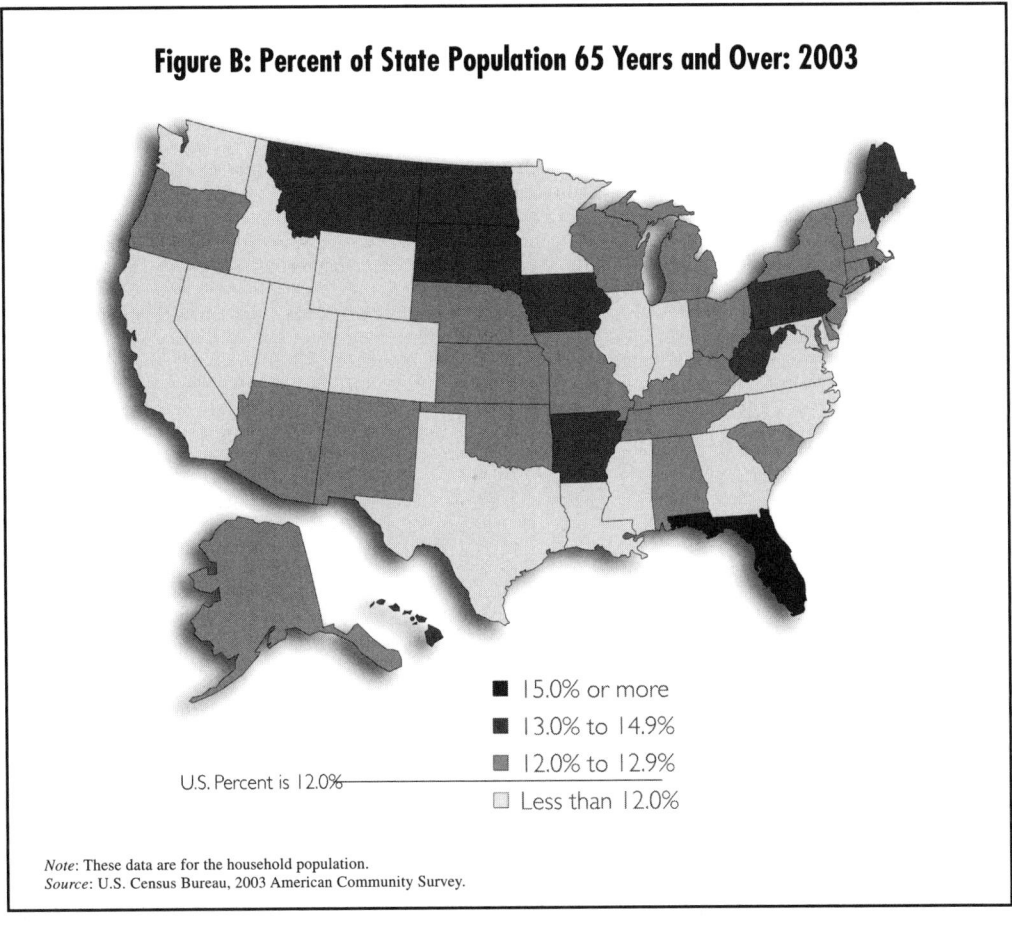

■ 15.0% or more

■ 13.0% to 14.9%

■ 12.0% to 12.9%

☐ Less than 12.0%

U.S. Percent is 12.0%

Note: These data are for the household population.
Source: U.S. Census Bureau, 2003 American Community Survey.

$31,705). Among the states, Mississippi had the lowest median income for households with an older householder ($20,973).

The older population was less likely than the total U.S. population to be in poverty in 2003 (9.8 percent compared with 12.7 percent). Nineteen states had proportions of older people in poverty that equaled or exceeded the national proportion of 9.8 percent. Nine of the 10 states with the highest proportions of older people in poverty are located in the South (Mississippi, 16.4 percent; Louisiana, 14.8 percent; the District of Columbia, 14.4 percent; Kentucky, 14.2 percent; Alabama, 13.7 percent; Georgia, 13.3 percent; Texas, 13 percent; and Arkansas and North Carolina, each with 12.9 percent) and one is in the West (New Mexico, 13.1 percent). The lowest proportion of older people in poverty was in Alaska (4.8 percent). The proportion of older people in poverty and the median income of households with an older householder

provide some insight into the economic situation of older Americans. Policy-makers can use these indicators when assessing the segments of the older population at the greatest risk of having inadequate basic needs such as food and housing.

Conclusion

The size of the older population will increase dramatically in the coming decades, far faster than the rest of the U.S. population. Policy-makers need current and relevant data to aid them in addressing the needs of this rapidly growing older population. These needs often reflect characteristics of the older population, including being predominantly female, commonly living alone, and typically reporting a disability.

Author's Note

This article is released to inform interested parties of ongoing research and to encourage discussion of work in progress. The views expressed on technical issues are those of the author and not necessarily those of the U.S. Census Bureau.

Notes

[1] In this article, the older population (or older people or older householders) is defined as people 65 years and over. Except where noted, age classification is based on the age of the person in complete years at the time of interview for the American Community Survey in 2003. Both age and date of birth are used in combination to calculate the most accurate age at the time of interview.

[2] Frank Hobbs and Nicole Stoops, U.S. Census Bureau, Census 2000 Special Reports, Series CENSR-4, *Demographic Trends in the 20th Century*, Washington, DC: U.S. Government Printing Office, 2002).

[3] U.S. Census Bureau, decennial census of population, 1900 and 2000. Median age splits the population into halves. One half of the population is older than the median age and the other half is younger.

[4] Frank Hobbs and Bonnie Damon, U.S. Census Bureau, Current Population Reports, Special Studies, P23-190, *65+ in the United States*, (Washington, DC: U.S. Government Printing Office, 1996).

[5] Federal Interagency Forum on Aging-Related Statistics, *Older Americans 2004: Key Indicators of Well-Being*, (Washington, DC: U.S. Government Printing Office, 2004).

[6] The data presented in the remainder of this paper are from the 2003 American Community Survey. The universe for this survey is the household population. Those in group quarters (e.g. nursing facilities, etc.) are not included in the universe.

[7] The West includes Alaska, Arizona, California, Colorado, Hawaii, Idaho, Montana, Nevada, New Mexico, Oregon, Utah, Washington and Wyoming. The South includes Alabama, Arkansas, Delaware, Washington, the District of Columbia, Florida, Georgia, Kentucky, Louisiana, Maryland, Mississippi, North Carolina, Oklahoma, South Carolina, Tennessee, Texas, Virginia and West Virginia. The Midwest includes Illinois, Indiana, Iowa, Kansas, Michigan, Minnesota, Missouri, Nebraska, North Dakota, Ohio, South Dakota and Wisconsin. The Northeast includes Connecticut, Maine, Massachusetts, New Hampshire, New Jersey, New York, Pennsylvania, Rhode Island and Vermont.

[8] For Census 2000 information about the older populations of counties, places, and cities, see Lisa Hetzel and Annetta Smith, 2001, *The 65 Years and Over Population: 2000*, Washington, DC, Census 2000 Brief, C2KBR/01-

10, U.S. Census Bureau. This report is available on the U.S. Census Bureau's Internet site at www.census.gov/prod/2001pubs/C2KBR01-10.pdf.

[9] The District of Columbia is treated as a state equivalent in this paper.

[10] The category "minority" includes people who identified themselves as Black, Asian, American Indian or Alaska Native, Native Hawaiian or Other Pacific Islander, Some other race, Two or more races, or Hispanic (who may be any race). People who identified themselves as non-Hispanic White only are not included in the minority population.

[11] Federal Interagency Forum on Aging-Related Statistics, *Older Americans 2004: Key Indicators of Well-Being*, (Washington, DC: U.S. Government Printing Office, 2004).

[12] Yvonne J. Gist and Lisa I. Hetzel, 2004, *We the People: Aging in the United States*, Washington, DC, Census 2000 Special Report, CENSR-19, U.S. Census Bureau.

[13] Federal Interagency Forum on Aging-Related Statistics, *Older Americans 2004: Key Indicators of Well-Being*, (Washington, DC: U.S. Government Printing Office, 2004).

[14] Federal Interagency Forum on Aging-Related Statistics, *Older Americans 2004: Key Indicators of Well-Being*, (Washington, DC: U.S. Government Printing Office, 2004).

[15] People aged 65 and over were classified as having a disability if they reported one or more of the following disabilities: 1) sensory disability; 2) physical disability; 3) mental disability; 4) self-care disability; 5) go-outside-home disability.

[16] Median household income in the last 12 months (2003 inflation-adjusted dollars) for households with a householder 65 years and over. Poverty status was determined for everyone except those in institutions, military group quarters, and college dormitories, and unrelated individuals under 15 years old. These groups were excluded from the denominator when calculating poverty rates.

About the Author

Karen Humes is a statistician with the U.S. Census Bureau. She received a B.A. in sociology from Eastern Michigan University and an M.A. degree in sociology from Western Michigan University. She began her career at the U.S. Census Bureau in 1998 in the Population Division where she focused on racial and ethnic group statistics. She currently manages the development and analysis of statistics related to age and gender.

TABLE A
DEMOGRAPHIC, SOCIAL, HEALTH AND ECONOMIC CHARACTERISTICS OF THE POPULATION 65 YEARS AND OVER FOR THE UNITED STATES AND STATES: 2003

State of jurisdiction	Population		Sex ratio (a)	Minority (b)		Widowed (c)		H.S. diploma or more (d)		Living alone		With a disability (e)		Median household income (f)	In poverty (g)	
	Number	% of pop.		Number	% of pop.	Number	% of pop.	Number	% of pop.	Number	% of pop.	Number	% of pop.		Number	% of pop.
Total U.S. Population (all ages) ...	282,909,885	100.0	95.8	91,141,238	32.2	13,824,645	6.2	154,181,509	83.6	29,090,016	10.3	37,458,292	14.3	43,564	35,846,289	12.7
65 Years and Over																
United States	33,896,172	12.0	73.7	6,097,304	18.0	10,548,288	31.1	23,979,708	70.7	10,091,191	29.8	13,526,817	39.9	26,736	3,319,167	9.8
Alabama	562,766	12.8	69.5	114,768	20.4	192,152	34.1	339,838	60.4	176,242	31.3	264,686	47.0	21,831	76,889	13.7
Alaska	39,600	6.3	97.8	10,904	27.5	9,862	24.9	30,692	77.5	10,906	27.5	17,934	45.3	37,540	1,896	4.8
Arizona	694,372	12.7	82.5	105,840	15.2	181,368	26.1	543,815	78.3	173,040	24.9	255,679	36.8	30,228	54,653	7.9
Arkansas	359,150	13.6	76.6	45,433	12.7	119,221	33.2	230,295	64.1	110,232	30.7	181,316	50.5	23,754	46,209	12.9
California	3,583,268	10.3	75.2	1,184,456	33.1	1,036,146	28.9	2,626,079	73.3	955,218	26.7	1,440,126	40.2	31,705	272,030	7.6
Colorado	420,597	9.5	78.0	62,126	14.8	111,808	26.6	337,636	80.3	127,909	30.4	160,706	38.2	27,258	40,135	9.5
Connecticut	432,715	12.8	71.3	37,339	8.6	129,219	29.9	321,326	74.3	126,998	29.3	149,327	34.5	32,306	23,241	5.4
Delaware	102,472	12.9	78.2	15,239	14.9	31,036	30.3	76,119	74.3	29,743	29.0	39,005	38.1	32,850	6,358	6.2
Florida	2,782,086	16.7	79.1	529,688	19.0	773,562	27.8	2,123,992	76.3	756,756	27.2	992,613	35.7	27,798	267,859	9.6
Georgia	774,936	9.2	70.6	166,697	21.5	249,566	32.2	474,330	61.2	226,317	29.2	353,424	45.6	24,774	103,269	13.3
Hawaii	163,517	13.4	78.6	127,701	78.1	47,134	28.8	117,686	72.0	35,805	21.9	56,213	34.4	39,378	12,200	7.5
Idaho	147,584	11.1	84.1	5,345	3.6	43,588	29.5	117,974	79.9	39,923	27.1	64,694	43.8	26,377	11,830	8.0
Illinois	1,411,495	11.4	70.8	251,927	17.8	464,877	32.9	998,261	70.7	446,838	31.7	549,012	38.9	27,311	132,054	9.4
Indiana	713,375	11.9	71.6	58,694	8.2	231,792	32.5	501,833	70.3	224,701	31.5	297,100	41.6	25,570	53,577	7.5
Iowa	397,122	14.0	73.7	8,729	2.2	115,164	29.0	311,722	78.5	126,812	31.9	146,734	36.9	25,032	30,376	7.6
Kansas	324,146	12.3	73.4	22,704	7.0	102,197	31.5	253,093	78.1	104,014	32.1	132,384	40.8	25,737	25,511	7.9
Kentucky	483,599	12.1	72.0	31,849	6.6	162,617	33.6	269,647	55.8	153,982	31.8	230,553	47.7	21,243	68,445	14.2
Louisiana	492,713	11.3	69.9	129,875	26.4	168,630	34.2	309,736	62.9	154,896	31.4	230,319	46.7	21,236	72,917	14.8
Maine	176,627	13.9	75.5	2,117	1.2	57,019	32.3	134,547	76.2	58,159	32.9	71,210	40.3	25,056	16,671	9.4
Maryland	594,609	11.1	71.5	145,684	24.5	189,957	31.9	420,506	70.7	166,513	28.0	231,065	38.9	33,203	51,954	8.7
Massachusetts	797,623	12.8	69.5	62,351	7.8	264,904	33.2	589,764	73.9	262,979	33.0	280,149	35.1	26,207	74,632	9.4
Michigan	1,177,082	12.0	73.1	155,342	13.2	366,192	31.1	831,524	70.6	362,541	30.8	474,500	40.3	26,501	98,727	8.4
Minnesota	563,090	11.4	75.6	20,906	3.7	166,119	29.5	427,568	75.9	179,016	31.8	195,997	34.8	27,990	47,302	8.4
Mississippi	328,868	11.8	65.5	87,454	26.6	117,736	35.8	200,786	61.1	105,367	32.0	178,321	54.2	20,973	53,920	16.4
Missouri	703,473	12.7	73.8	63,875	9.1	210,686	29.9	495,091	70.4	216,088	30.7	303,777	43.2	24,854	72,912	10.4
Montana	117,058	13.1	82.6	4,851	4.1	33,352	28.5	94,229	80.5	38,690	33.1	46,445	39.7	26,303	9,790	8.4
Nebraska	213,121	12.6	74.9	8,357	3.9	64,566	30.3	171,195	80.3	75,285	35.3	81,040	38.0	23,849	19,423	9.1
Nevada	245,844	11.1	87.2	43,260	17.6	70,380	28.6	193,379	78.7	67,856	27.6	88,450	36.0	29,418	19,659	8.0
New Hampshire	143,022	11.4	78.8	2,445	1.7	38,360	26.8	110,235	77.1	42,229	29.5	53,423	37.4	26,372	12,717	8.9
New Jersey	1,060,288	12.6	70.0	199,174	18.8	347,168	32.7	738,330	69.6	302,980	28.6	389,478	36.7	31,931	76,622	7.2
New Mexico	219,718	12.0	80.9	85,585	39.0	64,622	29.4	148,392	67.5	61,543	28.0	100,553	45.8	24,755	28,693	13.1
New York	2,343,263	12.6	69.4	558,602	23.8	767,424	32.8	1,614,154	68.9	727,434	31.0	886,578	37.8	26,908	280,128	12.0
North Carolina	953,129	11.7	70.9	170,573	17.9	319,104	33.5	584,158	61.3	286,936	30.1	418,899	43.9	24,425	122,492	12.9
North Dakota	85,646	14.1	76.3	1,698	2.0	26,023	30.4	58,443	68.2	29,673	34.6	33,400	39.0	21,683	10,834	12.6
Ohio	1,425,707	12.8	71.7	149,210	10.5	448,194	31.4	1,002,841	70.3	437,591	30.7	564,251	39.6	25,361	116,087	8.1

See footnotes at end of table

TABLE A
DEMOGRAPHIC, SOCIAL, HEALTH AND ECONOMIC CHARACTERISTICS OF THE POPULATION 65 YEARS AND OVER FOR THE UNITED STATES AND STATES: 2003 – CONTINUED

State of jurisdiction	Population Number	Population % of pop.	Sex ratio (a)	Minority (b) Number	Minority (b) % of pop.	Widowed (c) Number	Widowed (c) % of pop.	H.S. diploma or more (d) Number	H.S. diploma or more (d) % of pop.	Living alone Number	Living alone % of pop.	With a disability (e) Number	With a disability (e) % of pop.	Median household income (f)	In poverty (g) Number	In poverty (g) % of pop.
Oklahoma	428,874	12.6	75.2	56,455	13.2	130,847	30.5	305,937	71.3	140,278	32.7	186,894	43.6	24,190	48,269	11.3
Oregon	433,381	12.4	75.5	27,033	6.2	130,168	30.0	342,153	78.9	129,672	29.9	167,587	38.7	25,997	35,949	8.3
Pennsylvania	1,760,778	14.8	70.6	150,240	8.5	616,213	35.0	1,248,243	70.9	576,773	32.8	664,860	37.8	24,317	153,438	8.7
Rhode Island	141,420	13.6	69.6	10,137	7.2	51,543	36.4	88,621	62.7	49,096	34.7	56,994	40.3	23,212	14,978	10.6
South Carolina	488,162	12.2	73.2	115,259	23.6	153,572	31.5	320,044	65.6	132,989	27.2	195,707	40.1	26,593	59,273	12.1
South Dakota	99,781	13.6	76.6	1,688	1.7	30,255	30.3	72,499	72.7	32,952	33.0	37,693	37.8	24,042	10,729	10.8
Tennessee	683,271	12.0	70.8	81,009	11.9	226,794	33.2	430,501	63.0	209,696	30.7	304,920	44.6	23,697	84,659	12.4
Texas	2,062,327	9.6	75.4	651,641	31.6	646,663	31.4	1,352,673	65.6	581,419	28.2	875,493	42.5	25,403	267,633	13.0
Utah	196,568	8.5	82.3	14,581	7.4	53,073	27.0	165,108	84.0	48,708	24.8	75,869	38.6	32,754	15,007	7.6
Vermont	75,961	12.7	77.6	2,623	3.5	22,370	29.4	55,679	73.3	23,811	31.3	29,080	38.3	24,920	6,766	8.9
Virginia	788,419	11.0	73.2	155,154	19.7	250,330	31.8	538,141	68.3	224,700	28.5	302,056	38.3	31,863	71,190	9.0
Washington	656,630	11.0	77.0	67,822	10.3	194,665	29.6	538,467	82.0	204,912	31.2	253,253	38.6	31,882	44,934	6.8
West Virginia	263,926	14.9	72.2	9,396	3.6	85,660	32.5	156,614	59.3	83,365	31.6	131,573	49.9	21,467	33,581	12.7
Wisconsin	662,878	12.5	75.2	32,995	5.0	197,194	29.7	475,051	71.7	207,315	31.3	239,975	36.2	25,834	48,132	7.3
Wyoming	56,768	11.6	82.8	3,383	6.0	15,905	28.0	46,559	82.0	17,099	30.1	22,796	40.2	27,785	3,503	6.2
District of Columbia	63,347	12.0	60.7	47,090	74.3	21,291	33.6	44,202	69.8	27,194	42.9	22,706	35.8	31,198	9,114	14.4

Source: U.S. Census Bureau, 2003 American Community Survey.

Note: The universe for the 2003 American Community Survey is the household population. Those in group quarters (e.g. nursing facilities, etc.) are not included in the universe. Age classification is based on the age of the person in complete years at the time of interview for the American Community Survey in 2003. Both age and date of birth are used in combination to calculate the most accurate age at the time of interview.

(a) The sex ratio is the number of males per 100 females.

(b) The category minority includes people who identified themselves as Black, Asian, American Indian or Alaska Native, Native Hawaiian or Other Pacific Islander, Some other race, Two or more races, or Hispanic (may be of they reported one or more of the following disabilities: 1) sensory disability; 2) physical disability; 3) mental disability; 4) self-care disability; or 5) go-outside-home disability. For the total U.S. population with a disability, the universe is the population 5 years and over.

(f) Median household income in the last 12 months (2003 inflation-adjusted dollars) for households with a householder 65 years and over.

(g) Poverty status was determined for everyone except those in institutions, military group quarters, college dormitories, and unrelated individuals under 15 years old. These groups were excluded from the denominator when calculating poverty rates

Women in State Government:
Historical Overview and Current Trends
By Susan J. Carroll

In recent years the movement of women into state-level offices has slowed following several decades of gains, and the 2004 elections continued this pattern of stagnation, producing little change in the numbers of women officials. Efforts to actively recruit women for elective and appointive positions will be critical in determining what the future holds for women in state government.

In the history of our nation, women are relative newcomers among state elected and appointed officials. Women first entered state-level offices in the 1920s following passage and ratification of the 19th Amendment to the U.S. Constitution which granted women suffrage. However, significant growth in the numbers of women in office occurred only after the emergence of the contemporary women's movement during the late-1960s and early-1970s. Since the mid-1970s, as data collected by the Center for American Women and Politics show,[1] women have greatly increased their numbers among elected and appointed officials in state government. In recent years, however, progress has slowed, and nationwide statistics show a leveling off in the numbers of women serving in state-level offices. The 2004 elections continued the pattern of stagnation with the numbers of women nationwide showing little change following the elections.

Governors

Since the founding of our country, only 28 women (18 Democrats, 10 Republicans) have served as state governors (Table A), and only one woman has served as governor of a U.S. territory (Puerto Rico).[2] A majority of the states, 29, have never had a woman chief executive. Arizona is the only state to have had three women governors as well as the only state where a woman succeeded another as governor. Connecticut, Texas, Kansas, Washington and New Hampshire have each had two women governors although one of the governors of New Hampshire, Vesta Roy, served for only seven days following the death of an incumbent.

The first woman governor, Nellie Taylor Ross of Wyoming, was selected in a special election to succeed her deceased husband in 1925. Fifteen days later a second woman, Miriam "Ma" Ferguson, was inaugurated as governor of Texas, having been elected as a surrogate for her husband, a former governor who had been impeached and consequently was barred constitutionally from running again. Ferguson's campaign slogan was "Two governors for the price of one."[3] The third woman to serve as a governor, Lurleen Wallace of Alabama, who campaigned on the slogan, "Let George do it," was similarly elected to replace a husband who was constitutionally prohibited from seeking another term.[4]

The first woman elected in her own right (i.e., without following her husband) into the governorship was Ella Grasso, who presided over the state of Connecticut from 1975 to 1980. Eighteen of the women governors (including Grasso) who have served since the mid-1970s were elected in their own right. The other seven became governor through constitutional succession; only one of these seven was subsequently elected to a full term.

Eight women serve as governors in 2005, down from a record nine women who held governorships simultaneously at the end of 2004. Three states governed by women (Montana, Utah and Delaware) held elections in 2004. Of the three women governors of these states, only Ruth Ann Minner (D) of Delaware sought re-election,[5] and she won. Two other women in addition to Minner were gubernatorial candidates in 2004. Christine Gregoire (D) of Washington won her gubernatorial bid for an open seat by the slimmest of margins following a statewide manual recount. The other woman candidate, Claire McCaskill (D) of Missouri, lost her gubernatorial race. The eight women (6 Democrats, 2 Republicans) who serve as chief executives of their states in 2005 are: Ruth Ann Minner (D-Del.), Jennifer M. Granholm (D-Mich.), Linda Lingle (R-Hawaii), Janet Napolitano (D-Ariz.), Kathleen Sebelius (D-Kan.), Kathleen Blanco (D-La.), M. Jodi Rell (R-Conn.) and Christine Gregoire (D-Wash.).

Table A: Women Governors Throughout History

Name (party-state)	Dates served	Special circumstances
Nellie Tayloe Ross (D-WY)	1925–1927	Won special election to replace deceased husband.
Miriam "Ma" Ferguson (D-TX)	1925–1927, 1933–1935	Inaugurated 15 days after Ross; elected as surrogate for husband who could not succeed himself.
Lurleen Wallace (D-AL)	1967–1968	Elected as surrogate for husband who could not succeed himself.
Ella Grasso (D-CT)	1975–1980	First woman elected governor in her own right; resigned for health reasons.
Dixy Lee Ray (D-WA)	1977–1981	
Vesta Roy (R-NH)	1982–1983	Elected to state senate and chosen as senate president; served as governor for seven days when incumbent died.
Martha Layne Collins (D-KY)	1984–1987	
Madeleine Kunin (D-VT)	1985–1991	First woman to serve three terms as governor.
Kay Orr (R-NE)	1987–1991	First Republican woman governor and first woman to defeat another woman in a gubernatorial race.
Rose Mofford (D-AZ)	1988–1991	Elected as secretary of state, succeeded governor who was impeached and convicted.
Joan Finney (D-KS)	1991–1995	First woman to defeat an incumbent governor.
Ann Richards (D-TX)	1991–1995	
Barbara Roberts (D-OR)	1991–1995	
Christine Todd Whitman (R-NJ)	1994–2001	Resigned to take presidential appointment as commissioner of the Environmental Protection Agency.
Jeanne Shaheen (D-NH)	1997–2003	
Jane Dee Hull (R-AZ)	1997–2003	Elected as secretary of state, succeeded governor who resigned; later elected to a full term.
Nancy Hollister (R-OH)	1998–1999	Elected lieutenant governor; served as governor for 11 days when predecessor took U.S. Senate seat and successor had not yet been sworn in.
Jane Swift (R-MA)	2001–2003	Elected as lieutenant governor, succeeded governor who resigned for an ambassadorial appointment.
Judy Martz (R-MT)	2001–2005	
Olene Walker (R-UT)	2003–2005	Elected as lieutenant governor, succeeded governor who resigned to take a federal appointment.
Ruth Ann Minner (D-DE)	2001–present	
Jennifer M. Granholm (D-MI)	2003–present	
Linda Lingle (R-HI)	2003–present	
Janet Napolitano (D-AZ)	2003–present	First woman to succeed another woman as governor.
Kathleen Sebelius (D-KS)	2003–present	Father was governor of Ohio.
Kathleen Blanco (D-LA)	2004–present	
M. Jodi Rell (R-CT)	2004–present	Elected as lieutenant governor, succeeded governor who resigned.
Christine Gregoire (D-WA)	2005–present	

Source: Center for American Women and Politics, Eagleton Institute of Politics, Rutgers University.

Other Statewide Elected and Appointed Officials in the Executive Branch

The states vary greatly in their numbers of statewide elected and appointed officials. For example, Maine, New Hampshire and New Jersey have only one statewide elected official, the governor, while North Dakota, at the other extreme, has 12.

The first woman to ever hold a major statewide office was Soledad C. Chacon (D-N.M.) who was secretary of state in New Mexico from 1923–26;[6] Delaware, Kentucky, New York, South Dakota and Texas also had women secretaries of state in the 1920s. The first woman treasurer, Grace B. Urbahns (R-Indiana) also served during this time period, from 1926–1932.

Several more years passed before a woman became lieutenant governor. Matilda R. Wilson (R-Mich.) served briefly as lieutenant governor of Michigan in 1940 when she was appointed to fill an expiring term. However, the first woman elected as a lieutenant governor was Consuelo N. Bailey (R-Vt.) who served from 1955–1956. An additional three decades passed before a woman became attorney general of a state; the first was Arlene Violet (R-R.I.) who served from 1985–1987.

As evident from Figure A, the proportion of women among statewide elective officials has grown substantially over the past three decades. From 1971 to 1985 the increases were small and incremental. Then, between 1983 and 1995, a period of significant growth, the numbers and proportions of women serving in statewide office more than doubled. Since 1995, the numbers and proportions have leveled off.

The number of women serving in state-wide elective offices actually decreased by two as a result of the 2004 elections, and slightly fewer women, 79,[7] currently hold statewide offices than a decade ago when there were 84 women.

In early 2005, women hold 25.1 percent of the 315 statewide elective positions. In addition to the eight women governors, women serve as lieutenant governors in 16, or 37.2 percent, of the 43 states that elect lieutenant governors in statewide elections; this is the same number of women who served as lieutenant governor in 2004.[8] Other women statewide elected officials include: 12 secretaries of state, eight state treasurers, four attorney generals, 10 chief education officials, seven state auditors, four public service commissioners, three state comptroller/controllers, two chief agricultural officials, one commissioner of insurance, two commissioners of labor and two corporation commissioners. The women serving in statewide elective office include two African Americans (the lieutenant governor of Ohio and the state treasurer of Connecticut) as well as three Latinas (the secretary of state of New Mexico, the attorney general of New Mexico, and the superintendent of public instruction for Oregon).

Women are slightly better represented among top appointed officials in state government. According to nationwide data collected by the Center on Women in Government and Civil Society at SUNY-Albany, in the second half of 2004 women constituted 29.7 percent of department heads with major policy-making responsibilities (including heads of departments, agencies, offices, boards, commissions and authorities) who were appointed by governors. Similarly, women were 41.1 percent of the top appointed advisors in governors' offices. These 2004 figures represent a slight increase since 2003 and a more notable increase since 1998 when women were 23.7 percent of department heads and 39.6 percent of governors' top advisors. Women of color are also slightly better represented among these appointed officials than among statewide elective officials,[9] with women of color constitut-

Table B: Women Statewide Elected Officials, 2005

State	Governor	Lieutenant governor	Attorney general	Secretary of state	Treasurer
Alabama	★	W	★	W	W
Alaska	★	★	★	. . .	. . .
Arizona	W	. . .	★	W	★
Arkansas	★	★	★	★	★
California	★	★	★	★	★
Colorado	★	W	★	W	★
Connecticut	W	★	★	W	W
Delaware	W	★	W	. . .	★
Florida	★	W	★	. . .	. . .
Georgia	★	★	★	W	. . .
Hawaii	W	★	. . .	. . .	. . .
Idaho	★	★	★	★	★
Illinois	★	★	W	★	W
Indiana	★	W	★	★	★
Iowa	★	W	★	★	★
Kansas	W	★	★	★	W
Kentucky	★	★	★	★	★
Louisiana	W	★	★	★	★
Maine	★	. . .	. . .	. . .	. . .
Maryland	★	★	★	. . .	. . .
Massachusetts	★	W	★	★	★
Michigan	W	★	★	W	. . .
Minnesota	★	W	★	W	. . .
Mississippi	★	W	★	★	★
Missouri	★	★	★	W	W
Montana	★	★	★	★	. . .
Nebraska	★	★	★	★	. . .
Nevada	★	W	★	★	★
New Hampshire	★	. . .	. . .	. . .	. . .
New Jersey	★	. . .	. . .	. . .	. . .
New Mexico	★	W	W	W	★
New York	★	W	★	. . .	. . .
North Carolina	★	W	★	W	★
North Dakota	★	★	★	★	W
Ohio	★	W	★	★	★
Oklahoma	★	W	★	. . .	★
Oregon	★	. . .	★	★	★
Pennsylvania	★	W	★	. . .	W
Rhode Island	★	★	★	★	★
South Carolina	★	★	★	★	★
South Dakota	★	★	★	★	★
Tennessee	★	. . .	. . .	. . .	. . .
Texas	★	★	★	. . .	. . .
Utah	★	★	★	. . .	★
Vermont	★	★	★	W	★
Virginia	★	★	★	. . .	. . .
Washington	W	★	★	★	★
West Virginia	★	. . .	★	W	★
Wisconsin	★	W	W	★	★
Wyoming	★	. . .	. . .	★	W

Source: Data for elected officials are current as of January 2005 and have been provided by the Center for American Women and Politics, Eagleton Institute of Politics, Rutgers University.

Key:

★—Denotes that this position is filled through a statewide election.

W—Denotes that this position is filled through a statewide election and is held by a woman.

. . .—Denotes that this position is filled through methods other than a statewide election.

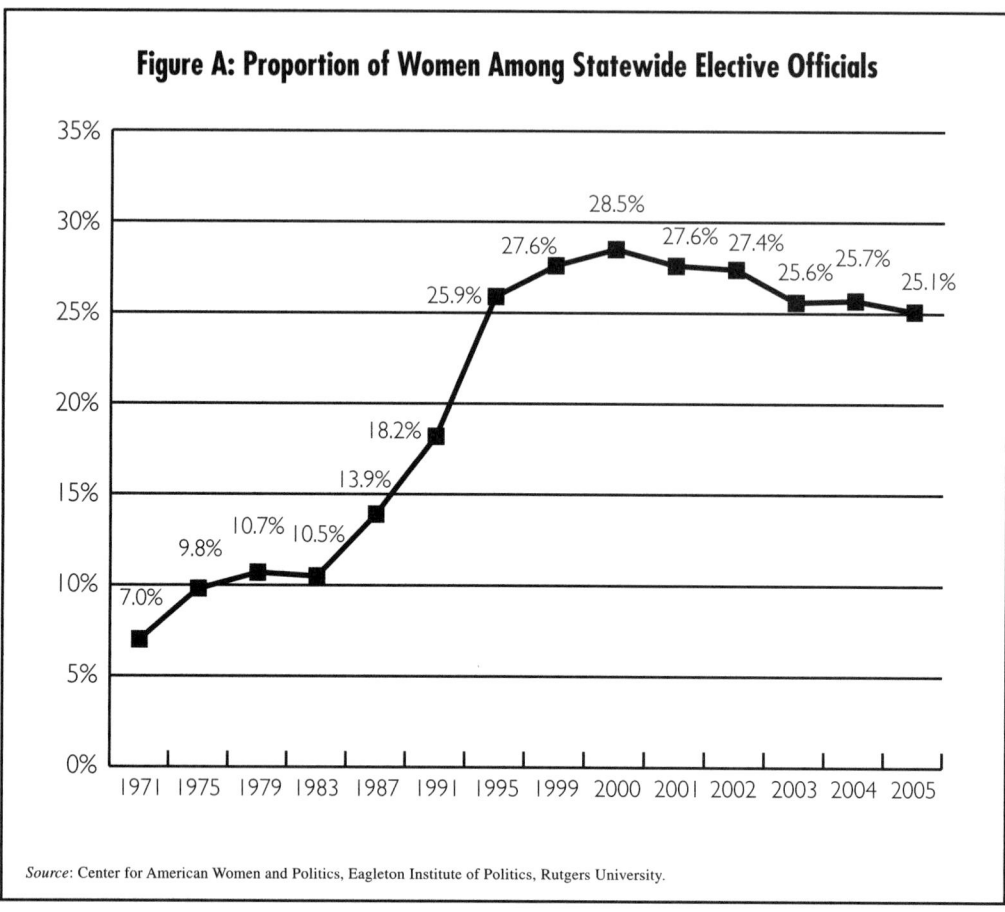

Figure A: Proportion of Women Among Statewide Elective Officials

Source: Center for American Women and Politics, Eagleton Institute of Politics, Rutgers University.

ing 5.8 percent of all department heads and 7.7 percent of top advisors in governors' offices.[10]

Justices on Courts of Last Resort

The first woman to win election to a state court of last resort was Florence E. Allen, who was elected to the Ohio Supreme Court in 1922 and re-elected in 1928. Nevertheless, it was not until 1960 that a second woman, Lorna Lockwood of Arizona, was elected to a state supreme court. In 1965 Lockwood's colleagues on the Arizona Supreme Court elected her chief justice, thereby also making her the first woman in history to preside over a state court of last resort.[11]

According to the National Center for State Courts, 95, or 28.2 percent, of the 337 justices on state courts of last resort in early 2005 are women. Of the 52 chief justices of these courts, 17, or 32.7 percent, are women. The current chief justice of the New Mexico Supreme Court, Petra Jimenez Maes, is the first Latina in the country to hold this position.

Women comprise a majority of justices on the courts of last resort in two states-New York and Ohio. Women constitute at least 40 percent of the justices (but less than a majority) on an additional 16 courts of last resort.

Legislators

Even before 1920 when women won the right to vote across the country, a few women had been elected to legislatures in states that had granted the franchise to women. By 1971 the proportion of women serving in state legislatures across the country had grown to 4.5 percent, and by 2005 this proportion had increased almost fivefold to 22.5 percent. As Figure B illustrates, the proportion of women among legislators grew throughout the 1970s and 1980s. The rate of growth slowed in the 1990s, and similar to the pattern for statewide elected officials, the numbers and proportions of women legislators nationally have leveled off since the late 1990s. In fact, the same number of women, 1664, serves in state legislatures at the beginning of 2005 as in 1999 when there were also 1664 women legislators.

Great variation exists across the states in the proportion of legislators who are women (see Table C). With 34.0 percent women in their legislatures, Maryland and Colorado are tied for first place among the states. They are closely followed by Delaware (33.9 percent), Arizona (33.3 percent), Nevada (33.3 percent), Vermont (33.3 percent) and Washington (33.3 percent). There seems to be no easy explanation for why these states have risen to the top, and indeed scholars who have statistically examined the variation among the states in the representation of women in their legislatures have found no simple patterns.[12]

At the other extreme, South Carolina with only 8.8 percent ranks last among the 50 states in the representation of women among its legislators. Accompanying South Carolina in the bottom five states are Alabama with 10.0 percent women, Ken-

tucky with 12.3 percent, Mississippi with 12.6 percent, and Pennsylvania with 12.6 percent. Six of the eight states with the lowest proportions of women are Southern or border states. No Southern state ranks among the top 20, and only Florida, with 23.8 percent women, is above the national average. These rankings suggest that the South lags behind the rest of the country in the representation of women within its legislatures.

In early 2005, women hold 402, or 20.4 percent, of all state senate seats and 1262, or 23.3 percent, of all state house seats across the country. Although state legislators nationally have become considerably more Republican over the last decade and a half with legislators now evenly divided between the two parties,[13] the same is not true for women legislators. In 2005 as in the past, Democrats substantially outnumber Republicans among women state legislators. Among women state senators nationwide, 63.8 percent are Democrats; among women state representatives, 62.2

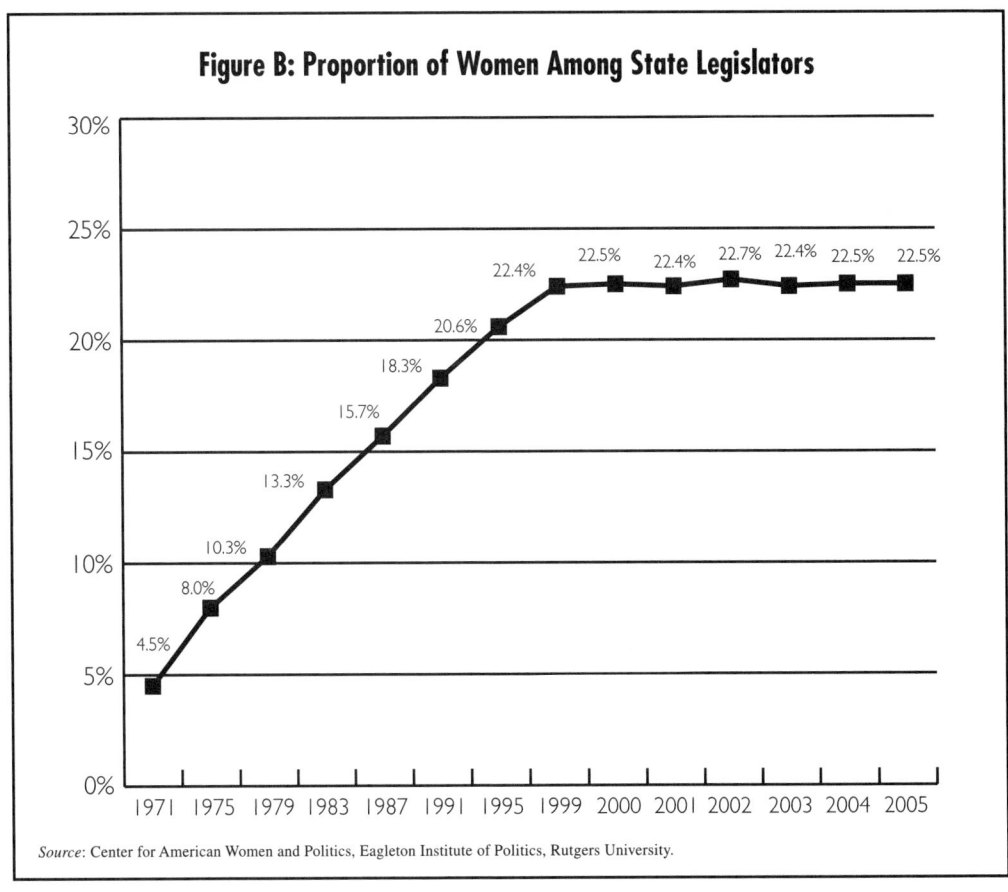

Figure B: Proportion of Women Among State Legislators

Source: Center for American Women and Politics, Eagleton Institute of Politics, Rutgers University.

Table C: Women in State Legislatures

State	Senate			House/Assembly			Legislature (both houses)	
	Democrats	Republicans	% Women	Democrats	Republicans	% Women	% Women	State rank
Alabama	2	1	8.6%	9	2	10.5%	10.0%	49
Alaska	2	1	15.0	4	4	20.0	18.3	32
Arizona	4	6	33.3	10	10	33.3	33.3	4
Arkansas	4	2	17.1	12	4	16.0	16.3	39
California	12	0	30.0	19	6	31.3	30.8	10
Colorado	9	2	31.4	19	4	35.4	34.0	1
Connecticut	7	2	25.0	27	18	29.8	28.9	13
Delaware	4	3	33.3	7	7	34.1	33.9	3
Florida	5	4	22.5	13	16	23.3	23.8	22
Georgia	5	2	12.5	26	10	20.0	18.2	33
Hawaii	6	0	24.0	9	6	29.4	27.6	16
Idaho	1	3	11.4	9	16	35.7	27.6	16
Illinois	9	5	23.7	24	11	29.7	27.7	15
Indiana	6	5	22.0	7	7	14.0	16.7	36
Iowa	1	4	10.0	17	8	25.0	20.0	29
Kansas	4	9	32.5	19	21	32.0	32.1	8
Kentucky	1	5	15.8	8	3	11.0	12.3	48
Louisiana	5	1	15.4	13	5	17.1	16.7	36
Maine	6	5	31.4	24	9	21.9	23.7	23
Maryland	12	3	31.9	38	11	34.8	34.0	1
Massachusetts	10	0	25.0	33	6	24.4	24.5	20
Michigan	5	6	28.9	13	9	17.3	20.3	27
Minnesota	11	11	34.3	26	11	27.6 (a)	29.9	12
Mississippi	4	0	7.7	13	5	14.8	12.6	46
Missouri	4	2	17.6	25	11	22.1	21.3	26
Montana	6	1	14.0	22	8	30.0	24.7	19
Nebraska (b)	—Nonpartisan—		24.5	—Unicameral—			24.5	20
Nevada	4	2	28.6	11	4	35.7	33.3	4
New Hampshire	4	1	20.8	72	53	31.3	30.7	11
New Jersey	4	2	15.0	10	3	16.3	15.8	42
New Mexico	7	4	26.2	12	12	34.4	31.3	9
New York	7	3	16.1	31	9	26.7	23.6	24
North Carolina	7	0	14.0	22	10	26.7	22.9	25
North Dakota	3	2	10.6	7	11	19.1	16.3	39
Ohio	3	2	15.2	13	8	21.2	19.7	31
Oklahoma	6	2	16.7	5	9	13.9	14.8	43
Oregon	8	1	30.0	9	8	28.3	28.9	13
Pennsylvania	4	4	16.0	9	15	11.8	12.6	46
Rhode Island	7	1	21.1	9	2	14.7	16.8	35
South Carolina	1	0	2.2	7	7	11.3	8.8	50
South Dakota	2	1	8.6	4	10	20.0	16.2	41
Tennessee	3	3	18.2	12	5	17.2	17.4	34
Texas	2	2	12.9	13	19	21.3	19.9	30
Utah	3	2	17.2	6	10	21.3	20.2	28
Vermont	8	2	33.3	36	14	33.3 (c)	33.3	4
Virginia	7	1	20.0	6	6	12.0	14.3	45
Washington	15	5	40.8	19	10	29.6	33.3	4
West Virginia	0	4	11.8	12	6	18.0	16.4	38
Wisconsin	3	5	24.2	12	14	26.3	25.8	18
Wyoming	3	1	13.3	4	5	15.0	14.4	44

Source: Center for American Women and Politics, Eagleton Institute of Politics, Rutgers University. Figures are as of January 2005.

Key:
(a)—Includes one member of the Independence Party.
(b)—Nebraska has a unicameral legislature with nonpartisan elections.
(c)—Includes two members of the Progressive Party.

percent are Democrats.

Almost one-fifth of women state legislators, 18.7 percent, are women of color. Of the 83 senators and 229 representatives serving in legislatures in early 2004, all but 18 are Democrats. African American women hold 56 seats in state senates and 158 seats in state houses across 39 states. Latinas are concentrated in 16 states; they hold 19 senate and 47 house seats. Asian American women count among their numbers six senators and 17 representatives in eight states while Native American women hold two senate and seven house seats in five states.

Looking Toward the Future

Although women have made substantial progress over time in increasing their presence in state government, the recent leveling off of women's numbers among statewide elective officials and state legislators is a puzzling, and for many a troubling, development. At a minimum, the leveling off is evidence that increases over time are not inevitable; there is no invisible hand at work to insure that more women will seek and be elected to office with each subsequent election.

The leveling off has implications for women's representation not only among state legislators and nongubernatorial statewide officeholders, but also among governors and members of Congress. Probably the most striking positive development for women in state government in recent years has been the increase in women governors. Of the 28 women in the entire history of our country who have served as governors, half (14) have served all or part of their terms during the first five years of the 21st century. Of the eight sitting governors, seven held statewide elective office before running for governor; three were lieutenant governors, three served as attorney generals and one was her state's insurance commissioner. Four of the current women governors also served in their state legislatures. Similarly, many of the women who run for Congress have gained experience and visibility in state government before seeking federal office. Of the 65 women members of the U.S. House, 29 served in their state houses, 17 in their state senates and two in statewide elective offices; of the 14 women U.S. senators, seven served in their state legislatures, two in statewide elective offices and one in an appointed state cabinet post.

Activists who are interested in increasing the numbers of women serving in office often refer to a political "pipeline" through which potential women candidates for higher level office come forward from amongst the pool of women who have gained experience at lower levels of office. Clearly, the pipeline has worked well in the case of the current women governors and members of Congress. But what will happen if the pool of candidates in statewide and state legislative office continues to stagnate or even decline? Then, the number of politically experienced women with the visibility and contacts necessary to step forward to run for governor or a seat in the U.S. House or Senate is also likely to stagnate or decline.

While several different factors may be responsible for the recent leveling off in the numbers of women in statewide elective and state legislative office, a lack of effective recruitment certainly is one of the most important. Statistics on the number of women candidates over time seem clearly to point to a problem with recruitment. For example, in 2004 a total of 2,220 women were general election candidates for 5,809 seats up for election in state legislatures. Although the number of state legislative seats up for election varies from year to year, fewer women ran for the state legislature in 2004 than in any year since 1990![14] Clearly, then, the number of women stepping forward to run for state legislative seats has not been increasing.

Research has found that women who run for office are less likely than their male counterparts to be "self-starters." Women more often than men seek office only after receiving encouragement from others. For example, one recent study of major party candidates in state legislative races found that only 11 percent of women, compared with 37 percent of men, said that it was entirely their own idea to run for the legislature; in contrast, 37 percent of women, compared with 18 percent of men, reported that they had not seriously thought about running until someone else suggested it.[15] Another recent study of people in the professions from which political candidates are most likely to emerge (i.e., law, business, education and politics) found that notably fewer women (43 percent) than men (59 percent) had ever considered running for office.[16]

Findings such as these suggest that the future for women in state government will depend, at least in part, upon the strength of efforts to actively recruit women for both elected and appointed positions. Legislative leaders, public officials, party leaders and advocacy organizations can help by renewing their commitment and augmenting their efforts to identify and offer support to potential women candidates, especially in winnable races with open seats or vulnerable incumbents. Recruitment efforts may well be the key to determining whether the numbers of women officials continue to stagnate (or even decline) or whether the numbers again begin to move steadily upward as they did in earlier decades.

Notes

[1] All statistical information in this essay, unless otherwise noted, has been provided by the Center for American Women and Politics (CAWP), Eagleton Institute of Politics, Rutgers University. Additional information is available at www.cawp.rutgers.edu. I would especially like to thank several of my colleagues at CAWP—Gilda Morales, Linda Phillips, Kathleen Casey and Amy Bain—for their assistance with the data for this essay.

[2] Sila Calderon (Popular Democratic Party) served as governor of Puerto Rico from 2001 to 2004.

[3] Martin Gruberg, *Women in American Politics* (Oshkosh, WI: Academia Press, 1968), 189.

[4] Ibid., 190.

[5] Judy Martz (R) of Montana did not seek re-election. Olene Walker (R) of Utah failed to win her party's nomination and thus was not a candidate in the general election. Sila Calderon (Popular Democratic Party), who served as governor of Puerto Rico in 2004, also did not seek re-election.

[6] Women did serve as superintendents of public instruction in a few states earlier than this.

[7] These 79 women serving in statewide elective office include 35 Democrats, 41 Republicans and 3 nonpartisans.

[8] Nine states held elections for lieutenant governor in 2004. One incumbent lieutenant governor was re-elected, one was defeated but replaced by a woman, and four other women candidates all lost. The net result was a slight partisan shift with one more Republican and one fewer Democrat (6 Democrats, 10 Republicans) serving in 2005 than in 2004,

[9] Women of color comprise less than 2 percent of all statewide elective officials.

[10] "Women's Leadership Profile 2004," A Report of the Center for Women in Government and Civil Society, (University at Albany, State University of New York, Fall 2004). http://www.cwig.albany.edu/2004leadershipprofile2004.pdf.

[11] See note 3 above, 190, 192.

[12] See, for example, Barbara Norrander and Clyde Wilcox, "The Geography of Gender Power: Women in State Legislatures," in Sue Thomas and Clyde Wilcox, ed., *Women and Elective Office: Past, Present, and Future*, (New York: Oxford University Press, 1998).

[13] Democrats did register gains in legislative races in the 2004 elections, and as a result, a slight Republican advantage among legislators in 2004 has disappeared, resulting in an even split between Democrats and Republicans nationally. See "Perfect Parity in Nation's State Legislatures," *NCSL News*, http://www.ncsl.org/programs/press/2004/pr041103a.htm.

[14] There were 2,375 women candidates for state legislative seats in 1992; 2,285 in 1994; 2,277 in 1996; 2,280 in 1998; 2,228 in 2000; and 2,348 in 2002.

[15] Gary Moncrief, Peverill Squire, and Malcolm Jewell, *Who Runs for the Legislature?* (New York: Prentice-Hall, 2001), Table 5.5, 102; see also Susan J. Carroll and Wendy S. Strimling, *Women's Routes to Elective Office: A Comparison With Men's* (New Brunswick, NJ: Center for the American Woman and Politics, 1983).

[16] Richard L. Fox and Jennifer Lawless, "Entering the Arena: Gender and the Initial Decision to Run for Office, *American Journal of Political Science*, forthcoming 2005.

About the Author

Susan J. Carroll is professor of Political Science and Women's and Gender Studies at Rutgers University and Senior Scholar at the Center for American Women and Politics (CAWP) of the Eagleton Institute of Politics. She has published numerous works on women public officials, women candidates, and various aspects of women's participation in American politics.

Chapter Eight

STATE MANAGEMENT AND ADMINISTRATION

Trends in State Information and Technology Management

By Chris Dixon, Drew Leatherby and Mary Gay Whitmer

State governments are becoming more disciplined in their approach to investing in and managing information technology, adopting an enterprise view with centralized oversight, common standards and shared solutions across agencies. The opportunities for improved service delivery, information sharing and economic growth through strategic technology deployment must be weighed against the potential privacy and security risks.

IT Governance

State chief information officers (CIOs) are typically asked to streamline state information technology (IT) budgets, justify IT spending and increase service delivery and efficiency, both internally and externally. CIOs address these issues through IT governance, which consists of the leadership, organizational structures, direction and processes that ensure information technology sustains and extends the enterprise's mission and objectives in a planned manner. IT governance frameworks can focus on IT organizational models, including reorganization and consolidation strategies, service delivery reform and shared services among agencies.

Reorganization strategies involve business process improvement and provide the framework for looking for redundancies in government services and work toward the consolidation of services that are redundant. Consolidation strategies ask and try to answer questions such as: is authority centralized; what are the roles of the different players; and, how are IT programs organized?

Service reform, another aspect of IT governance frameworks, involves both internal and external customers. Internal customer service reform focuses on ways of improving help to agencies. External customer service reform focuses on the citizen and their access to state government services, such as providing one-stop online services that can provide the experience of "seamless government" for the citizen customer. This process would be termed a shared services model; delivering transparent one-stop services to the public through cooperation with different levels of government and across agencies (e.g., by building an on-line application that all agencies can use to expedite the application for a business permit).

These IT governance framework models are typically organized around a steering committee or governing body made up of representatives from the various state agencies, or at higher levels, can even involve all three branches of government.

IT Procurement

States purchase a wide array of IT products and services ranging from desktop computers to elaborate financial and resource management systems. State IT procurement differs from the procurement of other types of products and services, since many IT systems are inherently complex and technology is evolving at an ever-accelerating pace. These differences have fueled a need to update state IT procurement processes to make them more flexible, especially for large IT procurements which may involve multiple contractors and the acquisition of both IT products and services. However, increased procurement flexibility must be balanced with the need to maintain or even improve the accountability, fairness and integrity of those processes. The benefits of increased procurement flexibility include: (1) improving the ability of contractors to provide their expertise to states regarding the types of solutions that could accomplish states' IT needs and (2) ensuring reasonable procurement timeframes so that technology is not obsolete by the time the procurement process has been completed. Well-written Requests for Proposals (RFPs) and good project management and contract administration are other ways of ensuring successful, flexible and accountable state IT procurement processes.

In updating their procurement processes, states also are re-examining their approaches to IT contract terms and conditions, such as liability limitations and intellectual property clauses, in order to ensure that they are fair and accurately reflect the true needs and risks of the state and contractor. In September 2004, the National Association of State Chief Information Officers (NASCIO) issued recommendations on liability limitations clauses and encourages states to consider limiting potential vendor liability in order to maximize the size and quality of the pool of potential contractors and to minimize the total contract price.[1]

The state CIO's role in IT procurement varies from state-to-state. Approximately one-fifth of CIOs have responsibility for statewide IT procurement (usually above a specified dollar threshold), while approximately half of the state CIOs share responsibility with their state's procurement office. While state CIOs' responsibility over IT procurement varies across the states, the state CIOs can play an important role in educating state policy-makers, procurement officials and attorneys, and others on the importance of the procurement process to ensure that the value of state IT systems and services is maximized.

Privacy

New technologies that are emerging in state government present opportunities to conduct business and provide citizen services in new and often more efficient ways. However, they can have unintended consequences that could place citizens' personal information, such as Social Security numbers, at risk. State CIOs can serve an important role in identifying and addressing those unintended consequences. By addressing potential privacy concerns early, states can foster citizens' trust that their personal information will be kept safe from unauthorized disclosure and use. Garnering citizens' trust is the key to facilitating the expansion and enhancement of e-government applications and systems.

Examples of emerging technologies include: camera phones, wireless devices, such as personal digital assistants, RFID (radio frequency identification) tags, data mining, and e-authentication.[2] New uses of existing technologies, such as email and spoofing of legitimate Web sites, also can create threats to citizens' privacy. Examples include: spam, spyware,

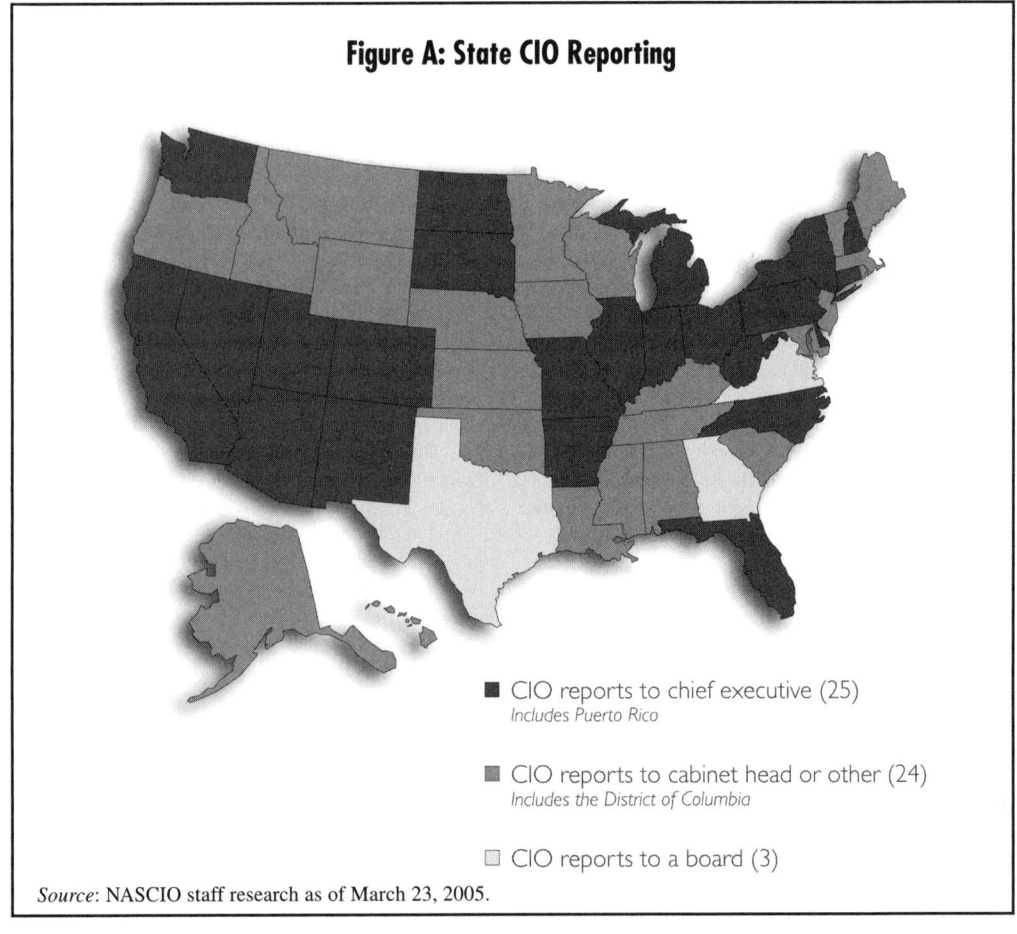

Figure A: State CIO Reporting

■ CIO reports to chief executive (25)
Includes Puerto Rico

■ CIO reports to cabinet head or other (24)
Includes the District of Columbia

☐ CIO reports to a board (3)

Source: NASCIO staff research as of March 23, 2005.

phishing, adware and malware. When introducing new technologies, states must identify potential unintended consequences to citizens' personal information and "bake privacy into" these technological solutions. Moreover, as states create new IT systems that handle citizens' personal information, they must ensure that any potential privacy concerns are addressed and integrated into the new system's development. Finally, states should not underestimate the ingenuity of state employees to bring new technologies, such as camera phones and other wireless devices, into the workplace and use them in a way that could compromise the privacy of citizens' personal information. The creation of sound workplace privacy policies can provide employees with guidance as to how and when they may use such technologies and what will happen if they misuse them. The Fair Information Use Principles, which include the concepts of notice, consent, access, security and enforcement, can provide states with guidance in creating such workplace privacy policies.[3]

The role of the state CIO is important to privacy, because the CIO has a broad view of the state enterprise and understands where privacy protections fit within the state's enterprise architecture and business processes. State CIOs also are in a position to educate policymakers who are seeking to ensure privacy protections through legislation or regulation.

Economic Development

Economic development is a perennial priority for the nation's elected officials. It receives even more attention during periods of economic downturn or re-adjustment. State CIOs, providing services that are integral to the Internet economy, have long been acutely aware of the role they play in growing opportunities for their states' citizens as the Internet economy continues to play havoc with Industrial Age business models.

The most pervasive contribution that many state CIOs make to economic development is in blazing the digital-government trail in their states. This puts them in the role of practice leader in the provision of on-line services and as promoter of the Internet economy. For example, providing online government-to-citizen (G2C) services can "market" the state to a "trendsetting technology elite" who are seeking quality of life and economic opportunities related to technology advances. Providing a coherent selection of online government-to-business (G2B) services helps to reduce the overhead costs for existing businesses within the state and facilitates the innovative start-ups that expect to plug-and-play in the Internet.

Government-to-government (G2G) services provide front-end (i.e., Web portal) and back-end (i.e., transaction engines, data repositories, telecommunications) infrastructure that local governments can either use freely or purchase at discounts in order to jumpstart their Internet Age presences.

When it comes to promoting adequate public access to the Internet, state CIOs are faced with a variety of options. While a consensus has emerged that pervasive high bandwidth connectivity will be integral-if not essential-to spurring the next wave of economic growth in the United States, there is still much debate as to the best way to foster pervasive access.[4] That decision will likely be made based on the practical realities such as cost and the philosophical leanings of decision makers. Options will range from direct provision of high-speed infrastructure by the state to more market-based approaches. Even where the state is relying more on market-based solutions, the state CIO will still be involved in the discussion in order to see that the chosen approach will further the goal of pervasive access in underserved or economically stressed areas.

State CIOs will be under pressure to leverage state spending to the benefit of the states' local workforces and taxpayers. The state CIO, as the operator of what is likely the state's largest IT enterprise, can bargain from a position of strength. Every penny saved in purchasing is a penny that can be used for worker retraining, economic development or tax cuts. Forrester research predicts the loss of U.S. IT jobs to overseas competitors will exceed 1 million in 2006 and reach 3.4 million by 2015.[5] What the economic and political ramifications of these losses will be nationally and within a particular state or the government sector remains to be seen. Therefore, when called upon to advise on sourcing issues the state CIO will tread cautiously into a very complex political debate with cross-cutting ideologies and demographic interests that won't fall into an easy partisan framework.

Homeland Security

The role of the state CIO in homeland security continued to evolve in 2004. State CIOs continued to push for more mature approaches to information security within state government, seeking the authority and resources needed to enforce a variety of policies governing the use and protection of state information systems. Many state CIOs received at least small sums of money from grants awarded to the states under the federal State Homeland Security Grant Program. In most cases these funds were used for risk assessments and the deployment of security technologies such as intrusion detection and prevention systems. State CIOs and state auditors also began working more closely to determine how best to leverage the strengths of their authorities and operations to best protect public information assets.

State CIOs also pushed for better inclusion of information (or "cyber") security in state homeland security assessment and strategy processes to ensure that the issue is adequately addressed in relation to chemical, biological, radiological, nuclear, and explosive (CBRNE) threats. State information and communications systems are vital to responding to CBRNE attacks. They are vulnerable to collateral damage from attacks on other targets as well as to direct cyber/physical attacks. Thus, state CIOs will continue to by the chief proponent of information security within state government. This role will continue to grow as decision makers increasingly rely on state CIOs to deploy new technologies that aggregate information from across state government for purposes of situational awareness and decision support on a daily basis and during crises.

Interoperability & Integration

Many state CIOs have responsibility for their states' voice and data communications infrastructure, including the systems that first responders use to communicate, and agencies use to share data across the enterprise. CIOs more and more are addressing issues related to public safety communications, spectrum management, data sharing and integration, seamless government and emerging enterprise technologies such as wireless and IP-based solutions. Questions state CIOs are facing regarding interoperability include, who needs to interoperate, and how; in real time, on demand, when needed, when authorized, etc.

Interoperability is important for government to deliver needed and life-saving services to the public, through public safety and public service organizations. Voice and/or data communication is integral to cooperative efforts. Public safety and public service are suffering from interoperability problems. The inoperability problem is both technical and cultural and must be addressed on both levels. State CIOs recognize the need for better and more refined governance over interoperability.

Good interoperability governance has value in improving services to the public. A suitable alignment and control framework allows efficient and responsible use of resources. Governance frameworks more and more will be used to align the state and local interoperability strategy with agencies' public

safety and public service strategies, and manage interoperability risks. Through these frameworks, CIOs can identify needs, evaluate priorities among needs, and take a leadership role in addressing a workable plan.

State CIOs will play a key role in efforts to achieve interoperability and improve the public safety communications infrastructure at the local, state and national levels. State leadership is essential to the development of a coordinated approach to this issue and CIOs are uniquely positioned to develop an interoperability architecture that provides a roadmap for all to follow.

Integration, unlike interoperability, is focused on the sharing of data across agencies and establishing enterprise data models and XML products to allow that information to be more readily shared. In addressing integration in their states, CIO's will also examine governance issues; data standards initiatives under way at the national level; the integration of data in justice and health & human services; the evolving role of state agencies as intelligence providers and not just data collectors; and drivers for integration, such as homeland security, E-911, and increasing customer demands.

Notes

[1]"Walking the Road to the Win-Win: NACIO Procurement Subcommittee's Recommendations on Liability Limitations for State IT Contracting," is available at *https://www.nacio.org/nascioCommittees/procurement*. NACIO anticipates releasing an additional set of recommendations on intellectual property clauses in early 2005. They will be available on NASCIO's Web site.

[2]NASCIO has published committee briefs on the privacy implications of data mining and e-authentication. They are entitled, "Think Before You Dig: The Privacy Implications of Data Mining and Aggregation" and "Who Are You? I Really Wanna Know: E-Authentication and its Privacy Implications" and are available at: *https://www.nascio.org/nascioCommittees/privacy/*.

[3]For more information about the Fair Information Use Principles, which serve as the foundation of many U.S. and other countries' privacy protection laws, please see NASCIO's "Information Privacy: A Spotlight on Key Issues," (February 2004). It is available at *https://www.nascio.org/nascioCommittees/privacy/* for NASCIO member download and purchase by non-members.

[4]Kathie Hackler and Ron Cowles, "Harnessing Broadband for Economic Growth," Gartner teleconference, June 24, 2003. *http://www4.gartner.com/2_events/audio conferences/2003/june/jun24tcm104.jsp*.

[5]W. David Gardner, "Offshore Outsourcers Said to Seek Risk Balance," *Information Week*, May 17, 2004. *http://www.informationweek.com/story/showArticle.jhtml?articleID=20301322*.

About the Authors

Chris Dixon is an issues coordinator for the National Association of Chief Information Officers (NASCIO) with responsibility for coordinating association activities in the areas of digital government, information security and economic development.

Drew Leatherby is an issues coordinator for the Na-

tional Association of Chief Information Officers (NASCIO) with responsibility for coordinating association activities in the areas of IT governance & service reform, interoperability & integration, and emerging technologies.

Mary Gay Whitmer is an issues coordinator for the National Association of Chief Information Officers (NASCIO) with responsibility for coordinating association activities in the areas of IT procurement and privacy.

Table A
STATEWIDE MANAGEMENT RESPONSIBILITIES OF THE CIO

State or other jurisdiction	Arch./ Std. Dev.	Budgeting	HR/ Hiring	Outsourcing	Perf. mgmt.	Personnel policy	Planning	Policies	Privacy policies	Procurement	Project mgmt.	Re-Engineering	Training
Alabama	RA	A	A	RA	A	RA	A	RAM	A	A	RA	A	RA
Alaska	N.A.	N.A.	N.A.	N.A.	N.A.	N.A.	N.A.	N.A.	N.A.	N.A.	N.A.	N.A.	
Arizona	RAM	RA	...	RA	...	RA	RAM	RAM	R	RA	RAM	RA	RAM
Arkansas	RAM	R	...	RAM	R	RAM	RAM	RAM	RAM	RM	RAM	R	RAM
California	RA	R	R	R	R	R	R	R	R	R	...	R	RA
Colorado	N.A.	N.A.	N.A.	N.A.	N.A.	N.A.	N.A.	N.A.	N.A.	N.A.	N.A.	N.A.	
Connecticut	RAM	RA	RA	RAM	RAM	R	RAM	RAM	RAM	RAM	RAM	RAM	RAM
Delaware	RAM	RAM	R	RAM	R	RA	RAM	RAM	RM	R	R	R	RAM
Florida	RA	R	...	R	...	R	RA	RA	...	...	R	...	RA
Georgia	RAM	RA	R	RAM	R	R	RAM	RAM	RAM	RAM	RAM	RAM	RAM
Hawaii	RAM			R	R	RM	RAM	RM	RM	R	R	R	RAM
Idaho	RA			R		RAM	RA	RAM	RAM	RA	R	R	RA
Illinois	N.A.	N.A.	N.A.	N.A.	N.A.	N.A.	N.A.	N.A.	N.A.	N.A.	N.A.	N.A.	
Indiana	N.A.	N.A.	N.A.	N.A.	N.A.	N.A.	N.A.	N.A.	N.A.	N.A.	N.A.	N.A.	
Iowa	RAM	...	...	RAM	R	R	RA	RAM	RA	R	R	R	RAM
Kansas	RAM	RAM	R	A	AM	R	RAM	RAM	RAM	RA	RAM	RAM	RAM
Kentucky	RAM	RA	...	RAM	R	RA	RAM	RA	RM	RA	RA	...	RAM
Louisiana	RA	R	...	RA	...	RA	RA	RA	R	RA	RA	...	RA
Maine	A	A	A	A	R	A	A	A	A	A	R	R	A
Maryland	A	RAM	R	RA	R	RA	RA	RA	A	RA	R	R	A
Massachusetts	RAM	RAM	R	RAM	RAM	R	RAM	RAM	RAM	R	RAM	R	RAM
Michigan	RAM	RAM	RAM	RAM	R	RAM	RAM	RAM	RAM	RAM	RAM	RAM	RAM
Minnesota	M	AM	RAM	A	RM	RAM	M	M	M	M	A	A	M
Mississippi	RAM	R	R	RAM	RA	RAM	RAM	R	RAM	RAM	R	RAM	RAM
Missouri	A	R	...	...	R	A	A	A	A	A	A	...	A
Montana	RA	R	...	A	RA	RA	RA	R	RAM	RA	RA	R	RA
Nebraska	RM	R	...	...	...	R	R	...	A	M	M	M	RM
Nevada	R	A	RA	RAM	R	RAM	RAM	RA	RA	RAM	A	R	R
New Hampshire	AM	R	AM	AM	AM	RAM	AM	AM	RA	AM	A	RAM	AM
New Jersey	RAM	RM		AM	R	RAM	RA	R	RAM	RAM	RM	RM	RAM
New Mexico	RAM	RM	RA	RA	RA	RAM	RM	RM	RA	RA	RAM	R	RAM
New York	RAM	R	...	R	R	RAM	RAM	RAM	RAM	RAM	M	RM	RAM
North Carolina	AM	A	...	R	...	A	AM	AM	RAM	AM	A	...	AM
North Dakota	RAM	RM	...	RAM	R	RA	RAM	RAM	RAM	RAM	RM	R	RAM
Ohio	RA	RAM	...	...	...	RAM	RAM	RAM	RAM	RAM	RA	...	RA
Oklahoma	N.A.	N.A.	N.A.	N.A.	N.A.	N.A.	N.A.	N.A.	N.A.	N.A.	N.A.	N.A.	
Oregon	RA	R	...	R	...	RAM	RAM	RAM	RA	RAM	...	...	RA
Pennsylvania	RAM	RAM	RAM	RAM	R	RAM	RAM	AM	R	RAM	RAM	R	RAM
Rhode Island	RAM	R	R	R	R	RAM	RAM	RAM	RA	R	R	R	RAM
South Carolina	R	A	...	...	R	A	R	A	AM	A	R	A	R
South Dakota	RAM	RAM	RAM	RAM	RAM	RAM	RAM	RAM	RAM	RAM	RAM	RAM	RAM
Tennessee	RAM	R	R	RA	...	R	R	RAM	R	RAM	RAM	...	RAM
Texas	RA	R	...	RAM	R	A	RA	RAM	RAM	R	...	RAM	RA
Utah	RAM	RA	R	RAM	RA	R	RAM	RAM	RA	RAM	RAM	R	RAM
Vermont	AM	RM	RA	RA	RAM	RAM	RAM	RAM	RA	RAM	RAM	RAM	AM
Virginia	AM	AM	RM	RAM	R	AM	AM	RA	AM	AM	AM	AM	AM
Washington	A	R				RM	M	M	RAM	RAM	...	...	A
West Virginia	RA			RA	R	RAM	RAM	R	RA	RA	RA	RA	RA
Wisconsin	RAM	RA	...	R	RAM	RA	RAM	RA	RAM	R	M	M	RAM
Wyoming	RAM	R	...	A	R	RA	RA	RA	RA	RA	...	RA	RAM
Dist. of Columbia	RAM	RAM	R	RAM	R	R	RAM	RAM	RAM	A	RAM	RAM	RAM
Count*	46	42	23	41	36	46	46	45	45	45	41	37	46

Source: National Association of State Chief Information Officers.
Note: This figure represents the number of states responding affirmatively (i.e., R, A, or M) in each category.

Key:
R—Recommend agency practices.
A—Approves agency practices.
M—Manage for agencies.
N.A. — Not available.
...—Not applicable.

Table B
COMPOSITION OF IT GOVERNING BOARDS

State or other jurisdiction	Number of representatives from each category								CIO role on board
	Agency	Elected officials	Judicial branch	Legislative branch	Local government	Public education	Private sector	Other	
Alabama	N.A.	N.A.	N.A.	N.A.	N.A.	N.A.	N.A.	N.A.	Chair or Leader
Alaska	N.A.	N.A.	N.A.	N.A.	N.A.	N.A.	N.A.	N.A.	N.A.
Arizona	4	...	1	2	1	1	4	1	Chair or Leader
Arkansas	9	...	...	...	1	...	...	6	Member (voting)
California	...Currently, there is no oversight board, but one is planned...								Chair or Leader
Colorado	N.A.	N.A.	N.A.	N.A.	N.A.	N.A.	N.A.	N.A.	N.A.
Connecticut	...	...	...	...	...	...	...	1	Chair or Leader
Delaware	2	1	1	1	...	...	...	4	Chair or Leader
Florida	N.A.	N.A.	N.A.	N.A.	N.A.	N.A.	N.A.	N.A.	N.A.
Georgia	...	...	1	4	...	...	7	...	Other leadership role
Hawaii	16	...	1	...	...	2	...	...	Other leadership role
Idaho	3	1	1	4	1	2	2	2	Chair or Leader
Illinois	N.A.	N.A.	N.A.	N.A.	N.A.	N.A.	N.A.	N.A.	N.A.
Indiana	N.A.	N.A.	N.A.	N.A.	N.A.	N.A.	N.A.	N.A.	N.A.
Iowa	2	...	1	4	...	1	5	1	Advisory capacity only
Kansas	4	...	2	1	2	1	3	4	Member (voting)
Kentucky	9	5	1	1	1	2	...	2	Chair or Leader
Louisiana	12	8	1	2	...	1	5	1	Other leadership role
Maine	N.A.	N.A.	N.A.	N.A.	N.A.	N.A.	N.A.	N.A.	Chair or Leader
Maryland	...	...	...	...	...	...	...	...	Other leadership role
Massachusetts	1	...	1	3	...	...	...	2	Other leadership role
Michigan	19	...	1	3	...	...	...	1	Chair or Leader
Minnesota	11	...	...	...	...	...	...	...	Member (voting)
Mississippi	...	...	...	2	...	...	...	5	Member (non-voting)
Missouri	16	4	2	2	...	...	...	...	Member (non-voting)
Montana	9	1	1	3	2	2	1	...	Member (voting)
Nebraska	...	1	...	...	1	2	5	...	Other leadership role
Nevada	N.A.	N.A.	N.A.	N.A.	N.A.	N.A.	N.A.	N.A.	Member (voting)
New Hampshire	7	...	...	2	2	...	...	...	Other leadership role
New Jersey	4	...	...	...	...	...	...	3	Chair or Leader
New Mexico	4	...	2	2	...	2	5	3	Advisory capacity only
New York	...	...	...	...	...	...	...	80	Chair or Leader
North Carolina	4	...	...	...	...	...	...	12	Other leadership role
North Dakota	9	3	1	2	...	1	2	...	Chair or Leader
Ohio	6	4	1	2	...	...	...	...	Chair or Leader
Oklahoma	N.A.	N.A.	N.A.	N.A.	N.A.	N.A.	N.A.	N.A.	N.A.
Oregon	...	...	...	...	...	...	...	...	Other leadership role
Pennsylvania	8	...	...	...	...	...	...	...	No data
Rhode Island	5	1	...	2	2	3	3	2	Chair or Leader
South Carolina	...	3	...	2	...	...	...	...	Advisory capacity only
South Dakota	6	...	...	...	...	...	...	2	Chair or Leader
Tennessee	2	...	1	7	...	...	2	3	Other leadership role
Texas	7	...	...	...	...	...	...	3	Other leadership role
Utah	...	...	...	...	...	...	...	...	Other leadership role
Vermont	7	...	...	...	...	...	...	...	Chair or Leader
Virginia	1	...	...	1	...	...	8	...	Advisory capacity only
Washington	1	...	1	4	...	2	2	5	Member (voting)
West Virginia	13	6	1	1	...	1	...	4	Other leadership role
Wisconsin	N.A.	N.A.	N.A.	N.A.	N.A.	N.A.	N.A.	N.A.	Advisory capacity only
Wyoming	6	1	...	...	...	...	2	...	Advisory capacity only
Dist. of Columbia	...	...	...	...	...	...	...	...	Other leadership role
Count*	30	13	19	23	9	14	16	21	

Source: National Association of Chief Information Officers.
Note: This total represents the number of states responding affirmatively in each category.
... . — Not applicable.
N.A. — Not available.

Table C
STATEWIDE IT PROCUREMENT RESPONSIBILITY

State or other jurisdiction	Hardware	Software	Services
Alabama	Shared	Shared	ITO
Alaska	N.A.	N.A.	N.A.
Arizona	CPO	CPO	CPO
Arkansas	Shared	Shared	Shared
California	CPO	CPO	CPO
Colorado	N.A.	N.A.	N.A.
Connecticut	ITO	ITO	ITO
Delaware	Shared	Shared	Shared
Florida	ITO	ITO	ITO
Georgia	ITO	ITO	ITO
Hawaii	Shared	Shared	Shared
Idaho	Shared	Shared	Shared
Illinois	N.A.	N.A.	N.A.
Indiana	N.A.	N.A.	N.A.
Iowa	ITO	ITO	ITO
Kansas	Shared	Shared	Shared
Kentucky	CPO	CPO	CPO
Louisiana	CPO	CPO	CPO
Maine	ITO	ITO	ITO
Maryland	Shared	Shared	Shared
Massachusetts	CPO	CPO	CPO
Michigan	Shared	Shared	Shared
Minnesota	Shared	Shared	ITO
Mississippi	ITO	ITO	ITO
Missouri	CPO	CPO	CPO
Montana	Shared	Shared	Shared
Nebraska	Shared	Shared	No data
Nevada	ITO	Shared	ITO
New Hampshire	CPO	CPO	CPO
New Jersey	Shared	Shared	Shared
New Mexico	Shared	Shared	Shared
New York	Shared	Shared	Shared
North Carolina	ITO	ITO	ITO
North Dakota	Shared	Shared	Shared
Ohio	ITO	ITO	ITO
Oklahoma	N.A.	N.A.	N.A.
Oregon	Shared	Shared	Shared
Pennsylvania	CPO	CPO	ITO
Rhode Island	CPO	CPO	CPO
South Carolina	Shared	Shared	Shared
South Dakota	Shared	Shared	Shared
Tennessee	ITO	CPO	ITO
Texas	ITO	ITO	ITO
Utah	CPO	CPO	CPO
Vermont	Shared	Shared	Shared
Virginia	ITO	ITO	ITO
Washington	Shared	Shared	Shared
West Virginia	Shared	Shared	Shared
Wisconsin	Shared	Shared	Shared
Wyoming	CPO	CPO	CPO
Dist. of Columbia	Shared	Shared	Shared

Source: The National Association of State Chief Information Officers
Key:
ITO—IT Office/Department.
CPO—Central Procurement Office.
Shared—Shared responsibilities between ITO and CPO.
N.A.—Not available.

Trends and Issues in State Libraries: Balancing Books and Bytes

By Thomas J. Hennen Jr.

Public libraries will continue to be buffeted by budget shortfalls at state and local levels. The rapid changes brought about by the Internet and electronic resources, as well as copyright, privacy issues, and censorship concerns, have presented major problems. Public libraries have adapted with new forms of service and new organizational structures.

No examination of the current and future status of library services can reasonably begin without noting this: library service in the United States is primarily a local affair. The federal and state governments provide funding and strategic planning, but, for the most part and in most states, public libraries are supported and governed locally.

In many Western countries, the national government is much more directly involved in funding and governing library services. Andrew Carnegie's gifts of millions of dollars for libraries in local communities at the beginning of the 20th century led U.S. public libraries to be far more local agencies than those found in many Western countries. The Carnegie grants encouraged local rather than district, regional or state library development. Wider units, on a county or regional basis, may have been wiser. That is something that even the Carnegie Endowment acknowledged, but libraries became and have mostly remained primarily local agencies.[1]

Copyright issues, especially the Digital Millennium Copyright Act (DMCA),[2] have added problems for all types of libraries. Libraries cannot make information available to their constituents if copyright restrictions are too restrictive. The tug and pull of publishers and copyright holders on the one hand, and librarians and other advocates of open access to information on the other hand will be a continuing trend. Nancy Kranich's paper on the Information Commons[3] does a remarkable job of illustrating the issues involved.

Although libraries are local agencies, the federal government continues to play a key role in setting the stage for library services. Each of the 50 states plays a commensurate role as well, as the next section demonstrates.

State Library Agencies

State library agencies vary throughout the United States, both in placement within the state government structure and in authority or funding ability. In some states, the state library agency runs an actual library with a collection and a building that everyone recognizes as "the state library." New York and Illinois are examples. The collection usually includes state documents and historical items as well as research items for the legislature and the public. In other states, like Minnesota, there is no state library building or collection and the agency is involved only in planning and distribution of funding.

The funding configurations also vary widely. Hawaii runs all libraries as a single system and Ohio provides the majority of funding for public libraries, but these are exceptions to the rule. A few other states, Mississippi, Pennsylvania and West Virginia, provide more than 20 percent of local library operating funds. The majority of states provide 5 percent or less of local library revenue. Many library agency operations are largely or completely funded by federal grants while they distribute state and/or federal funds to libraries. Most work on state legislation, literacy efforts, public relations, and provide for the smooth operation of interlibrary lending of materials. A few are involved with archives and state records. A few others provide certification programs for library staff and/or libraries.

Emerging Trends in State Library Operations

The most significant emerging trends for state library agencies are their involvement in full text databases, electronic network development, and massive budget cutting.

Many believe that everything on the Internet is free for the taking, but that is far from the truth. Full text databases are an example of an expensive resource that libraries provide. Full text databases are electronic databases that provide the full text of periodical and journal articles online. Users can read the article, print off a copy, or e-mail the text. Depend-

Table A: Types of Public Library Organization in the U.S.: 2003

Type of library organization	Number of states with this library type	States with this type	Percent of all U.S. libraries	Percent of U.S. population served	Total library expenditures	Per capita expenditures
Number			9,138	277,362,711	$8,026,123,397	
Municipal	44	All but: Ga., Hawaii, Ind., Ky., Md., Penn., Wyo.	54.2%	33.4%	34.51%	$28.44
County/parish	38	All but: Conn., D.C., Hawaii, Idaho, Ill., Ind., Maine, Mass., N.H., Penn., R.I., Vt., Wash.	10.4	33.6	31.58	29.91
Multi-jurisdictional	27	Ala., Alaska, Ark., Calif., Colo., Fla., Ga., Ind., Kan., Ky., La., Minn., Miss., Mo., Mont., N.H., N.J., N.M., N.C., N.D., Okla., S.D., Texas, Vt., Va., W.Va., Wis.	3.5	8.8	5.56	17.18
Special district	21	Ala., Ariz., Calif., Colo., Del., Fla., Idaho, Ill., Ind., Kan., Ky., La., Mich., Nev., N.M., N.Y., Ore., S.D., Texas, Vt., Wash.	11.2	10.6	12.54	34.39
Non-profit/agency	17	Alaska, Conn., Maine, Mass., N.H., N.J., N.M., N.Y., N.C., Ohio, Ore., Penn., R.I., S.D., Texas, Vt., Va.	14.9	6.9	6.76	23.5
City-county	16	Ala., Ark., Calif., Colo., Fla., La., Minn., Miss., Mo., Mont., N.C., N.D., S.D., Tenn., Texas, Utah	1	2.9	2.72	26.94
Miscellaneous	12	Ark., Hawaii, Iowa, Kan., Mass., Neb., N.M., N.Y., N.C., Penn., S.D., Texas	1	1.2	0.99	18.38
School district	8	Calif., Colo., Mich., N.Y., Ohio, Ore., W.Va, Wis.	3.4	2.6	5.29	59.40
Indian or tribal	7	Alaska, Ariz., N.J., N.M., N.Y., S.D, Wis.	0.4	0.1	0.05	27.17
Total/average			100.00%	100.00%	100.00%	$28.94

Source: Federal State Cooperative Service Data and Hennen's American Public Library Ratings.

ing on the publisher and the licensing arrangement, graphics or photos are sometimes included. Almost all states have entered into financial contracts with database providers to provide database content to state users, often at home as well as in the library. Individual libraries and cooperative library systems often supplement databases that are available statewide with ones that are specific to a geographic area. The provision of full text databases by states, regions and local libraries is a trend that is likely to accelerate as budgets become constrained and publishers learn to gauge the market better. In a budget pinch, libraries are increasingly deciding to drop print journals in favor of their electronic counterparts.

Nearly all state library agencies plan for electronic and Internet connections. The federal e-rate program advanced interest in network development. High-speed Internet connections are used for Web connections, circulation systems, video conferencing and much more, so it is no surprise that state library agencies have taken the lead in developing these networks on a statewide basis.

In the recent budget cutting that has engulfed most states, state governments have cut state library agencies at roughly the same rate as most other state pro-grams. In some states, such as California, Colorado, Florida, Iowa, Massachusetts, Minnesota and Washington, the cuts have been significantly higher.

Public libraries are often granted state aid, provided grant money, and subjected to certification and standards by state library agencies, so the health of the state's funding is important to them, even when most of their direct funding is provided locally, usually by property taxes. Among the major threats in the near term for libraries are public library dependence on state funding for all or most of their full text databases and library dependence on the state's Internet backbone for their Internet and circulation system connections. In the context of state budget cuts nationwide, this dependence causes vulnerabilities. The threat is all the more serious, of course, in those states that have a substantial state aid cash grant program for public libraries.

Legislative Implications

Since the beginning of the Clinton administration, a main thrust of the federal government has been to connect school and public libraries to the Internet. This goal has been largely achieved by using e-rate funds. These grants are generated by Universal Ser-

Table B: 2003 Average Library Revenue Per Capita in the 50 States

State	2003 public library revenue per capita					Ratio			
	Local	State	Federal	Other	Total	Local	State	Federal	Other
Alabama	$13.61	$0.95	$0.10	$1.31	$15.98	85.2%	6.0%	0.7%	8.2%
Alaska	33.03	1.41	1.43	1.63	37.50	88.1	3.8	3.8	4.3
Arizona	22.23	0.11	0.14	0.53	23.01	96.6	0.5	0.6	2.3
Arkansas	13.94	0.47	0.00	1.19	15.60	89.3	3.0	0.0	7.7
California	23.41	2.06	0.09	1.85	27.41	85.4	7.5	0.3	6.7
Colorado	38.67	0.51	0.04	2.92	42.14	91.8	1.2	0.1	6.9
Connecticut	36.33	0.50	0.36	7.16	44.34	91.9	1.1	0.8	16.1
Delaware	16.04	3.54	0.15	2.67	22.40	71.6	15.8	0.7	11.9
Florida	21.99	2.05	0.21	1.13	25.37	86.7	8.1	0.8	4.4
Georgia	14.69	3.72	0.20	0.99	19.59	75.0	19.0	1.0	5.1
Hawaii	0.00	18.50	0.45	1.76	20.71	0.0	89.3	2.2	8.5
Idaho	19.95	0.66	0.15	2.61	23.38	85.3	2.8	0.7	11.2
Illinois	43.26	3.36	0.28	4.37	51.28	84.4	6.6	0.6	8.5
Indiana	39.77	3.38	0.11	2.28	45.55	87.3	7.4	0.2	5.0
Iowa	23.25	0.76	0.15	2.24	26.40	88.1	2.9	0.6	8.5
Kansas	31.46	0.83	0.18	4.57	37.04	84.9	2.2	0.5	12.3
Kentucky	18.61	0.99	0.11	1.96	21.67	85.9	4.5	0.5	9.1
Louisiana	24.08	1.52	0.02	1.60	27.22	88.5	5.6	0.1	5.9
Maine	18.28	0.15	0.00	6.42	24.85	73.6	0.6	0.0	25.8
Maryland	25.52	5.03	0.38	5.99	36.92	69.1	13.6	1.0	16.2
Massachusetts	29.96	3.22	0.27	4.19	37.64	79.6	8.6	0.7	11.1
Michigan	29.96	1.22	0.05	2.59	33.81	88.6	3.6	0.1	7.6
Minnesota	28.29	1.65	0.21	1.96	32.12	88.1	5.1	0.7	6.1
Mississippi	9.81	2.64	0.24	1.02	13.72	71.5	19.3	1.8	7.4
Missouri	27.18	0.97	0.33	2.81	31.28	86.9	3.1	1.0	9.0
Montana	15.88	0.42	0.08	4.54	20.92	75.9	2.0	0.4	21.7
Nebraska	26.20	0.33	0.24	1.53	28.30	92.6	1.2	0.9	5.4
Nevada	19.95	0.64	0.27	8.52	29.38	67.9	2.2	0.9	29.0
New Hampshire	26.65	0.07	0.02	3.13	29.88	89.2	0.2	0.1	10.5
New Jersey	36.89	1.16	0.15	2.08	40.28	91.6	2.9	0.4	5.2
New Mexico	16.38	0.29	0.16	0.97	17.80	92.0	1.6	0.9	5.5
New York	36.50	2.65	0.32	7.27	46.74	78.1	5.7	0.7	15.6
North Carolina	15.66	1.73	0.13	1.43	18.96	82.6	9.1	0.7	7.6
North Dakota	13.21	1.07	0.03	2.34	16.64	79.4	6.4	0.2	14.1
Ohio	11.30	40.44	0.08	5.03	56.85	19.9	71.1	0.1	8.8
Oklahoma	21.26	0.64	0.09	1.46	23.45	90.7	2.7	0.4	6.2
Oregon	35.23	0.22	0.35	2.40	38.19	92.2	0.6	0.9	6.3
Pennsylvania	13.73	7.04	0.27	3.37	24.41	56.3	28.8	1.1	13.8
Rhode Island	23.19	6.05	0.25	8.57	38.06	60.9	15.9	0.7	22.5
South Carolina	16.99	1.47	0.15	1.00	19.61	86.7	7.5	0.8	5.1
South Dakota	26.06	0.00	0.18	2.30	28.54	91.3	0.0	0.6	8.0
Tennessee	13.26	0.00	0.10	1.00	14.36	92.3	0.0	0.7	7.0
Texas	16.36	0.28	0.14	0.65	17.42	93.9	1.6	0.8	3.7
Utah	26.00	0.40	0.11	1.41	27.90	93.2	1.4	0.4	5.0
Vermont	16.65	0.03	0.00	7.07	23.75	70.1	0.1	0.0	29.8
Virginia	24.17	2.88	0.18	1.54	28.77	84.0	10.0	0.6	5.4
Washington	38.78	0.27	0.16	1.64	40.86	94.9	0.7	0.4	5.0
West Virginia	8.72	5.04	0.07	1.24	15.07	57.9	33.4	0.5	8.2
Wisconsin	29.20	0.89	0.11	2.13	32.32	90.3	2.7	0.3	6.6
Wyoming	32.54	0.01	0.18	2.21	34.95	93.1	0.0	0.5	6.3
Average	24.45	3.62	0.17	2.69	30.93	79.0	11.7	0.6	8.7

Source: Federal State Cooperative Service and haplr-index.com.

vice Fund charges on consumer phone bills. Many school and public libraries receive substantial portions of their Internet connections from e-rate funds. The funding is targeted to communities with the least local financial resources. Recent federal legislation called the Child Internet Protection Act (CIPA)[4] limited e-rate funds to those libraries that use Internet filters to limit access to pornography and inappropriate materials.

The American Library Association and many local public libraries challenged CIPA in court on the grounds that the filters failed to work properly, often letting pornographic material through while restricting access to needed information. The Supreme Court ultimately ruled the legislation constitutional but noted that libraries needed to be in a position to turn off the filters if adults so requested.

An ironic result of the distribution formula for e-rate funds has been that libraries in wealthier communities have often found it is less expensive to forgo e-rate funds than to buy filters, while poorer communities have found themselves forced to provide filters.

Since the attacks of 9/11, the Patriot Act has added new issues for all types of libraries. Most states have existing privacy laws that prohibit the disclosure of library use records without a court order. The Patriot Act provides for disclosure with a far lower threshold, and many librarians have found this troublesome. The American Library Association resisted the provisions and called for their removal, citing constitutional and civil liberties issues. Former Attorney General Ashcroft maintained that the Patriot Act provisions had never been used in a library setting, a contention disputed by some librarians. Some members of Congress have tried to modify these provisions. It is likely that the debate will continue at both state and federal levels.[5]

Given the environment at the federal level with the Patriot Act and CIPA, state policy-makers should expect increasing challenges to privacy and free speech issues that may be at odds with existing state law. In some states, legislators have already proposed the requirement of Internet filters as a condition of state funding along the lines of the federal CIPA law. Policy-makers can expect resistance from free speech advocates. No filter companies can guarantee that their products work effectively 100 percent of the time. Many librarians charged that they either "over block," blocking useful materials that is not pornographic, or "under block," failing to block objectionable material, or usually both.

Policy-makers should not expect the censorship attempts to be limited to internet sources alone, of course. Videos, music CDs and, of course, print materials, will continue to be challenged both at the local and state levels. State library agencies and all the library literature urge libraries to have a written and specific materials selection policy and a process for re-consideration. Most states have laws giving library boards broad discretion in discharging their duties in conformance with local community standards, but state and federal changes are continuous. A 2004 election driven by values can be expected to drive further censorship/free speech legislation to the forefront.

States that do not have district laws on the books (see Table A) will want to consider writing them. The increased interest by local and state lawmakers in regional cooperation will fuel the trend. In fact, using Table A, policy-makers may want to consider whether forms of library operations of all kinds that are available in other states would be appropriate to their own.

Some have made the case that the formation of special districts for libraries runs a major public policy risk. Popular items like parks and libraries in "a la carte" districts can soak up public funds. That leaves less for important but non-attractive government functions like accounting or road building. The converse of this argument is that too often local government officials use the very popularity of library services to their own detriment. City mayors have used this strategy in local budget battles: threatening to close a branch library causes city council members to rally to the defense of their branches and voila—the budget is restored.

Wireless access points or "hot spots" are growing in popularity at airports, restaurants and libraries. Recent efforts in Philadelphia to make the entire city wireless ran into resistance from the private sector phone and cable distributors. Comparable arguments may arise over taxpayer supported, but free to the user, library wireless.

Policy-makers should also expect issues to arise over libraries and communities providing their own wiring for Internet and telecommunications infrastructure rather than buying the services from a phone or cable company.

A review of existing state statutes for libraries will usually uncover the need to establish new enabling legislation, re-consider funding formulas, and examine privacy and censorship issues.

Countercyclical Business

Public libraries are a traditionally counter-cyclical business. Library use increases when the economy sours, but as the economy gets worse, funding falls. By the time the economy recovers, library budget cuts have usually diminished libraries' resources so dramatically that many users in an expanding economy go elsewhere for service—only to return when the economy sours again. A recent study by the American Library Association re-affirmed the connection between the business cycle and library use.[6]

The budget problems in most states are causing problems for many libraries, of course, but the impact varies by the type of library program in a state. In late 2004 there were threats to close libraries completely in several areas of the country. Buffalo and Erie County Library in New York was among the most prominent of the threatened closures.[7] Because Colorado passed a constitutional limit on taxes called TABOR,[8] libraries there have been especially hard hit. Denver Public Library has slashed service radically and is attempting to establish itself as an independent library-taxing district.

Faced with large budget cuts from Ohio state funding, the Cuyahoga County treasurer is calling for consolidation of the county library system with the seven independent libraries in the county, including Cleveland. Similar calls for consolidation and wider units were heard recently in Broome County, New York; Scott County, Iowa; and Waukesha and Milwaukee Counties in Wisconsin. Calls to consolidate or form separate taxing districts are likely to increase in the near future, driven by budget problems and desires for efficiencies.

The fastest growing type of public library in the United States is the district library, a wider unit of service, often with elected boards and taxing authority. Only 40 percent of states provide for this type of service, however. Support for public libraries by the public at large is very high, even in a recessionary environment. Library Journal and American Libraries publish referendum reports annually. These referenda are for new buildings, higher rate authorizations, and so forth. The 2004 reports saw only a 50 percent success rate and this is very low by historic standards. In recent years, the success rate for library referenda has usually been closer to 85 percent. In fact, one of the reasons that some local officials oppose the development of separate library districts is the very popularity of libraries. A competing but more popular taxing authority is threatening to them.

For the next decade, public libraries will be challenged with the need to "balance the books and the bytes." Traditional library users expect print materials and readers' advisory assistance in a comfortable environment while new users expect the library to provide high speed, wireless Internet access, and the latest in technological services.

Table C: Library Visits and Library Spending Per Capita in the 50 States

State	Spending per capita	Visits per capita	Spending rank	Visit rank
Alabama	$15.68	3.0	46	47
Alaska	36.35	4.4	10	29
Arizona	22.11	3.7	34	38
Arkansas	13.75	2.9	49	49
California	25.38	4.1	26	32
Colorado	38.21	5.8	9	7
Connecticut	40.93	6.5	5	2
Delaware	19.87	3.7	37	37
Florida	22.92	4.0	32	34
Georgia	19.13	3.3	39	43
Hawaii	20.52	4.6	36	26
Idaho	22.85	5.8	33	6
Illinois	41.03	5.5	4	13
Indiana	42.41	6.3	3	3
Iowa	25.51	5.3	25	15
Kansas	36.14	5.8	11	8
Kentucky	19.00	3.6	40	39
Louisiana	23.20	2.9	31	48
Maine	24.36	5.0	29	22
Maryland	35.19	5.2	14	18
Massachusetts	35.71	5.5	12	14
Michigan	29.75	4.1	18	33
Minnesota	31.45	5.2	16	16
Mississippi	13.14	2.8	50	50
Missouri	27.56	4.5	22	27
Montana	16.62	4.0	44	35
Nebraska	26.45	5.2	24	19
Nevada	26.79	4.1	23	31
New Hampshire	28.93	4.7	19	24
New Jersey	39.02	5.1	7	20
New Mexico	18.32	3.3	41	44
New York	44.65	5.7	2	11
North Carolina	18.03	3.8	42	36
North Dakota	16.16	4.2	45	30
Ohio	53.93	6.9	1	1
Oklahoma	21.28	4.7	35	25
Oregon	38.94	5.9	8	4
Pennsylvania	24.18	3.4	30	41
Rhode Island	35.27	4.7	13	10
South Carolina	19.38	3.5	38	40
South Dakota	24.74	5.9	27	5
Tennessee	14.17	3.1	47	45
Texas	16.69	3.0	43	46
Utah	28.08	5.0	21	21
Vermont	24.38	5.2	28	17
Virginia	28.28	4.5	20	28
Washington	39.87	4.8	6	23
West Virginia	13.93	3.4	48	42
Wisconsin	31.30	5.7	17	9
Wyoming	32.81	5.6	15	12
Average	28.94	4.5		

Source: Federal State Cooperative Service and haplr-index.com.

Some elected officials and members of the public believe that since the Internet is now so pervasive and easy to use, the need for libraries is rapidly diminishing. In just 15 years, the Internet has gone from being a tool for researchers to a ubiquitous technology. In 1994, only one in 10 library systems provided Internet access. By 2004, the score was virtually 100 percent.

As Table C demonstrates, there is a very high correlation between the amount spent for library services on a per capita basis and the visits to libraries. Policy-makers must balance the public response with its willingness to pay.

Public libraries are seeing increasing challenges from all sides on the electronic information front. Each new medium presents librarians and policymakers with a new set of questions about how the medium can or should be integrated into the public library service profile. Many still question the validity of video in public libraries, arguing that they are entertainment only and compete with private business. Comparable arguments can and will be advanced regarding MP3s, of course.

Virtual reference is an attempt by libraries to provide online, real time answers to library user questions on the Internet. It is possible to provide 24/7 services by sharing librarians around various time zones. The trend towards digital preservation will undoubtedly continue. Many public libraries have unique local resources that can be preserved through digitization and placement on the Web. The costs are high and the technology changes rapidly.

Public librarians believe in libraries as public goods. Many fear the increasing commoditization of all forms of information from the for profit sector. This has led many to call for the libraries to be part of an "information commons."

The stress lines between the information commons and libraries as a public good on the one hand and profit-making inclinations of the information industry on the other, will engender much conflict that legislators at the state as well as federal levels will be called on to resolve in the next decade.

Notes

[1] A discussion of the relationship of Carnegie library grants as well as the federal government role in library development can be found in Chapter 3 of *Civic Space/ cyberspace: The American Public Library in the Information Age*, .By Redmond Kathleen Molz.

[2] The American Library Association provides balanced information on the DMCA on its Web site at: http:// www.ala.org/ala/washoff/WOissues/copyrightb/dmca/ guidedmca.htm.

[3] *The Information Commons: A Public Policy Report Free Expression Policy Project* is available on the Web at: http:/ /www.fepproject.org/policyreports/infocommons.content sexsum.htm.

[4] Information on CIPA is available from a number of sources, including the American Library Association Web site at: http://www.ala.org/ala/washoff/WOissues/ civilliberties/cipaweb/cipa.htm.

[5] The American Library Association provides balanced information on the Patriot Act on its Web site at: http:// www.ala.org/ala/oif/ifissues/usapatriotact.htm.

[6] The American Library Association Study of the relationship between library use and the economic cycle is available on the Web at: http://www.wcfls.lib.wi.us/ libstudies_pdf/ALALibraryUseData.pdf .

[7] "Buffalo Library System Saved, But Must Retrench," *Library Journal*, Dec. 13, 2004. http://www.libraryjournal .com/article/CA487351?display =breakingNews.

[8] TABOR is an acronym for the Taxpayer Bill of Rights. It passed in Colorado in 1992 and has had an impact on government spending throughout the state.

References

de la Peña McCook, Kathleen. *Introduction to Public Librarianship*. New York, NY: Neal-Schuman. 2004.

Hennen, Thomas J. Jr. *Hennen's Public Library Planner: A Manual and Interactive CD-ROM*. New York: Neal-Schuman, 2004 .

Kranich, Nancy. *The Information Commons: A Public Policy Report*. Free Expression Policy Project. http:// www.fepproject.org/policyreports/infocommons. contentsexsum.html.

McCabe, Ronald B. *Civic Librarianship: Renewing the Social Mission of the Public Library*, Scarecrow Press, 2001.

Molz, Redmond Kathleen, and Dain, Phyl. *Civic Space/ cyberspace: The American Public Library in the Information Age*. Cambridge, MA: MIT Press, 1999.

Agencies

ALA—American Library Association: www.ala.org

COSLA—Council of State Library Agencies: www.cosla.org/profiles

FSCS—Federal State Cooperative Service: nces.ed.gov/ surveys/libraries/FSCS.asp

HAPLR—Hennen's American Public Library Ratings: www.haplr-index.com

NCLIS—National Council on Libraries and Information Services: www.nclis.gov/index.cfm

NCES—National Commission on Educational Statistics: www.nclis.gov/statsurv/NCES/index.html

About the Author

Thomas J. Hennen Jr. is director of the Waukesha County Federated Library System in Wisconsin. He is the creator of the HAPLR Library Ratings (www.haplr-index.com), and author of *Hennen's Public Library Planner* (Neal-Schuman, 2004).

Professional Licensing
By Pam Brinegar

In an effort to contain costs while also providing better consumer service, government agencies throughout North America are developing business plans and restructuring professional and occupational regulatory agencies. Increased technology use is bringing new security problems along with enhanced access for all stakeholders. The professional licensing stakeholder community is expanding to include international regulators.

State professional licensing agencies are charged with protecting consumers from harm resulting from illegal or incompetent practitioner acts. They carry out their mission by ensuring that candidates for professional and occupational licensure, certification or registration meet all criteria mandated through statutes and regulations.[1] The agencies also renew licenses and administer continuing education and professional discipline programs. This context is expanding to include other countries where the system of professional licensing is most like that found in the United States (e.g., Western Europe, Canada, Australia, New Zealand and some Pacific Rim countries).

Agency Consolidation

In the late 1970s and early 1980s, there was a legislative trend to centralize state agencies based on statutory mission. As a result, most professions and occupations in 37 states and the District of Columbia are regulated by central agencies that share varying degrees of administrative tasks with the licensing boards. Some states (e.g. Indiana, Virginia, Washington) established two licensing agencies, one for regulation of health professions, and another for non-health.[2]

Agency consolidation is again occurring among the states, sometimes on a fairly large scale. In Illinois, the new Department of Financial and Professional Regulation (DFPR) combines the Departments of Professional Regulation, Insurance and Financial Institutions with the Offices of Banks and Real Estate. In Texas, 12 agencies are now combining into four departments under the Health and Human Services Commission. A proposed California reform would eliminate 118 boards and commissions, placing their functions in a Division of Commercial Licensing.[3]

One rationale for these agency restructurings is the presumed efficiency of grouping together all similar functions. Such agencies are considered not only less costly to operate, but much better providers of consumer service. For example, Oregon Business Plan's Objective 3 is to streamline regulatory processes and systems, with a focus on permits for de-velopment, regulation and registration of new businesses, and regulations that overlap between state agencies or between the state and local government.[4] The Oregon Office of Regulatory Streamlining claims "the nation's most comprehensive directory of state licenses, permits, registrations, certificates, authorizations, and charters."[5]

Professional Discipline

Every state has an administrative procedures act based in large part on the 1981 model act developed by the National Conference of Commissioners on Uniform State Laws (NCCUSL) that prescribes, among other things, disciplinary process.[6] Professional discipline is enormously costly, sometimes consuming up to 50 percent of an agency's resources. Agencies use increasingly efficient methods to handle their investigative case loads, such as permitting staff to handle minor complaints rather than involving the board or by employing alternative dispute resolution techniques, such as mediation, to reach a fairly rapid resolution for lesser offenses. No matter which approach is used, it is admittedly difficult to ensure that professional discipline is administered in a uniform and fair manner.

To introduce impartiality into the process, the Virginia Department of Health Professions has launched the first sanction reference point system for regulatory disciplinary cases. Using a point system developed from its own history of disciplinary actions over a six-year period, the Board of Medicine is the first of the state's boards to use the new method. All Virginia health licensing boards will eventually use the system, as reference points are developed based on the history of each board.[7]

Technology

The use of modern technology is now pervasive in professional regulation, supporting professional development, credentialing (licensing), service delivery and demonstration of continued competence. Now that candidates can prepare for and take their licensing examinations as well as apply for and renew their licenses online, security concerns are changing as well. Providers of computer based testing (CBT) find they must routinely check online discussion groups and other resources in an effort to detect security breaches.[8] Advantages of using CBT include candidate opportunities for continuous (or at least greatly expanded) access to licensing examinations, immediate scoring results, and the ability to generate varying versions of an examination.

Continuing Competence

Practitioner continuing competence remains a critical issue facing regulatory bodies. States frequently require mandatory continuing education programs designed to ensure that licensees maintain a level of minimally acceptable competence; however, initial licensure is typically granted for generic skills in a given profession or occupation. Depending on what tasks practitioners actually perform on a daily basis, state-mandated continuing education programs may or may not provide appropriate instruction for their individual competency needs. For that reason, there is a growing interest in requiring some additional demonstration of competence.

In Canada, the United Kingdom, Australia and New Zealand, it is now common for licensed health professionals to submit self-assessment tools such as practice portfolios that describe in detail their actual professional practice activities and propose individualized plans for remaining competent to practice. Although this system is based on the belief that it is up to professionals to maintain an appropriate level of competence, the ultimate responsibility for approving the proposed educational plans and for auditing randomly selected licensees in the workplace resides with the regulatory body. Online competence assessment resources are helping licensees learn to comply with the higher standards. For example, The Irish Nursing Board (an Board Altranais) provides an interactive e-learning center permitting its licensees the opportunity for peer-to-peer exchanges regarding competence as well as to review examples of actual competency assessment documents.[9]

The Mexican secretariat of education has established an Advisory Board for Professional Certification which is working toward the development of a national quality assurance system for the professions. Extraordinary features of this National System of Certification will include voluntary periodic recertification for both the certifying bodies and the professionals.[10]

Federal Initiatives

Federal activities bearing on professional licensing are often far-reaching and may take decades to fully implement. Three of these will likely receive increasing attention during the upcoming months.

Americans with Disabilities Act

The Americans With Disabilities Act (ADA) of 1990 "requires that credentialing agencies provide access to examination administration facilities, administer examinations for disabled candidates as often and in as timely a manner as examinations for nondisabled candidates, and provide examinations whose results measure candidates' level of knowledge and skill rather than their disabilities."[11] How the ADA should apply to individual candidates is still being worked out through state regulations and the courts.

Antitrust and the FTC

Twenty-five years ago, the Federal Trade Commission won its first antitrust case removing barriers to the competitive advertising of professional services. Such activity was considered unethical by physicians, attorneys and others since it was widely assumed that consumers who used the services of those advertising lower prices would unknowingly receive lower quality services. Five years ago the U.S. Supreme Court expressed discomfort with "permitting the market to operate in the 'learned professions,' including its own." A recent survey concludes that permitting such competition "yields major benefits to consumers in the form of lower prices, without adverse effects on quality." [12]

Trade Agreements

Services, including the professions and occupations, continue to represent the fastest growing global economy and, since 2000, have been included in multilateral trade negotiations for the General Agreement on Trade in Services which is under the supervision of the World Trade Organization .

The North American Free Trade Agreement also provides a structure through which individual professions and their regulatory bodies may reach agreement on the terms for mutual recognition of professional credentials. Under both treaties, agreements reached between countries are not binding on the states in the United States, which receive the agreement terms in the form of recommendations and which they individually may or may not incorporate into their statutes or regulations.[13]

The European Parliament is finalizing a Directive on Services in the Internal Market which provides a legal framework for the removal of unnecessary barriers to trade across the European member states.[14] Those American professionals who are licensed in any member state of the European Union stand to benefit under the proposed directive; however, there likely will be unequal treatment in their instance since the United States is unable to enforce any mutual recognition agreement because of states rights.[15]

Domestic Professional Mobility

As professional mobility is facilitated among other western countries, decades-old questions are resurfacing about why, if the function of state professional regulation is to protect the consumer, there are such varying standards among the states in America. It bears repeating that of the almost 1,000 professions regulated by the states, only a few dozen are regulated by all the states. Even for the most established of those few dozen, including such professions as nursing, medicine and engineering, individuals licensed to practice in any one state cannot practice in another without meeting different standards. Some reciprocity and endorsement agreements exist between states, but it is not a simple matter for a state to accept the standards established by another state.

In the late 1970s, Shimberg and Roederer pointed out that no consumer group has ever sought licensing for regulation, but that the push for regulation comes from the practitioners of a profession.[16] Why then do the professions that sought and gained state licensure not push for harmonization of state requirements? Sometimes they do, but it takes time and resources. Almost a decade ago, the National Council of State Boards of Nursing (NCSBN) began discussing a process for an interstate nurse licensure compact which would permit licensed nurses to practice in U.S. jurisdictions without meeting a variety of differing licensure requirements. The first nursing board agreed to participate in 2000 and, following a dedicated and determined effort on NCSBN's part, the number of participating agencies is now 20. The reluctance of many state regulators to participate in such compacts is based in part on concerns about how to effectively identify and discipline those relatively few licensees who do present a real threat to the consumer and who may gain the ability to move around more quickly in the states than the system can follow them.

Notes

[1] Licensure, the most restrictive form of state regulation, specifies that it is illegal to practice a state-licensed profession without meeting state-defined standards, usually consisting of at least educational and additional examination requirements. No one without a license may practice the profession as defined in a scope-of-practice act. Certification, also known as title protection, may use requirements similar to those for licensure, but it does not prevent individuals from performing the tasks of the profession as long as they do not use the regulated title. The term certification is widely used in the private sector as well, which is a source of considerable confusion not only for consumers, but for those involved with state and voluntary certification programs as well. Registration, the least restrictive form of state regulation, usually consists of little more than requiring individuals to file their names, addresses and qualifications with a designated state agency before performing the duties of the occupation.

There are several good primers on how professional and occupational licensing agencies are structured and what basic functions they perform. See for example Schmitt, K. and Shimberg, B., *Demystifying Occupational and Professional Regulation: Answers to Questions You May Have Been Afraid to Ask*, (Lexington, KY, The Council on Licensure, Enforcement and Regulation, 1996).

[2] Agency stakeholders include consumers, other professional and occupational regulatory agencies, the federal government, national associations of state and provincial boards, national professional associations, examination companies, other corporate interests, professional and occupational educators, voluntary (private) certifiers, legislators/legislative staffers, third-party reimbursors, legal system (civil and criminal), educational/facility accreditation, counties/municipalities, marketplace tensions among all stakeholders.

In particular, the relationship between educational institutions and regulators is not an easy one. Accrediting organizations help academic institutions develop curriculum content, while psychometricians conduct practice analyses to help licensing agencies determine the content of licensing examinations (J. Cote, "The Role of Accreditation in Licensure," Amelia Island, FL, Federation of Associations of Regulatory Boards Forum 2004).

[3] "Agency Consolidation is in the Air (Again)," *CLEAR News*, (Lexington, KY: Fall 2004) http://www.clearhq.org/fall_news_04_Consolidation.htm.

[4] http://www.oregonbusinessplan.org/regulatory_streamlining_objective3.html.

[5] http://lic.oregon.gov/cfmx/lic/index.cfm.

[6] An NCCUSL administrative procedures act revision draft was made available in November 2004, http://www.law.upenn.edu/bll/ulc/msapa/Nov2004Draft.htm.

[7] Virginia Department of Health Professions, Sanctioning Reference Points Instruction Manual, Board of Medicine, (Richmond, VA, 2004). http://www.dhp.virginia.gov/medicine/guidelines/85-11%20SRP%20BOM%20MANUAL%20JULY%202004.pdf.

[8] Sandy Greenberg, "Testing Across the Nation: Security Concerns—Perceived and Real," *CLEAR Exam Review*, Winter 2004.

[9] http://www.nursingboard.ie/elearning/Competency/html/orientation.htm.

[10] V.E. Beltran Corona, "International Negotiations of Professional Services in Mexico," (Kansas City, Missouri, September 29, 2004). http://www.clearhq.org/Beltran_2004.PDF.

[11] The Council on Licensure, Enforcement and Regulation, *The Americans With Disabilities Act: Information for Credentialing Examinations*, (Lexington, KY: CLEAR, 2004).

[12] J. Kwoka, "The Federal Trade Commission and the Professions: A Quarter Century of Accomplishment and Some New Challenges," September 2004 (Washington, DC, America Antitrust Institute working paper #04-04), *http://www.antitrustinstitute.org/recent2/354.pdf*. Publicly and privately credentialed professions subject to FTC antitrust action 1981 to date are accountants, anesthesiologists, arbitrators, automotive dealers, bid depositories, chiropractors, customs brokers, dentists, dermatologists, doctors, engineers (various), fashion designers, hotel associations, interpreters, language specialists, lawyers, movers (various), music dealers, obstetricians, optometrists, orthopedists, osteopathic physicians, pharmacists, physical therapists, podiatrists, psychologists, real estate agency, veterinarians.

[13] Some professions (notably accountants, architects, engineers, educator and attorneys) have worked with the World Trade Organization (WTO) and the Office of the United States Trade Representative to enter into or plan for agreements intended to facilitate mutual recognition of licensees among member countries. The WTO oversees the General Agreement on Trade in Services (GATS) which permits mutual recognition either through a harmonization of local regulations or direct agreement between member countries.

[14] *http://www.europa.eu.int/cgi-bin/eur-lex/udl.pl? REQUEST=Service-Search&LANGUAGE=en&GUILAN GUAGE=en&SERVICE =all&COLLECTION=com& DOCID=504PC0002.*

[15] B. Ascher, "Toward a Borderless Market for Professional Services," (Washington, D.C.: American Antitrust Institute, April 2004). *http://www.antitrustinstitute.org/recent2/316.cfm.*

[16] B. Shimberg and D. Roederer, *Questions a Legislator Should Ask*. 2d., K. Schmitt, ed., (Lexington, KY, The Council on Licensure, Enforcement and Regulation, 1994).

This influential pamphlet says that regulation should meet a public need, provide the minimum amount of oversight to meet that need, avoid overlap with other regulated services, provide for continued competence and professional discipline, and involve the public in the process. In other words, it educated legislators to understand that the only valid reason to regulate a profession is to protect consumers from any harm they may experience as a result of practice of the profession or occupation.

About the Author

Pam Brinegar is the executive director of The Council on Licensure, Enforcement and Regulation (CLEAR), which provides educational programs for professional licensing officials. CLEAR is an affiliate of The Council of State Governments.

Table A
STATE REGULATION OF SELECTED NON-HEALTH OCCUPATIONS AND PROFESSIONS: DECEMBER 2004

Column headings (left to right):
- State or other jurisdiction
- Accountant, certified public
- Agriculture inspector
- Architect
- Auctioneer
- Barber
- Cosmetologist
- Embalmer (a)
- Engineer, professional (b)
- Environmental science & protection tech.
- Forester
- Funeral director
- Geologist
- Hazardous materials removal worker
- Insurance agent
- Insurance broker
- Landscape architect
- Polygraph examiner
- Real estate agent
- Real estate broker
- Surveyor, land
- Water & liquid waste treatment plant/system operator

State or other jurisdiction rows:

Alabama
Alaska
Arizona
Arkansas
California

Colorado
Connecticut
Delaware
Florida
Georgia

Hawaii
Idaho
Illinois
Indiana
Iowa

Kansas
Kentucky
Louisiana
Maine
Maryland

Massachusetts
Michigan
Minnesota
Mississippi
Missouri

Montana
Nebraska
Nevada
New Hampshire
New Jersey

New Mexico
New York
North Carolina
North Dakota
Ohio

See footnotes at end of table.

STATE REGULATION OF SELECTED NON-HEALTH OCCUPATIONS AND PROFESSIONS: DECEMBER 2004 — Continued

State or other jurisdiction	Accountant certified public	Agriculture inspector	Architect	Auctioneer	Barber	Cosmetologist	Embalmer (a)	Engineer, professional (b)	Environmental science & protection tech.	Forester	Funeral director	Geologist	Hazardous materials removal worker	Insurance agent	Insurance broker	Landscape architect	Polygraph examiner	Real estate agent	Real estate broker	Surveyor, land	Water & liquid waste treatment plant/system operator
Oklahoma	L		L		L	L	L	L			L	L	L	L		L	L	L	L	L	L
Oregon	L		L		L	L	L	L	L		L	L	L	L	L	L		L	L	L	L
Pennsylvania	L		L	L	L	L	L	L	L		L			L	L	L		L	L	L	
Rhode Island	L	L	L	L	L	L	L	L	L		L	L	L	L	L	L	L	L	L	L	
South Carolina	L		L	L	L	L	L	L			L	L	L	L	L	L	L	L	L	L	L
South Dakota	L		L		L	L	L	L			L			L	L	L	L	L	L	L	L
Tennessee	L		L	L	L	L	L	L			L	L		L	L	L	L	L	L	L	L
Texas	L		L	L	L	L	L	L			L			L	L	L	L	L	L	L	
Utah	L		L	L	L	L	L	L	L		L		L	L	L	L	L	L	L	L	L
Vermont	L		L		L	L		L			L			L		C		L	L	L	L
Virginia	L	L	L	L	L	L	L	L			L	L	L	L	L	L	L	L	L	L	L
Washington	L		L	L	L	L	L	L			L		L	L	L	L		L	L	L	L
West Virginia	L	L	L	L	L	L	L	L		L	L	L	L	L	L	L	L	L	L	L	L
Wisconsin	L	L	L	L	L	L	L	L			L	L		L	L	L		L	L	L	L
Wyoming	L		L		L	L	L	L			L	L	L	L	L		L	L	L	L	L
Dist. of Columbia	L		L	L	L	L		L			L			L	L			L	L	L	

Source: Council on Licensure, Enforcement and Regulation, December 2004 and various national associations of state boards.

Key:
C—Certification
L—Licensure
R—Registration

(a) In some states, embalmers are not licensed separately from funeral directors; embalming is part of the funeral director's job.
(b) In addition to licensing professional engineers, some states regulate engineers by specific areas of expertise, such as civil engineers.

Table B
STATE REGULATION OF HEALTH OCCUPATIONS AND PROFESSIONS: DECEMBER 2004

State or other jurisdiction	Acupuncturist	Chiropractor	Counselor, professional (a)	Counselor, alcoholism	Counselor, drug	Counselor, pastoral	Counselor, substance abuse (b)	Dentist	Dental assistant (c)	Dental hygienist	Denturist	Dietitian	Emergency medical technician (d)	Hearing aid dealer & fitter
Alabama	...	L	L	...	...	...	...	L	...	L	...	L	L	L
Alaska	L	L	L	...	...	...	C	L	C	L	L	L	L	L
Arizona	L	L	C	C	C	...	...	L	R	L	...	...	L	L
Arkansas	L	L	L	...	...	...	...	L	L	L	...	R	L	L
California	L	L	L	C	C	...	L	L	...	L	...	C	L	L
Colorado	L	L	L	C	C	...	...	L	...	L	...	C	L	L
Connecticut	L	L	L	L	L	...	...	L	...	L	L	L	L	L
Delaware	...	L	L	C	C	...	...	L	C	L	...	L	L	L
Florida	L	L	L	...	...	...	C	L	...	L	...	C	L	L
Georgia	L	L	L	...	...	...	...	L	...	L	...	...	L	L
Hawaii	L	L	...	...	...	...	...	L	...	L	...	C	L	L
Idaho	L	L	L	...	...	...	C	L	...	L	...	L	L	L
Illinois	L	L	L	...	...	...	L	L	...	L	...	L	L	L
Indiana	L	L	L	...	...	...	L	L	...	L	...	C	L	L
Iowa	L	L	L	...	...	...	...	L	...	L	...	L	L	L
Kansas	...	L	L	C	C	...	C	L	...	L	...	L	L	L
Kentucky	L	L	L	L	L	C (e)	L	L	...	L	...	L	L	L
Louisiana	L	L	L	C-L	C-L	L	L	L	L	L	...	L	L	L
Maine	L	L	L	...	C-L	...	...	L	...	L	...	...	L	L
Maryland	L	L	C	...	...	...	...	L	L	L	...	L	L	L
Massachusetts	L	L	L	...	...	...	...	L	...	L	...	...	L	L
Michigan	L	L	L	...	...	...	...	L	...	L	...	...	L	L
Minnesota	...	L	L	...	...	...	...	L	...	L	...	L	L	L
Mississippi	L	L	L	...	...	...	...	L	L	L	...	L	L	L
Missouri	...	L	L	...	...	...	...	L	L	L	...	L	L	L
Montana	L	L	L	...	...	...	...	L	L	L	...	L	L	L
Nebraska	L	L	L	...	...	...	...	L	...	L	...	L	L	L
Nevada	L	L	C	C	C	C	C-L	L	...	L	L	L	L	L
New Hampshire	L	L	L	C	C	...	C	L	...	L	...	L	L	L
New Jersey	L	L	...	...	...	...	C	L	R	L	...	...	L	L
New Mexico	L	L	L	L	L	...	L	L	C	L	...	L	L	L
New York	L	L	L	L	L	...	C	L	L	L	...	L	L	L
North Carolina	L	L	L	...	L	...	L	L	L	L	...	...	L	L
North Dakota	...	L	L	...	...	...	L	L	L	L	...	L	L	L
Ohio	...	L	L	...	...	...	...	L	...	L	...	L	L	L

See footnotes at end of table.

STATE REGULATION OF HEALTH OCCUPATIONS AND PROFESSIONS: DECEMBER 2004 — Continued

State or other jurisdiction	Acupuncturist	Chiropractor	Counselor, professional (a)	Counselor, alcoholism	Counselor, drug	Counselor, pastoral	Counselor, substance abuse (b)	Dentist	Dental assistant (c)	Dental hygienist	Denturist	Dietitian	Emergency medical technician (d)	Hearing aid dealer & fitter
Oklahoma	...	L	L	...	...	...	...	L	C	L	...	L	L	L
Oregon	L	L	L	...	...	...	...	L	...	L	L	L	L	L
Pennsylvania	R	L	L(f)	...	...	...	...	L	...	L	...	C	L	L
Rhode Island	L	L	L	...	...	...	C	L	...	L	...	L	L	L
South Carolina	R	L	L	...	...	...	...	L	...	L	...	...	L	L
South Dakota	...	L	L	L	L	...	...	L	L	L	...	L	L	L
Tennessee	L	L	L	...	L	...	...	L	L	L	...	L	L	L
Utah	L	L	L	...	...	...	...	L	L	L	...	C	L	L
Vermont	L	L	L	L	L	...	...	L	...	L	...	L	L	L
Virginia	L	L	L	C	C	...	L	L	...	L	...	C	L	L
Washington	L	L	C	C	C	...	...	L	...	L	L	C	L	L
West Virginia	L	L	L	...	...	...	...	L	...	L	...	L	L	L
Wisconsin	...	L	C	...	...	...	...	L	...	L	...	C	L	L
Wyoming	...	L	L	...	...	...	L	L	L	L	...	...	L	L
Dist. of Columbia	L	L	L	...	...	...	R	L	...	L	...	L	L	...

Key:
C—Certification
L—Licensure
R—Registration
...—Not regulated

STATE REGULATION OF HEALTH OCCUPATIONS AND PROFESSIONS: DECEMBER 2004

State or other jurisdiction	Homeopath	Massage therapist	Nurse, licensed practical (g)	Nurse, midwife (g)	Nurse practitioner (g)	Nurse, registered (g)	Nursing home administrator	Occupational therapy	Occupational therapist assistant	Optician	Optometrist (h)	Osteopath	Pharmacist	Physical therapist
Alabama			L	L	L	L	L	L	L		L	L	L	L
Alaska	L		L	L	L	L	L	L	L	L	L	L	L	L
Arizona		L	L	L	L	L	L	L	L	L	L	L	L	L
Arkansas			L	L	L	L	L	L	L	L	L	L	L	L
California		C					L	C	C	C	L	L	L	L
Colorado			L	L	L	L	L	L	L	L	L	L	L	L
Connecticut	L	L	L	L	L	L	L	L	L	L	L	L	L	L
Delaware		L	L	L	L	L	L	L	L	L	L	L	L	L
Florida		L	L			L	L	L	L	L	L	L	L	L
Georgia			L			L	L	C	C		L	L	L	L
Hawaii			L			L	L				L	L	L	L
Idaho	L	L	L			L	L	L	L	L	L	L	L	L
Illinois		L	L			L	L	L	L		L	L	L	L
Indiana		L	L	L	L	L	L	C	C	L	L	L	L	L
Iowa		C	L			L	L	L	L		L	L	L	L
Kansas			L		L	L	L	L	L	L	L	L	L	L
Kentucky		L	L	L	L	L	L	L	L		L	L	L	L
Louisiana			L		C	L	L	L	L	L	L	L	L	L
Maine		L	L	C	C	L	L	L	L		L	L	L	L
Maryland		C	L	L	L	L	L	L	L	L	L	L	L	
Massachusetts			L			L	L	R	R		L	L	L	L
Michigan		L	L		L	L	L	L	L	L	L	L	L	L
Minnesota		C	L	C	L	L	L	L	L		L	L	L	L
Mississippi		L	L			L	L	L	L		L	L	L	L
Missouri		L	L	L		L	L	L	L	L	L	L	L	L
Montana			L			L	L	R	R		L	L	L	L
Nebraska	L	L	L	L	L	L	L	L	L	L	L	L	L	L
Nevada	L	C	L	L	L	L	L	L	L	L	L	L	L	L
New Hampshire	L	L	L	L	L	L	L	R	R	L	L	L	L	
New Jersey		L	L			L	L	L	L	L	L	L	L	L
New Mexico		L	L	L		L	L	L	L		L	L	L	L
New York		L	L	L	L	L	L	L	L	L	L	L	L	L
North Carolina		L	L	L	L	L	L	L	L		L	L	L	L
North Dakota		L	L	L	L	L	L	L	L		L	L	L	L
Ohio		L	L	L	L	L	L	L	L		L	L	L	L

See footnotes at end of table.

STATE REGULATION OF HEALTH OCCUPATIONS AND PROFESSIONS: DECEMBER 2004 – CONTINUED

State or other jurisdiction	Homeopath	Massage therapist	Nurse, licensed practical (g)	Nurse midwife (g)	Nurse practitioner (g)	Nurse, registered (g)	Nursing home administrator	Occupational therapy	Occupational therapist assistant	Optician	Optometrist (h)	Osteopath	Pharmacist	Physical therapist
Oklahoma	...	...	L	C	C	L	L	L	L	...	L	L	L	L
Oregon	...	L	L	L	C	L	L	L	L	...	L	L	L	L
Pennsylvania	...	...	L	L	L	L	L	L	L	...	L	L	L	L
Rhode Island	...	L	L	L	L	L	L	L	L	L	L	L	L	L
South Carolina	...	L	L	L	L	L	L	L	L	L	L	L	L	L
South Dakota	...	...	L	L	L	L	L	L	L	...	L	L	L	L
Tennessee	...	R	L	L	L	L	L	L	L	L	L	L	L	L
Texas	...	R	L	L	L	L	L	L	L	L	L	L	L	L
Utah	...	L	L	L	L	L	(i) L	L	L	L	L	L	L	L
Vermont	...	...	L	L	L	L	L	L	L	L	L	L	L	L
Virginia	...	C	L	L	L	L	L	L	L	L	L	L	L	L
Washington	...	L	L	L	L	L	L	L	...	L	L	L	L	L
West Virginia	...	L	L	L	L	L	L	L	L	L	L	L	L	L
Wisconsin	...	R	L	L	C	L	L	L	L	...	L	L	L	L
Wyoming	...	...	L	L	C	L	L	L	L	...	L	L	L	L
Dist. of Columbia	...	L	L	L	C	L	L	L	L	...	L	L	L	L

Key:
C—Certification
L—Licensure
R—Registration
. . .—Not regulated

STATE REGULATION OF HEALTH OCCUPATIONS AND PROFESSIONS: DECEMBER 2004 — Continued

State or other jurisdiction	Physical therapy assistant	Physician	Physician assistant	Podiatrist	Psychologist	Radiologic technologist	Radiation therapist	Respiratory therapist	Sanitarian	Social worker (f)	Speech-language pathologist & aud.	Therapist marriage & family	Veterinary	Veterinary technician
Alabama	L	L	L	L	L	…	…	…	…	L	L	L	L	L
Alaska	L	L	L	L	L	…	…	…	…	C	L	C	L	L
Arizona	L	L	C	L	L	C	L	L	R	L	L	L	L	L
Arkansas	L	L	L	L	L	C	L	L	R	L	L	L	L	R
California	…	L	L	L	L	C	…	L	…	L	L	L	L	C
Colorado	R	L	C	L	L	…	…	L	…	L	…	R	L	R
Connecticut	L	L	L	L	L	L	L	L	L	C	L	L	L	…
Delaware	L	L	L	L	L	L	L	L	L	L	L	L	L	R
Florida	L	L	L	L	L	L	L	…	R	L	L	C,L	L	L
Georgia	…	L	L	L	L	…	…	L	…	L	L	L	L	L
Hawaii	L	L	L	L	L	L	L	R	L	L	L	C	L	R
Idaho	L	L	L	L	L	C	…	C	R	L	L	L	L	R
Illinois	L	L	C	L	L	L	L	L	L	L	L	L	L	L
Indiana	L	L	C	L	L	L	L	L	L	L	L	L	L	L
Iowa	L	L	L	L	L	R	L	L	C	L	L	L	L	L
Kansas	L	L	L	L	L	…	L	L	L	L	L	L	L	R
Kentucky	L	L	L	L	L	L	…	R	R	C	L	L	L	L
Louisiana	L	L	L	L	L	L	…	L	R	L	L	L	L	L
Maine	L	L	C	L	L	R	…	R	L	L	L	C,L	L	R
Maryland	L	L	L	L	L	L	L	L	C	L	L	L	L	L
Massachusetts	L	L	L	L	L	R	L	R	L	L	L	R	L	R
Michigan	…	L	L	L	L	R	…	L	R	C	L	L	L	L
Minnesota	L	L	L	L	L	…	…	L	R	L	L	L	L	R
Mississippi	L	L	C	L	L	…	…	L	L	L	L	L	L	L
Missouri	L	L	L	L	L	…	L	L	C	L	L	L	L	…
Montana	L	C	L	L	L	…	…	…	L	L	L	C	L	…
Nebraska	C	L	L	L	L	C	…	L	R	C	L	L	L	L
Nevada	L	L	L	L	L	…	…	R	R	L	L	L	L	L
New Hampshire	L	L	L	L	L	…	…	L	…	C,L	L	L	L	L
New Jersey	L	L	L	L	L	…	…	…	…	L	L	L	L	…
New Mexico	L	L	L	L	L	…	…	…	…	C,L	L	C	L	L
New York	C	L	L	L	L	…	…	…	…	C,L	L	L	L	L
North Carolina	L	L	L	L	L	…	…	L	L	C,L	L	L	L	L
North Dakota	L	L	L	L	L	…	…	L	L	L	L	L	L	L
Ohio	L	L	L	L	L	L	L	L	L	L	L	…	L	L

See footnotes at end of table.

STATE REGULATION OF HEALTH OCCUPATIONS AND PROFESSIONS: DECEMBER 2004—Continued

State or other jurisdiction	Physical therapy assistant	Physician	Physician assistant	Podiatrist	Psychologist	Radiologic technologist	Radiation therapist	Respiratory therapist	Sanitarian	Social worker (f)	Speech-language pathologist & aud.	Therapist marriage & family	Veterinary	Veterinary technician
Oklahoma	L	L	L	L	L	…	…	L	L	C,L	L	L	L	L
Oregon	L	L	L	L	L	L	L	L	L	C,L	L	L	L	L
Pennsylvania	R	L	C	L	L	…	…	C	…	L(f)	L	L(f)	L	C
Rhode Island	L	L	L	L	L	…	…	L	R	L	L	L	L	…
South Carolina	L	L	L	L	L	C	C	L	R	L	L	L	L	L
South Dakota	L	L	L	L	L	…	…	L	…	L	L	L	L	L
Tennessee	L	L	L	L	L	…	L	L	C	L	L	L	L	L
Texas	…	L	L	L	L	L	L	L	L	L	…	L	L	…
Utah	L	L	C	L	L	…	L	L	L	L	L	L	L	R
Vermont	L	L	…	L	L	…	L	…	…	L	…	…	L	…
Virginia	L	L	L	L	L	L	L	L	…	L	L	L	L	L
Washington	…	L	L	L	L	C	C	L	…	L	L	…	L	L
West Virginia	L	L	L	L	L	L	L	L	L	C,L	L	…	L	L
Wisconsin	L	L	L	L	L	L	C	L	L	L	L	L	L	L
Wyoming	L	L	L	L	L	L	L	L	…	C,L	L	L	L	L
Dist. of Columbia	L	L	L	L	L	…	L	L	…	L	L	L	L	…

Source: Council on Licensure, Enforcement and Regulation, December 2004 and various national associations of state boards.

Key:
C—Certification
L—Licensure
R —Registration
… —Not regulated

(a) In some states, professional counselors can practice without a license as long as they do not use the title "licensed professional counselor."

(b) In some states, substance abuse counselors use the title "addiction counselor/therapist."

(c) In some states, certification is required for dental assistants to perform expanded functions and take x-rays.

(d) There are eight categories of emergency medical technicians, from basic to paramedic to task-specific certifications. No state regulates all categories, but every state regulates at least one category.

(e) In Kentucky, pastoral counselors must be certified only if their practice is fee-based.

(f) In Pennsylvania, professional counselors, social workers, and marriage and family therapists do not need a license to practice unless they hold themselves out to be licensed.

(g) Some states recognize various categories of advanced practice nurses (e.g. geriatric, school health, and women's health).

(h) In many states, opticians are not licensed separately from optometrists; making and selling eyeglasses is part of the optometrist's job.

(i) In Indiana and Utah, nursing home administrators are not licensed as such, but they are licensed more broadly as health facility administrators.

(j) In some states, social work practice is regulated at one or more of the following levels: basic, intermediate, advanced, and clinical. Certification may be required for practice at the lower levels and licensure required for practice at the higher levels.

Trends and Issues in State Motor Vehicle Agencies: More than Just a License

By Linda R. Lewis-Pickett

Recent events in our society have been the catalyst for rapid change in the way motor vehicle agencies do business. The need to balance highway safety, customer service and security of the homeland has created a challenge that very few industries will ever have to face.

The public servant who issued the first driver's license in the state of New York in 1903 probably had no inkling of the importance that small credential would some day come to hold. Initially intended simply to certify that an individual had earned the right to drive a motor vehicle, today drivers prefer to use it as a primary form of identification—giving its holder the ability to open bank accounts, purchase alcohol and cigarettes, access secure buildings and locations, purchase firearms, register to vote and even obtain a job. As use and dependence on the driver's license has increased, so has that of the automobile: it has gone from being a luxury item intended for the wealthy to a must-have for nearly every American over the age of 16, a status symbol and the key to job security and freedom. Both the driver's license and the automobile are now viewed as necessities for anyone who wants to live the American dream. As a result, some people will do just about anything to get a driver's license or a vehicle, including resorting to theft and fraud.

The agencies that administer driver's license and vehicle information and related highway safety laws increasingly must adjust their processes, networks and staffing to meet the challenges of a rapidly changing environment. Additionally, federal mandates ranging from homeland security to voter registration are stretching resources even further and changing the motor vehicle administration environment to the point that it barely resembles the framework that was initially set up to ensure driver safety.

Like it or not, the business of motor vehicle administration has changed. Commissioners of these state agencies have a greater responsibility than ever before. How well they anticipate issues and meet the challenges that have been thrust upon them will impact not only service to citizens, but also possibly their security.

Ensuring Identity

In the early to mid-1990s, motor vehicle administrators and law enforcement officials began to notice an increase in the number of cases of identity theft and identity fraud. Some of those cases were related to individuals who wished to enter or stay in the country illegally; others were individuals who were seeking to fabricate clean driving records or who wanted to use someone else's credit to make purchases. Nearly all cases involved an attempt to obtain a driver's license fraudulently.

Motor vehicle and law enforcement agencies began to work more closely together to combat the issues of identity theft and fraud. New processes were implemented, new networks were put into place and additional identity credentials were required in many states to help ensure that people applying for driver's licenses were who they said they were. Agencies also formed partnerships with retailers, credit institutions and others in the private sector to work on the problem together.

The motor vehicle landscape changed even more significantly after the terrorists attacks of September 11, 2001. Investigations indicate that the terrorists had obtained driver's licenses and used them as valid identification to move about society and ultimately to board the planes used as weapons.

The problem wasn't with the licenses themselves—most were issued according to existing guidelines. The problem was in both operational practices and the validity of the breeder documents, the documents applicants are required to produce to verify their identity when obtaining a driver's license. Breeder documents include birth certificates, Social Security cards, passports and immigration documents, among others.

Breeder documents have become the subject of intense scrutiny over the past four years, and rightly so. The challenge for motor vehicle agencies is that they are now being compelled to consider not only the validity of their own documents, but of those that are used to issue them. The challenge can be daunting, especially when you consider the sheer number of agencies that issue these documents. For example, there are some 14,000 different birth certificate formats that are issued in the United States. Determining whether the one the applicant is presenting is authentic can be nearly impossible.

Most states are now using or exploring the use of technology to assist in the verification process of some breeder documents and the information these documents display. The American Association of Motor Vehicle Administrators (AAMVA) provides a network to the Social Security Administration so agencies can access an online system to verify Social Security Numbers presented at the counter. The Bureau of Citizenship and Immigration Services has a similar system for authenticating immigration documents. To help ensure that applicants don't shop for the state that has the most lax identification practices, AAMVA has identified a list of verifiable identification resources that should be acceptable for proving identity, and has recommended that jurisdictions adopt the list to ensure uniformity across the country. These and other efforts to improve the security of the driver's license are likely to continue and to increase in scope over the next several years.

Crossing State Borders

The need for interoperability among states is one of the most critical issues facing motor vehicle administrators today. In the absence of states' ability to share information quickly and reliably, a small but dangerous percentage of the population will continue to shop around to find the easiest way to get the driver's license or even the vehicle title they seek.

Although standardization and interoperability are national issues, they are managed by the states, and therein lies the dilemma. Even if a state resolves its own issues, it has solved little if it means scofflaws are simply going to the next state over to obtain their documents fraudulently. A motor vehicle agency without technology that crosses state lines is ineffective in today's world. States must—and do—work together on these critical issues. On behalf of its member agencies, AAMVA is pushing for the establishment of more consistent ways to verify information and conduct business.

The business of motor vehicle administration is a multi-state process. The creation of interstate highways and public mobility has created this environment. For more than 40 years, a majority of states have voluntarily participated in two interstate compact agreements, the Driver's License Compact (DLC) and the Non-Resident Violator Compact (NRVC). Both compacts were established to provide guidelines to states on the licensing process and reciprocity in the treatment of traffic violations or convictions for out-of-state drivers.

Because of the increased need to verify identity in the driver's license application process, coupled with the increase in identity theft and fraud, the motor vehicle community has a renewed interest in multi-state reciprocity agreements and guidelines. The outcome of that interest was a new compact, the Driver's License Agreement (DLA), which provides a venue for states to verify and transmit driver and conviction information. The DLA combines the DLC/NRVC, adds identification verification practices and requirements, and has a goal of establishing one driver, one record and one identity.

Another multi-state led initiative is the National Motor Vehicle Title Information System (NMVTIS). Annually, criminals continue to produce multi-million dollars in profit due to vehicle theft, odometer rollback, and the misrepresentation of flooded or wrecked vehicles as being damaged. For this reason, we all suffer through increased insurance rates and threats to highway safety. Through NMVTIS, agencies can more easily determine if a vehicle is reported stolen or salvaged before issuing new titles. Law enforcement can be notified and vehicles recovered more quickly and frequently.

These are only a few examples of how states are working to improve the safety and security of documents. The progress in this area certainly will continue in the upcoming months and years. Efforts are underway to push for minimum standards for driver's licenses and issuance practices across states. While this concept is of concern to some states that see it as another federal mandate, it is a tool that will provide some of the greatest gains in the areas of law enforcement and document security. The federal government's encouragement in requiring states to meet at least minimum standards for issuing driver and vehicle documents would go a long way in helping to ensure the safety of citizens and their property.

Meeting Federal Mandates

Another issue that will continue to challenge motor vehicle administrators in the years to come is determining how to best handle federal mandates, especially those that come without funding. State budgets, like those in the private sector, have been severely impacted by the recent downturn in the economy. Motor vehicle agencies, already strapped for cash, must implement government mandates that often require expensive system changes and extensive training for employees. Agencies are reducing staff to offset expenses. The employees who remain are under greater pressure than ever due to their implied role in implementing social change.

Increasingly, federal mandates require motor vehicle administrators to stray farther away from the core mission of their agencies. Voter registration, payment of child support and even high school attendance are in some states being tied to obtaining or holding a driver's license. The challenge here is that to enact mandates such as these, agencies must find a way to communicate electronically with other state agencies.

The federal government can help ease these burdens by simply listening to and working closely with state officials on anticipated mandates. Funding must be addressed before mandates are imposed. The government also can look for ways to speed the promulgation of rules and support states' efforts to pass enacting legislation.

Addressing a Changing Society

Our society's transience is presenting yet another challenge for motor vehicle administrators. Increasingly, a larger number of customers speak little or no English, and may not understand our country's rules and systems that relate to driving. Administrators must find ways to educate and train their employees to provide these customers with the service they need. Some states have explored the use of incentives for hiring employees who speak other languages, while others have offered to train their employees to speak Spanish or other languages common to their customers. According to population projections, this challenge will continue to escalate and will not only impact the border states, but almost every other area of the country.

Baby Boomers are another group requiring motor vehicle administrators to think outside the box. This segment makes up a large part of our population and, as these drivers age, agencies are beginning to address the needs of the older driver, such as balancing independence with safe driving skills. The issue is one that will continue to impact motor vehicle agencies for at least the next few decades.

Meeting Societal Expectations

Motor vehicle agencies' challenges are not always the result of federal or state mandates, but often are due to the changing expectations of society. We live in a microwave, MTV, reality show society where people want and expect instant gratification. Motor vehicle agency customers want offices to be open late in the evening and on weekends to allow for their schedules. They want to walk into an office and walk out with a driver's license or vehicle title in a relatively short period of time. They look for immediate turnaround on permits they need to do their jobs. They expect prompt, courteous and professional service at all times. It is a challenge.

Facing the Challenge

E-government is helping administrators to meet many of the day-to-day challenges related to the balance between ensuring document validity and security and serving customers expediently. Many states now allow their customers to conduct transactions online, reducing wait time for customers who must visit an office in person and easing the burden on employees. Additionally, new interfaces between states and business partners will reduce paper handling and speed up the actual delivery of desired services. Both trends undoubtedly will escalate over the next several years as agencies continue to look for ways to do more with less.

In the decade ahead, motor vehicle administrators will continue to focus on developing and implementing systems and processes that will help increase the safety of our citizens. They will continue to grapple with the best ways to provide secure systems and outstanding service to their customers. They also will continue to look for opportunities to enhance service to citizens of our country even as their scope of responsibility expands well beyond that of verifying a person's ability to drive. Motor vehicle administration is not a job for the faint of heart. It is a champion's job. Each and every day, they will step up to the plate to balance the triad of priorities—highway safety, customer service and safety of our homeland.

About the Author

Linda R. Lewis-Pickett is president & CEO of the American Association of Motor Vehicle Administrators (AAMVA). AAMVA is voluntary, nonprofit, educational organization striving to develop model programs in motor vehicle administration, law enforcement and highway safety. The association's programs encourage uniformity and reciprocity among the states and provinces, and liaisons with other levels of government and the private sector. AAMVA's program development and research activities provide guidelines for more effective public service.

Table A
Member Status of Driver's License Compact (DLC) and Non-Resident Violator Compact (NRVC)

State or other jurisdiction	DLC/NRVC member status		
	Member of NRVC	Member of DLC	Member of neither
Alabama	★	★	. . .
Alaska		★	. . .
Arizona	★	★	. . .
Arkansas	★	★	. . .
California		★	. . .
Colorado	★	★	. . .
Connecticut	★	★	. . .
Delaware	★	★	. . .
Florida	★	★	. . .
Georgia	★	. . .	
Hawaii (a)	★	★	. . .
Idaho	★	★	. . .
Illinois	★	★	. . .
Indiana	★	★	. . .
Iowa	★	★	. . .
Kansas	★	★	. . .
Kentucky (a)	★	★	. . .
Louisiana	★	★	. . .
Maine	★	★	. . .
Maryland	★	★	. . .
Massachusetts	★		. . .
Michigan			★
Minnesota	★	★	. . .
Mississippi	★	★	. . .
Missouri	★	★	. . .
Montana		★	. . .
Nebraska	★	★	. . .
Nevada	★	★	. . .
New Hampshire	★	★	. . .
New Jersey	★	★	. . .
New Mexico	★	★	. . .
New York	★	★	. . .
North Carolina	★	★	. . .
North Dakota	★	★	. . .
Ohio	★	★	. . .
Oklahoma	★	★	. . .
Oregon	★		. . .
Pennsylvania	★	★	. . .
Rhode Island	★	★	. . .
South Carolina	★	★	. . .
South Dakota	★	★	. . .
Tennessee	★	(b)	
Texas	★	★	. . .
Utah	★	★	. . .
Vermont	★	★	. . .
Virginia	★	★	. . .
Washington	★	★	. . .
West Virginia	★	★	. . .
Wisconsin			★
Wyoming	★	★	. . .
Dist. of Columbia	★	★	. . .

Source: The American Association of Motor Vehicle Administrators (AAMVA), January 2005.
Key:
★—Yes
...—No
Note: Driver's License Compact (DLC) and the Non-Resident Violator Compact (NRVC). Both compacts were established to provide guidelines to states on the licensing process and reciprocity in the treatment of traffic violations or convictions for out-of-state drivers.
    (a) Newest members - Hawaii (NRVC), Effective date January 1, 1996;Kentucky (DLC), Effective date August 1996.
    (b) Inactive, Tennessee dropped out in 1997.

Table B
Driver's License Compact (DLC) and Non-Resident Violator Compact (NRVC) Member Joinder Dates

State or other jurisdiction	DLC/NRVC Compact member joinder dates	
	NRVC Effective date	DLC Effective date
Alabama	October 1981	1966
Alaska	Not a member	September 1996
Arizona	January 1993	1963
Arkansas	January 1986	1969
California	Not a member	1963
Colorado	January 1982	1965
Connecticut	January 1981	January 1993
Delaware	February 1979	1964
Florida	October 1981	1967
Georgia	February 1980	Not a member
Hawaii (a)	January 1996	1971
Idaho	October 1992	1963
Illinois	July 1984	1963
Indiana	January 1980	1967
Iowa	November 1980	1965
Kansas	January 1983	1965
Kentucky (a)	December 1978	August 1996
Louisiana	November 1979	1968
Maine	January 1982	1963
Maryland	July 1979	July 1978
Massachusetts	December 1987	Not a member
Michigan	Not a member	Not a member
Minnesota	October 1978	January 1990
Mississippi	March 1979	1962
Missouri	October 1980	October 1985
Montana	Not a member	1963
Nebraska	January 1982	1963
Nevada	February 1990	1961
New Hampshire	January 1982	October 1986
New Jersey	July 1983	1966
New Mexico	January 1985	1963
New York	June 1982	1965
North Carolina	September 1980	September 1993
North Dakota	July 1980	May 1986
Ohio	January 1985	October 1987
Oklahoma	July 1987	1967
Oregon	Not a member	1963
Pennsylvania	July 1979	October 1994
Rhode Island	April 1986	January 1987
South Carolina	January 1981	August 1987
South Dakota	May 1980	November 1987
Tennessee	September 1984	(a)
Texas	January 1982	September 1993
Utah	July 1985	1965
Vermont	October 1985	October 1987
Virginia	July 1980	1963
Washington	October 1993	1963
West Virginia	July 1978	July 1972
Wisconsin	Not a member	Not a member
Wyoming	July 1987	May 1987
Dist. of Columbia	August 1980	November 1985

Source: The American Association of Motor Vehicle Administrators (AAMVA), January 2005.

Note: Driver's License Compact (DLC) and the Non-Resident Violator Compact (NRVC). Both compacts were established to provide guidelines to states on the licensing process and reciprocity in the treatment of traffic violations or convictions for out-of-state drivers.

Key:
(a) Tennessee joined in 1965 and dropped out in 1997.

Trends in State Park Operations

By Daniel D. McLean and Traci Hogan

State park agencies have experienced significant growth during the last decade and made progress in personnel, funding and operations. The economy had an early positive impact on state parks during the mid to late parts of the last decade. Recent reductions in state revenues have begun to erode the progress made during the 1990s. State parks are challenged by reduced funding levels, decreases in visitation, and reduction in full-time staff. Entrepreneurship, external funding sources, and increased state park revenue generation are ongoing trends for state parks.

State park operations exist in various forms and structure across the United States. State parks predate national parks and are seen as a close to home recreation resource. State parks recorded more annual visits than the National Park Service and U.S. Forest Service combined. State parks represent less than 10 percent of combined state and federal park and recreation acreage and yet record almost 30 percent of all visits. As an outdoor recreation resource state parks are clearly important to Americans. During the 1990s and early parts of this decade, state parks and state government have seen dramatic shifts in funding, tax collection and revenue generation. The mid to late 1990s were characterized as a period of unparalleled economic growth while the early part of this decade resulted in some of the largest declines in state operating budgets and deficits since the 1930s.

Mission of State Parks

State parks were originally conceived in the latter-half of the 19th century and confirmed and structured in the early part of the 20th century. The National Conference on State Parks, organized in the early 1920s brought together the diversity of systems and provided common threads for state park administrators to work towards. In more recent years the diversity of the state park systems have found less commonality and more diversity, but as N.C. Landrum suggests, "state parks could serve as close-to-home substitutes for the national parks and provide a complementary alternative to the city parks. Filling that void between the outdoor recreational offerings of the national parks and those of the city parks thus became a major goal, and it is still valid—probably the *most* valid—purpose that state parks can serve today."

Methodology

Data for this report were collected from the National Association of State Park Directors (NASPD) Annual Information Exchange (AIX) for fiscal year (FY) 1994 through 2003. In most cases the entire 10-year period was used for data comparisons. In some few instances data is compared for the start point (FY1994), mid-point (FY1998) and end-point (FY2003).

The AIX is an annual report collected by NASPD and provided to its members. The report was first conceived in the 1970s and is the primary source of state park data available to state park directors and researchers. The AIX gathers data from seven areas including inventory of areas and acreage, types of facilities, visitation and use, capital improvements, financing, personnel and support groups.

The State Park Estate

In FY 2003 state park agencies managed 13,571,028 acres, an increase of 1.8 million acres since 1994 (Table A). Alaska makes the largest contribution to the state park system at 3.4 million acres. Without Alaska included in the total the state park system is a much more modest 10.2 million acres. State parks are not evenly distributed across the United States. The Western region has a proportionally larger portion of the acreage, and the Northeast ranks second in the acreage.

State park systems manage multiple types of areas. The AIX identifies nine such types of areas including state parks, recreation areas, natural areas, historic areas, environmental education areas, scientific areas, forests, fish and wildlife areas, and other areas. Within states the designations may vary and frequently are determined by legislatures and areas may be moved among agencies within the state. State park agencies managed 5,842 areas in FY 2003, up from 5,334 in FY 1994. The number of state park managed areas has grown slowly and is representative of a stable, mature system. Most states have had state park systems for sufficient length of time to recognize their importance to the state.

Table A
STATE PARK MANAGED ACRES: FISCAL YEARS 1994–2003

State	1994	1995	1996	1997	1998	1999	2000	2001	2002	2003
Alabama	49,710	49,710	49,710	49,710	49,710	49,710	49,710	49,710	49,710	49,710
Alaska	3,239,889	3,242,223	3,250,062	3,288,711	3,290,070	3,291,118	3,291,209	3,291,121	3,325,939	3,353,246
Arizona	42,703	42,703	46,351	46,356	46,356	58,526	58,528	58,491	58,512	60,921
Arkansas	50,893	50,904	50,926	51,003	51,407	51,292	50,945	50,375	51,293	52,248
California	1,333,267	1,334,362	1,345,213	1,355,639	1,372,040	1,375,779	1,412,825	1,416,221	1,456,732	1,480,699
Colorado	337,233	337,233	347,055	347,584	335,359	346,149	347,176	431,435	365,142	360,163
Connecticut	175,214	176,221	176,666	176,045	175,860	180,088	182,993	184,990	200,458	202,027
Delaware	15,576	15,528	17,290	17,425	18,189	20,039	21,142	21,395	22,039	24,049
Florida	432,879	437,473	454,481	510,529	525,809	512,538	547,020	571,212	591,525	602,006
Georgia	59,137	66,129	67,436	71,150	71,150	73,145	75,712	78,942	81,218	83,808
Hawaii	24,615	24,165	24,615	24,615	24,589	24,589	26,689	27,627	28,002	28,018
Idaho	41,848	41,848	41,867	41,867	41,039	43,048	43,456	42,917	44,643	44,643
Illinois	391,240	419,197	408,175	401,323	411,156	411,156	304,879	287,376	306,066	326,851
Indiana	54,221	59,292	174,96	178,277	178,507	177,886	178,315	178,665	178,937	179,181
Iowa	62,267	62,329	62,615	62,755	63,071	63,171	63,171	63,171	63,200	63,210
Kansas	353,742	324,177	29,000	29,000	32,300	52,300	32,300	32,300	32,300	32,300
Kentucky	42,594	42,748	43,110	43,110	43,310	43,310	43,508	43,508	44,290	44,525
Louisiana	38,751	39,007	39,049	39,053	39,136	36,119	36,099	37,329	38,267	41,204
Maine	83,940	74,973	567,069	587,206	587,558	94,604	94,970	93,634	96,686	98,814
Maryland	242,513	247,445	249,087	291,734	292,279	295,135	258,621	258,757	266,136	266,176
Massachusetts	290,927	314,026	276,338	277,498	285,264	287,163	288,801	290,601	293,821	295,211
Michigan	264,844	265,391	266,085	266,085	266,251	265,176	351,223	351,264	284,977	285,573
Minnesota	242,029	245,074	246,524	246,524	241,137	245,083	255,793	258,316	267,209	219,900
Mississippi	22,784	22,687	23,627	23,627	24,327	24,327	24,287	24,287	24,287	24,287
Missouri	132,142	133,632	136,811	134,889	135,738	136,791	137,120	138,357	138,522	139,731
Montana	52,241	52,469	48,733	51,014	51,115	54,494	64,916	65,182	65,839	70,868
Nebraska	133,367	133,455	133,455	133,360	133,024	133,044	133,044	134,230	134,200	134,681
Nevada	146,220	148,578	148,578	131,810	131,831	132,565	132,885	132,523	132,524	132,524
New Hampshire	74,554	153,214	153,520	153,520	74,471	74,471	74,471	78,849	84,547	85,709
New Jersey	308,216	321,143	327,359	334,254	341,301	343,419	345,425	357,805	376,532	380,036
New Mexico	120,793	120,193	90,901	90,901	90,693	90,693	90,693	90,693	90,693	90,693
New York	260,793	260,793	260,793	308,197	485,045	1,015,758	1,015,911	1,158,450	1,158,960	1,532,393
North Carolina	135,922	140,041	142,739	143,957	147,693	158,339	159,028	167,837	168,241	171,409
North Dakota	19,743	19,959	19,959	19,959	20,046	20,046	20,046	18,750	17,276	17,401
Ohio	202,913	204,274	204,274	204,317	204,852	204,871	205,047	204,445	204,557	163,918
Oklahoma	71,943	71,635	71,172	71,172	71,931	71,586	71,586	71,579	71,667	71,579
Oregon	91,656	92,277	91,605	91,638	92,606	94,331	94,869	94,937	95,463	95,129
Pennsylvania	282,500	282,500	282,500	282,675	283,001	283,383	288,486	288,795	289,362	289,893
Rhode Island	8,748	8,748	8,853	8,853	8,748	8,748	8,748	8,748	8,748	8,748
South Carolina	80,388	81,557	81,589	81,589	81,798	81,572	80,459	80,459	80,459	80,459
South Dakota	92,710	92,710	93,219	93,808	96,099	96,099	97,637	102,069	105,386	105,396
Tennessee	133,118	133,920	134,284	134,884	142,847	285,594	141,247	142,797	144,013	153,636
Texas	519,154	519,154	669,278	629,000	628,227	628,207	631,018	593,139	668,269	668,457
Utah	97,130	96,806	96,481	113,649	113,799	113,799	113,592	114,236	114,532	121,852
Vermont	64,035	64,101	64,888	65,080	77,631	83,617	81,529	68,677	68,859	68,776
Virginia	69,065	67,451	65,837	66,100	72,610	75,447	72,998	62,006	62,236	62,039
Washington	248,717	255,094	259,520	263,069	258,506	262,226	258,502	262,345	262,134	259,378
West Virginia	198,765	198,765	195,565	195,565	195,565	195,565	195,565	195,584	195,831	195,831
Wisconsin	127,424	128,097	139,545	127,063	127,811	128,578	129,353	132,238	132,725	132,456
Wyoming	119,864	119,866	119,866	126,897	120,707	120,930	121,170	121,170	119,266	119,266
Total	11,684,937	11,837,272	12,300,637	12,484,046	12,653,569	12,915,624	12,804,717	13,029,544	13,162,230	13,571,028
Less Alaska	8,445,048	8,595,049	9,050,575	9,195,335	9,363,499	9,624,506	9,513,508	9,738,423	9,836,291	10,217,782
Alaska percent	27.73%	27.39%	26.42%	26.34%	26.00%	25.48%	25.70%	25.26%	25.27%	24.71%

Source: Daniel McLean, *NASPD Annual Information Exchange Annual Report.*

Visitation at State Parks

Visitation in state parks remained steady over the reporting period showing a low of 745.7 million in FY 1995 and a high of 786.8 million in FY 2000. Since FY 2000 there has been an annual 2.2 percent decline in reported attendance in state parks. This is consistent with other studies reporting participation in outdoor recreation. It remains too early to determine if this represents a trend in outdoor recreation participation by Americans.

Day use represents 91.8 percent of all state park usage and for most states the peak usage is during

Table B
COMPARISON IMPACTS OF STATE PARK OPERATIONS

	Fiscal year		
	1993	1998	2003
Population	263,436,000	276,115,000	290,788,976
Visitation	752,266,297	760,829,945	735,004,031
Acreage	11,557,507	12,484,046	13,162,230
Operating budget	1,188,510,726	1,378,321,917	1,819,345,452
1994 dollars	1,188,510,726	1,286,112,181	1,551,719,736
Full time staff	18,844	18,533	20,603
Acres per 1000 population	43.87	45.21	45.26
Population per acre	22.79	22.12	22.09
Acres per 1000 visitors	15.36	16.41	17.91
Visitors per acre	65.09	60.94	55.84
Acres per full time staff	613.33	673.61	638.85
Expenditures per resident	$4.51	$4.99	$6.26
Expenditures per visitor	$1.58	$1.81	$2.48
Expenditures per acre	$102.83	$110.41	$138.22
Expenditures per resident—1994 $	$4.51	$4.66	$5.34
Expenditures per visitor—1994 $	$1.58	$1.69	$2.11
Expenditures per acre—1994 $	$102.83	$103.02	$117.89

Source: Daniel McLean, *NASPD Annual Information Exchange Annual Report.*

the summer. Overnight visitation has remained relatively constant over the reporting period, peaking in FY 2002 (72.2 million visitors).

State park visitation is affected by a variety of variables. In the past several years some states have had to close all or portions of some state parks due to financial problems. Weather appears to be the biggest determinant of visitation at state parks. A warm dry summer increases attendance while a cool wet summer decreases attendance. Since such seasonal variations are regional, attendance appears to adjust towards a mean on a national level. Severe weather can have a significant detrimental effect, as was the case with Florida in 2004 when almost every park was damaged by one or more hurricanes.

Funding of State Parks

Funding levels in state parks were viewed over the 10-year reporting period using FY 1994 as a base for comparison. Figure A illustrates changes in state park budgets looking at actual dollars, adjusted to 1994 dollars, and 1994 dollars adjusted for inflation. Using actual dollars, it appears that be-

tween FY 1998 and FY 2002 there were significant increases in state park budgets. This should not be interpreted to suggest that state park budgets grew at the expense of other state agencies, rather the state park budgets grew at a pace similar to that of state budgets and growth within other state agencies. In FY 1994 state expenditures on state parks represented 0.19 percent of the state budget. In FY 1998 it was 0.24 percent and in FY 2002 state parks share of state budgets was still 0.24 percent. State park budgets grew in relation to state revenues and state budgets, but the state park share of state budgets remained consistent over the period.

Figure A shows that from FY 1994 through FY 1998 state park operating budgets did not keep pace with inflation (2.23 percent growth). Beginning in FY 1999 and through FY 2002, operating budgets outpaced inflation, even during the early stages of the recession (5.53 percent growth). In FY 2003 the impact of inflation hit state park budgets and the actual dollars dropped for the first time and 1994 dollars dropped as precipitously, moving state park budgets level with inflation. Regardless, state park budgets grew (1994 dollars) from $1.19 billion to $1.47 billion after reaching a high of $1.56 billion. Based on reports from state park directors the trend began to reverse itself in

Figure A: State Park Operating Budgets: Fiscal Years 1994–2003
(In millions of dollars)

Table C
STATE PARK GENERATED REVENUES: FISCAL YEARS 1994–2003

State	1994	1995	1996	1997	1998	1999	2000	2001	2002	2003
Alabama	$25,371,387	$25,104,845	$24,723,792	$23,321,031	$23,065,581	$26,159,506	$25,213,099	$25,503,390	$24,094,767	$24,011,982
Alaska	1,339,850	1,724,639	1,957,318	1,929,958	1,937,708	2,105,772	2,011,922	2,343,504	2,340,817	2,290,487
Arizona	3,250,397	3,572,069	4,114,349	4,287,268	4,505,709	4,520,592	6,934,173	7,152,917	7,055,022	7,667,110
Arkansas	13,167,362	12,647,100	12,804,928	12,998,416	13,450,528	13,310,744	13,502,337	13,983,925	13,738,863	13,657,349
California	74,904,000	58,306,000	63,689,800	63,183,368	61,935,630	68,535,191	54,926,044	49,381,468	39,079,601	59,632,000
Colorado	8,499,526	8,061,593	10,707,556	10,264,145	11,683,703	12,040,322	12,127,312	14,315,644	15,164,684	16,558,008
Connecticut	3,877,012	3,345,317	3,570,600	3,610,921	3,428,297	3,725,981	3,204,719	3,144,679	3,740,903	4,263,925
Delaware	4,584,381	4,862,030	5,012,582	5,594,093	5,679,200	6,654,239	6,619,439	7,247,897	8,323,111	8,048,570
Florida	19,603,397	21,023,986	21,605,518	23,458,663	24,135,101	25,766,021	28,577,198	29,892,927	31,925,406	32,074,581
Georgia	19,049,713	15,080,647	16,916,897	16,926,897	17,182,325	19,822,858	18,171,785	20,516,081	26,037,139	28,513,609
Hawaii	368,894	0	0	265,821	0	275,345	771,100	1,792,758	1,795,197	1,995,000
Idaho	2,351,641	2,762,576	2,800,600	3,341,458	2,879,534	3,182,100	3,502,517	4,060,655	3,427,400	3,123,421
Illinois	6,269,200	5,250,550	4,281,995	5,368,781	4,744,092	950,714	5,199,583	5,435,150	6,019,589	5,857,655
Indiana	9,498,634	9,779,984	23,120,459	23,361,333	28,746,732	29,265,774	31,355,302	32,080,535	33,513,704	34,172,057
Iowa	2,500,000	2,800,000	2,700,000	2,900,000	2,025,959	3,265,000	3,234,000	3,130,410	3,386,109	3,431,038
Kansas	2,978,903	2,638,385	3,057,437	3,200,000	3,447,281	3,998,100	4,241,568	4,378,888	4,890,768	5,987,490
Kentucky	42,043,626	43,834,979	42,259,624	41,963,592	44,731,502	47,754,520	50,607,030	50,818,008	52,185,097	51,536,213
Louisiana	2,355,874	2,582,020	3,598,112	2,477,907	2,902,482	2,818,562	3,483,768	3,690,344	4,182,818	4,347,753
Maine	1,756,526	1,767,628	1,789,459	1,654,154	1,730,449	1,930,814	1,942,841	1,843,272	2,214,197	2,455,615
Maryland	9,770,392	11,131,232	11,162,748	9,613,668	11,979,262	13,847,396	14,202,135	14,749,818	15,065,042	14,548,253
Massachusetts	7,196,877	6,306,333	3,309,674	3,522,686	3,586,732	5,570,434	5,725,161	7,217,763	8,210,610	5,484,070
Michigan	23,869,753	24,143,049	24,143,049	32,511,314	29,556,984	17,723,606	32,346,662	29,431,947	32,848,145	33,239,617
Minnesota	8,400,000	9,190,000	9,201,000	10,250,000	10,611,000	10,705,000	10,939,000	11,351,000	12,118,000	11,665,000
Mississippi	5,136,567	5,313,088	5,441,881	5,994,375	10,297,457	6,706,072	7,266,094	6,260,457	6,644,844	6,541,571
Missouri	4,785,551	5,246,544	6,100,443	5,909,145	7,620,759	6,765,801	6,947,196	6,995,477	7,527,206	9,007,013
Montana	1,324,704	1,015,675	1,126,022	1,117,434	1,415,770	1,570,855	1,652,204	1,457,073	1,463,793	1,744,097
Nebraska	10,174,107	10,677,207	11,003,261	12,196,453	12,190,082	13,231,738	13,705,536	10,869,709	14,626,639	17,976,446
Nevada	832,725	1,095,681	1,362,004	1,531,525	1,707,201	1,822,182	1,902,662	1,991,071	2,018,778	2,179,328
New Hampshire	4,933,213	4,385,789	5,492,017	5,574,756	4,036,580	9,845,258	12,319,213	7,480,476	7,979,699	8,931,092
New Jersey	6,776,473	6,649,722	6,914,474	7,142,162	7,509,434	7,840,448	7,282,667	7,287,613	8,163,179	7,230,635
New Mexico	3,206,707	11,780,840	3,345,216	3,345,216	3,441,671	3,623,266	4,320,400	4,394,200	4,317,500	3,838,100
New York	37,677,478	36,930,909	42,298,725	54,106,000	55,156,500	58,924,072	63,254,371	63,421,947	65,994,458	69,286,337
North Carolina	2,263,132	2,848,586	2,481,371	2,540,912	3,298,564	3,439,904	3,499,641	3,623,932	3,712,559	3,186,593
North Dakota	719,826	717,996	803,188	718,572	808,035	923,329	1,167,775	1,183,470	1,170,276	1,245,276
Ohio	18,304,654	19,609,021	20,996,597	23,060,640	24,597,212	25,179,926	26,467,316	26,540,250	26,974,299	27,816,071
Oklahoma	17,831,274	19,077,362	16,679,489	20,582,514	20,250,204	21,234,176	22,804,143	23,897,358	24,007,738	22,988,827
Oregon	10,729,257	11,191,361	12,185,177	12,854,199	13,490,677	14,548,069	15,253,754	16,178,862	15,425,001	15,414,162
Pennsylvania	9,033,077	9,033,077	9,350,298	12,077,187	10,903,971	12,080,000	12,612,143	16,573,866	15,362,350	12,641,196
Rhode Island	2,922,066	2,791,560	3,039,065	3,039,065	2,251,585	3,684,049	3,237,144	3,125,885	3,839,332	4,291,517
South Carolina	13,125,394	14,263,721	14,431,180	14,629,534	15,104,228	15,264,641	16,057,457	15,970,410	16,537,120	15,058,144
South Dakota	5,473,158	5,879,639	5,923,367	6,235,044	6,876,449	7,522,196	7,153,532	7,694,016	8,472,801	9,826,343
Tennessee	22,086,565	23,328,255	24,538,121	23,921,206	23,841,606	26,192,000	28,451,337	30,324,800	32,403,451	28,751,266
Texas	15,745,552	19,522,133	18,822,008	12,897,352	15,479,948	26,028,040	21,247,524	24,269,227	25,428,235	26,130,106
Utah	4,373,896	4,395,232	5,493,559	6,565,382	6,559,424	7,706,824	7,848,800	7,929,200	8,212,500	7,991,100
Vermont	4,934,904	4,932,554	4,962,805	4,950,051	5,585,152	5,622,519	5,614,248	5,664,753	6,191,217	6,250,253
Virginia	2,717,812	3,624,673	3,977,880	3,877,079	5,134,455	7,258,399	6,476,873	7,911,583	8,583,791	8,726,989
Washington	8,342,436	9,128,054	9,337,401	10,905,142	39,519,134	10,367,941	10,573,593	12,122,366	13,818,288	15,703,194
West Virginia	16,221,628	14,960,636	15,250,168	15,559,233	16,435,865	17,364,166	18,035,815	18,852,238	19,214,102	18,928,398
Wisconsin	9,224,556	10,943,219	10,229,850	10,454,214	11,035,759	11,438,058	12,854,701	13,245,674	14,395,841	14,224,379
Wyoming	431,711	427,129	643,086	683,463	697,738	751,109	1,066,543	1,389,994	1,268,640	1,121,910
Total	532,335,768	535,684,625	558,756,150	588,473,329	639,191,251	650,863,629	677,911,377	690,118,887	715,110,626	741,591,146
1994 dollars	532,335,768	524,649,522	536,908,785	555,813,059	596,429,356	599,445,402	612,018,391	619,857,483	619,857,483	632,503,088
1994 inflated dollars	532,335,768	543,514,819	554,001,834	563,637,111	570,504,243	577,956,943	589,668,330	603,455,827	614,102,542	624,163,688

Source: Daniel McLean, *NASPD Annual Information Exchange Annual Report.*

FY 2003 and continues into FY 2004. In the short term state park budgets appear to be moving lower as state budgets move lower. There is no indication that state park share of state budgets is declining.

State park generated revenues (Figure B) come from services and sales in state parks and have be-come an increasingly important revenue source for state parks. State park generated revenue lagged in-flation growth through FY 1997. Beginning in FY 1998 and continuing through FY 2003 growth exceeded or kept pace with inflation. The FY 2002 data depicted a flat adjustment, losing ground to inflation and the FY 2003 report shows state park revenues keeping pace or experiencing a small growth, less than that lost by reductions in the general fund.

While total state park generated revenue has increased over the last 10 years the share of each revenue source has remained fairly constant. The AIX identifies 10 revenue sources. Camping has consistently been the largest source of income for state parks followed by entrance fees (combined accounting for over 40 percent of total revenue). As a share of growth in revenues camping showed an increase of 59.8 percent from FY 1994 to FY 2003 (actual dollars), lodges increased 54 percent, cabins and cottages increased 52.1 percent, and entrance fees increased 33.7 percent for the same period.

State park operating budget funding sources (Figure C) include state park revenue (that returned to the state park agency), general fund, dedicated sources, federal funds and other. The general fund is the single largest contributor of state park operating funds ranging from a low of 42.3 percent (FY 2003) to a high of 49.6 percent (FY 2001) and averaging 46.6 percent. State park generated revenue has contributed an average of 38.5 percent (high of 41.9 percent in FY 1996 and a low of 33.5 percent in FY 2001). Figure C suggests that as the general fund increases or decreases there is a corresponding shift in park revenues (in the opposite direction). These shifts appear to have remained fairly constant except for FY 2003 where general fund dollars declined at a rate higher than park revenue increased. This was offset, in part, by an almost 5 percent increase in dedicated funds in FY 2003—the highest recorded during this period.

It would seem, based on the data, that dependence on revenues as the primary source for operating state parks is not well founded. Park revenues are more volatile than the general fund and dependent upon a number of variables. There has been much discussion in the states about funding state parks from self-generated revenues and dedicated funds. No state park system has been successfully funded wholly from self-generated revenues. Combined with the decline in visitation, inability of state parks to easily adjust fees, and dependence on weather related challenges,

it is doubtful that any state park system could become self-sustaining without some type of dedicated fund. Missouri, for example, garners a portion of the state sales tax, a process which voters have renewed two times.

This does not suggest that state parks should back away from revenue sources, rather it suggests that in the light of decreasing financial support from states that state park systems must become more creative about revenue development, about the use of friends groups (nonprofits who support state parks), more creative partnering with public, private and nonprofit agencies, and building stronger constituencies. There are excellent examples of state park systems becoming more creative, finding new revenue sources, paying more attention to visitors, but there are also systems that struggle under the political structure that look upon state parks as a political reward or bureaucracies that are so tradition bound that movement forward is all but impossible.

Personnel

Full-time positions grew at an average rate of 1.1 percent for the reporting period with the largest number of full-time employees in FY 2002 at 21,148 full-time and 35,483 seasonal and part time employees. The lowest number of full-time employees was reported in FY 1996 at 18,772. FY 2003 showed a decrease in all three categories of employees and it is anticipated it will continue in the short term. Fourteen states reported permanent layoffs during FY 2003 and FY 2004. Reporting during FY 2004 19 states have had layoffs based on open positions that will not be filled.

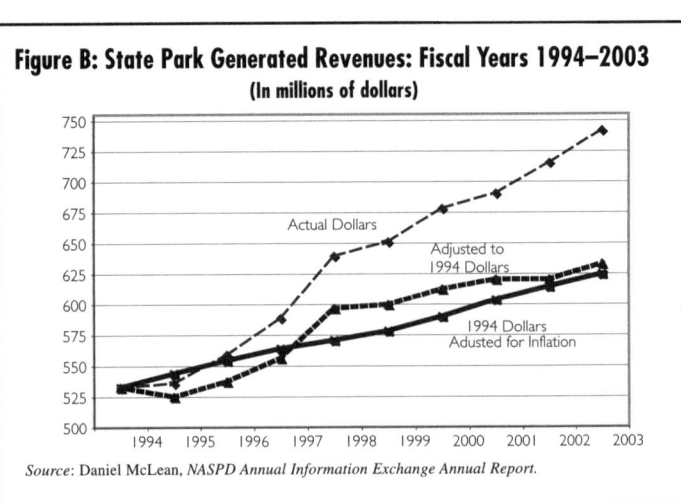

Figure B: State Park Generated Revenues: Fiscal Years 1994–2003
(In millions of dollars)

Source: Daniel McLean, *NASPD Annual Information Exchange Annual Report*.

Measures of Operations

There are no established standards for measuring state parks. Each state park system generates data as requested by its legislature or office of planning and budget. There are, however, common measures that multiple states employ. In most cases they will compare to either similar states or the system as a whole. For the purposes of this report, common standards that have seen use by various agencies and could be applied by states are presented in Table B.

Table B looks at comparisons of population, visitor, expenditure, full-time personnel and acres. During the period reported the acres per 1,000 population grew reflecting the growth of the state park estate. Visitors exceed the U. S. population by a factor of 2.5 (or each member of the U.S. population visited a state park 2.5 times during each year) and the density of use is recorded in visitors per acre. As expected, the visitors per acre declined over the period. Density of usage should be noted as a specific item of concern. Not all state parks receive equal numbers of visitors and not all visitation is distributed equally among state park acreage. Most attendance is present in relatively small built-up areas in state parks, thus confounding the problem of density of use as well as impact on the environment.

Seasonal and part-time staff are present in state parks as a support to the existing full-time staff. The report suggests that even as staff has increased over the period, it has been at a slower pace than land acquisition. In FY 2003 there are more acres per full-time staff than in FY 1994. It is likely this trend will continue in the short term as state park systems continue to experience declines in operating budgets and staff.

From a positive perspective expenditures have increased, whether viewed in actual dollars or in 1994 dollars. From the latter perspective growth has been less than state park managers might have desired, but nonetheless, growth has allowed state parks to make progress towards serving visitors.

Trends

The mission of state parks has remained fairly consistent over time. It has varied in some states, but state parks are a combined natural resource management agency and outdoor recreation provider. Urban parks, though not measured as a separate type of park, have become more common. Massachusetts, for example, joined with the Boston metro parks as a single state agency. New York's second busiest state park is located in New York City. Indiana has two urban state parks in Indianapolis, one a former military base and the other designated as a state park, but is not under the operation of the state park system. Most state park agencies operate under a traditional natural resources umbrella, yet a few are under tourism and there has been limited and slow growth in this area.

The dual mission of resource manager and outdoor recreation provider are not mutually exclusive but sometimes create conflict because the two missions are not compatible. State park managers are expected to be competent in resource management, maintenance management, administrative tasks, personnel management, community relations, planning, leadership and visitor services. The breadth of expectations of state park managers is continuing to grow and fund raising, entrepreneurship, and small business management are becoming essential, if previously unanticipated skills.

· Funding is at the core of state park operations. There is no national inventory of maintenance backlogs (unattended maintenance issues), but funding of state park maintenance will have to become less dependent upon general funds as a matter of course. For most, the disappearance of general fund support is not an alternative. While state parks have become more self-sufficient, the

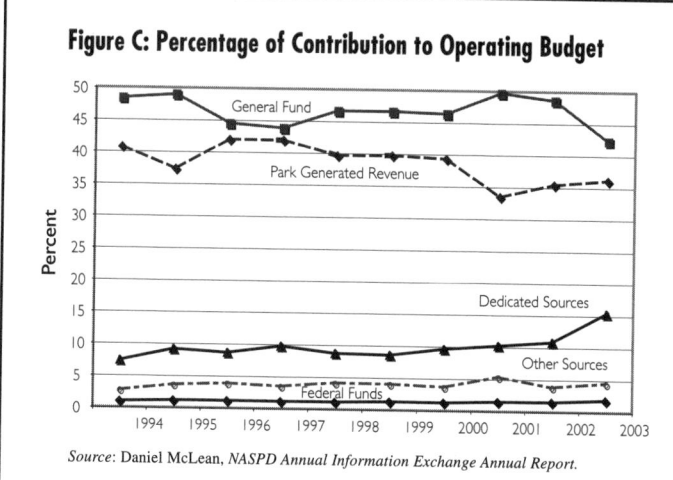

Figure C: Percentage of Contribution to Operating Budget

Source: Daniel McLean, *NASPD Annual Information Exchange Annual Report.*

data does not suggest revenue generation can continue to keep pace with inflation or replace the general fund as a significant source of operating funds. As attendance declines, so will state park generated income, especially as state parks are dependent upon legislatures and external boards to determine fee structures. In FY 2004, 27 states reported a self-funding component allowing fees and other revenues to go directly into their operating fund. Thirty-three states reported they see the self-funding initiative increasing. Allowing state parks to retain all or part of their generated revenue is a positive effort, but many legislatures prefer to have more rather than less control over spending. Dedicated sources of funds are growing and while it remains only a small part of the sources of operating funds, it may become an attractive source for some states as they struggle to maintain level revenues.

If attendance in outdoor recreation continues to decline, or if it stabilizes at a lower level, state parks will need to rethink who their audience is and how to attract new visitors. The growth of urban state parks is one tool that may introduce residents to outdoor recreation, but no studies have been done to determine if such efforts have a carry-over effect to more rural state parks.

States have reallocated some state park lands to municipal and county systems when it is apparent the lands are appropriately managed by that entity.

Twenty-four states report having done so in recent years. This is an ongoing trend highly dependent upon the legislature in most states.

Summary

State parks continue to provide a significant outdoor recreation resource close to many Americans. State parks are a part of the American fabric of life. Levels of participation in state parks remain high and will continue to do so in the future. Funding for state parks has always been problematic and current trends do not suggest this will change. State park managers have moved from traditional resource manager roles to more complex roles serving multiple constituencies and demanding an ever-increasing level of knowledge and sophistication.

Reference

Landrum, N. C. *The State Park Movement in America: A Critical Review.* Columbia: University of Missouri Press. 2004.

About the Authors

Daniel D. McLean is a professor and chairperson of the Department of Recreation and Sport Management at Indiana State University. He has served as the research director for the National Association of State Park Directors for nine years and manages the Annual Information Exchange.

Traci Hogan is a graduate student in the Department of Recreation and Sport Management at Indiana State University.

Telecommunications Policy: Life, Liberty and Data
By Wayne W. Hall Jr.

Telecommunications used to mean earnest debates about regulation, legislation and taxation, the instruments of government. It was about the telephone network. But popular demand for mobility and computing technology has forever changed that discussion. The communications technology industry is in the midst of a long-term transition away from the public switched telephone network towards always-on networks that use Internet and wireless technologies. Old distinctions no longer apply. These new networks are built as much around individuals as technology.

Success from Failure

This essay is about telecommunications, which for policy-makers means an earnest discussion about regulation, legislation and taxation, the instruments of government.

Much of the current policy struggle is really a very big fight over the various fees that show up on telephone bills. In 2005, legislators in Congress will re-write the 1996 telecommunications act, which, other than to encourage consolidation, generally failed to substantially alter the telecommunications and media landscape and has been rendered increasingly meaningless by developments in communications technology.

People are making different choices to communicate at home and in business, often using computer and wireless technologies to accomplish more than at any time in the past.

Access and universal service fees for example, though still important, are holdovers from an era when telecommunications meant "phone company." The phone company funded certain national goals such as universal service. Fine tuning the existing regulatory structure has proven to be an arduous task. Federal courts have consistently returned FCC rules back to the commission for more work.

The irony is that as these obligations have grown – universal service commitments are now at historic highs – the regulated portion of the communications marketplace is in decline. The long distance industry as a distinct market segment is rapidly vanishing. In an effort to rewrite telecommunications law, congressional leaders will have to account for an FCC that now appears ready to limit its own regulatory impulses. FCC commissioners consistently note that they are not in the business of picking technology winners and losers while simultaneously praising, for example, wireless technologies for bringing communications to the rural and urban poor in the nation. While not exactly laissez-faire, the direction is unmistakable.

Unwired

The Department of Commerce's Bureau of Economic Analysis shows that Information Technology (IT) as an industry led economic expansion in the late 1990s. And despite the subsequent stock market crash, IT remains an important driver of national— and international—economic growth.

According to survey data from the Pew Internet and American Life Project, more than a quarter of all Americans can now use wireless-enabled devices like notebook computers and cellular phones to connect to the Internet.[1] Many of these people will use free or cheap connections thanks in part to an effort by the FCC to make radio spectrum available for market experimentation.

One of the FCC's biggest achievements in recent years is the culmination of decision made 20 years ago to permit unlicensed devices to operate in so-called "junk" frequency bands—meaning not very valuable commercially—as long as they did not interfere with licensed services. For years, cordless phones and baby monitors filled that particular spectrum niche.

That has changed dramatically. Marketed by the computer industry as "WiFi," a relatively new wireless technology makes possible a broadband wireless connection of 100 feet or so, far enough, particularly in urban areas, to reach a high speed landline connection to the Web. WiFi access points have mushroomed all around the country thanks to a demand for these connections. The service is particularly attractive to on-the-go professionals who need to work in airports, coffee shops and hotel rooms.

Municipal governments have been quick to seize on this to expand the notion of economic development to include broadband communications services. Making use of city property such as lampposts, large municipalities such as Philadelphia have ambitious plans to use WiFi to connect entire cities to the Web with relatively little expenditure in money. Philadelphia recently worked out an agreement with Verizon to permit the municipality to build the infrastructure despite a statutory claim the carrier could make on the business.[2]

WiFi appears to have a cost advantage when it comes to building the infrastructure. For one thing, it avoids trenching and laying cable. And because it can raise funds and avoid state taxes, cities have some cost advantages to building such networks. While the cost recovery model may vary from place to place, new deals between carriers and municipalities to build these networks appear more and more likely.

Why should states care? The economic development benefits to state government from the expansion and development of broadband wireless infrastructure is crucial to luring business. Cities are important engines of growth and where, at least for now, the creative class chooses to live.

In addition, the federal government since 2002 has made spectrum policy and wireless broadband a priority.[3] The FCC will continue to push hard for policies that promote wireless development. Internally, after a series of management initiatives federal agencies have been ordered to make better use of the spectrum they do have.[4] Cabinet level agencies have a year to develop a comprehensive "spectrum needs plan" to address issues related, for example, to public safety. As with many federal initiatives, that effort will likely affect how states conduct business.

Blurring Distinctions

In existing circuit-switched networks, an open voice connection is maintained end-to-end. There is literally a continuous connection between handsets. Switches serve as the brains of this network, sorting out all the paths in between. Grossly simplified, it is not so far removed from a wire strung between two tin cans.

But in an Internet protocol (IP) network, transmissions are chopped into fragments, or packets, each with a home and destination address. Each packet is routed, along many separate paths if needed, until reassembled and interpreted by software at its destination as speech, data or video. The result is a "stateless" or "connectionless" network since no connection is maintained from beginning to end.

Voice calls today are increasingly made using computer-like appliances that while bearing the appearance of a phones, are in fact much closer to personal computers in the way they work. Conversations can be sliced, diced and synthesized like any other computer file and transported over Internet-like networks.

In this technological shift there is a powerful force. Time, distance and geographic boundaries are blurred if not eliminated.

This presents a problem for regulators at all levels of government, which has, unacknowledged until the recent past, been in the business of regulating a particular technology associated with copper circuits and the arrangements made to send and receive voice calls from a telephone wired to the kitchen counter.

Historically, there was a neat division of authority. State regulators regulated calls completed within the state. And federal regulators regulated calls between states. Just how the states will regulate these new arrangements where a customer's area code may not actually correspond to the geographic source of a call is being worked out now. But the bottom line is that the federal government will likely gain a great deal of clout.

State tax codes will need to be addressed too. New congressional legislation bans Internet access taxes, regardless of technology, until November 2007.[5] But in a nod to existing regulatory gray areas, the bill added that "any service that results in a telephone call, regardless of the technology behind it, can continue to be taxed (emphasis added)."

Meanwhile, the FCC moves ahead. In a February 2004 ruling, the commission decided that 'Net-only, or "computer-to-computer" calls, would be unregulated.[6] By making telephony another software application, Voice-over-IP (VoIP) attacks the billing models of traditional service because time and distance are largely irrelevant.

More recently, it has found that popular new calling services offered to consumers for use over home broadband connections are essentially interstate services, which removes such services from state regulatory oversight.

This decision is a brief stopover on the way to another regulatory destination: determining whether such calls are "telecommunications" or "information" services. The FCC has traditionally regulated telecommunications services, whereas information services have been unregulated. Again, this is a legacy distinction developed in an earlier age.

As of this writing, consumer all-you-can-talk VoIP deals can be had for about $25 per month. Because the real costs of the services are actually much lower than traditional phone offerings—thanks in part to fewer government mandated fees—they're more profitable.

It would be a mischaracterization to suggest that customers are fleeing traditional local phone service en masse. But there is a growing awareness that new ways of making phone calls are available and the industry, particularly AT&T and MCI, which were the most dependent on the long distance model, is working to position itself for a new age.

Can You Hear Me Now?

Without time or geographic constraints, the Internet is fast becoming the new communications platform of choice, functioning more like a public utility than private enterprise. Consumers plug into it like an electrical outlet. They receive information rather than electricity.

This utility is relentlessly efficient. It squeezes any market it touches by making the cost necessary to produce any item apparent to the consumer. Armed with this knowledge, consumers can wring savings from financial exchanges by going directly to the producer. Formerly profitable products and services become commodities.

One result of this brutal efficiency is the collapse of the long distance market. AT&T has left the consumer long distance market altogether. IBM will sell its personal computer division, an industry it virtually created, to a Chinese firm whose operating costs are undoubtedly lower.[7]

This reality is steadily reshaping the software industry. For example, open source software development is now more acceptable as an alternative to the Microsoft monopoly on the desktop. "Open source" is computer software for which the original code is in the public domain. Anyone can develop the code as long as they make their enhancements available to everyone else. The open source operating system Linux is one result of this kind of software development.

These efficiencies affect related businesses. Chipmaker Intel is getting behind Linux.[8] Other open source success stories like Firefox, a speedy and feature-rich Web browser, are gaining market share, which meets the test of open source acceptability: people want it.[9] Massachusetts now gives a purchasing preference to openly developed software. This issue also appears on the agenda of the National Association of State Chief Information Officers.

"We the Media"

The nature of information and communications technology is obviously changing the marketplace. Whereas telecommunications could once be managed, regulated and taxed as a discreet thing, it's a much different activity now. An industry in which every participant can in theory, if not in fact, effortlessly communicate across time, distance and geographic boundaries with any other member is far more challenging for government to address.

From a cultural viewpoint, the new world of telecommunications and information technology is as much about media as technology.[10] The ideas, interests and conversations of people are where a lot of money is made.

Like the open source movement, broadly successful technology now originates in the public sphere. For example, instant messaging keeps tabs on the people you've invited into your communications circle. Your "buddy list" lets you know at a glance which people are available to chat using a feature called "presence." Instant messaging is extremely popular among teenagers for whom the social network is paramount.

The technology of presence has business potential as well. Microsoft is investing heavily to field applications that will make instant messaging useful to business and government.[11]

This change affects the jobs of telecommunications and information technology professionals. Instead of acting as plumbers, they are just as likely now to talk about such issues as personal identity, authentication and reputation. By creating a national commons, communications technology is more than the sum of its hardware, whether it be wireless access points, handheld devices and notebook computers. It is not the sole domain of engineers and software developers.

Nor is it the property of the evening news. In a media-saturated culture, the one-to-many broadcast model used in television or print media is being overtaken by a society that can relate the news to each other. Given the ability to bring new facts to the table, a popular press is thriving.

In several recent instances print and broadcast media outlets have found themselves on the defensive by being careless with the public trust. This has prompted serious discussion between journalists and between marketing and advertising professionals over what instant information access means in their industries. As it turns out, ordinary people will fact-check what they hear. "We the media," indeed.

Some object that information ghettos have materialized, that given the choice citizens will consume only the information with which they agree. There are still areas beyond the reach of telecommunications and technology networks that must be reached. But the Pew Internet and American Life Project published research saying that assumption is wrong. Wired Americans are exposed to more points of view than non-wired citizens. Furthermore, they are not using the Web to consume only news with which they agree.[12]

State government, being in the business of safeguarding personal records, promoting economic development and providing for public health and safety, has not yet begun to grapple with how this phenomenon will affect it. Yet is has implications for the structure, management and flow of government and for how the governed will talk with their representatives.

Unfortunately, there is still a tendency to view telecommunications and information technology as simply the set of pipes necessary to move information around, that as elaborate and technically challenging as it has become, it's still just so much plumbing.

This is bound to change if for no other reason than the coming generation has other ideas. These technologies are for them the normal respiration of a free people in pursuit of life, liberty and data.

Notes

[1] Pew Internet & American Life Project, *http://www.pewinternet.org/pdfs/PIP_Wireless_Ready_Data_0504.pdf.*

[2] "Philly, Verizon Deal Lets WiFi Plan Go Forward," CNN.com, *http://www.cnn.com/2004/TECH/internet/12/01/wireless.philly.ap/index.html.*

[3] Michael K. Powell, "Broadband Migration III: New Directions in Wireless Policy," *http://www.fcc.gov/Speeches/Powell/2002/spmkp212.html.*

[4] "Bush orders agencies to define use of radio spectrum," *Government Computer News, http://www.gcn.com/vol11_no1/daily-updates/28018.html.*

[5] Jonathon Krim, "Moratorium on Web Tax Advances,"

Washington Post, http://www.washingtonpost.com/wp-dyn/articles/A58613-2004Nov17.html.

[6] A copy of the FCC's decision can be found online at *http://www.pulver.com/reports/pulver-decision.pdf.*

[7] "IBM Sells PC Unit to China's Lenovo," *Rueters, http://www.olympics.reuters.com/newArticle.jhtml?type=businessNews&storyID=7022724.*

[8] Cynthia L. Webb, "Linux Ready for Prime Time, Intel Says," *Washington Post Filter, http://www.washingtonpost.com/wp-dyn/articles/A9694-2004Nov24.html.*

[9] OneStat.com, (November 22, 2004), http://www.searchenginejournal.com/index.php?p=1082.

[10] *We the Media* is the title of a book by Dan Gillmor. A copy of the work is available online at *http://wethemedia.oreilly.com.*

[11] Om Malik, "Talking Turkey: Microsoft's Plan to Take Over IP Applications," *Business 2.0,* (November 16, 2004), *http://www.business2.com/b2/web/articles/0,17863,783501,00.html.*

[12] "The internet and democratic debate," Pew Internet & American Life Project, *http://www.pewinternet.org/pdfs/PIP_Political_Info_Report.pdf.*

About the Author

Wayne W. Hall Jr. has worked with the NASTD – Telecommunications and Technology Professionals Serving State Government – for 15 years. He is currently the Technology Analyst for NASTD.

Chapter Nine

SELECTED STATE POLICIES AND PROGRAMS

State Emergency Management and Homeland Security: A Changing Dynamic

By Trina R. Sheets

The discipline of emergency management is at a critical juncture in history. Even before the horrific events of September 11th, 2001, emergency management and other public safety disciplines had recognized the growing implications and reorganized to deal with the growing threat of terrorism. The national effort towards achieving "homeland security" is challenging the resources, relationships, organizational responsibilities and fundamental principles of the entire emergency response community. The relationships between the community of emergency management and the new and evolving dynamic we call homeland security is yet to mature or be defined so that a clear and achievable future path to greater national security and safety can be pursued.

Introduction

Three years following the terrorist attacks of September 11, 2001 the federal government remains keenly focused on developing national goals and strategies that will help enhance the nation's capability to prevent, prepare for, respond to and recover from incidents of terrorism. While no additional attacks have occurred on U.S. soil, the threat remains and federal, state and local governments continue to be vigilant and focused on keeping citizens, communities and the national infrastructure safe from harm. While federal funding and resources trend toward support of homeland security activities at the expense of all hazards emergency planning and day-to-day public safety programs, Mother Nature recently reminded us she's still our biggest threat when four major hurricanes struck the state of Florida in the span of a three month period in the fall of 2004. These four consecutive hurricanes required the largest deployment of federal, state and interstate resources in the nation's history. Yet terrorism remains the number one focus of the federal government. This newly defined national priority has created an incredibly new and dynamic interaction of local, state, and federal governments, the private sector and the international community.

Emergency Management Organizations

State emergency management agencies are responsible for developing emergency operations plans and procedures for all disasters and emergencies (including homeland security); training personnel; and conducting drills and exercises with local governments, other state agencies, volunteer agencies and the federal government. Emergency management agencies are also responsible for coordinating and facilitating the provision of resources and supplemen-

tal assistance to local governments when events exceed their capabilities. In the aftermath of a disaster or emergency, the emergency management agency coordinates public education, information and warning; conducts damage assessments, resource management and logistics; facilitates mutual aid, sheltering and mass care; manages transportation and evacuation; leads incident management; and oversees the emergency operations center.[1] In times of disaster, the nation's governors depend on the emergency management agency to provide damage estimates, assist the governor's office in crisis communications by providing accurate and realistic information, activate mutual aid agreements to move resources quickly and efficiently, and to coordinate with local volunteer organizations to manage donations and supplementary assistance.

The organization of state emergency management agencies varies widely. Currently, in 13 states, the emergency management agency is located within the department of public safety; in 20 states it is located within the military department under the auspices of the adjutant general; and in 11 states, it is located within the governor's office. Regardless of agencies' organizational structure for daily operations, emergency management ranks high among governors' priorities. In 29 states, the emergency management director is appointed by the governor. The position is appointed by the adjutant general in 12 states, and by the secretary of public safety in seven states.

Homeland Security Structures

The attacks on the World Trade Center and the Pentagon increased public awareness of the potential for domestic terrorism incidents and hastened preparedness efforts by all levels of government. The challenge states continue to face is to integrate homeland security planning and response activities into their existing emergency management and response systems.

All states have designated a homeland security point of contact. This position has become a critical component of a governor's staff and one that has an enormous responsibility to the public for preparing citizens, businesses and governments for the next emergency or large-scale disaster. To date, 17 states have established a unique position of homeland security director. In nine states, the emergency management director is the primary point of contact, and in eight states it is the adjutant general or director of the military department. Nine public safety secretaries also serve in the position. Several states have merged their emergency management and homeland security agencies and have named one individual to oversee both programmatic areas.

Increasingly, the homeland security director is becoming less a political appointment in the governor's office and more institutionalized in the organizational structure of state government. The number of homeland security offices, departments or agencies authorized through executive order or state statute has increased significantly over the last year. Funding and personnel for these offices has been on the rise as well, often matching and in many cases, surpassing the resources of the state emergency management agency and other state response agencies. The number of state personnel dedicated to homeland security activities ranges from two people to over 70 people. In several states, personnel from the emergency management agency have been transferred or reassigned to support homeland security functions. In others, homeland security functions have been an added responsibility for existing staff in the agency designated as the lead for homeland security. The majority of funding for homeland security offices comes from the federal government in the form of grants, although several states have appropriated their own funds to support counter terrorism. A popular and very necessary funding initiative among states to increase their preparedness levels is investing resources in statewide interoperable communications systems. Systems on the market today that allow the various emergency response disciplines to talk to each other through both voice and data cost several million dollars and require long-term financial investments by states and communities. There is not enough federal funding available to support such comprehensive interoper-able communications systems throughout the country.

Many states have undergone internal reorganiza-tions to adequately staff and fund homeland security offices and to appropriately realign their resources to accommodate the threat of terrorism. Seventeen states have recently completed or are planning a reorganization to address homeland security. Already, 15 states have combined the functions of emergency management and homeland security into one agency or department. In 16 states the two agencies have equal standing in the organizational structure. States are also employing regional approaches to homeland security. Regional coordination refers to defined areas within a given state or several states that have agreed to work together on common preparedness goals. These approaches provide for greater coordination and maximize state and federal funds. Mutual aid, or the sharing of resources across jurisdictional lines, is an important component of regional coordination. States can capitalize on the existing capabilities and years of experience and lessons learned from past disasters, which can be readily applied to domestic terrorism events. Emergency management is the central coordination point for all resources and assistance provided during disasters and emergencies, including acts of terrorism. Many states are building upon this experience and leveraging the ability of emergency management to bridge the gaps in communication and mobilize its resources to respond to any type of disaster, however unique, specialized or isolated.

Short-Term Investments for a Long-Term Problem

For the past several years, Congress and the federal government have provided billions of dollars to build a national capacity for domestic preparedness. Funding was provided through states for distribution to local governments in support of objectives identified in the statewide homeland security strategies required by the U.S. Department of Homeland Security. Congress requires that 80 percent of all funding be passed through to local governments leaving a much smaller amount for use by the state to coordinate the state strategy. Just three years into the funding cycle, homeland security money is being diverted from states to major metropolitan cities. There is no doubt that big cities are considered serious targets for terrorism and their resource needs are significant. Instead of increasing the overall funding level to accommodate major city needs, money is being shifted from one level of government to another. Developing isolated pockets of capability for counter terrorism does nothing to promote statewide or regional coordination. In addition, Congress is considering legislation that would change the funding allocation formula for states to receive federal homeland security grants, placing greater emphasis on risk and critical infrastructure vulnerability as opposed to the current approach of allocating dollars on a percentage plus population basis. Changes in funding allocations will have major impacts on smaller rural states that have become accustomed to receiving their share of terrorism preparedness monies. The terrorism response equipment purchased by states and localities, planning efforts and training conducted for thousands of state and local emergency response personnel require long-term support from the federal government for what can be characterized as a national security effort. Otherwise, the achievements that have been made thus far will fall to the wayside very quickly as day-to-day public safety needs consume the attention and resources of state and local governments. Among states and emergency response disciplines, there is a common concern regarding long-term sustainable federal funding for homeland security.

Traditional Funding is Losing Out

While money remains in the pipeline for such programs as bioterrorism preparedness, law enforcement prevention activities and terrorism response equipment purchase, funding for traditional programs such as the Predisaster Mitigation Program, the Hazard Mitigation Grant Program, and the Emergency Management Performance Grant is losing its foothold. These programs provide long term, critical operational funding for emergency management and the proven, successful programs that minimize the risk to property and life before a disaster occurs.

Earmarking funds for a particular need is a popular legislative strategy, but traditional funding for basic state emergency operations, grants management, non-homeland security related training, and public outreach has been lost in a wave of stovepipe funding for equipment, terrorism exercises, border and port security, and critical infrastructure protection. These are legitimate needs, but states and locals are struggling to simply maintain adequate staffing levels, pay overtime and administer the funds channeled through their agencies.

Funding for emergency management programs has been stagnant for over a decade, with only modest increases in state operating budgets despite the national focus on homeland security. State budget cuts due to revenue shortfalls have hit emergency management and public safety agencies at a time when more is expected from them. Increased responsibilities for homeland security and the loss of adequate

funding for basic operations have taken their toll. In fiscal year 2005, agency budgets ranged from $410,000 to $280 million, plus state disaster appropriations ranged from $20,000 to $560 million. The national average for state agency operating budgets was $12 million, and when disaster appropriations are included the national average increases to $26 million. This represents a significant decrease from fiscal year 2004. These budgets support an average of 70 full-time employees. Staffing levels in individual agencies range from 13 to 459 full-time employees.

Most new federal funds are being directed specifically toward homeland security activities, while ignoring the needs of basic public safety systems. The nation's emergency management and response system can support homeland security efforts, but must be made more robust and then maintained over the long-term. As their budgets allow, some states are doing their part by appropriating additional funds for homeland security related activities such as planning, training, and exercises; intelligence sharing and analysis; improvements to local emergency operations centers; critical infrastructure protection; increases in law enforcement personnel; support costs for homeland security staff; and matching funds to assist local jurisdictions in meeting federal grant requirements. However, more can be done. States need the flexibility to direct federal funds to fill the gaps where they cannot – whether it be to develop a specialized response capability to deal with particular threats or to enhance overall emergency preparedness within the state.

A New Strategy for Response

Homeland Security Presidential Directive #5 – Management of Domestic Incidents calls for the U.S. Department of Homeland Security to integrate the current family of federal domestic prevention, preparedness, response and recovery plans into a single all-hazards plan, and to develop a comprehensive national incident management system to respond to terrorist incidents and natural hazards.[2] The fundamental requirements of this *National Response Plan* (NRP) are to develop a consistent approach to domestic preparedness as well as to incident management across the life cycle of the incident—from awareness, through prevention and preparedness, and into response and recovery—and to improve the effective use of resources that are available to during each step of the this cycle.[3]

The NRP:

- Creates a single, all-hazards plan that is flexible enough to accommodate all types of disasters and applies to all of the disciplines involved in the response;

- Emphasizes the unity of effort among all levels of government, private industry, volunteer organizations, and the public;

- Places equal emphasis on awareness, prevention, preparedness, response and recovery; and

- Establishes federal authorities to coordinate federal response efforts and outlines involvement of the Department of Homeland Security in incident management.

The NRP is being rolled out by the Department of Homeland Security in early 2005. The plan has wide implications for state and local governments, as they work to rewrite their existing emergency operations plans to reflect new relationships and protocols identified in the NRP. State and local stakeholder organizations have provided a significant amount of input to ensure that the plan does not create a new system entirely, but rather, takes advantage of the best procedures states already have in place. The new approach will take time to implement and exercising of the system will be needed.

Mutual Aid Reaches New Heights

The Emergency Management Assistance Compact (EMAC) is a national interstate mutual aid agreement that allows states to share resources during times of disaster. EMAC has been in existence since 1992. To date, 48 states, two territories and the District of Columbia are signatories to EMAC. Membership requires that the compact legislation be enacted by the state legislature and signed into law by the governor.

The 2004 hurricane season required an extraordinary interstate mutual aid response to assist the impacted states of Florida, Alabama and West Virginia. EMAC reached a historic milestone when over 800 people from 38 states were deployed to help with disaster response and recovery efforts. EMAC assistance continued for over 85 straight days. The greatest needs were in the areas of 24 hour staffing for local emergency operations centers, managing donations, providing community outreach services to ensure disaster victims know where and how to access federal disaster assistance, and assisting the elderly and special needs population groups housed in emergency shelters. EMAC teams were also deployed to the Washington, D.C. headquarters of the Federal Emergency Management Agency (FEMA) where they worked for several weeks in coordination with FEMA and other federal agencies provid-

ing emergency support. This was the largest state to state utilization of mutual aid in history and the disaster threatened to overwhelm the federal government's response capability as well which made EMAC so valuable to the overall response.

As EMAC proved itself once again as the nation's premier interstate mutual aid mechanism, the Department of Homeland Security announced the rollout of the National Incident Management System (NIMS) which is intended to define a single comprehensive national approach to emergency and disaster prevention, preparedness, response and recovery. The overarching objective of NIMS is to ensure that all levels of government and the private sector are able to work together and communicate effectively. One of the main components of NIMS is mutual aid. All state and local governments are required to have mutual aid agreements in place by the end of fiscal year 2006 in order to be eligible to receive federal funding in the future.

States that are members of EMAC are ahead of the curve in the area of interstate mutual aid requirements by the federal government. At least 26 states have intrastate (local-to-local jurisdiction) mutual aid agreements in place and eight states are proposing such agreements be established. To date, approaches to implementing intrastate mutual aid have varied with 16 states making participation voluntary. Twelve states have mandated local mutual aid agreements through state statute and seven states require participation as a requirement for state/federal funding. The majority of agreements are cross-discipline allowing all first responders to participate i.e. fire, law enforcement, emergency medical services and others as determined appropriate by the participating mutual aid partners.

The National Emergency Management Association (NEMA) developed the National Model Intrastate Mutual Aid Legislation in 2004 and made it available to interested state and local governments. The model intrastate mutual aid agreement is based on EMAC and includes critical mutual aid provisions related to reimbursement, liability and workers compensation – all recommended in the NIMS document for inclusion in such agreements. Even those states with local mutual aid agreements already in place are now reviewing them against the national model and making revisions as needed to meet new requirements established through NIMS. At least 10 states plan to introduce the NEMA developed model into their 2005 state legislative sessions.

Notes

[1] National Emergency Management Association.

[2] The White House, *Homeland Security Presidential*

Directive #5 – Management of Domestic Incidents (Washington, D.C.: The White House, February 2003). *http://www.whitehouse.gov/news/releases/2003/02/20030228-9.html.*

[3] Department of Homeland Security, *National Response Plan*, (Washington, D.C.: Department of Homeland Security, 2004).

References

National Emergency Management Association Web site *http://www.nemaweb.org.*

Emergency Management Assistance Compact Web site *http://www.emacweb.org.*

National Emergency Management Association. *NEMA 2004 Biennial Report: Organizations, Operations and Funding for State Emergency Management and Homeland Security* (Lexington, KY: National Emergency Management Association).

National Emergency Management Association. *If Disaster Strikes Today—Are You Ready to Lead? A Governor's Primer on All-Hazards Emergency Management,* (Lexington, KY: The National Emergency Management Association, 2002).

About the Author

Trina R. Sheets is the executive director of the National Emergency Management Association, an affiliate of The Council of State Governments. She is responsible for organization management, strategic planning, tracking and reporting on national policy issues relating to emergency management and homeland security. Sheets is the author of several national emergency management and homeland security articles and publications.

Table A
STATE EMERGENCY MANAGEMENT: AGENCY STRUCTURE, BUDGET AND STAFFING

State or other jurisdiction	Position appointed	Appointed/ selected by	Reports to	Organizational structure	Agency operating budget FY 2004 ($ in thousands)	Full-time employee positions
Alabama	★	G	G	Governor's Office	$900	63
Alaska	★	G	ADJ	Adjutant General/Military Department	2,223	52
Arizona	★	ADJ	ADJ	Adjutant General/Military Department	1,349	50
Arkansas	★	G	G	Department of Emergency Management	1,183	77
California	★	G	G	Governor's Office	159,683	459
Colorado	...	CS	ED	Department of Local Affairs	595	27
Connecticut	★	G	C	Emergency Management/Homeland Security	120	70
Delaware	★	SPS	HSD	Safety & Homeland Security Agency	950	35
Florida	★	G	G	Department of Community Affairs	280,000	134
Georgia	★	G	HSD	Homeland Security Agency	3,000	100
Hawaii	★	ADJ	ADJ	Department of Defense	1,500	40
Idaho	★	ADJ	ADJ	Governor's Office/Military Division	1,302	38
Illinois	★	G	G	Governor's Office	30,000	267
Indiana	★	G	G	Governor's Office	987	46
Iowa	★	G	ADJ	Department of Public Defense	2,800	47
Kansas		ADJ	ADJ	Adjutant General/Military Department	550	28
Kentucky	★	G	ADJ	Adjutant General/Military Department	3,300	81
Louisiana	★	ADJ	ADJ	Adjutant General/Military Department	1,268	44
Maine	★	EM	ADJ	Adjutant General/Military Department	1,000	21
Maryland	★	G	ADJ	Adjutant General/Military Department	2,600	57
Massachusetts	★	G	PSS	Public Safety	3,368	70
Michigan	...	CS	SPS	State Police	4,200	75
Minnesota	★	G	PSS	Public Safety	2,903	59
Mississippi	★	G	G	Governor's Office	930	67
Missouri	★	ADJ	ADJ	Adjutant General/Military Department	3,000	69
Montana	...	ADJ	ADJ	Adjutant General/Military Department	454	21
Nebraska	★	ADJ	ADJ	Adjutant General/Military Department	1,260	34
Nevada	★	G	G	Public Safety	2,000	22
New Hampshire	★	SPS	PSS	Public Safety	3,570	40
New Jersey	★	SPS	SPS	State Police	7,100	56
New Mexico	★	G	PSS	Public Safety	1,100	34
New York	★	G	G	Adjutant General/Military Department	4,300	123
North Carolina	★	SPS	PSS	Public Safety	8,300	175
North Dakota	★	ADJ	ADJ	Adjutant General/Military Department	2,500	55
Ohio	★	G	PSS	Public Safety	3,853	99
Oklahoma	★	G	G	Governor's Office	680	32
Oregon	★	G	HS	Homeland Security	10,000	34
Pennsylvania	★	G	G	Governor's Office	17,000	162
Rhode Island	★	ADJ	ADJ	Adjutant General/Military Department	645	20
South Carolina	★	ADJ	ADJ	Adjutant General/Military Department	950	49
South Dakota	★	PSS	PSS	Public Safety	1,500	17
Tennessee	★	G	ADJ	Adjutant General/Military Department	2,300	107
Texas	★	HS	HS	Governor's Office	1,255	137
Utah	★	PSS	PSS	Public Safety	725	44
Vermont	★	PSS	PSS	Public Safety	410	13
Virginia	★	G	PSS	Public Safety	18,000	101
Washington	★	ADJ	ADJ	Adjutant General/Military Department	19,300	119
West Virginia	★	G	PSS	Public Safety	1,238	37
Wisconsin	★	G	ADJ	Adjutant General/Military Department	19,000	44
Wyoming	★	G	HSD	Governor's Office	1,006	24
District of Columbia	★	M	DM	Department of Public Safety	2,000	39
Puerto Rico	★	G	G	Governor's Office	3,600	
U.S. Virgin Islands	★	G	ADJ	Adjutant General/Military Department	576	20

Source: The National Emergency Management Association, December 2004.

Key:
★—Yes
...—No
G—Governor
GO—Governor's Office
ADJ—Adjutant General
M—Mayor

C—Commissioner
HSD—Homeland Security Director/Secretary
DM—Deputy Mayor
PSS—Public Safety Secretary/Commissioner/Director
SPS—State Police Superintendent/Commissioner
CS—Civil Service
PS—Public Safety
HS—Homeland Security
SP—State Police

Table B
STATE HOMELAND SECURITY STRUCTURES

State or other Jurisdiction	State homeland security advisor		Homeland security organizations	
	Designated contact	Operates under authority of	Designated department/agency	Full-time employee positions
Alabama	Homeland Security Director	SS	★	12
Alaska	Adjutant General	EO/SS	★	13
Arizona	EM Director	GA	★	13
Arkansas	EM Director	GA	★	13
California	Homeland Security Director	EO	★	33
Colorado	Public Safety Dir./Sec.	EO/SS	★	27
Connecticut	Commissioner/EM/HS	EO/SS	★	35
Delaware	Homeland Security Director	GA	★	35
Florida	Public Safety Dir./Sec.	SS	...	(a)
Georgia	Homeland Security Director	EO	★	(a)
Hawaii	Adjutant General	GA	★	4
Idaho	EM Director	EO/SS	★	38
Illinois	Special Assistant to Gov.	GA	★	8
Indiana	Homeland Security Director	SS	★	3
Iowa	EM Director	GA/SS	★	23.5
Kansas	Adjutant General	GA	...	...
Kentucky	Homeland Security Director	EO	★	20
Louisiana	Adjutant General	EO/SS	★	44
Maine	EM Director	GA	★	4
Maryland	Homeland Security Director	EO	★	4
Massachusetts	Public Safety Dir./Sec.	SS	...	...
Michigan	EM Director	EO	★	9
Minnesota	Public Safety Dir./Sec.	EO	...	...
Mississippi	Homeland Security Director	EO	★	12
Missouri	Homeland Security Director	EO	★	3
Montana	EM Director	SS	...	4
Nebraska	Lieutenant Governor	EO	★	34
Nevada	Adjutant General	GA	★	4
New Hampshire	EM Director	GA	...	...
New Jersey	Counter-Terrorism Ofc. Dir.	EO/SS	★	(a)
New Mexico	Special Assistant to Gov.	EO	★	4
New York	Homeland Security Director	SS	★	73
North Carolina	Public Safety Dir./Sec.	EO	★	14
North Dakota	EM Director	GA	★	55
Ohio	State Police Superintendent	GA	★	5
Oklahoma	Homeland Security Director	EO/SS	★	12
Oregon	Homeland Security Director	EO	★	2
Pennsylvania	Homeland Security Director	EO	...	4
Rhode Island	Public Safety Dir./Sec.	GA	(a)	(a)
South Carolina	State Police Superintendent	SS	...	...
South Dakota	Homeland Security Director	GA	★	3.5
Tennessee	Homeland Security Director	EO	★	19
Texas	Homeland Security Director	EO/SS	★	5
Utah	Public Safety Dir./Sec.	SS	★	40
Vermont	Public Safety Dir./Sec.	EO	★	7
Virginia	Special Assistant to Gov.	EO/SS	★	10
Washington	Adjutant General	GA	...	18
West Virginia	Public Safety Dir./Sec.	GA	★	(a)
Wisconsin	Adjutant General	SS	★	44
Wyoming	Homeland Security Director	SS	...	24.5
District of Columbia	Dep. Mayor, Public Safety	GA	(a)	(a)
U.S. Virgin Islands	Adjutant General	GA	★	2

Source: The National Emergency Management Association, December 2004.

Key:
★—Yes
...—No
GA—Gubernatorial authority
EO—Executive order
SS—State statute
HSD—Homeland Security Director
AH—Agency head
(a) Data not available.

The Impact of Terrorism on State Law Enforcement

By Chad Foster and Gary Cordner

Traditionally, state-level law enforcement has represented about 10 percent of total police employment in the United States. In keeping with this employment level, state law enforcement has traditionally played an important, but relatively small role in the overall picture of policing America. The information collected for this project, however, indicates an expanding role for state law enforcement since 2001, partly due to new roles and responsibilities associated with homeland security, and partly because state police are filling gaps and vacuums created by shifts in federal law enforcement priorities. Thus, while it is true that all types of police agencies have been significantly affected post Sept. 11, it seems that state law enforcement agencies have been affected the most.

In recent years, Arizona established the Arizona Counter Terrorism Information Center, a combined facility/information system that supports the analysis and sharing of law enforcement information. New York hired 120 new state troopers to guard critical infrastructure along the northern border. The state of Washington implemented an explosive detection canine program to provide additional security screening at terminals to its ferry system, the largest in the United States.[1]

These developments all suggest heightened roles for state law enforcement agencies since the September 11, 2001 terrorist attacks. Not only are state police organizations taking on these new terrorism-related responsibilities, they and their local counterparts are shouldering many new burdens because of shifting federal priorities.

In 2004, The Council of State Governments (CSG) and Eastern Kentucky University (EKU) conducted a 50-state survey of law enforcement agencies and convened an expert work group to examine how these changing conditions are affecting police and their traditional duties and to form recommendations for states. As state policy-makers and legislators seek policy improvements, results from this terrorism-prevention study and recently drafted guidance may help them understand current conditions and strategic directions for the future.

State Law Enforcement—
Yesterday and Today

Today, general purpose state law enforcement agencies exist in all states but Hawaii. General purpose agencies or departments typically fall under the rubric of state police, state patrol or highway patrol departments. One of the oldest and most well-known state police organizations is the Texas Rangers, es-

tablished in 1835.[2] Most state agencies, however, are relatively new. The proliferation of the interstate highway system during the mid-20th century and the need for traffic safety and enforcement forced most states to establish or expand their state law enforcement agency.

Although the structure and function of these agencies varies among states, similar characteristics exist. A common component of most state law enforcement agencies is a criminal investigation division. Roughly 50 percent of all states use a unified model or one that combines police/highway patrol function and investigation responsibilities into a single department. The other half of states have a separate bureau of criminal investigation that works independently or within the state attorney general's office.

In addition to highway safety and criminal investigations, general purpose agencies play many other lead and supporting roles in the states. For example, these agencies often provide states with: special weapons and tactics teams; search and rescue units; marine and aviation assets; crime labs; criminal history repositories; uniform crime reporting; statewide information systems; training for local law enforcement; and statewide communication, intelligence and analysis.

According to the Bureau of Justice Statistics,[3] there were roughly 700,000 full-time, sworn state and local law enforcement personnel in 2000. Within this total, state law enforcement agencies account for roughly 56,000 officers. The Federal Bureau of Investigation, on the other hand, employed just 11,523 special agents in 2000.[4] Law enforcement numbers substantially increase at all levels of government, especially at the state and federal levels, once special jurisdictions with arrest and firearm authorities are considered (e.g., alcoholic beverage control, fish and wildlife, state park services).

Local police departments and sheriffs' offices provide the bulk of law enforcement services to rural communities. As with many other services, however, rural areas are severely constrained by the lack of law enforcement resources. In 1999, for example, 52.4 percent of all local law enforcement agencies employed less than 10 sworn personnel while 5.7 percent employed just one sworn officer.[5] For this reason, state police departments often play enhanced roles in rural areas by providing critical support services to smaller local agencies.

Generally speaking, state law enforcement agencies existed in a fairly stable environment prior to Sept. 11, fulfilling traditional roles. The catastrophic events on Sept. 11 served as a wake-up call to the nation regarding the threat of terrorism. More specifically, it appeared to create and shift responsibilities and paradigms among all layers of law enforcement.

Changing Roles and Responsibilities

According to a 50-state survey by CSG and EKU in the spring of 2004, state law enforcement agencies are greatly involved in their state's homeland security initiatives, and are being stretched thin today due to these new roles and changing federal priorities.[6]

Roughly 75 percent of state agencies say they either have a great amount of involvement or serve as their state's leader in terrorism-related intelligence gathering, analysis and dissemination. In addition, more than 50 percent of state agencies report similar involvement in homeland security planning and coordination at the state level, conducting vulnerability assessments of critical infrastructure, providing protection for this infrastructure and dignitaries, and emergency response to terrorism-related incidents.

How are these responsibilities affecting state police in terms of resource allocation? In comparison to the period before Sept. 11, more than 70 percent of state agencies report allocating more or much more resources for: security of critical infrastructure, special events and dignitaries; intelligence gathering, analysis and sharing; and terrorism-related investigations. Furthermore, at least 50 percent of state police organizations say more or much more resources have been allocated for: airport, border and port security; commercial vehicle enforcement; high-tech/computer crime investigation; operational assistance to local agencies; and preventive patrols.

These resources are likely generated from a number of possible sources; the survey results and inter-

views suggest three. First, more than 10 percent of state agencies report allocating fewer resources for traditional criminal investigation and drug enforcement following Sept. 11. Therefore, it is likely that some resources have been shifted internally among competing public safety problems and priorities. Interviews with state officials in 2004 support the conclusion that other crime fighting efforts have suffered as a result of new terrorism-related demands. This may be especially troublesome for states experiencing problems with other types of crime, such as synthetic drugs (e.g., methamphetamines, prescription drug abuse), new violent gang activities, identity theft and cybercrimes.

Second, state police organizations are receiving funds and resources through a number of federal grant programs such as the State Homeland Security Program and Law Enforcement Terrorism Prevention Program. Although state law enforcement agencies will likely see a small portion of these funds, roughly $1.5 billion was allocated to states for these two programs in 2005.[7]

Third, interviews with state officials suggest they are simply doing more with less. For example, much of the overtime pay incurred during heightened levels of alert, participation on multijurisdictional task forces and working groups, and exhaustive planning and coordination have been absorbed internally. And, these new responsibilities come at a time when state police organizations, like local agencies across the country, face personnel shortfalls due to National Guard and reserve activations.

How do state law enforcement measure against local agencies? In general, law enforcement relationships and responsibilities continue to be assessed and redefined at all levels, and will evolve due to the changing nature of terrorist threats, prevention needs and transforming operations and tactics. The survey results do suggest, however, that certain responsibilities are more state or local in nature. State agencies were more likely to report allocating more or much more resources to the following operational responsibilities: intelligence gathering, analysis and sharing; security for critical infrastructure, special events and dignitaries; and commercial vehicle enforcement. Conversely, local agencies were more likely to indicate allocating more or much more resources to community policing, drug enforcement and traditional criminal investigation.

Shifting Federal Priorities

According to the *9/11 Commission Report* in 2004, "the concern with the FBI is that it has long favored

Table A: State Law Enforcement Agencies

Name of state agency	Sworn officers			Officers assigned to respond to calls		State population	Officers per 10,000 residents	Percent change in employees, 1996–2000		
	Total	Number	Percent of total	Number	Percent of total			Total	Sworn	Civilian
Alabama Department of Public Safety	1,201	628	52%	437	70%	4,447,100	14	1	8	(6)
Alaska State Troopers	409	232	57	155	67	626,932	37	(9)	(20)	12
Arizona Department of Public Safety	1,872	1,050	56	782	74	5,130,632	20	12	10	14
Arkansas State Police	913	559	61	330	59	2,673,400	21	28	7	86
California Highway Patrol	9,706	6,678	69	6,046	91	33,871,648	20	6	7	4
Colorado State Patrol	909	654	72	500	76	4,301,261	15	13	13	12
Connecticut State Police	1,692	1,135	67	585	52	3,405,565	33	9	11	6
Delaware State Police	827	580	70	280	48	783,600	74	9	7	12
Florida Highway Patrol	2,138	1,658	78	1,539	93	15,982,378	10	(3)	(5)	3
Georgia State Patrol	1,785	786	44	650	83	8,186,453	10	(38)	(10)	(50)
Hawaii (a)										
Idaho State Police	510	292	57	258	88	1,293,953	23	94	52	207
Illinois State Police	3,792	2,089	55	939	45	12,419,293	17	6	5	7
Indiana State Police	1,941	1,278	66	570	45	6,080,485	21	3	6	(2)
Iowa State Patrol	599	455	76	443	97	2,926,324	16	28	5	311
Kansas Highway Patrol	694	457	66	457	100	2,688,418	17	(8)	(17)	17
Kentucky State Police	1,670	937	56	481	51	4,041,769	23	(1)	(5)	5
Louisiana State Police	1,438	934	65	542	58	4,468,976	21	17	7	43
Maine State Police	495	325	66	225	69	1,274,923	25	4	(4)	24
Maryland State Police	2,328	1,575	68	1,575	100	5,296,486	30	(4)	(3)	(6)
Massachusetts State Police	2,590	2,221	86	2,221	100	6,349,097	35	(10)	(13)	15
Michigan State Police	3,189	2,102	66	1,310	62	9,938,444	21	2	(3)	12
Minnesota State Patrol	791	548	69	469	86	4,919,479	11	13	13	11
Mississippi Highway Safety Patrol	1,031	532	52	332	62	2,844,658	19	32	(1)	102
Missouri State Highway Patrol	2,170	1,080	50	753	70	5,595,211	21	4	8	0
Montana Highway Patrol	280	205	73	175	85	902,195	23	1	(3)	15
Nebraska State Patrol	640	462	72	382	83	1,711,263	27	0	0	2
Nevada Highway Patrol	597	414	69	414	100	1,998,257	21	14	10	22
New Hampshire State Police	389	315	81	237	75	1,235,786	25	17	29	(16)
New Jersey State Police	3,682	2,569	70	1,297	50	8,414,350	21	1	(5)	18
New Mexico State Police	649	525	81	350	67	1,819,046	29	(22)	21	(68)
New York State Police	4,948	4,112	83	2,439	59	18,976,457	22	6	4	21
North Carolina State Highway Patrol	1,810	1,416	78	1,133	80	8,049,313	18	3	3	6
North Dakota Highway Patrol	193	126	65	92	73	642,200	20	4	5	2
Ohio State Highway Patrol	2,552	1,382	54	1,151	83	11,353,140	12	7	(1)	17
Oklahoma Highway Patrol	1,420	782	55	555	71	3,450,654	23	6	3	10
Oregon State Police	1,409	826	59	450	54	3,421,399	24	13	0	39
Pennsylvania State Police	5,694	4,152	73	2,854	69	12,281,054	34	7	1	30
Rhode Island State Police	268	221	82	148	67	1,048,319	21	14	15	9
South Carolina Highway Patrol	1,220	977	80	977	100	4,012,012	24	11	10	15
South Dakota Highway Patrol	233	153	66	0	0	754,844	20	2	(1)	8
Tennessee Department of Safety	1,715	899	52	800	89	5,689,283	16	10	17	3
Texas Department of Public Safety	7,025	3,119	44	1,880	60	20,851,820	15	4	9	1
Utah Highway Patrol	441	397	90	257	65	2,233,169	18	10	12	(6)
Vermont State Police	513	304	59	239	79	608,827	50	15	5	35
Virginia State Police	2,511	1,883	75	1,464	78	7,078,515	27	12	13	7
Washington State Patrol	2,145	987	46	689	70	5,894,121	17	4	9	0
West Virginia State Police	1,044	681	65	502	74	1,808,344	38	15	14	15
Wisconsin State Patrol	665	508	76	340	67	5,363,675	9	(2)	2	(14)
Wyoming Highway Patrol	295	148	50	133	90	493,782	30	(2)	(2)	(2)

Source: Bureau of Justice Statistics, *Law Enforcement Management and Administrative Statistics, 2000: Data for Individual State and Local Agencies with 100 or More Officers* NCJ 203350, 2000 LEMAS survey, March 2, 2004

Note: Personnel data are for full-time employees during the pay period that included June 30, 2000. Population data are Bureau of the Census figures for April 1, 2000. Number of officers per 10,000 residents excludes part-time employees. Numbers in parentheses indicate a negative percent change in number of employees.

(a) Hawaii has no statewide law enforcement agency.

Table B: Operating Expenditures and Asset Forfeiture Receipts of State Law Enforcement Agencies, 2000

Name of agency	Annual operating expenditure				Estimated asset forfeiture receipts		
	Total	Per employee	Per officer	Per resident	Total	Per employee	Per officer
Alabama Department of Public Safety	$87,377,852	$72,754	$139,137	$20	$420,000	$350	$669
Alaska State Troopers	54,674,300	133,678	235,665	87	142,190	348	613
Arizona Department of Public Safety	123,655,000	66,055	117,767	24	2,440,824	1,304	2,325
Arkansas State Police	58,486,323	64,060	104,627	22	218,383	239	391
California Highway Patrol	917,355,000	94,054	137,370	27	1,467,323	150	220
Colorado State Patrol	66,223,000	72,733	101,258	15	282,028	310	431
Connecticut State Police	116,645,912	68,940	102,772	34	1,073,540	634	946
Delaware State Police	67,895,100	81,214	117,061	87	600,933	719	1,036
Florida Highway Patrol	141,237,296	66,060	85,185	9	1,649,453	771	995
Georgia State Patrol	112,846,027	62,849	143,570	14	2,082,929	1,160	2,650
Hawaii (a)							
Idaho State Police	47,000,000	90,385	160,959	36	0	0	0
Illinois State Police	373,040,400	98,376	178,574	30	4,334,554	1,143	2,075
Indiana State Police	105,917,669	54,569	82,878	17	616,455	318	482
Iowa State Patrol	36,047,438	59,681	79,225	12	119,894	199	264
Kansas Highway Patrol	24,720,000	35,517	54,092	9	942,252	1,354	2,062
Kentucky State Police	125,000,000	74,850	133,404	31	500,000	299	534
Louisiana State Police	126,863,639	88,222	135,828	28	757,194	527	811
Maine State Police	41,000,000	82,828	126,154	32	20,000	40	62
Maryland State Police	250,681,088	107,681	159,163	47	563,000	242	357
Massachusetts State Police	223,577,991	86,324	100,665	35	675,000	261	304
Michigan State Police	268,719,900	84,265	127,840	27	0	0	0
Minnesota State Patrol	60,226,000	76,139	109,901	12	21,886	28	40
Mississippi Highway Safety Patrol	49,200,000	47,721	92,481	17	234,054	227	440
Missouri State Highway Patrol	151,951,352	68,370	140,696	27	1,752,687	789	1,623
Montana Highway Patrol	17,000,000	59,649	82,927	19	250,000	877	1,220
Nebraska State Patrol	33,000,000	51,563	71,429	19	5,710,479	8,923	12,360
Nevada Highway Patrol	51,465,459	86,207	124,313	26	234,253	392	566
New Hampshire State Police	31,000,000	75,887	95,827	25	200,000	490	618
New Jersey State Police	203,087,000	55,157	79,053	24	3,784,000	1,028	1,473
New Mexico State Police	40,000,000	61,633	76,190	22	119,894	185	228
New York State Police	395,060,000	79,044	96,075	21	12,974,038	2,596	3,155
North Carolina State Highway Patrol	134,000,000	74,033	94,633	17	1,649,453	911	1,165
North Dakota Highway Patrol	12,000,000	62,176	95,238	19	4,000	21	32
Ohio State Highway Patrol	202,000,000	79,154	146,165	18	1,052,954	413	762
Oklahoma Highway Patrol	86,148,417	59,971	110,164	25	1,476,833	1,028	1,889
Oregon State Police	190,000,000	134,847	230,024	56	131,957	94	160
Pennsylvania State Police	511,795,000	89,883	123,265	42	4,042,325	710	974
Rhode Island State Police	37,724,490	140,763	170,699	36	232,600	868	1,052
South Carolina Highway Patrol	55,910,979	45,829	57,227	14	1,161,184	952	1,189
South Dakota Highway Patrol	13,300,000	56,596	86,928	18	119,894	510	784
Tennessee Department of Safety	139,538,000	81,363	155,215	25	544,420	317	606
Texas Department of Public Safety	350,560,935	49,902	112,395	17	7,500,000	1,068	2,405
Utah Highway Patrol	34,800,000	78,202	87,657	16	75,000	169	189
Vermont State Police	30,000,000	54,348	87,464	49	65,900	119	192
Virginia State Police	198,236,160	75,389	105,277	28	149,827,242	56,979	79,568
Washington State Patrol	157,193,811	73,284	159,264	27	288,289	134	292
West Virginia State Police	73,526,273	69,528	107,968	41	410,000	388	602
Wisconsin State Patrol	49,113,600	73,634	96,680	9	16,300	24	32
Wyoming Highway Patrol	15,800,000	53,469	106,757	32	0	0	0

Source: Bureau of Justice Statistics, *Law Enforcement Management and Administrative Statistics, 2000: Data for Individual State and Local Agencies with 100 or More Officers* NCJ 203350, 2000 LEMAS survey, March 2, 2004.

Note: Budget data are for the calendar or fiscal year that included June 30, 2000. Capital expenditures such as equipment purchases and construction costs are not included. Computation of per employee expenditure includes all agency employees with a weight of .5 assigned to part-time employees. Computation of per officer expenditure includes all sworn agency employees with a weight of .5 assigned to part-time officers. Computation of per resident expenditure is based on state population. In some cases, data are estimates provided by agency.

(a) Hawaii has no statewide law enforcement agency.

its criminal justice mission over its national security mission."[8] In 2002, the FBI announced a reshaping of priorities to guide future activities, with the new number one priority being "Protecting the United States from terrorist attacks."[9]

Shifting federal law enforcement priorities since Sept. 11 have forced state and local agencies to assume greater roles for those previously held federal responsibilities (e.g., financial crimes, bank robberies, organized crime, drug trafficking). These public safety and crime issues have not disappeared since Sept. 11, and state and local law enforcement agencies are obligated to address these deficiencies by assigning new personnel and shifting resources. Although the FBI may still be involved in these cases, they are much more selective today than before 2001.[10]

In addition to the strain on state resources, state officials are concerned that the shift by the FBI away from traditional crimes will cascade to the state and local levels, thus hindering efforts to screen and analyze possible precursor crimes for linkages to larger-scale terrorist activities. There is a strong indication that a nexus exists among types of criminal activity, including illegal drug operations, money laundering, fraud, identity theft and terrorism.[11]

Where Should States Focus Future Efforts?

CSG convened an expert work group in 2004 to explore these changing conditions and a broad range of alternatives to improve terrorism prevention at the state level. As states develop strategies concerning prevention and to a lesser extent, emergency response, they should consider the following recommendations.[12]

- *Intelligence fusion centers and analysts.* "Fusion centers are an integral part of a state's strategy regarding the prevention of terrorism," said Colonel Bart Johnson of the New York State Police. The centralization of intelligence sharing and analysis at the state level, through one physical center or network of facilities, provides a means to gather and analyze disparate networks of information more effectively and efficiently.

Arizona was one of a handful of states to establish an information fusion center after Sept. 11. The Arizona Counter Terrorism Information Center is nationally recognized for providing tactical and strategic intelligence support to law enforcement officials across the state and for being uniquely located with the FBI's Joint Terrorism Task Force.

According to the *National Criminal Intelligence Sharing Plan* released in 2004, "Analysis is the portion of the intelligence process that transforms the raw data into products that are useful...without this portion of the process, we are left with disjointed pieces of information to which no meaning has been attached."[13] Today,

---

Table C: Homeland Security Roles for State Law Enforcement

State law enforcement agencies level of involvement in their state's homeland security initiatives

	No involvement or very little involvement	Moderate involvement	Great amount or our agency is the leader
Source of homeland security announcements for the public	30.7%	35.5%	33.9%
Distribution of the state's federal homeland security funding	48.4	22.6	29.0
Coordinates homeland security activities in the state	16.1	30.7	53.2
Serves as state's primary contact to DHS and other federal agencies for homeland security	32.8	27.9	39.3
Conducting critical infrastructure, key asset and vulnerability assessments	9.7	33.9	56.5
Homeland security training for law enforcement	16.1	38.7	45.2
Homeland security education/training for the public	51.6	25.8	22.6
Homeland security planning for the state	11.3	27.4	61.3
Terrorism-related intelligence gathering, analysis and dissemination	4.9	19.7	75.4
Emergency response to terrorism-related incidents	16.4	27.9	55.7
Protection of dignitaries	12.9	29.0	58.1
Protection of critical infrastructure	22.6	24.2	53.2

Source: The Council of State Governments and Eastern Kentucky University National Survey of State and Local Law Enforcement Agencies, 2004.

Note: Total state law enforcement population = 73; number of collected surveys = 61; survey response rate = 84 percent.

---

terrorism and crime prevention missions require a much more proactive approach to identify terrorists before they act and interdict attacks that are occurring. To meet this new need, states should pursue specialized intelligence analysts and improved analytical tools. The Florida Legislature, for example, authorized more than 30 new intelligence analyst positions following Sept. 11 to address this need.

- *Collaboration among law enforcement partners.* "Terrorism prevention and response requires law enforcement agencies at all levels to work together, exchange information, train and coordinate efforts to a much greater extent than has ever occurred," said Sheriff Al Cannon of Charleston County, South Carolina.

The 9/11 Commission also recognized the importance of integrating law enforcement assets at all levels of government. They cite the nation's 66 Joint Terrorism Task Forces as a model intergovernmental approach. According to the Commission, state and local law enforcement agencies "need more training and work with federal agencies so that they can cooperate more effectively with those federal authorities in identifying terrorist suspects."[14]

To foster intergovernmental cooperation, the work group recommends that states: draft and implement a statewide counterterrorism program for the law enforcement community; develop standardized training programs and tools; build partnerships with key residential, commercial property owners and security personnel and provide them with resources and tools to identify and report suspicious activities; and develop and implement a public education and outreach plan that establishes and formalizes public information policies and procedures that relate to terrorism prevention and response.

- *Integration with the criminal justice system.* Not only must state agencies work closely with their local and federal counterparts, they must integrate terrorism prevention responsibilities into the criminal justice system at large. "It's now more important than ever to incorporate terrorism prevention into law enforcement's toolbox of crime fighting programs," said Representative John Millner of Illinois.

Law enforcement officials generally agree that an association exists among types of criminal

Table D: States' Allocation of Law Enforcement Resources

Change in state law enforcement agencies' allocations of resources since Sept. 11, 2001

	Fewer or much fewer resources	No change	More or many more resources
Airport security	0.0%	44.1%	55.9%
Border security	0.0	50.0	50.0
Commercial vehicle enforcement	0.0	43.1	56.9
Community policing	0.0	75.6	24.4
Drug enforcement and investigation	20.7	58.6	20.7
Forensic science/crime lab services	8.2	57.1	34.7
High tech/computer crime investigation	7.8	41.2	51.0
Intelligence gathering, anaylsis and sharing	3.2	4.8	91.9
Investigation of local agencies	3.9	88.2	7.8
Local agency operational assistance	8.3	38.3	53.3
Port security	0.0	43.8	56.3
Preventive patrol	3.8	37.7	58.5
Responding to calls for service	7.1	53.6	39.3
Security for critical infrastructure	1.9	3.7	94.4
Security for special events and dignitaries	1.7	13.6	84.8
Terrorism-related investigations	1.7	23.3	75.0
Tranditional criminal investigation	13.3	78.3	8.3
Traffic safety	7.7	73.1	19.2

Source: The Council of State Governments and Eastern Kentucky University National Survey of State and Local Law Enforcement Agencies, 2004.

Note: Total state law enforcement population = 73; number of collected surveys = 61; survey response rate = 84 percent.

activity and terrorism. "Some terrorist operations do not rely on outside sources of money and may now be self-funding, either through legitimate employment or low-level criminal activity," says the 9/11 Commission.[15] "Counter-terrorism investigations often overlap or are cued by other criminal investigations, such as money laundering or the smuggling of contraband. In the field, the close connection to criminal work has many benefits."[16]

Therefore, states should embrace an "all crimes" approach to terrorism prevention. This strategy ensures that possible precursor crimes are screened and analyzed for linkages to larger-scale terrorist activities. Also, states should develop and implement protocols to leverage all criminal justice and regulatory personnel, resources and systems, including: local law enforcement; probation and parole officers; court documents such as pre-sentence investigations; and other state and local regulatory agencies.

- *Governance and legal issues.* The work group addressed a number of state-level governance, planning and legal issues affecting state law enforcement and general terrorism prevention duties. First, states should consider regional approaches for homeland security planning and operational purposes. Creating or realigning existing regions or zones helps to remove or reduce local jurisdictional barriers for operational purposes and may enhance the distribution of federal grants.

States should also assign a principal point of oversight and review for homeland security through a legislative committee or multi-branch commission. In many states, disparate oversight is provided through individual disciplines and policy areas such as agriculture, military affairs, public health and public safety. Similarly, certain aspects of the homeland security mission should be codified into law, such as key terms and definitions, general duties and responsibilities for the primary state-level stakeholders, and strategic planning processes.

Finally, as a condition of accepting federal funds, states should ensure that state and local agencies have plans in place to sustain newly acquired equipment and capabilities for the long term. Future homeland security grant proposals and initiatives, therefore, should sufficiently demonstrate these long-term obligations, strategies and plans.

Today, state police organizations are taking many lead and supporting roles in the realm of terrorism prevention. They provide a critical information sharing and analysis capability at the state level and link between local and federal authorities. Their role is especially important in rural areas of states where resources are scarce. Thus, they provide a critical link among large and small local agencies.

In addition, state troopers patrol the interstate and state highways and serve as "eyes and ears" for suspicious activities, and would play a critical role in managing mass evacuations and aid for disaster areas. State police continue to play important roles guarding border crossings, seaports, airports and critical infrastructure. Furthermore, their specialized services (e.g., SWAT, canine units, air and marine assets) are often requested at the local levels, and are important assets to deter, interdict and respond to acts of terrorism.

State policy-makers should be informed about these changing conditions, as well as the risks that accompany them. For example, should drug enforcement resources be sacrificed at the expense of terrorism prevention? What new structures, capabilities, and resources benefit both responsibilities? Police organizations are becoming more proactive through new information-led policing initiatives and tools such as crime mapping. Can state-level fusion centers support these new general crime fighting initiatives?

"The fact remains that the Sept. 11 terrorists lived and shopped in small towns across the country, frequented bars and other establishments in these small towns, rented cars and drove across states, and took flying lessons at small regional airports," stressed Sheriff Cannon. "If not the state, then who should take the lead in establishing and maintaining the unprecedented cooperation required to prevent a future attack?"

Today, a tremendous opportunity exists for states to leverage their law enforcement resources to prevent future acts of terrorism, and improve overall public safety.

Authors' note:

This project was supported by Grant No. 2003-DT-CX-0004 awarded by the National Institute of Justice, Office of Justice Programs, U.S. Department of Justice. Points of view in this document are those of the authors and do not necessarily represent the official policies of the U.S. Department of Justice.

Notes

[1]The Council of State Governments and Eastern Kentucky University, National Study—The Impact of Terrorism on State Law Enforcement, 2004 (Through support from the National Institute of Justice). *http://www.csg.org*, keyword: protect.

[2]Texas Department of Public Safety, "Historical Developments," *http://www.txdps.state.tx.us/director_staff/texas_rangers.*

[3]Matthew J. Hickman and Brian A. Reaves, *Law Enforcement Management and Administrative Statistics, 2000: Data for Individual State and Local Agencies with 100 or More Officers*, (Washington, D.C.: Bureau of Justice Statistics, 2004), xiii.

[4]Matthew J. Hickman and Brian A. Reaves, *Federal Law Enforcement Officers*, 2000, (Washington, D.C.: Bureau of Justice Statistics, 2001), 2.

[5]Matthew J. Hickman and Brian A. Reaves, *Law Enforcement Management and Administrative Statistics: Local Police Departments*, 1999, (Washington, D.C.: Bureau of Justice Statistics, 2001), 2.

[6]See note 1 above.

[7]U.S. Department of Homeland Security, *Fiscal Year 2005 Homeland Security Grant Program: Program Guidelines and Application Kit*, 2.

[8]National Commission on Terrorist Attacks, *The 9/11 Commission Report*, (New York: W.W. Norton & Company, Inc., 2004), 423.

[9]The Federal Bureau of Investigation, "Facts and Figures 2003," *http://www.fbi.gov/priorities. priorities.htm.*

[10]See note 1 above.

[11]Ibid.

[12]Ibid.

[13]Global Intelligence Working Group, *The National Criminal Intelligence Sharing Plan*, 2004 Global Justice Information Sharing Initiative, (Washington, D.C.: Office of Justice Programs), 7.

[14]National Commission on Terrorist Attacks, *The 9/11 Commission Report*, (New York: W.W. Norton & Company, Inc., 2004), 390.

[15]Ibid., 383.

[16]Ibid., 424.

About the Authors

Chad Foster is a public safety and justice policy analyst with The Council of State Governments.

Gary Cordner, Ph.D., is a professor with the College of Justice & Safety at Eastern Kentucky University.

No Child Left Behind: A Perspective
By Ken Meyer

The bar has been raised in the United States and our system of public education must adapt to the new parameters of global competition. Public education in the United States has not necessarily declined; the rest of the world has caught up and is now providing a higher level of competition in the market place at all levels. The No Child Left Behind Act is meeting the challenge and has ushered in a new era in public education, focused on the fundamentals of accountability and results for schools all across the country.

Introduction

The Elementary and Secondary Education Act (ESEA) of 1965, known now as The No Child Left Behind Act (NCLB), while still young since its most recent reauthorization, is growing into a very dynamic piece of federal legislation, which characterizes the crucial link between the federal and state government cooperation and interrelationships. NCLB also promises to have a very positive impact on the education of all children in the United States as well as setting a high bar for educational proficiency and achievement for the rest of the world to follow. This federal/state partnership exemplifies the critical importance of meeting a national priority as set forth by the president and Congress through a strong cooperative effort at all levels of government. While not without controversy and even resistance, NCLB is already having a significant and positive impact all across the country. The achievement gap is beginning to narrow and overall achievement is now being scientifically measured, providing a critical tool in allowing new and dynamic instructional strategies to emerge and be developed to meet the challenges of competing in a global and highly technical economic environment of today and well into the future.

The primary objective of NCLB is to assist states with the closure of the chronic nationwide achievement gap, which has consistently existed for decades between low income, predominantly minority students, and the more affluent mostly majority white students in the country as well as raise overall achievement in reading, math and science for all students. This gap also exists between the majority student population and the limited English proficient students as well as special needs children. For proper perspective it is important to understand why this issue has been elevated to the status of national priority. According to recent studies, U.S. high school aged students consistently lag far behind peers in other peer industrialized countries as well as young

and growing capitalist economies in the very critical areas of math and science literacy and comprehension, the root of economic innovation and entrepreneurial expansion. As outlined over 20 years ago with the published report *A Nation at Risk,* in order to remain an economic leader in the future, the United States must improve educational skills in math and science.

Signed into law on January 8, 2002, NCLB established a set of accountability criteria for states to follow in order to continue participation in the ESEA programs, most notably the significant level of Title I funding flowing to the states for disadvantaged students.

Major Accomplishments and Successes

"Despite ongoing complaints, the federal No Child Left Behind Act has become implanted in the culture of America's public education system." Lynn Olson, *Education Week*, December 8, 2004

Often misunderstood and sometimes misrepresented, NCLB requires that every state establish its own set of academic performance standards against which all children in grades three through eight, and one time in high school, are to be tested. The states are then further required to set up a valid and reliable system of testing these students once a year for the purpose of gathering information to determine where there are significant problems, deficiencies and challenges and then directing resources to help solve those problems. The intended goal is to provide information to all stakeholders, including the public at large, on the condition of the level of effectiveness and success of all public schools in the country. As with any major reform effort, the challenge is in the details of implementing this law at the state level. In small print, NCLB is over 700 pages long and that does not include the voluminous regulations and guidance, which have been promulgated by the secretary of the U.S. Department of Education for the states to follow.

Despite the challenges and problems encountered,

however, with implementing the requirements of NCLB, to date every state is in compliance with this law and the culture of public education is slowly changing in this country to a system built on accountability and results (outputs), not just the amount of money being spent (inputs). This cultural shift is creating a dynamic new perspective on how children will be educated in this country well into the future. It is built on the premise that gathering solid information is the first step in identifying problems and then creating new solutions to the challenges of a changing world. Success is taking root.

Northeast. Fourth-grader Tiajha Battles, determined to pass the first round of state tests, did everything she could to prepare for the tough exams, and the Foxfire School faculty (Yonkers) did everything they could to help. She stayed after school three times a week for extra tutoring. She came to class on Saturday. She worked with a reading specialist. Her mother attended workshops so she could learn to help her struggling child achieve. Across Yonkers, thousands of students like Tiajha have moved up the academic ladder as the district infused new programs to boost achievement for all students. The new programs have resulted in higher test scores and the closing of an academic achievement gap. Back in 1999, nearly two-thirds of the city's African-American and Hispanic eighth-graders scored "1" on the state's four-point grading scale in the statewide math exam. Today, one in five black and Hispanic students scored "1" on that test. At Foxfire, in 1999, one in four students scored in the lowest level on the state's fourth-grade English exam. Today, that proportion plunged to one in 25. (*The Journal News*, 2/24/05)

Northwest. Six Oregon elementary schools and one rural school district were recently heralded by the state as models for closing the achievement gap. The schools, including Beaver Acres Elementary in Beaverton and Vernon Elementary in Portland, each get $2,000 to spend as they please and will share their successful strategies during a second annual "Closing the Gap" conference next month. Beaver Acres got its Latino and low-income students to pass the state math test at rates higher than white students statewide. At Vernon, African-American and Latino students perform nearly as well as Oregon's white students in reading and better than them in math. Several strategies were common to nearly all of the winning schools. They test students repeatedly during the year and act immediately on results, regrouping students, adding extra support, or changing curricula when necessary. They also set aside lots of time for teaching reading and math—75 minutes of math each day at Beaver Acres and two hours in reading and writing every day at Vernon—and treat that time as sacred. Nearly every certified educator in the school teaches reading so that reading groups can be small and tailored to students' particular level. (*The Oregonian*, 3/2/05)

Southeast. Calcedeaver Elementary School in Mobile County, Alabama, has 100 percent of its kindergarten and first-graders reading at or above grade level—and that's including special education students. Reading has improved drastically at Calcedeaver since August 2003, when the school adopted the Alabama Reading First Initiative. Students who participated in the program that first year read an average of 43 words per minute faster than students in the same grades did the year before, and, this year, many kindergarteners are reading on a second-grade level. Education officials say the Alabama Reading First Initiative and the better-known Alabama Reading Initiative, are proving their worth. Katherine Mitchell, the state's Assistant Superintendent for Reading, said the programs "are one and the same, but we have to name them according to their funding [streams]." (Federal grants under the *No Child Left Behind Act* pay for Reading First.) Nine of Mobile County's top 10 reading schools, with poverty levels averaging 85 percent in their student bodies, participate in one or both initiatives. (*The Mobile Register*, 2/27/05)

Southwest. Before the 2003–2004 school year, reading and math proficiency measured by the New Mexico Standards-based Assessment forced Desert View Elementary School into a probationary status. But Desert View's reading scores increased from 20 percent proficiency on the exam in 2002–2003 to 42 percent in 2003–2004, while math scores during the same period improved from 20 percent to 46 percent. The introduction of new teaching methods during the 2003–2004 school year prompted the striking improvements. And, the better scores have had a positive effect on the school. "You can see the uplifting of the instructional mood in the school," said Assistant Principal Fernando Carrasco. "Teachers and kids are not afraid to tackle the test now." And, in recognition of the turnaround, Principal Susan Yturralde and bilingual kindergarten teacher Lorna Clark flew to Washington, D.C., and were allowed to sit in the First Lady's box as the president gave his State of the Union Address. (*The El Paso Times*, 2/4/05)

While NCLB requires that every state create its own set of academic standards and system of testing against those standards, a further requirement is for every state to also participate in a random sampling of testing known as the National Assessment of Education Progress (NAEP). This test is often referred to as "The Nation's Report Card" as it gathers data from all across the country from every state and a reasonable comparison can be made between districts and states in terms of the level of success being achieved. This data also is collected and analyzed by education think tanks and other experts in psychometrics and education evaluation.

According to *Education Trust* and the most recent state scores, the nation's achievement gap is now beginning to close. NCLB is showing true signs of success.

Problems/Challenges

Communication

One of the biggest challenges which has confronted NCLB from its inception is the onerous task of communicating the intent of Congress and the specifics of the law to those most impacted by its implementation; educators, administrators and policy-makers. As such, very quickly after being signed into law, a great deal of misunderstanding, miscommunication and misinformation began to flow around the country regarding the true impact of NCLB at the state and local level creating a high level of tension across the country between policymakers and various constituent groups. This breakdown of communication, combined with the heightened level of political activism prior to and during a presidential election year created a very challenging environment for implementation of NCLB across the country. Any major reform in any law can cause anxiety. NCLB is no different.

Technical

NCLB requires that every child in the public school system in this country is to be tested once a year in reading, math and science in grades three through eight and one time in high school. These tests must be measured against a specific set of standards for each grade level as established by the state. For this purpose, students are not measured against their peers and placed in a percentage quartile on a bell curve, the measurement is against a state standard. Early on, this posed some of the most significant challenges for many states as each state, if not already in place, had to first create a set of standards and then create a valid and reliable system of testing against those standards. While there has been a lot of activity from education evaluators, think tanks and private vendors to accommodate the states' needs in this area, the fact that every state has its own set of standards

also means every state ultimately has a different set of tests. In the short run this caused a great deal of pressure on states as professional resources in this area were limited. Ultimately, with the guidance and assistance of the United States Department of Education, all 50 states created a system of accountability.

Political/Philosophical

Education has risen to the level of national debate in recent years due to the importance of the impact of education on the ability to compete in a global marketplace. This emphasis, however, has also created new debate in this country regarding the proper role of the federal government in the area of public education, which has historically been the primary responsibility of state and local governments. During the presidential election year of 2004, this debate rose to a level of national attention as a number of states, driven in part by political motivation, began to indicate a possible desire to not participate in, or opt-out of, the requirements of NCLB and actually forfeiting the significant funding associated with the law. These efforts generally grew out of the frustration state policy-makers were experiencing as they communicated with and received input from educators in their states and districts who were concerned about the impact of NCLB on their schools. A common theme began to emerge in some states which argued that the federal government had no right to dictate terms of public education at the local level. This argument evolved into a national debate of state sovereignty and resulted in the introduction of numerous resolutions and bills in state legislatures across the country expressing concern and discontent over the requirements of NCLB versus the level of funding associated with the requirements. However, although a few states took a serious look at pulling away from NCLB, in the end there was not one bill at the state legislative level which passed both houses and made it to a governor's desk for signature into law. As state policy-makers became more familiar with the actual requirements of the federal law as well as the level of funding their respective states were receiving to implement the law, while not necessarily in full agreement with the provisions of NCLB, realized that the level of funding was too important for the benefit of disadvantaged children than to forego its acceptance.

The debate will undoubtedly continue.

Funding

One of the most pronounced criticisms of NCLB and largely without merit is the question of funding.

Many critics have claimed that NCLB is an unfunded or under-funded mandate from the federal government to the state governments. The philosophical debate notwithstanding, the facts are clear that NCLB is very well funded relative to the requirements of the federal law. Since the inception of NCLB, total funding for the program has grown to almost $24 billion, an increase of 65 percent from FY 2001 to 2006. It is important to view these funds in terms of what is actually being required of the federal law. For example, while creating smaller classrooms may be a worthwhile endeavor for a state, school or district, it is not a requirement of NCLB. What is required under NCLB, including testing, school choice transportation, supplemental services, professional development, etc., is well funded. When measured against the actual federal requirements, funding is very strong for NCLB.

Furthermore, education funding in the United States has been and always will remain the primary responsibility of state and local governments. Any education program created by the federal government is intended to be supplemental to the overall effort, NCLB included. In addition, it is a grant program in which states may or may not choose to participate. As such, since it is voluntary on the part of states, it is incumbent upon state policy-makers to determine if the funding flow is adequate, relative to the requirements of the law.

IDEA/Special Ed

One of the biggest challenges in education has always been relative to providing instructional services to the special needs population, including those with the most severe cognitive limitations. As the special needs population has grown over the years, this has become of more significant concern to policy-makers. On April 7, 2005 Secretary of Education Margaret Spellings held a meeting of Chief State School Officers, invited from every state, to announce, among other things, a significant modification to the manner in which NCLB rules could potentially apply in the states to the special needs students across the country.

The modified requirements of academic achievement for students with persistent academic disabilities and served under the IDEA requirements has been well received in the states and underscores the Department of Education's commitment to listen, gather information and then create rules which and allow states more latitude to deal with the most significant problems.

Summary

Over the past several decades we have seen the dissolution of the Soviet Union and the emergence of many new free market economies and democracies across the globe. These new and growing economies are creating new challenges for the United States to maintain its prominence as the economic leader of the world. The world's economies are now inextricably linked together in a digital framework where the factors of production are no longer necessarily limited by geography, time and distance. This new economic world is based on technology the fundamentals of which being an educated workforce proficient in the areas of reading, math and science and motivated by an entrepreneurial drive for success and excellence. The bar has been raised and our system of public education must adapt to the new parameters of global competition. Public education in the United States has not necessarily declined, the rest of the world has caught up and is now providing a higher level of competition in the market place at all levels.

The No Child Left Behind Act is meeting the challenge and has ushered in a new era in public education focused on the fundamentals of accountability and results for schools all across the country. It is changing the culture of education. NCLB is empowering parents and arming them with valuable information about their childrens' schools and providing them with choices and options regarding how to hold schools accountable for success so that future generations can enjoy the same opportunity for prosperity as preceding generations of Americans. NCLB is having a positive impact and the achievement gap is narrowing.

About the Author

Ken Meyer is the deputy assistant secretary in the Office of Intergovernmental and Interagency Affairs, U.S. Department of Education. A graduate of the University of Tennessee at Chattanooga, Meyer is a former state legislator and businessman in Tennessee. He was asked to join the Bush administration in 2002 and works for the development and implementation of the communication effort for No Child Left Behind.

Issues in Faculty Salaries and Higher Education Financing

By John W. Curtis

This article provides an overview of several systematic factors contributing to the variation in faculty salaries. Institutional type is the most significant factor in determining faculty salaries overall; faculty members are also differentiated according to academic rank. Two other important factors are gender and region, and several individual factors are also identified. The article also discusses several policy issues related to the decline in state funding for higher education.

Faculty salaries, like much of American higher education itself, are widely differentiated according to several factors. The most significant sources of variation are institutional type (including both the level of degree offered and institutional affiliation) and academic rank. Two other important factors affecting salaries are gender and regional location. Finally, a number of factors affecting the salaries of individual faculty members are specific to each situation, even though commonalities can be observed across the spectrum. These individual factors include the faculty member's discipline, record of publications and scholarship, the presence of collective bargaining, and race or ethnicity. This article provides an overview of the most salient differences in faculty salaries, as identified above, and points to trends which should be of particular interest to policy-makers. In addition, it situates the consideration of faculty salaries within the context of broader issues in public higher education.

The source of primary data presented here is the annual Faculty Compensation Survey conducted by the American Association of University Professors (AAUP). The AAUP survey includes accredited institutions at all levels, both public and private. AAUP has collected and published faculty salary data in its "Annual Report on the Economic Status of the Profession" for nearly six decades. Table B reports average faculty salary at four-year institutions for academic year 2003-2004 by state, level and control of institution, and academic rank. (The AAUP collects data from Associate degree colleges as well, but the survey response for 2003-2004 did not provide sufficient cases for an accurate breakdown by state.)

In comparing faculty salaries between states, the most important factor—and perhaps the most significant source of variation in faculty salaries overall—is institutional type. Institutional type itself can be divided into two components: the level of institution, categorized in the AAUP survey by highest degree; and the control of the institution, generally dis-

tinguishing between public and private. Table A shows the variation in national average faculty salary by these two components of institutional type.

Approximately 70 percent of full-time faculty in the United States are employed at public institutions. However, as Table A indicates, faculty salaries at private-independent four-year institutions are 8 to 28 percent higher than those at public institutions. (Private-independent Associate degree institutions, by contrast, are few in number and tend to compensate their faculty at lower levels.) Table A distinguishes between two categories of institutions that are often lumped together as "private"—those that are independent and those that are affiliated with a religious denomination. Faculty salaries at institutions in the latter category are generally lower, although the average for church-related doctoral institutions is pushed upward by a relatively small group of large research universities that pay higher salaries. By contrast, in Table B average salaries for private baccalaureate colleges in some states are depressed by combining private-independent and church-related colleges into one category, since the proportion of church-related colleges is much larger in some states and most church-related colleges are in the baccalaureate category.

Tables A and B give an indication for the most current year of the primary issue of interest to state policy-makers: the divergence of faculty salaries between public and private sectors. At the national level, and in most states, faculty at public institutions receive lower salaries on average than do faculty at comparable private institutions. But this situation is not static. The AAUP annual report has followed the trend of public/private differentials for many years. As Ronald G. Ehrenberg summarized in a recent AAUP report:

> Several researchers have used AAUP data to document the decrease in the average salary of faculty members at public academic institutions relative to that of their peers at pri-

Table A: Average Full-Time Faculty Salary 2003–2004, By Institutional Category and Control

	Public		Private-Independent		Church-Related	
	Average salary 2003–2004	*Percent increase over 2002–2003*	*Average salary 2003–2004*	*Percent increaseover 2002–2003*	*Average salary 2003–2004*	*Percent increaseover 2002–2003*
Doctoral	$71,815	2.0%	$91,865	2.9%	$77,271	3.2%
Master's	58,668	0.5	63,252	3.2	58,563	2.4
Baccalaureate	53,666	1.4	63,236	3.9	50,475	2.8
Associate	50,958	0.4	39,168	n.d	36,048	n.d

Source: American Association of University Professors, Faculty Compensation Survey.
Notes:
Includes all full-time primarily instructional faculty, with or without academic rank.

Figures are weighted average (mean) salaries; salaries of faculty members on 12-month contracts have been adjusted to an academic year (9-month) equivalent.
n.d. = no data. There were too few responding institutions for meaningful analysis.

vate institutions that took place between 1978-1979 and 2001-2002. Most of the decline occurred before the mid-1990s; the relative salaries of faculty in the public and private sectors remained roughly constant between 1996-1997 and 2001-2002. ...[H]owever, average salaries in public institutions of higher education dropped this past year relative to those in private institutions.[1]

The public/private salary gap continued to widen in 2003-2004, as Table A indicates. The table shows the increase in average salary levels from 2002-2003, by institutional type. Overall, faculty salary levels at public institutions increased at or below the rate of inflation (measured at 1.9 percent from December 2002 to December 2003), while salary levels at private-independent institutions rose at substantially higher rates. Although these differences for a single year are small, the cumulative effect over time is stark: During the 1970-1971 academic year the average full professor at a private-independent doctoral university earned 10 percent more than his or her counterpart at a public doctoral university; by 2003-2004, that gap was 29 percent.

Although average faculty salary alone is not a sufficient indicator of institutional quality, it seems self-evident to observe that, given substantial and widening differences in pay over time, public colleges and universities will have difficulty attracting and keeping the most productive and innovative scholars and teachers. This becomes a public policy issue if we wish to make high-quality higher education accessible to large segments of the public, and not only to those who can pay the cost of and gain admission to private universities and colleges.

For the comparison of average faculty salaries between states, Table B also shows the important distinction between senior faculty members (holding the rank of professor) and generally entry-level faculty (assistant professors). Differences between states in average salary at either rank could indicate a disadvantage in attracting highly-qualified faculty, whether they be established scholars who bring immediate prestige and assume leadership of both scholarly projects and collegiate governance structures, or entry-level faculty who represent the potential for developing research and teaching.

A number of researchers have investigated the continuing salary differences between men and women faculty, differences which cut across institutional type and academic rank. The AAUP has collected institution-level data on average salaries by gender since the mid-1970s. An analysis of those data indicates a remarkably persistent salary disadvantage for women faculty over more than a quarter century. When faculty of the same rank are compared, average salaries for women are 7 to 12 percent lower than those of men. The greatest differences are at the rank of full professor. There are some variations in this comparison by institutional type, as average salaries are more equal in baccalaureate and Associate colleges, and are generally more equal at public colleges and universities. However, it is also the case that women faculty are more likely to hold positions that have lower salaries on average: they are more likely than men to be at public community colleges, they are less likely to achieve the rank of professor, and they are less likely to have tenure. (Women are also more likely than men to hold part-time faculty positions, but the AAUP survey includes salary data only for full-time faculty.) As a result, when the weighted average salaries of all women full-time faculty are compared with all full-time men, women receive only about 80 percent of the salary of men. The AAUP data indicate that this has been the case since the late 1970s, with surprisingly little change in the overall figure.

The AAUP data allow only for comparisons of institutional averages. Other investigators have utilized individual-level data to attempt to determine whether gender differences in salary can be attributed to differences in the distribution of women faculty according to other professional characteristics. A recent analysis of 1998 data by the U.S. Department of Education considered some 13 factors that might contribute to the salary difference between men and women faculty.[2] It concluded that, even when all of those factors are controlled in the analysis, men still earn 9.4 percent more than women, on average. Toutkoushian and Conley, in a recent comprehensive review and extension of various analytical models developed during the 1990s, found that progress appeared to have been made in narrowing the "unexplained" salary gap between men and women faculty—that not attributable to differences on observable factors—but that the gap remains at between 4 and 6 percent. As they point out, "[t]hese unexplained wage gaps are not only statistically significant, but are large in a practical sense especially when compounded over a woman's career. These inequities persist across most institution types and fields, and thus we should not lose focus on the fact that more improvement in the situation for women is needed."[3] What many statistical analyses fail to investigate, however, are the reasons why women continue to be overrepresented in the situations that result in lower average salary, as noted above. That, too, is a critical policy issue that remains to be addressed, if women are to participate fully in the academic profession.

Faculty salaries also vary by geographic region. The AAUP data, divided into nine regions, indicate that the highest overall average faculty salaries are found in New England,[4] a region dominated by private higher education institutions, and the Pacific,[5] heavily influenced by relatively high salaries in California. An analysis of regional salary trends over time indicates that the regional differences have also been widening. Growth in average salaries over the last 25 years has been most rapid in New England and in the South Atlantic,[6] with salaries in the latter region falling generally into the middle range nationally. Salary growth in the Middle Atlantic region[7] has also generally kept pace, while faculty salaries in the East North Central[8] and, especially, East South Central[9] regions have fallen further behind. The latter two regions are characterized by more public institutions, especially at the doctoral level, reflecting the public-private salary disparities discussed above.

In addition to the broad differences in faculty salaries by categories discussed above, salaries for individual faculty members also vary according to a number of specific aspects of the individual situation. In recent years, salary differences between faculty in different disciplines have emerged as a recurring topic for discussion, with the influence of "the market" often cited as the force driving widening disparities even within the same institution. Faculty in fields such as business, engineering or computer technologies, whose skills have been in demand in the private sector, have frequently been able to secure higher salaries than their colleagues in the humanities and social sciences. Analyses such as the two individual-level studies cited previously have also concluded that faculty members with a more substantial record of publications and scholarship earn higher salaries, even when other factors are taken into account. This likely reflects the continuing premium accorded to research among the several roles of faculty, an emphasis that appears to apply to faculty even in predominantly teaching institutions. Faculty salaries are also affected by the presence of collective bargaining, although a comprehensive recent analysis of the net impact of collective bargaining remains to be done. On the one hand, faculty collective bargaining may lead to higher salary levels for the faculty as a whole, and may lessen inequities within the compensation system; on the other hand, collective bargaining may act to preserve aspects of faculty self-governance and peer review, which can reinforce the differences by discipline and rank discussed above. Finally, the existence of systematic differences in faculty salary by race or ethnicity is a controversial topic, on which there is not conclusive evidence. The U.S. Department of Education analysis referenced above concluded that "…some racial/ethnic differences [in salary] existed in 1998. Compared with White faculty, Asian/Pacific Islander faculty had higher average salaries, were more likely to hold advanced degrees, and had greater representation at public doctoral, research and medical institutions. Black faculty had lower average salaries and were less likely to have advanced degrees or attain tenure or full professorship than White faculty."[10] However, the analysis concluded that when all factors were considered simultaneously, racial or ethnic category did not represent a statistically significant source of differences in faculty salaries.

In recent years, the issue of faculty compensation has increasingly been linked to other trends in higher education financing. Although space does not allow for a full consideration of these issues here, it is important to include them in order to place faculty salaries in their proper context.

The fundamental challenge facing higher education in the last few years has been a withdrawal of public funding. This has happened both directly and indirectly and at both state and federal levels. Direct funding of public higher education institutions from state sources has not kept pace with rising overall costs, so that states are now providing a smaller percentage of institutional revenues than ever before. According to figures compiled by the U.S. Department of Education, in FY 2001 state and local governments supplied 40 percent of current-fund revenues for public higher education institutions, down from 49 percent only 20 years previously.[11] And this figure is much lower at large research universities, where the proportion of state support now frequently falls below 20 percent.

Faced with a decline in state revenues, public institutions have raised tuition at an accelerated pace. Some observers have portrayed this as a shift to a "high tuition/high aid" model, in which rising tuition prices would be met with increased levels of financial aid, so that students with financial need would not be denied access to college. It does not appear that student financial aid has kept pace with increased tuition prices, however. The largest federal source of student financial aid is the Pell Grant program. The maximum Pell award has remained flat for several years, so that needy students must find additional sources for more of their tuition bills. At the same time, many states and institutions have shifted funding for student aid programs from need-based to merit-based awards. As Donald E. Heller notes, merit based awards increased from 9 percent of state grants awarded without consideration of need in 1981 to nearly 25 percent of those awards in 2001. And at the same time, non-need-based aid increased to 44 percent of all grant aid.[12] Thus, rising tuition prices threaten the ability of low-income students to afford higher education, because need-based financial aid has not kept pace with tuition increases.

Nor have tuition revenues fueled higher faculty salaries. As reported in the AAUP's 2003-2004 *Annual Report on the Economic Status of the Profession*, average faculty salaries have not kept pace with increasing tuition prices over the last 25 years. The report compared faculty salary data from the AAUP annual survey with figures on tuition from the College Board's annual report *Trends in College Pricing*. It concluded:

The bottom line is that although faculty

and staff salary increases obviously contribute to increases in tuition, other factors have played more important roles during the last quarter century. These factors include the escalating costs of benefits for all employees, reductions in state support of public institutions, growing institutional financial-aid costs, expansion of the science and research infrastructure at research universities, and the increasing costs of information technology. If tuition and fee increases had been held to the rate of average faculty salary increases during this period, average tuition and fees would be substantially lower today in both the public and private sectors.[13]

Seen in this broader context, rising tuition prices are a consequence of the trend also producing increased disparities in faculty salaries between public and private institutions: a withdrawal of public funding. If, at the same time, needy students do not receive aid sufficient to match increased tuition prices, enrollment patterns may shift as well. This complicated matrix points toward a single outcome, if trends remain on the same course: higher education will become increasingly differentiated in terms of quality, and will be increasingly less accessible to financially disadvantaged students—reversing four decades of developments in the American system of public higher education.

There are several thousand institutions of higher education in the United States, reflecting the wide variety of institutional traditions, missions and resources that is a central feature of the American system. Faculty in these institutions fill a number of roles and bring differing professional qualifications to their positions; with more than 600,000 full-time faculty employed in different institutional situations across the country, the variation in faculty salaries is tremendous. This article has provided an overview of the key factors differentiating faculty salaries. It has also identified critical issues facing state government policy-makers with regard to their public higher education sectors: the long-term decline in faculty salaries at public institutions, relative to those at private institutions; disadvantages for women faculty; and the consequences of a withdrawal of state funding for both quality and accessibility at public colleges and universities. States look to their higher education institutions to provide high-quality education in a range of rapidly changing fields of endeavor, as centers of innovation in science and technology, and as sources of solutions to pressing social needs. As enrollments continue to grow, and the need for expanded access to high-quality higher education becomes increasingly apparent, state policy-makers must identify sufficient resources to allow their higher education sectors to meet these new demands.

Notes

[1] Ronald G. Ehrenberg, "Unequal Progress: The Annual Report on the Economic Status of the Profession," *Academe* 89, no. 2 (March-April 2003): 26.

[2] U.S. Department of Education, National Center for Education Statistics. *The Condition of Education 2002.* (NCES 2002–025) Washington, DC: 103.

[3] Robert K Toutkoushian and Valerie Martin Conley. "Progress for Women in Academe, Yet Inequities Persist: Evidence from NSOPF: 99," *Research in Higher Education* 46, no. 1 (February 2005): 1-28.

[4] New England: Connecticut, Maine, Massachusetts, New Hampshire, Vermont and Rhode Island.

[5] Pacific: Alaska, California, Guam, Hawaii, Oregon and Washington.

[6] South Atlantic: Delaware, District of Columbia, Florida, Georgia, Maryland, North Carolina, Puerto Rico, South Carolina, Virginia and West Virginia.

[7] Middle Atlantic: New Jersey, New York and Pennsylvania.

[8] East North Central: Illinois, Indiana, Michigan, Ohio and Wisconsin.

[9] East South Central: Alabama, Kentucky, Mississippi and Tennessee.

[10] *Condition of Education 2002,* 103

[11] Figure for FY 2001 from U.S. Department of Education, National Center for Education Statistics. *Enrollment in Postsecondary Institutions, Fall 2001 and Financial Statistics, Fiscal Year 2001* (NCES 2004–155) Washington, DC: 57. Figure for FY 1981 from U.S. Department of Education, National Center for Education Statistics. *Digest of Education Statistics 2003.* (Available online at http://www.nces.ed.gov/programs/digest/d03_tf.asp) Table 334.

[12] Donald E. Heller, "The Changing Nature of Financial Aid," *Academe* 90, no. 4 (July-August 2004): 36-38.

[13] Ronald G. Ehrenberg, "Don't Blame Faculty for High Tuition: The Annual Report on the Economic Status of the Profession," *Academe* 90, no. 2 (March-April 2004): 30.

About the Author

John W. Curtis is director of research at the American Association of University Professors in Washington, D.C. He holds a Ph.D. in sociology from Johns Hopkins University, and has worked at colleges and universities in the United States, Germany and Kenya.

Note

Opinions expressed in this article are those of the author, and not of the AAUP.

Table B
AVERAGE FULL-TIME FACULTY SALARY IN FOUR-YEAR INSTITUTIONS 2003–2004, BY STATE, INSTITUTIONAL CONTROL, INSTITUTION CATEGORY, AND ACADEMIC

State or other jurisdiction	Public											
	Doctoral				Master's				Baccalaureate			
	Prof.	Assoc.	Asst.	All	Prof.	Assoc.	Asst.	All	Prof.	Assoc.	Asst.	All
United States	94,498	66,194	56,247	71,815	74,911	59,407	49,870	58,668	68,788	55,831	46,293	53,666
Alabama	82,413	61,045	51,135	63,946	65,172	53,476	46,210	51,343	...	...	...	...
Alaska	72,356	56,908	48,547	55,706	70,325	55,351	48,253	53,817	...	...	...	...
Arizona	88,910	61,979	54,857	69,757	85,654	65,651	52,326	61,305	...	...	...	...
Arkansas	81,900	61,036	53,160	63,950	66,307	56,335	46,262	51,237	61,130	52,717	42,662	46,818
California	112,304	71,683	61,634	89,475	83,503	67,574	55,174	69,736	85,362	74,348	67,114	67,225
Colorado	89,571	66,907	56,838	72,186	78,220	59,936	53,552	57,989	62,213	50,537	43,859	46,783
Connecticut	106,660	76,330	61,731	83,684	78,966	61,116	50,990	64,091	...	...	...	...
Delaware	105,821	73,390	60,060	79,385	71,262	59,119	50,113	56,672	...	...	...	...
Florida	88,609	63,393	54,998	66,653	75,938	59,540	51,430	57,092	74,047	58,249	43,932	57,755
Georgia	101,064	68,381	59,938	75,777	69,758	55,706	46,662	53,345	63,775	54,058	44,382	49,924
Hawaii	86,516	64,908	55,465	69,709	...	...	...	...	66,993	56,403	46,320	55,150
Idaho	70,733	56,731	48,101	57,328	63,523	53,169	45,320	50,64	53,780	45,083	36,097	43,734
Illinois	94,618	65,936	56,559	71,181	73,152	59,100	48,874	55,096	...	...	...	...
Indiana	92,382	65,365	54,633	70,263	75,615	60,470	50,198	56,204	68,771	56,115	44,484	50,675
Iowa	96,620	68,386	58,674	75,426	78,414	60,778	51,478	60,703	...	...	...	...
Kansas	81,959	60,985	51,744	64,517	68,394	55,261	45,519	53,712	...	...	...	...
Kentucky	88,547	63,103	53,399	69,382	70,311	56,159	48,166	52,738	...	...	...	...
Louisiana	84,788	61,722	53,359	60,994	62,377	52,506	44,661	48,390	48,256	42,634	34,807	40,498
Maine	72,467	61,566	48,494	59,673	75,913	58,500	46,629	59,259	57,434	47,730	39,831	47,950
Maryland	106,677	73,576	63,817	80,254	78,108	62,002	51,894	57,845	93,890	73,493	59,663	77,730
Massachusetts	89,190	70,784	57,854	73,812	80,735	63,757	55,118	68,096	65,558	53,473	43,601	57,601
Michigan	100,220	71,379	58,971	76,258	75,056	60,609	50,772	58,725	...	...	...	...
Minnesota	102,012	69,879	60,585	83,407	74,676	61,370	50,008	60,605	72,836	55,819	47,265	58,583
Mississippi	75,354	58,977	50,081	57,786	53,362	49,742	42,300	44,940	54,958	49,220	43,064	44,711
Missouri	89,857	64,145	53,195	68,404	65,119	52,562	44,125	51,156	62,598	50,058	42,627	48,690
Montana	69,490	53,817	47,231	55,381	59,286	48,028	45,940	47,665	58,197	50,051	43,978	49,192
Nebraska	90,872	65,381	56,156	72,417	68,722	56,876	48,343	55,438	60,596	44,768	39,848	48,096
Nevada	94,769	71,457	54,990	71,647	...	...	...	...	...	...	...	...
New Hampshire	90,603	68,483	56,054	74,121	68,786	55,083	45,997	57,456	...	...	...	...
New Jersey	112,533	79,908	63,592	87,110	92,679	72,745	57,584	73,906	90,986	71,433	54,187	71,809
New Mexico	78,046	59,580	51,199	62,252	58,294	48,728	42,889	46,333	...	...	...	...
New York	100,562	72,689	60,232	78,386	83,789	65,509	52,859	65,465	81,317	62,593	52,287	62,652
North Carolina	95,846	68,141	58,478	72,325	74,959	59,559	51,852	57,613	65,300	53,440	48,540	53,057
North Dakota	68,178	56,646	50,167	53,666	...	...	...	...	52,834	44,564	40,061	40,318
Ohio	91,074	64,833	53,225	68,399	76,575	60,499	50,119	63,941	64,765	55,173	42,691	51,488
Oklahoma	81,086	58,405	50,022	61,536	59,312	50,432	44,724	48,352	52,536	45,992	37,862	42,648
Oregon	79,232	60,524	51,752	60,066	58,590	48,482	40,662	47,777	55,646	47,874	41,056	46,900
Pennsylvania	104,271	72,391	61,070	75,164	86,705	69,859	57,105	66,691	77,603	62,457	51,991	56,177
Rhode Island	86,043	62,804	55,950	74,578	65,374	55,204	48,101	57,711	...	...	...	...
South Carolina	86,455	63,028	55,984	67,576	64,892	54,377	45,190	52,848	60,936	52,349	43,510	48,680
South Dakota	69,137	54,422	45,909	52,586	67,141	54,979	48,722	55,481	59,737	51,587	45,535	47,626
Tennessee	86,088	64,070	53,440	65,944	67,245	53,347	45,460	53,652	...	...	...	...
Texas	93,741	63,571	57,199	69,233	67,902	56,069	48,142	53,251	70,646	54,967	46,957	51,324
Utah	83,166	58,938	52,109	64,866	62,039	49,599	42,443	49,268	...	...	...	...
Vermont	82,762	62,980	52,064	60,313	...	...	...	...	54,919	46,562	36,729	46,921
Virginia	99,708	68,949	56,296	73,872	67,059	56,859	47,590	54,886	73,854	57,068	44,845	56,632
Washington	89,611	64,191	59,997	70,438	65,103	52,856	45,621	52,911	...	...	...	...
West Virginia	75,755	58,849	47,707	60,075	61,997	49,797	40,764	50,947	58,635	48,319	40,536	46,476
Wisconsin	93,283	68,747	60,468	77,314	66,864	54,843	47,534	56,045	...	...	...	...
Wyoming	77,708	58,574	55,432	61,910	...	...	...	...	...	...	...	...
District of Columbia	...	...	...	...	...	...	...	...	...	...	...	...
Puerto Rico	...	...	...	...	...	...	...	...	56,408	47,786	39,258	48,158

See footnotes at end of table.

AVERAGE FULL-TIME FACULTY SALARY IN FOUR-YEAR INSTITUTIONS 2003–2004, BY STATE, INSTITUTIONAL CONTROL, INSTITUTION CATEGORY, AND ACADEMIC RANK – Continued

State or other jurisdiction	Private Doctoral Prof.	Assoc.	Asst.	All	Master's Prof.	Assoc.	Asst.	All	Baccalaureate Prof.	Assoc.	Asst.	All
United States	118,735	76,740	66,039	88,308	79,130	61,237	50,289	61,115	72,617	55,290	46,002	56,472
Alabama	. . .	. . .	. . .	. . .	68,459	53,812	46,758	54,561	67,659	55,288	43,547	55,485
Alaska	. . .	. . .	. . .	. . .	. . .	. . .	. . .	. . .	. . .	. . .	. . .	. . .
Arizona	. . .	. . .	. . .	. . .	. . .	. . .	. . .	. . .	70,560	59,698	46,585	54,267
Arkansas	. . .	. . .	. . .	. . .	. . .	. . .	. . .	. . .	58,881	48,453	42,497	49,318
California	122,226	82,095	69,488	95,693	90,600	67,611	55,791	69,585	90,624	66,064	53,314	72,303
Colorado	88,239	66,959	55,354	68,935	. . .	. . .	. . .	. . .	90,453	64,710	51,400	70,484
Connecticut	138,830	78,450	66,514	102,291	90,347	66,328	55,326	69,212	91,737	68,524	52,922	70,460
Delaware	. . .	. . .	. . .	. . .	. . .	. . .	. . .	. . .	59,338	51,519	42,157	49,979
Florida	97,240	63,961	57,362	69,088	76,997	57,698	48,432	59,212	63,292	53,163	46,508	51,588
Georgia	126,457	81,124	72,325	96,945	77,149	57,851	47,991	57,300	64,173	52,662	42,584	50,640
Hawaii	. . .	. . .	. . .	. . .	. . .	. . .	. . .	. . .	61,878	55,497	44,398	50,425
Idaho	. . .	. . .	. . .	. . .	. . .	. . .	. . .	. . .	. . .	. . .	. . .	. . .
Illinois	124,460	77,585	67,640	91,556	67,766	57,744	47,805	56,720	64,339	52,248	44,524	51,627
Indiana	116,508	77,304	65,990	92,508	70,574	55,229	45,564	54,359	66,212	52,172	46,611	54,813
Iowa	. . .	. . .	. . .	. . .	80,181	56,517	48,926	61,452	62,506	51,027	43,579	51,421
Kansas	. . .	. . .	. . .	. . .	52,452	48,414	46,710	47,436	46,587	39,425	34,999	38,821
Kentucky	. . .	. . .	. . .	. . .	65,342	56,261	48,081	60,522	56,861	47,588	41,144	48,405
Louisiana	100,161	69,662	61,099	74,512	82,820	59,101	47,518	59,271	57,616	48,671	40,969	48,706
Maine	. . .	. . .	. . .	. . .	65,735	55,286	44,589	50,166	92,147	64,340	51,925	68,358
Maryland	111,770	78,209	63,223	81,800	79,522	61,025	51,709	60,497	69,145	56,107	45,637	56,805
Massachusetts	132,507	82,236	73,255	99,513	92,571	69,095	58,533	70,325	93,264	66,196	53,956	72,486
Michigan	. . .	. . .	. . .	. . .	58,768	49,067	41,085	47,372	64,463	52,782	44,418	54,140
Minnesota	78,936	64,745	54,879	64,426	70,704	53,273	42,118	49,968	73,661	56,162	47,054	57,488
Mississippi	. . .	. . .	. . .	. . .	61,217	53,023	41,677	48,164	69,855	52,284	46,498	52,933
Missouri	110,386	70,493	61,506	82,064	66,900	54,510	46,557	55,068	56,605	48,797	42,290	46,808
Montana	. . .	. . .	. . .	. . .	. . .	. . .	. . .	. . .	48,599	38,285	34,761	42,434
Nebraska	. . .	. . .	. . .	. . .	82,462	60,156	49,044	58,153	57,286	45,963	40,942	46,365
Nevada	. . .	. . .	. . .	. . .	. . .	. . .	. . .	. . .	. . .	. . .	. . .	. . .
New Hampshire	117,957	81,417	67,851	94,755	70,411	55,350	48,756	58,385	64,850	53,479	44,704	53,420
New Jersey	134,425	77,263	64,634	98,287	80,337	67,477	51,661	66,070	66,328	52,561	43,911	53,295
New Mexico	. . .	. . .	. . .	. . .	. . .	. . .	. . .	. . .	60,002	48,718	43,289	50,705
New York	117,529	78,977	66,785	88,585	81,744	64,540	53,718	64,024	84,301	62,326	50,103	64,076
North Carolina	128,604	85,354	74,642	103,948	80,389	61,474	47,358	60,754	59,808	47,800	40,749	47,391
North Dakota	. . .	. . .	. . .	. . .	. . .	. . .	. . .	. . .	44,957	41,442	39,202	40,354
Ohio	106,940	75,408	64,909	83,257	75,958	56,883	48,822	57,59	68,933	55,550	46,116	55,875
Oklahoma	. . .	. . .	. . .	. . .	74,344	55,137	46,846	55,538	46,742	42,169	36,525	39,249
Oregon	. . .	. . .	. . .	. . .	77,001	59,328	48,918	60,448	78,544	55,027	48,033	61,453
Pennsylvania	120,785	82,623	75,014	94,851	84,897	65,407	51,653	62,821	76,051	58,731	47,729	57,644
Rhode Island	116,912	73,695	65,518	93,930	77,453	57,806	49,971	55,107	90,943	72,721	61,169	76,553
South Carolina	. . .	. . .	. . .	. . .	. . .	. . .	. . .	. . .	66,613	49,432	43,451	51,420
South Dakota	. . .	. . .	. . .	. . .	. . .	. . .	. . .	. . .	55,464	47,239	40,324	44,334
Tennessee	117,125	76,206	64,336	85,847	60,414	53,058	44,187	51,182	57,878	45,944	39,638	45,366
Texas	101,681	70,397	62,871	74,046	72,694	55,281	45,725	56,538	59,395	52,165	41,893	48,881
Utah	. . .	. . .	. . .	. . .	. . .	. . .	. . .	. . .	68,014	56,981	48,564	55,680
Vermont	. . .	. . .	. . .	. . .	67,191	54,535	44,204	57,480	87,210	60,522	53,648	66,750
Virginia	. . .	. . .	. . .	. . .	67,958	55,487	46,041	55,161	69,430	53,845	44,069	55,037
Washington	. . .	. . .	. . .	. . .	71,908	60,502	47,919	58,015	69,879	54,409	47,728	57,077
West Virginia	. . .	. . .	. . .	. . .	. . .	. . .	. . .	. . .	52,041	46,257	37,673	43,747
Wisconsin	88,100	66,118	58,743	66,439	59,200	49,045	42,363	47,155	63,149	52,229	44,049	51,425
Wyoming	. . .	. . .	. . .	. . .	. . .	. . .	. . .	. . .	. . .	. . .	. . .	. . .
District of Columbia	103,076	72,199	58,279	76,894	99,109	73,050	55,795	79,079	62,371	49,805	41,094	49,178
Puerto Rico	. . .	. . .	. . .	. . .	39,784	34,896	31,419	33,599	42,489	30,724	29,545	30,376

Source: American Association of University Professors, Faculty Compensation Survey.

More extensive tables and complete definitions are in "The Annual Report on the Economic Status of the Profession 2003-04" *Academe* 90, no. 2 (March/April 2004).

Notes:

". . ." indicates no responses in that category.

"Prof"=Professor; "Assoc"=Associate Professor; "Asst"=Assistant Professor; "All" includes all full-time faculty, with or without academic rank.

Data include full-time primarily instructional faculty only.

Figures are weighted average (mean) salaries; salaries of faculty members on 12-month contracts have been adjusted to an academic year (9-month) equivalent.

Trends in Health Insurance Affordability

By Jenny Sewell

Exploding health care costs have created a health insurance affordability crisis in the United States. According to a Families USA analysis of U.S. Census Bureau data, roughly 81.8 million people under age 65, or one out of three, were without insurance for some or all of 2002 and 2003. Not only has the number of people without insurance increased, but even individuals who maintain their coverage have seen higher out-of-pocket expenses as employers and insurers have instituted additional cost-sharing mechanisms. Given the situation, it is not surprising that health care is a top priority for state policy-makers. As the 2005 legislative session begins, the search is on for solutions that will both stabilize health care spending and allow more people to access affordable insurance products.

According to data from the Centers for Medicare and Medicaid Services, overall health care spending increased 9.3 percent in 2002 and 7.7 percent in 2003.[1] While the 2003 figure represents the smallest rate of growth since 1997, it was still almost three percentage points greater than overall economic growth.[2] This trend has put tremendous pressure on payers to find ways to cut costs.

One solution has been to pass costs on to the employee. According to the Kaiser Family Foundation's 2004 Employer Health Benefit Survey, 44 percent of small firms (three to 199 employees) and 83 percent of large firms (200 or more employees) thought it somewhat likely or very likely they would increase the amount employees pay for health insurance in the next year. When asked if they planned to increase deductibles in order to save on costs, 42 percent of small firms and 52 percent of large firms indicated that it was somewhat or very likely.[3]

An analysis of insurance premiums and out-of-pocket expenses supports this data. Between 2000 and 2004, average monthly worker contributions for single employees went from $28 to $47. For families, costs increased from $135 to $222.[4] And, even as employers have asked their employees to foot more of the bill, benefits covered by insurance plans have declined. This is especially true for employees in the highest income categories (over $60,000) who reported in a Commonwealth Fund survey that 56 percent had seen new limits on their health benefits.[5]

Monitoring these trends is critical for state policy-makers, given the role employer-sponsored coverage plays in insuring Americans. In 2003, 175.3 million people in the United States were insured through their employers. This is greater than the number covered under Medicare, Medicaid, individual policies and military health care combined.[6] Even small changes in employer-sponsored coverage can affect a large number of people.

Making Health Insurance More Affordable

Just as states and state laws governing insurance vary, so do state strategies to improve health insurance affordability.

Reinsurance

Several states are using reinsurance to support the health care insurance market and keep premiums low. Reinsurance is insurance for insurers—it helps lower an insurance company's risk of having claims in excess of the amount paid in premiums. Lower risk means that a company can set premiums at a level that reflects what it usually costs to care for a plan member and not have to anticipate paying for those few who, because of accident, illness or disease, will cost significantly more. Two examples of state reinsurance programs are found in Arizona and New York.

Arizona's program, Healthcare Group of Arizona, is aimed at increasing the number of small businesses that offer employer-sponsored health care coverage (currently only 28 percent) by making plans less expensive. The state contracts with managed care organizations (MCOs) that then sell coverage to eligible small businesses. The state reinsures the MCOs for claims over $100,000 to protect them from the risk of high-cost medical cases and to assure financial stability. The state appropriates funds to pay for the program, which currently covers 11,200 individuals.[7]

The Healthy New York program reinsures participating HMO's by covering 90 percent of claims between $5,000 and $75,000 per member per year. The program targets small businesses with low-wage workers and individuals with lower incomes, and it currently insures 40,000 people. Like Arizona, New York pays for this program through state appropriation.[8]

Medicaid Expansion

Some states are also looking to insure more individuals by expanding public health insurance programs. For example, in 2002 the federal government approved a waiver submitted by New Mexico requesting permission to partially fund its State Coverage Initiative program using money from the state's children's health insurance program. New Mexico wants to create an affordable insurance product for employers who don't currently offer coverage. Premiums will be financed through a combination of employer, employee, state and federal contributions.[9]

Also through a waiver, Maryland offers Primary Care, a program for adults with chronic illnesses who are not eligible for Medicaid but are enrolled in the state's pharmacy assistance program. Services covered include office visits, diabetes treatment and maintenance drugs.[10]

Rhode Island has implemented RIte Share, a premium assistance program for families eligible for the state's Medicaid program but who also have access to approved employer-sponsor health plans. Instead of enrolling these families in Medicaid, the state instead pays the employee portion of the premium. The state estimates that for every 1,000 full-year RIte Share enrollees, it saves $1 million.[11]

Scaled-Back Benefits Policies

Many states have also sought to increase the number of affordable health insurance options available by allowing for the sale of scaled-back or "bare-bones" policies that do not have to include state-mandated benefits. Since 1999, 11 states have either considered or passed such laws but the success of such legislation is unclear. For example, one of the bare-bones policies for sale under Arkansas' Health Insurance Consumer Choice Act of 2001 is only 4 to 9 percent cheaper than policies that include all mandated benefits. This difference is not likely to be enough to entice employers who are currently offering care to switch, or to encourage employers not offering coverage to begin doing so.[12]

Employer Mandates

There are two types of employer mandates. The first requires all employers to provide health insurance for their employees. The second gives employers a choice: they either offer insurance benefits or are subject to an employer tax that will fund a public health plan. This second version is sometimes referred to as "play or pay." Proponents of mandates argue that when the mandate applies to all employers, no employer can gain a competitive advantage by not offering benefits.

Hawaii is the only state to have approved and implemented employer mandates. Since 1974, Hawaii has required employers to provide health insurance to employees who work more than 20 hours a week. Washington enacted a similar law in 1993 but repealed it in 1995. Massachusetts and Oregon both passed play-or-pay laws in the late 1980s but neither state enacted the legislation. In 1996, Massachusetts repealed the law. That same year, Oregon allowed the law to expire.

More recently, California passed the Health Insurance Act of 2003 (SB2) which established a pay-or-play employer mandate. Once implemented, this program would have expanded health insurance to about 1 million of California's uninsured. A referendum challenging the law was placed on the November 2004 ballot. By a slim margin of less than two percent, voters chose to repeal the law before it could be implemented.[13]

High-Risk Insurance Pools

Thirty-three states now have high-risk insurance pools.[14] While state programs vary, in general, to qualify for a program, an individual must have been rejected by an insurance company because of the high risk he or she poses. An individual may also qualify because of a specific health condition. Premiums for high-risk plans are higher than market average and states sometimes cap enrollment and/or lifetime benefits.

Some states are looking more favorably on these plans because the 2002 Trade Adjustment Act made money available to states for establishing high-risk insurance pools and to cover some of the losses associated with these plans. While the plans cover only a small group of individuals—less than 200,000 people—they are a critical source of coverage for this population, especially as health benefits for retirees vanishes and the need for insurance products that bridge the gap between employer coverage and Medicare increases.[15]

Certificate of Need

An increase in the number of specialty or "boutique" hospitals has reignited the debate over state's use of certificates of need (CON) to limit the number of hospitals or, in some cases, specialists in one area based on need. In Florida, one piece of legislation passed dealing with health insurance affordability included a ban on boutique hospitals. According to Alan Levine, secretary of Florida's Agency for Health Care Administration, this move was necessary to ensure competition occurs on a level playing field and that better paying patients aren't siphoned off leaving the safety net hospitals to care only for the poor.

Maine's Dirigo Health Reform Act also takes on CON. The act establishes the Commission to Study Maine's Hospitals, a nine-member board that will examine Maine's hospitals and make recommendations to the Legislature on how best to move forward. The commission will look at a wide variety of issues, including financing, reimbursements, assets, technology, and staffing.[16]

Association Health Plans

At the federal level, association health plans (AHP) are sometimes touted as a solution to the problem. Proponents argue that, "by uniting many small groups with similar interests across the country, AHPs could take full advantage of economies of scale to lower health care costs for their memberships."[17]

Risk segmentation and adverse selection are cited as major concerns if these types of plans are allowed, however. Healthier people might be attracted to such plans, exiting the small-group market and leaving those who remain with higher health care costs since the totals are spread over a smaller group. There is also the possibility that only people who feel they are likely to use such a benefit (i.e. those who are already sick) will purchase a policy, driving up costs.

Federal Response

The confirmation of Michael Leavitt to replace Tommy Thompson as head the U.S. Department of Health and Human Services has lead to speculation that significant changes in Medicaid and Medicare are on the way. When he was governor of Utah, Leavitt asked for and was given permission to pare back benefits in an effort to expand coverage to a larger group. Preparations are already underway to fight any attempts to cap state Medicaid payments for fear that this will leave states holding the bag if something were to happen to rapidly increase Medicaid enrollment.

No matter what happens with Medicaid and Medicare, however, it is likely the Bush administration will continue to promote at least one mechanism it says will help control rising health care costs: health savings accounts.

Health Savings Accounts

The 2003 Medicare Modernization Act included language creating health savings accounts, or HSAs. Just as an IRA allows an individual to shelter retirement savings, an HSA offers a tax-free way to save money for qualified health-related expenses. Any individual who is covered by a high-deductible health plan (defined as a minimum deductible of $1,000 for an individual or $2,000 for a family) may establish an HSA. The money contributed is portable and can roll over from year to year.

Contributions can be made in one of three ways. An employer can make contributions on which neither the employer nor the employee pays taxes. An individual or family member can make tax-deductible contributions even if the individual doesn't itemize deductions. Finally, an individual participating in a cafeteria plan, a plan that allows employees to choose benefits from a range of options, can contribute untaxed salary through a salary reduction plan.

Proponents of HSAs argue that these accounts give consumers a better understanding of how much health care costs and thus will lead to lower health care spending. Critics, however, worry that HSAs could have unintended consequences. If the accounts are primarily marketed to and purchased by healthy people, HSAs could damage the structure of shared risk upon which the health insurance industry is built.[18]

To date, less than 400,000 policies have been sold and a recent survey found that "less than a third of workers with insurance have heard of health savings accounts."[19] A second survey of employers found that few will be offering the policies this year although many more are considering adding it as an option in the future.[20]

Quality Matters

In addition to the strategies listed above, some states are looking at quality of care initiatives to improve access to affordable health care coverage. Preventing medical errors eliminates the unnecessary spending associated with such errors, including costly malpractice suits that sometimes follow.

Health Information Technology

Health information technology (HIT) has the potential to reduce medical error, improve quality of care, help doctors track important information about patients and give consumers more information about their providers, finances, and overall health status. And yet, a recent survey of physicians found that very few have embraced new technologies:

- Electronic billing is used by only 79 percent of physicians.

- Only 27 percent of physicians use electronic medical records and electronic ordering of tests, procedures or prescriptions.

- Only 6 percent of physicians routinely use electronic clinical decision support systems.

- Email is used by only 3 percent of doctors as a method of communicating with patients; 7 percent use it to communicate with other doctors.[21]

To help speed up implementation, several states are taking action. Delaware has formed a Health Information Network, a statewide, health information and electronic data interchange program that is managed under the Delaware Health Care Commission. Created in 1997, this initiative improves access to care by providing easy access to timely, reliable and relevant health care information.

Through a partnership with SureScripts, the Rhode Island Quality Institute has founded an e-prescribing initiative to modernize the prescribing process and improve accuracy for physicians, pharmacists and patients. Rhode Island is serving as a test site for implementing a state-wide electronic system between all retail pharmacies and all prescribers within a state.[22]

Florida's Medicaid program recently distributed personal digital assistants to its top 1,000 prescribing physicians. This allows doctors to know if the patient is being treated by other providers, if test have been ordered, and what prescriptions have been ordered and filled.

Conclusion

The steps states are taking to improve health insurance affordability are many and varied. Some seem to be having an immediate effect by increasing access to affordable insurance but other strategies are still hotly debated, including association health plans. What is not debatable is states' role as part of the solution. As insurance regulators and quality monitors, states should continue to seek answers to the question of health insurance affordability.

Notes

[1] Smith, Cynthia, *et. al.*, "Health Spending Growth Slows in 2003," *Health Affairs*, January/February 2005, Vol. 24, No. l, 185-94.

[2] Ibid.

[3] "2004 Employer Health Benefit Survey," Kaiser Family Foundation. *www.kff.org/insurance/7148/index.cfm.*

[4] Ibid.

[5] "The Affordability Crisis in U.S. Health Care: Findings from the Commonwealth Fund Biennial Health Insurance Survey," The Commonwealth Fund, March 2004. *www.cmwf.org/ programs/insurance/collins_affordability_723.asp.*

[6] Health Care Coverage in America: Understanding the Issues & Proposed Solutions," Cover the Uninsured, May 2004. *http://covertheuninsuredweek.org/materials/files/ IssuesGuide.pdf.*

[7] "Reinsurance Programs to Expand Small-Group Coverage," Presentation by Deborah Chollet of Mathematica,

June 2004. *www.statecoverage.net/0604/chollet.pdf.*

[8] Ibid.

[9] "New Mexico State Coverage Initiative." Presentation by Carolyn Ingram of New Mexico Human Services Department, June 2004. *www.statecoverage.net/0604/ ingram.ppt.*

[10] "Limited-Benefit Policies: Public and Private-Sector Experiences." State Coverage Initiatives, July 2004. *www.statecoverage.net/pdf/issuebrief704.pdf.*

[11] "RIte Share Premium Assistance Program: Then and Now." Presentation by Kate Brewster of RI Department of Human Services, June 2004. *www.statecoverage.net/0604/ brewster.ppt.*

[12] "Limited-Benefit Policies: Public and Private-Sector Experiences." State Coverage Initiatives, July 2004. *www.statecoverage.net/pdf/issuebrief704.pdf.*

[13] "State Employer Health Insurance Mandates: A Brief History." California Health Care Foundation, March 2004. *www.chcf.org/documents/insurance/sb2/employman/ EmployerInsuranceMandates.pdf* and "Proposition 72: Health Care Coverage." Institute of Governmental Studies, University of California. *http://igs.berkeley.edu/library/ htHealthCare.hmtl.*

[14] "State/Feds Try Out New Roles for High Risk Pools," *State Health Notes*, National Conference of State Legislatures, March 22, 2004.

[15] Ibid.

[16] "Dirigo Health Reform Act: Addressing Health Care Costs, Quality, and Access in Maine," National Association for State Health Policy, June 2004. *http:// statecoverage.net/statereports/me18.pdf.*

[17] "Insuring the Uninsured Through Association Health Plans," National Center for Policy Analysis, April 2003. *www.ncpa.org/pub/st/st259/.*

[18] "President Bush Purchases Health Savings Account." Kaiser Daily Health Policy Report, December 17, 2004. www.*kaisernetwork.org/daily_reports/rep_hpolicy_recent_ rep.cfm?dr_DateTime=12-17-04&show=yes.*

[19] Freudenheim, Milt. "Health Savings Accounts Off to Slow Start." *The New York Times*, January 11, 2005.

[20] "HSAs: A Market Under Construction, Maybe in Medicare Too." The Commonwealth Fund's Washington Health Policy Week In Review, December 20, 2004.

[21] Anne-Marie Audet, *et. al.* "Information Technologies: When Will They Make It into Physicians' Black Bags?" The Commonwealth Fund, December 2004. *www.cmwf.org/publications/publications_show. htm?doc_ id=251984.*

[22] Sarah Donta. "Upgrading Healthcare: State Plans for Health Information Technology." *Health Policy Monitor*, The Council of State Governments, Fall 2004.

About the Author

Jenny Sewell is a senior health policy analyst at The Council of State Governments. Her duties include writing, researching and planning conferences on a wide variety of health policy issues, including health literacy, health care quality, medical malpractice and health insurance affordability. She holds a Masters of Public Administration from the University of Kentucky.

Table 9.1
HEALTH INSURANCE COVERAGE STATUS BY STATE FOR ALL PEOPLE: 2003
(In thousands)

State or other jurisdiction	Total	Covered and not covered by health insurance during the year			
		Covered	Percent	Not covered	Percent
United States	288,280	243,320	84.4%	44,961	15.6%
Alabama	4,427	3,798	85.8	629	14.2
Alaska	645	523	81.1	122	18.9
Arizona	5,576	4,626	83.0	951	17.0
Arkansas	2,671	2,206	82.6	465	17.4
California	35,394	28,895	81.6	6,499	18.4
Colorado	4,480	3,708	82.8	772	17.2
Connecticut	3,421	3,065	89.6	357	10.4
Delaware	820	729	88.9	91	11.1
Florida	16,921	13,849	81.8	3,071	18.2
Georgia	8,571	7,162	83.6	1,409	16.4
Hawaii	1,253	1,126	89.9	127	10.1
Idaho	1,360	1,107	81.4	253	18.6
Illinois	12,628	10,810	85.6	1,818	14.4
Indiana	6,149	5,296	86.1	853	13.9
Iowa	2,921	2,593	88.7	329	11.3
Kansas	2,683	2,389	89.0	294	11.0
Kentucky	4,110	3,537	86.0	574	14.0
Louisiana	4,429	3,517	79.4	912	20.6
Maine	1,283	1,150	89.6	133	10.4
Maryland	5,493	4,731	86.1	762	13.9
Massachusetts	6,397	5,685	89.3	682	10.7
Michigan	9,918	8,838	89.1	1,080	10.9
Minnesota	5,076	4,633	91.3	444	8.7
Mississippi	2,854	2,343	82.1	511	17.9
Missouri	5,623	5,004	89.0	620	11.0
Montana	917	739	80.6	177	19.4
Nebraska	1,727	1,532	88.7	195	11.3
Nevada	2,250	1,824	81.1	426	18.9
New Hampshire	1,264	1,133	89.7	131	10.3
New Jersey	8,579	7,378	86.0	1,201	14.0
New Mexico	1,871	1,457	77.9	414	22.1
New York	18,970	16,104	84.9	2,866	15.1
North Carolina	8,253	6,829	82.7	1,424	17.3
North Dakota	631	563	89.1	69	10.9
Ohio	11,247	9,885	87.9	1,362	12.1
Oklahoma	3,438	2,737	79.6	701	20.4
Oregon	3,569	2,957	82.8	613	17.2
Pennsylvania	12,155	10,771	88.6	1,384	11.4
Rhode Island	1,053	946	89.8	108	10.2
South Carolina	4,064	3,481	85.6	584	14.4
South Dakota	751	659	87.8	91	12.2
Tennessee	5,909	5,131	86.8	778	13.2
Texas	21,858	16,484	75.4	5,374	24.6
Utah	2,352	2,055	87.3	298	12.7
Vermont	611	553	90.5	58	9.5
Virginia	7,386	6,424	87.0	962	13.0
Washington	6,091	5,147	84.5	944	15.5
West Virginia	1,787	1,491	83.4	296	16.6
Wisconsin	5,429	4,836	89.1	593	10.9
Wyoming	488	411	84.1	78	15.9
District. of Columbia	554	475	85.7	79	14.3

Source: U.S. Census Bureau, Current Population Survey, 2004 Annual Social and Economic Supplement. Revised June 25, 2004.

The 2025 Outlook for Oil and Gas
By James M. Kendell

Over the next 20 years U.S. consumption of oil and gas is expected to increase by at least one-third, while prices decline somewhat in real terms from today's high levels. Dependence on foreign imports of oil and gas is expected to increase as domestic production declines.

These projections are from the Energy Information Administration's *Annual Energy Outlook 2005 (AEO2005),* which provides projections of domestic energy consumption, supply, prices and carbon emissions. The Energy Information Administration (EIA) is an independent analytical and statistical agency within the U.S. Department of Energy. It does not represent any particular point of view on energy policy, and its views are not necessarily those of the Department or the Administration.

Assumptions are critical to any forecast. The projections are not statements of what will happen but of what might happen, given certain assumptions. The reference case projections are business-as-usual forecasts, given known technology and technological trends, demographic trends, and current laws and regulations. EIA does not propose, advocate, or speculate on changes in laws and regulations. So, one of the forecast's key assumptions is that all current laws and regulations remain as enacted. For *AEO2005,* that means, for example, that the provisions of proposed comprehensive energy legislation are not included in the forecast.

Petroleum Outlook

Since the beginning of 2004, high world oil prices have raised gasoline prices and unsettled consumers, but have not significantly reduced their driving. Despite higher prices, domestic crude oil production is expected to continue its historic decline, while consumption increases by 7.9 million barrels per day from 2003 to 2025. As a result, net imports are expected to grow by 7.9 million barrels per day between 2003 and 2025.

If world oil prices are higher than projected, the gap between supply and demand is expected to narrow, with higher oil prices spurring production and depressing demand.

Prices

World oil prices are one of the key assumptions in the *Annual Energy Outlook.* In addition to the reference case world oil price path, EIA normally pub-lishes a high and a low world oil price path. Because of recent crude oil price volatility, a futures case and a very high case were added to *AEO2005* (Figure A). World prices are defined as the "average refiners acquisition cost" of imported oil into the United States. This price is about $5-6 per barrel less than the often-quoted West Texas Intermediate price.

In the *Reference case,* prices in 2010 are projected to be about $10 per barrel lower than current prices in 2003 dollars. Between 2003 and 2010, crude oil prices are expected to decline as production from Russia and the Caspian area expands, new fields come on in West Africa, new oil sands production is initiated in Canada, new deepwater oil fields are brought into production in the Gulf of Mexico, and the Organization of Petroleum Exporting Countries (OPEC) expands production capacity. After 2010, oil prices are projected to rise to more than $30 per barrel in 2025. In the *October futures case,* prices in the near term rise through 2005, and then resume a growth trend similar to the reference case. This case is based on an extrapolation of oil prices loosely corresponding to the October 2004 NYMEX futures strip. In the October futures case, world crude oil prices are assumed to average $44 per barrel in 2005 before falling to about $31 per barrel in 2010 and then generally paralleling the rise in the reference case. In the *High A case,* prices are projected to remain at about $34 per barrel through 2015 and then increase to more than $39 per barrel in 2025. In the *High B case,* projected prices continue to increase through 2005 to $44 dollars per barrel, fall to $37 in 2010, and rise to $48 dollars per barrel by 2025. In the *Low case,* prices are projected to decline from their high in 2004 to $21 per barrel in 2009 and to remain at that level out to 2025.

Refined product prices are determined by crude oil costs, refining costs (including profits), marketing costs, and taxes. Whereas crude oil costs tend to increase refined product prices in the forecast, the assumption that Federal motor fuel taxes remain at nominal 2003 levels tends to reduce prices. Thus, gasoline price projections are relatively flat through-

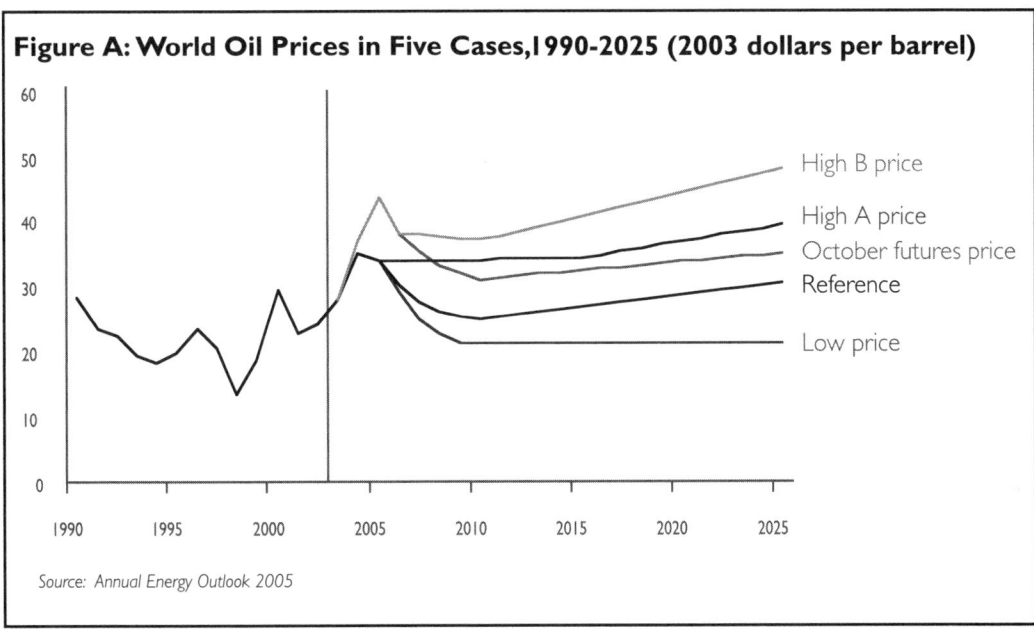

Figure A: World Oil Prices in Five Cases, 1990-2025 (2003 dollars per barrel)

High B price
High A price
October futures price
Reference
Low price

Source: *Annual Energy Outlook 2005*

out the projection period with gasoline at $1.59 per gallon in 2025 in the reference case.

Oil Consumption

In the reference case U.S. petroleum consumption is projected to increase by 7.9 million barrels per day from 2003 to 2025 (Figure B). However, a steep and prolonged rise in crude oil prices, as in the *High B case*, could reduce the growth in consumption to 6.2 million barrels per day, mainly because of lower growth in gasoline consumption.

About 92 percent of the projected reference case growth in petroleum consumption consists of "light products" (including gasoline, diesel, heating oil, jet fuel, kerosene, LPG and petrochemical feedstocks), which are more difficult and costly to produce than heavy products. Gasoline continues to make up nearly one-half of all petroleum used in the United States, increasing from 8.9 million barrels per day in 2003 to 12.9 million in 2025, mostly for transportation. Consumption of distillate fuel is also projected to increase, by 1.9 million barrels per day, from 2003 to 2025. Gasoline is used only in spark-ignition engines; distillate is used in furnaces, boilers, diesel engines and some turbines. Jet fuel consumption is projected to increase by 789,000 barrels per day from 2003 to 2025.

Residual fuel use, constrained by air quality regulations, increases by only 110,000 barrels per day from 2003 to 2025, including an increase of 79,000 barrels per day in residual fuel use for baseload electricity generation. More intensive refinery processing to maximize light product yield and minimize heavy product yield is expected to limit the availability of residual fuel.

The transportation sector accounted for two-thirds of U.S. petroleum use in 2003. In the forecast, population growth and economic growth cause miles traveled to increase across all modes of transit. Although improvements in vehicle technology yield reductions in fuel use per mile traveled, the increases in mileage outweigh increases in efficiency, leading to increases in consumption of gasoline, diesel and jet fuel.

The industrial sector currently accounts for 24 percent of U.S. petroleum demand. In the reference case, industrial consumption is projected to be 1.2 million barrels per day higher in 2025 than it was in 2003, and industrial consumption of liquefied petroleum gas (LPG), largely as a chemical feedstock, increases by about 490,000 barrels per day.

In the residential sector, distillate use is displaced by LPG, natural gas, and electricity for home heating toward the end of the forecast. As a result, residential oil use drops by 88,000 barrels per day from 2003 to 2025. Commercial use of heating oil grows from 246,000 barrels per day in 2003 to 362,000 barrels per day in 2025. The delivered price of dis-

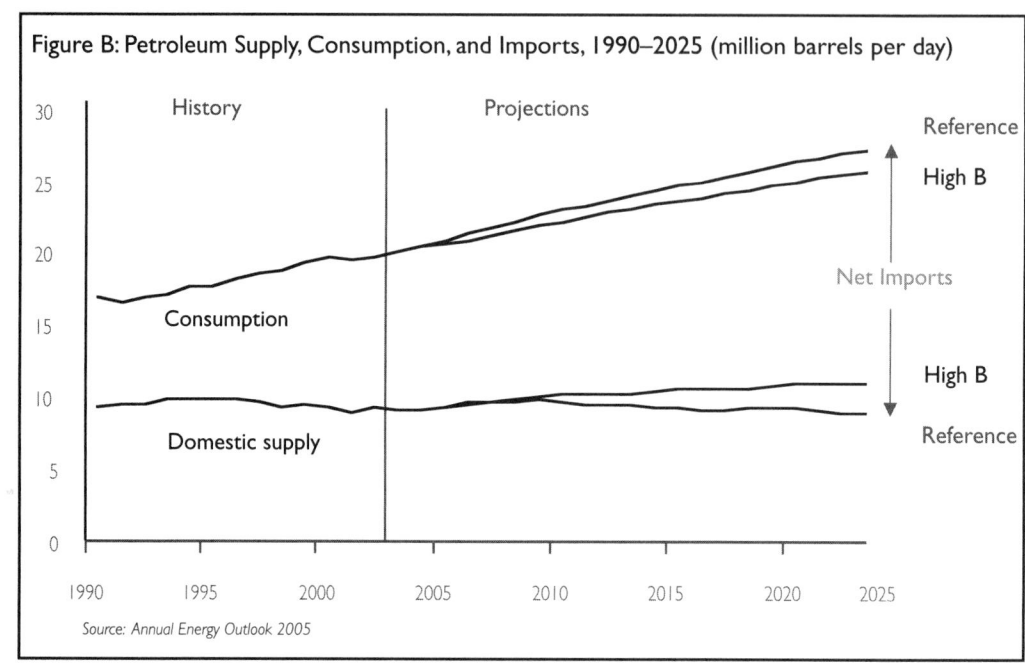

Figure B: Petroleum Supply, Consumption, and Imports, 1990–2025 (million barrels per day)

Source: Annual Energy Outlook 2005

tillate to commercial customers is projected to be lower than the price of natural gas throughout the forecast.

Only 3 percent of U.S. electricity is currently generated from refined petroleum, but the electricity sector nearly matches residential petroleum use by the end of the forecast. Consumption of residual and distillate fuel in the electric power sector increase modestly.

Oil Production

In the *AEO2005* reference case, U.S. crude oil production is projected to increase from 5.7 million barrels per day in 2003 to 6.2 million barrels per day in 2009 as a result of increased production offshore, predominantly from the deep waters of the Gulf of Mexico. Beginning in 2010, U.S. crude oil production begins to decline, falling to 4.7 million barrels per day in 2025. A steep and prolonged rise in crude oil prices, as in the *High B case*, could increase total domestic supply by 2.2 million barrels a day in 2025, including 1.2 million barrels per day from synthetic petroleum fuel produced from coal and natural gas (Figure B).

In the reference case, crude oil production from Alaska is expected to decline to about 810,000 barrels per day in 2010. After 2010, increased produc-

tion from the National Petroleum Reserve-Alaska (NPR-A) raises Alaska's total production to about 890,000 barrels per day in 2014. Depletion of the oil resource base in the North Slope, NPR-A, and southern Alaska oil fields is expected to lead to a decline in the State's total production to about 610,000 barrels per day in 2025.

Alaska crude oil production originates mainly from the North Slope, which includes the NPR-A and the state lands surrounding Prudhoe Bay. Because drilling is currently prohibited in the Arctic National Wildlife Refuge (ANWR), *AEO2005* does not project any production from ANWR.

Import Dependence

In 2003, net imports of petroleum climbed to a record 56 percent of domestic petroleum consumption. Dependence on petroleum imports is projected to reach 68 percent in 2025 in the reference case. (In the *High B case*, import dependence reaches only 58 percent in 2025.) The expected value of petroleum imports in the reference case in 2025 is projected to be $216 billion in 2003 dollars. Total annual U.S. expenditures for petroleum imports, which reached a historical peak of $148 billion in 1980, were $122 billion in 2003.

Net U.S. petroleum imports are projected to increase from 11.2 million barrels per day in 2003 to 19.1 million in 2025. Crude oil accounts for most of the increase in imports, because distillation capacity at U.S. refineries is expected to be more than 5.5 million barrels per day higher in 2025 than it was in 2003. Net imports of refined petroleum, including refined products, unfinished oils, and blending components, are expected to almost double by 2025, to 3.0 million barrels per day.

Crude oil imports from the North Sea are projected to decline gradually as North Sea production ebbs. Significant imports of petroleum from Canada and Mexico are expected to continue, with much of the Canadian contribution coming from the development of its enormous oil sands resource base. West Coast refiners are expected to import small volumes of crude oil from the Far East to replace the declining production of Alaska crude oil. The Persian Gulf share of total gross petroleum imports, 20.4 percent in 2003, is expected to increase to almost 30 percent in 2025; and the OPEC share of total gross imports, which was 42 percent in 2003, is expected to be above 60 percent in 2025. Vigorous growth in demand for lighter petroleum products in developing countries means that U.S. refin-

ers are likely to import smaller volumes of light, low-sulfur crude oils.

Most of the increase in refined product imports is projected to come from refiners in the Caribbean Basin, North Africa and the Middle East, where refining capacity is expected to expand significantly.

Natural Gas Outlook

Unlike oil, natural gas is still largely supplied from domestic sources. But over the forecast, imports are expected to more than double. Domestic natural gas production is expected to increase more slowly than consumption over the forecast, rising from 19.0 trillion cubic feet (Tcf) in 2003 to 21.8 Tcf in 2025. Growing production is supported by rising wellhead gas prices, relatively abundant gas resources, and improvements in technologies, particularly for unconventional gas. Economic conditions allow an Alaskan pipeline to begin moving gas to the lower 48 states in 2016.

Consumption is forecast to climb from 22.4 Tcf in 2003 to 30.7 Tcf by 2025. The increase is primarily due to the rapid growth in demand for electricity generation and industrial applications, which account for almost 75 percent of the growth. The difference be-

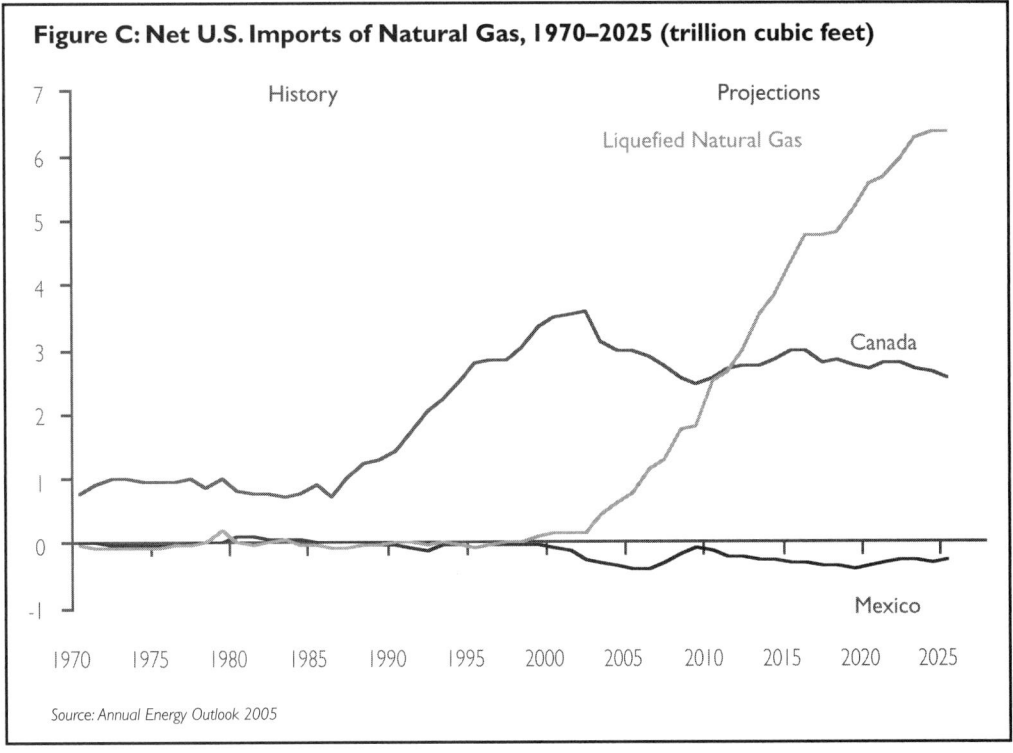

Figure C: Net U.S. Imports of Natural Gas, 1970–2025 (trillion cubic feet)

History   Projections

Liquefied Natural Gas

Canada

Mexico

Source: Annual Energy Outlook 2005

tween consumption and production is made up by increasing use of imports. In *AEO2005*, net imports grow from 3.3 Tcf in 2003 to 8.7 Tcf in 2025.

The national average wellhead price is projected to reach $4.16 per thousand cubic feet (mcf) in 2003 dollars in 2015 and $4.79 per mcf in 2025.

Consumption

The strongest growth in natural gas consumption is in the electric power sector, where consumption is projected to almost double, from 5.1 trillion cubic feet in 2003 to 9.4 trillion cubic feet in 2025. Demand by electricity generators is expected to account for 31 percent of total natural gas consumption in 2025, compared with about 23 percent in 2003. Electric power gas consumption growth results from both the construction of new gas-fired generation plants and from a higher capacity utilization of gas-fired generation plants. Most new electricity generation capacity is expected to be fueled by natural gas, because natural-gas-fired generators are projected to have advantages over coal-fired generators, including lower capital costs, higher fuel efficiency, shorter construction lead times, and lower emissions. Toward the end of the forecast, however, when natural gas prices rise substantially, coal-fired power plants are expected to be competitive for new capacity additions, and gas begins to lose market share to coal.

Industrial consumption (including lease and plant fuel) remains the largest consuming sector and is projected to increase from 8.3 trillion cubic feet in 2003 to 10.3 trillion cubic feet in 2025. Those industrial sectors projected to experience the greatest gas consumption growth from 2003 through 2025 include metal-based durables, petroleum refining, bulk chemicals, and food.

In the residential and commercial sectors, natural gas consumption is projected to increase by about 0.7 percent and 1.2 percent per year, respectively, from 2003 to 2025.

Production

Domestic gas production is expected to increase from 19.0 Tcf in 2003 to 21.8 Tcf in 2025. Increased U.S. natural gas production comes primarily from unconventional sources and from Alaska.

Unconventional gas production increases by 2.0 Tcf over the forecast period, mainly because of technological improvements, rising prices, and relatively

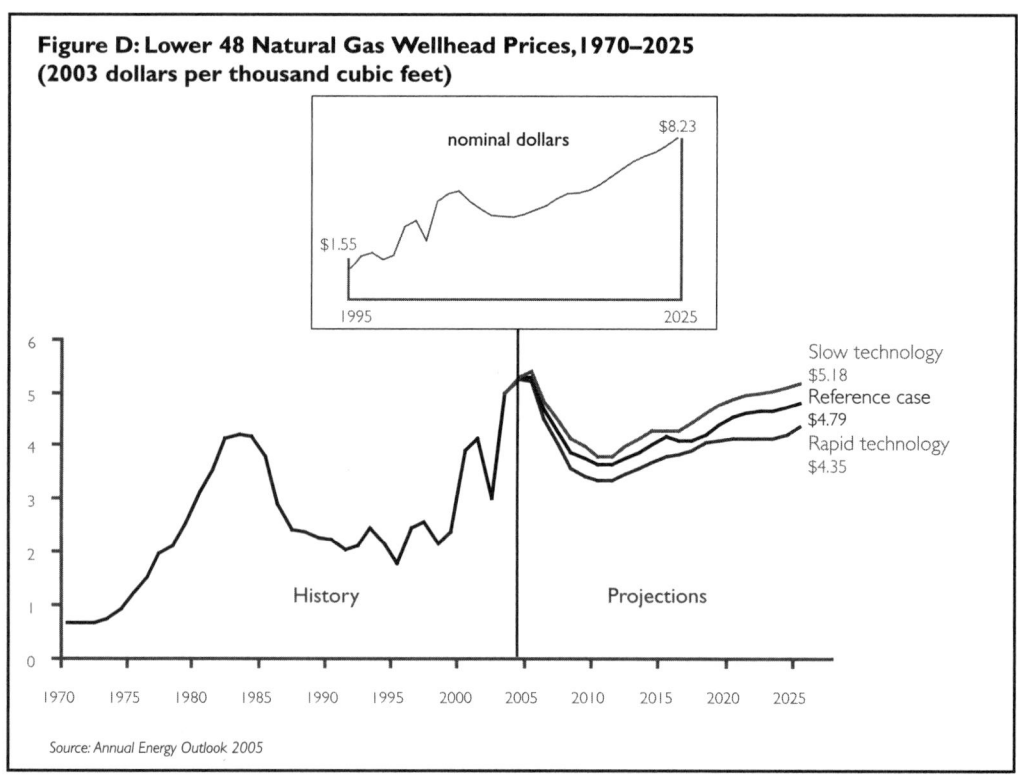

Figure D: Lower 48 Natural Gas Wellhead Prices, 1970–2025
(2003 dollars per thousand cubic feet)

nominal dollars
$8.23
$1.55
1995   2025

Slow technology
$5.18
Reference case
$4.79
Rapid technology
$4.35

History   Projections

Source: Annual Energy Outlook 2005

abundant unconventional sources (tight sands, shale and coalbed methane). Annual production from unconventional sources is expected to account for 44 percent of lower-48 production in 2025, compared to 35 percent in 2003.

Over the forecast, Alaska gas production accounts for most of the growth in domestic conventional gas production, growing by 1.8 Tcf over the forecast period. Alaska gas is projected to begin flowing to the lower-48 states in 2016. With subsequent expansion of this pipeline, Alaskan gas production reaches 2.2 Tcf in 2025, compared with 0.4 Tcf in 2003.

Lower-48 onshore and offshore non-associated conventional gas production is expected to decline by about 900 Bcf, as resource depletion causes exploration and development costs to increase.

Production of associated-dissolved (AD) natural gas from lower-48 crude oil reserves is projected to grow from 2.5 Tcf in 2003 to 3.1 Tcf in 2010. After 2010, both onshore and offshore AD gas production is expected to decline, with total AD gas production falling to 2.4 Tcf in 2025.

Imports

Imports are expected to be priced competitively with domestic sources of natural gas, and net imports of natural gas are expected to make up the difference between U.S. production and consumption. Liquefied natural gas (LNG) is expected to account for most of the projected increase in net imports (Figure C). One new LNG terminal started operation this year offshore Louisiana. By the end of the forecast, sufficient new LNG terminal capacity comes into operation to allow net LNG imports to increase from 440 bcf in 2003 to 6.4 trillion cubic feet in 2025. By 2025, net LNG imports are expected to equal 21 percent of total U.S. gas consumption, compared to 2 percent in 2003. Net LNG imports are expected to rise from 13 percent of net imports in 2003 to 74 percent in 2025.

Net imports of natural gas from Canada are projected to be 3.0 trillion cubic feet in 2005, and then decline gradually to 2.5 trillion cubic feet in 2009. A MacKenzie Delta natural gas pipeline is projected to begin transporting gas in 2010, and imports subsequently rise to 3.0 tcf in 2015. After 2015, net gas imports from Canada are projected to again decline, falling to 2.5 trillion cubic feet in 2025. Conventional production in the Western Sedimentary Basin is projected to decline throughout the projection, but unconventional gas production in Western Canada, conventional production in the MacKenzie Delta and Eastern Canada, and LNG imports are expected to more than offset the production decline in the Western Sedimen-

tary Basin. Towards the end of the forecast, imports from Canada decline as Canadian gas consumption increases faster than Canadian gas production.

Although Mexico has considerable natural gas resources, the United States historically has been a net exporter of gas to Mexico. Net exports of U.S. natural gas to Mexico are projected to grow until 2006, and subsequently decline after 2006 as LNG terminals in Baja California come online to serve both the Mexican and U.S. markets.

Prices

Average wellhead prices for natural gas are projected to increase from $4.88 per thousand cubic feet (2003 dollars) in 2003 to $5.30 per thousand cubic feet in 2005 (Figure D). After 2005, natural gas wellhead prices are projected to decline to $3.64 per thousand cubic feet in 2010 as the initial availability of new import sources and production from increased drilling expands available supply. After 2010, wellhead prices are projected to increase gradually, reaching $4.79 in 2025. The increase is in response to higher exploration and development costs associated with smaller and deeper gas deposits in the remaining domestic gas resource base.

Growth in unconventional sources, Alaska production, and LNG imports are not expected to increase enough to offset the impacts of resource depletion and increased demand.

Prices are projected to increase in an uneven fashion as new, large-volume supply projects temporarily depress prices when initially brought online. In nominal dollars, the 2025 price is the equivalent of $8.23 per thousand cubic feet.

The reference case forecast assumes known technology and technological trends. Wellhead natural gas price projections are more sensitive to variations in technological change than to the levels of natural gas production and consumption. And, prices vary significantly under alternate technology assumptions. Under the reference case, technologies are assumed to increase at historical rates. In the rapid and slow technology cases, the technology parameters in the model are increased and decreased by 50 percent.

The slow technology case projects a wellhead price of $5.18 per thousand cubic feet in constant 2003 dollars in 2025, which is 8 percent higher than the reference case price. In the rapid technology case, lower 48 natural gas wellhead prices are projected to reach $4.35 per thousand cubic feet in 2025, which is 9 percent lower than in the reference case.

Summary

Oil and gas prices are expected to decline in real terms through 2010, as current high prices spur the development of more foreign and domestic supplies and technological development continues. After 2010, prices are expected to rise steadily—though not as high as 2004 prices, as demand increases and resources continue to deplete.

Domestic consumption of oil and gas is expected to increase by at least one-third through 2025. In the face of declining oil and gas production by 2020, dependence on imports of oil and gas is expected to increase significantly. LNG is projected to meet most of the U.S. needs for additional natural gas imports.

About the Author

James M. Kendell is director of the Oil and Gas Division of the Office of Integrated Analysis and Forecasting at the U.S. Energy Information Administration (EIA). For the past 13 years he has managed natural gas and oil forecasting and analysis, and the development of the oil and gas models in the National Energy Modeling System (NEMS). Kendell graduated with an M.A. in Public Policy and Administration and a certificate in Energy Analysis and Policy from the University of Wisconsin-Madison in 1983. He received a B.S.J. with highest distinction from the University of Kansas in 1975.

State Economic Development Strategies: Job Growth and Retention in a Recovering Economy

By Jeffrey Finkle

Despite the slow turnaround of the economy, states are still faced with the challenge of maintaining and creating new jobs. Around the country state governments and economic development organizations are relying on proven programs and are challenging themselves to develop new ones in an effort to attract businesses to their areas and encourage expansion among existing local companies.

Economically, the year 2004 will go down in history as a mixed-bag, of sorts. The war in Iraq is technically over, but the multibillion-dollar price tag on our continued presence in the country and commitment to rebuilding it continues to soar. The recession that according to the Bureau of Economic Research, began in March 2001 and, technically, came to an end in November 2001 continues to leave its mark on the economy; although unemployment numbers have leveled off and are ever so slowly beginning to decrease. Despite any progress, the competition among states to create new jobs and retain existing ones is just as fierce as it was when the country was in the throes of a recession. States continue to struggle to retain and attract businesses that are, in their efforts to increase productivity, looking for more favorable conditions not only in other states, but in other countries as well. The International Economic Development Council, the largest economic development association in the United States, plays an important role in helping economic development entities to navigate the process of facilitating job growth, business development, and property development in a challenging climate.

From Vermont to California and all spots in between, states are all playing the same courting game—wooing new businesses to their area and coaxing existing companies to stay put and expand. The common thread in the states' approach to achieving the aforementioned goals is twofold, consisting of self-promotion and incentives. States have to sell their attributes, such as a highly-educated workforce or reasonably priced land. Additionally, they also frequently seal or sweeten the deal with new or existing businesses by offering incentives, ranging from tax breaks to job-training assistance. As for areas of focus, all states are pursuing high-technology businesses in an effort to expand and replace outdated sectors, while simultaneously cultivating successful existing industries.

What Kept Companies at Home in 2004: Old Programs with New Results

Vermont, which posted the lowest unemployment rate in the country at 3.1 percent in November 2004,[1] has employed a bevy of programs to help maintain and create new job opportunities for residents. One such endeavor that has proven successful is the Vermont Department of Economic Development's Vermont Training Program (VTP), which encourages expansion among industrial companies by providing training through individually tailored programs; the state covers as much as 50 percent of the training costs. The importance of educating and training local potential and existing employees is best expressed by one of the state's largest employer. "The field on which Vermont can compete successfully with other states is the quality of our workforce," John O'Kane, manager of governmental affairs for IBM in Vermont, noted in a report of the Vermont Workforce Education & Training Consortium. During FY 2004, VTM trained 1,694 employees at 153 businesses.[2] In November, VTP awarded $50,000 in training funds to Dirigo Paper Mill in Gilman, thereby allowing the manufacturer to create 25 new jobs. Recognizing the program's benefits and encouraging its continued success, the Vermont Legislature signed off on a 30 percent increase to $1.3 million in funding for the program in the 2005 budget.

While the state's key industries include financial services, technology and manufacturing, officials have not overlooked rural locales where the often struggling agricultural sector continues to generate $3 billion in revenue annually, with approximately 74 percent of that money being churned out by the state's 1,400 dairy farms.[3] And those dairy farms—with their laborers, milk transporters, processors, farm service firms and the like—provide thousands of jobs. In an effort to bolster the industry, the state Legislature in April 2003 approved the Vermont Economic Development Authority's Farm Operating

Loan Program, a fund of up to $20 million operated through the Vermont Agricultural Credit Corporation; it provides loans of up to $100,000 at below-market interest rates for dairy farms and $50,000 for non-dairy farms to cover a variety of annual operating expenses.

Training programs and targeted loans are just two commonly employed incentives used to keep businesses up and running or to help them expand. Another means to this end is the packaging of such incentives. In Pennsylvania, the Governor's Action Team (GAT) does just that. Comprised of high-level economic development leaders, GAT reports directly to Pennsylvania Gov. Edward G. Rendell and handholds companies in their growth pursuits by coordinating resources from various agencies and groups. "Their job is basically to work with companies that are already here in the state on projects that will create additional jobs by offering financial incentive bundles," says Kevin Ortiz, communications director for the Pennsylvania Department of Community and Economic Development. "The bundles can include tax credits, loan programs, the creation of opportunity grants, job creation tax credits." The results of the team's work speaks for itself. In 2004, the group assisted in creating and retaining thousands of jobs at 75 businesses. Among them, Aramark Corporation in Philadelphia where GAT played a prominent role in the managed services provider's decision to resist wooing by Delaware and New Jersey and stay at its 300,000 square foot headquarters in the 630,000 square foot aptly named Aramark Tower, thereby retaining over 1,400 jobs. GAT convinced the company to stay put with an $8.75 million incentives package that included such benefits as low-interest loans and tax credits.

Not only did the company decide to remain at its locale under a new 15-year lease agreement, it made plans to expand by an additional 50,000 square feet and to create 250 new positions. In another coup, GAT had a helping hand in 2,100 jobs at Bayer Corp., 3,700 at Sunoco Inc. and 1,500 and Towers Perrin.

Reeling Them In: Time-tested Programs and New Ideas Take States into the Future

With a successful program in place to assist in business growth and retention, Pennsylvania focused its attention in 2004 on stimulating economic development and improving communities through the newly established Governor's Economic Stimulus Plan. The $2 billion endeavor—expected to induce a target goal of $5 billion in private investment—consists of 19 programs designed to fuel business through a range of economic endeavors, including offering support for the establishment of new companies. To that end, the stimulus package includes the $60 million New Pennsylvania Venture Capital Investment Program, which provides funds for businesses willing to invest, through matching funds, in partnerships with start-up companies. Business in Our Sites is another one of programs under the governor's plan. This $300 million program provides communities with the monetary support needed to create viable, infrastructure-ready sites—particularly at under-utilized locations such as brownfields—to serve as homes for new companies. This particular endeavor allows communities to focus on luring new businesses to their areas in the immediate future, as well as in the long-term.

Other forms of partnership programs have already proven successful in other states. Ohio's Third Frontier Project, established in 2002 by Gov. Bob Taft and operated by the Ohio Department of Development, targets the universally burgeoning technology sector. The objective of the $1.1 billion, 10-year investment program is to utilize partnerships to further develop research capabilities, encourage new product development, and foster new manufacturing-centric technologies that will, in turn, fortify existing businesses. "We are creating a climate that entices companies to be interested in Ohio," Third Frontier Commission Staff Director Norman Chagnon explains. Case in point, Wright State University in Dayton and the Center of Innovation in Advanced Data Management and Analysis, an entity centered on the research and development of information technology services. Through the Third Frontier Project, Ohio contributed $11.1 million to the university in 2003 for the establishment of the center, which will create 500 new high-level positions over the next three years. The financial investment is having, as planned, a domino effect. "As a result of that investment a West Coast company, Alien Technology, is setting up a major presence in Dayton, Ohio," notes Chagnon. News of the plan was confirmed in the fall of 2004. "One of their big reasons for moving to Dayton was our investment in the Center." With the opening of the new Dayton location of the California-headquartered company will come with about 100 new high-level jobs.

Texas, riding high from its successful $300 million Texas Enterprise Fund (TEF) program, announced in December 2004 that it would turn a more focused eye toward courting the various businesses within the technology sector through the establishment of the Texas Emerging Technology Fund

(TETF);[4] suggested targeted industries range from nanotechnology to environmental sciences. Proposed by Gov. Rick Perry, the $300 million program would take a three-pronged approach to drawing new companies to the state; an endeavor that would also help build and maintain Texas's position as a competitive entity in the global economy. Half of TETF's funds would be spent on cultivating collaborations between universities and private businesses as a means of developing "Regional Centers of Innovation and Commercialization," such as Houston's Center for Advanced Diagnostic Imaging. Additionally, $75 million would go toward matching federal or private sector research grants that involve collaborations with local universities pursuing groundbreaking scientific achievements. Finally, the remaining $75 million would be used to entice celebrated research teams from other universities around the country to come to Texas and impart their wisdom to local public universities.

If the progress achieved through TEF is any indication of Texas's power to generate jobs through new business, then TETF will be an unqualified success. TEF has brought thousands of new positions to the state by luring companies and/or encouraging their local expansion. Perhaps the grandest achievement under the program is Calabasas, Calif.-based Countrywide Financial's decision, announced in mid-December, to expand its presence in Richardson, Texas through the addition of 7,500 new jobs over the next six years. The state secured Countrywide's commitment to grow at its Richardson site by offering an incentive package that included $20 million in TEF funding.

Focusing on a burgeoning industry has been one fruitful means of attracting new companies, promoting a state's unique assets is another. Acting through the Oregon Economic and Community Development Department (OECDD) in 2003, Oregon launched its Brand Oregon campaign, a statewide effort to stimulate the economy through the promotion of Oregon's local characteristics and products. The program began with the touting of a product for which the state has become known: seafood. Most recently, the state has seen great success by promoting a distinctive package of Oregon products that involved increasingly popular wines form local vineyards and Oregon specialty cheeses. As of late, however, the state's dedication to protecting the environment has become an equally viable indigenous asset to promote to new businesses. "We find that the organic—well, they call themselves specialty food processors—are very compatible with Oregon because we have such a high

value that we place on our environmental practices and that meshes very compliantly with organic food processors who share those values," says Michelle Godfrey, OECDD communications manager for the Oregon Economic and Community Development Department." A recent coup in this area involves Amy's Kitchen, a Santa Rosa, California-based family-operated natural and organic foods producer that settled on White City, a town in Southern Oregon, for the home of its new 400,000 square foot manufacturing plant after considering several other states; California made the biggest and seemingly strongest pitch for the facility. While the environment played a role in the company's decision, it was Oregon's traditional promotion of its comparably lower tax rates and workers' compensation rates, as well as its cost effective land prices and reasonable utility rates that sealed the deal.[5] Still, the fact that Amy's Kitchen took an interest in the state's environmentally-friendly climate has sparked new ideas. "We may be going after that segment in the next year ahead," Godfrey says.

Oregon's win as the site of California-based Amy's Kitchen's new manufacturing plant had more to do with Oregon than California, but Idaho relies on the direct comparison to California as one of its main tools for coaxing companies to relocate to the Potato State. "We're a low-cost area," explains Randy Shroll, sales and marketing manager for the Idaho Department of Commerce. "We don't have a large budget for programs so we target northern and southern California because it's such a high cost and regulated area to do business." In October of 2003, the Department of Commerce launched an advertising campaign, relying on funds from the department's meager $120,000 budget. The ads ran for four months in California business publications and the West Coast edition of the Wall Street Journal and touted the sizable potential savings in business operating expenses. Even before the ad campaign, however, Idaho had managed to lure away a bevy of big names, including El Cajon, California's Buck Knives, a sport-utility knife manufacturer that began building a new 128,000 square foot plant in Post Falls, Idaho in the spring of 2004.

States like Idaho and Nevada have spent the last few years directing their efforts to bring in new businesses at California-based companies that have grown weary of the state's comparatively high cost of living and other business challenges. Last year, however, California responded by putting some of its powerful Hollywood muscle to work. Governor Arnold Schwarzenegger—the celebrity action film star sworn into office in late 2003 following a special election[6]—initiated a billboard advertising campaign through the California Commission for Jobs and Economic Growth[7] featuring his world renowned visage and the catch phrase, "Arnold Says: California Wants Your Business." Placed on billboards in major metropolitan cities of competing states in the country, as well as such bustling East Coast locales as Times Square in New York City, the campaign was designed to stave off efforts by states to lure away California companies by touting the positive aspects of conducting business in the state. The "Arnold Says..." effort was even readapted for the governor's trade mission to Japan in an effort to promote the California business climate on an international level.[8]

The struggle to create new jobs persisted in 2004 as states—through new programs and existing ones— continued to tout their local amenities, woo the high-tech industry and peddle incentive packages. The economy may be on in the midst of a turnaround, but the persisting frenzy among the states to compete for jobs through the courting of new businesses and the encouragement of expansion among existing companies show no signs of being effected by any such change.

Notes

[1]Regional and State Employment and Unemployment Summary, Regional and State Employment and Unemployment: November 2004. (U.S. Department of Labor Bureau of Labor Statistics, 2004). *http://www.bls.gov/news.release/laus.nr0.htm.*

[2]Vermont Department of Economic Development,

Workforce Training: Vermont Training Program, *http://www.thinkvermont.com/workforce/vt_train.cfm.*

[3]House Concurrent Resolution (H.C.R. 240) Recognizing the Economic and Cultural Importance and Vitality of Vermont's Agricultural Community. 2003–2004, *http://www.leg.state.vt.us/docs/legdoc.cfm?RL =/docs/2004/acts/ACTR424.HTM.*

[4]Texas Emerging Technology Fund—White Paper, *http://www.utsystem.edu/news/2004/Emerging TechFundWhitePaper12-13-04.pdf.*

[5]Area Development—Site and Facility Planning, November 2004, *http://www.area-development.com/2005cd directory/pacific1.html*; Oregon Economic & Community Development Department, *http://www.econ.state.or. us/BIcosts.htm.*

[6]The State of California, *http://www.governor.ca. gov/state/govsite/gov_htmldisplay.jsp?BV_ SessionID= @ @ @ @ 0580427052.1103301742 @ @ @ @ &BV_ EngineID=cccgadddgehdlimcfngcfkmdffidfog.0&sFile Path=%2fgovsite%2fbiography%2fbio_arnold_schwarzeneggerhtml& sTitle=Arnold+Schwarzenegger+Biography&sCatTitle=Biographies.*

[7]California Commission for Jobs and Economic Growth, *http://4cajobs.com/press/20040803.*

[8]California Commission for Jobs and Economic Growth, *http://4cajobs.com/press/kit/roppongipress kit.pdf.*

About the Author

Jeffrey Finkle, a 20-year veteran in the world of economic development, is president and CEO of the Washington, D.C.-based Intentional Economic Development Council. Finkle, who earned a Bachelor of Science degree in communications form Ohio University and studied business administration at the graduate level at Ohio State University, also has a history in the public sector, having served as deputy assistant secretary of Community Planning and Development for program management with the United States Department of Housing and Urban Development.

Federal Incentives Ruling and the Corporate Attraction Process

By Adam Bruns

Economic developers and elected officials have long faced accusations of "corporate welfare" for the methods they use to lure companies to their turf. But a federal appeals court ruling in September 2004 that called certain Ohio tax breaks unconstitutional has also suddenly called everyone's turf into question. While companies and states alike scramble for certainty in making the case for projects, the legal case may eventually wind its way to the Supreme Court.

September 2004 saw hurricanes on two coasts and a major earthquake on another, but it was a federal appeals court decision in the U.S. heartland that packed an economic development wallop still awaiting measurement.

On Sept. 2, the U.S. Court of Appeals for the Sixth Circuit—whose jurisdiction encompasses automotive corridor states Michigan, Ohio, Kentucky and Tennessee—ruled after 19 months of deliberation that the State of Ohio's machinery and equipment investment tax credit program violates the Commerce Clause of the U.S. Constitution. Yet the same ruling determined that the state's property tax abatement program passed federal and state muster.

An immediate move was made to file an *en banc* petition, placing the case—*Charlotte Cuno, et al. v. DaimlerChrysler, Inc., et al*—before the entire 13 active judges on the Sixth Circuit's roster, rather than just the panel of three that issued the ruling. Whether ruling on that petition will be expedited remains to be seen. In the meantime, professionals on all sides of the site selection equation are scrambling to determine what the ruling means in the short and long term for projects either already under way or pending across the country. Many saw some confounding rationale in the 18-page court document.

"It's a very broad and troubling decision, based on peculiar legal reasoning," said Jay Biggins, managing director, national incentives, for Stadtmauer Bailkin Biggins, based in Princeton, N.J. "It injects uncertainty into a process that craves predictability. It's turned a lot of planning involving billions of dollars on its head."

Briefs of support for Ohio and DaimlerChrysler have been filed by a wide cross-section of industry players. That includes the United Auto Workers (UAW), whose membership includes 3,628 active members at the Jeep plant in Toledo, Ohio, where incentives related to its 1998 construction precipitated the lawsuit. The original project was a $1.2 bil-

lion blockbuster, and the incentives in question were valued at up to $90 million over seven years, of which the company has claimed a relatively small portion. Meanwhile, DaimlerChrysler, along with three major suppliers, just announced another $900 million investment in the complex in the summer of 2004.

"We don't expect it to derail the project," said Eileen Granata, interim COO for the Regional Growth Partnership (RGP) in Toledo in fall 2004, noting another ongoing expansion at Libbey Glass. In fact, Toledo industrial activity is churning at its highest level in years. As for other prospects, "it's early to say it's driving projects away," she said, but it "hasn't been a helpful part of those discussions, particularly against other states not in the sixth district. Look at projects in which we're competing with Indiana—we have seen that in a couple of those cases, we're significantly more at risk. From a manufacturing standpoint, one of your biggest tools is suddenly gone."

Indeed, not long after the ruling was issued, Indiana was the grateful recipient of a new automotive plant announcement from Canada's Magna International, as well as a $12.9 million investment from Illinois-based plumbing technology company Geberit Manufacturing, which also has operations in Ohio, as well as Wisconsin and Alabama.

The turmoil is taking place against the backdrop of a regional automotive industry economy that is unparalleled in its impact on the nation's economy at large: One in 10 jobs in the United States is in some way connected to the automotive industry. And if companies are subjected to increasing uncertainty about the financial conditions under which they operate, they immediately search out more stable ground. That could mean foreign ground, including NAFTA neighbor Canada, where it's one in seven jobs that are automotive-related. Coincidentally, that country has just stepped up to the incentives bargaining table after years of avoiding it, with both federal and Ontario incentive programs helping to stoke major project announcements from automotive OEMs in the fall of 2004.

In contrast to the court panel's apparent aim to level the proverbial playing field, UAW attorneys noted that the decision, by not taking into account the historical development of different states' economies, "creates a situation in which the playing field has not been leveled but rather has been tilted—even if unintentionally—in favor of some states."

The brief goes on to cite a 2003 study by the Center for Automotive Research. Because of differences in how their regional economies have developed, northern states offer incentive packages including 83 percent tax abatements and 13 percent infrastructure improvements, while southern states' packages included only 38 percent tax abatements, 44 percent infrastructure improvements and 18 percent employee training and recruitment. Other briefs in support come from Nissan North America and Ford Motor Co.

Prelude to Tax Reform?

"Stunned" was one adjective used by Bruce Johnson, director of the Ohio Department of Development, in describing his reaction to the ruling. "'Curious' would be another one," he said, "and frankly, reading the decision doesn't give me any more confidence."

Johnson appeared with other dignitaries in Columbus in September to honor Honda's 25 years of operations in the state, including five plants and a major R&D center. Part of the festivities was devoted to noting that for every dollar of the $27 million in direct incentives Honda has received in that time, the company has invested $226 in Ohio operations. The state was further relieved later in the fall when Honda, as part of a series of global project announcements, announced a further $100-million investment in its Russells Point, Ohio, operations.

But away from the spotlight, "the manufacturing community is extremely concerned about it," Johnson said of the ruling. "How do we handle our credits already offered? How is the state tax department going to handle various filings?"

An example of just such a quandary was offered up by Ohio Gov. Bob Taft's office on Sept. 7, when it announced various incentives for prospective projects. One was a pending $3.2-million, 25-job expansion by Jim Beam Brands Co. at its Cincinnati location, which currently employs 123 people. Part of the package was $360,000 in the form of a Manufacturing & Equipment (M&E) tax credit, the very program now deemed unconstitutional.

The incentive package for a new Dell fulfillment center in the Cincinnati suburb of West Chester does not include the suddenly illegal credits, but Melissa Koehler, director of West Chester Economic Development, said, "The credit was our top tool for helping existing manufacturers grow. The reason the tax credit was a good business retention stimulus is what I call 'silent growth' — existing companies that invest significantly in new machines and technology but are not physically expanding their buildings and don't make the news. For these companies, who often don't meet requirements for the big-bang programs like property tax abatements, the M&E credit was a 'cash back' deal that directly returned funds to them to reinvest in jobs and better technology."

"The only way to compete on a global basis is to keep costs down for these companies," said Michael Mullady, a Columbus-based senior associate with the Industrial Properties division of CB Richard Ellis. "Issues with labor rates or tax incentives are typically why we're losing. 'Our abatements are burning off, so we're moving' is a constant threat, but the states do a great job of balancing out each other on incentives."

As several experts point out, the language of the decision casts no aspersions on direct subsidies—"according to this decision, just handing them cash is okay," said Johnson. This and other aspects of incentives will no doubt be front and center on the agendas of several state legislatures.

"In the spring, the legislature will have to confront this," said Johnson, who is keen on comprehensive tax reform that addresses "lowering rates, broadening the base, reducing the penalty on capital expenditures and regulatory reform too." Meanwhile, he didn't want to exaggerate the impact of just one legal ruling on Ohio's competitiveness: "We think Ohio started out and continues to be competitive," he said. "The bottom line is how do we encourage people to make investments in our state? Some [incentives] create jobs and some just create productivity. Both are critically important."

Do Breaks Bring Boom?

In research published early in 2004, UCLA economist Enrico Moretti and MIT's Michael Greenstone used "million-dollar plant" stories and data from the archives of *Site Selection* to look at the ongoing economic vitality of 82 chosen communities vs. the runner-up cities. The study found that cities chosen for major projects have benefited from their arrangements, with concessions made up for by such factors as increased property values (averaging a 1.1 percent increase), higher public spending in areas like education and faster payroll growth in the plant's industry sector (an average 1.5 percent increase). The economists also noted the "spillover effect" of new plants, as neighboring towns saw job growth. "Overall," they wrote, "the results undermine the popular view that the provision of local subsidies to attract large industrial plants reduces local residents' welfare."

Such findings go against the grain of the Ohio case's plaintiffs, who were backed in large part by Ralph Nader. But the findings may actually fuel the legal argument against the Ohio subsidies rather than quell it, since they support the notion of concrete benefits attached to tax breaks, therefore providing evidence of competitive advantage vs. other states.

DaimlerChrysler and others are as worried about the effects of the ruling in other states as much as in Ohio, since about 40 states offer some version of machinery and equipment tax break. In fellow Sixth District state Michigan, for example, a machinery and equipment tax credit is part of the single business tax. Michigan Economic Development Corp. was indeed one of many filing briefs in support of the petition. And that's fitting, since its chief, Don Jakeway, was not only at the helm of RGP when the original Jeep deal was negotiated, but headed the Ohio Department of Development when the investment tax credit program under scrutiny came into being.

"This is the first real win for folks that really don't want anybody to do anything in this arena," he said. "I'm not pushing any panic buttons, and I'm not recommending anybody else do that. Yet it's very important we be proactive and step forward and be supportive, because the issues that are going to be addressed are very important issues, whether this is Ohio or Michigan or Arizona or Louisiana or Mississippi. This could represent a rather dramatic change in how economic development has taken place for at least as long as I've been doing it, over 20 years."

Jakeway is concerned about the level of risk now introduced into both past and prospective investment agreements. And he's concerned about a general setback for economic development professionals, who he says have come a long way in not only professionalizing their methods, but in making incentives performance-based — a detail often lost on incentives critics.

"These are the kind of programs that turned around Ohio's entire economy in the 1990s," he said. "Tax credits were used for people to spend their money

when we needed them to do it. They worked. Every company that got to take advantage of them would tell you that. And a lot of factors calculated into that ROI."

Indeed, when ROI and tracking of advantage are analyzed from the corporate or community point of view, a wide range of tax-related programs could conceivably find themselves in the crosshairs.

"The arguments they used for the interstate commerce clause being violated could have been applied to any tax structure a state has," said Brian Corde, director, location strategies, for New Jersey-based incentives negotiation and site selection firm Mintax. "In the state of Ohio, they use a multiple factor apportionment scheme. The argument would be 'If I build this facility in Ohio, by doing that I'd create tax, increase the factor, and increase tax in that state. Why shouldn't Ohio reduce my tax then?' They're just giving back a portion of what they're taking anyway." (Ohio's apportionment scheme is 60 percent sales, 20 percent payroll and 20 percent property.) Consulting firms like these are analyzing the ramifications for similar credits offered in more than 40 states, "and we are exploring alternative transaction structuring strategies which would safeguard projects from this uncertainty," said Biggins.

The Ultimate Authority

Several experts point out that tax systems themselves, with their varying apportionment formulas, create incentives to be in one state or another. In other words, it's not that big a leap from the particulars of this one case to the general principles that it calls into question. Granata, a licensed attorney in the state of Ohio with a background as an economist and financial officer, observed that apportionment factors have moved all over the board in recent years. A number of states have gone to a 100 percent sales basis for computation of corporate income or franchise taxes. How various factors are worked into taxation formulas "can have some peculiar impacts, particularly when companies are really multi-state," she said. "Tax systems themselves really create to some extent incentives to be in one state or another, and would treat you disparately based on whether you're in that state or outside that state."

But don't make the leap from the specifics of this case too fast, cautioned Corde. "The broad ramifications of this decision probably aren't as widespread as some people would like to believe," he said, describing how many companies may not reach the tax level that causes the credits to kick in that quickly. But the fact that the original case was backed by a Nader-affiliated group means the threat of similar suits in other circuits is very real. And Jay Biggins says the protracted length of time it may take the en banc petition to slog through the legal process only further destabilizes decision-making.

Allusions made in the ruling to Supreme Court statements prompt the question on many minds: Will the question of incentives—like the question of eminent domain currently before the justices— eventually get an answer from the country's highest judiciary authority? Jakeway and others say that's a possibility. If it does, Jay Biggins volunteered some historical context.

"Most litigation surrounding the Commerce Clause occurred within the first 50 years of its adoption," he says, "when all the states were still trying to get used to the pre-emptive power of the federal government. This is an anachronistic interpretation of the Commerce Clause."

The panel of judges, he continued, "purports to premise the decision on an economic reality test, when the economic reality is that any state that chooses to compete for incremental investment can do so. States determine where on the playing field they want to stand. Companies determine what states they want to locate in. It is an open, free, functioning and efficient market, best left alone."

About the Author

Adam Bruns is managing editor of *Site Selection*, a business publication published by Conway Data Inc. since 1954. Based in the Atlanta suburb of Norcross, the magazine covers the fields of corporate real estate and economic development.

Table A
FINANCIAL ASSISTANCE FOR INDUSTRY

State or other jurisdiction	State-sponsored industrial development authority	Privately sponsored development credit corporation	State authority or agency revenue bond financing	State authority or agency general obligation bond financing	City and/or county revenue bond financing	City and/or County General obligation bond financing	State loans for building construction	State loans for equipment machinery	City and/or county loans for building construction	City and/or county loans for equipment, machinery	State loan guarantees for building construction	State loan guarantees for equipment, machinery	City and/or county loan guarantees for building construction	City and/or county loan guarantees for equipment, machinery	State financing aid for existing plant expansion	State matching funds for city and/or county industrial financing programs	State incentive for establishing industrial plants in areas of high unemployment	City and/or county incentive for establishing industrial plants in areas of high unemployment
Alabama	★	★	★		★	★	★	★	★	★	★	★			★		★	★
Alaska	★		★	★	★	★	★	★	★	★	★	★			★	★	★	★
Arizona	★	★			★	★	★	★	★	★					★		★	★
Arkansas	★	★	★	★	★	★	★	★	★	★	★	★	★	★	★		★	★
California	★	★	★		★		★	★	★	★	★	★			★		★	★
Colorado	★	★	★		★	★			★	★					★	★	★	★
Connecticut	★	★	★	★	★	★	★	★	★	★	★	★	★	★	★	★	★	★
Delaware		★	★		★	★			★	★					★		★	★
Florida	★	★	★		★	★			★	★					★	★	★	★
Georgia	★		★		★	★			★	★					★	★	★	★
Hawaii		★	★	★	★	★	★	★	★	★	★	★	★	★	★	★	★	
Idaho	★				★	★			★	★					★		★	★
Illinois	★	★	★	★	★	★	★	★	★	★	★	★	★	★	★	★	★	★
Indiana	★	★	★		★	★			★	★					★	★	★	★
Iowa		★	★	★	★	★	★	★	★	★			★	★	★	★	★	★
Kansas		★	★	★	★	★	★	★	★	★	★	★	★	★	★	★	★	★
Kentucky	★	★	★	★	★	★	★	★	★	★			★	★	★	★	★	★
Louisiana	★		★	★	★	★	★	★	★	★	★	★	★	★	★	★	★	★
Maine	★	★	★	★	★	★	★	★	★	★	★	★	★	★	★	★	★	★
Maryland	★	★	★	★	★	★	★	★	★	★	★	★	★	★	★	★	★	★
Massachusetts	★	★	★	★	★	★	★	★	★	★	★	★	★	★	★	★	★	★
Michigan	★	★	★	★	★	★	★	★	★	★	★	★	★	★	★	★	★	★
Minnesota	★	★	★	★	★	★			★	★					★	★	★	★
Mississippi	★	★	★	★	★	★	★	★	★	★	★	★	★	★	★	★	★	★
Missouri	★		★		★	★	★	★	★	★	★	★	★	★	★	★	★	★
Montana	★	★	★	★	★	★	★	★	★	★	★	★	★	★	★		★	★
Nebraska		★	★		★	★			★	★					★		★	★
Nevada			★		★	★			★	★					★			★
New Hampshire	★	★	★	★	★	★	★	★	★	★	★	★	★	★	★		★	★
New Jersey	★	★	★		★	★	★	★	★	★	★	★	★	★	★		★	★
New Mexico	★	★	★	★	★	★			★	★					★		★	★
New York	★	★	★	★	★	★	★	★	★	★	★	★	★	★	★	★	★	★
North Carolina	★	★	★		★	★			★	★					★		★	★
North Dakota			★	★	★	★	★	★	★	★	★	★	★	★	★	★	★	★
Ohio	★	★	★		★	★	★	★	★	★	★	★	★	★	★	★	★	★

See footnotes at end of table.

FINANCIAL ASSISTANCE FOR INDUSTRY — Continued

State or other jurisdiction	State-sponsored industrial development authority	Privately sponsored development credit corporation	State authority or agency revenue bond financing	State authority or agency general obligation bond financing	City and/or county revenue bond financing	City and/or County General obligation bond financing	State loans for building construction	State loans for equipment machinery	City and/or county loans for building construction	City and/or county loans for equipment, machinery	State loan guarantees for building construction	State loan guarantees for equipment, machinery	City and/or county loan guarantees for building construction	City and/or county loan guarantees for equipment, machinery	State financing aid for existing plant expansion	State matching funds for city and/or county industrial financing programs	State incentive for establishing industrial plants in areas of high unemployment	City and/or county incentive for establishing industrial plants in areas of high unemployment
Oklahoma	★	...	★	★	★	★	★	★	★	★	★	★	★	★	★	★	★	★
Oregon	...	★	★	★	★	★	★	★	★	★	★	★	★	★	★	★	★	★
Pennsylvania	★	★	★	★	★	★	★	★	★	★	★	★	★	★	★	★	★	★
Rhode Island	★	★	★	★	★	...	★	★	★	★	...	★	...	...	★	★	★	★
South Carolina	★	★	★	...	★	★	★	★	★	★	★	...	★	★	★	...	★	...
South Dakota	★	...	★	★	★	★	★	★	★	★	...	...	...	...	★	★	...	...
Tennessee	...	...	★	★	★	★	★	★	★	★	...	★	...	...	★	★	★	★
Texas	★	★	★	★	★	★	★	★	★	★	★	★	★	★	★	★	★	★
Utah	★	★	...	...	★	★	...	...	★	★	...	★	...	...	...	...	★	...
Vermont	★	★	★	...	★	★	★	★	★	★	★	★	...	...	★	★	...	...
Virginia	★	★	★	...	★	★	★	★	...	...	...	★	...	...	★	★	★	★
Washington	★	★	★	...	★	...	★	★	★	★	...	★	...	...	...	★	★	...
West Virginia	★	★	★	...	★	★	★	★	★	★	★	★	★	★	★	★	...	...
Wisconsin	★	★	★	...	★	★	★	★	★	★	...	★	...	...	★	...	★	...
Wyoming	★	★	★	...	★	★	★	★	...	...	...	★	...	...	★	...	...	...
Puerto Rico	★	★	★	★	★	★	★	★	★	★	...	★	...	...	★	★	★	★

Source: Site Selection, November 2004.

Note: A significant number of footnotes are published with these charts in the November 2004 issue of *Site Selection* Magazine. For more information or to obtain a set of the footnotes, contact Editor Adam Bruns at adam.bruns@conway.com.

Key:
★ — Yes
. . .—No; or state/jurisdiction did not respond to survey.

Table B
TAX INCENTIVES FOR INDUSTRY

State or other jurisdiction	Corporate income tax exemption	Personal Income tax exemption	Excise tax exemption	Tax exemption or moratorium on land, capital improvements	Tax exemption or moratorium on equipment, machinery	Inventory tax exemption on goods in transit (freeport)	Tax exemption on manufacturers' inventories	Sales/use tax exemption on new equipment	Tax exemption on raw materials used in manufacturing	Tax incentive for creation of jobs	Tax incentive for industrial investment	Tax credits for use of specified state products	Tax stabilization agreements for specified industries	Tax exemption to encourage research and development	Accelerated depreciation of industrial equipment
Alabama	★	★	★	★	★	★	★	★	★	★	★			★	★
Alaska		★	★	★	★	★	★	★	★	★	★	★			★
Arizona	★	★	★	★	★	★	★	★	★	★	★			★	★
Arkansas	★			★	★	★	★	★	★	★	★	★		★	
California		★	★	★	★	★	★	★	★	★	★			★	★
Colorado	★		★	★	★	★	★	★	★	★	★				★
Connecticut	★	★	★	★	★	★	★	★	★	★	★		★	★	★
Delaware	★	★		★	★	★	★	★	★	★	★			★	★
Florida	★		★	★	★	★	★	★	★	★	★			★	★
Georgia	★	★		★	★	★	★	★	★	★	★			★	★
Hawaii	★	★	★	★	★	★	★	★	★	★	★		★	★	★
Idaho	★	★		★	★	★	★	★	★	★	★			★	★
Illinois	★	★	★	★	★	★	★	★	★	★	★			★	★
Indiana	★	★	★	★	★	★	★	★	★	★	★			★	★
Iowa	★				★	★	★	★	★	★	★				★
Kansas	★		★	★	★	★	★	★	★	★	★	★		★	★
Kentucky	★	★	★	★	★	★	★	★	★	★	★		★	★	★
Louisiana	★	★	★	★	★	★	★	★	★	★	★		★	★	★
Maine		★		★	★	★	★	★	★	★	★		★	★	★
Maryland	★	★	★	★	★	★	★	★	★	★	★			★	★
Massachusetts	★	★	★	★	★	★	★	★	★	★	★	★		★	★
Michigan	★	★	★	★	★	★	★	★	★	★	★			★	★
Minnesota	★	★	★	★	★	★	★	★	★	★	★			★	★
Mississippi	★	★	★	★	★	★	★	★	★	★	★		★	★	★
Missouri	★		★	★	★	★	★	★	★	★	★			★	★
Montana	★	★	★	★	★	★	★	★	★	★	★	★		★	★
Nebraska		★	★	★	★	★	★	★	★	★	★				★
Nevada	★					★	★	★	★	★	★				★
New Hampshire	★								★						
New Jersey	★	★	★	★	★	★	★	★	★	★	★			★	★
New Mexico								★	★						
New York	★	★		★	★	★	★	★	★	★	★	★		★	★
North Carolina	★		★	★	★	★	★	★	★	★	★			★	★
North Dakota					★	★	★	★	★	★	★			★	★
Ohio	★	★		★	★	★	★	★	★	★	★			★	★

See footnotes at end of table.

TAX INCENTIVES FOR INDUSTRY — Continued

State or other jurisdiction	Corporate income tax exemption	Personal Income tax exemption	Excise tax exemption	Tax exemption or moratorium on land, capital improvements	Tax exemption or moratorium on equipment, machinery	Inventory tax exemption on goods in transit (freeport)	Tax exemption on manufacturers' inventories	Sales/use tax exemption on new equipment	Tax exemption on raw materials used in manufacturing	Tax incentive for creation of jobs	Tax incentive for industrial investment	Tax credits for use of specified state products	Tax stabilization agreements for specified industries	Tax exemption to encourage research and development	Accelerated depreciation of industrial equipment
Oklahoma	★	★	★	★	★	★	★	★	★	★	★	★	★	★	★
Oregon	…	…	★	★	★	★	★	★	★	…	★	…	…	★	★
Pennsylvania	…	…	★	★	★	★	★	★	★	★	★	★	…	★	★
Rhode Island	★	…	★	★	★	★	★	★	★	★	★	★	★	★	★
South Carolina	★	★	…	★	★	★	★	★	★	★	★	…	…	★	★
South Dakota	★	★	★	★	…	★	★	★	★	★	★	…	…	★	★
Tennessee	★	★	★	★	★	★	★	★	★	★	★	…	…	★	★
Texas	…	…	…	★	★	★	…	★	★	★	★	…	…	★	…
Utah	★	…	★	…	★	★	★	★	★	★	…	…	★	…	★
Vermont	★	…	★	…	…	★	★	★	★	★	★	…	★	…	★
Virginia	★	★	★	★	★	★	★	★	★	★	★	…	…	★	★
Washington	★	★	…	…	★	★	★	★	★	★	★	★	…	★	…
West Virginia	★	…	…	★	…	★	…	★	★	★	★	…	…	★	★
Wisconsin	…	★	…	…	★	★	★	★	★	★	★	…	…	★	★
Wyoming	★	★	…	…	…	★	★	…	★	…	…	…	…	…	…
Puerto Rico	★	★	★	★	★	★	★	★	★	★	★	★	★	★	★

Source: Site Selection, November 2004.

Note: A significant number of footnotes are published with these charts in the November 2004 issue of Site Selection magazine. For more information or to obtain a set of the footnotes, contact Editor Adam Bruns at adam.bruns@conway.com.

Key:
★—Yes
…—No; or state/jurisdiction did not respond to survey.

State Science and Technology: Best Practices

By Marc Holzer and Richard Schwester

In a global economy it will be difficult for states to maintain an economic base as low-cost producers of goods and services. States must, therefore, foster innovation and entrepreneurship in order to bring advanced technologies to market ahead of their global competitors. If our country is to maintain its current standard of living, then government must support innovation, particularly in science and technology, where it already has a competitive advantage over other nations.

In a global economy it will be difficult for states to maintain an economic base as low-cost producers of goods and services. States must, therefore, foster innovation and entrepreneurship in order to bring advanced technologies to market ahead of their global competitors. If our country is to maintain its current standard of living, then government must support innovation, particularly in science and technology, where it already has a competitive advantage over other nations. This article begins with a comparative examination of science and technology efforts throughout Georgia, Maryland, Massachusetts, New Jersey, New York, North Carolina, Pennsylvania and Wisconsin. Emphasis is placed on programs dealing with university research and development (R&D), science and technology business assistance, in addition to collaborative efforts between university and industry leaders. All of these states recognize the opportunities for future economic growth inherent in R&D investments, and consequently have invested significant resources toward bolstering their respective science and technology infrastructures. This article further examines the governance structure of state science and technology entities, and concludes with recommendations that we hope will enable states to better harness their science and technology capabilities.

State Science and Technology Initiatives

University R&D and Industry Collaboration

The Georgia Research Alliance's Innovation Fund encourages research collaborations among the state's academic and business communities. The purpose is to foster technology development with commercial viability. The GRA's Innovation Fund fosters close collaboration between university scientists and their industry counterparts. The program provides direct linkages to the problems and interests of industry, and directs the capabilities of Georgia's research universities to specific industry needs, such as advanced communications, bioscience, nanoscience and advanced materials. Proposals are accepted from the University of Georgia, the Medical College of Georgia, Emory University, Clark Atlanta University, the Georgia Institute of Technology and Georgia State University. Innovation Fund recipients are awarded a maximum of $100,000, which must be matched by a Georgia-based industrial partner.

A primary focus of the New Jersey Commission on Science and Technology (NJCST) has been strengthening ties between university researchers and industry leaders through innovation zones. Innovation zones are geographic areas within close proximity to universities. Technology businesses located within these zones are eligible for financial incentives and support services (e.g. access to university facilities). Financial incentives include springboard funding (up to $300,000) for businesses working toward product development with commercial viability.

The New York State Office of Science, Technology, and Academic Research (NYSTAR) is an impressive model regarding university-based science and technology research. NYSTAR's Centers of Excellence, which are housed at universities throughout the state, are designed to focus on emerging technologies within high-growth markets. The 2002–2003 state budget allocated $250 million for further development of the Centers of Excellence, which focus on research pertaining to bioinformatics, environmental systems, nano-electronics, photonics and information technology. It is expected that the state's $250 million investment will leverage an addition $1 billion from private sector and federal government sources.

NYSTAR's Gen*NY*sis (Generating Employment through New York State Science) Center program provides the intellectual infrastructure necessary for the expansion of high technology research and the achievement of scientific breakthroughs. Gen*NY*sis Centers emphasize the life sciences, biotechnology, biomaterials and biomedical engineering research, which will help promote economic development through the creation of new bioscience and technology-based businesses. The 2002–2003 state budget allocated $225 million for the Gen*NY*sis Center program.

NYSTAR has further stressed the importance of moving the state's scientific and technological know how from the laboratory to the marketplace. NYSTAR's Centers for Advanced Technology (CATs) are designed to promote collaborative S&T research among the state's university and industry leaders. Emphasis is placed on R&D efforts that lead to commercially viable technologies and processes.

Science and Technology Business Assistance

The Massachusetts Technology Development Corporation (MTDC) represents a unique model in terms of science and technology business assistance. The MTDC is a state-controlled venture capital corporation that works to create technology-based employment, attract greater private investment in Massachusetts' technology companies, and encourage entrepreneurship. The MTDC operates three capital investment programs, the Traditional Investment Fund and two Commonwealth Investment Fund Programs. The Traditional Investment Fund is geared toward technology companies seeking between $1 and $3 million. The MTDC differs from the traditional venture capital corporation given its willingness to invest in start-up companies that have yet to establish a record of accomplishment. Approximately 80 percent of MTDC investments are made to start-ups. The MTDC typically provides between $300,000 and $500,000 of a total investment of $1 to $3 million. Private and co-investors provide the balance, and investments are made as equity, debt or a combination.

The Commonwealth Fund I was started in 1993 with $3 million from the MTDC and $1 million from two of the state's largest lending institutions, BancBoston and Fleet Bank. The Commonwealth Fund I makes investments ranging from $200,000 to $300,000 in follow-up financing for science and technology start-ups. The Commonwealth Fund Investment Program II established a $15 million investment pool. This investment program began in July 2000 with $12 million from MTDC, and an additional $2 million from BancBoston and $1 million from the Essex Regional Retirement Board. Initial investments range from $300,000 to $600,000.

From FY1980 through FY1999, early stage technology investments have yielded a 17 percent rate of return, which compares favorably to private seed and start-up venture capital funds. Since 1980, cumulative net equity gains from MTDC investments have totaled over $28 million. The MTDC has been a self-supporting state corporation since 1988. Through December 1999, 55 MTDC companies reported employing a total of 10,000 individuals, generating an annual payroll of approximately $500 million, and state tax revenues totaling more than $24 million.

The Ben Franklin Technology Partners (BFTP) in Pennsylvania is a regional network that offers direct assistance to technology-based companies and venture capital organizations that support tech-based companies throughout Pennsylvania. There are four regional technology partners, which are funded by the Pennsylvania Department of Economic Development. Base funding for the technology partners is approximately $27.5 million. The BFTP support the development and application of new products and technologies among entrepreneurs and companies. This results in the creation of jobs, the successful development of promising start-ups, and the growth of established companies.

The BFTP annually select a number of clients in which to invest. High priority is given to clients possessing the potential to create jobs. Interested client representatives must meet with Ben Franklin staff to discuss their vision and goals. If there is a match between the company's objectives and Ben Franklin's, the staff will discuss potential resources and services available. In cases where significant funds are needed, and the potential results of the assistance will produce sufficient benefits to the regional economy, the Ben Franklin Partners aid the client in preparing a formal request for funding. Investment recipients are expected to repay BFTP, which ensures the solvency of the program. In addition to providing direct funding support, BFTP draw upon outside sources of support. For example, a Ben Franklin Partner may solicit expert assistance from university faculty members or proven business professionals in areas such as strategy development, market positioning, acquiring capital, business planning, human resources and technical issues/opportunities.

The Technology Development Corporation of Maryland (TEDCO) has, in part, concentrated its efforts in the area of business incubation. TEDCO's incubator activities are guided by the assistance of a Business Incubator Technical Advisory Committee. TEDCO's board of directors appoints members to the committee who represent a cross-section of the state's business incubation, real estate and entrepreneurial communities. TEDCO further provides direct financial assistance to existing state incubators, operating under the assumption that TEDCO investments will help leverage additional resources. Similarly, the New Jersey Commission on Science and Technology has emphasized business incubation as part of its science and technology business development activities.

NYSTAR's Science and Technology Law Center provides resources for small and early stage companies working to succeed within an increasingly complex marketplace. The Law Center seeks to educate entrepreneurs and business owners about complex legal issues relevant to the protection of intellectual property, technology transfer, patent applications, licensing agreements, capital procurement and university/industrial partnerships. The Law Center further examines issues relevant to emerging industry sectors that could potentially influence New York companies and universities, and promotes economic development through university-based research and product commercialization in high technology industries.

Advisory Function

The North Carolina Board of Science and Technology (NBCST) was established to promote and support the growth of the state's scientific, engineering, and industrial research capabilities. The board does not run any projects or programs per se; rather, it serves in an advisory capacity to the governor and the General Assembly. The NCBST is charged with developing strategic plans. The most recent strategic plan, Vision 2030, outlines 10 recommendations. Each recommendation fits into the concept of economic development through a rededication to science and technology-based endeavors.

The Wisconsin Technology Council (WTC) is an independent, non-profit corporation created in 2001 by the state Legislature. The WTC performs a strategic planning function. For example, the WTC seeks to build Wisconsin's Technology Clusters, establish Research Centers of Excellence, and create an Institute for Interdisciplinary Research.

S&T Governance Structures

The Massachusetts Technology Development Cor-

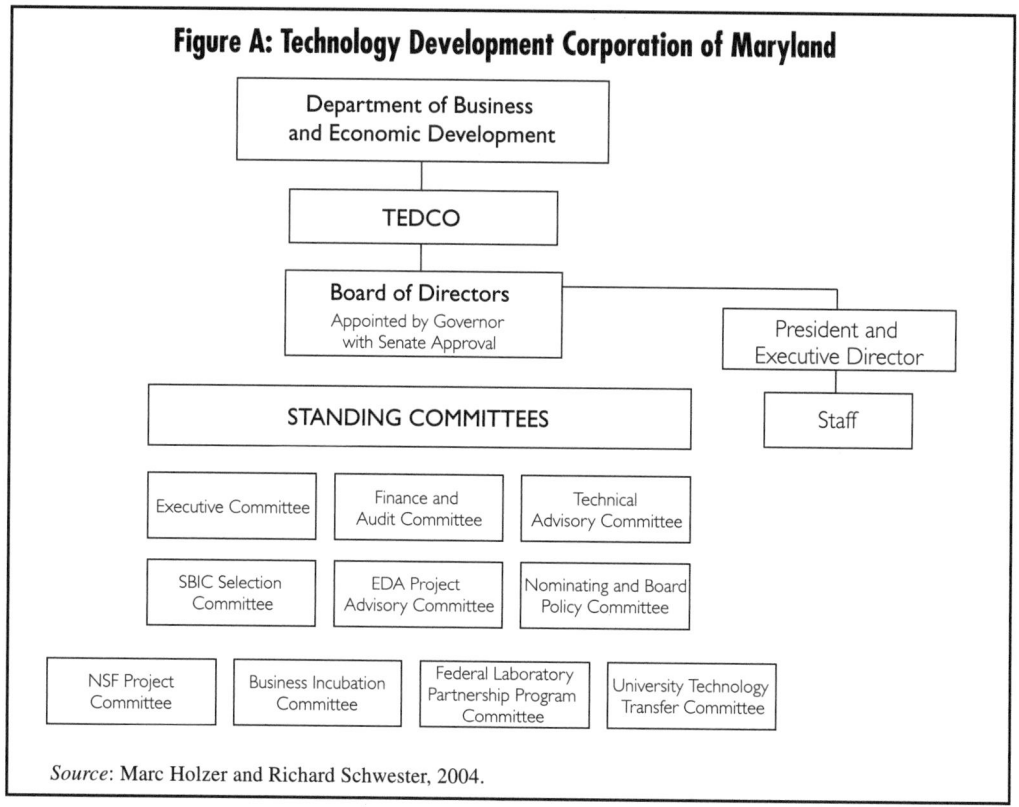

Figure A: Technology Development Corporation of Maryland

Source: Marc Holzer and Richard Schwester, 2004.

poration (MTDC) is a venture capital corporation created by the state legislature in 1978. The MTDC seeks to create technology-based jobs, attract greater private investment in the state's technology companies, and encourage entrepreneurship. An eleven-member board of directors governs the MTDC, which is responsible for approving all capital investments. MTDC Board members include private investors, legal experts, entrepreneurial management consultants, business leaders, academics, and government representatives.

Established in 1998, the Technology Development Corporation of Maryland (TEDCO) works to foster technology commercialization, create high technology businesses, and support university-based R&D. The Department of Business and Economic Development provides TEDCO with funding and legal council through the attorney general's office. TEDCO is governed by a 15-member board, which is appointed by the governor with advice and consent of the Senate. Board members must be residents of Maryland, representing the non-profit research sector, venture capital financing, technology-based businesses, the general public, and colleges and universities. The Board is geographically representative, and its responsibilities include: reviewing and auditing financial statements, approving a fiscal year budget for operations, program expenditures, and investments in technology development. Figure A shows the governance structure of TEDCO.

The New Jersey Commission on Science and Technology is consists of eight individuals representing the public, two individuals representing the state legislature, and two university presidents (New Jersey Institute of Technology and Princeton University). Three ex-officio members represent the Commerce and Economic Growth Commission, the Department of Education, and the Governor's Office. There are two standing committees of the Commission, the Technology Business Development Committee and the Scientific Fields Committee. They play a role in the determination of awards in their respective areas.

The New York State Office of Science, Technology, and Academic Research (NYSTAR) is a state agency within the Executive Department. Overseen by the governor, NYSTAR is headed by an executive director who is appointed by the governor and confirmed by the state Senate. The executive director supervises NYSTAR's programs and staff. The agency maintains an Advisory Council, headed by a chairman who is appointed by the governor. The governor, the majority leader of the Senate, or the speaker of the Assembly appoint the remaining members of NYSTAR's Advisory Council. The council works with NYSTAR to ensure that the NYSTAR's funding is channeled toward high-technology R&D having the potential to engender tangible economic benefits. The Advisory Council is comprised of academic, business, and scientific community leaders. Council members drawn from the public are expected to have at least five years of scientific or entrepreneurial experience with technologically oriented

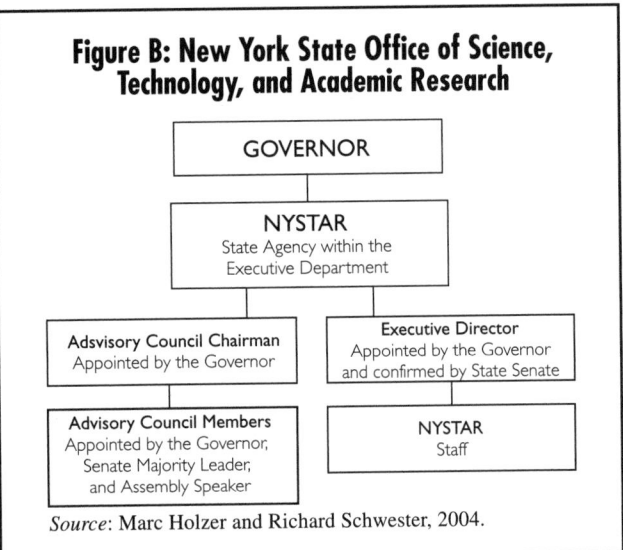

Figure B: New York State Office of Science, Technology, and Academic Research

GOVERNOR

NYSTAR
State Agency within the
Executive Department

Adsvisory Council Chairman
Appointed by the Governor

Executive Director
Appointed by the Governor
and confirmed by State Senate

Advisory Council Members
Appointed by the Governor,
Senate Majority Leader,
and Assembly Speaker

NYSTAR
Staff

Source: Marc Holzer and Richard Schwester, 2004.

business. NYSTAR's governance structure is presented below in Figure B.

The North Carolina Board of Science and Technology (NCBST) serves in an advisory capacity to the governor and the legislature. The NCBST is housed in the Department of Commerce, and its members are statutorily pre-determined. The NCBST's membership includes:

- The governor;
- The secretary of commerce;
- One member from the University of North Carolina at Chapel Hill;
- One member from North Carolina State University;

- Two members from other components of the University of North Carolina;
- One member from Duke University;
- One member from a private college or university other than Duke;
- One member from the Research Triangle Institute;
- One member from the Microelectronics Center of North Carolina;
- One member from the North Carolina Biotechnology Center;
- Four members from private industry in North Carolina;
- Two members from public agencies in North Carolina; and
- Two members appointed by the General Assembly.

By statutorily pre-determining the NCBST's makeup, there is a reasonable measure of assurance that the board is bipartisan and represents the interests of the state's academic and business communities. Similar to the NCBST, the Wisconsin Technology Council (WTC) is an independent organization created by the state legislature in 2001. The WTC serves in an advisory capacity to the governor and the legislature, and it consists of 41 individuals representing high-technology businesses, academic institutions, venture capital organizations and government. The president and

Executive Committee of the WTC manage the day-to-day operations.

The Ben Franklin Technology Development Authority governs the Ben Franklin Technology Partners. The director of statewide affairs for the BFTP is responsible for coordinating the technology partner's involvement in key initiatives undertaken by the state. The director of statewide affairs further serves as the primary liaison among the four Ben Franklin partners, implements opportunities for joint initiatives, and serves as liaison to the governor and the legislature. Each Ben Franklin Technology Partner maintains a board of directors. The boards are responsible for approving all funding and investment recommendations. Figure C below shows the governance structure of both the Ben Franklin Technology Development Authority and the Ben Franklin Technology Partners.

The Georgia Research Alliance (GRA) is a non-profit, independent company representing a public-private partnership. The GRA emphasizes economic development by better leveraging the research capabilities of the state's university infrastructure. The GRA further assists in the development of science and technology-based industry, commerce and businesses. This model is distinctive in that it is not a government entity, yet the GRA serves as the linchpin for a powerful partnership that includes government, academia, and

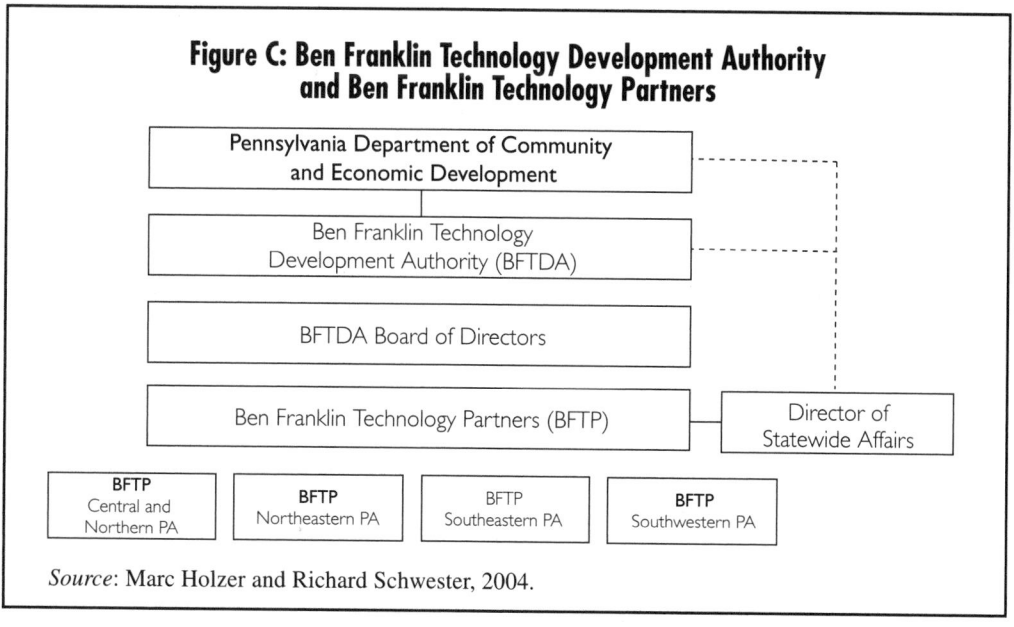

Figure C: Ben Franklin Technology Development Authority and Ben Franklin Technology Partners

Source: Marc Holzer and Richard Schwester, 2004.

the state's business community.

Recommendations Based Upon a Review of the Programs Above

Recommendation 1

Addressing the need for qualified policy advice and coordination of science and technology initiatives is imperative, and therefore we recommend the creation of a science and technology advisor in the office of the governor. This position would be similar to the national science advisor, who is appointed by the president to oversee the National Institute of Health, the National Science Foundation, and to advise the president on science and technology policy. The science and technology advisor should assist in coordination and priority setting, and he/she must have impeccable credentials in the areas of science and technology. We recommend that at a minimum the advisor have an earned doctorate in a relevant field of science and technology, a strong record of research and publications, and leadership experience in both the public and private sectors. The science and technology advisor should coordinate a statewide strategic planning process for science and technology. The strategic planning process should address the goals below. The science and technology advisor should articulate the specific goals and growth investment areas for state development after a due diligence process to identify such opportunities.

Recommendation 2

We recommend the creation of a Science and Technology Advisory Council to make strategic and policy recommendations to the governor in conjunction with the science and technology advisor. The Science and Technology Advisory Council should consist of apolitical, high profile scientists and university and industry leaders with knowledge of the implications of science and technology on public policy. The Science and Technology Advisory Council should consist of eight members, four with expertise in R&D in science and technology and four members to represent the leaders of science and technology industries. The advisory council should assist the governor in setting priorities for New Jersey's research and economic development priorities, and should provide guidance to the governor's science and technology advisor relating to the statewide strategic planning process.

Recommendation 3

A statewide strategic planning process, for all state agencies with an interest in economic and business development in science and technology, must be implemented. We recommend that the governor's science and technology advisor coordinate this strategic planning process. The statewide science and technology strategic plan process should be updated annually and should:

1. Identify the stakeholders in science and technology throughout the state and determine areas and initiatives that stakeholders deem to be a priority for New Jersey workers.

2. Identify the areas where the state deficient based on stakeholder views and other science and technology research.

3. Develop a timetable for what is necessary and feasible, and which may well incorporate objectives beyond mere incrementalism.

4. Identify goals, and how the state's science and technology programs might or should address those goals.

5. Require state agencies to benchmark their programs to these strategic goals.

6. Recognize that other states, and their public research universities, are competing for federal research dollars and private research funding.

The globalization of the American economy, increased commercial productivity from improved

Table A: State Science and Technology Models

State	S&T Entity	Model
Georgia	Georgia Research Alliance (GRA)	Non-profit Model
Massachusetts	Massachusetts Technology Development Corporation (MTDC)	Venture Capital Model
Maryland	Technology Development Corporation (TEDCO(	Business and University Assistance Model
New Jersey	New Jersey Commission on Science and Technology (NJCST)	Business and University Assistance Model
New York	New York State Office of Science, Technology and Academic Research (NYSTAR)	Business and University Assistance Model
North Carolina	North Carolina Board of Science and Technology	Advisory Model
Pennsylvania	Ben Franklin Technology Development Development Authority (BFTDA)	Business and University Assistance Model
Wisconsin	Wisconsin Technology Council (WTC)	Advisory Model

Source: Marc Holzer and Richard Schwester, 2004.

computer and information technologies and processes, as well as increased mobility have eroded many traditional employment opportunities throughout the United States. The continued prosperity of the United States since World War II has been enhanced by the recognition at the federal level of the role of longer-term scientific research in future economic development. To remain competitive in the emerging knowledge-based economy, states must continue to develop and maintain a world-class university research environment that will create innovations in technology. Those innovations can then be transferred to the commercial knowledge market.

References

BFTP (Ben Franklin Technology Partners). "Ben Franklin Program Overview." *http://www.nep.benfranklin. org/about/progWrks.cfm.*

GRA (Georgia Research Alliance). "Innovation Fund Program Announcement." *http://www.gra.org/documents/ FY05_Program_Announcement.doc.*

MTDC (Massachusetts Technology Development Corporation). 2000. "Annual Report." *http://www.mtdc.com/ annualreport.html.*

NCBST (North Carolina board of Science and Technology). *Mapping the Vision 2: Vision 2030. http://www. ncscienceandtechnology.com/PDF/Vision2030/Mapping TheVision2.pdf.*

NJCST (New Jersey Commission on Science and Technology). "Innovation Zones." *http://www.state.nj.us/ scitech/iz_what.html.*

NYSTAR (New York State Office of Science, Technology and Academic Research). "Centers for Advanced Technology." *http://www.nystar.state.ny.us/cats.htm.*

NYSTAR (New York State Office of Science, Technology and Academic Research). "Gen*NY*sis Centers." *http://www.nystar.state.ny.us/gennysis.htm.*

NYSTAR (New York State Office of Science, Technology and Academic Research). "Research Center Programs." *http://www.nystar.state.ny.us/research_programs.htm.*

NYSTAR (New York State Office of Science, Technology and Academic Research). "Science and Technology Law Center." *http://www.nystar.state.ny.us/stlc.htm.*

State Science and Technology Institute (SSTI). 2000. "SSTI Program Brief: Massachusetts Technology Development Corporation." March. http://www.ssti.org.

TEDCO (Maryland Technology Development Corporation). 2004. "Annual Report." *http://www.marylandtedco. org/resources/publication_pdfs/2004Report_Final.pdf.*

Wisconsin Technology Council. 2002. *Vision 2020: A Model Wisconsin Economy. http://www.wisconsin technologycouncil.com/vision_2020Vision_2020_ web2.pdf.*

About the Authors

Marc Holzer is chair and professor of the Graduate Department of Public Administration, Rutgers University-Newark and executive director of the National Center for Public Productivity. He holds a Ph.D. in Political Science and a Master of Public Administration degree, both from the University of Michigan. Holzer is a past president of the American Society for Public Administration (2000–2001) and a fellow of the National Academy of Public Administration.

Richard Schwester is a senior research associate for the National Center for Public Productivity in the Graduate Department of Public Administration, Rutgers University—Newark. Schwester received his B.A. from Johns Hopkins University and his M.A. from Rutgers University-Newark, both in political science.

The New Rural Development Challenge: Revitalizing Rural America

By Rob Atkinson

In the last decade, many rural areas have been left behind. Yet federal and state rural development efforts have not proven up to the task. As a result, it's time for a bold new approach to revitalizing rural America based on building competitive rural economies.

Fundamental changes in technology, markets and organizations are redrawing our nation's economic map and leaving many rural areas behind. Yet our de-facto federal rural policy—providing massive subsidies to a shrinking number of farmers—does little to help develop competitive rural economies or boost opportunity for most rural residents. Moreover, most states treat rural development as a poor stepchild to their core economic development efforts. As a result, it's time for a bold new approach to revitalizing rural America based on helping rural areas build competitive economies and enabling more Americans to fulfill their desire to live in less densely populated places.

To do this, we need a new national policy that weans rural areas off farm subsidies and instead invests the savings in rural development. We also need new state policies that make rural development a priority. Based on a recent report from the Progressive Policy Institute, this article examines what's happened to rural economies and discusses what states can do to revive rural growth.

How and Why Rural Economies Have Suffered

During the last two decades rural America has suffered. In 2001, 19.8 percent of Americans lived in non-metro areas, down from 21.8 percent in 1980. Jobs in rural areas grew 2.2 percentage points slower than metro areas in the 1980s and 3.6 percentage points slower in the 1990s (10.3 percent vs. 13.9 percent). In the 1990s almost half of rural counties lost both population and employment. Rural Americans now make on average $10,900 less annually than their urban counterparts, up from $5,893 less in 1978. This is not to say that some rural areas have not done well; many rural counties with retirement-based economies, regional trade centers, scenic amenities, or proximity to metro areas prospered. But most did not.

The result is a disturbing pattern in many states as "New Economy metropoles" have grown with rural areas lagging behind. For example, between 1989 and 1998 employment in the greater Atlanta region increased by 3.4 percent annually, compared to around 2.1 percent in rural Georgia. In North Carolina employment grew 16.3 percent in areas like Raleigh-Durham-Chapel Hill, but only 7.7 percent in rural areas. The Chicago metro area grew 12 percent in the 1990s, while rural Illinois grew 1 percent. As a result, many state leaders are calling attention to the problem of "two states"—a few prosperous and growing metro areas with stagnant areas in the remainder of the state.

There are a number of reasons why rural economies have suffered. Because key rural economic engines – farming, mining and manufacturing – have enjoyed significantly higher productivity growth, they employ a declining share of workers. In contrast, fast-growing knowledge and technology-based industries make up a much smaller share of rural economies than they do of metro economies. In part this is because as a group, rural workers have less education. For example, in the South, 28.1 percent of metro residents have a college degree compared to 15.1 percent of non-metro residents. Many rural areas have less of other key knowledge economy ingredients, including entrepreneurs, universities and colleges, high-speed data communications infrastructure, and frequent and inexpensive air service.

Finally, globalization threatens a core advantage rural areas have long relied on: low costs. For many decades rural regions have relied on the "filtering down" of more mature economic activities, especially branch manufacturing plants, from urban areas. However, globalization means that many establishments competing on costs instead "filter out" to developing nations. As a result, many rural regions find themselves squeezed between low-cost developing nations and high-skill metropolitan areas. This is one reason why since 1998, rural manufacturing jobs have decreased at a faster rate than urban manufacturing jobs. While these changes present challenges, the prospects for rural economies are not all bleak. In fact, many rural areas may be able to capitalize on a number of new developments. First, the digital economy is creating an ever-more footloose economy, which allows an increasing share of economic activity now located in high cost metro areas to relocate to lower cost areas, and not all these IT-enabled service jobs will go offshore. For example, Northwest Airlines recently opened a 600 person travel agency booking office in the small town of Minot, N.D. Second, as more people retire (35 million Americans are 50 to 59 years of age) many will choose rural life. Finally, as housing prices and traffic congestion grow in large metro areas, rural areas become more attractive for businesses and residents.

What Should States Do?

In the midst of these mixed set of forces, states are by no means helpless to advance rural economic development. But states would have a much easier time if Washington was doing its job. Unfortunately, federal rural policy is still seen as synonymous with farm policy, and expensive farm subsidies ($25 billion in 2001) now do little to create sustainable rural economies. As a result, states should call for the federal government to phase out farm subsidies, along with our major trading partners, and reinvest a portion of the savings in a new Rural Prosperity Corporation whose major activity would be to make matching grants to states for rural development efforts. However, states shouldn't hold their breath waiting for change from Washington. They can and should take a number of steps on their own.

1. Recognize That Balanced Growth is Good For Rural and Metro Areas

Because rural development is often viewed as social policy to help needy regions rather than as a key component of economic development policy, it is usually the poor stepchild when it comes to competing for resources. While states spend billions every year on economic development (including on tax incentives), little of it is focused on rural revitalization.

To generate support for robust rural development efforts state officials need to recognize that a more balanced distribution of economic activity helps not just rural areas, but also metropolitan economies. This is true because adding even more jobs and residents to metros like Boston, San Francisco-Oakland-San Jose, and Washington, D.C. will only raise costs there and hurt the quality of life of residents and competitive position of businesses. In contrast, encouraging growth in places like Springfield, Mass., Fresno, Calif., and Hagerstown, Md. would ease cost pressures in large metros while helping less populated regions. Rural growth acts as a relief valve,

reducing the growth of congestion and costs in large metropolitan areas, and making the entire state economy more competitive and able to grow with fewer of the problems stemming from growth.

2. Revamp State Economic Development Programs to Explicitly Focus on Boosting Rural Economies

Few states have developed comprehensive rural development strategies and of those that did, most are poorly linked to the state's overall economic development strategy. However, a few states have begun to develop more serious strategies for helping rural regions. Georgia's OneGeorgia Authority oversees economic development aimed at lagging parts of the state and provides grants and loans to 16 of the state's most economically distressed communities. North Carolina has created five types of regions, with tier one being the most economically distressed and tier five being the least economically distressed. Businesses in the lower tiers are eligible for more generous and more easily obtained business tax credits (e g., R&D credit).

3. Target Rural Development Efforts to a Smaller Number of Rural Centers With the Potential for Growth

In a knowledge-based economy where "critical mass" is increasingly central to success, some places that are too small or remote will find it difficult to succeed. Infrastructure providers, such as airlines and telecommunications companies, may not serve a place unless it is large enough to be economical. Moreover, companies employing skilled workers are unlikely to locate in a place without a pool of available trained workers. As a result, if states are to create the most jobs in rural regions, they should target development efforts to places with the potential to be the regional anchors for growth that surrounding rural residents can commute to for employment. The alternative—spreading out resources widely and thinly—while politically easier, is not likely to generate as many jobs in rural areas. These growth centers do not have to be metro areas. Towns of 10,000 to 20,000 people can serve as growth poles, especially if they have amenities to attract knowledge workers and have adequate infrastructure, especially high-speed telecommunications connections.

4. Co-fund New Economy Business Development Strategies

For rural America to prosper it will have to grow new businesses and expand existing ones, ideally ones providing better paying jobs. To do this, states need new approaches to economic development that stress new success factors, including workers' skills, entrepreneurial energy, and technology transfer.

Some states have already implemented innovative and effective initiatives in these areas. The Minnesota Technology Corporation Investment Fund, the Iowa Product Development Corporation, the Kentucky Rural Innovation Fund, and the Small Enterprise Growth Fund of Maine all focus at least part of their investments on rural areas. North Carolina's Institute for Rural Entrepreneurship helps spur business development in small towns losing jobs due to plant closures.

States can also help existing companies become more competitive. Kansas State University runs a technical assistance program to help agricultural co-ops develop value-added food processes. South Dakota's Value-Added Agriculture fund supports feasibility and marketing research for agricultural processing projects. The Vermont Sustainable Jobs Fund helps small business form business networks. One such network was the Vermont Quality Meats Cooperative, a 46-member co-op to produce, market, sell and transport meat directly to restaurants. In North Carolina, the Catawba County Hosiery Technology Center helps rural hosiery firms become more competitive through the adoption of new business practices.

States can also help spur new technologies that will lead to expanded rural-based production. South Dakota is working to boost wind energy production. Illinois' Renewable Fuels Development Program assists in the growth of renewable fuels plants. Minnesota's Natural Resource Research Institute conducts applied research and development to help develop new commercial applications for the state's natural resources, including timber and iron.

5. Facilitate Access to High-Speed Telecommunications

Access to high speed broadband telecommunications is critical if a region wants to grow and attract information-based businesses. However, for some rural areas, low levels of demand combined with higher costs means that companies often cannot make an adequate return on investment. As a result, states need to work to ensure that rural regions, particularly growth centers, have high-speed broadband connections.

States can do several things to help facilitate the rollout of broadband. Michigan preempts local authorities over rights-of-way for telecommunications use and reduces the fees that can be charged for access, while giving telecom providers tax credits for rights-of-ways fees. The Massachusetts Technology Collaborative sparked the creation of Berkshire Connect that aggregated demand for high-speed Internet services and used that demand to induce a private vendor chosen through a competitive proposal process to construct a high-speed data network.

6. Move Selected Government Jobs Out of High-Cost Metro Areas to Rural Growth Poles

While most of what states can do to influence rural growth patterns depends on indirect actions—for example, boosting skills of rural workers—there is one area that governments have direct control over—the location of government jobs. State governments employ over 5 million workers, most of them in state capitals and other metropolitan areas. These jobs can play an important role in rural economic development. Many government jobs, including routine "back office" government functions, are located in crowded, expensive metropolitan areas, even when there is no compelling business reason for them being there. These kinds of jobs can be relocated to rural growth poles, allowing governments to cut costs while maintaining the same level of service quality.

Conclusion

As we enter the 21st century it is time to recognize that the economic well-being of rural America is no longer synonymous with the well being of agriculture. If rural America is to prosper, it must develop new industries with sustainable competitive advantages. To help rural communities do that, we need new approaches to rural development from Congress and states.

About the Author

Rob Atkinson is vice president of the Progressive Policy Institute (PPI) and director of PPI's Technology and New Economy Project. He is also author, *The Past and Future of America's Economy: Waves of Innovation that Power Cycles of Growth* (Edward Elgar Press, 2005). While at PPI he has written groundbreaking reports on a wide range of new economy issues, including *"Reversing Rural America's Economic Decline,"* a report on how the New Economy is transforming rural America.

Trends and Issues in State Highways and Transportation

By John Horsley

State transportation departments that supply roads, bridges and transit face tough challenges. With the U.S. population projected to grow steadily, increasing vehicle miles traveled, and booming freight traffic, officials are squeezing efficiency from current funds even as they seek more. In coming years, it will be important to build a case for the value of transportation with the public and explore a variety of construction and financing approaches.

Providing the United States with the finest transportation system in the world has always been a challenge for the providers—chiefly the state departments of transportation, using a combination of state and federal funds. But several trends can be seen that may make the challenge more daunting in the future. These include population growth and surging freight traffic. In the short term, delayed action on a federal surface-transportation bill has cut some funding from the state-federal pipeline and introduced uncertainty, hampering states' ability to plan and proceed on needed projects.

Over the past 40 years, the United States funded and built the highways and bridges the nation's people and economy needed. Construction of the 47,000-mile Interstate Highway System surged from the 1960s through the 1980s. The 1980s and 1990s saw dramatic increases in investment in highways and transit by all levels of government.

During the period between 1982 and 2002, the nation's total capital investment more than doubled, according to the General Accounting Office (GAO)—but state and local highway investment during the period increased at twice the rate of federal investment. "Specifically, state and local investment increased 166 percent, from $14.1 billion to $37.6 billion in real terms, whereas the federal investment increased 83 percent from $15.5 billion to $28.3 billion."[1]

During the 1990s, state investment in transit increased substantially, with combined capital and operating spending rising from $5.17 billion in 1990 to $8.94 billion in 2000 (adjusted to 2003 dollars). During the same period, federal transit assistance increased from $3.84 billion to $5.52 billion, inflation-adjusted[2] (see Table A).

From 2002 to 2004, the states' relative share of total transportation spending dropped, largely due to the effects on overall state budgets of severe nationwide recession. As most state constitutions contain a ban on deficit spending, many states tapped their designated transportation trust funds in order to maintain balanced overall state budgets, pending the return of stronger tax revenues following the austerity period.

The National Association of State Budget Officers (NASBO), in its *2003 State Expenditure Report*, noted that the states appear to be fighting their way back from the trough of the recession, putting $92.9 billion into transportation spending in fiscal 2003, or 8.2 percent of all state expenditures—as compared with 3.5 percent in fiscal 2002.

However, "Following the fiscal downturn, states are still holding down spending on transportation projects," NASBO reported. "Estimates of fiscal 2004 total state transportation spending indicate growth of only 1.5 percent."[3]

The expiration of the six-year Transportation Equity Act for the 21st Century—the federal surface-transportation financing act—in September 2003 led to a series of short-term extensions of that act by Congress, but left the states for several months without a clear blueprint for anticipated federal funds. As federal funding typically covers about 80 percent of most highway projects built by states with federal support, many states found it necessary to delay or cancel projects.[4] Other states kept their projects' momentum going by increasing the proportion of state funds, leading the GAO to note that in 2002, state and local governments contributed 54 percent of the total U.S. capital investment in highways.[5]

Even as state transportation departments backed increased transit capacity and use technology to squeeze maximum efficiency out of existing assets, these trend lines point to an inescapable need for more highway capacity and to a need for greater reliability in the federal/state funding collaboration.

New Approaches by State DOTs

Several states, recognizing that transportation needs are great and can only become more serious if not addressed immediately, have increased their

Table A:
State Disbursements for Highways: Highway Statistics 1983 and 2003 (in thousands of dollars)

	Year of expenditure dollars	
State or other jurisdiction	1983	2003
Alabama	$ 628,732	$ 1,572,136
Alaska	323,665	618,077
Arizona	462,628	2,350,122
Arkansas	345,327	1,176,164
California	2,161,263	9,348,994
Colorado	440,598	1,787,710
Connecticut	457,321	1,361,653
Delaware	188,362	706,856
Florida	1,205,228	5,433,478
Georgia	944,552	1,949,804
Hawaii	160,247	329,954
Idaho	183,847	546,771
Illinois	1,594,964	4,423,094
Indiana	646,510	2,444,820
Iowa	551,003	1,419,474
Kansas	367,930	1,395,878
Kentucky	769,978	2,152,146
Louisiana	916,446	1,424,317
Maine	180,652	578,684
Maryland	836,680	1,792,279
Massachusetts	617,041	3,546,525
Michigan	988,644	2,798,807
Minnesota	734,958	1,959,322
Mississippi	456,108	1,014,057
Missouri	568,348	2,119,856
Montana	221,583	577,989
Nebraska	326,741	838,680
Nevada	208,125	806,564
New Hampshire	171,634	447,836
New Jersey	803,924	3,767,079
New Mexico	347,009	861,637
New York	1,876,156	5,829,420
North Carolina	744,572	3,012,676
North Dakota	186,619	379,015
Ohio	1,291,013	3,660,208
Oklahoma	603,056	1,286,597
Oregon	436,774	983,165
Pennsylvania	1,743,828	4,831,015
Rhode Island	92,103	277,873
South Carolina	340,448	1,151,233
South Dakota	164,883	441,222
Tennessee	653,962	1,660,505
Texas	1,761,665	6,515,831
Utah	247,402	878,816
Vermont	114,990	310,125
Virginia	908,685	2,998,344
Washington	836,616	2,220,022
West Virginia	467,210	1,107,307
Wisconsin	638,698	1,903,804
Wyoming	236,192	467,505
Dist. of Columbia	93,692	358,242
Total	$32,248,612	$101,833,691

Source: American Association of State Highway and Transportation Officials.

Note: Includes all federal, state and local funding disbursed within a state by all agencies.

transportation programs.

In Indiana, for example, the state's General Assembly approved a 3-cent gas tax increase effective Jan. 1, 2003. Two cents of that increase went to the state department of transportation, with 1 cent to be used for resurfacing and federal match and the other cent supporting a $450 million bonding program. The third cent went to local governments.

The bonded projects all have been let for bids, and Indiana has had a transportation construction program of $754 million in fiscal 2003 and $775 million in fiscal 2004.[6]

Kansas lawmakers—after a couple of years holding back funding from a 10-year comprehensive transportation program first adopted in 1999—restored full funding in 2004 to the $13.2 billion program following a recessionary need to meet a state constitutional requirement for a balanced budget.[7]

Maine's legislature has approved indexing the state gasoline tax to the Consumer Price Index starting in 2003, leading to a boost from 22 cents per gallon to 24.6 cents per gallon. State gasoline tax inflation indexing also is in effect in Florida, New York and Wisconsin.[8]

In Ohio, Gov. Robert Taft launched a long-range infrastructure investment plan dubbed "Access Ohio 2004-2030." It was supported by a 6-cent-per-gallon gas tax increase phased in over three years. A $5 billion, 10-year highway construction plan is its primary goal. Late last December, the state's Transportation Review Advisory Council gave the go-ahead for $3.7 billion in major highway work, setting in motion Ohio's largest transportation initiative since the creation of the Interstate Highway System.[9]

Washington state has more than 40 major highway projects planned using funds approved by the legislature in 2003 through a 5-cent increase in the state gasoline tax. The $4.2 billion package also will fund public transit, rail and ferry improvements.[10]

In Wisconsin, Gov. Jim Doyle has promoted economic investment through his "Grow Wisconsin" program, including signing a budget providing $1.8 billion for highway rehabilitation and construction during the 2003–2005 biennium.[11]

Tolling on the Upswing

Although the system that funds the national highway system and most state and local roads has always been a "user pays" approach—with gasoline taxes underpinning most road projects at all governmental levels—many states are finding tolling a way to accomplish expansion of capacity in crucial areas. Tolling is understood by the driving public to be a very obvious "user pays" approach, and in an environment in which raising gasoline taxes can be difficult, tolling often supplies the resources needed, especially for high-cost major capital improvements in high-volume metropolitan areas.

States are showing innovation in the use of tolls. For example, the Florida Turnpike has been engineered to have more electronic lanes that collect tolls without motorists having to stop—477 in all—than any other tolling network. Florida is also converting its Sawgrass Expressway into a fully automated system with no booths to interfere with traffic flow. Similarly, in New Jersey, two of every three transactions on the New Jersey Turnpike are handled electronically.[12]

In Texas, where the tradition of toll roads goes back half a century, there are now three regional tolling authorities, planning 331 new miles of roadway in the Houston area, 35 new tolled miles in the Dallas-Fort Worth area and a 65-mile toll road east of Austin. The roads are popular and use of highway-speed toll-deduction tags has surged.[13]

In addition, Virginia has decided to build toll-financed high-occupancy toll or "HOT" lanes on a 14-mile portion of the Capital Beltway. Carpools of three or more riders could travel the lanes for free, but others would pay tolls to use them. The lanes would also have changeable tolls that would increase as congestion did.[14]

A neighboring state, Maryland, is studying similar use of "express toll lanes" on portions of Interstate 95 north of Baltimore, I-95/I-495 on the Capital Beltway, I-270 and I-695 on the Baltimore Beltway.[15]

Increasing Commuter Contentment and Safety

To reduce construction's inconvenience for motorists and increase safety, several states also have planned and executed projects with lightning speed, compared to the rollout of similar work under traditional approaches. One increasing approach is termed "design-build," in which construction begins on already-designed portions of a project even as design continues on other portions of it.

The Colorado Department of Transportation has used design-build on its $1.7 billion renovation of Interstates 25 and 225 in the Denver area, a 5-1/2 year project that also will add light rail to the corridor. The 19-mile "T-Rex" project remains on schedule and on budget, with completion slated for September 2006.[16]

Another approach is full closure of an existing

roadway to traffic to allow its speedy rehabilitation. That angle has two goals: minimizing the inconvenience to the driving public of projects that go on and on, and increasing the safety of both motorists and workers by eliminating the need to perform reconstruction next to moving traffic.

In Indiana, Interstates 65 and 70 needed extensive repair—a job that normally would take many months. But the routes provided major access to the Indianapolis 500 and the Brickyard 400, a pair of events that brought millions of dollars in commerce to the area each year. So a decision was made—in the name of access, cost savings and heightened work-zone safety—to get the work done in the nine weeks between the first race, on Memorial Day of 2003, and the second, over the following Labor Day weekend. Work involved restoring and supporting bridge decks, widening lanes and resurfacing the roadway.[17]

Many states also are using incentives to contractors to complete work on a challenging schedule. When a river barge struck a support pillar, causing the partial collapse of an Interstate 40 bridge over the Arkansas River in Oklahoma, state transportation officials used financial incentives to get the bridge rebuilt in slightly more than two months—work that ordinarily would have taken three times that long.[18]

The Federal Picture

After six extensions, the 107th Congress adjourned without completing action on reauthorization of federal highway and transit programs. After the Senate passed its reauthorization bill at $318 billion in February 2004, and the House passed its version at $275 billion in April, a joint conference committee adjourned with a figure of $299 billion on the table as a possible compromise figure. State DOTs and industry will be pushing Congress to take up this measure as one of the first matters considered by the 109th Congress.

Coping with Increasing Transportation Demands

Over the past 40 years, the U.S. population grew by 100 million, reaching 295 million as of November 2004.[19] During the last decade, the United States grew by 32 million, 14 million of it from immigration. According to Census Bureau forecasts, over the next 40 years the United States will add another 110 million in population, growing to 392 million by 2040.[20]

In the closing 40 years of the past century, we invested heavily in our transportation infrastructure and created a system that has sustained the world's strongest economy. The question is what legacy will this generation leave the next.

Population growth is only part of the picture of increasing demand. The distances people tally up in their vehicles—a measure dubbed vehicle miles traveled (VMT)—has risen even more steeply than population has in the past 20 years. From 1980 to 2000, the population of the United States rose 24 percent,[21] but VMT grew 80 percent.[22] During this period the percentage of U.S. households owning cars increased from 86 percent to 92 percent.[23] VMT is expected to reach 3.35 trillion miles traveled per year by 2010.[24]

Another way of looking at it is to compare urban lane-miles constructed between 1980 and 2000 with vehicle miles traveled in the same period. Urban lane-miles built rose by 37 percent, but VMT grew by 80 percent.[25] With these statistics before us, the causes of congestion should not be a surprise.

Over the past decade, commuters have tended to drive alone more frequently and carpool less often, with the transit share of commuting remaining steady at 5 percent nationwide.[26] A result of these developments has been increasing traffic congestion.

The Texas Transportation Institute, in the latest version of its annual study of traffic congestion in urban areas, concluded in its 2004 report that U.S. commuters endured 3.5 billion hours of delay and wasted 5.7 billion gallons of fuel (burned while idling) at a cost of $63.2 billion.[27] States have responded with a variety of operational improvements; for example, "service patrols" that help motorists experiencing car trouble provide assistance in many states including California, Florida, Illinois, Ohio and Tennessee; real-time information about upcoming road conditions is provided by various means to motorists in Illinois, Michigan, New Mexico and Nebraska; and traffic-signal coordination is increasing across the nation.[28] Intelligent transportation systems (ITS) offer still more benefit in maximizing existing highway capacity.

Freight Demand

In 2000, the nation's freight system moved 14 billion tons of domestic freight valued at $11 trillion—78 percent by truck, 16 percent by rail, 6 percent by barge and 1 percent by air.[29] This ability to move goods is crucial to our economy, and domestic and international freight tonnage is expected to increase by 67 percent by 2020.[30] And that is excluding concerns that funding will not be adequate to maintain the current freight share held by rail, water and other non-road means. If those costs move over to the roads, the estimated cost to the highway system has

been pegged at $64 billion—conservatively estimated—over two decades.[31]

Keeping all modes of freight movement firing on all cylinders is crucial to our economy. Growth in international trade is now a key component of our gross domestic product—rising from 13 percent of GDP in 1990 to 26 percent in the year 2000, and projected to rise to 35 percent by the year 2020.[32] Significant growth will result in all freight modes—air, truck, rail and barge.

As these modes grow, they also change with the needs of the market. In the trucking industry, changes may spur more use of the highway infrastructure. Some of these include shorter hours of service for individual drivers, in the name of safety, which puts more drivers in more trucks on our roads. Other changes include "just-in-time" movement of supplies from warehouse to factory or end-user.

Providing the infrastructure to support these levels of freight movement is crucial not only to the overall economy, but to quality of life. There are few consumer items—from food, clothing and building materials to goods purchased on the Internet auction site E-Bay—that do not require freighting by road, rail or water before arriving in the consumer's hands.

Governments are addressing the intermodal challenge presented by freight transport in innovative ways. In California, port and trucking congestion was addressed by construction of the 20-mile, $2.4-billion Alameda Corridor, which created a freight-rail expressway between the ports of Los Angeles and Long Beach and destinations east. Opened in 2002, its key component is a below-ground railway 10 miles long that eliminated more than 200 at-grade railroad crossings. The project also halved the time needed to move cargo containers by train between the ports and downtown Los Angeles.[33]

In New Jersey, state officials in 2003 announced an $80 million public-private freight-rail improvement plan to upgrade access to the ports of Newark and Elizabeth and the Meadowlands area. The plan is expected to help slow the increase of truck traffic on the state's highways and preserve job growth in the shipping industry.[34]

And in Chicago, a site of significant freight-rail congestion, railroad industry experts proposed an action plan that will prepare the region for growth and help solidify its place as the nation's primary rail hub. The public-private plan, dubbed the dubbed the Chicago Region Environmental and Transportation Efficiency (CREATE) Project, would put $1.5 billion to work on a priority list of rail infrastructure improvements and grade-crossing eliminations.[35]

Conclusion

The task of those of us who believe in a superior transportation system is to convince our neighbors of the signal importance such a system has to our economy and their quality of life. Too few Americans link their ability to live a good life with the movement of freight on the rails and roads, or with the role a highway plays in taking them to work, to medical care or to their child's sporting events.

Transportation has been the economic edge that has kept U.S. goods competitive internationally—but other countries are gaining, and may surpass us unless we continue to improve and enhance our system. The state transportation departments are on the front lines in this competition, and must be involved in nationwide and regional solutions.

For our economy, for our freedom of travel and for a continuing high quality of life, the case must be made to support steps in the near future to finance the maintenance and improvement of our surface-transportation network.

Notes

[1]U.S. General Accounting Office, GAO-03-744R, *Trends in Federal and State Capital Investment in Highways*, (Washington, D.C.: U.S. General Accounting Office, June 2003). *http://frwebgate.access.gpo.gov/cgibin/ useftp.cgi?IPaddress=162.140.64.21&filename=d03744r.pdf&directory=/diskb/wais/data/gao*.

[2]American Public Transportation Association, *2004 Transit Fact Book*. (Washington, D.C.: American Public Transportation Association, 2004), Tables 18 and 19.

[3]National Association of State Budget Officers, *2003 State Expenditure Report*, (Washington, D.C.: National Association of State Budget Officers, October 2004), 66–72. *http://www.nasbo.org/Publications/PDFs/2003Expend Report.pdf*.

[4]American Association of State Highway and Transportation Officials, *TEA-21 Impacts of Delay: $2.1 Billion in Projects Delayed, 90,000 Jobs Lost*, (Washington, D.C.: September, 2003), 3–5. *http://downloads.transportation.org/TEA21Impacts.pdf*.

[5]JayEtta Z. Hecker, Steve Cohen, Jerry Fastrup et al, *Federal-Aid Highways: Trends, Effect on State Spending, and Options for Future Program Design* (Washington, D.C.: General Accounting Office, 2004).

[6]Tony Felts, spokesman for the Indiana Department of Transportation, November 30, 2004, telephone interview.

[7]Steven Schwartz, spokesman for the Kansas Department of Transportation, November 30, 2004, telephone interview.

[8]American Road & Transportation Builders Association, State Gas Tax Report, July 2004. *http://www.artba.org/economics_research/current_issues/ARTBA%20State%20Gas%20Tax%20Report%20July04.pdf* .

[9]Ohio Department of Transportation, "What is Access Ohio?" *http://www.dot.state.oh.us/planning/ACCESS%20OHIO/WhatIsACCESSOHIO.htm*.

[10]Washington State Department of Transportation, "Nickel Funding Package," *http://www.wsdot.wa.gov/projects/nickel/Default.htm*.

[11]State of Wisconsin, Office of the Governor, "Grow Wisconsin—Gov. Jim Doyle's Plan to Create Jobs." (Madison, Wisconsin, September 10, 2003.) *http://www.wisgov.state.wi.us/docs/Doyle_economic_package.pdf*.

[12]Ledyard King, "Tolls Used to Ramp Up Road Funds," *Detroit News on the Web*, November 9, 2004. *http://www.detnews.com/2004/commuting/0411/10/A11-899.htm*.

[13]Clint Shields, "Let's Play Tag—Electronic Tags to Work on All Texas Toll Roads," Window on State Government Web site, Texas Comptroller of Public Accounts, May 2004. *http://www.window.state.tx.us/comptrol/fnotes/fn0405/lets.html*.

[14]Steven Ginsberg, "Virginia to Build Beltway Toll Lanes." *Washington Post*, August 27, 2004 , A1.

[15]Steven Ginsberg, "Toll Lanes Seen as Fix for Lack of Road Funds," *Washington Post*, May 5, 2004, B1.

[16]Sharon McKone, "Colorado Turns to Tolls to Finance New Roads." *Better Roads for the Government/Contractor Project Team*, (October 2004). *http://www.betterroads.com/articles.oct04e.htm*.

[17]Indiana Department of Transportation, "About Hyperfix," *http://www.in.gov/dot/div/specialprojects/hyperfix/about/about.htm*.

[18]American Association of State Highway and Transportation Officials, Transportation.org Web site. *http://transportation.org/aashto/success.nsf/allpages/31-OKBridgeRebuild*.

[19]U.S. Bureau of the Census, *http:www.census.gov* (October 19, 2004).

[20]U.S. Bureau of the Census, *http://www.census.gov/ipc/www/usinterimproj/natprojtab02a.pdf* (October 15, 2004)

[21]Anthony Downs, *Traffic: Why It's Getting Worse, What Government Can Do*, (Washington, D.C., Brookings Institution, 2003). *http://www.brookings.edu/comm/policy briefs/pb128.htm*.

[22]Ibid.

[23]U.S. Bureau of the Census, cited by U.S. Department of Energy, *http://www.eere.energy.gov/vehiclesandfuels/facts/favorites/fcvt_fotw182.shtml*.

[24]American Association of State Highway and Transportation Officials, *Invest in America, the Bottom Line*, (Washington, D.C., American Association of State Highway and Transportation Officials, 2001), 3. *http://bottomline.transportation.org*.

[25]U.S. Bureau of Transportation Statistics, National Transportation Statistics tables 1–6 and 1–33. h*ttp://products.bts.gov/publications/national_transportation_statistics/2003/html/table_01_33.html and http://products.bts.gov/publications/national_transportation_statistics/2003/html/table_01_06.html*

[26]U.S. Bureau of the Census, 2000 journey-to-work statistics. *http://www.census.gov/population/socdemo/journey/usmode90.txt*.

[27]David Schrank and Tim Lomax, "The 2004 Urban Mobility Report," Texas Transportation Institute. (September, 2004) 1. *http://mobility.tamu.edu*.

[28]*Optimizing the System—Saving Lives, Saving Time*, (Washington, D.C.: American Association of State Highway and Transportation Officials, 2004) 17–45. *http://downloads.transportation.org/OptimizingTheSystem.pdf*.

[29]Lance R. Grenzeback and Alan Meyers, et al, *Freight-Rail Bottom Line Report*, (Washington, D.C.: American Association of State Highway and Transportation Officials, 2003) 13. *http://freight.transportation.org/doc/FreightRail Report.pdf*.

[30]Ibid., 45.

[31]Ibid., 27.

[32]U.S. Department of Commerce, Bureau of Economic Analysis at: *http://www.bea.doc.gov*.

[33]Alameda Corridor Transportation Authority at: *http://www.acta.org/newsroom_factsheet.htm*.

[34]New Jersey Department of Transportation news release, "Gov. McGreevey Announces $80 Million For Freight Rail Improvements." (April 28, 2003). *http://www.state.nj.us/transportation/press/2003releases/042903.htm*.

[35]Jeromie Winsor, "Railroads, transportation agencies release action plan to ease Chicago rail congestion." (Chicago, Campaign for Sensible Growth, 6 August 2003). *http://www.growingsensibly.org/news/releaseDetail.asp?objectID=1415*.

About the Author

John Horsley has been executive director of the American Association of State Highway and Transportation Officials (AASHTO) since 1999. AASHTO advocates policies and disseminates best practices in transportation. From 1993–1999 he was associate deputy secretary of the U.S. Department of Transportation, and earlier served on the county commission in Kitsap County, Washington. Horsley is a past president of the National Association of Counties.

Table 9.2
STATE REVENUES USED FOR HIGHWAYS, BY REGION: 2003 (In thousands of dollars)

State or other jurisdiction	Balance beginning of year (a)	Highway-user revenues	Appropriations from general funds (c)	Other state imposts	Miscellaneous	Bond proceeds Original issues	Bond proceeds Refunding issues	Payments from other governments Federal Funds FHA	Payments from other governments Other Agencies	Payments from other governments Local governments	Total receipts
United States	$39,280,834	$48,734,743	$3,399,724	$3,382,232	$2,748,979	$9,525,997	$7,562,991	$28,383,735	$796,715	$1,658,684	$106,193,800
Eastern Region											
Connecticut	813,943	447,112	107,735	65,529	89,661	264,432	381,575	407,569	9,471	5,632	1,778,716
Delaware	269,384	373,434	104,085	0	30,154	340,883	221,990	110,788	456	0	1,181,790
Maine	121,052	313,681	2,541	0	16,952	51,000	0	171,126	1,944	0	557,244
Massachusetts	1,108,360	1,199,477	636,957	0	192,635	916,474	0	508,637	9,084	0	3,463,264
New Hampshire	252,201	298,657	10,253	0	9,802	3,960	4,895	143,228	825	8,879	480,499
New Jersey	2,408,051	1,201,681	0	0	133,665	1,104,075	2,596,750	734,476	6,819	0	5,777,466
New York	-243,590	2,523,899	304,687	0	88,674	1,492,319	762,749	1,316,564	20,903	17,511	6,527,306
Pennsylvania	2,087,583	2,251,826	527,101	0	316,715	21,018	426,780	1,361,855	33,304	32,867	4,971,466
Rhode Island	43,498	93,512	0	0	17,297	30,000	21,211	137,563	3,133	0	302,716
Vermont	68,880	187,395	2,041	3,454	7,808	118	1,538	108,163	2,306	2,465	315,288
Regional average	692,936	889,067	169,450	6,898	90,336	422,428	441,749	499,997	8,825	6,735	2,535,576
Midwestern Region											
Illinois	1,783,219	2,511,681	54,048	0	31,665	429,160	172,331	836,519	14,406	45,217	4,095,027
Indiana	511,813	1,379,619	2,669	0	9,876	445,000	0	597,252	18,112	0	2,452,528
Iowa	45,362	753,503	60,077	245,731	7,441	0	495,500	343,791	5,893	0	1,416,436
Kansas	984,409	580,713	11,206	89,854	44,915	33,950	0	330,931	3,676	20,683	1,611,428
Michigan	1,156,371	1,776,862	165,999	0	67,227	0	0	592,450	13,270	31,237	2,647,045
Minnesota	1,036,796	1,117,068	16,128	184,957	74,976	28,477	0	330,300	7,188	22,218	1,781,312
Nebraska	105,555	357,156	33,614	135,315	27,981	0	0	210,107	1,282	58,753	824,208
North Dakota	46,529	154,065	11,875	5,711	382	0	0	198,301	3,959	12,501	386,794
Ohio	1,217,871	2,105,720	39,033	0	85,232	291,168	0	888,290	14,170	57,507	3,481,120
South Dakota	57,552	161,273	351	55,793	22,677	0	0	198,098	2,583	14,024	454,799
Wisconsin	325,522	1,118,729	0	0	31,913	213,182	0	563,295	9,775	87,136	2,024,030
Regional average	661,000	1,092,399	35,909	65,215	36,753	130,994	60,712	462,667	8,574	31,752	1,924,975
Southern Region											
Alabama	440,789	761,175	62,657	5,710	4,104	200,000	0	587,033	8,849	50,000	1,679,528
Arkansas	231,291	555,102	28,732	1,339	26,705	225,728	0	437,083	8,323	1,970	1,284,982
Florida	1,219,577	2,942,431	193,339	95,821	113,245	651,134	1,230,135	1,695,189	15,482	149,871	7,086,647
Georgia	1,305,174	676,337	203,744	217,296	90,067	0	0	792,804	11,767	0	1,992,015
Kentucky	1,103,023	1,054,649	192,527	0	56,585	0	0	513,357	10,450	0	1,827,568
Louisiana	644,603	737,833	101,176	0	25,334	278,734	73,510	483,710	7,875	0	1,744,184
Maryland	721,913	821,210	0	36,012	33,010	229,342	92,393	496,292	9,264	0	1,795,063
Mississippi	496,131	495,649	0	113,552	12,701	0	0	411,567	6,470	13,707	984,909
Missouri	632,212	899,193	19,705	44,815	26,562	0	0	732,290	8,067	13,162	1,916,074
North Carolina	972,506	1,359,861	0	217,095	81,721	0	0	791,500	13,078	10,424	2,640,069
Oklahoma	548,337	656,332	10,518	383,485	39,492	7,427	92,170	394,602	5,010	8,309	1,267,509
South Carolina	412,731	451,992	0	53,649	26,484	6,830	39,675	426,764	20,535	10,544	982,824
Tennessee	1,045,728	948,346	23,653	39,038	42,168	0	0	538,661	11,403	31,675	1,634,944
Texas	3,154,647	3,442,933	33,510	30,942	171,707	239,355	241,750	2,494,149	30,966	322,273	7,007,585
Virginia	1,192,845	1,227,310	101,978	411,991	77,307	686,588	420,808	656,374	19,537	39,685	3,641,578
West Virginia	252,324	589,025	14,995	0	9,186	1,416	61,280	407,254	15,787	0	1,098,943
Regional average	898,364	1,242,842	61,008	95,579	53,722	198,606	217,616	797,563	12,911	50,093	2,729,941

See footnotes at end of table.

STATE REVENUES USED FOR HIGHWAYS, BY REGION: 2003 (In thousands of dollars) — Continued

State or other jurisdiction	Balance beginning of year (a)	Highway-user revenues	Appropriations from general funds (c)	Other state imposts	Miscellaneous	Bond proceeds Original issues	Bond proceeds Refunding issues	Federal Funds FHA	Federal Funds Other Agencies	Local governments	Total receipts
Western Region											
Alaska	0	73,306	83,244	0	23,456	113,866	0	398,917	4,257	0	697,046
Arizona	736,846	850,797	43,533	579,148	1,995	349,172	103,045	447,986	11,127	41,967	2,428,770
California	6,403,743	4,039,730	5,411	264,838	283,379	0	0	2,481,325	76,051	513,258	7,663,992
Colorado	897,530	1,166,982	28,740	1,010	131,963	105,859	0	427,569	15,973	2,170	1,880,266
Hawaii	418,363	147,479	14,415	2,079	15,691	0	44,940	135,085	259	0	359,948
Idaho	206,268	329,330	0	0	0	0	0	207,684	16,257	2,413	555,684
Montana	101,374	247,708	0	0	2,807	0	0	307,434	13,852	625	572,426
Nevada	237,954	585,087	4,213	0	6,977	199,483	0	203,431	963	0	1,000,154
New Mexico	408,030	368,435	0	2,317	16,513	16,699	0	269,258	30,671	0	703,893
Oregon	342,594	643,370	37,215	9,745	15,246	0	0	366,640	111,578	0	1,183,794
Utah	442,817	405,681	69,708	38,031	40,484	161,597	0	223,395	20,721	0	959,617
Washington	417,312	1,096,840	10,474	27	59,490	373,580	68,405	587,235	30,266	25,073	2,251,390
Wyoming	32,665	132,744	0	11,301	6,011	0	0	226,448	77,385	4,928	458,817
Regional average	818,884	775,961	22,843	69,884	46,462	101,558	16,645	483,262	31,489	45,418	1,593,523
Regional average without California	304,020	443,707	23,891	53,638	26,719	110,021	18,033	316,757	27,776	6,431	1,087,650
Dist. of Columbia	61,146	120,813	25,837	36,647	941	13,971	9,561	153,396	1,933	0	363,099

Source: U.S. Department of Transportation, Federal Highway Administration, *Highway Statistics, 2003*, November 2004.

Note: Detail may not add to totals due to rounding. This table was compiled from reports of state authorities.

Key:

(a) Any differences between beginning balances and the closing balances on last year's information are the result of accounting adjustments, inclusion of funds not previously reported, etc.

(b) Amounts shown represent only those highway user revenues that were expended on state or local roads.

(c) Amounts shown represent gross general fund appropriations for highways reduced by the amount of highway-user revenues placed in the State General Fund.

Table 9.3
APPORTIONMENT OF FEDERAL-AID HIGHWAY FUNDS BY REGION: FISCAL YEAR 2004 (In thousands of dollars)

State or other jurisdiction	Interstate maintenance	National highway system	Surface transportation program	Bridge program	Congestion mitigation and air quality improvement	Appalachian development highway system	Recreation trails	Metropolitan planning	Minimum guarantee	Revenue aligned budget authority	Total (a)
United States Total	$4,623,245	$5,646,868	$6,612,124	$3,970,589	$1,618,091	$512,506	$57,657	$238,584	$7,252,725	$2,744,973	$33,277,362
Eastern Region											
Connecticut	47,666	44,141	61,695	76,807	32,211	0	675	3,375	169,814	47,878	484,262
Delaware	7,753	43,249	32,811	12,943	8,005	0	611	1,193	31,022	3,489	141,076
Maine	26,172	30,636	36,097	28,913	8,201	0	878	1,193	29,565	6,176	167,830
Massachusetts	81,299	81,467	115,571	146,159	62,270	0	937	6,677	73,260	26,702	594,342
New Hampshire	18,491	33,596	33,509	22,341	8,175	0	762	1,193	34,024	12,552	164,641
New Jersey	87,633	132,594	151,628	198,083	94,503	0	966	9,188	138,366	83,455	896,417
New York	163,828	190,396	254,640	396,669	149,873	12,174	1,377	18,373	325,707	133,314	1,646,351
Pennsylvania	173,369	190,915	237,435	402,417	84,589	140,113	1,403	9,730	214,245	136,617	1,590,833
Rhode Island	10,398	40,822	32,951	49,759	9,155	0	609	1,193	38,538	6,568	189,993
Vermont	15,639	36,015	33,230	25,478	8,107	0	704	1,193	20,952	4,509	145,827
Regional average	63,225	82,383	98,957	135,957	46,509	15,229	892	5,331	107,549	46,126	602,157
Midwestern Region											
Illinois	208,122	183,295	245,517	142,326	84,029	0	1,465	11,539	139,812	62,341	1,078,445
Indiana	120,463	126,487	155,990	41,893	15,085	0	959	4,042	219,994	67,280	752,191
Iowa	63,533	92,215	96,612	63,612	8,249	0	997	1,321	39,116	17,647	383,302
Kansas	60,363	83,602	106,243	59,404	8,261	0	992	1,431	35,568	17,775	373,640
Michigan	137,949	167,442	231,937	117,596	34,034	0	1,781	7,795	241,430	68,478	1,008,443
Minnesota	86,279	104,887	134,145	30,502	17,140	0	1,372	3,213	58,742	41,828	478,108
Nebraska	41,152	72,017	67,306	30,969	8,261	0	834	1,193	24,980	1,000	247,712
North Dakota	26,833	75,478	40,679	9,766	7,969	0	716	1,193	38,565	7,769	208,967
Ohio	193,760	178,737	230,364	121,892	52,020	25,241	1,367	8,664	214,907	110,305	1,137,257
South Dakota	31,841	62,878	44,819	14,040	7,957	0	724	1,193	47,630	16,890	227,972
Wisconsin	77,407	124,565	138,115	33,294	19,425	0	1,318	3,368	196,184	41,420	635,096
Regional average	95,246	115,600	135,612	60,481	23,857	2,295	1,139	4,087	114,266	41,158	593,739
Southern Region											
Alabama	90,138	102,254	131,709	77,780	8,106	56,582	1,128	2,300	134,649	41,705	646,352
Arkansas	63,041	77,596	90,170	46,637	7,904	0	934	1,193	94,920	38,983	421,378
Florida	180,339	256,640	305,847	65,166	40,416	0	1,932	15,962	608,741	151,046	1,626,091
Georgia	174,984	169,772	232,403	61,997	32,939	22,339	1,488	5,937	378,331	121,179	1,201,369
Kentucky	92,837	103,276	112,549	64,030	9,728	52,092	920	1,857	98,389	18,070	553,748
Louisiana	77,042	75,566	103,017	101,617	7,891	0	1,176	3,005	97,546	47,243	514,102
Maryland	80,288	88,116	108,096	73,558	48,435	8,953	820	5,096	95,174	48,538	557,073
Mississippi	58,674	81,598	93,153	51,596	7,991	6,255	1,151	1,193	63,834	30,536	395,981
Missouri	124,585	129,784	166,105	133,738	20,721	0	1,162	3,662	112,539	60,755	753,052
North Carolina	122,458	146,303	182,797	98,474	17,023	33,096	1,389	4,457	254,630	57,187	917,813
Oklahoma	85,188	106,299	131,582	94,797	8,247	0	1,071	1,758	49,936	50,231	529,111
South Carolina	80,662	81,370	113,715	54,805	7,871	2,692	879	2,220	160,233	48,459	552,907
Tennessee	118,259	121,609	146,120	66,485	14,224	62,438	1,082	3,513	131,744	64,448	729,925
Texas	360,453	456,184	545,406	153,547	96,045	0	2,534	17,533	803,010	308,890	2,743,602
Virginia	129,956	127,199	170,635	81,596	32,151	13,071	1,031	5,585	201,370	104,421	867,016
West Virginia	40,878	41,793	50,665	59,270	7,981	77,458	835	1,193	35,469	45,407	360,948
Regional average	117,486	135,335	167,748	80,318	22,980	20,936	1,221	4,779	207,532	77,319	835,654

See footnotes at end of table.

APPORTIONMENT OF FEDERAL-AID HIGHWAY FUNDS BY REGION: FISCAL YEAR 2004 (In thousands of dollars)—Continued

State or other jurisdiction	Interstate maintenance	National highway system	Surface transportation program	Bridge program	Congestion mitigation and air quality improvement	Appalachian development highway system	Recreation trails	Metropolitan planning	Minimum guarantee	Revenue aligned budget authority	Total (a)
Western Region											
Alaska	21,293	26,820	30,123	10,622	7,349	0	789	1,193	233,076	48,690	379,954
Arizona	92,543	100,206	113,571	11,412	33,173	0	1,245	4,631	181,799	56,372	594,953
California	412,855	529,273	646,100	319,659	352,511	0	4,024	35,573	548,626	252,160	3,100,780
Colorado	73,691	95,162	100,853	24,955	20,263	0	1,437	3,807	80,514	43,290	443,973
Hawaii	8,363	44,164	33,792	22,475	8,244	0	640	1,193	37,679	8,537	165,088
Idaho	35,315	47,121	40,470	15,207	8,023	0	958	1,193	70,811	27,020	246,117
Montana	46,785	64,508	39,511	13,292	7,590	0	959	1,193	119,029	23,755	316,623
Nevada	39,854	45,533	45,145	9,907	13,683	0	783	1,986	65,048	9,188	231,129
New Mexico	63,877	70,841	56,533	12,271	7,881	0	1,002	1,193	75,955	25,636	315,188
Oregon	61,688	80,058	87,190	49,970	11,464	0	990	2,342	59,574	35,224	388,500
Utah	65,224	47,390	55,829	27,137	10,822	0	990	2,071	27,795	16,806	254,063
Washington	91,963	102,415	131,087	109,705	25,635	0	1,373	5,100	70,241	32,492	570,011
Wyoming	47,205	81,573	31,999	9,567	7,807	0	891	1,193	28,410	13,014	221,658
Regional average	81,859	102,697	108,631	48,937	39,753	0	1,237	4,821	122,966	45,553	556,003
Regional average without California	53,983	67,149	63,842	26,377	13,495	0	1,005	2,258	87,494	28,335	343,938
Dist. of Columbia	2,857	51,013	34,656	24,457	8,455	0	594	1,193	1,231	1,695	126,152
American Samoa	0	0	3,015	0	0	0	0	0	0	0	3,015
Guam	0	0	9,592	0	0	0	0	0	0	0	9,592
No. Mariana Islands	0	0	3,015	0	0	0	0	0	0	0	3,015
Puerto Rico (b)	0	0	0	0	0	0	0	0	0	0	0
U.S. Virgin Islands	0	0	12,062	0	0	0	0	0	0	0	12,062

Source: U.S. Department of Transportation, Federal Highway Administration, *Highway Statistics, 2003* (Novemer 2004).

Note: Apportioned pursuant to the Transportation Efficiency Act of 1998 (TEA-21) as amended by the TEA-21 Restoration Act. Does not include funds from the Mass Transit Account of the Highway Trust Fund.

(a) Does not include funds from the following programs: emergency relief, Federal lands highway programs, Commonwealth of Puerto Rico highway programs,high priority projects, Woodrow Wilson Bridge, National Byways, construction of ferry boats and ferry terminal facilities, and intelligent vehicle-system,among others. These funds are allocated from the Highway Trust Fund.

(b) Under several extensions of TEA-21, Puerto Rico received a stand alone authorization of $72,974,214 for FY 2004.

Trends in Probation and Parole in the States
By William D. Burrell

Probation and parole play an essential and critical role in the administration of both criminal and juvenile justice. They supervise the vast majority of offenders, and their caseloads continue to grow. In response to the pressures of increased workload, static or declining budgets, and limited public and political support, six strategic trends have emerged. These trends characterize the efforts of probation and parole to meet their mandates and improve their effectiveness.

Introduction

Probation and parole are integral to criminal and juvenile justice in the states. They provide a wide variety of services that are critical to the effective and efficient operation of almost every aspect of the justice system, ranging from law enforcement to sentencing to the release of offenders from confinement into the community. While these community corrections agencies conduct investigations to support judicial and parole decision-making, operate residential and secure custodial facilities and provide free labor to local organizations through community service programs, probation and parole are best known for their role in the supervision of offenders in the community.

This community supervision function is responsible for the bulk of the correctional population in the United States. At the end of 2003, some 4.8 million adults were on probation and parole, compared with approximately 2.1 million adults in jail or prison. Seventy percent of the adult correctional population is under the jurisdiction of probation and parole officers.[1] Juvenile court statistics reveal that probation is imposed in 62 percent of adjudicated delinquency cases and that some 675,000 juveniles are under probation supervision.[2]

It is challenging to try to describe or discuss probation and parole in this country, not only because of the scope and scale of its operations, but also because of its structure and organization. The phrases "probation and parole," or "community corrections" are used routinely and would imply a single or unified system. Nothing could be farther from the truth. Probation and parole agencies are a fragmented, heterogeneous collection of organizations found at the federal, state, county and municipal levels, housed in the judicial and executive branches. There are even some private companies and non-profit organizations providing probation services. There are hundreds of departments and offices and thousands of staff committed to the mission of community corrections.

In addition, probation and parole agencies are part of a large, complex and interdependent array of gov-

ernmental, non-profit and private agencies and organizations that comprise the criminal and juvenile justice systems. Almost no aspect of the work of probation and parole can be considered in isolation, as they are affected by and have an impact on many other agencies.

Despite the challenge of this organizational diversity, it is possible to identify trends that are affecting probation and parole in the states. As with any endeavor, not every jurisdiction is affected or involved equally. The trends will be discussed in two major areas. The first involves trends in the overall operating environment of probation and parole. The second are trends that can best be described as the strategic responses of probation and parole as they strive to accomplish their mission.

Environmental Trends

The environmental factors that have an impact on probation and parole include organizational structure, workload, resources and funding and legislative/political initiatives and support.

The organizational structure of probation and parole is stable. Unlike the period of the late 1970s and early 1980s when parole came under attack and was abolished in 16 states,[3] no large scale efforts are underway in terms of significantly altering the organizational structure of these community-based correctional agencies.

The workload of probation and parole continues to grow. Since 1995, the number of adults on probation and parole has increased 29 percent, compared with 2.9 percent for prisons and 4 percent for jails. The adult probation population has grown steadily since 1990. The projection for adult probation populations is for continued slow but steady growth.[4]

The parole population has shown less annual growth over the past decade, but that is beginning to increase. The huge cohort of offenders incarcerated under the "get tough" sentencing laws passed in the 1980s is now approaching their release dates in large numbers. While the release of many of those inmates will be mandatory (not on parole), many will still be subject to post-release supervision of some type.[5] Overall, both probation and parole will continue to see modest growth for the foreseeable future.

Because of the complex organizational structure of these services, the resource and funding aspects of probation and parole are complex. The overall state of the economy contributes to the less than rosy picture as all levels of government are experiencing fiscal stress to some degree and money is generally tight. Probation and parole are not popular, high visibility programs with strong political support. Despite the fact that they handle the vast majority of the offender population, probation and parole receive less than 10 percent of the correctional funding from state and local governments.[6] Probation and parole supervision also lack the constitutional mandates and high public expectations that drive more adequate and stable funding, such as that provided for prisons and public schools.

The political/legislative arena is difficult to characterize in brief. The cost of incarceration is an immense burden on the states, which in turn is forcing changes in release practices. Many legislatures and governors are taking a hard look at alternatives, including sentencing reforms. Almost any conceivable response to the incarceration "problem" will lead to greater reliance on probation and parole. Depending on how extensive the changes are in sentencing or release practices, the impact on probation and parole caseloads case loads and resources could be substantial.

It is not just the legislatures and governors who are looking at this issue. In Arizona and California, voter referenda[7] on the handling of first time drug offenders resulted in significant changes in policy and increased referrals to probation. In California, 50,335 offenders agreed to participate in the alternative to incarceration program from July 1, 2002 to June 30, 2003. Ninety percent of those were sentenced to probation or were already on probation. The remaining 10 percent were parolees.[8] It is clear that sentencing reform to relieve the pressure of incarceration will have a substantial impact on probation and parole caseloads.

While the overall environment of probation and parole is stable, this should not be taken as a positive indicator. Workloads are generally too large and they are growing. Budgets are generally inadequate and getting tighter. The uncertain prospect of sentencing reform looms large over a system with little capacity to absorb additional workload without additional resources.

Strategic Trends

The pressure from the external environment obvi-ously only tells one part of the story. The responses of the probation and parole agencies to these pressures (and others) comprise the strategic trends in probation and parole. These are efforts designed to both cope with a large and often unmanageable workload and to improve the quality and effectiveness of services. The trends are strategic in that they are not case-based or a response to the challenges of one program, but redefine the missions and organizational culture of probation and parole. The six strategic trends are: collaboration and partnerships, results-driven management, re-emergence of rehabilitation, specialization, technology and community justice.

1. Collaboration and Partnerships. Probation and parole agencies are increasingly recognizing that they can not do it alone. They need the expertise and assistance of others. This is a trend that is emerging throughout all levels of government.[9] Ironically, line officers have been collaborating for years—with the police officers, drug counselors, teachers, psychologists, employment specialists and others—who were also involved with their clients. The critical difference today is that these partnerships are forged at a higher level and are more formal. They involve the sharing of important organizational commodities— staff time and resources, information, decision-making authority and political power. Important and influential decision-makers are involved on a regular basis in the operation of these collaborative programs.

The best example of these formal partnerships is the drug court and other specialty "treatment courts." Other examples of partnerships include school-based probation, police/probation partnerships, the offender reentry initiative, and collaborative case management and supervision for specific offender groups such as sex offenders, the mentally ill, DUI offenders and domestic violence offenders.

Implications—Collaborations and partnerships would seem to be an easy and smart thing to do. They do, however require some changes for those participating. Role's and responsibilities need to be discussed and revised to accommodate the new approach. The sharing of resources and decision-making authority can be a difficult concept for traditional bureaucrats. In some instances, statutory or rule changes may be necessary to allow information sharing, particularly with juvenile offenders.

2. Results-Driven Management. The mandate to demonstrate results is part of a larger national and international movement at all levels of government. It is another trend that is transforming government,[10] and probation and parole are no exception. Also known more generically as performance measurement, results-driven management requires that managers and their organizations be able to demonstrate both what they are doing (compliance and accountability) and what they are producing (outcomes or results). It is no longer good enough to be busy with large caseloads and hardworking staff. Agencies need to be productive, delivering the services as expected or required, and producing the results that matter, results that their constituents want. It is not enough to measure against internally set standards and goals —probation and parole must begin to address how they produce "public value."

Results-driven management requires a substantial investment of agency time and resources. The agency mission, goals and measures must be articulated and agreed upon. Resources, program rules and procedures must be aligned with the mission and goals. Managers and staff must engage in a regular examination and discussion of outcomes and must make those reports available to those outside the agency, who can use this outcome information in determining resource allocations.

Implications—Done well, results-driven management will produce more and better information about the agency's performance, both good and bad. This information will produce pressure for support of good programs and pressure to fix poor performers. Ultimately, the pressure could demand the elimination of poor performing programs. Information on agency and program performance will inform the budget process and make it more complex at the same time.

3. The Re-emergence of Rehabilitation. Probation and parole were established in this country in the middle of the 19th century. Both were founded on the principle that offenders could change and that the correctional system, and probation and parole officers in particular, had a central role in helping the offender change. In the 1970s, rehabilitation and correctional treatment were attacked as ineffective, and ultimately abandoned. The driving forces behind the attack were largely political (the "get tough on crime" movement), although a well-timed academic study was distorted to undermine the effectiveness of correctional treatment.[11] By the start of the 1980s, states were well on their way to erasing all traces of rehabilitation from corrections, including probation and parole.

At the same time, a small group of Canadian researchers was assembling a body of research that suggested that correctional rehabilitation was indeed effective, if done well. Over the decade of the 1980s and into the 1990s, this research continued to grow and provide increasing support for well designed treatment. The body of research became known as the "what works" literature. Increasingly, probation and parole agencies are becoming aware of this work and are adopting it.

The research is an important foundation for the effort to return to rehabilitation, but the bridge must be made to practical application if its full potential is to be reached. Two other developments have embraced the idea that correctional treatment works, and they are having a profound impact, having bridged the gap between theory and practice.

In 1989, the first drug court was established in Miami. Judge Stanley Goldstein and his colleagues developed the first drug court out of frustration for the revolving door that seemed to characterize his courtroom when dealing with drug offenders. The drug court is based on rehabilitation of the drug offender, not just incarceration. The success of the drug court model is widely known and the concept as spread across the country with great speed.[12] It was suddenly acceptable to talk openly about treatment and rehabilitation.

The second development is the prisoner reentry initiative, begun in the late 1990s. Re-entry is based on the recognition that hundreds of thousands of inmates who were incarcerated during the "get tough" era from 1980 on will soon be released from prison. What is noteworthy is that these inmates did not have the benefit of the correctional programs and treatment that formerly characterized a stay in prison. At best, these inmates will be no better off than when they went in, and more likely will pose a greater risk of re-offending as the result of their time inside the prison.[13]

The re-entry model views the period of incarceration as time when inmates should be participating in programs and treatment to better prepare them to return to the community. The incarceration should be followed by a graduated release back into the community, followed by supervision in the community by a parole officer, who is charged with assisting the offender with the transition to freedom. The re-entry concept embraces the rehabilitative model throughout all three phases.

Implications—Embracing the rehabilitative model requires a significant role redefinition and organizational change for probation and parole. An entire generation of staff has grown up in the field without exposure to treatment and rehabilitation. One of the key findings of the 'what works' research is that treatment cannot be done in a slip-shod manner and be effective. The large caseloads that currently epitomize probation and parole will significantly hinder the ability to officers to follow the principles of effective treatment. Additional resources or a realignment of resources will be necessary. Changing the mission of community corrections will also have political implications, for there are still many who believe strongly that incarceration is the most effective way to deal with criminals.

4. Specialization. As the problems facing society have grown more complex and challenging, so have the offenders who are sentenced to probation or released to parole. Today, the average agency caseload includes adult and juvenile offenders with alcohol and drug addictions, the mentally ill, sex offenders, drunk drivers, gang members, violent offenders and offenders with combinations of all of the above.

As the number of these "special needs" offenders grew, probation and parole agencies began to specialize their services. In the beginning, this meant putting all of the like offenders in one caseload. Staff assigned to those caseloads then began to develop experience and gained specialized expertise through training. As the knowledge about these cases grew, the nature and type of supervision changed. Caseloads were limited in size, and supervision was targeted to the special needs of the population. Officers began to consult with specialists and treatment providers from other agencies, providing more comprehensive services. Lastly, probation and parole agencies began to enter into formal partnerships with other agencies to provide more comprehensive supervision for these offenders.

Today it is commonplace to see a full array of specialized caseloads and even units in all but the smallest of probation and parole departments. This development is mirrored in the professional literature, which reflects an increased depth and sophistication about effective supervision and treatment strategies and techniques.

Implications—Specialization almost always requires additional resources for smaller caseloads, specialized training, purchase of treatment services and perhaps even hiring of specialists to provide services directly, if the numbers warrant. This approach poses particular problems for small departments, which have neither the number of cases to support specialization nor sufficient numbers of staff to specialize. Yet these departments still have the problematic offenders in their caseloads.

5. Technology. America's pursuit of the better mousetrap has penetrated probation and parole. The private sector is offering products that use a variety of electronic and chemical technologies to help monitor behavior and detect violations. Electronic monitoring is probably the best known, and includes global positioning satellite systems, the well-known ankle bracelet and voice verification systems. Vendors offer a full array of drug testing products that use urine, saliva and hair to detect drug use. The handheld breathalyzer can detect alcohol use, and that same technology has been incorporated into the ignition interlock, which prevents an intoxicated person from starting a vehicle. One product now on the market tests pupil response to determine if the subject is currently under the influence of drugs.

With sex offenders, software is available that can monitor the offender's computer use and report to the probation or parole officer what Internet sites the offender has visited. The polygraph is used frequently to monitor the truthfulness of sex offenders. Advances in computer software and improved interfaces between systems make it much easier for agencies to share information across jurisdictional and state lines.

Implications—As technology advances and becomes less expensive, it becomes more attractive and affordable to probation and parole. One big challenge that must be considered is how the system will respond to the increased ability to detect illegal behavior. With extra "eyes and ears" watching the offenders, officers will be confronted with additional violations. How will the system handle these cases? Are there effective strategies that can be used? Failure to respond effectively will undermine the effectiveness of the technology.

Technology almost always costs money. Some agencies pass the cost on the offender, but for some technologies (computer interfaces) and some offenders (those who are indigent), that is not possible. Any contract with a vendor raises concerns about the bidding and contracting process. There may be statutory and regulatory changes required allowing the use of certain technologies. Monitoring technologies raise a critical staffing issue. Notifications about violations can come from electronic monitoring systems at any hour of the day or night. Who will respond, or will there even be a response at 4:00AM? Real time monitoring does not fit into a traditional work schedule.

6. Community Justice. Dissatisfaction with the traditional justice system and its almost exclusive focus on the offender has generated a new paradigm called community justice. Under this approach, the justice system expands its focus beyond just finding and sanctioning the offender. The victim of the crime and the community itself are brought in to participate, and the process of justice expands from just sanctioning the offender to include restoring the victim and the community. The process also includes community-based problem-solving to prevent future crime. The justice system and the community join together to take a proactive, preventive and holistic approach to crime prevention.

A community justice system provides a role for the victim and dispositions of cases are likely to feature restitution and community service. It also provides a role for the community, and that can include advisory boards or something similar to Vermont's reparative boards, where citizens play a role in determining the disposition of the case.[14]

Implication—Adoption of a community justice model has profound implications for the justice system. It involves a fundamental re-tooling of the mission and roles of all components of the system, significant training requirements, partnerships with the community, and may require statutory changes to support its implementation.

Conclusion

The trends discussed above illustrate not only the forces that are affecting probation and parole, but also how the field is responding in an effort to accomplish its mission and improve its effectiveness. This is a critical point, because probation and parole play a critical role in achieving the fundamental purpose of the justice systems—preventing crime and ensuring the safety of citizens and the community. No matter whether the focus is probation or parole, adult or juvenile, county or state, the effectiveness of these agencies has implications throughout the justice system, the community and society as a whole. Several examples illustrate the impact of probation and parole:

1. Violations of probation or parole—offenders who violate the conditions of their supervision can be revoked and sentenced to jail or prison. A less effective program of supervision can result in more revocations and people sent to jail or prison, exacerbating the crowding in the correctional institutions.

2. Confidence of judges and paroling authorities—if the key decision-makers have confidence in the supervision provided, they will be more likely to sentence to probation or release to parole. This can reduce jail and prison crowding.

3. Demand for other justice services—if probation and parole are not effective in supervising and controlling their caseloads, the offenders will commit additional crimes and increase the demand on

police, prosecution, defense, courts and corrections.

4. Smooth functioning of the justice system – as noted at the outset, probation in particular and parole play a role in almost all aspects of the justice system. An effective and efficient system is reliant on probation and parole to carry out their role and work well with their partners.

5. Public confidence and expectations—the effectiveness of probation and parole can generate public confidence and garner political support if they meet the expectations of the citizens.

6. Community safety—probably the most important aspect of the effectiveness of probation and parole is that it can have a significant impact on public safety when it is done well.

All of the trends—environmental and strategic—clearly point to a continuing central role for probation in the criminal and juvenile justice systems. The consequences of these efforts are also clear. Improved performance of probation and parole will lead to less crime and increased safety. Investment in increased capacity and capability to deliver effective probation and parole services will provide a valuable return in justice and safety for the community.

Notes

[1] Lauren E. Glaze and Seri Pella, *Probation and Parole in the United States, 2003*, (Washington, D.C.: Bureau of Justice Statistics, July 2004).

[2] Charles Puzzanchera, et al, *Juvenile Court Statistics 1999*, (Pittsburgh, PA: National Center for Juvenile Justice. July 2003), 38.

[3] Joan Petersilia, *When Prisoners Come Home: Parole and Prisoners Reentry*, (New York: Oxford University Press, 2003), 65.

[4] Allen J. Beck, "Trends in Community Corrections," (Presentation to the Community Corrections Research Network, Washington, DC. October 19, 2004).

[5] Ibid.

[6] Joan Petersilia, "A Crime Control Rationale for Reinvesting in Community Corrections," *Prison Journal* 74, no. 3 (1995): 479-96.

[7] Proposition 200 in Arizona and Proposition 36 in California.

[8] Douglas Longshore, et al, *Evaluation of the Substance Abuse and Crime Prevention Act: 2003 Report*, (Los Angeles: UCLA Integrated Substance Abuse Programs, September 2004.)

[9] Mark A. Abramson, Jonathan D. Breul and John M. Kamensky, "Four Trends Transforming Government," *The Business of Government*, (Summer 2003): 17-18.

[10] Ibid., 12-13.

[11] Robert Martinson, "What Works? Questions and Answers About Prison Reform," *The Public Interest*, (Spring 1974): 22-54.

[12] James L. Nolan, Jr., *Reinventing Justice: The American Drug Court Movement*, (Princeton, NJ: Princeton University Press, 2001).

[13] Joan Petersilia, *When Prisoners Come Home: Parole and Prisoners Reentry*, (New York: Oxford University Press, 2003).

[14] David R. Karp, "Does Community Justice Work?" *Perspectives* 27, no. 1 (Winter 2003): 32-7

References

Abramson, Mark A., Jonathan D. Breul and John M. Kamensky. "Four Trends Transforming Government." *The Business of Government* (Summer 2003): 17-18.

Andrews, Don and James Bonta. *The Psychology of Criminal Conduct*, 3rd. ed. Cincinnati: Anderson Publishing, 2004

Bogue, Brad, et al. *Implementing Evidence-Based Principles in Community Corrections: Collaboration for Systemic Change in the Criminal Justice System.* Washington, DC: National Institute of Corrections, 2004.

Boone, Harry and Betsy Fulton. *Results-Driven Management.* Lexington, KY: American Probation and Parole Association, 1995.

Clear, Todd R. and David Karp. *The Community Justice Ideal: Preventing Crime and Achieving Justice.* Boulder, CO: Westview Press, 1999.

Crowe, Ann. *Intervening in Family Violence: A Resource Manual for Community Corrections Professionals.* Lexington, KY: American Probation and Parole Association, 1995.

Crowe, Ann. *Offender Supervision with Electronic Technology: A User's Guide.* Lexington, KY: American Probation and Parole Association, 2002.

The Council of State Governments. *Criminal Justice / Mental Health Consensus Project.* New York: The Council of State Governments, June 2002.

English, Kim, Suzanne Pullen and Linda Jones, eds. *Managing Adult Sex Offenders: A Containment Approach.* Lexington, KY: American Probation and Parole Association, 1996.

Fulton, Betsy. *Restoring Hope Through Community Partnerships: The Real Deal in Crime Control.* Lexington, KY: American Probation and Parole Association, 1996.

Goldsmith, Stephen and William D. Egggers. *Governing by Network: The New Shape of the Public Sector.* Washington, DC: The Brookings Institution, 2004.

Moore, Mark H. *Creating Public Value.* Cambridge, MA: Harvard University Press, 1995.

National Institute of Corrections. *Topics in Community Corrections: Collaboration – An Essential Strategy.* Washington, DC, 2001.

Nolan, James L., Jr. *Reinventing Justice: The American Drug Court Movement.* Princeton, NJ: Princeton University Press, 2001.

Petersilia, Joan. *When Prisoners Come Home: Parole and Prisoners Reentry.* New York: Oxford University Press, 2003.

Reinventing Probation Council. *Transforming Probation Through Leadership: The "Broken Windows" Model.* New York: The Manhattan Institute, 2000.

Robertson, Robyn D. and Herbert M. Simpson. *DWI System Improvements: Stopping the Revolving Door*, Ottawa, Canada, 2003.

About the Author

William D. Burrell is associate professor in the Department of Criminal Justice of Temple University in Philadelphia. In 2003, he retired as chief of probation services for the New Jersey state court system. He is chairman of the editorial committee for *Perspectives*, the journal of the American Probation and Parole Association, and writes a bimonthly column on management issues for *Community Corrections Report*.

Table 9.4
TRENDS IN STATE PRISON POPULATION BY REGION, 2002-2003

State or other jurisdiction	Total population			Percent chamge from -		Incarceration rate June 30, 2003 (a)
	June 30, 2003	December 31, 2003	June 30, 2002	June 30, 2002 to June 30, 2003	December 31, 2002 to June 30, 2003	
United States	1,460,920	1,437,807	1,419,937	2.9%	1.6%	480
Federal	170,461	163,528	161,681	5.4	4.2	51
State	1,290,459	1,274,279	1,258,256	2.6	1.3	429
Eastern Region						
Connecticut (b)	20,525	20,720	20,243	1.4	-0.9	403
Delaware (b)	6,879	6,778	6,957	-1.1	1.5	500
Maine	2,009	1,900	1,841	9.1	5.7	148
Massachusetts (c)	10,511	10,329	10,620	-1.0	1.8	235
New Hampshire	2,483	2,451	2,476	0.3	1.3	193
New Jersey (d)	28,213	27,891	28,054	0.6	1.2	327
New York	65,914	67,065	67,131	-1.8	-1.7	343
Pennsylvania	40,545	40,168	39,275	3.2	0.9	328
Rhode Island (b)	3,569	3,520	3,694	-3.4	1.4	187
Vermont (b)	1,984	1,863	1,768	12.2	6.5	226
Regional total	182,632	182,685	182,059	0.0	0.0	. . .
Midwestern Region						
Illinois (d)	43,186	42,693	43,142	0.1	1.2	341
Indiana	22,576	21,611	21,425	5.4	4.5	363
Iowa	8,395	8,398	8,172	2.7	0.0	285
Kansas (d)	9,009	8,935	8,758	2.9	0.8	331
Michigan	49,524	50,961	49,961	-0.9	-2.1	491
Minnesota	7,612	7,129	6,958	9.4	6.8	150
Nebraska	4,103	4,058	4,031	1.8	1.1	232
North Dakota	1,168	1,112	1,168	0.0	5.0	175
Ohio (d)	45,831	45,646	45,349	1.1	0.4	401
South Dakota	3,059	2,918	2,900	5.5	4.8	398
Wisconsin	22,366	22,133	21,963	1.8	1.1	393
Regional total	216,829	215,594	213,827	1.0	1.0	. . .
Southern Region						
Alabama	28,440	27,947	27,495	3.4	1.8	612
Arkansas	12,378	13,091	12,655	-2.2	-5.4	445
Florida (g)	80,352	75,210	73,553	(e)	(e)	472
Georgia (f)	47,004	47,445	46,417	1.3	-0.9	541
Kentucky	16,377	15,923	16,172	1.3	2.9	384
Louisiana	36,091	36,032	36,171	-0.2	0.2	803
Maryland	24,186	24,162	24,329	-0.6	0.1	427
Mississippi	20,542	19,923	19,287	6.5	3.1	688
Missouri	30,649	30,099	30,034	2.0	1.8	537
North Carolina	33,334	32,796	32,755	1.8	1.6	348
Oklahoma (d)	23,004	22,702	23,435	(e)	1.3	645
South Carolina	24,247	23,715	23,017	5.3	2.2	561
Tennessee	25,409	24,989	24,277	4.7	1.7	435
Texas	164,222	162,003	157,664	4.2	1.4	692
Virginia	34,733	34,973	32,739	(e)	-0.7	470
West Virginia	4,703	4,544	4,488	4.8	3.5	257
Regional total	605,671	595,554	584,488	4.0	2.0	. . .
Western Region						
Alaska (b)	4,431	4,398	4,205	5.4	0.8	399
Arizona (f)	30,741	29,359	29,103	5.6	4.7	502
California	163,361	161,361	160,315	1.9	1.2	455
Colorado (d)	19,085	18,833	18,320	4.2	1.3	419
Hawaii (b)	5,635	5,423	5,541	1.7	3.9	311
Idaho	5,825	6,203	5,802	0.4	-6.1	426
Montana	3,440	3,323	3,515	-2.1	3.5	375
Nevada	10,527	10,478	10,426	1.0	0.5	466
New Mexico	6,173	5,989	5,929	4.1	3.1	312
Oregon	12,422	12,085	11,812	5.2	2.8	349
Utah	5,594	5,565	5,353	4.5	0.5	234
Washington	16,284	16,062	15,829	2.9	1.4	262
Wyoming	1,809	1,737	1,732	4.4	4.1	361
Regional total	285,327	280,816	277,882	3.0	2.0	. . .
Regional total without California	121,966	119,455	117,567	4.0	2.0	. . .

Source: U.S. Department of Justice, Bureau of Justice Statistics, *Bulletin, Prisoners and Jail Inmates at Midyear 2003* (May 2004).

Key:
. . . - Not available.

(a) The number of prisoners with sentences of more than one year per 100,000 residents.

(b) Prisons and jails form one integrated system. Data include total jail and prison population.

(c) The incarceration rate includes an estimated 6,200 inmates sentenced to more than 1 year but held in local jails or houses of corrections.

(d) "Sentenced to more than 1 year" includes some inmates "sentenced to 1 year or less."

(e) Not calculated due to change in reporting.

(f) Population figures are based on custody counts.

(g) Population figures in 2003 are jurisdiction counts, not custody counts as in previous years.

Table 9.5
NUMBER OF SENTENCED PRISONERS ADMITTED AND RELEASED, BY REGION: 2000-2002

State or other jurisdiction	Admissions (a)				Releases (a)			
	2002	2001	2000	Percent change 2000-2002	2002	2001	2000	Percent change 2000-2002
United States	663,521	639,978	625,219	6.1%	632,183	628,626	604,858	4.5%
Federal	48,144	45,140	43,732	10.1	42,339	38,370	35,259	20.6
State	615,377	593,838	581,487	5.8	589,844	591,256	569,599	3.6
Eastern Region								
Connecticut	7,169	6,576	6,185	15.9	6,209	6,331	5,918	4.9
Delaware (b)	4,294	2,417	2,709	(c)	4,073	2,330	2,260	(c)
Maine	1,026	820	751	36.6	799	723	677	18.0
Massachusetts	1,833	2,215	2,062	-11.1	2,290	2,482	2,889	-14.8
New Hampshire	1,113	1,171	1,051	5.9	1,052	1,030	1	5.2
New Jersey	14,576	14,422	13,653	6.8	14,827	16,064	15,362	-3.5
New York	26,216	25,473	27,601	-5.0	26,829	28,101	28,828	-6.9
Pennsylvania	13,401	12,811	11,777	13.8	10,628	10,376	11,759	-9.6
Rhode Island	3,760	3,506	3,701	1.6	3,312	3,197	3,223	2.8
Vermont (b)	1,785	972	984	(c)	1,857	1,069	946	(c)
Regional total	75,713	70,383	70,474	7.0	61,594	63,042	63,685	3.0
Midwestern Region								
Illinois	34,467	35,289	29,344	17.5	36,162	36,313	28,876	25.2
Indiana	14,001	13,012	11,876	17.9	13,337	12,207	11,053	20.7
Iowa	5,516	4,826	4,656	18.5	5,748	5,357	4,379	31.3
Kansas	4,881	4,502	5,002	-2.4	4,524	4,270	5,231	-13.5
Michigan	14,411	13,105	12,169	18.4	12,771	11,928	10,874	17.4
Minnesota	5,265	4,620	4,406	19.5	4,706	4,250	4,244	10.9
Nebraska	1,934	1,783	1,688	14.6	1,840	1,738	1,503	22.4
North Dakota	768	747	605	26.9	770	715	598	28.8
Ohio	25,689	24,399	23,780	8.0	25,322	24,953	24,793	2.1
South Dakota	1,819	1,556	1,400	29.9	1,797	1,380	1,327	35.4
Wisconsin	7,990	7,442	8,396	-4.8	7,699	7,027	8,158	-5.6
Regional total	116,741	111,281	103,322	13.0	114,676	110,138	101,036	14.0
Southern Region								
Alabama	7,033	7,428	6,296	11.7	7,472	7,905	7,136	4.7
Arkansas	7,080	6,977	6,941	2.0	7,640	6,613	6,308	21.1
Florida	36,500	35,064	35,683	2.3	33,728	34,015	33,994	-0.8
Georgia	18,078	17,342	17,373	4.1	16,608	15,758	14,797	12.2
Kentucky	8,731	7,450	8,116	7.6	8,313	8,234	7,733	7.5
Louisiana	15,079	15,667	15,735	-4.2	14,847	15,031	14,536	2.1
Maryland	10,027	10,399	10,327	-2.9	9,617	10,050	10,004	-3.9
Mississippi	5,655	6,880	5,796	-2.4	5,592	5,685	4,940	13.2
Missouri	16,637	15,183	14,454	15.1	15,127	13,892	13,346	13.3
North Carolina	9,661	9,433	9,848	-1.9	8,606	8,935	9,687	-11.2
Oklahoma	8,269	7,872	7,426	11.4	8,375	8,265	6,628	26.4
South Carolina	9,834	9,218	8,460	16.2	8,604	8,627	8,676	-0.8
Tennessee	15,022	14,295	13,675	9.9	13,541	12,690	13,893	-2.5
Texas	63,446	61,276	58,197	9.0	64,720	66,228	59,776	8.3
Virginia	11,392	11,310	9,791	16.4	10,033	9,816	9,148	9.7
West Virginia	2,161	1,783	1,577	37.0	1,807	1,422	1,261	43.3
Regional total	244,605	237,577	229,695	6.0	234,630	233,166	221,863	6.0
Western Region								
Alaska	2,775	2,142	2,427	14.3	2,394	2,041	2,599	-7.9
Arizona	11,468	10,000	9,560	20.0	10,056	9,053	9,100	10.5
California	124,179	126,895	129,640	-4.2	119,683	129,982	129,621	-7.7
Colorado	7,953	7,252	7,036	13.0	6,588	6,634	5,881	12.0
Hawaii	1,892	1,700	1,594	18.7	1,735	1,581	1,379	25.8
Idaho	3,049	2,699	3,386	-10.0	2,855	2,539	2,697	5.9
Montana	1,510	1,472	1,202	25.6	1,518	1,246	1,031	47.2
Nevada	4,844	4,639	4,929	-1.7	4,734	4,480	4,374	8.2
New Mexico	4,009	2,545	3,161	26.8	3,809	3,194	3,383	12.6
Oregon	5,041	4,473	4,059	24.2	4,339	3,668	3,371	28.7
Utah	3,064	2,864	3,270	-6.3	2,864	3,151	2,897	-1.1
Washington (b)	8,305	7,185	7,094	(c)	7,401	6,957	6,764	(c)
Wyoming	769	731	638	20.5	686	723	697	-1.6
Regional total	178,858	174,597	177,996	0.0	168,662	175,249	173,794	-3.0
Regional total without California	54,679	47,702	48,356	13.0	48,979	45,267	44,173	11.0

Source: U.S. Department of Justice, Bureau of Justice Statistics, *Bulletin, Prisoners and Jail Inmates at Midyear 2003* (May 2004).
Note: Excludes AWOL's and transfers to or from other jurisdictions.
Key:
(a) Based on inmates under jurisdiction with a sentence of more than one year.

(b) Data may not be comparable from year to year due to changing reporting methods.
(c) Not calculated due to changes in reporting.

Table 9.6
ADULTS ON PROBATION BY REGION, 2003

State or other jurisdiction	Probation population				Percent change during 2003	Number on probation on 12/31/03 per 100,000 adult residents
	1/1/03	2003 Entries	2003 Exits	12/31/03		
United States	4,024,067	2,229,668	2,179,847	4,073,987	1.2%	1,876
Federal	31,330	13,989	14,449	30,599	-2.3	14
State	3,992,737	2,215,679	2,165,398	4,043,388	1.3	1,862
Eastern Region						
Connecticut	50,984	24,384	23,176	52,192	2.4	1,983
Delaware	20,201	13,962	15,242	18,921	-6.3	3,058
Maine	9,446	6,625	6,216	9,855	4.3	984
Massachusetts (a)(b)(c)	131,319	56,933	61,117	127,135	. . .	2,585
New Hampshire (d)	3,702	1,480	1,052	4,130	11.6	426
New Jersey	134,290	40,601	50,610	124,281	-7.5	1,907
New York (b)	132,966	39,590	48,261	124,295	-6.5	859
Pennsylvania (c)	130,786	52,072	45,652	137,206	4.9	1,454
Rhode Island	25,914	6,451	6,436	25,929	0.1	3,143
Vermont	10,096	4,908	5,202	9,802	-2.9	2,085
Regional total	649,704	247,006	262,964	633,746	-2.0	18,484
Midwestern Region						
Illinois	141,544	63,000	60,090	144,454	2.1	1,542
Indiana	114,209	94,741	97,324	111,626	-2.3	2,424
Iowa	19,970	14,600	13,685	20,885	4.6	945
Kansas (c)	15,217	23,315	23,981	14,551	-4.4	725
Michigan (c) (d)	174,577	130,857	129,029	176,392	1.0	2,364
Minnesota	122,692	59,517	71,484	110,725	-9.8	2,953
Nebraska	16,468	15,845	13,901	18,412	11.8	1,432
North Dakota	3,229	2,332	2,059	3,502	8.5	737
Ohio (c) (d)	215,186	146,723	142,616	219,658	2.1	2,573
South Dakota	5,088	3,261	3,129	5,236	2.9	933
Wisconsin	54,614	25,449	24,727	55,336	1.3	1,354
Regional total	882,794	579,640	582,025	880,777	0.2	17,982
Southern Region						
Alabama	39,713	15,152	15,213	39,652	-0.2	1,177
Arkansas	27,377	9,168	8,419	28,126	2.7	1,380
Florida (c)(d)	291,315	257,539	261,212	287,641	-1.3	2,169
Georgia (c)(e)	367,349	230,686	173,650	424,385	. . .	. . .
Kentucky (c)	24,480	16,165	11,949	28,696	17.2	921
Louisiana	36,257	13,875	13,455	36,677	1.2	1,120
Maryland	81,982	39,037	43,144	77,875	-5.0	1,890
Mississippi (c)(f)	16,633	8,773	6,290	18,116	14.9	911
Missouri	54,584	26,512	25,486	55610	1.9	1,305
North Carolina	112,900	60,782	60,521	113161	0.2	1,770
Oklahoma (d)	29,881	15,299	16,854	28,326	-5.2	1,082
South Carolina	41,574	14,760	16,287	40,047	-3.7	1,285
Tennessee (c)	42,712	24,256	24,132	42,836	0.3	968
Texas	434,486	200,450	202,947	431,989	-0.6	2,698
Virginia	40,359	30,669	29,365	41,663	3.2	743
West Virginia (c)	6,430	3,072	2,638	6,864	6.7	487
Regional total	1,648,032	966,195	911,562	1,701,664	3.2	19,906
Western Region						
Alaska	5,229	973	796	5,406	3.4	1,185
Arizona (d)	66,485	39,115	39,795	65,805	-1.0	1,586
California (d)	358,121	180,636	164,059	374,701	4.6	1,441
Colorado (c)(d)	57,328	28,954	30,985	55,297	-3.5	1,623
Hawaii	16,772	7,006	6,126	17,652	5.2	1,822
Idaho (d) (g)	31,361	25,360	24,501	32,220	2.7	. . .
Montana	6,703	3,898	3,687	6,914	3.1	1,006
Nevada	12,290	5,869	6,000	12,159	-1.1	716
New Mexico	16,287	7,662	7,813	16,136	-0.9	1,186
Oregon	45,397	16,275	16,847	44,825	-1.3	1,662
Utah	10,646	5,429	5,696	10,379	-2.5	646
Washington (c)(d)	171,603	93,132	91,921	172,814	0.7	3,767
Wyoming	4,596	1,932	1,866	4,662	1.4	1,255
Regional total	802	416,241	400,092	818,970	2.0	17,895
Regional total without California	444,697	235,605	236,033	444,269	-0.9	16,454
Dist. of Columbia (c)(d)	9,389	6,597	8,755	7,231	. . .	1,612

Source: U.S. Department of Justice, Bureau of Justice Statistics, *Probation and Parole in the United States, 2003*, (July 2004).

Note: Because of incomplete data, the population for some jurisdictions on December 31, 2003, does not equal the population on January 1, 2003, plus entries, minus exits.

Key:
. . . — Not calculated.
(a) Data are for June 30, 2002 and 2003. Some data for June 30, 2002 , were estimated.

(b) Due to changes in reporting criteria, data are not comparable to previous reports.
(c) Data for entries and exits were estimated for nonreporting agencies.
(d) All data were estimated.
(e) Counts include private agency cases and may overstate the number under supervision.
(f) Data are for year ending December 1, 2003.
(g) Counts include estimates for misdemeanors based on annual admissions.

Table 9.7
ADULTS ON PAROLE BY REGION, 2003

State or other jurisdiction	Parole population				Percent change during 2003	Number on parole on 12/31/03 per 100,000 adult residents
	1/1/2003	2003 Entries	2003 Exits	12/31/2003		
United States	750,934	492,727	470,538	774,588	0.0	357
Federal	83,063	33,590	31,088	86,459	4.1	40
State	667,871	459,137	439,450	688,129	3.0	317
Eastern Region						
Connecticut	2,186	3,260	2,847	2,599	18.9	99
Delaware	551	217	239	529	-4.0	85
Maine	32	0	0	32	0.0	3
Massachusetts	3,951	6,305	6,552	3,704	-6.3	370
New Hampshire (a)	963	719	482	1,200	24.6	124
New Jersey	12,576	10,322	9,650	13,248	5.3	203
New York	55,990	25,049	25,186	55,853	-0.2	386
Pennsylvania (b)	97,712	30,870	26,338	102,244	4.6	1,084
Rhode Island	384	456	448	392	2.1	48
Vermont	797	400	400	797	0.0	170
Regional total	175,142	77,598	72,142	180,598	3.1	2,572
Midwestern Region						
Illinois	35,458	32,476	32,926	35,008	-1.3	374
Indiana	5,877	7,304	6,162	7,019	19.4	152
Iowa (c)	2,787	2,787	2,475	3,099	11.2	140
Kansas (c)	3,990	4,146	3,991	4,145	3.9	207
Michigan	17,648	12,579	9,994	20,233	14.6	271
Minnesota	3,577	4,121	4,102	3,596	0.5	96
Nebraska	574	839	763	650	13.2	51
North Dakota	148	585	507	226	52.7	48
Ohio	17,853	11,670	11,096	18,427	3.2	216
South Dakota	1,640	1,451	1147	1,944	18.5	346
Wisconsin	11,088	6,877	5,999	11,966	7.9	293
Regional total	100,640	84,835	79,162	106,313	5.6	2,194
Southern Region						
Alabama	5,309	4,098	2,457	6,950	30.9	206
Arkansas	12,128	7,379	5,813	13,694	12.9	672
Florida	5,223	4,409	4,680	4,952	-5.2	37
Georgia	20,822	11,738	10,391	22,135	6.3	344
Kentucky (c)	5,968	4,719	3,115	7,572	26.9	243
Louisiana	23,049	13,468	11,452	25,065	8.7	766
Maryland	13,271	8,059	7,588	13,742	3.5	334
Mississippi (d)	1,816	1,103	963	1,816	0.0	87
Missouri	13,533	10,407	8,720	15,220	12.5	357
North Carolina	2,805	3,214	3,342	2,677	-4.6	42
Oklahoma (a)	3,573	1,995	1,521	4,047	. . .	155
South Carolina	3,491	1,025	1,306	3,210	-8.0	103
Tennessee	7,949	3,130	3,314	7,967	0.2	180
Texas (a)	103,068	32,847	33,644	102,271	-0.8	639
Virginia	4,530	2,779	2,475	4,834	6.7	86
West Virginia	999	826	682	1,143	14.4	81
Regional total	227,534	111,196	101,463	237,295	4.3	4332
Western Region						
Alaska (c)	900	614	587	927	. . .	203
Arizona (b)	4,587	8,895	8,115	5,367	17.0	129
California (c)	113,185	148,915	152,305	110,338	-2.5	424
Colorado	6,215	5,298	4,954	6,559	5.5	193
Hawaii	2,525	906	1,191	2,240	-11.3	231
Idaho	1,961	1,486	1,118	2,329	18.8	236
Montana (c)	845	601	631	815	-3.6	119
Nevada	3,971	2,956	2,801	4,126	3.9	243
New Mexico	1,962	1,977	1,532	2,407	22.7	177
Oregon	19,090	8,059	7,380	19,769	3.6	733
Utah	3,352	2,300	2,353	3,299	-1.6	205
Washington (a)	95	45	35	105	10.5	2
Wyoming	570	319	311	578	1.4	156
Regional total	159,258	182,371	183,313	158,859	-0.2	3,051
Regional total without California	44,372	30,278	25,366	49,282	5.3	2,627
Dist. of Columbia (a)(b)	5,297	3,136	3,369	5,064	. . .	1129

Source: U.S. Department of Justice, Bureau of Justice Statistics, *Probation and Parole in the United States, 2003* (July 2004).

Note: Because of incomplete data, the population on December 31, 2003, does not equal the population on January 1, 2003, plus entries, minus exits.

Key:
. . . —Number not calcualted.

(a) All data were estimated.
(b) Data for entries and exits were estimated for nonreporting agencies.
(c) Excludes parolees in one of the following categories: absconder, out of state, or inactive.
(d) Data are for the year ending December 1, 2003.

Table 9.8
CAPITAL PUNISHMENT (as of December 2003)

State or other jurisdiction	Capital offenses	Minimum age	Prisoners under sentence of death	Method of execution
Alabama	Intentional murder with 18 aggravating factors.	16	192	Electrocution or lethal injection
Alaska	. . .	. . .	. . .	. . .
Arizona	First degree murder accompanied by at least 1 of 10 aggravating factors. Capital sentencing excludes persons determined to be mentally retarded.	(l)	123	Lethal gas or lethal injection (a)
Arkansas	Capital murder with a finding of at least 1 of 10 aggravating circumstances; treason. Capital sentencing excludes persons determined to be mentally retarded.	14 (m)	40	Lethal injection or electrocution (b)
California	First-degree murder with special circumstances; train-wrecking; treason; perjury causing execution.	18	629	Lethal gas or lethal injection
Colorado	First-degree murder with at least 1 of 17 aggravating factors; treason. Capital sentencing excludes persons determined to be mentally retarded.	18	3	Lethal injection
Connecticut	Capital felony with 8 forms of aggravated homicide. Capital sentencing excludes persons determined to be mentally retarded.	18 (n)	7	Lethal injection
Delaware	First-degree murder with aggravating circumstances. Capital sentencing excludes persons determined to be mentally retarded.	16	16	Hanging or lethal injection (c)
Florida	First-degree murder; felony murder; capital drug-trafficking; capital sexual battery. Capital sentencing excludes persons determined to be mentally retarded.	17	364	Electrocution or lethal injection
Georgia	Murder; kidnapping with bodily injury or ransom when the victim dies; aircraft hijacking; treason. Capital sentencing excludes persons determined to be mentally retarded.	17	111	Lethal injection
Hawaii	. . .	. . .	. . .	. . .
Idaho	First-degree murder with aggravating factors; aggravated kidnapping.	(l)	19	Firing Squad or lethal injection
Illinois	First-degree murder with 1 of 21 aggravating circumstances.	18	2	Lethal injection
Indiana	Murder with 16 aggravating circumstances. Capital sentencing excludes persons determined to be mentally retarded.	18	35	Lethal injection
Iowa	. . .	. . .	. . .	. . .
Kansas	Capital murder with 8 aggravating circumstances. Capital sentencing excludes persons determined to be mentally retarded.	18	6	Lethal injection
Kentucky	Murder with aggravating factors; kidnapping with aggravating factors. Capital sentencing excludes persons determined to be mentally retarded.	16	35	Electrocution or lethal injection (d)
Louisiana	First-degree murder; aggravated rape of victim under age 12; treason.	(l)	87	Lethal injection
Maine	. . .	. . .	. . .	. . .
Maryland	First-degree murder, either premeditated or during the commission of a felony, provided that certain death eligibility requirements are satisfied. Capital sentencing excludes persons determined to be mentally retarded.	18	11	Lethal injection
Massachusetts	. . .	. . .	. . .	. . .
Michigan	. . .	. . .	. . .	. . .
Minnesota	. . .	. . .	. . .	. . .
Mississippi	Capital murder; aircraft piracy.	16 (o)	66	Lethal injection
Missouri	First-degree murder. Capital sentencing excludes persons determined to be mentally retarded.	18 (r)	52	Lethal injection or lethal gas
Montana	Capital murder with 1 of 9 aggravating circumstances; capital sexual assault.	(p)	5	Lethal injection
Nebraska	First-degree murder with a finding of at least 1 statutorily-defined aggravating circumstance. Capital sentencing excludes persons determined to be mentally retarded.	18	7	Electrocution
Nevada	First-degree murder with at least 1 of 14 aggravating circumstances.	16	84	Lethal injection
New Hampshire	Six categories of capital murder.	17	0	Lethal injection or hanging (e)
New Jersey	Murder by one's own conduct; committed in furtherance of a narcotics conspiracy, or during the commission of the crime of terrorism.	18	14	Lethal injection

See footnotes at end of table.

CAPITAL PUNISHMENT — Continued

State or other jurisdiction	Capital offenses	Minimum age	Prisoners under sentence of death	Method of execution
New Mexico	First-degree murder with at least 1 of 7 statutorily-defined aggravating circumstances. Capital sentencing excludes persons determined to be mentally retarded.	18	2	Lethal injection
New York	First-degree murder with 1 of 13 aggravating factors. Capital sentencing excludes persons determined to be mentally retarded.	18	5	Lethal injection
North Carolina	First-degree murder. Capital sentencing excludes persons determined to be mentally retarded.	17 (f)	195	Lethal injection
North Dakota	. . .	. . .	. . .	. . .
Ohio	Aggravated murder with at least 1 of 10 aggravating circumstances.	18	209	Lethal injection
Oklahoma	First-degree murder in conjunction with a finding of at least 1 of 8 statutorily-defined aggravating circumstances.	16	102	Lethal injection, electrocution or firing squad (g)
Oregon	Aggravated murder.	18	28	Lethal injection
Pennsylvania	First-degree murder with 18 aggravating circumstances.	(l)	230	Lethal injection
Rhode Island	. . .	. . .	. . .	. . .
South Carolina	Murder with 1 of 10 aggravating circumstances. (k)	(l)	71	Electrocution or lethal injection
South Dakota	First-degree murder with 1 of 10 aggravating circumstances; aggravated kidnapping. Capital sentencing excludes persons determined to be mentally retarded.	(q)	4	Lethal injection
Tennessee	First-degree murder with 1 of 15 aggravating circumstances. Capital sentencing excludes persons determined to be mentally retarded.	18	96	Lethal injection or electrocution (h)
Texas	Criminal homicide with 1 of 8 aggravating circumstances.	17	453	Lethal injection
Utah	Aggravated murder. Capital sentencing excludes persons determined to be mentally retarded.	14 (j)	10	Lethal injection or firing squad
Vermont	. . .	. . .	. . .	. . .
Virginia	First-degree murder with 1 of 13 aggravating circumstances. mentally retarded. Capital sentencing excludes persons determined to be mentally retarded.	14 (j)	27	Electrocution or lethal injection
Washington	Aggravated first-degree murder. Capital sentencing excludes persons determined to be mentally retarded.	18	10	Lethal injection or hanging
West Virginia	. . .	. . .	. . .	. . .
Wisconsin	. . .	. . .	. . .	. . .
Wyoming	First-degree murder.	16	1	Lethal injection or lethal gas (i)
Dist. of Columbia	. . .	. . .	. . .	. . .

Sources: U.S. Department of Justice, Bureau of Statistics, *Capital Punishment, 2003*(November 2004).

Note: There were seven prisoners sentenced to death in more than one state. They are included for each state in which they were sentenced to death.

Key:

. . . — No capital punishment statute.

(a) Arizona authorizes lethal injection for persons whose capital sentence was received after 11/15/92; for those sentenced before that date, the condemned may select lethal injection or lethal gas.

(b) Arkansas authorizes lethal injection for those whose capital offense occurred on or after 7/4/83; for those whose offense occurred before that date, the condemned may select lethal injection or electrocution.

(c) Delaware authorizes lethal injection for those whose capital offense occurred after 6/13/86; for those whose offense occurred before that date, the condemned may select lethal injection or hanging.

(d) Kentucky authorizes lethal injection for persons whose capital sentence was received on or after 3/31/98; for those sentenced before that date, the condemned may select lethal injection or electrocution.

(e) New Hampshire authorizes hanging only if lethal injection cannot be given.

(f) The age required is 17 unless the murderer was incarcerated for murder when a subsequent murder occurred; then the age may be 14.

(g) Oklahoma authorizes electrocution if lethal injection is ever held to

be unconstitutional, and firing squad if both lethal injection and electrocution are held unconstitutional.

(h) Tennessee authorizes lethal injection for those whose capital offense occurred after 12/31/98; those whose offense occurred before that date may select electrocution.

(i) Wyoming authorizes lethal gas if lethal injection is ever held to be unconstitutional.

(j) The minimum age for transfer to adult court by statute is 14, but the effective age is 16 based on interpretation of U.S. Supreme Court decisions by the state attorney general's office.

(k) Mental retardation is a mitigating factor.

(l) No age specified.

(m) See Arkansas Code Ann. 9-27-318(c)(2)(Supp. 2001).

(n) See Connecticut Gen. Stat. 53a-46a(g)(1).

(o) The minimum age defined by statute is 13, but the effective age is 16 based on interpretation of U.S. Supreme Court decisions by the Mississippi Supreme Court.

(p) Montana law specifies that offenders tried under the capital sexual assault statute be 18 or older. Age may be a mitigating factor for other capital crimes.

(q) Juveniles may be transferred to adult court. Age can be a mitigating factor.

(r) The minimum age defined by statute is 16, but the effective age is 18 based on interpretation of the 8th Amendment of the U. S. Constitution by the Missouri Supreme Court.

Trends in Welfare Programs
By Sheila R. Zedlewski and Jennifer Holland

Lawmakers on Capitol Hill have been stalemated in their attempts to reauthorize the nation's welfare bill. The stalemate between the House (following the administration's lead) and the Senate over work requirements, childcare dollars and superwaivers has left the original welfare bill unchanged through several "continuing resolutions." In the meantime, states' welfare programs have weathered an economic downturn. While nationwide caseloads continued to decline, some states experienced significant increases in their caseloads. While all states funded a broad array of services as well as basic assistance through their welfare programs, there was considerable variation in funding emphasis. States' flexibility could be curtailed in the future, however, if reauthorization proceeds along the lines proposed.

Recent Caseload Experience

Nationwide, Temporary Assistance for Needy Families (TANF) caseloads have dropped by more than half since passage of welfare reform in 1996. While most of the decline occurred in the first few years after the reforms passed, caseloads continued to decline following the 2000 recession and subsequent sluggish recovery. Caseloads fell below 2 million families in December 2003, the lowest level in over 30 years.

These national trends mask important differences across the states. Since 2000 caseloads have increased in 23 states (Table A); eight states experienced increases of 30 percent or more (Arizona, Colorado, Idaho, Indiana, Mississippi, Nevada, West Virginia and Wisconsin).

Caseload trends during this period of economic decline have stumped many scholars. Most would have predicted caseload increases in all states that experienced increased unemployment, but this did not happen. The national unemployment rate increased gradually between 2000 and 2003 (from 4 percent to 6 percent), but caseloads decreased. State unemployment rates tended to follow the national pattern, and states with the highest unemployment often did not experience rapid caseload growth. For example, state unemployment rates in 2003 ranged from about 4 percent (in Delaware, Georgia, Nebraska, New Hampshire, North Dakota, South Dakota, Virginia and Wyoming) to 8 percent (Alaska, Michigan, Oregon and Washington).[1] Three of the four states with the highest unemployment rates also experienced relatively fast growth in unemployment between 2000 and 2003 (Michigan, Oregon and Washington), but these states experienced either relatively modest or no growth in their TANF caseloads.

Other factors also affect caseloads, including states' TANF programs and their unemployment insurance programs. Some TANF programs discourage entry through diversion, work requirements, strict sanctions, and time limits. Research has shown that new program rules have reduced entry rates.[2] Eligible families are less likely to apply for welfare in the new system, making TANF less sensitive to unemployment rate changes.

The role that unemployment insurance has played in limiting caseload growth during this period of rising unemployment is not yet clear. Prior to passage of welfare reform, many studies showed that few adults leaving welfare gained eligibility for unemployment compensation. However, post-reform evidence suggests that a larger share of former welfare recipients should have qualified for unemployment insurance at least for some time.[3]

Another factor at play may be use of other safety net programs to tide former and potential welfare recipients over when jobs are scarce. In contrast to welfare, food stamp caseloads increased by about 30 percent between 2000 and 2003. A recent study found that a substantially larger share of former welfare recipients received these benefits in 2002 than in 1999. The author concludes that changes in states' administrative procedures that keep food stamp cases open after families leave welfare and new rules liberalizing the vehicle limits and recertification procedures played an important role in increasing food stamp participation among former welfare recipients.[4]

Caseload Work Participation

Caseload work participation rates also provide an important indicator of how states' welfare programs have weathered the recent economic downturn. Work participation rates have moderated somewhat since 1999. Thirty-three percent of the TANF caseload was engaged in work in 2002 (the latest data available), compared with 38 percent in 1999. Participation rates varied from a low of 8 percent in Georgia and Maryland to over 80 percent in Kansas, Montana and Wyoming (Table A). While the federal work participation target was 50 percent in 2002, all states met the target because of the caseload reduction credit.[5] After accounting for the credit, states only had to meet an average work participation rate of 6 percent, and only 11 states had to meet a work participation rate greater than 10 percent. States achieved substantially more than was required by the federal rules.

Comparisons of the work participation rates across the states can be somewhat misleading because the meaning of the rates varies across the states. Some states exclude families with a child younger than age one from work activities and their work participation rate calculation, and waivers that had been approved before 1996 were still in place in 11 states in 2002 can affect states' participation rate calculations. For example, Massachusetts' waiver allows them to exclude families from work requirements until they have received assistance for 24 months. Only 23 percent of the single-parent caseload is included in Massachusetts' work participation calculation. At the other extreme, all families are included in the participation rate calculation in Oregon and 95 percent or more are included in Maine, Utah and Montana.[6]

TANF Spending

States spent over $29 billion on TANF-related expenditures in 2003, including $2.7 billion in transfers to the Child Care Development Fund (CCDF) and the Social Services Block Grant (SSBG). Total TANF expenditures ($26.3 billion) were at the highest level since the program began.

Basic assistance only accounted for 35 percent of spending. Shares spent on other key areas include 9 percent on work activities, 18 percent on childcare, and 8 percent on administration (Table B). Expenditures in the "other category" accounted for 29 percent of the remaining spending and include transportation, separate state programs, tax credits, marriage and family formation, out-of-wedlock pregnancy prevention activities.

Individual states' spending patterns varied considerably from these national averages. Basic assistance accounted for half or more of spending in six states (Hawaii, Maine, Nebraska, New Hampshire, New Jersey and New Mexico). At the other extreme, six states spent less than 20 percent on basic (including Colorado, Idaho, Illinois, Maryland, Wisconsin and Wyoming). The share of total spending on work-related activities varied from 0 percent in 10 states (Colorado, Delaware, Maine, Oklahoma, Oregon, Vermont and West Virginia) to over 20 percent in Maryland, Utah and Virginia. South Carolina stands out because it spent one-third of its TANF expenditures on work-related activities.

Some states devoted more of their TANF monies to childcare services than other states. Nationwide over $5 billion in TANF dollars were spent for childcare in 2003. Nine states (Delaware, DC, Florida, Illinois, Massachusetts, North Carolina, Oklahoma, Washington and Wisconsin) spent at least three in 10 TANF dollars on this type of work support. Only a handful of states spent significantly more than the national average on administration. Colorado, Nevada, New Hampshire and Utah report spending more than twice the national average to administer their programs.

These spending patterns indicate the unique configurations of states' TANF programs. Particular combinations of spending (such as low basic assistance and high child care) do not tend to stand out. Instead, states focused on activities that fit their low-income families' needs and that fit with other spending programs in the state.

Congressional Action

Congressional proposals suggest that TANF reauthorization will reduce states' flexibility and sharpen the program's focus on work participation goals. Proposals in the House and the Senate would increase the share of the caseload required to work from today's 50 percent to 70 percent by 2010.[7] They disagree, however, on how work participation rates would be calculated. The House would maintain a caseload reduction credit, but base it on recent caseload experience. The Senate Finance Committee would move to an employment credit based on the employment rates of families leaving TANF. The House and Senate Finance proposals also differ on the number of weekly hours of work that should be required and the types of activity that can count as work. The House proposes requiring all mothers on welfare to work a 40 hour week—up from 30 hours under current law—and 24 hours would have to be in a paid or unpaid job rather than such work-related activities as training and education. The Senate Finance Committee proposes a 34 hour per week work requirement (24 hours for mothers of preschoolers) and gives states more flexibility to count education and training as work activities.

Both proposals would increase childcare funds. The House proposal would provide an additional $1 billion over five years (with a state match required), and they would authorize (but not guarantee) additional childcare dollars. The Senate Finance bill would add $6 billion in new child care funding over five years.

The added childcare dollars could provide important relief to the states as they comply with tougher work requirements. The Congressional Budget Office (CBO) estimated that the new work requirements in the House proposal would cost states between $3 billion and $9 billion over five years, and Senate Finance Committee's work provisions would cost from $1.1 and $1.5 billion.[8] Both proposals also earmark about $200 million of federal TANF monies for marriage activities over five years. Since the basic block grant would remain fixed at 1996 levels, most states would need to redirect TANF funds from current activities to meet the new requirements.

The remaining major disagreement between the House and the Senate Finance Committee concerns "superwaivers." The House proposal would allow states to waive federal rules for food stamps, public housing, and childcare and redirect these monies to low-income families in new ways. Senate Finance, in contrast, proposes a 10-state superwaiver demonstration limited to childcare, TANF, and Social Services Block grant.

Conclusion

The economic downturn had modest effects on the TANF program. Caseloads increased in 23 states, reversing stunning declines witnessed at the beginning of the program. Caseload work participation rates declined somewhat, although all states still met their targets because of the caseload reduction credits in the current law. Despite caseload increases, most states still spent a relatively small share of their TANF funds on basic assistance. States continued to focus TANF monies on childcare and other types of support services. Most spent relatively little directly on work-related activities in 2003.

Congressional proposals for TANF reauthorization would require many states to change their TANF programs. Areas of agreement between both Houses suggest that a final bill will toughen work requirements and change the participation rate offset either to one based on more recent caseload experience or a credit based on actual employment rates of welfare leavers. Most states will need to shift more spending towards work-related activities, and some may find it necessary to create jobs to meet the new requirements. The additional dollars for childcare in the Senate Finance bill would help states to meet the new requirements. However, the additional childcare dollars are far from certain. Federal budget deficit reduction goals may take precedence over helping states to meet new, tougher work requirements.

Notes

[1]Bureau of Labor Statistics, U.S. Department of Labor, "Over-the-Year Change in Unemployment Rates for States," downloaded from www.bls.gov, December 17, 2004.

[2]Greg Acs, Katherin Ross Phillips, and Sandi Nelson, "The Road Not Taken: Changes in Welfare Entry During the 1990s," December 2003).

[3]See Anu Rangarajan and Carol Razafindrakoto, "Unemployment Insurance as a Potential Safety Net for TANF Leavers: Evidence from Five States," Washington, D.C.: Mathematica Policy Research, 2004.

[4]See Sheila Zedlewski, "Recent Trends in Food Stamp Participation among Poor Families with Children," Washington, D.C.: The Urban Institute, Assessing the New Federalism Working Paper 04–03, 2004.

[5]The caseload reduction credit allows states to reduce participation rates by one percentage point for each percentage point decline in the caseload since fiscal year 1995.

[6]Pavetti, LaDonna, "The Challenge of Achieving High Work Participation Rates in Welfare Programs," Washington, D.C.: The Brookings Institution, Welfare Reform and Beyond Number 31, October 2004.

[7]The discussion reflects the 2005 proposal of the House Human Resources Subcommittee which mirrors the bill passed by the full House in 2004 and the bill passed by Senate Finance Committee in March 2005. Both the House and Senate expect to move these proposals to full floor action in 2005

[8]Congressional Budget Office, "Potential Cost to States of Meeting Proposed Work Requirement," (Washington, D.C.: CBO, September 2003).

About the Authors

Sheila R. Zedlewski is the director of the Income and Benefits Policy Center at the Urban Institute, a nonpartisan think tank located in Washington, D.C. She also manages the income and employment area of the Institute's Assessing the New Federalism project. Her recent work focuses on understanding low-income family participation in government programs. She has written extensively about the TANF program with a focus on families unable to move from welfare to work.

Jennifer Holland is a research assistant in the Income and Benefits Policy Center at the Urban Institute. Since completion of her B.A. at Vassar College in 2002, she has focused on issues related to the TANF program.

Table A
TRENDS IN TANF CASELOAD, 1996–2003

State or other jurisdiction	TANF family caseload			Percent change from		Work participation rates FY 2002 (b)
	December 2003 (a)	Average monthly FY 2000	Average monthly FY 1996	1996–2000	2000–2003	
Alabama	19,525	19,083	42,393	-55.0%	2.3%	37.3%
Alaska	4,900	7,347	12,253	-40.0	-33.3	39.6
Arizona	52,170	33,723	63,404	-46.8	54.7	25.9
Arkansas	10,695	12,354	22,747	-45.7	-13.4	21.4
California	449,132	498,414	895,960	-44.4	-9.9	27.3
Colorado	14,654	11,154	35,447	-68.5	31.4	35.9
Connecticut	20,975	28,095	58,117	-51.7	-25.3	26.6
Delaware	5,705	6,058	10,388	-41.7	-5.8	25.8
Florida	59,538	67,355	209,718	-67.9	-11.6	30.4
Georgia	57,359	52,928	130,387	-59.4	8.4	8.2
Hawaii	9,080	14,438	21,960	-34.3	-37.1	58.8
Idaho	1,844	1,275	9,008	-85.8	44.6	40.7
Illinois	34,856	83,917	224,148	-62.6	-58.5	58.4
Indiana	51,663	35,872	52,873	-32.2	44.0	62.6
Iowa	19,959	20,025	32,785	-38.9	-0.3	51.2
Kansas	16,156	12,585	25,148	-50.0	28.4	84.8
Kentucky	35,728	38,542	71,827	-46.3	-7.3	32.4
Louisiana	21,215	27,820	70,581	-60.6	-23.7	38.7
Maine	9,676	10,864	20,461	-46.9	-10.9	44.5
Maryland	26,850	29,313	74,106	-60.4	-8.4	8.3
Massachusetts	50,300	44,189	88,365	-50.0	13.8	60.9
Michigan	79,051	74,231	178,002	-58.3	6.5	28.9
Minnesota	34,571	39,040	58,250	-33.0	-11.4	40.4
Mississippi	19,769	14,970	47,954	-68.8	32.1	18.5
Missouri	41,586	46,776	82,717	-43.5	-11.1	25.4
Montana	5,349	4,555	10,836	-58.0	17.4	84.2
Nebraska	11,049	9,538	14,569	-34.5	15.8	28.1
Nevada	9,345	6,274	14,827	-57.7	79.0	21.6
New Hampshire	6,022	5,841	9,538	-38.8	3.1	41.8
New Jersey	43,589	51,630	105,504	-51.1	-15.6	36.4
New Mexico	17,606	23,655	33,852	-30.1	-25.6	42.7
New York	146,952	258,702	431,717	-40.1	-43.2	38.5
North Carolina	39,124	45,725	113,127	-59.6	-14.4	27.4
North Dakota	3,190	2,901	4,892	-40.7	10.0	30.4
Ohio	84,781	97,969	206,722	-52.6	-13.5	56.3
Oklahoma	14,921	14,316	38,809	-63.1	4.2	26.7
Oregon	18,223	17,058	33,444	-49.0	6.8	61.1
Pennsylvania	85,198	89,899	190,329	-52.8	-5.2	10.4
Rhode Island	12,693	16,324	21,226	-23.1	-22.2	24.6
South Carolina	18,931	17,502	45,770	-61.8	8.2	52.4
South Dakota	2,809	2,802	5,995	-53.3	0.3	42.5
Tennessee	72,162	56,148	99,096	-43.3	28.5	41.2
Texas	113,763	127,880	254,953	-49.8	-11.0	30.8
Utah	9,037	8,410	14,767	-43.1	7.5	27.9
Vermont	4,779	6,043	9,057	-33.3	-20.9	21.4
Virginia	9,185	31,864	64,937	-50.9	-71.2	42.9
Washington	54,763	57,008	98,933	-42.4	-3.9	49.8
West Virginia	16,340	12,146	36,562	-66.8	34.5	19.2
Wisconsin	22,043	16,719	60,058	-72.2	31.8	69.4
Wyoming	379	604	4,732	-87.2	-37.2	82.9
Dist. of Columbia	17,221	17,439	25,721	-32.2	-1.3	16.4
United States	1,986,411	2,229,315	4,488,974	-50.3	-10.9	33.4

Sources: U.S. Department of Health and Human Services, Administration for Children and Families, 2004. Total Number of TANF Families and Recipients Fiscal Year 2004 as of 7/31/04. http://www.acf.hhs.gov/news/press/ 2004/TANF_data.htm, and Temporary Assistance for Needy Families (TANF) Sixth Annual Report to Congress. http://www.acf.hhs.gov/programs/ofa/ annualreport6/ar6index.htm.

Key:
(a) Average monthly caseload for FY 2003 not available at time of publication. Most recent 2003 monthly caseload data included here.
(b) Work participation rate for all families, including two parent families. ACF/OFA: 4/25/03.

Table B
TANF SPENDING: COMBINED FEDERAL AND STATE, FY 2003

State or other jurisdiction	Total expenditures (federal and state) (a)	Percentage of basic assistance	Percentage of work related activities	Percentage of child care (b)	Percentage of administrative	Percentage of other
Alabama	201,718,633	23%	10%	31%	7%	29%
Alaska	107,977,794	46	12	23	6	12
Arizona	364,419,429	48	6	12	10	24
Arkansas	60,234,711	37	15	13	13	23
California	6,505,509,884	48	7	20	9	16
Colorado	273,392,839	19	0	9	16	56
Connecticut	476,612,663	28	7	8	5	52
Delaware	59,055,509	34	0	37	7	22
Florida	1,026,846,722	24	9	35	5	27
Georgia	551,615,768	31	19	10	3	37
Hawaii	155,010,178	59	7	17	10	7
Idaho	53,314,453	12	14	21	6	47
Illinois	1,009,914,813	11	10	37	3	39
Indiana	333,686,775	42	9	10	11	28
Iowa	195,556,172	41	9	20	6	24
Kansas	167,134,597	33	6	11	6	44
Kentucky	238,189,893	43	13	28	8	8
Louisiana	322,696,728	21	12	15	9	43
Maine	118,179,675	56	0	19	8	17
Maryland	437,716,868	7	23	17	9	44
Massachusetts	830,647,417	41	2	32	4	21
Michigan	1,224,872,767	32	4	25	8	31
Minnesota	527,545,540	37	15	23	11	14
Mississippi	139,335,300	26	18	21	5	30
Missouri	345,180,567	38	7	21	6	28
Montana	68,188,157	45	15	17	9	14
Nebraska	87,906,035	67	10	18	5	0
Nevada	85,768,264	56	3	5	21	15
New Hampshire	76,603,093	51	9	8	16	16
New Jersey	882,690,121	25	11	7	10	47
New Mexico	154,826,311	50	9	21	4	15
New York	4,747,187,210	34	6	3	10	48
North Carolina	535,841,382	25	13	34	7	21
North Dakota	41,915,124	43	5	9	10	33
Ohio	1,081,617,824	28	8	26	8	30
Oklahoma	249,405,396	23	0	41	4	31
Oregon	225,507,141	36	4	8	15	37
Pennsylvania	1,263,568,867	26	16	18	9	32
Rhode Island	171,402,209	48	5	24	8	14
South Carolina	155,004,530	31	33	3	9	23
South Dakota	30,478,987	37	10	8	10	35
Tenneessee	331,623,052	42	10	27	8	14
Texas	935,409,657	35	10	4	10	41
Utah	143,302,521	30	23	7	27	14
Vermont	80,569,398	43	1	21	10	26
Virginia	281,005,630	46	24	5	6	19
Washington	689,340,493	39	16	30	7	7
West Virginia	163,808,803	42	3	14	15	26
Wisconsin	567,873,780	19	11	42	7	20
Wyoming	90,874,725	16	7	15	7	55
Dist. of Columbia	188,805,540	36	13	32	9	10
United States	29,056,889,945	35	9	18	8	29

Source: U.S. Department of Health and Human Services, Administration for Children and Families, 2004. Fiscal Year 2003 TANF Financial Data. http://www.acf.hhs.gov/programs/ofs/data/tanf_2003.html.

Key:
(a) Includes transfers to the Child Care Development Fund (CCDF) and the Social Services Block Grant (SSBG).
(b) Includes the CCDF transfer.

U.S.-Mexico Trade: Trends and Issues

By Edgar Ruiz and Sujit M. CanagaRetna

One of the most crucial linkages in contemporary international relations involves the multifaceted and complex one shared between the United States and Mexico, a relationship that spans centuries and extends into myriad different arenas.

Introduction

One of the most crucial linkages in contemporary international relations involves the multifaceted and complex one shared between the United States and Mexico, a relationship that spans centuries and extends into myriad different arenas.

While the frequently referenced aspects of this complicated interaction include trade and agriculture, migration, border security, cooperation to combat drug trafficking, efforts to address labor, education, environment, housing, and transportation issues, personal relationships tightly unite the people of both nations. Table A provides a glimpse into several key economic and demographic indicators of the two countries.

U.S.-Mexico Trade Relationship

Any reference to global trading patterns in recent decades has to mention the North American Free Trade Agreement (NAFTA) enacted over 10 years ago. This revolutionary trade agreement, clinched between Mexico, Canada and the United States and implemented on January 1, 1994, created the world's largest free trade area involving more than 406 million people and weaving together the three countries through freer trade and investment. During this 10-year period, three-way trade among the countries escalated to over $623 billion, or approximately $1.7 billion each day, more than double the pre-NAFTA level of $306 billion. Similarly, between 1994 and 2003, cumulative foreign direct investment in the three countries increased by over $1.7 trillion.[1]

In terms of the United States-Mexico trading relationship between 1997 and 2003, the most recent year for which data is available, American exports grew by 37 percent from $71.4 billion to $97.5 billion. In 2000, just before the American economy lapsed into recession, exports to Mexico reached a record $111.7 billion, an impressive figure indeed. In terms of relative importance of exports to Mexico, a review of data for the 1997 to 2003 reveals that from 10 percent of total U.S. exports in 1997, the proportion escalated to 13 percent in 2003. While Mexico had been America's second largest trading partner for a number of years, particularly in the 1997–2003 review period, Mexico's most significant trading partner is the United States. In fact, Mexican exports to the United States grew by an outstanding 342 percent during the first 10 years of NAFTA, ballooning from $42.9 billion in 1993 to $146.8 billion in 2003.

While data on global exports to Mexico are useful, a state-by-state breakdown remains an even more important statistic. Table B provides information for the five states with the highest level of exports (in monetary terms) to Mexico in the 1999 to 2003 period. In dollar terms, Texas' $41.6 billion level reached in 2003 totally eclipsed every other state; California, in second place, stood at $14.9 billion. While almost two-thirds of the states experienced double digit growth rates in their exports to Mexico between 1999 and 2003, despite sluggish economic trends that swept across the United States in the 2001 to 2003 period, six states saw triple-digit growth levels in exports between 1999 and 2003 led by New Mexico (385 percent, $50 million to $242 million) and Maryland (222 percent, $93.4 million to $300.8 million).

Further exploration into exports to Mexico indicates that the major categories are manufacturing, agricultural and livestock products and other commodities. For all three categories in 2003, Texas occupies the top spot in the dollar value of exports while California retains second place in manufacturing and other commodity exports. For agricultural and livestock product exports in 2003, Louisiana secures the second spot. Manufacturing exports to Mexico in 2003 from Texas amounted to $39.5 billion while California's exports totaled $14.3 billion; some of the export items in this category included computers, electronic products and transportation equipment. In terms of agricultural and livestock product exports in 2003, exports to Mexico from Texas added up to $1.1 billion while Louisiana's exports totaled $909.7 million. Other commodity exports from Texas to Mexico in 2003 amounted to $968.5 million while California's exports involved $353.1 million. This

Table A: United States vs. Mexico

Categories	United States	Mexico
Population	290,809,777 in 2003 (U.S. Census Bureau 2003)	101,000,000 in 2002 (World Bank, World Development Report 2004)
Population growth	0.92% per year (2001 estimate, CIA World Fact Book)	1.5% per year (World Bank, World Development Indicators 2003)
Nominal GDP 2003	$10,987.9 billion (Bureau of Economic Analysis, 2001)	$637.2 billion (World Bank, World Development Indicators 2003)
GDP per capita 2002	$35,060 (World Bank, World Development Report 2004)	$5,910 (in 2001, World Bank, World Development Report 2004)
Area	3,717,792 miles	758,445.2 miles

Source: U.S. Embassy in Mexico, www.usembassy-mexico.gov.

Table B: Exports to Mexico: Top Five States, 1999–2003 (in thousands of dollars)

State	1999	2000	2001	2002	2003	Percent change
U.S. total	$87,044,038	$111,720,878	$101,509,075	$97,530,613	$97,457,420	11%
Texas	37,860,871	47,761,022	41,647,797	41,647,027	41,561,359	10
California	13,559,177	17,515,500	16,343,059	16,076,279	14,871,836	10
Michigan	2,387,992	3,970,824	4,790,885	4,238,982	4,006,426	68
Arizona	3,250,971	4,651,656	3,581,323	3,044,186	3,229,462	-1
Illinois	1,862,070	2,392,976	2,260,247	2,102,642	2,152,722	16

Source: International Trade Administration, U.S. Departement of Commerce.

surge in state exports to Mexico is the dominant reason for the rising number of states establishing trade, commercial and/or investment offices in Mexico; as of July 2004, 28 states had launched such offices in Mexico.[2]

In further examining the economic links between the United States and Mexico, the importance of the Partnership for Prosperity has to be mentioned. Launched in September 2001 by President Bush and Mexican President Vicente Fox, this is an effort to harness the resources of both the public and private sectors to create "an environment in which no Mexican feels compelled to leave his home for lack of jobs or opportunity."[3] Key measures in this effort to stimulate economic potential of people in parts of Mexico where growth has lagged and fueled immigration, include expanding and broadening access to capital, investment in small business, sharing best practices and technical expertise, building capacity for future growth, and linking institutions with shared goals.

The sustainability of the U.S.-Mexico trade relationship will depend on the establishment of binational, collaborative efforts among federal, state, and local governments in both countries, as well as the private sector, to enhance economic competitiveness, especially in the maquiladora sector thru value added trade. It will also require significant public and private investments in transportation, technology, and energy infrastructure along strategic trade corridors. These two areas will play a critical role for the future economic relations between the two countries and provide the underpinnings of the U.S.-Mexico relationship in general.

Economic Competitiveness and the Need to Attract Added Value Trade

The maquiladora industry is among the most visible aspects of the U.S.-Mexico trade relationship, especially along the 2,000-mile border shared by the two nations. Maquiladoras are manufacturing plants that process and assemble components imported into Mexico that are, in turn, exported, usually to the United States.[4] The industry uses relatively inexpensive Mexican labor to perform a range of manufacturing operations including assembly and processing. While the establishment of the maquiladora industry pre-dates the implementation of NAFTA, the industry has grown significantly since its enactment.

The maquiladora industry currently is the second largest source of export earnings in Mexico, and comprises a large sector of the U.S.-Mexico trade.[5] Today more than 3,000 maquiladora plants throughout the country employ more than 1 million workers. More than 2,000 of these plants are located in the border region. The industry is a leader in technology development, one of the main industrial engines for Mexico, one of the country's main employers, and one of the pillars for Mexican economic development.[6] Moreover, the maquiladora industry is very dependent on U.S. suppliers, thereby supporting American jobs outside the border region.

Recent global competition and outsourcing however, has impacted this sector. The maquiladora industry lost approximately 277,000 jobs between October 2000 and March 2002, with 187 plants closing or significantly downsizing since 2000.[7] Nearly a fifth of the factories fled to lower-cost locales in Central America, Southeast Asia and China.[8] In the U.S.-Mexico border region, where manufacturing and trade are so vital and is the foundation of the economy, such plant closures and employment loses can be devastating.

In an effort to ameliorate these job losses and investment, states and local governments on both sides of the border are jointly working to develop strategies to enhance the border region's economic competitiveness. Among the goals is to develop and coordinate policies and alliances between federal, state and local governments in the United States and Mexico. The Border Legislative Conference (BLC), a binational program of The Council of State Governments' western and southern regions, recently adopted recommendations to promote value added trade and for the creation of a seamless border that integrates the concepts of "secure, fast and smart" to expedite the crossing of legitimate people and commerce. The concept of "smart" is the utilization of broadband technology and state of the art business practices that permeate the region and the business community to reduce the cost of doing business.

A survey conducted by the College of the Northern Border (COLEF in Spanish) during the peak of the recent maquiladora crisis revealed that plants with the simplest production practices, such as factories involved in textile, clothing, and furniture manufacturing, were among the first to leave. The continued exodus of industries in these sectors to lower-cost countries such as China have made it clear that Mexico can no longer compete on the basis of cheap labor.[9]

The Mexican state of Baja California took steps to ensure the survival of its maquiladora operations by diversifying economic activity and focusing on attracting higher-grade manufacturing sectors less vulnerable to wage competition with other countries such as electronics, automotive and auto parts, aerospace, and medical products. The plants with the most sophisticated, most costly and highest value-added procedures weathered the economic crisis best.[10] Most recently, in the city of Mexicali, Baja California's capital, Mexican officials and U.S. investors announced plans to attract computer chip companies to build multibillion dollar factories at an industrial park instead of exporting production to Asia.[11]

Mexico's proximity to the United States, the world's largest consumer market, gives it a unique advantage over other countries. Its location is "ideal for designing and producing items for which proximity to the end user matters."[12] The maquiladora industry's long term prosperity, experts say, will depend on Mexico's ability to capitalize on this advantage with rapid-fire turn around that Asia and other countries can't match, while moving up the value chain to produce more complex products that aren't as dependent on rock-bottom factory wages.[13]

While the contribution of the maquiladora industry to the overall Mexican economy remains crucial, the role of the non-maquiladora investments remains substantially larger.[14] In fact, less than 15 percent of the $170 billion in foreign direct investment that flowed into Mexico since NAFTA involved maquiladora operations. In sum, both the maquiladora and non-maquiladora operations coalesced to significantly expand Mexico's economic potential by creating jobs, boosting competition and productivity, lowering prices, and expanding consumer choice.

Infrastructure and Trade Corridors

As the U.S. and Mexican economies further integrate and trade between the two countries flourishes, there will be a continual increase in commercial vehicular traffic at U.S.-Mexico ports of entry, as well as in interior highways in both countries. Given that most U.S.-Mexico trade moves across land via commercial vehicles, policy-makers at every level of government have to enact measures to accommodate these burgeoning trade volumes. In Texas alone, 23 international crossings serve as overland ports of entry for trade with Mexico. The state's ports of entry handle approximately 80 percent of U.S.-Mexico overland trade, of which 90 percent moves via commercial vehicle over NAFTA corridors that originate and end in the United States and Mexico. This percentage is not expected to change anytime in the foreseeable future. Rather the number of commercial vehicle crossings will grow exponentially over the next 10 to 15 years, creating choke points for trade.[15]

Commercial vehicles operating in the border region usually face long waits associated with government inspections, customs processing and increasingly, lack of adequate infrastructure at inspection facilities. These factors increase traffic congestion that impede commercial and non-commercial traffic in border communities and land border ports of entry, and have significant environmental impacts. Additionally, many state and local roads and highways leading to and from border ports of entry are not adequate to meet the growing demands of increased cross-border trade.

The increase in United States and Mexico over the last 10 years has not been matched by an increase in infrastructure investments by both countries. Since the enactment of NAFTA in 1994, state and local governments have provided much of the necessary infrastructure to facilitate the growing cross-border trade with limited federal support. According to the North American Development Bank (NADBank), a binational institution established under the auspices of NAFTA to finance environmental infrastructure projects, Mexico needs to invest $25 billion annually to meet their infrastructure needs. In addition, the U.S. Government Accountability Office's congressional report of March 2000 on U.S.-Mexico border infrastructure, concluded that despite the overall U.S.-Mexico policy for achieving closer economic integration, no clear strategy existed to ensure that the infrastructure and processes are in place to support such objective.

As a response to the growing coordination needs, in March 2002, Presidents Bush and Fox signed a 22-point smart border accord that focuses on secure infrastructure and the secure flow of people and goods. Among other things, the plan calls for long term planning, relief of bottlenecks, harmonization of ports of entry operations, financing, and electronic exchange of information. This action plan exemplifies the strategic partnerships developed by both countries and provides a conceptual framework and commitment of resources among both federal governments to improve cross-border infrastructure, as well as direction for state and local governments.

For their part, states on both side of the border have developed corridor strategies to facilitate national and international movement of goods, services, people and information. Among them is the joint effort by the U.S. states of Arizona, Nevada, Utah, Idaho and Montana to develop the CANAMEX Corridor Project. The CANAMEX Corridor Project extends from central Mexico to Alberta, Canada and focuses on the promotion of tourism, communications, key infrastructure investments, and the streamlining of international clearance at land border ports of entry. Similarly, the state of Texas has been working on the ongoing development of the Trans-Texas Corridor concept along Interstates 69 and 35 that would create a transportation and multi-modal system of more than 4,000 miles. The system would include toll roads, commercial vehicle lanes, rail lines, high speed rail and other services.

In the Mexican state of Nuevo Leon, home to the industrial city of Monterrey, the state is investing in the International Corridor for Border Security that connects from Monterrey to the Columbia port of entry along the Texas border, which provides access to U.S. markets. The corridor plans include plants for secure exportation that will have closed circuit, pavement, lighting, and secure entrances and exits. These efforts will not only increasing cross-border efficiency, but also to assist in both nations' efforts to combat terrorism by reducing the possibilities of contamination commercial vehicles with illegal substances or hazardous materials.

Local and regional governments have also been proactive in the development of regional strategies to address cross-border infrastructure needs. The San Diego Association of Governments has been working closely with officials in the neighboring City of Tijuana to develop cross-border plans that promote regional planning, identify of regional priorities, and jointly seek funding opportunities. Similar efforts have been established in El Paso, Texas—Ciudad Juarez, Chihuahua, and in the Laredo, Texas and Nuevo Laredo, Tamaulipas regions.

Conclusion

In conclusion, the U.S.-Mexico relationship spans so many different spheres though it could be argued that the trade relationship attracts the most attention given the sheer economic capacities involved. For this relationship to flourish, the active involvement of policy-makers at every level of government in both countries remains critical. To this end, programs such as the BLC perform a valuable function as they bring together policy-makers to resolve the challenges of today and prepare for the tests of tomorrow. Policy-makers can then debate and devise strategies that encourage the transition to higher-value-added operations, identify and tap into the comparative advantage of both countries, and forge ahead with reforms and infrastructure investments that create more competition, entrepreneurship, and flexibility in an ever increasing global economy.

Notes

[1] Information related to the impact of NAFTA since its inception a decade ago is extracted from Ambassador Robert B. Zoellick, United States Trade Representative, "NAFTA Free Trade Commission Joint Statement—A Decade of Achievement," July 16, 2004 and "NAFTA Highlights," U.S. Embassy in Mexico, www.usembassy-mexico.gov.

[2] Information provided by Chris Whatley, The Council of State Governments, DC Office.

[3] "U.S. and Mexico at a Glance," U.S. Embassy in Mexico, www.usembassy-mexico.gov.

[4] "The Maquiladora Industry," Made in Mexico Inc., www.madeinmexicoinc.com.

[5] Texas State Sen. Eliot Shapleigh, "Border 2020: Secure, Fast, Smart," Report presented to the Border Legislative Conference on July 9, 2004.

[6] Asociación de Maquiladoras de Nuevo León, A.C, PowerPoint Presentation, BLC meeting, Monterrey, Nuevo León, June 11, 2004.

[7] See note 5 above.

[8] "The Maquiladora Roars Back," The San Diego Union Tribune, June 29, 2004.

[9] "Chip Factories Envisioned for South of Border," *The Los Angeles Times*, Business Section, July 15, 2004.

[10] See note 8 above.

[11] See note 9 above.

[12] "Beyond Cheap Labor: Lessons for Developing Economies," The McKinsey Quarterly no. 1, 2005.

[13] See note 9 above.

[14] See note 12 above.

[15] See note 5 above.

About the Authors

Edgar Ruiz is the program director of the Border Legislative Conference in CSG's Western Regional Office. Prior to joining CSG in 2001, he served as management analyst in the Community Development Department of the city of Lake Forest, CA, and as legislative staff for then-Assemblywoman (now state Senator) Denise Moreno Ducheny in the California Legislature. He holds a Masters degree in Public Administration and a Bachelor of Arts degree in Political Science from State Diego State University.

Sujit M. CanagaRetna is currently the senior fiscal analyst at The Council of State Governments' Southern Office, the Southern Legislative Conference (SLC), where he has been since March 1998. He is responsible for tracking fiscal, economic development and transportation trends for CSG and SLC. CanagaRetna has a Bachelor of Arts degree from Bennington College, Vermont and graduate degrees (MIA/MPA) in International Affairs and Public Administration from Columbia University. Prior to joining CSG/SLC, CanagaRetna worked for the New York City Comptroller's Office.

Chapter Ten

STATE PAGES

Table 10.1
OFFICIAL NAMES OF STATES AND JURISDICTIONS, CAPITALS, ZIP CODES AND CENTRAL SWITCHBOARDS

State or other jurisdiction	Name of state capitol (a)	Capital	Zip code	Area code	Central switchboard
Alabama, State of	State House	Montgomery	36130	334	242-7100
Alaska, State of	State Capitol	Juneau	99801	907	465-4648
Arizona, State of	State Capitol	Phoenix	85007	602	542-4900
Arkansas, State of	State Capitol	Little Rock	72201	501	682-3000
California, State of	State Capitol	Sacramento	95814	916	657-9900
Colorado, State of	State Capitol	Denver	80203	303	866-5000
Connecticut, State of	State Capitol	Hartford	06106	860	240-0100
Delaware, State of	Legislative Hall	Dover	19903	302	739-4114
Florida, State of	The Capitol	Tallahassee	32399	850	488-4441
Georgia, State of	State Capitol	Atlanta	30334	404	656-2000
Hawaii, State of	State Capitol	Honolulu	96813	808	587-0221
Idaho, State of	State Capitol	Boise	83720	208	332-1000
Illinois, State of	State House	Springfield	62706	217	782-2000
Indiana, State of	State House	Indianapolis	46204	317	232-1000
Iowa, State of	State Capitol	Des Moines	50319	515	281-5011
Kansas, State of	Statehouse	Topeka	66612	785	296-0111
Kentucky, Commonwealth of	State Capitol	Frankfort	40601	502	564-3317
Louisiana, State of	State Capitol	Baton Rouge	70804	225	342-4479
Maine, State of	State House Station	Augusta	04333	207	287-6826
Maryland, State of	State House	Annapolis	21401	410	946-5400
Massachusetts, Commonwealth of	State House	Boston	02133	617	722-2000
Michigan, State of	State Capitol	Lansing	48909	517	373-0184
Minnesota, State of	State Capitol	St. Paul	55155	651	296-3962
Mississippi, State of	State Capitol	Jackson	39215	601	359-3770
Missouri, State of	State Capitol	Jefferson City	65101	573	751-2000
Montana, State of	State Capitol	Helena	59620	406	444-3111
Nebraska, State of	State Capitol	Lincoln	68509	402	471-2311
Nevada, State of	State Capitol	Carson City	89701	775	684-5670
New Hampshire, State of	State House	Concord	03301	603	271-1110
New Jersey, State of	State House	Trenton	08625	609	292-6000
New Mexico, State of	State Capitol	Santa Fe	87501	505	986-4600
New York, State of	State Capitol	Albany	12224	518	474-8390
North Carolina, State of	State Capitol	Raleigh	27601	919	733-4111
North Dakota, State of	State Capitol	Bismarck	58505	701	328-2000
Ohio, State of	Statehouse	Columbus	43215	614	466-2000
Oklahoma, State of	State Capitol	Oklahoma City	73105	405	521-2011
Oregon, State of	State Capitol	Salem	97310	503	986-1848
Pennsylvania, Commonwealth of	Main Capitol Building	Harrisburg	17120	717	787-2121
Rhode Island and Providence Plantations, State of	State House	Providence	02903	401	222-2653
South Carolina, State of	State House	Columbia	29211	803	212-6200
South Dakota, State of	State Capitol	Pierre	57501	605	773-3011
Tennessee, State of	State Capitol	Nashville	37243	615	741-2001
Texas, State of	State Capitol	Austin	78701	512	463-4630
Utah, State of	State Capitol	Salt Lake City	84114	801	538-3000
Vermont, State of	State House	Montpelier	05633	802	828-2231
Virginia, Commonwealth of	State Capitol	Richmond	23219	804	698-7410
Washington, State of	Legislative Building	Olympia	98504	360	635-9993
West Virginia, State of	State Capitol	Charleston	25305	304	558-3456
Wisconsin, State of	State Capitol	Madison	53702	608	266-0382
Wyoming, State of	State Capitol	Cheyenne	82002	307	777-7220
District of Columbia	District Building	. . .	20004	202	724-8000
American Samoa, Territory of	Maota Fono	Pago Pago	96799	684	633-4116
Guam, Territory of	Congress Building	Hagatna	96910	671	472-8931
No. Mariana Islands, Commonwealth of	Civic Center Building	Saipan	96950	670	664-0992
Puerto Rico, Commonwealth of	The Capitol	San Juan	00902	787	721-7000
U.S. Virgin Islands, Territory of	Capitol Building	Charlotte Amalie, St. Thomas	00804	340	774-0880

(a) In some instances the name is not official.

Table 10.2
HISTORICAL DATA ON THE STATES

State or other jurisdiction	Source of state lands	Date organized as territory	Date admitted to Union	Chronological order of admission to Union
Alabama	Mississippi Territory, 1798 (a)	March 3, 1817	Dec. 14, 1819	22
Alaska	Purchased from Russia, 1867	Aug. 24, 1912	Jan. 3, 1959	49
Arizona	Ceded by Mexico, 1848 (b)	Feb. 24, 1863	Feb. 14, 1912	48
Arkansas	Louisiana Purchase, 1803	March 2, 1819	June 15, 1836	25
California	Ceded by Mexico, 1848	(c)	Sept. 9, 1850	31
Colorado	Louisiana Purchase, 1803 (d)	Feb. 28, 1861	Aug. 1, 1876	38
Connecticut	Fundamental Orders, Jan. 14, 1638; Royal charter, April 23, 1662	(e)	Jan. 9, 1788 (f)	5
Delaware	Swedish charter, 1638; English charter, 1638	(e)	Dec. 7, 1787 (f)	1
Florida	Ceded by Spain, 1819	March 30, 1822	March 3, 1845	27
Georgia	Charter, 1732, from George II to Trustees for Establishing the Colony of Georgia	(e)	Jan. 2, 1788 (f)	4
Hawaii	Annexed, 1898	June 14, 1900	Aug. 21, 1959	50
Idaho	Treaty with Britain, 1846	March 4, 1863	July 3, 1890	43
Illinois	Northwest Territory, 1787	Feb. 3, 1809	Dec. 3, 1818	21
Indiana	Northwest Territory, 1787	May 7, 1800	Dec. 11, 1816	19
Iowa	Louisiana Purchase, 1803	June 12, 1838	Dec. 28, 1846	29
Kansas	Louisiana Purchase, 1803 (d)	May 30, 1854	Jan. 29, 1861	34
Kentucky	Part of Virginia until admitted as state	(c)	June 1, 1792	15
Louisiana	Louisiana Purchase, 1803 (g)	March 26, 1804	April 30, 1812	18
Maine	Part of Massachusetts until admitted as state	(c)	March 15, 1820	23
Maryland	Charter, 1632, from Charles I to Calvert	(e)	April 28, 1788 (f)	7
Massachusetts	Charter to Massachusetts Bay Company, 1629	(e)	Feb. 6, 1788 (f)	6
Michigan	Northwest Territory, 1787	Jan. 11, 1805	Jan. 26, 1837	26
Minnesota	Northwest Territory, 1787 (h)	March 3, 1849	May 11, 1858	32
Mississippi	Mississippi Territory (i)	April 7, 1798	Dec. 10, 1817	20
Missouri	Louisiana Purchase, 1803	June 4, 1812	Aug. 10, 1821	24
Montana	Louisiana Purchase, 1803 (j)	May 26, 1864	Nov. 8, 1889	41
Nebraska	Louisiana Purchase, 1803	May 30, 1854	March 1, 1867	37
Nevada	Ceded by Mexico, 1848	March 2, 1861	Oct. 31, 1864	36
New Hampshire	Grants from Council for New England, 1622 and 1629; made Royal province, 1679	(e)	June 21, 1788 (f)	9
New Jersey	Dutch settlement, 1618; English charter, 1664	(e)	Dec. 18, 1787 (f)	3
New Mexico	Ceded by Mexico, 1848 (b)	Sept. 9, 1850	Jan. 6, 1912	47
New York	Dutch settlement, 1623; English control, 1664	(e)	July 26, 1788 (f)	11
North Carolina	Charter, 1663, from Charles II	(e)	Nov. 21, 1789 (f)	12
North Dakota	Louisiana Purchase, 1803 (k)	March 2, 1861	Nov. 2, 1889	39
Ohio	Northwest Territory, 1787	May 7, 1800	March 1, 1803	17
Oklahoma	Louisiana Purchase, 1803	May 2, 1890	Nov. 16, 1907	46
Oregon	Settlement and treaty with Britain, 1846	Aug. 14, 1848	Feb. 14, 1859	33
Pennsylvania	Grant from Charles II to William Penn, 1681	(e)	Dec. 12, 1787 (f)	2
Rhode Island	Charter, 1663, from Charles II	(e)	May 29, 1790 (f)	13
South Carolina	Charter, 1663, from Charles II	(e)	May 23, 1788 (f)	8
South Dakota	Louisiana Purchase, 1803	March 2, 1861	Nov. 2, 1889	40
Tennessee	Part of North Carolina until land ceded to U.S. in 1789	June 8, 1790 (l)	June 1, 1796	16
Texas	Republic of Texas, 1845	(c)	Dec. 29, 1845	28
Utah	Ceded by Mexico, 1848	Sept. 9, 1850	Jan. 4, 1896	45
Vermont	From lands of New Hampshire and New York	(c)	March 4, 1791	14
Virginia	Charter, 1609, from James I to London Company	(e)	June 25, 1788 (f)	10
Washington	Oregon Territory, 1848	March 2, 1853	Nov. 11, 1889	42
West Virginia	Part of Virginia until admitted as state	(c)	June 20, 1863	35
Wisconsin	Northwest Territory, 1787	April 20, 1836	May 29, 1848	30
Wyoming	Louisiana Purchase, 1803 (d)(j)	July 25, 1868	July 10, 1890	44
Dist. of Columbia	Maryland (m)	. . .	. . .	. . .
American Samoa	Became a territory, 1900			
Guam	Ceded by Spain, 1898	Aug. 1, 1950	. . .	. . .
No. Mariana Islands	. . .	March 24, 1976	. . .	. . .
Puerto Rico	Ceded by Spain, 1898	. . .	July 25, 1952 (n)	. . .
U.S. Virgin Islands	Purchased from Denmark, March 31, 1917			

See footnotes at end of table.

HISTORICAL DATA ON THE STATES — Continued

Key:

(a) By the Treaty of Paris, 1783, England gave up claim to the 13 original Colonies, and to all land within an area extending along the present Canadian to the Lake of the Woods, down the Mississippi River to the 31st parallel, east to the Chattahoochee, down that river to the mouth of the Flint, border east to the source of the St. Mary's down that river to the ocean. The major part of Alabama was acquired by the Treaty of Paris, and the lower portion from Spain in 1813.

(b) Portion of land obtained by Gadsden Purchase, 1853.

(c) No territorial status before admission to Union.

(d) Portion of land ceded by Mexico, 1848.

(e) One of the original 13 Colonies.

(f) Date of ratification of U.S. Constitution.

(g) West Feliciana District (Baton Rouge) acquired from Spain, 1810; added to Louisiana, 1812.

(h) Portion of land obtained by Louisiana Purchase, 1803.

(i) See footnote (a). The lower portion of Mississippi also was acquired from Spain in 1813.

(j) Portion of land obtained from Oregon Territory, 1848.

(k) The northern portion of the Red River Valley was acquired by treaty with Great Britain in 1818.

(l) Date Southwest Territory (identical boundary as Tennessee's) was created.

(m) Area was originally 100 square miles, taken from Virginia and Maryland. Virginia's portion south of the Potomac was given back to that state in 1846. Site chosen in 1790, city incorporated 1802.

(n) On this date, Puerto Rico became a self-governing commonwealth by compact approved by the U.S. Congress and the voters of Puerto Rico as provided in U.S. Public Law 600 of 1950.

Table 10.3
STATE STATISTICS

| State or other jurisdiction | Land area | | Population | | Percentage change 2002 to 2003 | Density per square mile | No. of Representatives in Congress | Capital | Population | Largest city | Rank in state | Population |
	In square miles	Rank in nation	Size	Rank in nation								
Alabama	50,744	28	4,500,752	23	0.5	88.7	7	Montgomery	201,425	Birmingham	2	239,416
Alaska	571,951	1	648,818	47	1.1	1.1	1	Juneau	30,711	Anchorage	2	268,983
Arizona	113,635	6	5,580,811	18	2.6	49.1	8	Phoenix	1,371,960	Phoenix	1	1,371,960
Arkansas	52,068	27	2,725,714	32	0.7	52.3	4	Little Rock	184,055	Little Rock	1	184,055
California	155,959	3	35,484,453	1	1.4	227.5	53	Sacramento	435,245	Los Angeles	7	3,798,981
Colorado	103,718	8	4,550,688	22	1.1	43.9	7	Denver	560,415	Denver	1	560,415
Connecticut	4,845	48	3,483,372	29	0.7	719.0	5	Hartford	124,558	Bridgeport	3	140,104
Delaware	1,954	49	817,491	45	1.4	418.4	1	Dover	32,135	Wilmington	2	72,664
Florida	53,927	26	17,019,068	4	2.0	315.6	25	Tallahassee	155,171	Jacksonville	8	762,461
Georgia	57,906	21	8,684,715	9	1.6	150.0	13	Atlanta	424,868	Atlanta	1	424,868
Hawaii	6,423	47	1,257,608	42	1.4	195.8	2	Honolulu	378,155	Honolulu	1	378,155
Idaho	82,747	11	1,366,332	39	1.7	16.5	2	Boise	189,847	Boise	1	189,847
Illinois	55,584	24	12,653,544	5	0.5	227.6	19	Springfield	111,834	Chicago	6	2,886,251
Indiana	35,867	38	6,195,643	14	0.6	172.7	9	Indianapolis	783,612	Indianapolis	1	783,612
Iowa	55,869	23	2,944,062	30	0.3	52.7	5	Des Moines	198,076	Des Moines	1	198,076
Kansas	81,815	13	2,723,507	33	0.4	33.3	4	Topeka	122,103	Wichita	4	355,126
Kentucky	39,728	36	4,117,827	26	0.7	103.7	6	Frankfort	27,660	Louisville-Jefferson (b)	7	693,604
Louisiana	43,562	33	4,496,334	24	0.7	103.2	7	Baton Rouge	225,702	New Orleans	2	473,681
Maine	30,862	39	1,305,728	40	0.8	42.3	2	Augusta	18,560	Portland	9	64,249
Maryland	9,774	42	5,508,909	19	1.1	563.6	8	Annapolis	35,838	Baltimore	7	638,614
Massachusetts	7,840	45	6,433,422	13	0.2	820.6	10	Boston	589,281	Boston	1	589,281
Michigan	56,804	22	10,079,985	8	0.4	177.5	15	Lansing	118,588	Detroit	6	925,051
Minnesota	79,610	14	5,059,375	21	0.7	63.6	8	St. Paul	284,037	Minneapolis	2	375,635
Mississippi	46,907	31	2,881,281	31	0.5	61.4	4	Jackson	180,881	Jackson	1	180,881
Missouri	68,886	18	5,704,484	17	0.6	82.8	9	Jefferson City	39,636	Kansas City	15	443,471
Montana	145,552	4	917,621	44	0.8	6.3	1	Helena	25,780	Billings	6	89,847
Nebraska	76,872	15	1,739,291	38	0.7	22.6	3	Lincoln	232,362	Omaha	2	399,357
Nevada	109,826	7	2,241,154	35	3.4	20.4	3	Carson City	52,457	Las Vegas	6	508,604
New Hampshire	8,968	44	1,287,687	41	1.0	143.6	2	Concord	40,687	Manchester	3	108,398
New Jersey	7,417	46	8,638,396	10	0.7	1,164.7	13	Trenton	85,403	Newark	9	277,000
New Mexico	121,356	5	1,874,614	36	1.2	15.4	3	Santa Fe	62,203	Albuquerque	6	463,874
New York	47,214	30	19,190,115	3	0.3	406.4	29	Albany	95,658	New York City	6	8,084,316
North Carolina	48,711	29	8,407,248	11	1.2	172.6	13	Raleigh	306,944	Charlotte	2	580,597
North Dakota	68,976	17	633,837	48	0.0	9.2	1	Bismarck	55,532	Fargo	2	90,599
Ohio	40,948	35	11,435,798	7	0.2	279.3	18	Columbus	725,228	Columbus	1	725,228
Oklahoma	68,667	19	3,511,532	28	0.6	51.1	5	Oklahoma City	519,034	Oklahoma City	1	519,034
Oregon	95,997	10	3,559,596	27	1.1	37.1	5	Salem	140,977	Portland	3	539,438
Pennsylvania	44,817	32	12,365,455	6	0.3	275.9	19	Harrisburg	48,950	Philadelphia	13	1,492,231
Rhode Island	1,045	50	1,076,164	43	0.7	1,029.8	2	Providence	175,901	Providence	1	175,901
South Carolina	30,110	40	4,147,152	25	1.1	137.7	6	Columbia	117,394	Columbia	1	117,394

See footnotes at end of table.

STATE STATISTICS — Continued

State or other jurisdiction	Land area — In square miles	Land area — Rank in nation	Population — Size	Population — Rank in nation	Percentage change 2002 to 2003	Density per square mile	No. of Representatives in Congress	Capital	Capital — Population	Capital — Rank in state	Largest city	Largest city — Population
South Dakota	75,885	16	764,309	46	0.5	10.1	1	Pierre	13,876	7	Sioux Falls	130,491
Tennessee	41,217	34	5,841,748	16	0.9	141.7	9	Nashville	545,915 (c)	2	Memphis	648,882
Texas	261,797	2	22,118,509	2	1.8	84.5	32	Austin	671,873	4	Houston	2,009,834
Utah	82,144	12	2,351,467	34	1.4	28.6	3	Salt Lake City	181,266	1	Salt Lake City	181,266
Vermont	9,250	43	619,107	49	0.4	66.9	1	Montpelier	8,035	13	Burlington	38,889
Virginia	39,594	37	7,386,330	12	1.4	186.6	11	Richmond	197,456	4	Virginia Beach	433,934
Washington	66,544	20	6,131,445	15	1.1	92.1	9	Olympia	42,514	18	Seattle	570,898
West Virginia	24,078	41	1,810,354	37	0.3	75.2	3	Charleston	53,421	1	Charleston	53,421
Wisconsin	54,310	25	5,472,299	20	0.6	100.8	8	Madison	215,211	2	Milwaukee	590,895
Wyoming	97,100	9	501,242	51	0.5	5.2	1	Cheyenne	53,011	1	Cheyenne	53,011
District of Columbia ...	63	...	563,384	50	-1.0	8,942.6	1 (a)	...	...	...	...	...
American Samoa (d) ...	77	...	57,291	...	22.0	...	1 (a)	Pago Pago	4,278	3	Tafuna	8,409
Guam (d)	210	...	154,805	...	...	...	1 (a)	Hagåtña	1,100	18	Dededo	42,980
No. Mariana Islands (d)	181	...	69,221	...	...	...	...	Saipan	62,392	1	Saipan	62,392
Puerto Rico (d)	3,427	...	3,878,523	...	0.5	1,131.8	1 (a)	San Juan	421,958	1	San Juan	421,958
U.S. Virgin Islands (d) ..	134	...	108,612	...	...	...	1 (a)	Charlotte Amalie, St. Thomas	11,004	1	Charlotte Amalie, St. Thomas	11,004

Source: U.S. Census Bureau, July 2003.

Key:
. . . — Not applicable
(a) Delegate with privileges to vote in committees and the Committee of the Whole.
(b) Coextensive with Jefferson County.
(c) This city is part of a consolidated city-county government and is coextensive with Davidson County.
(d) Information for territories and cities with a population under 100,000 is from the U.S. Census Bureau, Census 2000.

Alabama

Nickname .... The Heart of Dixie
Motto .... *Aldemus Jura Nostra Defendere*
(We Dare Defend Our Rights)
Flower .... Camellia
Bird .... Yellowhammer
Tree .... Southern (Longleaf) Pine
Song .... *Alabama*
Entered the Union .... December 14, 1819
Capital .... Montgomery

STATISTICS

Land Area (square miles) 50,744
    Rank in Nation 28th
Population 4,500,752
    Rank in Nation 23rd
    Density per square mile 88.7
Capital City .... Montgomery
    Population 201,425
    Rank in State 2nd
Largest City .... Birmingham
    Population 239,416
Number of Representatives in Congress 7
Number of Counties 67
Number of Municipal Governments 451
Number of 2004 Electoral Votes 9
Number of School Districts 128
Number of Special Districts 525

STATE INTERNET ADDRESSES

Official State Website .... http://www.alabama.gov
Governor's Website .... http://www.governor.state.al.us
State Legislative Website .... http://www.legislature.state.al.us
State Judicial Website .... http://www.judicial.state.al.us

Alaska

Nickname .... The Last Frontier
Motto .... *North to the Future*
Flower .... Forget-Me-Not
Bird .... Willow Ptarmigan
Tree .... Sitka Spruce
Song .... *Alaska's Flag*
Entered the Union .... January 3, 1959
Capital .... Juneau

STATISTICS

Land Area (square miles) 571,951
    Rank in Nation 1st
Population 648,818
    Rank in Nation 47th
    Density per square mile 1.1
Capital City .... Juneau
    Population 31,283
    Rank in State 2nd
Largest City .... Anchorage
    Population 268,983
Number of Representatives in Congress 1
Number of Counties 27
Number of Municipal Governments 149
Number of 2004 Electoral Votes 3
Number of School Districts 53
Number of Special Districts 14

STATE INTERNET ADDRESSES

Official State Website .... http://www.state.ak.us
Governor's Website .... http://www.gov.state.ak.us
State Legislative Website .... http://www.legis.state.ak.us
State Judicial Website .... http://www.state.ak.us/courts

Arizona

Nickname .... The Grand Canyon State
Motto .... *Ditat Deus (God Enriches)*
Flower .... Blossom of the Saguaro Cactus
Bird .... Cactus Wren
Tree .... Palo Verde
Songs .... *Arizona March Song and Arizona*
Entered the Union .... February 14, 1912
Capital .... Phoenix

STATISTICS

Land Area (square miles) 113,635
    Rank in Nation 6th
Population 5,580,811
    Rank in Nation 18th
    Density per square mile 49.1
Capital City .... Phoenix
    Population 1,371,960
    Rank in State 1st
Largest City .... Phoenix
Number of Representatives in Congress 8
Number of Counties 15
Number of Municipal Governments 87
Number of 2004 Electoral Votes 10
Number of School Districts 410
Number of Special Districts 305

STATE INTERNET ADDRESSES

Official State Website .... http://www.az.gov
Governor's Website .... http://www.governor.state.az.us
State Legislative Website .... http://www.azleg.state.az.us
State Judicial Website .... http://www.supreme.state.az.us

Arkansas

Nickname .... The Natural State
Motto .... *Regnat Populus (The People Rule)*
Flower .... Apple Blossom
Bird .... Mockingbird
Tree .... Pine
Song .... *Arkansas*
Entered the Union .... June 15, 1836
Capital .... Little Rock

STATISTICS

Land Area (square miles) 52,068
    Rank in Nation 27th
Population 2,725,714
    Rank in Nation 32nd
    Density per square mile 52.3
Capital City .... Little Rock
    Population 184,055
    Rank in State 1st
Largest City .... Little Rock
Number of Representatives in Congress 4
Number of Counties 75
Number of Municipal Governments 499
Number of 2004 Electoral Votes 6
Number of School Districts 310
Number of Special Districts 704

STATE INTERNET ADDRESSES

Official State Website .... http://www.state.ar.us
Governor's Website .... http://www.state.ar.us/governor
State Legislative Website .... http://www.arkleg.state.ar.us
State Judicial Website .... http://courts.state.ar.us

California

Nickname .... The Golden State
Motto .... *Eureka* (I Have Found It)
Flower .... Golden Poppy
Bird .... California Valley Quail
Tree .... California Redwood
Song .... *I Love You, California*
Entered the Union .... September 9, 1850
Capital .... Sacramento

STATISTICS

Land Area (square miles) 155,959
    Rank in Nation 3rd
Population 35,484,453
    Rank in Nation 1st
    Density per Square Mile 227.5
Capital City .... Sacramento
    Population 435,245
    Rank in State 7th
Largest City .... Los Angeles
    Population 3,728,981
Number of Representatives in Congress 53
Number of Counties 58
Number of Municipal Governments 475
Number of 2004 Electoral Votes 55
Number of School Districts 985
Number of Special Districts 2,830

STATE INTERNET ADDRESSES

Official State Website .... http://www.ca.gov
Governor's Website .... http://www.governor.ca.gov
State Legislative Website .... http://www.leginfo.ca.gov
State Judicial Website .... http://www.courtinfo.ca.gov

Colorado

Nickname .... The Centennial State
Motto .... *Nil Sine Numine*
(Nothing Without
Providence)
Flower .... Columbine
Bird .... Lark Bunting
Tree .... Blue Spruce
Song .... *Where the Columbines Grow*
Entered the Union .... August 1, 1876
Capital .... Denver

STATISTICS

Land Area (square miles) 103,718
    Rank in Nation 8th
Population 4,550,688
    Rank in Nation 22nd
    Density per square mile 43.9
Capital City .... Denver
    Population 560,415
    Rank in State 1st
Largest City .... Denver
Number of Representatives in Congress 7
Number of Counties 63
Number of Municipal Governments 270
Number of 2004 Electoral Votes 9
Number of School Districts 176
Number of Special Districts 1,414

STATE INTERNET ADDRESSES

Official State Website .... http://www.state.co.us
Governor's Website...http://www.state.co.us/gov_dir/governor_office.html
State Legislative Website .... http://www.leg.state.co.us
State Judicial Website .... http://www.courts.state.co.us

Connecticut

Nickname .... The Constitution State
Motto .... *Qui Transtulit Sustinet*
(He Who Transplanted Still
Sustains)
Flower .... Mountain Laurel
Bird .... American Robin
Tree .... White Oak
Song .... *Yankee Doodle*
Entered the Union .... January 9, 1788
Capital .... Hartford

STATISTICS

Land Area (square miles) 4,845
    Rank in Nation 48th
Population 3,483,372
    Rank in Nation 29th
    Density per square mile 719.0
Capital City .... Hartford
    Population 124,558
    Rank in State 3rd
Largest City .... Bridgeport
    Population 140,104
Number of Representatives in Congress 5
Number of Counties 8
Number of Municipal Governments 30
Number of 2004 Electoral Votes 7
Number of School Districts 166
Number of Special Districts 384

STATE INTERNET ADDRESSES

Official State Website .... http://www.state.ct.us
Governor's Website .... http://www.state.ct.us/governor
State Legislative Website .... http://www.cga.state.ct.us
State Judicial Website .... http://www.jud.state.ct.us

Delaware

Nickname .... The First State
Motto .... *Liberty and Independence*
Flower .... Peach Blossom
Bird .... Blue Hen Chicken
Tree .... American Holly
Song .... *Our Delaware*
Entered the Union .... December 7, 1787
Capital .... Dover

STATISTICS

Land Area (square miles) 1,954
    Rank in Nation 49th
Population 817,491
    Rank in Nation 45th
Density per square mile 418.4
Capital City .... Dover
    Population 32,581
    Rank in State 2nd
Largest City .... Wilmington
    Population 73,135
Number of Representatives in Congress 1
Number of Counties 3
Number of Municipal Governments 57
Number of 2004 Electoral Votes 3
Number of School Districts 19
Number of Special Districts 260

STATE INTERNET ADDRESSES

Official State Website .... http://delaware.gov
Governor's Website .... http://www.state.de.us/governor
State Legislative Website .... http://www.legis.state.de.us
State Judicial Website .... http://courts.state.de.us

Florida

Nickname .... The Sunshine State
Motto .... *In God We Trust*
Flower .... Orange Blossom
Bird .... Mockingbird
Tree .... Sabal Palmetto Palm
Song .... *The Swannee River (Old Folks at Home)*
Entered the Union .... March 3, 1845
Capital .... Tallahassee

STATISTICS

Land Area (square miles) 53,927
    Rank in Nation 26th
Population 17,019,068
    Rank in Nation 4th
    Density per square mile 315.6
Capital City .... Tallahassee
    Population 155,171
    Rank in State 8th
Largest City .... Jacksonville
    Population 762,461
Number of Representatives in Congress 25
Number of Counties 67
Number of Municipal Governments 404
Number of 2004 Electoral Votes 27
Number of School Districts 67
Number of Special Districts 626

STATE INTERNET ADDRESSES

Official State Website .... http://www.myflorida.com
Governor's Website .... http://www.state.fl.us/eog
State Legislative Website .... http://www.leg.state.fl.us
State Judicial Website .... http://www.flcourts.org

Hawaii

Nickname .... The Aloha State
Motto .... *Ua Mau Ke Ea O Ka Aina I Ka Pono*
    (The Life of the Land Is Perpetuated in Righteousness)
Flower .... Native Yellow Hibiscus
Bird .... Hawaiian Goose (Nene)
Tree .... *Kukue Tree (Candlenut)*
Song .... *Hawaii Ponoi*
Entered the Union .... August 21, 1959
Capital .... Honolulu

STATISTICS

Land Area (square miles) 6,423
    Rank in Nation 47th
Population 1,257,608
    Rank in Nation 42nd
    Density per square mile 195.8
Capital City .... Honolulu
    Population 378,155
    Rank in State 1st
Largest City .... Honolulu
Number of Representatives in Congress 2
Number of Counties 5
Number of Municipal Governments 1
Number of 2004 Electoral Votes 4
Number of School Districts 1
Number of Special Districts 15

STATE INTERNET ADDRESSES

Official State Website .... http://www.hawaii.gov
Governor's Website .... http://gov.state.hi.us
State Legislative Website .... http://www.capitol.hawaii.gov
State Judicial Website .... http://www.courts.hi.us

Georgia

Nickname .... The Empire State of the South
Motto .... *Wisdom, Justice and Moderation*
Flower .... Cherokee Rose
Bird .... Brown Thrasher
Tree .... Live Oak
Song .... *Georgia on My Mind*
Entered the Union .... January 2, 1788
Capital .... Atlanta

STATISTICS

Land Area (square miles) 57,906
    Rank in Nation 21st
Population 8,684,715
    Rank in Nation 9th
    Density per square mile 150.0
Capital City .... Atlanta
    Population 424,868
    Rank in State 1st
Largest City .... Atlanta
Number of Representatives in Congress 13
Number of Counties 159
Number of Municipal Governments 531
Number of 2004 Electoral Votes 15
Number of School Districts 180
Number of Special Districts 581

STATE INTERNET ADDRESSES

Official State Website .... http://www.state.ga.us
Governor's Website .... http://gov.state.ga.us/
State Legislative Website .... http://www.legis.state.ga.us
State Judicial Website .... http://www.georgiacourts.org

Idaho

Nickname .... The Gem State
Motto .... *Esto Perpetua* (Let It Be Perpetual)
Flower .... Syringa
Bird .... Mountain Bluebird
Tree .... Western White Pine
Song .... *Here We Have Idaho*
Entered the Union .... July 3, 1890
Capital .... Boise

STATISTICS

Land Area (square miles) 82,747
    Rank in Nation 11th
Population 1,366,332
    Rank in Nation 39th
Density per square mile 16.5
Capital City .... Boise
    Population 189,847
    Rank in State 1st
Largest City .... Boise
Number of Representatives in Congress 2
Number of Counties 44
Number of Municipal Governments 200
Number of 2004 Electoral Votes 4
Number of School Districts 115
Number of Special Districts 798

STATE INTERNET ADDRESSES

Official State Website .... http://www.state.id.us
Governor's Website http://www2.state.id.us/gov
State Legislative Website http://www2.state.id.us/legislat
State Judicial Website http://www2.state.id.us/judicial

Illinois

Nickname .... The Prairie State
Motto .... *State Sovereignty-National Union*
Flower .... Native Violet
Bird .... Cardinal
Tree .... White Oak
Song .... *Illinois*
Entered the Union .... December 3, 1818
Capital .... Springfield

STATISTICS

Land Area (square miles) 55,584
   Rank in Nation 24th
Population 12,653,544
   Rank in Nation 5th
   Density per square mile 227.6
Capital City .... Springfield
   Population 111,834
   Rank in State 6th
Largest City .... Chicago
   Population 2,886,251
Number of Representatives in Congress 19
Number of Counties 102
Number of Municipal Governments 1,291
Number of 2004 Electoral Votes 21
Number of School Districts 894
Number of Special Districts 3,145

STATE INTERNET ADDRESSES

Official State Website .... http://www.state.il.us
Governor's Website .... http://www.state.il.us/gov
State Legislative Website .... http://www.legis.state.il.us
State Judicial Website .... http://www.state.il.us/court

Indiana

Nickname .... The Hoosier State
Motto .... *Crossroads of America*
Flower .... Peony
Bird .... Cardinal
Tree .... Tulip Poplar
Song .... *On the Banks of the Wabash, Far Away*
Entered the Union .... December 11, 1816
Capital .... Indianapolis

STATISTICS

Land Area (square miles) 35,867
   Rank in Nation 38th
Population 6,195,643
   Rank in Nation 14th
   Density per square mile 172.7
Capital City .... Indianapolis
   Population 783,612
   Rank in State 1st
Largest City .... Indianapolis
Number of Representatives in Congress 9
Number of Counties 92
Number of Municipal Governments 567
Number of 2004 Electoral Votes 11
Number of School Districts 295
Number of Special Districts 1,125

STATE INTERNET ADDRESSES

Official State Website .... http://www.state.in.us
Governor's Website .... http://www.in.gov/gov
State Legislative Website .... http://www.in.gov/legislative
State Judicial Website .... http://www.in.gov/judiciary

Iowa

Nickname .... The Hawkeye State
Motto .... *Our Liberties We Prize and*
Our Rights We Will Maintain
Flower .... Wild Rose
Bird .... Eastern Goldfinch
Tree .... Oak
Song .... *The Song of Iowa*
Entered the Union .... December 28, 1846
Capital .... Des Moines

STATISTICS

Land Area (square mile) 55,869
   Rank in Nation 23rd
Population 2,944,062
   Rank in Nation 30th
   Density per square mile 52.7
Capital City .... Des Moines
   Population 198,076
   Rank in State 1st
Largest City .... Des Moines
Number of Representatives in Congress 5
Number of Counties 99
Number of Municipal Governments 948
Number of 2004 Electoral Votes 7
Number of School Districts 374
Number of Special Districts 542

STATE INTERNET ADDRESSES

Official State Website .... http://www.state.ia.us
Governor's Website .... http://www.governor.state.ia.us
State Legislative Website .... http://www.legis.state.ia.us
State Judicial Website .... http://www.judicial.state.ia.us

Kansas

Nickname .... The Sunflower State
Motto .... *Ad Astra per Aspera*
(To the Stars through Difficulties)
Flower .... Wild Native Sunflower
Bird .... Western Meadowlark
Tree .... Cottonwood
Song .... *Home on the Range*
Entered the Union .... January 29, 1861
Capital .... Topeka

STATISTICS

Land Area (square miles) 81,815
   Rank in Nation 13th
Population 2,723,507
   Rank in Nation 33rd
   Density per square mile 33.3
Capital City .... Topeka
   Population 122,103
   Rank in State 4th
Largest City .... Wichita
Population 355,126
Number of Representatives in Congress 4
Number of Counties 105
Number of Municipal Governments 627
Number of 2004 Electoral Votes 6
Number of School Districts 304
Number of Special Districts 1,533

STATE INTERNET ADDRESSES

Official State Website .... http://www.accesskansas.org
Governor's Website .... http://www.ksgovernor.org
State Legislative Website .... http://www.kslegislature.org
State Judicial Website .... http://www.kscourts.org

Kentucky

Nickname .... The Bluegrass State
Motto .... *United We Stand, Divided We Fall*
Flower .... Goldenrod
Bird .... Cardinal
Tree .... Tulip Poplar
Song .... *My Old Kentucky Home*
Entered the Union .... June 1, 1792
Capital .... Frankfort

STATISTICS

Land Area (square miles) 39,728
    Rank in Nation 36th
Population 4,117,827
    Rank in Nation 26th
    Density per square mile 103.7
Capital City .... Frankfort
    Population 27,741
    Rank in State 7th
Largest City .... Louisville-Jefferson Co.
    Population 693,604
Number of Representatives in Congress 6
Number of Counties 120
Number of Municipal Governments 424
Number of 2004 Electoral Votes 8
Number of School Districts 176
Number of Special Districts 720

STATE INTERNET ADDRESSES

Official State Website .... http://kentucky.gov
Governor's Website .... http://governor.ky.gov
Legislative Website .... http://www.lrc.state.ky.us
Judicial Website .... http://www.kycourts.net

Louisiana

Nickname .... The Pelican State
Motto .... *Union, Justice and Confidence*
Flower .... Magnolia
Bird .... Eastern Brown Pelican
Tree .... Bald Cypress
Songs .... *Give Me Louisiana* and
You Are My Sunshine
Entered the Union .... April 30, 1812
Capital .... Baton Rouge

STATISTICS

Land Area (square miles) 43,562
    Rank in Nation 33rd
Population 4,496,334
    Rank in Nation 24th
    Density per square mile 103.2
Capital City .... Baton Rouge
    Population 225,702
    Rank in State 2nd
Largest City .... New Orleans
    Population 473,681
Number of Representatives in Congress 7
Number of Parishes 64
Number of Municipal Governments 302
Number of 2004 Electoral Votes 9
Number of School Districts 78
Number of Special Districts 45

STATE INTERNET ADDRESSES

Official State Website .... http://www.state.la.us
Governor's Website .... http://www.gov.state.la.us
Legislative Website .... http://www.legis.state.la.us
Judicial Website .... http://www.state.la.us/gov_judicial.htm

Maine

Nickname .... The Pine Tree State
Motto .... *Dirigo* (I Direct or I Lead)
Flower .... White Pine Cone and Tassel
Bird .... Chickadee
Tree .... White Pine
Song .... *State of Maine Song*
Entered the Union .... March 15, 1820
Capital .... Augusta

STATISTICS

Land Area (square miles) 30,862
    Rank in Nation 39th
Population 1,305,728
    Rank in Nation 40th
    Density per square mile 42.3
Capital City .... Augusta
    Population 18,560
    Rank in State 9th
Largest City .... Portland
    Population 64,249
Number of Representatives in Congress 2
Number of Counties 16
Number of Municipal Governments 22
Number of 2004 Electoral Votes 4
Number of School Districts 282
Number of Special Districts 222

STATE INTERNET ADDRESSES

Official State Website .... http://www.state.me.us
Governor's Website .... http://www.state.me.us/governor
Legislative Website .... http://janus.state.me.us/legis
Judicial Website .... http://www.courts.state.me.us

Maryland

Nicknames .... The Old Line State and Free State
Motto .... *Fatti Maschii, Parole Femine*
(Manly Deeds, Womanly Words)
Flower .... Black-eyed Susan
Bird.. .... Baltimore Oriole
Tree .... White Oak
Song .... *Maryland, My Maryland*
Entered the Union .... April 28, 1788
Capital .... Annapolis

STATISTICS

Land Area (square miles) 9,774
Rank in Nation 42nd
Population 5,508,909
    Rank in Nation 19th
    Density per square mile 563.6
Capital City .... Annapolis
    Population 35,838
    Rank in State 22nd
Largest City .... Baltimore
    Population 638,614
Number of Representatives in Congress 8
Number of Counties 24
Number of Municipal Governments 157
Number of 2004 Electoral Votes 10
Number of School Districts 24
Number of Special Districts 85

STATE INTERNET ADDRESSES

Official State Website .... http://www.maryand.gov
Governor's Website .... http://www.gov.state.md.us
Legislative Website .... http://www.mlis.state.md.us
Judicial Website .... http://www.courts.state.md.us

Massachusetts

Nickname .... The Bay State
Motto .... *Ense Petit Placidam Sub Libertate Quietem*
(By the Sword We Seek Peace, but Peace Only under Liberty)
Flower .... Mayflower
Bird .... Chickadee
Tree .... American Elm
Song .... *All Hail to Massachusetts*
Entered the Union .... February 6, 1788
Capital .... Boston

STATISTICS

Land Area (square miles) 7,840
   Rank in Nation 45th
Population 6,433,422
   Rank in Nation 13th
   Density per square mile 820.6
Capital City .... Boston
   Population 589,281
   Rank in State 1st
Largest City .... Boston
Number of Representatives in Congress 10
Number of Counties 14
Number of Municipal Governments 45
Number of 2004 Electoral Votes 12
Number of School Districts 349
Number of Special Districts 403

STATE INTERNET ADDRESSES

Official State Website .... http://www.mass.gov
Governor's Website .... http://www.state.ma.us/gov
Legislative Website .... http://www.state.ma.us/legis
Judicial Website .... http://www.state.ma.us/courts

Minnesota

Nickname .... The North Star State
Motto .... *L'Etoile du Nord* (The North Star)
Flower .... Pink and White Lady-Slipper
Bird .... Common Loon
Tree .... Red Pine
Song .... *Hail! Minnesota*
Entered the Union .... May 11, 1858
Capital .... St. Paul

STATISTICS

Land Area (square miles) 79,610
   Rank in Nation 14th
Population 5,059,375
   Rank in Nation 21st
   Density per square mile 63.6
Capital City .... St. Paul
   Population 284,037
   Rank in State 2nd
Largest City .... Minneapolis
   Population 375,635
Number of Representatives in Congress 8
Number of Counties 87
Number of Municipal Governments 854
Number of 2004 Electoral Votes 10
Number of School Districts 415
Number of Special Districts 403

STATE INTERNET ADDRESSES

Official State Website .... http://www.state.mn.us
Governor's Website .... http://www.governor.state.mn.us
Legislative Website .... http://www.leg.state.mn.us
Judicial Website .... http://www.courts.state.mn.us/home

Michigan

Nickname .... The Wolverine State
Motto .... *Si Quaeris Peninsulam Amoenam Circumspice*
(If You Seek a Pleasant Peninsula, Look About You)
Flower .... Apple Blossom
Bird .... Robin
Tree .... White Pine
Song .... *Michigan, My Michigan*
Entered the Union .... January 26, 1837
Capital .... Lansing

STATISTICS

Land Area (square miles) 56,804
   Rank in Nation 22nd
Population 10,079,985
   Rank in Nation 8th
   Density per square mile 177.5
Capital City .... Lansing
   Population 118,588
   Rank in State 6th
Largest City .... Detroit
   Population 925,051
Number of Representatives in Congress 15
Number of Counties 83
Number of Municipal Governments 533
Number of 2004 Electoral Votes 17
Number of School Districts 734
Number of Special Districts 366

STATE INTERNET ADDRESSES

Official State Website .... http://www.michigan.gov
Governor's Website .... http://www.michigan.gov/gov
Legislative Website .... http://www.michiganlegislature.org
Judicial Website .... http://www.courts.michigan.gov

Mississippi

Nickname .... The Magnolia State
Motto .... *Virtute et Armis* (By Valor and Arms)
Flower .... Magnolia
Bird .... Mockingbird
Tree .... Magnolia
Song .... *Go, Mississippi*
Entered the Union .... December 10, 1817
Capital .... Jackson

STATISTICS

Land Area (square miles) 46,907
   Rank in Nation 31st
Population 2,881,281
   Rank in Nation 31st
   Density per square mile 61.4
Capital City .... Jackson
   Population 180,881
   Rank in State 1st
Largest City .... Jackson
Number of Representatives in Congress 4
Number of Counties 82
Number of Municipal Governments 296
Number of 2004 Electoral Votes 6
Number of School Districts 152
Number of Special Districts 458

STATE INTERNET ADDRESSES

Official State Website .... http://www.ms.gov
Governor's Website .... http://www.governor.state.ms.us
Legislative Website .... http://www.ls.state.ms.us
Judicial Website .... http://www.mssc.state.ms.us

Missouri

Nickname .... The Show Me State
Motto .... *Salus Populi Suprema Lex Esto*
(The Welfare of the People Shall Be the Supreme Law)
Flower .... White Hawthorn Blossom
Bird .... Bluebird
Tree .... Flowering Dogwood
Song .... *Missouri Waltz*
Entered the Union .... August 10, 1821
Capital .... Jefferson City

STATISTICS

Land Area (square miles) 68,886
    Rank in Nation 18th
Population 5,704,484
    Rank in Nation 17th
    Density per square mile 82.8
Capital City .... Jefferson City
    Population 39,636
    Rank in State 15th
Largest City .... Kansas City
    Population 443,471
Number of Representatives in Congress 9
Number of Counties 115
Number of Municipal Governments 946
Number of 2004 Electoral Votes 11
Number of School Districts 524
Number of Special Districts 1,514

STATE INTERNET ADDRESSES

Official State Website .... http://www.state.mo.us
Governor's Website .... http://www.gov.state.mo.us
Legislative Website .... http://www.moga.state.mo.us
Judicial Website .... http://www.osca.state.mo.us

Montana

Nickname .... The Treasure State
Motto .... *Oro y Plata* (Gold and Silver)
Flower .... Bitterroot
Bird .... Western Meadowlark
Tree .... Ponderosa Pine
Song .... *Montana*
Entered the Union .... November 8, 1889
Capital .... Helena

STATISTICS

Land Area (square miles) 145,552
    Rank in Nation 4th
Population 917,621
    Rank in Nation 44th
    Density per square mile 6.3
Capital City .... Helena
    Population 25,780
    Rank in State 6th
Largest City .... Billings
    Population 89,847
Number of Representatives in Congress 1
Number of Counties 56
Number of Municipal Governments 129
Number of 2004 Electoral Votes 3
Number of School Districts 453
Number of Special Districts 592

STATE INTERNET ADDRESSES

Official State Website .... http://www.state.mt.us
Governor's Website http://www.discoveringmontana.com/gov2
Legislative Website .... http://leg.state.mt.us
Judicial Website .... http://www.lawlibrary.state.mt.us

Nebraska

Nickname .... The Cornhusker State
Motto .... *Equality Before the Law*
Flower .... Goldenrod
Bird .... Western Meadowlark
Tree .... Western Cottonwood
Song .... *Beautiful Nebraska*
Entered the Union .... March 1, 1867
Capital .... Lincoln

STATISTICS

Land Area (square miles) 76,872
    Rank in Nation 15th
Population 1,739,291
    Rank in Nation 38th
    Density per square mile 22.6
Capital City .... Lincoln
    Population 232,362
    Rank in State 2nd
Largest City .... Omaha
    Population 399,357
Number of Representatives in Congress 3
Number of Counties 93
Number of Municipal Governments 531
Number of 2004 Electoral Votes 5
Number of School Districts 576
Number of Special Districts 1,146

STATE INTERNET ADDRESSES

Official State Website .... http://www.state.ne.us
Governor's Website .... http://gov.nol.org
Legislative Website .... http://www.unicam.state.ne.us
Judicial Website .... http://court.nol.org

Nevada

Nickname .... The Silver State
Motto .... *All for Our Country*
Flower .... Sagebrush
Bird .... Mountain Bluebird
Tree .... Bristlecone Pine and Single-leaf Pinon
Song .... *Home Means Nevada*
Entered the Union .... October 31, 1864
Capital .... Carson City

STATISTICS

Land Area (square miles) 109,826
    Rank in Nation 7th
Population 2,241,154
    Rank in Nation 35th
    Density per square mile 20.4
Capital City .... Carson City
    Population 52,457
    Rank in State 6th
Largest City .... Las Vegas
    Population 508,604
Number of Representatives in Congress 3
Number of Counties 17
Number of Municipal Governments 19
Number of 2004 Electoral Votes 5
Number of School Districts 17
Number of Special Districts 158

STATE INTERNET ADDRESSES

Official State Website .... http://www.nv.gov
Governor's Website .... http://www.gov.state.nv.us
Legislative Website .... http://www.leg.state.nv.us
Judicial Website .... http://silver.state.nv.us/elec_judicial.htm

New Hampshire

Nickname .... The Granite State
Motto .... *Live Free or Die*
Flower .... Purple Lilac
Bird .... Purple Finch
Tree .... White Birch
Song .... *Old New Hampshire*
Entered the Union .... June 21, 1788
Capital .... Concord

STATISTICS

Land Area (square miles) 8,968
   Rank in Nation 44th
Population 1,287,687
   Rank in Nation 41st
   Density per square mile 143.6
Capital City .... Concord
   Population 40,687
   Rank in State 3rd
Largest City .... Manchester
   Population 108,398
Number of Representatives in Congress 2
Number of Counties 10
Number of Municipal Governments 13
Number of 2004 Electoral Votes 4
Number of School Districts 178
Number of Special Districts 148

STATE INTERNET ADDRESSES

Official State Website .... http://www.state.nh.us
Governor's Website .... http://www.nh.gov/governor
Legislative Website .... http://www.gencourt.state.nh.us
Judicial Website .... http://www.courts.state.nh.us

New Jersey

Nickname .... The Garden State
Motto .... *Liberty and Prosperity*
Flower .... Violet
Bird .... Eastern Goldfinch
Tree .... Red Oak
Song .... *I'm From New Jersey*
Entered the Union .... December 18, 1787
Capital .... Trenton

STATISTICS

Land Area (square miles) 7,417
   Rank in Nation 46th
Population 8,638,396
   Rank in Nation 10th
   Density per square mile 1,164.7
Capital City .... Trenton
   Population 85,650
   Rank in State 9th
Largest City .... Newark
   Population 277,000
Number of Representatives in Congress 13
Number of Counties 21
Number of Municipal Governments 324
Number of 2004 Electoral Votes 15
Number of School Districts 604
Number of Special Districts 276

STATE INTERNET ADDRESSES

Official State Website .... http://www.state.nj.us
Governor's Website .... http://www.state.nj.us/governor
Legislative Website .... http://www.njleg.state.nj.us
Judicial Website .... http://www.judiciary.state.nj.us

New Mexico

Nickname .... The Land of Enchantment
Motto .... *Crescit Eundo* (It Grows As It Goes)
Flower .... Yucca (Our Lord's Candles)
Bird .... Chaparral Bird
Tree .... Pinon
Songs .... *Asi es Nuevo Mexico and
O, Fair New Mexico*
Entered the Union .... January 6, 1912
Capital .... Santa Fe

STATISTICS

Land Area (square miles) 121,356
   Rank in Nation 5th
Population 1,874,614
   Rank in Nation 36th
   Density per square mile 15.4
Capital City .... Santa Fe
   Population 62,203
   Rank in State 3rd
Largest City .... Albuquerque
   Population 463,874
Number of Representatives in Congress 3
Number of Counties 33
Number of Municipal Governments 101
Number of 2004 Electoral Votes 5
Number of School Districts 89
Number of Special Districts 628

STATE INTERNET ADDRESSES

Official State Website .... http://www.state.nm.us
Governor's Website .... http://www.governor.state.nm.us
Legislative Website .... http://legis.state.nm.us
Judicial Website .... http://www.nmcourts.com

New York

Nickname .... The Empire State
Motto .... *Excelsior* (Ever Upward)
Flower .... Rose
Bird .... Bluebird
Tree .... Sugar Maple
Song .... *I Love New York*
Entered the Union .... July 26, 1788
Capital .... Albany

STATISTICS

Land Area (square miles) 47,214
   Rank in Nation 30th
Population 19,190,115
   Rank in Nation 3rd
   Density per square mile 406.4
Capital City .... Albany
   Population 95,658
   Rank in State 6th
Largest City .... New York City
   Population 8,084,316
Number of Representatives in Congress 29
Number of Counties 62
Number of Municipal Governments 616
Number of 2004 Electoral Votes 31
Number of School Districts 703
Number of Special Districts 1,135

STATE INTERNET ADDRESSES

Official State Website .... http://www.state.ny.us
Governor's Website .... http://www.state.ny.us/governor
Senate Website .... http://www.senate.state.ny.us
Assembly Website .... http://assembly.state.ny.us
Judicial Website .... http://www.courts.state.ny.us

North Carolina

Nickname .... The Tar Heel State and Old North State
Motto .... *Esse Quam Videri*
(To Be Rather Than to Seem)
Flower .... Dogwood
Bird .... Cardinal
Tree .... Long Leaf Pine
Song .... *The Old North State*
Entered the United States .... November 21, 1789
Capital .... Raleigh

STATISTICS

Land Area (square miles) 48,711
  Rank in Nation 29th
Population 8,407,248
  Rank in Nation 11th
  Density per square mile 172.6
Capital City .... Raleigh
  Population 306,944
  Rank in State 2nd
Largest City .... Charlotte
  Population 580,597
Number of Representatives in Congress 13
Number of Counties 100
Number of Municipal Governments 541
Number of 2004 Electoral Votes 15
Number of School Districts 120
Number of Special Districts 319

STATE INTERNET ADDRESSES

Official State Website .... http://www.ncgov.com
Governor's Website .... http://www.governor.state.nc.us
Legislative Website .... http://www.ncleg.net
Judicial Website .... http://www.nccourts.org

North Dakota

Nickname .... Peace Garden State
Motto .... *Liberty and Union, Now and Forever,*
One and Inseparable
Flower .... Wild Prairie Rose
Bird .... Western Meadowlark
Tree .... American Elm
Song .... *North Dakota Hymn*
Entered the Union .... November 2, 1889
Capital .... Bismarck

STATISTICS

Land Area (square miles) 68,976
  Rank in Nation 17th
Population 633,837
  Rank in Nation 48th
  Density per square mile 9.2
Capital City .... Bismarck
Population 55,532
  Rank in State 2nd
Largest City .... Fargo
  Population 90,599
Number of Representatives in Congress 1
Number of Counties 53
Number of Municipal Governments 360
Number of 2004 Electoral Votes 3
Number of School Districts 230
Number of Special Districts 764

STATE INTERNET ADDRESSES

Official State Website .... http://discovernd.com
Governor's Website .... http://www.governor.state.nd.us
Legislative Website .... http://www.state.nd.us/lr
Judicial Website .... http://www.court.state.nd.us

Ohio

Nickname .... The Buckeye State
Motto .... *With God, All Things Are Possible*
Flower .... Scarlet Carnation
Bird .... Cardinal
Tree .... Buckeye
Song .... *Beautiful Ohio*
Entered the Union .... March 1, 1803
Capital .... Columbus

STATISTICS

Land Area (square miles) 40,948
  Rank in Nation 35th
Population 11,435,798
  Rank in Nation 7th
  Density per square mile 279.3
Capital City .... Columbus
Population 725,228
  Rank in State 1st
Largest City .... Columbus
Number of Representatives in Congress 18
Number of Counties 88
Number of Municipal Governments 942
Number of 2004 Electoral Votes 20
Number of School Districts 662
Number of Special Districts 631

STATE INTERNET ADDRESSES

Official State Website .... http://www.state.oh.us
Governor's Website .... http://governor.ohio.gov
Legislative Website .... http://www.ohio.gov/ohio/GovState.stm#ohleg
Judicial Website .... http://www.sconet.state.oh.us

Oklahoma

Nickname .... The Sooner State
Motto .... *Labor Omnia Vincit* (Labor Conquers All Things)
Flower .... Mistletoe
Bird .... Scissor-tailed Flycatcher
Tree .... Redbud
Song .... *Oklahoma*
Entered the Union .... November 16, 1907
Capital .... Oklahoma City

STATISTICS

Land Area (square miles) 68,667
  Rank in Nation 19th
Population 3,511,532
  Rank in Nation 28th
  Density per square mile 51.1
Capital City .... Oklahoma City
Population 519,034
  Rank in State 1st
Largest City .... Oklahoma City
Number of Representatives in Congress 5
Number of Counties 77
Number of Municipal Governments 590
Number of 2004 Electoral Votes 7
Number of School Districts 544
Number of Special Districts 560

STATE INTERNET ADDRESSES

Official State Website .... http://www.state.ok.us
Governor's Website .... http://www.governor.state.ok.us/
Legislative Website .... http://www.lsb.state.ok.us
Judicial Website .... http://www.oscn.net

Oregon

Nickname .... The Beaver State
Motto .... *She Flies with Her Own Wings*
Flower .... Oregon Grape
Bird .... Western Meadowlark
Tree .... Douglas Fir
Song .... *Oregon, My Oregon*
Entered the Union .... February 14, 1859
Capital .... Salem

STATISTICS

Land Area (square miles) 95,997
    Rank in Nation 10th
Population 3,559,596
    Rank in Nation 27th
    Density per square mile 37.1
Capital City .... Salem
    Population 140,977
    Rank in State 3rd
Largest City .... Portland
    Population 539,438
Number of Representatives in Congress 5
Number of Counties 36
Number of Municipal Governments 240
Number of 2004 Electoral Votes 7
Number of School Districts 197
Number of Special Districts 927

STATE INTERNET ADDRESSES

Official State Website .... http://www.oregon.gov
Governor's Website .... http://www.governor.state.or.us
Legislative Website .... http://www.leg.state.or.us
Judicial Website .... http://www.ojd.state.or.us

Pennsylvania

Nickname .... The Keystone State
Motto .... *Virtue, Liberty and Independence*
Animal .... White-tailed Deer
Flower .... Mountain Laurel
Tree .... Hemlock
Song .... Pennsylvania
Entered the Union .... December 12, 1787
Capital .... Harrisburg

STATISTICS

Land Area (square miles) 44,817
    Rank in Nation 32nd
Population 12,365,455
    Rank in Nation 6th
    Density per square mile 275.9
Capital City .... Harrisburg
    Population 48,540
    Rank in State 13th
Largest City .... Philadelphia
    Population 1,492,231
Number of Representatives in Congress 19
Number of Counties 67
Number of Municipal Governments 1,018
Number of 2004 Electoral Votes 21
Number of School Districts 501
Number of Special Districts 1,885

STATE INTERNET ADDRESSES

Official State Website .... http://www.state.pa.us
Governor's Website .... http://www.governor.state.pa.us
Legislative Website .... http://www.legis.state.pa.us
Judicial Website .... http://www.courts.state.pa.us

Rhode Island

Nicknames .... Little Rhody and Ocean State
Motto .... *Hope*
Flower .... Violet
Bird .... Rhode Island Red
Tree .... Red Maple
Song .... *Rhode Island*
Entered the Union .... May 29, 1790
Capital .... Providence

STATISTICS

Land Area (square mile) 1,045
    Rank in Nation 50th
Population 1,076,164
    Rank in Nation 43rd
    Density per square mile 1,029.8
Capital City .... Providence
Population 175,901
    Rank in State 1st
Largest City .... Providence
Number of Representatives in Congress 2
Number of Counties 5
Number of Municipal Governments 8
Number of 2004 Electoral Votes 4
Number of School Districts 36
Number of Special Districts 75

STATE INTERNET ADDRESSES

Official State Website .... http://www.state.ri.us
Governor's Website .... http://www.governor.state.ri.us
Legislative Website .... http://www.rilin.state.ri.us
Judicial Website .... http://www.courts.state.ri.us

South Carolina

Nickname .... The Palmetto State
Motto .... *Animis Opibusque Parati*
    (Prepared in Mind and Resources) and
    Dum Spiro Spero (While I breathe, I Hope)
Flower .... Yellow Jessamine
Bird .... Carolina Wren
Tree .... Palmetto
Songs .... *Carolina* and *South Carolina on My Mind*
Entered the Union .... May 23, 1788
Capital .... Columbia

STATISTICS

Land Area (square miles) 30,110
    Rank in Nation 40th
Population 4,147,152
    Rank in Nation 25th
    Density per square mile 137.7
Capital City .... Columbia

Population 117,394
    Rank in State 1st
Largest City .... Columbia
Number of Representatives in Congress 6
Number of Counties 46
Number of Municipal Governments 269
Number of 2004 Electoral Votes 8
Number of School Districts 90
Number of Special Districts 301

STATE INTERNET ADDRESSES

Official State Website .... http://www.myscgov.com
Governor's Website .... http://www.scgovernor.com/
Legislative Website .... http://www.scstatehouse.net
Judicial Website .... http://www.judicial.state.sc.us

South Dakota

Nicknames .... The Mt. Rushmore State
Motto .... *Under God the People Rule*
Flower .... American Pasque
Bird .... Chinese ring-necked pheasant
Tree .... Black Hills Spruce
Song .... *Hail, South Dakota*
Entered the Union .... November 2, 1889
Capital .... Pierre

STATISTICS

Land Area (square miles) 75,885
    Rank in Nation 16th
Population 764,309
    Rank in Nation 46th
    Density per square mile 10.1
Capital City .... Pierre
    Population 13,876
    Rank in State 7th
Largest City .... Sioux Falls
    Population 130,491
Number of Representatives in Congress 1
Number of Counties 66
Number of Municipal Governments 308
Number of 2004 Electoral Votes 3
Number of School Districts 176
Number of Special Districts 376

STATE INTERNET ADDRESSES

Official State Website .... http://www.state.sd.us
Governor's Website .... http://www.state.sd.us/governor
Legislative Website .... http://legis.state.sd.us
Judicial Website .... http://www.sdjudicial.com

Tennessee

Nickname .... The Volunteer State
Motto .... *Agriculture and Commerce*
Flower .... Iris
Bird .... Mockingbird
Tree .... Tulip Poplar
Songs .... *When It's Iris Time in Tennessee;*
The Tennessee Waltz; My Homeland, Tennessee
My Tennessee; and *Rocky Top*
Entered the Union .... June 1, 1796
Capital .... Nashville

STATISTICS

Land Area (square miles) 41,217
    Rank in Nation 34th
Population 5,841,748
    Rank in Nation 16th
    Density per square mile 141.7
Capital City .... Nashville
    Population 545,915
Rank in State 2nd
Largest City .... Memphis
    Population 648,882
Number of Representatives in Congress 9
Number of Counties 95
Number of Municipal Governments 349
Number of 2004 Electoral Votes 11
Number of School Districts 138
Number of Special Districts 475

STATE INTERNET ADDRESSES

Official State Website .... http://www.state.tn.us
Governor's Website .... http://www.state.tn.us/governor
Legislative Website .... http://www.legislature.state.tn.us
Judicial Website .... http://www.tsc.state.tn.us

Texas

Nickname .... The Lone Star State
Motto .... *Friendship*
Flower .... Bluebonnet (Buffalo Clover, Wolf Flower)
Bird .... Mockingbird
Tree .... Pecan
Song .... *Texas, Our Texas*
Entered the Union .... December 29, 1845
Capital .... Austin

STATISTICS

Land Area (square miles) 261,797
    Rank in Nation 2nd
Population 22,118,509
    Rank in Nation 2nd
    Density per square mile 84.5
Capital City .... Austin
    Population 671,873
    Rank in State 4th
Largest City .... Houston
    Population 2,009,834
Number of Representatives in Congress 32
Number of Counties 254
Number of Municipal Governments 1,196
Number of 2004 Electoral Votes 34
Number of School Districts 1,040
Number of Special Districts 2,245

STATE INTERNET ADDRESSES

Official State Website .... http://www.state.tx.us
Governor's Website .... http://www.governor.state.tx.us
Legislative Website .... http://www.capitol.state.tx.us
Judicial Website .... http://www.courts.state.tx.us

Utah

Nickname .... The Beehive State
Motto .... *Industry*
Flower .... Sego Lily
Bird .... California Seagull
Tree .... Blue Spruce
Song .... *Utah, We Love Thee*
Entered the Union .... January 4, 1896
Capital .... Salt Lake City

STATISTICS

Land Area (square miles) 82,144
    Rank in Nation 12th
Population 2,351,467
    Rank in Nation 34th
    Density per square mile 28.6
Capital City .... Salt Lake City
    Population 181,266
    Rank in State 1st
Largest City .... Salt Lake City
Number of Representatives in Congress 3
Number of Counties 29
Number of Municipal Governments 236
Number of 2004 Electoral Votes 5
Number of School Districts 40
Number of Special Districts 300

STATE INTERNET ADDRESSES

Official State Website .... http://www.utah.gov
Governor's Website .... http://www.utah.gov/governor
Legislative Website .... http://www.le.state.ut.us
Judicial Website .... http://utcourts.gov

Vermont

Nickname .... The Green Mountain State
Motto .... *Freedom and Unity*
Flower .... Red Clover
Bird .... Hermit Thrush
Tree .... Sugar Maple
Song .... *Hail, Vermont!*
Entered the Union .... March 4, 1791
Capital .... Montpelier

STATISTICS

Land Area (square miles) 9,250
   Rank in Nation 43rd
Population 619,107
   Rank in Nation 49th
   Density per square mile 66.9
Capital City .... Montpelier
   Population 8,035
   Rank in State 13th
Largest City .... Burlington
Population 38,889
Number of Representatives in Congress 1
Number of Counties 14
Number of Municipal Governments 47
Number of 2004 Electoral Votes 3
Number of School Districts 288
Number of Special Districts 152

STATE INTERNET ADDRESSES

Official State Website .... http://vermont.gov
Governor's Website .... http://www.vermont.gov/governor
Legislative Website .... http://www.leg.state.vt.us
Judicial Website .... http://www.vermontjudiciary.org

Virginia

Nickname .... The Old Dominion
Motto .... *Sic Semper Tyrannis* (Thus Always to Tyrants)
Flower .... Dogwood
Bird .... Cardinal
Tree .... Dogwood
Song .... *Carry Me Back to Old Virginia*
Entered the Union .... June 25, 1788
Capital .... Richmond

STATISTICS

Land Area (square miles) 39,594
   Rank in Nation 37th
Population 7,386,330
   Rank in Nation 12th
   Density per square miles 186.6
Capital City .... Richmond
   Population 197,456
   Rank in State 4th
Largest City .... Virginia Beach
Population 433,934
Number of Representatives in Congress 11
Number of Counties 135
Number of Municipal Governments 229
Number of 2004 Electoral Votes 13
Number of School Districts 135
Number of Special Districts 196

STATE INTERNET ADDRESSES

Official State Website .... http://www.virginia.gov
Governor's Website .... http://www.governor.state.va.us
Legislative Website .... http://legis.state.va.us
Judicial Website .... http://www.courts.state.va.us

Washington

Nickname .... The Evergreen State
Motto .... *Alki* (Chinook Indian word meaning By and By)
Flower .... Coast Rhododendron
Bird .... Willow Goldfinch
Tree .... Western Hemlock
Song .... *Washington, My Home*
Entered the Union .... November 11, 1889
Capital .... Olympia

STATISTICS

Land Area (square miles) 66,544
   Rank in Nation 20th
Population 6,131,445
   Rank in Nation 15th
   Density per square mile 92.1
Capital City .... Olympia
   Population 42,530
   Rank in State 18th
Largest City .... Seattle
   Population 570,426
Number of Representatives in Congress 9
Number of Counties 39
Number of Municipal Governments 279
Number of 2004 Electoral Votes 11
Number of School Districts 296
Number of Special Districts 1,173

STATE INTERNET ADDRESSES

Official State Website .... http://access.wa.gov
Governor's Website .... http://www.governor.wa.gov
Legislative Website .... http://www.leg.wa.gov
Judicial Website .... http://www.courts.wa.gov

West Virginia

Nickname .... The Mountain State
Motto .... *Montani Semper Liberi*
(Mountaineers Are Always Free)
Flower .... Rhododendron
Bird .... Cardinal
Tree .... Sugar Maple
Songs .... *West Virginia, My Home Sweet Home;*
The West Virginia Hills;
and *This is My West Virginia*
Entered the Union .... June 20, 1863
Capital .... Charleston

STATISTICS

Land Area (square miles) 24,078
   Rank in Nation 41st
Population 1,810,354
   Rank in Nation 37th
   Density per square mile 75.2
Capital City .... Charleston
   Population 53,421
   Rank in State 1st
Largest City .... Charleston
Number of Representatives in Congress 3
Number of Counties 55
Number of Municipal Governments 234
Number of 2004 Electoral Votes 5
Number of School Districts 55
Number of Special Districts 342

STATE INTERNET ADDRESSES

Official State Website .... http://www.wv.gov
Governor's Website .... http://www.state.wv.us/governor
Legislative Website .... http://www.legis.state.wv.us/legishp.html
Judicial Website .... http://www.state.wv.us/wvsca

Wisconsin

Nickname*	The Badger State
Motto	*Forward*
Flower	Wood Violet
Bird	Robin
Tree	Sugar Maple
Song	*On, Wisconsin!*
Entered the Union	May 29, 1848
Capitol	Madison

STATISTICS

Land Area (square miles)	54,310
Rank in Nation	25th
Population	5,472,299
Rank in Nation	20th
Density per square mile	100.8
Capital City	Madison
Population	215,211
Rank in State	2nd
Largest City	Milwaukee
Population	590,895
Number of Representatives in Congress	8
Number of Counties	72
Number of Municipal Governments	585
Number of 2004 Electoral Votes	10
Number of School Districts	431
Number of Special Districts	684

STATE INTERNET ADDRESSES

Official State Website	http://www.wisconsin.gov
Governor's Website	http://www.wisgov.state.wi.us
Legislative Website	http://www.legis.state.wi.us
Judicial Website	http://www.courts.state.wi.us

*unofficial

Wyoming

Nicknames	The Equality State and The Cowboy State
Motto	*Equal Rights*
Flower	Indian Paintbrush
Bird	Western Meadowlark
Tree	Cottonwood
Song	*Wyoming*
Entered the Union	July 10, 1890
Capital	Cheyenne

STATISTICS

Land Area (square miles)	97,100
Rank in Nation	9th
Population	501,242
Rank in Nation	51st
Density per square mile	5.2
Capital City	Cheyenne
Population	53,658
Rank in State	1st
Largest City	Cheyenne
Number of Representatives in Congress	1
Number of Counties	23
Number of Municipal Governments	98
Number of 2004 Electoral Votes	3
Number of School Districts	48
Number of Special Districts	546

STATE INTERNET ADDRESSES

Official State Website	http://www.state.wy.us
Governor'sWebsite	http://wyoming.gov/governor/governor_home.asp
Legislative Website	http://legisweb.state.wy.us
Judicial Website	http://www.courts.state.wy.us

District of Columbia

Motto	*Justitia Omnibus* (Justice to All)
Flower	American Beauty Rose
Bird	Wood Thrush
Tree	Scarlet Oak
Became U.S. Capital	December 1, 1800

STATISTICS

Land Area (square miles)	63
Population	563,384
Density per square mile	9378.0
Delegate to Congress*	1
Number of Municipal Governments	1
Number of 2004 Electoral Votes	3
Number of School Districts	2
Number of Special Districts	1

*Committee voting privileges only.

INTERNET ADDRESSES

Official Website	http://www.washingtondc.gov
Mayor's Website	http://dc.gov/mayor/index.shtm
Legislative Website	http://www.dccouncil.washington.dc.us
Judicial Website	http://www.dcbar.org

American Samoa

Motto	*Samoa-Maumua le Atua* (Samoa, God Is First)
Flower	Paogo (Ula-fala)
Plant	Ava
Song	*Amerika Samoa*
Became a Territory of the United States	1900
Capital	Pago Pago

STATISTICS

Land Area (square miles)	77
Population	57,291
Density per square mile	744.0
Capital City	Pago Pago
Population	4,100
Rank in Territory	3rd
Largest City	Tafuna
Population	8,409
Delegate to Congress	1
Number of School Districts	1

INTERNET ADDRESSES

Official Website	http://www.asg-gov.com
Governor's Website	http://www.government.as/gov.htm
Legislative Website	http://www.government.as/legislative.htm
Judicial Website	http://www.government.as/highcourt.htm

Guam

Nickname .... Hub of the Pacific
Flower .... Puti Tai Nobio (Bougainvillea)
Bird .... Toto (Fruit Dove)
Tree .... Ifit (Intsiabijuga)
Song .... *Stand Ye Guamanians*
Stone .... Latte
Animal .... Iguana
Ceded to the United States by Spain .... December 10, 1898
Became a Territory .... August 1, 1950
Request to become a Commonwealth Plebiscite .... November 1987
Capital .... Hagatna

STATISTICS

Land Area (square miles) 210
Population 154,805
    Density per square mile 737.1
Capital .... Hagatna
    Population 1,122
    Rank in Territory 18th
Largest City .... Dededo
Population 42,980
Delegate to Congress 1
Number of School Districts 1

INTERNET ADDRESSES

Official Website .... http://ns.gov.gu
Governor's Website .... http://ns.gov.gu/webtax/govoff.html
Legislative Website .... http://www.guam.net/gov/senate
Judicial Website .... http://www.justice.gov.gu

Northern Mariana Islands

Flower .... Plumeria
Bird .... Marianas Fruit Dove
Tree Flame Tree
Song .... *Gi TaloGi Halom Tasi*
Administered by the United States
    a trusteeship for the United Nations .... July 18, 1947
Voters approved a proposed constitution .... June 1975
U.S. president signed covenant agreeing to
    commonwealth status for the islands .... March 24, 1976
Became a self-governing Commonwealth .... January 9, 1978
Capital .... Saipan

STATISTICS

Land Area (square miles) 181
Population 69,221
    Density per square mile 382.4
Capital City .... Saipan
    Population 62,392
Largest City .... Saipan
Delegate to Congress 1
Number of School Districts 1

INTERNET ADDRESSES

Official Website .... http://www.saipan.com/gov
Governor's Website .... http://www.mariana-islands.gov.mp
Legislative Website .... http://www.saipan.com/gov/branches/senate
Judicial Website http://cnmilaw.org/htmlpage/hpg34.htm

Puerto Rico

Nickname .... Island of Enchantment
Motto .... *Joannes Est Nomen Ejus*
(John is Thy Name)
Flower .... Maga
Bird .... Reinita
Tree .... Ceiba
Song .... *La Borinquena*
Became a Territory of the United States .... December 10, 1898
Became a self-governing Commonwealth .... July 25, 1952
Capital .... San Juan

STATISTICS

Land Area (square miles) 3,427
Population 3,878,532
    Density per square mile 1,111.3
Capital City .... San Juan
    Population 442,447
Largest City .... San Juan
Delegate to Congress* 1
Number of School Districts 1

    *Committee voting privileges only

INTERNET ADDRESSES

Official State Website .... http://www.puertorico.pr
Governor's Website .... http://www.fortaleza.gobierno.pr
Senate Website .... http://www.camaradepuertorico.org
House Website .... http://www.camaradepuertorico.org
Judicial Website .... http://www.tribunalpr.org

U.S. Virgin Islands

Nickname .... The American Paradise
Motto .... United in Pride and Hope
Flower .... The Yellow Cedar
Bird .... Yellow Breast or Banana Quit
Song .... *Virgin Islands March*
Purchased from Denmark .... March 31, 1917
Capital .... Charlotte Amalie, St. Thomas

STATISTICS

Land Area (square miles)* 134
Population 108,612
    Density per square mile 810.5
Capital City .... Charlotte Amalie, St. Thomas
    Population 12,500
Largest City .... Charlotte Amalie, St. Thomas
Delegate to Congress** 1
Number of School Districts 1

    *The U.S. Virgin Islands is comprised of three large islands (St. Croix, St. John, and St. Thomas) and 50 smaller islands and cays.
    **Committee voting privileges only.

INTERNET ADDRESSES

Official Website .... http://www.usvi.org
Governor's Website .... http://www.usvi.org
Legislative Website .... http://www.senate.gov.vi
Judicial Website .... http://www.vid.uscourts.gov

Index

INDEX

—X–Y–Z—